Western Civilization

THE CONTINUING EXPERIMENT

Western Civilization

THE CONTINUING EXPERIMENT

FOURTH EDITION

VOLUME II
SINCE 1560

Thomas F. X. Noble
University of Notre Dame

Barry Strauss
Cornell University

Duane J. Osheim
University of Virginia

Kristen B. Neuschel
Duke University

William B. Cohen
Late of Indiana University

David D. Roberts
University of Georgia

Rachel G. Fuchs
Arizona State University

Houghton Mifflin Company   Boston New York

Publisher: Charles Hartford
Editor-in-Chief: Jean L. Woy
Senior Sponsoring Editor: Nancy Blaine
Senior Development Editor: Julie Dunn
Editorial Associate: Annette Fantasia
Senior Project Editor: Christina M. Horn
Editorial Assistant: Teresa Huang
Senior Art and Design Coordinator: Jill Haber
Senior Photo Editor: Jennifer Meyer Dare
Senior Composition Buyer: Sarah Ambrose
Senior Designer: Henry Rachlin
Senior Manufacturing Coordinator: Marie Barnes
Senior Marketing Manager: Sandra McGuire
Marketing Assistant: Ilana Gordon

Volume II cover image: *Church Goers in a Boat,* 1909 (oil on canvas), by Carl Wilhelm Wilhelmson (1866–1928). Photograph: Nationalmuseum, Stockholm, Sweden/Bridgeman Art Library, London/N.Y.

Illustration credits: Global Encounters: © Corbis Images; The Continuing Experiment: © Getty Images; Weighing the Evidence: Library of Congress.

Text credits: Page 907: Excerpts from *A Room of One's Own* by Virginia Woolf, copyright 1929 by Harcourt, Inc., and renewed 1957 by Leonard Woolf. Reprinted by permission of the publisher.

Printed in the U.S.A.

Library of Congress Control Number: 2003110158

ISBN: 0-618-43278-7

23456789-VH-08 07 06 05

In Memoriam
William Benjamin Cohen
1941–2002

BILL COHEN was born in Jakobstad, Finland, amid the horrors of World War II. His parents were German Jews who had fled Hitler's regime. Bill's father was a doctor, and his connection with an influential patient saved the family when Nazi sympathizers among the Finns began rounding up German Jews. When Bill was 2, his family moved to Sweden. Three years later they moved to Ethiopia, and then eight years later back to Sweden. One enduring result of Bill's peregrinations was that he learned six languages: Swedish, German, Amharic, Italian, French, and English. He always joked that he spoke six languages with an accent. Remarkably, Bill's maternal great-grandfather had served in the U.S. Civil War in Texas, and his grandfather was permitted to immigrate to the United States during World War II. Bill's father died when Bill was 16, and his mother moved the family to southern California. Bill acclimated himself quickly enough to earn substantial winnings on a game show and to complete high school early. He won a scholarship to Pomona College and then undertook graduate study in history at Stanford. Bill taught briefly at Northwestern and then moved to Indiana University, which was to be his professional home and where he chaired the history department on two occasions. Through a long series of distinguished publications, Bill became one of the world's pre-eminent historians of modern France and French colonialism. Almost never without one of his prodigious collection of hats, Bill was a connoisseur of fine foods, a formidable critic of music, a voracious reader, a world traveler, a cunning wit, and a deeply sympathetic person. A friend said of him, "He was a multinational, multicultural, multilingual being, who crossed borders of all kinds effortlessly as a natural dimension of life." Bill's untimely death in November 2002, at the height of his intellectual powers and in the happiest moments of his life, was an inconsolable loss to all who knew him.

Brief Contents

Contents

CHAPTER 30

The West and the World Since 1989   1023

Maps

Documents

Weighing the Evidence

Information Technology

Preface

Chance discoveries reveal that fifteen centuries ago, boys in Ireland and in what is now Afghanistan were copying the biblical psalms with a view to memorizing them. Young Christians were learning these Latin and Greek translations of ancient Hebrew poems. This arresting development points to three big themes that inform this book and that contribute to an understanding of why we should study Western Civilization in the early twenty-first century.

First, what or where is the "West"? The West is sometimes understood geographically and sometimes culturally. For most people, the West means western Europe. And yet western Europe itself is the heir of the peoples and cultures of antiquity, including the Sumerians, Egyptians, Persians, Greeks, Romans, Jews, Christians, and Muslims. In fact, Europe is the heir of even earlier civilizations in Asia and Africa.

Let us turn back to the psalm-learning boys of Ireland and Afghanistan. Although Ireland is now considered European, it was not part of the classical world. In fact, the Romans placed the island "at the end of the world." Christian missionaries prepared Ireland's entry into Western Civilization, and it has been at the heart of the West for more than a millennium. Consider Saint Patrick, the exuberant beauty of Celtic art, the English entanglement with Ireland, the poetry of William Butler Yeats or Seamus Heaney, and the novels of James Joyce—all of these are part of our Western heritage. The question of Afghanistan is trickier. Persians touched this land, as did the soldiers of Alexander the Great. The Silk Road—that great artery of objects and ideas—passed through it. A few years ago, to the horror of the world, the Taliban, radical Muslims, destroyed two monumental Buddha statues at Bamiyan. The psalm-learning boys, their psalms, and their heirs had religious competitors. But those statues had unmistakably Greek features, and today Western troops police much of Afghanistan. It would be a fascinating thought exercise to ask whether Afghanistan is "East" or "West."

As a cultural phenomenon, "Western" implies many things: freedom and free, participatory political institutions; economic initiative and opportunity; monotheistic religious faiths (Judaism, Christianity, and Islam); rationalism and ordered thought in the social, political, and philosophical realms; an aesthetic sensibility that aspires to a universal sense of beauty. But the West has felt free to evoke tradition as its guiding light and also to innovate brilliantly; to accommodate slavery and freedom simultaneously; to esteem original thought and to persecute people who deviate from the norm. "Western" indeed has meant many things in various places at different times. This book constantly and explicitly attempts to situate its readers in place, time, and tradition.

Second, what exactly is civilization? No definition can win universal acceptance, but certain elements of a definition are widely accepted. Cities are crucial; with cities emerge complex social organizations that involve at least a minimal division of labor. Some people work in the fields, some in the home. Soldiers defend the city, and artisans provide its daily goods. Governing institutions have a wide measure of acceptance and have the ability to enforce their will. Complex cultures also develop religious ideas and authorities; a literature and law that may be oral or written; monumental architecture, especially fortifications, palaces, and temples; and arts such as music, painting, and sculpture.

Western Civilization has had an influence on almost every person alive today. The West deserves to be studied because its tale is compelling, but it demands to be studied because its story has been so central to the development of the world in which we live. Many of the world's dominant institutions are Western in their origin and in their contemporary manifestations—most notably parliamentary democracy. Commercial capitalism, a Western construct, is the world's dominant form of economic organization, and even its greatest rival, communism, is fundamentally Western: its theoreticians were Europeans who drew on utopian ideals, classical economics, Enlightenment doctrines, and the ideologies of the French Revolution. Western styles in architecture dominate the skyline of every major city in the world. Western popular culture, from movies and music to fast food, may be found everywhere. Communications technologies, from cell phones to e-mail, are as global in spread as they are Western in origin.

It must be said that some people, inside and outside the West, have grave reservations about the extent of Western influence in the modern world. Were those boys of fifteen centuries ago heirs and beneficiaries of a great tradition? Or were they dupes and victims of Western cultural aggression? Some critics challenge Western religious, philosophical, political, and economic ideas at their core. Others have no quarrel with Western ideas as such but regret that local cultures around the globe are vanishing before a relentless Western onslaught. Still others wonder why Western achievements in political stability and economic prosperity cannot be more widely shared. In other words, to say that the West is dominant is only to state the obvious, not to insist that such domination is inevitable or desirable. But the sheer, unassailable fact of that domination makes the careful study of the West essential for informed, responsible participation in the modern world. And such study can help us understand and appreciate an impressive cultural heritage.

Third, the subtitle of this book, "The Continuing Experiment," was chosen to signal our third theme, contingency or unpredictability. This subtitle conveys our resolve to avoid a deterministic approach. For students and teachers, an appreciation of continuity and change, or unity and diversity, can foster sympathetic participation in this often-bewildering world. We try to give individual actors, moments, and movements the sense of drama, possibility, and contingency that they actually possessed. We, with faultless hindsight, always know how things came out. Contemporaries often did not have a clue. We respect them. Much of the fascination, and the reward, of studying Western Civilization lies precisely in its richness, diversity, changeability, and unpredictability. No one in Israel in 500 B.C. or in Rome a millennium later could have predicted that Irish and Afghan boys would simultaneously cultivate a new and similar religious sensibility by reading Jewish poems in the Christianized versions of the classical languages. Who, a generation ago, could have predicted the collapse of the Soviet Union or the rise of Osama bin Laden? The experiment continues.

Basic Approach

More than a decade ago the six authors of *Western Civilization: The Continuing Experiment* set out to create a textbook that would play a role in a course that will, as a total effort, inform students about essential developments within a tradition that has powerfully, though not always positively, affected everyone in the contemporary world. Although each of us found something to admire in all of the existing textbooks, none of us was fully happy with any of them. We were disappointed with

books that claimed "balance," but actually stressed a single kind of history. We regretted that so many texts were uneven in their command of recent scholarship. Although we were convinced of both the inherent interest of Western Civilization and the importance of teaching the subject, we were disconcerted by the celebratory tone of some books, which portrayed the West as resting on its laurels instead of creatively facing its future.

We decided to produce a book that is balanced and coherent; that addresses the full range of subjects that a Western Civilization book needs to address; that provides the student reader with interesting, timely material; that is up-to-date in terms of scholarship and approach; and that is handsome to look at—in short, a book that helps the instructor to teach and the student to learn. We have kept our common vision fresh through frequent meetings, correspondence, critical mutual readings, and expert editorial guidance. We have come together as one, and because each of us has focused on his or her own area of specialization, we believe that we have attained a rare blend of competence, confidence, and enthusiasm. Moreover, in moving from plans for a first edition to the preparation of a fourth, we have been able to profit from the experience of using the book, the advice and criticism of dozens of colleagues, and the reactions of thousands of students.

Western Civilization is a story. Therefore, we aimed at a strong chronological narrative line. Our experience as teachers tells us that students appreciate this clear but gentle orientation. Our experience tells us, too, that an approach that is broadly chronological will leave instructors plenty of room to adapt our narrative to their preferred organization, or to supplement our narrative with one of their own.

Although we maintain the familiar, large-scale divisions of a Western Civilization book, we also present some innovative adjustments in arrangement. For instance, Chapter 2 treats early Greece together with the whole eastern Mediterranean region in the period from about 1500 to 750 B.C. This approach both links kindred cultures and respects chronological flow better than customary treatments, which take western Asia to a certain point and then backtrack to deal with early Greece. We incorporate a single chapter on Late Antiquity, the tumultuous and fascinating period from about A.D. 300 to 600 that witnessed the transformation of the Roman Empire into three successors: Byzantine, Islamic, and European. One chapter studies those three successors, thereby permitting careful comparisons. But we also assign chapters to some of the greatest issues in Western Civilization, such as the Renaissance, the age of European exploration and conquest, the Scientific Revolution, and the industrial transformation. Our twentieth-century chapters reflect an understanding of the last century formed in its closing years rather than in its middle decades. What is new in our organization represents adjustments grounded in the best scholarship, and what is old represents time-tested approaches.

In fashioning our picture of the West, we took two unusual steps. First, our West is itself bigger than the one found in most textbooks. We treat the Celtic world, Scandinavia, and the Slavic world as integral parts of the story. We look often at the lands that border the West—Anatolia/Turkey, western Asia, North Africa, the Eurasian steppes—in order to show the to-and-fro of peoples, ideas, technologies, and products. Second, we continually situate the West in its global context. We must be clear: this is not a world history book. But just as we recognize that the West has influenced the rest of the world, we also carefully acknowledge how the rest of the world has influenced the West. We begin this story of mutual interaction with the Greeks and Romans, carry it through the European Middle Ages, focus on it in the age of European exploration and conquest, and analyze it closely in the modern world of industry, diplomacy, empire, immigration, and questions of citizenship and identity.

Another approach that runs like a ribbon throughout this textbook involves balance and integration. Teachers and students, just like the authors of this book, have their particular interests and emphases. In the large and diverse American academy, that is as it should be. But a textbook, if it is to be helpful and useful, should incorporate as many interests and emphases as possible. For a long time, some said, Western Civilization books devoted excessive coverage to high politics—"the public deeds of great men," as an ancient Greek writer defined the historian's subject. Others felt that high culture—all the Aristotles and Mozarts—were included to the exclusion of supposedly lesser figures and ordinary men and women. In the 1970s books began to emphasize social history. Some applauded this new emphasis even as they debated fiercely over what to include under this heading.

In this book, we attempt to capture the Western tradition in its full contours, to hear the voices of all those who have made durable contributions. But because we cannot say everything about everybody at every moment, we have had to make choices about how and where to array key topics within our narrative. Above all, we have tried to be integrative. For example, when we talk about government and politics, we present the institutional structures through which power was exercised, the people who possessed power as well as the people who did not, the ideological foundations for the use of power, and the material conditions that fostered or hindered the real or the would-be powerful. In other words, instead of treating old-fashioned "high politics" in abstract and descriptive ways, we take an approach that is organic and analytical: How did things work? Our approach to the history of women is another example. A glance at this book's table of contents and then at its index is revealing. The former reveals very few sections devoted explicitly and exclusively to women. The latter shows that women appear constantly in every section of this book. Is there a contradiction here? Not at all. Women and men have not been historical actors in isolation from one another. Yet gender is an important variable that has shaped individual and collective experience. Hence we seek to explain why certain political, economic, or social circumstances had differing impacts on men and women, and how such conditions led them to make different choices.

Similarly, when we talk of great ideas, we describe the antecedent ideas from which seemingly new ones were built up, and we ask about the consequences of those ideas. We explore the social positions of the authors of those ideas to see if this helps us to explain the ideas themselves or to gauge their influence. We try to understand how ideas in one field of human endeavor proved to be influential in other fields. For instance, gender is viewed as connected to and part of the larger fabric of ideas including power, culture, and piety.

We invite the reader to look at our narrative as if it were a mosaic. Taken as a whole, our narrative contains a coherent picture. Viewed more closely, it is made up of countless tiny bits that may have their individual interest but do not even hint at the larger picture of which they are parts. Finally, just as the viewer of a mosaic may find his or her eye drawn especially to one area, feature, color, or style, so too the reader of this book will find some parts more engaging or compelling than others. But it is only because there is, in this book as in a mosaic, a complete picture that the individual sections make sense, command our attention, excite our interest.

One word sums up our approach in this book: "balance." We tell a good story, but we pause often to reflect on that story, to analyze it. We devote substantial coverage to the typical areas of Greece, Rome, Italy, France, Great Britain, and so forth, but we say more about western Europe's frontiers than any other book. We do not try to disguise our Western Civilization book as a world history book, but we take great pains to locate the West within its global context. And we always assume that context means mutuality and reciprocity. We have high politics and big ideas alongside household management and popular culture. We think that part of the fascination of the past lies in its capacity to suggest understandings of the present and possibilities for the future.

DISTINCTIVE FEATURES

To make this book as accessible as possible to students, we have constantly been aware of its place in a program of teaching and learning. Each chapter begins with a vignette that is directly tied to an accompanying picture. These vignettes introduce the reader to one or more of the key aspects of the chapter. Then the reader encounters a thematic introduction that evokes interest while pointing clearly and in some detail to what follows.

To make our chapter introductions more effective, which means to give students greater confidence as they proceed through the book, we have taken five steps. First, for this as for past editions, we reviewed and revised our opening vignettes to connect text and picture more closely and to use both to invite the reader into the chapter.

Second, we place on the first page of each chapter a succinct outline that immediately and dramatically tells the reader what he or she is going to encounter in the following pages.

Third, we put at the end of each chapter's introduction a list of Questions to Consider that are designed to work with the introduction and outline to give the student a clear orientation to what will follow.

Fourth, we include a list of Terms to Know that also alert the student to people or issues that demand special attention. As a complement to text coverage, a ready reference, and a potential study guide, all of the Terms to Know are gathered into a Glossary at the back of the book.

Fifth, as the student begins to read the chapter proper, he or she will see a Chronology, which serves as yet another orientation to the material contained in the chapter. Subject-specific chronologies still appear in various parts of the book, but we felt that readers would benefit from a chronological orientation to each chapter.

In addition to this fundamental attention to the chapter opening, we also sought to improve the book's teachability by adding a pronunciation guide. Whenever we use an unfamiliar name or term, we show the reader how to pronounce it. Instead of using the intricate rules of phonetics, we provide commonsense guides to pronunciation at the foot of the page.

Careful chapter summaries draw together major topics and themes and link the present chapter to the one that follows. To encourage students to strike out on their own historical discoveries, each chapter offers a few carefully selected suggestions for further reading.

We have been conscious of how the book *looks* to the reader from the very beginning. Attractively laid-out pages, a handsome full-color design, engaging maps, and beautifully reproduced pictures enhance the book's appearance. In keeping with our desire to integrate the components of the book into a coherent whole, we carefully anchor the maps and pictures into the volume. The authors chose the maps in this book, labeled them to complement its text, and captioned them to advance its teaching role. The same is true of the pictures: the authors selected them, worked with the book's designers to place them advantageously (and not just decoratively), and wrote all the captions. All the maps are cross-referenced in the text, some of them several times, and the text often refers directly to the pictures. Our diverse boxed documents—usually five per chapter—are referred to and tightly anchored in the text and support the surrounding discussion. As with the maps, familiar documents are blended with pleasing newcomers.

Another important component of this book is the two-page feature Weighing the Evidence, presented at the end of each chapter. This feature introduces students to the fascinating array of sources that historians use and invites them to think critically about the nature of historical information and inquiry. Each opens with a description of the evidence presented in the feature—topics ranging from images of Cleopatra, the Ravenna mosaics, and Renaissance marriage chests to eighteenth-century political symbols, the layout of the British Museum, and postmodern architecture—and then discusses how the professional historian examines this evidence to reconstruct the past. When Samuel Butler said that God cannot change history but that historians can and often do, he meant that history itself arises from new or different acts of interpretation. With Weighing the Evidence, students look over the shoulder of the historian to become active participants in this interpretive process. The sources examined are interesting and instructive in their own right, but the Weighing the Evidence also contributes to the teaching program of the book. As always, these boxes are carefully integrated into the text. There are references to them at appropriate points in the narrative, they contain cross-references to other sections or illustrations, and they support ongoing discussions.

Many textbooks have boxed documents. In four different respects, we have taken special care with our documents for this edition. First, we have included more than fifty new documents as this book has proceeded through its four editions. Second, we have included in most chapters at least one document that permits a gendered analysis of a key historical person or problem. Third, we have included in each chapter one Global Encounters box. The documents under this heading depict either a Western person commenting on the non-Western world, or a non-Western person commenting on the Western world. They further our intention to situate our story in its global context. Fourth, because some documents cry out for more discussion or context than we can provide on the page, we have supplied web activities in the *Student Study Companion,* a website that grows continually but that, right away, expands on some of the documents included in our text—at least one per chapter. (See the Supplements section later in this Preface for more information about the *Student Study Companion.*)

This book is flexible in format as well as substantive organization. Because schools use different academic calendars, organize Western Civilization courses according to different chronologies, and require or recommend different parts of the course, we issue this book in three formats:

- **One-volume hardcover edition** (Chapters 1–30)
- **Two-volume paperback edition:** Volume I, To 1715 (Chapters 1–17); Volume II, Since 1560 (Chapters 15–30)
- **Three-volume paperback edition:** Volume A, To 1500 (Chapters 1–12); Volume B, 1300–1815 (Chapters 11–19); Volume C, Since 1789 (Chapters 19–30)

Volume II begins with a comprehensive Introduction that situates the student reader in the late sixteenth century and surveys the course of Western Civilization from ancient times to the early centuries of the modern era. This Introduction is designed particularly for students who did not take the first semester of the course or who are new to this book.

CHANGES IN THE NEW EDITION

In preparing our fourth edition, we thought hard about our own experiences in using the book and paid strict attention to the advice given to us by many instructors, including both those who use the book and those who do not. Two main lines of revision guided our changes.

The Continuing Experiment

Helpful advice suggested to us that our "Continuing Experiment" theme was welcome but less fully developed than it might have been. Accordingly, each chapter now has a boxed document called The Continuing Experiment. The authors have chosen a document that shows contingency, possibility, or uncertainty. The document is carefully introduced and then followed by a series of focus questions that are designed to invite the reader to imagine how things might have been different. Readers will encounter topics such as Egypt's startling religious experimentation, Archimedes' anticipation of the scientific method, Charlemagne's attempts to reform education, the stupendous achievement of Brunelleschi's dome for Florence's cathedral, France's premature efforts at religious toleration, the ambiguous appeal of Marxism, the complexities of Keynesian economics, and the varying outcomes of "women's liberation." Again and again, readers are encouraged to think imaginatively and creatively.

Organization and Content Changes

As always, we have paid close attention to how our chapters "work." Accordingly, Chapter 5 includes revised material on Roman politics and the conflict of the orders, as well as material on the Roman household and the connection between family and government. Chapter 7 has reorganized material on the Catholic Church, and Chapter 9 has expanded coverage of the Crusades. The material on the Thirty Years' War in Chapter 15 has been fully reworked and now includes a section on the developments in eastern and central Europe. New material on the slave trade has been added to Chapter 18. In Chapter 23, a new discussion of women and charity has been added, focusing on Josephine Grey Butler, Annie Wood Besant, and others. Chapter 28 incorporates new scholarship on the role of Pope Pius XII during the Holocaust, as well as an expanded account of the Warsaw uprising. Finally, in light of the drastic changes in the world since this book was last revised, Chapter 30 has been thoroughly reworked to include coverage of the Iraq War, recent environmental issues, the expanding European Union, the changing demographics of Europe, and the issues of unilateralism and Western responsibility in an increasingly global community.

SUPPLEMENTS

We have assembled with care an array of supplements to aid students in learning and instructors in teaching. These supplements include the new *History Companion,* the *Instructor's Resource Manual, Test Items,* WebCT and Blackboard course cartridges, and a collection of map transparencies for Western Civilization courses.

The new *Houghton Mifflin History Companion* is a collection of resources designed to complement the use of this edition. It is organized according to the chapters in the text and has three parts—the *Instructor Companion,* the *Student Research Companion,* and the *Student Study Companion.* The *Instructor Companion* is a free, searchable CD-ROM featuring hundreds of historical images and maps in PowerPoint format. Each image is accompanied by notes that place it in its proper historical context. The maps and images are correlated to the text's table of contents and are also searchable by other criteria. They are formatted for easy presentation in the classroom. The CD-ROM also includes the *HM Testing* program, a computerized version of the *Test Items* to enable instructors to alter, replace, or add questions, as well as resources from the *Instructor's Resource Manual.*

The *Student Research Companion* is a free web-based tool with one hundred interactive maps and hundreds of primary sources. The primary sources include headnotes that provide pertinent background information and questions that students can answer and e-mail to their instructors. This website also provides students and teachers with additional information for the documents that are featured in the text. It has lengthy, searchable bibliographies that permit students to launch research assignments or pursue personal interests while giving teachers an outstanding opportunity to get directed guidance to the best historical literature in fields outside their own areas of expertise.

The *Student Study Companion* is a free, online study guide to accompany our text. It contains a variety of tutorial resources, including self-tests (ACE questions) with feedback, chronological exercises, flash cards to test vocabulary, and web activities that correspond to the chapter features. In addition, the site features an electronic *Study Guide* containing chapter outlines, chapter summaries, review questions, and more. This versatile, interactive study tool satisfies different learning styles and can improve students' chances of success.

The print *Instructor's Resource Manual,* written by Matthew Lenoe, includes learning objectives, annotated outlines, suggested lecture topics, discussion questions, classroom activities, and paper topics for each chapter of the text. It also features suggestions for integrating the web exercises into your teaching. Each chapter of the print *Test Items,* by Diane Moczar, offers key terms, short-answer and essay questions, map questions, and multiple-choice questions. An answer key for the multiple-choice questions is located at the end of the *Test Items.*

ACKNOWLEDGMENTS

The authors have benefited throughout the process of revision from the acute and helpful criticisms of numerous colleagues. We thank in particular: **James Burns,** Clemson University; **Eleanor A. Congdon,** Youngstown State University; **Eugene Cruz-Uribe,** Northern Arizona University; **Janusz Duzinkiewicz,** Purdue University North Central; **Ann R. Higginbotham,** Eastern Connecticut State University; **Vejas Gabriel Liulevicius,** University of Tennessee; **David A. Reid,** University of North Florida; and **Alice N. Walters,** University of Massachusetts, Lowell.

Each of us has also benefited from the close readings and careful criticisms of our coauthors, although we all assume responsibility for our own chapters. Barry Strauss has written Chapters 1–6; Thomas Noble, 7–10; Duane Osheim, 11–14; Kristen Neuschel, 15–19; William Cohen, 20–24; and David Roberts, 25–30.

Many colleagues, friends, and family members have helped us develop this work as well. Thomas Noble wishes to thank Linda Noble for her patience and good humor. He is also grateful to John Contreni, Wendy Davies, Thomas Head, Elizabeth Meyer, Julia Smith, Richard Sullivan, John Van Engen, Robert Wilken, and Ian Wood.

Barry Strauss is grateful to colleagues at Cornell and at other universities who offered advice and encouragement and responded to scholarly questions. He would also like to thank the people at Cornell who provided technical assistance and support. Most important have been the support and forbearance of his family. His daughter, Sylvie; his son, Michael; and, above all, his wife, Marcia, have truly been sources of inspiration.

Duane Osheim wishes to thank his family for support during the writing and revising of this book. He is also grateful to colleagues at the University of Virginia, who helped to clarify the many connections between Western Civilization and the wider world. He would specifically like to thank Erik Midelfort, Arthur Field, Janis Gibbs, and Beth Plummer for comments and advice.

Kristen Neuschel thanks her colleagues at Duke University for sharing their expertise. She is especially grateful to Sy Mauskopf, Bill Reddy, John Richards, Tom Robisheaux, and Alex Roland. She also thanks her husband and fellow historian, Alan Williams, for his wisdom about Western Civilization and his support throughout the project, and her children, Jesse and Rachel, for their patience, joy, and curiosity.

Rachel Fuchs wishes to thank two of her graduate students, Ute E. Chamberlin and Richard S. Hopkins, for their enthusiasm for this project and their very able assistance.

David Roberts wishes to thank Bonnie Cary, Linda Green, and Nancy Heaton for their able assistance and Timothy Cleaveland, Joshua Cole, Karl Friday, Thomas Ganschow, John Haag, Michael Kwass, John Morrow, Douglas Northrup, Miranda Pollard, Eve Trout Powell, Judith Rohrer, William Stueck, and Kirk Willis for sharing their expertise in response to questions. He also thanks Beth Roberts for her constant support and interest and her exceedingly critical eye.

The first plans for this book were laid in 1988, and over the course of fifteen years, there has been remarkable stability in the core group of people who have been responsible for its growth and development. The author team suffered the loss of a member, but Rachel Fuchs, a student of Bill Cohen's, joined us to revise the chapters dealing with the nineteenth century. Our gratitude to Rachel is as immense as our pleasure at the quality of her work. Our original sponsoring editor, Jean Woy, has become Editor-in-Chief for History and Political Science but has never missed a meeting with us or weakened in her interest in and commitment to this book. Christina Horn, our Senior Project Editor, has been the wizard behind the curtain for all four editions. She understood from the beginning our desire to have maps, pictures, and boxes closely integrated with their pertinent text, and she has never let us down. Our picture researcher, Carole Frohlich, also has been with us from the start, and she has always understood the spirit of this book and the wishes of its authors. Our sponsoring editor, Nancy Blaine, has imparted wisdom and encouragement, sympathy and understanding. We have been fortunate in our editors: Elizabeth Welch, Jennifer Sutherland, and Julie Dunn. They have been by turns friends, confidantes, critics, advisers, and cheerleaders. We are a team, a veteran team, a team with what sports enthusiasts call "good chemistry." We authors are grateful to all the people who have taught us so much and who have prodded us to do better than we could possibly have done on our own or under the guidance of anyone else.

Thomas F. X. Noble

About the Authors

Thomas F. X. Noble   After receiving his Ph.D. from Michigan State University, Thomas Noble taught at Albion College, Michigan State University, Texas Tech University, and the University of Virginia. In 1999 he received the University of Virginia's highest award for teaching excellence. In 2001 he became Robert M. Conway Director of the Medieval Institute at the University of Notre Dame. He is the author of *The Republic of St. Peter: The Birth of the Papal State, 680–825; Religion, Culture and Society in the Early Middle Ages; Soldiers of Christ: Saints and Saints' Lives from Late Antiquity and the Early Middle Ages;* and *Images and the Carolingians: Tradition, Order, and Worship.* Noble's articles and reviews have appeared in many leading journals, including the *American Historical Review, Byzantinische Zeitschrift, Catholic Historical Review, Revue d'histoire ecclésiastique, Speculum,* and *Studi medievali.* He has also contributed chapters to several books and articles to three encyclopedias. He was a member of the Institute for Advanced Study in 1994 and the Netherlands Institute for Advanced Study in 1999–2000. He has been awarded fellowships by the National Endowment for the Humanities (twice) and the American Philosophical Society.

Barry S. Strauss   Professor of history and Classics at Cornell University, Barry Strauss holds a Ph.D. from Yale. He has been awarded fellowships by the National Endowment for the Humanities, the American School of Classical Studies at Athens, the MacDowell Colony for the Arts, the Korea Foundation, and the Killam Foundation of Canada. He is the recipient of the Clark Award for excellence in teaching from Cornell. He served as Director of Cornell's Peace Studies Program. His many publications include *Athens After the Peloponnesian War: Class, Faction, and Policy, 403–386 B.C.; Fathers and Sons in Athens: Ideology and Society in the Era of the Peloponnesian War; The Anatomy of Error: Ancient Military Disasters and Their Lessons for Modern Strategists* (with Josiah Ober); *Hegemonic Rivalry from Thucydides to the Nuclear Age* (co-edited with R. Ned Lebow); *War and Democracy: A Comparative Study of the Korean War and the Peloponnesian War* (co-edited with David R. McCann); *Rowing Against the Current: On Learning to Scull at Forty;* and *The Battle of Salamis, the Naval Encounter That Saved Greece—and Western Civilization.*

Duane J. Osheim   A Fellow of the American Academy in Rome with a Ph.D. in history from the University of California, Davis, Duane Osheim is a professor of history at the University of Virginia. A specialist in late medieval and Renaissance social and institutional history, he is the author and editor of *A Tuscan Monastery and Its Social World, An Italian Lordship: The Bishopric of Lucca in the Late Middle Ages,* and *Beyond Florence: The Contours of Medieval and Early Modern Italy.*

Kristen B. Neuschel   After receiving her Ph.D. from Brown University, Kristen Neuschel taught at Denison University and Duke University, where she is currently associate professor of history. She is a specialist in early modern French history and is the author of *Word of Honor: Interpreting Noble Culture in Sixteenth-Century France* and articles on French social history and European women's history. She has received grants from the National Endowment for the Humanities and the American Council of Learned Societies. She has also received the Alumni Distinguished Undergraduate Teaching Award, which is awarded annually on the basis of student nominations for excellence in teaching at Duke. She is currently Director of Undergraduate Studies for the History Department.

William B. Cohen   After receiving his Ph.D. at Stanford University, William Cohen taught at Northwestern University and Indiana University, where he was professor of history. At Indiana, he served as chairman of the West European Studies and History Departments and was Director of Graduate Studies for the History Department. A previous president of the Society of French Historical Studies, Cohen received several academic fellowships, including a National Endowment for the Humanities and a Fulbright fellowship. He was the author of many works on French history and his research focused on the Algerian war and French memory.

David D. Roberts   After taking his Ph.D. in modern European history at the University of California, Berkeley, David Roberts taught at the Universities of Virginia and Rochester before becoming professor of history at the University of Georgia in 1988. At Rochester he chaired the Humanities Department of the Eastman School of Music, and he chaired the History Department at Georgia from 1993 to 1998. A recipient of Woodrow Wilson and Rockefeller Foundation fellowships, he is the author of *The Syndicalist Tradition and Italian Fascism; Benedetto Croce and the Uses of Historicism;* and *Nothing but History: Reconstruction and Extremity After Metaphysics,* as well as two books in Italian and numerous articles and reviews. He is currently the Albert Berry Saye Professor of History at Georgia.

The West Before 1560

HISTORIANS sometimes say that "History begins at Sumer," a region of ancient Mesopotamia located in the south of modern Iraq. For the reader of Volume II of *Western Civilization: The Continuing Experiment*, history begins forty-five hundred years after Sumer, in the last decades of the sixteenth-century European world. Some orientation may therefore be helpful to situate the start of this volume in time and place.

"Western civilization" is the traditional name for the history you will encounter in these pages. Before we go back to Sumer, let us reflect a little on these two words. The "West" is sometimes understood geographically and sometimes culturally. Each understanding is complex. For most people, the "West" means western Europe. And yet western Europe was itself the heir of the peoples and cultures of the Mediterranean world of antiquity. These included Mesopotamians—people such as the Sumerians—and Egyptians, Greeks and Romans, Jews and Christians. Moreover, through exploration, war, and commerce, the "West" gradually imposed its influence on the whole globe. Concerning Europe itself, one view might encompass Rome, Paris, and London whereas another might stretch from Dublin to Moscow.

As a cultural phenomenon, "Western" implies many things: freedom and free, participatory political institutions; economic initiative and opportunity; monotheistic religious faiths (Judaism, Christianity, and Islam); rationalism and ordered thought in the social, political, and philosophical realms; an aesthetic sensibility that aspires to a universal sense of truth and beauty. But the West has felt free both to evoke tradition as its guiding light *and* to innovate brilliantly; to accommodate slavery and freedom simultaneously; to esteem original thought and to persecute people who deviate from the norm. "Western" has different meanings depending on time, place, and circumstance.

What, then, is civilization? No definition has won universal acceptance, but certain elements are seen in almost every civilization.

Cities are crucial. Cities require complex social organizations that involve at least a minimal division of labor: Some people work in the fields, some in the home. Soldiers defend the city, and artisans provide its handcrafted goods. Governing institutions have a wide measure of acceptance and the wherewithal to enforce their wills. Cultures grow more complex and exhibit such traits as religious ideas and authorities; a literature and law that may be oral or written; monumental architecture, especially fortifications, palaces, and temples; and arts such as music, painting, and sculpture.

Civilization emerged in the West over a long time after about 3500 B.C. It appears that a slowly but steadily increasing population made it imperative to secure a predictable food supply. This need led to agriculture and animal husbandry, the taming of fields and flocks to the needs of a human community. The many processes involved in agriculture led to specialization of labor. The sharper definition of social and economic roles led to the delineation of gender roles. Communities defined certain tasks—government and war, for example—as essentially male, while reserving domestic responsibilities and some religious duties for women. The interests of self-sufficiency became subordinated to the needs of the community.

THE ANCIENT WORLD, CA. 3500–323 B.C.

HISTORIANS usually begin their accounts of Western civilization with the Sumerians and Egyptians because they were, between about 3500 and 3000 B.C., the first peoples to attain civilization within the orbit of the West.

Western Asia

Sumer lies in *Mesopotamia*, the land "between the rivers" Tigris and Euphrates. After the Sumerians, a succession of peoples in Mesopotamia itself—Akkadians, Babylonians, and Assyrians, for example—and many other peoples in the lands bordering Mesopotamia—Medes and Persians to the east, Hittites to the north, Phoenicians, Canaanites, and Hebrews to the west—also crossed the line that marks the beginnings of civilization.

All of these peoples are interesting and important in their own rights, but they concern the continuing course of Western civilization in one particularly important way: they were the cultural ancestors of the founders of the West, the Greeks and the Romans. The Greeks were a millennium behind them in developing civilization; the Romans were another millennium behind the Greeks. Western Asia (often called "the Middle East") contributed religious ideas, artistic norms, mathematical concepts, ways of reckoning time, and even the alphabet. Ideas, technologies, and practices from western Asia radiated far beyond the Greek and Roman worlds and helped spark the rise of civilization in Europe, where the Neolithic period (the "new stone" age, the time of carefully fashioned stone tools) gave way to civilization more slowly than in the Mediterranean world.

Egypt

The Greek historian Herodotus (480–425 B.C.) called Egypt "the gift of the Nile." Historical Egypt is a fertile strip of land, ranging from 5 to 15 miles wide, that hugs the Nile River along its 750-mile course. Whereas the Tigris and Euphrates flood irregularly, sometimes violently, the Nile usually floods annually and beneficently. Efforts to manage irrigation, grain production, and storage along the course of the river led to an early (just before 3000 B.C.) replacement of local autonomy by a unified monarchy under god-kings called pharaohs.

Under the pharaohs of the period that historians now call the "Old Kingdom" (2695–2160 B.C.), Egypt faced no foreign threats and built up its central institutions. The great monuments of this time, the pyramids—pharaonic tombs—symbolize the power, wealth, and security of Egypt. An invasion brought an end to the Old Kingdom, but the eventual overthrow of the invaders ushered in the Middle Kingdom (1963–1786 B.C.), a time of political innovation—pharaohs had to share power with aristocrats—and cultural stimulation from Mesopotamian sources. The Middle Kingdom yielded in turn to the New Kingdom (1550–1070 B.C.), when Egypt became an imperial state whose reach extended all the way to Mesopotamia. The treasures of Tutankhamon ("King Tut") exemplify the wealth and sophistication of this age. Imperial Egypt was eventually ground down in a series of wars with the Hittites, an Indo-European-speaking people who settled in Anatolia (present-day Turkey).

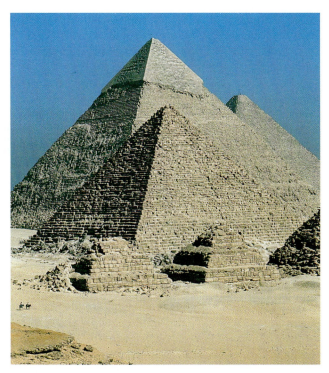

Great Pyramids of Giza   Royal funerary monuments of three Egyptian kings of the twenty-sixth century B.C., the pyramids symbolize the power and ambition of the Old Kingdom.
(*Michael Holford*)

Small Kingdoms and Great Empires

After the Egyptians and Hittites wore each other out, western Asia experienced a time of smaller, independent states. Phoenicia (roughly today's Lebanon) emerged as a major commercial power. The Phoenicians gathered up goods bought from Asia and Arabia via long-established overland trade routes and exchanged them for products acquired in their colonies all over the Mediterranean. Phoenician commerce thus initiated the cultural unification of the Mediterranean world.

Another small state of immense importance was the kingdom created by the Hebrews. Oral traditions and much later writings suggest that as early as 2000 B.C. a band of Hebrews under their tribal leader Abraham migrated from Mesopotamia to Palestine, on the eastern shore of the Mediterranean. Neither numerous nor united nor powerful, the Hebrews were often victimized by stronger neighbors. Around 1200 B.C. a group of Hebrews, slaves and workers in Egypt, cast off their bondage and returned to Palestine. This formative experience, remembered as the Exodus ("journey out" in Greek), forged a nation. For a century after 1000 B.C.,

Kings Saul, David, and Solomon built a state that was a match for its neighbors. Later, fierce rivalries among the Hebrews led to the disintegration of the unified monarchy, and the fragmented Hebrew communities were eventually conquered by powerful enemies.

The unique religious vision of the Hebrews makes them key founders of the Western tradition. The Jewish faith is very much alive today and serves as the basis for two other major religious traditions: Christianity and Islam.

The Hebrew religious vision is revealed to us in the Hebrew Bible, a large collection of writings that Christians call the Old Testament. The Hebrew Bible consists of historical writings on the unfolding relationship of the Hebrews with their God, legal books that lay down rules for personal conduct and social organization, prophetic books that express some of humanity's deepest spiritual insights, and wisdom literature that is full of humane guidance for daily life.

The central truth revealed by these Scriptures is exclusive monotheism. There is only one God. With this God the Hebrews have a covenant, a special pact. As long as the Hebrews do God's will by observing the Law and heeding His prophets, they will enjoy God's blessings and protection.

The period of small states was concluded by the creation, one after another, of ever larger states culminating in the Persian Empire (ca. 550–334 B.C.), which was centered in modern Iran. The Persians spread ideas and institutions through their vast empire, the largest the world had yet seen. The Persians were finally conquered by the armies of Alexander the Great (r. 336–323 B.C.), from Macedon in the northern Balkans.

This long succession of states and peoples led to the diffusion of many ideas and practices. We have remarked on one example already: the religious vision of the Hebrews. Another is a style of rulership that we call "theocratic." In a "theocracy," rulers are placed in office by, and are answerable only to, a god. In Mesopotamia rulers were generally believed to be the agents of the gods; in Egypt rulers were believed to *be* gods. In Alexander and his successors, notably Roman emperors, theocratic rulership had a long run. Egyptian ideas of a last judgment and of life after death circulated widely. Scientific and mathematical advances are another legacy of the ancient kingdoms and empires. In building huge monuments such as pyramids, in preserving human remains by mummification, in measuring fields, in observing the heavens, people in Mesopotamia and Egypt laid up a huge store of practical information from which later peoples, especially the Greeks, drew enthusiastically.

CLASSICAL ANTIQUITY, CA. 1000 B.C.–A.D. 284

CLASSICAL means normative, a standard by which to judge. In the nineteenth century, intellectuals were fond of saying to one another, "You were born in Greece." Such an assertion insisted that many cultural and aesthetic standards still prevalent in their own day had arisen in ancient Greece. So powerful has been the hold of Greece over architecture and sculpture, for example, that some modern movements have been deliberately "anticlassical." The Romans were the great interpreters of Greek culture, but they also added their own distinctive contributions to Western civilization.

Ancient Greece

The Greeks made fundamental—classical—contributions in two areas: political ideas and institutions, and culture. Homer's epic poems, the *Iliad* and the *Odyssey*, probably composed not long after 800 B.C. but the products of a long oral development, open before us the course of Greek political development. The poems purport to tell of Greece in the days of the Trojan Wars. Greek memory fixed those wars in about 1200 B.C., when undoubtedly the Greeks engaged in some nasty commercial squabbles with their neighbors in the Aegean basin. It is grand to imagine, with Homer, that the beauty of Helen of Troy launched a thousand Greek ships. It is unlikely, however, that it is historically accurate to think so.

The *Iliad* and the *Odyssey* profess to describe actual events in the Greek world in the Mycenaean period, so called because Mycenae was the greatest city of that time. Between about 1500 and 1200 B.C., several remarkable cities were built in the Greek lands by peoples who were the ancestors of the Greeks of the classical period. Before the Mycenaeans a remarkable culture had flourished, then faded, on the island of Crete. Historians call this culture "Minoan" after the legendary King Minos. But there is nothing legendary about the spectacular Minoan palaces, whose ruins are still impressive, or about the exquisite artistic remains of Minoan culture. The Minoan and Mycenaean periods played a key role in connecting the Greeks with the realms of western Asia and Egypt. The *Iliad*, after all, is a tale about a Greek expedition to Anatolia.

Homer sings of a world of kings and aristocrats. Huge armies are mustered on his pages; individual warriors are described in minute detail. A common soldier could be flogged for speaking in the presence of his betters. This regal, aristocratic society, whose leaders were *Eupatrids,* "well-fathered men," dominated Greece for centuries.

Slowly the polis, the city-state, the basic Greek political institution, began to emerge. The people of rugged, craggy Greece clustered in small territories; as a result, many independent poleis arose in a land smaller than most American states. Each polis had a central urban zone and an agricultural hinterland. Often the urban zone featured an easily fortified hill: an *acropolis.* The acropolis sheltered people in times of attack and served as a meeting place for the conduct of civic and religious affairs.

Many poleis outstripped the locally available food supplies and looked enviously at their neighbors' provisions. Weaker poleis had to see to their defenses just as stronger ones had to beef up their capacity for attack. This competition resulted in the expansion of political and social participation in the public life of the polis. The infantryman, known as the hoplite, gained a role in defending his city and then insisted on a role in its government. Some cities, most notably Athens, moved toward greater and greater participation until *demokratia,* the rule of the people, was achieved. In Athens, all adult male citizens could vote and hold any of the key offices in the city. Sparta, however, became a military juggernaut in which the rights of all were subordinated to the dictates of a small number of the oldest, most conservative citizens. Corinth, where large landowners invested in trade, became a commercial oligarchy. In all cases, expanded or redefined participation belonged only to men. Women were excluded from participation in political life. Yet in Sparta women exercised effective daily control over the private lands allotted to soldiers, and in Athens women played leading roles in public religious celebrations.

As their populations exceeded the available resources of their tiny homelands, many Greek cities exported surplus population to colonies all over the Mediterranean world. As well as defusing Greek tensions, these colonies spread Greek culture far and wide.

While they were creating their basic political institutions between about 750 and 500 B.C., the Greeks also began to reflect systematically on political organization. Indeed, much of our political vocabulary is Greek in origin. Politics, after all, is what people do publicly in a polis.

Although Athens invented democracy, most Greek political thinkers were hostile to democratic ideas. They argued that democracy elevated the rabble over the best citizens and permitted the masses to satisfy their immediate desires, cast aside restraint, and neglect the long-

The Parthenon
The temple of Athena Parthenos ("the Maiden") on the Athenian Acropolis, the Parthenon was dedicated in 438 B.C. The partially restored ruins symbolize the wealth, power, and greatness of classical Greece. *(William Katz/Photo Researchers)*

term needs of the community. In one way or another, every Greek political thinker addressed an issue that has been critical in Western political discourse ever since: How can a person reconcile personal interests with the needs of the community?

The second Greek achievement lies in the realm of culture—in art, architecture, literature, science, and philosophy. Generalizations are difficult, but it may be fair to say that the Greeks, or at least the elite among them, set out very early to pursue truth and beauty. The Greeks were not unique in this quest. What sets them apart is the way they defined their objectives.

To a Greek thinker, beauty existed in the balance, order, and harmony that seemed to underlie everything really good. Greek scientific writers looked for a single, unchanging substance behind everything in existence. Failing in this search, they looked for overarching theories capable of explaining everything. Failing in this, they explored the nature of thought and language to see what could be known and communicated. In relative terms, the Greeks added rather few concrete details to the huge fund of Mesopotamian and Egyptian discoveries. What the Greeks contributed was a vast mental framework designed to systematize and explain what is known. In Classical Greece we see the birth of both science and philosophy.

Greek literature is full of memorable characters who present the reader, or the theater audience, with dilemmas of conscience. Oedipus, the main character of *Oedipus the Tyrant* by Sophocles (ca. 495–406 B.C.), whom Shakespeare called "the most tragic of poets," kills his father and marries his mother. He has absolutely no idea that he has done so. Is he nevertheless guilty of a hideous offense? It is to Greek literature that we must turn for insights into the roles of women, for they were excluded

from formal, public positions. Antigone, the central character in Sophocles' *Antigone,* is one of the most memorable women in literature. She struggles courageously to reconcile the conflicting demands of political allegiance and family ties. What is justice; what does it mean to be just; is it possible to be just? Can a rule apply to one person alone, or must it apply to everyone? Do rules exist at all? Reading the best of Greek literature today evokes the same feelings it did then: gut-wrenching agony over life choices.

To look at a fine Greek statue or building is, first of all, to admire the astonishing technical skill that went into making it. Second, the viewer is moved by its beauty. Another look will usually prove disconcerting. The object in our gaze is *too* perfectly executed, *too* beautiful. It is like nothing we have ever seen, although it is vaguely like everything we see all the time. It is as if the object is meant less to remind us of things in this world than to provide a glimpse of a better, purer world.

Greek art opens up a vista on the greatest Greek philosophers. Plato (427–348 B.C.) distrusted the senses as guides to truth or reality. He believed that we are all prisoners of the world and of our human limitations. According to Plato, ultimate reality exists not here and now but in a transcendent world. In our world, and in this life, we can gain only hints of what really exists. His greatest pupil was Aristotle (384–322 B.C.), whose mania for classification has been the despair of many a biology student. Aristotle reminds us of the technical artistry of the Greek sculptor. For Aristotle, knowledge was possible in this world. But knowledge was the result of knowing what you wanted to find out, of working immensely hard to discover truth, and of living with the consequences of the truths you found.

Fame and success are not the same. Greek political ideas, institutions, and terminology have been famous for ages, but the Greeks were, finally, unsuccessful at politics. Only during the Persian Wars (490–479 B.C.) were the Greeks able to rally together, and even then they quarreled over strategy and leadership. Individual Greek states were notoriously unstable and violent, and most of the time the poleis of Greece found themselves forced to accept membership in leagues and alliances. Between 431 and 404 B.C., Sparta's Peloponnesian League and the Athenian Empire—an involuntary association of the Greek states that had fought against Persia—convulsed the whole Greek world in the Peloponnesian War.

Philip II of Macedon, an increasingly powerful and well-organized kingdom to the north of Greece, conquered the Greeks in 338 B.C. and bequeathed his prize to his remarkable son, Alexander the Great. After securing the Balkans, Alexander set off on a tour of military conquest unrivaled before his time. He conquered the Persian Empire and much more besides. His conquests ushered in a period that historians call "Hellenistic."

Hellenistic, the customary name for the period following Alexander's death, roughly 323 to 30 B.C., when Greek language and culture dominated the Mediterranean world, means "Greeklike," as opposed to *Hellenic,* "purely Greek," the term applied to the preceding period from about 750 to 323 B.C. Alexander's generals carved his vast empire into many smaller states that survived despite many struggles, until one by one they fell to Rome. Greek leaders and elites mixed with local populations of many traditions to produce a rich, international culture that was everywhere recognizably, but nowhere purely, Greek.

The expanding, fluid nature of Hellenistic culture and states provided unprecedented opportunities for women in commerce and in government. Unlike cities, which reserved offices to men, monarchies had courts in which women could be influential advisers and sometimes actual rulers. Cleopatra of Egypt (r. 51–30 B.C.) is the most famous but by no means the only powerful Hellenistic woman.

The Roman Republic and Empire

The Roman poet Horace (65–8 B.C.) once said that "Captive Greece took her captor captive." His clever epigram is an apt transition from Greek to Roman history. But what did he mean? First, to be sure, the Romans conquered Greece—and many more lands. Second, Greek culture deeply influenced the Romans, who in general were not as original and creative as the Greeks.

The Romans considered their history to have begun with the founding of Rome itself, an event that they dated to what we call 753 B.C. Actually, the historical Romans were in Rome's neighborhood long before that date, and Rome's familiar society and institutions arose long after it.

From 509 B.C., when the Romans believed that their Republic had been instituted, until 27 B.C., when that Republic was definitively transformed into a military monarchy, Rome was remarkably stable. That stability was partly institutional. Rome had several magistrates with differing degrees of power, responsibility, and prestige, and several representative institutions with varying areas of authority. All adult men participated in important but very different ways. In addition, Rome's stability was partly cultural. In society and politics, Rome was hierarchical and deferential in equal measure. Rome accorded responsibility for running the Republic to a small number of men. As in Greece, women in Rome were systematically excluded from public life. Roman literature depicts women as domestic and submissive.

Prominent Romans ruled through office and assembly and also through patronage and private influence. Leading Romans were firmly opposed to innovation. The only good ways were the old ways, they believed. A Roman speech almost always began with an appeal to the "way our ancestors would have done things." Thus, it took a long time for the Roman system to emerge, and it seemed unchanged and unchanging.

Slowly the Romans conquered their neighbors in Italy (509–265 B.C.). Then victory in wars (264–146 B.C.) against Carthage, an old Phoenician colony, gave Rome dominance in the western Mediterranean. Finally, a series of wars against the Hellenistic monarchies (200–31 B.C.) left Rome in control of the whole Mediterranean world. It is easy to appreciate the old saying, "All roads lead to Rome."

Rome's wars came at a high price. Political and social stability was destroyed as personal and imperial ambition became regular weapons in domestic politics. Generals came to count for more than statesmen. Vast wealth, new and unevenly distributed, fractured the old structures of social deference that had long organized Roman society. Great fortunes and shifting social realities also created unprecedented opportunities for women to influence public life through family politics and artistic patronage. The culture of the Hellenistic world, as Horace correctly saw, overwhelmed the earnest Romans, who were less bumpkinish than they pretended but less sophisticated than most of their neighbors.

The Republic collapsed in a century of civil wars. Augustus Caesar (r. 31 B.C.–A.D. 14) created a dramatically changed regime. He inaugurated a two-century-long period, the *pax Romana* (the Roman peace), that brought the Mediterranean world as close as it has ever come to unity. Peace and prosperity, good government, spectacular building projects, and a process of cultural diffusion now called "Romanization" also characterized the pax Romana.

Augustus took the title *Princeps* ("First Citizen"). The Augustan Principate rested on a few basic notions. Rome's ruler was now an emperor whose power depended on his control of the military. The Roman Empire was now less and less an exclusively Roman entity: People from all over Italy and from the provinces shared in the benefits of empire. Augustus and the emperors who succeeded him forged a partnership with local elites everywhere. For instance, the Herods of Judea are villains in the Christian Scriptures, but from the Roman point of view, they were loyal, pliable, competent servants. And they were hardly alone. One of the ways in which such people showed their loyalty to Rome was by adopting the trappings of Roman culture—that is, by Romanizing.

Although the Romans were less innovative than the Greeks, they were by no means uncreative. Roman architecture achieved heights of complexity and sophistication. Roman law remains influential to this day. Cities from England to Mesopotamia still reveal their Roman street plans, and highway systems all over Europe lie atop Roman roads. Roman writers were learned, technically expert, verbally adroit, and at their best they ranged from moving to hilarious. Virgil's *Aeneid*, the story of Aeneas, one of the defeated at Troy and the legendary founder of Rome, presents the archetypal Roman hero: strong, familial, humble, loyal, and, above all else, perseverant.

The third century A.D. brought the Augustan Principate and the classical order to a close. From one end of the Roman Empire to the other, both the forms and the feelings of classical literature vanished. Large-scale building ceased. New religions, perhaps capable of explaining the difficulties of the age, proliferated. One prominent historian speaks of an "age of anxiety." What happened?

First, as the Roman historian Tacitus dryly observed in the first century A.D., "the army made the emperor." And, we might add, unmade him too, with alarming frequency. Civil wars between military commanders competing for the imperial office became endemic. Civil strife undermined the empire's ability to meet military threats along its exposed frontiers. Military and civil unrest contributed to a loosening of the old ties between the imperial government and the provincial elites. The economy was disrupted by political turmoil and was further weakened by uncontrollable inflation. At the end of the third century, Rome's prospects looked grim.

Augustus of Prima Porta   Named for the place where it was found, this statue (early first century A.D.) depicts an idealized and heroic Augustus. Scenes of victory, peace, and prosperity—symbols of the Principate—decorate his breastplate.   *(Alinari/Art Resource, NY)*

THE WORLD OF LATE ANTIQUITY, 284–CA. 600

THE years from about 284 to 600, now usually called Late Antiquity, witnessed changes in the structure of Roman institutions, alterations in the composition and functions of the social and political elite, and the elaboration of a Christian culture and an undivided, universal—that is, catholic—church.

The Transformation of the Roman Empire

To preserve the empire, Diocletian (r. 284–305) and Constantine (r. 306–337) radically expanded the imperial bureaucracy and army. Constantine established a second capital for the empire at Byzantium on the Bosphorus, which he renamed after himself: Constantinople. These reforms were costly in several senses. They necessitated higher taxes and more vigilant tax collecting. Roman officials seemed more intrusive and, quite often, less honest. A larger army solved neither border problems nor political ones. The armies themselves were increasingly recruited from Germanic peoples living along the frontiers. Some of these people were loyal to Rome; others sought to profit from its weakness. Not only the legions but the military leaders in the fourth and fifth centuries were likely to be Germanic. These men were usually loyal and competent, but divided allegiance could be a problem for them in ways unknown to the sturdy Romans of old.

The greatest change in the political landscape of Late Antiquity can be seen on a map. In 300 the western half of the Roman Empire consisted of a number of provinces governed by a hierarchy of Roman officials. In 600 a number of Germanic kingdoms had replaced those provinces. One might suppose that Rome had "fallen," that the ancient world had ended. It is true that after 476 there were no more emperors in the western half of the empire. But a closer look at those supplanting kingdoms reveals some interesting continuities.

The earliest kingdoms were actually founded by Roman-Germanic collaboration, and their kings continued to cultivate close relations with the eastern Roman Empire headquartered at Constantinople. Kings covered themselves with Roman titles, adapted Roman public ceremonies, and acted like imperial magistrates. They issued laws and recorded documents in Latin and maintained, under their own authority, features of Roman local administration. Given that most Germanic kings were the descendants of late antique Roman military officers, it is unlikely that most people detected much difference between Roman and Germanic rule.

Who were these Germanic kings and their followers? The lands beyond the Rhine and Danube, the two rivers that formed Rome's northern frontier, held innumerable peoples with whom the Romans had long, complex relationships. Rome traded with, fought against, allied with, and recruited many Germanic peoples at one time or another. The Germanic peoples were confederations, not ethnic groups. "Frank," the name of one Germanic people, applies not only to persons who were Frankish but also to their relatives by marriage, clients, allies, defeated foes, and hangers-on. Such peoples created kingdoms by violent encounters and by peaceful settlement, by usurpation and by delegation. One might say that the kingdoms were Germanized and militarized versions of formerly Roman provinces. In other words, Rome provided the framework within which its own transformation took place.

The Triumph of Christian Culture

Continuity and change are also evident in the most important cultural transformation of Late Antiquity: the triumph of Christianity. Christianity arose in first-century Palestine among a dedicated band of followers of Jesus of Nazareth. Jesus, a Jewish teacher of great charisma and compassion, preached an uncompromising morality, a need for repentance, and preparation for a coming kingdom of God. Jesus's teachings were intimately connected to venerable strains in Jewish thought and life. His followers believed him to be the Son of God.

From unpromising beginnings among a minority sect of Jews in a small, poor province, Christianity rose by the end of the fourth century to become the dominant religion in the Roman world. Fundamental teachings, the basic message of Jesus as related in the New Testament books of Matthew, Mark, Luke, and John—four accounts of Jesus's life and teachings written a generation or two after his death—were critical to this success. Jesus's teachings were universal, addressed to men and women, people of every land, persons of every status.

Christianity spread initially through towns. In each town, communities of believers installed officials whose customary titles in English are *bishop, priest*, and *deacon*. Bishops—the word means "overseers"—gradually came to have administrative, moral, and intellectual responsibilities in their towns. They controlled the local church and its property, recruited and trained priests and deacons, disciplined heretics (dissenters from official doctrine), and preached. A growing Christian church adapted the administrative geography of the Roman Empire. Bishops from towns and provinces began to meet in councils to decide complex matters of theology and ordinary matters of Christian living.

Christians were at times persecuted, but in 314 Constantine granted Christianity legal equality with all other religions. By 400 the most eminent local personage in almost every town of the empire was the bishop. Bishops came from the same families that had long given Rome its greatest citizens. Following the lead of the bishops was not difficult for local populations. Leading people from the pulpit was easy for men accustomed to authority and respect.

Christians were invited both to change the world around themselves and also to flee that world and its temptations. The church's public institutions represented an effort to respond to the first of these invitations. Another institution, monasticism, responded to the second. All over the Roman world, groups of men and women settled as monks or nuns in communities dedicated to prayer, study, self-denial, and work. Monasticism attracted people from every region, class, and level of education. This powerful spiritual force was one of Late Antiquity's most enduring legacies.

Christianity touched the lives of women in a variety of ways. Church teachings held out two models to women. There was Eve, the eternal temptress, who had tricked Adam and cost humanity the joys of paradise. Then there was Mary, the holy, obedient, and exemplary mother of Jesus. Women were gradually denied clerical positions in the church but gained great prominence in monasticism. Generally, Christian teachings accorded women more respect and dignity than secular laws did.

The bishop of Rome attained special prominence. This status owed something to the doctrine of apostolic succession, according to which all bishops inherited the teaching authority of the apostles, the twelve most prominent original followers of Jesus. In the Roman version of this doctrine, Peter had been the leader of the apostles and Peter's successors, the bishops of Rome—they began to be called popes in the third century—were the leaders of the church as a whole. Roman prominence is also attributable to the connection between the popes and the city of Rome itself, the capital of the empire to which all roads led. Finally, papal leadership matured during bitter theological struggles in the Christian community. Popes routinely intervened on behalf of, or entertained appeals from, persons they supported. As the popes attained leadership and defined dogmas, they laid the foundations for the Roman Catholic Church.

The quarrels were many but tended to focus on two key issues: the problem of the Trinity and the person of Jesus. The majority of Christian thinkers argued that God was triune, three persons—Father, Son, and Holy Spirit—in one. Christian tradition also maintained that the second person of the Trinity, Jesus Christ, was true God and true man.

Between about 350 and 450, Christian thinkers all over the Mediterranean world addressed themselves to solving such theological problems, to explaining both the Jewish and the Christian Scriptures (which Christians call the Old and the New Testaments), and to defining practical rules for living. We call such thinkers "Church Fathers" and their age "patristic" (from *pater*, the Latin word for "father"). The most famous of the Latin Church Fathers was Augustine (354–430), a North African who became a professor of rhetoric and converted to Christianity as an adult. Augustine's writings chronicled his own spiritual quest and commented on the religious issues of his day.

The Church Fathers are among the most learned, prolific, accomplished, and influential writers in all of history. They were products of the Roman world, but they did not suppose, as Virgil had, that time would last only as long as Rome. For them, the source and goal of human existence was in heaven, not on earth.

MEDIEVAL CIVILIZATIONS, 600–1300

THE Roman world left not one but three heirs. The first comprised the Germanic kingdoms that replaced Rome's western provinces. The second was the eastern Roman Empire centered in Constantinople. The third was a surprising development that no one in Late Antiquity could have predicted: the emergence of the Islamic faith and the Muslim empire.

Islam and the Arabs

Islam arose in Arabia, a large, barren land in western Asia deeply influenced by all the currents of ancient culture but never wholly conquered by any ancient people. In 570 Islam's pivotal figure, Muhammad, was born in Mecca, a great commercial city. Tradition holds that when Muhammad was a young man, his spiritual sensibilities were awakened by visits from the archangel Gabriel, who commanded him to "recite" a holy text. That text revolved around one great truth: "There is no God but Allah, and Muhammad is his prophet."

Like many religious leaders, Muhammad gained both followers and foes. Enemies forced Muhammad to flee in 622 to Medina, a city about 200 miles from Mecca. There he gave full force to his religious and social vision. Before he died in 632, Muhammad saw that vision triumph in Mecca and throughout Arabia.

The faith of Muhammad is revealed in the Quran, a collection of Allah's revelations to the prophet. Muhammad's religion demands absolute surrender to Allah: *al-Islam*, "the surrender," whence the name of the faith. Like Judaism, Islam has two central components: faith and community. The faith is simple, direct, uncompromising. There is no God but Allah, the creator and ruler of all. Islam had no creeds, no statements of religious belief, and no hierarchical clergy. The community, the *umma muslima*, was the totality of those who had surrendered to Allah. Class, status, occupation, gender, ethnicity—none of these mattered at all.

After Muhammad's death, his followers rallied to the standard of the caliph, the successor to the prophet and commander of the faithful, and in a century created an empire that extended from France to the frontiers of China. That empire, the caliphate, centering on Arabia plus the ancient lands of Mesopotamia and Egypt, hugged the Mediterranean. Over time Muslim scholars reflected on the Judeo-Christian and the Greco-Roman heritages, and their writings proved influential when western Europeans discovered them in the twelfth and thirteenth centuries. As it expanded, the caliphate also absorbed rich cultural ingredients from Persia, India, Africa, and Asia.

Internal rivalries and external threats eventually pulled the caliphate apart. Spain broke away first, then a series of small states across North Africa, then Egypt, then parts of Anatolia. Caliphs sat on their jeweled thrones until 1258 while a succession of foreigners dominated the state. Byzantines, Italian merchants, and Turkish mercenaries were among the most prominent of the caliphate's external foes until the Mongols over-

Justinian and His Courtiers   This magnificent mosaic from Ravenna depicts Emperor Justinian in all his power and majesty.   *(Scala/Art Resource, NY)*

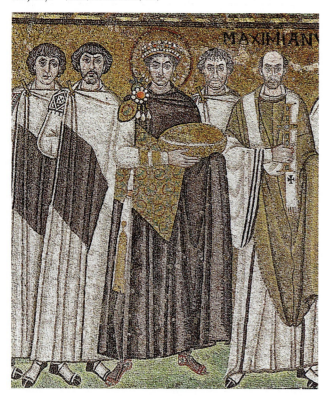

whelmed the caliphate in that year in their bid for world domination. A collection of peoples from the frontiers of Mongolia and China, the Mongols turned the Islamic world so that its back was to the Mediterranean and its face to Asia. Until then, the Islamic world had been very much a part of the West. Since that time, neither the Islamic world nor the West has been quite sure about their relationship.

The Byzantine Empire

As the western Roman Empire was being parceled into kingdoms, the eastern half survived almost intact. In the sixth century, the Roman emperor Justinian (r. 527–565), based in Constantinople, regained several of Rome's former western provinces, reformed the imperial administration, issued a major codification of Roman law, and regulated ecclesiastical affairs. In the next two centuries his successors created new military and administrative institutions to address Muslim threats in the east and Slavic threats in the Balkans.

In 726 Emperor Leo III (r. 717–741) issued the first major revision of Roman law since Justinian's. Leo's code, a drastically abbreviated version of Justinian's, provided a simplified, unified body of law for provincial judges in the empire. In religion, the Orthodox tradition of Christianity began clearly to emerge, based on the writings of the Greek Church Fathers, Greek forms of worship and church discipline, and a close partnership between the emperors and the patriarchs of Constantinople, the highest religious officers. For almost a thousand years this eastern incarnation of the Roman Empire, usually called the Byzantine Empire, preserved the Roman legacy.

In 867 a new and highly talented dynasty, the Macedonian, came to the throne in the person of Basil I (r. 867–886). Until 1025, rulers from this family expanded the empire's frontiers, carried out impressive legal and government reforms, and continued a close partnership with the Orthodox Church. This period proved the high point of Byzantine political, military, and diplomatic influence.

The years after 1025 brought short reigns, disputed successions, aristocratic and ecclesiastical factionalism, a bitter feud with the papacy in Rome over theology and worship, and, worst of all, military threats from the Turks. In 1071 the Byzantines suffered a devastating defeat by the Turks at Manzikert in central Anatolia. Appeals to western Europe for assistance brought not mercenaries to recapture Anatolia from the Turks but Crusaders intent on liberating the Holy Land—the Palestine of Jesus—from the Muslims. In 1204 a crusading army conquered Constantinople, and until 1261 a "Latin Empire" held sway in the east. The Byzantines eventually rallied, expelled the Latins, and restored independent rule. Down to the fall of Constantinople to the Turks in 1453, however, Byzantium was a shadow of its former self.

Western Europe

In Late Antiquity the Roman West had been divided among several Germanic kingdoms. Those that did not confront more powerful neighbors, that experienced reasonable religious harmony, and that had room to expand managed to succeed. Thus, the late antique heritage fell to the Franks in Gaul and the Anglo-Saxons in Britain.

By the middle of the eighth century, continental Europe was dominated by a single family whom we call "Carolingian" from *Carolus Magnus,* Charles the Great (or Charlemagne). Charlemagne's dynasty united France, the Low Countries, most of Germany, northern Italy, and northeastern Spain into a single empire that lasted in reality for a few generations—and in memory for a millennium—as "Christendom." In 800 Charlemagne was crowned emperor in Rome by the pope. By force of will the Carolingians imposed standards of worship, education, law, and institutions throughout Christendom. Their success was very uneven, but much of the similarity in the later history of the western European countries derives from their common Carolingian past.

In Britain, Germanic Anglo-Saxons from continental Europe jostled with local Celts, especially in Wales and Scotland. Anglo-Saxon, or English, Britain was moving toward unity, as were Wales and Scotland, until attacks by the Vikings. These seaborne raiders from Scandinavia provoked a crisis of authority in Britain that was resolved to the advantage of the central government only in Scotland. In 1013 and again in 1066, bands of Northmen conquered England. Bands of Vikings called Varangians founded the beginnings of a new state near Kiev in Ukraine. Vikings attacked the Continent too, but so did Muslims in the south and Magyars, the ancestors of the Hungarians, in the east. The Carolingian Empire, already weakened by struggles among Charlemagne's descendants, succumbed to these attacks and crumbled into a number of kingdoms and smaller political entities.

For more than two centuries social and political development was more creative at the local than at the central level. Powerful men (lords) forced lesser men (vassals) into bonds of dependence that we usually refer to as feudalism. Vassals pledged homage (honor), fealty (fidelity),

and service; lords promised maintenance and protection. To maintain their vassals, lords sometimes gave them fiefs—estates consisting of farms and peasants.

Between the collapse of the Carolingian Empire around 900 and the renewal of central authority around 1150, Europe experienced effective government only at the local level. In fact, counties, duchies, principalities, and cities displayed an amazing institutional creativity. The population of Europe expanded dramatically, perhaps doubling in two and a half centuries. Trade expanded everywhere. In a sense, Europe grew physically. New states emerged in the Celtic world (Ireland, Scotland, Wales), in Scandinavia (Denmark, Norway, Sweden), and in the Slavic regions (Poland, Bohemia, Serbia, Hungary, Bulgaria, Kievan Rus). The Crusades extended Europe's frontier to Muslim Palestine. People everywhere felled forests, drained marshes, and brought new land into cultivation.

Twelfth- and thirteenth-century Europe was marked by a series of struggles for authority between secular and religious rulers. If, as all seemed to agree, government existed to promote eternal salvation, who was to have final authority: the pope and the ecclesiastical hierarchy or the emperor and other secular rulers? No land in Europe escaped these battles between 1050 and 1300. The Catholic Church, with its elaborate administration, its sophisticated canon law, and its command of people's spiritual loyalties, won most of the early battles. Then, slowly, secular governments began to define their responsibilities in nonreligious terms and to treat churches as subordinate institutions. By 1300 the church was exhausted from decades of struggles with a variety of rulers, European society had become more secular, and public institutions were growing more effective. The advantageous position the church had enjoyed in, say, 1100 or 1200 had been reversed by 1300.

Central governments gained strength as kings promoted themselves through ceremonies, built up their financial resources, won key military victories, reduced great aristocrats to submission, and allied themselves to rising urban and commercial movements. But Europe was a complex place, and the governments were fragile. England, France, and Spain were headed toward centralization by 1300 but then suffered reverses and differed sharply in their basic institutional structures. Imperial and royal power collapsed in Germany. Italy remained disunited but its many urban communes produced regimes of infinite variety and robust creativity. In 1300 Europe was teeming in its political complexity.

European culture was likewise rich and complex. Latin culture was primarily religious culture, fostered by

Romanesque Interior, Saint Sernin, Toulouse   The interior space of Saint Sernin is elegant, high, and well-ordered. But its typical Romanesque effect—from "barrel" vaulting—is that of a tunnel. Massive piers support the gallery and roofing above.   *(Éditions Gaud)*

the church. The church needed educated clergy to carry out its tasks of preaching and teaching. Moreover, religious leaders were conscious of belonging to a rich intellectual tradition that needed to be mastered and transmitted.

Schools and libraries were found in cathedrals, bishops' churches, and monasteries. Monasteries preserved books and learning while serving as witnesses to a holy way of living. Many convents of nuns were also intellectual centers and places where women could attain a control over their lives that was denied them in the male world of lords and vassals. Gradually a new kind of religious intellectual establishment, the university, achieved prominence. Though changed in important ways since its twelfth-century origins, the university has

never lost its position as the paramount intellectual institution in the West.

Although medicine and law were important courses of study in some places, university teaching and research were focused primarily on the key texts of the Christian tradition. The approach to those texts was increasingly through the logic of the Greek philosopher Aristotle. Scholasticism is the name for this encounter between Greek logic and Christian revelation. Thomas Aquinas (1225–1274), prolific author, immensely learned scholar, and Paris professor, was the greatest of the Scholastics.

A vernacular culture flourished alongside the Latin culture of the Catholic Church. Literature in Welsh and Irish had appeared already in the seventh century; Old English literature, capped by the epic poem *Beowulf,* came only a little later. French literature produced an epic—*The Song of Roland*—around 1100, then romances and adventures. German literature preceded French but took longer to reach a high standard. Italian emerged last but was the first to produce a true masterpiece, Dante's *Divine Comedy* of the early fourteenth century. More and more literatures appeared, especially in Scandinavian and Slavic lands. In addition to imaginative literature, lawbooks, ordinary legal documents, and commercial texts were written in languages other than Latin.

Architecture produced two stunning leaps forward. In Romanesque (after 1050) and Gothic (after 1150) cathedrals, all existing forms were recombined in buoyant new styles that have lost none of their power to move and inspire. Romanesque façades saw the reappearance of large-scale sculpture, lost since antiquity, and freestanding sculpture reappeared. Gothic stained glass was one of medieval Europe's crowning achievements.

Medieval Europe remained a challenging place for women. Public power was generally reserved for men in a society that prized military qualities. Except in convents, church offices were confined to men, as were student and teaching positions in schools and universities. Nevertheless, on Europe's many expanding frontiers, where old conventions were observed less strictly, women had opportunities for social and political power. Bustling, innovative cities accorded women a wide range of occupations. Some women, such as the gifted theologian Hildegard of Bingen (1098–1179), made distinguished contributions to Latin literature, and a number of women, such as Marie de France (active ca. 1170), became prominent as vernacular authors. Women played key roles in the many new religious movements of the Middle Ages. The thirteenth-century Beguines made up the first religious movement created by and only for women in the history of Christianity.

FROM MEDIEVAL TO RENAISSANCE EUROPE, 1300–1500

THE biblical Book of Revelation depicts Four Horsemen of the Apocalypse: war, slaughter, famine, and death. Those grim riders trod hard on fourteenth-century Europe.

Crisis and Recovery

Old hostilities dragged France and England into the conflict now known as the "Hundred Years' War" (1337–1453), which, before it ended, drained the talent and treasure of many parts of Europe. This conflict was only one of the age's struggles. Trade wars rocked the Baltic and North Seas, religious and ethnic battles flared in the Holy Roman Empire (as the German Empire came to be called), Christian-Muslim struggles continued in Spain, peasants rebelled in France and England, and workers staged revolts in Flanders and Italy. Violence seemed to be the norm.

To all this slaughter must be added economic dislocation. Several problems combined to produce economic and social crisis. Population began leveling off in the thirteenth century. The weather turned foul. And in 1348 Europe was visited by an outbreak of bubonic plague that carried off perhaps one-third of the population and worked its cruelest ravages on the cities that were Europe's most creative, productive areas. The epidemic of 1348–1349 was only the first of many recurrences of the plague.

A sense of despair fell over a Christian society convinced that God was punishing it. But for what? Moralists complained about dissolute living, and ecclesiastical powers worried about heresy. Jews sometimes became scapegoats as people sought to blame others for their own misfortunes.

The church could not salve Europe's wounds because it too was going through deep struggles. By the end of the thirteenth century the papacy seemed focused more on political power than on spiritual leadership. From 1305 to 1378 the popes resided not in Rome but in Avignon, in the south of what is now France. They had settled there temporarily to settle some outstanding controversies with the French monarchy but scandalized people all over Europe by staying for three-quarters of a century. When the popes tried to return to Rome, the college of cardinals, the aristocrats of the church, split into factions. From 1378 to 1417 the Catholic Church suffered the Great Schism, as two or more men claimed to be the legitimate pope. The schism was healed and the pope restored to Rome only after a council proclaimed a new vision of church government: "conciliarism" maintained that the church was not a monarchy under the pope but a collegial body of all bishops. Churchmen argued for years over the implications of this pronouncement.

After surmounting these trials, western Europe began to recover in the fifteenth and early sixteenth centuries. France emerged from its long war with England with a greatly strengthened royal government that could raise armies, collect taxes, and control nobles. England suffered through a civil war after the Hundred Years' War but then, after 1485, began a long, steady process of political consolidation under the Tudor dynasty. Major compromises in 1356 provided the Holy Roman Empire with a formula not for unity but at least for stability. The Spanish monarchies grew stronger by the year. In Italy a profusion of independent cities deferred, by choice or by force, to Florence, Milan, or Venice.

The Renaissance

The years from 1300 to about 1550 were both constructive and destructive in the political and material realms but were boundlessly creative in the cultural realms. This was the Renaissance (from a French word meaning "rebirth"). Its pioneers were Italians, who believed that they were calling back to life the spirit, the ideals, of classical Greece and Rome. They sought out works of classical literature and combed through them for models of style and for long-lost gems of practical wisdom and guidance. Though by no means irreligious, Renaissance writers were more concerned with the ancient world, and their own world, than they were the next. We call them "humanists" because of their interest in the humane disciplines. The "study of humanity" (*studia humanitatis*) that was central to the Renaissance was grounded in the seven so-called liberal arts—grammar, rhetoric, logic, arithmetic, astronomy, geometry, and music—that had formed the core of Western education since antiquity. The "arts" were the skills or methods used by the "liberal"—literally, the free—in the conduct of their affairs in society. Armed with the liberal arts, the humanists sought beauty and harmony; they cultivated elegance in the spoken and written word. Their achievements in literature, art, and architecture represent for many the dawn of a new age.

"They," however, were mostly men. A great historian has asked whether women had a Renaissance at all.

The Pietà   Michelangelo sculpted three versions of Mary holding the crucified Jesus. This late, unfinished work reveals Michelangelo's desire to show the suffering of Christ. *(Scala/Art Resource, NY)*

Some women humanists have come to light, and the importance of vernacular writers such as Christine de Pizan (1364–1430) and Marguerite de Navarre (1492–1549) has long been acknowledged. But women's daily lives do not seem to have changed much during the Renaissance.

The Renaissance was disseminated from Italy—first by northerners who had studied in the south and then, after 1454, by printing, which made books and ideas more accessible than ever before. In northern Europe, Renaissance scholars turned to the sources of the Christian tradition—to the Scriptures and the Church Fathers—with the same zeal and scholarship that the Italians had applied to classical sources. Such study led some figures to harsh criticism of the institutional, intellectual, and moral failings of the late medieval Catholic Church.

GLOBALIZATION, RELIGIOUS REFORMATION, POLITICAL TRANSFORMATION, 1500–1560

AS the Renaissance was wending its way through European space and consciousness, other momentous changes began to appear. Spanish and Portuguese explorers and conquerors had begun building vast overseas empires in North and South America and in the Indian Ocean basin. The whole globe was being brought within the orbit of Western civilization. The European world was riven by religious differences that reflected old political and cultural divisions and generated new tensions. The late medieval state system was marked by ever larger empires and ever more intricate, and fickle, alliances.

Europe and the Wider World

A glance at a map of the world today will show that Europe is not especially well placed for global domination. It is smaller than other continents, its population is modest, and its material resources are unexceptional. One of the important questions in world history is why it was Europeans, of all peoples, who succeeded in exploring and exploiting the rest of the world.

Europeans long had had contacts with non-Europeans. From ancient times, trade routes running across Africa and Asia had brought the products of the whole world to Europe's markets. Occasional bursts of crusading ferocity or missionary zeal carried Europeans beyond their own frontiers. Travelers, such as the renowned Italian Marco Polo (1254–1324), were sometimes drawn by an irresistible urge to know what lay beyond the horizon. Nevertheless, most Europeans traveled little and knew almost nothing about the world.

In the fifteenth century an accumulation of factors changed forever Europe's place on earth. Travel literature aroused some people's curiosity. Real and imagined threats from the Turks fanned the remaining embers of crusading and missionary zeal. Above all, the Italian stranglehold on Mediterranean trade encouraged other nations to seek alternative commercial routes. New technologies for sailing and navigation made possible long voyages beyond the security of familiar coastlines. Better maps and charts and improved ship and sail designs—some of the latter borrowed from the non-European world—gave Europeans distinct advantages. The consolidation of powerful states such as Spain and, a century later, France and England put financial

The Holy Household   One of the most popular ideas among Protestants was that true religion should be taught and preserved in the Christian family, presided over by the father.   *(The Shakespeare Birthplace Trust)*

resources at the disposal of brave and ambitious seamen.

From modest explorations of the West African coast sponsored by the Portuguese royal family, European involvement with the rest of the world expanded to the creation of vast empires. By 1560 the Spanish had conquered southwestern North America, Central America, and South America, except for Brazil, which fell to Portugal. The Portuguese had established military and commercial bases in the Indian Ocean and the South China Sea. The Dutch would eventually contest Portuguese control of the seas and islands lying to the south of China, as well as land colonists in southern Africa and North America. Yet the Dutch presence in North America would pale into insignificance before the territorial acquisitions of France and England.

Did Europeans bring real benefits to the rest of the world, or were they merely cruel exploiters? How did the non-Western world influence the West? People continue to argue over these questions. What cannot be denied is that during the 1500s, Western civilization assumed a role in world history that it had never held before.

Religious Divisions

For hundreds of years after Charlemagne (r. 768–814), many people held up the ideal of Europe as "Christendom." Christianity was seen as a badge of citizenship in a world where the purpose of governments—indeed of organized societies—was to assist people in their quest for eternal salvation.

A truly Christian political order that transcended national boundaries never existed in the Middle Ages, but a fundamentally Christian society certainly did. The beliefs of ordinary people were not their own affair. Deviation from official beliefs brought swift punishment. "Correct" belief was nurtured, imposed, and reinforced in countless ways. Most schools were run by the church to promote religious learning and culture. The major turning points of life—birth, baptism, marriage, death— were attended by religious ceremonies. Celebrations, from royal feasts to humble village revels, were held on saints' days. Christianity, and churchmen, were literally and figuratively inescapable.

In the sixteenth century western Europe's religious life was sundered in unprecedented ways by a series of developments that are usually called the Protestant Reformation. The reformers shared fundamental beliefs. The first was that everything necessary for salvation had been revealed by God in the Bible; thus, the teachings of the Catholic Church were as nothing compared to the word of God. The second was that salvation resulted from faith in God and from God's grace; thus, good works and upright behavior were no guarantees of salvation. The name *Protestant* was coined in 1529 and has become a common designation for many groups of people who both dissented from the Catholic Church and embraced devout views of their own.

Protestant reformers such as the German Martin Luther (1483–1546) and the French-born John Calvin (1509–1564) sought to restore Christianity to the form they believed it had possessed in the first centuries of its existence. Royal reformers such as Henry VIII of England (r. 1509–1547) decreed the reform of the church in their lands. Fiery radicals wished to cast down the existing order of society in the name of a purified religion, and humble pietists sought to withdraw from all social and political entanglements. The Catholic Church corrected many of the abuses that had offended its critics but reaffirmed its basic teachings at the Council of Trent (1545–1563). There was no longer a possibility of attaining or enforcing a single pattern of belief. The Roman Catholic Church and Catholic rulers had permanently lost their control of England and Scotland, Scandinavia, the Netherlands, Switzerland, and northern Germany.

Many of the political and diplomatic controversies of the sixteenth century were related to religious issues. The English crown vastly strengthened itself by promoting religious reform, while bitter religious quarrels threatened more than once to destroy the French monarchy. Spain set itself up as the guardian of Catholic orthodoxy but usually lacked the power to impose its will in matters of religion. Since the Holy Roman emperors were Catholic, and most northern German rulers were Protestant, religious divisions worsened old antagonisms and generated new ones.

The Protestant Reformation did not dramatically alter the roles of women in European society or in the Christian churches. From the beginning, ambivalence marked women's participation in the Christian religion. On the one hand, the teachings of Jesus proclaimed the essential equality of women and men and opened heaven equally to both. On the other hand, both Protestant and Catholic Churches denied official and educational roles to women. The reformers were not social revolutionaries. They said, for example, that a housewife was as pleasing to God as a nun, but they refused to suppose that a woman could be a minister. And the Protestants' closing of convents denied some women the intellectual and administrative opportunities long available in those houses.

States and Empires

Europe's state system was dominated by two multiethnic empires. Through marriage alliances, the Habsburg family, originally from Switzerland, had established extensive claims: to Spain and its overseas empire, to parts of Italy and much of Austria, to the crown of the Holy Roman Empire, to Burgundy, and to the Netherlands. The Habsburg dominions literally surrounded France. The chief dynamic in western Europe was continuing rivalry between the Habsburgs and the Valois rulers of France. At the opposite end of Europe, the empire of the Muslim Ottoman Turks reached from central Asia to the gates of Vienna.

Other states in Europe sought a place alongside the greater ones. Scandinavia was dominated by Sweden, whose rulers continually entered the complicated politics of northern Germany. Those complications, and Sweden's opportunities, were directly tied to the fluctuating influence of the Holy Roman emperors. Prussia, a small Baltic state founded by German knights and adventurers, was hemmed in by other German states, Sweden, Lithuania, and, on occasion, Russia. In the fifteenth century, the Russians threw off the yoke of the Mongols and began expanding to the east, without ever losing sight of their western frontier with Germanic and Slavic Europe or their southern frontier with the Turks. The Turks threatened, or at least contemporaries perceived them to threaten, the Holy Roman Empire in the northern Balkans, Russia in the Black Sea region, and Italian merchants all over the Mediterranean. The traders of Venice and Genoa, in particular, were anxious about their old commercial superiority after the Portuguese and the Spanish opened vast new economic opportunities as a result of their commercial exploitation of the Americas, Africa, and the Indian Ocean basin.

In the fourteenth century the Florentine man of letters Francesco Petrarch (1304–1374) and his contemporaries, the earliest humanists, explicitly stated their feeling that they were unlike the people and times that had just preceded them and were instead similar to the ancient Romans. Petrarch and the others created the traditional tripartite division of Western history into ancient, modern, and the part in the middle—the so-called Middle Ages, or Dark Ages.

Scholars today do not think Petrarch was right either in his dismissal of the medieval period as the "Dark Ages" or in his claim that he and his contemporaries resembled the Romans. His argument reveals more about how people thought in his period than about the realities of the past. Modern historians do not see sharp breaks between historical periods. Historians now talk about continuity and change operating in tandem. Nevertheless, the old three-part division persists because it represents the major way in which we in the West have reflected on our history and because broad chronological divisions accommodate academic programs of study. In this volume, you will explore the possibilities and paradoxes, triumphs and tragedies, indeed the *Continuing Experiment*, of the modern phase of Western civilization.

Thomas F. X. Noble

CHAPTER 15

Europe in the Age of Religious Wars 1560–1648

THREE well-dressed gentlemen stand over a mutilated body; one of them holds up the severed head. Elsewhere sword-wielding men engage in indiscriminate slaughter, even of babies. Corpses are piled up in the background. This painting memorializes the grisly events of August 24, 1572. A band of Catholic noblemen accompanied by the personal guard of the king of France had hunted down a hundred Protestant nobles, asleep in their lodgings in and around the royal palace, and murdered them in cold blood. The king and his counselors had planned the murders as a preemptive political strike because they feared that other Protestant nobles were gathering an army outside Paris. But the calculated attack became a general massacre when ordinary Parisians, overwhelmingly Catholic and believing they were acting in the king's name, turned on their neighbors. About three thousand Protestants were slain in Paris over the next three days.

This massacre came to be called the Saint Bartholomew's Day Massacre for the Catholic saint on whose feast day it fell. Though particularly horrible in its scope, the slaughter was not unusual in the deadly combination of religious and political antagonisms it reflected. Religious conflicts were by definition intractable political conflicts since virtually every religious group felt that all others were heretics who could not be tolerated and must be eliminated. Rulers of all faiths looked to divine authority and religious institutions to uphold their power.

In the decades after 1560 existing political tensions contributed to instability and violence, especially when newly reinforced by religious differences. Royal governments continued to consolidate authority, but resistance to royal power by provinces, nobles, or towns accustomed to independence now might have a religious sanction.

The Saint Bartholomew's Day Massacre.
(Musée Cantonal des Beaux-Arts, Lausanne)

Economic Change and Social Tensions

Imperial Spain and the Limits of Royal Power

Religious and Political Conflict in France and England

Religious and Political Conflict in Central and Eastern Europe

Writing, Drama, and Art in an Age of Upheaval

Warfare over these issues had consumed the Holy Roman Empire in the first half of the sixteenth century. The conflict had now spilled over into France and the Netherlands and threatened to erupt in England. In the early seventeenth century the Holy Roman Empire once again was wracked by a war simultaneously religious and political in origin. Regardless of its roots, warfare itself had become more destructive than ever before thanks to innovations in military technology and campaign tactics. Tensions everywhere were also worsened by economic changes, especially soaring prices and grinding unemployment.

A period of tension, even extraordinary violence, in political and social life, the era of the late sixteenth and early seventeenth centuries was also distinguished by great creativity in some areas of cultural and intellectual life. The plays of Shakespeare, for example, mirrored the passions but also reflected on the dilemmas of the day and helped to analyze Europeans' circumstances with a new degree of sophistication.

QUESTIONS TO CONSIDER

- How did ordinary people cope with the economic stresses of these decades?

- In what ways was the most powerful state of the era—Spain—exceptional among western European monarchies, and in what ways was it typical of them?

- Why did war break out again in the Holy Roman Empire, and what was the significance of the conflict?

- In what ways do the literature and art of this period reflect the political, social, and religious tensions of the age?

TERMS TO KNOW

price revolution	Elizabeth I
gentry	Puritans
Philip II	Thirty Years' War
the Armada	Peace of Westphalia
Huguenots	Ivan IV, the "Terrible"
Edict of Nantes	baroque

ECONOMIC CHANGE AND SOCIAL TENSIONS

RELIGIOUS strife, warfare, and economic change disrupted the everyday lives of whole communities as well as individuals in the late sixteenth and early seventeenth centuries. Wars were devastating to many areas of western Europe and contributed to especially severe economic decline in parts of the Low Countries (the Netherlands), France, and the Holy Roman Empire. But other factors, most notably a steady rise in prices, also played a role in the dramatic economic and social changes of the century after 1550. A series of economic changes altered power relations in cities, in the countryside, and in the relationship of both to central governments. Ordinary people managed their economic difficulties in a variety of ways: they sought new sources of work; they protested against burdensome taxes; sometimes they found scapegoats for their distress among their neighbors.

Economic Transformation and the New Elites

The most obvious economic change was an unrelenting rise in prices, which resulted in the concentration of wealth in fewer and fewer hands. Sixteenth-century observers attributed rising prices to the inflationary effects of the influx of precious metals from Spanish territories in the New World. Historians now believe that European causes may also have helped trigger this "price revolution." Steady population growth caused a relative shortage of goods, particularly food, and the result was higher prices. Both the amount and the effect of price changes were highly localized, depending on factors such as the structure of local economies and the success of harvests. Between 1550 and 1600, however, the price of grain may have risen between 50 and 100 percent, and sometimes more, in cities throughout Europe—including eastern Europe, the breadbasket for growing urban areas to the west. Wages did not keep pace with prices; historians estimate that wages lost between one-tenth and one-fourth of their value by the end of the century. The political and religious struggles of the era thus took place against a background of increasing want, and economic distress was often expressed in both political and religious terms.

These economic changes affected the wealthy as well as the poor. During this period monarchs were making new accommodations with the hereditary aristocracy—with the Crown usually emerging stronger, if only through concessions to aristocrats' economic interests. Underlying this new symbiosis of monarchy and traditional warrior-nobles were the effects of the widespread economic changes. These changes would eventually blur lines between the old noble families and the new elites and would simplify power relationships within the state. Conditions in the countryside, where there were fewer resources to feed more mouths, grew less favorable. But at the same time, more capital became available to wealthy urban or landholding families to invest in the countryside, by buying land outright on which to live like gentry or by making loans to desperate peasants. This capital came from profits from expanded production and trade and was also an effect of the scarcity of land as population and prices rose. Enterprising landholders raised ground rents wherever they could, or they converted land to the production of wool, grain, and other cash crops destined for distant markets.

As a result, a stratum of wealthy, educated, and socially ambitious "new gentry," as these families were called in England, began growing and solidifying. Many of the men of these families were royal officeholders. Where the practice existed, many bought titles outright or were granted nobility as a benefit of their offices. They often lent money to royal governments. The monumental expense of wars made becoming a lender to government, as well as to individuals, an attractive way to live off personal capital.

No one would have confused this up-and-coming gentry with warrior-aristocrats from old families, but the social distinctions between them are less important (to us) than what they had in common: legal privilege, the security of landownership, a cooperative relationship with the monarchy. Monarchs deliberately favored the new gentry as counterweights to independent aristocrats.

City governments also changed character as wealth accumulated in the hands of formerly commercial families. Town councils became dominated by successive generations of privileged families, now more likely to live from landed than from commercial wealth. By the beginning of the seventeenth century traditional guild control of government had been subverted in many places. Towns became more closely tied to royal interests by means of the mutual interests of Crown and town elites.

CHRONOLOGY

1556–1598	Reign of Philip II
1558–1603	Reign of Elizabeth I
1559	Act of Supremacy (England)
1562–1598	Religious wars in France
1565	Netherlands city councils and nobility ignore Philip II's law against heresy
1566	Calvinist "iconoclastic fury" begins in the Netherlands
1567	Duke of Alba arrives in the Netherlands
1571	Defeat of Turkish navy at Lepanto
1576	Sack of Antwerp
1579	Union of Utrecht
1588	Defeat of Spanish Armada
1589–1610	Reign of Henry IV
1598	Edict of Nantes (France)
1609	Truce between Spain and the Netherlands is declared
1618–1648	Thirty Years' War
1620	Catholic victory at Battle of White Mountain
1621	Truce between Spain and the Netherlands expires; war between Spain and the Netherlands begins
1629	Peace of Alais
1631	Swedes under Gustav Adolf defeat imperial forces
1635	Peace of Prague
1640–1653	"Long Parliament" in session in England
1648	Peace of Westphalia

The long medieval tradition of towns serving as independent corporate bodies had come to an end.

Economic Change and the Common People

The growth of markets around Europe and in Spanish possessions overseas, as well as population growth within

Europe, had a marked effect on patterns of production and the lives of artisans and laborers. Production of cloth on a large scale for export, for example, now required huge amounts of capital—much more than a typical guild craftsman could amass. Cloth production was increasingly controlled by new investor-producers with enormous resources and access to distant markets. These entrepreneurs bought up large amounts of wool and hired it out to be cleaned, spun into thread, and woven into cloth by wage laborers in urban workshops or by piece-workers in their homes. Thousands of women and men in the countryside around urban centers helped to support themselves and their families in this way.

The new entrepreneurs had sufficient capital entirely to bypass guild production. In towns guilds still regulated most trades but could not accommodate the numbers of artisans who sought to join them. Fewer and fewer apprentices and journeymen could expect to become master artisans. The masters began to treat apprentices virtually as wage laborers, at times letting them go during slow periods. The household mode of production, in which apprentices and journeymen had worked and lived side by side with the master's family, also began to break down, with profound economic, social, and political consequences.

One of the first reflections of the dire circumstances faced by artisans was an attempt to reduce competition at the expense of the artisans' own mothers, sisters, daughters, and sons. Increasingly, widows were forbidden to continue practicing their husbands' enterprises, though they headed from 10 to 15 percent of households in many trades. Women had traditionally learned and practiced many trades but rarely followed the formal progress from apprenticeship to master status. A woman usually combined work of this kind with household production, with selling her products and those of her husband, and with bearing and nursing children. Outright exclusion of women from guild organization appeared as early as the thirteenth century but now began regularly to appear in guild statutes. In addition, town governments tried to restrict women's participation in work such as selling in markets, which they had long dominated. Even midwives had to defend their practices, even though as part of housewifery women were expected to know about herbal remedies and practical medicine. Working women thus began to have difficulty supporting themselves if single or widowed and difficulty supporting their children. In the changing position of such women we can see the distress of the entire stratum of society that they represent.

Wealth in the countryside was also becoming more stratified. Population growth caused many peasant farms to be subdivided for numerous children, creating tiny plots that could not support the families who lived on them. Countless peasants lost what lands they had to wealthy investors—many of them newly wealthy gentry—who lent them money for renting more land or for purchasing seed and tools, and then reclaimed the land when the peasants failed to repay. Other peasants were simply unable to rent land as rents rose. To survive, some sought work as day laborers on the land of rich landlords or more prosperous farmers. But with the shrinking opportunities for farming, this option became less feasible. Many found their way to cities, where they swelled the ranks of the poor. Others, like some of their urban counterparts, coped by becoming part of the newly expanding network of cloth production, combining spinning and weaving with subsistence farming. However, one bad harvest might send them out on the roads begging or odd-jobbing; many did not long survive such a life.

In eastern Europe peasants faced other dilemmas, for their lands had a different relationship to the wider European economy. The more densely urbanized western Europe, whose wealth controlled the patterns of trade, sought bulk goods, particularly grain, from eastern Germany, Poland, and Lithuania. Thus there was an economic incentive for landowners in eastern Europe to bind peasants to the land just as the desire of their rulers for greater cooperation had granted the landlords more power. Serfdom now spread in eastern Europe, while precisely the opposite condition—a more mobile labor force—grew in the West.

Coping with Poverty and Violence

The common people of Europe did not submit passively to either the economic difficulties or the religious and political crises of their day. Whatever their religion, common people took the initiative in attacking members of other faiths to rid their communities of them. Heretics were considered to be spiritual pollution that might provoke God's wrath, and ordinary citizens believed that they had to eliminate heretics if the state failed to do so. Common people, as well as elites and governments, were thus responsible for the violence that sometimes occurred in the name of religion.

Ordinary people fought in wars not only from conviction but also from the need for self-defense and from economic choice. It was ordinary people who defended the walls of towns, dug siege works, and manned artillery batteries. Although nobles remained military leaders, armies consisted mostly of infantry made up of common people, not mounted knights. Women were part of armies, too. Much of the day-to-day work of finding food and firewood, cleaning guns, and endlessly repairing inadequate clothing was done by women looking after their husbands and lovers among the troops.

Many men joined the armies and navies of their rulers because, given the alternatives, the military seemed a reasonable way of life. Landless farm hands, day laborers, and out-of-work artisans found the prospect of employment in the army attractive enough to outweigh the dangers of military life. Desertion was common; nothing more than the rumor that a soldier's home village was threatened might prompt a man to abandon his post. Battle-hardened troops could threaten their commanders not only with desertion but with mutiny. A mutiny of Spanish soldiers in 1574 was a well-organized affair, for example, somewhat like a strike. Occasionally mutinies were brutally suppressed; more often they were successful and troops received some of their back wages.

Townspeople and country people participated in riots and rebellions to protest their circumstances when the situation was particularly dire or when other means of action had failed. The devastation of religious war led to both peasant rebellions and urban uprisings. Former soldiers, prosperous farmers, or even noble landlords whose economic fortunes were tied to peasant profits might lead rural revolts. Urban protests could begin spontaneously when new grievances worsened existing problems. In 1585 food riots in Naples were provoked not simply by a shortage of grain but also by a government decision to raise the price of bread during the shortage. Rebels sometimes seized property—for example, they might distribute looted bread among themselves—and occasionally killed officials. Their protests rarely generated lasting political change and were usually brutally quashed.

Governments at all levels tried to cope with the increasing problem of poverty by changing the administration and scale of poor relief. In both Catholic and Protestant Europe caring for the poor became more institutionalized and systematic, and more removed from religious impulses. In the second half of the sixteenth century, governments established public almshouses and poorhouses to dispense food or to care for orphans or the destitute in towns throughout Catholic and Protestant Europe. Initially these institutions reflected an optimistic

Soldiers and Civilians   This contemporary painting of a military camp illustrates the presence of women and even children among the troops. Common people were the majority of combatants in wartime.   *(Kunsthistorisches Museum, Vienna/Art Resource, NY)*

vision of an ideal Christian community attentive to material want. But by 1600 the charitable distribution of food was accompanied by attempts to distinguish "deserving" from "undeserving" poor, by an insistence that the poor work for their ration of food, and even by an effort to compel the poor to live in almshouses and poorhouses.

These efforts were not uniformly successful. Begging was outlawed by Catholic and Protestant city governments alike, but never thoroughly suppressed. Catholic religious orders and parishes often resisted efforts at regulating their charitable work—even when they were imposed by Catholic governments. Nonetheless, the trend was clear. From viewing poverty as a fact of life and as an occasional lesson in Christian humility, European elites were beginning to see it as a social problem. And they saw the poor as people in need of control and institutional discipline.

The Hunt for Witches

Between approximately 1550 and 1650 Europe saw a dramatic increase in the persecution of women and men for witchcraft. Approximately one hundred thousand people were tried and about sixty thousand executed. The surge in witch-hunting was closely linked to communities' religious concerns and also to the social tensions that resulted from economic difficulties.

Certain types of witchcraft had long existed in Europe. So-called black magic of various kinds—one peasant casting a spell on another peasant's cow—had been common since the Middle Ages. What now made the practice seem particularly menacing, especially to elites, were theories linking black magic to Devil worship. Catholic leaders and legal scholars began to advance such theories in the fifteenth century, and by the late sixteenth century both Catholic and Protestant elites viewed a witch not only as someone who might cast harmful spells but also as a heretic.

The impetus for most individual accusations of witchcraft came from within the communities where the "witch" lived—that is, from common people. Usually targeted were solitary or unpopular people whose difficult relationships with fellow villagers made them seem likely sources of evil. Often such a person had practiced black magic (or had been suspected of doing so) for years, and the villagers took action only when faced with a community crisis, such as an epidemic.

The majority of accused witches were women. Lacking legal, social, and political resources, women may have been more likely than men to use black magic for self-protection or advancement. Women's work often made them vulnerable to charges of witchcraft since families'

food supplies and routine medicines passed through women's hands. The deaths of young children or of domestic animals, such as a milk cow, were among the most common triggers for witchcraft accusation. The increase in poverty during the late sixteenth and early seventeenth centuries made poor women frequent targets of witch-hunts. It was easier to find such a woman menacing—and to accuse her of wrongdoing—than to feel guilty because of her evident need.

Both Christian dogma and humanistic writing portrayed women as morally weaker than men and thus more susceptible to the Devil's enticements. Writings on witchcraft described Devil worship in sexual terms, and the prosecution of witches had a voyeuristic, sexual dimension. The bodies of accused witches were searched for the "Devil's mark"—a blemish thought to be Satan's imprint. In some regions women accounted for 80 percent of those prosecuted and executed. A dynamic of gender stereotyping was not always at work, however; in other regions prosecutions were more evenly divided between men and women, and occasionally men made up the majority of those accused.

Because they were often prompted by village disasters or tragedies, individual accusations of witchcraft increased in these decades in response to the crises that beset many communities. In addition, isolated accusations often started localized frenzies of active hunting for other witches. Dozens of "witches" might be identified and executed before the whirlwind subsided. These more widespread hunts were driven in part by the anxieties of local elites about disorder and heresy and were facilitated by contemporary legal procedures that they applied. These procedures permitted lax rules of evidence and the use of torture to extract confessions. Torture or the threat of torture led most of those accused of witchcraft to "confess" and to name accomplices or other "witches." In this way a single initial accusation could lead to dozens of prosecutions. In regions where procedures for appealing convictions and sentences were fragile or nonexistent, witch-hunts could expand with alarming speed. Aggressive hunts were common, for example, in the small principalities and imperial cities of the Holy Roman Empire, which were largely independent of higher political authority. (See the box "Reading Sources: A City Official Worries About Witch-Hunting.")

The widespread witch-hunts virtually ended by the late seventeenth century, in part because the intellectual energies of elites shifted from religious to scientific thought. The practice of witchcraft continued among common folk, although accusations of one neighbor by another never again reached the level of these crisis-ridden decades.

READING SOURCES

A City Official Worries About Witch-Hunting

In this letter written in 1629, the chancellor to the prince-bishop of the German city of Würzburg confides to a friend his doubts about the wisdom of zealous witch-hunting. Note that he mentions the deaths of many young people and many members of the elite. The persecutions seem to have taken on a life of their own. Note that the chancellor's revulsion at the effects of witch-hunting have not yet led him to reject the whole notion of witchcraft, however.

As to the affair of the witches . . . it has started up afresh, and no words can do justice to it. Ah, the woe and misery of it—there are still four hundred in the city, high and low, of every rank and sex . . . so strongly accused that they may be arrested at any hour. It is true that, of the people of my Gracious Prince here, some out of all the offices and faculties must be executed: clerics, elected councilors and doctors, city officials . . . several of whom [you] know. There are law students to be arrested. The Prince-Bishop has over forty students who are soon to be pastors; among them thirteen or fourteen are said to be witches. . . . The notary of our Church consistory, a very learned man, was yesterday arrested and put to the torture. In a word, a third part of the city is surely involved. The richest, most attractive, most prominent of the clergy are already executed. A week ago a maiden of nineteen was executed, of whom it is everywhere said that she was the fairest in the whole city, and was held by everybody a girl of singular modesty and purity. . . . To conclude this wretched matter, there are children of three or four years . . . who are said to have had intercourse with the Devil. I have seen put to death children of seven, promising students of ten, twelve, fourteen and fifteen. Of the nobles—but I cannot and must not write more of this misery. . . .

P.S. Though there are many . . . terrible things happening it is beyond doubt that, at a place called the Fraw-Rengberg, the Devil in person, with eight thousand of his followers, held an assembly and celebrated mass before them all. . . . There took place not only foul but most horrible and hideous blasphemies, whereof I shudder to write.

Source: Alan C. Kors and Edward Peters, eds., *Witchcraft in Europe, 1100–1700: A Documentary History* (Philadelphia: University of Pennsylvania, 1972), pp. 251–252. Reprinted by permission of the University of Pennsylvania Press.

Imperial Spain and the Limits of Royal Power

To contemporary observers, no political fact of the late sixteenth century was more obvious than the ascendancy of Spain. Philip II (r. 1556–1598) ruled Spanish conquests in the New World as well as wealthy territories in Europe, including the Netherlands and parts of Italy. Yet imperial Spain did not escape the political, social, and religious turmoil of the era. Explosive combinations of religious dissent and political disaffection led to revolt against Spain in the Netherlands. This conflict revealed the endemic tensions of sixteenth-century political life: nobles, towns, and provinces trying to safeguard remnants of medieval autonomy against efforts at greater centralization—with the added complications of economic strain and religious division. The revolt also demonstrated the material limits of royal power, since even with treasure from the American conquests pouring in, Philip could at times barely afford to keep armies in the field. As American silver dwindled in the seventeenth century, Philip's successors faced severe financial and political strains even in their Spanish domains.

The Revolt of the Netherlands

Philip's power stemmed in part from the far-flung territories he inherited from his father, the Habsburg king of Spain and Holy Roman emperor Charles V: Spain, the Low Countries (the Netherlands), the duchy of Milan, the kingdom of Naples, the conquered lands in the Americas, and the Philippine Islands in Asia. (Control of Charles's Austrian lands had passed to his brother, Ferdinand, Philip's uncle; see Map 15.1.) Treasure fleets bearing precious metals from the New World began to reach Spain regularly during Philip's reign. Spain was now the engine powering a trading economy unlike any that had existed

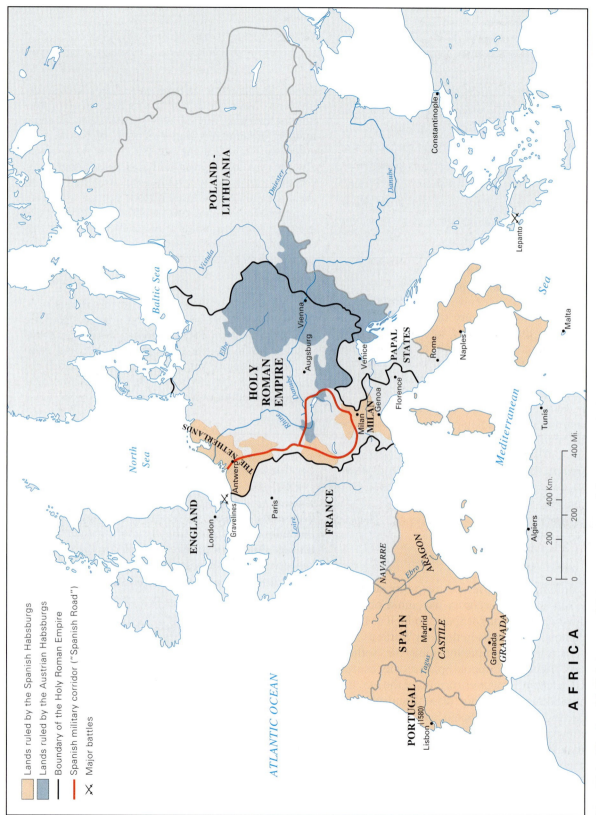

Map 15.1 The Spanish Habsburgs and Europe, ca. 1556 Philip II's control of territories in northern Italy permitted the overland access of Spanish troops to the Netherlands and heightened the Spanish threat to France. Lands bordering the western Mediterranean made the sea a natural sphere of Spanish influence as well. Habsburg lands in central Europe were controlled after 1556 by Charles V's brother Ferdinand and his descendants.

The City of Antwerp   Antwerp, in the southern Netherlands, was the point of sale for Portuguese spices brought around Africa from India; the selling and transshipping center for Baltic goods, including timber, fur, and grain; and the source for manufactured goods such as cloth.   *(Musées royaux des Beaux-Arts de Belgique)*

in Europe before. To supply its colonies Spain needed timber and other shipbuilding materials from the hinterlands of the Baltic Sea. Grain from the Baltic fed the urban populations of Spain (where wool was the principal cash crop) and the Netherlands, while the Netherlands, in turn, was a source of finished goods, such as cloth. The major exchange point for all of these goods was the city of Antwerp in the Netherlands, the leading trading center of all of Europe by 1550.

The Netherlands were the jewel among Philip's European possessions. These seventeen provinces (constituting mostly the modern nations of Belgium and the Netherlands) had been centers of trade and manufacture since the twelfth century. In the fourteenth and fifteenth centuries they had enjoyed political importance and a period of cultural innovation under the control of the dukes of Burgundy. By the time Philip inherited the provinces from his father, a sort of federal system of government had evolved to accommodate the various centers of power. Each province had an assembly (Estates) in which representatives of leading nobility and towns authorized taxation, but each also acknowledged a central administration in Brussels that represented Philip. Heading the council of state in Brussels was a governor-general, Philip's half sister, Margaret of Parma.

Philip's clumsy efforts to adjust this distribution of power in his favor pushed his subjects in the Netherlands into revolt. Though conscientious to a fault, Philip was a rigid, unimaginative man. Born and raised in Spain, he had little real familiarity with the densely populated, linguistically diverse Netherlands, and he never visited there after 1559. Early in Philip's reign, tensions in the Netherlands arose over taxation and Spanish insistence on maintaining tight control. Bad harvests and commercial disruptions occasioned by wars in the Baltic region in the 1560s depressed the Netherlands' economy and made it difficult for the provinces to pay taxes demanded by Spain. When the Peace of Cateau-Cambrésis° of 1559

Cateau-Cambrésis (kah-toe kam-bray-SEE)

Philip II in 1583 Dressed in the austere black in fashion at the Spanish court, Philip holds a rosary and wears the Order of the Golden Fleece, an order of knighthood, around his neck. At age 56 Philip has outlived four wives and most of his children. *(Museo del Prado, Madrid)*

brought an end to the long struggle between the Habsburgs and the Valois° kings of France, the people of the Netherlands had reason to hope for lower taxes and reduced levels of Spanish control, yet neither was forthcoming. Indeed, Philip had named to the council of state officials who were Spaniards themselves or had close ties to the Spanish court, bypassing local nobles who had fought for Philip and his father before 1559 and who expected positions of influence in his government.

Philip only added to the economic and political discontent by unleashing an invigorated repression of heresy. Unlike his father, Philip directed the hunt for heretics not just at lower-class dissenters but also at well-to-do Calvinists—followers of the French Protestant religious reformer John Calvin—whose numbers were considerable. Punishment for heresy now included confiscation of family property along with execution of the individ-

ual. By 1565 municipal councils in the Netherlands were routinely refusing to enforce Philip's religious policies, believing that urban prosperity—as well as their personal security—depended on restraint in the prosecution of heresy. Leading nobles also stopped enforcing the policies on their estates.

Encouraged by greater tolerance, Protestants by 1566 had begun to hold open-air meetings and attract new converts in many towns. In a series of actions called the "iconoclastic fury," townsfolk around the provinces stripped Catholic churches of the relics and statues deemed idolatrous by Calvinist doctrine. At the same time, reflecting the economic strain of these years, some townsfolk rioted to protest the price of bread. One prominent nobleman warned Philip, "All trade has come to a standstill, so that there are 100,000 men begging for their bread who used to earn it . . . which is [important] since poverty can force people to do things which otherwise they would never think of doing."[1]

In early 1567 armed bands of Calvinist insurgents seized two towns in the southern Netherlands by force of arms in hopes of stirring a general revolt that would secure freedom of worship. Margaret of Parma quelled the uprisings by rallying city governments and loyal nobles, now fearful for their own property and power. But by then, far away in Spain, a decision had been made to send in the Spanish duke of Alba with an army of ten thousand men.

Alba arrived in August 1567 and, to bolster his own shaky standing at the Spanish court, acted more like a conqueror than a peacemaker. He billeted troops in friendly cities, established new courts to try rebels, arrested thousands of people, executed about a thousand rebels (including Catholics as well as prominent Protestants), and imposed heavy new taxes to support his army. Thus Alba repeated every mistake of Spanish policy that had triggered rebellion in the first place.

Margaret of Parma resigned in disgust and left the Netherlands. Protestants from rebellious towns escaped into exile, where they were joined by nobles who had been declared traitors for resisting Alba's extreme policies. The most important of these was William of Nassau°, prince of Orange (1533–1584), whose lands outside the Netherlands, in France and the Holy Roman Empire, lay beyond Spanish reach and so could be used to finance continued warfare against Spain. A significant community with military capability began to grow in exile.

In 1572 ships of exiled Calvinist privateers known as the "Sea Beggars" began preying on Spanish shipping and coastal fortresses from bases in the northern provinces.

Valois (val-WAH)

Nassau (NAS-saw)

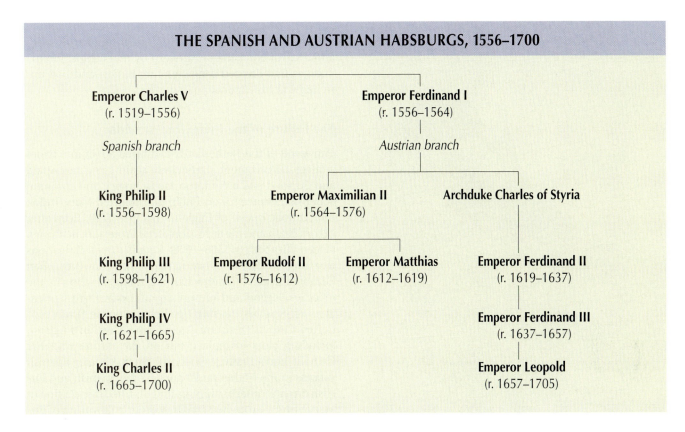

THE SPANISH AND AUSTRIAN HABSBURGS, 1556–1700

Emperor Charles V (r. 1519–1556)

Spanish branch

Emperor Ferdinand I (r. 1556–1564)

Austrian branch

King Philip II (r. 1556–1598)

Emperor Maximilian II (r. 1564–1576)

Archduke Charles of Styria

King Philip III (r. 1598–1621)

Emperor Rudolf II (r. 1576–1612)

Emperor Matthias (r. 1612–1619)

Emperor Ferdinand II (r. 1619–1637)

King Philip IV (r. 1621–1665)

Emperor Ferdinand III (r. 1637–1657)

King Charles II (r. 1665–1700)

Emperor Leopold (r. 1657–1705)

These provinces, increasingly Calvinist, became the center of opposition to the Spanish, who concentrated their efforts against rebellion in the wealthier southern provinces. Occasionally the French and English lent aid to the rebels.

The war in the Netherlands was a showcase for the new and costly technology of warfare in this period. Many towns were (or came to be, as a consequence of the revolt) equipped with "bastions," newly designed walled defenses that could resist artillery fire; such cities could not be taken by storm. Where bastions had been built, military campaigns consisted of grueling sieges, skirmishes in surrounding areas for control of supplies, and occasional pitched battles between besiegers and forces attempting to break the siege. Vast numbers of men were required both for effective besieging forces and for garrisoning the many fortresses that controlled the countryside and defended access to major towns.

In an attempt to supply the Netherlands with seasoned veterans and materiel from Spain and Spanish territories in Italy, the Spanish developed the "Spanish Road," an innovative string of supply depots where provisions could be gathered in advance of troops marching to the Netherlands (see Map 15.1). Maintaining its large armies, however, taxed Spain's resources to the breaking point. Even with American silver at hand, Philip could at times barely afford to keep armies in the field. Inevitably, large numbers of troops also exhausted the countryside, and both soldiers and civilians suffered great privations. On occasion Spanish troops reacted violently to difficult conditions and to delayed pay (American treasure dwindled badly between 1572 and 1578). In 1576 Spanish troops sacked the hitherto loyal city of Antwerp and massacred about eight thousand people. This event was bitterly remembered afterward as the "Spanish Fury."

The massacre prompted leaders in the southern provinces to raise their own armies to protect themselves against the Spanish. Late in 1576 they concluded an alliance with William of Orange and the northern rebels. But the northern and southern provinces were increasingly divided by religion, and their differences were skillfully exploited by Philip's new commander, Margaret's son Alexander Farnese°, duke of Parma. With galleons from America filling the king's coffers again, Parma wooed the Catholic elites of the southern provinces back into loyalty to Philip, in return for promises to respect their provincial liberties and safeguard their property from troops.

Farnese (far-NAY-zee)

Map 15.2 The Netherlands, 1559–1609 The seventeen provinces of the Netherlands were strikingly diverse politically, economically, and culturally. Like his father, Philip was, technically, the ruler of each province separately—that is, he was count of Flanders, duke of Brabant, and so forth.

In 1579 the northern provinces united in a defensive alliance, the Union of Utrecht°, against the increasingly unified south. Parma's forces could not surmount the natural barrier of the Rhine River that bisects the Low Countries (see Map 15.2) or meet the increasing costs of siege warfare in waterlogged terrain, particularly as Spain diverted money to conflicts with England in 1588 and France after 1589. In 1609 a truce was finally concluded between Spain and the northern provinces. This truce did not formally recognize the "United Provinces" as an independent entity, though in fact they were. The modern nations of Belgium (the Spanish provinces) and the Netherlands are the distant result of this truce.

The independent United Provinces (usually called, simply, the Netherlands) was a fragile state, an accident of warfare at first. But commercial prosperity began to emerge as its greatest strength. Much of the economic activity of Antwerp had shifted north to Amsterdam in the province of Holland because of fighting in the south and a naval blockade of Antwerp by rebel ships. Philip's policies had created a new enemy nation and had enriched it at his expense.

The Failure of the Invincible Armada

The revolt of the Netherlands had lured Spain into wider strategic involvement, particularly against England. Spain and England had a common foe in France and common economic interests, and Philip had married Mary Tudor, the Catholic queen of England (r. 1553–1558). Even after Mary's death and the accession of her Protestant half sister, Queen Elizabeth (r. 1558–1603), Spanish-English relations remained cordial. Relations started to sour, however, when Elizabeth began tolerating the use of English ports by the rebel Sea Beggars and authorizing attacks by English privateers on Spanish treasure fleets. In response Spain supported Catholic resistance to Elizabeth within England, including plots to replace her on the throne with her Catholic cousin, Mary, Queen of Scots. Greater Spanish success in the Netherlands, raids by the Spanish and English on each other's shipping, and Elizabeth's execution of Mary in 1587 prompted Philip to order an invasion of England. A fleet (*armada*) of Spanish warships sailed in 1588.

"The enterprise of England," as the plan was called in Spain, represented an astounding logistical effort. The Armada was supposed to clear the English Channel of English ships in order to permit an invading force—troops under Parma in the Netherlands—to cross on barges. The sheer number of ships required for the undertaking—about 130—meant that some, inevitably, were slower supply ships, or vessels designed for the more protected waters of the Mediterranean. The English also had the advantage in arms, since they had better long-range artillery and better-trained gunners.

When the Armada entered the Channel on July 29, the English harassed the Spanish with artillery from a distance without sustaining much damage themselves. Parma could not get his men readied on their barges quickly enough once the fleet's presence in the Channel had been confirmed by messenger, nor could the fleet protect itself while waiting offshore. On the night of August 7 the English launched eight fire ships—burning vessels set adrift to deliver arson—into the anchored Spanish fleet. At dawn on the next day, they attacked the weakened fleet off Gravelines°, sank many ships, and dispersed what remained. (See the box "Reading Sources: Secret Dispatches from the Venetian Ambassador in Spain.")

Utrecht (OO-trekt)

Gravelines (grahv-LEEN)

Because it so heavily depended on its trading empire, Venice closely monitored developments at foreign courts. The Venetian ambassador at the Spanish court sent these reports back about the Spanish Armada. Note that the most sensitive material (in italics here) was sent in code. What differences do you notice between the encoded dispatches and the others? What seems to be the ambassador's attitude toward Philip and his invincible fleet? What can you learn from these dispatches about how fast and how accurately news traveled in sixteenth-century Europe?

April 30, 1588

Day by day we are expecting news that the Armada has sailed. It has drawn down the river to Belem at the mouth of the port, three miles from Lisbon. The blessing of the standard [flag] was performed with great pomp and many salvos of artillery. . . . Here in all the churches they make constant prayers; and the king himself is on his knees two or three hours every day before the sacrament. Everyone hopes that the greater the difficulties, humanly speaking, the greater will be the favor of God.

June 4, 1588

The Armada set sail from Lisbon at length on the twenty-ninth of last month, a Sunday. . . . They are now waiting the news of its arrival at Corunna to embark more troops, and then to sail. I have from time to time reported the great preparations which have been made; but we here must expect news of its progress from other quarters now, unless the peace is effected in Flanders.

July 12, 1588

The wiser wonder what can induce the king to insist, quite against his natural temper, that the Armada shall give battle to the English, who are known to be awaiting the attack with eager courage, and so they surmise that, over and above the belief that God will be on his side, two motives urge the king to this course; first, that he has some secret understandings which will fail if there is any delay; secondly, that these expenses of a million of gold a month cannot be supported for long, and so he has resolved to try his fortune. . . .

August 20, 1588

Don Bernardino de Mendoza [the Spanish ambassador in France] announces from France, in letters of the second of August, that the Armada has given battle to the English, sunk some of their ships, won a great victory and passed on to join the duke of Parma; but the report is so confused, and that ambassador is so accustomed to deceive himself, that they are waiting confirmation of the news. . . .

September 6, 1588

The bad news received in dispatches from the duke of Parma, and dated the tenth of August . . . pain the king and the court all the more that they were unexpected, and moreover quite contrary to the news sent by [Mendoza], who by three different couriers had confirmed . . . that [the Armada] had sunk many of the enemy and was on the point of effecting a junction with the Duke of Parma. . . . It is a blessing that the bad news did not reach Spain while the king was suffering from fever, for though His Majesty professes to allow no occurrence to disturb his equanimity, yet this war moves him in such a way as to prove clearly that on other occasions he was only acting and that now he is unable to do so, perhaps because this war is entirely conducted by himself alone and that it should not succeed brings to light all his anxiety.

Source: *The Pursuit of Power: Venetian Ambassadors' Reports on Turkey, France and Spain in the Age of Philip II, 1560–1600,* by James C. Davis, editor and translator. English translation copyright © 1970 by James C. Davis. Reprinted by permission of HarperCollins Publishers, Inc.

 For additional information on this topic, go to college.hmco.com/students.

The Battle at Gravelines was the first major artillery battle by sailing ships and helped set the future course of naval warfare. It was a disaster for Philip's hopes and for thousands of sailors and soldiers in Spanish pay. Many of the surviving ships sank in bad weather or were forced into hostile harbors as the Armada sailed for home around the northern tip of the British Isles (see Map 15.1). Less than half of Philip's great fleet made it back to Spain.

Successes at Home and Around the Mediterranean

Despite his bountiful overseas empire and his preoccupation with the Netherlands, many of Philip's interests still centered on the Mediterranean. Spain and the kingdom of Naples had exchanged trade for centuries. Newer ties had been forged with the duchy of Milan and the city-

The Battle of Lepanto   On October 7, 1571, vessels of the Holy League (Spain, Venice, and the papacy) defeated the Ottoman fleet off the coast of Greece. It was the last great battle between galleys—the oared warships that had dominated Mediterranean waters since ancient times. The Ottomans never again contested for power in the western Mediterranean, but they rebounded to eclipse Venice in the east.   *(Courtesy, National Maritime Museum)*

state of Genoa, whose bankers were financiers to the Spanish monarchy. It was in his kingdoms of Spain and their Mediterranean sphere of interest that Philip made his power felt more effectively, though not without effort.

Philip's father, Charles V, had tried to secure the western Mediterranean against the Turks and their client states along the African coast, but it was under Philip that the Turkish challenge in the western Mediterranean receded. The Spanish allied temporarily with the papacy and Venice—both were concerned with Turkish naval power in the Mediterranean—and their combined navies inflicted a massive defeat on the Turkish navy at Lepanto, off the coast of Greece, in October 1571 (see Map 15.1). The Turks remained the leading power in the eastern Mediterranean, but their ability to threaten Spain and Spanish possessions in the West was over.

To Philip and his advisers, the Turks represented a potential internal threat as well, since it was feared that they might incite rebellion among his Muslim subjects. These were the nominally Christian descendants of the Muslims of Granada, who had been conquered by the Spanish in 1492. Called *moriscos,* they had been forced

to convert to Christianity in 1504 or be expelled from Spain. Yet no serious effort had been made to teach them Christian beliefs in their own language (Arabic), and they had not been assimilated into Spanish society. Philip inaugurated a new wave of persecution and provoked a massive rebellion by the moriscos that began on Christmas Day in 1568. The revolt took two years to suppress. After it was crushed, the moriscos of Granada were forcibly exiled and dispersed farther north in Spain.

Philip's power in each of his Spanish kingdoms was limited by the traditional privileges of towns, nobility, and clergy. In Aragon, for example, he could raise revenues only by appealing to local assemblies, the Cortes°. Philip made significant inroads into Aragonese independence by the end of his reign, however. Noble feuds and peasant rebellions in Aragon during the 1580s provided a pretext for sending in veteran troops from the Netherlands campaigns to establish firmer royal control. Philip was successful in the long run in Aragon, as he had not been in the Netherlands, because he used ade-

---

Cortes (core-TEZ)

quate force but tempered it afterward with constitutional changes that were cleverly moderate. He cemented the peace by appearing in Aragon in person, in the words of a contemporary, "like a rainbow at the end of a storm."[2]

In Castile, the arid kingdom in the center of the Iberian Peninsula, the king was able to levy taxes with greater ease but only because of concessions that gave nobles undisputed authority over their peasants. Philip established his permanent capital, Madrid, and his principal residence, the Escorial, there. The Spanish Empire became more and more Castilian as the reign progressed, with royal advisers and counselors increasingly drawn only from the Castilian elite. Yet the rural economy of Castile was stunted by the dual oppression of landholders and royal tax collectors.

Philip also invaded and annexed Portugal in 1580, temporarily unifying the Iberian Peninsula. The annexation was ensured by armed force but had been preceded by careful negotiation to guarantee that Philip's claim to the throne—through his mother—would find some support within the country. When Philip died in 1598, he was old and ill, a man for whom daily life had become a painful burden. His Armada had been crushed; the Netherlands had slipped through his fingers. Yet he had learned from his mistakes and had been more successful, by his own standards, in other regions that he ruled.

Spain in Decline, 1600–1648

Spain steadily lost ground economically and strategically after the turn of the century. Imports of silver declined. The American mines were exhausted, and the natives forced to work in them were decimated by European diseases and brutal treatment. Spain's economic health was further threatened by the very success of its colonies: local industries in the Americas began to produce goods formerly obtained from Spain. The increasing presence of English, French, and Dutch shipping in the Americas provided colonists with rival sources for the goods they needed. Often these competitors could offer their goods more cheaply than the Spanish, for Spanish productivity was low and prices were high because of the inflationary effects of the influx of precious metals.

Spain renewed hostilities with the United Provinces in 1621, after the truce of 1609 had expired. Philip IV (r. 1621–1665) also aided his Habsburg cousins in the Thirty Years' War in the Holy Roman Empire (see page 523). Squeezed for troops and revenue for these commitments, other Spanish territories revolted. The uprisings reflected both economic distress and unresolved issues of regional autonomy. Castile bore the brunt of the financial support of the state. The chief minister to Philip IV, Gaspar de Guzmán, Count Olivares° (1587–1645), was an energetic Castilian aristocrat determined to distribute the burdens of government more equitably among the various regions of Spain. His policies provoked rebellions in Catalonia and Portugal.

In Catalonia, a province of the kingdom of Aragon, the revolt began as a popular uprising against the billeting of troops. At one point Catalan leaders invited French troops to defend them and solemnly transferred their loyalty to the French king in the hope that he would respect their autonomy. Spain resumed control only in 1652, after years of military struggle and promises to respect Catalan liberties.

In Portugal a war of independence began in 1640, also launched by popular revolt. The Spanish government tried to restore order with troops under the command of a leading Portuguese prince, John, duke of Braganza. The duke, however, was the nearest living relative to the last king of Portugal, and he seized this opportunity to claim the crown of Portugal for himself. Although war dragged on until 1668, the Portuguese under John IV (r. 1640–1656) succeeded in winning independence from Spain.

As a result of these uprisings, Count Olivares resigned in disgrace in 1643. In 1647 upheaval would shake Spain's Italian possessions of Sicily and Naples. By mid-century Spain had lost its position as the pre-eminent state in Europe.

RELIGIOUS AND POLITICAL CONFLICT IN FRANCE AND ENGLAND

IN the second half of the sixteenth century France was convulsed by civil war that had both religious and political causes. Although a temporary resolution was achieved by 1598, the kingdom was still divided by religion and by military and political challenges to royal authority. England, in contrast, was spared political and religious upheaval in the second half of the century, in part because of the talents and long life of its ruler, Elizabeth I. But in the seventeenth century constitutional and religious dissent began to reinforce each other in new ways and dramatically threatened royal power.

Olivares (oh-lih-VAR-ez)

The French Religious Wars, 1562–1598

Civil war wracked France from 1562 until 1598. As in the Netherlands, the conflicts in France had religious and political origins and international ramifications. The French monarch, like Philip, was unable to monopolize military power. In 1559 the king of France, Henry II (r. 1547–1559), had concluded the Peace of Cateau-Cambrésis with Philip II, ending the Habsburg-Valois Wars, but had died in July of that year from wounds suffered at a tournament held to celebrate the new treaty. His death was a political disaster. Great noble families vied for influence over his 15-year-old son, Francis II (r. 1559–1560). The queen mother, Catherine de' Medici° (1519–1589), worked carefully and intelligently to balance the nobles' interests. She gained greater authority when, in late 1560, the sickly Francis died and was succeeded by his brother, Charles IX—a 10-year-old for whom Catherine was officially the regent. But keeping the conflicts among the great courtiers from boiling over into civil war proved impossible.

In France, as elsewhere, noble conflict invariably had a violent component. Noblemen carried swords and daggers and were accompanied by armed entourages. Although they relied on patronage and army commands from the Crown, the Crown depended on their services. Provincial landholdings, together with the royal offices they enjoyed, afforded enough resources to support private warfare, and the nobles assumed the right to wage it.

In addition, religious tension was rising throughout France. (Henry II had welcomed the 1559 treaty in part because he wanted to turn his attention to "heresy.") Public preaching by and secret meetings of Protestants (known as "Huguenots°" in France) were causing unrest in towns. At court members of leading noble families—including the Bourbons, who were princes of royal blood—had converted to Protestantism and worshiped openly in their rooms in the palace. In 1561 Catherine convened a national religious council, known as the Colloquy of Poissy°, to reconcile the two faiths. When it failed, she chose provisional religious toleration as the only practical course and issued a limited edict of toleration in the name of the king in January 1562.

The edict led only to further unrest. Ignoring its restrictions, Protestants armed themselves, while townspeople of both faiths insulted and attacked one another at worship sites and religious festivals. In March 1562 the armed retainers of a Catholic duke killed a few dozen

Protestants gathered in worship at Vassy°, near one of the duke's estates. The killing, in bringing the military power of the nobility to bear on the broader problem of religious division, sparked the first of six civil wars. In some ways the initial conflict was decisive. The Protestant army lost the principal pitched battle of the war in December 1562. This defeat checked the growth of the Protestant movement by reducing the appeal of the movement to nobles. The peace edict granted in 1563 curtailed the reach of the Huguenot movement; the limited rights granted to Protestants in the Crown's edict made it difficult for Protestants in towns—where the vast majority of them lived—to worship. But if the Protestants were not powerful enough to win, neither were they weak enough to be decisively beaten.

The turning point most obvious to contemporaries came a decade later. The Protestant faction was still represented at court by the Bourbon princes and by the very able and influential nobleman Gaspard de Coligny°, related to the Bourbons by marriage. Coligny was pressing the king for a war against Spain in order to aid Protestant rebels in the Netherlands. Opposed to entanglement in another war against Spain and alarmed by rumors of Huguenot armies massing outside Paris, Charles IX (r. 1560–1574) and his mother authorized royal guards to murder Coligny and other Protestant leaders on August 24, 1572—Saint Bartholomew's Day. Coligny's murder touched off a massacre of Protestants throughout Paris and, once news from Paris had spread, throughout the kingdom.

The Saint Bartholomew's Day Massacre revealed the degree to which religious differences had strained the fabric of community life. Neighbor murdered neighbor in an effort to rid the community of heretical pollution; bodies of the dead, including Coligny's, were mutilated. Gathered in the south of France, the remaining Huguenot forces vowed "never [to] trust those who have so often and so treacherously broken faith and the public peace."[3] Huguenot writers published tracts arguing that royal power was by nature limited and that rebellion was justified against tyrants who overstepped their legitimate authority.

Further war produced the inevitable truces and limited toleration, but many Catholics also renounced reconciliation. Some noblemen formed a Catholic league to fight in place of the weakened monarchy. Charles's brother, Henry III (r. 1574–1589), was another king of limited abilities. Middle-aged, Henry had no children. The heir to his throne was the Protestant Henry of Navarre, and the

---

de' Medici (day MAY-di-chi)   **Huguenots** (HEW-guh-nots)
Poissy (pwa-SEE)

Vassy (vah-SEE)
Gaspard de Coligny (gas-PAR duh koh-leen-YEE)

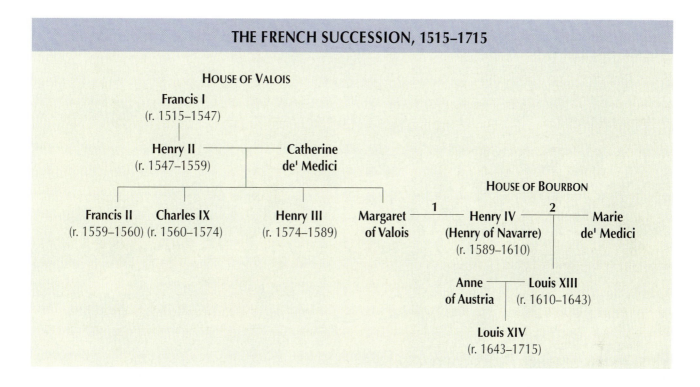

THE FRENCH SUCCESSION, 1515–1715

HOUSE OF VALOIS

Francis I
(r. 1515–1547)

Henry II ——— **Catherine**
(r. 1547–1559)   **de' Medici**

HOUSE OF BOURBON

Francis II **Charles IX**   **Henry III**   **Margaret** —1— **Henry IV** —2— **Marie**
(r. 1559–1560) (r. 1560–1574)   (r. 1574–1589)   **of Valois**   **(Henry of Navarre)**   **de' Medici**
                                                                  (r. 1589–1610)

Anne ——— **Louis XIII**
of Austria (r. 1610–1643)

Louis XIV
(r. 1643–1715)

assumption of the throne by a Protestant was unimaginable to the zealous Catholic faction at court and to many ordinary Catholics. By the end of Henry III's reign, the king had almost no royal authority left to wield. He was forced to cooperate with first one of the warring parties and then another. In December 1588 he resorted to murdering two courtiers who led the ultra-Catholic faction; in turn he was murdered by a priest in early 1589.

Henry of Navarre, the Bourbon prince who became Henry IV (r. 1589–1610), had to fight for his throne. He faced Catholic armies now subsidized by Philip II of Spain, an extremist Catholic city government in Paris, and subjects who were tired of war but mainly Catholic, and he could count on only meager support from Protestants abroad. Given these obstacles, the politically astute Henry agreed to convert to Catholicism.

After his conversion in 1593, the wars continued for a time, but after thirty years of civil strife many of Henry's subjects believed that only rallying to the monarchy could save France from chaos. Nobles grew increasingly disposed, for both psychological and practical reasons, to cooperate with the Crown. Service to a successful king could be a source of glory, and Henry was personally esteemed because he was a talented general and brave, gregarious, and charming. The nobility forced the citizens of Paris and other cities to accept Henry's authority.

The civil war period thus proved to be an important phase in the incremental accommodation of the nobility to the power of the state.

In April 1598 Henry granted toleration for the Huguenot minority in a royal edict proclaimed in the city of Nantes°. The Edict of Nantes was primarily a repetition of provisions from the most generous edicts that had ended the various civil wars. Nobles were allowed to practice the Protestant faith on their estates; townspeople were granted more limited rights to worship in selected towns in each region. Protestants were also guaranteed rights of self-defense—specifically, the right to maintain garrisons in about two hundred towns. About half of these garrisons would be paid for by the Crown. (See the box "The Continuing Experiment: Tolerating Religious Diversity: The Edict of Nantes.")

The problem was that the Edict of Nantes, like any royal edict, could be revoked by the king at any time. Moreover, the provision allowing Protestants to keep garrisoned towns reflected concessions to Protestant aristocrats, who could support their followers by paid garrison duty. It also reflected the assumption that living peacefully amid religious diversity might prove to be impossible. Thus, although Henry IV ended the French religious wars, he

Nantes (NAHNT)

The Entry of Henry IV into Paris After the Religious Wars   The king is depicted here as the magnanimous victor, and the residents of the city are shown as both submissive and grateful.   *(Réunion des Musées Nationaux/Art Resource, NY)*

had not solved the problem of religious and political division within France.

The Consolidation of Royal Authority in France, 1598–1643

During Henry IV's reign, France recovered from the long years of civil war. Population and productivity began to grow; the Crown encouraged internal improvements to facilitate commerce. Henry's chief minister, Maximilien de Béthune°, duke of Sully° (1560–1641), increased royal revenue by nibbling away at traditional local self-

---

Béthune (bay-TOON)   **Sully** (soo-LEE)

government and control of taxation. He succeeded in creating a budget surplus and in extending mechanisms of centralized government.

Yet Henry's regime was stable only in comparison with the preceding years of civil war. The power of the great nobility had not been definitively broken. Moreover, the king had agreed to a provision, known as the *paulette* (named for the functionary who first administered it), that allowed royal officeholders not merely to own their offices but also to pass on those offices to their heirs in return for the payment of an annual fee. Primarily a device to raise revenue after decades of civil war, the paulette also helped cement the loyalty of royal bureaucrats at a critical time, particularly that of the royal

Tolerating Religious Diversity: The Edict of Nantes

Henry IV of France proclaimed this edict of toleration in 1598 in order to end all pretext for civil war over the issue of religion. The Edict of Nantes ensured that Catholicism would remain pre-eminent but tried also to guarantee the rights of Protestants within France. The effort at toleration proved very fragile, however. Some of the privileges granted Protestants were withdrawn by Henry's son, and the entire edict was revoked in 1685 by Henry's grandson. Full civil equality for Protestants and Jews in France was not achieved until almost two hundred years after Henry's edict.

Henry, by the grace of God king of France . . . to all to whom these presents come, greeting: . . .

We have, by this perpetual and irrevocable edict, established and proclaimed. . . . First, that the recollection of everything done by one party or the other [in the later civil wars] . . . and during all the preceding period of troubles, remain obliterated and forgotten, as if no such things had ever happened.

We ordain that the Catholic Apostolic and Roman religion shall be restored and reestablished in all places and localities of this our kingdom . . . where the exercise of the same has been interrupted, . . . forbidding very expressly all persons, of whatsoever estate, quality, or condition, from troubling, molesting, or disturbing ecclesiastics in the celebration of divine service, in the enjoyment or collections of tithes, fruits or revenues of their benefices. . . .

And in order to leave no occasion for troubles or differences between our subjects, we . . . herewith permit, those of the said religion called Reformed [Protestants] to live and abide in all the cities and places of this our kingdom . . . without being annoyed, molested, or compelled to do anything in the matter of religion contrary to their consciences. . . .

We very expressly forbid to all those of the said religion its exercise, either in respect to ministry, regulation, discipline, or the public instruction of children . . . otherwise than in the places permitted and granted by the present edict. . . .

We also forbid all our subjects . . . from carrying off by force or persuasion, against the will of their parents, the children of the said religion, in order to cause them to be baptized or confirmed in the Catholic Apostolic and Roman Church; and the same is forbidden to those of the said religion called Reformed. . . .

Books concerning the said religion called Reformed may not be printed and publicly sold, except in cities and places where the public exercise of the said religion is permitted.

We ordain that there shall be no difference . . . made in respect to the said religion, in receiving pupils to be instructed in universities, colleges, and schools; nor in receiving the sick and poor into hospitals, retreats, and public charities.

QUESTIONS

1. In what ways and to what degree does the edict establish mutual toleration of the two religions?

2. What barriers to civil and religious peace does the edict seem to anticipate?

SOURCE: James Harvey Robinson, *Readings in European History,* vol. 2 (Boston and New York: Ginn, 1906), pp. 183–185.

judges of the supreme law court, the Parlement of Paris, who had recently agreed to register the Edict of Nantes only under duress. However, the paulette made royal officeholders largely immune from royal control since their posts were now in effect property, like the landed property of the traditional nobility.

In 1610 a fanatical Catholic assassinated Henry IV. Henry's death brought his 9-year-old son, Louis XIII (r. 1610–1643), to the throne with Louis's mother, Marie de' Medici, serving as regent. Marie was disgraced when her unpopular leading minister—resented for monopolizing patronage—was assassinated with Louis's approval in 1617.

Four years later Louis faced a major rebellion by his Huguenot subjects in southwestern France. Huguenots felt that Louis's recent marriage to a Spanish princess and other ominous policies meant that royal support for toleration was wavering. Certain Huguenot nobles initiated fighting as a show of force against the king. The wars persisted, on and off, for eight years, as the French royal troops, like the Spanish in the Netherlands, had difficulty breaching the defenses of even small fortress towns. The main Huguenot stronghold was the well-fortified port city of La Rochelle, which had grown wealthy from European and overseas trade. Not until the king took the city, after a siege lasting more than a year and costing thousands of lives, did the Protestants accept a peace on royal terms.

The Peace of Alais° (1629) reaffirmed the policy of religious toleration but rescinded the Protestants' military and political privileges. It was a political triumph for the Crown because it deprived French Protestants of the means for further rebellion while reinforcing their dependence on the Crown for religious toleration. Most of the remaining great noble leaders began to convert to Catholicism.

The Peace of Alais was also a personal triumph for the king's leading minister, who crafted the treaty and who had directed the bloody siege that made it possible. Armand-Jean du Plessis° (1585–1642), Cardinal Richelieu°, came from a provincial noble family and rose in the service of the queen mother. He was admired and feared for his skill in the political game of seeking and bestowing patronage—a crucial skill in an age when elites received offices and honors through carefully cultivated relationships at court. His control of many lucrative church posts gave him the resources to build up a large network of clients. He and the king—whose sensitive temperament Richelieu handled adeptly—formed a lasting partnership that had a decisive impact not only on French policy but also on the entire shape of the French state.

Richelieu favored an aggressive foreign policy to counter what he believed still to be the greatest threat to the French crown: the Spanish Habsburgs. When war resumed between the Netherlands and Spain after their truce expired in 1621 (see page 526), Richelieu sent troops to attack Spanish possessions in Italy. In the 1630s, with the king's full confidence, he superintended large-scale fighting against Spain in the Netherlands itself, as well as in Italy, and he began subsidizing Swedish and German Protestant armies fighting the Habsburgs in Germany.

Richelieu's policies were opposed by many people, who saw taxes double, then triple, in just a few years. Many courtiers and provincial elites favored keeping a tenuous peace with Spain, a fellow Catholic state, and objected to alliances with German Protestants. They were alarmed by the increasing taxes and by the famine, disease, and, above all, the revolts that accompanied the peasants' distress. Their own status was also directly

threatened by Richelieu's monopoly of royal patronage and by his creation of new offices, which diluted and undermined their power. In 1632, for example, Richelieu created the office of *intendant*. Intendants had wide powers for defense and administration in the provinces that overrode the established bureaucracy.

By 1640 Richelieu's ambitious foreign policy seemed to be bearing fruit. The French had won territory along their northern and eastern borders by their successes against Habsburg forces. But when Richelieu and Louis XIII died within five months of each other, in December 1642 and May 1643, Richelieu's legacy was tested. Louis XIII was succeeded by his 5-year-old son, and the warrior-nobility, as well as royal bureaucrats, would waste little time before challenging the Crown's new authority.

Precarious Stability in England: The Reign of Elizabeth I, 1558–1603

England experienced no civil wars during the second half of the sixteenth century, but religious dissent challenged the stability of the monarchy. In Elizabeth I (r. 1558–1603), England—in stark contrast to France—possessed an able and long-lived ruler. Elizabeth was well educated in the humanistic tradition and was already an adroit politician at the age of 25, when she acceded to the throne at the death of her Catholic half sister, Mary Tudor (r. 1553–1558).

Elizabeth faced the urgent problem of reaching a policy of consensus in religious matters. Her father, Henry VIII (r. 1509–1547), had broken away from the Catholic Church for political reasons but had retained many Catholic doctrines and practices. A Calvinist-inspired Protestantism had been prescribed for the Church of England by the advisers of Henry's successor, Elizabeth's young half brother, Edward VI (r. 1547–1553). True Catholicism, such as Mary had tried to reimpose, was out of the question. The Roman church had never recognized Henry VIII's self-made divorce and thus regarded Elizabeth as a bastard with no right to the throne.

Elizabeth adopted a cleverly moderate solution and used force, where necessary, to maintain it. In 1559 Parliament passed a new Act of Supremacy, which restored the monarch as head of the Church of England. Elizabeth dealt with opposition to the act by arresting bishops and lords whose votes would have blocked its passage by Parliament. Elizabeth and most of her ministers, all moderate realists, were willing to accept some flexibility in personal belief. For example, the official prayer book in use in Edward's day was revised to include elements of both traditional and radical interpretations of Commu-

---

Alais (ah-LAY)   **du Plessis** (doo pleh-SEE)
Richelieu (RISH-el-yeuh)

Elizabeth I: The Armada Portrait
Both serene and resolute, Elizabeth is flanked by "before" and "after" glimpses of the Spanish fleet; her hand rests on the globe in a gesture of dominion that also memorializes the circumnavigation of the globe by her famous captain, Sir Francis Drake, some years before.
(By kind permission of Marquess of Tavistock and Trustees of Bedford Estate)

nion. But church liturgy, clerical vestments, and, above all, the hierarchical structure of the clergy closely resembled Catholic practices. The Act of Uniformity required all worship to be conducted according to the new prayer book. Although uniformity was required in worship, Elizabeth was careful, in her words, not to "shine beacons into her subjects' souls."

Catholicism continued to be practiced, especially by otherwise loyal nobility and gentry in the north of England, who worshiped privately on their estates. But priests returning from exile beginning in the 1570s, most newly imbued with the proselytizing zeal of the Counter-Reformation (the Catholic response to the Protestant Reformation), practiced it more visibly and were zealously prosecuted for their boldness. In the last twenty years of Elizabeth's reign, approximately 180 Catholics were executed for treason, two-thirds of them priests. (By 1585 being a Catholic priest in itself was a crime.)

In the long run, the greater threat to the English crown came from the most radical Protestants in the realm, known (by their enemies initially) as Puritans. Puritanism was a broad movement for reform of church practice along familiar Protestant lines: an emphasis on Bible reading, preaching, and private scrutiny of conscience; a de-emphasis on institutional ritual and clerical authority. Most Puritans had accepted Elizabeth's religious compromise for practical reasons but grew increasingly alienated by her insistence on clerical authority and her refusal to change any elements of the original religious settlement. A significant Presbyterian underground movement began to form among them. Presbyterians wanted to dismantle the episcopacy—the hierarchy of priests and bishops—and to govern the church instead with councils, called "presbyteries," that included lay members of the congregation. Laws were passed late in the queen's reign to enable the Crown to prosecute more easily, and even to force into exile, anyone who attended "nonconformist" (non-Anglican) services.

The greatest challenge Elizabeth faced from Puritans came in Parliament, where they were well represented by many literate gentry. Parliament met only when called by the monarch, and in theory members could merely voice opinions and complaints. Initiating legislation and prescribing policy were beyond its purview. However, only Parliament could vote taxes. Further, since it had in effect helped constitute royal authority by means of the two Acts of Supremacy, Parliament's supposedly consultative role had been expanded by the monarchy itself. During Elizabeth's reign, Puritans capitalized on Parliament's enlarged scope, using meetings to press for further religious reform. In 1586 they went so far as to introduce bills calling for an end to the episcopacy and the Anglican prayer book. Elizabeth had to resort to imprisoning one Puritan leader to end debate on the issue and on Parliament's right to address it.

Also during Elizabeth's reign, efforts at English expansion in the New World began, in the form of unsuccessful attempts at colonization and successful raids on Spanish possessions. However, the main focus of her foreign policy remained Europe itself. Elizabeth, like all her forebears, felt her interests tightly linked to the independence of the Netherlands, whose towns were a major outlet for English wool. Philip II's aggressive policy in the Netherlands increasingly alarmed her, especially in view of France's weakness. She began to send small sums of money to the rebels and allowed their ships access to southern English ports, from which they could raid Spanish-held towns on the Netherlands' coast. In 1585, in the wake of the duke of Parma's successes against the rebellions, she committed troops to help the rebels.

Her decision was a reaction not only to the threat of a single continental power dominating the Netherlands but also to the threat of Catholicism. From 1579 to 1583 the Spanish had helped the Irish fight English domination and were involved in several plots to replace Elizabeth with her Catholic cousin, Mary, Queen of Scots. These threats occurred as the return of Catholic exiles to England peaked. The victory over the Spanish Armada in 1588 was quite rightly celebrated, for it ended any Catholic threat to Elizabeth's rule.

The success against the Armada has tended to overshadow other aspects of Elizabeth's foreign policy, particularly with regard to Ireland. Since the twelfth century an Anglo-Irish state dominated by great princely families had been loosely supervised from England, but most of Ireland remained under the control of Gaelic chieftains. Just as Charles V and Philip II attempted to tighten their governing mechanisms in the Netherlands, so did Henry VIII's minister, Thomas Cromwell, streamline control of outlying areas such as Wales and Anglo-Ireland. Cromwell proposed that the whole of Ireland be brought under English control partly by the established mechanism of feudal ties: the Irish chieftains were to pay homage as vassals to the king of England.

Under Elizabeth this legalistic approach gave way to virtual conquest. Elizabeth's governor, Sir Henry Sidney, appointed in 1565, inaugurated a policy whereby Gaelic lords, by means of various technicalities, could be entirely dispossessed of their lands. Any Englishman capable of raising a private force could help enforce these dispossessions and settle his conquered lands as he saw

fit. This policy provoked stiff Irish resistance, which was viewed as rebellion and provided the rationale for further military action, more confiscations of lands, and more new English settlers. Eventually the Irish, with Spanish assistance, mounted a major rebellion, consciously Catholic and aimed against the "heretic" queen. The rebellion gave the English an excuse for brutal suppression and massive transfers of lands to English control. The political domination of the Irish was complete with the defeat, in 1601, of the Gaelic chieftain Hugh O'Neill, lord of Tyrone, who had controlled most of the northern quarter of the island. Although the English were unable to impose Protestantism on the conquered Irish, to Elizabeth and her English subjects the conquests in Ireland seemed as significant as the victory over the Spanish Armada.

The English enjoyed relative peace at home during Elizabeth's reign. However, her reign ended on a note of strain. The foreign involvements, particularly in Ireland, had been very expensive. Taxation granted by Parliament more than doubled during her reign, and local taxes further burdened the people. Price inflation related to government spending, social problems caused by returned unemployed soldiers, and a series of bad harvests heightened popular resentment against taxation. Despite her achievements, therefore, Elizabeth passed two problems on to her successors: unresolved religious tensions and financial instability. Elizabeth's successors would also find in Parliament an increasing focus of opposition to their policies.

Rising Tensions in England, 1603–1642

In 1603 Queen Elizabeth died, and James VI of Scotland, the Protestant son of Mary, Queen of Scots, ascended to the English throne as James I (r. 1603–1625). Religious tensions between Anglicans and Puritans were temporarily quieted under James because of a plot, in 1605, by Catholic dissenters. The Gunpowder Plot, as it was called, was a conspiracy to blow up the palace housing both king and Parliament at Westminster. Protestants of all stripes once again focused not on their differences but on their common enemy, Catholics.

Financial problems were James's most pressing concern. Court life became more elaborate and an increasing drain on the monarchy's resources. James's extravagance was partly to blame for his financial problems, but so were pressures for patronage from courtiers. Added to the debts left from the Irish conflicts and wars with Spain were new military expenses as James helped defend the claims of his daughter and her husband, a German prince, to rule Bohemia (see page 525).

When James summoned Parliament to ask for funds in 1621, Parliament used the occasion to protest court corruption and the king's financial measures. The members revived the medieval procedure of impeachment and removed two royal ministers from office. In 1624, still faced with expensive commitments to Protestants abroad and in failing health, James again called Parliament, which voted new taxes but also openly debated the wisdom of the king's foreign policy.

Tensions between Crown and Parliament increased under James's son, Charles I (r. 1625–1649). One reason was the growing financial strain of foreign policy as well as the policies themselves. Charles declared war on Spain and supported the Huguenot rebels in France. Many wealthy merchants opposed this aggressive foreign policy because it disrupted trade. In 1626 Parliament was dissolved without granting any monies, in order to stifle its objections to royal policies. Instead, Charles levied a forced loan and did not hesitate to imprison gentry who refused to lend their money to the government.

Above all, Charles's religious policies were a source of controversy. Charles was personally inclined toward "high church" practices: an emphasis on ceremony and sacrament reminiscent of Catholic ritual. He also was a believer in Arminianism, a school of thought that rejected the Calvinist notion that God's grace cannot be earned, and hence emphasized the importance of the sacraments and the authority of the clergy. Charles's attempt to fashion the Church of England into an instrument that would reflect and justify royal claims to power put him on a collision course with gentry and aristocrats who leaned toward Puritanism.

Charles's views were supported by William Laud° (1573–1645), archbishop of Canterbury from 1633 and thus leader of the Church of England. He tried to impose changes in worship, spread Arminian ideas, and censor opposing views. He also challenged the redistribution of church property, which had occurred in the Reformation of the sixteenth century, and thereby alienated the gentry on economic as well as religious grounds.

Charles's style of rule worsened religious, political, and economic tensions. Cold and intensely private, he did not inspire confidence or have the charm or the political skills to disarm his opponents. His court was ruled by formal protocol, and access to the king was highly restricted—a serious problem in an age when proximity to the monarch was a guarantee of political power.

Revenue and religion dominated debate in the Parliament of 1628–1629, which Charles had called, once

Criticism of Monopolies Holders of royally granted monopolies were bitterly resented by English consumers and tradespeople alike, as this contemporary print reveals. The greedy beast pictured here controls even ordinary commodities such as pins, soap, and butter. *(Courtesy of the Trustees of the British Museum)*

To raise revenue without Parliament's consent, James relied on sources of income that the Crown had enjoyed since medieval times: customs duties, wardship (the right to manage and liberally borrow from the estates of minor nobles), and the sale of monopolies, which conveyed the right to be sole agent for a particular kind of goods. To rebuild his treasury James increased the number of monopolies for sale and even created a new noble title—baronet—which he sold to socially ambitious commoners.

The monopolies were widely resented. Merchants objected to the arbitrary restriction of production and trade; common people found that they could no longer afford certain ordinary commodities, such as soap. Resentments among the nobility were sharpened, and general criticism of the court escalated, as James indulged in extreme favoritism of certain courtiers, including the corrupt George Villiers° (1592–1628), duke of Buckingham, who served as the king's first minister.

Villiers (VIL-yerz)

Laud (LAWD)

again, to get funds for his foreign wars. In 1628 Parliament presented the king with a document called the Petition of Right, which protested his financial policies as well as arbitrary imprisonment. (Seventeen members of Parliament had been imprisoned for refusing loans to the Crown.) Though couched conservatively as a restatement of customary practice, the petition in fact claimed a tradition of expanded parliamentary participation in government. Charles dissolved Parliament in March 1629, having decided that the money he might extract was not worth the risk.

For eleven years Charles ruled without Parliament. When he was forced by necessity to summon it again in 1640, the kingdom was in crisis. Royal finances were in desperate straits, even though Charles had pressed collection of revenues far beyond traditional bounds. In 1634, for example, he had revived annual collection of "ship money"—a medieval tax levied on coastal districts to help support the navy during war. England, however, was not at war at that time, and the tax was levied not only on seaports but on inland areas, too.

The immediate crisis in 1640—and the reason for Charles's desperate need for money—was a rebellion in Scotland. Like Philip II in the Netherlands, Charles tried to rule in Scotland through a small council of men who did not represent the local elite. Worse, he also tried to force his "high church" practices on the Scots. The Scottish Church had been more dramatically reshaped during the Reformation and now was largely Presbyterian in structure. The result of Charles's policies was riots and rebellion. Unable to suppress the revolt in a first campaign in 1639, Charles was forced to summon Parliament to obtain funds to raise a more effective army.

But the Parliament that assembled in the spring of 1640 provided no help. Instead, members questioned the war with the Scots and other royal policies. Charles's political skills were far too limited for him to re-establish a workable relationship with Parliament under the circumstances. Charles dissolved this body, which is now known as the "Short Parliament," after just three weeks. Even more stinging than Charles's dissolution of the Parliament was the lack of respect he had shown the members: a number of them were harassed or arrested. Mistrust fomented by the eleven years in which Charles had ruled without Parliament thus increased.

Another humiliating and decisive defeat at the hands of the Scots later in 1640 made summoning another Parliament imperative. Members of the "Long Parliament" (it sat from 1640 to 1653) took full advantage of the king's predicament. Charles was forced to agree not to dissolve or adjourn Parliament without the members' consent and to summon Parliament at least every three years. Parliament abolished many of his unorthodox and traditional sources of revenue and impeached and removed from office his leading ministers, including Archbishop Laud. The royal commander deemed responsible for the Scottish fiasco, Thomas Wentworth, earl of Strafford, was executed without trial in May 1641.

The execution of Strafford shocked many aristocrats in the House of Lords (the upper house of Parliament), as well as some moderate members of the House of Commons. Meanwhile, Parliament began debating the perennially thorny religious question. A bare majority of members favored abolition of Anglican bishops as a first step in thoroughgoing religious reform. Working people in London, kept apprised of the issues by the regular publication of parliamentary debates, demonstrated in support of that majority. Moderate members of Parliament, in contrast, favored checking the king's power but not upsetting the Elizabethan religious compromise.

An event that unified public and parliamentary opinion at a crucial time—a revolt against English rule in Ireland in October 1641—temporarily eclipsed these divisions and once again focused suspicion on the king. The broad consensus of anti-Catholicism once again became the temporary driving force in politics. Fearing that Charles would use Irish soldiers against his English subjects, Parliament demanded that it have control of the army to put down the rebellion. In November the Puritan majority introduced a document known as the "Grand Remonstrance," an appeal to the people and a long catalog of parliamentary grievances against the king. It was passed by a narrow margin, further setting public opinion in London against Charles. The king's remaining support in Parliament eroded in January 1642 when he attempted to arrest five leading members on charges of treason. The five escaped, and the stage was set for wider violence. The king withdrew from London, unsure he could defend himself there, and began to raise an army. In mid-1642 the kingdom stood at the brink of civil war.

RELIGIOUS AND POLITICAL CONFLICT IN CENTRAL AND EASTERN EUROPE

THE Holy Roman Empire enjoyed a period of comparative quiet after the Peace of Augsburg halted religious and political wars in 1555. The 1555 agreement, which permitted rulers of the various states within the empire to impose either Catholicism or Lutheranism in their lands, proved to be a workable solution, for a time, to the problem of religious division. By the early seventeenth century, however, fresh causes of instability brought about renewed fighting. One factor was the rise of Calvinism, for which no provision had been necessary in 1555. Especially destabilizing was the drive by the Austrian Habsburgs to reverse the successes of Protestantism both in their own lands and in the empire at large and to solidify their control of their diverse personal territories. The result was a devastating conflict known as the Thirty Years' War (1618–1648).

Like conflicts elsewhere in Europe, the Thirty Years' War reflects religious tensions, regionalism versus centralizing forces, and dynastic and strategic rivalries between rulers. The war was particularly destructive because of the size of the armies and the degree to which army commanders evaded control by the states for which they fought. As a result of the war, the empire was eclipsed as a political unit by the regional powers that composed it. Meanwhile, a Polish state resembling the Habsburg territories in its regional diversity remained the dominant state in northeastern Europe. But it would soon face challenges, particularly from a powerful new state being crafted in Russia.

Fragile Peace in the Holy Roman Empire, 1556–1618

The Austrian Habsburgs ruled over a diverse group of territories in the Holy Roman Empire, as well as northwestern Hungary (see Map 15.3). On his abdication in 1556, Emperor Charles V granted Habsburg lands in central Europe to his brother, Ferdinand (see the chart on page 509), who had long been the actual ruler there in Charles's stead. On Charles's death in 1558, Ferdinand was duly crowned emperor.

Though largely contiguous, Ferdinand's territories comprised independent duchies and kingdoms, each with its own institutional structure, and included speakers of Italian, German, and Czech, plus a few other languages. The non-German lands of Bohemia (the core of the modern Czech Republic) and Hungary had been distinct kingdoms since the High Middle Ages. Both states bestowed their crowns by election and had chosen Ferdinand, the first Habsburg to rule them, in separate elections in the 1520s and 1530s. Most of Hungary was now under Ottoman domination, but Bohemia, with its rich capital, Prague, was a wealthy center of population and culture.

Unlike the Netherlands, these linguistically and culturally diverse lands were still governed by highly decentralized institutions. Moreover, unlike their Spanish cousins, the Austrian Habsburgs made no attempt to impose religious uniformity in the late sixteenth century. Ferdinand was firmly Catholic but tolerant of reform efforts within the church. Both he and his son, Maximilian II (r. 1564–1576), believed that an eventual reunion of the Catholic and Protestant faiths might be possible. During his reign Maximilian worked to keep religious peace in the empire as a whole and granted limited rights of worship to Protestant subjects within his ancestral lands (separate territories more or less equivalent to modern Austria in extent). Catholicism and many strands of Protestantism flourished side by side in Maximilian's domains, above all in Hungary and, especially, Bohemia, which had experienced its own religious reform movement under Jan Hus in the fifteenth century.

Maximilian's son, Rudolf II (r. 1576–1612), shared the religious style of his father and grandfather. He was an energetic patron of the arts and humanist education and sponsored the work of scientists. Yet Rudolf was a weak leader politically and was challenged by his brother and ambitious cousins for control both of Habsburg lands and the empire itself. Meanwhile, the resurgence of Catholicism in the wake of the Council of Trent (1545–1563) had begun to shift the religious balance. Members of the Jesuit order arrived in Habsburg lands in the reign of Maximilian. Tough-minded and well trained, they established Catholic schools and became confessors and preachers to the upper classes. Self-confident Catholicism emerged as one form of cultural identity among the German-speaking ruling classes, and thus as a religious impetus to further political consolidation of all the Habsburg territories.

Resurgent Catholicism was evident, too, in the empire as a whole, where certain princes were confident they might now eliminate Protestantism, as their ancestors had failed to do. In the face of this challenge, certain Protestant princes formed a defensive pact known as the Evangelical Union in 1608. In response Catholic princes formed an alliance, the Holy League, the next year. A major war between the two alliances over a disputed territory was narrowly averted the following year. Like the English under Elizabeth, Habsburg subjects and peoples in the empire had enjoyed a period of calm in political and religious matters. Now, as in England, the stage was set for conflict of both kinds.

The Thirty Years' War, 1618–1648

The Thirty Years' War was touched off in 1618 by a revolt against Habsburg rule in the kingdom of Bohemia. Bohemia was populous and prosperous; Rudolf II had made its bustling capital, Prague, his imperial capital. Its powerful and diverse Protestant community had wrested formal recognition of its right to worship from Rudolf and his younger brother, Matthias (r. 1612–1619).

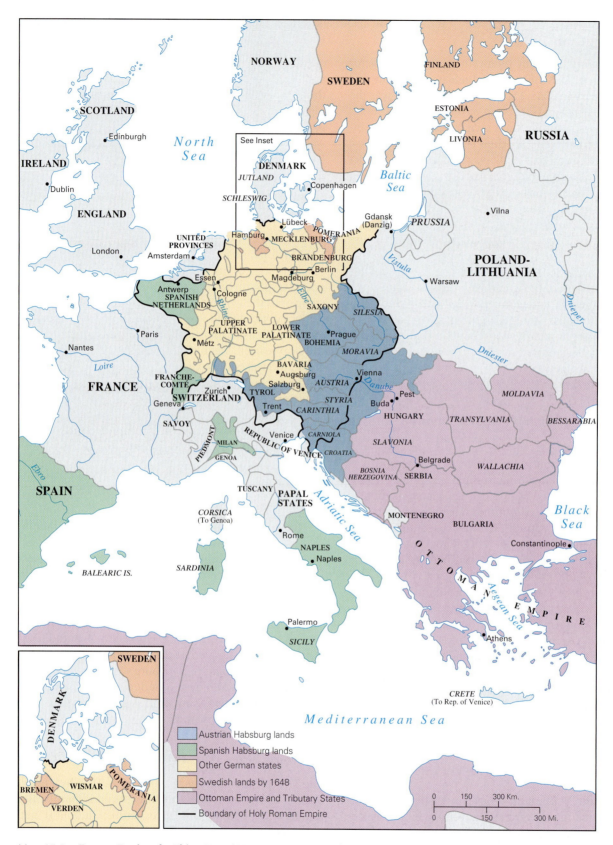

Map 15.3 Europe During the Thirty Years' War, 1618–1648 The Thirty Years' War was fought largely within the borders of the Holy Roman Empire. It was the result of conflicts within the empire as well as the meddling of neighbors for their own strategic advantages.

Austrian Habsburg lands
Spanish Habsburg lands
Other German states
Swedish lands by 1648
Ottoman Empire and Tributary States
Boundary of Holy Roman Empire

Matthias was quickly succeeded by his cousin Ferdinand II (r. 1619–1637), who was the ideal Counter-Reformation prince and unlikely to honor these agreements. Educated by the Jesuits, Ferdinand sincerely believed that reimposing Catholicism was his Christian duty; he once stated that he would "sooner beg than rule over heretics."[4] He had virtually eliminated Protestantism, by persuasion as well as by compulsion, in the small duchy in southern Austria he had governed before assuming the throne.

Ferdinand would not tolerate the political independence of nobles and towns in Bohemia or the religious pluralism that independence defended. As Philip II had done in the Netherlands, Ferdinand appointed a regency council to govern in his name. That council enforced unpopular policies: the right to build new Protestant churches was denied, Bohemian crown lands were given to the Catholic Church, and non-Catholics were barred from serving in government.

On May 23, 1618, delegates to a Protestant assembly that had unsuccessfully petitioned Ferdinand to end his violations of earlier guarantees marched to the palace in Prague where the royal officials met. After a confrontation over their demands, the delegates "tried" the officials on the spot for treason and, literally, threw them out of the palace window. The incident became known as the "Defenestration of Prague" (from the Latin *fenestra*, or "window"). (The officials' lives were saved only because they fell into a pile of refuse in the moat.) The rebels proceeded to set up their own government.

This upstart Bohemian government officially deposed Ferdinand and elected a new Protestant king in 1619: Frederick, elector of the Palatinate and a Calvinist prince. His election had implications for the Holy Roman Empire as a whole because his role as leader of the territories in west-central Germany called the Lower and Upper Palatinate conveyed the right to be one of the seven electors who chose the emperor.

Emboldened by these events, Protestant subjects in other Habsburg lands asked for guarantees of freedom of worship similar to those enjoyed by Protestants in Bohemia. Other princes saw their chance to make political gains. For example, rival claimants to Habsburg rule in Hungary took up arms against Ferdinand.

The revolt in Bohemia set off a wider war because foreign rulers also felt their interests to be involved. The English king, James I, supported Frederick because Frederick was married to his daughter. Spain's supply routes north from Italy to the Netherlands passed next to Frederick's lands in western Germany. France's first interest was its rivalry with Spain; thus France kept its eye on the border principalities that were strategically important to Spain. In addition, France desired to keep Protestant as well as Catholic princes within the empire strong enough to thwart Austrian Habsburg ambitions. Thus, from the outset, the war was a conflict not only over the Habsburgs'

The Defenestration of Prague
This contemporary print memorializes the events of May 23, 1618. Bohemian Protestants tried two imperial officials for violating agreements that safeguarded their religious liberties. The two officials and their secretary were thrown out of the windows of Prague castle. *(Corbis)*

power in their own lands but also over the balance of religious and political power in the empire and in Europe (see Map 15.3).

Ferdinand secured aid from the Catholic duke of Bavaria and from his cousin, King Philip III (r. 1598–1621) of Spain, by promising them Frederick's lands in the Palatinate. By the fall of 1620 a Catholic army was closing in on Bohemia. On November 8, on a hillside near Prague, the Catholic force faced a Bohemian army that had received little aid from its Protestant allies. The Battle of White Mountain was a complete Catholic victory.

Despite the rout, fighting did not cease but instead became more widespread. The truce between Spain and the Netherlands, established in 1609, expired in 1621, and the nearby Lower Palatinate, now in Spanish hands, offered a staging point for Spanish forces and thus threatened the peace in that corner of the empire. Claiming to be a Protestant champion, the Protestant king of Denmark, Christian IV (r. 1588–1648), who was also duke of Holstein in northern Germany, sought to conquer additional German territory. His goals were to gain greater control over profitable German Baltic seaports and to defend himself against any Catholic attempt to seize northern German territory. Christian received little help from fellow Protestants, however. The Dutch were busy with Spain, the English were wary of fighting after Frederick's defeat, and Denmark's regional rivals, the Swedes, were uninterested in furthering Danish ambitions in the Baltic.

The confusing blend of politics and religion that motivated the Protestant rulers was also evident on the Catholic side. When imperial forces defeated Christian's armies in 1626, Catholic princes became alarmed at the possibility of greater imperial power in northern Germany. Led by the duke of Bavaria, they arranged a truce that resulted in Denmark's withdrawal from the fighting on relatively generous terms. At the same time, Protestants outside Bohemia saw the potential consequences of imperial victory and took up arms. As his armies defeated Christian, Ferdinand issued new edicts that in effect voided the religious settlement in place since 1555. His victorious armies brutally enforced his edicts wherever they passed.

Christian's rival, Gustav Adolf, king of Sweden (r. 1611–1632), now assumed the role of Protestant leader. An innovative military leader, Gustav Adolf hoped to gain territory along the Baltic seacoast, but personal aggrandizement also was one of his goals. His campaigns were capped by a victory over an imperial army at Breitenfeld°,

in Saxony, in 1631. After he was killed in battle in 1632, however, the tide turned in favor of Ferdinand's forces. A decisive imperial victory over a combined Swedish and German Protestant army at Nördlingen° in 1634 led to the Peace of Prague (1635), a general peace treaty favorable to Catholics.

The Peace of Prague brought only a temporary peace, however, because Ferdinand died shortly thereafter and French involvement increased now that other anti-Habsburg forces had been eclipsed. France tried to seize imperial territory along its own eastern border and generously subsidized continued fighting within the empire by channeling monies to Protestant princes and mercenaries there. The fighting dragged on. By the end of the Thirty Years' War order had disintegrated so completely in the wake of the marauding armies that both staunchly Catholic rulers and firmly Protestant ones allied with religious enemies to safeguard their states.

A comprehensive peace treaty became possible when France withdrew its sponsorship of the fighting in order to concentrate on its conflict with Spain. The French wanted only a workable balance of power in the empire, which was achieved once they and their allies convincingly defeated imperial forces in 1645. More urgent to the French was the continued rivalry with the Spanish Habsburgs for control of territory along France's eastern and northern borders and in Italy. A defeat by France in the Spanish Netherlands in 1643 had convinced Spain to concentrate on that rivalry, too, and fighting between them continued separately until 1659. Negotiations for peace had begun in 1643 among war-weary states of the empire and resulted in a group of agreements known as the Peace of Westphalia° in 1648.

The Effects of the War

The Thirty Years' War ruined the economy and decimated the population in many parts of the empire and had long-term political consequences for the empire as a whole. One reason for the war's devastation was a novel application of firepower to warfare that increased both the size of armies and their deadly force in battle. This was the use of volley fire, the arrangement of foot soldiers in parallel lines so that one line of men could fire while another reloaded. This tactic, pioneered in the Netherlands around the turn of the century, was further refined by Gustav Adolf of Sweden. Gustav Adolf amassed large numbers of troops and increased the rate of fire so that a virtually continuous barrage was maintained. He

---

Breitenfeld (BRIGHT-un-feld)

Nördlingen (NERD-ling-un) Westphalia (west-FAIL-yuh)

The Horrors of War This painting by a seventeenth-century artist depicts an attack on a supply convoy by opposing troops. Control of supplies to feed and equip the increasing numbers of troops was one of the most important aspects of warfare. *(Staatsgalerie Aschaffenburg [Schloss], Bayerische Staatsgemäldesammlungen/ Godwin Alfen-ARTOTHEK)*

also used maneuverable field artillery to protect the massed infantry from cavalry charges.

Following Gustav Adolf's lead, armies of all the major states adopted these new offensive tactics. But defensive expertise—as in holding fortresses—also remained important, and pitched battles, such as at Nördlingen in 1634, still tended to be part of sieges. The costs in resources and human life of this kind of warfare reached unheard-of dimensions. Popular printed literature and court drama both condemned the horrors of the war.

Where fighting had been concentrated, as in parts of Saxony, between one-third and one-half of the inhabitants of rural villages and major towns may have disappeared. Many starved, were caught in the fighting, or were killed by marauding soldiers. The most notorious atrocity occurred in the aftermath of the siege of Magdeburg° in 1631. After the city surrendered to besieging Catholic

Magdeburg (MAHG-duh-boorg)

forces, long-deprived soldiers ate and drank themselves into a frenzy, raped and killed indiscriminately, and set fires that destroyed the town. Some victims of war migrated to other regions in search of peaceful conditions and work. Some joined the armies in order to survive. Others formed armed bands to fight off the soldiers or to steal back enough goods to live on.

Compounding these effects of war were the actions of armies hired by enterprising mercenary generals for whom loyalty to the princes who paid them took a back seat to personal advancement. They contracted to provide, supply, and lead troops and thus were more willing than the princes would have been to allow troops to live "economically" on plunder. States thus managed to field large armies but had not yet evolved the mechanisms fully to fund, and thus control, them.

The Peace of Westphalia, which ended fighting in the empire, was one of the most important outcomes of the war. The various treaties composing the peace effectively put an end to religious war in the empire. Calvinism was recognized as a tolerated religion. The requirement that all subjects must follow their ruler's faith was retained, but some leeway was allowed for those who now found themselves under new rulers.

In political matters the treaties reflected some of the recent successes of the Swedes by granting them territory on the Baltic coast. France gained the important towns of Metz, Toul, and Verdun on its eastern border. Spain formally recognized the independence of the Netherlands.

The most important political outcome of the peace was a new balance of power in the empire. Most of the major Catholic and Protestant rulers extended their territories at the expense of smaller principalities and cities. The son of Frederick, Protestant king of Bohemia, received back the smaller of the two Palatine territories that his father had held. The Upper Palatinate—as well as the right to be a new elector of the emperor—was given to the powerful duke of Bavaria. The principalities within the empire were acknowledged, in the peace, to be virtually autonomous, both from the emperor and from one another. In addition, the constitution of the empire was changed to make it very difficult for one prince or a group of princes to disrupt the peace in their own interests. As a result, the agreements at Westphalia were the beginning of one hundred years of peace within the Holy Roman Empire.

Another outcome was that the Habsburgs, though weakened as emperors, were strengthened as rulers of their own hereditary lands on the eastern fringes of the empire. Except in Hungary, Protestantism—and its contrary political baggage—had been eliminated early in the wars, and the peace did not alter these circumstances. The Habsburgs moved their capital back to Vienna from Prague, and the government of their hereditary lands gained in importance as administration of the empire waned.

Stability and Dynamism in Eastern Europe

On the southern frontier of Austrian Habsburg lands, the empire of the Ottoman Turks continued to control southeastern Europe in the late sixteenth and early seventeenth centuries. The Ottoman state had reached the practical limits of its expansion with the conquests of Suleiman I (r. 1520–1566), known to Europeans as "the Magnificent." Sporadic fighting between the Ottomans and the Habsburgs continued in Hungary, which the Ottomans largely controlled, but the fighting there was secondary to the Ottomans' rivalry with the Safavid rulers of Persia. The Ottomans succeeded in extending their territory

eastward into modern Iraq, Azerbaijan, and Georgia at Safavid expense. Despite the Ottomans' many commitments and a succession of weak rulers, their presence in southeastern Europe remained secure, partly because they respected the cultural and religious diversity of their Christian subjects. Aristocratic and regional independence were factors, too: Christian princes, particularly in the Hungarian borderlands, found distant Turkish overlords more palatable than closer Habsburg ones. The naval defeat at Lepanto in 1571 (see page 512) had been a setback for the Ottomans, but they quickly rebuilt their fleet and re-established supremacy in the eastern Mediterranean.

Ottoman power was a constant presence in European affairs, but a more dynamic state in the late sixteenth century was the newly proclaimed empire in Russia (see Map 15.4). Through the late Middle Ages Muscovite princes had accumulated land and authority as they vied for pre-eminence with other principalities after the decline of Kievan Rus (modern Ukraine). Ivan III (r. 1462–1505) absorbed neighboring Russian principalities and ended Moscow's subservience to Mongol overlords. He then took the title of "Tsar," Russian for "Caesar." In 1547 his grandson, Ivan IV (r. 1533–1584), was officially proclaimed "Tsar of All the Russias" and became the first ruler to routinely use the title. For Russians this title placed Ivan IV in higher esteem than the neighboring Polish-Lithuanian and Swedish kings.

Ivan's use of the title reflects his imperial intentions, as he continued Moscow's push south, into lands that were once part of Kievan Rus, and east, against the Tatar states of Astrakhan, Kazan, and Sibir (Siberia). Within his expanding empire Ivan ruled as an autocrat. The practice of gathering tribute money for Mongol overlords had concentrated many resources in the hands of Muscovite princes. Ivan was able to bypass noble participation and intensify the centralization of government by creating ranks of officials loyal only to him. Part of his authority stemmed from his personality. He was willing, perhaps because of mental imbalance, to use ruthless methods—including torture and the murder of thousands of subjects—to enforce his will.

Ivan came to be called "the Terrible," from a Russian word meaning "awe-inspiring." Although a period of disputed succession to the throne known as the "Time of Troubles" followed Ivan's death in 1584, the foundations of the large and cohesive state he had built survived until a new dynasty of rulers was established in the seventeenth century.

Checking Russian expansion to the west was the commonwealth of Poland-Lithuania, a large, multi-ethnic state at the height of its power (see Map 15.4). The duchy

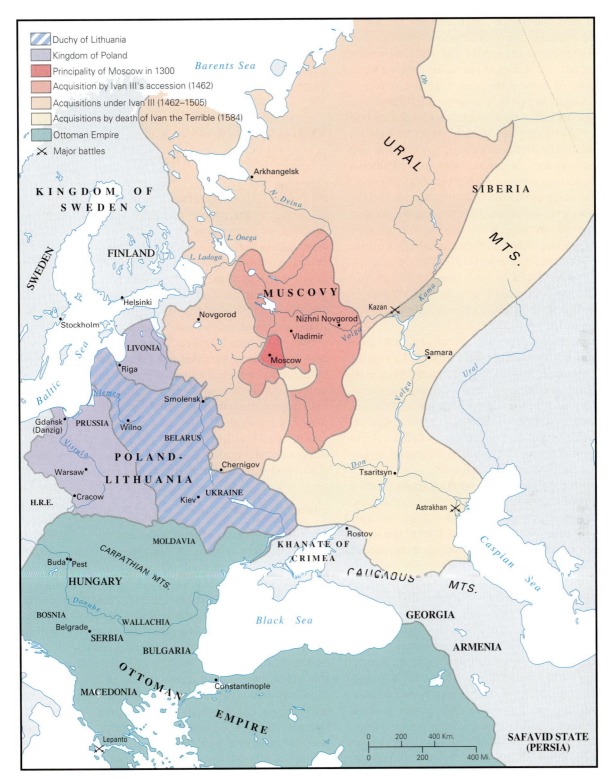

Map 15.4 Two Empires in Eastern Europe, ca. 1600 Poland-Lithuania dominated the Baltic coast and its productive hinterland in the sixteenth century, but it would face increasing challenges for control of its eastern territories by the expanding Russian state.

of Lithuania had conquered the territories known as Ruthenia (comprising most of modern Belarus and Ukraine) in the fourteenth century. Then in 1386 a marriage had brought the duchy of Lithuania and the kingdom of Poland under a joint ruler. Like the union of Castile and Aragon in Spain, the union of Poland and Lithuania was initially only dynastic. But two hundred years later, in 1569, they were brought under a single set of institutions by the Treaty of Lublin. Even so, the two states retained distinct traditions. Poles spoke Polish, a Slavic language, and were primarily Catholic, although there were also large minorities of Protestants, Orthodox Christians, and Jews in Poland. Lithuanians, whose language was only distantly related to the Slavic languages, were mostly Catholic as well, although Orthodox Christianity predominated among the Ruthenians, who spoke a Slavic language related to both Russian and Polish. Poland-Lithuania was unusual among European states in that religious toleration was a long-standing practice and was even enshrined in law in 1573.

Valuable resources such as grain, timber, and other naval stores passed through Polish-controlled ports on the Baltic Sea on their way to western Europe. Poland itself also became an increasingly important source of grain for Spanish, French, and English cities. Russia and Sweden, however, challenged Polish control of the lucrative Baltic coast. Polish forces were able to defeat efforts by Ivan the Terrible to control Livonia (modern Latvia), with its important port of Riga°, and briefly placed a Polish claimant on the Russian throne during the Time of Troubles. They were not as successful against the Swedes, who, under the expansionist Gustav Adolf, took Riga and the Baltic coast to its north in 1621 (as part of the same drive for Baltic territory that lay behind his involvement in the Thirty Years' War). The Turks also were a constant threat to Poland-Lithuania on its southern border.

In addition to the foreign challenges it faced by virtue of its geography, Poland-Lithuania had internal weaknesses. It was a republic of the nobility, with a weak elected king at its head. (The elective crown was a tradition that had developed over centuries when the throne had been contested by rival claimants from within Poland or from other states.) The great nobles, whose fortunes increased with the grain trade, ran the affairs of state through the national parliament, the Sejm°, as well as local assemblies and various lifelong offices. They drastically limited the ability of the Crown to tax and to grant new titles of nobility, as was the practice throughout Europe. These limitations meant that the king could not re-

ward and reinforce the loyalty of wealthy gentry or the small numbers of urban elites so that they might be a counterweight to noble power. Limited funds also meant that the Polish crown would be hard put to defend its vast territories later in the seventeenth century.

WRITING, DRAMA, AND ART IN AN AGE OF UPHEAVAL

BOTH imaginative literature and speculative writing, such as political theory, bear the stamp of their times. In the late sixteenth and early seventeenth centuries, political speculation often concerned questions of the legitimacy of rulers and of the relationship of political power to divine authority—urgent problems in an age when religious division threatened the very foundations of states. Authors and rulers alike often relied on still-prevalent oral modes of communication to convey their ideas. Indeed, some of the greatest literature and some of the most effective political statements of the period were presented as drama and not conveyed in print. Nevertheless, literacy continued to spread and led to greater opportunities for knowledge and reflection. The medium of print became increasingly important to political life. In the visual arts, the dramatic impulse was wedded to religious purposes to create works that conveyed both power and emotion.

Literacy and Literature

Traditional oral culture changed slowly under the impact of the spread of printing, education, and literacy. Works of literature from the late sixteenth and early seventeenth centuries incorporate material from traditional folktales, consciously reflecting the coexistence of oral and literate culture. In *Don Quixote*°, by Spain's Miguel de Cervantes° (1547–1616), the title character and his companion, Sancho Panza, have a long discussion about oral and literate traditions. The squire Panza speaks in the style that was customary in oral culture—a rather roundabout and repetitive style, which enabled the speaker and listener to remember what was said. Much of the richness of *Don Quixote* is due to the interweaving of prose styles and topical concerns from throughout Cervantes' culture—from the oral world of peasants to the refined world of court life. Yet the perspective that enabled Cervantes to accomplish this rich portrayal came

---

Riga (REE-guh)   **Sejm** (SAME)

Quixote (key-HO-tay)   **Cervantes** (sair-VAHN-tayz)

from his own highly developed literacy and the awareness of language that literacy made possible.

The spread of education and literacy in the late sixteenth century had a dramatic impact on attitudes toward literature and on literature itself. The value of education—particularly of the continuing humanist recovery of ancient wisdom—was reflected in much of the literature of the period. Writers found in humanistic education a vision of what it meant to be cultivated and disciplined men of the world. This vision provided the beginnings of a new self-image for members of the warrior class.

It is customary to regard the French author Michel de Montaigne° (1533–1592) as the epitome of the reflective—and, more important, the *self*-reflective—gentleman. Montaigne was a judge in the parlement (law court) of Bordeaux. In 1570 he resigned from the court and retired to his small château, where he wrote his *Essais* (from which we derive the word *essays*), a collection of short reflections that were revolutionary in both form and content. Montaigne invented writing in the form of a sketch, an "attempt" (the literal meaning of *essai*) that enabled him to combine self-reflection with formal analysis.

Montaigne's reflections range from the destructiveness of the French civil wars to the consequences of European exploration of the New World. Toward all of these events and circumstances, Montaigne was able to achieve an analytic detachment remarkable for his day. For example, he noted an irony in Europeans labeling New World peoples "savages," given Europeans' seemingly endless and wanton violence against those "savages" and one another. (See the box "Global Encounters: Montaigne Discusses Barbarity in the New World and the Old.") Owing to the spread of printing and literacy, Montaigne had—in addition to his own effort and the resources of leisure—a virtually unparalleled opportunity to reflect on the world through reading the wide variety of printed texts available to him. For the first time it was possible for a leisured lay reader to consider and compare different events, values, and cultures.

Montaigne's essays also reveal a distancing from himself. This distancing was another result of literacy—not simply the ability to read and write but the capacity to enjoy long periods of solitude and reflection in the company of other solitary, book-bound voices. Montaigne's works mark the beginning of what we know as the "invention" of private life, in which an individual is known more by internal character and personality traits than by social role and past behavior.

Montaigne (mon-TEN-yuh)

The works of the great English poet and playwright William Shakespeare (1564–1616) are still compelling to us because of the profundity of the questions he asked about love, honor, and political legitimacy, but he asked these questions in terms appropriate to his own day. One of his favorite themes—evident in *Hamlet* and *Macbeth*—is the legitimacy of rulers. He was at his most skilled, perhaps, when exploring the contradictions in values between the growing commercial world he saw around him and the older, seemingly more stable world of feudal society. Subtle political commentary distinguishes Shakespeare's later plays, written near and shortly after the death of Queen Elizabeth in 1603, when political and economic problems were becoming increasingly visible and troublesome. Shakespeare explored not only the duties of rulers but also the rights of their subjects. In *Coriolanus* he portrays commoners as poor but neither ignorant nor wretched; they are in fact fully rational and capable of analyzing their situation—perhaps more capable, Shakespeare hints, than their ruler is. The play is safely set in ancient Rome, but the social and political tensions it depicts clearly applied to the Elizabethan present.

Shakespeare, Cervantes, and other writers of their day were also representatives of what were starting to be self-consciously distinct national literatures. The spread of humanism added a historical dimension to their awareness of their own languages and to their distinct subject matter: each one's own society and its past. This kind of self-consciousness is evident in Shakespeare's historical plays, such as *Henry V* and *Richard II*. In *Richard II* he depicts the kingdom in terms that reflect the Elizabethan sense of England as a separate and self-contained nation:

> This royal throne of kings, this scept'red isle,
> This earth of majesty, this seat of Mars,
> This other Eden, demi-paradise,
> This fortress built by Nature for herself
> Against infection and the hand of war,
> This happy breed of men, this little world,
> This precious stone set in the silver sea . . .
> This blessed plot, this earth, this realm, this
>   England . . .
> (*Richard II*, act 2, sc. 1, lines 40–50)[5]

The Great Age of Theater

Shakespeare's extraordinary career was possible because his life coincided with the rise of professional theater. In the capitals of England and Spain professional theaters first opened in the 1570s. Some drama was produced at court or in aristocratic households, but most

Montaigne Discusses Barbarity in the New World and the Old

In one of his most famous essays, the French jurist and essayist Michel de Montaigne (1533–1592) ironically compares the customs of Native Americans with the customs of his own society. Information about Native Americans came from published reports of European voyages and from news of individual Native Americans who had journeyed (usually forcibly) to Europe. Europeans' encounters with peoples in the New World gave Montaigne a vantage point from which to criticize his own society.

They have their wars with [other] nations, to which they go quite naked, with no other arms than bows or wooden spears. . . . It is astonishing that firmness they show in their combats, which never end but in slaughter and bloodshed; for, as to routs and terror, they know nothing of either.

Each man brings back as his trophy the head of the enemy he has killed. . . . After they have treated their prisoner well for a long time with all the hospitality they can think of . . . they kill him with their swords. This done, they roast him and eat him in common and send some pieces to their absent friends.

I am not sorry that we notice the barbarous horror of such acts, but am heartily sorry that . . . we should be so blind to our own. I think there is more barbarity . . . in tearing by tortures and the rack a body still full of feeling, in roasting a man bit by bit, having him bitten and mangled by dogs (as we have not only read but seen within fresh mem-

ory . . . among neighbors and fellow citizens, and what is worse, on the pretext of piety and religion).

Three of these men (were brought to France) . . . and [someone] wanted to know what they had found most amazing. . . . They said that in the first place they thought it very strange that so many grown men, bearded, strong and armed who were around the king . . . should submit to obey a child [the young French king]. . . . Second (they have a way in their language of speaking of men as halves of one another), they had noticed that there were among us men full and gorged with all sorts of good things, and that their other halves were beggars at their doors, emaciated with hunger and poverty; and they thought it strange that these needy halves could endure such injustice.

QUESTIONS

1. What practices in the two cultures is Montaigne commenting on in this excerpt?

2. In what ways does he find Native American culture admirable by comparison to his own? What aspects of his own culture is he criticizing?

3. How are contemporary events and conditions reflected in Montaigne's remarks?

SOURCE: Donald M. Frame, trans., *The Complete Essays of Montaigne* (Stanford, Calif.: Stanford University Press, 1948), pp. 153, 155–159. Reprinted by permission of the publisher.

---

public theaters drew large and very mixed audiences, including the poorest city dwellers. Playwrights, including Shakespeare, often wrote in teams under great pressure to keep acting companies supplied with material. The best-known dramatist in Spain, Lope de Vega° (1562–1635), wrote more than fifteen hundred works on a wide range of topics. Although religious themes remained popular in Spanish theater, as an echo of medieval drama, most plays in England and Spain treated secular subjects and, as in *Coriolanus,* safely disguised political commentary.

Over time theater became increasingly restricted to aristocratic circles. In England Puritan criticism of the "immorality" of public performance drove actors and playwrights to seek royal patronage. The first professional

theater to open in Paris, in 1629, as political and religious turmoil quieted, quickly became dependent on Cardinal Richelieu's patronage. Inevitably, as court patronage grew in importance, the wide range of subjects treated in plays began to narrow to those of aristocratic concern, such as family honor and martial glory. These themes are depicted in the works of the Spaniard Pedro Calderón° (1600–1681), who wrote for his enthusiastic patron, Philip IV, and of the Frenchman Pierre Corneille° (1606–1684), whose great tragedy of aristocratic life, *Le Cid,* was one of the early successes of the seventeenth-century French theater.

Drama's significance as an art form is reflected in its impact on the development of music: the opera, which weds drama to music, was invented in Italy in the early

---

Lope de Vega (LOW-pah day VAY-guh)

Calderón (kall-day-ROHN)   **Corneille** (kore-NAY)

seventeenth century. The first great work in this genre is generally acknowledged to be *Orfeo* (*Orpheus,* 1607) by Claudio Monteverdi° (1567–1643). Opera, like drama, reflected the influence of humanism in its secular themes and in its emulation of Greek drama, which had used both words and music. The practice of music itself changed under the dramatic impulse. Monteverdi was the first master of a new musical style known as "monody," which emphasizes the progression of chords. Monodic music is inherently dramatic, creating a sense of forward movement, expectation, and resolution.

Sovereignty in Ceremony, Image, and Word

Whether produced on a public stage or at court or in a less formal setting, drama was a favored method of communication in this era because people responded to and made extensive use of the spoken word. Dramatic gesture and storytelling to get a message across were commonplace and were important components of politics.

What we might call "street drama" was an ordinary occurrence. When great noble governors entered major towns, such as when Margaret of Parma entered Brussels, a solemn yet ostentatious formal "entry" was often staged. The dignitary would ride through the main gate, usually beneath a canopy made of luxurious cloth. The event might include staged tableaux in the town's streets, with costumed townspeople acting out brief symbolic vignettes, such as David and Goliath, and it might end with an elaborate banquet. A remnant of these proceedings survives today in the ceremony by which distinguished visitors are given "the keys to the city," which, in the sixteenth century, really were functional.

Royalty made deliberate and careful use of dramatic ceremony. Royal entries into towns took on an added weight, as did royal funerals and other such occasions. These dramas reinforced political and constitutional assumptions in the minds of witnesses and participants. Thus over time we can see changes in the representations of royal power. In France, for example, the ritual entry of the king into Paris had originally stressed the participation of the leading guilds, judges, and administrators, symbolizing their active role in governing the city and the kingdom. But in the last half of the sixteenth century the procession began to glorify the king alone. Speculation about and celebration of power, as well as dramatic emotion, also occurred in the visual arts—most notably in painting and architecture, in the style now known as "baroque°." Baroque style was a new kind of visual language that could project power and grandeur and simultaneously engage viewers' senses. (See the feature "Weighing the Evidence: Baroque Art" on pages 536–537.)

The very fact that rulers experimented self-consciously with self-representation suggests that issues pertaining to the nature and extent of royal power were profoundly important and far from settled. Queen Elizabeth I had the particular burden of assuming the throne in a period of great instability. Hence she paid a great deal of attention to the image of herself that she conveyed in words and authorized to be fashioned in painting. Elizabeth

An Image of Royalty   This dramatic painting of Charles I on horseback was executed by the baroque artist Anthony Van Dyck in about 1633. It was one of several paintings of himself and the royal family that Charles commissioned from Van Dyck. This painting was originally hung at the end of a long gallery in one of the royal palaces, next to similarly triumphal images of Roman emperors.   *(The Royal Collection © 2003, Her Majesty Queen Elizabeth II)*

Monteverdi (mon-tay-VAIR-dee)   **baroque** (ba-ROKE)

READING SOURCES

ELIZABETH I ADDRESSES HER TROOPS

The day after English ships dispersed the Spanish Armada in 1588, Elizabeth addressed a contingent of her troops. She used the opportunity to fashion an image of herself as a warrior above all but also as the beloved familiar of her people, unafraid of potential plots against her. Note her willingness to portray herself as androgynous—that is, embodying both female and male qualities.

My loving people, we have been persuaded by some that are careful of our safety, to take heed how we commit ourselves to armed multitudes, for fear of treachery. But I assure you, I do not desire to live to distrust my faithful and loving people. Let tyrants fear. I have always so behaved myself that, under God, I have placed my chiefest strength in the loyal hearts and good will of my subjects; and therefore I am come amongst you, as you see, at this time, not for my reaction or disport, but being resolved, in the midst and heat of the battle, to live or die amongst you all, to lay down for my God, and for my kingdom, and for my people, my honor and my blood, even in the dust. I know I have the body of a weak and feeble woman, but I have the heart and the stomach of a king, and of a king of England too, and think foul scorn that Parma or Spain, or any prince of Europe should dare to invade the borders of my realm; to which, rather than any dishonor shall grow by me, I myself will take up arms, I myself will be your general, judge, and rewarder of every one of your virtues in the field.

Source: J. E. Neale, *Queen Elizabeth I* (New York: Anchor, 1957), pp. 308–309.

styled herself variously as mother to her people and as a warrior-queen (drawing on ancient myths of Amazon women). She made artful use of the image of her virginity to buttress each of these images—as the wholly devoted, self-sacrificing mother (which, of course, had religious tradition behind it) or as an androgynous ruler, woman but doing the bodily work of man. (See the box "Reading Sources: Elizabeth I Addresses Her Troops.")

More formal speculation about constitutional matters also resulted from the tumult of the sixteenth and seventeenth centuries. As we have seen, the Protestant faction in France advanced an elaborate argument for the limitation of royal power. Alternative theories enhancing royal authority were offered, principally in support of the Catholic position though also simply to buttress the beleaguered monarchy itself. The most famous of these appeared in *The Six Books of the Republic* (1576), by the legal scholar Jean Bodin° (1530–1596). Bodin was a Catholic but offered a fundamentally secular perspective on the purposes and source of power within a state. His special contribution was a vision of a truly sovereign monarch. Bodin offered a theoretical understanding that is essential to states today and is the ground on which people can claim rights and protection from the state—namely, that there is a final sovereign authority. For Bodin that authority was the king. He recognized that in practice royal power was constrained by limitations, but he was intrigued more by the theoretical grounding for royal authority than by its practical application.

Contract theory devised by French Protestants to legitimize resistance to the monarchy had to be abandoned when Henry IV granted toleration to the Huguenots in 1598. In England theoretical justification of resistance to Charles I was initially limited to invoking tradition and precedent. Contract theory, as well as other sweeping claims regarding subjects' rights, would be more fully developed later in the century.

Bodin's theory of sovereignty, however, was immediately echoed in other theoretical works, most notably that of Hugo Grotius° (1583–1645). A Dutch jurist and diplomat, Grotius developed the first principles of modern international law. He accepted the existence of sovereign states that owed no loyalty to higher authority (such as the papacy) and thus needed new principles to govern their interactions. His major work, *De Jure Belli ac Pacis* (*On the Law of War and Peace*, 1625), was written in response to the turmoil of the Thirty Years' War. Grotius argued that relations between states could be based on

Bodin (bo-DAHN)

Grotius (GROW-shus)

respect for treaties voluntarily reached between them. In perhaps his boldest move he argued that war must be justified, and he developed criteria to distinguish just from unjust wars.

SUMMARY

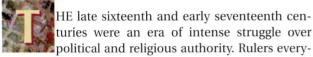 HE late sixteenth and early seventeenth centuries were an era of intense struggle over political and religious authority. Rulers everywhere, through a variety of expedients, tried to buttress and expand royal power. They were resisted by traditional centers of power, such as independent-minded nobles. But they were also resisted by the novel challenge of religious dissent, which empowered subjects both to claim a greater right to question authority and to risk more in their attempts to oppose it. In some areas of Europe, such as the Holy Roman Empire, the struggles reached some resolution. In other areas, such as England, decades of bloody conflict still lay ahead.

On the whole these conflicts did little to improve the lives of ordinary people since for the most part victorious elites decided matters of religion and governance in their own interests. In addition, the difficult economic circumstances of these decades meant that working people, desperate for a secure livelihood, rioted or took up arms out of economic as well as religious concerns.

Yet however grim the circumstances people faced, the technology of print and the spread of literacy helped spur speculative and creative works by providing the means for reflection and the audiences to receive and appreciate it. Ironically, the increased importance and grandeur of court life, though a cause of political strain, resulted in a new wave of patronage for art, literature, and drama. Some of the works we still value portray the splendid ambience of royal courts. Other works, such as Shakespeare's plays, both reflect and reflect on the tensions and contradictions in the society of the day: for example, the importance of the stability provided by royal authority as opposed to the dignity and wisdom of ordinary people, who had no claim to power at all.

■ Notes

1. Geoffrey Parker, *The Dutch Revolt* (London: Penguin, 1985), p. 288, n. 5.
2. Quoted in A. W. Lovett, *Early Habsburg Spain, 1517–1598* (Oxford: Oxford University Press, 1986), p. 212.

3. Quoted in R. J. Knecht, *The French Wars of Religion, 1559–1598* (London: Longman, 1989), p. 109.
4. Quoted in Jean Berenger, *A History of the Habsburg Empire, 1273–1700,* trans. C. A. Simpson (London and New York: Longman, 1990), p. 239.
5. *The Riverside Shakespeare,* ed. G. Blakemore Evans, 2d ed. (Boston: Houghton Mifflin, 1997), p. 855. Copyright © 1997 by Houghton Mifflin Company. Reprinted by permission of the publisher.

■ Suggested Reading

Berenger, Jean. *A History of the Habsburg Empire, 1273–1700,* trans. C. A. Simpson. 1990. A detailed treatment of Habsburg rule in the Holy Roman Empire and in their own principalities. Considers economic and cultural changes as well as political ones.

Bonney, Richard. *The European Dynastic States, 1494–1660.* 1991. A rich survey of the period that is solid on eastern as well as western Europe. Written from an English point of view, it does not consider England as part of Europe.

Eagleton, Terry. *William Shakespeare.* 1986. A brief and highly readable interpretation of Shakespeare that emphasizes the tensions in the plays caused by language and by ideas from the new world of bourgeois commercial life.

Edwards, Philip. *The Making of the Modern English State.* 2001. A readable survey of political and religious developments in England that incorporates much new scholarship.

Holt, Mack P. *The French Wars of Religion, 1562–1629.* 1995. An up-to-date synthesis that evaluates social and political context while not slighting the importance of religion.

Lynch, John. *Spain, 1516–1598: From Nation-State to World Empire.* 1991. A survey covering the reign of Philip II by a leading scholar of Spanish history.

Parker, Geoffrey. *The Military Revolution.* 1988; and Black, Jeremy. *A Military Revolution?* 1991. Two works that disagree about the nature and extent of the changes in military practices and their significance for military, political, and social history. Black tries to refute claims of a dramatic military "revolution."

Parker, Geoffrey. *The Dutch Revolt.* 2d ed. 1985. The best survey of the revolt available in English.

Wiesner, Merry. *Women and Gender in Early Modern Europe.* 1993. Discusses all aspects of women's experience, including their working lives.

 For a searchable list of additional readings for this chapter, go to college.hmco.com/students.

Baroque Art

If today you were to walk through the cathedral in the Belgian city of Antwerp and notice this painting, titled *The Raising of the Cross,* it might not strike you as remarkable. The crucifixion of Jesus is a frequent subject of religious painting, after all. But let us look at the image more carefully. First of all, this is a portrayal not of Jesus on the cross but rather of the *raising* of the cross. In other words, it captures a moment of action, not its aftermath. The frame of the painting is filled with action as well. The figures on the left and at the center support the cross and push it up. At the bottom right we see figures straining at ropes as they pull the cross upright. Our eye is drawn to the movement in the painting partly by the use of light, which floods the figure of Jesus. We also note the unexpected diagonal position of the crucified figure, and we survey the image in order to make sense of it.

This is a dynamic painting, and simultaneously an emotionally engaging one. We encounter Jesus not as a static, perhaps already dying, figure on the cross, but at the very moment of his crucifixion. There is also a striking similarity between the figure of Jesus and those of the men who are working hard to accomplish his crucifixion: they are all men, whose muscled bodies are more alike than not. The human pathos of the moment is brought to life.

The image you see before you is one of three panels in a triptych, or three-paneled altarpiece. The left-hand panel depicts Saint John, the Virgin Mary, and others witnessing Jesus's crucifixion. The panel on the right shows a Roman officer watching over his soldiers as they crucify two thieves. Whereas most triptychs of the period contained three unrelated images, here the panels combine to form a single story of the crucifixion.

This altarpiece was executed in 1610 by the influential painter Peter Paul Rubens (1577–1640), a native of Antwerp, in the southern Netherlands. Rubens was one of the great masters of what came to be called the baroque style. Baroque techniques were pioneered in the late sixteenth century in Italy, first in church design, and spread slowly, with many regional variations, especially throughout Catholic Europe, during the seventeenth century. The origin of the term *baroque* has been debated; it may have come from the Portuguese *barroco,* used to describe irregularly shaped pearls. The term as applied to the arts was initially derogatory, denoting distortion, illogic, and irregularity. Baroque painting was distinguished by the dramatic use of color and shading and

by the dynamic energy of figures. Baroque artists based their work on Renaissance achievements in representing the human form in a convincing three-dimensional space. But with the strong use of light, movement, and more robust and realistic human figures, these artists enhanced the drama and emotional impact of what they depicted.

Like baroque artists, baroque architects modified the precision, symmetry, and orderliness of Renaissance architecture to produce a sense of greater dynamism in space. Baroque churches, for example, were impressively grand and monumental yet emotionally engaging at the same time. Façades and interiors were both massive and, through the clever use of architectural and decorative components, suggestive of movement. A good example of this is the work of Gianlorenzo Bernini° (1598–1680), who designed the portico outside Saint Peter's Basilica in Rome, as well as the highly ornate bronze canopy over the altar inside the basilica. Dramatic illusion in the interior of buildings—such as painting a chapel ceiling with figures receding as if ascending to heaven—was a common device in baroque architecture. One of the primary purposes of baroque architecture and art was to create simultaneously a display of power and an invitation to sensory experience. Baroque art encouraged piety that was not only emotionally involved, and thus satisfying, but also awe-inspired. In this way it reflected the aims of the Counter-Reformation church, whose leaders were among its most important patrons.

Peter Paul Rubens's early training in Italy shaped him as an artist and established his secondary career as a diplomat. Throughout his life he undertook diplomatic missions for the Habsburg viceroys in the Spanish Netherlands, gaining artistic commissions wherever he went. Rubens's subject matter varied widely, including church design and decoration, portraiture, and landscape painting, reflecting the fact that baroque art also had important secular applications. Indeed, magnificent baroque palaces symbolized the wealth and power of the elites (see the photos on pages 545 and 554).

Rulers began to employ artists as portrait painters, such as Rubens's pupil Anthony Van Dyck (1599–1641), whose painting of Charles I of England appears on page 533. Because portraits have become so common, we

---

Bernini (bare-NEE-nee)

Rubens: The Raising of the Cross
(Onze Lieve Vrouwkwerk, Antwerp Cathedral,
Belgium/Peter Willi/Bridgeman Art Library)

cannot fully appreciate how arresting this image would have been in its day. Like Rubens's *Raising of the Cross,* Van Dyck's image of Charles was a novel rendering of familiar elements. The image of a ruler on horseback was well known, but it had never been exploited as fully by English monarchs as it had been by rulers on the Continent. This large portrait of the king was designed to be hung at the end of a long palace corridor so that, from a distance, a courtier would have the illusion of actually seeing the king riding proudly through a triumphal arch. This effect was similar to that achieved by artists who painted church ceilings with receding angels and cherubs, giving the faithful the illusion of gazing up toward heaven.* Compare this portrait with the much more stilted one of Elizabeth I on page 519. It is striking how effective the technical and stylistic innovations of baroque art and architecture were in expressing secular as well as spiritual power.

---

*This discussion draws on the work of Roy Strong, *Van Dyck: Charles I on Horseback* (New York: Viking, 1972), pp. 20–25.

Europe in the Age of Louis XIV ca. 1640–1715

THE portrait of King Louis XIV of France as a triumphant warrior, to the left, was one of hundreds of such images of the king that decorated his palace at Versailles and other sites around his kingdom—where they made his subjects aware of his presence, regardless of whether he was in residence. Louis is dressed as a Roman warrior, and his power is represented by a mixture of other symbols—Christian and pagan, ancient and contemporary. An angel crowns him with a victor's laurel wreath and carries a banner bearing the image of the sun. In his hand Louis holds a marshal's baton—a symbol of military command—covered with the royal emblem of the fleur-de-lys°. In the background, behind the "Roman" troops following Louis, is an idealized city.

These trappings symbolized the significant expansion of royal power during Louis's reign. He faced down the challenges of warrior-nobles, suppressed religious dissent, and tapped the nation's wealth to wage a series of wars of conquest. A period of cultural brilliance early in his reign and the spectacle of an elaborate court life crowned his achievements. In his prime, his regime was supported by a consensus of elites; such harmony was made possible by the lack of institutional brakes on royal authority. However, as his attention to symbolism suggests, Louis's power was not unchallenged. By the end of the Sun King's reign the glow was fading: France was struggling under economic distress brought on by the many wars fought for his glory and had missed opportunities for commercial success abroad. Elites throughout France who had once accepted, even welcomed, his rule became trenchant critics, and common people outright rebels.

---

fleur-de-lys (flur–duh–LEE)

Louis XIV in Roman armor, by the contemporary artist Charles Le Brun. (Scala/Art Resource, NY)

France in the Age of Absolutism

English Civil War and Its Aftermath

New Powers in Central and Eastern Europe

The Expansion of Overseas Trade and Settlement

After the Thirty Years' War, vigorous rulers in central and eastern Europe undertook a program of territorial expansion and state building that led to the dominance in the region of Austria, Brandenburg-Prussia, and Russia. The power of these states derived, in part, from the economic relationship of their lands to the wider European economy. In all the major states of continental Europe, princely governments were able to monopolize military power for the first time, in return for economic and political concessions to noble landholders. In England, by contrast, the Crown faced rebellion by subjects claiming religious authority and political legitimacy for their causes. Resistance to the expansion of royal authority, led by Parliament, resulted in the execution of the king and the establishment of a short-lived republic, the Commonwealth. Although the monarchy was restored, the civil war had long-term consequences for royal power in England.

The seventeenth century also witnessed a dynamic phase of European expansion overseas, following on the successes of the Portuguese and the Spanish in the fifteenth and sixteenth centuries. Eager migrants settled in the Americas in ever increasing numbers, while forced migrants—enslaved Africans—were transported by the thousands to work on the profitable plantations of European colonizers. Aristocrats, merchants, and peasants back in Europe jockeyed to take advantage of—or to mitigate the effects of—the local political and economic impact of Europe's expansion.

QUESTIONS TO CONSIDER

- ✑ How did Louis XIV successfully expand royal power in France?

- ✑ What were the long-term consequences of the English civil war?

- ✑ What economic and political interests led to war in eastern Europe?

- ✑ How did the expansion of international trade and colonization affect European states and communities?

TERMS TO KNOW

Louis XIV	Treaty of Carlowitz
absolutism	Brandenburg-Prussia
mercantilism	Cossacks
Parliament	Peter the Great
Oliver Cromwell	Dutch East India Company
Glorious Revolution	plantation system

FRANCE IN THE AGE OF ABSOLUTISM

ABSOLUTISM is a term often used to describe the extraordinary concentration of power in royal hands achieved by the kings of France, most notably Louis XIV (r. 1643–1715), in the seventeenth century. Louis continued the expansion of state power begun by his father's minister, Cardinal Richelieu (see page 518). The extension of royal power, under Louis as well as his predecessor, was accelerated by the desire to sustain an expensive and aggressive foreign policy. The policy itself was partly traditional—fighting the perpetual enemy, the Habsburgs, and seeking military glory—and partly new—expanding the borders of France. Louis XIV's successes in these undertakings made him both envied and emulated by other rulers: the French court became a model of culture and refinement. But increased royal authority was not accepted without protest: common French people as well as elites dug in their heels.

The Last Challenge to Absolutism: The Fronde, 1648–1653

Louis came to the throne as a 5-year-old child in 1643. Acting as his regent, his mother, Anne of Austria (1601–1666), had to defuse a serious challenge to royal authority during her son's minority. Together with her chief minister and personal friend, Cardinal Jules Mazarin°

Mazarin (mah-zah-RAHN)

(1602–1661), she faced opposition from royal bureaucrats and the traditional nobility as well as the common people.

Revolts against the concentration of power in royal hands and against the exorbitant taxation that had prevailed under Louis's father began immediately. In one province a group of armed peasants cornered the intendant and forced him to agree to lower taxes; elsewhere provincial parlements tried to abolish special ranks of officials, especially the intendants, created by Richelieu. In 1648, after several more years of foreign war and the financial expedients to sustain it, the most serious revolt began, led by the Parlement° of Paris and the other sovereign law courts in the capital.

The source of the Parlement's leverage over the monarchy was its traditional right to register laws and edicts, which amounted to judicial review. Now the Parlement, as a guardian of royal authority, attempted to extend this power by debating and even initiating government policy. The sovereign courts sitting together drew up a reform program abolishing most of the machinery of government established under Richelieu and calling for consent to future taxation. The citizens of Paris rose to defend the courts when royal troops were sent against them in October.

Mazarin was forced to accept the proposed reform of government, at least in theory. He also had to avert challenges by great nobles for control of the young king's council. Civil war waxed and waned around France from 1648 to 1653. The main combatants were conventionally ambitious great nobles, but reform-minded urban dwellers often made common cause with them, to benefit from their military power. Meanwhile, middling nobles in the region around Paris began to devise a thoroughgoing reform program and to prepare for a meeting of the Estates General—a representative assembly—to enact it.

These revolts begun in 1648 were derided with the name "Fronde°," which was a popular children's game. However, the Fronde was not child's play; it constituted a serious challenge to the legacy of royal government as it had developed under Richelieu. It ended without a noteworthy impact on the growth of royal power for several reasons. First, Mazarin methodically regained control of the kingdom through armed force and artful concessions to individual aristocrats, who were always eager to trade their loyalty for the fruits of royal service. Meanwhile, the Parlement of Paris, as well as many citizens of the capital, welcomed a return to royal authority when civil war caused starvation as well as political unrest.

Moreover, the Parlement of Paris was a law court, not a representative assembly. Its legitimacy derived from

Parlement (par-luh-MAWNH)   Fronde (FRAWND)

CHRONOLOGY

1602	Dutch East India Company formed
1607	Jamestown colony founded in Virginia
1608	Champlain founds Quebec City
1613	Michael becomes first Romanov tsar in Russia
1620	Pilgrims settle at Plymouth (Massachusetts)
1642–1648	Civil war in England
1643	Louis XIV becomes king of France
1648–1653	Fronde revolts in France
1649	Execution of Charles I
1649–1660	English Commonwealth
1659	Peace of the Pyrenees
1660	Monarchy restored in England
1661	Louis XIV assumes full control of government
1672–1678	Dutch War
1682	Peter the Great becomes tsar of Russia
1685	Edict of Nantes revoked
1688	Glorious Revolution
1699	Treaty of Carlowitz
1700–1721	Great Northern War
1701–1714	War of the Spanish Succession
1713	Peace of Utrecht
1715	Death of Louis XIV

its role as upholder of royal law, and it could not, over time, challenge the king on the pretext of upholding royal tradition in his name. Parlementaires tended to see the Estates General as a rival institution and helped quash the proposed meeting of representatives. Above all, they wanted to avert reforms such as the abolition of the paulette, a fee guaranteeing the hereditary right to royal office (see page 516).

Unlike in England, there was in France no single institutional focus for resistance to royal power. A strong-willed and able ruler, as Louis XIV proved to be, could obstruct or override challenges to royal power, particularly when he satisfied the ambitions of aristocrats and those bureaucrats who profited from the expansion of royal power. Moreover, the young Louis had been traumatized by the uprisings of the Fronde and grew up determined never to allow another such challenge to his absolute sovereignty.

France Under Louis XIV, 1661–1715

Louis XIV fully assumed control of government at Mazarin's death in 1661. It was a propitious moment. The Peace of the Pyrenees in 1659 had ended in France's favor the wars with Spain that had dragged on since the end of the Thirty Years' War. As part of the peace agreement, Louis married a Spanish princess, Maria Theresa. In the first ten years of his active reign Louis achieved a degree of control over the mechanisms of government unparalleled in the history of monarchy in France or anywhere else in Europe. Louis was extremely vigorous and proved a diligent king. He put in hours a day at a desk while sustaining the ceremonial life of the court, with its elaborate hunts, balls, and other public events.

Louis did not invent any new bureaucratic devices but rather used existing ranks of officials in new ways that increased government efficiency and further centralized control. He radically reduced the number of men in his High Council, the advisory body closest to the king, to include only three or four great ministers of state affairs. This intimate group, with Louis's active participation, handled all policymaking. The ministers of state, war, and finance were chosen exclusively from non-noble men of bourgeois background whose training and experience fitted them for such positions. Jean-Baptiste Colbert° (1619–1683), perhaps the greatest of them, served as minister of finance and supervised most domestic policy from 1665 until his death. He was from a merchant family and had served for years under Mazarin.

Several dozen other officials, picked from the ranks of up-and-coming lawyers and administrators, drew up laws and regulations and passed them to the intendants for execution at the provincial level. Sometimes these officials at the center were sent to the provinces on short-term supervisory missions. The effect of this system was to bypass many entrenched provincial bureaucrats, particularly those known as tax farmers. Tax farmers were freelance businessmen who bid for the right to collect taxes in a region in return for a negotiated fee they paid to the Crown. The Crown, in short, did not control its own tax revenues. The money Louis's regime saved by the more efficient collection of taxes (revenues almost doubled in some areas) enabled the government to streamline the bureaucracy: dozens of the offices created over the years to bring cash in were bought back by the Crown from their owners.

The system still relied on the bonds of patronage and personal service—political bonds borrowed from aristocratic life. Officials rose through the ranks by means of service to the great, and family connection and personal loyalty still were essential. Of the seventeen different men who were part of Louis XIV's High Council during his reign, five were members of the Colbert family, for example. In the provinces important local families vied for minor posts, which at least provided prestige and some income.

Further benefits of centralized administration can be seen in certain achievements of the early years of Louis's regime. Colbert actively encouraged France's economic development. He reduced the internal tolls and customs barriers, which were relics of medieval decentralization—for example, the right of a landholder to charge a toll on all boats along a river under his control. He encouraged industry with state subsidies and protective tariffs. He set up state-sponsored trading companies—the two most important being the East India Company and the West India Company, established in 1664.

Mercantilism is the term historians use to describe the theory behind Colbert's efforts. This economic theory stressed self-sufficiency in manufactured goods, tight control of trade to foster the domestic economy, and the absolute value of bullion. Both capital for development—in the form of hard currency, known as bullion—and the amount of world trade were presumed to be limited in quantity. Therefore state intervention in the form of protectionist policies was believed necessary to guarantee a favorable balance of payments.

This static model of national wealth did not wholly fit the facts of growing international trade in the seventeenth century. Nevertheless, mercantilist philosophy was helpful to France. France became self-sufficient in the all-important production of woolen cloth, and French industry expanded notably in other sectors. Colbert's greatest success was the systematic expansion of the navy and merchant marine. By 1677 the navy had increased almost sixfold, to 144 ships. By the end of Louis XIV's reign the French navy was virtually the equal of the English navy.

Colbert and the other ministers began to develop the kind of planned government policymaking that we now take for granted. Partly by means of their itinerant

---

Colbert (coal-BEAR)

supervisory officials, they tried to formulate and execute policy based on carefully collected information. How many men of military age were available? How abundant was this year's harvest? Answers to such questions enabled not only the formulation of economic policy but also the deliberate management of production and services to achieve certain goals—above all, the recruitment and supply of the king's vast armies.

Beginning in 1673 Louis tried to bring the religious life of the realm more fully under royal control, claiming for himself—with mixed success—some of the church revenues and powers of ecclesiastical appointment that still remained to the pope. Partly to bolster his position with the pope, he also began to attack the Huguenot community in France. First he offered financial inducements for conversion to Catholicism. Then he took more drastic steps, such as destroying Protestant churches and quartering troops in Huguenots' homes to force them to convert. In 1685 he declared that France would no longer abide any Protestant community, and he revoked the Edict of Nantes. A hundred thousand Protestant subjects—including some six hundred army and navy officers—refused even nominal conversion to Catholicism and chose to emigrate.

Meanwhile, Louis faced resistance to his claims against the pope from within the ranks of French clergy. These churchmen represented a movement within French Catholicism known as Jansenism, after Cornelius Jansen, a professor of theology whose writings were its inspiration. Jansenists practiced an austere style of Catholic religiosity that, in its notions about human will and sinfulness, was akin to some Protestant doctrine. Louis was suspicious of Jansenism because its adherents included many of his political enemies, particularly among families of parlement officials. Louis was wary of any threat to the institutional—or symbolic—unity of his regime, such as Protestants and Jansenists represented. At the end of Louis's long reign another pope obligingly declared many Jansenist doctrines to be heretical as part of a compromise agreement with Louis on matters of church governance and finance. Louis's efforts to exert greater control over the church had brought him modest practical gains, but at the price of weakening the religious basis of his authority in the eyes of many sincere Catholics.

By modern standards the power of the Crown was still greatly limited. The "divine right" of kingship, a notion formulated by Louis's chief apologist, Bishop Jacques Bossuet° (1627–1704), did not mean unlimited power to rule; rather it meant that hereditary monarchy was the divinely ordained form of government, best suited to human needs. *Absolutism* was not ironfisted control of the realm but rather the successful focusing of energy, loyalties, and symbolic authority in the Crown. The government functioned well in the opening decades of Louis's reign because his role as the focal point of power and loyalty was both logical, after the preceding years of unrest, and skillfully exploited. Much of the glue holding together the absolutist state lay in informal mechanisms such as patronage and court life, as well as in the traditional hunt for military glory—all of which Louis amply supplied.

The Life of the Court

An observer comparing the lives of prominent noble families in the mid-sixteenth and mid-seventeenth centuries would have noticed striking differences. By the second half of the seventeenth century, most sovereigns or territorial princes had the power to crush revolts, and the heirs of the feudal nobility had to accommodate themselves to the increased power of the Crown. The nobility relinquished its former independence but retained economic and social supremacy and, as a consequence, considerable political clout. Nobles also developed new ways to symbolize their privilege by means of cultural refinement. This process was particularly dramatic in France as a strong Crown won out over a proud nobility.

One sign of Louis's success in marshaling the loyalty of the aristocracy was the brilliant court life that his regime sustained. No longer able to wield independent political power, aristocrats lived at court whenever they could. There they endlessly jostled for patronage and prestige—for commands in the royal army and for honorific positions at court itself. (See the box "Reading Sources: A Courtier Criticizes the King.") A favored courtier might, for example, participate in the elaborate daily *lever* (arising) of the king; he might be allowed to hand the king his shirt—a demeaning task, yet a coveted one for the attention by the king that it implied and guaranteed. Courtiers now defended their honor with private duels, not warfare, and more routinely relied on elegant ceremonial, precise etiquette, and clever conversation to demarcate their political and social distinctiveness. (See the feature "Weighing the Evidence: Table Manners" on pages 570–571.)

As literacy became more widespread and the power of educated bureaucrats of even humble origin became more obvious, nobles from the traditional aristocracy began increasingly to use reading and writing as a means to think critically about their behavior—in the case of men, to re-imagine themselves as gentlemen rather than warriors. Noblewomen and noblemen alike began to reflect

---

Bossuet (BOS-soo-way)

READING SOURCES

A COURTIER CRITICIZES THE KING

Louis de Rouvroy, duke of Saint-Simon (1675–1755), was a favored courtier but one critical of Louis XIV on a number of counts. In this excerpt from his memoirs, Saint-Simon evaluates the character of the king and criticizes his reliance on men of bourgeois background for his leading ministers. As a member of the traditional aristocracy, Saint-Simon certainly had a reason for disliking this policy. However, this testimony does have the ring of unbiased authenticity in some important respects.

The king's] ministers, general, mistresses and courtiers learned soon after he became their master that glory, to him, was a foible rather than an ambition. They therefore flattered him to the top of his bent, and in so doing, spoiled him. Praise, or better, adulation . . . were the only road to his favour and those whom he liked owed his friendship to choosing their moments well and never ceasing in their attentions. That is what gave his ministers their power, for they had endless opportunities of flattering his vanity, especially by suggesting that he was the source of all their ideas. . . .

He was well aware that though he might crush a nobleman with the weight of his displeasure, he could not destroy him or his line, whereas a secretary of state or other such minister could be reduced together with his whole family to those depths of nothingness from which he had been elevated. . . . Therein lay the reason for the watchful, jealous attitude of his ministers, who made it difficult for the King to hear any but themselves, although he pleased to think that he was an easy man to approach.

Nevertheless, in spite of the fact that the King had been so spoiled with false notions of majesty and power, that every other thought was stifled in him, there was much to be gained from a private audience, if it might be obtained, and if one knew how to conduct oneself with all the respect due to his dignity and habits. Once in his study, however prejudiced he might be . . . he would listen patiently, good-naturedly, and with a real desire to be informed. You could see that he had a sense of justice and a will to get at the truth. . . . It is therefore enough to make one weep to think of the wickedness of an education designed solely to suppress the . . . intelligence of that prince, and the insidious poison of barefaced flattery which make him a kind of god in the very heart of Christendom.

Source: Louis, duc de Saint-Simon, *Versailles, the Court and Louis XIV,* ed. Lucy Norton (New York: Harper and Row, 1966), pp. 248–251. Reprinted by permission of the Estate of Lucy Norton.

---

on their new roles in letters, memoirs, and the first novels. A prominent theme of these works is the increasing necessity for a truly private life of affection and trust, with which to counterbalance the public façade necessary to an aspiring courtier. The most influential early French novel was *The Princess of Cleves* by Marie-Madeleine Pioche de la Vergne (1634–1693), best known by her title, Madame de Lafayette. Mme. de Lafayette's novel treats the particular difficulties faced by aristocratic women who, without military careers to bring glory and provide distraction, were more vulnerable than men to gossip and slander at court and more trapped by their arranged marriages.

Louis XIV's court is usually associated with the palace he built at Versailles°, southwest of Paris. Some of the greatest talent of the day worked on the design and construction of Versailles from 1670 through the 1680s. It became a masterpiece of luxurious but restrained baroque style—a model for royal and aristocratic palaces throughout Europe for the next one hundred years.

Before Louis's court in his later years withdrew to Versailles, it traveled among the king's several châteaux around the kingdom, and in this itinerant period of the reign, court life was actually at its most creative and productive. These early years of Louis's personal reign were the heyday of French drama. The comedian Jean-Baptiste Poquelin, known as Molière° (1622–1673), impressed the young Louis with his productions in the late 1650s and was rewarded with the use of a theater in the main royal palace in Paris. Like Shakespeare earlier in the century, Molière explored the social and political tensions of his day. He satirized the pretensions of the aristocracy, the social climbing of the bourgeoisie, and the self-righteous piety of clerics. Some of his plays were banned from performance, but most were not only tolerated but extremely

---

Versailles (vare-SIGH)

Molière (mole-YARE)

The Château of Versailles   This view of the central section of the palace is taken from the gardens. The reflecting pools you see here are on the first level of an immense terraced garden that, to someone exiting the château, seems to stretch to the horizon. The apparent openness of the king's residence (notice the rows of floor-length windows on the ground floor) is in stark contrast to a fortified castle and was a dramatic statement of a new kind of royal power.   *(Château de Versailles, France/Peter Willi/The Bridgeman Art Library)*

popular with the elite audiences they mocked. Their popularity is testimony to the confidence of Louis's regime in its early days.

Also popular at court were the tragedies of Jean Racine[6] (1639–1699), who was to the French theater what Shakespeare was to the English: the master of poetic language. His plays, which treat familiar classical stories, focus on the emotional and psychological lives of the characters and often stress the unpredictable, usually unhappy, role of fate, even among royalty. The pessimism in Racine foreshadowed the less successful second half of Louis's reign.

The Burdens of War and the Limits of Power

Wars initiated by Louis XIV dominated the attention of most European states in the second half of the seventeenth century. Louis's wars sprang from traditional causes: the importance of the glory and dynastic aggrandizement

---

Racine (rah-SEEN)

of the king and the preoccupation of the aristocracy with military life. But if Louis's wars were spurred by familiar concerns about territorial and economic advantage, they were far more demanding on state resources than any previous wars.

In France and elsewhere the size of armies grew markedly. And with the countryside still smarting from the rampaging armies of the Thirty Years' War, so did the need for greater management of troops. Louis XIV's victories in the second half of the century are partly traceable to his regime's attention to the bureaucratic tasks of recruitment, training, and supply, which together constituted another phase of the "military revolution." The new offensive tactics developed during the Thirty Years' War (see page 526) changed the character of armies in ways that demanded more resources for training. A higher proportion of soldiers became gunners, and their effectiveness lay in how well they operated as a unit. Armies began to train seriously off the field of battle because drill and discipline were vital to success. France was the

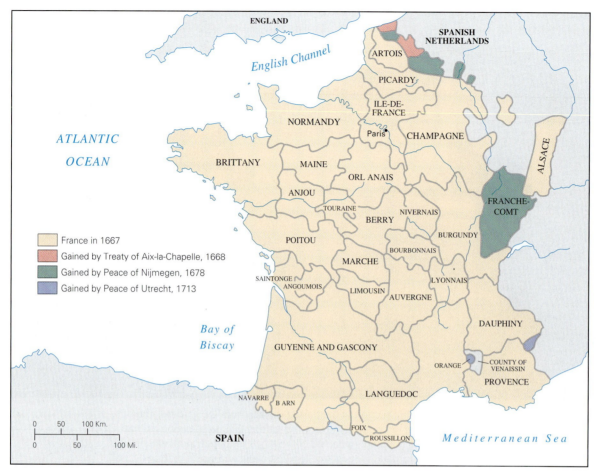

Map 16.1   Territorial Gains of Louis XIV, 1667–1715   Louis's wars, though enormously expensive for France, produced only modest gains of territory along France's eastern and northern frontiers.

first to provide its soldiers with uniforms, which boosted morale and improved discipline. The numbers of men on the battlefield increased somewhat as training increased the effectiveness of large numbers of infantry, but the total numbers of men in arms supported by the state at any time increased dramatically once the organization to support them was in place. Late in the century France kept more than 300,000 men in arms when at war (which was most of the time).

Louis's first war, in 1667, reflects the continuing French preoccupation with Spanish power on French frontiers. Louis invoked rather dubious dynastic claims to demand from Spain lands in the Spanish Netherlands and the large independent county on France's eastern border called the Franche-Comté° (see Map 16.1). After a

brief conflict, the French obtained only some towns in the Spanish Netherlands by the terms of the Treaty of Aix-la-Chapelle. Louis had already begun to negotiate with the Austrian Habsburgs over the eventual division of Spanish Habsburg lands, for it seemed likely that the Spanish king, Charles II (r. 1665–1700), would die without an heir. So, for the moment, Louis was content with modest gains at Spain's expense, confident that he would get much more in the future.

Louis's focus then shifted to a new enemy, the Dutch. The Dutch had been allied with France since the beginning of their existence as provinces in rebellion against Spain. The French now turned against the Dutch for reasons that reflect the growth of the international trading economy: Dutch dominance of seaborne trade. The French at first tried to offset the Dutch advantage in trade with tariff barriers against Dutch goods. But confidence in the

---

Franche-Comté (FRAWNSH–con-TAY)

French army led Louis's generals to urge action against the vulnerable Dutch lands. "It is impossible that his Majesty should tolerate any longer the insolence and arrogance of that nation," rationalized the usually pragmatic Colbert in 1670.[1]

The Dutch War began in 1672, with Louis personally leading one of the largest armies ever fielded in Europe— perhaps 120,000 men. At the same time, the Dutch were challenged at sea by England. The English had fought the Dutch over trade in the 1650s; now Louis secretly sent the English king, Charles II, a pension to secure an alliance against the Dutch.

At first the French were spectacularly successful against the tiny Dutch army. However, the Dutch opened dikes and flooded the countryside, and what had begun as a rout became a soggy stalemate. Moreover, the Dutch were beating combined English and French forces at sea and were gathering allies who felt threatened by Louis's aggression. The French soon faced German and Austrian forces along their frontier, and by 1674 the English had joined the alliance against France as well.

Nonetheless, the French managed to hold their own, and the Peace of Nijmegen° in 1678 gave the illusion of a French victory. Not only had the French met the challenge of an enemy coalition, but Spain ceded them further border areas in the Spanish Netherlands as well as control of the Franche-Comté.

Ensconced at Versailles since 1682, Louis seemed to be at the height of his powers. Yet the Dutch War had in fact cost him more than he had gained. Meeting the alliance against him had meant fielding ever increasing numbers of men. Internal reforms in government and finance ended under the pressure of paying for war, and old financial expedients of borrowing money and selling privileges were revived. Other government obligations, such as encouraging overseas trade, were neglected. Colbert's death in 1683 dramatically symbolized the end of an era of innovation in the French regime.

Louis's unforgiving Dutch opponent, William of Orange, king of England from 1689 to 1702, renewed and stirred up anti-French alliances. The war, now known as the Nine Years' War, or King William's War, was touched off late in 1688 by French aggression—an invasion of Germany to claim an inheritance there. In his ongoing dispute with the pope, Louis seized the papal territory of Avignon° in southern France. Boldest of all, he helped the exiled Catholic claimant to the English crown mount an invasion to reclaim his throne.

A widespread war began with all the major powers— Spain, the Netherlands, England, Austria, the major German states—ranged against France. The French also carried the fighting abroad by seizing English territory in Canada. As with the Dutch War, the Nine Years' War was costly and, on most fronts, inconclusive. This time, though, there was no illusion of victory for Louis. In the Treaty of Ryswick (1697) Louis gave up most of the territories in Germany, the Spanish Netherlands, and northern Spain that he managed to occupy by war's end. Avignon went back to the pope, and Louis relinquished his contentious claim to papal revenues. The terrible burden of war taxes combined with crop failures in 1693 and 1694 caused widespread starvation in the countryside. French courtiers began to criticize Louis openly.

The final major war of Louis's reign, called the War of the Spanish Succession, broke out in 1701. In some ways it was a straightforward dynastic clash between France and its perennial nemesis, the Habsburgs. Both Louis and Habsburg Holy Roman emperor Leopold I (r. 1657–1705) hoped to claim for their heirs the throne of Spain, left open at the death in 1700 of the last Spanish Habsburg, Charles II. Leopold represented the Austrian branch of the Habsburg family (see page 509), but Charles II bequeathed the throne to Louis's grandson, Philip of Anjou°, by reason of Louis's marriage to the Spanish princess Maria Theresa. Philip quickly proceeded to enter Spain and claim his new kingdom. War was made inevitable when Louis renounced one of the conditions of Charles's will: Philip's accession to the throne of Spain, Louis insisted, did not preclude his becoming king of France as well. This declaration was an act of sheer belligerence, for Philip was only third in line for the French throne. The Dutch and English responded to the prospect of so great a disruption of the balance of power in Europe by joining the emperor in a formal Great Alliance in 1701. The Dutch and English also wanted to defend their colonial interests since the French had already begun to profit from new trading opportunities with the Spanish colonies.

Again the French fought a major war on several fronts on land and at sea. Again the people of France felt the cost in crushing taxes worsened by harvest failures. Major revolts inside France forced Louis to divert troops from the war. For a time it seemed that the French would be soundly defeated, but they were saved by the superior organization of their forces and by dynastic accident: unexpected deaths in the Habsburg family meant that the Austrian claimant to the Spanish throne suddenly

---

Nijmegen (NIME-ay-gehn)   **Avignon** (ah-veen-YOHN)   **Anjou** (ahn-ZHOO)

was poised to inherit rule of Austria and the empire as well. The English, more afraid of a revival of unified Habsburg control of Spain and Austria than of French domination of Spain, quickly called for peace negotiations.

The Peace of Utrecht in 1713 resolved long-standing political conflicts and helped to set the agenda of European politics for the eighteenth century. Philip of Anjou was recognized as Philip V, the first Bourbon king of Spain, but on the condition that the Spanish and French crowns would never be worn by the same monarch. To maintain the balance of power against French interests, the Spanish Netherlands and Spanish territories in Italy were ceded by a second treaty in 1714 to Austria, which for many decades would be France's major continental rival. The Peace of Utrecht also marked the beginning of England's dominance of overseas trade and colonization. The French gave to England lands in Canada and the Caribbean and renounced any privileged relationship with Spanish colonies. England was allowed to control the highly profitable slave trade with Spanish colonies.

Louis XIV had added small amounts of strategically valuable territory along France's eastern border (see Map 16.1), and a Bourbon ruled in Spain. But the costs in human life and resources were great for the slim results achieved. Moreover, the army and navy had swallowed up capital that might have fueled investment and trade; strategic opportunities overseas were lost, never to be regained. Louis's government had been innovative in its early years but remained constrained by traditional ways of imagining the interest of the state.

ENGLISH CIVIL WAR AND ITS AFTERMATH

IN England, unlike in France, a representative institution—Parliament—became an effective, permanent brake on royal authority. The process by which Parliament gained a secure role in governing the kingdom was neither easy nor peaceful, however. As we saw in Chapter 15, conflicts between the English crown and its subjects, culminating in the Crown-Parliament conflict, concerned control over taxation and the direction of religious reform. Beginning in 1642 England was beset by civil war between royal and parliamentary forces. The king was eventually defeated and executed, and for a time the monarchy was abolished altogether. It was restored in 1660, but Parliament retained a crucial role in governing the kingdom—a role that was confirmed when, in 1688, it again deposed a monarch whose fiscal and religious policies became unacceptable to its members.

Civil War and Regicide, 1642–1649

Fighting broke out between the armies of Charles I and parliamentary armies in the late summer of 1642. The Long Parliament (see page 522) continued to represent a broad coalition of critics and opponents of the monarchy, ranging from aristocrats concerned primarily with abuses of royal prerogative to radical Puritans eager for thorough religious reform and determined to defeat the king. Fighting was halfhearted initially, and the tide of war at first favored Charles.

In 1643, however, the scope of the war broadened. Charles made peace with Irish rebels and brought Irish troops to England to bolster his armies. Parliament in turn sought military aid from the Scots in exchange for promises that Presbyterianism would become the religion of England. Meanwhile, Oliver Cromwell (1599–1658), a Puritan member of the Long Parliament and a cavalry officer, helped reorganize parliamentary forces. The eleven-hundred-man cavalry trained by Cromwell and known as the "Ironsides," supported by parliamentary and Scottish infantry, defeated the king's troops at Marston Moor in July 1644. The victory made Cromwell famous.

Shortly afterward Parliament further improved its forces and created the New Model Army, rigorously trained like Cromwell's Ironsides. Sitting members of Parliament were barred from commanding troops; hence upper-class control of the army was reduced. This army played a decisive role not only in the war but also in the political settlement that followed the fighting.

The New Model Army won a convincing victory over royal forces at Naseby in 1645. In the spring of 1646 Charles surrendered to a Scottish army in the north. In January 1647 Parliament paid the Scots for their services in the war and took the king into custody. In the negotiations that followed, Charles tried to play his opponents off against one another, and, as he had hoped, divisions among them widened.

Most members of Parliament were Presbyterians, Puritans who favored a strongly unified and controlled state church along Calvinist lines. They wanted peace with the king in return for acceptance of the new church structure and parliamentary control of standing militias for a specified period. They did not favor expanding the right to vote or other dramatic constitutional or legal change. These men were increasingly alarmed by the rise of sectarian differences and the actual religious freedom that

Oliver Cromwell   Cromwell had seen his own family's income decline under the weight of Charles I's exactions. Elected to Parliament in 1628 and again in 1640, he also brought a long-standing religious zeal to his public life. His opposition to the "tyranny and usurpation" of the Anglican Church hierachy first prompted him to criticize royal government.   *(In the collection of the Duke of Buccleuch and Queensberry KT)*

many ordinary people were claiming for themselves. With the weakening of royal authority and the disruption of civil war, censorship was relaxed, and public preaching by ordinary men and even women who felt divinely inspired was becoming commonplace.

Above all, Presbyterian gentry in Parliament feared more radical groups in the army and in London who had supported them up to this point but who favored more thoroughgoing reform. Most officers of the New Model Army, such as Cromwell, were Independents, Puritans who favored a decentralized church, a degree of religious toleration, and a wider sharing of political power among men of property, not just among the very wealthy gentry. In London a well-organized artisans' movement known as the "Levellers" favored universal manhood suffrage, law reform, better access to education, and decentralized churches—in short, the separation of political power from wealth and virtual freedom of religion. Many of the rank and file of the army were deeply influenced by Leveller ideas.

In May 1647 the majority in Parliament voted to offer terms to the king and to disband the New Model Army—without first paying most of the soldiers' back wages. This move provoked the first direct intervention by the army in politics. Representatives of the soldiers were chosen to present grievances to Parliament; when this failed, the army seized the king and, in August, occupied Westminster, Parliament's meeting place. Independent and Leveller elements in the army debated the direction of possible reform to be imposed on Parliament. (See the box "The Continuing Experiment: The Putney Debates.")

In November Charles escaped from his captors and raised a new army among his erstwhile enemies, the Scots, who were also alarmed by the growing radicalism in England. Civil war began again early in 1648. Although it ended quickly with a victory by Cromwell and the New Model Army in August, the renewed war further hardened political divisions and enhanced the power of the army. The king was widely blamed for the renewed bloodshed, and the army did not trust him to keep any agreement he might now sign. When Parliament, still dominated by Presbyterians, once again voted to negotiate with the king, army troops under Colonel Thomas Pride prevented members who favored Presbyterianism or the king from attending sessions. The "Rump" Parliament that remained after "Pride's Purge" voted to try the king. A hasty trial ensued, and Charles I was executed for "treason, tyranny and bloodshed" against his people on January 30, 1649.

The Interregnum, 1649–1660

A Commonwealth—a republic—was declared. Executive power resided in a council of state. The House of Lords having been abolished, legislative power resided in the one-chamber Rump Parliament. Declaring a republic proved far easier than running one, however. The execution of the king shocked most English and Scots and alienated many elites from the new regime. The legitimacy of the Commonwealth government would always be in question.

The tasks of making and implementing policy were hindered by the narrow political base on which the government now rested. Excluded were the majority of the reformist gentry who had been purged from Parliament. Also excluded were the more radical Levellers; Leveller leaders in London were arrested when they published tracts critical of the new government. Within a few years

The Putney Debates

In October 1647 representatives of the Leveller movement in the army ranks confronted Independents—largely comprising the officer corps—in formally staged debates in a church at Putney, outside London. In this exchange, the Leveller representative, Thomas Rainsborough, advocates universal manhood suffrage, whereas Cromwell's fellow officer, Henry Ireton, argues for a more restricted franchise. The staging of the debates reflects the importance of the army in deciding the scope of constitutional change in England at this moment of extraordinary political fluidity. Even more important were the views that were aired at the debates, which had in common the assertion that government should exist only by the consent of the governed. These ideas became reality very slowly. The poorest men (and all women) did not get the vote in Britain until the twentieth century.

Rainsborough: . . . Really I think that the poorest he that is in England hath a life to live as the greatest he; and therefore truly, sir, I think it's clear, that every man that is to live under a government ought first by his own consent to put himself under that government; and I do think that the poorest man in England is not at all bound in a strict sense to that government that he hath not had a voice to put himself under; and I am confident that, when I have heard the reasons against it, that something will be said to answer those reasons, insomuch that I should doubt whether I was an Englishman or no, that should doubt of these things.

Ireton: . . . I think that no person hath a right to an interest or share in the disposing of the affairs of the kingdom, and in determining or choosing those that shall determine what laws we shall be ruled by here, no person hath a right to this that hath not a permanent fixed interest in this kingdom, and those persons together are properly the represented of this kingdom, who taken together, and consequently are to make up the represented of this kingdom, are the representers, who taken together do comprehend whatsoever is of real or permanent interest in the kingdom, and I am sure there is otherwise (I cannot tell what), otherwise any man can say why a foreigner coming in amongst us, or as many as will be coming in amongst us, or by force or otherwise settling themselves here, or at least by our permission having a being here, why they should not as well lay claim to it as any other. We talk of birthright. Truly birthright there is thus much claim: men may justly have by birthright, by their very being born in England, that we should not seclude them out of England. That we should not refuse to give them air and place and ground, and the freedom of the highways and other things, to live amongst us, not any man that is born here, though he in birth, or by his birth there come nothing at all that is part of the permanent interest of this kingdom to him. That I think is due to a man by birth. But that by a man's being born here he shall have a share in that power that shall dispose of the lands here, and of all things here, I do not think it a sufficient ground, but I am sure if we look upon that which is the utmost, within man's view, of what was originally the constitution of this kingdom, upon that which is most radical and fundamental, and which if you take away, there is no man hath any land, any goods, you take away any civil interest, and that is this: that those that choose the representers for the making of laws by which this state and kingdom are to be governed, are the persons who taken together, do comprehend the local interest of this kingdom; that is, the persons in whom all land lies, and those in corporations in whom all trading lies. This is the most fundamental constitution of this kingdom, and which if you do not allow, you allow none at all.

QUESTIONS

1. On what grounds does Henry Ireton argue for restricting the right to participate in government? How does he counter Rainsborough's more sweeping claim that all men should be governed only with their own consent?

2. What social, religious, economic, and political conditions prevalent in seventeenth-century England help us to explain the origins of these ideas?

3. In what ways might the Putney debates have been important, even though the ideas aired in them were not enacted, in the main, for centuries to come?

Source: G. E. Aylmer, ed., *The Levellers in the English Revolution* (Ithaca, N.Y.: Cornell University Press, 1975), pp. 100–101. Copyright Thames & Hudson Ltd. Reprinted by permission of Thames & Hudson Ltd.

many disillusioned Levellers would join a new religious movement called the Society of Friends, or Quakers, which espoused complete religious autonomy. Quakers declined all oaths or service to the state, and they refused to acknowledge social rank.

Above all, the new government was vulnerable to the power of the army, which had created it. In 1649 and 1650 Cromwell led expeditions to Ireland and Scotland, partly for sheer revenge and partly to put down resistance to Commonwealth authority. In Ireland Cromwell's forces acted with shameful ruthlessness. English control there was strengthened by more dispossession of Irish landholders, which also served to pay off the army's wages. Meanwhile, Parliament could not agree on systematic reforms, particularly the one reform Independents in the army insisted on: more broadly based elections for a new Parliament. Fresh from his victories, Cromwell led his armies to London and dissolved Parliament in the spring of 1652.

In 1653 a cadre of army officers drew up the "Instrument of Government," England's first and only written constitution. It provided for an executive, the Lord Protector, and a Parliament to be based on somewhat wider male suffrage. Cromwell was the natural choice for Lord Protector, and whatever success the government of the Protectorate had was due largely to him.

Cromwell was an extremely able leader who was not averse to compromise. Although he had used force against Parliament in 1648, he had worked hard to reconcile the Rump Parliament and the army before marching on London in 1652. He believed in a state church, but one that allowed for control, including choice of minister, by local congregations. He also believed in toleration for other Protestant sects, as well as for Catholics and Jews, as long as no one disturbed the peace.

As Lord Protector, Cromwell oversaw impressive reforms in law that testify to his belief in the limits of governing authority. For example, contrary to the practice of his day, he opposed capital punishment for petty crimes. The government of the Protectorate, however, accomplished little given Parliament's internal divisions and opposition to Cromwell's initiatives. The population at large still harbored royalist sympathizers; after a royalist uprising in 1655, Cromwell divided England into military districts and vested governing authority in army generals.

In the end the Protectorate could not survive the strains over policy and the challenges to its legitimacy. When Cromwell died of a sudden illness in September 1658, the Protectorate did not long survive him. In February 1660 the decisive action of one army general en-

Popular Preaching in England   Many women took advantage of the collapse of royal authority to preach in public—a radical activity for women at the time. This print satirizes the Quakers, a religious movement that attracted many women. *(Mary Evans Picture Library)*

abled all the surviving members of the Long Parliament to rejoin the Rump. The Parliament summarily dissolved itself and called for new elections. The newly elected Parliament recalled Charles II, son of Charles I, from exile abroad and restored the monarchy. The chaos and radicalism of the late civil war and "interregnum"—the period between reigns, as the years from 1649 to 1660 came to be called—now spawned a conservative reaction.

The Restoration, 1660–1685

Charles II (r. 1660–1685) claimed his throne at the age of 30. He had learned from his years of uncertain exile and from the fate of his father. He did not seek retribution but rather offered a general pardon to all but a few rebels (mostly those who had signed his father's death warrant), and he suggested to Parliament a relatively tolerant religious settlement that would include Anglicans as well as Presbyterians. He was far more politically adept than his father and far more willing to compromise.

That the re-established royal government was not more tolerant than it turned out to be was not Charles's doing but Parliament's. During the 1660s, the "Cavalier" Parliament, named for royalists in the civil war, passed harsh laws aimed at religious dissenters. Anglican orthodoxy was reimposed, including the re-establishment of bishops and the Anglican *Book of Common Prayer*. All officeholders and clergy were required to swear oaths of obedience to the king and to the established church. As a result, hundreds were forced out of office and pulpits. Holding nonconformist religious services became illegal, and Parliament passed a "five-mile" act to prevent dissenting ministers from traveling near their former congregations. Property laws were tightened and the criminal codes made more severe.

The king's behavior in turn began to mimic prerevolutionary royalist positions. Charles II began to flirt with Catholicism, and his brother and heir, James, openly converted. Charles promulgated a declaration of tolerance that would have included Catholics as well as nonconformist Protestants, but Parliament would not accept it. Anti-Catholic feeling still united all Protestants. In 1678 Charles's secret treaties with the French became known (see page 547), and rumors of a Catholic plot to murder Charles and reimpose Catholicism became widespread. No evidence of any plot was ever unearthed, although thirty-five people were executed for alleged participation. Parliament focused its attention on anti-Catholicism, passing the Test Act, which barred all but Anglicans from public office. As a result, the Catholic James was forced to resign as Lord High Admiral.

When Parliament moved to exclude James from succession to the throne, Charles dissolved it. A subsequent Parliament, worried by the specter of a new civil war, backed down. But the legacy of the civil war was a potent one. First, despite the harsh laws, to silence all dissent was not possible. After two decades of religious pluralism and broadly based political activity, it was impossible to reimpose conformity; well-established communities of various sects and self-confidence bred vigorous resistance. The clearest reflection of the legacy of events was the power of Parliament. Though reluctant to press too far, Parliament had tried to assert its policies against the desires of the king.

Nevertheless, by the end of his reign Charles was financially independent of Parliament, thanks to increased revenue from overseas trade and secret subsidies from France, his recent ally against Dutch trading rivals. This financial independence and firm political tactics enabled Charles to regain, and retain, a great deal of power. If he had been followed by an able successor, Parliament might have lost a good measure of its confidence and independence. But his brother James's reign and its aftermath further enhanced Parliament's power.

The Glorious Revolution, 1688

When James II (r. 1685–1689) succeeded Charles, Parliament's royalist leanings were at first evident. James was granted customs duties for life and was also given funds to suppress a rebellion by one of Charles's illegitimate sons. James did not try to impose Catholicism on England as some had feared, but he did try to achieve toleration for Catholics in two declarations of indulgence in 1687 and 1688. However admirable his goal—toleration—he had essentially changed the law of the realm without Parliament's consent and further undermined his position with heavy-handed tactics. When several leading Anglican bishops refused to read the declarations from their pulpits, he had them imprisoned and tried for seditious libel. However, a sympathetic jury acquitted them.

James also failed because of the coincidence of other events. In 1685, at the outset of James's reign, Louis XIV of France had revoked the Edict of Nantes. The possibility that subjects and monarchs in France and, by extension, elsewhere could be of different faiths seemed increasingly unlikely. Popular fears of James's Catholicism were thus heightened early in his reign, and his later declarations of tolerance, though benefiting Protestant dissenters, were viewed with suspicion. In 1688 not only were the Anglican bishops acquitted but the king's second wife, who was Catholic, gave birth to a son. The birth raised the specter of a Catholic succession.

In June 1688, to put pressure on James, leading members of Parliament invited William of Orange, husband of James's Protestant daughter, Mary, to come to England. William mounted an invasion that became a rout when James refused to defend his throne. James simply abandoned England and went to France. William called Parliament, which declared James to have abdicated and offered the throne jointly to William and Mary. With French support James eventually invaded Ireland in 1690—bound for Westminster—but was defeated by William at the Battle of Boyne that year.

The substitution of William (r. 1689–1702) and Mary (r. 1689–1694) for James, known as the "Glorious Revolution," was engineered by Parliament and confirmed its power. Parliament presented the new sovereigns with a

Declaration of Rights upon their accession and, later that year, with a Bill of Rights that defended freedom of speech, called for frequent Parliaments, and required subsequent monarchs to be Protestant. The effectiveness of these documents was reinforced by Parliament's power of the purse. Parliament's role in the political process was ensured by William's interests in funding his ambitious military efforts, particularly the Netherlands' ongoing wars with France.

The issues that had faced the English since the beginning of the century were common to all European states: religious division and elite power, fiscal strains and resistance to taxation. Yet the cataclysmic events in England—the interregnum, the Commonwealth, the Restoration, the Glorious Revolution—had set it apart from other states. Consequently, the incremental assumption of authority by a well-established institution, Parliament, made challenge of the English monarchy more legitimate and more effective.

NEW POWERS IN CENTRAL AND EASTERN EUROPE

B Y the end of the seventeenth century three states dominated central and eastern Europe: Austria, Brandenburg-Prussia, and Russia. After the Thirty Years' War the Habsburgs' dominance in the splintering empire waned, and they focused on expanding and consolidating their power in their hereditary possessions. Brandenburg-Prussia, in northeastern Germany, emerged from obscurity to rival the Habsburg state. The rulers of Brandenburg-Prussia had gained lands in the Peace of Westphalia, and astute management transformed their relatively small and scattered holdings into one of the most powerful states in Europe. Russia's new stature in eastern Europe resulted in part from the weakness of its greatest rival, Poland, and the determination of one leader, Peter the Great, to assume a major role in European affairs. Sweden controlled valuable Baltic territory through much of the century but eventually was also eclipsed by Russia as a force in the region.

The internal political development of these states was dramatically shaped by their relationship to the wider European economy: they were sources of grain and raw materials for the more densely urbanized West. The development of and the competition among states in central and eastern Europe were closely linked to developments in western Europe.

The Consolidation of Austria

The Thirty Years' War (see pages 523–528) weakened the Habsburgs as emperors but strengthened them in their own lands. The main Habsburg lands in 1648 were a collection of principalities comprising modern Austria, the kingdom of Hungary (largely in Turkish hands), and the kingdom of Bohemia (see Map 16.2). In 1714 Austria acquired the Spanish Netherlands, which were renamed the Austrian Netherlands. Although language and ethnic differences prevented an absolutist state along French lines, Leopold I (r. 1657–1705) instituted political and institutional changes that enabled the Habsburg state to become one of the most powerful in Europe through the eighteenth century.

Much of the coherence that already existed in Leopold's lands had been achieved by his predecessors in the wake of the Thirty Years' War. The lands of rebels in Bohemia had been confiscated and redistributed among loyal, mostly Austrian, families. In return for political and military support for the emperor, these families were given the right to exploit their newly acquired land and the peasants who worked it. The desire to recover population and productivity after the destruction of the Thirty Years' War gave landlords further incentive to curtail peasants' autonomy, particularly in devastated Bohemia. Austrian landlords throughout the Habsburg domains provided grain and timber for the export market and foodstuffs for the Austrian armies, while elite families provided the army with officers. This political-economic arrangement provoked numerous serious peasant revolts, but the peasants were not able to force changes in a system that suited both the elites and the central authority.

Although Leopold had lost much influence within the empire itself, an imperial government made up of various councils, a war ministry, financial officials, and the like still functioned in his capital, Vienna. Leopold worked to extricate the government of his own lands from the apparatus of imperial institutions, which were staffed largely by Germans more loyal to imperial than to Habsburg interests. In addition, Leopold used the Catholic Church as an institutional and ideological support for the Habsburg state.

Leopold's personal ambition was to re-establish devout Catholicism throughout his territories. Acceptance of Catholicism became the litmus test of loyalty to the Habsburg regime, and Protestantism vanished among elites. Leopold encouraged the work of Jesuit teachers and members of other Catholic orders. These men and women helped staff his government and administered religious life down to the most local levels.

Baroque Splendor in Austria   The Belvedere Palace (whose name means "beautiful view") was built near Vienna as the summer residence of the great aristocratic general Prince Eugene of Savoy, who had successfully led Habsburg armies against the Turks and had reaped many rewards from Leopold and his successors. The palace shares many features in common with Louis XIV's palace of Versailles (see page 545).   *(Erich Lessing/Art Resource, NY)*

Leopold's most dramatic success, as a Habsburg and a religious leader, was his reconquest of the kingdom of Hungary from the Ottoman Empire. Since the mid-sixteenth century the Habsburgs had controlled only a narrow strip of the kingdom. Preoccupied with countering Louis XIV's aggression, Leopold did not himself choose to begin a reconquest. His centralizing policies, however, alienated nobles and townspeople in the portion of Hungary he did control, as did his repression of Protestantism, which had flourished in Hungary. Hungarian nobles began a revolt, aided by the Turks, aiming for a reunited Hungary under Ottoman protection.

The Habsburgs emerged victorious in part because they received help from the Venetians, the Russians, and especially the Poles, whose lands in Ukraine were threatened by the Turks. The Turks overreached their supply lines to besiege Vienna in 1683. When the siege failed, Habsburg armies slowly pressed east and south, recovering Buda, the capital of Hungary, in 1686 and Belgrade (modern Serbia) in 1688. The Danube basin lay once

again in Christian hands. The Treaty of Carlowitz ended the fighting in 1699, after the first conference where European allies jointly dictated terms to a weakening Ottoman Empire. Austria's allies had also gained at the Ottomans' expense: the Poles recovered the threatened Ukraine, and the Russians gained a vital foothold on the Black Sea.

Leopold gave land in the reclaimed lands to Austrian officers who he believed were loyal to him. The traditions of Hungarian separatism, however, were strong, and the great magnates—whether they had defended the Habsburgs against Turkish encroachment or guarded the frontier for Turkish overlords—retained their independence. The peasantry, as elsewhere, suffered a decline in status as a result of the Crown's efforts to ensure the loyalty of elites. In the long run Hungarian independence weakened the Habsburg state, but in the short run Leopold's victory over the Turks and the recovery of Hungary itself were momentous events, confirming the Habsburgs as the pre-eminent power in central Europe.

The Rise of Brandenburg-Prussia

Three German states, in addition to Austria, gained territory and stature after the Thirty Years' War: Bavaria, Saxony, and Brandenburg-Prussia. By the end of the seventeenth century the strongest was Brandenburg-Prussia, a conglomeration of small territories held, by dynastic accident, by the Hohenzollern family. The two principal territories were electoral Brandenburg, in northeastern Germany, with its capital, Berlin, and the duchy of Prussia, a fief of the Polish crown along the Baltic coast east of Poland proper (see Map 16.2). In addition, the Hohenzollerns ruled a handful of small principalities near the Netherlands. The manipulation of resources and power that enabled these unpromising lands to become a powerful state was primarily the work of Frederick William, known as "the Great Elector" (r. 1640–1688).

Frederick William used the occasion of a war to effect a permanent change in the structure of government. He took advantage of a war between Poland and its rivals, Sweden and Russia (described in the next section), to win independence for the duchy of Prussia from Polish overlordship. When his involvement in the war ended in 1657, he kept intact the general war commissariat, a combined civilian and military body that had efficiently directed the war effort, bypassing traditional councils and representative bodies. He also used the standing army to force the payment of high taxes. Most significantly, he established a positive relationship with the Junkers°, hereditary landholders, which ensured him both revenue and loyalty. He agreed to allow the Junkers virtually total control of their own lands in return for their agreement to support his government—in short, they surrendered their accustomed political independence in exchange for greater economic and social power over the peasants who worked their lands.

Peasants and townspeople were taxed, but nobles were not. The freedom to control their estates led many nobles to invest in profitable agriculture for the export market. The peasants were serfs who received no benefits from the increased productivity of the land. Frederick William further enhanced his state's power by sponsoring state industries. These industries did not have to fear competition from urban producers because the towns had been frozen out of the political process and saddled with heavy taxes. Though an oppressive place for many Germans, Brandenburg-Prussia attracted many skilled refugees, such as Huguenot artisans fleeing Louis XIV's France.

Bavaria and Saxony, in contrast to Brandenburg-Prussia, had vibrant towns, largely free peasantries, and weaker aristocracies but were relative nonentities in international affairs. Power on the European stage depended on military force. Such power, whether in a large state like France or in a small one like Brandenburg-Prussia, usually came at the expense of the people.

Competition Around the Baltic: The Decline of Poland and the Zenith of Swedish Power

The rivers and port cities of the Baltic coast were conduits for the growing trade between the Baltic hinterland and the rest of Europe. In 1600 a large portion of the Baltic hinterland lay under the control of Poland-Lithuania, a vast and diverse state at the height of its power, but one that would prove an exception to the pattern of expanding royal power in the seventeenth century. Wars in the middle of the century were extremely destructive in regard not only to lives and property but also, unlike in neighboring Prussia, to the coherence of the state as well.

Internal strains began to mount in Poland-Lithuania in the late sixteenth century. The spread of the Counter-Reformation, encouraged by the Crown, created tensions with both Protestant and Orthodox subjects in the diverse kingdom. The greatest source of political instability was the power of landholding nobles, whose fortunes grew as Poland became the granary of western Europe. Impoverished peasants were bound to the land, and lesser gentry, particularly in the Ruthenian lands of Lithuania, were shut out of political power by Polish aristocrats. In Ukraine communities of Cossacks, nomadic farmer-warriors, grew as Polish and Lithuanian peasants fled harsh conditions to join them. The Cossacks had long been tolerated because they served as a military buffer against the Ottoman Turks to the south, but now Polish landlords wanted to reincorporate the Cossacks into the profitable political-economic system they controlled.

In 1648 the Polish crown faced revolt and invasion that it could not fully counter. The Cossacks led a major uprising, which included Ukrainian gentry as well as peasants. The Cossacks held their own against the Polish armies. Meanwhile, the Crown's efforts to reach a peace agreement were blocked by the noble landlords against whom the revolt had been directed. In 1654 the Cossacks tried to assure their autonomy by transferring their allegiance to Moscow. They became part of a Russian invasion of Poland-Lithuania that by the next year had engulfed much of the eastern half of the dual state. At the same time, Poland's perennial rival, Sweden, seized central Poland in a military campaign marked by extreme brutality. Many

---

Junkers (YUNG-kurz)

Map 16.2 New Powers in Central and Eastern Europe, to 1725   The balance of power in central and eastern Europe shifted with the strengthening of Austria, the rise of Brandenburg-Prussia, and the expansion of Russia at the expense of Poland and Sweden.

Polish and Lithuanian aristocrats continued to act like independent warlords and cooperated with the invaders to preserve their own local power.

Operating with slim resources, Polish royal armies eventually managed to recover much territory—most important, the western half of Ukraine (see Map 16.2). But the invasions and subsequent fighting were disastrous. These wars were afterward referred to as "the deluge," and with good reason. The population of Poland declined by as much as 40 percent, and vital urban economies were in ruins. The Catholic identity of the Polish heartland had been a rallying point for resistance to the Protestant Swedes and the Orthodox Russians, but the religious tolerance that had distinguished the Polish kingdom and had been mandated in its constitution was now abandoned. In addition, much of its recovery of Lithuanian territory was only nominal.

The elective Polish crown passed in 1674 to the military hero Jan Sobieski° (r. 1674–1696), known as "Vanquisher of the Turks" for his role in raising the siege of Vienna in 1683. Given Poland's internal weakness, however, Sobieski's victories in the long run helped the Ottomans' other foes—Austria and Russia—more than they helped the Poles. Moreover, though a brilliant tactician, he was a master of an increasingly outmoded form of warfare that was almost wholly reliant on cavalry. He was unable to force reforms that would have led to increased royal revenue and a more up-to-date royal army. After his death Poland would be vulnerable to the political ambitions of its more powerful neighbors. Augustus II of Saxony (r. 1697–1704, 1709–1733) dragged Poland back into war, from which Russia would emerge the clear winner in the power struggle in eastern Europe.

The Swedes, meanwhile, had successfully vied with the Poles and other competitors for control of the lucrative Baltic coast. Swedish efforts to control Baltic territory began in the sixteenth century, first to counter the power of its perennial rival, Denmark, in the western Baltic. It then competed with Poland to control Livonia (modern Latvia), whose principal city, Riga, was an important trading center for goods from both Lithuania and Russia. By 1617, under Gustav Adolf, the Swedes gained the lands to the north surrounding the Gulf of Finland (the most direct outlet for Russian goods), and in 1621 they displaced the Poles in Livonia itself. Swedish intervention in the Thirty Years' War came when imperial successes against Denmark both threatened the Baltic coast and created an opportunity to strike at Sweden's old enemy. The Treaty of Westphalia (1648) confirmed Sweden's earlier gains and added control of further coastal territory, mostly at Denmark's expense.

The port cities held by Sweden were profitable but simply served to pay for the costly wars necessary to seize and defend them. Indeed, Sweden's efforts to hold Baltic territory were driven by dynastic and strategic needs as much as economic objectives. The ruling dynasty struggled against Denmark's control of western Baltic territory in order to safeguard its independence from the Danes, who had ruled the combined kingdoms until 1523. Similarly, competition with Poland for the eastern Baltic was part of a dynastic struggle after 1592. Sigismund Vasa, son of the king of Sweden, had been elected king of Poland in 1587 but also inherited the Swedish throne in 1592. Other members of the Vasa family fought him successfully to regain rule over Sweden and extricate Swedish interests from Poland's continental preoccupations. Although Sigismund ruled Poland until his death in 1632, a Vasa uncle replaced him on the Swedish throne in 1604.

The one permanent gain that Sweden realized from its aggression against Poland in the 1650s was the renunciation of the Polish Vasa line to any claim to the Swedish crown. Owing to its earlier gains, Sweden reigned supreme on the Baltic coast until the end of the century, when it was supplanted by the powerful Russian state.

Russia Under Peter the Great

The Russian state expanded dramatically through the sixteenth century under Ivan IV and weathered the period of disputed succession known as the "Time of Troubles" (see pages 528–530). The foundations of the large and cohesive state laid by Ivan enabled Michael Romanov° to rebuild autocratic government with ease after being chosen tsar in 1613.

The Romanovs were an eminent aristocratic family related to Ivan's. Michael (r. 1613–1645) was selected to rule by an assembly of aristocrats, gentry, and commoners who were more alarmed at the civil wars and recent Polish incursions than at the prospect of a return to strong tsarist rule. Michael was succeeded by his son, Alexis (r. 1645–1676), who presided over the extension of Russian control to eastern Ukraine in 1654 following the wars in Poland and developed an interest in cultivating relationships with the West.

Shifting the balance of power in eastern Europe and the Baltic in Russia's favor was also the work of Alexis's son, Peter I (r. 1682–1725), "the Great." Peter accomplished this by military successes against his enemies and by

Sobieski (so-BYESS-key)

Romanov (ROH-man-off)

Peter the Great   This portrait by a Dutch artist captures the tsar's "westernizing" mission by showing Peter in military dress according to European fashions of the day.
(Rijksmuseum-Stichting, Amsterdam)

forcibly reorienting Russian government and society toward involvement with the rest of Europe.

Peter was almost literally larger than life. Nearly 7 feet tall, he towered over most of his contemporaries and had physical and mental energy to match his size. He set himself to learning trades and studied soldiering by rising through the ranks of the military like a common soldier. He traveled abroad to learn as much as he could about western European economies and governments. He wanted the revenue, manufacturing output, technology and trade, and, above all, up-to-date army and navy that other rulers enjoyed. In short Peter sought for Russia a more evolved state system because of the strength it would give him.

Immediately on his accession to power, Peter initiated a bold series of changes in Russian society. His travels had taught him that European monarchs coexisted with a privileged but educated aristocracy and that a brilliant court life symbolized and reinforced their authority. So he set out to refashion Russian society in what amounted

to an enforced cultural revolution. He provoked a direct confrontation with Russia's traditional aristocracy over everything from education to matters of dress. He elevated numerous new families to the ranks of gentry and created an official ranking system for the nobility to encourage and reward service to his government.

Peter's effort to reorient his nation culturally, economically, and politically toward Europe was most apparent in the construction of the city of St. Petersburg on the Gulf of Finland, which provided access to the Baltic Sea (see Map 16.2). In stark contrast to Moscow, dominated by the medieval fortress of the Kremlin and churches in the traditional Russian style, St. Petersburg was a modern European city with wide avenues and palaces designed for a sophisticated court life.

Although Peter was highly intelligent, practical, and determined to create a more productive and better-governed society, he was also cruel and authoritarian. Peasants already were bearing the brunt of taxation, but their tax burden worsened when they were assessed arbitrarily by head and not by output of the land. The building of St. Petersburg cost staggering sums in both money and workers' lives. Peter's entire reform system was carried out tyrannically; resistance was brutally suppressed. Victims of Peter's oppression included his son, Alexis, who died after torture while awaiting execution for questioning his father's policies.

Peter faced elite as well as populist rebellions against the exactions and the cultural changes of his regime. The most serious challenge was the revolt in 1707 of the Cossacks in the Don River region against the regime's tightened controls. (See the box "Reading Sources: Resistance to Peter the Great.") A major reason for the high cost of Peter's government to the Russian people was his ambition for territorial gain—hence his emphasis on an improved, and costly, army and navy. Working side by side with workers and technicians, many of whom he had recruited while abroad, Peter created the Russian navy from scratch. At first ships were built in the south to contest Turkish control of the Black Sea. Later they were built in the north to secure and defend the Baltic. Peter also modernized the Russian army by employing tactics, training, and discipline he had observed in the West. He introduced military conscription and munitions plants. By 1709 Russia was able to manufacture most of the up-to-date firearms its army needed.

Russia waged war virtually throughout Peter's reign. Initially with some success, he struck at the Ottomans and their client state in the Crimea. Later phases of these conflicts brought reverses, however. Peter was spectacularly successful against his northern competitor, Sweden, for control of the weakened Polish state and the Baltic

READING SOURCES   RESISTANCE TO PETER THE GREAT

Many of Peter's subjects resisted his policies, including nobles who despised the enforced cultural changes and peasants who chafed under his more traditional demand of heavy taxes. This letter from July 1705 reflects the efforts of one group of resisters, city dwellers from Astrakhan, a port on the Caspian Sea, to join forces with the Cossacks of the Don River region to their west. Many citizens of Astrakhan had been at odds with the tsars over church reforms since the seventeenth century. Note that their objections to Peter's cultural reforms, which included European dress and other matters of style (such as being clean-shaven and using tobacco), are thus couched in religious terms. What other concerns does this document reveal? Why might the citizens of Astrakhan have forged an alliance with the Cossacks?

To [the Chief] and to all the Don Cossack Host, we . . . all the city folk of Astrakhan . . . send our greetings. We wish to inform you of what has happened in Astrakhan on account of our Christian faith, because of beard-shaving, German dress, and tobacco; how we, our wives and our children were not admitted into churches in our old Russian dress; how men and women who entered the holy church had their clothes shorn and were expelled and thrown out. . . . Moreover, in the last year, they imposed on us and collected a [new] tax: one ruble "bath money" apiece; and they also ordered us to pay [a certain tax] per seven feet of cellar space. . . . The [local governor] together with other men in authority, colonels and captains, took away all of our firearms and wanted to kill us. . . . They also took away from us, without orders, our bread allowance and forbade that it be issued to us. We endured all this for a long time. [At last,] after taking counsel among ourselves . . . moved by our great distress, for we could endure it no more to be in danger of losing our Christian faith, we resisted: we killed some of them and have put some others in prison. You, the Cossack [Chief] and all the Host of the Don, please deliberate among yourselves and stand up together with us to defend the Christian faith, and send a message about your decision to us at Astrakhan. We are awaiting you . . . and we rely upon you.

Source: Alfred J. Andrea and James H. Overfield, *The Human Record: Sources of Global History,* vol. 2: *Since 1500,* 2d ed. (Boston: Houghton Mifflin, 1994), pp. 168–169.

Sea. The conflicts between Sweden and Russia, known as the Great Northern War, raged from 1700 to 1709 and, in a less intense phase, lasted until 1721. By the Treaty of Nystadt in 1721, Russia gained its present-day territory in the Gulf of Finland near St. Petersburg, plus Livonia and Estonia. These acquisitions gave Russia a secure window on the Baltic and, in combination with its gains of Lithuanian territory earlier in the century, made Russia the pre-eminent Baltic power, at Sweden's and Poland's expense.

THE EXPANSION OF OVERSEAS TRADE AND SETTLEMENT

BY the beginning of the seventeenth century competition from the Dutch, French, and English was disrupting the Spanish and Portuguese trading empires in Asia and the New World. During the seventeenth century European trade and colonization expanded and changed dramatically. The Dutch not only became masters of the spice trade but broadened the market to include many other commodities. In the Americas a new trading system linking Europe, Africa, and the New World came into being with the expansion of tobacco and, later, sugar production. French and English colonists began settling in North America in increasing numbers. By the end of the century trading and colonial outposts around the world figured regularly as bargaining chips in disagreements between European states. More important, overseas trade had a crucial impact on life within Europe: on patterns of production and consumption, on social stratification, and on the distribution of wealth.

The Growth of Trading Empires: The Success of the Dutch

By the end of the sixteenth century the Dutch and the English were making incursions into the Portuguese-controlled spice trade with areas of India, Ceylon, and

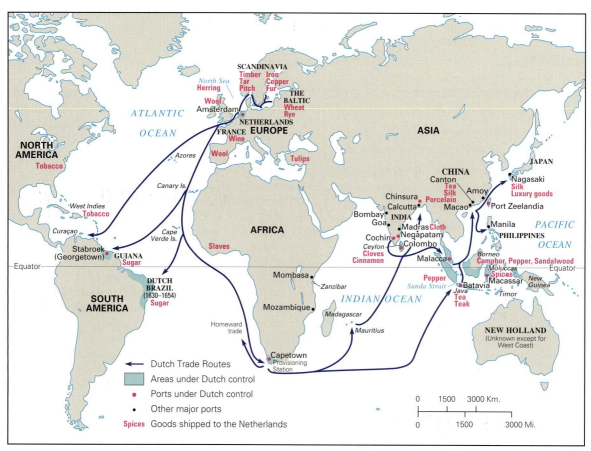

Map 16.3 Dutch Commerce in the Seventeenth Century The Dutch supplanted Portuguese control of trade with Asia and dominated seaborne trade within Europe.

the East Indies. Spain had annexed Portugal in 1580, but the drain on Spain's resources from its wars with the Dutch and French prevented Spain from adequately defending its enlarged trading empire in Asia. The Dutch and, to a lesser degree, the English rapidly supplanted Portuguese control of this lucrative trade (see Map 16.3).

The Dutch were particularly well placed to be successful competitors in overseas trade. They already dominated seaborne trade within Europe, including the most important long-distance trade, which linked Spain and Portugal—with their wine and salt, as well as spices, hides, and gold from abroad—with the Baltic seacoast, where these products were sold for grain and timber produced in Germany, Poland-Lithuania, and Scandinavia. The geographic position of the Netherlands and the fact that the Dutch consumed more Baltic grain than any other area, because of their large urban population, help to explain their dominance of this trade. In addition, the Dutch had improved the design of their mer-

chant ships to maximize their profits. By 1600 they were building the *fluitschip* (flyship) to transport cargo economically; it was a vessel with a long, flat hull, simple rigging, and cheap construction.

The Dutch were successful in Asia because of institutional as well as technological innovations. In 1602 the Dutch East India Company was formed. The company combined government management of trade, typical of the period, with both public and private investment. In the past groups of investors had funded single voyages or small numbers of ships on a one-time basis. The formation of the Dutch East India Company created a permanent pool of capital to sustain trade. After 1612 investments in the company were negotiable as stock. These greater assets allowed proprietors to spread the risks and delays of longer voyages among larger numbers of investors. In addition, more money was available for warehouses, docks, and ships. The English East India Company, founded in 1607, also supported trade, but more modestly. It had

Dutch Strength at Sea   This painting by the Dutch artist Van der Velde the Younger celebrates a Dutch victory over a combined French and English fleet in 1673. The Dutch had fought their primary commercial rivals, the English, during the 1650s and had built up their fleet of warships in response. Like most major sea battles of the era, this one was fought close to home, off the Dutch coast near the sea-lanes to Amsterdam.   *(HarperCollins Publishers/The Art Archive)*

one-tenth the capital of the Dutch company and did not use the same system of permanent capital held as stock by investors until 1657. The Bank of Amsterdam, founded in 1609, became the depository for the bullion that flowed into the Netherlands with the flood of trade. The bank established currency exchange rates and issued paper money and instruments of credit to facilitate commerce.

A dramatic expansion of trade with Asia resulted from the Dutch innovations, so much so that by 1650 the European market for spices was glutted, and traders' profits had begun to fall. To control the supply of spices, the Dutch seized some of the areas where they were produced. The Dutch and English further responded to the oversupply of spices by diversifying their trade. The proportion of spices in cargoes from the East fell from about 70 percent at midcentury to just over 20 percent by the century's end. New consumer goods such as tea, coffee, and silk and cotton fabrics took their place. The demand of ordinary people for inexpensive yet serviceable Indian cottons grew steadily. Eventually the Dutch and the English, alert for fresh opportunities in the East, entered the local carrying trade among Asian states. Doing so enabled them to make profits even without purchasing goods, and it slowed the drain of hard currency from Europe—

currency in increasingly short supply as silver mines in the Americas were depleted.

The "Golden Age" of the Netherlands

The prosperity occasioned by the Netherlands' "mother trade" within Europe and its burgeoning overseas commerce helped foster social and political conditions unique among European states. The concentration of trade and shipping sustained a healthy merchant oligarchy and also an extensive and prosperous artisanal sector. Disparities of wealth were smaller here than anywhere else in Europe. The shipbuilding and fishing trades, among others, supported large numbers of workers with a high standard of living for the age.

The Netherlands appeared to contemporaries to be an astonishing exception to the normal structures of politics. Political decentralization in the Netherlands persisted. The Estates General (representative assembly) for the Netherlands as a whole had no independent powers of taxation. Each of the seven provinces retained considerable autonomy. Wealthy merchants in the Estates of the province of Holland, in fact, constituted the government for the entire nation for long periods because of

Vermeer: The Soldier and the Laughing Girl   This is an early work by one of the great artists of the Dutch "Golden Age." Dutch art was distinguished by its treatment of common, rather than heroic, subjects. The masterful use of light and perspective in paintings such as this one would not be equaled until the invention of photography.   *(Copyright The Frick Collection, New York)*

Holland's economic dominance. The head of government was the executive secretary, known as the pensionary, of Holland's Estates.

Holland's only competition in the running of affairs came from the House of Orange, aristocratic leaders of the revolt against Spain (see pages 508–510). They exercised what control they had by means of the office of *stadholder°*—a kind of military governorship—to which they were elected in individual provinces. Their principal

interest was the traditional one of military glory and self-promotion. Therein lay a portion of their influence, for they continued to lead the defense of the Netherlands against Spanish attempts at reconquest until the Peace of Westphalia in 1648 and against French aggression after 1672. Their power also came from their status as the only counterweight within the Netherlands to the dominance of Amsterdam's (in Holland) mercantile interests. Small towns dependent on land-based trade or rural areas dominated by farmers and gentry looked to the stadholders of the Orange family to defend their interests.

stadholder (STAHT-hole-der)

As elsewhere, religion was a source of political conflict. The stadholders and the leading families of Holland, known as regents, vied for control of the state church. Pensionaries and regents of Holland generally favored a less rigid and austere form of Calvinism than did the stadholders. Their view reflected the needs of the diverse urban communities of Holland, where thousands of Jews, as well as Catholics and various Protestants, lived. Foreign policy was also disputed: Hollanders desired peace in order to foster commerce, whereas stadholders willingly engaged in warfare for territory and dynastic advantage.

These differences notwithstanding, Dutch commercial dominance involved the Netherlands in costly wars throughout the second half of the century. Between 1657 and 1660 the Dutch defended Denmark against Swedish ambitions in order to safeguard the sea-lanes and port cities of the Baltic. More costly conflicts arose because of rivalry with the more powerful England and France. Under Cromwell the English attempted to close their ports to the Dutch carrying trade. In 1672 the English under Charles II allied with the French, assuming that together they could destroy Dutch power and perhaps even divide the Netherlands' territory between them. The Dutch navy, rebuilt since Cromwell's challenge, soon forced England out of the alliance.

Owing largely to the land war with France, the Estates in Holland lost control of policy to William of Nassau (d. 1702), prince of Orange after 1672. William drew the Netherlands into his family's long-standing close relationship with England. Like other members of his family before him, William had married into the English royal family: his wife was Mary, daughter of James II.

Ironically, after William and Mary assumed the English throne, Dutch commerce suffered more in alliance with England than in its previous rivalry. William used Dutch resources for the land war against Louis XIV and reserved for the English navy the fight at sea. By the end of the century Dutch maritime strength was being eclipsed by English sea power.

The Growth of Atlantic Colonies and Commerce

In the seventeenth century the Dutch, the English, and the French joined the Spanish as colonial and commercial powers in the Americas. The Spanish colonial empire, in theory a trading system closed to outsiders, was in fact vulnerable to incursion by other European traders. Spanish treasure fleets were themselves a glittering attraction. In 1628, for example, a Dutch captain seized the entire fleet. But by then Spain's goals and those of its competitors had begun to shift. The limits of an economy based on the extraction, rather than the production, of wealth became clear with the declining output of the Spanish silver mines during the 1620s. In response the Spanish and their Dutch, French, and English competitors expanded the production of the cash crops of tobacco, dyestuffs, and, above all, sugar.

The European demand for tobacco and sugar, both addictive substances, grew steadily in the seventeenth century. The plantation system—the use of forced labor to produce cash crops on vast tracts of land—had been developed on Mediterranean islands in the Middle Ages by European entrepreneurs, using slaves procured in Black Sea ports by Venetian and Genoese traders. Sugar production by this system had been established on Atlantic islands, such as the Cape Verde Islands, using African labor, and then in the Americas by the Spanish and Portuguese. Sugar production in the New World grew from about 20,000 tons in 1600 to about 200,000 tons by 1770.

In the 1620s, while the Dutch were exploiting Portuguese weakness in the Eastern spice trade, they were also seizing sugar regions in Brazil and replacing the Portuguese in slaving ports in Africa. The Portuguese were able to retake most of their Brazilian territory in the 1650s. But the Dutch, because they monopolized the carrying trade, were able to become the official supplier of slaves to Spanish plantations in the New World and the chief supplier of slaves as well as other goods to most other regions. (See the box "Global Encounters: Journal of a Dutch Slave Ship.") The Dutch were able to make handsome profits dealing in human cargo until the end of the seventeenth century, when they were supplanted by the British.

The Dutch introduced sugar cultivation to the French and English after learning it themselves in Brazil. Sugar plantations began to supplant tobacco cultivation, as well as subsistence farming, on the Caribbean islands the English and French controlled. Beginning in the late sixteenth century English and French seamen had seized island territories to serve as provisioning stations and staging points for raids against or commerce with Spanish colonies. Some island outposts had expanded into colonies and attracted European settlers—some, as in North America, coming as indentured servants—to work the land. Sugar cultivation, though potentially more profitable than tobacco, demanded huge outlays of capital and continual supplies of unskilled labor, and it drastically transformed the settlements' characters. Large plantations owned by wealthy, often absentee landlords and dependent on slave labor replaced smaller-scale independent farming. The most profitable sugar colonies were, for the French, the islands of

Sugar Manufacture in Caribbean Colonies   Production of sugar required large capital outlays, in part because the raw cane had to be processed quickly, on-site, to avoid spoilage. This scene depicts enslaved workers operating a small sugar mill on the island of Barbados in the seventeenth century. In the background a press crushes the cane; in the foreground the juice from the cane is boiled down until sugar begins to crystallize.   *(Mary Evans Picture Library)*

Martinique° and Guadeloupe° and, for the English, Barbados° and Jamaica.

Aware of the overwhelming Spanish territorial advantage in the New World, and yet still hoping for treasures such as the Spanish had found, the English, French, and Dutch were also eager to explore and settle North America. From the early sixteenth century on, French, Dutch, English, and Portuguese seamen had fished and traded off Newfoundland. By 1630 small French and Scottish settlements in Acadia (near modern Nova Scotia) and on the St. Lawrence River and English settlements in Newfoundland were established to systematically exploit the timber, fish, and fur of the north Atlantic coasts.

In England rising unemployment and religious discontent created a large pool of potential colonists, some of whom were initially attracted to the Caribbean. The

Martinique (mar-tih-NEEK)
Guadeloupe (gwah-dah-LOO-puh)
Barbados (bar-BAY-dose)

first of the English settlements to endure in what was to become the United States was established at Jamestown, named for James I, in Virginia in 1607. ("Virginia," named for Elizabeth I, the "Virgin Queen," was an extremely vague designation for the Atlantic coast of North America and its hinterland.)

The Crown encouraged colonization, but a private company similar to those that financed long-distance trade was established to organize the enterprise. The directors of the Virginia Company were London businessmen. Investors and would-be colonists purchased shares. Shareholders among the colonists could participate in a colonial assembly, although the governor appointed by the company was the final authority.

The colonists arrived in Virginia with ambitious and optimistic instructions. They were to open mines, establish profitable cultivation, and search for sea routes to Asia. But at first they struggled merely to survive. (See the box "Reading Sources: The Disappointments of the Virginia Colony.") The indigenous peoples in Virginia, un-

Journal of a Dutch Slave Ship

These excerpts from a journal kept by the captain of the Dutch ship *St. Jan* record a 1659 slave-trading voyage that began in Africa and ended on Curaçao, a Dutch island colony in the Caribbean.

The 8th [of March]. We arrived with our ship on Saturday before Arda [in modern Benin] to take on board the surgeon's mate, and tamarinds as refreshment for the slaves. We set sail the next day to continue our voyage to Rio Reael.

The 22nd [of May]. We weighed anchor again and sailed out of the Rio Reael. . . . We acquired there in trade two hundred and nineteen slaves, men and women, boys as well as girls; and we set our course for [islands in the Gulf of Biafra] in order to seek food for the slaves, because nothing was to be had in Rio Reael.

The 26th ditto. On Monday we arrived [on the islands]. We spent seven days there looking but barely obtained enough for the slaves' daily consumption; therefore we decided to sail [up a nearby river] to see whether any food could be found there.

The 29th [of June]. On Sunday we decided to continue our voyage because there was also little food [up the river mouth] for the slaves because of the heavy rain which we had daily and because many slaves were suffering from dysentery caused by the bad food supplied to us at [St. George del Mina, a Dutch fort established to serve the slave trade]. . . .

The 11th [of August]. We lay sixteen days at Cape Lopez [modern Gabon] in order to take on water and firewood. Among the water barrels some forty were taken apart to be repaired because our cooper died . . . [and] we had no one who could repair them.

The 24th [of September]. On Friday we arrived at the island of Tobago [in the Caribbean] where we took on water and also bought some bread for our crew because for three weeks they have had no rations.

The 1st of November. We lost our ship on the reef [east of Curaçao] and our crew fled in the boat immediately. There was no chance to save the slaves because we had to abandon the ship on account of heavy surf.

The 4th ditto. We arrived with the boat at . . . Curaçao. The [governor] dispatched two sloops to retrieve the slaves from the shipwreck. One of the sloops was taken by a pirate together with eighty-four slaves.

QUESTIONS

1. Note the dates in the captain's journal. How much time was devoted to trade and provisioning in Africa? How much time to the transatlantic journey?

2. The voyage seems to have been very poorly planned, particularly regarding provisioning. Is this a fair interpretation of the document?

3. A companion document reveals that 110 of the 219 captive men, women, and children died during the voyage across the Atlantic. Note the fate of those who were still alive by journey's end. Why was a pirate able to escape with so many of the slaves?

SOURCE: Charles T. Gehring and J. A. Schiltkamp, eds., *New Netherlands Documents,* vol. 17 (Interlaken, N.Y.: Heart of the Lakes Publishing, 1987), pp. 128–131. Used by permission from the *New Netherland Project,* The New York State Library.

 For additional information on this topic, go to college.hmco.com/students.

like those in Spanish-held territories, were not organized in urbanized, rigidly hierarchical societies that, after conquest, could provide the invaders with a labor force. Indeed, much of the local native population was quickly wiped out by European diseases. The introduction of tobacco as a cash crop a few years later saved the colonists economically—although the Virginia Company had already gone bankrupt and the Crown had assumed control of the colony. With the cultivation of tobacco, the Virginia colony, like the Caribbean islands, became dependent on forced, eventually slave, labor.

Among the Virginia colonists were impoverished men and women who came as servants indentured to those who had paid their passage—that is, they were bound by contract to pay off their debts by several years of labor. Colonies established to the north, in what was called "New England," also drew people from the margins of English society. Early settlers there were religious

READING SOURCES

THE DISAPPOINTMENTS OF THE VIRGINIA COLONY

In this letter sent to the Virginia Company back in London in 1608, Captain John Smith (1580–1631) explains somewhat angrily that the colony cannot produce the profits that the investors had hoped for. He notes the folly of carrying boats west over the fall line of the Virginia rivers—where, it had been assumed, they might sight the Pacific Ocean as the Spaniards had done in Panama. He reports no sign of the colony of Sir Walter Raleigh, which vanished after being planted in North Carolina in 1585. He also notes the difficulties of mere survival, let alone extracting wealth.

I have received your letter, wherein you write that . . . we feed you but with ifs and ands and hopes, and some few proofs . . . and that we must expressly follow your instructions sent by Captain Newport [the commander of the supply ship], the charge of whose voyage . . . we cannot defray.

For the quartered boat to be borne by the soldiers over the falls, Newport had 120 of the best men. . . . If he had burned her to ashes, one might have carried her in a bag, but as she is, five hundred cannot, to a navigable place above the falls. And for him, at that time to find in the South Sea a mine of gold, or any of them sent by Sir Walter Raleigh, at our consultation I told them was as likely as the rest. . . . In their absence I followed the new begun works of pitch and tar, glass, [potash, and lumber], whereof some small quantities we have sent you. But if you rightly consider, what an infinite toil it is in Russia and [Sweden], where the woods are proper for naught else [and where] there be the help of both man and beast . . . yet thousands of those poor people can scarce get necessaries to live. . . .

From your ship we had not provision in victuals worth twenty pound, and we are more than two hundred to live upon this. . . . Though there be fish in the sea, fowls in the air, and beasts in the woods . . . they are so wild and we so weak and ignorant, we cannot much trouble them.

Source: Philip L. Barbour, ed., *The Complete Works of Captain John Smith (1580–1631)*, vol. 2 (Chapel Hill: University of North Carolina Press, 1986), pp. 187–189.

---

dissidents. The first to arrive were the Pilgrims, who arrived at Plymouth (modern Massachusetts) in 1620. They were a community of religious Separatists who had originally immigrated to the Netherlands from England for freedom of conscience.

Following the Pilgrims came Puritans escaping escalating persecution under Charles I. The first, in 1629, settled under the auspices of another royally chartered company, the Massachusetts Bay Company. Among their number were many prosperous Puritan merchants and landholders. Independence from investors in London allowed them an unprecedented degree of self-government once the Massachusetts Bay colony was established.

Nevertheless, the colonies in North America were disappointments to England because they generated much less wealth than expected. Shipping timber back to Europe proved too expensive, although New England forests did supply some of the Caribbean colonists' needs. The fur trade became less lucrative as English settlement pushed the Native Americans who did most of the trapping west and as French trappers to the north encroached on the trade. Certain colonists profited enormously from the tobacco economy, but the mother country did so only moderately because the demand in Europe for tobacco never grew as quickly as the demand for sugar. The English settlements did continue to attract more migrants than other colonizers' outposts. By 1640 Massachusetts had some fourteen thousand European inhabitants. Through most of the next century the growth of colonial populations in North America would result in an English advantage over the French in control of New World territory.

The French began their settlement of North America at the same time as the English, in the same push to compensate for their mutual weakness vis-à-vis the Spanish (see Map 16.4). The French efforts, however, had very different results, owing partly to the sites of their settlements but mostly to the relationship between the mother country and the colonies. The French hold on territory was always tenuous because of the scant num-

Map 16.4   The English and French in North America, ca. 1700   By 1700 a veritable ring of French-claimed territory encircled the coastal colonies of England. English-claimed areas, however, were more densely settled and more economically viable.

ber of colonists who could be lured from home. There seems to have been less economic impetus for colonization from France than from England. And after the French crown took over the colonies, any religious impetus evaporated, for only Catholics were allowed to settle in New France. Moreover, control by the Crown forced a traditional hierarchical political organization on the French colonies. A royal governor directed the colony, and large tracts of land were set aside for privileged investors. Thus North America offered little to tempt French people of modest means who were seeking a better life.

The first successful French colony was established in Acadia in 1605. This settlement was an exception among the French efforts because it was founded by Huguenots, not by Catholics. A few years later the explorer Samuel de Champlain (1567?–1635) navigated the

St. Lawrence River and founded Quebec City (1608). He convinced the royal government, emerging from its preoccupations with religious wars at home, to promote the development of the colony. French explorers went on to establish Montreal, farther inland on the St. Lawrence (1642), and to explore the Great Lakes and the Mississippi River basin (see Map 16.4).

Such investment as the French crown was able to attract went into profitable trade, mainly in furs, and not into the difficult business of colonization. French trappers and traders who ventured into wilderness areas were renowned for their hardiness and adaptability, but they did not bring their families and establish settled, European-style towns. Quebec remained more of a trading station, dependent on shipments of food from France, than a growing urban community. Added to the commercial dimension of New France was the church's interest: much of the energy of French colonization was expended by men and women of religious orders—the "Black Robes"—bringing their zeal to new frontiers. By the middle of the seventeenth century all of New France had only about three thousand European inhabitants.

The seeming weakness of the French colonial effort in North America was not much noticed at the time. French and English fishermen, trappers, and traders competed intensely, and the French often reaped the greater share of profits, owing to their closer ties with Native American trading systems. Outright battles occasionally erupted between English and French settlements. But for both England and France the major profits and strategic interests in the New World lay to the south, in the Caribbean. The Dutch experience reveals the degree to which North America, for all colonial powers, was of secondary importance to the plantation profits farther south. In 1624 the Dutch founded a trading center, New Amsterdam, at the site of modern-day New York City. Fifty years later they relinquished New Amsterdam—the cornerstone of their northern enterprise—to the English in return for recognition of the Dutch claims to sugar-producing Guiana (modern Suriname°) in South America.

Consequently, by far the largest group of migrants to European-held territories in the Americas were forced migrants: African men and women sold into slavery and transported across the Atlantic to work the plantations established by Europeans. A conservative estimate is that approximately 1.35 million Africans were forcibly transported as slave labor to the New World during the seventeenth century.

Suriname (SIR-ih-nam)

The Beginning of the End of Traditional Society

Within Europe the economic impact of overseas trade was profound. Merchants and investors in a few of Europe's largest cities reaped great profits. Mediterranean ports such as Venice, once the heart of European trade, did not share in the bonanza from the new trade with Asia or the Americas. Atlantic ports such as Seville, through which most Spanish commerce with the New World flowed, and, above all, Amsterdam began to flourish. The population of Amsterdam increased from about 30,000 to 200,000 in the course of the seventeenth century.

All capital cities, however, not just seaports, grew substantially during the 1600s. Increasing numbers of government functionaries, courtiers and their hangers-on, and people involved in trade lived and worked in capital cities. These cities also grew indirectly from the demand such people generated for services and products, ranging from fashionable clothing to exotic foodstuffs. For the first time cities employed vast numbers of country people. Perhaps as much as one-fifth of the population of England passed through London at one time or another, creating the mobile, volatile community so active in the English civil war and its aftermath.

The economy became more productive and flexible as it expanded, but social stratification intensified. Patterns of consumption in cities reflected the economic gulfs between residents. Most people could not afford to buy imported pepper or sugar. Poverty increased in cities, even in vibrant Amsterdam, because cities attracted people fleeing rural unemployment with few skills and fewer resources. As growing central governments heaped tax burdens on peasants, many rural people were caught in a cycle of debt; the only escape was to abandon farming and flock to cities.

Peasant rebellions occurred throughout the century as a result of depressed economic conditions and heavy taxation, reflecting the expansion of royal power and expensive royal military ambitions. Some small-scale revolts involved direct action, such as seizing the tax collector's grain or stopping the movement of grain to the great cities. Urban demand often caused severe food shortages in rural areas in western Europe, despite the booming trade in grain with eastern Europe via the Baltic.

The typical peasant revolt in western Europe during the seventeenth century, however, was directed against escalating taxation. Tax rebellions often formed spontaneously, perhaps as tax officials passed through a village, but they were not mere chaotic gatherings of rabble. Country folk were accustomed to defending themselves as communities—against brigands and marauding sol-diers, for example. Local gentry or prosperous farmers who ordinarily fulfilled the function of local constable led such revolts from time to time, convinced that they represented the legitimate interests of the community against rapacious officials higher up. The scale of peasant violence meant that thousands of troops sometimes had to be diverted from a state's foreign wars. As a matter of routine, soldiers accompanied tax officials and enforced collection all over Europe. Thus, as the ambitions of rulers grew, so too did the resistance of ordinary people to the exactions of the state.

SUMMARY

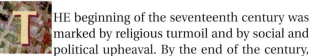 HE beginning of the seventeenth century was marked by religious turmoil and by social and political upheaval. By the end of the century, the former had faded as a source of collective anxiety, and the latter was largely resolved. States troubled by religious and political turmoil or on the political margins early in the century had evolved into secure and dynamic centers of power: the Netherlands, the Habsburg domains, Brandenburg-Prussia, and Russia. Following the most powerful monarchy in Europe, France, most states had moved from internal division—with independent provinces and aristocrats going their own way—to greater coherence. This stability was both cause and consequence of rulers' desires to make war on an ever larger scale. By the end of the century only those states able to field massive armies were competitive on the European stage. The Netherlands, a stark exception to the pattern of centralized royal control, began more closely to resemble other states under the pressure of warfare by century's end.

At the beginning of the century, overseas trade and colonization had been the near monopoly of Spain and Portugal. At the end of the century the English, French, and Dutch had supplanted the Iberian states in controlling trade with Asia and were reaping many profits in the Americas, especially from the extension of plantation agriculture. Beneath all these developments lay subtle but significant economic, social, and cultural shifts. One effect of the increased wealth generated by overseas trade and the increased power of governments to tax their subjects was a widening gulf between rich and poor. New styles of behavior and patterns of consumption highlighted differences between social classes. Long-term effects of overseas voyages on Old World attitudes, as well as fundamental changes in world-views that were paving the way for modern science, would have a revolutionary impact on Europeans and their cultures.

■ Notes

1. Quoted in D. H. Pennington, *Europe in the Seventeenth Century*, 2d ed. (London: Longman, 1989), p. 508.

■ Suggested Reading

Collins, James B. *The State in Early Modern France*. 1995. An up-to-date synthesis by one of the leading scholars of French absolutism.

Howard, Michael. *War in European History*. 1976. A general study of warfare emphasizing the relationship between war making and state development.

Ingrao, Charles. *The Habsburg Monarchy, 1618–1815*. 1994. A treatment of the Austrian Habsburgs that stresses the distinctiveness of the Habsburg state.

Kishlansky, Mark. *A Monarchy Transformed*. 1996. The most recent full scholarly treatment of political events in England.

Musgrave, Peter. *The Early Modern European Economy*. 1999. A recent survey of the scholarship on the expanding European economy.

Oakley, Stewart P. *War and Peace in the Baltic, 1560–1790*. 1992. An excellent survey of the Baltic region in the early modern period.

Pennington, D. H. *Europe in the Seventeenth Century*. 2d ed. 1989. A general history of the century.

Riasanovsky, Nicolas V. *A History of Russia*. 6th ed. 2000. A reliable and readable survey of Russian history from medieval times; includes an extensive bibliography of major works available in English.

Schama, Simon. *The Embarrassment of Riches: An Interpretation of Dutch Culture in the Golden Age*. 1997. An innovative study of Dutch culture that explores the social and psychological tensions created by its growing wealth in the seventeenth century.

Wolf, Eric R. *Europe and the People Without History*. 1982. A survey of European contact with and conquest of peoples after 1400; includes extensive treatments of non-European societies and detailed explanations of the economic and political interests of the Europeans.

 For a searchable list of additional readings for this chapter, go to college.hmco.com/students.

Table Manners

If you were to sit down in a fancy restaurant, order a juicy steak, and then eat it with your bare hands, other diners would undoubtedly stare, shocked by your bad manners. It has not always been the case that table manners meant very much—were able to signal social status, for example. It was not always the case that table manners existed at all in the sense that we know them. How did they evolve? How did they come to have the importance that they do? And why should historians pay any attention to them?

Imagine that you have been invited to dinner at a noble estate in the year 1500. As you sit down, you notice that there are no knives, forks, and spoons at your place, and no napkins either. A servant (a young girl from a neighboring village) sets a roast of meat in front of you and your fellow diners. The lords and ladies on either side of you hack off pieces of meat with the knives that they always carry with them, and then they eat the meat with their fingers. Hunks of bread on the table in front of them catch the dripping juices.

One hundred fifty years later, in 1650, dinner is a much more "civilized" meal. Notice the well-to-do women dining in this engraving by the French artist Abraham Bosse (1602–1676). The table setting, with tablecloths, napkins, plates, and silverware, is recognizable to us. The lady at the extreme right holds up her fork and napkin in a somewhat forced and obvious gesture. These diners have the utensils that we take for granted, but the artist does not take them for granted: they are intended to be noticed by Bosse's elite audience.

In the seventeenth century aristocrats and gentry signaled their political and social privilege with behavior that distinguished them from the lower classes in ways their more powerful ancestors had found unnecessary. Historians have called this the invention of civility. As we have seen, proper courtesy to one's superiors at court was considered essential. It marked the fact that rituals of honor and deference were increasingly taking the place of armed conflict as the routine behavior of the upper classes. Also essential, however, were certain standards of physical privacy and delicacy. Something as seemingly trivial as the use of a fork became charged with symbolic significance. As the actual power of the aristocrats was circumscribed by the state, they found new expressions of status. Since the sixteenth century new kinds of manners had been touted in handbooks,

reflecting changes that already had occurred at Italian courts. During the seventeenth century these practices became more widespread and opened up a gulf between upper- and lower-class behavior.

Some of the new behaviors concerned bodily privacy and discretion. A nobleman now used a handkerchief instead of his fingers or coat sleeve, and he did not urinate in public. The new "rules" about eating are particularly interesting. Why did eating with a fork seem refined and desirable to aristocrats trying to buttress their own self-images? As any 3-year-old knows, eating with a fork is remarkably inefficient.

Using a fork kept you at a distance—literal and symbolic—from the animal you were eating. Napkins wiped away all trace of bloody juices from your lips. Interestingly, as diners began to use utensils, other eating arrangements changed in parallel ways. Sideboards had been in use for a long time, but pieces of meat were now discreetly carved on the sideboard and presented to diners in individual portions. The carcass was brought to the sideboard cut into roasts instead of unmistakably whole, and it was often decorated—as it is today—to further disguise it.

The new aristocrat was increasingly separated from the world of brute physical force, both in daily life and on the battlefield. In warfare brute force was no longer adequate. Training, discipline, and tactical knowledge were more important and heightened the significance of rank, which separated officers from the vast numbers of common soldiers (see page 545). Aristocrats now lived in a privileged world where violence—except for an occasional duel—was no longer a fact of life. Their new behavior codes signaled their new invulnerability to others. Above all, they worked to transform a loss—of the independence that had gone hand in hand with a more violent life—into a gain: a privileged immunity to violence.

Specific manners became important, then, because they were symbols of power. The symbolic distance between the powerful and the humble was reinforced by other changes in habits and behavior. A sixteenth-century warrior customarily traveled on horseback and often went from place to place within a city on foot, attended by his retinue. A seventeenth-century aristocrat was more likely to travel in a horse-drawn carriage. The presence of special commodities from abroad—such as sugar—in the seventeenth century created further possibilities for signaling status.

Table Manners of the Upper Class in the Seventeenth Century *(Courtesy of the Trustees of the British Museum)*

It is interesting to note that other personal habits still diverged dramatically from what we would consider acceptable today. Notice the large, stately bed in the same room as the dining table in Bosse's engraving. Interior space was still undifferentiated by our standards, and it was common for eating, talking, sleeping, and estate management all to go on in a single room. The grand bed is in the picture because, like the fork, it is a mark of status. Like virtually everything else, what is "proper" varies with historical circumstance.

571

CHAPTER 17

A Revolution in World-View

THE year is 1649. Queen Christina of Sweden welcomes us with her gaze and her gesture to witness a science lesson at her court. Her illustrious instructor, the French philosopher René Descartes, clutches a compass and points to an astronomical drawing. The young queen, twenty-three years old at the time, was already well known as a patron of artists and scholars. Christina had invited Descartes to her court because of his achievements in physics and philosophy. This painting depicts the fact that during Christina's lifetime, new theories in the field of astronomy revolutionized the sciences and required new definitions of matter to explain them. Descartes earned fame both for his novel theories about matter and for his systematic approach to the application of human reason to understanding the universe. This painting celebrates both Descartes's work and Christina's sponsorship of it.

The revolution within the sciences had been initiated in the sixteenth century by the astronomical calculations and hypotheses of Nicholas Copernicus, who posited that the earth moves around the sun. The work of the Italian mathematician and astronomer Galileo Galilei, as well as others, added evidence to support this hypothesis. Their work overturned principles of physics and philosophy that had held sway since ancient times. Later generations of scientists and philosophers, beginning with Descartes, labored to construct new principles to explain the way the physical universe behaves. The readiness of scientists, their patrons, and educated laypeople to push Copernicus's hypothesis to these conclusions came from several sources: their exposure to the intellectual innovations of Renaissance thought, the intellectual challenges and material opportunities represented by the discovery of the New World, and the challenge to authority embodied in the Reformation. Also, the new science offered

René Descartes (*second from the right*) instructs Queen Christina of Sweden and her courtiers.
(Réunion des Musées Nationaux/Art Resource, NY)

The Revolution in Astronomy, 1543–1632

The Scientific Revolution Generalized, ca. 1600–1700

The New Science: Society, Politics, and Religion

prestige and technological advances to the rulers, such as Christina, who sponsored it.

By the end of the seventeenth century a vision of an infinite but orderly cosmos appealing to human reason had, among educated Europeans, largely replaced the medieval vision of a closed universe centered on the earth and suffused with Christian purpose. Religion became an increasingly subordinate ally of science as confidence in an open-ended, experimental approach to knowledge came to be as strongly held as religious conviction. It is because of this larger shift in world-view, not simply because of particular scientific discoveries, that the seventeenth century may be labeled the era of the Scientific Revolution.

Because religious significance had been attached to previous explanations and religious authority defended them, the new astronomy automatically led to an enduring debate about the compatibility of science and religion. But the revolution in world-view was not confined to astronomy or even to science generally. As philosophers gained confidence in human reason and the intelligibility of the world, they turned to new speculation about human affairs. They began to challenge traditional justifica-

tions for the hierarchical nature of society and the sanctity of authority just as energetically as Copernicus and his followers had overthrown old views about the cosmos.

QUESTIONS TO CONSIDER

- Why did new theories about astronomy lead to a broader Scientific Revolution?

- What were some of the features of the new "mechanistic" world-view?

- How did religious, political, and social conditions shape the work of scientists?

- What were the implications for political thought of the new scientific approach to the world?

TERMS TO KNOW

Nicholas Copernicus	René Descartes
heliocentric theory	mechanistic world-view
Johannes Kepler	Isaac Newton
Galileo Galilei	laws of motion
Francis Bacon	Thomas Hobbes
empirical method	John Locke

THE REVOLUTION IN ASTRONOMY, 1543–1632

THE origins of the seventeenth-century revolution in world-view lie, for the most part, in developments in astronomy. Because of astronomy's role in the explanations of the world and human life that had been devised by ancient and medieval scientists and philosophers, any advances in astronomy were bound to have widespread intellectual repercussions. By the early part of the seventeenth century fundamental astronomical beliefs had been successfully challenged. The consequence was the undermining of both the material (physics) and the philosophical (metaphysics) explanations of the world that had been standing for centuries.

The Inherited World-View and the Sixteenth-Century Context

Ancient and medieval astronomy accepted the perspective on the universe that unaided human senses support—namely, that the earth is fixed at the center of the universe and the celestial bodies rotate around it. The regular movements of heavenly bodies and the obvious importance of the sun for life on earth made astronomy a vital undertaking for both scientific and religious purposes in many ancient societies. Astronomers in ancient Greece carefully observed the heavens and learned to calculate and to predict the seemingly circular motion of the stars and the sun about the earth. The orbits of the planets were more difficult to explain, for the planets seemed to travel both east and west across the sky at various times and with no regularity that could be mathematically understood. Indeed, the very word *planet* comes from a Greek word meaning "wanderer."

We now know that all the planets simultaneously orbit the sun at different speeds in paths that are at different distances from the sun. The relative positions of the planets constantly change; sometimes other planets are "ahead" of the earth and sometimes "behind." In the second century A.D. the Greek astronomer Ptolemy° attempted to explain the planets' occasional "backward" motion by attributing it to "epicycles"—small circular orbits within the larger orbit. Ptolemy's mathematical explanations of the imagined epicycles were extremely complex, but neither Ptolemy nor medieval mathematicians and astronomers were ever able fully to account for planetary motion.

Ancient physics, most notably the work of the Greek philosopher Aristotle° (384–322 B.C.), explained the fact that some objects (such as cannonballs) fall to earth but others (stars and planets) seem weightless relative to earth because of their composition: different kinds of matter have different inherent tendencies and properties. In this view all earthbound matter (like cannonballs) falls because it is naturally attracted to earth—heaviness being a property of earthbound things.

In the Christian era the Aristotelian explanation of the universe was infused with Christian meaning and purpose. The heavens were said to be made of different, pure matter because they were the abode of the angels. Both the earth and the humans who inhabited it were changeable and corruptible. Yet God had given human beings a unique and special place in the universe, which was thought to be a closed world with the stationary earth at the center. Revolving around the earth in circular orbits were the sun, moon, stars, and planets. The motion of all lesser bodies was caused by the rotation of all the stars together in the vast crystal-like sphere in which they were embedded.

A few ancient astronomers theorized that the earth moved about the sun. Some medieval philosophers also adopted this heliocentric thesis (*helios* is the Greek word for "sun"), but it remained a minority view because it seemed to contradict both common sense and observed data. The sun and stars *appeared* to move around the earth with great regularity. Moreover, how could objects fall to earth if the earth was moving beneath them? Also, astronomers detected no difference in angles from which observers on earth viewed the stars at different times. Such differences would exist, they thought, if the earth changed positions by moving around the sun. It was in-

conceivable that the universe could be so large and the stars so distant that the earth's movement would produce no measurable change in the earth's position with respect to the stars.

Several conditions of intellectual life in the sixteenth century encouraged new work in astronomy and led to the revision of the earth-centered world-view. The most important was the work of Renaissance humanists in recovering and interpreting ancient texts. Now able to work with new Greek versions of Ptolemy, mathematicians and astronomers noted that his explanations for the motion

---

Ptolemy (TOL-eh-mee)   **Aristotle** (AIR-is-tot-il)

CHRONOLOGY

1543	Copernicus, *De Revolutionibus Orbium Caelestium;* Vesalius, *On the Fabric of the Human Body*
1576	Construction of Brahe's observatory begins
1603	Accadèmia dei Lincei founded in Rome
1609	Kepler's third law of motion
1610	Galileo, *The Starry Messenger*
1620	Bacon, *Novum Organum*
1628	Harvey, *On the Motion of the Heart*
1632	Galileo, *Dialogue on the Two Chief Systems of the World*
1633	Galileo condemned and sentenced to house arrest
1637	Descartes, *Discourse on Method*
1651	Hobbes, *Leviathan*
1660	Boyle, *New Experiments Physico-Mechanical* Royal Society of London founded
1666	Académie Royale des Sciences founded in France
1686	Fontenelle, *Conversations on the Plurality of Worlds*
1687	Newton, *Principia* (*Mathematical Principles of Natural Philosophy*)
1690	Locke, *Two Treatises of Government* and *Essay on Human Understanding*
1702	Bayle, *Historical and Critical Dictionary*

The Traditional Universe In this print from around 1600 heavenly bodies are depicted orbiting the earth in perfectly circular paths. In fact, the ancient astronomer Ptolemy believed that the planets followed complex orbits within orbits, known as *epicycles,* moving around the stationary earth. *(Hulton Archive/Getty Images)*

of the planets were imperfect and not simply inadequately transmitted, as they had long believed. Also, the discovery of the New World dramatically undercut the assumption that ancient knowledge was superior. The existence of the Americas specifically undermined Ptolemy's authority once again, for it disproved many of the assertions in his *Geography,* which had just been recovered in Europe the previous century.

The desire to explain heavenly movements better was still loaded with religious significance in the sixteenth century and was heightened by the immediate need for reform of the Julian calendar (named for Julius Caesar). Ancient observations of the movement of the sun, though remarkably accurate, could not measure the precise length of the solar year. By the sixteenth century the cumulative error of this calendar had resulted in a change of ten days: the spring equinox fell on March 11

instead of March 21. An accurate and uniform system of dating was necessary for all rulers and their tax collectors and recordkeepers. And because the calculation of the date of Easter was at stake, a reliable calendar was the particular project of the church.

Impetus for new and better astronomical observations and calculations arose from other features of the intellectual and political landscape as well. Increasingly, as the century went on, princely courts became important sources of patronage for and sites of scientific activity. Rulers eager to buttress their own power by symbolically linking it to dominion over nature sponsored investigations of the world, as Ferdinand and Isabella had so successfully done, and displayed the marvels of nature at their courts. Sponsoring scientific inquiry also yielded practical benefits: better mapping of the ruler's domains and better technology for mining, gunnery, and navigation.

Finally, schools of thought fashionable at the time, encouraged by the humanists' critique of received tradition, hinted at the possibilities of alternative physical and metaphysical systems. The ancient doctrine of Hermeticism (named for the mythical originator of the ideas, Hermes Trismegistos), revived since the Renaissance, claimed that matter is universally imbued with divine (or magical) spirit. Drawing on Hermeticism was Paracelsianism, named for the Swiss physician Philippus von Hohenheim (1493–1541), who called himself Paracelsus° (literally "beyond Celsus," an acclaimed Roman physician whose works had just been recovered). Paracelsus scoffed at the notion that ancient authorities were the final word on the workings of nature. "He who is born in imagination," he wrote, "discovers the latent forces of nature."[1] Paracelsus offered an alternative to accepted medical theory, put forth by the physician Galen° (ca. 131–201), the premier medical authority of antiquity, now as revered as Aristotle. Galen believed that an imbalance of bodily "humors" caused illness. Paracelsus substituted a theory of chemical imbalance that was a forerunner of modern understandings of pathology. He was wildly popular wherever he taught because of the success of his treatments of illness and his willingness to lecture openly to laymen.

Neo-Platonism, another school of thought, had a more systematic and far-reaching impact. Neo-Platonism was a revival, primarily in Italian humanist circles, of certain aspects of Plato's thought. It contributed directly to innovation in science because it emphasized the abstract nature of true knowledge and thus encouraged mathematical investigation. This provided a spur to astronomical studies, which, since ancient times, had been concerned more with mathematical analysis of heavenly movements than with physical explanations for them. Also, like Hermeticism and Paracelsianism, Neo-Platonism had a mystical dimension that fostered creative speculation about the nature of matter and the organization of the universe. Neo-Platonists were particularly fascinated by the sun as a symbol of the one divine mind or soul at the heart of all creation.

The Copernican Challenge

Nicholas Copernicus° (1473–1543), son of a German merchant family in Poland, pursued wide-ranging university studies in philosophy, law, astronomy, mathematics, and medicine—first in Cracow in Poland and then in Bologna and Padua in Italy. In Italy he was exposed to Neo-Platonic ideas. He took a degree in canon (church) law in 1503 and became a cathedral canon (a member of the cathedral staff) in the city of Frauenburg (modern Poland), where he pursued his own interests in astronomy while carrying out administrative duties. When the pope asked Copernicus to assist with the reform of the Julian calendar, he replied that reform of the calendar required reform in astronomy. His major work, *De Revolutionibus Orbium Caelestium* (*On the Revolution of Heavenly Bodies,* 1543), was dedicated to the pope in the hopes that it would help with the task of calendar reform—as indeed it did. The Gregorian calendar, issued in 1582 during the pontificate of Gregory XIII (r. 1572–1585), was based on Copernicus's calculations.

Copernicus postulated that the earth and all the other planets orbit the sun. He did not assert that the earth does in fact move around the sun but offered the heliocentric system as a mathematical construct, useful for predicting the movements of planets, stars, and the sun. However, he walked a thin line between making claims for a mathematical construct on the one hand and physical reality on the other. Scholars now believe that Copernicus was himself persuaded that the heliocentric theory was correct. He had searched in ancient sources for thinkers who believed the earth moved. Other astronomers familiar with his work and reputation urged him to publish the results of his calculations. But not until 1542, twelve years after finishing the work, did he send *De Revolutionibus* to be published. He received a copy just before his death the next year. (See the box "Reading Sources: Copernicus Justifies His Work to the Pope.")

By affirming the earth's movement around the sun while also salvaging features of the old system, Copernicus faced burdens of explanation not faced by Ptolemy. For example, Copernicus still assumed that the planets traveled in circular orbits, so he was forced to retain some epicycles in his schema to account for the circular motion. In general, however, the Copernican account of planetary motion was simpler than the Ptolemaic account. It appealed to other astronomers of the age because it was useful and because it highlighted the harmony of heavenly motion, which remained a fundamental physical and metaphysical principle. Inaccessible except to other astronomers, Copernicus's work only slowly led to conceptual revolution, as scientists worked with his calculations and assembled other evidence to support the heliocentric theory.

The most important reason that fundamental conceptual change followed Copernican theory so gradually was that Copernicus did not resolve the physical problems his ideas raised. If Copernicus were right, the earth

---

Paracelsus (pair-uh-SEL-sus)   Galen (GAY-len)
Copernicus (kuh-PURR-nih-kus)

READING SOURCES

COPERNICUS JUSTIFIES HIS WORK TO THE POPE

In this dedicatory letter to the pope that prefaced On the Revolution of Heavenly Bodies, *Nicholas Copernicus expresses his desire to assist with calendar reform. Principally, however, he seeks to justify his novel conclusions. Note that he not only cites ancient authority for the movement of the earth but also stresses the mathematical (not metaphysical) nature of the problem and of his solution to it.*

To the Most Holy Lord, Pope Paul III

I may well presume, most Holy Father, that certain people, as soon as they hear that in this book about the Revolutions of the Spheres of the Universe I ascribe movement to the earthly globe, will cry out that, holding such views, I should at once be hissed off the stage. . . . How I came to dare to conceive such motion of the Earth, contrary to the received opinion of the Mathematicians and indeed contrary to the impression of the senses, is what your Holiness will rather expect to hear. So I should like your Holiness to know that I was induced to think of a method of computing the motions of the spheres by nothing else than the knowledge that the Mathematicians are inconsistent in these investigations. . . . Mathematicians are so unsure of the movements of the Sun and the Moon that they cannot even explain . . . the constant length of the seasonal year.

. . . I pondered long upon this uncertainty of mathematical tradition. I . . . read again the works of all the philosophers on whom I could lay a hand to seek out whether any of them had ever supposed that the motions of the spheres were other[wise]. I found first in Cicero that Hicetas [of Syracuse, fifth century B.C.] had realized that the earth moved. . . . Mathematics are for mathematicians, and they, if I be not wholly deceived, will hold that my labors contribute somewhat . . . to the Church. . . . For under Leo X, the question of correcting the ecclesiastical calendar was . . . left undecided.

Source: Thomas S. Kuhn, *The Copernican Revolution* (Cambridge, Mass.: Harvard University Press, 1985), pp. 137–143.

would have to be made of the same material as other planets. How, then, would Copernicus explain the motion of objects on earth—the fact that they fall to earth—if it was not in their nature to fall toward the heavy, stationary earth? In Copernicus's system, the movement of the earth caused the *apparent* motion of the stars. But if the stars did not rotate in their crystalline sphere, what made all other heavenly bodies move?

Copernicus was not as troubled by these questions as we might expect him to be. Since ancient times, mathematical astronomy—the science of measuring and predicting the movements of heavenly bodies—had been far more important than, and had proceeded independently of, physical explanations of observed motion. Nevertheless, as Copernicus's own efforts to support his hypothesis reveal, his theories directly contradicted many of the supposed laws of motion. The usefulness of his theories to other astronomers meant that the contradictions between mathematical and physical models for the universe would have to be resolved. Copernicus himself might be best understood as the last Ptolemaic astronomer, working within inherited questions and with known tools. His work itself did not constitute a revolution, but it did initiate one.

The First Copernican Astronomers

In the first generation of astronomers after the publication of *De Revolutionibus* in 1543 we can see the effects of Copernicus's work. His impressive computations rapidly won converts among fellow astronomers. Several particularly gifted astronomers continued to develop the Copernican system. Thus, by the second quarter of the seventeenth century, they and many others accepted the heliocentric theory as a reality and not just as a useful mathematical fiction. The three most important astronomers to build on Copernican assumptions, and on the work of one another, were the Dane Tycho Brahe (1546–1601), the German Johannes Kepler (1571–1630), and the Italian Galileo Galilei (1564–1642).

Like generations of observers before him, Tycho Brahe° had been stirred by the majesty of the regular

Brahe (BRAH)

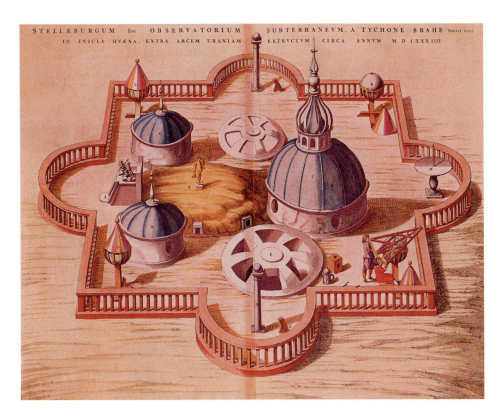

STELLÆBURGUM sive OBSERVATORIUM SUBTERRANEVM, A TYCHONE BRAHE Nobili Dano
IN INSULA HVÆNA, EXTRA ARCEM URANIAM, EXTRVCTVM CIRCA ANNVM M D LXXXIIII.

Tycho Brahe's Observatory
A gifted artist and craftsman as well as an astronomer, Brahe gathered the best talent, including German instrument makers and Italian architects, to build his state-of-the-art observatory near Copenhagen. Brahe named the complex Uraniborg, for Urania, the muse of astronomy.
(The Fotomas Index)

movements of heavenly bodies. After witnessing a partial eclipse of the sun, he abandoned a career in government befitting his noble status and became an astronomer. Brahe was the first truly post-Ptolemaic astronomer because he was the first to improve on the data that the ancients and all subsequent astronomers had used. Ironically, no theory of planetary motion could have reconciled the data that Copernicus had used: they were simply too inaccurate, based as they were on naked-eye observations, even when errors of translation and copying, accumulated over centuries, had been corrected.

In 1576 the king of Denmark showered Brahe with properties and pensions enabling him to build an observatory, Uraniborg, on an island near Copenhagen. At Uraniborg Brahe improved on ancient observations with large and very finely calibrated instruments that permitted precise measurements of celestial movements by the naked eye. His attention to precision and frequency of observation produced results that were twice as accurate as any previous data had been.

As a result of his observations, Brahe agreed with Copernicus that the various planets did rotate around the sun, not around the earth. He still could not be persuaded that the earth itself moved, for none of his data

supported such a notion. Brahe's lasting and crucial contribution was his astronomical data. They would become obsolete as soon as data from telescopic observations were accumulated about a century later. But in the meantime they were used by Johannes Kepler to further develop Copernicus's model and arrive at a more accurate heliocentric theory.

Kepler was young enough to be exposed to Copernican ideas from the outset of his training, and he quickly recognized in Brahe's data the means of resolving the problems in Copernican analysis. Though trained in his native Germany, Kepler went to Prague, where Brahe spent the last years of his life at the court of the Holy Roman emperor after a quarrel with the Danish king. There Kepler became something of an apprentice to Brahe. After Brahe's death in 1601, Kepler kept his mentor's records of astronomical observations and continued to work at the imperial court as Rudolf II's court mathematician.

Kepler's contribution to the new astronomy, like that of Copernicus, was fundamentally mathematical. In it we can see the stamp of the Neo-Platonic conviction about the purity of mathematical explanation. Kepler spent ten years working to apply Brahe's data to the most intricate of all the celestial movements—the motion of the planet Mars—as a key to explaining all planetary motion. Mars is close to the earth, but its orbital path is farther from the sun. This combination produces very puzzling and dramatic variations in the apparent movement of Mars to an earthly observer.

The result of Kepler's work was laws of planetary motion that, in the main, are still in use. First, Kepler eliminated the need for epicycles by correctly asserting that planets follow elliptical and not circular orbits. Elliptical orbits could account, both mathematically and visually, for the motion of the planets when combined with Kepler's second law, which describes the *rate* of a planet's motion around its orbital path. Kepler noted that the speed of a planet in its orbit slows proportionally as the planet's distance from the sun increases. A third law demonstrates that the distance of each planet from the sun and the time it takes each planet to orbit the sun are in a constant ratio.

Kepler's work was a breakthrough because it mathematically confirmed the Copernican heliocentric hypothesis. In so doing, the work directly challenged the ancient world-view, in which heavenly bodies constantly moved in circular orbits around a stationary earth. Hence Kepler's laws invited speculation about the properties and movements of heavenly and terrestrial bodies alike. A new physics would be required to explain the novel motion that Kepler had posited. Kepler himself, in Neo-Platonic fashion, attributed planetary motion to the sun: "[The sun] is a fountain of light, rich in fruitful heat, most fair, limpid and pure . . . called king of the planets for his motion, heart of the world for his power. . . . Who would hesitate to confer the votes of the celestial motions on him who has been administering all other movements and changes by the benefit of the light which is entirely his possession?"[2]

Galileo and the Triumph of Copernicanism

Galileo Galilei° holds a pre-eminent position in the development of astronomy because, first, he provided compelling new evidence to support Copernican theory and, second, he contributed to the development of a new physics—or, more precisely, mechanics—that could account for the movements of bodies in new terms. In short he began to close the gap between the new astronomy and new explanations for the behavior of matter. Just as important, his efforts to publicize his findings and his condemnation by the church spurred popular debate

---

Galileo Galilei (gal-ih-LAY-oh gal-ih-LAY-ee)

Galileo Galilei This portrait of Galileo appeared as the frontispiece in two of his publications. He is identified as "philosopher and mathematician of the grand duke of Tuscany." The cherubs above the portrait hold a military compass and a telescope—two of Galileo's inventions that he gave to his patrons. *(Image Select International)*

about Copernican ideas in literate society and helped to determine the course science would take.

Galileo's career also illustrates, in dramatic fashion, the dependence of scientists on and their vulnerability to patronage relationships. Born to a minor Florentine noble family, Galileo began studying medicine at the nearby University of Pisa at the age of 17 but became intrigued by problems of mechanics and mathematics. He began studying those disciplines at Pisa under the tutelage of a Florentine court mathematician and became a lecturer in mathematics there in 1589, at age 25, after publishing promising work in mechanics. Three years later, well-connected fellow mathematicians helped him secure a more lucrative and prestigious professorship at the University of Padua, where Copernicus had once studied. Galileo skillfully cultivated the learned Venetian aristocrats (Venice ruled Padua at this time) who controlled academic appointments and secured renewals and salary raises over the next eighteen years.

During his years at Pisa and Padua, Galileo pursued his revolutionary work in mechanics, although he did not publish the results of his experiments until much later. Galileo's principal contribution to mechanics lay in his working out of an early theory of inertia. As a result of a number of experiments with falling bodies (balls rolling on carefully constructed inclines—not free-falling objects that, according to myth, he dropped from the Leaning Tower of Pisa), Galileo ventured a new view of what is "natural" to objects. Galileo's view was that uniform motion is as natural as a state of rest. In the ancient and medieval universe, all motion needed a cause, and all motion could be explained in terms of purpose. "I hold," Galileo countered, "that there exists nothing in external bodies . . . but size, shape, quantity and motion."[3] Galileo retained the old assumption that motion was somehow naturally circular. Nevertheless, his theory was a crucial step in explaining motion according to new principles and in fashioning a world-view that accepted a mechanical universe devoid of metaphysical purpose.

The results of this work were, for the most part, not published until the end of his life. In the meantime, Galileo became famous for his astronomical observations, which he began in 1609 and which he parlayed into a position back at the Florentine court. Early that year Galileo learned of the invention of a primitive telescope (which could magnify distant objects only three times) and quickly improved on it to make the first astronomically useful instrument. In *Sidereus Nuncius* (*The Starry Messenger*, 1610) he described his scrutiny of the heavens with his telescope in lay language. He documented sighting previously undetectable stars, as well as moons orbiting the planet Jupiter. In another blow to ancient descriptions of the universe, he noted craters and other "imperfections" on the surface of the moon. Three years later he published his solar observations in *Letters on Sunspots*. Sunspots are regions of relatively cool gaseous material that appear as dark spots on the sun's surface. For Galileo sunspots and craters on the moon proved that the heavens are not perfect and changeless but rather are like the supposedly "corrupt" and changeable earth. His telescopic observations also provided further support for Copernican heliocentrism. Indeed, Galileo's own acceptance of Copernicanism can be dated to this point because magnification revealed that each heavenly body rotates on its axis: sunspots, for example, can be tracked across the visible surface of the sun as the sun rotates.

Galileo had already been approached by various Italian princes and in turn sought to woo their support with gifts of some of his earlier inventions, such as a military compass. He aimed his *Starry Messenger* at the Medici dukes of Florence, naming Jupiter's moons the "Medicean Stars" and publishing the work to coincide with the accession of the young Cosimo II, whom he had tutored as a youth. In 1610 he returned in triumph to his native Tuscany as court philosopher to the grand duke. Soon, however, his own fame and the increasing acceptance of Copernicanism, especially vindicated by his work on sunspots, aroused opposition. In 1615 Galileo was denounced to the Inquisition by a Florentine friar. (See the box "The Continuing Experiment: Galileo Asserts Science and Religion Are Compatible.") After an investigation, the geokinetic theory (that the earth moves) was declared heretical, but Galileo himself was not condemned. He could continue to use Copernican theory, but only as a theory. Indeed, a number of the most fervent practitioners of the new science continued to be clergymen who followed Galileo's work with interest. A new pope, elected in 1623, was a Tuscan aristocrat and an old friend of Galileo. Galileo dedicated his work on comets, *The Assayer* (1624), to Urban VIII in honor of his election.

Now in his 60s, Galileo began to work on a book that summarized his life's work—*Dialogue on the Two Chief Systems of the World* (1632), structured as a conversation among three characters debating the merits of Copernican theory. Given the work's sensitive subject matter, Galileo obtained explicit permission from the pope to write it and cleared some portions with censors before publication. The work was the most important single source in its day for the popularization of Copernican theory, but it led to renewed concerns in Rome. Galileo had clearly overstepped the bounds of discussing Copernicanism in theory only and appeared to advocate it. Simplicio, the character representing the old world-view, was, as his name suggests, an example of ignorance, not wisdom.

Moreover, the larger political context affecting Galileo's patrons and friends had changed. The pope was being threatened by the Spanish and Austrian Habsburgs for his tepid support in the Thirty Years' War, in which Catholic forces were now losing to Protestant armies, and he could no longer be indulgent with his friend. (The pope tended to favor French foreign policy as a counterweight to the enormous power of the Habsburgs.) Galileo was forced to stand trial for heresy in Rome in 1633. When, in a kind of plea-bargain arrangement, he pled guilty to a lesser charge of inadvertently

Galileo Asserts Science and Religion Are Compatible

After Galileo Galilei's work on sunspots was released, many learned followers grew anxious about the implications of the new science. In the letter excerpted here, published in 1615 and widely circulated, Galileo reassures the mother of Cosimo II, the dowager grand duchess of Tuscany, that the new science does not contradict Christianity. The Catholic Church would eventually condemn Galileo for his beliefs, arguing that it was wrong to contradict established knowledge about the heavens. Although the church's actions constrained the development of science in some (predominantly Catholic) regions, throughout Europe investigators continued to find ways to make the new science fully compatible with their faiths.

Some years ago, as Your Serene Highness well knows, I discovered in the heavens many things that had not been seen there before our own age. The novelty of these things, as well as some consequences which followed from them . . . stirred up against me no small number of professors—as if I had placed these things in the sky with my own hands in order to upset nature and overturn the sciences. . . . [These professors] go about invoking the Bible, which they would have minister to their deceitful purposes. Contrary to the sense of the Bible and the intention of the holy Fathers, if I am not mistaken, they would extend such authorities until even in purely physical matters—where faith is not involved—they would have us altogether abandon reason and the evidence of our own senses in favor of some biblical passage, though under the surface meaning of its words this passage may contain a different sense. . . .

I think that in discussions of physical problems we ought to begin not from the authority of scriptural passages, but from sense experience and necessary demonstrations. . . . I should judge that the authority of the Bible was designed to persuade men of those articles and propositions which, surpassing all human reasoning, could not be made credible by science, or by any means other than through the very mouth of the Holy Spirit. . . .

But I do not feel obliged to believe that the same God who has endowed us with senses, reason and intellect has intended to forgo their use and by some other means to give us knowledge which we can attain by them. He would not require us to deny sense and reason in physical matters which are set before our eyes and minds by direct experience or necessary demonstrations. This must be especially true in those sciences of which but the faintest trace . . . is to be found in the Bible. Of astronomy, for instance, so little is found that none of the planets except Venus are so much as mentioned. . . .

Now, if the Holy Spirit has purposely neglected to teach us propositions of this sort as irrelevant to the highest goal (that is, to our salvation), how can anyone affirm that it is obligatory to take sides on them, and that one belief is required by faith, while another side is erroneous? . . . I would assert here something that was heard from [a respected cleric]: . . . "the intention of the Holy Ghost is to teach us how to go to heaven, not how heaven goes." . . . [And] in St. Augustine we read: "If anyone shall set the authority of Holy Writ against clear and manifest reason, . . . he opposes to the truth not the meaning of the Bible, which is beyond his comprehension, but rather his own interpretation. . . ."

Moreover, we are unable to affirm that all interpreters of the Bible speak with divine inspiration, for if that were so there would exist no differences between them about the sense of a given passage. Hence [it would be wise] not to permit anyone to usurp scriptural texts and force them in some way to maintain any physical conclusion to be true, when at some future time the senses . . . may show the contrary. Who indeed will set bounds to human ingenuity? Who will assert that everything in the universe capable of being perceived is already discovered and known?

QUESTIONS

1. How does Galileo justify pursuing scientific investigation against certain claims of faith? What is the tone of his argument? Is he confident about the future progress of science?

2. Do you think that Galileo's arguments would have been reassuring to the grand duchess? Why or why not?

3. Why might the arguments have further angered those church officials already hostile toward Galileo's work?

SOURCE: *Discoveries and Opinions of Galileo*, by Galileo Galilei, translated by Stillman Drake, copyright © 1957 by Stillman Drake. Used by permission of Doubleday, a division of Random House, Inc.

advocating Copernicanism, Pope Urban intervened to insist on a weightier penalty. Galileo's book was banned, he was forced to formally renounce his "error," and he was sentenced to house arrest. Galileo lived confined and guarded, continuing his investigations of mechanics, until his death seven years later.

THE SCIENTIFIC REVOLUTION GENERALIZED, CA. 1600–1700

GALILEO'S work found such a willing audience in part because Galileo, like Kepler and Brahe, was not working alone. Dozens of other scientists were examining old problems from the fresh perspective offered by the breakthroughs in astronomy. Some analyzed the nature of matter, now that it appeared that all matter in the universe was somehow the same despite its varying appearances. Many of these thinkers addressed the metaphysical issues that their investigations inevitably raised. They began the complex intellectual and psychological journey toward a new world-view, one that accepted the existence of an infinitely large universe of undifferentiated matter with no obvious place in it for humans.

The Promise of the New Science

No less a man than Francis Bacon (1561–1626), lord chancellor of England during the reign of James I, wrote a utopian essay extolling the benefits of science for a peaceful society and for human happiness. In *New Atlantis*, published one year after his death, Bacon argued that science would produce "things of use and practice for man's life."[4] In *New Atlantis* and *Novum Organum* (1620) Bacon reveals his faith in science by advocating patient, systematic observation and experimentation to accumulate knowledge about the world. He argues that the proper method of investigation "derives axioms from . . . particulars, rising by gradual and unbroken ascent, so that it arrives at the most general axioms of all. This is the true way but untried."[5]

Bacon himself did not undertake experiments, although his widely read works were influential in encouraging both the empirical method (relying on observation and experimentation) and inductive reasoning (deriving general principles from particular facts). Indeed, Bacon was a visionary. Given the early date of his writings, it might seem difficult to account for his enthusiasm and confidence. In fact, Bacon's writings reflect the widespread

interest and confidence in science within his elite milieu, an interest actively encouraged by the state. In another of his writings he argues that a successful state should concentrate on effective "rule in religion *and nature,* as well as civil administration."[6]

Bacon's pronouncements reflect the fact that an interest in exploring nature's secrets and exercising "dominion over nature" had become an indispensable part of princely rule. Princely courts were the main sources of financial support for science and the primary sites of scientific work during Bacon's lifetime. Part of the impetus for this development had come from the civic humanism of the Italian Renaissance, which had celebrated the state and service to it and had provided models both for educated rulers and for cultivated courtiers. Attention to science and to its benefits for the state also reflect the scope, and pragmatism, of princely resources and ambitions: the desire of rulers for technical expertise in armaments, fortification, construction, navigation, and mapmaking. (See the feature "Weighing the Evidence: Modern Maps" on pages 600–601.)

The promise of the New World and the drive for overseas trade and exploration especially encouraged princely support of scientific investigation. A renowned patron of geographic investigation, from mapmaking to navigation, was Henry, prince of Wales (d. 1612), eldest son of James I. Prince Henry patronized technical experts such as experienced gunners and seamen, as well as those with broader and more theoretical expertise. One geographer at his court worked on the vital problem of calculating longitude, sketched the moon after reading and emulating Galileo's work with the telescope, and, in the spirit of empiricism often associated with Bacon, compiled information about the new territory Virginia, including the first dictionary of any Native American language.

Science was an ideological as well as a practical tool for power. Most courts housed collections of marvels, specimens of exotic plants and animals, and mechanical contrivances. These demonstrated the ruler's interest in investigation of the world—in other words, his or her status as an educated individual. These collections and the work of court experts also enhanced the ruler's reputation as a patron and person of power. Galileo was playing off such expectations when he named his newly discovered moons of Jupiter "Medicean Stars." Like all patronage relationships, the status was shared by both partners; indeed, the attention of a patron was a guarantee of the researcher's scientific credibility.

By the beginning of the seventeenth century, private salons and academies where investigators might meet on their own were another significant milieu of scientific

A Collection of Naturalia   Displays of exotica, such as these specimens in Naples, symbolized the ruler's authority by suggesting his or her power over nature.   *(From Ferrante Imperato,* Dell' Historia Naturale *[Naples, 1599]. By permission of the Houghton Library, Harvard University)*

investigation. These, too, had their roots in the humanist culture of Italy, where circles of scholars without university affiliations had formed. Though also dependent on private resources, these associations were an important alternative to princely patronage, since a ruler's funds might wax and wane according to his or her other commitments. Private organizations could avoid the stark distinctions of rank that were inevitable at courts yet mimicked courts in the blend of scholars and educated courtiers they embraced. This more collegial but still privileged environment also fostered a sense of legitimacy for the science pursued there: legitimacy came from the recognition of fellow members and, in many cases, from publication of work by the society itself.

The earliest academy dedicated to scientific study was the *Accadèmia Segreta* (Secret Academy) founded in Naples in the 1540s. The members pursued experiments together in order, in the words of one member, "to make a true anatomy of the things and operations of nature it-

self."[7] During the remainder of the sixteenth century and on into the seventeenth, such academies sprang up in many cities. The most celebrated was the *Accadèmia dei Lincei°*, founded in Rome by an aristocrat in 1603. Its most famous member, Galileo, joined in 1611. The name "Lincei," from *lynx,* was chosen because of the legendary keen sight of that animal, an appropriate mascot for "searchers of secrets."

Galileo's notoriety and the importance of his discoveries forced all such learned societies to take a stand for or against Copernicanism. Throughout the seventeenth century, specific investigation of natural phenomena would continue in increasingly sophisticated institutional settings. The flowering of scientific thought in the seventeenth century occurred because of the specific innovations in astronomy and the general spread of

---

Accadèmia dei Lincei (ack-uh-DAY-mee-uh day-ee lin-CHAY-ee)

scientific investigation that had been achieved by the end of Bacon's life.

Scientific Thought in France: Descartes and a New Cosmology

Philosophers, mathematicians, and educated elites engaged in lively debate and practical investigation throughout Europe in the first half of the seventeenth century. In France the great questions about cosmic order were being posed, ironically, at a time of political disorder. The years following the religious wars saw the murder of Henry IV, another regency, and further civil war in the 1620s (see pages 516–518). In this environment questions about order in the universe and the possibilities of human knowledge took on particular urgency. It is not surprising that a Frenchman, René Descartes° (1596–1650), created the first fully articulated alternative world-view.

Descartes's thinking was developed and refined in dialogue with a circle of other French thinkers. His work became more influential among philosophers and laypeople than the work of some of his equally talented contemporaries because of its thoroughness and rigor, grounded in Descartes's mathematical expertise, and because of its graceful, readable French. His system was fully presented in his *Discours de la méthode* (*Discourse on Method*, 1637). Descartes described some of his intellectual crises in his later work, *Meditations* (1641).

Descartes accepted Galileo's conclusion that the heavens and the earth are made of the same elements. In his theorizing about the composition of matter he drew on ancient atomic models that previously had not been generally accepted. His theory that all matter is made up of identical bits, which he named "corpuscles," is a forerunner of modern atomic and quantum theories. Descartes believed that all the different appearances and behaviors of matter (for example, why stone is always hard and water is always wet) could be explained solely by the size, shape, and motion of these "corpuscles." Descartes's was an extremely mechanistic explanation of the universe. It nevertheless permitted new, more specific observations and hypotheses and greater understanding of inertia. For example, because he re-imagined the universe as being filled with "corpuscles" free to move in any direction, "natural" motion no longer seemed either circular (Galileo's idea) or toward the center of the earth (Aristotle's idea). The new understanding of motion would be crucial to Isaac Newton's formulations later in the century.

In his various works Descartes depicts and then firmly resolves the crisis of confidence that the new discoveries about the universe had produced. The collapse of the old explanations about the world made Descartes and other investigators doubt not only what they knew but also their capacity to know anything at all. Their physical senses—which denied that the earth moved, for example—had been proved untrustworthy. Descartes's solution was to re-envision the human rational capacity, the mind, as completely distinct from the world—that is, as distinct from the human body—and the unreliable perceptions it offers the senses. In a leap of faith Descartes presumed that he could count on the fact that God would not have given humans a mind if that mind consistently misled them. For Descartes, God became the guarantor of human reasoning capacity, and humans were distinguished by that capacity. This is the significance of his famous claim "I think, therefore I am." (See the box "Reading Sources: Descartes: 'I think, therefore I am.'")

Descartes thus achieved a resolution of the terrifying doubt about the world—a resolution that exalted the role of the human knower. The Cartesian universe was one of mechanical motion, not purpose or mystical meaning, and the Cartesian human being was pre-eminently a mind that could apprehend that universe. In what came to be known as "Cartesian dualism," Descartes proposed that the human mind is detached from the world and yet at the same time can objectively analyze the world.

Descartes's ambitious view of human reason emphasizes deductive reasoning (a process of reasoning in which the conclusion follows necessarily from the stated premises), a natural consequence of his philosophical rejection of sense data. The limits of deductive reasoning for scientific investigation would be realized and much of Cartesian physics supplanted by the end of the century. Nevertheless, Descartes's assumption about the objectivity of the observer would become an enduring part of scientific practice. In Descartes's day the most radical aspect of his thought was the reduction of God to the role of guarantor of knowledge. Many fellow scientists and interested laypeople were fearful of Descartes's system because it seemed to encourage "atheism." In fact, a profound faith in God was necessary for Descartes's creativity in imagining his new world system—but the system did work without God.

Although Descartes would have been surprised and offended by charges of atheism, he knew that his work would antagonize the church. He moved to the Netherlands to study in 1628, and his *Discourse* was first published there. He had lived in the Netherlands and in

---

Descartes (day-KART)

READING SOURCES

DESCARTES: "I THINK, THEREFORE I AM"

In the passages leading up to this one in his Discourse on Method, *René Descartes has made it clear that he does not advocate, or anticipate, any social or political upheaval as a consequence of his search for truth. On the contrary, he acknowledges his duty to abide by the tenets of religion and the laws of his country. The only status quo he wants to challenge is the habits of his own mind, in order to build a sure foundation for reasoning. Notice that he assumes his senses may deceive him and therefore sure knowledge cannot be based on sensory data.*

For a long time I had remarked that it is sometimes requisite in common life to follow opinions which one knows to be most uncertain, as [I have stated] above. But because in this case I wished to give myself entirely to the search for Truth, I thought that it was necessary for me to take an apparently opposite course, and to reject as absolutely false everything as to which I could imagine the least ground of doubt, in order to see afterwards if there remained anything in my belief that was entirely certain. Thus, because our senses sometimes deceive us, I wished to suppose that nothing is just as they cause us to imagine . . . and judging that I was as subject to error as was any other [man], I rejected as false all the reason formerly accepted by me as demonstrations. . . . I resolved to assume that everything that ever entered into my mind was no more true than the illusions of my dreams. But immediately afterwards I noticed that whilst I thus wished to think all things false, it was absolutely essential that the "I" who thought this should be somewhat, and remarking that this truth, "I think, therefore I am" was so certain and so assured that all the most extravagant suppositions brought forward by the skeptics were incapable of shaking it, I came to the conclusion that I could receive it without scruple as the first principle of the Philosophy for which I was seeking.

Source: René Descartes, *Discourse on the Method of Rightly Conducting the Reason,* trans. Elizabeth S. Haldane and G. R. T. Ross, in *Great Books of the Western World,* vol. 28, ed. Mortimer Adler (Chicago: Encyclopaedia Britannica, 1990), p. 275.

Germany earlier in his life; fearful of the tense atmosphere during the renewed war against French Protestants, he now left France virtually for good. Unlike Galileo, Descartes enjoyed personal wealth that enabled him to travel widely, work in solitude, and sample the intellectual environment of courts and universities without depending on powerful patrons. Long residence in the Netherlands led him to advocate religious toleration late in his life. In 1649, at the urging of an influential friend with contacts at the Swedish court, Descartes accepted the invitation of Queen Christina to visit there. Christina was an eager but demanding patron, who required Descartes to lecture on scientific topics at 5:00 a.m. each day. The long hours of work and harsh winter weather took their toll on his health, and Descartes died of pneumonia after only a few months in Sweden.

A contemporary of Descartes, fellow Frenchman Blaise Pascal° (1623–1662), drew attention in his writings and in his life to the limits of scientific knowledge. The son of a royal official, Pascal was perhaps the most brilliant mind of his generation. A mathematician like Descartes, he stressed the importance of mathematical representations of phenomena, built one of the first calculating machines, and invented probability theory. He also carried out experiments to investigate air pressure, the behavior of liquids, and the existence of vacuums.

Pascal's career alternated between periods of intense scientific work and religious retreat. Today he is well known for his writings justifying the austere Catholicism known as Jansenism (see page 543) and explored the human soul and psyche. His *Pensées* (*Thoughts,* 1657) consists of the published fragments of his defense of Christian faith, which remained unfinished at the time of his death. Pascal's appeal for generations after him may lie in his attention to matters of faith and of feeling. His most famous statement, "The heart has its reasons which reason knows not," can be read as a declaration of the limits of the Cartesian world-view.

Pascal (pahss-KAHL)

Science and Revolution in England

The new science had adherents and practitioners throughout Europe by 1650. Dutch scientists in the commercial milieu of the Netherlands, for example, had the freedom to pursue practical and experimental interests. The Dutch investigator Christiaan Huygens° (1629–1695) worked on a great variety of problems, including air pressure and optics. In 1657 he invented and patented the pendulum clock, the first device to measure accurately small units of time, essential for a variety of measurements.

England proved a unique environment for the development of science in the middle of the century. In a society torn by civil war, differing positions on science became part and parcel of disputes over Puritanism, church hierarchy, and royal power. Scientific investigation and speculation were spurred by the urgency of religious and political agendas. Scientific, along with political and religious, debate was generally encouraged by the collapse of censorship beginning in the 1640s.

During the 1640s natural philosophers with Puritan leanings were encouraged in their investigations by dreams that science, of the practical Baconian sort, could be the means by which the perfection of life on earth could be brought about and the end of history—the reign of the saints preceding the return of Christ—could be accelerated. Their concerns ranged from improved production of gunpowder (for the armies fighting against Charles I) to surveying and mapmaking. Perhaps the best-known member of this group was Robert Boyle (1627–1691). In his career we can trace the evolution of English science through the second half of the seventeenth century.

Boyle and his colleagues were theoretically eclectic, drawing on Cartesian mechanics and even Paracelsian chemical theories. They attacked the English university system, still under the sway of Aristotelianism, and proposed widespread reform of education. They were forced to moderate many of their positions, however, as the English civil wars proceeded. Radical groups such as the Levellers used Hermeticism and the related Paracelsianism as part of their political and religious tenets. The Levellers and other radical groups drew on the Hermetic notion that matter is imbued with divine spirit; they believed that each person was capable of divine knowledge and a godly life without the coercive hierarchy of church and state officials.

Boyle and his colleagues responded to these challenges. They gained institutional power, accepting positions at Oxford and Cambridge. They formed the core of the Royal Society of London, which they persuaded Charles II to recognize and charter on his accession to the throne in the Restoration of 1660. They worked to articulate a theoretical position that combined the orderliness of mechanism, a continued divine presence in the world, and a Baconian emphasis on scientific progress. This unwieldy set of notions was attractive to the educated elite of their day, who embraced the certainties of science but also clung to certain authoritarian aspects of the old Christian world-view.

Their most creative contribution, both to their own cause and to the advancement of science, was their emphasis on and refinement of experimental philosophy and practice. In 1660 Boyle published *New Experiments Physico-Mechanical*. The work describes the results of his experiments with an air pump he had designed, and it lays out general rules for experimental procedure. Descartes had accounted for motion by postulating that "corpuscles" of matter interact, thereby eliminating the possibility of a vacuum in nature. Recent experiments on air pressure suggested otherwise, however, and Boyle tried to confirm their findings with his air pump.

Boyle's efforts to demonstrate that a vacuum could exist—by evacuating a sealed chamber with his pump—were not successes by modern standards because they could not readily be replicated. Boyle tied the validity of experimental results to the agreement of witnesses to the experiment—a problematic solution, for only investigators sympathetic to his hypothesis and convinced of his credibility usually witnessed the results. In response to a Cambridge scholar who criticized his interpretation of one of his experiments, Boyle replied that he could not understand his critic's objections, "the experiment having been tried both before our whole society [the Royal Society of London], and very critically, by its royal founder, his majesty himself."[8] Rather than debate differing interpretations, Boyle appealed to the authority and prestige of the participants. In English science of the mid-seventeenth century, therefore, we have a further example of the fact that new truths, new procedures for determining truth, and new criteria for practitioners were all being established simultaneously.

The Newtonian Synthesis: The Copernican Revolution Completed

The Copernican revolution reached its high point with the work of the Englishman Isaac Newton (1643–1727), born one year almost to the day after Galileo died. Newton completed the new explanation for motion in the

---

Huygens (HI-ghenz)

Isaac Newton   Pictured here about fifteen years after the publication of *Principia,* Newton was also one of the developers of calculus. The cumbersome mathematics he still relied on, however, has led one scholar to ponder: "What manner of man he was who could use as a weapon what we can scarcely lift as a burden."[9]   *(By courtesy of the National Portrait Gallery, London)*

heavens and on earth that Copernicus's work had initiated and that Kepler, Galileo, and others had sought.

After a difficult childhood and an indifferent education, Newton entered Cambridge University as a student in 1661. Copernicanism and Cartesianism were being hotly debated, though not yet officially studied. Newton made use of Descartes's work in mathematics to develop his skill on his own, and by 1669 he had invented calculus. (He did not publish his work at the time, and another mathematician, Gottfried von Leibniz°, later independently developed calculus and vied with Newton for credit.)

Newton was elected to a fellowship at Cambridge in 1667 and was made a professor of mathematics in 1669 at the recommendation of a retiring professor with whom he had shared his work on calculus. With less demanding teaching assignments, he was able to devote

much of the next decade to work on optics—an important area of study for testing Descartes's corpuscular theory of matter.

In the 1680s Newton experienced a period of self-imposed isolation from other scientists after a particularly heated exchange with one colleague, provoked by Newton's difficult temperament. During this decade he returned to the study of alternative theories about matter. As a student at Cambridge he had been strongly influenced by the work of a group of Neo-Platonists who were critical of Cartesian dualism. This controversial theory posited God as a cause of all matter and motion but removed God, or any other unknown or unknowable force, as an explanation for the behavior of matter. The Neo-Platonists' concerns were both religious and scientific. As Newton says in some of his early writing while a student, "However we cast about we find almost no other reason for atheism than this [Cartesian] notion of bodies having . . . a complete, absolute and independent reality."[10]

Newton now read treatises in alchemy and Hermetic tracts and began to imagine explanations for the behavior of matter (such as for bits of cloth fluttered from a distance by static electricity) that Cartesian corpuscular theory could not readily explain. Precisely what the forces were that caused such behavior he was not sure, but his eclectic mind and his religious convictions enabled him to accept their existence.

It was this leap that allowed him to propose the existence of gravity—a mysterious force that accounts for the movements of heavenly bodies in the vacuum of space. Others had speculated about the existence of gravity; indeed, the concept of inertia as so far elaborated by Galileo, Descartes, and others suggested the need for the concept of gravity. Otherwise, if a planet were "pushed" (say, in Kepler's view, by the "motive force" of the sun), it would continue along that course forever unless "pulled back" by something else.

Newton's extraordinary contribution to a new mechanistic understanding of the universe was the mathematical computation of the laws of gravity and planetary motion, which he combined with a fully developed concept of inertia. In 1687 Newton published *Philosophia Naturalis Principia Mathematica* (*Mathematical Principles of Natural Philosophy;* usually called *Principia*). In this mathematical treatise—so intricate that it was baffling to laypeople, even those able to read Latin—Newton laid out his laws of motion and expressed them as mathematical theorems that can be used to test future observations of moving bodies. Then he demonstrated that these laws also apply to the solar system, confirming the data already gathered about the planets and even predicting the

---

Leibniz (LIBE-nits)

existence of an as yet unseen planet. His supreme achievement was his law of gravitation, with which he could predict the discovery of the invisible planet. This law states that every body, indeed every bit of matter, in the universe exerts over every other body an attractive force proportional to the product of their masses and inversely proportional to the square of the distance between them. Newton not only accounted for motion but definitively united heaven and earth in a single scheme and created a convincing picture of an orderly nature.

Neither Newton nor anyone else claimed that his theorems resolved all questions about motion and matter. Exactly what gravity is and how it operates were not clear, as they still are not. Newton's laws of motion are taught today because they still adequately account for most problems of motion. The fact that so fundamental a principle as gravity remains unexplained in no way diminishes Newton's achievement but is clear evidence of the nature of scientific understanding: science provides explanatory schemas that account for many—but not all—observed phenomena. No schema explains everything, and each schema contains open doorways that lead both to further discoveries and to blind alleys. Newton, for example, assumed that the forces that accounted for gravity would mysteriously work on metals so that, as alchemists predicted, they might "quickly pass into gold."[11]

After the publication of *Principia* Newton was more of a celebrated public figure than a practicing scientist. He helped lead resistance to James II's Catholicizing policies in the university, and he became the familiar of many other leading minds of his day, such as John Locke (see page 596). Newton became the president of the Royal Academy of Sciences in 1703 and was knighted in 1705, the first scientist to be so distinguished. By the end of his life universities in England were dominated by men who acclaimed and built on his work. The transformation of the institutional structure of science in England was complete.

Other Branches of Science

The innovations in astronomy that led to the new mechanistic view of the behavior of matter did not automatically spill over to other branches of science. In astronomy innovation came after the ancient and medieval inheritance had been fully assimilated and its errors disclosed. Other branches of science followed their own paths, though all were strongly influenced by the mechanistic world-view.

In chemistry the mechanistic assumption that all matter was composed of small, equivalent parts was crucial to understanding the properties and behaviors of compounds (combinations of elements). But knowledge of these small units of matter was not yet detailed enough to be of much use in advancing chemistry conceptually. Nevertheless, the flawed conceptual schema did not hold back all chemical discovery and development. Lack of understanding of gases, and of the specific elements in their makeup, for example, did not prevent the development and improvement of gunpowder. Indeed, unlike the innovations in astronomy, eventual conceptual innovation in chemistry and biology owed a great deal to the results of plodding experiment and the slow accumulation of data.

A conceptual leap forward was made in biology in the sixteenth and seventeenth centuries. Because biological knowledge was mostly a byproduct of the practice of medicine, biological studies remained very practical and experimental. The recent discovery of *On Anatomical Procedures,* a treatise by the ancient physician Galen, encouraged dissection and other practical research. Andreas Vesalius° (1514–1564), in particular, made important advances by following Galen's exhortation to anatomical research. Born in Brussels, Vesalius studied at the nearby University of Louvain and then at Padua, where he was appointed professor of surgery. He ended his career as physician to Emperor Charles V and his son, Philip II of Spain. In his teaching at Padua Vesalius acted on the newly recovered Galenic teachings by doing dissections himself rather than giving the work to technicians. In 1543 he published versions of his lectures as an illustrated compendium of anatomy, *De Humani Corporis Fabrica (On the Fabric of the Human Body).*

The results of his dissections of human corpses, revealed in this work, demonstrated a number of errors in Galen's knowledge of human anatomy, much of which had been derived from dissection of animals. Neither Vesalius nor his immediate successors, however, questioned overall Galenic theory about the functioning of the human body, any more than Copernicus had utterly rejected Aristotelian physics.

The slow movement from new observation to changed explanation is clearly illustrated in the career of the Englishman William Harvey (1578–1657). Much like Vesalius, Harvey was educated first in his own land and then at Padua, where he benefited from the tradition of anatomical research. He also had a career as a practicing physician in London and at the courts of James I and Charles I.

Harvey postulated the circulation of the blood—postulated rather than discovered, because owing to the

Vesalius (vuh-SAY-lee-us)

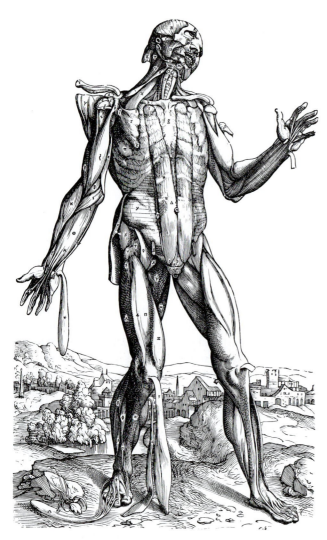

Vesalius on Human Anatomy The meticulous illustrations in Vesalius's work helped ensure its success. The medium of print was essential for accurate reproduction of scientific drawings. *(Courtesy, Dover Publications)*

technology of the day, he could not observe the tiny capillaries where the movement of arterial blood into the veins occurs. After conducting vivisectional experiments on animals that revealed the actual functioning of the heart and lungs, he reasoned that circulation must occur. He carefully described his experiments and his conclusions in *Exercitatio Anatomica de Motu Cordis et Sanguinis in Animalibus* (1628), usually shortened to *De Motu Cordis* (*On the Motion of the Heart*).

Harvey's work challenged Galenic anatomy and, like Copernicus's discoveries, created new burdens of expla-

nation. According to Galenic theory, the heart and lungs helped each other to function. The heart sent nourishment to the lungs through the pulmonary artery, and the lungs provided raw material for the "vital spirit," which the heart gave to the blood to sustain life. The lungs also helped the heart sustain its "heat." This heat was understood to be an innate property of organs, just as "heaviness," in traditional physics, had been considered an innate property of earthbound objects.

From his observations Harvey came to think of the heart in terms consonant with the new mechanistic notions about nature: as a pump to circulate the blood. But he adjusted, rather than abandoned, Galenic theories concerning "heat" and "vital spirit." The lungs had been thought to "ventilate" the heart by providing air to maintain "heat," just as a bellows aerates a fire. In light of his discovery of the pulmonary transit (that all of the blood is pumped through the lungs and back through the heart), Harvey suggested instead that the lungs carried out some of these functions for the blood, helping it to concoct the "vital spirit." Only in this sense did he think of the heart as a machine, circulating this life-giving material throughout the body.

Harvey's explanation of bodily functions in light of his new knowledge did not constitute a rupture with Galenic tradition. But by the end of his life Harvey's own adjustments of Galenic theory were suggesting new conceptual possibilities. His work inspired additional research in physiology, chemistry, and physics. Robert Boyle's efforts to understand vacuums can be traced in part to questions Harvey raised about the function of the lungs and the properties of air.

THE NEW SCIENCE: SOCIETY, POLITICS, AND RELIGION

SCIENTISTS wrestled with questions about God and human capacity every bit as intently as they attempted to find new explanations for the behavior of matter and the motion of the heavens. Eventually the profound implications of the new scientific world-view would affect thought and behavior throughout society. Once people no longer thought of the universe in hierarchical terms, they could question the hierarchical organization of society. Once people questioned the authority of traditional knowledge about the universe, the way was clear for them to begin to question traditional views of the state, the social order, and even the divine order. Such profound changes of perspective took hold very gradually, however. The advances in science did lead to revolutionary cultural change, but until the end of the seventeenth century traditional institutions and ideologies limited its extent.

The Beginnings of Scientific Professionalism

Institutions both old and new supported the new science developing in the sixteenth and seventeenth centuries. Some universities were the setting for scientific breakthroughs, but court patronage, a well-established institution, also sponsored scientific activity. The development of the Accadèmia dei Lincei, to which Galileo belonged, and other academies was a step toward modern professional societies of scholars, although these new organizations depended on patronage.

In England and France, royally sponsored scientific societies were founded in the third quarter of the century. The Royal Society of London, inaugurated in 1660, received royal recognition but no money and remained an informal institution sponsoring amateur scientific interests as well as specialized independent research. The Académie Royale des Sciences in France, established in 1666 by Jean-Baptiste Colbert, Louis XIV's minister of finance (see page 542), sponsored research and supported chosen scientists with pensions. These associations were extensions to science of traditional kinds of royal recognition and patronage. Thus the French Académie was well funded but tightly controlled by the government of Louis XIV, and the Royal Society of London received little of Charles II's scarce resources or precious political capital. Like the earlier academies, these royally sponsored societies published their fellows' work; in England the *Philosophical Transactions of the Royal Society* began in 1665.

The practice of seventeenth-century science took place in so many diverse institutions—academies, universities, royal courts—that neither *science* nor *scientist* was rigorously defined. Science as a discipline was not yet detached from broad metaphysical questions. Boyle, Newton, Pascal, and Descartes all concerned themselves with questions of religion, and all thought of themselves not as scientists but, like their medieval forebears, as natural philosophers. These natural philosophers were still members of an elite who met in aristocratic salons to discuss literature, politics, or science with equal ease and interest. Nevertheless, the beginnings of a narrowing of the practice of science to a tightly defined, truly professional community are evident in these institutions.

The importance of court life and patronage to the new science had at first enabled women to be actively

Astronomers Elisabetha and Johannes Hevelius   The Heveliuses were one of many collaborating couples among the scientists of the seventeenth century. Women were usually denied pensions and support for their research when they worked alone, however.   *(From Hevelius, Machinae coelestis. By permission of the Houghton Library, Harvard University)*

involved. Women ran important salons in France; aristocratic women everywhere were indispensable sources of patronage for scientists; and women themselves were scientists, combining, as did men, science with other pursuits. Noblewomen and daughters of gentry families had access to education in their homes, and a number of such women were active scientists—astronomers, mathematicians, and botanists. The astronomer Maria Cunitz° (1610–1664), from Silesia (a Habsburg-controlled province, now in modern Poland), learned six languages

Cunitz (KOO-nits)

READING SOURCES

MARGARET CAVENDISH CHALLENGES MALE SCIENTISTS

In her preface to her earliest scientific work, The Philosophical and Physical Opinions *(1655), Margaret Cavendish addresses scholars at Oxford and Cambridge Universities with deceptive humility. She implies that the seeming limitations of women's abilities are in fact the consequence of their exclusion from education and from participation in worldly affairs.*

Most Famously Learned,

I here present to you this philosophical work, not that I can hope wise school-men and industrious laborious students should value it for any worth, but to receive it without scorn, for the good encouragement of our sex, lest in time we should grow irrational as idiots, by the dejectedness of our spirits, through the careless neglects and despisements of the masculine sex to the female, thinking it impossible we should have either learning or understanding, wit or judgment, as if we had not rational souls as well as men, and we out of a custom of dejectedness think so too, which makes us quit all industry towards profitable knowledge, being imployed only in low and petty imployments which take away not only our abilities towards arts but higher capacities in speculations, so that we are become like worms, that only live in the dull earth of ignorance, winding ourselves sometimes out by the help of some refreshing rain of good education, which seldome is given us, for we are kept like birds in cages, to hop up and down in our houses . . . ; thus by an opinion, which I hope is but an erroneous one in men, we are shut out of all power and authority by reason we are never imployed either in civil or martial affairs, our counsels are despised and laughed at and the best of our actions are trodden down with scorn, by the overweening conceit men have of themselves and through a despisement of us.

Source: Moira Ferguson, ed., *First Feminists: British Women Writers, 1578–1799* (Bloomington and New York: Indiana University Press and The Feminist Press, 1985), pp. 85–86.

---

with the encouragement of her father, who was a medical doctor. Later she published a useful simplification of some of Kepler's mathematical calculations. Women from artisanal families might also receive useful training at home. Such was the case of the German entomologist Maria Sibylla Merian (1647–1717). Merian learned the techniques of illustration in the workshop of her father, an artist in Frankfurt. She later used her artistic training and her refined powers of observation to study and record the features and behaviors of insects and plants in the New World.

Margaret Cavendish, duchess of Newcastle (1623–1673), wrote several major philosophical works, including *Grounds of Natural Philosophy* (1668). She was a Cartesian but was influenced by Neo-Platonism. She believed matter to have "intelligence" and thus disagreed with Cartesian dualism, but she criticized fellow English philosophers on the grounds that, like Descartes, she distrusted sensory knowledge as a guide to philosophy.

Women were routinely accepted as members of Italian academies, but they were excluded from formal membership in the academies in London and Paris, although they could use the academies' facilities and received prizes from the societies for their work. One reason that women were barred was the purse: the amount of available patronage was limited, and coveted positions automatically went to men. Moreover, the hierarchical distinction signified by gender made the exclusion of women a useful way to define the academies as special and privileged.

Margaret Cavendish was aware of the degree to which her participation in scientific life depended on informal networks and on the resources available to her because of her aristocratic status. (See the box "Reading Sources: Margaret Cavendish Challenges Male Scientists.") Women scientists from more modest backgrounds, without Cavendish's resources, had to fight for the right to employment as public institutions gained importance as settings for the pursuit of science. The German astronomer Maria Winkelman° (1670–1720), for example,

---

Winkelman (VINK-el-mahn)

tried to succeed her late husband in an official position in the Berlin Academy of Sciences in 1710, after working as his unofficial partner during his tenure as astronomer to the academy. The academy withheld an official position from Winkelman after her husband's death, however, despite her experience and accomplishments (she had discovered a new comet, for example, in 1702). The secretary of the academy stated: "That she be kept on in an official capacity to work on the calendar or to continue with observations simply will not do. Already during her husband's lifetime the society was burdened with ridicule because its calendar was prepared by a woman. If she were now to be kept on in such a capacity, mouths would gape even wider."[12]

Winkelman worked in private observatories but was able to return to the Berlin Academy only as the unofficial assistant to her own son, whose training she herself had supervised. As the new science gained in prestige, women scientists often found themselves marginalized.

The New Science, the State, and the Church

The new natural philosophy had implications for traditional notions about the state. The new world-view that all matter was identical and answerable to discernible natural laws gradually undermined political systems resting on a belief in the inherent inequality of persons and on royal prerogative. By the middle of the eighteenth century a fully formed alternative political philosophy would argue for more "rational" government in keeping with the rational, natural order of things. But the change came slowly, and while it was coming, traditional rulers found much to admire and utilize in the new science.

Technological possibilities of the new science were very attractive to governments. Experiments with vacuum pumps had important applications in the mining industry, for example. Governments also sponsored pure, and not only applied, scientific research. A French naval expedition to Cayenne, in French Guiana, led to refinements of the pendulum clock but had as its main purpose progressive observations of the sun to permit the calculation of the earth's distance from the sun. Members of the elite saw the opportunity not only for practical advances but also for prestige and, most important, confirmation of the orderliness of nature. It is hard to overestimate the psychological impact and intellectual power of this fundamental tenet of the new science—namely, that nature is an inanimate machine that reflects God's design not through its purposes but simply by its orderliness. Thus, in the short run, the new science

supported a vision of order that was very pleasing even to a monarch of absolutist pretensions such as Louis XIV.

As we have seen, scientists themselves flourished in close relationships with princes and actively sought their patronage for its many benefits. Christiaan Huygens left the Netherlands to accept the patronage of Louis XIV, producing in France some of his most important work in optics and mechanics. Huygens had learned from his father, secretary to the princes of Orange in the Netherlands, that a princely court not only offered steady support but also opened doors to other royal academies and salons. Huygens published some of his early research through the Royal Society in London, thanks to contacts his father had established. When Galileo left his position at Padua for the Medici court in Florence, he wrote to a friend, "It is not possible to receive a salary from a Republic [Venice] . . . without serving the public, because to get something from the public one must satisfy it and not just one particular person; . . . no one can exempt me from the burden while leaving me the income; and in sum I cannot hope for such a benefit from anyone but an absolute prince."[13]

Scientists and scientific thought also remained closely tied to religion in both practical and institutional ways during the seventeenth century. Both religion and the Catholic Church as an institution were involved with scientific advancement from the time of Copernicus. Copernicus himself was a cleric, as were many philosophers and scientists after him. This is not surprising, for most research in the sciences to this point had occurred within universities sponsored and staffed by members of religious orders, who had the education, time, and resources necessary for scientific investigation. Some of Descartes's closest collaborators were clerics, as were certain of Galileo's aristocratic patrons and his own proteges. Moreover, religious and metaphysical concerns were central to the work of virtually every scientist. The entire Cartesian edifice of reasoning about the world, for example, was grounded in Descartes's certainty about God. Copernicus, Kepler, Newton, and others perceived God's purpose in the mathematical regularity of nature.

The notion that religion was the opponent of science in this era is a result of Galileo's trial, and represents a distortion even of that event. It is true that the new astronomy and mechanics challenged traditional interpretations of Scripture, as well as the fundamentals of physics and metaphysics that were taught in universities. Thus, in its sponsorship of universities, the church was literally invested in the old view, even though individual clerics investigated and taught Copernican ideas.

Science and Royal Power   This painting memorializes the founding of the French Académie des Sciences and the building of the royal observatory in Paris. Louis himself is at the center of the painting, reflecting the symbolic importance of royal power in the sponsorship of science. *(Château de Versailles/Laurie Platt Winfrey, Inc.)*

The rigid response of the church hierarchy to Galileo is partially explained by the aftermath of the Protestant Reformation, which, in the minds of many churchmen— including Galileo's accusers and some of his judges— had demonstrated the need for a firm response to any challenge to the church's authority. Galileo seemed particularly threatening because he was well known, wrote for a wide audience, and, like the Protestants, presumed to interpret the Scriptures. Galileo may well have escaped punishment entirely had it not been for the political predicament faced by the pope coincident with his trial, however.

The condemnation of Galileo shocked many clerics, including the three who had voted for leniency at his trial. Clerics who were also scientists continued to study and teach the new science where and when they could. Copernicanism was taught by Catholic missionaries abroad. (See the box "Global Encounters: Jesuits and Astronomy in China.") To be sure, Galileo's trial did have a chilling effect on scientific investigation in most Catholic regions of Europe. Investigators could and did continue their research, but many could publish results only by smuggling manuscripts to Protestant lands. Many of the most important empirical and theoretical innovations in science occurred in Protestant regions after the middle of the seventeenth century.

Protestant leaders, however, were also not initially receptive to Copernican ideas because they defied scrip-

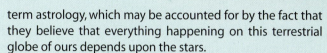

Jesuits and Astronomy in China

The Italian Matteo Ricci (1552–1610) was one of the first Jesuit missionaries to establish himself at the imperial court in China. Ricci's willingness to learn the Chinese language and his own scientific knowledge was crucial to his acceptance at the Chinese court. Jesuit missionaries who followed Ricci in the seventeenth century found their scientific expertise equally valued, and several openly taught Copernican theory in the East. Chinese interest in European knowledge was itself new. In previous centuries Europeans had eagerly borrowed from China, including knowledge of papermaking and printing.

The Chinese have not only made considerable progress in moral philosophy but in astronomy and in many branches of mathematics as well. At one time they were quite proficient in arithmetic and geometry, but in the study and teaching of these branches of learning they labored with more or less confusion. They divide the heavens into constellations in a manner somewhat different from that which we employ. Their count of the stars outnumbers the calculations of our astronomers by fully four hundred, because they include in it many of the fainter stars which are not always visible. And yet with all this, the Chinese astronomers take no pains whatever to reduce the phenomena of celestial bodies to the discipline of mathematics. Much of their time is spent in determining the moment of eclipses and the mass of the planets and the stars, but here, too, their deductions are spoiled by innumerable errors. Finally they center their whole attention on that phase of astronomy which our scientists term astrology, which may be accounted for by the fact that they believe that everything happening on this terrestrial globe of ours depends upon the stars.

Some knowledge of the science of mathematics was given to the Chinese by the Saracens [Mongols], who penetrated into their country from the West, but very little of this knowledge was based upon definite mathematical proofs. What the Saracens left them, for the most part, consisted of certain tables of rules by which the Chinese regulated their calendar and to which they reduced their calculations of planets and the movements of the heavenly bodies in general. The founder of the family which at present regulates the study of astrology prohibited anyone from indulging in the study of this science unless he were chosen for it by hereditary right. The prohibition was founded upon fear, lest he who should acquire a knowledge of the stars might become capable of disrupting the order of the empire and seek an opportunity to do so.

QUESTIONS

1. In what ways is Ricci both appreciative and critical of Chinese science?

2. What do Ricci's comments about Chinese science reveal about his own assumptions concerning astronomy and mathematics and how to study them appropriately?

Source: Louis J. Gallagher, trans., *China in the Sixteenth Century: The Journals of Matthew Ricci: 1583–1610* (New York: Random House, 1953), pp. 30–31. Copyright 1942, 1953 and renewed 1970 by Louis J. Gallagher, S.J. Used by permission of Random House, Inc.

tural authority as well as common sense. In 1549 one of Martin Luther's associates wrote: "The eyes are witnesses that the heavens revolve in the space of twenty-four hours. But certain men, either from love of novelty or to make a display of ingenuity, have concluded that the earth moves. . . . Now it is want of honesty and decency to assert such notions publicly and the example is pernicious. It is part of a good mind to accept the truth as revealed by God and to acquiesce in it."[14]

Protestant thinkers were also as troubled as Catholics by the metaphysical dilemmas that the new theories seemed to raise. In 1611, one year after Galileo's *Starry Messenger* appeared, the English poet John Donne (1573–1631) reflected on the confusion that now reigned in human affairs, with the heavenly hierarchy dismantled:

> [The] new Philosophy calls all in doubt,
> The Element of fire is quite put out;
> The Sun is lost, and th'earth, and no man's wit
> Can well direct him where to look for it.
> . . . .
> Tis all in pieces, all coherence gone;
> All just supply, and all Relation:
> Prince, Subject, Father, Son, are things forgot,
> For every man alone thinks he hath got
> To be a Phoenix, and that then can be
> None of that kinde, of which he is, but he.[15]

The challenge of accounting in religious terms for the ideas of Copernicus and Descartes became more urgent for Protestants as the ideas acquired an anti-Catholic status after the trial of Galileo in 1633 and as they became common scientific currency by about 1640. A religious certainty about divine force that could account for the motion of bodies in a vacuum enabled Newton to develop his theories on motion and gravity. In short, religion did not merely remain in the scientists' panoply of explanations; it remained a fundamental building block of scientific thought and central to most scientists' lives, whether they were Catholic or Protestant.

The New Science and Human Affairs at the End of the Seventeenth Century

Traditional institutions and ideologies checked the potential effects of the new science for a time, but by the middle of the seventeenth century political theory was beginning to reflect the impact of the mechanistic world-view. Political philosophers began to doubt that either the world or human society was an organic whole in which each part was distinguished in nature and function from the rest. Thomas Hobbes, John Locke, and others recast the bonds that link citizens to one another and to their rulers.

Because of the political turmoil in England, Thomas Hobbes (1588–1679) spent much of his productive life on the Continent. After the beginnings of the parliamentary rebellion he joined a group of royalist émigrés in France. He met Galileo and lived for extended periods in Paris, in contact with the circle of French thinkers that included Descartes. Like Descartes, he theorized about the nature and behavior of matter and published a treatise on his views in 1655.

Hobbes is best known today for *Leviathan*° (1651), his treatise on political philosophy. *Leviathan* applies to the world of human beings Hobbes's mostly Cartesian view of nature as composed of "self-motivated," atom-like structures. Hobbes viewed people as mechanistically as he viewed the rest of nature. In his view, people are made up of appetites of various sorts—the same kind of innate forces that drive all matter. The ideal state, he concluded, is one in which a strong sovereign controls the disorder that inevitably arises from the clash of desires. Unlike medieval philosophers, Hobbes did not draw analogies between the state and the human body (the king as head, judges and magistrates as arms, and so

forth). Instead, he compared the state to a machine that "ran" by means of laws and was kept in good working order by a skilled technician—the ruler.

Hobbes's pessimism about human behavior and his insistence on the need for restraint imposed from above reflect, as does the work of Descartes, a concern for order in the wake of political turmoil. This concern was one reason he was welcomed into the community of French philosophers, who were naturally comfortable with royalty as a powerful guarantor of order. But Hobbes's work, like theirs, was a radical departure because it envisioned citizens as potentially equal and constrained neither by morality nor by natural obedience to authority.

Another Englishman, John Locke (1632–1704), offered an entirely different vision of natural equality among people and, consequently, of social order. Locke's major works, *Essay on Human Understanding* (1690) and *Two Treatises of Government* (1690), reflect the experimentalism of Robert Boyle, the systematizing rationality of Descartes, and other strands of the new scientific thought. In his *Essay* Locke provides a view of human knowledge more pragmatic and utilitarian than the rigorous mathematical model of certainty used by many other philosophers. He argues that human knowledge is largely the product of experience. He agrees with Descartes that reason orders and explains human experience, but unlike Descartes, he doubts that human reason had unlimited potential to comprehend the universe. Locke, however, offered a more optimistic vision of the possible uses of reason. Whereas Descartes was interested in mentally ordering and understanding the world, Locke was interested in actually functioning *in* the world.

Locke's treatises on government reflect his notion of knowledge based on experience, as well as his particular experiences as a member of elite circles following the Restoration in England. Trained in medicine, he served as personal physician and general political assistant to one of the members of Parliament most opposed to Charles II's pretensions to absolutist government. When James II acceded to the throne in 1685, Locke remained in the Netherlands, where he had fled to avoid prosecution for treason. He became an adviser to William of Orange and returned to England with William and Mary in 1688. Locke's view of the principles of good government came to reflect the pro-parliamentary stance of his political milieu.

Unlike Hobbes, Locke argued that people are capable of self-restraint and mutual respect in their pursuit of self-interest. The state arises, he believed, from a contract that individuals freely enter into to protect themselves, their property, and their happiness from possible

---

Leviathan (luh-VIE-uh-thun)

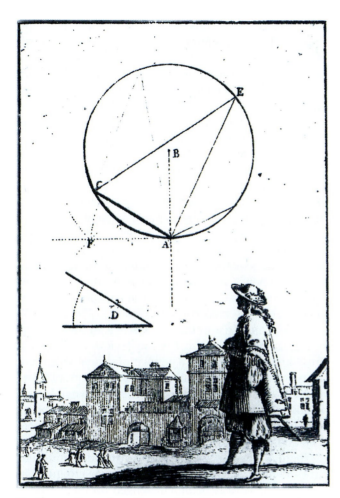

Gentleman Surveying a Town   This illustration appears in a seventeenth-century book on surveying by a mathematician who helped design the gardens at Versailles. The book aimed to teach elites the math necessary for precise measurements of landscapes—for example, for the purpose of siege warfare. The presence of the gentleman in the foreground, estimating the proportions of the town by sight, reveals that the author expected his audience to be interested in the mathematical computations he sought to teach them.   *(Bibliothèque nationale de France)*

aggression by others. They can invest the executive and legislative authority to carry out this protection in monarchy or any other governing institution, though Locke believed that the English Parliament was the best available model. Because sovereignty resides with the people who enter into the contract, rebellion against the abuse of power is justified. At the core of Locke's schema is thus a revolutionary vision of political society based on human rights.

Locke's experience as an English gentleman is apparent in his emphasis on private property, which he considered a fundamental human right. Nature, he believed, cannot benefit humankind unless it is worked by human hands, as on a farm, for example. Private ownership of property guarantees its productivity and entitles the owner to participate in Locke's imagined contract. Indeed, Locke's political vision is unequivocal, and unbending, on the nature of property. Locke even found a justification for slavery. He also did not consider women to be political beings in the same way as men. The family, he felt, is a separate domain from the state, not bound by the same contractual obligations.

Locke and many other seventeenth-century thinkers were unable to imagine a new physical or political reality without invoking a notion of gender as a "natural" principle of order and hierarchy. Although Margaret Cavendish (see page 592) and other women disputed the validity of such gender distinctions, men frequently used them. Locke's use of gender as an arbitrary organizing principle gave his bold new vision of rights for certain men a claim to being "natural." The use of gender-specific vocabulary to describe nature itself had the effect of making the new objective attitude toward the world seem "natural." Works by seventeenth-century scientists are filled with references to nature as a woman who must be "conquered," "subdued," or "penetrated."

Traditional gender distinctions limited and reinforced most facets of political thought, but in other areas the fact of uncertainty and the need for tolerance were embraced. Another of Locke's influential works was the impassioned *Letter on Toleration* (1689). In it he argues that religious belief is fundamentally private and that only the most basic Christian principles need be accepted by everyone. Others went further than Locke by entirely removing traditional religion as necessary to morality and public order. Fostering this climate of religious skepticism were religious pluralism in England and the self-defeating religious intolerance of Louis XIV's persecution of Protestants.

Pierre Bayle° (1647–1706), a Frenchman of Protestant origins, argued that morality can be wholly detached from traditional religion. Indeed, Bayle concluded, one need hardly be a Christian to be a moral being. Bayle cited as an example of morality the philosopher Baruch Spinoza° (1632–1677), a Dutch Jew who had been cast out of his local synagogue for supposed atheism. Even so, Spinoza believed the state to have a moral purpose and human happiness to have spiritual roots.

Bayle (BAIL)   **Spinoza** (spin-OH-za)

Bayle's skepticism toward traditional knowledge was more wide-ranging than his views on religion. His best-known work, *Dictionnaire historique et critique (Historical and Critical Dictionary,* 1702), was a compendium of observations about and criticisms of virtually every thinker whose works were known at the time, including such recent and lionized figures as Descartes and Newton. Bayle was the first systematic skeptic, and he relentlessly exposed errors and shortcomings in all received knowledge. His works were very popular with elite lay readers.

Bayle's countryman Bernard de Fontenelle° (1657–1757), secretary to the Académie des Sciences from 1699 to 1741, was the greatest popularizer of the new science of his time. His *Entretiens sur la Pluralités des Mondes (Conversations on the Plurality of Worlds,* 1686) was, as the title implies, an informally presented description of the infinite universe of matter. A great success, it went through numerous editions and translations. As secretary to the Académie, Fontenelle continued his work as popularizer by publishing descriptions of the work of the Académie's scientists. At his death (at age 99) in 1757, it was said that "the Philosophic spirit, today so much in evidence, owes its beginnings to Monsieur de Fontenelle."[16]

SUMMARY

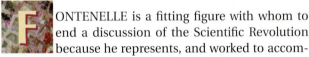

FONTENELLE is a fitting figure with whom to end a discussion of the Scientific Revolution because he represents, and worked to accomplish, the transference of the new natural philosophy into political and social philosophy—a movement we know as the "Enlightenment." The Scientific Revolution began, as innovation in scientific thinking often does, with a specific research problem whose answer led in unexpected directions. Copernicus's response to traditional astronomical problems led to scientific and philosophical innovation because of his solution and because of the context in which it was received. Recent recoveries of new ancient texts in the Renaissance and the discovery of previously unknown lands in the New World made it possible to imagine challenging ancient scientific authority. The interest of princes in both the prestige and the practical use of science helped support the work of scientists.

Other scientists, following Copernicus, built on his theories, culminating in the work of Galileo, who sup-

Fontenelle (fon-tuh-NEL)

ported Copernican theory with additional data and widely published his findings. The Frenchman Descartes was the first to fashion a systematic explanation for the operations of nature to replace the medieval view. The political and intellectual climate in England, meanwhile, encouraged the development of experimental science and inductive reasoning. Isaac Newton provided new theories to explain the behavior of matter and expressed them in mathematical terms that could apply to either the earth or the cosmos. With his work traditional astronomy and physics were overturned, replaced by a vision of a universe of matter that behaves not according to a higher purpose but rather as a machine. New institutions in the form of private as well as officially sponsored scientific societies rose up to support scientists' work. These societies were particularly important before the new science became accepted in universities, although they excluded some practitioners of the new science, particularly women.

Rulers made use of the new science for the practical results it offered despite the ideological challenges it presented to their power. The relationship of religion to the new science was equally complex and contrary. Some religious leaders scorned the new science; most scientists, whether Catholic or Protestant, worked to accommodate both the new science and their religious beliefs. Indeed, religious faith—in the case of Newton, for example—was a spur to innovation. By the end of the seventeenth century, the hierarchical Christian world-view grounded in the old science was being challenged on many fronts, most notably in the work of the political philosophers Hobbes and Locke. A fully articulated secular world-view would be the product of the Enlightenment in the next century.

■ **Notes**

1. Quoted in *Encyclopaedia Britannica,* 15th ed., vol. 9, p. 135.
2. Quoted in Thomas S. Kuhn, *The Copernican Revolution* (Cambridge, Mass.: Harvard University Press, 1985), p. 131.
3. Quoted in Margaret C. Jacob, *The Cultural Meaning of the Scientific Revolution* (Philadelphia: Temple University Press, 1988), p. 18.
4. Quoted ibid., p. 33.
5. Quoted in Alan G. R. Smith, *Science and Society in the Sixteenth and Seventeenth Centuries* (New York: Science History Publications, 1972), p. 72.
6. Quoted in Jacob, p. 32 (emphasis added).
7. Quoted in Bruce T. Moran, ed., *Patronage and Institutions: Science, Technology and Medicine at the European Court* (Rochester, N.Y.: Boyden Press, 1991), p. 43.
8. Quoted in Steven Shapin, *A Social History of Truth* (Chicago: University of Chicago Press, 1994), p. 298.

9. Quoted in Smith, p. 130.
10. Quoted in Jacob, p. 89.
11. Quoted ibid., p. 25.
12. Quoted in Londa Schiebinger, *The Mind Has No Sex?* (Cambridge, Mass.: Harvard University Press, 1989), p. 92.
13. Quoted in Richard S. Westfall, "Science and Patronage," *ISIS* 76 (1985): 16.
14. Quoted in Kuhn, p. 191.
15. *Complete Poetry and Selected Prose of John Donne,* ed. John Hayward (Bloomsbury, England: Nonesuch Press, 1929), p. 365, quoted in Kuhn, p. 194.
16. Quoted in Paul Edwards, ed., *The Encyclopedia of Philosophy,* vol. 3 (New York: Macmillan, 1967), p. 209.

■ Suggested Reading

Biagioli, Mario. *Galileo, Courtier.* 1993. A study that stresses the power of patronage relations to shape scientific process.

Dear, Peter. *Revolutionizing the Sciences: European Knowledge and Its Ambitions, 1500–1700.* 2001. An excellent general overview of the era of the Scientific Revolution.

Kuhn, Thomas. *The Copernican Revolution.* 1985. A classic treatment of the revolution in astronomy that lucidly explains the Aristotelian world-view; to understand the Copernican revolution, start here.

Schiebinger, Londa. *The Mind Has No Sex?* 1989. An examination of the participation of women in the practice of science and an explanation of how science began to reflect the exclusion of women in its values and objects of study—above all, in its claims about scientific "facts" about women themselves.

Shapin, Steven, and Simon Schaffer. *Leviathan and the Air-Pump.* 1985. One of the most important studies of seventeenth-century science; traces the conflict between Cartesian science, as represented by Hobbes, and experimental science, in the work of Boyle; shows the relationship of Hobbes and Boyle to their respective contexts and the widespread philosophical implications of each school of thought.

Westfall, Richard S. *Never at Rest: A Biography of Isaac Newton.* 1993. A biography by one of the best-known historians of science.

For a searchable list of additional readings for this chapter, go to college.hmco.com/students.

Modern Maps

We take for granted that contemporary maps will provide accurate representations of geography and present information in standardized ways we can easily read. But how did these standards of clarity and accuracy come about?

Modern mapping was developed during the Scientific Revolution. Like most of the changes we have labeled the "Scientific Revolution," changes in mapping were the result of several influences: innovations in Renaissance art, knowledge gleaned from voyages of exploration, the impact of new astronomical discoveries, and the interest and support of princely patrons. All of these factors enabled Europeans of this era to have a literally new view of their world.

Let us look at Christopher Saxton's map of Somerset, a county in England. This map was printed in 1579 in one of the first atlases ever published. We might be struck by how different this map appears from contemporary maps; many of its features seem decorative or even quaint. Ships, not drawn to scale, ride at anchor or sail off the coast. Towns are represented not by dots of various sizes but by miniature town buildings. Relief in the landscape is depicted with hills drawn, like the town buildings, from a side view inconsistent with the aerial perspective of the map as a whole. The large royal coat of arms that occupies the upper left quadrant of the map seems the most antiquated and irrelevant feature.

But is it irrelevant? Let us try to appreciate what a striking and powerful image this map must have been for its original viewers. Because the features are represented in ways that we consider decorative, it is easy for us to overlook the fact that this map illustrates a revolutionary method of depicting space. Saxton provides an aerial view of an entire county, with all locales arrayed in accurate spatial relationship to one another. This accurate rendering of space was, first, the result of the discovery of linear perspective by Renaissance artists. This discovery, which enabled space to be imagined from the perspective of a distanced observer, created the illusion of three-dimensional space in Renaissance paintings. Saxton's maps—and the few others published at about the same time—represented the first time Europeans could take

The County of Somerset, England, 1579   *(British Library)*

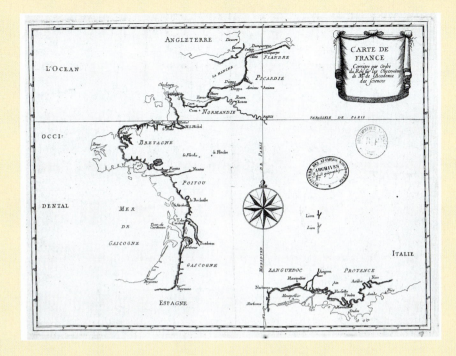

The French Coastline, 1693
(Bibliothèque nationale de France)

"visual possession" of the land they lived in, in the way we now take for granted whenever we buy a road map.*

Precise measurement of landforms—the location of hills in this map, for example—still relied on the established craft of systematic surveying. And here is where the royal coat of arms enters the picture, literally. Saxton's surveying and the production of his atlas were sponsored by the government of Queen Elizabeth. Thus just as this map enabled contemporary observers to envision for the first time, in its entirety, the land they lived in, it simultaneously marked royal power over that land.

Now let us look at a 1693 map of the coastline of France. We immediately note that most decorative elements are gone: no ships sail the abundant seas, for example. The figure of a compass marks the Paris meridian—the site of the city, we are shown, has been precisely determined by means of its longitude and latitude. More accurate calculation of longitude had been made possible by the work of Johannes Kepler and Galileo Galilei, whose mapping of heavenly bodies provided known points in the night sky from which to calculate the longitude of the observer's position on earth. (Calculation of latitude had

always been easier, since it involved only determining the angle of the sun above the horizon, but it was also improved by better instrumentation in the seventeenth century.) After 1650 French cartographers, among others, systematically collected astronomical observations from around the world so they could map all known lands more precisely.

This map superimposes a corrected view (the darker line) of the coastline of France over an older rendering. The power of this coastline map lies in the way it dramatically advertises the progress of mapmaking itself. Royal power remains connected to scientific effort: the title reads, "Map of France, corrected by order of the King by the observations of Messieurs of the Academy of Sciences."

Thus both of these maps glorify royal power: one by linking it with a new visualization of the land it ruled, the other by presenting royalty as a patron and guarantor of knowledge. But in the second map royal identity is no longer pictured along with the land it claims. Instead, the king is mentioned discreetly, in what came to be a standardized label.

Like all innovations of the Scientific Revolution, those in mapmaking had unintended consequences. Claims to royal power articulated on maps lost their force as the information the maps conveyed was increasingly valued for itself. Royal power had many practical and ideological uses for the new science but in the end would be undermined by the world-view the new science made possible.

---

*Richard Helgerson, "The Land Speaks: Cartography, Chorography, and Subversion in Renaissance England," *Representations* 16 (Fall 1986): 51. This discussion of Saxton's map and the evolution of mapmaking is drawn from Helgerson and from Norman J. W. Thrower, *Maps and Civilization* (Chicago: University of Chicago Press, 1996), chaps. 5 and 6.

CHAPTER 18

Europe on the Threshold of Modernity ca. 1715–1789

DRINKS are set before these gentlemen on their table, but something tells us this is more than just a social gathering. The men are absorbed in intense conversation. One man raises his hand, perhaps to emphasize his point, while another listens with a skeptical smirk. Several others eagerly follow their conversation. Other animated discussions go on at nearby tables. The setting depicted here was altogether new in the eighteenth century, when this picture was made, and a caption that originally accompanied the illustration speaks to its importance: "Establishment of the new philosophy: our cradle was the café."

Cafés were one of the new settings in which literate elites could discuss the "new philosophy"—what we now call Enlightenment philosophy—and could explore its implications for social and political life. Men gathered in clubs and cafés; women directed private gatherings known as salons. Both men and women read more widely than ever before. The Enlightenment was the extension into political and social thought of the intellectual revolution that had already occurred in the physical sciences. Hence it constituted a revolution in political philosophy, but it was also much more. The era witnessed the emergence of an informed body of public opinion, critical of the prevailing political system. The relationship between governments and the governed had begun to change: subjects of monarchs were becoming citizens of nations.

The notion that human beings, using their rational faculties, could not only understand nature but might also transform their

Café society in the eighteenth century.
(G. Dagli Orti/The Art Archive)

societies was appealing to rulers as well, in part for the traditional reason—strengthening state power. Frederick the Great of Prussia, Catherine the Great of Russia, and other monarchs self-consciously tried to use Enlightenment precepts to guide their efforts at governing. They had mixed success because powerful interests opposed their efforts at reform and because, ultimately, their own hereditary and autocratic power was incompatible with Enlightenment perspectives.

Profound changes in economic and social life accompanied this revolution in intellectual and political spheres. Economic growth spurred population growth, which in turn stimulated industry and trade. The increasing economic and strategic importance of overseas colonies made them important focal points of international conflict. As the century closed, Europe was on the threshold of truly revolutionary changes in politics and production that had their roots in the intellectual, economic, and social ferment of eighteenth-century life.

QUESTIONS TO CONSIDER

- What were the most important notions in Enlightenment thought, and what were some of the intellectual, social, and political conditions that favored its development?

- To what extent did the activities of "enlightened despots" reflect Enlightenment precepts, and to what extent did they reflect traditional concerns of state power?

- How did warfare itself, and the causes of war, change in the eighteenth century?

- How was European agriculture transformed in this era, and what further transformations did it bring in its wake?

TERMS TO KNOW

philosophes	Maria Theresa
Voltaire	Catherine the Great
Adam Smith	Seven Years' War
Jean-Jacques Rousseau	slave trade
salon, salonnière	agricultural revolution
enlightened despotism	putting-out system
Frederick the Great	

THE ENLIGHTENMENT

THE Enlightenment was an intellectual movement that applied to political and social thought the confidence in the intelligibility of natural law that Newton and other scientists had recently achieved. Following Descartes and Locke, Enlightenment thinkers believed that human beings could discern and work in concert with the laws of nature for the betterment of human life. Perhaps the most significant effect of this confidence was the questioning of traditional social and political bonds. A belief grew that society must be grounded on rational foundations to be determined by humans, not arbitrary foundations determined by tradition and justified by religious authority.

The Enlightenment was a social and cultural movement: Enlightenment thought was received and debated in the context of increasingly widespread publications and new opportunities for exchanging views in literary societies, salons, and cafés. This context shaped the potential radicalism of the Enlightenment by helping to ensure that informed public opinion would become a new force in political and cultural life. Given this broad base, Enlightenment thinking was certain to challenge the very foundations of social and political order.

Voltaire: The Quintessential Philosophe

A wide range of thinkers participated in the Enlightenment. In France they were known as *philosophes°*, a term meaning not a formal philosopher but rather a thinker and critic. The most famous of the philosophes was Voltaire (1694–1778). A prolific writer, critic, and reformer, Voltaire was lionized by admirers throughout Europe, including several rulers. Born François-Marie Arouet to a middle-class family, he took the pen name

---

philosophes (fee-low-ZOHFS)

Voltaire in 1718, after one of his early plays was a critical success. Like many philosophes, Voltaire moved in courtly circles but was often on its margins. His mockery of the regent for the young French king earned him a year's imprisonment in 1717, and an exchange of insults with a leading courtier some years later led to enforced exile in Great Britain for two years.

After returning from Britain, Voltaire published his first major philosophical work. *Lettres philosophiques* (*Philosophical Letters*, 1734) revealed the influence of his British sojourn and helped to popularize Newton's achievement. To confidence in the laws governing nature Voltaire added cautious confidence in humans' attempts to discern truth. From Locke's work (see page 596) he was persuaded to trust human educability tempered by awareness of the finite nature of the human mind. These elements gave Voltaire's philosophy both its passionate conviction and its sensible practicality.

Voltaire portrayed Great Britain as a more rational society than France. He was particularly impressed with the relative religious and intellectual toleration evident across the Channel. The British government had a more workable set of institutions; the economy was less crippled by the remnants of feudal privilege, and education was not in the hands of the church. (See the box "Reading Sources: Voltaire on Britain's Commercial Success.") Voltaire was one of many French thinkers who singled out the Catholic Church as the archenemy of progressive thought. Philosophes constantly collided with the church's negative views of human nature and resented its control over most education and its still strong sway in political life. Typical of Voltaire's castigation of the church is his stinging satire of the clerics who condemned Galileo: "I desire that there be engraved on the door of your holy office: Here seven cardinals assisted by minor brethren had the master of thought of Italy thrown into prison at the age of seventy, made him fast on bread and water, because he instructed the human race."

After the publication of his audacious *Letters,* Voltaire was again forced into exile from Paris, and he resided for some years in the country home of a woman with whom he shared a remarkable intellectual and emotional relationship: Emilie, marquise du Châtelet° (1706–1749). Châtelet was a mathematician and a scientist. She prepared a French translation of Newton's *Principia* while Voltaire worked at his accustomed variety of writing, which included a commentary on Newton's work. Because of Châtelet's tutelage, Voltaire became more knowledgeable about the sciences and more serious in

Châtelet (shot-uh-LAY)

CHRONOLOGY

1715–1774	Reign of Louis XV in France
1722–1741	Walpole first British "prime minister"
1734	Voltaire, *Philosophical Letters*
1740–1748	War of the Austrian Succession
1740–1780	Reign of Maria Theresa of Austria
1740–1786	Reign of Frederick the Great of Prussia
1746	Battle of Culloden
1748	Montesquieu, *The Spirit of the Laws* Hume, *Essay Concerning Human Understanding*
1751–1765	Diderot, *The Encyclopedia*
1756–1763	Seven Years' War
1758	Voltaire, *Candide*
1762	Rousseau, *The Social Contract*
1762–1796	Reign of Catherine the Great of Russia
1772	First partition of Poland
1776	Smith, *The Wealth of Nations*
1780–1790	Reign of Joseph II of Austria
1792	Wollstonecraft, *A Vindication of the Rights of Woman*

his efforts to apply scientific rationality to human affairs. He was devastated by her sudden death in 1749.

Shortly afterward he accepted the invitation of the king of Prussia, Frederick II, to visit Berlin. His stay was stormy and brief because of disagreements with other court philosophers. He resided for a time in Geneva, until his criticisms of the city's moral codes forced yet another exile on him. He spent most of the last twenty years of his life at his estates on the Franco-Swiss border, where he could be relatively free from interference by any government. These were productive years. He produced his best-known satirical novelette, *Candide,* in 1758. It criticized aristocratic privilege and the power of clerics as well as the naiveté of philosophers who took "natural law" to mean that the world was already operating as it should.

READING SOURCES

VOLTAIRE ON BRITAIN'S COMMERCIAL SUCCESS

In this excerpt from Philosophical Letters, *Voltaire compares British trade and sea power with the commercial activities of the German and French elites, who scorned trade in order to engage in aristocratic pretentiousness and court politics. Voltaire's admiration for England and his penchant for criticizing irrationalities of all sorts are evident, as is his famed wit. Wit and irony were important tools for Voltaire, enabling him to advance trenchant criticism when seeming only to poke fun.*

Commerce, which has brought wealth to the citizenry of England, has helped to make them free, and freedom has developed commerce in its turn. By means of it the nation has grown great; it is commerce that little by little has strengthened the naval forces that make the English the masters of the seas. . . . Posterity may learn with some surprise that a little island with nothing of its own but a bit of lead, tin . . . and coarse wool became, by means of its commerce, powerful enough to send three fleets at one time to three different ends of the earth.

All this makes the English merchant justly proud; moreover, the younger brother of a peer of the realm does not scorn to enter into trade. . . . [In Germany], they are unable to imagine how [an aristocrat could enter trade since they have] as many as thirty Highnesses of the same name, with nothing to show for it but pride and a coat of arms.

In France anybody who wants to can [act the part of marquis] and whoever arrives in Paris with money to spend and a [plausible name] may indulge in such phrases as "a man of my rank and quality" and with sovereign eye look down upon a wholesaler. . . . Yet I don't know which is the more useful to a state, a well-powdered lord who knows precisely what time the king gets up in the morning . . . and who gives himself airs of grandeur while playing the role of slave in a minister's antechamber, or a great merchant who enriches his country.

Source: *Voltaire: Philosophical Letters,* edited and translated by Ernest Dilworth. Copyright © 1961. Reprinted by permission of Prentice-Hall, Inc., Upper Saddle River, N.J.

Voltaire's belief that only by struggle are the accumulated habits of centuries overturned is also reflected in his political activity. He became involved in several celebrated legal cases in which individuals were pitted against the authority of the church, which was still backed by the authority of the state. In pursuit of justice in these cases and in relentless criticism of the church, Voltaire added a stream of straightforward political pamphlets to his literary output. He also worked closer to home, initiating agricultural reform on his estates and working to improve the status of peasants in the vicinity.

Voltaire died in Paris in May 1778, after a triumphal welcome for the staging of one of his plays. By then he was no longer leader of the Enlightenment in strictly intellectual terms. Thinkers and writers more radical than he had earned prominence during his long life and had dismissed some of his beliefs, such as the notion that a monarch could introduce reform. But Voltaire had provided a crucial stimulus to French thought with his *Philosophical Letters.* His importance lies also in his embodiment of the critical spirit of eighteenth-century rationalism: its confidence, its increasingly practical bent, its wit and sophistication. Until the end of his life, Voltaire remained a bridge between the increasingly diverse body of Enlightenment thought and the literate elite audience.

The Variety of Enlightenment Thought

Differences among philosophes grew as the century progressed. In the matter of religion, for example, there was virtual unanimity of opposition to the Catholic Church among French thinkers, but no unanimity about God. Voltaire was a theist—believing firmly in God, creator of the universe, but not a specifically Christian God. To some later thinkers, God was irrelevant—the creator of the world, but a world that ran continuously according to established laws. Some philosophes were atheists, arguing that a universe operating according to discoverable laws needs no higher purpose and no divine pres-

Voltaire Visits Frederick the Great of Prussia   Voltaire leans forward, at left, to discuss a point of philosophy with Frederick. Skill at witty conversation enabled philosophes such as Voltaire to advance fundamental criticisms of society even to elite audiences.   *(Bildarchiv Preussischer Kulturbesitz/Art Resource, NY)*

ence to explain, run, or justify its existence. In Protestant areas of Europe, in contrast to France, Enlightenment thought was often less hostile to Christianity.

Questions about social and political order, as well as about human rationality, also were pondered. Charles de Secondat (1689–1755), baron of Montesquieu°, a French judge and legal philosopher, combined the belief that human institutions must be rational with Locke's assumption of human educability. Montesquieu's treatise *De L'Esprit des lois* (*The Spirit of the Laws*, 1748) was pub-

lished in twenty-two printings within two years. In it Montesquieu maintained that laws were not meant to be arbitrary rules but derived naturally from human society: the more evolved a society was, the more liberal were its laws. This notion that progress is possible within society and government deflated Europeans' pretensions with regard to other societies, for a variety of laws could be equally "rational" given different conditions. Montesquieu is perhaps best known to Americans as the advocate of the separation of legislative, executive, and judicial powers that later became enshrined in the U.S. Constitution. To Montesquieu this scheme seemed to

---

Montesquieu (mawn-tess-KYUH)

parallel in human government the balance of forces observable in nature; moreover, the arrangement seemed best to guarantee liberty.

Enlightenment philosophers also investigated the "laws" of economic life. In France economic thinkers known as *physiocrats* proposed ending "artificial" control over land use in order to free productive capacity and permit the flow of produce to market. Their target was traditional forms of land tenure, including collective control of village lands by peasants and seigneurial rights over land and labor by landlords. The freeing of restrictions on agriculture, manufacture, and trade was proposed by the Scotsman Adam Smith in his treatise *An Inquiry into the Nature and Causes of the Wealth of Nations* (1776).

Smith (1723–1790), a professor at the University of Glasgow, is best known in modern times as the originator of "laissez-faire" economics. *Laissez faire,* or "let it run on its own," assumes that an economy will regulate itself, without interference by government and, of more concern to Smith, without the monopolies and other economic privileges common in his day. Smith's schema for economic growth was not merely a rigid application of natural law to economics. His ideas grew out of an optimistic view of human nature and rationality that was heavily indebted to Locke. Humans, Smith believed, have drives and passions that they can direct and govern by means of reason and inherent mutual sympathy. Thus, Smith suggested, in seeking their own achievement and well-being, people are often "led by an invisible hand" simultaneously to benefit society as a whole.

Throughout the century, philosophers of various stripes disagreed about the nature and the limits of human reason. Smith's countryman and friend David Hume (1711–1776) was perhaps the most radical in his critique of the human capacity for knowing. He was the archskeptic, taking Locke's view of the limitations on pure reason to the point of doubting the efficacy of any sensory data. His major exposition of these views, *Essay Concerning Human Understanding* (1748), led to important innovations later in the century in the work of the German philosopher Immanuel Kant. At the time, though, Hume's arguments were almost contrary to the prevailing spirit that embraced empirical knowledge. Hume himself separated this work from his other efforts in moral, political, and economic philosophy, which were more in tune with contemporary views.

Mainstream confidence in empirical knowledge and in the intelligibility of the world is evident in the production of the *Encyclopédie* (*Encyclopedia*). This seventeen-volume compendium of knowledge, criticism, and philosophy

was assembled by leading philosophes in France and published there between 1751 and 1765. The volumes were designed to contain state-of-the-art knowledge about arts, sciences, technology, and philosophy. The guiding philosophy of the project, set forth by its chief editor, Denis Diderot° (1713–1784), was a belief in the advancement of human happiness through the advancement of knowledge. The *Encyclopedia* was a history of the march of knowledge as well as a compendium of known achievements. It was revolutionary in that it not only intrigued and inspired intellectuals but also assisted thousands of government officials and professionals.

The encyclopedia project illustrates the political context of Enlightenment thought as well as its philosophical premises. The Catholic Church placed the work on the *Index of Prohibited Books,* and the French government might have barred its publication but for the fact that the official who would have made the decision was himself drawn to Enlightenment thinking. Many other officials, however, worked to suppress it. By the late 1750s, losses in wars overseas had made French officials highly sensitive to political challenges of any kind. Thus, like Voltaire, the major contributors to the *Encyclopedia* were admired by certain segments of the elite and persecuted by others in their official functions.

The *Encyclopedia* reflects the complexities and limitations of Enlightenment thought on another score—the position of women. One might expect that the Enlightenment penchant for challenging received knowledge and traditional hierarchies would lead to revised views of women's abilities and rights. Indeed, some contributors blamed women's inequality with men not on inherent gender differences but rather on the customs and laws that had kept women from education and the development of their abilities. However, other contributors blamed women, and not society, for their plight, or they argued that women had talents that fit them only for the domestic sphere.

Both positions were represented in Enlightenment thought as a whole. The assumption of the natural equality of all people provided a powerful ground for arguing the equality of women with men. Some thinkers, such as Mary Astell (1666–1731), challenged Locke's separation of family life from the public world of free, contractual relationships. "If absolute authority be not necessary in a state," she reasoned, "how comes it to be so in a family?" Most such thinkers advocated increased education for women, if only to make them more fit to raise enlightened children. By 1800 the most radical think-

---

Diderot (DEED-uh-row)

An Enlightenment Thinker Argues for the Equality of Women

Mary Wollstonecraft was not alone among thinkers in the eighteenth century to argue for the equality of women with men. She was more radical than most, however, when she argued that even to be good wives and mothers, women must be economically independent. She was extending to women the connection between independence and virtue that John Locke and Jean-Jacques Rousseau, among others, applied to men. Locke's and Rousseau's assumptions that only men could exercise political rights or be independent beings won out in the short term but have been vigorously contested since Wollstonecraft's day.

It is vain to expect virtue from women till they are in some degree independent from men; nay, it is vain to expect that strength of natural affection which would make them good wives and mothers. Whilst they are absolutely dependent on their husbands, they will be cunning, mean and selfish. . . . Yet whilst wealth enervates men, and women live, as it were, by their personal charms, how can we expect them to discharge those ennobling duties which equally require exertion and self-denial? . . . The society is not properly organized which does not compel men and women to discharge their respective duties, by making it the only way to acquire that countenance [respect] from their fellow creatures which every human being wishes some way to attain. . . .

But to render [woman] really virtuous and useful, she must not . . . want, individually, the protection of civil laws; she must not be dependent on her husband's bounty for her subsistence during his life or support after his death—for how can a being be generous who has nothing of its own? Or virtuous, who is not free? . . .

Business of various kinds they might likewise pursue, if they were educated in a more orderly manner. . . . Women would not then marry for a support, as men accept of places under government, and neglect the implied duties; nor would an attempt to earn their own subsistence . . . sink them almost to the level of those poor abandoned creatures who live by prostitution.

QUESTIONS

1. How does Wollstonecraft connect independence with virtuous behavior? Why do you think she framed her argument for the equality of women in these terms?

2. What attributes does an independent woman bring to the roles of wife and mother, according to Wollstonecraft?

SOURCE: Moira Ferguson, ed., *First Feminists: British Women Writers, 1578–1799* (Bloomington: Indiana University Press, 1985), pp. 423–429.

For additional information on this topic, go to college.hmco.com/students.

---

ers were advocating full citizenship rights for women and equal rights to property, along with enhanced education.

The best-known proponent of those views was an Englishwoman, Mary Wollstonecraft (1759–1797), who wrote *A Vindication of the Rights of Woman* (1792). She assumed that most elite women would devote themselves to domestic duties, but she argued that without the responsibilities of citizenship, the leavening of education, and economic independence, women could be neither fully formed individuals nor worthy of their duties. Working women, she concluded, needed these rights simply to survive. (See the box "The Continuing Experiment: An Enlightenment Thinker Argues for the Equality of Women.")

A more limited view of women's capacities was one element in the influential work of Jean-Jacques Rousseau° (1712–1778). Like Locke, Rousseau could conceive of the free individual only as male, and he grounded his scorn of the old order and his novel political ideas in an arbitrary division of gender roles. Rousseau's view of women was linked to a critique of the artificiality of elite, cosmopolitan society in which Enlightenment thought was then flourishing, and in which aristocratic women were fully involved. Rousseau believed in the educability of men but was as concerned with issues of character and emotional life as with cognitive knowledge. Society—particularly the artificial courtly

---

Rousseau (roo-SO)

READING SOURCES

ROUSSEAU DISCUSSES THE BENEFITS OF SUBMITTING TO THE GENERAL WILL

In this excerpt from his Social Contract, *Rousseau describes the relationship of individuals to the general will. Notice the wider-ranging benefits Rousseau believes men will enjoy in society as he envisions it. Rousseau is clearly interested in intellectual, moral, and emotional well-being.*

I assume that men reach a point where the obstacles to their preservation in a state of nature prove greater than the strength that each man has to preserve himself in that state. Beyond this point, the primitive condition cannot endure, for then the human race will perish if it does not change its mode of existence. . . .

"How to find a form of association which will defend the person and goods of each member with the collective force of all, and under which each individual, while uniting himself with the others, obeys no one but himself, and remains as free as before." This is the fundamental problem to which the social contract holds the solution. . . .

The passing from the state of nature to the civil society produces a remarkable change in man; it puts justice as a rule of conduct in the place of instinct, and gives his actions the moral quality they previously lacked. . . . And although in civil society man surrenders some of the advantages that belong to the state of nature, he gains in return far greater ones; his faculties are so exercised and developed, his mind is so enlarged, his sentiments so ennobled, and his whole spirit so elevated that . . . he should constantly bless the happy hour that lifted him for ever from the state of nature and from a stupid, limited animal made a creature of intelligence and a man. . . .

For every individual as a man may have a private will contrary to, or different from, the general will that he has as a citizen. His private interest may speak with a very different voice from that of the public interest; his absolute and naturally independent existence may make him regard what he owes to the common cause as a gratuitous contribution, the loss of which would be less painful for others than the payment is onerous for him; and fancying that the artificial person which constitutes the state is a mere fictitious entity (since it is not a man), he might seek to enjoy the rights of a citizen without doing the duties of a subject. The growth of this kind of injustice would bring about the ruin of the body politic.

Hence, in order that the social pact shall not be an empty formula, it is tacitly implied in that commitment—which alone can give force to all others—that whoever refuses to obey the general will shall be constrained to do so by the whole body, which means nothing other than that he shall be forced to be free; for this is the necessary condition which, by giving each citizen to the nation, secures him against all personal dependence, it is the condition which shapes both the design and the working of the political machine, and which alone bestows justice on civil contracts—without it, such contracts would be absurd, tyrannical and liable to the grossest abuse.

Source: Jean-Jacques Rousseau, *The Social Contract*, translated by Maurice Cranston. Reprinted by permission of PFD on behalf of The Estate of Maurice Cranston. Copyright © 1968 by Maurice Cranston.

---

society—was corrupting, he believed. The true citizen had to cultivate virtue and sensibility, not manners, taste, or refinement. Rousseau designated women as guarantors of the "natural" virtues of children and as nurturers of the emotional life and character of men—but not as fully formed beings in their own right.

Rousseau's emphasis on the education and virtue of citizens was the underpinning of his larger political vision, set forth in *Du Contrat social* (*The Social Contract*, 1762). He imagined an egalitarian republic—possible particularly in small states such as his native Geneva—in which men would consent to be governed because the government would determine and act in accordance with the "general will" of the citizens. The "general will" was not majority opinion but rather what each citizen *would* want if he were fully informed and were acting in accordance with his highest nature. The "general will" became apparent whenever the citizens met as a body and made collective decisions, and it could be imposed on all inhabitants. (See the box "Reading Sources: Rousseau Discusses the Benefits of Submitting to the General Will.") This was a breathtaking vision of direct

The Growth of the Book Trade   Book ownership dramatically increased in the eighteenth century, and a wide range of secular works—from racy novelettes to philosophical tracts—was available in print. In this rendering of a bookshop, shipments of books have arrived from around Europe. Notice the artist's optimism in the great variety of persons, from the peasant with a scythe to a white-robed cleric, who are drawn to the shop by "Minerva" (the Roman goddess of wisdom).   *(Musée des Beaux-Arts de Dijon)*

democracy—but one with ominous possibilities, for Rousseau rejected the institutional checks on state authority proposed by Locke and Montesquieu.

Rousseau's emphasis on private emotional life anticipated the romanticism of the early nineteenth century. It also reflected Rousseau's own experience as the son of a humble family, always sensing himself an outcast in the brilliant world of Parisian salons. He had a love-hate relationship with this life, remaining attached to several aristocratic women patrons even as he decried their influence. His own personal life did not match his prescriptions for others. He completely neglected to give his four children the nurture and education that he argued were vital; indeed, he abandoned them all to a foundling home. He was nevertheless influential as a critic of an elite society still dominated by status, patron-

age, and privilege. Rousseau's work reflects to an extreme degree the tensions in Enlightenment thought generally: it was part of elite culture as well as its principal critic.

The Growth of Public Opinion

It is impossible to appreciate the significance of the Enlightenment without understanding the degree to which it was a part of public life. Most of the philosophes were of modest origin. They influenced the privileged elite of their day because of the social and political environment in which their ideas were elaborated. Indeed, the clearest distinguishing feature of the Enlightenment may be the creation of an informed body of public opinion that stood apart from court society.

Increased literacy and access to books and other printed materials are an important part of the story. Perhaps more important, the kinds of reading that people favored began to change. We know from inventories made of people's belongings at the time of their deaths (required for inheritance laws) that books in the homes of ordinary people were no longer just traditional works such as devotional literature. Ordinary people now read secular and contemporary philosophical works. As the availability of such works increased, reading itself evolved from a reverential encounter with old ideas to a critical encounter with new ideas. Solitary reading for reflection and pleasure became more widespread.

Habits of reading and responding to written material changed not only because of these increased opportunities to read but also because of changes in the social environment. In the eighteenth century, forerunners of the modern lending libraries made their debut. In Paris, for a fee, one could join a *salle de lecture*° (literally, a "reading room") where the latest works were available to any member. Booksellers, whose numbers increased dramatically, found ways to meet readers' demands for inexpensive access to reading matter. One might pay for the right to read a book in the bookshop itself. In short, new venues encouraged people to see themselves not just as readers but as members of a reading public.

Among the most famous and most important of these venues were the Parisian salons, regular gatherings in private homes, where Voltaire and others read their works in progress aloud and discussed them. Several Parisian women—mostly wealthy, but of modest social status—invited courtiers, bureaucrats, and intellectuals to meet in their homes at regular times each week. The *salonnières*° (salon leaders) themselves read widely in order to facilitate the exchange of ideas among their guests. This mediating function was crucial to the success of the salons. Manners and polite conversation had been a defining feature of aristocratic life since the seventeenth century, but they had largely been means of displaying status and safeguarding honor. The leadership of the salonnières and the protected environment they provided away from court life enabled a further evolution of "polite society" to occur: anyone with appropriate manners could participate in conversation as an equal. The assumption of equality in turn enabled conversation to turn away from maintaining the status quo to questioning it.

The influence of salons was extended by the wide correspondence networks the salonnières maintained.

Perhaps the most famous salonnière in her day, Marie-Thérèse Geoffrin° (1699–1777) corresponded with Catherine the Great, the reform-minded empress of Russia, as well as with philosophes outside Paris and with interested would-be members of her circle. The ambassador of Naples regularly attended her salon while in Paris and exchanged weekly letters with her when home in Italy. He reflected on the importance of salon leaders such as Geoffrin when he wrote from Naples lamenting, "[Our gatherings here] are getting farther away from the character and tone of those of France, despite all [our] efforts. . . . There is no way to make Naples resemble Paris unless we find a woman to guide us, organize us, *Geoffrinise* us."[1]

Various clubs, local academies, and learned and secret societies, such as Masonic lodges, copied some features of the salons of Paris. Hardly any municipality was without a private society that functioned both as a forum for political and philosophical discussion and as an elite social club. Here mingled doctors, lawyers, local officials—some of whom enjoyed the fruits of the political system in offices and patronage. In Scotland universities were flourishing centers of Enlightenment thought, but political clubs in Glasgow and Edinburgh enriched debate and the development of ideas.

Ideas circulated beyond the membership of the multitude of clubs by means of print. Newsletters reporting the goings-on at salons in Paris were produced by some participants. Regularly published periodicals in Great Britain, France, and Italy also served as important means for the dissemination of enlightened opinion in the form of reviews, essays, and published correspondence. Some of these journals had been in existence since the second half of the seventeenth century, when they had begun as a means to circulate the new scientific work. Now subscribers included Americans anxious to keep up with intellectual life in Europe. Europeans who could not afford the annual subscriptions could peruse the journals in the newly opened reading rooms and libraries. In addition to newsletters and journals, newspapers, which were regularly published even in small cities throughout western and central Europe, circulated ideas. (See the feature "Information Technology: Newspapers.")

In all these arenas Enlightenment ideas encouraged, and lent legitimacy to, a type of far-reaching political debate that had never before existed, except possibly in England during the seventeenth century. The greatest impact of the Enlightenment, particularly in France, was not

---

salle de lecture (sahl-duh-lek-TOOR)
salonnières (sal-on-YAIR)

Geoffrin (zhoh-FRAN)

The Cult of Sensibility in Art   This painting, *The Swing*, by Frenchman Fragonard, depicts a moment of playful and sensuous intimacy. This style of painting was an elaboration of baroque style known as "rococo." It began to be considered too excessive and lighthearted and was replaced by the more serious neoclassical style as the century wore on.   *(Wallace Collection, London/ Art Resource, NY)*

the creation of any specific program for political or social change. Rather its supreme legacy was an informed body of public opinion that could generate change.

Art in the Age of Reason

The Enlightenment reverberated throughout all aspects of cultural life. Just as the market for books and the reading public expanded, so did the audience for works of art in the growing leisured urban circles of Paris and other great cities. The modern cultured public—a public of concertgoers and art gallery enthusiasts—began to make its first appearance and constituted another arena in which public opinion was shaped. The brilliant and sophisticated courts around Europe continued to sponsor composers, musicians, and painters by providing both patronage and audiences. Yet some performances of concerts and operas began to take place in theaters and halls outside the courts in venues more accessible to the public.

Beginning in 1737 one section of the Louvre° palace in Paris was devoted annually to public exhibitions of

painting and sculpture (though by royally sponsored and approved artists). In both France and Britain, public discussion of art began to take place in published reviews and criticisms: the role of art critic was born. Works of art were also sold by public means, such as auctions. As works became more available, demand grew and production increased.

In subject matter and style these various art forms exhibited greater variety than works in preceding centuries had shown. We can nevertheless discern certain patterns and tendencies in both the content and the form of eighteenth-century European art. Late baroque painters contributed to an exploration of private life and emotion sometimes called the "cult of sensibility." Frequently they depicted private scenes of upper-class life, especially moments of intimate conversation or flirtation.

The cult of sensibility was fostered by literature as well. The private life of emotion was nurtured by increased

Louvre (LOO-vruh)

Newspapers

The invention of printing in the fifteenth century greatly expanded the kinds of information available to Europeans. In addition to books, thousands of pamphlets and single-page "reports" of startling news appeared, such as the 1513 "Trew Encountre" describing a battle between the English and Scots and detailing the heroic deeds of the combatants. Along with these other short, occasional publications, the newspaper was born in the seventeenth century. By the eighteenth century, newspapers had become firmly established as a means of spreading news of European and world affairs, as well as of local concerns, within European society. Newspapers represented an application of printing technology that, under new conditions and for new purposes, constituted a real innovation in communication—and one with long-term consequences.

News had commercial as well as entertainment value. Even before printing technology had taken hold, the agents of great merchant families dispatched detailed news of products and harvests, as well as of timely political issues. In the sixteenth century, the Venetian government charged citizens a small fee to hear official news of battles against its great rival, the Turks. (A common name for newspaper—gazette—comes from *gazetta,* the coin Venetians used to pay for their news.) One of the first true newspapers was the Dutch paper *Nieuwe Tidjingen*. It began publication in the early seventeenth century about the same time the Dutch East India Company was formed. The same ships that brought goods back from abroad brought news of the world, too.

Dutch publishers had an advantage over many other publishers around Europe because the Netherlands' highly decentralized political system made its censorship laws very difficult to enforce. Throughout Europe in the seventeenth century, governments began recognizing the revolutionary potential of the free press and began requiring licenses of newspapers—to control who was able to publish news. Another tactic, in France and elsewhere on the Continent from the 1630s onward, was for governments to sponsor official newspapers. These state publications met the increasing demand for news but always supported the government's views of the events of the day.

By the eighteenth century new conditions allowed newspapers to flourish as never before. First, demand for news increased as Europe's commercial and political interests spread around the globe. Merchants in London, Liverpool, or Glasgow, for example, depended on early news of Caribbean harvests and gains and losses in colonial wars. Europe's growing commercial strength also increased distribution networks for newspapers. There were more and better roads, and more carters who could deliver newspapers in cities and convey them to outlying towns. Newspaper publishers made use of the many new sites where the public expected to read, as newspapers were delivered to cafés and sold or delivered by booksellers.

Second, many European states had established effective postal systems by the eighteenth century. It was through the mail that readers outside major cities and their environs—and virtually all readers in areas where press censorship was exercised firmly—received their newspapers. One of the most successful newspapers in Europe was a French-language paper (one of the many known as "la Gazette") published in Leiden, in the Netherlands, which boasted a wide readership in France and among elites throughout Europe. Censorship thus had a dwindling effect on well-educated readers anywhere in Europe.

Finally, press censorship faltered in one of the most important markets for news—England—at the turn of the eighteenth century. After the Glorious Revolution, debates raged about whether Parliament or the Crown had the right to control the press, and in the confusion the press flourished. The emergence of political parties further hampered control of the press because political decisions in Parliament now always involved compromise and many members believed that an active press was useful to that process. British control of the press was reduced to a tax (one of the

literacy, greater access to books, and the need to retreat from the elaborate artifice of court life. The novel became an increasingly important genre as a means of exploring social problems and human relationships. In English literature the novels of Samuel Richardson (1689–1761)—*Pamela* (1740) and *Clarissa* (1747–1748)—explored personal psychology and passion. Other novelists, such as Daniel Defoe in *Robinson Crusoe* (1717), used realism for purposes of social commentary.

Rousseau followed Richardson's lead in structuring his own novels, *La Nouvelle Héloïse* (1761) and *Emile* (1762). The cult of sensibility was not mere entertainment; it also carried the political and philosophical message that honest emotion was a "natural" virtue and

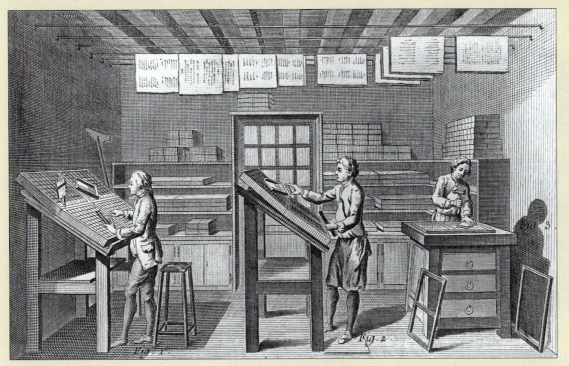

Producing a Newspaper   This illustration of the process of typesetting by hand in a newspaper printshop appears in Diderot's *Encyclopedia*. Notice the finished printed sheets drying above the workers' heads.   *(Division of Rare & Manuscript Collections/Cornell University Library)*

Stamp Acts so hated by American colonists) that drove some papers out of business.

Eighteenth-century newspapers were modest products by our standards. Many were published only once or twice a week instead of every day, in editions of only a few thousand copies. Each newspaper was generally only four pages long. Illustrations were rare, and headlines had not yet been invented. Hand-operated wooden presses were used to print the papers, just as they had been used to print pamphlets and books since the invention of printing in the fifteenth century.

Yet these newspapers had a dramatic impact on their reading public. Regular production of newspapers (especially of many competing newspapers) meant that news was presented to the public at regular intervals and in manageable amounts. Even strange and threatening news from around the world became increasingly easy for readers to absorb and interpret. The more sophisticated reader of the eighteenth century would respond to news more skeptically than had readers of the harrowing "Trew Encountre."

Newspaper readers also felt themselves part of the public life about which they were reading. This was true partly because newspapers, available in public reading rooms and in cafés, were one kind of reading that occupied an increasingly self-aware and literate audience. Newspapers also were uniquely responsive to their readers. They began to carry advertisements, which both produced revenue for papers and widened readers' exposure to their own communities. Even more important was the inauguration of letters to the editor. Newspapers thus became venues for the often rapid exchange of news and opinions. They were a vital tool of Europe's "enlightened" citizenries.

that courtly manners, by contrast, were irrational and degrading. The enormous popularity of Rousseau's novels, for example, came from the fact that their intense emotional appeal was simultaneously felt to be uplifting.

A revival of classical subjects and styles after the middle of the century evoked what were thought to be the pure and timeless values of classical heroes. This re-

vival revealed the influence of Enlightenment thought because the artists assumed the educability of their audience by means of example. Classical revival architecture illustrated a belief in order, symmetry, and proportion. Americans are familiar with its evocations because it has been the architecture of their republic, but even churches were built in this style in eighteenth-century

The Moralizing Message of Neoclassical Art   The French painter Jacques-Louis David portrays the mourning of the Trojan hero Hector by his wife, Andromache. David was well known for depicting his subjects with simple gestures—such as the extended arm of Andromache here—that were intended to portray honest and sincere emotion.   *(Private Collection/The Stapleton Collection/Bridgeman Art Library International)*

Europe. The classical movement in music reflected both the cult of sensibility and the classicizing styles in the visual arts. Embodied in the works of Austrians Franz Josef Haydn (1732–1809) and Wolfgang Amadeus Mozart (1756–1791), this movement saw the clarification of musical structures, such as the modern sonata and symphony, and enabled melody to take center stage.

Another trend in art and literature was a fascination with nature and with the seemingly "natural" in human culture—less "developed" or more historically distant societies. One of the most popular printed works in the

middle of the century was the alleged translation of the poems of Ossian°, a third-century Scots Highland poet. Early English, German, Norse, and other folktales were also "discovered" (in some cases invented) and published, some in several editions during the century. Folk life, other cultures, and untamed nature itself thus began to be celebrated at the very time they were being more definitively conquered. (See the feature "Weighing the

---

Ossian (AHSH-un)

Evidence: Gardens" on pages 638–639.) Ossian, for example, was celebrated just as the Scottish Highlands were being punished and pacified by the English after the clans' support for a rival claimant to the English throne. Once purged of any threat, the exotic image of another culture (even the folk culture of one's own society) could be a spur to the imagination. Thus the remote became romantic, offering a sense of distance from which to measure one's own sophistication and superiority.

EUROPEAN STATES IN THE AGE OF ENLIGHTENMENT

MINDFUL of the lessons to be learned from the civil war in England and the achievements of Louis XIV, European rulers in the eighteenth century continued their efforts to govern with greater effectiveness. Some, like the rulers of Prussia and Russia, were encouraged in their efforts by Enlightenment ideas that stressed the need for reforms in law, economy, and government. In the main they, like Voltaire, believed that monarchs could be agents for change. In Austria significant reforms, including the abolition of serfdom, were enacted. The changes were uneven, however, and at times owed as much to traditional efforts at better government as to enlightened persuasion.

In all cases, rulers' efforts to govern more effectively meant continual readjustments in relationships with traditional elites. Whether or not elites had formal roles in the governing process by means of established institutions such as the English Parliament, royal governments everywhere depended on their participation. However limited their "enlightened" policies, monarchs were changing their views of themselves and their public images from diligent but self-aggrandizing absolutist to servant of the state. In this way, monarchs actually undermined their dynastic claims to rule by re-founding their regimes on a utilitarian basis. The state was increasingly seen as separate from the ruler, with dramatic consequences for the future.

France During the Enlightenment

It is one of the seeming paradoxes of the era of the Enlightenment that critical thought about society and politics flourished in France, an autocratic state. Yet France was blessed with a well-educated elite, a tradition of scientific inquiry, and a legacy of cultured court life that, since the early days of Louis XIV, had become the model for all Europe (see pages 543–545). French was the international intellectual language, and France was the most fertile center of cultural life. Both Adam Smith and David Hume, for example, spent portions of their careers in Paris and were welcomed into Parisian salons. In fact, the French capital was an environment that encouraged debate and dissent precisely because of the juxtaposition of the new intellectual climate with the difficulties the French state was facing and the institutional rigidities of its political system. In France access to power was wholly through patronage and privilege, a system that excluded many talented and productive members of the elite.

The French state continued to embody fundamental contradictions. As under Louis XIV, the Crown sponsored scientific research, subsidized commerce and exploration, and tried to rationalize the royal administration. Royal administrators tried to chip away at the privileges, accrued since the Middle Ages, that hampered effective government—such as the exemption most nobles enjoyed from taxation. However, the Crown also continued to claim the right to govern autocratically, and the king was supported both ideologically and institutionally by the Catholic Church. A merchant in the bustling port of Bordeaux might be glad of the royal navy's protection of the colonies, and of the Crown's efforts to build better roads for the movement of goods within France. However, with his fellow Masons, he would fume when church officials publicly burned the works of Rousseau and be continually frustrated over his exclusion from any formal role in the political process.

The problems facing the French government were made worse by two circumstances: first, the strength of the privileged elites' defense of the old order, and second, mounting state debt from foreign wars that made fiscal reform increasingly urgent. Louis XIV was followed on the throne by his 5-year-old great-grandson, Louis XV (r. 1715–1774). During the regency early in his reign, the supreme law courts, the parlements, reclaimed the right of remonstrance—that is, the right to object to royal edicts and thus to exercise some control over the enactment of law. Throughout Louis XV's reign, his administration often locked horns with the parlements, particularly as royal ministers tried various expedients to cope with financial crises.

The power of the parlements came not only from their routine role in government but also from the fact that parlementaires were all legally noble and owned their offices just as a great nobleman owned his country estate. In addition, the parlements were the only institutions that could legitimately check royal power. As such, the parlements were often supported in their opposition to royal policies by the weight of public opinion. On the one hand, enlightened opinion believed in the rationality of doing away with privileges such as the ownership of offices. On the other hand, the role of consultative bodies and the separation of powers touted by Montesquieu, himself a parlementaire, were much prized. And even our Bordeaux merchant, who had little in common with privileged officeholders, might nevertheless see the parlementaires' resistance as his best protection from royal tyranny. The parlementaires, however, usually used their power for protecting the status quo.

Further hampering reform efforts was the character of the king himself. Louis XV displayed none of the kingly qualities of his great-grandfather. He was neither pleasant nor affable, and he was lazy. By the end of his reign, he was roundly despised. He did not give the "rationality" of royal government a good name. By the late 1760s the weight of government debt from foreign wars finally forced the king into action. He threw his support behind the reforming schemes of his chancellor, Nicolas de Maupeou°, who dissolved the parlements early in 1771 and created new law courts whose judges would not enjoy independent power.

The Crown lost control of reform when Louis died soon after, in 1774. His 20-year-old grandson, Louis XVI, well-meaning but insecure, allowed the complete restoration of the parlements. Further reform efforts, sponsored by the king and several talented ministers, came to naught because of parlementary opposition. Not surprisingly, from about the middle of the century, there had been calls to revive the moribund Estates General, the representative assembly last convened in 1614, as well as for the establishment of new councils—local, decentralized representative assemblies. By the time an Estates General was finally called in the wake of further financial problems in 1788, the enlightened elites' habit of carrying on political analysis and criticism outside the actual corridors of power, as well as their accumulated mistrust of the Crown, had given rise to a volatile situation.

Monarchy and Constitutional Government in Great Britain

After the deaths of William (d. 1702) and Mary (d. 1694), the British crown passed to Mary's sister, Anne (r. 1702–1714), and then to a collateral line descended from Elizabeth Stuart (d. 1662), sister of the beheaded Charles I. Elizabeth had married Frederick, elector of the Palati-

nate (and had reigned with him briefly in Bohemia at the outset of the Thirty Years' War; see page 525), and her descendants were Germans, now electors of Hanover. The new British sovereign in 1714, George I (r. 1714–1727), was both a foreigner and a man of mediocre abilities. Moreover, his claim to the throne was immediately contested by Catholic descendants of James II (see page 552), who attempted to depose him in 1715 and later his son, George II (r. 1727–1760), in 1745.

The 1745 attempt to depose the Hanoverian kings was more nearly successful. The son of the Stuart claimant to the throne, Charles (known in legend as Bonnie Prince Charlie), landed on the west coast of Scotland, with French assistance, and marched south into England. Most of the British army, and George II himself, was on the Continent, fighting in the War of the Austrian Succession (see page 625). Scotland had been formally united with England in 1707 (hence the term *Great Britain* after that time), and Charles found some support among Scots dissatisfied with the economic and political results of that union.

But the vast majority of Britons did not want the civil war that Charles's challenge inevitably meant, especially on behalf of a Catholic pretender who relied on support from Britain's great rival, France. Charles's army, made up mostly of poor Highland clansmen, was destroyed at the Battle of Culloden° in April 1746 by regular army units returned from abroad. Charles fled back to France, and the British government used the failed uprising as justification for the brutal and forceful integration of the still-remote Highlands into the British state.

Traditional practices, from wearing tartans to playing bagpipes, were forbidden. Control of land was redistributed to break the social and economic bonds of clan society. Thousands of Highlanders died at the battle itself, in prisons or on deportation ships, or by deliberate extermination at the hands of British troops after the battle.

Despite this serious challenge to the new dynasty and the harsh response it occasioned, the British state, overall, enjoyed a period of relative stability as well as innovation in the eighteenth century. The events of the seventeenth century had reaffirmed both the need for a strong monarchy and the role of Parliament in defending elite interests. The power of Parliament had recently been reinforced by the Act of Settlement, by which the Protestant heir to Queen Anne had been chosen in 1701. By excluding the Catholic Stuarts from the throne and establishing the line of succession, this document re-

---

Maupeou (mo-POO)

Culloden (cull-AH-dun)

asserted that Parliament determined the legitimacy of the monarchy. In addition, the act claimed greater parliamentary authority over foreign and domestic policy in the wake of the bellicose William's rule (see page 563).

Noteworthy in the eighteenth century were the ways in which cooperation evolved between monarchy and Parliament as Parliament became a more sophisticated and secure institution. Political parties—that is, distinct groups within the elite favoring certain foreign and domestic policies—came into existence. Two groups, the Whigs and the Tories, had begun to form during the reign of Charles II (d. 1685). The Whigs (named derisively by their opponents with a Scottish term for horse thieves) had resisted Charles's pro-French policies and his efforts to tolerate Catholicism and had wholly opposed his brother and successor, James II. Initially, the Whigs favored an aggressive foreign policy against continental opponents, particularly France. The Tories (whose name was also a taunt, referring to Irish cattle rustlers) tended to be staunch Anglicans uninterested in Protestant anti-Catholic agitation. They leaned toward a conservative view of their own role, favoring isolationism in foreign affairs and deference toward monarchical authority. Whigs generally represented the interests of the great aristocrats or wealthy merchants or gentry. Tories more often represented the interests of provincial gentry and the traditional concerns of landholding and local administration.

The Whigs were the dominant influence in government through most of the century to 1770. William and Mary, as well as Queen Anne, favored Whig religious and foreign policy interests. The loyalty of many Tories was called into question by their support for a Stuart, not Hanoverian, succession at Anne's death in 1714. The long Whig dominance of government was also ensured by the talents of Robert Walpole, a member of Parliament who functioned virtually as a prime minister from 1722 to 1742.

Walpole (1676–1745) was from a minor gentry family and was brought into government in 1714 with other Whig ministers in George I's new regime. An extremely talented politician, he took advantage of the mistakes of other ministers over the years and, in 1722, became both the first lord of the treasury and chancellor of the exchequer. No post or title of "prime minister" yet existed, but

Political Satire in England   This gruesome image, showing England being disemboweled by members of the government, criticizes the government's acceptance of a treaty with France. Satirical images such as this one were increasingly part of the lively and more open political life in eighteenth-century England.   *(Courtesy of the Trustees of the British Museum)*

the great contribution of Walpole's tenure was to create that office in fact, if not officially. He chose to maintain peace abroad when and where he could and thus presided over a period of recovery and relative prosperity that enhanced the stability of government.

Initially, Walpole was helped in his role as go-between for king and Parliament by George I's own limitations. The king rarely attended meetings of his own council of ministers and, in any case, was hampered by his limited command of English. Gradually, the Privy Council of the king became something resembling a modern cabinet dominated by a prime minister. By the end of the century the notions of "loyal opposition" to the Crown within Parliament and parliamentary responsibility for policy had taken root.

In some respects, the maturation of political life in Parliament resembled the lively political debates in the salons of Paris. In both cases, political life was being legitimized on a new basis. In England, however, that legitimation was enshrined in a legislative institution, which made it especially effective and resilient.

Parliament was not yet in any sense representative of the British population, however. Because of strict property qualifications, only about 200,000 adult men could vote. In addition, representation was very uneven, heavily favoring traditional landed wealth. Some constituencies with only a few dozen voters sent members to Parliament. Many of these "pocket boroughs" were under the control of (in the pockets of) powerful local families who could intimidate the local electorate, particularly in the absence of secret ballots.

Movements for reform of representation in Parliament began in the late 1760s as professionals, such as doctors and lawyers, with movable (as opposed to landed) property and merchants in booming but underrepresented cities began to demand the vote. As the burden of taxation grew—the result of the recently concluded Seven Years' War (discussed later in this chapter)—these groups felt increasingly deprived of representation. Indeed, many felt kinship and sympathy with the American colonists who opposed increased taxation by the British government on these same grounds and revolted in 1775.

However, the reform movement faltered over the issue of religion. In 1780 a tentative effort by Parliament to extend some civil rights to British Catholics provoked rioting in London (known as the Gordon Riots, after one of the leaders). The riots lasted for eight days and claimed three hundred lives. Pressure for parliamentary reform had been building as Britain met with reversals in its war against the American rebels, but this specter of a popular movement out of control temporarily ended the drive for reform by disenfranchised elites.

"Enlightened" Monarchy

Arbitrary monarchical power might seem antithetical to Enlightenment thought. After all, the Enlightenment stressed the reasonableness of human beings and their capacity to discern and act in accord with natural law. Yet monarchy seemed an ideal instrument of reform to Voltaire and to many of his contemporaries. The work of curtailing the influence of the church, reforming legal codes, and eliminating barriers to economic activity might be done more efficiently by a powerful monarch than by other available means. Historians have labeled a number of rulers of this era "enlightened despots" because of the arbitrary nature of their power and the enlightened or reformist uses to which they put it.

"Enlightened despotism" aptly describes certain developments in the Scandinavian kingdoms in the late eighteenth century. In Denmark the Crown had governed without significant challenge from the landholding nobility since the mid-seventeenth century. The nobility, however, like its counterparts in eastern Europe, had guaranteed its supremacy by means of ironclad domination of the peasantry. In 1784 a reform-minded group of nobles, led by the young crown prince Frederick (governing on behalf of his mentally ill father), began to apply Enlightenment remedies to the kingdom's economic problems. The reformers encouraged freer trade and sought, above all, to improve agriculture by elevating the status of the peasantry. With improved legal status and with land reform, which enabled some peasants to own the land they worked for the first time, agricultural productivity in Denmark rose dramatically. These reforms constitute some of the clearest achievements of any of the "enlightened" rulers.

In Sweden in 1772, Gustav III (r. 1771–1796) staged a coup with army support that overturned the dominance of the Swedish parliament, the Diet. In contrast to Denmark, Sweden had a relatively unbroken tradition of noble involvement in government, stemming in part from its marginal economy and the consequent interest of the nobility in participation in the Crown's aggressive foreign policy. Since Sweden's eclipse as a major power after the Great Northern War (see page 559), factions of the Diet, not unlike the rudimentary political parties in Great Britain, had fought over the reins of government. After reasserting his control, Gustav III began an ambitious program of reform of the government. Bureaucrats more loyal to parliamentary patrons than to the Crown were replaced, restrictions on trade in grain and other economic controls were liberalized, the legal system was rationalized, the death penalty was strictly limited, and legal torture was abolished.

Despite his abilities, Gustav III suffered the consequences of the contradictory position of advancing reform by autocratic means in a kingdom with a strong tradition of representative government. Gustav eventually tried to deflect the criticisms of the nobility by reviving grandiose—but completely untenable—schemes for the reconquest of Baltic territory. However, in 1796 he was mortally wounded by an assassin hired by disgruntled nobles.

Another claimant to the title "enlightened despot" was Frederick II of Prussia (r. 1740–1786), known as Frederick the Great. Much of the time, Frederick resided in his imperial electorate of Brandenburg, near its capital, Berlin. His scattered states, which he extended by seizing new lands, are referred to as Prussia rather than Brandenburg-Prussia because members of his family were now kings of Prussia thanks to their ambitions and the weakness of the Polish state, of which Prussia had once been a dependent duchy. In many ways, the Prussian state *was* its military victories, for Frederick's bold moves and the policies of his father, grandfather, and great-grandfather committed the state's resources to a military presence of dramatic proportions. Prussia was on the European stage at all only because of that driving commitment.

The institutions that constituted the state and linked the various provinces under one administration were dominated by the needs of the military. Frederick II's father, Frederick William (r. 1713–1740), had added an efficient provincial recruiting system to the state's central institutions, which he also further consolidated. But in many other respects, the Prussian state was in its infancy. There was no tradition of political participation—even by elites—and little chance of cultivating any. Nor was there any political or social room for maneuver at the lower part of the social scale. The rulers of Prussia had long ago acceded to the aristocracy's demand for tighter control over peasant labor on their own lands in return for their support of the monarchy. The rulers relied on the nobles for local administration and army commands. Thus the kinds of social, judicial, or political reforms that Frederick could hope to carry out without undermining his own power were starkly limited.

Frederick tried to modernize agricultural methods and simultaneously to improve the condition of the peasants, but he met stiff resistance from the noble landholders. He did succeed in abolishing serfdom in some regions. He tried to stimulate the economy by sponsoring state industries and trading monopolies, but too few resources and too little initiative from the tightly controlled merchant communities stymied his plans. Simplifying and codifying the inherited jumble of local laws was a goal of every ruler. A law code published in 1794, after Frederick's death, was partly the product of his efforts.

Frederick's views of the role of Enlightenment thought reflect the limitations of his situation. One doesn't have to lead a frontal assault on prejudices consecrated by time, he thought; instead, one must be tolerant of superstition because it will always have a hold on the masses. Perhaps his most distinctive "enlightened" characteristic was the seriousness with which he took his task as ruler. He was energetic and disciplined to a fault. In his book *Anti-Machiavel* (1741), he argued that a ruler has a moral obligation to work for the betterment of the state. He styled himself as the "first servant" or steward of the state. However superficial this claim may appear, Frederick compares favorably with Louis XV of France, who, having a far more wealthy and flexible society to work with, did much less.

Enlightenment and Tradition: The Case of Austria

One of the most effective rulers of the eighteenth century was the Habsburg ruler Maria Theresa of Austria (r. 1740–1780). A devout Catholic, she was guided more by traditional concerns for effective rule and compassion for her subjects than by Enlightenment ideas. After surviving the near dismemberment of Austrian territories in the War of the Austrian Succession (see page 625), she embarked on an energetic program of reform to remedy the weaknesses in the state that the war had revealed. "Austria," it must be remembered, is a term of convenience; the state was a very medieval-looking hodgepodge that included present-day Austria, the kingdoms of Bohemia and Hungary, the Austrian Netherlands, and lands in northern Italy. In addition, since the sixteenth century a male member of the Habsburg family had almost always been elected emperor of the Holy Roman Empire.

Maria Theresa streamlined and centralized administration, finances, and defense, particularly in Bohemia and Austria, where she was able to exercise her authority relatively unchecked, compared with her other domains. Above all, she reformed the assessment and collection of taxes to tap the wealth of her subjects more effectively and thus better defend all her domains. She improved her subjects' access to justice and limited the exploitation of serfs by landlords. She made primary schooling universal and compulsory, in order better to train peasants for the army. Although the policy was far from fully implemented at the time of her death (only about half of Austrian children were in school, and far fewer in Hungary and elsewhere), hers was the first European state with so ambitious an education policy. Maria Theresa accomplished all of this without being particularly "enlightened" personally. For example, she had a traditional fear of freedom of the press and cherished orthodoxy in religious matters.

Maria Theresa's policies were implemented by a group of ministers, bureaucrats, and officers who shared her concern for effective government and defense, and who were well versed in "enlightened" ideas for reform. The diverse character of the Habsburg lands meant that some members of the governing elite came from the Netherlands and from Italy, where sympathy for the Enlightenment was well rooted by comparison with the relatively poorer and more rural society of the Austrian hinterland. Moreover, the language of the Habsburg court was French (Maria Theresa spoke it fluently); thus no amount of local censorship—which, in any case, Maria Theresa relaxed—could prevent the governing class from reading and absorbing Enlightenment philosophy in its original language.

Maria Theresa was followed on the throne by her two sons, Joseph II (r. 1780–1790) and Leopold II (r. 1790–1792). Each son counted himself a follower of the Enlightenment, and each, as was the family custom, served a period of "apprenticeship" governing Habsburg territories where he could attempt to implement reform. After his mother's death, Joseph II carried out a variety of bold initiatives that she had not attempted, including freedom of the press, significant freedom of religion, and the abolition of serfdom in Habsburg lands. During his ten-year reign, the political climate in Vienna began to resemble that in Paris, London, and other capitals where political life was no longer confined to the royal court.

Like Frederick the Great, Joseph regarded himself as a servant of the state. Also like Frederick, he was limited in his reform program by the economic and social rigidities of the society he ruled. Austria had but a small middle class to insist on reform, and Joseph could not directly assault the privileges of great landholders, on whose wealth the state depended. In addition, Joseph was by temperament an inflexible autocrat, whose methods antagonized many of these powerful subjects. Joseph's policies provoked simmering opposition, even open revolt, and some of his reforms were repealed even before his death. His more able brother, Leopold, had implemented many reforms while ruling as grand duke in Tuscany (Italy) before assuming the throne in 1790. Much of his two-year reign was spent dexterously saving reforms enacted by his mother and brother in the face of mounting opposition.

Catherine the Great and the Empire of Russia

Another ruler with a claim to the title "enlightened despot" was Catherine, empress of Russia (r. 1762–1796).

Catherine the Great Catherine was a German princess who had been brought to Russia to marry another German, Peter of Holstein-Gottorp, who was being groomed as heir to the Russian throne. Russia had crowned several monarchs of mixed Russian and German parentage since the time of Peter the Great's deliberate interest in and ties with other European states. *(The Wernher Collection)*

Catherine the Great, as she came to be called, was the true heir of Peter the Great in her abilities, policies, and ambitions. Her determination and political acumen were obvious early in her life at the Russian court, where she had been brought from her native Germany in 1745. Brutally treated by her husband, Tsar Peter III, Catherine engineered a coup in which he was killed, then ruled alone for more than thirty years.

Like any successful ruler of her age, Catherine counted territorial aggrandizement among her chief achievements. With regard to the major European powers, Russia tended to ally with Britain (with which it had important trading connections, including the provi-

Map 10.1   The Partition of Poland and the Expansion of Russia   Catherine the Great acquired present-day Lithuania, Belarus, and Ukraine, which had once constituted the duchy of Lithuania, part of the multi-ethnic Polish kingdom.

sion of timber for British shipbuilding) and with Austria (against their common nemesis, Turkey), and against France, Poland, and Prussia. In 1768 Catherine initiated a war against the Turks from which Russia gained much of the Crimean coast. She also continued Peter's efforts to dominate the weakened Poland. She was aided in this goal by Frederick the Great, who proposed the deliberate partitioning of Poland to satisfy his own territorial ambitions as well as those of his competitors, Russia and Austria. In 1772 portions of Poland were gobbled up in the first of three successive "grabs" of territory (see Map

18.1). Warsaw eventually landed in Prussian hands, but Catherine gained all of Belarus, Ukraine, and modern Lithuania—which had constituted the duchy of Lithuania.

Nevertheless, Catherine counted herself a sincere follower of the Enlightenment. While young, she had received an education that bore the strong stamp of the Enlightenment. Like Frederick, she attempted to take an active role in the European intellectual community, corresponding with Voltaire over the course of many years and acting as patron to the encyclopedist Diderot. One of Catherine's boldest political moves was the secularization of church lands. Although Peter the Great had extended government control of the Russian Orthodox Church, he had not touched church lands. Catherine also licensed private publishing houses and permitted a burgeoning periodical press. The number of books published in Russia tripled during her reign. This enriched cultural life was one of the principal causes of the flowering of Russian literature that began in the early nineteenth century.

The stamp of the Enlightenment on Catherine's policies is also clearly visible in her attempts at legal reform. In 1767 she convened a legislative commission and provided it with a guiding document, the *Instruction,* which she had penned. The commission was remarkable because it included representatives of all classes, including peasants, and provided a place for the airing of general grievances. Catherine hoped for a general codification of law as well as reforms such as the abolition of torture and capital punishment—reforms that made the *Instruction* radical enough to be banned from publication in other countries. She did not propose changing the legal status of serfs, however, and class differences made the commission unworkable in the end. Most legal reforms were accomplished piecemeal and favored the interests of landed gentry.

Like the Austrian rulers, Catherine undertook far-reaching administrative reform to create more effective local units of government. Here again, political imperatives were fundamental, and reforms in local government strengthened the hand of the gentry. The legal subjection of peasants in serfdom was also extended as a matter of state policy to help win the allegiance of landholders in newly acquired areas—such as Ukrainian territory gained in the partition of Poland. Gentry in general and court favorites in particular, on whom the stability of her government depended, were rewarded with estates and serfs to work them.

In Russia, as in Prussia and Austria, oppression of the peasantry was perpetuated because the monarch wanted to ensure the allegiance of the elites who lived from the peasants' labor. Catherine particularly valued the cooperation of elites because the Russian state was in a formative stage in another sense as well. It was trying to incorporate new peoples, such as the Tatars in the Crimea, and to manage its relationships with border peoples such as the Cossacks. Catherine's reign was marked by one of the most massive and best-organized peasant rebellions of the century. Occurring in 1773, the rebellion expressed the grievances of the thousands of peasants who joined its ranks and called for the abolition of serfdom. The revolt took its name, however, from

its Cossack leader, Emelian Pugachev° (d. 1775), and reflected the dissatisfaction with the Russian government of this semi-autonomous people.

The dramatic dilemmas faced by Catherine illustrate both the promise and the costs of state formation throughout Europe. State consolidation permitted the imposition of internal peace, coordinated economic policy, and reform of justice, but it came at the price of greater—in some cases much greater—control and coercion of the population. Thus we can see from the alternative perspective of Russia the importance of the political sphere that was opening up in France and was being consolidated in England. It was in that environment, rather than in Russia, that the Enlightenment philosophy could find its most fertile ground.

THE WIDENING SCOPE OF COMMERCE AND WARFARE

IN the eighteenth century a new constellation of states emerged to dominate politics in Europe. Alongside the traditional powers of England, France, and Austria were Prussia in central Europe and Russia to the east (see Map 18.1); these five states would dominate European politics until the twentieth century. Certain characteristics common to all these states account for their dominance. None is more crucial than their various abilities to field effective armies. In the eighteenth century most wars were launched to satisfy traditional territorial ambitions. Now, however, the increasing significance of overseas trade and colonization also made international expansion an important source of conflict, particularly between England and France. As warfare widened in scope, governments increasingly focused on recruiting and maintaining large navies and armies, with increasingly devastating effects on ordinary people.

A Century of Warfare: Circumstances and Rationales

The large and small states of Europe continued to make war on one another for both strategic and dynastic reasons. States fought over territory that had obvious economic and strategic value. War over the Baltic coastline,

---

Pugachev (poo-guh-CHOFF)

for example, absorbed Sweden and Russia early in the century. Dynastic claims, however, were still major causes of war. Indeed, the fundamental instability caused by hereditary rule accounts for many of the major wars of the eighteenth century. The century opened with the War of the Spanish Succession, and later the succession of the Austrian Habsburgs provoked a continent-wide war. Often these conflicts were carried out in arbitrary ways that reflected a dynastic, rather than wholly strategic, view of territory. Although rational and defensible "national" borders were important, collecting isolated bits of territory was also still the norm. The wars between European powers thus became extremely complex strategically. France, for example, might choose to strike a blow against Austria by invading an Italian state in order to use the conquered Italian territory as a bargaining chip in eventual negotiations. Wars were preceded and carried out with complex systems of alliances and were followed by the adjustments of many borders and the changing control of small, scattered territories. Rulers of lesser states in Germany and Italy, particularly, remained important as allies and as potential rivals of the Great Powers. The rise of Prussia, after all, had demonstrated the benefits of zealous ambition.

The state of military technology, tactics, and organization shaped the outcomes of conflicts as well as the character of the leading states themselves. In the eighteenth century weapons and tactics became increasingly refined. More reliable muskets were introduced. A bayonet that could slip over a musket barrel without blocking the muzzle was invented. Coordinated use of bayonets required even more careful drill of troops than did volley fire alone to ensure disciplined action in the face of enemy fire and charges. Artillery and cavalry forces also were subjected to greater standardization of training and discipline in action. Increased discipline of forces meant that commanders could exercise meaningful control over a battle for the first time. But such battles were not necessarily decisive, especially when waged against a comparable force. Indeed, training now was so costly that commanders were at times ironically reluctant to hazard their fine troops in battle at all.

One sure result of the new equipment and tactics was that war became a more expensive proposition than ever before and an ever greater burden on a state's resources and administration. It became increasingly difficult for small states, such as Sweden, to compete with the forces that others could mount. Small and relatively poor states, such as Prussia, that were able to support large forces did so by means of an extraordinary bending of civil society to the economic and social needs of the

army. In Prussia twice as many people were in the armed forces, proportionally, as in other states, and a staggering 80 percent of its meager state revenue went to sustain the army.

Most states introduced some form of conscription in the eighteenth century. In all regions, the very poor often volunteered for army service to improve their lives. However, conscription of peasants, throughout Europe but particularly in Prussia and Russia, imposed a significant burden on peasant communities and a sacrifice of productive members to the state. Governments everywhere supplemented volunteers and conscripts with mercenaries and even criminals, as necessary, to fill the ranks without tapping the wealthier elements of the community. Thus common soldiers were increasingly seen not as members of society but as its rejects. Said Frederick II, "useful hardworking people should [not be conscripted but rather] be guarded as the apple of one's eye," and a French war minister agreed that armies had to consist of the "scum of people and of all those for whom society has no use."[2] Brutality became an accepted tool for governments to use to manage such groups of men. From the eighteenth century on, the army increasingly became an instrument of social control used to contain and make use of individuals who otherwise might disrupt their own communities.

The costs of maintaining these forces had other outcomes as well. Wars could still be won or lost not on the battlefield but on the supply line. Incentive still existed to bleed civilian populations and exploit the countryside. Moreover, when supply lines were disrupted and soldiers not equipped or fed, the armies of a major power could be vulnerable to smaller, less disciplined armies of minor states. Finally, even supplies, training, and sophisticated tactics could not guarantee success. Not until 1746, at Culloden, could the British army decisively defeat the fierce charge and hand-to-hand fighting of Highland clansmen by holding its position and using disciplined volley fire and bayonet tactics. Warfare became increasingly professional but was still an uncertain business with unpredictable results, despite its staggering cost.

The Power of Austria and Prussia

Major wars during the mid-eighteenth century decided the balance of power in German-speaking Europe for the next hundred years. Prussia emerged as the equal of Austria in the region. The first of these wars, now known as the War of the Austrian Succession, began shortly after the death of the emperor Charles VI in 1740. Charles died without a male heir, and his daughter, Maria Theresa, succeeded him. Charles VI had worked to shore up his daughter's position as his heir (versus other female relatives who also had claims) by means of an act called the Pragmatic Sanction, which he had painstakingly persuaded allies and potential opponents to accept. When Charles VI died, rival heiresses and their husbands challenged Maria Theresa for control of her various lands. They were supported by France, the Habsburgs' perennial rival.

The Austrian lands were threatened with dismemberment. Indeed, Charles had negotiated away the wealthy Bohemian province of Silesia°, promising it to Prussia in return for acceptance of his heir (see Map 18.1), and had not left his armies or his treasury well equipped to fight a war to defend it. When Frederick the Great's troops marched into Silesia in 1740, Maria Theresa's rivals saw their chance and invaded other Habsburg territories.

Maria Theresa proved a more tenacious opponent than anyone had anticipated, and she was helped by Great Britain, which saw the possibility of gains against its colonial rival, France. Fighting eventually spread throughout Habsburg territories, including the Netherlands and in Italy, as well as abroad to British and French colonies. In a preliminary peace signed in 1745, Frederick the Great was confirmed in possession of Silesia, but the throne of the Holy Roman Empire was returned to the Habsburgs—given to Maria Theresa's husband, Francis (Franz) I (r. 1745–1765). A final treaty in 1748 ended all the fighting that had continued since 1745, mostly by France and Britain overseas. The Austrian state had survived dismemberment, but Maria Theresa now embarked on the administrative and military reforms necessary to make her state less vulnerable in the future. Prussia, because of the annexation of Silesia and the psychological imprint of victory, emerged as a power of virtually equal rank to the Habsburgs.

The unprecedented threat that Austria now felt from Prussia led to a revolution in alliances across Europe. To isolate Prussia, Maria Theresa agreed to an alliance with France, the Habsburgs' long-standing enemy. Sweden and Russia, with territory to gain at Prussia's expense, joined as well.

Frederick the Great initiated what came to be known as the Seven Years' War in 1756, hoping to prevent consolidation of the new alliances. Instead, he found that he had started a war against overwhelming odds. What saved him in part was limited English aid. The English,

engaged with France in the overseas conflict that Americans call the French and Indian War, wanted France to be heavily committed on the Continent. Prussia managed to emerge intact—though strained economically and demographically. Prussia and Austria were confirmed as the two states of European rank in German-speaking Europe. Their rivalry would dominate German history until the late nineteenth century. Austria's and Prussia's narrow escapes from being reduced to second-class status reveal how fragile even successful states could be; Prussia's emergence as a major power was by no means assured.

The Atlantic World: Expanding Commerce and the Slave Trade

The importance of international trade and colonial possessions to the states of western Europe grew enormously in the eighteenth century (see Map 18.2). Between 1715 and 1785 Britain's trade with North America rose from 19 to 34 percent of its total trade, and its trade with Asia and Africa rose from 7 to 19 percent of the total. By the end of the century more than half of all British trade was carried on outside Europe; for France the figure was more than a third.

European commercial and colonial energies were concentrated in the Atlantic world in the eighteenth century because the profits were greatest there. The population of British North America grew from about 250,000 in 1700 to about 1.7 million by 1760. The densely settled New England colonies provided a market for manufactured goods from the mother country, although they produced little by way of raw materials or bulk goods on which traders could make a profit. The colonies of Maryland and Virginia produced tobacco, the Carolinas rice and indigo (a dyestuff). England re-exported all three throughout Europe at considerable profit.

The French in New France, only 56,000 in 1740, were vastly outnumbered by British colonists. Nevertheless, the French had successfully expanded their control of territory in Canada. Settlements sprang up between the outposts of Montreal and Quebec on the St. Lawrence River. Despite resistance, the French extended their fur trapping—the source of most of the profits New France generated—west and north along the Great Lakes, con-

Map 18.2 The Atlantic Economy, ca. 1750   The triangle trade linked Europe, Africa, and European colonies in the Americas. The most important component of this trade for Europe was the plantation agriculture of the Caribbean islands, which depended on enslaved Africans for labor.

Silesia (sigh-LEE-zhee-uh)

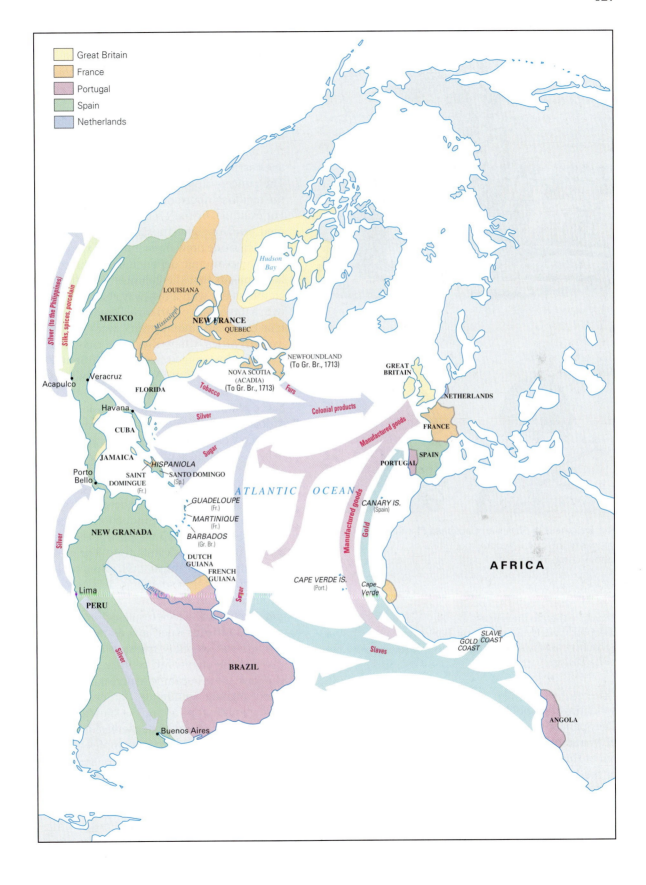

Great Britain
France
Portugal
Spain
Netherlands

Silver (to the Philippines)
Silks, spices, porcelain

LOUISIANA

Hudson Bay

MEXICO

NEW FRANCE
QUEBEC

NEWFOUNDLAND
(To Gr. Br., 1713)

NOVA SCOTIA
(ACADIA)
(To Gr. Br., 1713)

GREAT
BRITAIN

NETHERLANDS

Veracruz

Acapulco

FLORIDA

Tobacco

Furs

FRANCE

Havana

Silver

Colonial products

Manufactured goods

SPAIN

PORTUGAL

CUBA

Sugar

JAMAICA

Porto Bello

SAINT
DOMINGUE
(Fr.)

HISPANIOLA
SANTO DOMINGO
(Sp.)

ATLANTIC OCEAN

GUADELOUPE
(Fr.)

CANARY IS.
(Spain)

AFRICA

MARTINIQUE
(Fr.)

Silver

NEW GRANADA

BARBADOS
(Gr. Br.)

DUTCH
GUIANA

Manufactured goods

Gold

FRENCH
GUIANA

Lima

PERU

Amazon

Sugar

CAPE VERDE IS.
(Port.)

Cape
Verde

Silver

Slaves

GOLD
COAST

SLAVE
COAST

BRAZIL

ANGOLA

Buenos Aires

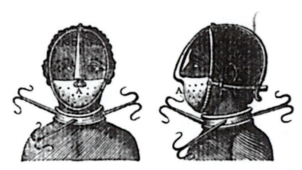

The Treatment of Slaves on Carribean Plantations   These images of the brutal treatment of slaves on West Indian plantations come from a report published in England designed to convince the British public of the horrors of slavery. At top, a husband and wife are violently separated after being sold to different slaveowners. At bottom, a mouthpiece and neck guard are used to prevent escape. The treatment of slaves described here is also documented in other surviving accounts from the eighteenth century.   *(New York Public Library/ Art Resource, NY)*

The commercial importance of these North American holdings, as well as those in Asia, was dwarfed by the European states' Caribbean possessions, however. The British held Jamaica, Barbados, and the Leeward Islands; the French, Guadeloupe and Martinique; the Spanish, Cuba and Santo Domingo; and the Dutch, a few small islands. Sugar produced on plantations by slave labor was the major source of profits, along with other cash crops such as coffee, indigo, and cochineal (another dyestuff). The concentration of shipping to this region indicates the region's importance in the European trading system. For example, by the 1760s the British China trade occupied seven or eight ships. In the 1730s British trade with Jamaica alone drew three hundred ships.

The economic dependence of the colonies on slave labor meant that the colonies were tied to their home countries not with a two-way commercial exchange but with a three-way, or "triangle," trade (see Map 18.2). Certain European manufactures were shipped to ports in western Africa, where they were traded for slaves. Captive Africans were transported to South America, the Caribbean, or North America, where planters bought and paid for them with profits from their sugar and tobacco plantations. (See the box "Global Encounters: An African Recalls the Horrors of the Slave Ship.") Sugar and tobacco were then shipped back to the mother country to be re-exported at great profit throughout Europe.

This plantation economy in the Caribbean was vulnerable to slave revolts, as well as to competition among the Europeans. Often wars over control of the islands significantly disrupted production and lessened profits for the European planters on the islands and for their trading partners back in Europe. The growing demands by Europeans for sugar and other products kept the plantation system expanding, despite these challenges, throughout the eighteenth century. The slave trade grew dramatically as a result. Approximately five times as many Africans—perhaps as many as seven million people—were forcibly transported to the Americas as slaves in the eighteenth century as in the seventeenth. The slave trade became an increasingly specialized form of oceangoing commerce (for example, slave traders throughout Europe adopted a standardized ship design) and, at the same time, one increasingly linked to the rest of European commerce by complex trade and financial ties. In England, London merchants who imported Asian goods, exported European manufactures, or distributed Caribbean sugar could provide credit for slave traders based in the northern city of Liverpool to fund their journeys to Africa and then the Americas.

solidating their hold by building forts at strategic points. They penetrated as far as the modern Canadian province of Manitoba, where they cut into the British trade run out of Hudson Bay. The French also contested the mouth of the St. Lawrence River and the Gulf of St. Lawrence with the British. The British held Nova Scotia and Newfoundland, the French controlled parts of Cape Breton Island, and both states fished the surrounding waters.

An African Recalls the Horrors of the Slave Ship

Olaudah Equiano (ca. 1750–1797) was an Ibo from the Niger region of West Africa. He first experienced slavery as a boy when kidnapped from his village by other Africans, but nothing prepared him for the brutality of the Europeans who bought and shipped him to Barbados, in the British West Indies. His narration of the horrors of the "Middle Passage" between Africa and the Americas may represent a composite story of others' experiences as well as his own. Nevertheless, his account remains one of the few written records by an African survivor of a slave ship.

The first object which saluted my eyes when I arrived on the [African] coast was the sea and a slave ship, which was then riding at anchor, and waiting for its cargo. . . . When I was carried on board I was immediately handled, and tossed up, to see if I were sound, by some of the crew. . . . When I looked around the ship . . . and saw . . . a multitude of black people of every description chained together, every one of their countenances expressing dejection and sorrow, I no longer doubted of my fate. . . .

I was not long suffered to indulge my grief; I was soon put down under the decks, and there I received such a salutation in the nostrils as I had never experienced in my life; so that with the loathsomeness of the stench . . . I became so sick and low that I was not able to eat. . . . I now wished for the last friend, death, to relieve me; but soon, to my grief, two of the white men offered me eatables; and, on my refusing to eat, one of them held me fast by the hands and laid me across, I think, the windlass, and tied my feet while the other flogged me severely.

One day, when we had a smooth sea and a moderate wind, two of my wearied countrymen, who were chained together . . . , preferring death to such a life of misery, somehow made through the nettings and jumped into the sea; immediately another dejected fellow who [was ill and so not in irons] followed their example; and I believe many more would very soon have done the same, if they had not been prevented by the ship's crew who were instantly alarmed. Those of us that were the most active were in a minute put down under the deck; and there was such a noise and confusion amongst the people of the ship as I have never heard before, to stop her, and get the boat to go after the slaves. However, two of the wretches were drowned, but they got the other and afterwards flogged him unmercifully for thus attempting to prefer death to slavery. In this manner we continued to undergo more hardships than I can now relate; hardships which are inseparable from this accursed trade.

QUESTIONS

1. What particular horrors of the Middle Passage seem to stand out in Equiano's mind? What is the significance of these vignettes?

2. What clues in this excerpt reveal the audience Equiano had in mind for his narrative?

SOURCE: *The Interesting Narrative of the Life of Olaudah Equiano, or Gustavus Vassa, the African* (London, 1793); reprinted in David Northrup, ed., *The Atlantic Slave Trade* (Boston: Houghton Mifflin, 2002), pp. 68–70.

Great Britain and France: Wars Overseas

The proximity and growth of French and British settlements in North America ensured conflict (see Map 18.3). The Caribbean and the coasts of Central and South America were strategic flashpoints as well. At the beginning of the eighteenth century, several substantial islands remained unclaimed by any power. The British were making incursions along the coastline claimed by Spain and were trying to break into the monopoly of trade between Spain and its vast possessions in the region. Public opinion in both Britain and France became increasingly sensitive to colonial issues. For the first time, tensions abroad fueled major conflicts between two European states.

During this century England became the dominant naval power in Europe. Its navy protected its far-flung trading networks, its merchant fleet, and the coast of England itself. England's strategic interests on the Continent lay in promoting a variety of powers there, none of which (or no combination of which) posed too great a threat to England or to its widespread trading system. A second, dynastic consideration in continental affairs was the electorate of Hanover, the large principality in western Germany that was the native territory of the

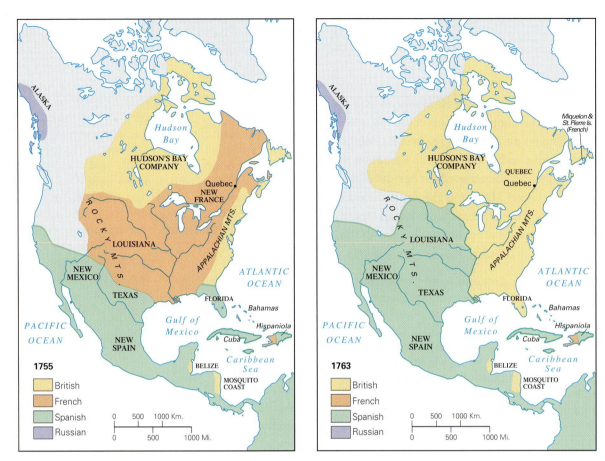

Map 18.3   British Gains in North America   The British colonies on the Atlantic coast were effective staging posts for the armies that ousted the French from North America by 1763. However, taxes imposed on the colonies to pay the costs of the Seven Years' War helped spark revolt—the American Revolution—a decade later.

Hanoverian kings of England. Early in the century especially, the interests of this German territory were a significant factor in British foreign policy. Unable to field a large army, given their maritime interests, the British sought protection for Hanover in alliances and subsidies for allies' armies on the Continent and paid for these ventures with the profits on trade.

After the death of Louis XIV in 1715, England's energies centered on colonial rivalries with France, its greatest competitor overseas. Conflict between England and France in colonial regions played out in three major phases. The first two were concurrent with the major land wars in Europe: the War of the Austrian Succession (1740–1748) and the Seven Years' War (1756–1763). The third phase coincided with the rebellion of British colonies in North America—the American Revolution—beginning in the 1770s. France was inevitably more

committed to affairs on the Continent than were the British. The French were able to hold their own successfully in both arenas during the 1740s, but by 1763, though pre-eminent on the Continent, they had lost many of their colonial possessions to the English.

In the 1740s France was heavily involved in the War of the Austrian Succession, while Britain vied with Spain for certain Caribbean territories. Both France and England also tested each other's strength in scattered colonial fighting, which produced a few well-balanced gains and losses. Their conquests were traded back when peace was made in 1748.

Tension was renewed almost immediately at many of the strategic points in North America. French and British naval forces harassed each other's shipping in the Gulf of St. Lawrence. The French reinforced their encirclement of British colonies with more forts along the

The Death of General Wolfe at Quebec   General Wolfe commanded British troops that in 1759 defeated the French at Quebec in Canada. Wolfe's death at the battle was memorialized ten years later by American-born artist Benjamin West. This image became widely popular after West sold cheap engraved versions. Notice West's sympathetic treatment of the Native American earnestly focused, like his British allies, on the death of the commander.   *(National Gallery of Canada, Ottawa, Transfer from the Canadian War Memorials)*

Great Lakes and the Ohio River. When British troops (at one point led by the colonial commander George Washington) attempted to strike at these forts beginning in 1754, open fighting between the French and the English began.

In India, meanwhile, both the French and the British attempted to strengthen their commercial footholds by making military and political alliances with local Indian rulers. The disintegration of the Mogul Empire heightened competition among regional Indian rulers and sparked a new level of ambition on the part of the European powers with interests in Asia. A British attack on a French convoy provoked a declaration of war by France in May 1756, three months before fighting in the Seven Years' War broke out in Europe. For the first time, a major war between European nations had started and would be fought in their empires, signifying a profound change in the relation of these nations to the world.

The French had already committed themselves to an alliance with Austria and were increasingly involved on the Continent after Frederick II initiated war there in August 1756. Slowly, the drain of sustaining war both on the Continent and abroad began to tell, and Britain scored major victories against French forces after an initial period of balanced successes and failures. The French lost a number of fortresses on the Mississippi and Ohio Rivers and on the Great Lakes, and then they also lost the interior of Canada with the fall of Quebec and of Montreal in 1759 and 1760, respectively (see Map 18.3).

In the Caribbean, the British seized Guadeloupe, a vital sugar-producing island. Superior resources in India enabled the British to take several French outposts there, including Pondicherry°, the most important. The cost of involvement on so many fronts meant that French troops were short of money and supplies. They were particularly vulnerable to both supply and personnel shortages—especially in North America—because they were weaker than the British at sea and because New France remained sparsely settled and dependent on the mother country for food.

By the terms of the Peace of Paris in 1763, France regained Guadeloupe, the most profitable of its American colonies, although Britain gained control of several smaller, previously neutral Caribbean islands to add to its own sugar-producing colonies of Jamaica and Barbados. In India, France retained many of its trading stations but lost its political and military clout. British power in India was dramatically enhanced not only by French losses but also by victories over Indian rulers who had allied with the French. In the interior, Britain now controlled lands that had never before been under the control of any European power. British political rule in India, as opposed to merely a mercantile presence, began at this time. The British also held Canada. They emerged from the Seven Years' War as the pre-eminent world power among European states. The dramatic gains led some Britons to speak of the "British Empire" overseas.

ECONOMIC EXPANSION AND SOCIAL CHANGE

THE eighteenth century was an era of dramatic change, although that change was not always apparent to those who lived through it. The intellectual and cultural ferment of the Enlightenment laid the groundwork for domestic political changes to come, just as British victories in the Seven Years' War shifted the balance of power abroad. More subtle and potentially more profound changes were occurring in the European countryside, however. Population, production, and consumption were beginning to grow beyond the bounds

---

Pondicherry (pon-dih-CHAIR-ee)

that all preceding generations had lived within and taken for granted.

More Food and More People

Throughout European history, a delicate balance had existed between available food and numbers of people to feed. Population growth had accompanied increases in the amount of land under cultivation. From time to time, however, population growth surpassed the ability of the land to produce food, and people became malnourished and prey to disease. In 1348 the epidemic outbreak of the plague known as the Black Death struck just such a vulnerable population in decline.

Europeans had few options for increasing the productivity of the land. Peasants safeguarded its fertility by alternately cultivating some portions while letting others lie fallow or using them as pasture. Manure provided fertilizer, but during the winter months livestock could not be kept alive in large numbers. Limited food for livestock meant limited fertilizer, which in turn meant limited production of food for both humans and animals.

After a devastating decline in the fourteenth century, the European population experienced a prolonged recovery, and in the eighteenth century the balance that had previously been reached began to be exceeded for the first time. Infant mortality remained as high as ever. No less privileged a person than Queen Anne of England outlived every one of the seventeen children she bore, and all but one of them died in infancy. But population growth occurred because of a decline in the death rate for adults and a simultaneous increase in the birthrate in some areas owing to earlier marriages.

Adults began to live longer partly because of a decline in the incidence of plague. However, the primary reason adults were living longer, despite the presence of various epidemic diseases, was that they were better nourished and thus better able to resist disease. More and different kinds of food began to be produced. The increase in the food supply also meant that more new families could be started.

Food production increased because of the introduction of new crops and other changes in agricultural practices. The cumulative effect of these changes was so dramatic that historians have called them an "agricultural revolution." The new crops included fodder, such as clover, legumes, and turnips, which did not deplete the soil and could be fed to livestock over the winter. The greater availability of animal manure in turn boosted grain production. In addition, the potato, introduced from the Americas in the sixteenth century, is nutrient-

Gérard Dou: The Vegetable Seller
The specialization of agriculture meant that a more varied diet was available to increasing numbers of Europeans. *(Musée des Beaux-Arts, Nimes/Giraudon/Art Resource, NY)*

dense and can feed more people per acre than can grain. In certain areas, farming families produced potatoes to feed themselves while they grew grain to be sold and shipped elsewhere.

More food being produced meant more food available for purchase. The opportunity to buy food freed up land and labor. A family that could purchase food might decide to convert its farm to specialized use, such as raising dairy cattle. In such a case, many families might be supported by a piece of land that had previously supported only one. Over a generation or two, a number of children might share the inheritance of what had previously been a single farm, yet each could make a living from his or her share, and population could grow as it had not done before.

Farmers had known about and experimented with many of the crops used for fodder for centuries. However, the widespread planting of these crops, as well as other changes, was long in coming and happened in scattered areas. A farmer had to have control over land in order to implement change. In the traditional open-field system, peasants had split up all the land in each community so that each family might have a piece of each field. Making effective changes was hard when an entire community had to act together. Most important, changing agriculture required capital for seed and fertilizer and for the greater number of people and animals needed to cultivate the new crops. Only prosperous farmers had spare capital. Few were inclined to take risks with the production of food and to trust the workings of the market. The bad condition of roads was reason enough not to rely on distant markets.

Yet where both decent roads and growing urban markets existed, some farmers—even entire villages working together—were willing to produce for urban populations. Capital cities, such as London and Amsterdam, and trading centers, such as Glasgow and Bordeaux, were booming. These growing cities demanded not only grain but also specialized produce such as dairy products and fruits and vegetables. Thus farmers had an incentive to make changes. Urbanization and improved transportation networks also encouraged agriculture because human waste produced by city dwellers—known as "night soil"—could be collected and distributed in the surrounding agricultural regions as fertilizer. By the late eighteenth century, pockets of intensive, diversified agriculture existed in England, northern France, the Rhineland in Germany, the Po Valley in Italy, and Catalonia in Spain.

In some areas, changes in agriculture were accompanied by a shift in power in the countryside. Wealthy landlords began to invest in change in order to reap the profits of producing for the new markets. Where the traditional authority of the village to regulate agriculture was weak, peasants were vulnerable. In England a combination of weak village structure and the attraction of urban markets created a climate that encouraged landlords to treat land speculatively. To make their holdings more profitable, they raised the rents that farmers paid. They changed cultivation patterns on the land that they controlled directly. They appropriated the village common lands, a process known as "enclosure," and used them for cash crops such as sheep (raised for their wool) or beef cattle. Among other ramifications, the clans of Scotland completely disintegrated as meaningful social units as markets for beef, wool, and other Highland commodities drew chieftains' resources and turned what remained of their traditional clan relationships into exploitative commercial ones.

Thus, although the agricultural revolution increased the food supply to sustain more people in Europe generally, it did not create general prosperity. The growth of population did not mean that most people were better off. Indeed, many rural people were driven off the land or made destitute by the loss of the resources of common lands. Peasants in eastern Europe produced grain for export to the growing urban centers in western Europe, but usually by traditional methods. In both eastern and western Europe, the power and profits of landlords were a major force in structuring the rural economy.

The Growth of Industry

Agricultural changes fostered change in other areas of economic and social life. As more food was grown with less labor, that labor was freed to take on other productive work. If enough people could be kept employed making useful commodities, the nonagricultural population could continue to grow. If population grew, more and more consumers would be born, and the demand for more goods would help continue the cycle of population growth, changes in production, and economic expansion. This is precisely what happened in the eighteenth century. A combination of forces increased the numbers of people who worked at producing a few essential materials and products (see Map 18.4).

Especially significant was the expansion in the putting-out system. Also known as cottage industry, putting out involved the production in the countryside of thread and cloth by spinners and weavers working in their own homes for an entrepreneur who bought raw materials and "put them out" to be finished by individual workers. The putting-out system expanded in the eighteenth century as the agricultural economy was transformed. All agricultural work was seasonal, demanding intensive effort and many hands at certain times but not others. The labor demands of the new crops meant that an even larger number of people might periodically need work away from the fields to make ends meet. Rural poverty, whether as a result of traditional or new agricultural methods, made manufacturing work in the home attractive to more and more people.

Overseas trade also stimulated the expansion of production by spurring the demand in Europe's colonies for cloth and other finished products and increasing the demand at home for manufactured items, such as nails to build the ships that carried the trade. The production of cloth also expanded because heightened demand led to changes in the way cloth was made. Wool was increasingly combined with other fibers to make less expensive fabrics. By the end of the century, wholly cotton fabrics were being made cheaply in Europe from cotton grown in America by slave labor.

Steady innovation in textile production allowed woven goods to be aimed at broader markets. In the Middle Ages, weavers produced luxury-quality cloth, and their profits came not from demand, which was relatively low, but from the high price that affluent consumers paid. In the eighteenth century, cloth production became a spur to a transformed industrial economy because cheaper kinds of cloth were made for mass consumption. Pro-

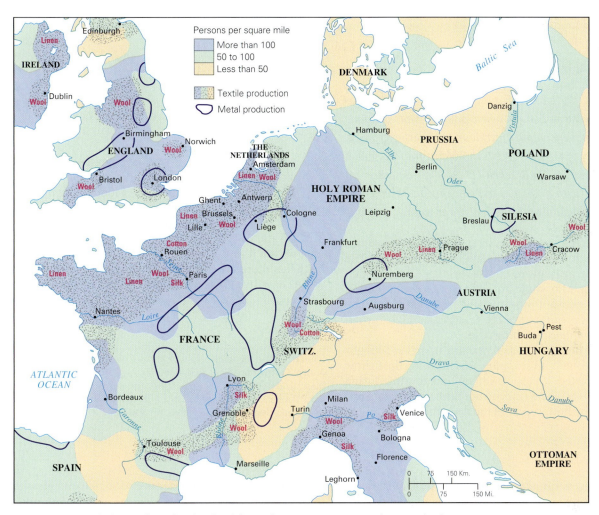

Map 18.4   Population and Production in Eighteenth-Century Europe   The growth of cottage industry helped to support a growing population. With changes in agriculture, more land-poor workers were available in the countryside to accept work as spinners, knitters, and weavers.

ducing in great quantities became important, and innovations that promoted productivity were welcomed.

A crucial innovation was increased mechanization. The invention of machines to spin thread in the late eighteenth century brought a marked increase in the rate of production. Machines likewise brought profound changes to the lives of rural workers who had been juggling agricultural and textile work according to season and need. The selected areas of England, France, and the Low Countries where the new technologies were introduced stood, by the end of the century, on the verge of a massive industrial transformation that would have unprecedented social consequences.

Control and Resistance

The economic changes of the century produced both resistance and adaptation by ordinary people and, at times, direct action by state authorities. (See the box "Reading Sources: A Peasant Protests Forced Labor.") Sometimes ordinary people coped in ways that revealed their desperation. In many cities numbers of abandoned children rose greatly because urban families, particularly recent immigrants from the countryside, could not support all their offspring. The major cities of Europe put increasing resources into police forces and city lighting schemes. Charitable institutions run by cities, churches,

READING SOURCES

A PEASANT PROTESTS FORCED LABOR

Generally, the condition of agricultural workers was worst in eastern Europe, where political and economic forces kept them bound in serfdom. In A Journey from St. Petersburg to Moscow *(1790), the reform-minded nobleman Alexander Radishchev (1749–1802) describes an encounter with a Russian serf who, like most serfs, was forced to work the lord's lands at the expense of his own.*

A few steps from the road I saw a peasant plowing a field. It was now Sunday, [about midday]. The ploughing peasant, of course, belonged to a landed proprietor, who would not let him pay a commutation tax. The peasant was plowing very carefully. The field . . . was not part of the master's land. He turned the plow with astonishing ease.

"God help you," I said, walking up to the ploughman, who, without stopping, was finishing the furrow he had started. . . . "Have you no time to work during the week, then, and can you not have any rest on Sundays, in the hottest part of the day, at that?"

"In a week, sir, there are six days, and we go six times a week to work on the master's field; in the evening, if the weather is good, we haul to the master's house the hay that is left in the woods. . . . God grant that it rains this evening. If you have peasants of your own, sir, they are praying for the same thing."

"But how do you manage to get food enough [for your family] if you have only the holidays free?"

"Not only the holidays, the nights are ours too."

"Do you work the same way for your master?"

"No, sir, it would be a sin to work the same way. On his fields there are a hundred hands for one mouth, while I have two for seven mouths: you can figure it out for yourself."

Source: Alexander Radishchev, *A Journey from St. Petersburg to Moscow,* trans. Leo Wiener, ed. Roderick Page Thaler (Cambridge, Mass.: Harvard University Press, 1958), quoted in Robert and Elborg Forster, eds., *European Society in the Eighteenth Century* (New York: Harper and Row, 1969), pp. 136–139.

and central governments expanded. By 1789, for example, there were more than two thousand *hôpitaux*°— poorhouses for the destitute and ill—in France. The poor received food and shelter but were forced to work for the city or to live in poorhouses against their will. Men were sometimes taken out of poorhouses and forced to become soldiers.

Resistance and adaptation were particularly visible wherever the needs of common people conflicted with the states' desire for order and revenue. This scenario was evident on the high seas, for example, in the crusade to suppress piracy. Piracy had been a way of life for hundreds of Europeans and colonial settlers since the sixteenth century. From the earliest days of exploration, European rulers had authorized men known as privateers to commit acts of war against specific targets. The Crown took little risk and was spared the cost of arming the ships but shared in the plunder. True piracy— outright robbery on the high seas—was illegal, but in practice the difference between piracy and privateering

was negligible. As governments and merchants grew to prefer regular trade over the irregular profits of plunder, and as national navies developed in the late seventeenth century, a concerted effort to eliminate piracy began.

Life on the seas became an increasingly vital part of western European economic life in the eighteenth century. English-speaking seamen alone numbered about thirty thousand around the middle of the century. Sea life began to resemble life on land in the amount of compulsion it entailed. Sailors in port were always vulnerable to forcible enlistment in the navy by impressment gangs, particularly during wartime. A drowsy sailor sleeping off a rowdy night in port could wake up to find himself aboard a navy ship. Press gangs operated throughout England and not just in major ports, for authorities were as interested in controlling "vagrancy" as in staffing the navy. Merchant captains occasionally filled their crews by such means, particularly when sailing unpopular routes.

Like soldiers in the growing eighteenth-century armies, sailors in the merchant marine as well as the navy could be subjected to brutal discipline and appalling conditions. Merchant seamen attempted to improve their lot by trying

hôpitaux (oh-pee-TOE)

An Idle Apprentice Is Sent to Sea, 1747   In one of a series of moralizing engravings by William Hogarth, the lazy apprentice, Tom, is sent away to a life at sea. The experienced seamen in the boat introduce him to some of its terrors: on the left one dangles a cat-o'nine-tails—the instrument used for flogging—and on the distant promontory is a gallows, where pirates and mutineers meet their fate.   *(From the Collections of Lauinger Library, Georgetown University)*

to regulate their relationship with ships' captains. Contracts for pay on merchant ships became more regularized, and seamen often negotiated their terms very carefully, including, for example, details about how rations were to be allotted. Sailors might even take bold collective action aboard ship. The modern term for a work stoppage, *strike*, comes from the sailing expression "to strike sail," meaning to loosen the sails so that they cannot fill with wind. Its use dates from the eighteenth century, from "strikes" of sailors protesting unfair shipboard conditions.

Seafaring men were an unusually large and somewhat self-conscious community of wage workers. Not until industrialization came into full swing a century later would a similar group of workers exist within Eu-

rope itself (see Chapter 21). But economic and political protests by ordinary people on the Continent also showed interesting parallel changes. Peasant revolts in the past had ranged from small-scale actions against local tax collectors to massive uprisings that only an army could suppress. The immediate goals of the rebels were usually practical. For example, they aimed not to eliminate taxation altogether but perhaps to protest the collection of a particularly burdensome tax. The political rationale behind such actions was not a hope that the system would disappear but rather a hope that it would operate more fairly, as it presumably had in the past.

(continued on page 640)

Gardens

What is a garden? We first think of intensely cultivated flower gardens, such as the famous Rose Garden at the White House. We usually don't think of the yards around houses as gardens, yet that is what they are. The landscaping around most ordinary American homes derives from English landscape gardening of the eighteenth century and after—a fact that is reflected in the British custom of calling the "yards" around their homes "gardens." Like most of the art forms that we see habitually, the garden, reproduced in the American backyard, is difficult to analyze or even to think of as an art form. Like the buildings they surround, however, gardens have much to tell us about human habits and values. Let us examine their eighteenth-century ancestors for evidence of contemporaries' attitudes toward nature and their relationship with it.

Look at the two English-style gardens illustrated here. The first is next to the Governor's Mansion in Williamsburg, the capital of the English colony of Virginia. Construction of this garden began at the end of the seventeenth century; the photograph shows the restored gardens that tourists may visit today. The second garden, from the private estate of West Wycombe in England, looks very different—much more like a natural landscape. The engraving reproduced here dates from the 1770s. The two gardens represent distinct epochs in the development of the garden, hence the differences between them. However, each of these gardens in its own way celebrates human domination of nature.

This symbolic domination of nature is more obvious to us in the Williamsburg garden. The lawns and hedges are trimmed in precise geometrical shapes and are laid out, with the walkways, in straight lines. This "palace garden" was a small English variant of the classical garden developed in France—most spectacularly at the Versailles Palace—and then imitated throughout Europe during the seventeenth century. The garden at Versailles is so vast that at many points, all of nature visible to the eye is nature disciplined by humans.

We can think of such gardens as pieces of architecture, because that is how they were originally conceived. The design originated in the enclosed courtyard gardens of the homes of classical antiquity. The straight lines and square shapes of these gardens mimic the buildings they are attached to. In fact, these seventeenth- and eighteenth-century gardens were usually laid out as an extension of the buildings themselves. Notice the wide staircase that descends from the central axis of the Governor's Mansion into the central walkway of the garden. Other architectural details, such as the benches positioned at the ends of various walkways, add to the sense of the garden as an exterior room. Elsewhere, this sense was enhanced by the construction of devices such as grottoes, such as that at Versailles. The garden symbolizes the taming of nature into a pleasing vision of order and regularity.

The later eighteenth-century garden represents even greater confidence in the human relationship with nature, although it does not appear to do so at first glance. The extensive garden at first seems to be nature itself plus a few added details, such as the statuary, and a few improvements, such as the grass kept trim by the workers in the foreground. Our familiarity with such landscapes—in our own suburban yards—keeps us from immediately perceiving how contrived such a landscape is. Nature, however, does not intersperse dense stands of trees or clumps of shrubbery with green expanses of lawns. Nor does nature conveniently leave portions of a hillside bare of trees to provide a view of the water from a palatial house on the hill. Note also that the waterfall cascading over rocks and statuary flows from an artificial lake, neatly bordered by a path.

This kind of garden reflects Enlightenment optimism about humans' ability to understand and work with nature. Such gardens were asymmetrical: Paths were usually curved, and lakes and ponds were irregularly shaped, as they would be in nature. Trees and shrubs were allowed to maintain their natural form. Nevertheless, this landscaping conveys a powerful message of order. Humans cannot bend or distort nature to their own ends, but they can live in harmony with it as they manage it and enjoy its beneficence. People were freed from regarding nature as hostile and needing to be fought. In this garden, one lives with nature but improves on it. The workers cutting the grass do not detract from the engraving but rather make the scene more compelling.

This brand of landscape gardening appeared in the English colonies across the Atlantic by the end of the eighteenth century. One of the best examples is at Monticello, Thomas Jefferson's Virginia estate, first designed in the 1770s and constructed and improved over the remainder of Jefferson's life (1743–1826). If you tour Monticello, you will notice a curving garden path bordered by

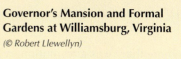

Governor's Mansion and Formal Gardens at Williamsburg, Virginia
(© Robert Llewellyn)

Landscape Garden at West Wycombe, England
(Courtesy of the Trustees of the British Museum)

flowers in season, with mature trees scattered here and there. Jefferson planned every inch of this largely random-looking outdoor space, just as he planned the regimented fruit and vegetable garden that borders it. The older, classical style of the Williamsburg garden is partly explained by its earlier date and also because this more aggressively controlling style lasted longer in the American colonies than in Europe, perhaps because "nature" seemed more wild and more formidable in the New World. You might wish to consider the curious blend of "nature" and order that is evident in the landscapes we create and live with today.

639

Where there was a revolutionary vision, it was usually a utopian one—a political system with no kings, landlords, taxes, or state of any kind.

Peasant revolts continued to follow those patterns in the eighteenth century. They were also driven by the localized unemployment caused by agricultural reforms or by objections to press gangs. In certain cases, however, peasants, like sailors, began to confront the state in new ways. Peasants often attacked not state power but the remnants of landlords' power, wielded over them in the shape of forced labor and compulsory use of landlords' mills. As weapons, they increasingly marshaled legal devices to maintain control over their land and to thwart landlords' efforts to enclose fields and cultivate cash crops. This change, though subtle, was important because it signaled an effort to bring permanent structural change to the system and was not simply a temporary redress of grievances. In part the trend toward "enlightened" revolt reflects increased access to information and the circulation of ideas about reform. A major peasant rebellion in 1775 in Austrian lands, for example, followed several years of bad harvests but specifically protested the delay in implementing changes—the subject of earnest debate among elites—in compulsory labor by peasants.

SUMMARY

T is important not to exaggerate the degree to which circumstances of life changed in the eighteenth century. The economy was expanding and the population growing beyond previous limits, and the system of production was being restructured. But these developments occurred incrementally over many decades and were not recognized for the fundamental changes they were.

Most of the long-familiar material constraints were still in place. Roads, on which much commerce depended, were generally impassable in bad weather. Shipping was relatively dependable and economical—but only relatively. Military life likewise reflected traditional constraints. Despite technological changes and developments of the administrative and economic resources of the state to equip, train, and enforce discipline, the conduct of war was still hampered by problems of transport and supply that would have been familiar to warriors two centuries before.

Similarly, though some rulers were inspired by precepts of the Enlightenment, all were guided by traditional concerns of dynastic aggrandizement and strategic advantage. One new dimension of relations between states was the importance of conflict over colonies abroad, but the full economic and strategic impact of British colonial gains would not be felt until the next century.

The most visible change would happen first in politics, where goals and expectations nurtured by Enlightenment philosophy clashed with the rigid structure of the French state and triggered the French Revolution. The Enlightenment was not simply an intellectual movement that found fault with society. It also encompassed the public and private settings in which "enlightened" opinion flourished. The revolutionary potential of Enlightenment thought came from belief in its rationality and from the fact that it was both critical of its society and fashionable to practice.

■ Notes

1. Quoted in Dena Goodman, *The Republic of Letters: A Cultural History of the French Enlightenment* (Ithaca, N.Y.: Cornell University Press, 1994), p. 89.
2. Quoted in M. S. Anderson, *Europe in the Eighteenth Century, 1713–1783*, 3d ed. (London: Longman, 1987), pp. 218–219.

■ Suggested Reading

Anderson, M. S. *Europe in the Eighteenth Century, 1713–1783.* 4th ed. 2000. A general history covering political, economic, social, and cultural developments.

Black, Jeremy. *European Warfare, 1660–1815.* 1994. One of several recent books by this military historian known particularly for his studies of the seventeenth and eighteenth centuries.

Cipolla, Carlo. *Before the Industrial Revolution.* 1976. A comprehensive treatment of the development of the European economy and technology through this period.

Colley, Linda. *Britons: Forging the Nation, 1707–1837.* 1992. A history of the British that emphasizes the interrelationships of political, social, and cultural history.

Goodman, Dena. *The Republic of Letters: A Cultural History of the French Enlightenment.* 1994. Useful for understanding the social context of the Enlightenment, especially the role of women as salon leaders.

Kennedy, Paul. *The Rise and Fall of British Naval Mastery.* 1976. A comprehensive work on the rise of British sea power from the sixteenth century to modern times.

Porter, Roy. *The Enlightenment.* 1990. A brief introduction.

Roche, Daniel. *France in the Enlightenment.* 1998. A study of state and society in France by an eminent French scholar.

www. **For a searchable list of additional readings for this chapter, go to college.hmco.com/students.**

CHAPTER 19

An Age of Revolution 1789–1815

THESE militiamen marching off to defend France against the invader in September 1792 appear to be heroes already. Adoring women in the crowd hand them laurel wreaths as they pass; the men march by, resolute and triumphant. Symbols of the ongoing revolution stand out as well: the prominent tricolor flag, the tricolor cockade in each man's hat. In fact, that September France's citizen armies for the first time defeated the army of a foreign monarch poised to breach its borders and snuff out its revolution. The painting celebrates this triumph about to happen and thereby inspires confidence in the Revolution and pride in its citizen-soldiers.

Today the French Revolution is considered the initiation of modern European as well as modern French history. The most powerful monarch in Europe was forced to accept constitutional limits to his power by subjects convinced of their right to demand them. Eventually, the king was overthrown and executed, and the monarchy abolished. Events in France reverberated throughout Europe because the overthrow of one absolute monarchy threatened fellow royals elsewhere. Revolutionary fervor on the part of ordinary soldiers enabled France's armies unexpectedly to best many of their opponents. By the late 1790s the armies of France would be led in outright conquest of other European states by one of the most talented generals in European history: Napoleon Bonaparte. He brought to the continental European nations that his armies eventually conquered a mixture of imperial aggression and revolutionary change. Europe was transformed

The National Guard of Paris leaves to join the army, September 1792 (detail). (Photos12.com-ARJ)

The Beginnings of Revolution, 1775–1789

The Phases of the Revolution, 1789–1799

The Napoleonic Era and the Legacy of Revolution, 1799–1815

both by the shifting balance of power and by the spread of revolutionary ideas.

Understanding the French Revolution means understanding not only its origins but also its complicated course of events, and their significance. Challenges to the power of the king were not new, but the Revolution overthrew his right to rule at all. The notion that the people constituted the nation, were responsible as citizens, and had some right to representation in government became irresistible. The republican system it conjured up replaced a government by inherited privilege. Louis XVI was transformed from the divinely appointed father of his people to an enemy of the people, worthy only of execution. Central to the Revolution was the complex process by which public opinion was shaped and, in turn, shaped events. Change was driven in part by the power of symbols—flags, rallying cries, inspiring art—to challenge an old political order and legitimize a new one.

QUESTIONS TO CONSIDER

- What factors led to the beginning of revolution in France in 1789?
- Why did the Revolution take a more radical direction from 1792 to 1794?
- What was the impact of Napoleon's rule on France?
- What were the major effects of the French Revolution and Napoleonic rule on the rest of Europe and overseas?

TERMS TO KNOW

Third Estate	Maximilien Robespierre
National Assembly	the Terror
Tennis Court Oath	Society of Revolutionary
Declaration of the	Republican Women
Rights of Man	Directory
and the Citizen	Napoleon Bonaparte
sans-culottes	Civil Code
Jacobins	François Toussaint-Louverture

THE BEGINNINGS OF REVOLUTION, 1775–1789

I AM a citizen of the world," wrote John Paul Jones, captain in the fledgling U.S. Navy, in 1778. He was writing to a Scottish aristocrat, apologizing for raiding the lord's estate while marauding along the British coast during the American Revolution. Jones (1747–1792), himself born a Scotsman, was one of the thousands of cosmopolitan Europeans who were familiar with European cultures on both sides of the Atlantic. As a sailor, Jones literally knew his way around the Atlantic world, but he was a "citizen of the world" in another sense as well. When the Scotsman wrote back to Jones, he expressed surprise that his home had been raided because he was sympathetic to the American colonists. Like Jones, he said, he was a man of "liberal sentiments."[1] Both Jones and the Scottish lord felt they belonged to an international society of gentlemen who recognized certain Enlightenment principles regarding just and rational government.

In the Atlantic world of the late eighteenth century, both practical links of commerce and shared ideals about "liberty" were important shaping forces. The strategic interests of the great European powers were also always involved. Thus when the American colonists actively resisted British rule and then in 1776 declared their independence from Britain, the consequences were widespread and varied: British trading interests were challenged, French appetites for gains at British expense were whetted, and illusive notions about "liberty" seemed more plausible. The victory of the American colonies in 1783, followed by the creation of the U.S. Constitution in 1787, further heightened the appeal of liberal ideas elsewhere. Attempts at liberal reform were mounted in several states, including Ireland, the Netherlands, and Poland. However, the American Revolution had the most direct impact on later events in France because the French had been directly involved in the American effort.

Revolutionary Movements in Europe

While the British government was facing the revolt of the American colonies, it also confronted trouble closer to home. The war against the American colonies was not firmly supported by Britons. Like many Americans, many Britons had divided loyalties, and many who did favor armed force to subdue the rebellion were convinced that the war was being mismanaged. The prosecution of the war against the American colonies proceeded amid calls for reform of the ministerial government. In this setting, a reform movement sprang up in Ireland in 1779. The reformers demanded greater autonomy from Britain. Like the Americans, Irish elites felt like disadvantaged junior partners in the British Empire. They chafed over British policies that favored British imperial interests over those of the Irish ruling class: for example, the exclusion of Irish ports in favor of English and Scottish trading stops and the granting of political rights to Irish Catholics so that they might fight in Britain's overseas armies.

Protestant Irish landlords, threatened by such policies, expressed their opposition not only in parliamentary debates but also in military defiance. Following the example of the American rebels, middle- and upperclass Anglo-Irish set up a system of locally sponsored voluntary militia to resist British troops if necessary. The Volunteer Movement was neutralized when greater parliamentary autonomy for Ireland was granted in 1782, following the repeal of many restrictions on Irish commerce. Unlike the Americans, the Irish elites faced an internal challenge to their own authority—the Catholic population whom they had for centuries dominated. That challenge forced them to reach an accommodation with the British government.

Meanwhile, a political crisis with constitutional overtones was also brewing in the Netherlands. Tensions between the aristocratic stadholders of the House of Orange and the merchant oligarchies of the major cities deepened during the American Revolution. The Dutch were then engaged in a commercial war against the British, to whom the stadholder was supposed to be sympathetic. The conflict ceased to be wholly traditional for two reasons. First, the representatives of the various cities, calling themselves the Dutch "Patriot" Party, defended their position on the grounds of traditional balance of power within the Netherlands and invoked wider claims to American-style "liberty." Second, the challenge to traditional political arrangements widened when middling urban dwellers, long disenfranchised by these oligarchies, demanded "liberty," too—that is, political enfranchisement within the cities—and briefly took over the Patriot movement. Just as many Irish rebels accepted the concessions of 1782, many Patriot oligarchs in the Netherlands did nothing to resist an invasion in 1787 that restored the power of the stadholder, the prince of Orange, and thereby ended the challenge to their own control of urban government.

Both the Irish volunteers and the Dutch Patriots, though members of very limited movements, echoed

CHRONOLOGY

1775–1783	American Revolutionary War
1779–1782	Irish Volunteer Movement
1788	U.S. Constitution ratified
	Reform movement begins in Poland
	"Patriot" movement ends in the Netherlands
1789	French Estates General meets at Versailles (May)
	Third Estate declares itself the National Assembly (June)
	Storming of the Bastille (July)
1790	Polish constitution
1791	French king Louis XVI captured attempting to flee (June)
	Slave revolt begins in Saint Domingue
1792	France declares war on Austria; revolutionary wars begin (April)
	Louis XVI arrested; France declared a republic (August–September)
1793	Louis XVI guillotined
1793–1794	Reign of Terror in France
1799	Napoleon seizes power in France
1801	Concordat with pope
1804	Napoleon crowned emperor
	Napoleonic Civil Code
	Independence of Haiti (Saint Domingue) declared
1805	Battle of Trafalgar
	Battle of Austerlitz
1806	Dissolution of Holy Roman Empire
1812	French invasion of Russia
1814	Napoleon abdicates and is exiled
	French monarchy restored
1815	Hundred Days (February–June)
	Battle of Waterloo

the American rebels in practical and ideological ways. Both were influenced by the economic and political consequences of Britain's relationship with its colonies. Both were inspired by the success of the American rebels and their thoroughgoing claims for political self-determination.

Desire for political reform flared in Poland as well during this period. Reform along lines suggested by Enlightenment precepts was accepted as a necessity by Polish leaders after the first partition of Poland in 1772 had left the remnant state without some of its wealthiest territories (see Map 18.1 on page 623). Beginning in 1788, however, reforming gentry in the *Sejm*° (representative assembly) went further; they established a commission to write a constitution, following the American example. The resulting document, known as the May 3 (1791) Constitution, was the first codified constitution in Europe; it was read and admired by George Washington.

Poles thus established a constitutional monarchy in which representatives of major towns as well as gentry and nobility could sit as deputies. The *liberum veto*, which had allowed great magnates to obstruct royal authority at will, was abolished. However, Catherine the Great, empress of Russia, would not tolerate a constitutional government operating so close to her own autocratic regime; she ordered an invasion of Poland in 1792. The unsuccessful defense of Poland was led by, among others, a Polish veteran of the American Revolution, Tadeusz Kosciuszko° (1746–1817). The second, more extensive partition of Poland followed, to be answered in turn in 1794 by a widespread insurrection against Russian rule, spearheaded by Kosciuszko. The uprising was mercilessly suppressed by an alliance of Russian and Prussian troops. Unlike the U.S. Constitution from which they drew inspiration, the Poles' constitutional experiment was doomed by the power of its neighbors.

The American Revolution and the Kingdom of France

As Britain's greatest commercial and political rival, France naturally was drawn into Britain's struggle with its North American colonies. In the Seven Years' War (1756–1763), the French had lost many of their colonial settlements and trading outposts to the English (see page 632). Stung by this outcome, certain French courtiers and ministers pressed for an aggressive colonial policy that would regain for France some of the riches in trade that Britain now threatened to monopolize. The American Revolu-

tion seemed to offer the perfect opportunity. The French extended covert aid to the Americans from the very beginning of the conflict in 1775. After the first major defeat of British troops by the Americans—at the Battle of Saratoga in 1777—France formally recognized the independent United States and established an alliance with it. The French then committed troops as well as funds for the American cause. John Paul Jones's most famous ship, the *Bonhomme Richard*°, was purchased and outfitted in France at French government expense, as were many other American naval vessels during the war. French support was decisive. In 1781 the French fleet kept reinforcements from reaching the British force besieged by George Washington at Yorktown. The American victory at Yorktown effectively ended the war; the colonies' independence was formally recognized by the Treaty of Paris in 1783.

The consequences for France of its American alliance were momentous. Aid for the Americans saddled France with a debt of about 1 billion *livres* (pounds), which represented as much as one-quarter of the total debt that the French government was trying to service. A less tangible impact of the American Revolution derived from the direct participation of about nine thousand French soldiers, sailors, and aristocrats. The best known is the Marquis de Lafayette°, who became an aide to George Washington and helped command American troops. For many humble men, the war was simply employment. For others, it was a quest of sorts. For them, the promise of the Enlightenment—belief in human rationality, natural rights, and universal laws by which society should be organized—was brought to life in America.

Exposure to the American conflict occurred at the French court, too. Beginning in 1775, a permanent American mission to Versailles lobbied hard for aid and later managed the flow of that assistance. The chief emissary of the Americans was Benjamin Franklin (1706–1790), a philosophe by French standards whose writings and scientific experiments were already known to European elites. His talents—among them, a skillful exploitation of a simple, Quaker-like demeanor—succeeded in promoting the idealization of America at the French court.

The U.S. Constitution, the various state constitutions, and the debates surrounding their ratification were all published in Paris and much discussed in salons and at court, where lively debate about reform of French institutions had been going on for decades. America became the prototype of the rational republic—the em-

---

Sejm (SAME)
Tadeusz Kosciuszko (tah-DAY-oosh kos-USE-ko)

Bonhomme Richard (bon-OHM ree-SHARD)
Marquis de Lafayette (mar-KEE duh la-fye-ET)

The Common People Crushed by Privilege   In this contemporary cartoon, a nobleman in military dress and a clergyman crush a commoner under the rock of burdensome taxes and forced labor (*corvées*). The victim's situation reflects that of the peasantry, but his stylish clothes would allow affluent townspeople to identify with him. *(Musée Carnavalet, Paris/Giraudon/Art Resource, NY)*

bodiment of Enlightenment philosophy. It was hailed as the place where the irrationalities of inherited privilege did not prevail. A British observer, Arthur Young (1741–1820), believed that "the American revolution has laid the foundation of another in France, if [the French] government does not take care of itself."[2]

By the mid-1780s there was no longer a question of whether the French regime would experience reform but rather what form the reform would take. The royal government was almost bankrupt. A significant minority of the politically active elite was convinced of the fundamental irrationality of France's system of government. Nevertheless, a dissatisfied elite and a financial crisis—even fanned by a successful revolt elsewhere—do not necessarily lead to revolution. Why did the French government—the *Ancien Régime°*, or "Old Regime," as it became known after the Revolution—not "take care of itself"?

The Crisis of the Old Regime

The Old Regime was brought to the point of crisis in the late 1780s by three factors: (1) heavy debts that dwarfed an antiquated system for collecting revenue; (2) institu-

tional constraints on the monarchy that defended privileged interests; and (3) public opinion that envisioned thoroughgoing reform and pushed the monarchy in that direction. Another factor was the ineptitude of the king, Louis XVI (r. 1774–1793).

Louis came to the throne in 1774, a year before the American Revolution began. He was a kind, well-meaning man better suited to carry out the finite responsibilities of a petty bureaucrat than to be king. The queen, the Austrian Marie Antoinette (1755–1793), was unpopular. She was regarded with suspicion by the many who despised the "unnatural" alliance with Austria the marriage had sealed. She, too, was politically inept, unable to negotiate the complexities of court life and widely rumored to be selfishly wasteful of royal resources despite the realm's financial crises.

The fiscal crisis of the monarchy had been a long time in the making and was an outgrowth of the system in which the greatest wealth was protected by traditional privileges. At the top of the social and political pyramid were the nobles, a legal grouping that included warriors and royal officials. In France nobility conferred exemption from much taxation. Thus the royal government could not directly tax its wealthiest subjects.

This situation existed throughout much of Europe, a legacy of the individual contractual relationships that had formed the political and economic framework of medieval

---

Ancien Régime (ahn-SYEN ray-ZHEEM)

Europe. Unique to France, however, was the strength of the institutions that defended this system. Of particular importance were the royal law courts, the parlements°, which claimed a right of judicial review over royal edicts. All the parlementaires—well-educated lawyers and judges—were noble and loudly defended the traditional privileges of all nobles. Louis XV (d. 1774), near the end of his life, had successfully undermined the power of the parlements by a bold series of moves. Louis XVI, immediately after coming to the throne, buckled under pressure and restored the parlements to full strength.

Deficit financing had been a way of life for the monarchy for centuries. After early efforts at reform, Louis XIV (d. 1715) had reverted to common fund-raising expedients such as selling offices, which only added to the weight of privileged investment in the old order. England had established a national bank to free its government from the problem, but the comparable French effort early in the century had been undercapitalized and had failed. Late in the 1780s, under Louis XVI, one-fourth of the annual operating expenses of the government was borrowed, and half of all government expenditure went to paying interest on its debt. Short-term economic crises, such as disastrous harvests, added to the cumulative problem of government finance.

The king employed able finance ministers who tried to institute fundamental reforms, such as replacing the tangle of taxes with a simpler system in which all would pay and eliminating local tariffs, which were stifling commerce. The parlements and many courtiers and aristocrats, as well as ordinary people, resisted these policies. Peasants and townsfolk did not trust the "free market" (free from traditional trade controls) for grain; most feared that speculators would buy up the grain supply and people would starve. Trying to implement such reforms in times of grain shortage almost guaranteed their failure. Moreover, many supported the parlements simply because they were the only institution capable of standing up to the monarchy. Yet not all members of the elite joined the parlements in opposing reform. The imprint of "enlightened" public opinion was apparent in the thinking of some courtiers and thousands of educated commoners who believed that the government and the economy had to change and openly debated the nature and extent of reform needed.

In 1787 the king called an "Assembly of Notables"—an ad hoc group of elites—to support him in facing down the parlements and proceeding with some changes. He found little support even among men known to be sympathetic to reform. Some did not support particular proposals, and many were reluctant to allow the monarchy free rein. Others, reflecting the influence of the American Revolution, maintained that a "constitutional" body such as the Estates General, which had not been called since 1614, needed to make these decisions.

Ironically, nobles and clergy who were opposed to reform supported the call for the Estates General, confident they could control its deliberations. The three Estates met and voted separately by "order"—clergy (First Estate), nobles (Second Estate), and commoners (Third Estate). The combined votes of the clergy and nobles would presumably nullify whatever the Third Estate might propose.

In 1788 popular resistance to reform in the streets of Paris and mounting pressure from Louis's courtiers and bureaucrats induced the king to summon the Estates General. On Louis's orders, deputies were to be elected by local assemblies, which were chosen in turn by wide male suffrage. Louis mistakenly assumed he had widespread support in the provinces, and he wished to tap into it by means of this grass-roots voting. Louis also agreed that the Third Estate should have twice as many deputies as the other two Estates, but he did not authorize voting by head rather than by order, which would have brought about the dominance of the Third Estate. Nevertheless, the king hoped that the specter of drastic proposals put forth by the Third Estate would frighten the aristocrats and clergy into accepting some of his reforms. (See the box "Reading Sources: List of Grievances for the Estates General.")

Louis's situation was precarious when the Estates General convened in May 1789. As ever, he faced immediate financial crisis. He also faced a constitutional crisis. Already a groundswell of sentiment confirmed the legitimacy of the Estates General, the role of the Third Estate, and the authority of the Third Estate to enact change. Political pamphlets abounded arguing that the Third Estate deserved enhanced power because it carried the mandate of the people. The most important of these was *What Is the Third Estate?* (1789) by Joseph Emmanuel Sieyès° (1748–1836), a church official from the diocese of Chartres. The sympathies of Abbé Sieyès, as he was known, were with the Third Estate: his career had suffered and stalled because he was not noble. Sieyès argued that the Third Estate represented the nation because it did not reflect special privilege.

Among the deputies of the first two Estates—clergy and nobility—were men, such as the Marquis de Lafayette

---

parlements (par-luh-MAWHN)

Sieyès (say-EZ)

READING
SOURCES

LISTS OF GRIEVANCES FOR THE ESTATES GENERAL

In preparation for the meeting of an Estates General, communities throughout France prepared lists of grievances that they hoped the deputies would address. Among the following petitions compiled by a town in Normandy in 1789, we can note deference to the king but also radical proposals reflecting the impact of Enlightenment thought. The document denounces certain special privileges associated with nobility, in particular the burdensome remnants of medieval property control, and clearly recognizes the Estates as the legitimate voice of the nation. Note also the initial demand that, contrary to the king's plans, voting in the Estates should occur by head.

The inhabitants decreed that their wishes were:

1. That in the assembly of the Estates-General, opinions be counted by head and not by order. . . .

2. That only the assembled nation may consent to taxes, loans and new offices, and no corporation, organization, not even provincial estates will be allowed to represent the nation.

3. That, in keeping with his majesty's promise, the Estates-General will assemble at fixed and determined periods, that taxes may only be consented to by the Estates until the period of their next meeting, and that each new assembly of estates will be preceded by a new choosing of deputies, so that no citizen can perpetually represent the nation. . . .

7. That all privileges and pecuniary exemptions be abolished, and taxes be collected without discrimination in the same proportion from all orders within the province.

8. That, to facilitate commerce, tollgates be removed to the frontiers of the realm, that his majesty be entreated to remedy the obstacles to commerce occasioned by differences in weights and measures. . . .

10. That the right of *franc fief* [fee payable by commoners to the king for the right of holding a noble fief] be suppressed, as humiliating to the Third Estate.

11. That, at the same time, his majesty be humbly entreated to recall that decision . . . which excludes from his majesty's service all citizens who cannot prove four degrees of nobility; that his majesty equally be entreated to bring about a reform of the [Parlement's] decisions whereby a gentleman is sought for an office which confers nobility before a candidate's merits are considered, in consequence of which merit will become sufficient grounds to enter the different estates.

Source: Annales du Centre Régional de Documentation Pédagogique de Caen, *Les Cahiers de Doléances de 1789 dans le Calvados.* Nouvelle série #6. Service Éducatif des Archives départementales du Calvados. Translated by Laura Mason. Reprinted in Laura Mason and Tracey Rizzo, eds., *The French Revolution: A Document Collection*, pp. 56–57. Copyright © 1999 Houghton Mifflin Company. Reprinted by permission.

(1757–1834), who were sympathetic to reform. More important, however, the elections had returned to the Third Estate a large majority of deputies who reflected the most radical political thought possible for men of their standing. Most were lawyers and other professionals who were functionaries in the government but, like Sieyès, of low social rank. They frequented provincial academies, salons, and political societies. They were convinced of the validity of their viewpoints and determined on reform, and they had little stake in the system as it was. When this group convened and met with resistance from the First and Second Estates and from Louis himself, they seized the reins of government and a revolution began.

1789: A Revolution Begins

As soon as the three Estates convened at the royal palace at Versailles, conflicts surfaced. The ineptness of the Crown was immediately clear. On the first day of the meetings in May, Louis and his ministers failed to introduce a program of reforms for the deputies to consider. This failure raised doubt about the monarchy's commitment to reform. More important, it allowed the political initiative to pass to the Third Estate. The deputies challenged the Crown's insistence that the three Estates meet and vote separately. Deputies to the Third Estate refused to be certified (that is, to have their credentials officially recognized) as members of only the Third

The Tennis Court Oath   It was raining on June 20, 1789, when the deputies found themselves barred from their meeting hall and sought shelter in the royal tennis court. Their defiance created one of the turning points of the Revolution; the significance was recognized several years later by the creator of this painting.   *(Réunion des Musées Nationaux/Art Resource, NY)*

Estate rather than as members of the Estates General as a whole.

For six weeks the Estates General was unable to meet officially, and the king did nothing to break the impasse. During this interlude, the determination of the deputies of the Third Estate strengthened. More and more deputies were won over to the notion that the three Estates must begin in the most systematic way: France must have a written constitution.

By the middle of June, more than thirty reformist members of the clergy were sitting jointly with the Third Estate, which had invited all deputies from all three Estates to meet and be certified together. On June 17 the Third Estate simply declared itself the National Assembly of France. At first the king did nothing, but when the deputies arrived to meet on the morning of June 20, they discovered they had been locked out of the hall. Undaunted, they assembled instead in a nearby indoor tennis court and produced the document that has come to

be known as the "Tennis Court Oath." It was a collective pledge to meet until a written constitution had been achieved. Only one deputy refused to support it. Sure of their mandate, the deputies had assumed the reins of government.

The king continued to handle the situation with both ill-timed self-assertion and feeble attempts at compromise. As more and more deputies from the First and Second Estates joined the National Assembly, Louis "ordered" the remaining loyal deputies to join it, too. Simultaneously, however, he ordered troops to come to Paris. He feared disorder in the wake of the recent disturbances throughout France and believed that any challenge to the legitimacy of arbitrary monarchical authority would be disastrous.

This appeal for armed assistance stirred unrest in the capital. Paris, with a population of about 600,000 in 1789, was one of the largest cities in Europe. It was the political nerve center of the nation—the site of the publishing industry, salons, the homes of parlementaires and royal ministers. It was also a working city, with thousands of laborers of all trades plus thousands more—perhaps one-tenth of the inhabitants—jobless recent immigrants from the countryside. The city was both extremely volatile and extremely important to the stability of royal power. The king's call for troops aroused Parisians' suspicions. Some assumed a plot was afoot to starve Paris and destroy the National Assembly. Already they considered the Assembly to be a guarantor of acceptable government.

It took little—the announcement of the dismissal of a reformist finance minister—for Paris to erupt in demonstrations and looting. Crowds besieged City Hall and the royal armory, where they seized thousands of weapons. A popular militia formed as citizens armed themselves. Armed crowds assailed other sites of royal authority, including the huge fortified prison, the Bastille, on the morning of July 14. The Bastille now held only a handful of petty criminals, but it still remained a potent symbol of royal power and, it was assumed, held large supplies of arms. Like the troops at the armory, the garrison at the Bastille had received no firm orders to fire on the crowds if necessary. The garrison commander at first mounted a hesitant defense, then decided to surrender after citizens managed to secure cannon and drag them to face the prison. Most of the garrison were allowed to go free, although the commander and several officers were murdered by the crowd.

The citizens' victory was a great embarrassment to royal authority. The king immediately had to embrace the popular movement. He came to Paris and in front of crowds at City Hall donned the red and blue cockade worn by the militia and ordinary folk as a badge of resolve and defiance. This symbolic action signaled the reversal of the Old Regime—politics would now be based on new principles.

Encouraged by events in Paris, inhabitants of cities and towns around France staged similar uprisings. In

Storming the Bastille   The crowd was convinced that the Bastille held political prisoners as well as a large supply of arms. In fact, it held neither. Thousands of Parisians—including artisans and shopkeepers, and not merely desperate rabble—surrounded the fortress and forced the garrison to surrender.   *(akg-images)*

many areas, the machinery of royal government completely broke down. City councils, officials, and even parlementaires were thrown out of office. Popular militias took control of the streets. A simultaneous wave of uprisings shook the countryside. Most of them were the result of food shortages, but their timing added momentum to the more strictly political protests in cities. These events forced the members of the National Assembly to work energetically on the constitution and to pass legislation to satisfy popular protests against economic and political privileges.

On August 4 the Assembly issued a set of decrees abolishing the remnants of powers that landlords had enjoyed since the Middle Ages, including the right to co-opt peasant labor and the bondage of serfdom itself. Although largely symbolic, because serfdom and forced labor had been eliminated in much of France, these changes represented a dramatic inroad into the property rights of the elite as they had been traditionally construed. The repeals were hailed as the "end of feudalism." A blow was also struck at established religion by eliminating the tithe. At the end of August, the Assembly issued the Declaration of the Rights of Man and the Citizen. It was a bold assertion of the foundations of a newly conceived government, closely modeled on portions of the U.S. Constitution. Its preamble declared "that [since] the ignorance, neglect or contempt of the rights of man are the sole cause of public calamities and the corruption of governments," the deputies were "determined to set forth in a solemn declaration the natural, inalienable and sacred rights of man."[3]

In September the deputies debated the king's role in a new constitutional government. Monarchists favored a government rather like England's, with a two-house legislature, including an upper house representing the hereditary aristocracy and a royal right to veto legislation. More radical deputies favored a single legislative chamber and no veto power for the king. After deliberation, the Assembly reached a compromise. The king was given a three-year suspensive veto—the power to suspend legislation for the sitting of two legislatures. This was still a formidable amount of power but a drastic curtailment of his formerly absolute sovereignty.

Again Louis resorted to troops. This time he called them directly to Versailles, where the Assembly sat. News of the troops' arrival provoked outrage, which height-

Women's March on Versailles, October 1789   Parisian marketwomen marched the 12 miles to the king's palace at Versailles, some provisioning themselves with tools or weapons as they left the capital.   *(Réunion des Musées Nationaux/Art Resource, NY)*

ened with the threat of another grain shortage. Early on the morning of October 5, women in the Paris street markets saw the empty grocers' stalls and took immediate collective action. "We want bread!" they shouted at the steps of City Hall. Because they were responsible for procuring their families' food, women often led protests over bread shortages. This protest, however, went far beyond the ordinary. A crowd of thousands gathered and decided to walk all the way to Versailles, accompanied by the popular militia (now called the "National Guard"), to petition the king directly for sustenance.

At Versailles they presented a delegation to the National Assembly, and a joint delegation of the women and deputies was dispatched to see the king. Some of the women fell at the feet of the king with their tales of hardship, certain that the "father of the people" would alleviate their suffering. He did order stored grain supplies distributed in Paris, and he also agreed to accept the constitutional role that the Assembly had voted for him.

That very night members of the National Guard, which had replaced the royal guard around the person of the king, saved Louis's life. A mob broke into the palace and managed to kill two members of the royal guard still in attendance outside the queen's chamber. The king agreed to return to Paris so that he could reassure the people. But the procession back to the city was a curious one. The royal family was escorted by militia and bread protesters, and the severed heads of the dead royal guardsmen were carried on pikes.

The king was now in the hands of his people. Already, dramatic change had occurred as a result of a complex dynamic among the three Estates, the Crown, and the people of Paris. The king was still assumed to be the fatherly guardian of his people's well-being, but his powers were now limited, and his authority was badly shaken. The Assembly had begun to govern in the name of the "nation" and so far had the support of the people.

THE PHASES OF THE REVOLUTION, 1789–1799

THE French Revolution was a complicated affair. It was a series of changes, in a sense a series of revolutions, driven not by one group of people but by several groups. Even among elites convinced of the need for reform, the range of opinion was wide. The people of Paris continued to be an important force for change. Country people also became active, primarily in resisting changes forced on them by the central government.

All of the wrangling within France was complicated by foreign reaction. Managing foreign war soon became a routine burden for the fragile revolutionary governments. In addition, they had to cope with the continuing problems that had precipitated the Revolution in the first place: the government's chronic indebtedness, economic difficulties, and recurrent grain shortages. Finally, the Revolution itself was an issue in that, once the traditional arrangements of royal government had been altered, momentum for further change was unleashed.

The First Phase Completed, 1789–1791

At the end of 1789 Paris was in ferment, but for a time forward progress blunted the threat of disastrous divisions between king and Assembly and between either of those and the people of Paris. The capital continued to be the center of lively political debate. Salons continued to meet; academies and private societies proliferated. Deputies to the Assembly swelled the ranks of these societies or helped to found new ones. Several would be important throughout the Revolution—particularly the Jacobin° Club, named for the monastic order whose buildings the members used as a meeting hall.

These clubs represented the gamut of revolutionary opinion. Some, in which ordinary Parisians were well represented, focused on economic policies that would directly benefit common people. Women were active in a few of the more radical groups. Monarchists dominated other clubs. At first similar to the salons and debating societies of the Enlightenment era, the clubs quickly became both sites of political action and sources of political pressure on the government. A bevy of popular newspapers also contributed to the vigorous political life in the capital.

The broad front of revolutionary consensus began to break apart as the Assembly forged ahead with decisions about the constitution and with policies necessary to remedy France's still-desperate financial situation. The largest portion of the untapped wealth of the nation lay with the Catholic Church, an obvious target of anticlerical reformers. The deputies did not propose to dismantle the church, but they did make sweeping changes: They kept church buildings intact and retained the clergy as salaried officials of the state. They abolished all monasteries and pensioned the monks and nuns to permit them to continue as nurses and teachers where possible. With the depleted treasury in mind, the Assembly seized most of the vast lands of the church and declared them national property (*biens nationaux*) to be sold for revenue.

Jacobin (JACK-oh-bin)

CHRONOLOGY

The French Revolution

May 5, 1789	Estates General meets in Versailles
June 17, 1789	Third Estate declares itself the National Assembly
June 20, 1789	Tennis Court Oath
July 14, 1789	Storming of the Bastille
August 27, 1789	Declaration of the Rights of Man and the Citizen
October 5–6, 1789	Women's march on Versailles Louis XVI returns to Paris
July 1790	Civil Constitution of the Clergy
June 1791	Louis XVI captured attempting to flee
August 1791	Declaration of Pillnitz
September 1791	New constitution implemented
October 1791	Legislative Assembly begins to meet
April 1792	France declares war on Austria
August 10, 1792	Storming of the Tuileries; Louis XVI arrested
September 21, 1792	National Convention declares France a republic
January 21, 1793	Louis XVI guillotined
May 1793	First Law of the Maximum
July 1793	Terror inaugurated
July 1794	Robespierre guillotined; Terror ends
October 1795	Directory established
November 1799	Napoleon seizes power

Economic and political problems ensued. Revenue was needed faster than the property could be inventoried and sold, so government bonds (*assignats°*) were issued against the eventual sale of church properties.

Unfortunately, in the cash-strapped economy, the bonds were treated like money, their value became inflated, and the government never realized the hoped-for profits. A greater problem was the political divisiveness generated by the restructuring of the church. Many members of the lower clergy, living as they did near ordinary citizens, were among the most reform-minded of the deputies. These clergy were willing to go along with many changes, but the required oath of loyalty to the state made a mockery of clerical independence.

The Civil Constitution of the Clergy, as these measures were called, was passed by the Assembly in July 1790 because the clerical deputies opposing it were outvoted. More than half of the churchmen did take the oath of loyalty. Those who refused, concentrated among the higher clergy, were in theory thrown out of their offices. A year later (April 1791) the pope declared that clergy who had taken the oath were suspended from their offices. Antirevolutionary sentiment grew among thousands of French people, particularly in outlying regions, to whom the church was still vital as a source of charity and a center of community life. This religious opposition worked to undermine the legitimacy of the new government.

Meanwhile, the Assembly proceeded with administrative and judicial reform. The deputies abolished the medieval provinces as administrative districts and replaced them with uniform *départements* (departments). They declared that local officials would be elected—a revolutionary dispersal of power that had previously belonged to the king.

As work on the constitution drew to a close in the spring of 1791, the king decided that he had had enough. Royal authority, as he knew it, had been virtually dismantled. Louis himself was now a virtual prisoner in the Tuileries° Palace in the very heart of Paris. Afraid for himself and his family, he and a few loyal aides worked out a plan to flee France. The king and the members of his immediate family set out in disguise on June 20, 1791. However, the party missed a rendezvous with a troop escort and was stopped—and recognized—in the town of Varennes°, near the eastern border of the kingdom.

Louis and his family were returned to Paris and held under lightly disguised house arrest. The circumstances of his flight were quickly discovered. He and the queen had sent money abroad ahead of themselves. He had left behind a document condemning the constitution. His intention was to invade France with Austrian troops if necessary. Thus in July 1791, just as the Assembly was

---

assignats (ah-see-NYAH)

Tuileries (TWEE-lair-ee)   Varennes (vah-REN)

completing its proposal for a constitutional monarchy, the constitution it had created began to seem unworkable because the monarch was not to be trusted.

Editorials and protests against the monarchy increased. In one incident known as the Massacre of the Champ (Field) de Mars°, government troops led by Lafayette fired on citizens at an antimonarchy demonstration that certain Parisian clubs had organized; about fifty men and women died. This inflammatory incident both reflected and heightened tensions between moderate reformers satisfied with the constitutional monarchy, such as Lafayette, and outspoken republicans who wanted to eliminate the monarchy altogether.

On September 14 the king swore to uphold the constitution. He had no choice. The event became an occasion for celebration, but the tension between the interests of the Parisians and the provisions of the new constitution could not be glossed over. Though a liberal document for its day, the constitution reflected the views of the elite deputies who had created it. The right to vote, based on a minimal property qualification, was given to about half of all adult men. However, these men only chose electors, for whom the property qualifications were higher. The electors in turn chose deputies to national bodies as well as local officials. Although in theory any eligible voter could be an elected deputy or official, the fact that elite electors determined every officeholder meant that few ordinary citizens would become deputies or local administrators. The new Declaration of Rights that accompanied the constitution reflected a fear of the masses that had not existed when the Declaration of the Rights of Man and the Citizen was first promulgated in 1789. Freedom of the press and freedom of assembly, for example, were not fully guaranteed.

Further, no political rights were accorded to women. Educated women had joined Parisian clubs such as the *Cercle sociale* (Social Circle), where opinion favored extending rights to women. Through such clubs, these women had tried to influence the National Assembly. But the Assembly granted neither political rights nor legal equality to women, nor did it pass other laws beneficial to women, such as legalizing divorce or mandating female education. The prevailing view of women among deputies seemed to reflect those of the Enlightenment philosophe Jean-Jacques Rousseau, who imagined women's competence to be entirely circumscribed within the family. The Declaration of the Rights of Woman was drafted by a woman named Olympe de Gouges° to draw attention to the treatment of women in the constitution. (See the box "Reading Sources: Declaration of the Rights of Woman.")

Very soon after the constitution was implemented, the fragility of the new system became clear. The National Assembly declared that its members could not serve in the first assembly to be elected under the constitution. Thus the members of the newly elected Legislative Assembly, which began to meet in October 1791, lacked any of the cohesiveness that would have come from collective experience. Also, unlike the previous National Assembly, they did not represent a broad range of opinion but were mostly republicans.

In fact, the Legislative Assembly was dominated by republican members of the Jacobin Club. They were known as Girondins°, after the region in southwestern France from which many of the club's leaders came. The policies of these new deputies and continued pressure from the ordinary citizens of Paris would cause the constitutional monarchy to collapse in less than a year.

The Second Phase and Foreign War, 1791–1793

An additional pressure on the new regime soon arose: a threat of foreign invasion and a war to counter the threat. Antirevolutionary aristocratic émigrés, including the king's brothers, had taken refuge in nearby German states and were planning to invade France. The emperor and other German rulers did little actively to aid the plotters. Austria and Prussia, however, in the Declaration of Pillnitz of August 1791, declared, as a concession to the émigrés, that they would intervene if necessary to support the monarchy in France.

The threat of invasion, when coupled with distrust of the royal family, seemed more real to the revolutionaries in Paris than it may actually have been. Indeed, many deputies hoped for war. They assumed that the outcome would be a French defeat, which would lead to a popular uprising that would rid them, at last, of the monarchy. In April 1792, under pressure from the Assembly, Louis XVI declared war against Austria. From this point on, foreign war would be an ongoing factor in the Revolution.

At first the war was a disaster for France. The army had not been reorganized into an effective fighting force after the loss of many aristocratic officers and the addition of newly self-aware citizens. On one occasion troops insisted on putting an officer's command to a vote. The French lost early battles in the Austrian Netherlands, but the Austrians did not press their advantage and invade

---

Champ de Mars (SHOM duh MARSS)
Olympe de Gouges (oh-LAMP duh GOOZH)

Girondins (zhih-ron-DEHN)

READING SOURCES

DECLARATION OF THE RIGHTS OF WOMAN

This retort to the new constitution, in which rights for women were conspicuously absent, was written in 1791 by Olympe de Gouges (1748?–1793), a self-educated butcher's daughter from southwestern France. The document reflects the complexity of political life during the Revolution. Gouges's declaration urges the extension to women of the Revolution's broad-based challenge to tradition. Yet Gouges dedicates the declaration to the queen, Marie Antoinette, drawing on the tradition of aristocratic patronage. Ironically, given Article 10, Gouges died on the scaffold for her revolutionary sympathies.

Man, are you capable of being just? It is a woman who poses the question; at least you will not take away this right. Tell me, what gives you the sovereign empire to oppress my sex? Your strength? Your talents? Observe the Creator in his wisdom; look at nature in all her grandeur, with whom you seem to want to be in harmony, and give me, if you dare, an example of this tyrannical empire. . . . Bizarre, blind, bloated with science and degenerated—in a century of light and wisdom—in the crassest ignorance, he wants to command as a despot a sex which has received all intellectual faculties; he pretends to enjoy the Revolution and reclaim his rights to equality only to say nothing more about it.

1. Woman is born free and lives equal to man in her rights. Social distinctions may be founded only upon common utility.

2. The purpose of any political association is the conservation of the natural and imprescriptible rights of woman and man; these rights are liberty, property, security, and above all resistance to oppression.

3. The principle of all sovereignty resides essentially in the Nation, which is nothing other than the union of woman and man: no body, no individual can exercise authority which does not emanate from it.

4. Liberty and justice consist of rendering all that belongs to others; thus, the exercise of the natural rights of woman has only been limited by the perpetual tyranny that man opposes to them; these limits should be reformed by the laws of nature and reason. . . .

10. No one should be troubled for holding basic opinions; woman has the right to mount the scaffold; she must equally have the right to mount the podium.

Source: Olympe de Gouges, *Écrits politiques, 1788–1791* (Paris: Côte-femmes, 1993), pp. 204–210. Translated by Tracey Rizzo. Reprinted in Laura Mason and Tracey Rizzo, eds., *The French Revolution: A Document Collection*, pp. 110–112. Copyright © 1999 Houghton Mifflin Company. Reprinted by permission.

France because they were preoccupied with problems in eastern Europe.

The defeats emboldened critics of the monarchy, who demanded action. Under the direction of the Girondins, the Legislative Assembly began to press for the deportation of priests who had been leading demonstrations against the government. The Assembly abolished the personal guard of the king and summoned provincial National Guardsmen to Paris. The king's resistance to these measures, as well as fears of acute grain shortages owing to a poor harvest and the needs of the armies, created further unrest. Crowds staged boisterous marches near the royal palace, physically confronted the king, and forced him to don the "liberty cap," a symbol of republicanism. The king's authority and prestige were now thoroughly undermined.

By July 1792 tensions had become acute. The grain shortage was severe, Austrian and Prussian troops committed to saving the royal family were threatening to invade, and, most important, the populace was better organized and more determined than ever before. In each of the forty-eight "sections"—administrative wards—of Paris, a miniature popular assembly thrashed out all the events and issues of the day just as deputies in the nationwide Legislative Assembly did. Derisively called *sans-culottes*° ("without knee pants") because they could not afford elite fashions, the ordinary Parisians in the section assemblies included shopkeepers, artisans, and laborers. Their political organization enhanced their in-

---

sans-culottes (sahn–koo-LOT)

Louis XVI in 1792   The king, though a kindly man, had neither the character nor the convictions necessary to refashion royal authority symbolically as the Revolution proceeded. When Parisian crowds forced him to wear the "liberty cap," the monarchy was close to collapse.   *(Metropolitan Museum of Art, The Elisha Whittelsey Collection, The Elisha Whittelsey Fund, 1962)*

fluence with the Assembly, the clubs, and the newspapers in the capital. By late July most sections of the city had approved a petition calling for the exile of the king, the election of new city officials, the exemption of the poor from taxation, and other radical measures.

In August the sans-culottes took matters into their own hands. On the night of August 9, after careful preparations, representatives of the section assemblies constituted themselves as a new city government with the aim of "saving the state." They then assaulted the Tuileries Palace, where the royal family was living. In the bloody confrontation, hundreds of royal guards and citizens died. After briefly taking refuge in the Legislative Assembly, the king and his family were imprisoned in one of the fortified towers in the city, under guard of the popularly controlled city government.

The storming of the Tuileries inaugurated the second major phase of the Revolution: the establishment of republican government in place of the monarchy. By their intimidating numbers, the people of Paris now controlled the Legislative Assembly. Some deputies had fled. Those who remained agreed under pressure to dissolve the Assembly and make way for another body to be elected by universal manhood suffrage. On September 20 that assembly, known as the National Convention, began to meet. The next day the Convention declared the end of the monarchy and set to work crafting a constitution for the new republic.

Coincidentally, that same September day, French forces won their first genuine victory over the allied Austrian and Prussian invasion forces. Though not a decisive battle, it was a profound psychological triumph. A citizen army had defeated the professional force of a ruling prince. The victory bolstered the republican government and encouraged it to put more energy into the wars. Indeed, maintaining armies in the field became a weighty factor in the delicate equilibrium of revolutionary government. The new republican regime let it be known that its armies were not merely for self-defense but for the liberation of all peoples in the "name of the French Nation."

The Convention faced the divisive issue of what to do with the king. Louis had not done anything truly treasonous, but some of the king's correspondence, discovered after the storming of the Tuileries, provided the pretext for charges of treason. The Convention held a trial for him, lasting from December 11, 1792, through January 15, 1793. He was found guilty of treason by an overwhelming vote (683 to 39); the republican government would not compromise with monarchy. Less lopsided was the sentence: Louis was condemned to death by a narrow majority, 387 to 334.

The consequences for the king were immediate. On January 21, 1793, Louis mounted the scaffold in a public square near the Tuileries and was beheaded. The execution split the ranks of the Convention and soon resulted in the breakdown of the institution itself.

The Faltering Republic and the Terror, 1793–1794

In February 1793 the republic was at war with virtually every state in Europe; the only exceptions were the Scandinavian kingdoms and Russia. Moreover, the regime faced massive and widespread counterrevolutionary uprisings within France. Vigilance against internal and external enemies became a top priority. The Convention established an executive body, the Committee of Public Safety. In theory, this executive council was answerable

Robespierre the Incorruptible   A lawyer who had often championed the poor, Robespierre was elected to the Estates General in 1789 and was a consistent advocate of republican government from the beginning of the Revolution. His unswerving loyalty to his political principles earned him the nickname "the Incorruptible."   *(Musée des Beaux-Arts, Lille)*

to the Convention as a whole. As the months passed, however, it acted with greater and greater autonomy not only to institute policies but also to eradicate enemies. The broadly based republican government represented by the Convention began to disintegrate.

The first major narrowing of control came in June 1793. Pushed by the Parisian sections, a group of extreme Jacobins purged the Girondin deputies from the Convention, arresting many of them. The Girondins were republicans who favored an activist government in the people's behalf, but they were less radical than their fellow Jacobins who now moved against them, less insistent on central control of the Revolution, and less willing to share power with the citizens of Paris. After the purge, the Convention still met, but most authority lay with the Committee of Public Safety.

New uprisings against the regime began. Added to counterrevolutionary revolts by peasants and aristocrats

were new revolts by Girondin sympathizers. As resistance to the government mounted and the foreign threat continued, a dramatic event in Paris led the Committee of Public Safety officially to adopt a policy of political repression. A well-known figure of the Revolution, Jean Paul Marat (1743–1793), publisher of a radical republican newspaper very popular with ordinary Parisians, was murdered on July 13 by Charlotte Corday (1768–1793), a young aristocratic woman who had asked to meet with him. Shortly afterward, a longtime member of the Jacobin Club, Maximilien Robespierre° (1758–1794), joined the Committee and called for "Terror"—the systematic repression of internal enemies. He was not alone in his views. Members of the section assemblies of Paris led demonstrations to pressure the government into making Terror the order of the day.

Since the previous autumn, the guillotine had been at work against identified enemies of the regime, but now a more energetic apparatus of Terror was instituted. A Law of Suspects was passed that allowed citizens to be arrested simply on vague suspicion of counterrevolutionary sympathies. Revolutionary tribunals and an oversight committee made arbitrary arrests and rendered summary judgments. In October a steady stream of executions began, beginning with the queen, imprisoned since the storming of the Tuileries the year before. The imprisoned Girondin deputies followed, and then the beheadings continued relentlessly. Paris witnessed about 2,600 executions from 1793 to 1794.

Around France the verdicts of revolutionary tribunals led to approximately 14,000 executions. Another 10,000 to 12,000 people died in prison. Ten thousand or more were killed, usually by summary execution, after the defeat of counterrevolutionary uprisings. For example, 2,000 people were summarily executed in Lyon when a Girondin revolt collapsed there in October. The aim of the Terror was not merely to stifle active resistance; it was also to silence simple dissent. The victims in Paris included not only aristocrats or former deputies but also sans-culottes. The radical Jacobins wanted to seize control of the Revolution from the Parisian citizens who had lifted them to power.

Robespierre embodied all the contradictions of the policy of Terror. He was an austere, almost prim man who lived very modestly—a model, of sorts, of the virtuous, disinterested citizen. The policies followed by the government during the year of his greatest influence, from July 1793 to July 1794, included generous, rational, and humane actions to benefit ordinary citizens as well

Robespierre (ROBES-pee-air)

Robespierre Justifies Terror Against Enemies of the Revolution

In this excerpt from a speech before the National Convention in December 1793, Robespierre justifies the revolutionary government's need to act in an extraconstitutional manner in order to defend itself from challenges within and without. This policy of Terror ended in France when the threat of foreign invasion declined and the government's policies of arbitrary arrest, imprisonment, and execution seemed too threatening to be tolerable. However, the question of how far a government may go to ensure safety for all while infringing on the rights of some of its citizens remained far from settled. Can a government declare some citizens to be enemies of the state and not merely political opponents?

The defenders of the Republic must adopt Caesar's maxim, for they believe that "nothing has been done so long as anything remains to be done." Enough dangers still face us to engage all our efforts. It has not fully extended the valor of our Republican soldiers to conquer a few Englishmen and a few traitors. A task no less important, and one more difficult, now awaits us: to sustain an energy sufficient to defeat the constant intrigues of all the enemies of our freedom and to bring to a triumphant realization the principles that must be the cornerstone of public welfare. . . . Revolution is the war waged by liberty against its enemies; a constitution . . . crowns the edifice of freedom once victory has been won and the nation is at peace. . . . The principal concern of a constitutional government is civil liberty; that of a revolutionary government, public liberty. [A] revolutionary government is obliged to defend the state itself against the factions that assail it from every quarter. To good citizens revolutionary government owes the full protection of the state; to the enemies of the people it owes only death.

Is a revolutionary government the less just and the less legitimate because it must be more vigorous in its actions and freer in its movement than ordinary government? . . . It also has its rules, all based on justice and public order. . . . It has nothing in common with arbitrary rule; it is public interest which governs it and not the whims of private individuals.

Thanks to five years of treason and tyranny, thanks to our credulity and lack of foresight . . . Austria and England, Russia, Prussia, and Italy had time to set up in our country a secret government to challenge the authority of our own. . . . We shall strike terror, not in the hearts of patriots, but in the haunts of foreign brigands.

QUESTIONS

1. How does Robespierre describe the differences between constitutional and revolutionary government?

2. How does Robespierre defend the legitimacy of revolutionary government?

SOURCE: Reprinted with permission of Simon & Schuster Adult Publishing Group, from *Robespierre,* by George Rudé. Copyright © 1967 by Prentice-Hall, Inc., copyright renewed © 1995 by George Rudé.

---

as the atrocities of official Terror. (See the box "The Continuing Experiment: Robespierre Justifies Terror Against Enemies of the Revolution.") Indeed, the Terror notwithstanding, the government of the Committee of Public Safety was effective in providing direction for the nation at a critical time. In August 1793 it instituted the first mass conscription of citizens into the army (*levée en masse°*), and a consistently effective popular army came into existence. In the autumn of 1793 this army won impressive victories. In May the Convention had instituted the Law of the Maximum, which controlled the price of grain so that city people could afford their staple food—bread. In September the Committee extended the law to apply to other necessary commodities. Extensive plans were made for a system of free and universal primary education. Slavery in the French colonies was abolished in February 1794. Divorce, first legalized in 1792, was made easier for women to obtain.

In the name of "reason," traditional rituals and rhythms of life were changed. One reform of long-term significance was the introduction of the metric system of weights and measures. Although people continued to use the old, familiar measures for a very long time, the change was eventually accomplished, leading the way for standardization throughout Europe. Equally "rational" but not as successful was the elimination of the traditional

---

levée en masse (leh-VAY ohn MAHSS)

calendar; weeks and months were replaced by forty-day months and *decadi* (ten-day weeks with one day of rest), and all saints' days and Christian holidays were eliminated. The years had already been changed—Year I had been declared with the founding of the republic in the autumn of 1792.

Churches were rededicated as "temples of reason." Believing that outright atheism left people with no basis for personal or national morality, Robespierre sought instead to promote a cult of the Supreme Being. The new public festivals were solemn civic ceremonies intended to ritualize and legitimize the new political order. These and other innovations of the regime were not necessarily welcomed. The French people generally resented the elimination of the traditional calendar. In the countryside massive peasant uprisings protested the loss of poor relief, community life, and familiar ritual.

Divorce law and economic regulation were a boon, especially to urban women, but women's participation in sectional assemblies and in all organized political activity—which had been energetic and widespread—was banned in October 1793. The particular target of the regime was the Society of Revolutionary Republican Women, a powerful club representing the interests of female sans-culottes. By banning women from political life, the regime helped to ground its legitimacy, since the seemingly "natural" exclusion of women might make the new system of government appear part of the "natural" order. (See the feature "Weighing the Evidence: Political Symbols" on pages 674–675.) Outlawing women's clubs and barring women from section assemblies also eliminated a source of popular power, from which the regime was now trying to distance itself.

The Committee and the Convention were divided over religious and other policies, but the main policy differences concerned economic matters: how far to go to assist the poor, the unemployed, and the landless. Several of the temperate critics of Robespierre and his allies were guillotined for disagreeing with these policies and for doubting the continuing need for the Terror itself. Their deaths helped precipitate the end of the Terror by causing Robespierre's power base to shrink so much that it had no further legitimacy.

Deputies to the Convention finally dared to move against Robespierre in July 1794. French armies had scored a major victory over Austrian troops on June 26, so there was no longer any need for the emergency status that the Terror had thrived on. In late July the Convention voted to arrest Robespierre, the head of the revolutionary tribunal in Paris, and their closest associates and allies in the city government. On July 28 and 29

Robespierre and the others—about a hundred in all—were guillotined, and the Terror ended.

The Thermidorian Reaction and the Directory, 1794–1799

After the death of Robespierre, the Convention reclaimed many of the executive powers that the Committee of Public Safety had seized. The Convention dismantled the apparatus of the Terror, repealed the Law of Suspects, and forced the revolutionary tribunals to adopt ordinary legal procedures. The Convention also passed into law some initiatives, such as expanded public education, that had been proposed in the preceding year but not enacted. This post-Terror phase of the Revolution is called the "Thermidorian Reaction" because it began in the revolutionary month of Thermidor (July 19–August 17).

Lacking the weapons of the Terror, the Convention was unable to enforce controls on the supply and price of bread. Thus economic difficulties and a hard winter produced famine by the spring of 1795. The people of Paris tried to retain influence with the new government. In May crowds marched on the Convention chanting "Bread and the Constitution of '93," referring to the republican constitution drafted by the Convention but never implemented because of the Terror. The demonstrations were met with force and were dispersed.

Members of the Convention remained fearful of a renewed, popularly supported Terror, on the one hand, or a royalist uprising, on the other. Counterrevolutionary uprisings had erupted in the fall of 1794, and landings on French territory by émigré forces occurred the following spring. The Convention drafted a new constitution that limited popular participation in government, as had the first constitution of 1791. The new plan allowed fairly widespread (but not universal) male suffrage, but only for electors, who would choose deputies for the two houses of the legislature. The property qualifications for being an elector were very high, so all but elite citizens were effectively disenfranchised. The Convention also decreed, at the last minute, that two-thirds of its members must serve in the new legislature, regardless of the outcome of elections. Although this maneuver enhanced the stability of the new regime, it undermined the credibility of the new ballot.

Governance under the provisions of the new constitution, beginning in the fall of 1795, was called the Directory, for the executive council of five men chosen by the upper house of the new legislature. To avoid the concentration of authority that had produced the Terror, the members of the Convention had tried to enshrine separation of powers in the new system. However, the governments under the Directory were never free from attempted coups or from their own extraconstitutional maneuvering.

The most spectacular external challenge, the Conspiracy of Equals, was led by extreme Jacobins who wanted to restore popular government and aggressive economic and social policy on behalf of the common people. The conspiracy ended with arrests and executions in 1797. When elections in 1797 and 1798 returned many royalist as well as Jacobin deputies, the Directory abrogated the constitution to forestall challenges to its authority. Many undesirable deputies were arrested, sent into exile, or denied seats.

The armies of the republic did enjoy some spectacular successes during these years, for the first time carrying the fighting—and the effects of the Revolution—onto foreign soil. French armies conquered the Dutch in 1795. In 1796–1797 French armies led by the young general Napoleon Bonaparte° wrested control of northern Italy from the Austrians. Both regions were transformed into "sister" republics, governed by local revolutionaries but under French protection. By 1799, however, conditions had once again reached a critical juncture. The demands of the war effort, together with rising prices and the continued decline in the value of the assignats, brought the government again to the brink of bankruptcy. The government also seemed to be losing control of the French countryside; there were continued royalist uprisings, local political vendettas between moderates and Jacobins, and outright banditry.

Members of the Directory had often turned to sympathetic army commanders to suppress dissent and to carry out arrests and purges of the legislature. They now invited General Bonaparte to help them form a government that they could more strictly control. Two members of the Directory plotted with Napoleon and his brother, Louis Bonaparte, to seize power on November 9, 1799.

THE NAPOLEONIC ERA AND THE LEGACY OF REVOLUTION, 1799–1815

TALENTED, charming, and ruthless, Napoleon Bonaparte (1769–1821) was the kind of person who gives rise to myths. His audacity, determination, and personal magnetism enabled him to profit from the political instability and confusion in France

---

Napoleon Bonaparte (nuh-POLE-ee-un BONE-uh-part)

and to ensconce himself in power. Once in power, he temporarily stabilized the political scene by fixing in law the more conservative gains of the Revolution. He also used his power and his remarkable abilities as a general to continue wars of conquest against France's neighbors, which helped deflect political tensions at home.

Napoleon's troops in effect exported the Revolution as they conquered most of Europe. In most states that came under French control, law codes were reformed, governing elites were opened to talent, and public works were upgraded. Yet French conquest also meant domination, pure and simple, and involvement in France's rivalry with Britain. The Napoleonic era left Europe an ambiguous legacy—war and its complex aftermath, yet also revolution and its goad to further change.

Napoleon: From Soldier to Emperor, 1799–1804

Napoleon was from Corsica, a Mediterranean island that had passed from Genoese to French control in the eighteenth century. The second son of a large gentry family, he was educated at military academies in France, and he married the politically well-connected widow Joséphine de Beauharnais (1763–1814), whose aristocratic husband had been a victim of the Terror.

Napoleon steered a careful course through the political turmoil of the Revolution. By 1799 his military victories had won him much praise and fame. He had demonstrated his reliability and ruthlessness in 1795 when he ordered troops guarding the Convention to fire on a Parisian crowd. He had capped his successful Italian campaign of 1796–1797 with an invasion of Egypt in an attempt to strike at British influence and trade connections in the eastern Mediterranean. The Egyptian campaign failed in its goals, but individual spectacular victories during the campaign ensured Napoleon's military reputation. In addition, Napoleon had demonstrated his widening ambitions. He had taken leading scientists and skilled administrators with him to Egypt in order to export the seeming benefits of French civilization—and to install a more lasting bureaucratic authority.

Napoleon's partners in the new government after the November 1799 coup soon learned of his great political ambition and skill. In theory, the new system was to be a streamlined version of the Directory: Napoleon was to be first among equals in a three-man executive— "First Consul," according to borrowed Roman terminology. But Napoleon quickly asserted his primacy among them and began not only to dominate executive functions but also to bypass the authority of the regime's various legislative bodies.

Napoleon Crossing the Great St. Bernard   This stirring portrait by the great neoclassical painter Jacques-Louis David memorializes Napoleon's 1796 crossing of the Alps before his victorious Italian campaign, as a general under the Directory. In part because it was executed in 1801–1802, the painting depicts the moment heroically rather than realistically. (In truth, Napoleon wisely crossed the Alps on a sure-footed mule, not a stallion.) Napoleon, as First Consul, wanted images of himself that would justify his increasingly ambitious claims to power.   *(Réunion des Musées Nationaux/Art Resource, NY)*

Perhaps most important to the success of his increasingly authoritarian rule was his effort to include men of many political stripes—Jacobins, reforming liberals, even former Old Regime bureaucrats—among his ministers, advisers, and bureaucrats. He welcomed many exiles back to France, including all but the most ardent royalists. He thus stabilized his regime by healing some of the rifts among ruling elites. Napoleon combined toleration with ruthlessness, however. Between 1800 and 1804 he imprisoned, executed, or exiled dozens of individuals for alleged Jacobin agitation or royalist sympathies. His final gesture to intimidate royalist opposition came in 1804, when he kidnapped and coldly murdered a Bourbon prince who had been living in exile in Germany.

Under Napoleon's regime, any semblance of free political life ended. Legislative bodies lost all initiative in the governing process, becoming rubber stamps for the consuls' policies. In any case, there were no meaningful elections. Voters chose only candidates for a kind of pool of potential legislators, from which occasional replacements were chosen by members of the Senate, an advisory body entirely appointed by Napoleon himself. Political clubs were banned; the vibrant press of the revolutionary years wilted under heavy censorship. Napoleon also further centralized the administrative system, set up by the first wave of revolutionaries in 1789, by establishing the office of prefect to govern the départements. All prefects and their subordinates were appointed by Napoleon, thus extending the range of his power and undermining autonomous local government.

Certain administrative changes that enhanced central control, such as for tax collection, were more uniformly positive in their effects. Napoleon oversaw the establishment of the Bank of France, modeled on the Bank of England. The bank provided capital for investment and helped the state stabilize the French currency. Perhaps the most important achievement early in his regime was the Concordat of 1801. The aim of this treaty with the pope was to solve the problem of church-state relations that for years had provoked counterrevolutionary rebellions. The agreement allowed for the resumption of Catholic worship and the continued support of the clergy by the state, but also accepted the more dramatic changes accomplished by the Revolution. Church lands that had been sold were guaranteed to their new owners. Although Catholicism was recognized as the "religion of the majority of Frenchmen," Protestant churches also were allowed, and their clergy were paid. Later, Napoleon granted new rights to Jews as well. Nonetheless, the Concordat removed one of the most important grounds for counterrevolutionary upheaval in the countryside and defused royalist resistance from abroad.

The law code that Napoleon established in 1804 was much like his accommodation with the church in its limited acceptance of revolutionary gains. His Civil Code (also known as the *code napoléon*, or Napoleonic Code) honored the revolutionary legacy in its guarantee of equality before the law and its requirement for the taxation of all social classes; it also enshrined modern forms of property ownership and civil contracts. Neither the code nor Napoleon's political regime fostered individual rights, especially for women. Fathers' control over their families was enhanced. Divorce was no longer permitted except in rare instances. Women lost all property rights when they married, and they generally faced legal domination by fathers and husbands.

Napoleon was careful, though, to avoid heavy-handed displays of power. He cleverly sought ratification of each stage of his assumption of power through national plebiscites (referendums in which all eligible voters could vote for or against proposals)—one plebiscite for a new constitution in 1800 and another when he claimed consulship for life in 1802. He approached his final political coup—declaring himself emperor—with similar dexterity. Long before he claimed the imperial title, Napoleon had begun to sponsor an active court life appropriate to imperial pretensions. The empire was proclaimed in May 1804 with the approval of the Senate; it was also endorsed by another plebiscite. Members of Napoleon's family were given princely status, and a number of his favorites received various titles and honors. The titles brought no legal privilege but signaled social and political distinctions of great importance. Old nobles were allowed to use their titles on this basis.

Many members of the elite, whatever their persuasions, tolerated Napoleon's claims to power because he safeguarded fundamental revolutionary gains yet reconfirmed their own status. War soon resumed against political and economic enemies—principally Britain, Austria, and Russia—and for a time Napoleon's success on the battlefield continued. Because military glory was central to the political purpose and self-esteem of elites, Napoleon's early successes as emperor further enhanced his power.

Conquering Europe, 1805–1810

Napoleon maintained relatively peaceful relations with other nations while he consolidated power at home, but the truces did not last. Tensions with the British quickly re-escalated when Britain resumed aggression against French shipping in 1803, and Napoleon countered by seizing Hanover, the ancestral German home of the English king. England was at war on the high seas with Spain and the Netherlands, which Napoleon had forced to enter the fray. Napoleon began to gather a large French force on the northern coast of France; his objective was to invade England.

The British fleet, commanded by Horatio Nelson (1758–1805), intercepted the combined French and Spanish fleets that were to have been the invasion flotilla and inflicted a devastating defeat off Cape Trafalgar in southern Spain (see Map 19.1) on October 21, 1805. The victory ensured British mastery of the seas and, in the long run, contributed to Napoleon's demise. In the short run, the defeat at Trafalgar paled for the French beside Napoleon's impressive victories on land. Even as the French admirals were preparing for battle, Napoleon had abandoned the plans to invade England and in August had begun to march his army east through Germany to confront the great continental powers, Austria and Russia.

In December 1805, after some preliminary, small-scale victories, Napoleon's army routed a combined Austrian and Russian force near Austerlitz°, north of Vienna (see Map 19.1). The Battle of Austerlitz was Napoleon's most spectacular victory. Austria sued for peace. In further battles in 1806, French forces defeated Prussian as well as Russian armies once again. Prussia was virtually dismembered by the subsequent Treaty of Tilsit (1807), but Napoleon tried to remake Russia into a contented ally. His hold on central Europe would not be secure with a hostile Russia, nor would the anti-British economic system that he envisioned—the Continental System (see page 666)—be workable without Russian participation.

Austerlitz (AW-stir-lits)

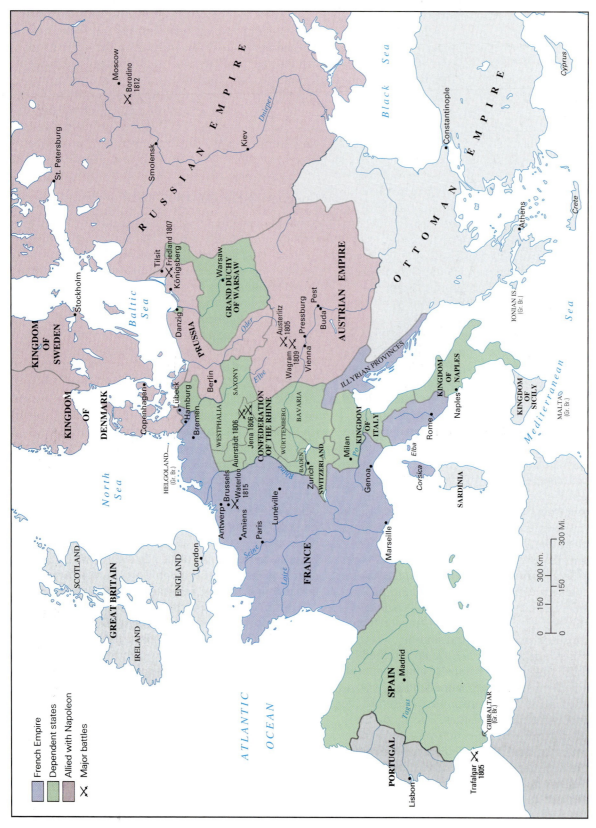

Map 19.1 Napoleonic Europe, ca. 1810 France dominated continental Europe after Napoleon's victories.

"And It Cannot Be Changed"
This horrifying scene of an execution of rebels against French rule in Spain was one of a series of etchings by Madrid artist Francisco Goya. In the 1810 series, titled "The Disasters of War," Goya was severely critical of French actions, as well as of barbarities committed by the British-backed Spaniards. *(Foto Marburg/Art Resource, NY)*

French forces were still trying to prevail in Spain, which had been a client state since its defeat by revolutionary armies in 1795 but was resisting outright rule by a French-imposed king. In 1808, however, Napoleon turned his attention to more fully subduing Austria. Napoleon won the Battle of Wagram° in July 1809, and Austria, like Russia, accepted French political and economic hegemony in a sort of alliance. By 1810 Napoleon had transformed most of Europe into allied or dependent states (see Map 19.1). The only exceptions were Britain and the parts of Spain and Portugal that continued, with British help, to resist France.

The states least affected by French hegemony were its reluctant allies: Austria, Russia, and the Scandinavian countries. Denmark had allied with France in 1807 only for help in fending off British naval supremacy in the Baltic. Sweden had reluctantly made peace in 1810 after losing control of Finland to Napoleon's ally, Russia, and only minimally participated in the Continental System. At the other extreme were territories that had been incorporated into France. These included the Austrian Netherlands, territory along the Rhineland, and sections of Italy that bordered France. These regions were occupied by French troops and were treated as though they were départements of France itself.

In most other areas, some form of French-controlled government was in place, usually headed by a member of Napoleon's family. In both northern Italy and the Netherlands, where "sister" republics had been established after French conquests under the Directory, Napoleon imposed monarchies. Rulers were also installed in the kingdom of Naples and in Spain. Western German states of the Holy Roman Empire that had allied with Napoleon against Austria were organized into the Confederation of the Rhine, with Napoleon as its "Protector." After a thousand years, the Holy Roman Empire ceased to exist. Two further states were created, largely out of the defeated Prussia's territory: the kingdom of Westphalia in western Germany and the Grand Duchy of Warsaw in the east (see Map 19.1).

Napoleon's domination of these various regions had complex, and at times contradictory, consequences. On the one hand, Napoleonic armies essentially exported the French Revolution, in that French domination

---

Wagram (VAHG-rahm)

brought with it the Napoleonic Civil Code, and with it political and economic reform akin to that of the early phases of the Revolution. Equality before the law was decreed following the French example. This meant the end of noble exemption from taxation in the many areas where it existed. In general, the complex snarl of medieval taxes and tolls was replaced with straightforward property taxes that were universally applied. As a consequence, tax revenues rose dramatically—by 50 percent in the kingdom of Italy, for example. Serfdom and forced labor also were abolished, as they had been in France in August 1789.

In most Catholic regions the church was subjected to the terms of the Concordat of 1801. The tithe was abolished, church property was seized and sold, and religious orders were dissolved. Although Catholicism remained the state-supported religion in these areas, Protestantism was tolerated, and Jews were granted rights of citizenship. Secular education, at least for males, was encouraged.

On the other hand, Napoleon would countenance in the empire only those aspects of France's revolutionary legacy that he tolerated in France itself. Just as he had suppressed any meaningful participatory government in France, so too did he suppress it in conquered regions. This came as a blow in states such as the Netherlands, which had experienced its own democratizing "Patriot" movement and which had enjoyed republican self-government after invasion by French armies during the Revolution itself. Throughout Napoleon's empire, many of the benefits of streamlined administration and taxation were offset by the drain of continual warfare. Deficits rose three- and fourfold, despite increased revenues. In addition, one of the inevitable costs of empire was political compromise to secure allies. In the Grand Duchy of Warsaw, reconstituted from lands Prussia had seized in the eighteenth century, Napoleon tampered little with either noble privileges or the power of the church. And throughout Europe he randomly allotted lands to reward his greatest generals and ministers, thereby exempting those lands from taxation and control by his own bureaucracy.

If true self-government was not allowed, a broad segment of the elite in all regions was nevertheless won over to cooperation with Napoleon by being welcomed into his bureaucracy or into the large multinational army, called the *Grande Armée*°. Their loyalty was cemented when they bought confiscated church lands.

The impact of Napoleon's Continental System was equally mixed. Under this system the Continent was in theory closed to all British shipping and goods. The effects were widespread but uneven, and smuggling to evade controls on British goods became a major enterprise. Regions heavily involved in trade with Britain or its colonies or dependent on British shipping suffered in the new system, as did overseas trade in general when Britain gained dominance of the seas after Trafalgar. However, the closing of the Continent to British trade, combined with increases in demand to supply Napoleon's armies, spurred the development of continental industries, at least in the short run. This industrial growth, enhanced by the improvement of roads, canals, and the like, formed the basis for further industrial development.

Defeat and Abdication, 1812–1815

Whatever its achievements, Napoleon's empire was ultimately precarious because of the hostility of Austria and Russia, as well as the belligerence of Britain. Russia was a particularly weak link in the chain of alliances and subject states because Russian landowners and merchants were angered when their vital trade in timber for the British navy was interrupted and when supplies of luxury goods, brought in British ships, began to dwindle. A century of close alliances with German ruling houses made alliance with a French ruler an extremely difficult political option for Tsar Alexander I.

It was Napoleon, however, who ended the alliance by provoking a breach with Russia. He suddenly backed away from an arrangement to marry one of Alexander's sisters and accepted the Austrian princess Marie Louise instead. (He had reluctantly divorced Joséphine in 1809 because their marriage had not produced an heir.) Also, he seized lands along the German Baltic seacoast belonging to a member of Alexander's family. When Alexander threatened rupture of the alliance if the lands were not returned, Napoleon mounted an invasion. Advisers warned him about the magnitude of the task he seemed so eager to undertake—particularly about the preparations needed for winter fighting in Russia—but their alarms went unheard.

Napoleon's previous military successes had stemmed from a combination of strategic innovations and pure audacity. Napoleon divided his forces into independent corps. Each corps included infantry, cavalry, and artillery. Organized in these workable units, his armies could travel quickly by several separate routes and converge in massive force to face the enemy. Leadership on the battlefield came from a loyal and extremely talented officer corps that had grown up since army commands had been thrown open to nonaristocrats during the Rev-

---

Grande Armée (grawnd are-MAY)

A NAPOLEONIC SOLDIER RECOUNTS THE HORRORS OF THE RUSSIAN CAMPAIGN

Jakob Walter, a stonemason from western Germany, was conscripted in 1806 into the army of a German prince, an ally of Napoleon against Prussia and Austria. In 1812, at age 24, he marched into Russia with the massive Grande Armée and was one of the lucky few to survive the campaign. Some years afterward, Walter recorded his memoirs of military life in the citizen army—including its appalling dehumanization. In this passage he describes the fleeing army's crossing of the Berezina River (in modern Belarus). Thousands managed to ford the Berezina, thanks to the heroic work of French engineers, many of whom died constructing the bridges. But the horror of the crossing, in Walter's experience, almost overshadows the fact that part of the army was saved. This excerpt also provides a glimpse of the extreme privation that the soldiers endured.

When I had gone somewhat further . . . I met a man who had a sack of raw bran in which there was hardly a dust of flour. I begged him ceaselessly to sell me a little of the bran, pressing a silver ruble into his hand; so he put a few handfuls in my little cloth. . . . When I and my master came closer to the Beresina, we camped on a near-by hill and by contributing wood I obtained a place at the fire. I immediately mixed some snow with my bran . . . [and]

allowed it to heat red on the outside in order to obtain something like bread from the inside. . . .

After a time . . . the Russians pressed nearer and nearer from every side, and the murdering and torturing seemed to annihilate everyone. . . . When it became day again, we stood near the stream approximately a thousand paces from the two bridges. . . . However, one could not see the bridges because of the crowd of people, horses and wagons. Everyone crowded together into a solid mass, and nowhere could one see a way out or a means of rescue. From morning til night we stood unprotected from the cannonballs and grenades which the Russians hurled at us from two sides. . . . I had to kneel on [my horse] in order not to have my feet crushed off, for everything was so closely packed that in a quarter of an hour one could move only four or five steps forward. To be on foot was to lose all hope of rescue. . . . Everyone was screaming under the feet of the horses, and everywhere was the cry, "Shoot me. . . ." Finally, toward four o'clock in the evening, when it was almost dark, I came to the bridge. . . . Now it is with horror, but at that time it was with a dull, indifferent feeling, that I looked at the masses of horses and people that lay dead, piled upon the bridge.

SOURCE: Jakob Walter, *The Diary of a Napoleonic Footsoldier,* ed. Marc Raeff (New York: Random House).

 For additional information on this topic, go to college.hmco.com/students.

olution. The final ingredient in the success formula was the high morale of French troops. Since the first victory of the revolutionary armies in September 1792, citizen-soldiers had proved their worth. Complicated troop movements and bravery on the battlefield were possible when troops felt they were fighting for their *nation,* not merely their ruling dynasty. Napoleon's reputation as a winning general added a further measure of self-confidence.

The campaign against Russia began in June 1812. It was a spectacular failure. (See the box "Reading Sources: A Napoleonic Soldier Recounts the Horrors of the Rus-

sian Campaign.") Napoleon had gathered a force of about 700,000 men—about half from France and half from allied states—a force twice as large as Russia's. The strategy of quickly moving independent corps and assembling massive forces could not be implemented: simply mustering so many men along the border was already the equivalent of gathering them for battle. Bold victories had often enabled Napoleon's troops to live off the countryside while they waited for supplies to catch up to the front line. But when the enemy attacked supply lines, the distances traveled were very great, the countryside was impoverished, or battles were not decisive,

Napoleon's ambitious strategies proved futile. In varying degrees, these conditions prevailed in Russia.

By the time the French faced the Russians in the principal battle of the Russian campaign—at Borodino°, west of Moscow (see Map 19.1)—the Grande Armée had been on the march for two and a half months and stood at less than half its original strength. After the indecisive but bloody battle, the French occupied and pillaged Moscow but found scarcely enough food and supplies to sustain them. When Napoleon finally led his troops out of Moscow late in October, the fate of the French forces was all but sealed. As they retreated, French and allied soldiers who had not died in battle died of exposure or starvation or were killed by Russian peasants when they wandered away from their units. The talents of generals and the determination of troops were focused on sheer survival. Of the original 700,000 troops of the Grand Armée, fewer than 100,000 made it out of Russia.

Napoleon left his army before it was fully out of Russia. A coup attempt in Paris prompted him to return to his governing duties before the French people realized the extent of the disaster in the East. The collapse of his reign had begun, spurred by a coincidental defeat in Spain. Since 1808 Spain had been largely under French domination, with Napoleon's brother, Joseph, as king. A rebel Cortes (national representative assembly), however, continued to meet in territory that the French did not control, and British troops were never expelled from the Iberian Peninsula. In 1812, as Napoleon was advancing against Russia, the collapse of French control accelerated. By the time Napoleon reached Paris at the turn of the new year, Joseph had been expelled from Spain, and an Anglo-Spanish force led by the duke of Wellington was poised to invade France.

Napoleon lost his last chance to stave off a coalition of all major powers against him when he refused an Austrian offer of peace for the return of conquered Austrian territories. With Britain willing to subsidize the allied armies, Tsar Alexander determined to destroy Napoleon, and the Austrians now anxious to share the spoils, Napoleon's empire began to crumble. Imperial forces—many now raw recruits—were crushed in the massive "Battle of Nations" near Leipzig in October 1813, during which some troops from German satellite states deserted him on the battlefield. The allies invaded France and forced Napoleon to abdicate on April 6, 1814.

Napoleon was exiled to the island of Elba, off France's Mediterranean coast, but was still treated somewhat royally. He was installed as the island's ruler and was given an

income drawn on the French treasury. Meanwhile, however, the restored French king was having his own troubles. Louis XVIII (r. 1814–1824) was the brother of the executed Louis XVI (he took the number eighteen out of respect for Louis XVI's son, who had died in prison in 1795). The new monarch had been out of the country and out of touch with its circumstances since the beginning of the Revolution. In addition to the delicate task of establishing his own legitimacy, he faced enormous practical problems, including pensioning off thousands of soldiers now unemployed and still loyal to Napoleon.

Napoleon, bored and almost penniless in his island kingdom (the promised French pension never materialized), took advantage of the circumstances and returned surreptitiously to France on February 26, 1815. His small band of attendants was joined by the soldiers sent by the king to halt his progress. Louis XVIII abandoned Paris to the returned emperor.

Napoleon's triumphant return lasted only one hundred days, however. Though many soldiers welcomed his return, many members of the elite were reluctant to throw in their lot with Napoleon again. Many ordinary French citizens had also become disenchanted with him since the defeat in Russia and with the high costs, in conscription and taxation, of raising new armies. In any case, Napoleon's reappearance galvanized the divided allies, who had been haggling over a peace settlement, into unity. Napoleon tried to strike first, but he lost against English and Prussian troops in his first major battle, at Waterloo (in modern Belgium; see Map 19.1) on June 18, 1815. When Napoleon arrived in Paris after the defeat, he discovered the government in the hands of an ad hoc committee that included the Marquis de Lafayette. Under pressure, he abdicated once again. This time he was exiled to the tiny, remote island of St. Helena in the South Atlantic, from which escape would be impossible. He died there in 1821.

The Legacy of Revolution for France and the World

The process of change in France between 1789 and 1815 was so complex that it is easy to overlook the overall impact of the Revolution. Superficially, the changes seemed to come full circle—with first Louis XVI on the throne, then Napoleon as emperor, and then Louis XVIII on the throne. Even though the monarchy was restored, however, the Revolution had discredited absolute monarchy in theory and practice. Louis XVIII had to recognize the right of "the people," however narrowly defined, to participate in government and to enjoy due process of

---

Borodino (bore-uh-DEE-no)

law. Another critical legacy of the Revolution and the Napoleonic era was a centralized political system of départements rather than a patchwork of provinces. For the first time, a single code of law applied to all French people. Most officials—from département administrators to city mayors—were appointed by the central government until the late twentieth century. The conscientious attention of the government, at various stages of the Revolution, to advances for France generally reflects the positive side of this centralization. The government sponsored national scientific societies, a national library and archives, and a system of teachers' colleges and universities. Particularly under Napoleon, a spate of canal- and road-building projects drastically improved transport systems.

Napoleon's legacy, like that of the Revolution itself, was mixed. His self-serving reconciliation of aristocratic pretensions with the opening of careers to men of talent ensured the long-term success of revolutionary principles from which the elite as a whole profited. His reconciliation of the state with the Catholic Church helped to stabilize his regime and cemented some revolutionary gains. The restored monarchy could not renege on these gains. Yet whatever his achievements, Napoleon's overthrow of constitutional principles worsened the problem of political instability. His brief return to power in 1815 reflects the degree to which his power had always been rooted in military adventurism and in the loyalty of soldiers and officers. Similarly, the swiftness of his collapse suggests that although the empire under Napoleon may have seemed an enduring solution to the political instability of the late 1790s, it was no more secure than any of the other revolutionary governments.

Although Louis XVIII acknowledged the principle of constitutionalism at the end of the Revolution, the particular configuration of his regime rested on fragile footing. Indeed, the fragility of new political systems was one of the most profound lessons of the Revolution. There was division over policies, but even greater division over legitimacy—that is, the acceptance by a significant portion of the politically active citizenry of a particular government's right to rule. Before the Revolution started, notions about political legitimacy had undergone a significant shift. The deputies who declared themselves to be the National Assembly in June 1789 already believed that they had a right to do so. In their view, they represented "the nation," and their voice had legitimacy for that reason. The shift reflects not the innate power of ideas but the power of ideas in context. These deputies brought to Versailles not only their individual convictions that "reason" should be applied to the political system but also their experience in social settings where those ideas were well received. In their salons, clubs, and literary societies, they had experienced the familiarity, trust, and sense of community that are essential to effective political action.

The deputies' attempt to transplant their sense of community into national politics was not wholly successful. Factions, competing interests, and clashes of personality can be fatal to an insecure system. The National Assembly had scarcely been inaugurated when its deputies guaranteed its failure by disqualifying themselves from standing for office under the new constitution. The king also actively undermined the system because he disagreed with it in principle. The British parliamentary system, by comparison, though every bit as elitist as the narrowest of the representative systems during the French Revolution, had a long history as a workable institution for lords, commoners, and rulers. This shared experience was an important counterweight to differences over fundamental issues, so that Parliament as an institution both survived political crises and helped resolve them. The Revolution thus left a powerful yet ambiguous legacy for France. Politics was established on new principles, yet still lacking were the practical means to achieve the promise inherent in those principles.

Throughout Europe and overseas, the Revolution left a powerful and equally complex legacy. France's continental conquests were the least enduring of the changes of the revolutionary era. Nevertheless, French domination had certain lasting effects: elites were exposed to modern bureaucratic management, and equality under the law transformed social and political relationships. Although national self-determination had an enemy in Napoleon, the breaking down of ancient political divisions provided important practical grounding for later cooperation among elites in nationalist movements. In Napoleon's kingdom of Italy, for example, a tax collector from Florence for the first time worked side by side with one from Milan. The most important legacy of the revolutionary wars, however, was the change in warfare itself made possible by the citizen armies of the French. Citizen-soldiers who identified closely with their nation, even when conscripts, proved able to maneuver and attack on the battlefield in ways that the brutishly disciplined poor conscripts in royal armies would not. In response, other states tried to build competing armies; the mass national armies that fought the world wars of the twentieth century were the result.

Naturally, the most important legacy of the French Revolution, as of the American, was the success of the Revolution itself. The most powerful absolute monarchy in Europe had succumbed to the demands of its people for dramatic social and political reforms. Throughout Europe in the nineteenth century, ruling dynasties faced revolutionary movements that demanded constitutional government, among other changes, and resorted to force to achieve it. European colonies overseas felt the impact of the Revolution and subsequent European wars in several ways. The British tried to take advantage of Napoleon's preoccupation with continental affairs by seizing French colonies and the colonies of the French-dominated Dutch. In 1806 they seized the Dutch colony of Cape Town—crucial for support of trade around Africa—as well as French bases along the African coast. In 1811 they grabbed the island of Java. In the Caribbean, the French sugar-producing islands of Martinique and Guadeloupe were particularly vulnerable to English sea power while Napoleon was executing his brilliant victories on the Continent after 1805. On the most productive of the French-controlled Caribbean islands, Saint Domingue°, the Revolution inspired a successful rebellion by the enslaved plantation workers.

The National Assembly in Paris had delayed abolishing slavery in French colonies, despite the moral appeal of such a move, because of pressure from the white planters and out of fear that the financially strapped French government would lose some of its profitable sugar trade. But the example of revolutionary daring in Paris and confusion about ruling authority as the Assembly and the king wrangled did not go unnoticed in the colonies—in either plantation mansions or slave quarters. White planters on Saint Domingue simply hoped for political and economic "liberty" from the French government and its mercantilist trade policies. White planter rule was challenged, in turn, by wealthy people of mixed European and African descent who wanted equal citizenship, hitherto denied them. A civil war broke out between these upper classes and was followed by a full-fledged slave rebellion, beginning in 1791. (See the box "Global Encounters: A Planter's Wife on the Haitian Slave Revolt.") Britain sent aid to the rebels when it went to war against the French revolutionary government in 1793. Only when the republic was declared in Paris and the Convention abolished slavery did the rebels abandon alliances with France's enemies and attempt to govern in concert with the mother country.

Although it recovered other colonies from the British, France never regained control of Saint Domingue. Led by a former slave, François Dominique Toussaint-Louverture°

Saint Domingue (SAHN dome-ANGUE)
Toussaint-Louverture (too-SAHN–loo-ver-TOUR)

Haitian Leader Toussaint-Louverture   Son of an educated slave, Toussaint-Louverture had himself been freed in 1777 but took on a leadership role when the slave revolt began on Saint Domingue in 1791. His military skill and political acumen were vital to the success of the revolt and to ruling the island's diverse population afterward.   *(Stock Montage, Inc.)*

(1743–1803), the new government of the island tried to run its own affairs, though without formally declaring independence from France. Napoleon, early in his rule, decided to tighten control of the profitable colonies by reinstituting slavery and ousting the independent government of Saint Domingue. In 1802 French forces fought their way onto the island. They captured Toussaint-Louverture, who died shortly thereafter in prison. But in 1803 another rebellion, provoked by the threat of renewed slavery, expelled French forces for good. A former aide of Toussaint's declared the independence of the colony under the name Haiti—the island's Native American name—on January 1, 1804.

The French Revolution and Napoleonic rule, and the example of the Haitian revolution, had a notable impact on Spanish colonies in the Americas. Like other Ameri-

A Planter's Wife on the Haitian Slave Revolt

Following are excerpts from two letters of Madame de Rouvray, a wealthy planter's wife living in the French colony of Saint Domingue (the western half of the island of Hispaniola), to her married daughter in France. The decree of May 15, 1791, that Madame de Rouvray mentions in her first letter granted civil rights to free persons of mixed race. The decree affected only a few hundred persons on Saint Domingue (many of whom themselves owned slaves), but white planters feared any breach in the barriers between the races. Tensions between white planters, on the one hand, and mulattoes and modest white settlers who favored revolutionary changes, on the other, enabled the well-organized slave rebellion to be dramatically successful. It began in late August 1791 and is the backdrop to Madame de Rouvray's second letter. Madame de Rouvray and her husband fled the island for the United States in 1793.

July 30, 1791

I am writing to you from Cap [a city on the island] where I came to find out what the general mood is here. . . . All the deputies who make up the general assembly [of the colony] left here the day before yesterday to gather at Léogane [another city]. If they conduct themselves wisely their first action should be to send emissaries to all the powers who have colonies with slaves in order to tell them of the decree [of May 15] and of the consequences that will follow from it, and ask for help from them in case it happens that the National Assembly actually abolishes slavery too, which they will surely do. After their decree of May 15, one cannot doubt that that is their plan. And you understand that all the powers who have slave colonies have a common interest in

opposing such a crazy plan because the contagion of liberty will soon infect their colonies too, especially in nearby Jamaica. It is said that [the English] will send a ship and troops [which] would be wonderful for us. Your father thinks it won't be long before the English take control here.

September 4, 1791

If news of the horrors that have happened here since the 23rd of last month have reached you, you must have been very worried. Luckily, we are all safe. We can't say whether our fortunes are also safe because we are still at war with the slaves who revolted [and] who have slaughtered and torched much of the countryside hereabouts. . . . All of this will gravely damage our revenues for this year and for the future, because how can we stay in a country where slaves have raised their hands against their masters? . . . You have no idea, my dear, of the state of this colony; it would make you tremble. Don't breathe a word of this to anyone but your father is determined, once the rebels have been defeated, to take refuge in Havana.

QUESTIONS

1. What is Madame de Rouvray's attitude toward the changes proposed by the National Assembly in Paris? What glimpses does she provide of the political life of the planter class in the Caribbean?

2. Why might she want her husband's plan to take refuge in Havana kept secret?

SOURCE: M. E. McIntosh and B. C. Weber, *Une Correspondance familiale au temps des troubles de Saint-Domingue* (Paris: Société de l'Histoire des Colonies Françaises et Librairie Larose, 1959), pp. 22–23, 26–28. Translated by Kristen B. Neuschel.

can colonies, the Spanish colonies wanted to loosen the closed economic ties the mother country tried to impose. In addition, the liberal ideas that had helped spawn the French Revolution spurred moves toward independence in Spanish America. Taking advantage of the confusion of authority in Spain, some of these colonies were already governing themselves independently in all but name. Echoes of radical republican ideology and of the Haitian experience resounded in some corners. For example, participants in two major rebellions in Mexico espoused

the end of slavery and championed the interests of the poor against local and Spanish elites. The leaders of these self-declared revolutions were executed (in 1811 and 1815), and their movements were crushed by local elites in alliance with Spanish troops. The efforts of local elites to become self-governing—the attempted liberal revolutions—were little more successful. Only Argentina and Paraguay broke away from Spain at this time.

But as in Europe, a legacy remained of both limited and more radical revolutionary activity, and of its risks.

Slave rebellions rocked British Caribbean islands in subsequent decades. Other colonies had learned a lesson from the Haitian revolution and were determined to avoid the horrors that had surrounded that struggle for freedom. In some regions dominated by plantations, such as some British possessions and the Spanish island of Cuba, planters were reluctant to disturb the prevailing order with any liberal political demands.

The View from Britain

Today the city of Paris is dotted with public monuments that celebrate Napoleon's victories. In London another hero and other victories are celebrated. In Trafalgar Square stands a statue of Lord Nelson, the British naval commander whose fleet destroyed a combined French and Spanish navy in 1805. Horatio Nelson was a brilliant tactician, whose innovations in maneuvering ships in the battle line resulted in stunning victories at Trafalgar and, in 1798, at the Nile Delta, which limited French ambitions in Egypt and the eastern Mediterranean. Trafalgar looms large in British history because it ensured British mastery of the seas, which then forced Napoleon into economic policies that strained French ties to France's allies and satellites. Virtually unchallenged sea power enabled the British to seize colonies formerly ruled by France and its allies.

Britain's maritime supremacy and seizure of French possessions expanded British trading networks overseas—though in some cases only temporarily—and closer to home, particularly in the Mediterranean. As long as the British had been involved in trade with India, the Mediterranean had been important for economic and strategic reasons: it marked the end of the land route for trade from the Indian Ocean. Especially after Napoleon's aggression in Egypt, the British redoubled their efforts to control strategic outposts in the Mediterranean, such as ports in southern Italy and on the island of Malta.

The British economy would expand dramatically in the nineteenth century as industrial production soared. The roots for growth were laid in this period in the countryside of Britain, where changes in agriculture and in pro-

The Battle of Trafalgar   Admiral Nelson's bold strategy of dividing his fleet to break through the line of the French-Spanish fleet at Trafalgar resembled Napoleon's successful strategies in land warfare. Nelson's maneuver isolated portions of the enemy fleet, which could then be attacked in strength. Nelson's intense naval engagements, like Napoleon's battles, caused many casualties, even for the victorious side.   *(The Bridgeman Art Library International)*

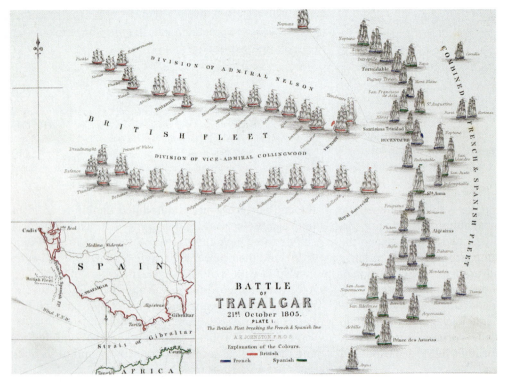

duction were occurring. These roots were also laid in Britain's overseas possessions as tighter control of foreign sources of raw materials, notably raw Indian cotton, meant rising fortunes back in Britain. In regions of India, the East India Company was increasing its political domination, and hence its economic stranglehold on Indian commodities. The export of Indian cotton rose significantly during the revolutionary period as part of an expanding trading system that included China, the source of tea.

However, economic expansion was not the sole motive for British aggression. In fact, economic expansion was often a byproduct of increased British control of particular regions or sea-lanes, and the reasons for it were as much strategic as economic. Not every conquest had direct economic payoffs, but British elites were sure that strategic domination was a desirable step, wherever it could be managed. One Scottish landholder, writing in the opening years of the nineteenth century, spoke for many when he said that Britain needed an empire to ensure its greatness and that an empire of the sea was an effective counterweight to Napoleon's empire on land. Much as the French were at that moment exporting features of their own political system, the British, he said, could export their constitution wherever they conquered territory.

Thus England and France were engaged in similar phases of expansion in this period. In both, the desire for power and profit drove policy. In each, myths about heroes and about the supposed benefits of domination masked the state's self-interest. For both, the effects of conquest would become a fundamental shaping force in the nineteenth century.

SUMMARY

 HE French Revolution was a watershed in European history because it successfully challenged the principles of hereditary rule and political privilege by which all European states had hitherto been governed. The Revolution began when a financial crisis forced the monarchy to confront the desire for political reform by a segment of the French elite. Political philosophy emerging from the Enlightenment and the example of the American Revolution moved the French reformers to action. In its initial phase the French Revolution established the principle of constitutional government and ended many of the traditional political privileges of the Old Regime.

Then, because of the intransigence of the king, the threat of foreign invasion, and the actions of republican

legislators and Parisian citizens, the Revolution moved in more radical directions. Its most extremist phase, the Terror, produced the most effective legislation for ordinary citizens but also the worst violence of the Revolution. A period of unstable conservative rule that followed the Terror ended when Napoleon seized power.

Although Napoleonic rule solidified some of the gains of the Revolution, it also subjected France and most of Europe to the great costs of wars of conquest. After Napoleon the French monarchy was restored, but henceforth its power would not be absolute—and the people would not be refused a voice in government—as a result of the Revolution. Indeed, hereditary rule and traditional social hierarchies remained in place in much of Europe, but they would not be secure in the future. The legacy of revolutionary change would prove impossible to contain in France or anywhere else.

■ Notes

1. Quoted in Samuel Eliot Morrison, *John Paul Jones: A Sailor's Biography* (Boston: Little, Brown, 1959), pp. 149–154.
2. Quoted in Owen Connelly, *The French Revolution and the Napoleonic Era* (New York: Holt, Rinehart, and Winston, 1979), p. 32.
3. James Harvey Robinson, *Readings in European History* (Boston: Ginn, 1906), p. 409.

■ Suggested Reading

Baker, Keith Michael. *Inventing the French Revolution.* 1990. A series of essays situating the Revolution amid the dramatic changes in eighteenth-century political culture.

Hunt, Lynn. *The French Revolution and Human Rights: A Brief Documentary History.* 1996. A well-presented short collection of documents, useful for a greater understanding of the impact of the Revolution on the development of human rights.

Jordan, D. P. *The King's Trial.* 1979. An engaging study of Louis XVI's trial and its importance for the Revolution.

Landes, Joan. *Women and the Public Sphere in the Age of the French Revolution.* 1988. An analysis of the uses of gender ideology to fashion the new political world of the revolutionaries.

Langley, Lester D. *The Americas in the Age of Revolution, 1750–1850.* 1996. A survey of all the American states and colonies and the impact of the Atlantic revolutions.

Popkin, Jeremy. *A Short History of the French Revolution.* 1995. A compact and readable recent synthesis of research.

For a searchable list of additional readings for this chapter, go to college.hmco.com/students.

Political Symbols

An Armed Citizen, ca. 1792 *(Bibliothèque nationale de France)*

During the French Revolution, thousands of illustrations in support of various revolutionary (or counterrevolutionary) ideas were reproduced on posters, on handbills, and in pamphlets. Some satirized their subjects, such as Marie Antoinette, or celebrated revolutionary milestones, such as the fall of the Bastille. The etching here of the woman armed with a pike, dating from 1792, falls into this category. Other pictures, such as the representation from 1795 of Liberty as a young woman wearing the liberty cap, symbolized or reinforced various revolutionary ideals.*

Political images like these are an invaluable though problematic source for historians. Let us examine these two images of women and consider how French people during the Revolution might have responded to them. To understand what they meant to contemporaries, we must know something about the other images that these would have been compared to. We must also view the images in the context of the events of the Revolution itself. Immediately, then, we are presented with an interpretive agenda. How ordinary and acceptable was this image of an armed woman? If women were not citizens coequal with men, how could a woman be a symbol of liberty? What, in short, do these political images reveal about the spectrum of political life in their society?

The woman holding the pike stares determinedly at the viewer. Many details confirm what the original caption announced: This is a French woman who has become free. In her hat she wears one of the symbols of revolutionary nationhood: the tricolor cockade. The badge around her waist celebrates a defining moment for the revolutionary nation: the fall of the Bastille. Her pike itself is inscribed with the words "Liberty or death."

*This discussion draws on the work of Joan Landes, "Representing the Body Politic: The Paradox of Gender in the Graphic Politics of the French Revolution," and Darlene Gay Levy and Harriet B. Applewhite, "Women and Militant Citizenship in Revolutionary Paris," in Sara E. Melzer and Leslie W. Rabine, eds., *Rebel Daughters: Women and the French Revolution* (New York: Oxford University Press, 1992), pp. 15–37, 79–101.

The woman appears to be serving not merely as a symbol of free women. She comes close to being the generic image of a free citizen, willing and able to fight for liberty—an astonishing symbolic possibility in a time when women were not yet treated equally under the law or granted the same political rights as the men of their class. Other images prevalent at the time echo this possibility. Many contemporary representations of the women's march on Versailles in 1789 show women carrying arms, active in advancing the Revolution. By the time this image was created (most likely in 1792), many other demonstrations and violent confrontations by ordinary people had resulted in the creation of dozens of popular prints and engravings that showed women acting in the same ways as men.

Repeatedly during 1792, women proposed to the revolutionary government that they be granted the right to bear arms. Their request was denied, but it was not dismissed out of hand. There was debate, and the issue was in effect tabled. Nevertheless, women's actions in the Revolution had created at least the possibility of envisaging citizenship with a female face.

The image of Liberty from 1795 does not reflect the actions of women but rather represents their exclusion from political participation. It is one of a number of images of Liberty that portray this ideal as a passive, innocent woman, here garbed in ancient dress, surrounded by a glow that in the past had been reserved for saints. Liberty here is envisaged as a pure and lofty goal, symbolized as a pure young woman.

Late in 1793, during the Terror, women were excluded from formal participation in politics with the disbanding of women's organizations. Nor did they gain political rights under the Directory, which re-established some of the limited gains of the first phase of the Revolution. The justification offered for their exclusion in 1793 was borrowed from Jean-Jacques Rousseau: it is contrary to nature for women to be in public life (see page 609). Women "belong" in the private world of the family, where they will nurture male citizens. Women embody ideal qualities such as patience and self-sacrifice; they are not fully formed beings capable of action in their own right.

Such notions made it easy to use images of women to embody ideals for public purposes. A woman could represent liberty precisely because actual women were not able to be political players.

The two images shown here thus demonstrate that political symbols can have varying relationships to "real-

"Liberty" as a Young Woman, ca. 1795 *(S. P. Avery Collection, Miriam and Ira D. Wallach Division of Arts, Prints, and Photographs, The New York Public Library, Astor, Lenox, and Tilden Foundations/Art Resource, NY)*

ity." The pike-bearing citizen is the more "real." Her image reflects the way of thinking about politics that became possible for the first time because of their actions. The other woman reflects not the attributes of actual women but an ideal type spawned by the use of arbitrary gender distinctions to legitimize political power. In these images we can see modern political life taking shape: the sophistication of its symbolic language, the importance of abstract ideas such as liberty and nationhood—as well as the grounding of much political life in rigid distinctions between public and private, male and female.

 For additional information on this topic, go to college.hmco.com/students.

CHAPTER 20

W ITH fires spewing from factory chimneys, it was hard to distinguish day from night. At night the sky was so lit up it might be daytime. During the day smoke and smog so obscured the sunlight that it might be night. Shropshire, England, a region previously renowned for its natural beauty, was transformed by industrial activity by 1788, when this painting was made. Containing in proximity both coal and iron deposits, Shropshire was the ideal site for establishing ironworks. Here Abraham Darby (1676–1717) and his descendants built one of the largest and most important concentrations of ironworks in Britain. The dramatic rise in the use of new machinery, which led to previously unheard-of levels in the production of iron and textiles, struck contemporaries. In the 1830s the French socialist Louis Blanqui° (see page 719) proposed a descriptive term, suggesting that just as France had recently experienced a political revolution, so Britain was undergoing an "industrial revolution." Eventually, that expression entered the general vocabulary to describe the advances in production that occurred first in England and then dominated most of western Europe by the end of the nineteenth century. Many economic historians now emphasize how gradual and cumulative the changes were and question the appropriateness of the term. Indeed, it seems best to discuss the changes not as an industrial revolution but as a continuous process of economic transformation.

Industrial development left its mark on just about every sphere of human activity. Scientific and rational methods altered production. Economic activity became increasingly specialized. The unit of production changed from the family to a larger and less personal group.

Blanqui (blahn-KEE)

George Robertson, *Nat-Y-Glo Iron Works.*
(National Museums & Galleries of Wales)

The Industrial Transformation of Europe 1750–1850

Setting the Stage for Industrialization

Industrialization and European Production

The Transformation of Europe and Its Environment

Responses to Industrialization

Significant numbers of workers left farming to enter mining and manufacturing, and major portions of the population moved from rural to urban environments. Machines replaced or supplemented manual labor.[1]

The economic changes brought about by industrial development physically transformed Europe. Greater levels of production were achieved, and more wealth was created, than ever before. Factory chimneys belched soot into the air. Miners in search of coal, iron ore, and other minerals cut deep gashes into the earth. Cities, spurred by industrialization, grew quickly, and Europe became increasingly urban.

Industrialization simultaneously created unprecedented advancement and opportunity as well as unprecedented hardships and social problems. Workers, with a growing sense of solidarity, struggled to protect and advance their interests.

QUESTIONS TO CONSIDER

- Why did Europe industrialize before the rest of the world?
- Which inventions appear to have been the most important in launching industrialization?
- What impact did industrialization have on the environment?
- What did workers gain and what did they lose as a result of industrialization?

TERMS TO KNOW

industrialization	mass production
steam engine	urbanization
factories	friendly societies
entrepreneurs	proletariat
primogeniture	Luddites

SETTING THE STAGE FOR INDUSTRIALIZATION

NO one can say with certainty what conditions were necessary for the industrialization of Europe. Nevertheless, we do know why industrialization did not spread widely to the rest of the world in the nineteenth century. A certain combination of conditions—geographic, cultural, economic, demographic—helped make industrialization possible in Europe.

Why Europe?

A unique set of circumstances seems to explain why Europe was the stage for industrial development. With the development of legal due process, rich merchants did not run the risk of having their wealth confiscated—as they did, for instance, in the Ottoman Empire, where sultans and corrupt officials on a whim grabbed wealth. Hence in the West, accumulating wealth was a worthwhile endeavor. The unfolding of state power in Europe reduced the frequency of highway robbery—still common in many parts of the world—and thus encouraged trade.

In Europe disparities of wealth, though serious, were less extreme than in other parts of the world; thus there was a better market for goods. At the time western Europe industrialized, the average yearly income per person was equivalent to $500—more than the amount in many non-Western societies even today. And nearly half of the population was literate, again a very high proportion compared with non-Western societies.

Although Europe's population grew during the eighteenth century, late marriages and limited family sizes kept its rise in check. European society was, therefore, rarely overwhelmed by population pressure. Because all of Europe's energies were not absorbed in feeding its people, it could mobilize for other production.

Compared with Asia, Europe enjoyed greater cultural, political, and social diversity. Challenges to dominant religious and political powers had brought some diversity—a rarity in Asia, where large territories tended to be dominated by a single ruler and faith. Diversity encouraged a culture that tolerated and eventually promoted innovation. Competitiveness drove states to try to outdo one another. Governments actively encouraged industries and commerce to enrich their countries and make them more powerful than their neighbors. None of these factors alone explains why industrialization occurred, but a combination of factors seems to have facilitated the process when it did.[2]

The industrialization of Europe radically transformed power relationships between the industrial West and nonindustrial Africa, Asia, and South America. By 1900 the West had overwhelmed the other regions with its economic and military power. Within Europe power shifted to the most industrial nation. Britain, the first to industrialize, was the dominant political power throughout the nineteenth century. The rest of Europe admired Britain and regarded it not only as an economic model but also as a political and cultural one. As France had been the dominant power in the eighteenth century, so Britain dominated the nineteenth, a stellar accomplishment for a small island nation.

Transformations Accompanying Industrialization

A number of transformations preceded or accompanied and helped define the industrializing era. Changes in commerce, agriculture, transportation, and behavior of the population, if not always creating the preconditions of industrial development directly, were at least the major stimuli making them possible.

Changes in agriculture increased the productivity of the land. Farmers more frequently used fertilizer and improved the rotation of their crops, easing the exhaustion of the soil. New, more efficient plows enabled them to cultivate more land than ever before. In the eighteenth century, new crops that provided high yields even in poor soil—maize (corn) and potatoes—were introduced into Europe from the Americas. The wealth created by agriculture allowed for investment in industry and for expenditures on infrastructure, such as roads and canal systems, useful to industry. More prosperous farmers could purchase manufactured goods such as iron plows and even machine-woven textiles, thus providing an impetus for industry. Most important, the new crops and the more efficient cultivation of traditional ones increased the capacity to feed a growing population and freed many people to go to the city and work in the industries.

In the seventeenth and eighteenth centuries, European trade had grown significantly, enriching entrepreneurs and making them aware of the fortunes to be made by marketing high-demand goods not just locally but even far away. A new dynamic ethos inspired entre-

CHRONOLOGY

1712	Newcomen invents steam-operated water pump
1733	Kay invents flying shuttle
1750–1800	Three million Africans are brought to the Americas as slaves
1753	First steam engine in the Americas
1760s	Hargreaves invents spinning jenny
1765	Watt improves steam engine with separate condenser
1769	Arkwright invents water frame
1777	Watt and Arkwright build power loom
1793	Whitney invents cotton gin
1804	Jacquard invents automatic loom
1811–1812	Luddites organize
1825	Börsig builds first steam engine in Germany
1831, 1834	Workers' uprising in Lyon
1832	Cholera epidemic
1834	Creation of German customs union, the Zollverein
1844	Workers' uprising in Silesia
1851	Majority of Britain's population becomes urban

preneurs to venture into untried fields of economic endeavor.

During the years of the industrial transformation, population grew enough to promote industrialization, yet not so much as to put a brake on economic expansion. The first spurt in population growth occurred in the mid-eighteenth century, before the effects of industrialization could be widely felt. Thereafter the population of Europe increased dramatically throughout the industrial era, doubling between 1750 and 1850.

This growth was partly due to a lowering of the death rate. Infant mortality had been very high from diseases such as smallpox, diphtheria, and tuberculosis. Although none of these diseases had been medically conquered,

First Railroad, from Manchester to Liverpool, England   The engineer George Stephenson (1781–1848) first built engines that could pull coal at mines, then in 1821 he constructed the first "locomotive" for public transportation. Four years later the first regular railroad line, connecting Manchester with Liverpool, was erected.   *(Private Collection/Bridgeman Art Library International)*

improved standards of living after 1750, such as improved food intake, enabled children to better resist killer diseases. New employment opportunities led to earlier marriages and thus higher fertility. This growing group of people supplied the labor force for the new industries and provided the large surge in consumers of various industrial goods.

In the countryside industrialization was foreshadowed by a form of production that had developed beginning in the seventeenth century—the putting-out system, or cottage industry. During the winter and at other slack times, peasants took in handwork such as spinning, weaving, or dyeing. Often they were marginal agriculturists, frequently women, who on a part-time basis could augment the family income. Entrepreneurs discovered that some individuals were better than others at specific tasks. Rather than have one household process the wool through all the steps of production until it was a finished piece, the entrepreneur would buy wool from one family, then take it to another to spin, a third to dye, a fourth to weave, and so on. Some historians believe that this form of production, also called protoindustrialization, laid the basis for industrial manufacture. Both

protoindustrialization and industrial manufacture depended on specialization; both supplied goods to a market beyond the producers' needs. Although cottage industry was an important contributor to industrialization in some regions, that was not the case everywhere.

A less ambiguous prerequisite for industry was a good transportation network. Transportation improved significantly in the eighteenth century. Better roads were built; new coaches and carriages could travel faster and carry heavier loads. Government and private companies built canals linking rivers to each other or to lakes. Road- and canal-building were important preconditions for industrialization, hastening and cheapening transportation and making possible the movement of raw materials to manufacture and products to market without too great an increase in the price of the finished goods. In Great Britain these transformations occurred simultaneously with industrialization; on the Continent they were actual precursors to economic change.

In Britain industrialization preceded the development of railroads. Yet once railroad expansion occurred, beginning in the 1830s, the order for iron rails, steam engines, and wagons sustained and advanced industrial

A Persian Discovers the British Rail System

In 1836 a delegation of three Persian princes visited England. Traveling widely, they had the opportunity to meet important Englishmen and to inspect and experience some of the country's latest technological advances, including the railroad. One of the princes, Najaf-Kuli Mirza, wrote down his observations. In this entry on the new British rail system, he attempts to describe its workings to fellow Persians.

All the wonderful arts which require strong power are carried on by means of steam, which has rendered immense profits and advantages. The English then began to think of steam coaches, which are especially applicable to their country, because it is small, but contains an enormous population. Therefore, in order to do away with the necessity for horses, and that the land which is sown with horse-corn [rye] should be cultivated with wheat, so as to cause it to become much more plentiful (as it is the most important article of food), and that England might thereby support a much greater population, they have with their ingenious skill invented this miraculous wonder, so as to have railroads from the capital to all parts of the kingdom.

Thus, by geometrical wisdom, they have made roads of iron, and where it was necessary these roads are elevated on arches. The roads on which the coaches are placed and fixed are made of iron bars. The coach is so fixed that no air or wind can do it any harm and twenty or thirty coaches may be fixed to the first in the train, and these one after the other.

All that seems to draw these coaches is a box of iron, in which they put water to boil, as in a fire-place; underneath this iron box is like an urn, and from it rises the steam which gives the wonderful force: when the steam rises up, the wheels take their motion, the coach spreads its wings, and the travellers become like birds. In this way these coaches go the incredible distance of forty miles an hour.

We actually travelled in this coach, and we found it very agreeable, and it does not give more but even less motion than horses; whenever we came to the sight of a distant place, in a second we passed it. The little steam engine possesses the power of eighteen horses.

QUESTIONS

1. What does the Persian traveler identify as some of the benefits of rail technology in England? Can you tell whether he believes that the railroad would be a useful innovation for his country?

2. What does the prince's report tell you about scientific knowledge and technology in Persia? Who is his intended audience?

SOURCE: Najaf-Kuli Mirza, *Journal of a Residence in England and of a Journey to and from Syria*, vol. 2 (London, 1839; repr., Farnborough, England: Gregg International Publishers, 1971), pp. 11–12.

---

growth. (See the box "Global Encounters: A Persian Discovers the British Rail System.") On the Continent, notably in Germany and later in Italy, rail-building stimulated industrialization.

INDUSTRIALIZATION AND EUROPEAN PRODUCTION

SEVERAL important technological advances powered European industry, and breakthroughs in one field often led to breakthroughs in others. The first two industries to be affected by major technological breakthroughs were textiles and iron. New forms of energy drove the machinery; novel methods of directing labor and organizing management

further enhanced production. At first limited to the British Isles, industry spread to the Continent, a development that occurred unevenly in various regions and at different times.

Advances in the Cotton Industry

A series of inventions in the eighteenth century led to the mass production of textiles. One of the earliest was the flying shuttle, introduced in Britain in 1733 by John Kay (1704–1764). (A shuttle carries the thread back and forth on a loom.) Kay's flying shuttle accelerated the weaving process to such an extent that it increased the demand for thread. This need was met in the 1760s by James Hargreaves (d. 1778), who invented the spinning jenny, a device that spun thread from wool or cotton. Improvements in spinning thread, such as the mule of Samuel

Crompton (1753–1827), made the spinning jenny increasingly efficient, and by 1812 one jenny could produce as much yarn as two hundred hand spinners. In 1769 Richard Arkwright (1732–1792), a barber and wigmaker, invented the water frame. It was installed in a single establishment with three hundred employees, forming the first modern factory. The frame was originally powered by horses or by a waterfall, but in 1777 Arkwright had James Watt construct a steam engine to operate it, making it the first power loom. With these innovations, cotton manufacturing was fully mechanized; the industry's output increased 130-fold between 1770 and 1841.

The cotton manufacturing industry in Great Britain was an important departure from traditional production. For the first time in history a staple industry was based on a natural resource that was not domestically produced. Grown mainly in the U.S. South, cotton was transformed into cloth in Britain. Manufactured cotton was comfortable to wear and easy to wash; it became so cheap that it competed effectively with all handmade textiles. The popularity of cotton may have improved public health as well, for it enabled people to own several changes of clothing and keep them clean. Everyone was eager to buy British cottons. The higher demand for raw material put pressure on cotton growers in the U.S. South, who opened up new land.

In 1793 the American Eli Whitney (1765–1825) invented the cotton gin, a device that mechanically removed the seeds from cotton, formerly a laborious hand process. The cotton gin meant that more cotton could be processed and thus more could be grown. Almost overnight the machine heightened the profitability of the

British Cotton Manufacture   Machines simultaneously performed various functions. The carding machine (*front left*) separated cotton fibers, readying them for spinning. The roving machine (*front right*) wound the cotton onto spools. The drawing machine (*rear left*) wove patterns into the cloth. Rich in machines, this factory needed relatively few employees; most were women and children. *(The Granger Collection, New York)*

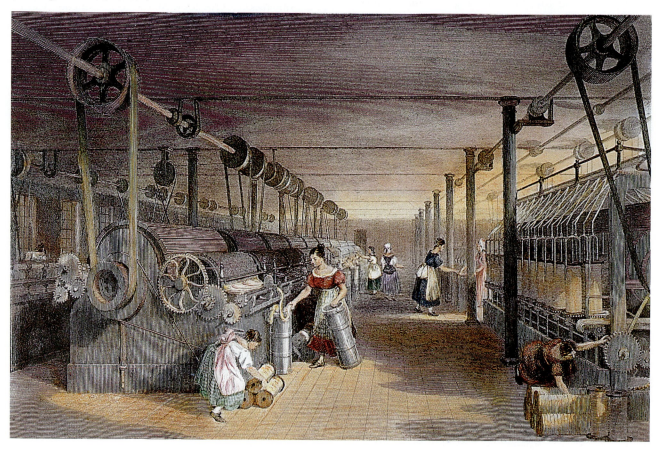

United States' southern plantation economy, and that situation increased the attractiveness of slave labor.

Between 1750 and 1800 approximately three million Africans were forcibly transported to the New World. The demographic loss to Africa was great; at least 10 percent of the captives died in the Middle Passage while being transported to the Americas, and an unknown number died in the wars triggered by slavers. Since predominantly young men were enslaved, villages were often left without their most productive workers and became vulnerable to famine, which also may have decimated the population.

The slave economy in the Americas influenced Britain's economy in several ways. Sugar produced by slave labor in the West Indies and cotton in the American South shifted Britain's trade patterns from Asia to the Atlantic. The sophisticated administrative skills that went into organizing and operating the slave trade provided invaluable management experience to the more conventional sectors of the British economy. Although some historians have argued that Britain's industrialization was founded on the wealth generated by the traffic in humans, the evidence is far from conclusive. Yet once Britain's economy was industrialized, it benefited enormously from the processing of sugar and cotton, staples produced by slaves.

In ways beneficial and not, people were interconnected by the cotton trade. Later, other products would also link the economies of various nations and peoples. No longer, as in preindustrial trade, were all goods locally made, nor did the consumers meet the producers and buy from them. Increasingly, specialization became the norm. Those most skilled performed a particular function efficiently and productively. The results were high production and low prices for finished textile products. Hand sewing and needlework, usually done by young women, completed the garment-making process. (See the box "Reading Sources: A French Woman Goes to Work.")

Iron, Steam, and Factories

Industrial production was facilitated by the use of a new energy source, coal. Traditionally, charcoal had fueled the smelting of iron. Britain, however, ran low on wood—the source of charcoal—before other European countries did and needed an alternative fuel. There was plenty of coal, but it contained impurities, particularly sulfur, which contaminated the materials with which it came into contact. In 1708 the English ironmaster Abraham Darby discovered that coal in a blast furnace could smelt iron without these attending complications. His

discovery triggered the iron industry's use of coal. In 1777 the introduction of a steam engine to operate the blast furnace considerably increased efficiency. In 1783 a steam engine was first used to drive a forge hammer to shape the iron; three years later steam-driven rollers flattened the iron into sheets. With these innovations, the output of the English iron industry doubled between 1788 and 1796 and again in the following eight years.

The greater supply of iron stimulated other changes. Relatively cheap and durable iron machines replaced wooden machines, which wore out rapidly. The new machines opened the door to further advances. Improvements in manufacturing methods and techniques led to the production of ever larger amounts of goods, usually at lower prices. Industrial change started with cotton, but breakthroughs in the use of iron and coal continued and sustained these changes.

Before the age of industry, the basic sources of power were humans, animals, wind, and water. Humans and animals were limited in their capacities to drive the large mills needed to grind grain or cut wood. Wind was unreliable because it was not constant. Water-driven mills depended on the seasons—streams dried up in the summer and froze in the winter. And water mills could be placed only where a downward flow of water was strong enough to drive a mill. Clearly the infant industries needed a power source that was constant and not confined to riverbanks. The steam engine, invented and improved on in Britain, met that need and stoked the island's industrial growth. As late as the 1860s, people, animals, and wind- and water-operated machines still supplied more than half of the energy needs of manufacturing in Great Britain and the United States. But the steam engine was clearly the wave of the future.

The steam engine was first used to pump water out of coal mines. As mining shafts were dug ever deeper through groundwater, drainage became a critical factor. In 1712 Thomas Newcomen (1663–1729) invented a steam-operated water pump. Its use spread rapidly. The first steam engine in the Americas was a Newcomen engine installed in New Jersey in 1753. James Watt (1736–1819) improved on the Newcomen engine considerably, making it twice as efficient in energy output. Eventually, by developing a separate condenser, Watt devised an engine that enabled the steam engine to power a variety of machines. Thus steam engines could operate mills that had previously been powered by water or wind. The high-pressure steam engine was even more powerful and energy-efficient. The use of steam engines spread in Britain and then to the Continent and the United States.

READING SOURCES

A FRENCH WOMAN GOES TO WORK

The new cotton mills presented several obstacles to women workers. They had to negotiate the machinery while wearing the petticoats and aprons that custom required. Such dress could catch in the machinery, causing broken limbs and loss of a job, if not of life. At work and on their way to and from work in the British mills or at the less mechanized garment workshops of France, women had to pass dangerous places, where some experienced sexual harassment. Suzanne Voilquin (ca. 1801–ca. 1876), forced to go out to work to help her parents, took a job not at a mill or a factory, as was common in England, but as an embroiderer in a small workshop in Paris. In this selection she writes of her experiences as a young woman from about 1823 to 1825.

We had to be at our looms at seven o'clock sharp and, even before setting out on the long race to get there on time, we had to carry out all our little household duties as quickly as we could. If certain details made us late, Mrs. Martin [her employer] would accept no excuses and offer no reprieve. We had to pay in kind, that is to say, make good those few minutes at the end of the day's work. When our days were prolonged in this way, I had a horrible fear of meeting on my return one of those contemptible men who make a game of accosting young working women and frightening them with disgraceful remarks. When this happened, my nerves were always on edge and I lacked all physical courage. It was quite otherwise with . . . Adrienne [her younger sister]. She would say to me, . . . "Dear Sister, aren't I here?" (She was barely fifteen.) "If the occasion arises, why then you'll see that *a person's worth is not measured in years!*" And indeed, one evening, she gave me positive proof. Around nine o'clock . . . we were stopped by the vulgar words and filthy gestures of some poor wretch. As always, I stood there trembling and unable to speak before this reviler. Adrienne, on the contrary, experienced a moment of sublime energy. She managed to find such a tone of resolve, while brandishing an enormous key before his eyes, that he backed away, and, when we reached the corner of the main street, we were delivered from his insolent remarks.

Mrs. Martin seemed satisfied with our work, and we were accepted as regular employees. And so, at the end of the first week, we were very proud to deposit on our father's mantelpiece the eighteen francs we earned as wages. It was the same each week.

Source: Suzanne Voilquin, "Recollections of a Daughter of the People," in Mark Traugott, ed. and trans., *The French Worker: Autobiographies from the Early Industrial Era.* Copyright © 1993 The Regents of the University of California. Reprinted by permission of The University of California Press.

The steam engine centralized the workplace. With the machine as a central power source, it became practical and commonplace to organize work in a factory. Locating a manufacturing plant where it was most convenient eliminated the expense of transporting raw materials to be worked on at a natural but fixed power source such as a waterfall. The central factory also reinforced work discipline. These factories were large, austere edifices, sometimes inspired by military architecture and therefore resembling barracks. With the introduction of blast furnaces and other heat-producing manufacturing methods, the tall factory chimney became a common sight on the industrial landscape.

The steam engine powered a dramatic growth in production. It increased the force of blast furnaces and the mechanical power of machinery used to forge iron and to produce equipment for spinning and weaving. Assisted by machines, workers were enormously more productive than when they depended solely on hand-operated tools. In 1700 spinning 100 pounds of cotton took 50,000 worker-hours; by 1825 it took only 135 worker-hours—a 370-fold increase in productivity capacity per worker.

Inventors and Entrepreneurs

Inventions triggered the industrial age, and the continued flow of new ones sustained it. People were seeing in their lifetimes sizable growth in productivity, both in the factory and on the farm. Rather than cling to traditional methods, many entrepreneurs persistently challenged tradition and attempted to find new ways of improving production. In this age of invention, innovation was prized as never before.

The early inventors and industrialists came from a variety of backgrounds. In Britain very few were landed nobles, industrial workers, or artisans. A large number of the early manufacturers were university educated, a fact suggesting that even in the early stages of industry, scientific knowledge was valuable. Most came from the merchant class, since also in these early years the possession of capital was a distinct advantage in launching an industrial enterprise. In France Joseph-Marie Jacquard (1752–1834), the son of a weaver, invented the Jacquard loom in 1804, which used a punched-card system to automate silk weaving. Within his lifetime industrialists in France and England adopted his loom, which later became the model for early computers using punched cards.

Entrepreneurs such as Arkwright and Watt pioneered innovations and became famous, but most who advanced the cause of industrial production were not particularly inventive. They just replicated methods of production that had proved profitable to others. Truly successful entrepreneurs, however, seemed to share one attribute: they were driven by a nearly insatiable appetite for innovation, work, and profit.

Entrepreneurs took the financial risk of investing in new types of enterprises. Most industrialists ran a single plant by themselves or with a partner, but even in the early stages, some ran several plants. In 1788 Richard Arkwright and his partners ran eight mills. Some enterprises were vertically integrated, controlling production at many stages. The Peels in Britain owned operations ranging from spinning to printing and even banking. The entrepreneurs' dynamism and boldness fostered the growth of the British industrial system, making that small nation the workshop of the world.

Britain's Lead in Industrial Innovation

Britain led the way industrially for many reasons. It was the first European country to have a standard currency, tax, and tariff system. Although Britain was by no means an egalitarian society, it accommodated some movement between the classes. Ideas and experiments were readily communicated among entrepreneurs, workers, and scientists.

In addition, England had gained an increasing share of international trade since the seventeenth century. This trade provided capital for investment in industrial

Augusta Ada Byron, Countess of Lovelace (1815–1852)
Daughter of the poet Lord Byron (see page 714), Ada was tutored at home in many subjects and became an accomplished mathematician. At a London party she met Charles Babbage (1792–1871), who was demonstrating his new invention, the Analytical Engine—considered the earliest computer—which she compared to the Jacquard loom. She subsequently described how to program the machine to perform calculations, and she is considered the first computer programmer.   *(Queen's Printer and Controller of HMSO, 2002. UK Government Art Collection)*

plants. The world trade network also ensured that Britain had a market beyond its borders, and because total demand was relatively high, mass manufacture was feasible. The international trade network also enabled Britain to import raw materials for its industry, the most important of which was cotton.

Earlier than its competitors, Britain had a national banking system that could finance industries in areas where private funding fell short. In addition to numerous London banks lending mainly in the capital, six hundred provincial banks serviced the economy by 1810. The banking system reflected the growth of the economy as much as it contributed to it. Banking could flourish because Britons had wide experience in trade, had accumulated considerable amounts of wealth, and had found a constant demand for credit.

Geographically, Britain was also fortunate. Coal and iron were located close to each other (see Map 20.1). Because Britain is a relatively narrow island, virtually all of it has easy access to the sea—no part of the country is more than 70 miles from the coast. This was a strategic advantage, for water was by far the cheapest means of transportation. Compared with the Continent, Britain

had few tolls, and moving goods was relatively easy and inexpensive.

On the whole, British workers were better off than their continental counterparts. They were more skilled, earned higher wages, and had discretionary income to spend on the manufactured goods now for sale. But because labor was more costly than on the Continent, British business owners had an incentive to find labor-saving devices and reduce the number of workers needed for production.

The population of Great Britain increased by 8 percent in each decade from 1750 to 1800, in part as a result of industrial growth. This swelling population expanded the market for goods. The most rapid growth occurred in the countryside, causing a steady movement of people from rural to urban areas. The presence of this work force was another contributing factor in Britain's readiness for change.

Britain was far more open to dissent than were other European countries at the time. The lack of conformity was reflected in religion and also in a willingness to try new methods of production. In fact, the two often went together. A large proportion of British entrepreneurs were Quakers or belonged to one of the dissenting (non-Anglican) religious groups. Among these were the iron-making Darby family; the engineer of the steam engine, James Watt; and the inventor of the spinning mule, Samuel Crompton. Perhaps dissenters were accustomed to questioning authority and treading new paths. They were also well educated and, as a result of common religious bonds, inclined to provide mutual aid, including financial support.

The timing of the industrial transformation in Britain was also influenced by plentiful harvests in the years 1715 to 1750, creating low food prices and thus making possible low industrial wages. The demand for industrial goods was reasonably high. Farmers with good earnings could afford to order the new manufactured iron plows. It is likely that income from farming helped bring about changes associated with industrialization, such as population growth, improvements to the transportation system, and the growing availability of capital for investment. Thus each change triggered more change; the cumulative effect was staggering.

Map 20.1 The Industrial Transformation in England, ca. 1850 Industry developed in the areas rich in coal and iron fields. Important cities sprang up nearby and were soon linked by a growing rail network.

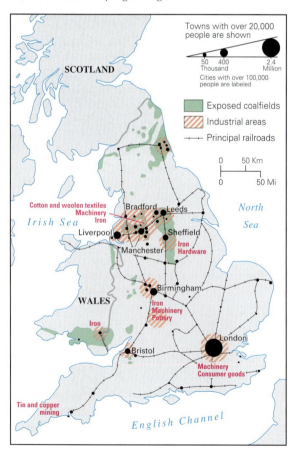

The Spread of Industry to the Continent

The ideas and methods that were changing industry in Britain spread to the Continent by direct contact and by emulation. Visitors came to Britain, studied local methods of production, and returned home to set up blast

The Börsig Ironworks in the 1840s   August Börsig, an artisan, founded these ironworks in Berlin. The factory expanded to meet the needs of the burgeoning German rail system. By the time of Börsig's death in 1854, his factory had built five hundred locomotives.   *(Bildarchiv Preussischer Kulturbesitz/Art Resource, NY)*

furnaces and spinning works inspired by British design. The German engineer August Börsig° (1804–1854), after studying steam engines in Britain, built the first German steam engine in 1825 and the first German locomotive in 1842. Some visitors even resorted to industrial espionage, smuggling blueprints of machines out of Britain. Although a British law forbade local artisans to emigrate, some did leave, including entrepreneurs who helped set up industrial plants in France and Belgium. By the 1820s British technicians were all over Europe—in Belgium, France, Germany, and Austria.

In the eighteenth century, France had seemed a more likely candidate for economic growth than Britain. France's overseas trade was growing faster than Britain's. In 1780 France's industrial output was greater than

Britain's, though production per person was less. In the nineteenth century, however, while Britain's industry boomed and it became the workshop of the world, France lagged behind. Why?

Historians have suggested several reasons. The wars and revolutions of the late eighteenth century were certainly contributing factors. They slowed economic growth and cut France off from the flow of information and new techniques from Britain. Moreover, in the 1790s, when the French peasants pressured for legislation to ease their situation, the revolutionaries responded positively. Thus the misery of the peasantry was somewhat relieved, and the peasants were comfortable enough to feel no urgency to leave the land and provide the kind of cheap and ready labor that Britain had. Further, the Napoleonic Code of 1804 abolished primogeniture, so that when a peasant died, his younger sons were not forced off the land.

Börsig (BEUR-sick)

Population figures suggest another reason for France's relatively low economic growth. Between 1800 and 1914 the population of France grew at half the average rate experienced by the rest of the Continent. In Britain during this period, much of the labor that left the land and worked the factories and mills came from the rural population explosion. But no such phenomenon occurred in the French countryside, and thus the labor force in France was not poised for industrial growth.

Traditionally, France had produced high-quality luxury goods, and French entrepreneurs who sought to emulate British accomplishments faced serious difficulties. Iron and coal deposits in France were not close together (see Map 20.2). Because labor was still quite cheap, many goods could be manufactured inexpensively by hand; thus the incentive to invest in laborsaving devices was absent. Soon, however, French manufacturers found themselves facing British competition. By being the first

to industrialize, the British had the advantage of being able to manufacture goods and to corner markets efficiently and relatively cheaply. The French were the first to feel the negative effects of being industrial latecomers.

The invasions of Germany by Napoleon caused considerable destruction, but they also brought some positive economic benefits. The example of the French Revolution led to important socioeconomic changes. Restrictive guilds declined. The French occupiers suppressed the small German states with their many tariffs and taxes, established a single unified legal system— which survived even after 1815—and introduced a single standard of measurement based on the metric system.

Government in Germany played an important role in the adoption of improved methods of manufacturing. The Prussian state, eager for industrial development, sent an official to Britain to observe the puddling process (the method by which iron is freed of carbon) and

Map 20.2 Continental Industrialization, ca. 1850   Industry was still sparse on the Continent, but important regions had developed near major coal deposits in Liège, the Ruhr, and Silesia.

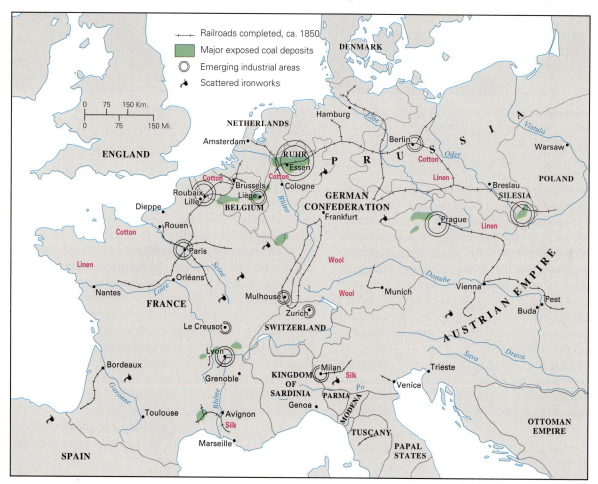

bring that know-how back home. The Prussian government promoted industrial growth by investing in a transportation network to carry raw materials for processing and finished goods to their markets. To spur both trade and industrial growth, Prussia took the lead in creating a customs union, the *Zollverein°*, which abolished tariffs among its members. By 1834 a German market embracing eighteen German states with a population of 23 million had been created.

German industrial growth accelerated dramatically in the 1850s. Massive expenditures on railways created a large demand for metal, which pressured German manufacturers to enlarge their plant capacities and increase efficiency. The German states were not yet politically unified, but the German middle classes saw economic growth as the means by which their country could win a prominent place among Europe's nation-states.

Germany's growth was phenomenal. It successfully emulated Britain, overtook France, and toward the end of the nineteenth century pioneered in the electrical engineering and chemical industries. If France experienced the disadvantages of being a latecomer, Germany reaped the benefits of that status. The Germans were able to avoid costly and inefficient early experimentation and to adopt the latest, proven methods; moreover, Germany entered fields that Britain had neglected.

Even by the end of the century, however, progress remained slow in many areas of Europe. As long as Russia retained serfdom (until 1861), it would lack the mobile labor force needed for industrial growth. And until late in the century, the ruling Russian aristocracy hesitated to adopt an economic system in which wealth was not based on land. In Austria, Bohemia was the only important industrial center; otherwise, Austria remained heavily agrarian (see Map 20.2).

The impoverished southern Mediterranean countries experienced little economic growth. With mostly poor soil, their agriculture yielded only a meager surplus. Spain, lacking coal and access to other energy sources, could not easily diversify its economic base. Some industry emerged in Catalonia, especially around Barcelona, but it was limited in scope and did not have much impact on the rest of the country. The Italian peninsula was still industrially underdeveloped in the middle of the nineteenth century. There were modest advances, but growth was too slow to have a measurable positive impact on the Italian economy. In 1871, 61 percent of the population of Italy was still agrarian.

Although by midcentury only a few European nations had experienced industrialization to any great extent, many more would do so by the end of the century, pressured by vigorous competition from their more advanced neighbors (see Figure 20.1). The potential threat was political and military as well as economic, for the industrialized nations had the backing of military might and superiority. Compared with the rest of the world, the European continent in the nineteenth century had acquired a distinct material culture that was increasingly based on machine manufacture or was in the process of becoming so. The possession of "skillful industry," one Victorian writer exulted, was "ever a proof of superior civilization." Although only some regions of Europe were

Figure 20.1   The Increase in Gross National Product per Capita in Principal European Countries, 1830–1913   The countries that industrialized rapidly—such as the United Kingdom in particular, and also Belgium, France, and Germany—experienced dramatic increases in per capita income during the nineteenth century. Other countries, such as Greece and Portugal, economically trailed the industrial leaders, and per capita income there remained essentially flat.   *(Source: Norman J. G. Pounds, An Historical Geography of Europe, 1800–1914 [New York: Cambridge University Press, 1985], p. 32. Used by permission of the publisher.)*

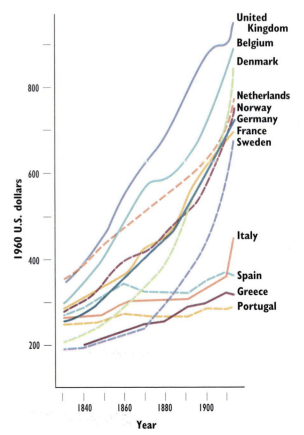

Zollverein (TZOLL-fair-eyn)

industrialized, many Europeans came to view themselves as obviously "superior," while deeming all other races inferior.

THE TRANSFORMATION OF EUROPE AND ITS ENVIRONMENT

INDUSTRY changed the traditional methods of agriculture, commerce, trade, and manufacture. It also transformed people's lives, individually and collectively. It altered how they made a livelihood, where and how they lived, even how they thought of themselves. Industry's need of people with specialized skills created new occupations. Because industry required specialization, the range of occupations that people adopted expanded dramatically.

The advent of industry transformed the way society functioned. Until the eighteenth century, the basis of influence and power was hereditary privilege, which meant aristocratic birth and land. The aristocracy did not disappear overnight. From the late eighteenth century on, however, it was challenged by a rising class of people whose wealth was self-made and whose influence was based on economic contributions to society rather than on bloodlines. Increased social mobility opened opportunities even for some workers. Industrialization transformed both the social and the natural environment. Cities experienced extraordinary growth as a result of industrialization. Europeans faced not only urban problems but also the dangerous pollution of their air and water.

Urbanization and Its Discontents

A sociologist at the end of the nineteenth century observed, "The most remarkable social phenomenon of the present century is the concentration of population in cities."[3] The number and size of cities grew as never before. The major impetus for urban growth was the concentration of industry in cities and the resulting need of large numbers of urban workers and their families for goods and services (see Map 20.3).

Industrialization was not the only catalyst. France provides many examples of urban growth with little industry. Increased commercial, trading, and administrative functions led to the growth of cities such as Toulouse, Bordeaux, and Nancy. Neither Holland, Italy, nor Switzerland witnessed much industrial development in the first half of the nineteenth century, yet their cities grew. In

general, however, industry transformed people from rural to urban inhabitants. People wanted to live near their work, and as industries concentrated in cities, so did populations.

Urban growth in some places was explosive. In the entire eighteenth century, London grew by only 200,000; but in the first half of the nineteenth century, it grew by 1.4 million, more than doubling its size. Liverpool and Manchester experienced similar growth in the same period. Census figures show that by 1851 Britain was a predominantly urban society, the first country to have as many people living in cities as in the countryside. For Germany that date was 1891, and for France it was not until 1931. Although the proportion of people who were urban varied from place to place, the trend was clear and has continued.

As the pace of industry governed in part urban growth, it was fueled in turn by urbanization. Large cities provided convenient markets for goods and a labor pool for manufacturing. The concentration of people encouraged the exchange of ideas. A large city was likely to have scientific societies and laboratories where engineers and scientists could share new ideas and new inventions that would encourage industrial production. After midcentury, industrialization was driven more and more by scientific and technological breakthroughs made in urban environments.

Cities pulled in people from near and far. Usually the larger the city, the stronger its ability to attract migrants from great distances. The medium-sized French town of Saint-Etienne° drew resettlers from the nearby mountains, whereas Paris drew from the entire country. Industrial centers even attracted people from beyond the nation's borders. The Irish arrived in large numbers to work in the factories of Lancashire, in northwestern England; Belgians came for mine work in northern France; and Poles sought employment in the Ruhr Valley of western Germany. Industrial activity stimulated the growth of world trade and shipping across the seas, taking merchant sailors far from home. Many large cities were marked by heterogeneous populations, which included people with different native languages, religions, and national origins, as well as, in some cases, people of different races. Africans and Asians inhabited port cities such as Amsterdam, Marseille, and Liverpool.

With the growth of cities came a multitude of urban ills. In the first half of the nineteenth century, mortality rates were higher in the cities than in the countryside. In

---

Saint-Etienne (sen-et-YEN)

the 1840s Britain as a whole had a death rate of 22 per thousand, but Liverpool averaged 39.2 and Manchester 33.1. In France national mortality rates were around 22 per thousand, but in some French cities the rate was as high as 35 per thousand. Social inequality in the face of death was startling. Including the high child mortality rate, the average age at death for members of gentry families in Liverpool in 1842 was 35; for members of laborers' families it was 15. In 1800 boys living in urban slums were 8 inches shorter than the sons of rich urban dwellers.

The rapid growth of the cities caught local authorities unprepared, and in the early stages of industrialization, city life was particularly severe for the poor. Urban slums developed. The most notorious London slum was St. Giles, which became a tourist attraction because of its squalor. In many cities large numbers of people were crammed into small areas. The houses were built back to back on small lots and had insufficient lighting and ventilation. Overcrowding was the norm. (See the box "Reading Sources: A Slum in Manchester.")

Sanitation was rudimentary or nonexistent. A single privy in a courtyard was likely to serve dozens of tenants—in some notorious cases in Britain and France, a few hundred. Waste from the privy might drain through open sewers to a nearby river, which was likely to be the local source of drinking water. Or the privy might be connected to a cesspool, from which wastewater would seep and contaminate nearby wells. Some tenants lacked toilets and relieved themselves in the streets. In the 1830s

Map 20.3   Cities Reaching Population Level of 100,000 by 1750, 1800, and 1850   In 1750 the largest cities owed their existence to factors other than industry, but thereafter the development of industry often determined the growth of cities. England, the leading industrial nation, contained many of the largest cities.   *(Source: Data from Tertius Chandler,* Four Thousand Years of Urban Growth: An Historical Census *[Lewistown, N.Y.: St. David's University Press, 1987], pp. 22–24.)*

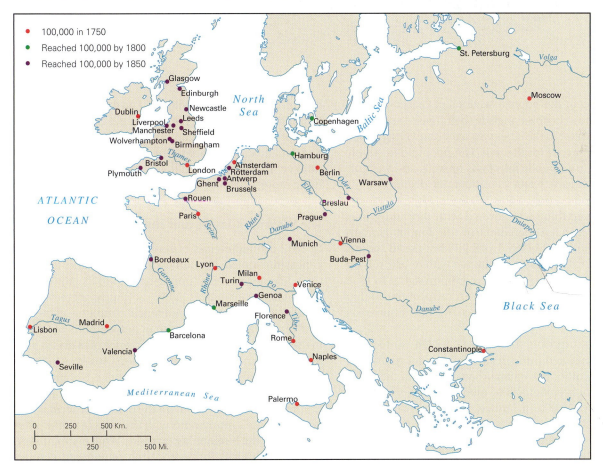

St. Giles   The most notorious London slum was St. Giles, whose human squalor made it a tourist attraction.   *(From Thomas Beames,* The Rookeries of London. *Photo: Harvard Imaging Service)*

people living in the poorest sections of Glasgow stored human waste in heaps alongside their houses and sold it as manure. Water in the cities was scarce and filthy. Piped water was reserved for the rich. The poor had to supply themselves from public fountains or wells and were often obliged to carry water a considerable distance.

In manufacturing towns factory chimneys spewed soot, and everything was covered with dirt and grime. Smoke was a major ingredient of the famous London fog, which not only reduced visibility but posed serious health risks. City streets were littered with refuse; rotting corpses of dogs and horses were common sights. In 1858 the stench from sewage and other rot was so putrid that the British House of Commons was forced to suspend its sessions.

It is not surprising that cholera, a highly infectious disease transmitted through contaminated water, swept London and other European urban centers. In the 1830s one of the first epidemics of modern times struck Europe, killing 100,000 in France, 50,000 in Britain, and 238,000 in Russia. A generation later the cholera epidemic of 1854 killed 150,000 in France. Typhoid fever, also an acute infectious disease, struck mostly the poor but did not spare the privileged. Queen Victoria of Great Britain nearly died of it; her husband, Prince Albert, did.

For most of its denizens, the city provided a crowded and squalid environment. Only in the second half of the nineteenth century would any attempts be made to bring order to the chaos of urban life.

The Working Classes and Their Lot

In 1842 a middle-class observer traveling in industrial Lancashire noted that around the mills and factories there had developed a "population [that] like the system to which it belongs is NEW . . . hourly increasing in breadth and strength."[4] A French countess, using the pen name Daniel Stern, wrote in her memoirs of France in the 1830s and 1840s of the emergence of "a class apart, as if it were a nation within the nation," working in factories and mines, called "by a new name: the industrial proletariat."[5] Originally used to designate the poorest propertyless wretches in Roman society, the term *proletariat* became synonymous with the class of workers developing in the burgeoning factories. What distinguished this growing class throughout the nineteenth century

READING SOURCES

A SLUM IN MANCHESTER

The terrible conditions in urban slums were captured by the physician James Philips Kay, who practiced medicine in the newly industrialized city of Manchester, England. The dizzying pace of growth made it impossible for the city to provide basic sanitary facilities for its inhabitants. At the time Kay wrote, in 1832, the causes of many diseases, such as typhus and tuberculosis, were not known. He attributed the unhealthiness of the city to dirt, and, in a way, he was right. In the dirt, dampness, and darkness of crowded tenements and polluted streets, the fleas that communicated typhus and tuberculosis bacteria thrived.

Manchester, properly so called, is chiefly inhabited by shopkeepers and the labouring classes. Those districts where the poor dwell are of very recent origin. The rapid growth of the cotton manufacture has attracted hither operatives from every part of the kingdom, and Ireland has poured forth the most destitute of her hordes to supply the constantly increasing demand for labour. . . .

The state of the streets powerfully affects the health of their inhabitants. Sporadic cases of typhus chiefly appear in those which are narrow, ill ventilated, unpaved, or which contain heaps of refuse, or stagnant pools. The confined air and noxious exhalations, which abound in such places, depress the health of the people. And on this account contagious diseases are also most rapidly propagated there. The operation of these causes is exceedingly promoted by their reflex influence on the manners. The houses, in such situations, are unclean, ill provided with furniture; an air of discomfort if not of squalid and loathsome wretchedness pervades them, they are often dilapidated, badly drained, damp; and the habits of their tenants are gross—they are ill-fed, ill-clothed. . . .

A whole family is often accommodated on a single bed, and sometimes a heap of filthy straw and a covering of old sacking hide them in one undistinguished heap, debased alike by penury, want of economy and dissolute habits. Frequently, the inspectors found two or more families crowded into one small house, containing only two apartments, one in which they slept, and another in which they eat; and often more than one family lived in a damp cellar, containing only one room, in whose pestilential atmosphere from twelve to sixteen persons were crowded. To these fertile sources of disease were sometimes added the keeping of pigs and other animals in the house, with other nuisances of the most revolting character.

Source: J. P. Kay, *The Moral and Physical Condition of the Working Classes Employed in the Cotton Manufacture in Manchester* (London: James Ridgway, 1832), pp. 6, 14–15, 19.

---

was that it was relatively unskilled and totally dependent on the factory owners for its livelihood. In earlier eras apprentices appear to have occupied a similar situation. But guild rules and traditions gave apprentices some protection from arbitrariness, and they could escape their lowly position by eventually becoming master artisans themselves, owning their own tools and being masters of their own time—a possibility denied the members of the working classes.

As industry advanced and spread, more and more people depended on it for a livelihood. In the putting-out system, during an agricultural downturn, a cottager could spend more time on hand labor; when demand for piecework slacked off, the cottager could devote more time to the land. But people living in industrial cities had no such backup. And neither skilled nor unskilled work-

ers were assured of regular employment: any downturn in the economy translated into layoffs or job losses.

In addition, the introduction of new industries often devastated laborers in older forms of production. The mechanization of cotton production reduced the earning power of weavers in England and in Flanders, for instance. The production of linen was mechanized in Belgium by the 1840s, but cotton production was so much cheaper that in order to price their wares competitively, linen producers drastically reduced their workers' wages.

Most factory work was dirty and laborious in grim plants with heavy, noisy machinery. Sixteen-hour workdays were common. Child labor was widespread. With no safety provisions, the workers were prone to accidents. Few factory owners protected their workers against dangerous substances or circumstances. Mercury

Children Toiling in Mines Able to crawl in narrow mine shafts, many children were employed underground. In this woodcut, a woman joins a child in his labor. Often whole families worked together and were paid a fixed price for the amount of coal extracted. *(Hulton Archive/Getty Images)*

used in hat manufacturing gradually poisoned the hatmakers and often led to dementia, hence the term "mad hatters." Lead used in paints and pottery also had a devastating impact on workers' health.

Usually physically lighter than boys and often underfed, young girls were faced with heavy labor that undermined their health. In 1842, 18-year-old Ann Eggley, a mineworker since the age of 7, hauled carriages loaded with ore weighing 800 pounds for twelve hours a day. She testified to a parliamentary commission that she was so tired from her work that when she came home, she often fell asleep before even going to bed. Isabel Wilson, another mineworker, testified that she had given birth to ten children and had suffered five miscarriages. These women were overworked, exhausted, and vulnerable to disease, and they faced premature death.

Did industrialization improve the workers' lot? Perhaps this question is best answered by another question: What would the workers have done without industrial employment? A population explosion meant that many did not have enough land to make a living, and more efficient farming methods lessened the need for farm hands. It is not clear that these workers could have made a better living, or any at all, if they had remained in the country.

Until the mid-nineteenth century, information on workers' income and expenses is incomplete. The best evidence comes from Britain, where an average family of five needed at least 21 shillings a week to fend off poverty. Skilled workers, who were in demand, might earn as much as 30 shillings a week, but most workers were unskilled. And even skilled workers enjoyed little security: if they became less productive because of illness or old age, their wages fell. If women and children did not always need to work to help the family meet its minimum needs, at some point they usually did have to pitch in. Women, even when they were the main breadwinners, almost never received wages sufficient to meet a family's total needs.

Incomes were so low that workers normally spent between two-thirds and three-fourths of their budget on food. Those who lived in rural areas might raise chickens or pigs or have a plot of potatoes. Bread was the largest single item consumed, varying between one and two pounds a day per person. In Britain and Germany people also ate a lot of potatoes. A little bacon or other meat gave flavor to the soup in which people dipped their bread or potatoes, but meat was rarely consumed as a main course. Because men were the chief breadwinners and tended to have the most strenuous occupations, they received the choice piece of meat and the largest amount of food. Women and children ate what was left.

From the beginning, industrialization increased society's wealth. But did it benefit workers? "Optimist" historians argue that some of the new wealth trickled down to the lower levels of society. "Pessimist" historians say that a downward flow did not necessarily occur. Statistics suggest that by the 1840s workers' lives in Britain did improve. Their real income rose by 40 percent between 1800 and 1850.

Factory workers benefited not only from increased earnings but from the relatively low prices of many basic goods. In London the price of 4 pounds of household bread fell from 15 pennies at the beginning of the nineteenth century to 8½ pennies in the 1830s. As the cost of cloth declined, the dress of working-class people noticeably improved. On the Continent, the lot of workers improved a little later than in Britain, but the process followed the same pattern. (See the feature "Weighing the Evidence: Workers' Wages" on pages 704–705.)

Industrialization and the Family

Industrialization dramatically changed the character of the working-class family and household. Job segregation reserved the best-paying jobs for men; men were supervisors and ran machinery such as the jenny. Especially in the textile industries, factory owners employed children and women in the lowliest positions. They were thought to be more pliable than men, and their wages were considerably lower. Women generally received from 30 to 50 percent of men's wages, children from 5 to 25 percent. In 1839 Thomas Heath, a weaver in Spitalfields, a London neighborhood, earned 15 shillings a week, his wife but 3 shillings.

Factory work often undermined the ability of women to take care of their children. As farmers or cottagers, women had been able simultaneously to work and to supervise their children. The factory, however, often separated mothers from their children. Many children were given heavy responsibilities at an early age, and it was not uncommon for an older child, sometimes only 5 or 6 years old, to be entrusted with the care of a younger sibling.

Urban and rural women, usually unmarried domestic servants, sometimes resorted to more dangerous methods of child-care. In England they might send newborns to "babyfarms," run by individuals in the countryside who were paid to take care of infants. In France and Italy poor mothers abandoned their infants at foundling homes, which in turn sent them to women in the countryside to breast-feed them. Very often these babies were neglected, and their mortality rate was extremely high. In many cases babyfarming was no more than a camouflaged form of infanticide. Mothers who kept their children but were obliged to leave them unwatched at home during factory hours sometimes pacified the children by drugging them with mixtures of opium, readily available from the local apothecary.

Working-class women carried an exhausting burden in the family. In addition to sometimes working outside the home, they were responsible for running the household, managing the family income, and taking care of the children, providing most of the nurture and supervision they required.

Because of the many demands on married women, their employment pattern often was affected by the life cycle. Young women might work before marriage or before giving birth, stay home until the children were older, and then return to work. Factory work had a harsh impact on women's lives, but it should be remembered that relatively few women were in the wage market—by 1850 only about a quarter in both Britain and France. Of that quarter, few worked in factories; far more were in agriculture, crafts industries (which still flourished despite poor working conditions), and domestic service. Some sectors of industry, such as textiles, employed a large proportion of women. Other sectors, such as the metal and mining industries, were heavily male-dominated.

The textile industry found employment for children once they were over the age of 5 or 6. Their size and agility made them useful for certain jobs, such as reaching under machines to pick up loose cotton. Because of their small hands they were also hired as "doffers," taking bobbins off frames and replacing them. Elizabeth Bentley began work as a doffer in 1815 at the age of 6. At the age of 23, when she testified before a parliamentary commission, she was "considerably deformed . . . in consequence of this labor." (See the box "Reading Sources: The Young Girl in the Factory.") Child labor certainly did not start with the industrial transformation; it had always existed. What was new was the stern industrial discipline imposed on the very young. Children were subject to the clock, closely supervised and prevented from taking long breaks or mixing work and play—as had been possible in an earlier era.

Although children were common in British textile industries, overall less than 10 percent of working children were in industry. Most were in agriculture or the service sector. In the early stages of industrialization, children were primarily employed in textile mills to pick up waste and repair broken threads. As technological advances relieved both problems, the need for children lessened.

Improved technology and the growth of industries other than textiles increased the employment of adult men. In iron and later steel plants, physical strength was essential. Despite the higher labor costs that resulted when men were employed, managers had no choice but to hire them. However, in France, where textiles were still the predominant product after the turn of the nineteenth

READING SOURCES

THE YOUNG GIRL IN THE FACTORY

Reformers in Parliament, among them Michael Sadler, denounced the appalling conditions in the factories. Sadler was appointed to head the commission that investigated the matter. Workers who appeared before the panel gave vivid descriptions of their lot. Public and parliamentary outrage at the conditions revealed by these hearings led to the Factory Act of 1833. Among the witnesses was Elizabeth Bentley, a 23-year-old weaving machine operative, who gave the following testimony. Note the extent to which the questions and answers deal with time. Both employers and employees had developed a strong sense of time. As Bentley's testimony shows, employees who ignored the clock risked retribution.

What age are you?—23. . . .

What time did you begin to work in a factory?—When I was 6 years old. . . .

What were your hours of labor? . . . —From 5 in the morning till 9 at night, when they were thronged [busy].

For how long have you worked that excessive length of time?—For about half a year.

What were your usual hours of labor when they were not so thronged?—From 6 in the morning till 7 at night.

What time was allowed for your meals?—40 minutes at noon. . . .

Your labor is very excessive?—Yes, you have not time for anything.

Suppose you flagged a little, or were too late, what would they do?—Strap us. . . .

Girls as well as boys?—Yes.

Severely?—Yes.

Could you eat your food well in that factory?—No, indeed, I had not much to eat, and the little I had I could not eat it, my appetite was so poor, and being covered with dust; and it was no use taking it home, I could not eat it. . . .

Did you live far from the mill?—Yes, two miles.

Had you a clock?—No, we had not. . . .

Were you generally there in time?—Yes; my mother has been up at four o'clock in the morning and at two o'clock; the colliers used to go to their work at about three or four o'clock, and when she heard them stirring she has got up out of her warm bed, and gone out and asked them the time; and I have sometimes been at Hunslet Car at 2 o'clock when it was steaming down with rain, and we have had to stay till the mill was opened [at 5 A.M.].

Source: House of Commons, *Sessional Papers, 1831–32*, hearing of 4 June 1832, vol. 15, pp. 195–197.

 For additional information on this topic, go to college.hmco.com/students.

---

century, women made up two-thirds of the textile industry work force as late as 1906.

In some cases industrialization meant a transformation in the authority structure of workers' households, undermining the influence of the male as head of the household. A woman could make a living independently of her spouse, and children at a reasonably early age could emancipate themselves from their parents and make a go of it working in a factory or a mine. These options were not possible in agriculture or in the putting-out system. As in the putting-out system, however, often

whole families were hired as a group to perform a specific function. Contemporaries sometimes denounced industry for dissolving family bonds, but the family remained an effective work unit.

If not participating in the wage market, wives and children contributed in other ways to the household budget—by making clothes, raising a pig, tending a potato patch, and performing daily household chores. Grandparents often moved from the country to live with the family and take care of the children. When industrial workers married, they frequently settled with their spouses on the same street or in the same neighborhood where their parents lived. Although industry had the potential to break up traditional family structures, the historical evidence is that the family adjusted and survived the challenges posed by the new economic system.

The Land, the Water, and the Air

Industrialization seriously disturbed the environment, transforming the surface of the earth, the water, and the air. To run the new machinery, coal was mined in increasing amounts (see Table 20.1). Iron and other minerals were also in great demand. The exploitation of coal ushered in the modern age of energy use, in which massive amounts of nonrenewable resources are consumed.

To extract coal and other minerals, miners dug deep tunnels, removing millions of tons of earth, rock, and other debris. This material, plus slag and other waste from the factories, was heaped up in mounds that at times covered acres of land, creating new geological formations.

With axes and saws people cut down trees, depleting forests to supply the wood needed to build shafts for coal, iron, and tin mines, or to make the charcoal necessary for glassmaking. Between 1750 and 1900 industrial and agricultural needs led to the clearing of 50 percent of all the forests ever cleared. Many of Europe's major forests disappeared or were seriously diminished. Deforestation in turn sped up soil erosion.

Industry changed the physical environment in which people lived. Forests, lakes, rivers, and air—as well as people themselves—showed the harmful effects of industry. Centrifugal pumps drained large marshes in the Fenland in eastern England. A contemporary lamented, "The wind which, in the autumn of 1851 was curling the blue water of the lake, in the autumn of 1853 was blowing in the same place over fields of yellow corn." Factories dumped waste ash into rivers, changing their channels and making them considerably shallower. Because of pollution from industrial and human waste, by 1850 no fish could survive in the lower Thames River. Some rivers were so polluted that their water could be used as ink. Alkali, used for making glass, when released into the atmosphere killed trees for several miles around. Smoke and soot darkened the skies, intensifying the fog over London and other cities. Foul odors from factories could be detected at several miles' distance. Not merely unpleasant, various air pollutants caused cancer and lung diseases, though the connection between pollutants and disease was not yet understood.

A Letter Written with Polluted Water   In 1868 an irate Englishman wrote the health board, using water drawn from the Calder River in northern England to make his point about the condition of the river. As the letter writer points out, readers of the missive will miss one dimension of the situation—the river's stench.   *(The British Library)*

Table 20.1	Coal Production in Industrializing Nations	
	Millions of Tons	Kilograms per Inhabitant
1700	4	26
1750	7	16
1800	16	76
1830	30	120
1860	129	390

Source: Based on B. R. Mitchell, "Statistical Appendix, 1700–1914," in *The Fontana Economic History of Europe*, ed. Carlo Cippola, vol. 4 (London: Collins, 1973), pp. 747, 770; and Norman J. G. Pounds, *An Historical Geography of Europe, 1500–1840* (New York: Cambridge University Press, 1979), pp. 268–269.

A Changing Sense of Time

In agrarian societies time was measured in terms of natural occurrences, such as sunrise and sunset, or the time it might take to milk a cow. With industrialization, punctuality became essential. Shifts of labor had to be rotated to keep the smelters going; they could not stop, or the molten iron would harden at the bottom of the hearths. The interactive nature of industrial production, in which workers with differing specialties each performed a particular task in finishing a product, made it necessary for employees to be at the factory at an appointed time. They could not be late.

Clocks were installed in church towers and municipal buildings as early as the fourteenth century, but they were not very reliable until the eighteenth century. Watches were commonly owned by men of property and even by some artisans. By the mid-nineteenth century, at least in Britain, as the price of watches came down, many workers could afford them. And even when workers did not own timepieces, they were intensely aware of time. Those who ignored time were fined or fired from their jobs. People listened for the church bell or factory whistle, or asked a neighbor or passerby for the time. (See the box "The Continuing Experiment: The New Discipline of the Factory System." See also "The Young Girl in the Factory" on page 696.) Western societies increasingly regularized and internalized the sense of time.

RESPONSES TO INDUSTRIALIZATION

PEOPLE in the new industrial classes living at subsistence levels were disquieting evidence of the impact of industrialization. What should be done about the working classes—or for them? These new classes developed their own sense of a common interest and fate. The result was a resounding cry for political and social democracy that began in the first half of the nineteenth century and became increasingly insistent. Many solutions were proffered.

Manchester, England, 1851   A small, unimportant town of 20,000 in the 1750s, Manchester—as a result of industrialization—had 400,000 inhabitants in 1850. In this 1851 painting, the polluted industrial city is contrasted with its idealized pastoral suburb.   *(The Royal Collection © 2003 Her Majesty Queen Elizabeth II)*

The New Discipline of the Factory System

As industries change, employers and employees encounter different methods and locations of work. The new factories regimented work by time, requiring workers to obey the clock and factory regulations rather than the seasons and sun that governed agricultural work and cottage crafts. In separating the home and workplace, the factory system began a long-lasting experiment in the organization of work. This document lists some of the regulations of the Berlin Foundry and Engineering Works of the Royal Overseas Trading Company of 1844. Note how obsessed with the efficient use of time the factory rules are.

The normal working day begins at all seasons at 6 A.M. precisely and ends, after the usual break of half an hour for breakfast, an hour for dinner, and half an hour for tea, at 7 P.M., and it shall be strictly observed.

Five minutes before the beginning of the stated hours of work until their actual commencement, a bell shall ring and indicate that every worker employed in the concern has to proceed to his place of work, in order to start as soon as the bell stops.

The doorkeeper shall lock the door punctually at 6 A.M., 8:30 A.M., 1 P.M., and 4:30 P.M.

Workers arriving 2 minutes late shall lose half an hour's wages; whoever is more than 2 minutes late may not start work until after the next break, or at least shall lose his wages until then. . . .

Repeated irregular arrival at work shall lead to dismissal. This shall also apply to those who are found idling by an official or overseer, and refuse to obey their order to resume work. . . .

All conversation with fellow-workers is prohibited. . . .

Smoking in the workshops or in the yard is prohibited during working-hours; anyone caught smoking shall be fined five silver groschen for the sick fund.

Natural functions must be performed at the appropriate places. . . .

It goes without saying that all overseers and officials of the firm shall be obeyed without question, and shall be treated with due deference. Disobedience will be punished by dismissal.

Immediate dismissal shall also be the fate of anyone found drunk in any of the workshops. . . .

The gatekeeper and the watchman, as well as every official, are entitled to search the baskets, parcels, aprons, etc. of the women and children who are taking the dinners into the works, on their departure, as well as search any worker suspected of stealing any article whatever. . . .

A free copy of these rules is handed to every workman, but whoever loses it and requires a new one, or cannot produce it on leaving, shall be fined 2½ silver groschen.

QUESTIONS

1. The new factory discipline was strict and did not allow room for personal initiative. What might have been the advantages and disadvantages of this system for the employer or worker?

2. What would it have meant for the workers to organize their time in terms of the clock? How might that have affected their concepts of work and leisure and the structure of their daily lives?

3. Do workplaces today differ from the disciplined environment of the early nineteenth century? In what ways are workers still regimented, and what are some examples of new freedoms and benefits workers receive today? Do you find today's workplaces better or worse than the one described in this document?

SOURCE: S. Pollard and C. Holmes, eds., *Documents of European Economic History*, vol. 1 (New York: St. Martin's Press, 1968), pp. 534–536.

The Growth of Working-Class Solidarity

Hardest hit by economic changes, workers sought to improve their conditions by organizing and articulating their needs. In the preindustrial economy, artisans and craftsmen lived in an accepted hierarchy with prescribed rules. They began by serving for a certain number of years as apprentices to a master, next became journeymen, and finally with hard work and good fortune became masters of their trades. As tradesmen with common

Leisure Activity for the Working Poor   Some harsh forms of entertainment turned up in the industrial period. Scores of working-class spectators came to see the celebrated dog "Billy" kill a hundred rats at one time at the Westminster Pit in London in 1822.   *(The British Library)*

interests, they tended to band together into brother-hoods, promising one another help and trying to improve their working conditions.

With industrialization, guilds declined. Unlike the skilled handicrafts that required years of apprenticeship, few aspects of industrial production demanded extensive training. The system of dependence between apprentice and master became irrelevant. Guilds trying to protect their members often resisted new technologies and came to be seen as a hindrance to economic development. Liberals viewed guilds as constraints on trade and the free flow of labor. In France the revolutionaries abolished the guilds and all workers' coalitions. Throughout the eighteenth century, the British Parliament passed various acts against "combinations" by workmen.

While guilds faded in importance, the solidarity and language born of the guild continued to shape workers' attitudes throughout much of the nineteenth century. New experiences also reinforced the sense of belonging to a group and sharing common aspirations.

Cultural forces fostered workers' sense of solidarity. The common language of religion and shared religious practice united workers. Religious sects flourished in an environment of despair punctuated by hopes of deliverance. Some historians believe that the growth of Methodism in England in the 1790s (see page 713) was a response to grim economic conditions. Emphasis on equality before God fueled the sense of injustice in a world where a privileged few lived in luxury while others were condemned to work along with their children for a pittance. Joanna, a self-proclaimed prophet active in the 1810s in England, announced both salvation and the coming of a new world of material well-being. In France workers believed the new society would come about by their martyrdom; like Jesus, the workers would suffer, and from their suffering would emerge a new, better society. Ideas of social justice were linked in the countryside with religious broadsides speaking of "Jesus the worker." Religious themes and language continued to be important in labor organization for many years.

Other cultural and social factors created bonds among workers. Housing was increasingly segregated. Workers lived in low-rent areas—in slums in the center of cities or in outlying areas near the factories. Thus urban workers lived close together, in similar conditions of squalor and hardship. Workers grew close by spending their leisure time together, drinking in pubs, attending theaters and new forms of popular entertainment such as the circus, or watching traditional blood sports such as boxing or cockfights. Sports became popular as both spectator and participatory events in the 1880s. Soccer, which developed in England at this time, drew players and fans overwhelmingly from the working classes.

Social institutions also encouraged class unity. In the eighteenth century, both husband and wife were usually in the same craft. By 1900 it became more common for workers to marry across their crafts, thereby strengthening the sense of solidarity that encompassed the working classes as a whole.

Faced with the uncertainties of unemployment and job-related accidents, in addition to disease and other natural catastrophes, workers formed so-called friendly societies in which they pooled their resources to provide mutual aid. These societies, descendants of benefit organizations of the Middle Ages and Renaissance, combined business activity with feasts, drinking bouts, and other social functions.

Friendly societies had existed as early as the seventeenth century, but they became increasingly popular and important after industrialization. Their strength in a region often reflected the degree to which the area was industrialized. First started to provide aid for workers in a particular trade, they soon included members in several crafts. In time they federated into national organizations, so that a worker who moved to a new town could continue membership in the new locale. Connected by common membership in friendly societies, workers expressed a feeling of group solidarity beyond their individual occupations. Though far from solidified, a working class was in the making.

Collective Action

Militant and in some cases violent action strengthened workers' solidarity. In politics workers expressed common grievances, and some of their disappointments in the political arena underscored their common situation.

In the face of hardships, artisans organized for collective action. In 1811 and 1812 British hand weavers, faced with competition from mechanized looms, organized in groups claiming to be led by a mythical General Ned Ludd. In the name of economic justice and to protect their livelihood, the "Luddites," as the general's followers were called, smashed machines or threatened to do so. In Saxony, in eastern Germany, in the 1830s and 1840s, weavers went on machine-crushing campaigns. These movements revealed the militance of labor and its willingness to resort to violence.

In Lyon, France, in 1831 and 1834, workers led uprisings demanding fair wages for piecework. Angered when the silk merchants lowered the amount they would pay, the workers marched in the streets bearing banners proclaiming "Live Working or Die Fighting." Troops were brought in to restore order to the riot-torn city. Although conditions of the silk trade had been the immediate impetus for the uprising, the workers appealed for help to their fellow workers in other trades, who joined in the protests.

Labor agitation in much of Europe increased in the 1840s. A major strike wave involving twenty thousand workers broke out in Paris in 1840. In the summer of 1842 an industrial downturn in England led to massive unemployment and rioting. During the summer of 1844 in Silesia, in eastern Prussia, linen hand-loom weavers, desperate because of worsening conditions brought on

Unionization   This certificate signifies membership in the first professional union in Britain, the Amalgamated Society of Engineers. With references to classical antiquity, British inventors, and various trades, the document highlights the nobility of the trade.   *(The Art Archive)*

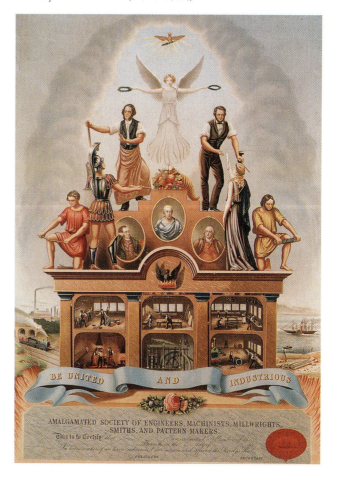

by competition from machine-made cotton fabrics, attacked the homes of the wealthy. In 1855 in Barcelona, the government tried to dissolve unions, and fifty thousand workers went on strike, carrying placards that warned "Association or Death."

Workers had to conform to severe discipline and rigid rules not only in the workplace but also away from it. Workers in some factories were forbidden to read certain newspapers, had to attend religious services, and could marry only with the owners' permission. Workers resisted these attempts at control and resented employers' intrusiveness.

Workers' actions in the early nineteenth century clearly showed that they wanted both freedom from intrusive regulation by their employers and the security of employment at a decent wage. Unions provided a means to these goals.

Many of the friendly societies struggled to improve their members' working conditions, acting very much as labor unions would. They organized strikes and provided support to members during work stoppages. The advantages offered by unions were well understood—by both sides. Unions were illegal in Britain until 1825, in Prussia until 1859, and in France until the 1860s. As a French workers' paper declared in 1847, "If workers came together and organized . . . nothing would be able to stop them." An organized force could threaten to withhold labor if the employer did not grant decent wages and acceptable conditions. Unions made workers a countervailing force to factory owners.

The process of unionization was difficult. By 1850 many countries had passed laws supporting employers against workers. Censorship and the use of force against organized strikes were not uncommon. Population growth made it difficult for workers to withhold labor lest they be replaced by others only too willing to take their places. Foreign workers—for example, the Irish who streamed into England and the Belgians and Italians who migrated to France—were often desperate for work and not well informed about local conditions.

In many countries workers formed unions before unions were legalized. Although there were early attempts in Britain to organize unions on a national basis, most were centered on a single craft or a single industry. Because labor unions originated in the crafts tradition, the earliest members were skilled craftsmen who organized to protect their livelihoods from the challenge that industrialization posed. These craftsmen were usually literate and longtime residents of their communities. They provided the labor movement with much of its leadership and organization. Skilled craft workers also played a

strong role in developing a sense of class-consciousness. The language and institutions that they had developed over decades, and sometimes over centuries, became the common heritage of workers in general.

Workers looked to political action as the means to improve their situations. In the 1830s and 1840s British and French workers agitated for the right to vote; they saw voting as a way to put themselves on equal footing with the privileged and to win better conditions. Their disappointment at their failure to win political representation strengthened their class solidarity against the wealthy, privileged upper classes. Politically, organized workers played a major role in the revolutions that would rock Europe in 1848 (see pages 732–735), sometimes helping to instigate the uprisings, often influencing their course. However vague their ideas, European workers showed that their organizations were legitimate representatives of the people and that the lot of the worker should be the concern of government. In general, workers upheld the ideal of a moral economy—one in which all who labored got a just wage and every person was assured a minimum level of well-being.

The working classes were never a monolithic group. They consisted of people with varying skills, responsibilities, and incomes. Artisans with valuable skills were the segment that employers most respected and favored in pay and in working conditions. In contrast, unskilled workers were poorly paid, harshly treated, and often given only temporary work. Many skilled workers looked with contempt on the unskilled.

If both sexes worked side by side, it created little solidarity between them. Men worried that women were undermining their earning power by accepting lower wages. They often excluded women from their unions. Men even went on strike to force employers to discharge women.

Nor was there solidarity across nationalities. Foreign workers were heartily despised. British workers were hostile toward their Irish colleagues, the French toward the Belgians and Italians in their midst. The hostility often led to fisticuffs. In London anti-Irish riots were common. Many forces fostered dissension among the working classes in the nineteenth century, and unity among workers was far from achieved. Nevertheless, various experiences, including the spread of industry, broadened and deepened workers' sense of a shared fate and common goal.

The middle classes came to believe that all workers formed a single class. By the mid-nineteenth century, they had developed a clear fear of workers, not only as individuals but as a group, as a class. It was not unusual for members of the elite to refer to workers as "the swinish multitude" or, as the title of a popular English book put it, *The Great Unwashed* (1868). In France reference was alternately made to "the dangerous classes" and "the laboring classes." Not just workers but even the privileged seemed to see relations between the groups as a form of class war.

Summary

INDUSTRIAL transformation altered the face of Europe. This process, which started around 1750 in parts of England, spread by 1850 to other states of Europe. Material and cultural factors, combined with a number of fortuitous circumstances, explain why industrial production originated in England. The proximity of coal and iron, the relative ease of domestic transportation, a culture open to innovation and entrepreneurship, and the existence of an already relatively dynamic economy help explain why Britain was the first nation to industrialize.

Economies based on industry changed power relations within Europe and altered the relationship of Europe to the rest of the world. As a result of the transformation in its economy, Britain became in the nineteenth century the most powerful nation in Europe and achieved worldwide influence. Although Europe was industrialized only in certain areas, many Europeans came to think of their continent as economically and technologically superior to the rest of the world. For many, being industrial became synonymous with Europe's identity.

Industry changed the nature of work for large numbers of Europeans. Machines replaced human energy in the workplace. By the application of science and technology, manufacturing productivity increased significantly. A decreasing number of people worked in agriculture, and more entered manufacturing. Population patterns changed; cities grew dramatically, and for the first time European cities had over a million inhabitants.

The massing of workers in factories and urban areas aggravated their misery but called attention to their potential power. Eager to improve their lives and working conditions, workers began to express their solidarity. They organized into associations that were more broadly based and therefore more powerful than workers' groups of the past. As workers began to think of themselves as a class, the dominant elites within society began to perceive them as such. The new proletarian class, shaped by industrialization, was a growing force that would challenge the existing order throughout the nineteenth century and much of the next.

■ Notes

1. Phyllis Deane, *The First Industrial Revolution* (Cambridge: Cambridge University Press, 1965), p. 1.
2. These ideas are provocatively developed in E. L. Jones, *The European Miracle: Environments, Economies and Geopolitics of Europe and Asia* (Cambridge: Cambridge University Press, 1981).
3. Adna Ferrin Weber, *The Growth of Cities in the Nineteenth Century: A Study in Statistics* (New York: Macmillan, 1899; repr., Ithaca, N.Y.: Cornell University Press, 1963), p. 1.
4. Cooke Taylor, *Notes of a Tour in the Manufacturing Districts of Lancashire, in a Series of Letters to His Grace the Archbishop of Dublin* (London, 1842), pp. 4–6, quoted in E. P. Thompson, *The Making of the English Working Class* (New York: Vintage, 1963), p. 191.
5. Marie de Flavigny d'Agoult [Daniel Stern], *Histoire de la Révolution de 1848*, 2d ed., vol. 1 (Paris, 1862), p. 7, quoted in Theodore S. Hamerow, *The Birth of a New Europe: State and Society in the Nineteenth Century* (Chapel Hill: University of North Carolina Press, 1983), pp. 206–207.

■ Suggested Reading

Chinn, Carl. *Poverty Amidst Prosperity: The Urban Poor in England, 1834–1914.* 1995. Concentrates on the harsher aspects of industrialization.

Clark, Anna. *The Struggle for the Breeches: Gender and the Making of the British Working Class.* 1995. An examination of the role of working women and gender conflicts in domestic life, work, and politics.

Hopkins, Eric. *Industrialisation and Society.* 2000. A survey that considers the social and political impact of industry on British society.

Landes, David S. *The Wealth and Poverty of Nations.* 1999. Explores why Europe industrialized as compared with the rest of the world.

Mokyr, Joel. *The Lever of Riches: Technological Creativity and Economic Progress.* 1990. A comparative study of Western and Chinese technology, emphasizing cultural elements as explanations for the industrialization of the West.

Sylla, Richard, and Gianni Toniolo, eds. *Patterns of European Industrialization.* 1991. A comparative perspective on the patterns of industrialization.

Thompson, E. P. *The Making of the English Working Class.* 1963. Emphasizes the cultural factors that encouraged the development of working-class consciousness in England.

For a searchable list of additional readings for this chapter, go to college.hmco.com/students.

Workers' Wages

In 1869 the Chamber of Commerce of Verviers°, a town in eastern Belgium, published a report on workers' wages. In the seventeenth century, Verviers, located on the Vesdre° River, had become a major producer of woolens. The river provided water for power, for washing the cloth, and for carrying away industrial waste. Thus, the site was ideal for finishing textiles, and the merchants of Verviers drew on the labor of spinners and weavers in the surrounding farm areas. With a population of 4,500 in the mid-seventeenth century, Verviers had 10,000 inhabitants by the end of the eighteenth century.

Two local entrepreneurs brought the Englishman John Cockerill to town. He set up the first spinning machine on the Continent in 1802 and the first steam engine in Belgium in 1816. Thirty years later Verviers boasted forty factories, and the population had increased to 23,000.

Industrialization transformed the people's lives in many ways. The table of wages reveals the existence of a variegated, hierarchical work force with clear, separate functions and specified salaries. It indicates the uneven ways in which people benefited from industry, depending on their skills, age, and gender.

For example, this list allows us to compare the wages of industrial workers and artisans. Industry made it difficult for the artisans to survive; unable to compete with machine manufacture, many had to give up their trades or tighten their belts to make ends meet. The new machine age, however, created an increased demand for the services of some artisans. Early in the nineteenth century, the new machines eliminated hand spinning, for example, but inexpensive yarn at first increased the demand for hand-loom weavers. Notice that hand-loom weavers ("hand weavers" in the table) were relatively well paid in 1836. This is due to the uneven introduction of mechanical production. Weaving of high-quality woolens proved to be more difficult to mechanize than cotton goods. Power looms did not become common in Verviers until the 1860s, and we see the relative wages of hand-loom weavers decline in 1869. Joiners and ironsmiths not only did the work they had traditionally done but also found new opportunities building and repairing machines. The ironsmiths, joiners, and carpenters of Verviers were all paid better than other workers.

Verviers (ver-VYAY)   Vesdre (VEH-druh)

Even among the factory workers, we find some significant wage discrepancies. Compare, for example, the wages of the nonspecialized laborer to the wages of the other, specialized industrial workers.

Changes in technology, productivity, labor supply, and market demand for certain goods increased the relative wages of workers over time. Thus the relative wages of jobs changed between 1836 and 1869. Notice that a wool washer in 1869 was making 174 percent more than a wool washer made in 1836, but in the same period the wages paid to a warper had increased by 300 percent.

Let us next consider women in the labor force. Notice that the list is divided into "male occupations," "female occupations," and finally "children's occupation." Work is divided according to gender and age. Look at the list of women's industrial occupations. The absence of female spinners in this list is significant. Spinning had been a female occupation since antiquity, but the spinning machines in Verviers were tended by men. Notice how little differentiation is evident among women's work; far fewer industrial occupations are listed for women than for men. Also look at the wages. Women's wages were all equally depressed, but the most highly paid occupation for women (mender) climbed 200 percent from 1836 to 1869, finally reaching the level of the lowest paid man's occupation (wool washer) in that year. For men, the wages of the most highly paid skilled artisans in 1869 (ironsmiths) had risen 124 percent since 1836. The spread of wages among men's occupations was far greater than among women's. In 1869 the highest paid men (ironsmiths) received 72 percent more than the lowest paid men (wool washers), while the highest paid women (menders) earned 39 percent more than the lowest paid women (scourers).

Some male artisans—carpenters, for example—consistently received wages higher than the wages of many machine operators. But notice the one female artisan occupation: seamstress. Although some seamstresses were probably quite skilled, others were not and did repetitive stitching in their rooms. In general, seamstresses were paid no more than the women in factories. Special crafts, still prized for some men, were not given much monetary value when practiced by women. Note the wage differences overall between male and female workers. In 1836 the average female worker received wages equivalent to 53.2 percent of the average male worker's wages. By 1869 there was some improvement:

Wage Differentials in Verviers, Belgium, 1836–1869

		Wages (francs per day)				
		1836	**1846**	**1856**	**1863**	**1869**
Male Occupations	Ironsmith*	1.73	2.25	2.50	3.00	3.87
	Carpenter*	1.90	2.25	2.65	2.87	3.50
	Dyer	1.40	1.46	1.60	2.60	3.37
	Spinner	1.80	1.90	2.90	3.12	3.40
	Carder	1.47	1.75	2.30	3.25	3.30
	Tanner*	1.83	2.00	2.25	3.00	3.25
	Warper	0.80	0.95	1.57	1.65	3.25
	Hand weaver*	1.97	1.70	2.85	3.00	3.00
	Joiner*	1.98	2.00	2.25	2.75	3.00
	Tenterer	—	1.25	1.40	2.34	3.00
	Presser	1.47	1.78	1.78	2.15	3.00
	Machine weaver	—	—	—	—	2.75
	Comber	0.84	1.27	1.50	1.75	2.65
	Fuller	1.40	1.50	1.75	2.30	2.67
	Laborer	—	1.25	1.50	1.87	2.50
	Wool washer	1.15	1.25	1.40	1.75	2.25
Female Occupations	Mender	0.73	0.80	1.10	1.40	2.25
	Wool sorter	0.98	1.08	1.70	1.85	2.00
	Gigger	0.75	0.80	0.80	1.25	2.00
	Burler	0.77	1.00	1.20	1.70	1.80
	Seamstress*	0.73	0.80	1.10	1.40	—
	Scourer	0.70	0.75	0.85	1.35	1.62
Children's Occupation	Piecener	—	0.70	0.90	1.10	1.60

*Artisans. (Those not starred were industrial workers.)

Source: Chamber of Commerce of Verviers, *Rapport général sur la situation du commerce et de l'industrie en 1868* (Verviers, 1869), p. 69; reprinted in George Alter, *Family and the Female Life Course: The Women of Verviers, Belgium, 1849–1880* (Madison: University of Wisconsin Press, 1988), p. 103. © 1988. Reprinted by permission of The University of Wisconsin Press.

the difference had declined, but women still earned only 64 percent of what men earned.

The table lists only one occupation for children: piecener. Small and nimble, children were paid to splice broken threads. They worked in many other capacities as well. Some were paid wages by their employers; others helped their parents in a factory or workshop. The wages of some adults probably included compensation for their children's labor.

We can learn much from a statistical table such as this about the impact of industrialization on the labor force. Some workers benefited, and others were harmed by the adoption of industry; over time workers experi-

enced changes in their circumstances. If statistical tables are informative on such issues, they also have their limits. They do not tell us how workers interpreted and understood their experience. As workers suffered daily hardships, they had to try to make sense of their changing world, an effort no table can count.

 For additional information on this topic, go to college.hmco.com/students.

CHAPTER 21

Restoration, Reform, and Revolution 1814–1848

REVOLUTION struck Berlin in March 1848. King Friedrich Wilhelm IV (r. 1840–1861), who initially opposed the revolutionaries' demands for political liberties and a unified nation, surprised his subjects on March 21 by announcing support for a united, free, constitutional Germany. This print, distributed by the thousands, shows the king on horseback, being acclaimed by a grateful people. The black, red, and gold flags, the symbol of German unity since the Napoleonic Wars, are prominently displayed. The king is preceded by a businessman he had appointed as chief minister. People from most walks of life appear united in purpose. Notice the depiction of well-dressed middle-class citizens as well as humble artisans. The print captures a moment of hope and great possibilities. Soon, however, the forces that made the revolution possible fell into disunion, and the Prussian king was able to turn back the tide of change. As in Prussia, the first moments of exhilarating possibilities in the rest of Europe nearly always were followed by failure and disappointment as the forces of reaction won the upper hand.

In 1848 Europe experienced a revolutionary wave, unprecedented in over a half century since the heady days of the French Revolution. These revolutions erupted in protest against the reactionary regimes established after the fall of Napoleon. The political order in western Europe started changing by the 1830s. The pace of change was slower, however, in eastern Europe.

Despite European statesmen's dogged attempts to set the clock back, the forces unleashed by the French Revolution proved irrepressible. Conservatism attempted to bolster the old order, but new ideologies such as romanticism, nationalism, liberalism, and socialism challenged it. (An ideology is a structured, organized set of ideas that reflects a group's thinking about life or society.) The forces revealing

King Friedrich Wilhelm IV (*center*) announcing his devotion to German unity (*detail*).
(Germanisches National Museum Nuremberg)

The Search for Stability: The Congress of Vienna, 1814–1815

Ideological Confrontations

Restoration, Reform, and Reaction

The Revolutions of 1848

themselves in 1848 suggested the outline of Europe's development in the second half of the century.

At the end of the Napoleonic Wars, in 1815, the victorious Great Powers—Austria, Great Britain, Prussia, and Russia—tried to re-establish as much of the old European state system as possible. The international arrangements they carved out at the Congress of Vienna were soon shaken by outbreaks of nationalist fervor. Nationalists aimed either to create larger political units, as in Italy and Germany, or to win independence from foreign rule, as in Greece.

The attempt to set the clock back had only limited success. The conservatism of European rulers and their opposition to change were at odds with the new dynamism of European society. Between 1800 and 1850 Europe's population increased by nearly 50 percent, from around 190 million to 280 million. Population growth and surging industrialization had turned small towns into large cities. Factory manufacturing was on the rise, promising to reshape class structures and the lives of workers. Romanticism, liberalism, and other systems of thought were redefining the relationship of the individual to society. Sporadic outbreaks of collective violence reached a crescendo when the revolutions of 1848 swept most of Europe, undermining the es-

tablished order in state after state. Revolutionaries did not win all their goals, and in many cases the forces of order crushed them. Yet by midcentury major intellectual, social, and political changes had occurred.

QUESTIONS TO CONSIDER

- What were the goals of the restorations that followed the Napoleonic era?

- What major ideologies developed in the first half of the nineteenth century?

- What were the main causes of the revolutions of 1848, and what roles did nationalism and liberalism play in inciting and sustaining revolution?

- What new and permanent features were created by the revolutions of 1848?

TERMS TO KNOW

Congress of Vienna	socialism
romanticism	Marxism
conservatism	July Revolution
nationalism	Great Reform Bill
liberalism	Chartism
laissez faire	Decembrists
Utilitarian	Frankfurt Assembly

THE SEARCH FOR STABILITY: THE CONGRESS OF VIENNA, 1814–1815

THE defeat of Napoleon put an end to French dominance in Europe. In September 1814 the victorious Great Powers—Austria, Great Britain, Prussia, and Russia—convened an international conference in Vienna to negotiate the terms of peace. The victors sought to draw territorial boundaries advantageous to themselves and to provide long-term stability on the European continent. Although many small powers attended the Congress of Vienna, their role was reduced to ratifying the large states' decisions. Having

faced a powerful France, which had mobilized popular forces with revolutionary principles, the victors decided to erect an international system that would remove such threats. One method was to restore the European order that had existed before the French Revolution. Thus, following principles of "legitimacy and compensation," they redrew the map of Europe (see Map 21.1). Rulers who had been overthrown were restored to their thrones. The eldest surviving brother of Louis XVI of France became King Louis XVIII. In Spain Ferdinand VII was restored to the throne from which Napoleon had toppled him and his father. The restoration, however, was not so complete as its proponents claimed. After the French Revolution certain new realities had to be recognized. For example,

Metternich   A consummate statesman and aristocrat, the Austrian prince Metternich tried to quell revolution at home and abroad. Some called his era the Metternichean age.
(The Royal Collection © 2003 Her Majesty Queen Elizabeth II)

CHRONOLOGY

1808	Beethoven, *Pastoral* Symphony
1814–1815	Congress of Vienna
1819	Peterloo Massacre Carlsbad Decrees
1821	Spanish revolt Greek Revolution
1821–1825	Spanish colonies in the Americas win independence
1823	Monroe Doctrine
1824	Owen establishes New Harmony
1825	Decembrists in Russia
1830	July Revolution in France Ottoman Empire recognizes Serbian autonomy
1832	Great Reform Bill in Britain
1833	Abolition of slavery in British colonies
1834	Turner, *Fire at Sea*
1838	"People's charter" in Great Britain
1839	Anti–Corn Law League
1845–1848	Hungry '40s
1848	Marx and Engels, *Communist Manifesto* Revolutions of 1848

Napoleon had consolidated the German and Italian states; the process was acknowledged in the former with the creation of a loose German Confederation. In Italy the number of independent states had shrunk to nine. Also, unlike earlier French kings, Louis XVIII could not be an absolute monarch.

Negotiations at the Congress of Vienna strengthened the territories bordering France, enlarged Prussia and created the kingdom of Piedmont-Sardinia, joined Belgium to Holland, and provided the victors with spoils and compensation for territories bartered away. Austria received Venetia and Lombardy in northern Italy to compensate for the loss of Belgium (to the Netherlands) and parts of Poland (to Russia) and to strengthen its position in general. Prussia was also allowed annexations in compensation for giving up parts of Poland. England acquired a number of colonies and naval outposts. Thus with one hand these conservative statesmen swore their loyalty to the prerevolutionary past, and with the other they nevertheless changed the map of Europe.

The leading personality at the Congress of Vienna was the Austrian foreign minister, Prince Clemens von Metternich° (1773–1859), who presided over the meetings. An aristocrat in exile from the Rhineland, which had been annexed by revolutionary France, he had gone into the service of the Habsburg empire and risen to become its highest official. Personal charm, tact, and representation of a state that for the time being was satisfied with its territories made Metternich seem a disinterested statesman. His influence at the congress was great.

Because it was Napoleon's belligerent imperialism that had brought the powers together in Vienna, France

---

Metternich (MEH-ter-nick)

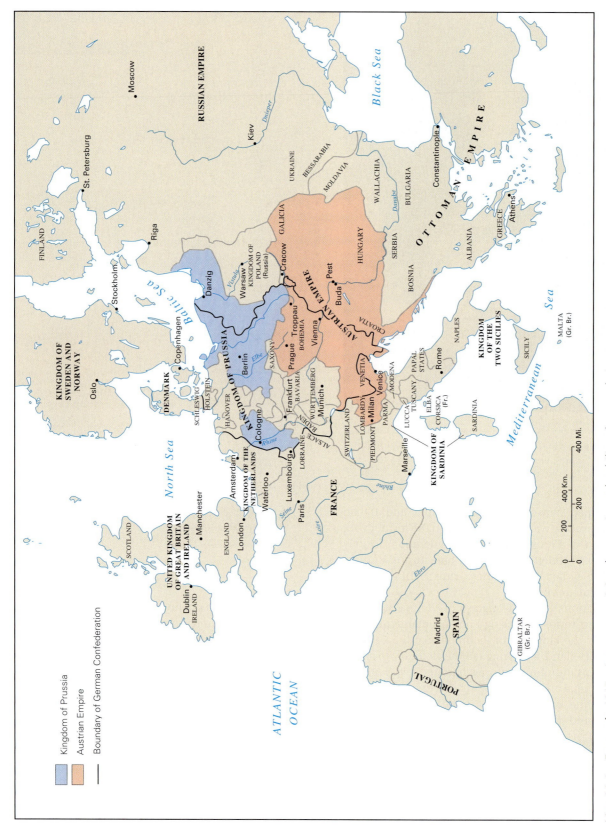

Map 21.1 **Europe in 1815** Intent on regaining the security and stability of prerevolutionary years, the Great Powers redrew the map of Europe at the Congress of Vienna.

was at first treated as an enemy at the conference. By the end, however, France managed to join the other states and be included with them as one of the five Great Powers jointly known as the "Concert of Europe." The Concert continued to function for nearly forty years, meeting and resolving international crises and preventing any major European war from breaking out. Underlying the states' cooperation was the principle of a common European destiny.

IDEOLOGICAL CONFRONTATIONS

THE international and domestic political system established in 1815 was modified by a series of challenges, even revolts, culminating in revolutions throughout Europe in 1848. The order established in 1815 was inspired by conservatism. Its challengers advocated competing ideologies: romanticism, nationalism, liberalism, and socialism.

Conservatism

The architects of the restoration justified their policies with doctrines based on the ideology of conservatism, emphasizing the need to preserve the existing order of monarchies, aristocracy, and an established church. As a coherent movement, conservatism sprang up during and after the French Revolution to resist the forces of change. Before the American and French Revolutions, the existing political institutions appeared to be permanent. When the old order faced serious challenges in the late eighteenth and early nineteenth centuries, an ideology justifying traditional authority emerged.

Edmund Burke (1729–1797), a British statesman and political theorist, launched one of the first intellectual assaults on the French Revolution. The revolutionary National Assembly had asserted that ancient prerogatives were superseded by the rights of man and principles of human equality based on appeals to natural law. In *Reflections on the Revolution in France* (1790), Burke countered that such claims were abstract and dangerous and that the belief in human equality undermined the social order. Government should be anchored in tradition, he argued. No matter how poorly the French monarchy and its institutions had served the nation, they should be preserved; their very longevity proved their usefulness. Burke's writings were widely read and influential on the Continent.

In the English-speaking world, one of the most popular writers was Hannah More (1745–1833), who with her four sisters ran a prosperous school. More saw piety as a rampart against rebellion. In a series of pamphlets titled *Cheap Repository Tracts,* she advocated the acceptance of the existing order and the solace of religious faith. Costing but a penny, the moral tracts were often handed out by the rich together with alms or food to the poor. More was the first writer in history to sell over a million copies; within three years her sales doubled. Conservative values thus spread to a very large audience in both Britain and the United States, where one of her works appeared in thirty editions.

A more extreme version of conservatism was the counterrevolutionary or ultraroyalist ideology. Unlike Burke, who was willing to tolerate some change, counterrevolutionaries wanted to restore society to its prerevolutionary condition. The most extreme counterrevolutionaries were those with personal experience of the upheavals of the Revolution. Count Joseph de Maistre° (1753–1821), a Savoyard (from the Franco-Italian border region) nobleman whose estates were occupied by the invading French, described monarchy as a God-given form of government in his *Considerations on France* (1796). Any attempt to abolish or even limit it was a violation of divine law. According to de Maistre and his fellow reactionaries, the authority of church and state was necessary to prevent human beings from falling into evil ways. De Maistre advocated stern government control, including the generous use of the death penalty, to keep people loyal to throne and altar.

Conservatism was also influenced by romanticism, with its glorification of the past, taste for pageantry, and belief in the organic unity of society. Nor were conservative ideas limited to intellectual circles; at times they had mass appeal, even to the conservative peasantry in Spain and elsewhere.

Romanticism

The long-lived romantic movement had emerged in the 1760s as a rebellion against rationalism and persisted until the 1840s. It was primarily a movement in the arts. Writers, painters, composers, and others consciously rebelled against the Enlightenment and its rationalist values. In contrast to the philosophes and their emphasis on reason (see Chapter 18), the romantics praised emotion and feeling. Jean-Jacques Rousseau's strong appeal to sentiment was taken up by the German writer Johann Wolfgang von Goethe° (1749–1832), who declared, "Feeling is everything." Goethe's *Sorrows of Young Werther* (1774), the most widely read book of the era—Napoleon

---

Maistre (MESS-treh)   **Goethe** (GOE-teh)

Caspar David Friedrich: The Chalk Cliffs on Rügen (ca. 1825–1826)   The foremost German romantic painter evokes nature in all its fearsome mystery and majesty. The three figures at the edge of a dangerous and bold precipice experience the power of nature from the smallest blades of grass, to the stark white jagged cliffs, to the arching trees that almost make a heart shape, to the vast expanse of the sea. Two men and a woman rest at the dangerous abyss. As the woman points out the chasm or perhaps the small flowers, one man is on his knees face-to-face with the details of nature while the other man distractedly gazes away from the other two figures, out into eternity. The romantics often invoked the awe-inspiring marvels of nature and loved mysterious, half-seen figures on distant horizons and dreamlike figures. Goethe remarked that if this painting were turned upside down, it would heighten the ambiguity, whereby the dark water and white cliffs would reveal a jagged mysterious mountain peak. *(Courtesy, Museum Oskar Reinhard am Stadtgarten, Winterthur)*

had a copy by his bedside—depicted the passions of the hero, who, depressed over unrequited love, kills himself. Many young men dressed in "Werther clothes"—tight black pants, long blue jacket, and buff yellow leather vest—which exemplified the clothing of tradesmen and provided a visual protest by young intellectuals against the frivolous dress of the upper classes. In some cases they emulated the tragic hero by committing suicide.

Whereas the Enlightenment had studied nature for the principles it could impart, the romantics worshiped nature for its inherent beauty. The German composer Ludwig van Beethoven° (1770–1827) wrote his *Pastoral* Symphony in praise of idyllic nature, depicting the pas-

sions one might feel in contemplating its loveliness and serenity. The English poets William Wordsworth (1770–1850) and Samuel Taylor Coleridge (1772–1834) treated untamed wilderness as a particular subject of wonder. Fellow Englishman Joseph Mallord William Turner (1775–1851) displayed the raw passions of the sea in such paintings as *Fire at Sea* (1834) and *Snowstorm: Steamboat off a Harbour's Mouth* (1842). Before painting the latter, Turner is said to have tied himself to a ship's mast and braved a snowstorm for four hours.

In pursuit of the authentic and the ancient, of feeling rather than rationality, many romantics rediscovered religion. In some areas of Europe, popular religion had anticipated the artists' and intellectuals' romantic sensibilities. France experienced a revival of Catholicism. In

Beethoven (BATE-ho-ven)

the German states, pietism, which had emerged in the seventeenth and eighteenth centuries, stressed the personal relationship between the individual and God, unimpeded by theological formalities or religious authorities. The influence of pietism, with its emphasis on spirituality and emotion, spread throughout central Europe in schools and churches.

In England emotionalism in religion expressed itself in the popularity of Methodism. Founded in the 1730s by the English preacher John Wesley (1703–1791), this movement emphasized salvation by a faith made active in one's life, a method of living. Appealing especially to the poor and desperate, Methodism by the 1790s had gained seventy thousand members; within a generation it quadrupled its flock.

The classicism of the Enlightenment had required an audience well versed in the traditional texts. Since the mid-eighteenth century, however, the reading public had grown to include people without access to elite culture. Appeals to emotion and sentiment were congenial to these new audiences, and a new interest developed in folklore and rustic life. In his short but productive life, Franz Schubert (1797–1828) composed, among other forms of music, over 600 *lieder*°, or songs, that echo the simplicity of folk tunes. Although living in Paris, Frédéric Chopin° (1810–1849) composed works influenced by the peasant music of his native Poland.

Whereas the philosophes had decried the Middle Ages, the romantics celebrated the medieval period. Painters frequently took Gothic buildings or ruins as their theme. Architects imitated the Gothic style in both private and public buildings. Sir Walter Scott (1771–1832) in Scotland and Victor Hugo° (1802–1885) in France recaptured chivalry and the age of faith in such popular works as *Ivanhoe* (1819) and *The Hunchback of Notre Dame* (1831). The opera *William Tell* by Gioacchini Rossini (1792–1868) is based on the legendary tale of a freedom-loving peasant who supposedly lived in thirteenth-century Switzerland. Thus it also had a liberal and nationalistic appeal.

The romantics sought displacement not only in time but also in place. The exotic had great appeal to them. Recently conquered Algeria in North Africa provided exotic scenes for French painters, among them Eugène Delacroix° (1798–1863) and Jean Ingres° (1780–1867). Senegal, in West Africa, which the French recovered from the British in 1815, offered the setting for Théodore Géricault's° powerful *Raft of the "Medusa."* (See the feature

"Weighing the Evidence: Raft of the 'Medusa'" on pages 738–739.) In music Franz Liszt (1811–1886) composed Hungarian rhapsodies that were considered exotic since they were based on gypsy music.

Romanticism exalted mythical figures as embodiments of human energy and passion. In the dramatic poem *Faust*, Goethe retold the legend of a man who sells his soul to the Devil in exchange for worldly success. Several composers set that story to powerful music. In the poetic drama *Prometheus Unbound*, the English romantic poet Percy Bysshe Shelley (1792–1822) celebrated Prometheus°, who, according to Greek mythology stole fire from the gods and gave it to human beings. In much the same spirit, many romantics lionized Napoleon, who had overthrown kings and states. Delacroix, who witnessed the July Revolution of 1830 in Paris (see pages 722–723), celebrated the heroism and passion of the revolutionaries in his huge canvas *Liberty Leading the People* (1830).

Romantics often challenged existing power relations, including relations between the sexes. The French writer Amandine-Aurore Dupin° (1804–1876), better known by her pen name, George Sand°, spoke for the emancipation of women from the oppressive supervision of their husbands, fathers, and brothers. In her personal life Sand practiced the freedom she preached, dressing like a man, smoking cigars, and openly pursuing affairs with a number of well-known artists. The English writer Mary Ann Evans (1819–1892), like George Sand, adopted a male pseudonym, George Eliot. She conducted her life in a nonconformist manner, living with a married man. The use of male pen names by both writers attests to the hostility that intellectual women still faced.

After the French Revolution nobles and monarchs ceased sponsoring art on a grand scale and were expected to conduct their lives soberly. Cut off from royal patronage, artists had to depend on members of the new middle classes to buy paintings and books and attend plays and musical performances. If earning a livelihood had often been difficult for artists in the past, it now became even more so. Forced to live marginally, they cultivated the image of the artist as unconventional. In their lifestyles and their work, they deliberately rejected the norms of society. The romantic period gave rise to the notion of the starving genius, alienated from society and loyal only to his all-consuming art.

Romantics of many stripes declared their determination to overthrow the smug present and create a new world. Victor Hugo called for "no more rules, no more

---

lieder (LEE-der)   **Chopin** (sho-PEHN)   **Hugo** (U-go)
Delacroix (de-la-KRWAH)   **Ingres** (AENG-reh)
Géricault (jair-ih-KO)

Prometheus (pro-MEETH-ee-us)   **Amandine-Aurore Dupin**
(ah-man-DEEN–oh-ROR du-PAEN)   **Sand** (SAN)

models" to constrain the human imagination. Romantic painters and musicians consciously turned their backs on the classical tradition in both subject matter and style. Old methods were discarded for new ones. The English poet George Gordon, Lord Byron (1788–1824), declared war on kings, on established religion, and on the international order. A nationalist as well as a romantic, he died while fighting for the independence of Greece.

Nationalism

The ideology of nationalism emerged in, and partly shaped, this era. Nationalism is the belief that people derive their identity from their nation and owe it their primary loyalty. A list of criteria for nationhood is likely to include a common language, religion, and political authority, as well as common traditions and shared historical experiences. Some nineteenth-century nationalists found any one of those criteria sufficient. Others insisted

that all of them had to be present before a group could consider itself a nation.

In an era that saw the undermining of traditional religious values, nationalism offered a new locus of faith. To people who experienced the social turmoil brought about by the erosion of the old order, nationalism held out the promise of a new community. Nationalism became an ideal espoused as strongly as religion. The Italian nationalist Giuseppe Mazzini° (1805–1872) declared that nationalism was "a faith and mission" ordained by God. The Polish romantic poet and nationalist Adam Mickiewicz° (1798–1855) compared perpetually carved-up Poland to the crucified Christ. The religious intensity of nationalism helps explain its widespread appeal.

Many forces shaped nationalism. Its earliest manifestation, cultural nationalism, had its origins in Rousseau's ideas of the organic nature of a people. Johann Gottfried Herder (1744–1833), Rousseau's German disciple, elaborated on his mentor's ideas, declaring that every people has a "national spirit." To explore the unique nature of this spirit, intellectuals all over Europe began collecting local folk poems, songs, and tales. In an effort to document the spirit of the German people, the Grimm brothers, Jacob (1785–1863) and Wilhelm (1786–1859), compiled fairy tales and published them between 1812 and 1818; among the better known are "Little Red Riding Hood" and "Snow White."

Political nationalism, born in the era of the French Revolution, injected urgency and passion into the new ideology. In the 1770s French aristocrats resisted attempts by the French monarchy to impose taxes, claiming that they embodied the rights of "the nation" and could not be taxed without its consent. Thus the concept of nation was given general currency. When revolutionary France was attacked by neighboring countries, which were ruled by kings and dukes, the Legislative Assembly called on the French people to rise and save the nation. The realm of the king of France had become the French nation.

In reaction to the French threat, intellectuals in Germany and Italy embraced the spirit of nationalism. In Germany the philosopher Johann Gottlieb Fichte° (1762–1814) delivered his series of *Addresses to the German Nation* after the Prussian defeat at Jena, calling on all Germans to stand firm against Napoleon. He argued that Germans were endowed with a special genius that had to be safeguarded for the well-being of all humankind. In Italy the writer Vittorio Alfieri (1749–1803) challenged France's claim to the right to lead the peoples of Europe.

Lord Byron in Albanian Costume   The British romantic poet had himself painted in exotic garb. Romantics were attracted to what were believed to be the mysteries of the East, representing a truer, more authentic existence.   *(Courtesy of the National Portrait Gallery, London)*

Mazzini (mat-SEE-nee)   Mickiewicz (MISS-kyev-ich)
Fichte (FISH-te)

That right, Alfieri insisted, properly belonged to Italians, the descendants and heirs of ancient Rome.

For the most part, however, after the French Revolution and the Napoleonic era, early-nineteenth-century nationalism was generous and cosmopolitan in its outlook. Herder and Mazzini believed that each of Europe's peoples was destined to achieve nationhood by forming its own political identity and that the nations of Europe would then live peacefully side by side. The members of dedicated nationalist groups such as Young Germany and Young Italy were also members of Young Europe. Many nationalists in the 1830s and 1840s were likewise committed to the ideal of a "Europe of free peoples." Victor Hugo even envisioned a "European republic" with its own parliament.

It is important to remember, however, that although many intellectuals found nationalism attractive, in the first half of the nineteenth century most people were likely to feel local and regional affinities more than national identities. Only as the result of several decades of propaganda by nationalists and governments was this ideology to win wide support, and only then did it become natural for Europeans to think of dying for their nations.

Liberalism

Liberalism was a direct descendant of the Enlightenment's critique of eighteenth-century absolutism. Nineteenth-century liberals believed that individual freedom was best safeguarded by reducing government powers to a minimum. They wanted to impose constitutional limits on government, to establish the rule of law, to sweep away all restrictions on individual enterprise—specifically, state regulation of the economy—and to ensure a voice in government for men of property and education. Liberalism was influenced by romanticism, with its emphasis on individual freedom and the imperative of the human personality to develop to its full potential. Liberalism was also affected by nationalism, especially in multinational autocratic states such as Austria, Russia, and the Ottoman Empire, in which free institutions could be established only if political independence were wrested from, respectively, Vienna, St. Petersburg, and Istanbul. (Nationalism challenged the established order in the first half of the century, but in the second half conservatives were to use nationalism as a means to stabilize their rule.)

Liberalism was both an economic and a political theory. In 1776 Adam Smith (1723–1790), the influential Scottish economist, published *An Inquiry into the Na-*

ture and Causes of the Wealth of Nations, a systematic study of the economic knowledge of his era. Smith advocated freeing national economies from the fetters of the state. (See the box "Reading Sources: Adam Smith Describes the Workings of the Market Economy.") Under the mercantilist system, prevalent throughout Europe until about 1800, the state regulated the prices and conditions of manufacture. Smith argued for letting the free forces of the marketplace shape economic decisions. He believed that economics was subject to basic unalterable laws that could be discerned and applied in the same fashion as natural laws. Chief among them, in Smith's view, was the compatibility of economic self-interest and the general good. He argued that entrepreneurs who lower prices sell more products, thus increasing their own profits *and* providing the community with affordable wares. In this way an individual's drive for profit benefits society as a whole. The economy is driven as if "by an invisible hand." This competitive drive for profits, Smith predicted, would expand the "wealth of nations." In France advocates of nonintervention by government in the economy were called supporters of *laissez faire* (meaning "to leave alone, to let run on its own").

Smith and his disciples formed what came to be known as the school of classical economy, emphasizing the importance of laissez faire. Smith had been relatively optimistic about the capacities of the free market. Those who followed him, and who witnessed more of the negative results of industrialization, were more gloomy. Thomas Malthus (1766–1834), a parson, published in 1798 *An Essay on the Principle of Population,* which suggested that population was outstripping resources. Unless people voluntarily limited their family sizes, they would suffer starvation. By their failure to exercise sexual restraint, the poor, Malthus declared, "are themselves the cause of their own poverty." The laws of economics suggested to Malthus that factory owners could not improve their workers' lot by increasing wages or providing charity because higher living standards would lead to more births, which in turn would depress wages and bring greater misery.

David Ricardo (1772–1823) made his fortune in the stock market, retired young, and wrote on economics, his best-known work being *Principles of Political Economy* (1817). Ricardo argued that capitalists' profits depended on wages paid to workers; to be profitable, industrialists had to compete in limiting the wages they offered. The capitalist offering the lowest wages was likely to be most successful. The "iron law of wages" seemed to provide, as had Malthus, scientific justification for the exploitation of workers.

READING SOURCES

ADAM SMITH DESCRIBES THE WORKINGS OF THE MARKET ECONOMY

In An Inquiry into the Nature and Causes of the Wealth of Nations, *Adam Smith explained how individuals working to maximize their own interests cause the economy as a whole to expand and society to benefit. Among the various economic activities, trade and specialization particularly contribute to the well-being of both society and the individual. Notice the reciprocal nature of self-interest. Smith is building a model, characterized by a mixture of theory and down-to-earth examples, which he believed applied to all societies and at all times.*

In almost every other race of animals each individual, when it is grown up to maturity, is entirely independent, and in its state has occasion for the assistance of no other living creature. But man has almost constant occasion for the help of his brethren, and it is in vain for him to expect it from their benevolence only. He will be more likely to prevail, if he can interest their self-love in his favour, and shew them that it is for their advantage to do for him what he requires of them. Whoever offers to another a bargain of any kind, proposes to do this. Give me that which I want, and you shall have this which you want, is the meaning of every such offer; and it is in this manner that we obtain from one another the far greater part of those good offices which we stand in need of. It is not from the benevolence of the butcher, the brewer, or the baker, that we expect our dinner, but from their regard to their own interest. We address ourselves, not to their humanity, but to their self-love, and never talk to them of our own necessities, but of their advantages. Nobody but a beggar chooses to depend chiefly upon the benevolence of his fellow-citizens. . . .

So it is this same trucking [trading] disposition which originally gives occasion to the division of labour. In a tribe of hunters or shepherds a particular person makes bows and arrows, for example, with more readiness and dexterity than any other. He frequently exchanges them for cattle or venison with his companions; and he finds at last that he can in this manner get more cattle and venison, than if he himself went to the field to catch them. From a regard to his own interest, therefore, the making of bows and arrows grows to be his chief business, and he becomes a sort of armourer. Another excels in making the frames and covers of their little huts or moveable houses. He is accustomed to be of use in this way to his neighbours, who reward him in the same manner with cattle and with venison, till at last he finds it in his interest to dedicate himself entirely to this employment, and to become a sort of house-carpenter. In the same manner a third becomes a smith or a brazier, a fourth a tanner or dresser of hides of skin, the principal part of the clothing of savages. And thus the certainty of being able to exchange all that surplus part of the produce of his own labour, which is over and above his own consumption, for such parts of the produce of other men's labour as he may have occasion for, encourages every man to apply himself to a particular occupation.

Source: Adam Smith, *An Inquiry into the Nature and Causes of the Wealth of Nations* (London: W. Strahan, 1776), pp. 17–18.

Even supporters of laissez faire had some reservations about the market economy. In France in the first half of the nineteenth century, commentators on the factory system, including industrialists, expressed fear that factory work would undermine the stability of family life and hence of society itself. Philanthropic intervention, they hoped, would resolve the problems they had identified.

Even some of the British classical economists doubted the wisdom of allowing the market economy to operate entirely without regulation and of trusting it to provide for human happiness. Smith warned that the market tended to form monopolies, and he suggested that government intervene to prevent this occurrence. According to Smith, the marketplace could not provide for all human needs; the government needed to supply education, road systems, and an equitable system of justice.

John Stuart Mill (1806–1873), the leading British economic and political thinker at midcentury, voiced strong support for laissez-faire economics in the first edition of his *Principles of Political Economy* (1848). If left alone, the individual could carry on economic functions better than the government, Mill insisted. In subsequent editions, however, he remarked that the state had an obligation to relieve human misery. Nor could the free market satisfactorily address every human need. Once wealth was produced, he noted, its distribution was subject to traditions and to decisions made by those in power. Thus, presumably, wealth could be shared by society as a whole. Toward the end of his life, Mill seemed to be leaning toward socialism.

Mill's about-face reflected and presaged changing attitudes among the proponents of laissez faire. In the face of unsanitary urban conditions, child labor, stark inequities in wealth, and other alarming results of industrialization, at least some liberals around midcentury called on the state to intervene in areas of concern that would have been unthinkable a half century earlier.

In their political positions, liberals were firm throughout the century, constant in their support for limiting government power to prevent despotism. Enlightened eighteenth-century monarchs had declared that the purpose of their rule was to promote the public good. In even more ringing terms, the French Revolution had proclaimed that the purpose of government is to ensure the happiness of humankind. As Thomas Jefferson (1743–1826), another child of the Enlightenment, asserted in the Declaration of Independence (1776), among the "unalienable rights" of individuals are "life, liberty, and the pursuit of happiness." The purpose of government is to safeguard and promote those rights.

The Enlightenment had posited natural law as the basis of government. French liberals in the nineteenth century continued to see human liberty as founded on natural law, but their English counterparts were less theoretical in outlook. Jeremy Bentham (1748–1832) argued that the purpose of government is to provide "the greatest happiness of the greatest number" and that governments should be judged on that basis. Bentham and his disciples believed that the test of government is its usefulness; thus they were known as "Utilitarians."

Democracy was implicit in Bentham's philosophy: the greatest number could ensure its own happiness only by voting for its rulers. John Stuart Mill, a disciple of Bentham, was the foremost proponent of liberalism, seeing it as guaranteeing the development of a free society. Individuals could best develop their talents if they were unhampered by state interference. In his essay *On Liberty*, one of the fundamental documents of nineteenth-century liberalism, Mill argued for the free circulation of ideas—even false ideas. For in the free marketplace of ideas, false ideas will be defeated, and truth vindicated, in open debate. Mill also asserted that a free society should be free for all its members. Influenced by his wife, Harriet Taylor Mill (1807–1856), he wrote in *On the Subjection of Women* (1861) that women should be permitted to vote and should have access to equal educational opportunities and the professions. Such equality not only would be just but also would have the advantage of "doubling the mass of mental faculties available for the higher service of humanity." Mill, the foremost male proponent of women's rights in his generation, helped win a broader audience for the principle of equality between the sexes.

Despite Mill's influence, many liberals, especially in the early nineteenth century, feared the masses and therefore vigorously opposed democracy. They feared that the common people, uneducated and supposedly gullible, would easily be swayed by demagogues who might become despotic or who, in a desire to curry favor with the poor, might attack the privileges of the wealthy. The French liberal Benjamin Constant denounced democracy as "the vulgarization of despotism"; the vote, he declared, should be reserved for the affluent and educated. When less fortunate Frenchmen denounced the property requirements that prevented them from voting, the liberal statesman François Guizot (1787–1874) smugly replied, "Get rich."

In the twelfth and thirteenth centuries, a new wealthy class based on urban occupations emerged; its members were called "burgers" or "bourgeois." This class fully developed in the nineteenth century. If unsympathetic to extending suffrage to the lower classes, the *bourgeoisie*° championed liberalism, which justified its own right to participate in governance. Economic liberalism was also attractive to merchants and manufacturers, who wished to gather wealth without state interference.

If originating in and justifying middle-class interests, the basic tenets of liberalism—the belief in the sanctity of human rights, freedom of speech and freedom to organize, the rule of law and equality before the law—eventually became so widely accepted that even conservative and socialist opponents of liberalism accepted them as fundamental rights.

Socialism

The notion that human happiness can best be ensured by the common ownership of property had been suggested in earlier times by individuals as different as the Greek philosopher Plato (427?–347 B.C.) and Sir Thomas More (1478–1535), the English author of *Utopia*. Troubled

---

bourgeoisie (boor-zhwa-ZEE)

by the harsh condition of the working classes, thinkers in Britain and France came to espouse theories that, beginning in the 1820s, were called "socialist." Socialists believed that the "social" ownership of property, unlike private ownership, would benefit society as a whole. During the first half of the nineteenth century, most workers, even in industrializing England, where manufacturing was increasingly large scale, were artisans. It was in a later era that socialism would address the issues raised by industry.

In 1796, during the French Revolution, Gracchus Babeuf° (1760–1797), a minor civil servant, participated in the Conspiracy of Equals (see page 661). The Revolution, however haltingly, had proclaimed political equality for its citizens, but it had failed to bring economic equality. Babeuf decided to resort to revolution to bring about a "communist" society—a society in which all property would be owned in common and private property would be abolished. Work would be provided for everyone; medical services and education would be free to all. Babeuf's plot was discovered, and he was guillotined, but his theories and example of conspiratorial revolutionary action would influence later socialists.

Several other important French thinkers made contributions to European socialism. Curiously, it was a French aristocrat, Henri de Saint-Simon° (1760–1825), who emphasized the need "to ameliorate as promptly and as quickly as possible the moral and physical existence of the most numerous class." The proper role for the state, Saint-Simon declared, was to ensure the welfare of the masses. The course of history, he suggested, was in the direction of expertise. No longer could people rule solely on the basis of their birth. Rather, Europe should come to be governed by a council of qualified artists and scientists who would oversee the economy and ensure that everyone enjoyed a minimum level of well-being. Many women, including those of the working classes, supported the views of Saint-Simon. (See the box "Reading Sources: A Call to Women.")

Another vital contribution to socialist thought came from thinkers who tried to imagine an ideal world. They were later derisively dismissed as dreamers, as builders of utopias, fantasy worlds (the Greek word *utopia* means "nowhere"). Their schemes varied, but they shared the view that property should be owned in common and used for the common good. They also believed that society should rest on principles of cooperation rather than competitive individualism.

One of the earliest and most notable utopians was the Welsh mill owner Robert Owen (1771–1859). Beginning in 1800 he ran a prosperous cotton mill in New Lanark, Scotland. He also provided generously for his workers, guaranteeing them jobs and their children a decent education. In his writings Owen suggested the establishment of self-governing communities owning the means of production. Essentials would be distributed to all members according to their needs. Owen's ideas for the new society included equal rights for women. Owen received little support from fellow manufacturers and political leaders, and his own attempt in 1824 to establish an ideal society in the United States at New Harmony, Indiana, ended in failure after four years.

Another influential contributor to early socialist theory was the Frenchman Charles Fourier° (1772–1837). A clerk and salesman, Fourier wrote out in great detail his vision of the ideal future society. It would consist of cooperative organizations called "phalansteries," each with sixteen hundred inhabitants who would live in harmony with nature and with one another. Everyone would be assured gainful employment, which would be made enjoyable by rotating jobs. Because cooperative communes often faced the issue of who would carry out the distasteful tasks, everyone would share the pleasant *and* unpleasant work. Fourier thought that because children enjoy playing with dirt, they should be put in charge of picking up garbage.

Fourier had an important female following because of his belief in the equality of the sexes, and some of these women tried to put his ideas into action. In Belgium the activist Zoé Gatti de Gamond° (1806–1854) co-founded a phalanstery for women. She believed that if women could be assured of economic well-being, other rights would follow. Also inspired by Fourier, Flora Tristan (1801–1844) was an effective advocate for workers' rights. In her book *Union Ouvrière* (*Workers' Union*), she suggested that all workers should contribute to establish a "Workers' Palace" in every town. In the palace, the sick and disabled would have shelter, and the workers' children could receive a free education. Crossing France on foot, she spread the word of workers' solidarity and self-help.

There were other approaches. The French socialist journalist Louis Blanc° (1811–1882) saw in democracy the means of bringing into existence a socialist state. By securing the vote, the common people could win control over the state and require it to serve their needs. The state could be induced to buy up banks, insurance com-

---

Gracchus Babeuf (GRAH-kus bah-BOEF)
Saint-Simon (saen–see-MON)

Fourier (foor-YAY)   **Gamond** (gay-MON)   **Blanc** (BLAHN)

READING SOURCES

A CALL TO WOMEN

From 1832 to 1834 an intellectually sophisticated group of Saint-Simonian women published a journal, first under the title La Femme libre *(The Free Woman) and then under the title* La Femme nouvelle *(The New Woman). They called for gender equality in their private lives as well as in the political arena. Referring to the subjugation of women to men as slavery, they sought to unify women of all social classes to further equal civil rights for all.*

While all the people stir themselves up in the name of *Liberty,* and the proletariat demands enfranchisement, we women remain passive before this great movement of social emancipation that is occurring before our eyes.

Is our lot so happy that we have nothing to demand as well? Women . . . have been exploited, tyrannized. This tyranny, this exploitation must end. We are born free like men; and half of the human race may not, without injustice, enslave the other half.

Let us understand then our rights; understand our power; we have an attractive power, the power of charm—the irresistible weapon, let us know how to use it.

Let us refuse as husbands any man who is not generous enough to share his power; we no longer want this formula: *Woman, submit to your husband!*

We want marriage based on equality. . . . Celibacy rather than slavery!

We are free and equal to men. . . .

Liberty, equality . . . that is to say free and equal opportunity to develop our faculties: there is the conquest we must achieve, and we can only obtain it through a united front, let us no longer form two camps to which our interests bind us; those of women of the people and women of privilege. . . .

Women of the privileged class, you who are young, rich and beautiful, you believe yourselves to be happy while in your salons you breathe the fragrance of flattery that protects you from those that surround you; you reign: your reign is short lived; it ends with the ball. Returning to your home, you become slaves again, you find a master who makes you feel his power and you forget all the pleasures that you have tasted.

Women of all classes, you have a powerful action to exercise, you are called to spread the feeling of order and harmony everywhere. Turn to the profit of society the irresistible charm of your beauty, the sweetness of your captivating word, which must make men march for a similar cause. . . . Signed: Jeanne-Victoire [*omitting her patronymic*]

Source: *La Femme libre,* no. 1 (1832), p. 1. Translated by R. S. Hopkins.

---

panies, and railway systems and set up a commercial and retail chain that would provide jobs for workers and offer goods and services at prices unaffected by the profit motive. Once the workers controlled the state by the ballot, the state in turn would establish social workshops in which the workers would be responsible for production and supervision of business matters. Society should be established according to (from the socialist viewpoint) fundamental fairness: "Let each produce according to his aptitudes and strength; let each consume according to his need."

Blanc's contemporary Louis Blanqui° (1805–1882) suggested a more violent mode of action. He advocated

Blanqui (blahn-KEE)

seizure of the state by a small, dedicated band of men who were devoted to the welfare of the working class and who would install communism, for the equality of all. Blanqui was a perpetual conspirator, confined to state prisons for much of his long life. His ideas strengthened the notion of class warfare, and his own life served as a symbol of this struggle. The thought and example of Blanqui and the other socialists would play a major role in shaping the thinking of the most important socialist of the nineteenth century, Karl Marx.

Karl Marx (1818–1883), the son of a lawyer, grew up in the Rhineland, in western Germany, an industrializing area that was particularly open to political ideas and agitation. The Rhineland had been influenced by the ideas of the French Revolution and was primed for political radicalism. As a young man, Marx studied philosophy at the University of Berlin and joined a group known as the "Young Hegelians," self-declared disciples of the idealist philosopher G. W. F. Hegel (1770–1831). Hegel taught that reality is mainly based on the ability of the mind to conceive of it. Marx, by contrast, was a materialist, believing that material realities impose themselves on the mind.

Marx showed an early interest in political liberty and socialism. In 1842–1843 he edited a newspaper that spoke out for freedom and democracy in Germany. The following year, in Paris, he met several of the French socialist writers. Even when he was a young man, his contemporaries perceived him as bright but unyielding in his determination.

Because of his radical journalism, he was exiled from the Rhineland and lived briefly in Paris, then Brus-

Karl Marx   Through his writings and agitation, Marx transformed the socialism of his day and created an ideology that helped shape the nineteenth and twentieth centuries.   *(Corbis)*

sels. In 1849 he settled in London, where he lived for the rest of his life, dedicated to establishing his ideas on what he viewed as scientific bases. Deriving a modest income from writing for the *New York Daily Tribune* and from funds provided by his friend and collaborator Friedrich Engels (1820–1895), Marx was never able to provide well for his family, which constantly lived on the edge of poverty. Of the six children born to the Marx household, three died in infancy.

In 1848 Marx and Engels published the *Communist Manifesto*. A pamphlet written for the Communist League, a group of Germans living in exile, the Manifesto was an appeal to the working classes of the world. The league deliberately called itself "Communist" rather than "Socialist." Communism was a radical program, bent on changing property relations by violence; socialism was associated with more peaceful means of transformation. The pamphlet laid out Marx's basic ideas, calling on the proletariat to rise—"You have nothing to lose but your chains"—and create a society that would end the exploitation of man by man. (See the box "The Continuing Experiment: Marxism and the Working Classes.")

A number of political and polemical works flowed from Marx's pen, but most of them remained unpublished during his lifetime. The first volume of his major work, *Capital*, was published in 1867; subsequent volumes appeared posthumously. Marxism, the body of Marx's thought, is complex and sometimes contradictory. *Capital* is written in an obscure style and difficult to penetrate, but certain basic concepts resound throughout and were embraced by Marx's followers.

Marx agreed with Hegel and many of his contemporaries that human history has a direction and a goal. Hegel believed that the goal was the realization of the world spirit. Marx believed that it was the abolition of capitalism, the victory of the proletariat, the disappearance of the state, and the ultimate liberation of all humankind.

Whereas Hegel thought that ideas govern the world, Marx insisted that material conditions determine it. Hegel said that history evolves by the "dialectic": a principle, say despotism, has within it ideas that oppose it; in the struggle between despotism and its opposite, a higher ideal emerges—freedom, the ultimate goal of history. Following Hegel, Marx posited a world of change but insisted that it was embedded in material conditions, not in a clash of ideas. Hence the process of history was grounded on the notion of "dialectical materialism." Ideas, to Marx, were but a reflection of the material world.

Marx grouped human beings into classes based on their relationship to the means of production. Capitalists were one class because they owned the means of pro-

Marxism and the Working Classes

By the 1840s workers labored long hours each day in unsanitary and dangerous conditions. Moreover, the gap between the rich and the poor had become vast, prompting critics to propose ways to ameliorate the condition of the working classes. In the *Communist Manifesto,* Karl Marx views history as a class struggle and calls on the workers of the world to unite and rise up to help themselves. His idea of an international workers' movement contrasted with the dominant currents of capitalism and nationalism. Marx's appeal to workers met with limited success. The Manifesto inspired workers and revolutionary leaders alike, often resulting in significant political and economic gains. However, with the development of capitalism, many Marxist movements in industrialized European nations agitated for reform rather than revolution. Despite the creation of international Marxist organizations, and some victorious revolutions, workers never united on a large scale to stage violent successful communist or socialist revolutions that would destroy the bourgeoisie as Marx had envisioned.

The history of all hitherto existing society is the history of class struggles.

Freeman and slave, patrician and plebeian, lord and serf, guild-master and journeyman, in a word, oppressor and oppressed, stood in constant opposition to one another, carried on an uninterrupted, now hidden, now open fight, that each time ended, either in a revolutionary reconstitution of society at large, or in the common ruin of the contending classes. . . .

In ancient Rome we have patricians, knights, plebeians, slaves; in the Middle Ages, feudal lords, vassals, guild-masters, journeymen, apprentices, serfs; in almost all of these classes, again, subordinate gradations.

The modern bourgeois society that has sprouted from the ruins of feudal society, has not done away with class antagonisms. It has but established new classes, new conditions of oppression, new forms of struggle in place of the old ones. . . .

Society as a whole is more and more splitting up into two great hostile camps, into two great classes directly facing each other: Bourgeoisie and Proletariat. . . .

With the development of industry the proletariat not only increases in number; it becomes concentrated in greater masses, its strength grows and it feels that strength more. . . . [T]he collisions between individual workmen and individual bourgeois take more and more the character of collisions between two classes. . . .

Of all the classes that stand face to face with the bourgeoisie today, the proletariat alone is a really revolutionary class. The other classes decay and finally disappear in the face of modern industry; the proletariat is its special and essential product.

All previous historical movements were movements of minorities. The proletarian movement is the self-conscious, independent movement of the immense majority. The proletariat, the stratum of our present society, cannot stir, cannot raise itself up, without the whole superincumbent strata of official society being sprung into the air. . . .

. . . The development of modern industry, therefore, cuts from under its feet the very foundation on which the bourgeoisie produces and appropriates products. What the bourgeoisie therefore produces, above all, are its own grave-diggers. Its fall and the victory of the proletariat are equally inevitable.

QUESTIONS

1. In what ways was Marxism, as expressed in the *Communist Manifesto,* a revolutionary doctrine? To whom might Marxism have appealed, and how do you account for that appeal?

2. In what ways are the ideas of Marx a product of their time, applicable to industrial Europe in the mid-nineteenth century and the first wave of industrialization? What were the roles and responsibilities of the bourgeoisie and the proletariat?

3. Marx viewed economics as the driving force of the historical process and centered his argument on the concept of class conflict. How might this be problematic?

SOURCE: Karl Marx and Friedrich Engels, *Communist Manifesto* (1848; repr., New York: International Publishers, 1948), pp. 9, 17, 20–21.

duction. Workers were a separate class—the proletariat—because they did not own any of the means of production and their income came only from their own hands. Because these two classes had different relationships to the means of production, they had different—in fact, antagonistic—interests and were destined (Marx believed) to engage in a class struggle.

Some of Marx's contemporaries lamented the increasing hostility between workers and capitalists. Marx, however, saw the conflict as necessary to advance human history, and he sought to validate his thesis by the study of the past. In the Middle Ages, he pointed out, the feudal class dominated society but eventually lost the struggle to the commercial classes. Now, in turn, the capitalists were destined to be overwhelmed by the rising proletariat.

In his study of history and economics, Marx found not only justification for but irrefutable proof of the "scientific" basis of his ideas. Capitalism was itself creating the forces that would supplant it. The large industrial plants necessitated an ever greater work force with a growing sense of class interest. The inherently competitive nature of capitalism would inevitably drive an increasing number of enterprises out of business, and a form of monopoly capitalism would emerge, abusive of both consumers and workers. As a result of ever more savage competition, more businesses would fail, and consequently more workers would become unemployed. Angered and frustrated by their lot, workers would overthrow the system that had abused them for so long: "The knell of private property has sounded. The expropriators will be expropriated." The proletariat would take power and, to solidify its rule, would temporarily exercise the "dictatorship of the proletariat." Once that had taken place, the state would wither away. With the coming to power of the proletariat, the history of class war would end and the ideal society would prevail. Ironically, Marx, who spent his life writing about the nature and history of social change, envisaged a time when change would cease, when history, as it were, would stop.

Many protested the evils of industrialism, but Marx described economic change in dramatic terms as a necessary stage for humankind to traverse on its way to liberation. The suffering of the workers was not in vain. Rather, it was a necessary process, part of the drama that would finally lead to human emancipation. Unlike some of the utopians who deplored industrialism, Marx accepted it and saw it as part of the path that history was fated to follow.

Marx's study of economics and history proved to him that the coming of socialism was not only desirable—as the utopians had thought—but inevitable. The laws of history dictated that capitalism, having created the rising proletariat, would collapse. By labeling his brand of socialism as scientific, Marx gave it the aura it needed to become the faith of millions of people. To declare ideas scientific in the nineteenth century, when science was held in such high esteem, was to ensure their popularity.

RESTORATION, REFORM, AND REACTION

DESPITE the new ideologies that emerged to challenge the existing order, efforts at restoration appeared successful until at least 1830. Indeed, in central and eastern Europe, from the German states to Russia and the Ottoman Empire, the political systems established in 1815 would persist virtually unchanged until midcentury. In western Europe, however, important transformations would occur by the 1830s as reaction gave way to reform. Then in 1848 widespread revolutions would break out on much of the Continent. The language of liberalism and nationalism, and even the newer idiom of socialism, would be heard on the barricades, in popular assemblies, and in parliamentary halls.

Western Europe: From Reaction to Liberalism, 1815–1830

Most of Europe until the 1830s experienced the heavy hand of reaction. Then western Europe saw more liberal regimes come into their own. Revolution and the threat of revolution helped dismantle the worst features of the restored regimes. The more liberal western European states faced continuing discontents of various sorts—mainly social and political—which they managed to negotiate with varying degrees of success.

The most dramatic restoration of the older order occurred in France. The restored Bourbons turned the clock back, not to 1789 but closer to 1791, when the country had briefly enjoyed a constitutional monarchy, and it went beyond that in maintaining the Napoleonic Code, with its provisions of legal equality. The Bourbon constitution provided for a parliament with an elected lower house, the Chamber of Deputies, and an appointed upper house, the Chamber of Peers. Although suffrage to the Chamber of Deputies was limited to a small elite of men with landed property—100,000 voters, about 0.2 percent of the population—this constitution was a concession to representative government that had not existed in the Old Regime (see page 647). Louis XVIII (r. 1814–1824) stands out among European rulers because he realized that it would be necessary to compromise on the principles of popular sovereignty proclaimed by the French Revolution. His intention was to "popularize the monarchy" and "royalize the nation." A moderate, Louis was succeeded by his ultrareactionary brother, Charles X (r. 1824–1830), who alienated the middle classes. More general disenchantment came with an economic downturn in 1827, marked by poor harvests and increased unemployment in the cities. Discontent brought to Parliament a liberal majority that refused to accept the reactionary ministers the king appointed. On July 26, 1830, after the humiliating defeat of his party at the polls, the king issued a set of decrees suspend-ing freedom of the press, dissolving the Chamber of Deputies, and stiffening property qualifications for voters in subsequent elections. The king appeared to be engineering a coup against the existing political system.

The first to protest were the Parisian journalists and typesetters, directly threatened by the censorship laws. On July 28 others joined the protest and began erecting barricades across many streets. After killing several hundred protesters, the king's forces lost control of the city. This July Revolution, also known as "the three glorious days," drove the king into exile.

Alarmed by the crowds' clamor for a republic, the liberal opposition—consisting of some of the leading newspaper editors and sympathetic deputies—quickly drafted the duke of Orléans, Louis Philippe (r. 1830–1848), known for his liberal opinions, to occupy the throne.

Louis XVIII as Military Leader   The French king, returned to his throne by France's foreign enemies, had no military glory attached to his reign. But in 1823 France successfully invaded Spain, helping its reactionary king suppress a liberal revolt. This painting celebrates the return of the victorious French troops.   *(Château de Versailles/Laurie Platt Winfrey, Inc.)*

"Peterloo" Massacre In August 1819 at St. Peter's Fields in Manchester, England, a crowd demanding parliamentary reform was charged by government troops, leading to bloodshed. Many English people derided the event and called it "Peterloo." *(The National Archives, Public Record Office)*

Compared with the rest of Europe, Great Britain enjoyed considerable constitutional guarantees and a parliamentary regime. Yet liberals and radicals found their government retrograde and repressive. Traumatized by the French Revolution, the ruling class clung to the past, certain that advocates for change were Jacobins in disguise. Change seemed to invite revolution.

Social unrest beset Britain as it faced serious economic dislocation. The arrival of peace in 1815 led to a sudden drop in government expenditures, the return into the economy of several hundred thousand men who had been away at war, financial disarray, and plummeting prices. The poor and the middle classes were especially incensed over the clear economic advantages that the landed classes, dominating Parliament, had secured for themselves in 1815 in passing the Corn Law. This legislation imposed high tariffs on imported "corn"—that is, various forms of grain. It thus shielded the domestic market from international competition and allowed landowners to reap huge profits at the expense of consumers. All these issues were cause for demonstrations, petitions, protest marches, and other challenges to the authorities.

In August 1819, sixty thousand people gathered in St. Peter's Fields in Manchester to demand universal suf-

frage for men and women alike, an annual Parliament, and other democratic reforms. The crowd was peaceful and unarmed, yet mounted soldiers charged, killing eleven and wounding four hundred. Using military force against the people as if against the French at Waterloo was seen as wrong, and the confrontation was branded "the battle of Peterloo," or more often "the Peterloo Massacre." The British public was shocked by this use of violence against peaceful demonstrators; Parliament responded by passing the so-called Six Acts, which outlawed freedom of assembly and effectively imposed censorship. Through much of the 1820s Britain appeared resistant to reform until news of revolution across the channel in 1830 brought about change.

The term *liberal* was first coined in Spain, where the fate of liberals prefigured what would happen elsewhere in continental Europe. In 1812 a national parliament, the Cortes, elected during the Napoleonic occupation, issued a democratic constitution that provided for universal manhood suffrage and a unicameral legislature with control over government policy. Supporters and admirers of the constitution in Spain and elsewhere were known as "liberals," or friends of liberty.

Napoleon had ousted the Bourbon king of Spain, Ferdinand VII (r. 1808, 1814–1833). Ferdinand returned to power in 1814, promising to respect the liberal 1812 constitution. But Ferdinand was by temperament hostile to the new order, and he was a believer in the divine right of kings. He drew his support from the aristocracy and from segments of the general population still loyal to the call of throne and altar. Liberals were arrested or driven into exile.

Ferdinand's plan to restore Spain to its earlier prominence included a reassertion of control over its American colonies. The Spanish dominions had grown restless in the eighteenth century, for they had witnessed the advent of an independent United States and the French occupation of Spain itself. Spain's emboldened colonies had refused to recognize the Napoleonic regime in Madrid and became increasingly self-reliant. Their attitude did not change when French control of Spain ended. Ferdinand refused to compromise with the overseas territories. Instead, he gathered an army to subdue them. Some liberal junior officers, declaring the army's loyalty to the constitution of 1812, won support from the rank and file, who balked at going overseas. This military mutiny coincided with a sympathetic provincial uprising to produce the "revolution of 1820," the first major assault on the European order established in 1815 at the Congress of Vienna. Ferdinand appealed to the European powers for help. France intervened on his behalf and crushed the uprising.

Ferdinand restored his reactionary regime but could not regain Spain's American colonies. The British, sympathetic to the cause of Latin American independence and eager for commercial access to the region, opposed reconquest, and their naval dominance of the seas kept Spain in its place. The United States, meanwhile, had recognized the independence of the Latin American republics and wished to see their independence maintained. In 1823 President James Monroe issued the statement known as the Monroe Doctrine, prohibiting European colonization or intervention in the affairs of independent republics in the Americas. Of course, the United States had no military muscle to back this proclamation, but the British navy effectively enforced it. By 1825 all of Spain's colonies on the mainland in Central and South America had won their freedom.

The newly independent states patterned their regimes on models of Spanish liberalism; all had constitutions stipulating separation of powers and guaranteeing human rights. Brazil, the Portuguese empire in the Americas, was a monarchy for most of the rest of the nineteenth century, as was Mexico for a short time, but all the other states became republics, opting for what was then an unusual form of government. Although most of the Latin regimes eventually became dictatorships, they continued to pay lip service to liberal values.

Western Europe, 1830–1848

For the political systems of western Europe, the 1830s marked a time of modification. The threat, and occasionally the sting, of revolt produced more liberal regimes, but except for Britain and Spain, most governments were unable to stem the tide of discontent, which became revolution in 1848.

As a result of the 1830 revolution in Paris, a more liberal regime was installed in France. Louis Philippe proclaimed himself "King of the French," thus acknowledging that he reigned at the behest of the people. Freedom of the press was reinstated. Suffrage was extended to twice as many voters as before, 200,000 men. The July Monarchy, named after the month in which it was established by revolution, justified itself by celebrating the great Revolution of 1789. Louis Philippe commissioned huge canvases glorifying great moments of the Revolution. On the site where the Bastille had been razed in 1789, the government erected a large column with the names of the victims of the July 1830 revolution, thus suggesting a continuity between those who had fought tyranny in 1789 and 1830.

Identification with the Revolution appeared to legitimize the regime but also had the potential to subvert it. Fearful that the cult of revolution would encourage violence against the new monarchy, the regime censored artistic production, promoting only works that extolled the period from 1789 to 1791, when the revolutionaries had attempted to found a constitutional monarchy. Now that the revolution of 1830 had established a constitutional monarchy, the regime was suggesting, any further uprisings were illegitimate. If the July Monarchy turned out not to be as liberal as its founders had hoped, foreign visitors coming from more authoritarian societies were nonetheless impressed by France's apparently liberal institutions. (See the box "Global Encounters: A Moroccan Describes French Freedom of the Press.") Many French liberals, however, saw the regime as a travesty of the hopes and promises it had represented on coming to power in 1830.

The major political problem facing Britain in the early nineteenth century was the composition of Parliament, which did not reflect the dramatic population shifts that had occurred since the seventeenth century. Industrialization had transformed mere villages into major cities—Manchester, Birmingham, Leeds, Sheffield—but those cities had no representation in Parliament.

A Moroccan Describes French Freedom of the Press

In 1845–1846 a Moroccan diplomatic mission visited Paris. The ambassador's secretary, Muhammad as-Saffar (d. 1881), wrote an account of the visit. Impressed by many aspects of French society, he praises France's press in the following passage. The "Sultan" as-Saffar refers to is King Louis Philippe. To this Moroccan observer, the extent to which the French enjoyed constitutional government was striking.

The people of Paris, like all the French indeed, like all of [Europe] are eager to know the latest news and events that are taking place in other parts [of the world]. For this purpose they have the gazette. [In] these papers . . . they write all the news that has reached them that day about events in their own country and in other lands both near and far.

This is the way it is done. The owner of a newspaper dispatches his people to collect everything they see or hear in the way of important events or unusual happenings. Among the places where they collect the news are the two Chambers, the Great and the Small, where they come together to make their laws. When the members of the Chamber meet to deliberate, the men of the gazette sit nearby and write down everything that is said, for all debating and ratifying of laws is matter for the gazette and is known to everyone. No one can prevent them from doing this. . . .

. . . [I]f someone has an idea about a subject but he is not a member of the press, he may write about it in the gazette and make it known to others, so that the leaders of opinion learn about it. If the idea is worthy they may follow it, and if its author was out of favor it may bring him recognition.

No person in France is prohibited from expressing his opinion or from writing it and printing it, on condition that he does not violate the law. . . .

In the newspapers they write rejoinders to the men of the two Chambers about the laws they are making. If their Sultan demands gifts from the notables or goes against the law in any way, they write about that too, saying that he is a tyrant and in the wrong. He cannot confront them or cause them harm. Also, if someone behaves out of the ordinary, they write about that too, making it common knowledge among people of every rank. If his deeds were admirable, they praise and delight in him, lauding his example; but if he behaved badly, they revile him to discourage the like.

Moreover, if someone is being oppressed by another, they write about that too, so that everyone will know the story from both sides just as it happened, until it is decided in court. One can also read in it what their courts have decided.

QUESTIONS

1. Based on the diplomat's reaction to the French system, what can you deduce about freedom of the press and the expression of public opinion in Morocco?

2. Do you think this observer has a positive opinion of the French press? Why or why not?

Source: Susan Gilson Miller, ed. and trans., *Disorienting Encounters: Travels of a Moroccan Scholar in France in 1845–1846; The Voyage of Muhammad as-Saffar.* Copyright © 1992 Regents of the University of California. Reprinted by permission of the University of California Press.

Localities that had lost population, however, were still represented. In districts known as "pocket boroughs," single individuals owned the right to a seat in Parliament. In districts known as "rotten boroughs," a handful of voters elected a representative.

News of the July 1830 revolution in Paris encouraged British liberals to push for reform. Fearing the same fate as the hapless Charles X, some conservatives silently yielded. The government introduced a reform bill abolishing or reducing representation for sparsely populated areas while granting seats for the populous and unrepresented cities. The bill also widened the franchise by lowering property qualifications to include many middle-class men. Following a prolonged, bitter political battle between the government and middle classes on one side and the aristocracy on the other, the House of Lords finally passed what came to be known as the Great Reform Bill of 1832.

The reform was not particularly radical. Only the upper layers of the male middle class were enfranchised, or one in seven adult men. By establishing national criteria for the vote and eliminating local variations, some people, including some women, actually lost the vote. Yet despite its shortcomings, the reform demonstrated the willingness of the political leaders to acknowledge the increasing economic importance of manufacturing. Parliament became a more representative forum whose makeup better reflected the shift of economic power from agricultural landowners to the industrial and commercial classes. The bill passed as a result of nationwide agitation, evidence that the political system could respond to grievances and bring about reform peacefully.

Parliament justified the population's newfound faith in its efficacy by undertaking several more reforms. In 1835 Parliament passed the Municipal Corporation Act, which provided for more representative municipal councils with increased decision-making powers in local affairs.

A series of colonial reforms also showed Parliament's willingness to adapt to changing circumstances. Opposition to slavery had been voiced since the 1780s. (See the box "Reading Sources: A Plea to Abolish Slavery in the British Colonies.") Slavery, the very opposite of human freedom, was an affront to liberal principles. Moreover, its persistence threatened the empire—in 1831 sixty thousand slaves rebelled in Jamaica. Parliament heeded the call for change and in 1833 abolished slavery throughout the British Empire.

In addition, the British began to review their imperial administration. Their control over Canada had been challenged in an uprising in 1837. London sent out a fact-finding mission headed by Lord Durham (1806–1848). As a result of the *Durham Report,* the British government promulgated self-government for Canada in 1839 and 1841. Eventually all the British colonies with a majority of white settlers were given similar rights of self-rule. The idea of self-government for nonwhites in the colonies was as yet an unimaginable proposition.

Reforms solidified Britain's influence overseas. In Canada they reduced opposition to British rule. The antislavery campaign led to the extension of British power into Africa. Having abolished the slave trade in 1807, the British worked to compel other nations to end the trade. With the largest navy in the world, Britain was well equipped to patrol the coast of West Africa, trying to suppress the traffic in humans and hinder its colonial rivals from benefiting from the trade. Needing bases for these patrols, the British established a number of minor settlements in West Africa, becoming the predominant European power along the coast. Although unimportant when acquired, these possessions foreshadowed the increasing European intrusion into African affairs.

Parliament's reforming zeal stimulated support for Chartism, a movement intended to transform Britain from essentially an oligarchy—rule by a few—into a democracy. In 1838 political radicals with working-class support drew up a "people's charter" calling for universal male suffrage, electoral districts with equal population, salaries and the abolition of property qualifications for members of Parliament, the secret ballot, and annual general elections. The Chartists hoped that giving workers the vote would end the dominance of the much smaller upper classes in Parliament and ensure an improvement in the workers' lot.

Chartism won wide support among men and women in the working class, sparking demonstrations and petition drives of unprecedented size. Women participated to a larger extent than in any other political movement of the day, founding over a hundred female Chartist chapters. Some Chartists, especially female members, asked for women's suffrage, but this demand failed to gain overall adherence from the membership. Winning mass support during particularly hard economic years, Chartism lost followers during a temporary economic upswing. The movement also fell under the sway of advocates of violence, who scared off many artisans and potential middle-class supporters. It lost credibility too by criticizing British institutions for being unresponsive to the needs of the working class, whereas in fact Parliament had introduced a number of significant reforms, including the Factory Act of 1833, which provided some protection to laborers. Lacking popular support, Chartism failed as a political movement; yet it drew public attention to an integrated democratic program whose main provisions (except for yearly elections) would be adopted piecemeal over the next half century.

In 1839 urban businessmen founded the Anti–Corn Law League for the purpose of abolishing the Corn Law of 1815, which was increasing the price of grain. The Corn Law was unpopular with manufacturers, who knew that low food prices would allow them to pay low wages. It was also unpopular with workers, who wanted bread at a price they could afford. The anti–Corn Law movement proved more effective than Chartism because it had the support of the middle classes. Alarmed by the threat of famine after the poor harvest of 1845, Parliament repealed the Corn Law in 1846.

In the end this action did not affect the price of grain. Nevertheless, repeal of the Corn Law was a milestone in British history, demonstrating the extent to which organized groups could bring about economic improvements. A popular, mass organization had been able to shape public policy—a far cry from the days of Peterloo, when the government had not only ignored the public but attacked it with bayonets fixed.

READING SOURCES

A Plea to Abolish Slavery in the British Colonies

Among the causes that British reformers embraced was the abolition of slavery. The slave trade had been abolished in 1807; one more step was left—ending in the colonies the institution of slavery itself. In this petition to Parliament in 1823, the Society for the Mitigation and Gradual Abolition of Slavery Throughout the British Dominions explains the harsh and degrading nature of the institution. Trading in slaves had already been abolished as immoral and unnatural; here the petitioners remind Parliament that holding slaves is no less abhorrent. Under the pressure of this type of agitation, Parliament in 1833 abolished slavery in the British Empire.

In the colonies of Great Britain there are at this moment upwards of 800,000 human beings in a state of degrading personal slavery.

These unhappy persons, whether young or old, male or female, are the absolute property of their master, who may sell or transfer them at his pleasure, and who may also regulate according to his discretion (within certain limits) the measure of their labour, their food, and their punishment.

Many of the slaves are (and all may be) branded like cattle, by means of a hot iron, on the shoulder or other conspicuous part of the body, with the initials of their master's name; and thus bear about them in indelible characters the proof of their debased and servile state. . . .

It can hardly be alleged that any man can have a right to obtain his fellow creatures in a state so miserable and degrading as has been described. And the absence of such right will be still more apparent, if we consider how these slaves were originally obtained. They, or their parents, were the victims of the Slave Trade. They were obtained, not by lawful means, or under any colourable pretext, but by the most undisguised rapine, and the most atrocious fraud. Torn from their homes and from every dear relation in life, barbarously manacled, driven like herds of cattle to the sea-shore, crowded into the potential holds of slave-ships, they were transported to our colonies and there sold in bondage. . . .

The Government and Legislature of this country have on various occasions, and in the most solemn and unequivocal terms denounced the Slave Trade as immoral, inhuman, and unjust; but the legal perpetuation of that state of slavery, which has been produced by it, is surely, in its principle, no less immoral, inhuman and unjust, than the trade itself. . . .

Source: Reprinted in *Circular Letters of the Society for the Mitigation and Gradual Abolition of Slavery Throughout the British Dominions* (April 1823).

 For additional information on this topic, go to college.hmco.com/students.

The Absolutist States of Central and Eastern Europe, 1815–1848

Having seen the turmoil unleashed by the French Revolution and suffered at the hands of the Grande Armée, the states of central and eastern Europe were particularly committed to maintaining absolute government. In contrast to many parts of western Europe, which saw important political changes in the 1830s, the absolutist states were able to preserve themselves essentially unchanged until 1848—and in some cases even beyond.

The Austrian Empire's far-flung territories seemed to its Habsburg rulers to require a firm hand (see Map 21.1). Liberalism, which challenged imperial power, could not be countenanced. Nor, in this multinational empire, could nationalism be tolerated. The emperor, Francis I (r. 1792–1835), was opposed to any change; his motto was "Rule and change nothing." Prince Metternich, Francis's chief minister, viewed the French Revolution of 1789 and its aftermath as a disaster and believed his task was to hold the line against the threat of revolution. Quick to interpret protests or the desire for change as a threat to the fundamental order, Metternich established a network of secret police and informers to spy on the imperial subjects and keep them in check.

In most of the German states, the political order was authoritarian and inflexible. The states of Baden and Württemberg in the southwest and Bavaria in the south had granted their subjects constitutions, although effective power remained in the hands of the ruling houses.

The king of Prussia had repeatedly promised a constitution, but none had materialized. A central, representative Diet would not meet there until 1847. Prussia was ruled by an alliance of the king and the *Junkers°*, the landowning aristocrats who staffed the officer corps and the bureaucracy. Both the officer corps and the bureaucracy were efficient enough to serve as models for the rest of Europe. Where Prussia lagged by liberal standards was in its political institutions.

Throughout the German states, the urban middle classes, intellectuals, journalists, university professors, and students were frustrated with the existing system. They were disappointed by the lack of free institutions and the failure of the patriotic wars against Napoleon to create a united Germany. University students formed *Burschenschaften°*, or brotherhoods, whose slogan was "Honor, Liberty, Fatherland." Metternich imposed a policy of reaction on the German Confederation and pushed through the Carlsbad Decrees in July 1819, establishing close supervision over the universities, censorship of the press, and dissolution of the youth groups. Wholesale persecution of liberals and nationalists followed. The Prussian king dismissed his more enlightened officials. (See the box "Reading Sources: The Carlsbad Decrees and University Students.")

The outbreak of revolution in Paris in 1830 inspired further political agitation and repression in several German states. Mounting opposition to local despots and agitation for national unity led to the prosecution of outspoken liberals. Many associated with the nationalist "Young Germany" movement fled abroad, particularly to Paris.

Renewed nationalist agitation swept the German states in the 1840s. A mass outpouring of patriotic sentiment erupted in response to possible French ambitions on the Rhine during a diplomatic crisis in 1840. Two patriotic songs were penned: "The Watch on the Rhine" and *"Deutschland, Deutschland über alles"* ("Germany, Germany Above All"), the latter becoming Germany's national anthem half a century later. German rulers, who in the past had been reluctant to support the national idea, now attempted to co-opt it. In Bavaria the crown prince, who later became King Ludwig I (r. 1825–1848), built Walhalla, named after the hall in which fallen heroes gather in Germanic lore. Ludwig's Walhalla was to be a "sacred monument" to German unity, adorned with statues of famous Germans. Cologne's unfinished cathedral became a symbol of German enthusiasm; from all over Germany donations poured in to finish it. These events suggested a broadening base for nationhood, which potentially could replace the existing system of a fragmented Germany. But with minor exceptions, the system established in 1815 prevailed until 1848.

Austria exercised considerable power over Italy through its possession of Italian territory, by dynastic ties to several ruling houses in the central part of the peninsula, and by political alliances with others, including the papacy. The only ruling house free of Austrian ties—and hence eventually looked to by nationalists as a possible rallying point for the independence of the peninsula—was the Savoy dynasty of Piedmont-Sardinia.

Italy consisted of eight political states, and it was in Austria's interest to maintain disunity. Many Italian governments—notably the papacy, the kingdom of Naples, and the central Italian duchies—imposed repressive policies, knowing that they could count on Austrian assistance to squelch any uprising. Indeed, Metternich did crush rebellions that were intended to bring about freer institutions and a unified Italy. His interventions generated hatred of Austria among Italian liberals and nationalists.

By far the most autocratic of the European states was tsarist Russia. Since 1801 Alexander I (r. 1801–1825) had been tsar. An enigmatic character whose domestic policy vacillated between liberalism and reaction and whose foreign policy wavered between brutal power politics and apparently selfless idealism, Alexander puzzled his contemporaries. When the Congress of Vienna gave additional Polish lands to the tsar, establishing the Kingdom of Poland, he demonstrated his liberalism to the world (and curried favor with his new subjects) by granting Poland a liberal constitution. But he offered no such constitution to his own people and within a few years violated the Polish constitution, refusing to call the Diet into session. Alexander and his council discussed terms for the abolition of serfdom in Russia in 1803 and again in 1812, but like so many of his plans, this one was not implemented. Although he earnestly desired freedom for the serfs, the tsar was unwilling to impose any policy detrimental to the interests and privileges of the landed gentry.

Toward the end of his rule, Alexander became increasingly authoritarian and repressive, probably in response to growing opposition. Western liberal ideas, including constitutionalism, were adopted by Russian military officers who had served in western Europe, by Russian Freemasons who had corresponded with Masonic lodges in western Europe, and by Russian intellectuals who read Western liberal political tracts. These

Junkers (YUNG-kurz)
Burschenschaften (BOOR-shen-shaft-en)

READING SOURCES

THE CARLSBAD DECREES AND UNIVERSITY STUDENTS

Universities have long been institutions of open discussion and the free exchange of ideas. In nineteenth-century Europe they were also places of political unrest and demonstrations. In 1819, as an effort to eliminate intellectual discussions that might have been hostile to the Austrian regime, Metternich obtained the approval of a set of decrees restricting freedom of expression and association for students and professors.

1. A special representative of the ruler of each state shall be appointed for each university, with appropriate instructions and extended powers, and shall reside in the place where the university is situated. . . .

The function of this agent shall be to see to the strictest enforcement of existing laws and disciplinary regulations; to observe carefully the spirit which is shown by the instructors in the university in their public lectures and regular courses, and, without directly interfering in scientific matters or in the methods of teaching, to give a salutary direction to the instruction, having in view the future attitude of the students. Lastly, he shall devote unceasing attention to everything that may promote morality, good order, and outward propriety among the students. . . .

2. The confederated governments mutually pledge themselves to remove from the universities or other public educational institutions all teachers who, by obvious deviation from their duty, or by exceeding the limits of their functions, or by the abuse of their legitimate influence over the youthful minds, or by propagating harmful doctrines hostile to public order or subversive of existing governmental institutions, shall have unmistakably proved their unfitness for the important office entrusted to them. . . .

No teacher who shall have been removed in this manner shall be again appointed to a position in any public institution of learning in another state of the union.

3. Those laws which have for a long period been directed against secret and unauthorized societies in the universities shall be strictly enforced. These laws apply especially to that association established some years since under the name Universal Students' Union (*Allgemeine Burschenschaft*) since the very conception of the society implies the utterly unallowable plan of permanent fellowship and constant communication between the various universities. The duty of especial watchfulness in this matter should be impressed upon the special agents of the government.

The governments mutually agree that such persons as shall hereafter be shown to have remained in secret or unauthorized associations, or shall have entered such associations, shall not be admitted to any public office.

Source: J. H. Robinson, ed., *Readings in European History* (Boston: Ginn, 1906), vol. 2, pp. 547–550. Scanned, edited, and reproduced at http://history.hanover.edu/texts/carlsbad.htm.

---

groups formed secret societies with varying agendas. Some envisioned Russia as a republic, others as a constitutional monarchy, but all shared a commitment to the abolition of serfdom and the establishment of a freer society.

Alexander died in December 1825, without designating which of his brothers would succeed him. Taking advantage of the confusion, the military conspirators declared in favor of the older brother, Constantine, in the belief that he favored a constitutional government. The younger brother, Nicholas, claimed to be the legal heir. The St. Petersburg garrison rallied to the conspirators' cause. Taking their cue from the Spanish uprising of 1820, the officers little doubted that the military could bring about change on its own in a country in which popular participation in governance was unknown.

The "Decembrist uprising," as it is known, quickly failed. The military revolt in the Russian capital was badly coordinated with uprisings planned in the countryside, and Nicholas moved quickly to crush the rebellion. He had the leaders, called the Decembrists, executed, sent to Siberia, or exiled. In spite of its tragic end, throughout the nineteenth century the Decembrist uprising served as an inspiration to Russians resisting tsarist oppression.

Coming to the throne under such circumstances, Nicholas I (r. 1825–1855) was obsessed with the danger of revolution and determined to suppress all challenges to his authority. The declared goal of his rule was to uphold "orthodoxy, autocracy, and nationality." Nicholas created a stern, centralized bureaucracy to control all facets of Russian life. He originated the modern Russian secret police, called the "Third Section"; a state within the state, it was above the law. Believing in the divine right of monarchs, Nicholas refused to accept limits to his imperial powers. The tsar supported the primacy of the Russian Orthodox Church within Russian society; the church in turn upheld the powers of the state. Nicholas also used nationalism to strengthen the state, exalting the country's past and trying to "Russify" non-Russian peoples. After a nationalist rebellion in 1831 in Poland attempted to shake loose Russian control, Nicholas abrogated the kingdom's constitution and tried to impose the Russian language on its Polish subjects.

Russia's single most overwhelming problem was serfdom. Economically, serfdom had little to recommend it; free labor was far more efficient. Moreover, public safety was threatened by the serfs' dissatisfaction with their lot. Nicholas's thirty-year reign was checkered with over six hundred peasant uprisings, half of them put down by the military. Nicholas understood that serfdom had to be abolished for Russia's own good, but he could envision no clear alternative to it. Emancipation, he believed, would only sow further disorder. Except for a few minor reforms, he did nothing. Nicholas's death, followed by Russia's defeat in the Crimean War (see page 743), eventually brought to an end the institution that had held nearly half of the Russian people in bondage.

In its sheer mass, the Ottoman Empire continued to be a world empire. It extended over three continents. In Africa it ran across the whole North African coast. In Europe it stretched from Dalmatia (on the Adriatic coast) to Istanbul. In Asia it extended from Mesopotamia (present-day Iraq) to Anatolia (present-day Turkey). But it was an empire in decline, seriously challenged from inside by nationalist movements and from outside by foreign threats.

The Ottoman bureaucracy, once the mainstay of the government, had fallen into decay. In the past officials had been recruited and advanced by merit; now lacking funds, Constantinople sold government offices. Tax collectors ruthlessly squeezed the peasantry. By the eighteenth century, the Janissaries, formerly an elite military force, had become an undisciplined band that menaced the peoples of the Ottoman Empire—especially those located at great distances from the close control of the capital. The reform-minded Sultan Selim III (r. 1789–1807) sought to curb the army, but he was killed by rebellious Janissaries, who forced the new ruler, Mahmud II (r. 1808–1839), to retract most of the previous improvements. The worst features of the declining empire were restored.

Most of the Ottoman Empire was inhabited by Muslims, but in the Balkans Christians were in the majority. Ottoman officials usually treated religious minorities such as Jews and Orthodox Christians with tolerance. But the Christian subject peoples found in their religion a means of collectively resisting a harsh and at times capricious rule. Some Christian peoples in the Balkans looked back nostalgically to earlier eras—the Greeks to their great Classical civilization or the Serbs to their era of self-rule. The ideas of nationalism and liberty that triggered changes in western Europe also stirred the peoples of the Balkans.

The Serbs were the first people to revolt successfully against Ottoman rule. A poor, mountainous region, Serbia suffered greatly from the rapaciousness of the Janissaries. In protest, a revolt broke out in 1804. At first the Ottomans were able to contain the insurrection, but in 1815 they had to recognize one of its leaders, Milosh Obrenovich (r. 1815–1839), as governor and allow the formation of a national assembly. In 1830, under pressure from Russia, which took an interest in fellow Slavs and members of the Orthodox faith, Constantinople recognized Milosh as hereditary ruler over an autonomous Serbia.

The Greeks' struggle led to complete independence from Ottoman rule. Greeks served as administrators throughout the Ottoman lands and, as merchants and seafarers, traveled widely throughout the Mediterranean world and beyond. They had encountered the ideas of the French Revolution and, in the 1790s, were affected by the nationalism spreading in Europe. Adamantios Koraïs° (1748–1833), an educator living in revolutionary Paris, reformed written Greek to make it more consonant with ancient Greek by removing foreign accretions. Koraïs created a new, more elegant Greek and edited Greek classics to connect his fellow countrymen with their ancient and illustrious past. Greek cultural nationalism found an echo among some intellectuals. The *Philike Hetairia* (Society of Friends), a conspiratorial group founded in 1814, dedicated itself to restoring Greek independence by political means.

Greek peasants were not particularly interested in politics, but they were hostile to the Ottoman Turks, who had accumulated vast landholdings at their expense. This in part motivated Greek peasants to join the anti-Turkish revolt that began in 1821. Greeks killed large numbers of defenseless Turks in the Morea, a region in

Koraïs (KOOR-ay-iss)

Mehemet Ali Painted by the famed British artist Sir David Wilkie, this portrait depicts the Egyptian leader at the height of his powers. Mehemet challenged the Ottoman Empire, winning for Egypt virtual independence and bringing Syria under his control. *(Tate Gallery, London/Art Resource, NY)*

central Greece. The Turkish authorities hanged the patriarch, the leader of the Orthodox Church, in Constantinople and massacred or sold into slavery the population of the Aegean island of Chios. The war continued fitfully. By 1827 the Ottomans, aided by their vassal Mehemet Ali (1769–1849) of Egypt, controlled most of the Balkan peninsula. The rest of Europe, excited by the idea of an independent Greece restored to its past greatness, widely supported the Greek movement for freedom. The Great Powers intervened in 1827, sending their navies to intercept supplies intended for the Ottoman forces. At Navarino Bay, in the southwest of the Peloponnesus, the Ottoman navy fired on the allies, who returned fire and sank the Turkish ships. The destruction of Ottoman power ensured the independence of Greece. In 1830 an international agreement spelled out Greek independence.

Losing influence in the Balkans, the Ottoman Empire was also challenged elsewhere. In Egypt Mehemet Ali, nominally subordinate to Constantinople, actually ruled Egypt as if it were independent. He wrested Syria away in 1831 and threatened to march against his over-

lord, the sultan. Britain and Russia, concerned that an Ottoman collapse would upset the region's balance of power, intervened on the empire's behalf. Constantinople won back Syria but in 1841 had to acknowledge Mehemet Ali as the hereditary ruler of Egypt. The survival of the Ottoman Empire was beginning to depend on the goodwill—or self-interest—of the Great Powers.

THE REVOLUTIONS OF 1848

FROM France in the west to Poland in the east, at least fifty separate revolts and uprisings shook the Continent in 1848, the most extensive outbreak of popular violence in nineteenth-century Europe (see Map 21.2). The revolt had an impact far beyond Europe's borders. Inspired by the example of the European revolutions, Brazilians rose up against their government. In Bogota, Colombia, church bells rang, and in New York public demonstrations enthusiastically greeted the announcement of a republic in France. And as a result of the Parisian revolution, slaves in French colonies were emancipated.

Roots of Rebellion

At no time since 1800 had so many Europeans been involved in collective action. Many reasons account for this widespread outbreak of discontent. In the countryside restrictions in access to land such as enclosure frustrated peasants. Although in the past many had enjoyed free access to village commons, these were coming increasingly under private control, or the peasants faced competition for their use. Formerly a peasant might have grazed sheep in the commons, but now a peasant's two or three animals competed with herds of sometimes hundreds of sheep owned by a rich farmer. Also, the poor once had relatively free access to forests to forage for firewood, but the limitation of this right also now led to frequent conflicts.

Points of friction were made worse by growing populations that put pressure on available resources. In the urban environment a crisis erupted in the handicrafts industry, which dominated city economies. Urban artisans were being undercut by the putting-out system or cottage industry, in which capitalists had goods produced in the countryside by cottagers—part-time artisans who supported themselves partly through agriculture and were thus willing to work for lower wages. Crises in the crafts hurt the journeymen who wanted to be masters; they had to serve far longer apprenticeships and in many

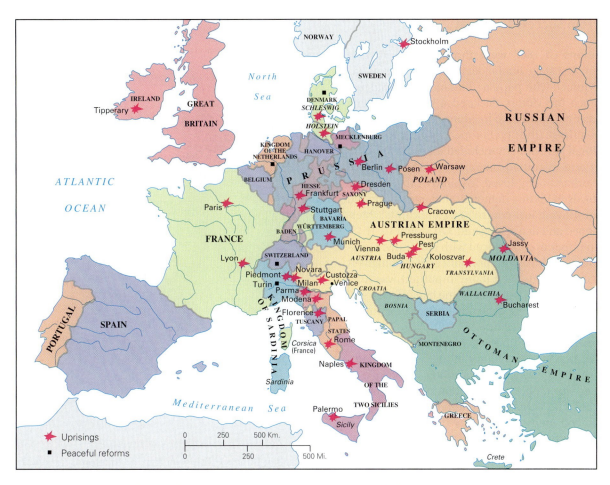

Map 21.2   Major Uprisings and Reforms, 1848–1849   In no other year had as many revolts broken out simultaneously. In many cases the revolutions led to reforms and new constitutions.

cases could never expect promotion. Where the guild system still existed, it was in decline, unable to protect the economic interests of artisans anxious about their futures.

These developing concerns came to a crisis point as a result of the economic depression of 1845–1846. In 1845 a crop disaster, including the spread of potato blight, destroyed the basic food of the poor in northern Europe. The most notorious catastrophe was in Ireland. In the last famine in western Europe, one million Irish starved to death between 1844 and 1851 as a result of the blight. The poor harvests doubled the price of food from the 1840 level. An industrial downturn accompanied these agricultural disasters, creating massive unemployment. Municipal and national governments seemed unable to deal with the crowding, disease, and unsanitary conditions that were worsening already high tensions in the cities, the sites of national governments. People were ready to heed those who called for the overthrow of the existing regimes. The established political and administrative elites were disoriented and found they could not count on their traditional sources of support. Revolts were triggered not only by discontent but also by the hope for change.

The revolutions of 1848 were sparked by the revolution in Paris in February. News of the fall of Louis Philippe triggered a ripple effect, spreading turbulence to over fifty localities in Europe. In France the revolution was for political and social rights. In several other countries, another issue was added to the combustible situation—nationalism. Once the revolution in the Germanies had started, the demands arose for national unification. Throughout the Italian peninsula national unity was the goal; northern Italians added their desire for independence from the Habsburg empire. In other Habsburg lands the cry went out for national independence: the Hungarians, Poles, and Czechs all wanted to be masters of their own destinies and free from Vienna's control.

Liberals: From Success to Defeat

The revolutions of 1848 went through a number of stages. In the first stage liberal demands for more political liberties joined with popular demands for social justice. In France the victors declared a republic, which provided basic constitutional freedoms and granted universal male suffrage (the first European regime to do so). The provisional government included a working man in the cabinet and instituted national workshops to give work to the urban unemployed. Inspired by the example of Paris, crowds in Vienna demonstrated and petitioned the emperor. Having lost control over the capital, Metternich resigned and fled to England. On March 15, 1848, the Austrian imperial court, faced with continued agitation by students and workers, announced its willingness to issue a constitution. Even more important was Austria's decision to abolish serfdom. Some had feared a serf uprising, but the relatively generous terms of the emancipation mollified the peasantry.

In Germany news of the February uprising in Paris also acted as a catalyst for change in the German states. The forces of change seemed irresistible. As the king of Württemberg observed, "I cannot mount on horseback against ideas." The wisest course appeared to be compromise. He and many of his fellow dukes and princes changed their governments, dismissing their cabinets and instituting constitutions.

Up to this point Prussia was conspicuous for being untouched by the revolutionary wave. But when news of Metternich's fall reached Berlin on March 16, middle-class liberals and artisans demonstrated for reforms. To appease his subjects, King Friedrich Wilhelm IV appointed the liberal Rhenish businessman who in the ceremonial march through Berlin (see the illustration on page 706) walked ahead of the king. Representative government was introduced, and suffrage was extended, though it was still restricted to men of property. No longer the exclusive preserve of the aristocracy, government was opened to men from the liberal professions and the business classes. As in Austria, the German countryside was appeased by reducing some of the feudal arrangements that still existed in many areas.

The second stage of the revolution marked a breakdown in the unity that had initially formed against the old regimes. With the enemy defeated or compliant, the middle classes, peasants, and workers discovered that they no longer shared a common goal. In France the peasants, who at least had not opposed the revolution, by April 1848 were hostile to the new republic. They decried the additional taxes that had to be levied to pay for the national workshops supporting unemployed urban

Ballots, Not Bullets This print from 1848 informs the revolutionary on the barricades to put away his rifle and trust the democratic process. Pointing to the rifle, our French revolutionary announces, "This is for the external enemy." "As for the internal ones," he says, indicating the election urn, "this is how one fights them loyally." *(Harlingue-Viollet/Getty Images)*

workers. Armed with the vote, the peasants elected conservative landowners, lawyers, and notaries—a group nearly identical to the pre-1848 deputies. In June the new parliament decided to terminate the costly national workshops. The workers, in despair, revolted. The government carried out a bloody repression, killing 1,500 and arresting 12,000. The re-election of conservative forces revealed that universal suffrage could serve as a means to mobilize moderate public opinion against radicalism in Paris. The advent of railroads allowed the government to muster military support from outside the city. Thereafter it would be far more difficult for radical Parisian crowds to dictate policies to the rest of the country.

The propertied classes, feeling menaced by the poor, looked to authority for security. Of the several candidates for president in 1848, Louis Napoleon (1808–1873), a nephew of Napoleon Bonaparte, appealed to the largest cross section of the population. The middle class was attracted by the promise of authority and order. Peasants, disillusioned by the tax policies of the republic, remained loyal to the memory of Napoleonic glory. Workers embittered by the government's repression of the June uprisings were impressed by Louis Napoleon's vaguely socialistic program. Louis Napoleon was elected president. Three years later he dissolved the National Assembly by force and established a personal dictatorship. In 1852 he declared himself Emperor Napoleon III.

In Austria and Germany the middle classes became wary of the lower classes; the class conflict in Paris intensified their concern. Once the peasants had won their freedom from feudal dues in Germany and from serfdom in the Austrian Empire, they were no longer interested in what was occurring in the capital. Thus the alliance in favor of change disappeared, and it could not even serve as a bulwark against the return of conservative forces. In Austria the reactionary forces around the court, led by General Windischgrätz, reconquered Vienna in October 1848 for the emperor and suspended the liberals' constitution. In December the king of Prussia, who had appeared to bow to liberal opinion, regained his courage and dismissed the elected assembly. Most of the liberal forces were spent and overcome by the end of the year.

The Nationalist Impulse

The revolutions did not break out because of nationalism, but once they erupted, the nationalist cause helped shape the outcome in several regions. Faced with internal turmoil, Prussia and Austria—which both opposed German unification lest it undermine their power—could not prevent the question of a united Germany from coming to the fore. In March 1848 a self-appointed national committee invited five hundred prominent German liberals to convene in Frankfurt to begin the process of national unification. In addition to fulfilling a long-standing liberal dream, a united German nation would consolidate the liberal victory over absolutism. The gathering called for suffrage based on property qualifications, thus excluding most Germans from the political process and alienating them from the evolving new order. The first all-German elected legislature met in May 1848 in Frankfurt to pursue unification. It faced the thorny issue of the shape of this new Germany: which regions should be included and which excluded? The most ambitious plan envisioned a *Grossdeutschland°*, or large

Germany, consisting of all the members of the German Confederation, including the German-speaking parts of Austria and the German parts of Bohemia. Such a solution would include many non-Germans, including Poles, Czechs, and Danes. The proponents of *Kleindeutschland°*, or small Germany, which would exclude Austria and its possessions, saw their solution as a more likely scenario, although it would exclude many Germans. They succeeded in the end, largely because the reassertion of Austrian imperial power in the fall of 1848 put the non-German areas under Vienna's control out of reach.

The Prussian reassertion of royal power, though partial, was a signal for other German rulers in late 1848 to dismiss their liberal ministers. The moment for liberalism and national unification to triumph had passed by the time the Frankfurt Assembly drew up a constitution in the spring of 1849. Having opted for the *Kleindeutsch* solution, the parliament offered the throne to Friedrich Wilhelm IV, king of Prussia. Although the king was not a liberal, he ruled the largest state within the designated empire. If power could promote and protect German unity, he possessed it in the form of the Prussian army. But Friedrich Wilhelm feared that accepting the throne would lead to war with Austria. Believing in the principle of monarchy, he also did not want an office offered by representatives of the people, and so he refused the offer. Lacking an alternative plan, most members of the Frankfurt Assembly went home. A rump parliament and a series of uprisings in favor of German unity were crushed by the Prussian army. So German unification failed. Liberalism alone was unable to bring about German unity; other means would be required to do so.

In Italy, too, nationalist aspirations emerged once a revolt triggered by social and economic grievances had broken out. In the years before 1848 nationalists and liberals hoped somehow to see their program of a united and free Italy implemented. News of the Paris uprising in February galvanized revolutions in Italy. Italians under Austrian rule forced the Austrians to evacuate their Italian possessions. Revolts and mass protests in several Italian states led rulers to grant, or at least promise, a constitution. The king of Piedmont, Charles Albert (r. 1831–1849), granted his people a constitution, the Statuto. Charles Albert hoped to play a major part in unifying Italy. In Austrian Italy the middle classes, although eager to be free of foreign rule, feared radical elements among the laborers. They believed that annexation to nearby Piedmont would provide security from both Austria and the troublesome lower classes. The king of

---

Grossdeutschland (Grose-doyt-shlant)   Kleindeutschland (Kline-doyt-shlant)

Constitutional Government in Denmark   On March 21, 1848, fifteen thousand Danes, inspired by the example of Paris, marched on the palace to demand constitutional rights. Unlike the French capital, however, this event was peaceful and led to the establishment of a constitutional government. This painting honors the new parliament that came into being after the liberal constitution was adopted in 1849.   *(Statens Museum for Kunst, Copenhagen)*

Piedmont decided to unite Italy under his throne if doing so would prevent the spread of radicalism to his kingdom. On March 24, 1848, he declared war on Austria but was defeated in July and had to sue for an armistice. The continued spread of nationalist and revolutionary sentiment tempted Charles Albert to declare war on Austria once again, in March 1849. The outcome for Piedmont was even worse than it had been a year earlier. Within six days its army was defeated. Humiliated, Charles Albert resigned his throne to his son, Victor Emmanuel II (r. 1849–1878). The Austrians quickly reconquered their lost provinces and reinstated their puppet governments. The dream of a united Italy was dashed.

In the multinational empire of the Habsburgs, nationalism manifested itself in the form of demands for national independence from foreign rule. With Austria's power temporarily weakened as a result of revolution in Vienna, nationalist revolts broke out not only in Italy, but simultaneously in Hungary, the Czech lands, and Croatia. The Austrian emperor yielded in Hungary, giving it virtual independence; it was joined to the empire solely by personal union to the ruler. Constitutional government was established in Hungary, but participation in the political process was limited to Magyars, who were the single largest ethnic group, constituting 40 percent of the population. The other nationalities in Hungary—Romanians, Slovaks, Croats, and Slovenes—preferred the more distant rule of Austrian Vienna to Magyar authority. The Czech lands also witnessed agitation, but there and elsewhere the tide favoring the nationalists turned. The revolt against the empire was not coordinated, and the nationalisms were often in conflict with one another. Once the emperor re-established his power in Vienna, he could move against his rebellious subjects. The Austrian Empire practiced a policy of divide and rule; it re-established its authority in Italy, bombarded Prague into submission, and with Russian help brought Hungary to heel. If the nationalist fires had been quenched, the dangers nationalism posed to the survival of the Habsburg empire were also revealed.

In the large sweep of revolutions that washed across Europe, three major countries were spared. In Great Britain the government had proven sufficiently capable of adjusting to some of the major popular demands; revolution seemed unnecessary. In Russia the repressive tsarist system prevented any defiance from escalating into an opposition mass movement. Successive military officers governed in Spain, including General Ramón Narváez° (1799–1868), who brutally ran the country from 1844 to 1851. When he was on his deathbed, the priest asked him whether he forgave his enemies. He answered, "I have no enemies. I have shot them all!" So in 1848, no revolution disturbed Spain.

SUMMARY

THE revolutions of 1848 released many of the forces for change that had been gathering strength since 1815. In spite of the Congress of Vienna's effort to restore the old order after Napoleon's fall, the generation after 1815 established a new order. The ideas of change that had powered the French Revolution of 1789 continued to shape an era that claimed to be rolling history back to prerevolutionary times. Liberalism contested authoritarianism.

Reform-minded regimes in Europe improved the lives of people in colonies overseas, abolishing slavery in British and then French colonies and providing self-rule for Canada. Some states even turned away from monarchy and experimented with republicanism, a form of government that until then many had thought fit only for small states. All of the Latin American colonies except Mexico and Brazil became republics on gaining independence. In Europe during 1848–1849, the French, German, Hungarian, and Roman republics were proclaimed. Although they did not last, these experiments suggested new modes of political organization that were to become common in the following century.

The generation after 1815 experienced revolutions frequently and broadly. These uprisings usually failed, and the forces of order in most cases were able to recapture power. Yet the status quo was altered. In many cases absolutist rulers had to grant constitutions and accept ministers who were not their choices. Even though most of these arrangements were temporary, they established an important precedent. If unusual in the first half of the century, constitutions became the norm in the second half.

Nationalism arose in these years. The desire for national independence and unity found expression in Italy, Germany, Hungary, Poland, and the land of the Czechs. To free themselves from Madrid's rule, the Spanish colonies in the Americas employed a nationalist discourse borrowed from Europe. In the second half of the century, Europe would have to contend more rigorously with the forces of nationalism that first appeared after 1814.

Socialist ideas challenged private property. In 1848 some might have pointed to the institution of the temporary workshops in Paris as an effort to realize a part of the socialist program. But that was a modest effort; socialist ideas would come into full expression—and their power become formidable—toward the end of the century.

The middle classes found their position strengthened after 1848. They did not dominate the political system, but their influence increased with the growth of entrepreneurship. Middle-class professionals were recruited into the civil services of states determined to streamline their operations in order to withstand revolution more effectively. Revolutionary fervor waned after 1848, but the current of economic and social change continued to transform Europe.

■ Suggested Reading

Broers, Michael. *Europe After Napoleon: Revolution, Reaction, and Romanticism, 1815–1848.* 1996. Evaluates the era from the point of view of the participants.

Hobsbawm, E. J. *The Age of Revolution, 1789–1848.* 1962. Presents compelling arguments that the era was dominated by two simultaneous revolutions, the French Revolution and the industrial transformation.

Johnson, Paul. *The Birth of the Modern World Society, 1815–1830.* 1991. A weighty but readable book providing a panoramic view of the era; includes biographical sketches of some of the major figures of the time.

Laven, David, and Lucy Riall, eds. *Napoleon's Legacy: Problems of Government in Restoration Europe.* 2000. Essays on the restoration experience in different European countries.

Sperber, Jonathan. *The European Revolutions, 1848–1851.* 1994. The best up-to-date synthesis, which includes some new emphases, such as the role of rural and religious discontent in shaping the revolts.

Wheen, Francis. *Karl Marx: A Life.* 2000. A lively biography that, in addition to discussing Marxian thought, emphasizes the man's personal life.

Narváez (Nar-va-yes)

 For a searchable list of additional readings for this chapter, go to college.hmco.com/students.

Raft of the "Medusa"

In September 1816 the French were shocked at the news of the disaster that had befallen the government ship *Méduse* (Medusa) as it headed for Senegal in West Africa the previous July. Including the ship's crew, 400 passengers had boarded the vessel.

The captain of the ship was a nobleman, Duroys de Chaumareys°, whom the restoration government had appointed solely on the basis of his family and political connections. Inexperienced as a seaman, the captain clumsily ran his ship aground on the Mauritanian coast, off West Africa, on July 2. The *Medusa* had only 6 lifeboats, capable of carrying a total of 250 people. For the rest of the passengers, a raft was rigged with planks, beams, and ropes. The captain and his officers forcibly took over the lifeboats, abandoning 150 passengers, including one woman, to the less secure raft. With no navigational tools and insufficient food and water, the passengers of the raft were at the mercy of stormy seas and a brutal sun. Anger at officers for having abandoned them led seamen on the raft to murder some of their superiors. By the third day, driven by thirst and hunger, some passengers ate their dead companions—killed by exposure or drowned by huge waves. On the sixth day the strongest among the survivors, fearing that their rations were dwindling, banded together and murdered the weaker ones. On the thirteenth day the French frigate *Argus* spotted the raft and rescued 15 survivors. Five died soon after, leaving only 10 survivors out of the raft's original 150 passengers.

Although the government tried to suppress information about the event, the French press exposed the incompetence and cowardice of Captain de Chaumareys. The event was understood to reflect the weakness of the regime that had appointed him. The selfish act of the captain and his fellow officers suggested the narrow class interest of the restoration government, favoring aristocracy at the cost of the common people.

The French painter Théodore Géricault (1791–1824) befriended the ship's surgeon, Henri Savigny, one of the lucky ten who survived the harrowing experience on the raft. In addition to press reports, Géricault thus had a direct eyewitness account of the event. The painter shared Savigny's sense of outrage against the government for

Duroys de Chaumareys (du-RWAH duh sho-mah-RAY)

having appointed the incompetent captain and for having treated the survivors callously. (At one point the government arrested Savigny for publicizing the tragedy.) The light prison sentence imposed on the captain was another source of grievance.

Since 1815 the French government had sought to bring distinction to itself by displaying art in salon expositions. That of 1819 was intended to be larger and more glorious than any previous one. Among its paintings was Géricault's huge canvas—the largest in that year's exposition—measuring 16 feet high by 24 feet wide and innocently titled "Scene of Shipwreck." Carelessly, the regime had wanted to gain glory for itself by exhibiting this impressive artwork while at the same time keeping hidden its real subject. But the stratagem failed; everyone recognized the painting to be the *Raft of the "Medusa"* and an attack on the Bourbon regime.

The painting, reproduced here, depicts the moment the survivors spotted the frigate *Argus,* barely visible on the horizon. Notice the figure of an African standing at the fore of the raft, waving a red and white cloth to attract the ship's attention. In this painting the nobility and symbol of hope the African symbolizes is an attack on the slave trade, which Britain had abolished but which France was still engaged in. By including the African, the artist was implicitly criticizing the restoration regime for sanctioning commerce in humans. Just as the *Argus* is coming to the rescue of the shipwrecked, the painting appears to suggest, so Africans will see the day when their enslavement will be ended.

Historians often regard the *Raft of the "Medusa"* as the most important painting of French romanticism, and it includes nearly all the major themes of the movement. By locating the scene off the coast of Africa, Géricault incorporated an element of exoticism. Nature—cruel and unforgiving—is central to the scene, reflected in the turbulent sea, dark clouds, and imperiled raft. The canvas includes an extraordinary range of passions. Observe, for example, the inconsolable grief of the figure at the bottom left, a father cradling the dead body of his son. Other figures express despair and terror, and still others limitless hope. The painting evokes the dark passions lurking in the human heart. Although it does not show the scenes of insanity, murder, and cannibalism that the survivors had witnessed, they undoubtedly came to the minds of the viewers, who were familiar with the

Géricault: Raft of the "Medusa" *(Erich Lessing/Art Resource, NY)*

tragic events. The painting is a powerful indictment of Enlightenment faith in humans as creatures of reason and balance.

Romantic artists wanted to engage the passions of those viewing, reading, or hearing their works. *Raft of the "Medusa"* purposely stages the events in the foreground in order to pull viewers into the picture and make them participants in the drama. They thus share in the alternating feelings of terror and hope that swept the raft.

The fate of the painting and the artist followed a romantic script. When Géricault started the painting, he intended it as an indictment of the restoration government. He poured energy into it in an effort to take his mind off a disastrous love affair. As his work proceeded, he came to see the painting as an allegory of larger human passions and concerns. Yet when it was displayed, much to his disappointment, the painting was understood mainly in political terms. Disillusioned by this re-

action, Géricault thereafter painted no major works. He grew sickly, rarely bestirred himself, and died of bone tuberculosis in 1824 at age 33. He illustrates the romantics' view of a heroic life—the genius who performs a major feat and then dies young, before realizing his potential. To the romantics, human intent and effort often appeared thwarted by larger forces. This painting, originally meant to criticize the regime, was purchased after Géricault's death by the restoration government and hung in France's national museum, the Louvre.

CHAPTER 22

Nationalism and Political Reform 1850–1880

I N 1885, on the occasion of the seventieth birthday of the German chancellor Otto von Bismarck, Kaiser Wilhelm I gave the chancellor this painting, depicting the proclamation of German unification in the Hall of Mirrors at the palace of Versailles in 1871. On the podium, standing just behind the newly declared kaiser, is Crown Prince Friedrich Wilhelm (later Kaiser Friedrich III). To the kaiser's left, with his arm upraised, is the grand duke of Baden. In the middle of the scene, resplendent in his white uniform, is Bismarck, the political architect of German unification. On the right nearby is Field Marshal Helmuth von Moltke°, the military genius who provided the series of military victories allowing Prussia to unify Germany under its aegis. The new state was proclaimed by the crowned heads of Germany; no popular vote or parliament sanctioned the founding event. By war, Germany had become a united nation. Wars and the threat of wars brought about the emergence of several new states on the European scene: Italy, Romania, and Bulgaria. In the generation after 1850 the contours of European politics were being changed—new states appeared on the map, and within their national borders a good number of states reformed their political institutions. As Europe changed, a much enlarged and more powerful United States and a united Canada also emerged.

To meet the demand for popular participation in government so forcefully expressed in 1848, every European state except the Ottoman and Russian Empires found it necessary to have a parliament. Rare before midcentury, such institutions became common thereafter. No longer was the demand for popular participation seen as a

---

von Moltke (fon molt-KEH)

Wilhelm I is proclaimed ruler of the German Empire at Versailles, 1871. (Bismarck Museum/akg-images)

741

threat to the existing political and social order. In fact, popular participation, or the appearance of it, gave the existing order a legitimacy it had not enjoyed since before the French Revolution. Nationalism flourished during this period, emerging as a decisive force in European affairs and in the United States, where it promoted territorial expansion and fired a determination to preserve the Union.

These political transformations occurred in an era of unprecedented economic growth and prosperity. Industrial production expanded the economy; the discovery of gold in California in 1848 led to the expansion of credit (since currencies were backed by gold), which led to the founding of new banks and mass investments in growing industries. The standard of living rose significantly in industrializing nations. Between 1850 and 1880 industrial production increased by 90 percent in Great Britain and by 50 percent in France. The middle classes expanded dramatically.

In the first half of the century, international relations had been dominated by the congress system, in which representatives of the major European states met periodically to refine and preserve the balance of power. This system disappeared in the second half of the century, as political leaders pursued the narrow interests of their respective states. Instead of negotiating with one another, a new generation of leaders employed brute military force—

or the threat of its use—to resolve international conflicts. The new age was dominated not by ideals but by force, announced Bismarck, the main practitioner of what became known as *Realpolitik,* a policy in which war became a regular instrument of statecraft.

QUESTIONS TO CONSIDER

- ✑ How did the Crimean War affect international relations?

- ✑ How did political leaders in Prussia and Piedmont harness the forces of nationalism to achieve German and Italian national unity?

- ✑ Why did Russia abolish serfdom, and what was the impact of this action?

- ✑ Why was comprehensive political reform, especially the expansion of democracy, possible in some countries but only limited reform possible in others?

TERMS TO KNOW

congress system	Tanzimat
Realpolitik	Young Turks
risorgimento	glasnost
trasformismo	mir
Otto von Bismarck	manifest destiny
February Patent	Second Reform Bill
Compromise of 1867	Paris Commune

THE CHANGING NATURE OF INTERNATIONAL RELATIONS

THE Crimean War and its aftermath shaped European international relations for several decades. Following the 1815 Congress of Vienna (see Chapter 21), European states attempted to work out their differences by negotiation, avoiding situations in which one state triumphed at the cost of another. The Crimean War and subsequent realignments

raised mutual suspicions, leading nations to act in their own self-interests and to ignore the concerns of the other major players in the international system. This reorientation facilitated the emergence of nation-states.

The Crimean War, 1854–1856

The Crimean War had many causes. Principally, however, it was ignited by the decision of French and British statesmen to contain Russian power in the Balkans and keep it from encroaching on the weakening Ottoman

Empire. Russian claims to have the right to intervene on behalf of Ottoman Christians had led to war between the two states in October 1853. The defeat of the Ottoman navy at Sinope° in November left the Ottoman Empire defenseless.

British and French statesmen had considerable interest in the conflict. Britain had long feared that the collapse of the Ottoman Empire would lead Russia to seek territorial gains in the Mediterranean. Such a move would challenge Britain's supremacy. An explosion of public sentiment against Russia also obliged the British government to take an aggressive stance. Meanwhile, the French emperor, Napoleon III, viewed defeat of Russia as a way to eclipse one of the states most dedicated to preserving the current European borders. He wanted to undermine existing power relations, hoping that a new order would lead to increased French power and influence. Napoleon also imagined that fighting side by side with Britain could lay the foundation for Anglo-French friendship. And so England and France rushed to defend the Ottoman Empire and declared war on Russia in March 1854.

The war was poorly fought on all sides. Leadership was woefully inadequate, and five times more casualties resulted from disease than from enemy fire. Although the Russians had a standing army of a million men, their poor communications and supply systems prevented them from ever fielding more than a quarter of their forces. In Britain, the press and members of Parliament denounced their side's inadequate materiel and incompetent leadership. For the first time, the press played an active role in reporting war, and photography brought to readers at home the gruesome realities of battle. One of the few heroic figures to emerge from this conflict was the English nurse Florence Nightingale (1820–1910), who organized a nursing service to care for the British sick and wounded. Later her wartime experience allowed her to pioneer nursing as a professional calling. (See the box "Reading Sources: Florence Nightingale in the Crimean War.")

After almost two years of fighting in the Balkans and the Crimean peninsula, Russia abandoned the key fortress of Sevastopol in September 1855. Militarily defeated, the Russians also were alarmed at Austria's posture. Tsar Nicholas I had expected Austrian assistance in the war in return for his help in crushing the Hungarian rebellion in 1849. Instead, Austria's leaders not only withheld aid but even threatened to join the Western alliance.

Sinope (see-NO-pay)

CHRONOLOGY

1840s	Tanzimat in the Ottoman Empire
1851	Louis Napoleon's coup d'état
1854–1856	Crimean War
1860	Italy united under Piedmontese rule
1861	Great Reforms in Russia
1861–1865	U.S. Civil War
1862	Bismarck appointed minister president of Prussia
1864	Austria and Prussia attack Denmark and occupy Schleswig-Holstein
1866	Austro-Prussian War Abolition of estate system in Sweden
1867	Second Reform Bill in England North America Act creates Canadian federation Austro-Hungarian compromise
1870	Franco-Prussian War Rome, joined to Italy, becomes its capital Declaration of French Third Republic
1871	Unification of German Empire Paris Commune
1876	Bulgarian horrors
1878	Congress of Berlin

The Crimean conflict killed three-quarters of a million people—more than any European war between the end of the Napoleonic Wars and World War I. It was a particularly futile, senseless war whose most important consequence was political: it unleashed dramatic new changes in the international order that allowed for the emergence of the new nation-states.

The Congress of Paris, 1856

The former combatants met in Paris in February 1856 to work out a peace treaty. Their decisions—which pleased no one—shaped relations among European states for the next half century. Russian statesmen were especially

Crimean War This photograph shows the interior of the Sevastapol fortress after it had been battered into surrender. The Crimean War was the first conflict to be documented by photographers. *(Courtesy of the Board of Trustees of the Victoria & Albert Museum)*

discontented, as their country was forbidden to have a fleet in the Black Sea. Nor did French leaders feel that their nation had benefited. Although holding the congress in Paris flattered the emperor, no other clear advantages emerged for France. The north Italian state of Piedmont°, which had joined the allies, gained from the congress only a vague statement on the unsatisfactory nature of the existing situation in Italy. Prussia was invited to attend the congress only as an afterthought and hence also felt slighted.

Although the war seemed to have sustained the integrity of the Ottoman Empire, the peace settlement weakened it indirectly by dictating reforms in the treatment of its Christian populations. These reforms impaired the empire's ability to repress the growing nationalist movements in the Balkans. British political

Florence Nightingale This photograph was taken in 1856, shortly after Nightingale returned to England from the Crimean War. Her privileged background provided the official connections that helped her nursing services succeed. *(Courtesy, Florence Nightingale Museum, St. Thomas' Hospital, London. Photo: London Metropolitan Archives)*

Piedmont (PEED-mont)

READING SOURCES

FLORENCE NIGHTINGALE IN THE CRIMEAN WAR

Florence Nightingale used her influential family connections to win an appointment to the Crimean battlefield. Once there, she organized nursing for the wounded and was able to secure additional personnel and medical supplies for her hospital. Women were supposed to be sheltered from the harsh realities of the outside world, but as this letter indicates, Nightingale was not spared war in its cruelest aspects.

We have no room for corpses in the wards. The Surgeons pass on to the next, an excision of the shoulder-joint—beautifully performed and going on well—[cannon] ball lodged just in the head of the joint, and fracture starred all round. The next poor fellow has two stumps for arms—and the next has lost an arm and leg. As for the balls, they go in where they like, and do as much harm as they can in passing. That is the only rule they have. The next case has one eye put out, and paralysis of the iris of the other. He can neither see nor understand. But all who can walk come into us for Tobacco, but I tell them that we have not a bit to put into our own mouths. Not a sponge, nor a rag of linen, not anything have I left. Everything is gone to make slings and stump pillows and shirts. These poor fellows have not had a clean shirt nor been washed for two months before they came here, and the state in which they arrive from the transport is literally crawling. I hope in a few days we shall establish a little cleanliness. But we have not a basin nor a towel nor a bit of soap nor a broom—I have ordered 300 scrubbing brushes. But one half the Barrack is so sadly out of repair that it is impossible to use a drop of water on the stone floors, which are all laid upon rotten wood, and would give our men fever in no time. . . .

I am getting a screen now for the Amputations, for when one poor fellow, who is to be amputated tomorrow, sees his comrade today die under the knife it makes an impression—and diminishes his chance. But, anyway, among these exhausted frames the mortality of the operations is frightful.

Source: Letter to Dr. William Bowman, November 14, 1854, in *"I Have Done My Duty": Florence Nightingale in the Crimean War, 1854–56*, ed. Sue M. Goldie (Iowa City: University of Iowa Press, 1987), pp. 37–38.

---

leaders, galled by the heavy sacrifices of the war, moved toward isolationism in foreign policy. Austrian policymakers, who had hoped to gain the aid of Britain and France in preserving the Habsburg empire, found them hostile instead, a stance that encouraged the forces undermining Habsburg hegemony. At the time the peace treaty was signed, few people foresaw the enormous results that would flow from it.

In the first half of the century, the congress system had tried to ensure that no major state was dissatisfied enough to subvert the existing distribution of power. The international order had been upheld in part by the cooperation of the rulers of the conservative Eastern powers: Russia, Austria, and Prussia. Now these powers were rivals, and their competition contributed to growing instability in the international system. By and large, the decisions reached in Paris would be disregarded or unilaterally revised. This new international climate also allowed new states to take shape without international sanction.

ITALIAN UNIFICATION, 1859–1870

N Metternich's memorable phrase, Italy at midcentury was nothing but a "geographic expression." The revolution of 1848 (see pages 735–737) had revealed an interest in national unification, but the attempt had failed. Within a dozen years, however, what many believed to be impossible would come to pass. Idealists such as Giuseppe Mazzini (see page 714) had preached that Italy would be unified not by its rulers but by its people, who would rise and establish a free republic. Instead, the deed was done by royalty, by war, and with the help of a foreign state. Although ideals were not absent from the process of unification, cynical manipulation and scheming also came into play.

Since the late eighteenth century, some Italians had been calling for a *risorgimento*°, a political and cultural renewal of Italy. By the mid-nineteenth century, the idea was actively supported by a small, elite group consisting of the educated middle class, urban property owners, and members of the professions. For merchants, industrialists, and professionals, a unified state would provide a larger stage on which to pursue their ambitions.

Cavour Plots Unification

After the failed 1848 revolution, most Italian rulers resorted to repression. Only the northern Italian kingdom of Piedmont kept the liberal constitution adopted during the 1848 revolution, and it welcomed political refugees from other Italian states. Not only politically but economically, it was a beacon to the rest of Italy, establishing modern banks and laying half the rail lines on the peninsula.

The statesman who was to catapult Piedmont into a position of leadership in the dramatic events leading to Italian unification was Count Camillo di Cavour° (1810–1861). The son of a Piedmontese nobleman and high government official, he grew up speaking French, the language of the royal court and formal education in Piedmont, and mastered Italian only as an adult. Cosmopolitan in his interests, Cavour knew more about Britain and France than about Italy. He was sympathetic to the aspirations of the middle class and saw in Britain and France models of what Italy ought to become, a liberal and economically advanced society.

Short, fat, and nearsighted, Cavour hardly cut a heroic figure. Yet he was ambitious, hard-working, and driven to succeed. A well-known journalist and the editor of the newspaper *Risorgimento*, he joined the government in 1850. Two years later King Victor Emmanuel appointed him prime minister. He shared the enthusiasm of the middle classes for an Italian nation, but his vision did not include the entire Italian peninsula, only its north and center, which then could dominate the rest of the peninsula in a loose federation. One lesson he had learned from the failures of 1848 was that foreign help, especially French assistance, would be necessary to expel the Austrians from the peninsula.

When the Crimean War broke out in 1854, Cavour steered Piedmont to the allied side, hoping to advance his cause. He sent twenty thousand troops to the Crimea, one-tenth of whom died. This act gained him a seat at the Congress of Paris, where his presence boosted the kingdom's prestige—and where he and Napoleon III had an opportunity to meet and size up each other.

Napoleon III favored the cause of Italian liberation from Austrian rule and some form of unification of the peninsula. Austria had been France's traditional opponent; destroying Austria's power in Italy might strengthen France. Thus in July 1858 the French emperor and the Piedmontese prime minister met secretly at Plombières°, a French spa, to discuss how Italian unity could be achieved. They agreed that Piedmont would stir up trouble in one of Austria's Italian territories in an effort to goad the Austrians into war. France would help the Piedmontese expel Austria from the peninsula, and the new Piedmont, doubled in size, would become part of a confederation under the papacy. In exchange, the French emperor demanded the Piedmontese provinces of Nice° and Savoy, which bordered France.

This demand presented difficulties: Savoy was the heartland of the Piedmont kingdom, the ancestral home of the royal family; and Nice had a mostly Italian, not French, population. Napoleon's other condition was that the king of Piedmont, who headed the oldest reigning house in Europe, the Savoy, allow his 15-year-old daughter to marry the emperor's 38-year-old dissipated cousin. To accept these terms seemed a betrayal of national honor and conventional morality. But scruples gave way to political ambition, and Cavour assented. (See the box "Reading Sources: Cavour Outlines a Deal with Napoleon III.")

War between Austria and Piedmont broke out in April 1859. By June the combined Piedmontese and French forces had routed the Austrians at Magenta and Solferino (see Map 22.1). The bloodiness of these battles impressed contemporaries: the color magenta was named after the deep red of the soaked battlefield, and when a Swiss humanitarian, Henri Dunant° (1828–1901), organized emergency services for both French and Austrians wounded at Solferino, he proposed the founding of voluntary relief societies in every nation, called the Red Cross.

Instead of pressing on after these two victories, Napoleon III decided to end the fighting. He was shocked by the bloodshed he had witnessed and alarmed by the Prussian mobilization on the Rhine on behalf of Austria. In addition, his plan for Italy was threatening to develop in unforeseen directions. Several states in central Italy

---

Plombières (plom-bee-YAIR)   **Nice** (NEECE)
Dunant (dew-NAN)

---

risorgimento (ree-sor-djee-MEN-toe)   **Cavour** (kah-VOOR)

READING SOURCES — CAVOUR OUTLINES A DEAL WITH NAPOLEON III

In July 1858 Count Camillo di Cavour and Napoleon III met at Plombières in France to plot war against Austria. In this note written to the military aide of the king of Savoy, Cavour reports on the negotiations. The king's young daughter was to be given in marriage to cement the Piedmontese-French alliance. Notice the lack of concern for the 15-year-old princess; she is to be sacrificed on the altar of Realpolitik.

The Emperor entered into many particulars on the problems of the war, which it is my duty to tell you about, and which I shall report to you orally. He seemed to me to have studied the matter rather better than his generals, and to have sensible ideas in that regard. He talked of direct command questions—of how to manage the Pope—of the administrative system for stabilizing the occupied countries—of methods of finance. In a word of all the essential things for our grand project. We were in accord on everything.

The only undefined point is that of the marriage of the Princess Clotilde. The King had authorized me to agree to that, but only in the case that the Emperor had made it a condition *sine qua non* of the alliance. The Emperor not having pushed his insistence to that extreme, I did not, as a gentleman, undertake pledges. But I remain convinced that he lays very great importance on the matrimonial question, and that on it depends, if not the alliance, then its final outcome. It would be an error and a very grave error to commit oneself to the Emperor and at the same time to give him an affront which would never fade. . . . I have written strongly to the King not to risk the finest undertaking of modern times out of sour aristocratic scruples. I beg you, if he consults you, to join your voice to mine. Perhaps this enterprise should not be attempted, in which the crown of our King and the fate of our people are jeopardized; but if it is attempted, then for the love of heaven let nothing be neglected which could decide the final outcome.

I left Plombières in very serene spirits. If the King consents to the marriage I am confident, let me say almost certain, that within two years you will enter Vienna at the head of our victorious columns.

Source: Letter from Cavour to La Marmora, July 24, 1858, reprinted in *Plombières: Secret Diplomacy and the Rebirth of Italy,* ed. Mack Walker, p. 227. Copyright © 1968 by Oxford University Press, Inc. Used by permission of Oxford University Press, Inc.

had appealed for annexation to Piedmont, which would have resulted in a larger independent state than Napoleon III had anticipated. These factors led Napoleon to sign an armistice with the Austrians, allowing Austria to remain in northern Italy and participate in an Italian confederation. Cavour was outraged by Napoleon's betrayal and resigned as prime minister; he returned to office, however, in January 1860.

Unification Achieved, 1860

Cavour had envisioned no more than a united northern Italy. Unexpected events in the south, however, dramatically expanded that vision. The centuries-old misgovernment of the kingdom of Naples led to an uprising in Sicily in April 1860. The revolutionary firebrand Giuseppe Garibaldi° (1807–1882), a rival of Cavour, set sail for Sicily in May 1860 with but a thousand poorly armed, red-shirted followers to help the island overthrow its Bourbon ruler. Winning that struggle, Garibaldi's forces crossed to the mainland in August. Victory followed victory, and enthusiasm for Garibaldi grew. His army swelled to 57,000 men, and he won the entire kingdom of Naples.

Threatened by the advance of Garibaldi's power and fearing its reach into the Papal States, Cavour sent his army into the area in September 1860. Many Catholics viewed this brutal attack on a weak state that had not harmed Piedmont as aggression against the pope and the church. However, as Cavour explained to his parliament, political necessity required it. Morality was less important than the interests of Piedmont and the about-to-be-born Italy. Although Garibaldi was a republican, he was convinced that Italy could best achieve unity under the king of Piedmont, and he willingly submitted the southern part of Italy, which he controlled, to the king,

Garibaldi (gar-ih-BALL-dee)

Map 22.1 **The Unification of Italy, 1859–1870** Piedmontese leadership and nationalist fervor united Italy.

Victor Emmanuel II (r. 1849–1878). Thus by November 1860 Italy had been united under Piedmontese rule (see Map 22.1). The territories that had come under Piedmont's control affirmed their desire to be part of the new Italy in plebiscites based on universal male suffrage. The 1848 constitution of Piedmont became the constitution of the newly united Italy. The statesman who had engi-

neered the nation's unification lived to relish his handiwork for only a few months, as he died of an undiagnosed illness in May 1861. Cavour's last words were "Italy is made—all is safe."

Still to be joined to the new state were Austrian-held Venetia in the northeast and Rome and its environs, held by the pope with the support of a French garrison. But

Garibaldi Leading His "Red Shirts" to Victory over the Neapolitan Army, May 1860   Garibaldi's conquests in the south and Cavour's in the north opened the way for Italian unification.   *(Museo di Risorgimento, Milan/Scala/Art Resource, NY)*

within a decade, a favorable international situation enabled the fledgling country to acquire both key areas. After Austria was defeated in the Austro-Prussian War in 1866, it ceded Venetia to Italy. Then the Franco-Prussian War forced the French to evacuate Rome, which they had occupied since 1849. Rome was joined to Italy and became its capital in 1870. With that event unification was complete.

The Problems of a Unified Italy

National unity had been achieved, but it was frail. The uprisings in the south that had led to its inclusion in a united Italy were motivated more by hatred of the Bourbons than by fervor for national union. And once the union was achieved, the north behaved like a conquering state—sending its officials to the south, raising taxes, and imposing its laws. In 1861 an uprising of disbanded Neapolitan soldiers and brigands broke out. To crush the

revolt, half the Italian army was sent south; the civil war lasted five years and produced more casualties than the entire effort of unification.

Other major divisions remained. In 1861 only 2.5 percent of the population spoke the national language, Florentine Italian. The economy also remained divided. The north was far more industrialized than the rural south. In the south child mortality was higher, life expectancy was lower, and illiteracy was close to 90 percent. The two regions seemed to belong to two different nations. Piedmont imposed strong central control, resolutely refusing a federal system of government, which many Italians in an earlier era had hoped for. This choice reflected the determination of Piedmont to project its power onto the rest of the peninsula, as well as fear that any other form of government might lead to disintegration of the new state. The United States, with its federal system of government, was wracked by secessionism so strident that in early 1861 it led to the Civil War (see page 763). Piedmont wanted to save the new Italian state from such a fate.

Piedmont imposed its constitution on unified Italy, which limited suffrage to men of property and education—less than 2 percent of the population. Further, although parliamentarism was enshrined in the constitution, Cavour's maneuvering as prime minister had kept governments from being answerable to the parliament. Instead of parliamentary majorities designating the government, Cavour created majorities in parliament to support the cabinet. He cajoled and bribed parliamentarians, transforming previous foes into supporters. This system of manipulation, known as *trasformismo°*, would characterize Italian government for the next several decades. Nevertheless, the new unified Italy was a liberal state that guaranteed legal equality and freedom of association, and provided more freedom for its citizens than the Italian people had seen for centuries.

The Catholic Church remained hostile to the new Italian state. The popes, left to rule a tiny domain—a few square blocks around the papal palace known as the Vatican—considered themselves prisoners. They denounced their "captor" and all its supporters, including anyone who participated in elections. Thus many Italian Catholics refused to recognize the new state for decades, thwarting its legitimacy. With its 27 million people in 1870, Italy was the sixth most populous European nation. It was too small to be a great power and too large to accept being a small state. Italian statesmen found it difficult to define their country's role in international politics, and they lacked a firm consensus on Italy's future.

German Unification, 1850–1871

L IKE Italy, Germany had long been a collection of states. Since 1815 the thirty-eight German states had been loosely organized in the German Confederation. Like Piedmont in Italy, one German state, powerful Prussia, led the unification movement. And just as Italy had in Cavour a strong leader who imposed his will, so did German unification have a ruthless and cunning champion: Otto von Bismarck, minister president of Prussia. But whereas Cavour, for all his wiliness, was committed to establishing a liberal state, Bismarck was wedded to autocratic rule.

The revolutionaries of 1848 had failed in their attempt to achieve German unification when the king of Prussia refused to accept a throne offered by the elected Frankfurt Assembly. As the painting at the beginning of this chapter illustrates, German unification was ratified not by the ballot, as it was in Italy, but by the acclamation of the crowned heads of Germany. The nation was united by the use of military force and the imposition of Prussian absolutism over the whole country.

The Rise of Bismarck

Austria under Metternich had always treated Prussia as a privileged junior partner. After Metternich's fall in 1848, however, rivalry erupted between the two German states. Each tried to manipulate for its own benefit the desire for national unity that had become manifest during the revolution of 1848.

In March 1850 a number of German states met in Erfurt to consider unification under Prussian sponsorship. Austria, which had been excluded, insisted that the "Erfurt Union" be dissolved and that Prussia remain in the German Confederation. Austrian leaders, supported by Russia, threatened war. Since the Prussian military was not strong enough to challenge Austria, Prussia agreed to scuttle the Erfurt Union and accept Austrian leadership in Germany. The new Prussian king, Wilhelm I (r. 1861–1888), was determined to strengthen Prussia by expanding the size and effectiveness of the army. He wanted to reduce the reserve army, increase the professional army, and expand the training period from two to three years. These measures needed parliamentary approval, but the parliament, which was dominated by liberals, opposed the increased costs.

When the parliament refused to accept the king's proposals, he dissolved it. But new elections produced an even stronger liberal majority. The issue was not purely military, but rather one of who should govern the country—the king or the elected representatives. To get his way, the king appointed Count Otto von Bismarck as minister president.

Bismarck was a Junker, a Prussian aristocrat known for his reactionary views, who had opposed the liberal movement in 1848. As Prussian emissary to the German Confederation, he had challenged Austrian primacy. Devoted to his monarch, Bismarck sought to heighten Prussian power in Germany and throughout Europe. He faced down the parliament, telling the Budget Commission in 1862, "The position of Prussia in Germany will be decided not by its liberalism but by its power . . . not through speeches and majority decisions are the great questions of the day decided—that was the mistake of 1848 and 1849—but by iron and blood."[1]

---

trasformismo (trass-for-MEES-mo)

Bismarck tried to win over the liberals by suggesting that with military force at its disposal, Prussia could lead German unification. But the liberals resisted, and the parliament voted against the military reforms. Unfazed, Bismarck carried out the military measures anyway and ordered the collection of the necessary taxes. The citizens acquiesced and paid to upgrade their army. Prussia was not going to submit to parliamentarism as Britain had.

German liberals faced a dilemma: which did they value more punctuation here unclear—the goal of nationhood or the principles of liberty? Fellow liberals elsewhere lived in existing nation-states in which statehood had preceded the development of liberalism. In Italy unification had been led by the liberal state of Piedmont. That was not the case in Germany, where the natural leader, Prussia, had a long tradition of militarism and authoritarianism. To oppose Bismarck effectively, German liberals knew they would have to join with the working classes, but they feared the workers and forestalled such an alliance. Germany appeared embarked on an illiberal course.

Bismarck's genius was to exploit the growing desire for German unification. During the Franco-Austrian War of 1859, which launched Italian unification, Germans had feared that the French would attack across the Rhine River. Many came to believe that only a strong, united Germany could give its inhabitants security. Economically, a united Germany was developing under Prussian leadership with the *Zollverein,* a customs union of most German states, excluding Austria. Founded in 1834, the customs union had become more extensive with the passage of time; even states that were politically hostile to Prussia joined to protect their economic interests. Germans began to think in all-German terms. Professional and cultural organizations often extended beyond a single state to the wider, "national" context: the German Commercial Association, the Congress of German Jurists, and the German Sharpshooters League, for example. Although the idea of a united Germany had yet to find much resonance among the lower classes, it had gained a substantial audience by the 1860s.

Prussian Wars and German Unity

Having established the supremacy of royal power in Prussia, Bismarck was ready to enlarge Prussia's role in Germany at the expense of Austria. A crisis over Schleswig-Holstein° (see Map 22.2) gave him an opening. These two provinces, ethnically and linguistically German (except for northern Schleswig), were ruled by the king of Denmark. Historically and by previous treaty agreements, Schleswig and Holstein were legally inseparable. When in 1863 the Danish king, contrary to earlier treaty obligations, attempted to annex Schleswig to Denmark, Holstein felt threatened. Holstein was a member of the German Confederation, so it called on the confederation for protection. Acting on behalf of the confederation, Prussia and Austria intervened, sending troops that won a quick, cheap victory. Prussia occupied Schleswig, and Austria took Holstein.

Prussia and Austria continued to be bitter rivals for the domination of Germany. Bismarck believed that war was the only means to win this contest, and conflicts over the administration of Schleswig and Holstein served as a pretext. With no declaration of war, Prussia attacked Austrian-administered Holstein in June 1866. The Austro-Prussian War lasted a scant seven weeks. The decisive victory of the new, reformed Prussian army was the Battle of Sadowa° on July 3. With a much more advanced industry than Austria, Prussia had equipped its soldiers with the new breech-loading rifles, known as needle guns. Their advantage was that troops could fire from a prone position, while the Austrians, with their muzzle loaders, had to stand up to shoot. Prussia's superiority in arms and Moltke's superb military leadership defeated Austria, forcing it to accept peace on Prussian terms.

Prussia annexed its smaller neighbors, which had supported Austria, creating a contiguous state linking Prussia with the Rhineland. In Bismarck's scheme this enlarged Prussia would dominate the newly formed North German Confederation, comprising all the states north of the Main° River. From now on, Austria was excluded from German affairs.

The triumph of Sadowa made Bismarck a popular hero. Elections held on the day of the battle returned a conservative pro-Bismarck majority to the Prussian parliament. The legislature, including a large number of liberals mesmerized by the military victory, voted to legalize retroactively the illegal taxes that had been levied since 1862 to upgrade the military. Enthusiastic at the prospect of achieving German unity at last, most liberals compromised their principles. They rationalized that national unity ought to be gained first, with liberal constitutional institutions secured later. Their optimism proved to be a miscalculation.

The unification of Germany, like that of Italy, was facilitated by a favorable international situation. The Crimean War had estranged Russia from Austria. In 1850

Schleswig (SHLES-vik)   **Holstein** (HOLL-shteyn)

Sadowa (SAH-doe-wah)   **Main** (MINE)

Map 22.2 The Unification of Germany, 1866–1871 A series of military victories made it possible for Prussia to unite Germany under its domain.

Austrian resistance to Prussian attempts to lead Germany had been backed by Russia, but by the time the Austro-Prussian War broke out in 1866, Austria stood alone. Although it would have been opportune for France to intervene on the Austrian side, the French emperor was indecisive and in the end did nothing. He also had been lulled into inaction by vague Prussian prom-ises of support for French plans to annex Luxembourg. Once the war was won, Bismarck reneged on these promises. France was left with the problem of a strong, enlarged Prussia on its eastern border, which threatened France's position as a Great Power. British leaders like-wise did not intervene in the unification process. Disillu-sioned by the results of the Crimean War, they were in an isolationist mood. Moreover, Britain's government was sympathetic to the rise of a fellow Protestant power.

Bismarck's design was almost complete. Only the southern German states remained outside the North German Confederation. He obliged them to sign a military treaty with Prussia and established a customs parliament for all the members of the Zollverein (the customs union), including the southern German states. The southern states, which were Catholic and sympathetic to Austria, were reluctant to see German unity advance any further. Only some dramatic event could remove their resistance.

The Franco-Prussian War and Unification, 1870–1871

French leaders were also determined to prevent German unity. They feared the loss of influence in the southern German states that had traditionally been France's allies. Moreover, since the mid-seventeenth century, French security had relied on a weak and divided Germany.

Both Berlin and Paris anticipated war, which came soon enough, precipitated by a crisis over the Spanish succession. In 1868 a military coup had overthrown the Spanish queen Isabella, and the provisional government offered the throne to a Catholic member of the Hohenzollerns°, the reigning Prussian monarch's family. The French viewed this candidacy as an unacceptable expansion of Prussian power and influence. Fearing a two-front war with Prussia in the east and Spain in the south, they insisted that the Hohenzollerns refuse the proffered throne. As passions heated, Bismarck was elated at the prospect of war, but King Wilhelm was not. On July 12, 1870, Wilhelm engineered the withdrawal of the young prince's candidacy, removing the cause for war. Bismarck was bitterly disappointed.

Not content with this diplomatic victory, the French pushed their luck further. On July 13 the French ambassador met the king of Prussia at Ems and demanded guarantees that no Hohenzollern would ever again be a candidate for the Spanish throne. Unable to provide any more concessions without a serious loss of prestige, the Prussian king refused the French petition.

Wilhelm telegraphed an account of his meeting to Bismarck. The chancellor immediately seized the opportunity this message provided. He edited what became known as the Ems dispatch, making the exchange between king and ambassador seem more curt than it actually had been; then he released it to the press. As he

hoped, the French interpreted the report as a deliberate snub to their ambassador and overreacted. Napoleon III was deluged with emotional demands that he avenge the imagined slight to French national honor, and on July 15 he declared war.

The Prussians led a well-planned campaign. An army of 384,000 Prussians was rushed by rail to confront a force of 270,000 Frenchmen. The French had the advantage of better rifles, but the Prussians were equipped with heavier cannon, which could pulverize French positions from a distance. Within a few weeks Prussia won a decisive victory at Sedan°, taking the French emperor prisoner on September 2. The French continued the struggle, despite difficult odds. Infuriated by the continuation of the war, the Prussians resorted to extreme measures. They took hostages and burned down whole villages, and they laid siege to Paris, starving and bombarding its beleaguered population.

Throughout Germany the outbreak of the war aroused general enthusiasm for the Prussian cause. Exploiting this popular feeling, Bismarck called on leaders of the southern German states to accept the unification of Germany under the Prussian king. Reluctant princes, such as the king of Bavaria, were bought off with bribes. On January 18, 1871, the German princes met in the Hall of Mirrors at the palace of Versailles, symbol of past French greatness, and acclaimed the Prussian king as German emperor, Kaiser Wilhelm I.

In May 1871 the Treaty of Frankfurt established the peace terms (see Map 22.1). France was forced to give up the provinces of Alsace and Lorraine and to pay Germany a heavy indemnity of five billion francs. These harsh terms embittered the French, leading many to desire revenge and establishing a formidable barrier to future Franco-German relations.

The Character of the New Germany

German unity had been won through a series of wars—against Denmark in 1864, Austria in 1866, and France in 1870. The military had played a key role in forging German unity, and it remained a dominant force in the new nation. Italian unity had been sanctioned by plebiscites and a vote by an elected assembly accepting the popular verdict. The founding act of the new German state, as the opening illustration to this chapter shows, was the acclamation of the German emperor by German rulers on the soil of a defeated neighbor. Thus the rulers placed themselves above elected assemblies and popular sanction.

On the surface, the constitution of the new Germany was remarkably democratic. It provided for an upper,

---

Hohenzollerns (HO-en-tsoll-ernz)   **Sedan** (seh-DAEN)

Women and Citizenship in Emerging Nations

The governments formed in the 1870s did not include women as equal citizens, nor did they grant them national voting rights. Politicians feared that women's religious ties would lead to the undue influence of established churches in the new secular governments. Hedwig Dohm (1833–1919), a social democrat, worked toward universal suffrage in post-unification Germany. Her 1873 proposal, shown here, uses the concept of natural law to argue that freedom and citizenship should not belong only to men and that women also should have the right to exercise their citizenship by voting. Between 1917 and 1919 women in Austria, Czechoslovakia, Germany, the Netherlands, Poland, Russia, and the United Kingdom received the right to vote. Women in France and Italy had to wait until 1945.

The most fluent speaker claims that women's votes would produce a political reaction because they are strongly influenced by the church. And who would be responsible if women were to cast their votes under priestly guidance? Who created religious conditions? Who invented confession? To this day women have not invented a religion. Men have driven women to churches by excluding them from all other areas of spiritual life. This clerical influence will diminish in proportion to women's being permitted to participate in higher duties. . . .

Everyone agrees that the municipal vote for Englishwomen is nothing but a precursor of general national voting rights. The principle is thereby accepted; we are concerned now with a broadening of the practice.

Other precursors of general enfranchisement are the women who in some American states already exercise the right to vote. . . .

It may be true that at present only a minority of German women are concerned with the liberation of women and demand radical reform. Many women are deterred from participating in the agitation for the reforms by a simple reasoning. They say to themselves: I eat well and drink well, I have elegant clothes, I frequent theaters, balls, etc. . . . I have what I need—why concern myself about others? . . .

It is not modesty nor the recognition of an unchangeable decision of nature that restrains thousands upon thousands of women from the great revolutionary movement; it is common selfishness. . . .

"Are you perchance demanding that women should eventually sit in the chambers of parliaments?" suggests a sarcastic voice. Why not? Even though the liberal statesman to whom we mentioned this possibility felt that it could never come to pass—since, as he argued, many capable men would find their voting and political resolve confused by feelings of love. . . .

As a matter of fact, gentlemen, one must ask: Are women in this world only in order to eliminate all possible obstacles to male virtue? Could not men themselves occasionally do something for their own virtue? In my opinion the interests of half of humanity are of greater importance than the danger that some weak-minded representatives might lose their political acumen along with their hearts.

QUESTIONS

1. Dohm calls attention to England and America. What does the choice of these two countries signify?

2. What are the similarities and differences between Dohm's argument and the one made forty years earlier by the woman writing in *La Femme libre* (see page 719) and the one made in 1908 by Emmeline Pankhurst (see page 829). How do you account for the differences in their arguments and their appeal? Why might some men and women have objected to Dohm's argument?

3. Women in England, France, and Italy also argued for their civil and legal rights from the 1860s through the 1880s. Why might this period have been an opportune time for women to press for their rights, and why did they not succeed at this time?

SOURCE: Excerpts from Susan Groag Bell and Karen M. Offen, eds., *Women, the Family, and Freedom: The Debate in Documents*, Volume One: 1750–1880 (Stanford, Calif.: Stanford University Press, 1983), pp. 507–508. Translated by Susan Groag Bell. Copyright © 1983 by the Board of Trustees of the Leland Stanford Junior University. Used with permission of Stanford University Press, www.sup.org.

appointed house, the *Bundesrat*°, representing the individual German states, and a lower house, the *Reichstag*°, which was elected by universal manhood suffrage. The latter might seem a surprising concession from Bismarck, the authoritarian aristocrat. But he knew the liberals lacked mass support and gambled that, with appropriate appeals, he would be able to create majorities that could be manipulated for his purposes. (See the box "The Continuing Experiment: Women and Citizenship in Emerging Nations.")

The dominant state in the new Germany was, of course, Prussia, which was home to two-thirds of its population. The king of Prussia occupied the post of emperor, and the chancellor and other cabinet members were responsible not to parliament but to him. Only the emperor could make foreign policy and war, command the army, and interpret the constitution. The authoritarianism of Prussia had been projected onto all of Germany.

The emergence of a strong, united Germany shattered the European balance of power. In February 1871 the British political leader Benjamin Disraeli° observed that the unification of Germany was a "greater political event than the French revolution of last century. . . . There is not a diplomatic tradition which has not been swept away. You have a new world. . . . The balance of power has been entirely destroyed."[2] Germany had become the dominant power on the Continent.

PRECARIOUS EMPIRES

THE three large empires of central and eastern Europe, battered by aggressive behavior from other European states and challenged by internal tensions, attempted to weather the endless crises they confronted. The Austrian, Ottoman, and Russian Empires labored to fortify their regimes with political reforms, restructuring their institutions, but only Austria tried to accommodate democratic impulses by establishing a parliament. The Ottoman sultans and the Russian tsars clung tenaciously to their autocratic traditions.

The Dual Monarchy in Austria-Hungary

Emperor Franz Joseph (r. 1848–1916) had come to the throne as an 18-year-old in that year of crisis, 1848. He was a well-meaning monarch who took his duties seri-

ously. His upbringing was German, he lived in German-speaking Vienna, and he headed an army and a bureaucracy that was mostly German. But Franz Joseph was markedly cosmopolitan. He spoke several of his subjects' languages and thought of himself as the emperor of all his peoples. A much-loved, regal figure, Franz Joseph provided a visible symbol of the state. He lacked imagination, however, and did little more than try to conserve a disintegrating empire coping with the modern forces of liberalism and nationalism.

After the war with Piedmont and France (see page 746), Austrian statesmen sensed the vulnerability of their empire. To give the government credibility, in February 1861 Franz Joseph issued what became known as the February Patent, which guaranteed civil liberties and provided for local self-government and a parliament elected by eligible males.

The need to safeguard the remaining territories was clear. By 1866 the Austrian Habsburgs were no longer a German or an Italian power (Venetia had been handed over to a united Italy). The strongest challenge to Habsburg rule came from Hungary, where the Magyars insisted on self-rule, a claim based on age-old rights and Vienna's initial acceptance of autonomy in 1848. Since Magyar cooperation was crucial for the well-being of the Habsburg empire, the government entered into lengthy negotiations with Magyar leaders in 1867. Empress Elizabeth, sympathetic to the Magyars, helped convince the emperor to take a conciliatory stance. The outcome was the Compromise of 1867, creating new structures for the empire that lasted until 1918. The agreement divided the Habsburg holdings into Austria in the west and Hungary in the east (see Map 22.3). Each was independent, but they were linked by the person of the emperor of Austria, Franz Joseph, who was also king of Hungary. Hungary had full internal autonomy and participated jointly in imperial affairs—state finance, defense, and foreign relations. The new state created in 1867 was known as the dual monarchy of Austria-Hungary.

The compromise confirmed Magyar dominance in Hungary. Although numerically a minority, the Magyars controlled the Hungarian parliament, the army, the bureaucracy, and other state institutions. They opposed self-rule by the Croats, Serbs, Slovaks, Romanians, and others in the kingdom and attempted a policy of Magyarization—teaching only Magyar in the schools, conducting all government business in Magyar, and giving access to government positions only to those fully assimilated in Magyar culture. This arrangement created frustrations and resistance among the various nationalities under their rule.

Bundesrat (BOON-tes-raht)   **Reichstag** (RYSH-stak)
Disraeli (diz-RAY-lee)

756

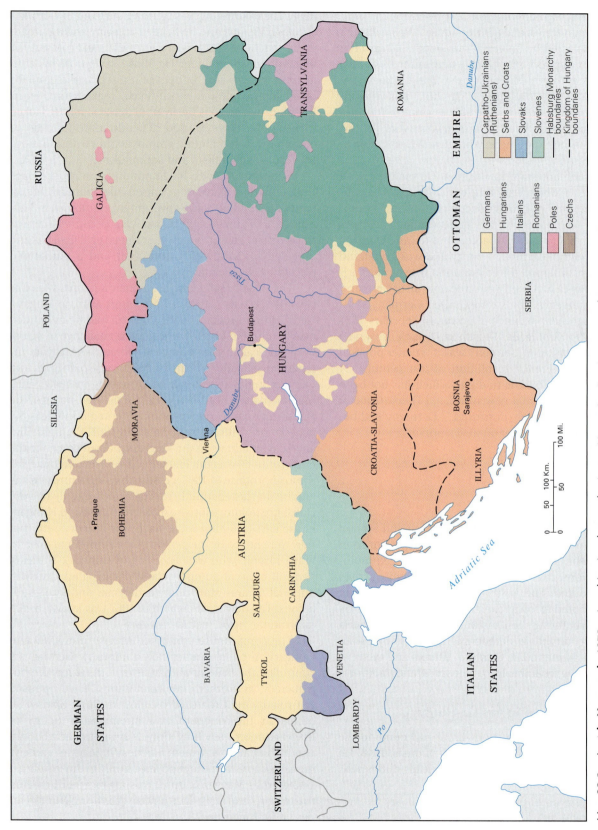

Map 22.3   Austria-Hungary in 1878   A multinational state, the Austro-Hungarian Empire occupied Bosnia in 1878, bringing more dissatisfied peoples under its rule. Tensions in the Balkans would lead to the outbreak of world war in 1914.

The terms of the compromise also gave the Hungarians a voice in imperial foreign policy. The Magyars feared that Slavic groups outside the empire, who planned to form independent states or had already done so, would inspire fellow Slavs in Austria-Hungary to revolt. To prevent that, the Hungarians favored an expansionist foreign policy in the Balkans, which the monarchy embraced (see Map 22.3). Having lost its influence in Germany, Austria-Hungary saw the Balkans as an area in which it could assert itself. The policy was fraught with risks and, by bringing more discontented Slavs into the empire, led to hostilities with other states.

The Ailing Ottoman Empire

At midcentury the Ottoman Empire was still one of the largest European powers, but it faced unrest within its borders and threats from the expansionist designs of its neighbors. The ailing empire was commonly referred to as "the sick man of Europe." Over the next twenty-five years the empire shed some of its territory and modernized its government, but nothing could save it from decline in the face of nationalist uprisings in its Balkan possessions.

As early as the 1840s, the Ottoman Empire had begun various reform movements to bring more security to its subjects. Known as the *Tanzimat*°, these changes were initiated by Sultan Abdul Mejid° (r. 1839–1861), with the help of his able prime minister, Reshid Mustafa Pasha° (1800–1858). Reshid had served as the Ottoman ambassador in London and Paris and was familiar with Western institutions, which he admired and wished to emulate. The reforms introduced security of property, equity in taxation, and equality before the law regardless of religion. Government officials—who previously had been free to collect taxes arbitrarily, sending the required amount to the central government and keeping the rest—were given fixed salaries and subjected to regular inspections.

These reforms were strengthened after the Crimean War by further imperial edicts. Contacts with the West encouraged Turks to think of transforming their empire into a more modern, Westernized state. Many young intellectuals were impatient with the pace of change, however, and critical of the sultan. Unable freely to express their opinions at home, some went into exile in Paris and London in the late 1860s. Their hosts called them the "Young Turks," an expression that became synonymous with activists for change and improvement.

Alarmed by challenges to its authority, the central government began to turn away from reform, and in 1871 the sultan decided to assert his personal rule. His inability to wage war successfully and to hold on to the empire led to dissatisfaction, and in the spring of 1876 rioters demanded and won the establishment of constitutional government. Within a year, however, the new sultan, Abdul Hamid II (r. 1876–1909), dismissed the constitutional government and reverted to personal rule.

Part of the administration's problem was financial. The Crimean War had forced the empire to borrow money abroad. The easy terms of foreign credit lured the sultan into taking out huge loans to finance extravagant projects. By 1875 more than half the annual income of the empire went to pay the interest on the debt. In spite of drought and famine, the authorities raised taxes, fostering widespread discontent.

Opposition to the government increased, fueled by nationalist fervor. The empire tolerated religious diversity and did not persecute people because of their religion. But the central administration had lost control over its provincial officials, who were often corrupt and tyrannical. Christians, the majority population in the Balkans, blamed their suffering on Islamic rule, and many were inspired by the 1821 Greek war of independence and the revolutions of 1848 to seek their own independence.

The Romanians, who lived mainly in the adjoining provinces of Moldavia in the north and Wallachia° in the south, began to express nationalist sentiments in the late eighteenth century. These sentiments were nurtured by Western-educated students, who claimed for their countrymen illustrious descent from Roman settlers of antiquity. News of the 1848 revolution in Paris helped trigger a revolt in both provinces by those demanding unification and independence. This uprising was quickly crushed by the Turks.

In 1856 the Congress of Paris removed Russia's right of protection over Moldavia and Wallachia and provided for a referendum to determine their future. In 1859 the two provinces chose a local military officer, Alexander Cuza° (r. 1859–1866), as the ruler of each territory. In 1862 the Ottoman Empire recognized the union of the two principalities in the single, autonomous state of Romania. At the Congress of Berlin in 1878, Romania's full independence was recognized. Thus, in less than a quarter century, two provinces of the Ottoman Empire had gained full sovereignty.

The path to independence was much more violent for the Bulgarians. Influenced by neighboring Serbia and

---

Tanzimat (tan-zee-MAT)
Abdul Mejid (Ab-DOOL med-JEED)
Reshid Mustafa Pasha (ray-SHEED moo-STAH-fah PAH-shah)

Wallachia (vall-AK-yah)   **Cuza** (KOO-sah)

Nationalistic Uprising in Bulgaria   In this 1879 lithograph, Bulgaria is depicted in the form of a maiden—protected by the Russian eagle, breaking her chains, and winning liberty from the Ottoman Empire.   *(St. Cyril and Methodius National Library, Sofia)*

encouraged by the Russians, revolutionary committees spread propaganda and agitated against Ottoman rule. An uprising in Bulgaria broke out in May 1876. The Christian rebels attacked not only symbols of Ottoman authority but also peaceable Turks living in their midst. The imperial army, aided by local Turkish volunteers, quickly re-established Ottoman authority. Incensed by the massacre of fellow Muslims, the volunteers resorted to mass killing, looting, and burning of Christian villages. The "Bulgarian horrors" shocked Europe and made the continuation of Turkish rule unacceptable.

The Bulgarian crisis was resolved by the Balkan wars of 1876 to 1878, which were provoked by the uprising of the westernmost Ottoman provinces of Bosnia and Herzegovina. Since many of the inhabitants of these two provinces were Serbs, they had the sympathy of Serbia, which hoped to unify the southern Slavs. Serbia and the neighboring mountain state of Montenegro then declared war on the Ottoman Empire, which savagely defeated them.

Russia, which saw itself as the protector of the Slavic peoples, reacted to the Bulgarian horrors by declaring war on the Ottoman Empire in April 1877. At first progress was slow, then the Russians broke through the Turkish lines and forced the sultan to sue for peace. The resulting Treaty of San Stefano, signed in March 1878, created a huge, independent Bulgaria as essentially a Russian protectorate.

The British, Austrians, and French were shocked at the extent to which the San Stefano treaty favored Russia. Under their pressure, the European powers met in Berlin in 1878 to reconsider the treaty. The Congress of Berlin reduced the size of the Bulgarian territory, returning the rest to the Ottomans. Bosnia and Herzegovina were removed from Ottoman rule, henceforth to be administered by Austria-Hungary (see Map 24.4 on page 838). The sultan was forced to acknowledge the legal independence of Serbia, Montenegro, and Romania and the autonomy of Bulgaria. The British insisted on being allowed to administer the island of Cyprus, in the eastern Mediterranean, as an outpost for checking further Russian challenges to the existing balance of power.

Thus Turkey was plundered not only by its enemies but also by powers that had intervened on its behalf. When France complained that it received no compensation, it was given the chance to grab Tunisia, another land under Ottoman rule. Russia, which had signed an alliance with Romania and promised to respect Russia's territorial integrity, ignored its obligations and took southern Bessarabia from its ally. The devious work of the Congress of Berlin reflected the power politics that now characterized international affairs. Statesmen shamelessly used force against both foe and friend for the aggrandizement of their own states. Neither morality nor international law restrained ambition.

Russia and the Great Reforms

Russia's defeat in the Crimean War and its distrust of the Western powers forced the tsar to consider ways of strengthening Russia by restructuring its institutions. Beginning in 1861, a series of measures known collectively as the Great Reforms began to change the face of Russia.

Already by the 1840s concern about the archaic nature and structure of Russian government was mount-

READING SOURCES

THE TSAR DEMANDS THE FREEING OF THE SERFS

In January 1861 Tsar Alexander II addressed the Council of State, an advisory body that he had asked four years earlier to prepare a draft law emancipating the serfs. After this forceful speech, a workable proposal emerged that was implemented six weeks later. Notice that the council's opinion is only advisory; the tsar is indicating his "absolute will." Although he gives lip service to the serfs' interests, the power of Russia and the future of the tsarist regime are Alexander's prime concerns.

The matter of the liberation of the serfs, which has been submitted for the consideration of the State Council, I consider to be a vital question for Russia, upon which will depend the development of her strength and power. . . . [T]his matter cannot be postponed . . . I repeat—and this is my absolute will—that this matter should be finished right away. . . .

You will assure yourselves that all that can be done for the protection of the interests of the nobility has been done . . . but I ask you only not to forget that the basis of the whole work must be the improvement of the life of the peasants—an improvement not in words alone or on paper but in actual fact. . . .

My predecessors felt all the evils of serfdom and continually endeavored, if not to destroy it completely, to work toward the gradual limitation of the arbitrary power of the estate owners.

Already in 1856, before the coronation, while in Moscow I called the attention of the leaders of the nobility of the Moscow *guberniia* [region] to the necessity for them to occupy themselves with improving the life of the serfs, adding that serfdom could not continue forever and that it would therefore be better if the transformation took place from above rather than from below. . . .

I have the right to demand one thing from you: that you, putting aside all personal interests, act not like estate owners but like imperial statesmen invested with my trust. Approaching this important matter I have not concealed from myself all those difficulties that awaited us and I do not conceal them now.

Source: Speech of January 28, 1861, in *A Sourcebook for Russian History from Early Times to 1917*, ed. George Vernadsky et al., vol. 3. Copyright © 1972. Reprinted by permission of the publisher, Yale University Press.

ing. Many officials lamented the tendency of a timid bureaucracy to lie to and mislead the public. Defeat in the Crimean War widened the critique of Russian institutions. Calls for *glasnost*—greater openness—became the leading motif in the Great Reforms. The chief problem that needed resolution was serfdom. Educated opinion had long denounced serfdom as immoral, but conscience was not the principal reason for its abolition. Serfdom was abolished because it presented clear disadvantages in both the domestic and international domains. The new tsar, Alexander II (r. 1855–1881), feared that if serfdom was not abolished from above, it would be overthrown from below—by a serf rebellion that would sweep away everything in its path, including the autocracy itself.

Serfdom also held Russia back in its competition with the rest of the world. Defeat in the Crimean War by Britain and France suggested that soldiers with a stake in their society fought harder than men bound to lifetime

servitude. In addition, the victorious Western states had won in part because their industrial might translated into more and better guns, ammunition, and transportation. Industrial progress required a mobile labor force, not one tied to the soil by serfdom. With a free labor force, rural populations, as in the West, could become the abundant labor supply that drove industrial production. Many educated Russians felt that the defeat in the Crimea had revealed Russia's general backwardness. To catch up with the West, they argued, Russia needed to shed its timeworn institutions, particularly serfdom.

In April 1861 Alexander II issued a decree freeing the serfs. (See the box "Reading Sources: The Tsar Demands the Freeing of the Serfs.") With one stroke, he emancipated 22 million people from a system that allowed them to be bought and sold, separated from their families, and treated in the cruelest ways imaginable. Emancipation represented a compromise with the gentry, which had reluctantly agreed to liberate its serfs but insisted on

A Critique of Russian Serfdom   The French artist Gustave Doré reveals how landowners viewed their serfs as mere property that could be won and lost with a draw of the cards.
(Miriam and Ira D. Wallach Division of Art, Prints and Photographs, The New York Public Library, Astor, Lenox and Tilden Foundations/Art Resource, NY)

compensation. As a result, the newly liberated peasants had to reimburse the government with mortgage payments lasting fifty years. The peasants received some land, but its value was vastly overrated and its quantity insufficient for peasant families. To make ends meet, most freed peasants continued working for their former masters.

The local commune, or *mir°*, handled the mortgage payments and taxes that the central government imposed on the peasants. The mir determined how the land was to be used, and it paid collectively for the mortgage and taxes on the land. As a consequence, the commune was reluctant for the peasants to leave the land, and they could do so only with its permission. Freed from serfdom, the peasants still suffered many constraints. In fact, the emancipation declaration was accompanied by massive peasant uprisings that had to be put down by force.

The tsar and his advisers feared the large mass of uneducated peasants as a potential source of anarchy and rebellion. They depended on the mir to preserve control even though the commune system had some inherent economic disadvantages. Since increased productivity benefited the commune as much as the individual peasant, there was little incentive for peasants to improve their land, and agricultural yields remained low.

Alexander, lauded as the "tsar emancipator" by his contemporaries, remained wedded to the principles of autocracy. His aim in abolishing serfdom and introducing other reforms was to modernize and strengthen Russia and stabilize his divinely mandated rule. Like most Russians, Alexander believed that only the firm hand of autocracy could hold together a large, ethnically diverse country. The peasant uprisings that accompanied emancipation only confirmed his beliefs. Clearly, however, the sudden freedom of 22 million illiterate peasants threatened to overwhelm existing institutions, and some changes had to be made. Although he surrendered no

mir (MEER)

powers, Alexander did institute a number of reforms, altering the government and the judicial and military systems so they could deal more effectively with the totally remodeled Russian society.

Government reform had paramount importance. Between 1800 and 1850 the Russian population had increased from 36 million to 59 million, and administering this vast country had become more and more difficult. Overcentralized, with a poorly trained civil service, the government was unable to cope effectively with the problems of its people. Emancipation of the serfs greatly exacerbated this situation. Thus in 1864 a law was passed providing for local governments, or *zemstvos*°, at the village and regional levels, giving Russians the authority and the opportunity to use initiative in local matters.

The zemstvos were largely controlled by the gentry and not particularly democratic. They were forbidden to debate political issues, and their decisions could be overridden or ignored by local officials appointed by the tsar. Some hoped that zemstvos could become the basis for self-government at the national level and looked for the creation of an all-Russian zemstvo, but such hopes were firmly squelched by the tsar, who jealously insisted on undivided and undiminished autocracy. Nonetheless, the zemstvos were a viable attempt to modernize an overburdened central government.

The tsar also created an independent judiciary that ensured equality before the law, public jury trials, and uniform sentences. Russian political leaders recognized that public confidence in the judiciary and the rule of law was a prerequisite for the development of commerce and industry. Businessmen would no longer fear arbitrary intervention by capricious officials and could develop enterprises in greater security.

In addition, censorship of the press was abolished. Under the previous tsar, Nicholas I, all ideas that did not conform to government policy were censored. Such censorship prevented the central government from being well informed about public opinion or about the effects of its policies on the country. Under Alexander openness in the press was viewed as a remedy for corruption and misuse of power. People could be punished only for specific violations after publication, and they would face trial in an independent court.

Reform also extended to the Russian army. Its structure and methods became more Western. Military service, previously limited to peasants, became the obligation of all Russian men, who submitted to a lottery. Those with an "unlucky" number entered the service. In an effort to make military service more attractive, the length of service was drastically cut and corporal punishment was abolished. Access to the officer corps was to be by merit rather than by social connection. The Ministry of War also improved the system of reserves, enabling Russia to mobilize a larger army with more modern weapons in case of war.

The Great Reforms represented considerable change for Russia. Serfdom had been abolished, self-government was established on the local level, the rule of law was adopted, and army service was made more humane. But above the change, the tsarist regime remained autocratic and repressive, flexible only to the degree that its rulers had the will and wisdom to be.

THE EMERGENCE OF NEW POLITICAL FORMS IN THE UNITED STATES AND CANADA, 1840–1880

ACROSS the sea, a new power emerged in these years, the United States. It enlarged its territories, strengthened its national government, and broadened its democracy by including a large category of people previously excluded from the political process—African Americans. But these achievements were the result of the bloodiest conflict in U.S. history, the Civil War.

Territorial Expansion and Slavery

In the early years of its existence, the United States was confined to the land east of the Mississippi River, but in the nineteenth century it gained much territory through westward expansion (see Map 22.4). In 1803 President Thomas Jefferson secured the Louisiana Purchase from the French, which nearly doubled the size of the United States. In 1819 Florida was acquired from Spain. Some Americans looked even farther west and began to insist that the United States had a "manifest destiny" to occupy the whole North American continent from coast to coast.

The U.S. government used the settlements of American citizens in Mexican- and British-held territories as pretexts for expansion. In 1845 Congress voted to annex Texas, which had gained independence from Mexico in 1836. As a result of negotiation with Britain, the United States in 1846 acquired the Oregon Country south of the forty-ninth parallel. Declaring war on Mexico that same year, and quickly winning, the United States added

---

zemstvos (SEMST-vose)

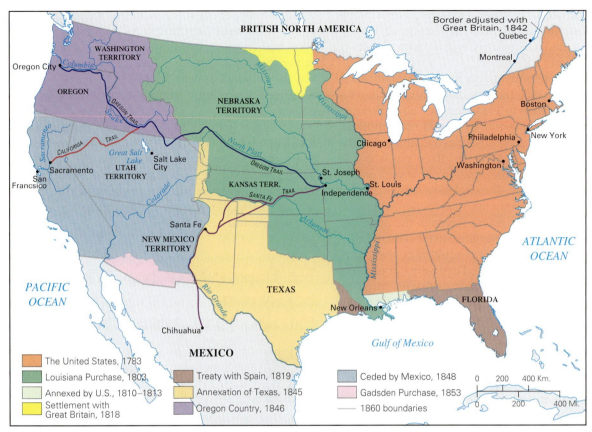

Map 22.4 U.S. Expansion Through 1853   In just eight years, from 1845 to 1853, the United States increased its territory by a third. The principle of manifest destiny appeared to be fulfilled, as the United States now stretched from the Atlantic to the Pacific.

California and the Southwest in 1848. Manifest destiny or not, the United States now spanned the continent from the Atlantic to the Pacific.

Beginning in the 1820s, the United States saw serious sectional clashes between East and West as well as North and South. The latter were more important. Many issues divided the two regions, notably a conflict between the industrial interests of the North and the agrarian interests of the South. What sharpened this divide, however, was the issue of slavery. As the United States annexed new territories, the question of whether they would be slave or free divided the nation. The North opposed the extension of the "peculiar institution," while much of the South favored it. Southerners believed that if the new areas were closed to slavery, the institution would weaken in the South; slaveholding would eventually disappear, and with it Southern prosperity. They would then be unable to withstand the political and eco-

nomic pressure of an economically richer and more populous North, which was unsympathetic to slavery.

The issue of slavery was passionately debated for decades. Some Americans wanted slavery abolished throughout the United States. If that could not be done, some of the most committed abolitionists, especially in New England, advocated the secession of free states from the Union. On the other side, Southerners threatened that if their way of life—meaning a society based on slavery—were not assured, then the South would secede. The threat of secession was lightly and frequently made by partisans of various causes for many decades.

In November 1860 Illinois Republican Abraham Lincoln (1809–1865) was elected president in a highly contested four-way race. Lincoln opposed the spread of slavery beyond its existing borders and hence appeared to threaten its future in the South. For many Southerners his election to the highest office was the final straw.

Beginning in December 1860, most Southern state legislatures voted to secede from the Union, forming in February 1861 the Confederate States of America. The South defined its cause as defending states' rights, claiming that the people of each state had the right to determine their destiny, free from what they viewed as the tyranny of the national government. The Southern states seized federal funds and property, and in April 1861 the Confederates bombarded federally held Fort Sumter, South Carolina. Lincoln, inaugurated in March 1861, was determined to preserve the Union and to put down the insurrection. The long-dreaded Civil War had begun.

Civil War and National Unity, 1861–1865

The North had many advantages. It had nearly three times as many people as the South, a strong industrial base that could supply an endless stream of weapons, and a far more extensive rail system for transporting men and materiel to the front. Although blue and gray armies clashed in a number of important military engagements, the North effectively blockaded the South, leading it, toward the end of the war, to be desperately short of men, money, and supplies.

During the war, Lincoln's government took measures that centralized power in Washington, changing the nation from a loose federation of states to a more centrally governed entity. The federal government intruded into areas of life from which it had before been absent. With the National Banking Act of 1863, state banks were driven out of business and replaced by a uniform national banking system. The federal government provided massive subsidies for a national railroad system. Lincoln established the National Academy of Sciences to advise him on scientific matters. The word *national* came into increasing use. Senator John Sherman of Ohio declared during the war that "the policy of this country ought to be to make everything national as far as possible."

When the main Confederate army surrendered in 1865, the principle of state sovereignty, proclaimed by the South, was roundly defeated. With the passage of the Thirteenth Amendment to the U.S. Constitution the same year, slaves, previously considered property, were declared to be free. The North occupied the South in an attempt to "reconstruct" it. Reconstruction included efforts to root out the Confederate leadership and ensure full civil and political rights for the newly emancipated African Americans. The government also embarked on a short-lived campaign to provide freed slaves with

enough land to ensure them a livelihood—another example of federal authority at work. At the end of Reconstruction, federal power retreated and many states denied African Americans their rights. But certainly the nation was more centralized and its citizens were more enfranchised after the Civil War than before.

The Frontiers of Democracy

One of the major transformations in the United States from the 1820s through the 1860s was the inclusion of an ever greater number of people in the political process. By the late 1820s, as a result of popular pressure, states abandoned restrictions on voting, and most adult white men received the vote. Symbolic of this new "age of the common man" was the election of Andrew Jackson as U.S. president in 1828. All his predecessors had been men of education and property—some were even described as "Virginia aristocrats"—but Jackson represented himself as a self-made man, a rugged frontiersman. State legislatures had in the past elected members to the presidential Electoral College, but in response to public calls for change, state legislatures altered the system so that Electoral College members were selected by direct popular vote.

National presidential campaigns became rough-and-tumble affairs, with emotional appeals to the public. Scurrilous attacks, many untrue, were mounted against opponents. In 1828, for instance, during President John Quincy Adams's re-election campaign, his opponents charged him with corruption, although once he was defeated, they admitted he had been one of the nation's most honest officeholders. Campaigns began to revolve around easily grasped symbols, and when William Henry Harrison ran for president in 1840, he was depicted as a simple frontiersman. His supporters wore log-cabin badges, sang log-cabin songs, and dragged log-cabin replicas on floats in parades. Such paraphernalia became a common sight in American elections. If some contemporary observers, such as the Frenchman Alexis de Tocqueville (1805–1859), were disappointed at the lack of a thoughtful and deliberate process in choosing political leaders, they recognized that democracy was nowhere in the world as fully developed as in the United States, where it foreshadowed the future of other societies.

When Abraham Lincoln was elected U.S. president in 1860, nobody of his social standing occupied an equivalent position in Europe. At the news of his assassination in 1865, workmen and artisans, seeing in the dead president a kindred spirit, stood for hours in line outside

Bingham: The Verdict of the People   In George Caleb Bingham's 1855 painting set in the American West, voters await election results. Unlike in Europe, where religious and property barriers to suffrage continued throughout the nineteenth century, many U.S. states had universal white male suffrage by the 1820s.   *(From the Art Collection of NationsBank)*

the U.S. legation in London and the consul general's office in Lyon (France) to sign a book of condolence to express their sorrow. It was also a form of tribute to the nation that had elected a backwoodsman, born in a log cabin, to its highest office.

The frontiers of democracy appeared to have widened after the Civil War when amendments to the U.S. Constitution granted African Americans full equality with whites. Slavery was forbidden throughout the United States, and regardless of "race, color, or previous condition of servitude," all Americans were declared to be citizens. During the first few years of Reconstruction, whites who had supported the Confederacy were deprived of the right to vote, and African Americans represented a voting bloc in the South. As a result, for the first

time the United States saw the election of blacks to positions as varied as lieutenant governor, U.S. senator, congressman, postmaster, and innumerable county and town offices. After the end of military occupation of the South, however, local white power reasserted itself, and the rights of African Americans were sharply curtailed. Yet compared with their status before the Civil War, African Americans had advanced significantly. They were no longer slaves but citizens, they were free to move where they wanted, and in some places they were able to participate in the political process.

By 1880 the United States not only had seen four decades of territorial expansion but had been transformed by the ordeal of the Civil War, which brought about the extension of federal authority and—however

Map 22.5 Dominion of Canada, 1873 By 1873 Canada had become a vast nation with the addition of the western territories. Like the United States, Canada reached from the Atlantic to the Pacific.

hesitatingly—of the rights of citizenship to new groups. A large, powerful democracy had arisen in the North American continent.

The United States' Northern Neighbor: Canada

Just north of the United States, in Canada, some similar processes unfolded during the 1800s that also resulted in a larger, freer, and more centralized society. Though Canada was spared a civil war, a popular uprising did occur as citizens chafed under the oligarchical grip of British colonial rule, in which authority was in the hands of a few families. Lord Durham, the new governor, suggested in 1839 a series of reforms (see page 727) that in the end were implemented, uniting Upper and Lower Canada and providing for an elected assembly and a government responsible to it. The British North America Act in 1867 created a federal system of government, with each province exercising considerable autonomy. With the purchase of the Northwest Territories from the pri-

vate Hudson's Bay Company in 1869 and the gradual attachment of other provinces, Canada gained in size. By 1871 the country stretched from the Maritime Provinces in the east to the Pacific Ocean in the west (see Map 22.5). The building of a transcontinental railroad in the 1880s helped unite the huge nation. By the end of the nineteenth century, Canada was virtually self-governing, having full control over all its affairs, except for defense and foreign affairs.

THE DEVELOPMENT OF WESTERN DEMOCRACIES

IN the generation after 1850 Britain, France, and several smaller states in northern Europe made major strides forward in creating democratic political systems and cultures. Although universal manhood suffrage had been instituted only in France, all

A Japanese View of the British Parliament

In 1862 the Japanese government sent its first diplomatic mission to Europe. Accompanying the delegation was a young translator, Fukuzawa Yukichi (1835–1901). Intrigued by what he saw and eager to interest his fellow Japanese in the West, Fukuzawa published several books. In fact, all books about the West in Japan came to be known as "Fukuzawa-bon." Toward the end of his life, in his *Autobiography,* he described how, while in London, he had tried to understand the workings of the British Parliament.

Of political situations at that time, I tried to learn as much as I could from various persons that I met in London . . . though it was often difficult to understand things clearly as I was as yet unfamiliar with the history of Europe. . . . A perplexing institution was representative government. When I asked a gentleman what the "election law" was and what kind of an institution the Parliament really was, he simply replied with a smile, meaning I suppose that no intelligent person was expected to ask such questions. But these were the things most difficult of all for me to understand. In this connection, I learned that there were different political parties—the Liberal and the Conservative—who were always "fighting" against each other in the government.

For some time it was beyond my comprehension to understand what they were "fighting" for, and what was meant, anyway, by "fighting" in peace time. "This man and that man are 'enemies' in the House," they would tell me. But these "enemies" were to be seen at the same table, eating and drinking with each other. I felt as if I could not make much out of this. It took me a long time, with some tedious thinking, before I could gather a general notion of these separate mysterious facts. In some of the more complicated matters, I might achieve an understanding five or ten days after they were explained to me. But all in all, I learned much from this initial tour of Europe.

QUESTIONS

1. Why might the Japanese visitor have been puzzled by the use of the words "fighting" and "enemies" in this context?

2. Would Japanese readers have obtained a good idea of the British parliamentary system based on this report?

SOURCE: *The Autobiography of Fukuzawa Yukichi,* trans. Eiichi Kiyooka (Tokyo: Hokuseida Press, 1948), pp. 138, 143–144.

 For additional information on this topic, go to college.hmco.com/students.

---

these countries' governments were responsible to elected representatives of the voters. Lincoln had spoken of the United States enjoying "government of the people, by the people, for the people." As a result of a series of political reforms, this goal was in the process of being attained in many European countries.

Victorian Britain

The mid-nineteenth century was a period of exceptional wealth and security for Britain, as the population as a whole began to share in the economic benefits of industrialization. Britain enjoyed both social and political peace. The political system was not challenged as it had been in the generation after the Napoleonic Wars. A self-assured, even smug, elite—merchants, industrialists, and landowners—developed a political system reflecting liberal values.

Although suffrage was still restricted to propertied Christian men before the 1850s, the parliamentary system was firmly established, with government clearly responsible to the electorate. The importance of Parliament was symbolized by the new building in which it met, finished in 1850 on the site of previous parliamentary buildings but of unprecedented splendor and size. The form of government developed in its halls after mid-century aroused the curiosity and envy of much of the world. (See the box "Global Encounters: A Japanese View of the British Parliament.")

In the twenty years after 1846 five different political parties vied for power. Depending on the issue, parties and factions coalesced to support particular policies. After 1867, however, a clear two-party system emerged: Liberal and Conservative (Tory), both with strong leadership. This development gave the electorate a distinct choice. The Conservatives were committed to preserving traditional institutions and practices, whereas the Liberals were more open to change.

Heading these parties were the two strong-minded individuals who dominated British political life for over a generation: William E. Gladstone (1809–1898), a Liberal, and Benjamin Disraeli (1804–1881), a Conservative. Gladstone came from a family of industrialists and married into the aristocracy; Disraeli was the son of a Jewish man of letters who had converted to Christianity. His father's conversion made his career possible—before the 1850s Jews were barred from Parliament. Prior to heading their parties, Gladstone and Disraeli both served in important cabinet positions. They were master debaters; Parliament and the press hung on their every word. Each was capable of making speeches lasting five hours or more and of conducting debates that kept the house in session until 4:00 A.M. The rivalry between the two men thrilled the nation and made politics a popular pastime.

The Conservatives' electoral base came from the landed classes, from Anglicans, and from England, rather than the rest of the United Kingdom (consisting of Scotland, Wales, and Ireland). The Liberals' base came from the middle classes, from Christian groups other than the Church of England, and from Scotland and Wales. In the House of Commons both parties had a large number of members from the landed aristocracy, but cabinet members were increasingly chosen for political competence rather than family background. Aristocratic birth was no longer a requirement for reaching the pinnacle of power, as Gladstone and Disraeli so clearly illustrated.

The competition for power between the Liberals and the Conservatives led to an extension of suffrage in 1867. The Second Reform Bill lowered property qualifications, extending the vote from 1.4 million to 2.5 million people out of a population of 22 million, and gave new urban areas better representation by equalizing the electoral districts—henceforth the same size population was required for each district sending a member to Parliament. Although some in Parliament feared that these changes would lead to the masses capturing political power—"a leap into the dark," one member called it—in fact no radical change ensued. Extending the vote to clerks, artisans, and other skilled workers made them feel more a part of society and thus bolstered the existing system. John Stuart Mill, then a member of Parliament, along with his colleague and wife, Harriet Taylor Mill (1807–1856), championed the cause of women's suffrage, but he had few allies in Parliament, and that effort failed.

As the extension of voting rights increased the size of the electorate, parties became larger and stronger. Strong party systems meant alternation of power be-

Disraeli and Gladstone: Victorian Political Rivals   This 1868 cartoon from *Punch* magazine captures the politicians' personalities. Disraeli was known as vain and theatrical, while Gladstone was dour and moralistic.   *(Mary Evans Picture Library)*

tween the Liberals and the Conservatives. With an obvious majority and minority party, the monarch could no longer play favorites in choosing a prime minister. The leader of the majority party had to be asked to form a government. Thus even though Queen Victoria (r. 1837–1901) detested Gladstone, she had to ask him to form governments when the Liberals won parliamentary elections. (See the feature "Weighing the Evidence: An Engraving of the British Royal Family" on pages 772–773.)

The creation of a broad-based electorate also meant that politicians had to make clear appeals to the public and its interests. In the past, oratory had been limited to the halls of Parliament, but after the electoral reforms, it occurred in the public arena as well. Public election campaigns became part of the political scene in Britain. The democratic, "American" style of campaigning appealed to the common man. Also borrowed from abroad was the "Australian ballot"—the secret ballot—adopted in 1872. This protected lower-class voters from intimidation by their employers, landowners, or other social superiors. In 1874 the first two working-class members of Parliament were elected, sitting as Liberals. Although their victory represented a very modest gain for workers' representation, it presaged the increasingly democratic turn England was to take.

France: From Empire to Republic

Unlike Britain, which was transformed gradually into a parliamentary democracy, France took a more tumultuous path. Revolutions and wars overthrew existing political systems and inaugurated new ones. Each time the French seemed to have democracy within reach, the opportunity slipped away.

The constitution of the Second French Republic provided for a single four-year presidential term. Frustrated by this limitation of power, Louis Napoleon extended his presidency to a ten-year term by a coup d'état in 1851. The following year he called for a plebiscite to confirm him as Napoleon III (r. 1852–1870), emperor of the French. Both of these moves were resisted in the countryside, particularly in the south, but the resistance was put down by massive repression.

In the rest of the country huge majorities of voters endorsed first the prolonged presidency and then the imperial title. The new emperor seemed different from his predecessors. He believed in the principle of popular sovereignty (he maintained universal male suffrage, introduced in 1848), he did not pretend to reign by divine right, and he repeatedly tested his right to rule by an appeal to the popular vote. He seemed to combine order and authority with the promises of the Revolution—equality before the law, careers open to talent, and the abolition of hereditary rights.

The mid-nineteenth century was a period of prosperity for most Frenchmen, including urban workers and peasants. Louis Napoleon, in his youth the author of a book on pauperism, introduced measures congenial to labor. On the one hand, workers were required to keep a booklet in which employers recorded their conduct. On the other hand, workers were granted limited rights to strike, and labor unions were virtually legalized. The emperor expressed his desire to improve the workers' lot, and the government initiated a few concrete measures, such as providing some public housing. Although slum clearance during the rebuilding of Paris drove many from their homes to the outskirts of the city, it did provide healthier towns for those who stayed behind, and the ambitious urban projects provided work for many

Napoleon III This is an example of official art glorifying the emperor. Napoleon is framed by a Roman statue on his right and the imperial eagle on his left, both symbols of strength and glory. *(Giraudon/Art Resource, NY)*

(see page 791). Other public works projects, such as ports, roads, railroads, and monumental public buildings, also created jobs. Railroad mileage in France increased tenfold, enabling peasants to market their harvests more widely. If some peasants had initially opposed Louis Napoleon, most supported him once he was in power. Not only were they a cautious group, preferring stable authority, but they saw in the emperor—the heir to the great Napoleon—an incarnation of national glory.

Not all the French supported the emperor; many republicans could not forget that he had usurped the constitution of 1848. In protest, some had gone into exile, including the poet Victor Hugo. Trying to win over the opposition, Napoleon made some concessions in 1860, easing censorship and making his government more accountable to the parliament. Instead of winning him new support, however, liberalization allowed the expression of mounting opposition. A coordinated republican opposition strongly criticized the economic policies of the empire, notably the decision to sign a free-trade treaty with England. Free trade helped wine and silk exporters, but it left iron and textile manufacturers unprotected. Businessmen in these fields rallied their workers against the imperial regime.

A number of other issues—including widespread hostility toward the influence of the Catholic Church and the desire for more extensive freedom of expression and assembly—also helped forge a republican alliance of the middle classes and workers. This alliance was strongest in the large cities and in some southern regions notorious for their opposition to central government control. Republicanism was better organized than in earlier years and had a more explicit program. Moreover, its proponents were now better prepared to take over the government, if the opportunity arose.

By 1869 the regime of Napoleon III, which declared itself a "liberal empire," had evolved into a constitutional monarchy, responsible to the Legislative Corps, the lower house of the parliament. In a plebiscite in May 1870, Frenchmen supported the liberal empire by a vote of five to one. It might have endured had Napoleon III not rashly declared war against Prussia two months later in a huff over the supposedly insulting Ems dispatch (see page 753). Defeat at the hands of Bismarck brought down the empire. In September, at news of the emperor's capture, the republican opposition in the Legislative Corps declared a republic. It continued the war but had to sign an armistice in January 1871.

The leader of the new government was an old prime minister of Louis Philippe, Adolphe Thiers° (1797–1877). Before signing a definitive peace, the provisional government held elections. The liberals, known as republicans since they favored a republic, were identified with continuing the war; the conservatives, mostly royalists, favored peace. Mainly because of their position on this issue, the royalists won a majority from a country discouraged by defeat.

The new regime had no time to establish itself before a workers' uprising in the spring of 1871 shook France, while reminding the rest of Europe of revolutionary dangers. The uprising was called the Paris Com-

mune, a name that harked back to 1792 to 1794, when the Paris crowds had dictated to the government. The Commune insisted on its right to home rule. Radicals and conservatives greeted the Commune as a workers' revolt intended to establish a workers' government. Marx described it as the "bold champion of the emancipation of labor." To an even larger degree than during the revolution of 1848, women took an active part, fighting on the barricades, pouring scalding water on soldiers, posting revolutionary broadsides. The main woman's leader was Louise Michel (1830–1905), a schoolteacher who, while agitating for both socialism and women's rights, took an active part in the fighting.

Although labor discontent played a role in the Paris Commune, other forces also contributed, notably the Prussian siege of Paris during the Franco-Prussian War. Paris had become radicalized during the siege: the rich had evacuated the city, leaving a power vacuum quickly filled by the lower classes. Parisians suffered much because of the siege, and angered that their economic needs went unmet and their courage against the Prussians unnoticed, they rose up against the new French government. Food was the paramount issue sparking the massive women's participation in the uprising. The Commune, composed largely of artisans, now governed the city.

In March 1871 the Commune declared itself free to carry out policies independent of the central government in Versailles. Its goals were quite moderate: it sought free universal education, a fairer taxation system, a minimum wage, and disestablishment of the official Catholic Church. But this was too radical for the conservative French government, which sent in the army. It suppressed the Commune, massacring 25,000 people, arresting 40,000, and deporting several thousand more.

The crushing of the Paris Commune and some of its sister communes in southern France, which had also asserted local autonomy, signified the increasing power of the centralized governments. One mark of the emerging modern state was its capacity to squelch popular revolts that, in the past, had constituted serious threats. Western Europe would not again witness a popular uprising of this magnitude.

Despite its brutality, the suppression of the Commune reassured many Frenchmen. "The Republic will be conservative, or it will not be," declared Thiers. The question now at hand was what form the new government would take. The monarchist majority offered the throne to the Bourbon pretender. However, he insisted he would become king only if the *tricouleur*—the blue, white, and red flag of the Revolution, which long since

Thiers (tee-YAIR)

had become a cherished national symbol—were discarded and replaced by the white flag of the house of Bourbon. This was unacceptable, so France remained a republic. The republic, as Thiers put it, "is the regime which divides us the least."

By 1875 the parliament had approved a set of basic laws that became the constitution of the Third Republic. Ironically, a monarchist parliament had created a liberal, democratic parliamentary regime. A century after the French Revolution, the republican system of government in France was firmly launched.

Scandinavia and the Low Countries

France and especially Britain served as models of parliamentary democracy for the smaller states in northern Europe. Denmark, Sweden, Norway, Holland, and Belgium recast their political institutions at midcentury. Several of the states were affected by the revolutions of 1848. That year Denmark saw a peaceful protest demanding enlarged political participation (see page 736), Sweden saw minor riots, and the king of the Netherlands (after 1830 Holland and the Netherlands refer to the same country) feared that his country would be affected by revolution as in the neighboring German states. In Copenhagen King Frederick VII (r. 1848–1863), who had no stomach for a confrontation, yielded and accepted a constitution providing for parliamentary government. "Now I can sleep as long as I like," he is reputed to have said.

Sweden's parliamentary system, established in the Middle Ages, had representation by estates—noble, clergy, burgher, and peasant. The 11,000 nobles were given the same weight as the 2.5 million to 3 million peasants. After the riots of 1848 liberal aristocrats recognized that abolition of the estates system would best preserve their privileges, removing the major issue that had provoked popular resentments. With some delays, this conviction was finally carried out in 1866. The estates were replaced by a parliament with two houses. The upper house was restricted to the wealthiest landowners and the lower house to men of property, providing the vote to 20 percent of adult men. Although the king was not constitutionally obligated to choose a government reflecting parliamentary currents, he usually did so in an effort to avoid conflict.

Norway had been joined to Sweden in 1814 under the Swedish king, but it had a separate parliament and made its own laws. Swedish rule rankled the Norwegians, however, and in the 1850s the Norwegian Liberal Party began to insist that the king should not have the final word in governance. Instead, they argued, the parliament, representative of the Norwegian people, should be

supreme. In 1883 the principle that government officials are responsible to parliament won out. In 1905 Norway peacefully separated from Sweden and became an independent state.

In the Netherlands, as a result of the revolutions of 1848, the king recognized the need to strengthen support for his crown by acceding to liberals' demands for parliamentary government. By midcentury, government officials in the Netherlands were responsible to the parliament rather than to the king. A new constitution guaranteed the principles of freedom of speech, assembly, and religion.

Belgium had enjoyed a liberal constitution from the time it became an independent state after the Belgian Revolution of 1830, but because no strong party system materialized, the king was able to appoint to government whom he pleased. In the 1840s the liberals organized, and the king, reluctantly, had to invite them to govern in 1848. The new government reduced property qualifications for voting, thus increasing the electorate. Unlike the reforms that had followed the revolutions of 1848, only to be rolled back in conservative backlashes, these sweeping reforms in northern European states became the basis for their evolution into full democracies. For full democracy to take hold, the electorate had to be broadened. These years witnessed much agitation for universal male suffrage. Property qualifications, wherever they were instituted, were questioned and resisted. For instance, in Sweden the stipulation that a man had to earn 800 crowns a year to be a voter unleashed a pamphlet war: What if a man earned only 799 crowns? Did that make him less qualified? What if a man qualified one year but, through no fault of his own—for instance, because of a natural disaster—did not earn that much the following year? Should he then be barred from voting? In the 1880s Belgium saw a mass movement in favor of universal suffrage. The letters "SU," standing for universal suffrage in French, became emblematic of the masses' hope for a better life. Although suffrage still remained limited in these countries, it was only a matter of time before democracy would be achieved.

Summary

NOVEL configurations of power appeared on the West's chessboard in the period from about 1850 to 1880, as new or enlarged states were created through warfare or the threat of force. Liberal nationalists in the early nineteenth century had believed that Europe would be freer and more peaceful if each people had a separate nation, but they were now proved wrong. The Crimean War and its aftermath replaced the congress system, which had sought a balance of power among partners, with a system of rival states in pursuit of their own self-interests. The international order was severely shaken as Italy and Germany emerged from the center of Europe and as Romania and Bulgaria were carved out of the Ottoman Empire in the East.

Both new and existing states faced a choice between federalism and centralized rule. In the process of unification, Italy and Germany could have opted for a loose federal union, but both Piedmont and Prussia chose central control. In France the crushing of the Paris Commune spelled doom for those who wanted a nation of decentralized self-governing units. Indeed, strong, centralized governments increasingly became the norm. That was also the case across the ocean in the United States, where North and South fought the bloody Civil War over the issues of slavery and state sovereignty, and the victorious federal government imposed its will on the rebellious states. Canada became a large state, stretching across the continent, and acquired self-government.

To achieve legitimacy, however, governments had to appear to be enjoying the consent of their peoples. Hence all European rulers, except those of the Ottoman and Russian Empires, found it necessary to have a parliament. France, Britain, and several northern European states became increasingly democratic, answerable to a growing electorate. In other states, parliaments had only limited powers, but once they were in place, it could be argued—and was—that more power should be shifted to them and that they should be chosen by an expanded electorate. In the United States whites already enjoyed freer and more open institutions than existed elsewhere, and the post–Civil War era marked a further enlargement of political participation when African American men were granted the right to vote.

Two major changes that liberals had agitated for in 1848 had become a reality: freer political institutions and the organization of nation-states. Although neither of these changes was fully implemented everywhere, both appeared to have been generally established. Many Europeans could easily believe that they were living in an age of optimism.

■ Notes

1. Quoted in Otto Pflanze, *Bismarck and the Development of Germany*, vol. 1 (Princeton, N.J.: Princeton University Press, 1990), p. 184.
2. Quoted in William Flavelle Monypenny and George Earle Buckle, *The Life of Benjamin Disraeli: Earl of Beaconsfield*, vol. 2 (London: John Murray, 1929), pp. 473–474.

■ Suggested Reading

Alter, Peter. *The German Question and Europe: A History*. 2000. Explains the international context within which German unity was possible and its impact on European diplomacy.

Blackbourn, David. *The Long Nineteenth Century: A History of Germany, 1780–1918*. 1998. Particularly strong on the social aspects and consequences of German unification.

Gullickson, Gay. *Unruly Women of Paris*. 1996. Discusses the activities of women during the Paris Commune, the myths about them, and how others represented them.

Lewis, Bernard. *The Emergence of Modern Turkey*. 2001. The foremost historian on Turkey and the modern Middle East provides an important survey of the Ottoman Empire.

Lincoln, W. Bruce. *Great Reforms*. 1990. Shows the reforms to be part of a general program of modernization.

Matthew, Colin, ed. *The Nineteenth Century: The British Isles, 1815–1901*. 2000. An up-to-date collection of articles on major themes in British history.

 For a searchable list of additional readings for this chapter, go to college.hmco.com/students.

An Engraving of the British Royal Family

Why were Queen Victoria and her family depicted in the manner shown in this popular engraving? The illustration might well have been of an upper-middle-class family. Note the family's attire. The queen is plainly dressed; her husband, Prince Albert, wears a dark business suit; the children are clothed in simple outfits. The image extends from the royal family to the rest of England, depicted as a quaint farm, some cottages, and a grouping of common people. Notice the crown hovering over this idyllic scene. Victoria's reign was the longest of any British monarch; the manner in which she conducted herself and her subjects' image of her shaped the monarchy and people's expectations of it.

Illustrations of this type familiarized the British with their monarch. Surrounded by her husband and children, the queen seemed to have an endearing common touch. In the past, representations of the monarchy had suggested power and intimidation. The aura of the close-knit, nuclear royal family, not unlike the families of the queen's middle-class subjects, suggested a serenity that was reassuring to those subjects.

Victoria cultivated the image of herself as contented mother, but in reality she resented much about motherhood. She complained of the extent to which her pregnancies interfered with her daily routines, preventing her from traveling and from being with her beloved Albert as much as she would have liked. She described childbearing as an "annoyance" that made her feel "so pinned down—one's wings clipped." She also refused to romanticize birthing, seeing it as an animal-like act that reduced a woman to "a cow or a dog." Biology put women in an inauspicious position, she thought, and she lamented, "I think our sex a most unenviable one." Victoria continued to view her children, once they were no longer babies, as a burden, describing them as "an awful plague and anxiety for which they show one so little gratitude very often!" But such views were expressed strictly privately, and the public never suspected Victoria's ambivalence regarding her role as mother.

Whatever her complaints about children, Victoria's family life was in strong contrast to that of her predecessors, projecting a new image of the monarchy. Her grandfather George III (r. 1760–1820) had been plagued with bouts of insanity. Her uncle George IV (r. 1820–1830) was a notorious philanderer. George IV and his brothers, the duke of Clarence (later to be William IV [r. 1830–1837]) and the duke of Kent (Victoria's father), were bigamists. They fathered a large brood of illegitimate children and were implicated in numerous public scandals.

The character of Victoria's three predecessors and of the various other men in line to the throne had strengthened opposition to the monarchy. Public outrage at their excesses had led to a call for the abolition of the institution. When the 18-year-old Victoria came to the throne, it would have been difficult to imagine that she would on her death leave the monarchy considerably strengthened.

The image of Victoria shown here intentionally contrasts her reign with those of her predecessors. Victoria is surrounded by four of her children (eventually she would have nine). Her predecessors had died leaving no legitimate direct heirs and thus endangering the regular succession to the throne. The engraving announced that the royal line was assured. English people wary of a female ruler could find solace in knowing that Victoria would be succeeded by one of her sons. Later Victoria's children and their progeny would intermarry with the rest of Europe's royalty, and by the end of her reign most of Europe's crowned heads would be related to one another.

Although Victoria's uncles and father were wastrels and bankrupts, the queen and her husband lived frugally by royal standards and conducted an exemplary family life. Under the wise administration of Prince Albert, royal wealth increased, as he carefully administered various royal estates and investments. Instead of being subject to various debtors, the British royal house became one of the wealthiest landowners in Great Britain, achieving financial independence and winning social prestige. Among the large landowning magnates of Britain, the royal house became the most prominent.

The model royal family appealed to the growing middle class of Victorian society. Consider how the simple terms in which the monarch is depicted here and in many other illustrations reflect the increasingly democratic spirit of the era. The ruler and her family appear in a common scene. Victoria is queen, but she is also mother and wife. There is no sign here of pomp and ceremony.

Given the disrepute into which the monarchy had fallen and the rise of republican sentiment, the coming to the throne of a woman in 1837 may have substantially lessened antimonarchical sentiment. The last woman to

ILLUSTRATED BOOK OF BRITISH SONG.

THY CHOICEST GIFTS IN STORE ON HER BE PLEASED TO POUR.

GOD SAVE THE QUEEN.

rule England, Elizabeth I (r. 1558–1603), had been one of its greatest monarchs, who had provided stability and brought glory to her kingdom. As a young, seemingly frail woman coming to the throne, Victoria lent a certain gallantry to the royal household. Also, because of her gender, Victoria was seen as less of a threat to constitutional liberties.

Under Victoria's rule, Britain completed the process of becoming a constitutional monarchy. Although her predecessors had been openly partisan, the queen cultivated the image of being above party, a symbol of national unity and the state. Fellow monarchs in central and eastern Europe exercised greater power, but after World War I they were all toppled. In Britain, monarchy in its constitutional form endured. Victoria established a pattern of public and private behavior by which members of subsequent generations of the British royal family were to be judged.

www. **For additional information on this topic, go to college.hmco.com/students.**

CHAPTER 23

The Age of Optimism

1850–1880

THE first department store in Paris, which served as a model for others in France and abroad, *Le Bon Marché* (the "good buy") opened its doors in the 1850s. The store bought goods in mass quantities and thus could sell them at low prices. Constructed of glass and iron, Le Bon Marché represented the new, modern age. It combined under one roof a large range of products that previously had been available only in separate specialty shops—a timesaving convenience in an increasingly harried age. The store also had a large catalog sales department for customers too busy or distant to shop in person. Filled with toys, bed linens, furniture, crystal, and other items, the department store was a symbol of the new opulence of the middle classes.

This new type of store would not have been possible in an earlier age. It serves as a summary of the various technological and social changes that the more prosperous regions of the West experienced as industrialization advanced in the second half of the nineteenth century. Industrial innovation had lowered the price of glass and steel, so that these new, huge commercial emporiums could be built at reasonable cost. Railroads brought into the city large quantities of increasingly mass-produced goods, as well as out-of-town customers. In town, trams and omnibuses transported shoppers to the store. The penny press provided advertising for the department store, which in turn supported the emergence of this new medium. The expansion of the postal system facilitated catalog sales and the mailing of parcels

Felix Valloton, *Le Bon Marché.*
(Private Collection/Edimedia)

Industrial Growth and Acceleration

Changing Conditions Among Social Groups

Urban Problems and Solutions

Social and Political Initiatives

Culture in an Age of Optimism

to customers. And the higher incomes available to many people allowed them to purchase more than just the necessities. A phenomenon began that would become predominant in the West a century later—the consumer society.

As industrialization spread throughout western Europe, rising productivity brought greater wealth to more social groups and nations. This wealth not only led to more consumer spending but also contributed to a change in attitudes. The second half of the nineteenth century was an era shaped to a large extent by the growing middle classes, who were filled with optimism and convinced they were living in an age of progress. John Stuart Mill proclaimed that in his era "the general tendency is and will continue to be . . . one of improvement—a tendency towards a better and happier state." Across the Channel in France, the social thinker Auguste Comte° (1798–1857) concurred, confidently stating, "Human development brings . . . an ever growing amelioration." The successful application of science and technology to social problems gave many men and women confidence in the human ability to improve the world. People controlled their environments to a degree never before possible. On farms they increased the fertility of the soil; to the burgeoning cities they brought greater order. Scientists used new methods to study and combat disease. Public authorities founded schools, trained teachers, and reduced illiteracy. Transportation and communication rapidly improved.

In reality, not all of society benefited from the fruits of progress. The new wealth was far from equally shared. Eastern and southern Europe changed little, and even in the western regions a large part of the population still lived in great misery. If some cities carried out ambitious programs of urban renewal, others continued to neglect slums. Public sanitation programs did not affect the majority of Europeans who lived in rural areas. Despite spectacular advances in science, much of the population maintained a traditional belief in divine intervention. Many intellectuals strongly denounced the materialism and smugness of the age, stressing the meanness and ignorance that lay just beneath the surface.

Still, the tone of the age was set by the ascendant middle classes in western Europe, which embraced change and believed that the era was heading toward even more remarkable improvements. Their optimism was all the greater because the ultimate effects of the social and technological changes taking place in Europe were not yet known. Of the major processes that unfolded between 1850 and 1880, many were still in their infancy in 1880. What lay beyond the horizon would certainly be even more wonderful.

QUESTIONS TO CONSIDER

- What technological changes led to the expansion of the European economy after the mid-nineteenth century?

- How did the economic expansion affect the various social classes, and city versus rural areas, differently?

- In what ways did the state increasingly intervene in people's daily lives?

- How did Charles Darwin both reflect and shape the intellectual trends of his era?

TERMS TO KNOW

second industrial revolution	solidarism
bourgeois century	social Catholics
professionalization	positivism
Victorian morality	Darwinism
separate spheres	Social Darwinism
	impressionism

Auguste Comte (oh-GOOST KONT)

INDUSTRIAL GROWTH AND ACCELERATION

BEGINNING in the 1850s, western Europe experienced an unprecedented level of economic expansion. Manufacturers created new products and harnessed new sources of energy. An enlarged banking system provided more abundant credit to fund this expansion. Scientific research was systematically employed to improve methods of manufacture. A revolution in transportation speedily delivered goods and services to distant places. For many Europeans daily life was profoundly changed by technological innovations.

The "Second Industrial Revolution"

The interrelated cluster of economic changes that began in the generation after 1850 is often called the "second industrial revolution." It was characterized by a significant speedup in production and by the introduction of new materials such as mass-produced steel, synthetic dyes, and aluminum. Manufacturers replaced the traditional steam engine with stronger steam-powered turbines or with machines powered by new forms of energy—petroleum and electricity.

The invention of new products and methods of manufacture spurred this industrial expansion. The second half of the nineteenth century has often been called the "age of steel." Up to then, steel production had been limited by the expense involved in its manufacture, but in 1856 Sir Henry Bessemer (1813–1898) discovered a much cheaper method, which produced in twenty minutes the same amount of steel previously produced in twenty-four hours. Ten years later William Siemens° (1823–1883) in England and Pierre Martin (1824–1915) in France developed an even more efficient technique of steel production, the open-hearth process. The Thomas-Gilchrist method, invented in 1878, made possible the use of phosphor-laden iron ore, which previously had been economically unfeasible.

The results were dramatic. In Great Britain steel production increased fourfold, and the price of steel fell by more than 50 percent between the early 1870s and the following decade. Greater steel production made possible the expansion of the rail system, the creation of a steamship fleet, and an explosive growth in the building industry. No longer was steel a rare alloy used only for

Siemens (SEE-menz)

CHRONOLOGY	
1818	Gas streetlamps in London
1820s	Omnibuses introduced in France
1829	Stephenson runs the *Rocket*
1830	Lyell founds the principles of modern geology
1831	Faraday discovers electromagnetic induction
1833	Telegraph invented
1840	Penny stamp introduced
1848	England adopts first national health legislation
1850s	Age of clipper ships Trams added to public transportation systems
1851	Crystal Palace
1852–1870	Rebuilding of Paris
1859	Darwin, *On the Origin of Species*
1863	Europe's first underground railroad, in London
1864	Pope Pius IX issues *Syllabus of Errors*
1865	Transoceanic telegraph cable installed Lister initiates antiseptic surgery University of Zurich admits women
1869	Opening of Suez Canal Mendeleev produces periodic table of elements
1874	Impressionist exhibition
1875	Bell invents telephone Electric lights in Paris
1881	Pasteur proposes germ theory of disease
1891	Pope Leo XIII issues *Rerum novarum*

the finest swords and knives; it became the material that defined the age.

Significant changes in the supply of credit further stimulated economic expansion. Discovery of gold in California and Australia led to the inflow of huge

The Suez Canal Opened in 1869, the canal significantly shortened the voyage by ship from Europe to East Asia. The Suez Canal exemplified the speeding up of transportation and communication in the second half of the nineteenth century. *(akg-images)*

amounts of the precious metal to Europe, expanding the supply of money and credit. This led to the establishment of the modern banking system.

Each advance made possible additional changes. Increased wealth and credit accelerated further expansion of industrial plants and the financing of an ambitious infrastructure of roads, railroads, and steamships, which in turn boosted trade. Between 1800 and 1840 the value of world trade had doubled. In the twenty years following 1850, it increased by 260 percent.

By the 1880s important scientific discoveries fueled industrial improvements. Electricity began to be more widely used, replacing coal as a source of energy. Synthetic dyes revolutionized the textile industry, as did alkali in the manufacture of soap and glass. Dynamite, invented by the Swedish chemist Alfred Nobel° (1833–1896) in the 1860s, made it possible to level hills and blast tunnels through mountains, facilitating construction. Five years after Nobel's death, his will established a prestigious prize, named after its donor, to honor significant contributions to science and peace.

Nobel (no-BELL)

Transportation and Communication

The rail system grew dramatically in the middle decades of the nineteenth century. When the English engineer Robert Stephenson (1803–1859) demonstrated the feasibility of his steam locomotive, the *Rocket,* in 1829, it ran at 5 miles per hour on a track that was 1½ miles long. By 1880 total European railroad mileage was 102,000 (see Map 23.1). In 1888 the Orient Express line opened, linking Constantinople to Vienna and thus to the rest of Europe. Distance was conquered by speed as well. By midcentury trains ran 50 miles per hour, ten times as fast as when they were invented. The cost of rail transport steadily decreased, allowing for its greater use. Between 1850 and 1880 in Germany, the number of rail passengers increased tenfold and the volume of goods eightyfold. In France and Great Britain the increases were nearly as impressive.

Ocean transportation was also revolutionized. In 1869 the French built the Suez Canal across Egyptian territory, linking the Mediterranean to the Red Sea and the Indian Ocean. The canal reduced by 40 percent the thirty-five-day journey between London and Bombay. More efficient ships were developed. By midcentury the so-

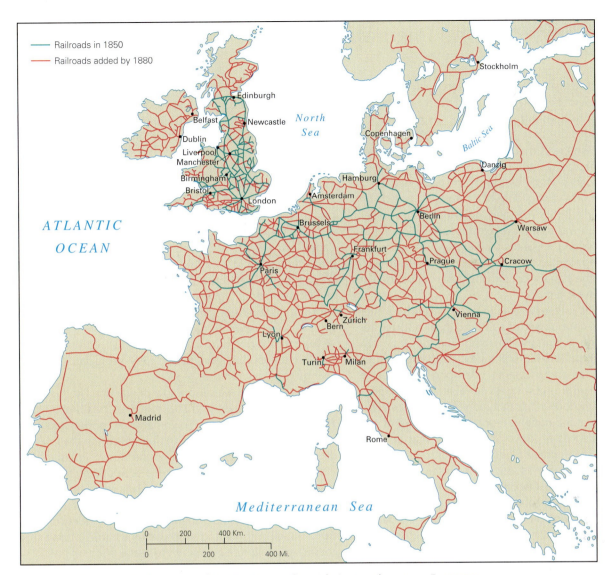

Map 23.1   European Rails, 1850 and 1880   During the mid-nineteenth century, European states built railroads at an increasing rate, creating a dense network by the 1880s.   *(Adapted from Norman J. G. Pounds, An Historical Geography of Europe, 1800–1914 [New York: Cambridge University Press, 1985]. Used by permission of the publisher.)*

called clipper ship could cross the Atlantic in fourteen days, half the previous length of time. Steamships also were built, although they did not dominate ocean traffic until the 1890s. By 1880 European shipping carried nearly three times the cargo it had thirty years earlier.

The optimism born of conquering vast distances was reflected in a popular novel by the French writer Jules Verne° (1828–1905), *Around the World in Eighty Days* (1873). The hero, Phineas Fogg, travels by balloon, llama,

and ostrich, as well as by the modern steam locomotive and steamship, to accomplish in eighty days a feat that, only thirty years earlier, would have taken at least eleven months. In 1889 the New York newspaper the *World,* in a publicity gambit to increase readership, sent its reporter Nellie Bly (1867–1922) on an around-the-world trip to see if she could beat Phineas Fogg's record. Readers breathlessly kept up with reports of her progress. She circled the globe in 72 days, 6 hours, 11 minutes, and 14 seconds. Such was the impact of the steamship, the locomotive, the Suez Canal—and the newspaper.

Jules Verne (DJOOL VAIRN)

The Telegraph

The telegraph radically altered the speed with which information could be collected and spread around the world. In 1793 two young Frenchmen, Claude Chappe (1763–1805) and his brother, Ignace (1760–1829), built a device with large wooden arms that, by their location, designated letters of the alphabet in a prearranged code. A lookout, equipped with a telescope and stationed on a tower mounted on a tall building or a hill, would take down the message and relay it to the next lookout, as far as 6 miles away. The system was called the *telegraph,* meaning "far or long-distance writing" in Greek. This system was cumbersome, depending as it did on the messengers' ability to read and retransmit the signals. It could obviously not be used at night or in bad weather.

The Chappes' invention was to be replaced by something that was more powerful and functional but that retained the name "telegraph." In the 1830s the American Samuel F. B. Morse (1791–1872) surmised that electricity could be used to send messages over long distances. In 1844, with funding from Congress, he built a line 40 miles long from Washington, D.C., to Baltimore. Morse sent electrical impulses in combinations representing letters of the alphabet—sequences of "dots" and "dashes" that became known as the Morse code. A clerk would transcribe the signals into the alphabetical letters they represented, spelling out a message, and have it delivered to the recipient.

In England two events popularized the telegraph, showing its benefits. In 1844, forty minutes after the palace announced that Queen Victoria had given birth to her second son, the *Times* was able to share the happy news with the nation. The following year a man named John Tawell murdered his mistress in Slough. Fleeing the police there, he boarded the train for London. Alerted by telegraph, the police in London arrested the murderer as he got off the train in Paddington Station. The utility of the telegraph had been convincingly demonstrated.

Telegraph wires were rapidly expanded. In the 1850s the telegraph in Britain crossed the English Channel. The following decade the telegraph spread across the North American continent and then connected it with Europe via the transatlantic cable. From a few dozen miles in the 1840s, telegraph lines extended 650,000 miles within thirty years, connecting twenty thousand towns and villages around the world.

Newspapers prided themselves on being "wired" and so able to give their readers the latest news. Many newspapers adopted names such as the *Daily Telegraph.* In the 1840s newspapers printed news from overseas that was at best outrageously outdated. In the *London Times* news from Cape Town, South Africa, was eight weeks old and from Brazil six weeks old. A couple of decades later, thanks to the telegraph, international news could be printed the next day.

Governments found the telegraph useful in collecting information and issuing orders to subordinates. Imperial authority over distant territories was better assured. In the 1840s it took ten weeks for a message and a reply to go from London to Bombay and back. Thirty years later the exchange took four minutes.

The telegraph was also a tool of warfare. The first conflict in which it played a crucial role was the Crimean War. The British and French high commands in London and Paris were able to communicate with their officers in the Crimea, directing operations from afar. In the Austro-Prussian War the Prussians directed their pincer attack leading to the victory at Sadowa by telegraph. Battle plans could be modified quickly as telegrams informed commanders of how the fighting was developing. The telegraph was widely used in the U.S. Civil War, helping shape many a battle. During that conflict six million telegrams were sent.

The most common early use of the telegraph was to coordinate railroads. Still in their infancy, most rail lines had single tracks, and collisions were frequent. Now stations could inform each other of a train's departure so that the managers could decide which train had the right of way and take appropriate precautions. The telegraph spread with the rail lines, usually built alongside them. Train travel became safer and faster, for with good communications between stations, trains could be more readily dispatched.

Along with the new speed, advances in refrigeration changed food transport. Formerly, refrigeration could be achieved only with natural ice, cut from frozen ponds and lakes, but this changed in the 1870s with the introduction of mechanical ice-making machines. By the 1880s dairy products and meat were being transported vast distances by rail and even across the seas by ship. Thanks to these advances, the surplus food of the Americas and Australia, rich in grasslands, could offer Europe a cheaper and far more varied diet.

Regular postal service was also a child of the new era of improved transportation. In 1840 Britain insti-

The Telegraph and War
Although the telegraph served mainly civilian purposes, it was repeatedly used in warfare after its invention in the 1840s, notably in the U.S. Civil War. Here linemen string wire for the Union army near Brandy Station, Virginia, in 1864. The belligerents used 16,000 miles of telegraph wire during the Civil War. *(National Archives, NWDNS-165-SP-62)*

Even so, railroads found it impossible to schedule trains traveling across large nations because each area had its own local time. The setting of a standard time was facilitated by the telegraph. At a given moment, a telegraphic message indicated the exact time to the second, and every town along the line was able to set its time accordingly.

Until the advent of the telegraph, it was difficult for merchants to know trade conditions in distant lands. With the new device, business people could collect market information, such as the cheapest price of commodities, and offer their wares competitively to potential buyers around the world. The telegraph brought instant information to merchants, allowing them to expand their markets and lower their costs, thus fostering the development of the consumer society.

Used by governments and businesses, the telegram also became a means for frequent and immediate communication between individuals. Lovers sent each other messages, parents proudly announced children's births, and people shared the sad news of a death in the family. Telegraph operators in the dead of night when there was no traffic on the wires would share jokes or play chess. With greater use, the cost of sending telegrams went down. By 1885 in Britain, a short message was priced at 6 pence, an amount within the reach of most people. Lower cost allowed for greater use. During the second half of the 1800s, the number of telegrams sent each year in Britain rose from 100,000 to over 90 million.

Along with the train and the steamship, the telegraph was one of the technological advances that conquered distances during the nineteenth century. Charles Dickens described the telegraph as "of all our modern wonders the most wonderful." Even more than improved transportation, it transformed the world into an instant, global village. As the governor of New York said at a commemorative event a generation after Samuel Morse's invention, "Men speak to one another now, though separated by the width of the earth, with lightning's speed and as if standing face to face."

tuted a postage system based on standard rates. Replacing the earlier practice in which the recipient paid for the delivery of a letter, the British system enabled the sender to buy a stamp—priced at just one penny—and drop the letter into a mailbox. It was collected, transported speedily by the new railroads, and delivered. The efficiency and low cost of mail led to a huge increase in use.

The post combined with transoceanic telegraphs and the invention of the telephone to transform the world of information. The telegraph was invented in the late 1830s, and by 1864, 80,000 miles of telegraph wire had been laid on the European continent. (See the feature "Information Technology: The Telegraph.") In 1875 the American inventor Alexander Graham Bell (1847–1922) invented a machine capable of transmitting the human voice by electrical impulses; in 1879 the first telephones were installed in Germany; two years later they appeared in France. At first a curiosity, used to listen to a musical or theatrical production at a distance, the phone began to be installed in homes for people to communicate with each other.

CHANGING CONDITIONS AMONG SOCIAL GROUPS

INDUSTRIAL advances transformed the traditional structure of European society. Fewer people worked the land; more worked in industry. The social and political influence of the landed aristocracy waned as wealth became far less dependent on property ownership. To varying degrees, this influence now had to be shared with the growing middle classes. Generally, life for both industrial and farm workers improved in this period. However, great disparities persisted, and many people continued to suffer from profound deprivation.

The Declining Aristocracy

Always a small, exclusive group, the European aristocracy in the nineteenth century represented less than 1 percent of the population. Many of those of noble birth were quite poor and economically indistinguishable from their non-noble neighbors. Others owned vast estates and were fabulously wealthy.

Some ennoblements were of recent origin. In England most titles were less than a hundred years old, having originally been conferred on individuals in recognition of service to the state, the arts, or the economy. In France both Napoleons had bestowed titles on persons they wished to honor. In Germany Chancellor Otto von Bismarck ennobled the Jewish banker Gerson Bleichröder° (1822–1893) for helping finance the wars of the Prussian state and for relieving the German chancellor of personal financial worries by making profitable investments for him. Distinctions between aristocrats and members of the upper middle class became increasingly

---

Bleichröder (BLY-shro-der)

blurred. Noble families in financial straits often married their children to the offspring of wealthy merchants. And many nobles who previously had shunned manufacture participated in the new economy by becoming industrialists and bankers. Idle members of the nobility were now somewhat rare. Although many aristocrats still enjoyed a lavish lifestyle, others had adopted the habits of successful business people.

Despite the theories of egalitarianism sweeping Europe in the aftermath of the French Revolution and the rapidly changing social structure engendered by industrialization, the power of the aristocracy did not disappear altogether. In Prussia some of the wealthiest industrialists came from the highest aristocracy. The heavily aristocratic officer corps played an important role in running the Prussian state and unified Germany. In France about 20 to 25 percent of officers and many diplomats were aristocrats. In Britain officers, diplomats, and high-ranking civil servants were usually of noble birth. In Austria and Russia, aristocratic origin was the norm for government service.

Nonetheless, nobles no longer asserted privileges based exclusively on birth. In most European states, such claims had become anachronisms.

The Expanding Middle Classes

Up to the eighteenth century, society had been divided into legally separate orders on the basis of birth. In the nineteenth century, it became more customary to classify people by their economic functions. The "middle class" belonged neither to the nobility nor to the peasantry nor to the industrial working class. It included such people as wealthy manufacturers, country physicians, and bank tellers. Given this diversity, it has become common to use the plural and think of all these people as forming the "middle classes." Another term frequently used to describe these people is *bourgeois*.

The nineteenth century has often been described as the "bourgeois century." Although such a label may be too broad, after the midcentury mark it is appropriate enough to use as a shorthand term to describe the dominance of the bourgeois elites. This situation was especially prevalent in western Europe, where the middle classes helped fashion much of society.

The middle classes expanded dramatically in the wake of industrialization. More trade and manufacture meant more entrepreneurs and managers, while the increasingly complex society called for more engineers, lawyers, accountants, and bankers. New standards of comfort and health demanded more merchants and doc-

Interior of a Danish Middle-Class Home   With its stuffed furniture, lace curtains and tablecloths, and gilt-edged framed paintings, this living room provided a comfortable and pleasing escape from the grimy exterior of the industrial city. *(National Museum of Denmark)*

meant a need for fewer additional laborers and more clerks and bureaucrats. Large import-export businesses, insurance companies, and department stores provided opportunities of this kind. So did the expansion of government services.

The social impact of job growth was great. The men and women staffing these new positions often came from modest backgrounds. For the son or daughter of peasants to become village postmaster, schoolteacher, or clerk in a major firm signified social ascension, however modest. And for the family such a position, even more than income, meant joining the lower stratum of the middle classes. Accessibility to its ranks was certainly one of the strengths of the bourgeoisie, an ever growing group whose promise of social respectability and material comfort exercised a compelling force of attraction over the lower classes.

A widening subgroup of the middle classes consisted of members of the professions, those whose prestige rested on the claim of exclusive expertise in a particular field. In the early nineteenth century, requirements for exercising a profession varied, depending on the country. In France and Prussia, for example, government regulation stipulated the necessary qualifications to practice medicine; in England only the Royal Colleges did. Medicine in the United States was unregulated by either government or medical schools. As the professions attempted to create a monopoly for themselves and eliminate rivals, they established stricter standards. Medical doctors, for instance, began requiring specialized education to distinguish themselves from herbalists, midwives, bonesetters, healers, and other competitors, and they insisted on their exclusive right to exercise their profession. The medical profession controlled access to its ranks by establishing powerful professional associations—for example, the British Medical Association (1832) and the German Medical Association (1872).

Although the professionalization of medicine did not create better doctors immediately, as the science of medicine taught at universities improved, so did the preparation and expertise of doctors. Similarly, in other professions, such as law, architecture, and engineering, common standards and requirements encouraged professional practice and expertise. By midcentury either professional associations or the state itself accredited members of the professions. Women had limited access to these professions; typically their opportunities were confined to lower teaching positions. After the Crimean War, as a result of Florence Nightingale's efforts (see page 743), nursing became an increasingly popular profession for women. Even so, the dominant culture generally

tors. Urban improvements in the generation after 1850 created a need for architects and contractors, among other professionals.

The middle and lower levels of middle-class society grew most rapidly as business, the professions, and government administration created more jobs. In the 1870s about 10 percent of urban working-class people reached lower-middle-class status by becoming storekeepers, lower civil servants, clerks, or salespeople. Faster growth occurred for white-collar workers than for their blue-collar counterparts. As industries matured, the increasing use of machinery and better industrial organization

opposed middle-class women's salaried employment outside the home.

The growing role of the state in society led to bureaucratic expansion. More and more, civil servants were selected by merit rather than through patronage. By the eighteenth century, Prussia had instituted a civil service examination system. After the Revolution, France instituted educational requirements for certain government corps, and by the 1880s it established civil service exams for all government positions. Beginning in 1870 Britain introduced the civil service examination and eliminated patronage.

Middle-Class Lifestyles

The standard of living of the growing middle classes varied considerably, from the wealthy entrepreneur who bought a château, or built one, to the bourgeois who dwelled in a modest apartment. But all lived in new standards of comfort. Their homes had running water, upholstered furniture, and enough space to provide separate sleeping and living quarters. They owned several changes of clothing and consumed a varied diet that included meat and dairy products, sugar, coffee, and tea. They read books and subscribed to newspapers and journals. Having at least one servant was a requisite for anyone who wished to be counted among the middle classes in the mid-nineteenth century.

By 1900 servants were still common among bourgeois households, but they were fewer in proportion to the population as a whole. As service industries developed, the need for servants decreased. With the growth of cab services, for instance, a family could dispense with a coachman and groom. Toward the end of the century, domestics' wages rose as competing forms of employment vied for their service, and households below the upper layers of the bourgeoisie found it difficult to afford domestic help.

In some areas suburban living became fashionable. The wealthy lived in large, imposing houses; those who were less well-off lived in smaller houses with a garden for privacy and quiet. Some people owned two homes—

The Crystal Palace   Built in 1851, this building was the largest glass and steel structure of its time. Site of the first great international exposition, the Crystal Palace displayed the inventiveness and opulence of the age.   *(Courtesy of the Trustees of the British Museum)*

one in the city and one in the countryside, providing a respite from the hectic urban environment.

For further relief from the crowded cities, visits to resorts became popular. Throughout Europe resort towns sprang up, devoted principally to the amusement of the well-off. It became fashionable to "take the waters"—to bathe in hot springs and drink the mineral waters thought to have special attributes—and to gamble in resorts such as Baden-Baden in Germany and Vichy in France. For the first time, tourism became big business. Thomas Cook (1808–1892), an Englishman, organized tours to the Crystal Palace exhibition of 1851 in London, the largest world exposition, which highlighted industrial accomplishments. Discovering the large market for guided travel, Cook began running tours in England and on the Continent. In the eighteenth century, the European tour had been a custom of the aristocracy, but now many men and even some women of the middle classes demanded this experience as well.

New wealth and leisure time led to more hotels, restaurants, and cafés. In 1869 Paris had 20,000 cafés and 4,000 hotels and lodging houses; the largest hotel offered 700 well-appointed rooms to discriminating guests. Vienna's National Hotel, with 300 rooms, had steam heat, spring water on every floor, and an icehouse providing cool drinks. For the traveler's convenience, many hotels, such as the monumental Charing Cross Hotel in London, were located next to train stations. At home or away, the bourgeoisie valued comfort.

The middle classes shared certain attitudes about the conduct of their lives. They believed their successes were due not to birth but to talent and effort. They wanted to be judged by their merits, and they expected their members to abide by strict moral principles. Their lives were supposed to be disciplined, especially with regard to sex and drink. The age was called "Victorian" because the middle classes in Britain saw in the queen who reigned for two-thirds of the century a reflection of their own values. (See the feature "Weighing the Evidence: An Engraving of the British Royal Family" on pages 772–773 in Chapter 22.) "Victorian morality," widely preached but not always practiced, was often viewed as hypocritical by social critics. Yet as the middle classes came to dominate society, their values became the social norms. Public drunkenness was discouraged, and anti-alcohol movements vigorously campaigned against drinking. Public festivals were regulated, making them more respectable and less rowdy.

In spite of their differences in education, wealth, and social standing, most of the bourgeoisie resembled one another in dress, habits of speech, and deportment.

Bourgeois men dressed somberly, in dark colors, avoiding any outward signs of luxury. Their clothing fit closely and lacked decoration—an adjustment to the machine age, in which elaborate dress hampered activity. It also reflected a conscious attempt to emphasize the frugal and achievement-oriented attitudes of the bourgeoisie in contrast to what was seen as the frivolous nobility.

Bourgeois conventions regarding women's dress were less reserved. Extravagant amounts of colorful fabrics used to fashion huge, beribboned hoop dresses reflected the newfound wealth of the middle classes and confirmed their view of women as ornaments whose lives were to be limited to the home and made easier by servants. The language and paraphernalia of idealized domesticity dominated this era. While the man was out in the secular world earning a living and advancing his career, the bourgeois woman was supposed to run her household, providing her family with an orderly, comfortable shelter from the storms of daily life. In 1861 Isabella Mary Mayson Beeton, a London housewife, published *Mrs. Beeton's Book of Household Management*, which in Britain was outsold only by the Bible. Her popular book provided British middle-class women with advice on running their households and reflected their values, fostering discipline, frugality, and cleanliness. The ideal woman decorated the rooms, changed the curtains with the seasons and styles, supervised the servants, kept the accounts, oversaw the children's homework and religious education, and involved herself in charitable works. In the decades around midcentury, the notion of two separate spheres—one male and public, the other female and private—reached its height.

In spite of the relatively passive role assigned to bourgeois women, many were very active. Some helped their husbands or fathers in the office, the business, or the writing of scientific treatises. Others achieved success on their own terms, running their own businesses, writing, painting, or teaching.

The expectation that middle-class women would be married and taken care of by their husbands led to the provision of inferior education for girls and young women. Even bright and intellectually curious young girls most often could not receive as good an education as their brothers, nor as a consequence could they pursue as interesting a career—a situation that had prevailed for centuries.

Various liberal movements in the nineteenth century insisted on legal equality among men, removing disabilities aimed at members of a particular social class or religion. Such discrimination, many had insisted, should also not be based on gender. Proponents of

Ladies' Bicycling Fashion   This new mode of transportation suggested possibilities for female emancipation. Free on her bicycle, the young woman is contrasted with the man, who rides only a tricycle.   *(From Karin Helm [ed.],* Rosinen aus der Gartenlaube *[Gutersloh: Signum Verlag, n.d.]. Reproduced with permission.)*

Telephone Operators in London   New technologies opened up new employment opportunities for women. Telephone operators formed a completely feminized profession.   *(Roger-Viollet/Getty Images)*

women's rights demanded equal access to education and the professions. Slowly, secondary and university education was made available to young women. On the European continent the University of Zurich was the first university to admit women, in 1865. Although British universities admitted women, the University of London did not grant them degrees until after 1878, and the most prestigious British institutions, Oxford and Cambridge, did not grant degrees to women until after World War I. (See the box "Reading Sources: Women Enter the University.") In spite of discriminatory laws, harassment by male students, and initial obstruction by professional and accrediting groups, a few female doctors and lawyers practiced in England by the 1870s and on the Continent in the following decades.

Women more easily penetrated the lower levels of middle-class occupations. Expanding school systems, civil services, and businesses provided new employment opportunities for women. By the 1890s two-thirds of pri-

mary school teachers in England and half the post office staff in France were women. By 1914 nearly half a million women worked as shop assistants in England. Some new technologies created jobs that became heavily feminized, such as the positions of typist and telephone operator.

The Workers' Lot

The increased prosperity and greater productivity of the period gradually improved the conditions of both female and male workers in the generation after 1850. Their wages and standards of living rose, and they enjoyed more job security. In Britain the earning power of the average worker rose by one-third between 1850 and 1875. For the first time, workers were able to put money aside to tide them over in hard times.

The workers' increased income permitted a better diet. In France the average number of calories consumed

WOMEN ENTER THE UNIVERSITY

Women's activism resulted in some advances in higher education for women. They were now able to get an education for their own independence and self-fulfillment rather than as preparation for motherhood. Louisa Lumsden (1840–1935) was among the first women to take the honors exams at Cambridge University, although she had to take them unofficially and apart from the male students, under the eye of a chaperone. She attended Hitchin College, which in 1869 became Girton College of Cambridge University, the first residential college for women. She passed her honors exams but could not receive her degree until after Cambridge started to award degrees to women in 1921. Emily Davies (1830–1921), who assisted Lumsden, pioneered university education for women, enabling them to take courses and examinations at Cambridge. Here Lumsden writes of resistance to women in higher education and of how they persevered.

We had one lecture every day which everybody attended, the length of this lecture being fixed neither by our capacities of taking in knowledge nor by the convenience of the lecturer, but by the hours of railway trains. . . . We had two Latin lectures a week, two mathematical, one English and one Divinity. . . .

This plain statement of the oddity of our lecture arrangements at Hitchin fitly introduces the great Tripos [honors] question. . . . I had studied a copy of the Cambridge Calendar . . . and I rose from this study with the settled determination to attempt the Classical Tripos. Gradually most of my fellow students formed similar resolutions. . . . But an unlooked for difficulty arose.

The committee [which governed Hitchin College] was displeased. I think the truth was that never having seen us students, they forgot that we were not mere schoolgirls, altogether destitute of culture. . . . To them we seemed simply ungrateful for the good things offered to us, careless of culture, mere imitators of men. It was difficult even for our lecturers to grasp our position. . . .

How well I remember the first morning [of the exams]. We settled down in our sitting-room, pen in hand, expectant of the [examination] paper, while Miss [Emily] Davies knitted away steadily by the fire. . . . But minute after minute slipped away and still, until a whole hour had gone by, no paper came.

Miss Davies said nothing, but she must have despaired, for she knew, though she had considerably hidden it from us, that some of the examiners were dead against admitting us to the examination at all. For my part I grew desperate—had the examiners at the eleventh hour refused the paper? When at last the messenger came, he had, it appeared, been sent first to a wrong address. My nerves were all in a quiver and work was almost impossible. . . . That morning was far the worst bit of the week. . . . There were certainly moments of depression when we sat on the bridge behind King's [College at Cambridge] and thought as we looked down upon the slowly sliding Cam [River] that, had the water not been so muddy, one plunge might have ended all! . . . The kindness of friends and two very pleasant dinner parties cheered us, however, and the ordeal came to an end at last. I was visiting friends when the news that we had passed came to Hitchin, so I cannot relate what happened there as an eyewitness. But I have been told that the students in their triumph climbed to the roof of "the College" and set the fire bell a-tolling, to proclaim the news to all the world, and that the good folks of Hitchin were properly amazed and no doubt disgusted by the noise.

Source: Louisa Lumsden, *Yellow Leaves: Memories of a Long Life* (William Blackwell and Sons, 1935). Edited and reprinted in Janet Murray, *Strong-Minded Women and Other Lost Voices from Nineteenth-Century England.* Copyright © 1982 by Janet Murray. Used by permission of Pantheon Books, a division of Random House, Inc.

 For additional information on this topic, go to college.hmco.com/students.

per adult male increased by one-third between 1840 and 1890. In Britain per capita consumption of tea tripled and that of sugar quadrupled between 1844 and 1876. The quality of food also improved, as people consumed more meat, fish, eggs, and dairy products.

Legislation gradually reduced the length of the workweek. The British workweek, typically 73 hours in the 1840s, was reduced to 56 hours in 1874. In France it was reduced to 10 hours a day, in Germany to 11. But these improvements were accompanied by an increased emphasis on efficiency in the workplace. Fewer informal breaks were allowed as industrialists insisted on greater worker productivity. New machines increased the tempo of work, frequently leading to exhaustion and accidents.

As workers had more time and money, their leisure patterns changed. Some leisure activities that previously had been limited to the upper classes became available to workers. The introduction of rail connections to resort towns such as Brighton in England or Trouville and Dieppe in France enabled workers to visit such places. New music and dance halls, popular theaters, and other forms of public entertainment sprang up to claim workers' increased spending money.

Although most workers believed that their lot had improved, they were also aware that a vast gulf remained between them and the middle and upper classes. In the 1880s in the northern French industrial city of Lille, the combined property of twenty thousand workers equaled the estate of one average industrialist. Life expectancies still varied dramatically according to income. In Bordeaux in 1853, the life expectancy of a male bourgeois was twenty years greater than that of a male laborer.

The disparity between rich and poor was especially striking in the case of domestics. Most servants were female, and they led tiring and restricted lives under the close supervision of their employers. Their hours were overly long, as they often worked six and a half days a week. Housed in either the basement or the attic, servants experienced extremes of cold, heat, and humidity. Sometimes they were subjected to physical or sexual abuse by the master of the house, his sons, or the head of the domestic staff. And yet, for impoverished rural women with little chance of finding better work, domestic service was a risky but often necessary option. It provided free housing, food, and clothing and sometimes allowed a servant to save an annual sum equivalent to an amount between one-third and one-half of a worker's yearly wages. These savings often served as a dowry and could enable a young woman to make an advantageous marriage. Two out of five female wage earners in England were in domestic employment in 1851.

Although a few members of the working class managed to enter the lower levels of the middle classes, most remained mired in the same occupations as their grandparents. Poverty was still pervasive. In the 1880s about one-third of Londoners were living at or below the subsistence level. Industrial and urban diseases, such as tuberculosis, were common among workers. Compared with the healthier, better-fed, and better-housed middle classes, the workers continued living in shabby and limited circumstances.

The Transformation of the Countryside

Before the nineteenth century, the countryside had hardly changed at all, but beginning at midcentury it was radically transformed. Especially in western Europe, an increasing number of people left the land. In 1850, 20 percent of the people in Britain were agricultural workers; by 1881 only 11 percent were. The decrease of the agricultural population led in many places to labor shortages and therefore higher wages for farm hands.

Agriculture became increasingly efficient, and the food supply grew significantly. More land was put under the plow. Not only was more land cultivated, but the yield per acre increased. In 1760 an agricultural worker in England could feed himself and one other person; by 1841 he could feed himself and 2.7 others. The population of Europe nearly doubled between 1800 and 1880, and yet it was nourished better than ever before.

Higher yields were the result of an increased use of manure, augmented in the 1870s by saltpeter imported from Chile and, beginning in the 1880s, by chemical fertilizers manufactured in Europe. Innovations in tools also improved productivity. The sickle, which required the laborer to crouch to cut grass or wheat, was replaced by the long-handled scythe, which allowed the field hand to stand and use the full weight of the body to swing the instrument through the grain. This new method increased efficiency fourfold. In the 1850s steam-driven threshing machinery was introduced in some parts of western Europe. Organizational techniques borrowed from industrial labor, including specialization and regular schedules, also contributed to greater productivity on the land.

Improved roads and dramatically expanded rail lines enabled farmers to extend their markets. No longer did they need to produce only for the local area; they could depend on a national market and beyond for customers.

While the prices of farm products rose, those of industrial products fell, allowing farmers to purchase ma-

Steam-Powered Thresher   This image shows the thresher being operated in the French countryside in 1860. It would be decades before this kind of technology became a common sight in Europe, but it was a harbinger of the change coming to the rural world.   *(Bibliothèque nationale de France)*

chinery to work the land as well as items providing personal convenience, such as cast-iron stoves. Owners of medium and large farms did particularly well. For the first time, many qualified for credit, and the availability of fire and weather insurance buffered some from the unpredictability of farming.

Life in the countryside became less insular. Not only did rail lines connect farms to cities, but national school systems brought teachers into the villages. Local dialects, and in some cases even distinct languages that peasants had spoken for generations, were replaced by a standardized national language. Local provincial costumes became less common as styles fashionable in the cities spread to the countryside via mail order catalogs. The farm girls who went to the cities as maids to work in middle-class homes returned to their villages with urban and middle-class ideals. The military draft brought the young men of the village into contact with urban folk and further spread urban values to the countryside.

Even so, the rural world remained very distinct from urban society. Many of the forces seen as contributing to modernity actually aggravated rural conditions. The expansion of manufacturing in cities contributed to the decline of cottage industry in rural areas, where agricultural workers had relied on the putting-out system to provide supplementary income. Thus farmworkers were idle during slack seasons, and rural unemployment grew. In many cases railroads bringing goods made elsewhere wiped out some of the local markets on which these cottage industries had depended. The steamship lowered the cost of transporting freight, including grain from distant Canada and Argentina, which often undersold wheat grown in Europe. The resultant crisis, worsened by a rural population explosion, led to the emigration of millions, who left the land for towns and cities or even migrated across the seas to the Americas and Australia (see page 820). Although this process was painful for large segments of the rural population, the situation eventually improved for those who were able to remain on the land.

These trends had a striking effect in the rural areas of western Europe. Eastern Europe, in contrast, was hardly touched by them. In Russia agriculture remained backward; the average yield per acre in 1880 was one-quarter that in Great Britain. The land sheltered a large surplus population that was underemployed and contributed little to the rural economy. In the Balkans, most peasants were landless and heavily indebted.

URBAN PROBLEMS AND SOLUTIONS

B Y 1851 the majority of English people lived in cities; by 1891 the majority of Germans did as well. To cope with urban growth and its attendant problems—epidemics, crowding, traffic jams—cities developed public health measures and introduced plan-

ning and rebuilding programs. They adapted the new technologies to provide such urban amenities as streetlights, public transportation, and water and sewer systems, and they established large, more efficient police forces. Cities gradually became safer and more pleasant places to live, although for a long time city dwellers continued to suffer high mortality rates.

City Planning and Urban Renovation

Most of Europe's cities had begun as medieval walled cities and had grown haphazardly into major industrial

Pissarro: L'avenue de l'Opéra, Sunlight, Winter Morning   Camille Pissarro, one of the leading impressionists, portrayed the broad new Parisian avenue designed by Baron Haussmann. The avenue leads to the new opera, in the background, also planned during the Second Empire.   *(Musée Saint-Denis, Reims/Giraudon/Art Resource, NY)*

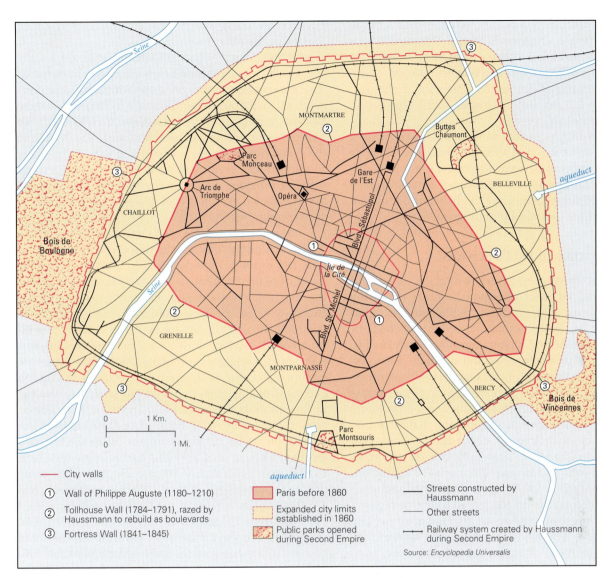

Map 23.2   Haussmann's Paris, 1850–1870   During the reign of Napoleon III, Baron Georges Haussmann reshaped the city of Paris, replacing its narrow medieval streets with a system of broad avenues and public parks and encircling the city with a railway.

centers. Their narrow, crooked streets could not accommodate the increased trade and daily movement of goods and people, and traffic snarls were common. City officials began to recognize that broad, straight avenues would help relieve the congestion and also bring sunlight and fresh air into the narrow and perpetually dank lanes and alleys. In the 1820s London saw the first ambitious street-widening initiative. On Regency Street old hovels were torn down and replaced with fancy new houses; the poor were displaced. Later projects followed this pattern. (See the feature "Weighing the Evidence: The Modern City and Photography" on pages 806–807.)

The most extensive program of urban rebuilding took place in midcentury Paris. Over a period of eighteen years Napoleon III and his aide Baron Georges Haussmann (1809–1891) transformed Paris from a dirty medieval city to a beautiful modern one (see Map 23.2). Haussmann and his engineers carved broad, straight avenues through what had been overcrowded areas. They built elegant apartment houses on the new tree-lined avenues. Public monuments and buildings, such as the new opera house, enhanced the city. The tremendous costs of this ambitious scheme kept Paris in debt for decades. In addition, the urban renewal program drove tens of thousands of the poorest Parisians to the outskirts of the city, leading to greater social segregation than had previously existed.

Haussmann's extensive work in Paris served as a model for other cities, and although none was rebuilt as extensively, many underwent significant improvements. The cities of Europe began to display an expansive grace and sense of order, supporting the belief of the middle classes that theirs was an age of progress.

The Introduction of Public Services

Beginning at midcentury, government at the central and local levels helped make cities more livable by legislating sanitary reforms and providing public transportation and lighting. Medical practitioners in the 1820s had observed that disease and higher mortality were related to dirt and lack of clean air, water, and sunshine. Since diseases spreading from the poorer quarters of town threatened the rich and powerful, there was a general interest in improving public health by clearing slums, broadening streets, and supplying clean air and water to the cities.

Reform began in England, where the lawyer and civil servant Edwin Chadwick (1800–1895) drafted important plans for reform that became the basis for legislation. The Public Health Bill of 1848 established national standards for urban sanitation and required cities to regulate the installation of sewers and the disposal of refuse. The 1875 Health Act mandated certain basic health standards for water and drainage. Armed with these laws, cities and towns took the initiative: Birmingham cleared 50 acres of slums in the 1870s, for example.

London was also a leader in supplying public water, a service later adopted by Paris and many other cities. Berlin had a municipal water system in 1850, but it would be several decades before clean water was available in every household. As late as the 1870s, Berlin's sewage was carried in open pipes. In Paris, which typically led France in innovations, 60 percent of the houses had running water in 1882. The French capital did not have a unitary sewer system until the 1890s, however.

As running water in the home became a standard rather than a luxury, bathing became more common. The English upper classes had learned the habit of daily baths from their colonial experience in India; on the Continent it did not become the custom until about the third quarter of the nineteenth century. The French artist

Edgar Degas° (1834–1917) frequently painted bath scenes, portraying the new European habit.

All these changes had a direct impact on the lives of city dwellers. Life became healthier, more comfortable, and more orderly. Between the 1840s and 1880, London's death rate fell from 26 per thousand to 20 per thousand. In Paris during the same period, the decline was from 29.3 per thousand to 23.7 per thousand. The decline in the incidence of diseases associated with filthy living conditions was even more immediate. Improved water supplies provided a cleaner environment and reduced the prevalence of waterborne diseases such as cholera and typhoid.

Other improvements also contributed to a better quality of life. With the introduction of urban transportation, city dwellers no longer had to live within walking distance of their workplaces. An early example of public transportation was the French omnibus service of the 1820s—a system of horse-drawn carriages available to the public on fixed routes. In the 1850s the tram was introduced. A carriage drawn on a rail line by horses, a tram could pull larger loads of passengers faster than the omnibus. Because of the many rail stations in London and the difficulty of getting from one station to another in time to make a connection, London built an underground railway in 1863, the predecessor of the subway system. Technological improvements made the bicycle a serious means of transportation for some city dwellers. By the mid-1880s nearly 100,000 bicycles were being pedaled around Great Britain. A decade later there were 375,000 bicycles in France, and by 1900 1 million.

Improvements in public transportation and urban renewal projects led workers to move out of the inner city and into the less dense and less expensive suburbs. This trend in turn led to a decrease in urban population density and eventually helped make the city a healthier place to live.

Gaslights also improved city life, making it easier and safer to be outside at night. (Prior to gaslights, city dwellers depended mainly on moonlight or, rarely, expensive and time-consuming oil lamps—which had to be lit one at a time.) In 1813 London was the first city to be illuminated by gas; Berlin followed in 1816. Electrical lights were introduced in Paris in 1875, although they were not common until the end of the century.

Cities also significantly expanded police forces to impose order, control criminal activity, and discourage behavior deemed undesirable, such as dumping garbage on the street, relieving oneself in public, and carousing

---

Degas (Duh-GAH)

late at night. In 1850 London was the best-policed city in Europe, with a 5,000-man force. Paris had around 3,000 police officers.

SOCIAL AND POLITICAL INITIATIVES

SEVERAL institutions and groups emerged to tackle the unequal distribution of wealth and critical urban problems that followed in the wake of economic growth. The state intervened in the economy in new ways. Private charitable groups, which had existed for decades, continued to administer to a few of the poor, and new charities developed. Socialist political parties, exclusively dedicated to improving the workers' lot, gained in numbers and strength.

State Intervention in Welfare

The difficult conditions industry imposed on workers led to debates in several countries about the need for the state to protect the workers. The growing militancy of organized labor also forced the established authority to consider ways to meet the workers' needs. While some rejected government intervention in the free operation of market forces, others argued that the laws of supply and demand had caused the exploitation of many who ought to have been protected—especially very young children and pregnant women. Britain led the way with the Factory Acts, regulating child and female labor. Similar acts were passed later in Prussia and France. In much of Europe, however, the state did little to improve the welfare of the working class. In eastern Europe, where industry was still in its infancy, workers had no protection.

Fear of social upheaval, a desire to prevent depopulation, and the rising strength of socialist political parties prompted some governments to act. In France moderate bourgeois liberals attempted to defuse class war by advocating "solidarism." With the motto "Every man, his neighbor's debtor," solidarism insisted on the mutual responsibility of classes and individuals for one another's well-being. Guided by such sentiments, French republicans passed a number of laws toward the end of the century that improved the lot of the working class, especially women and children. In newly unified Germany, the government wanted to impress workers with state benefits so they would abandon the growing Socialist Party and back the kaiser's authoritarian government. Chancellor Otto von Bismarck embarked on a deliberate program to tame the workers and win their support for the existing political and economic institutions. Thus in the 1880s the new German government provided a comprehensive welfare plan that included health insurance and old-age pensions. In addition to the welfare initiatives by state and city governments, the middle and upper classes also worked to better the workers' lot. Concern among these groups and individuals arose from a mixture of pity for workers' conditions, religious teachings about their responsibilities for the less fortunate, and fear of the consequences of unrelieved misery.

Women engaged in charity and social reform. In Sweden by the 1880s, women had founded refuges for the destitute, old-age homes, a children's hospital, an asylum for the mentally handicapped, and various societies to promote female industry. By the end of the nineteenth century, as many as half a million English women contributed their time to provide for the less fortunate, either in charities or in trying to enact social legislation. Among them was Josephine Grey Butler (1828–1906), who fought for the education of impoverished women.

Josephine Grey Butler   An important Victorian reformer, Butler agitated for several causes, most notably abolition of the Contagious Diseases Acts. These acts empowered the police to arrest any woman it suspected of prostitution and to force her to be examined for venereal disease. Largely as a result of Butler's efforts, these acts were repealed in 1886. *(Fawcett Library/Mary Evans Picture Library)*

Annie Besant Argues for the Right of Free Discussion

Speaking on behalf of the poor in her 1877 trial for publishing a pamphlet on birth control, Annie Wood Besant (1847–1933) decries a lack of open discussion on social subjects. Although politicians and reformers had often discussed social subjects, they had usually framed them in moral terms. Besant, and others in England and on the Continent, sought to recast the social question into one they could address both through social reform and by providing information to the poor. This excerpt is Besant's response to the prosecution's charge that the dissemination of information about birth control was obscene. Besant focused her defense on "the right to public discussion by means of publication." At issue was freedom of expression on birth control, which fit into the larger debates about freedom to disseminate information, the right to open discussion, and freedom to present differences of opinion—ideas that have occupied the minds of many.

Do you, gentlemen, think for one moment that myself and my co-defendant are fighting the simple question of the sale or publication of this sixpenny volume . . . ? No, it is nothing of the sort; we have a much larger interest at stake, and one of vital interest to the public, one which we shall spend our whole lives in trying to uphold. The question really is one of the right to public discussion by means of publication. . . . I sell it so long as the detective police spies and secret agents of a society calling itself a Vice Society resort to the practices that they do to get respectable booksellers into trouble; so long as that goes on, so long shall we endeavour to uphold those principles which we maintain with reference to the right of public discussion, by fighting this great battle until we win ultimate success.

This pamphlet is valuable to us just as is the piece of silk to the soldier who wins the battle for his country; it is the flag which represents the cause we have at stake. It is with that feeling—and that feeling alone—that we stand here today to uphold the right to publish this pamphlet, and I fight that I may make here the right of open and free discussion on a great and important social subject. There are various rights of speech which the public enjoy. The right of discussion in theology is won; the right of publicly discussing politics is won, but as to discussion on social subjects, there is at present no right. . . . If your verdict is in our favour, . . . you may depend upon it, that verdict once given no one will ever go against it; everyone will then feel free to discuss a point of vital interest to society; but till that verdict, that right is not one which can be exercised with impunity. . . .

Difference of opinion is not to be taken as proof of obscenity against any particular subject. . . . I want you, by your verdict, to lay down this great and just principle—that opinion, honestly given opinion, honestly expressed opinion, freely and fairly published, shall not be prevented public expression because a police officer does not agree with the opinion so expressed upon matters in which probably he is not at all informed.

I have in my hand the opinion of Mr. John Stuart Mill, in which he treats of the right of free discussion; he says, in his *Essay on Liberty:* "If all mankind, minus one, were of one opinion, and only one person were of the contrary opinion, mankind would be no more justified in silencing that one person than he, if he had the power, would be justified in silencing mankind."

QUESTIONS

1. Why was the right of free expression on the issue of birth control so problematic? When public authorities prohibit the dissemination of birth control information and prevent public expression of such ideas, does that indicate state regulation of people's private lives?

2. Do you agree that there was free discussion of religious and political issues but not of social subjects? How might you account for the different treatment of different subjects?

3. What might Besant have hoped to gain by invoking John Stuart Mill? Why is the right of free discussion important in a liberal, democratic society?

SOURCE: Annie Besant, "Defense of Dr. Knowlton's *The Fruits of Philosophy,*" in *Sharing the State: Biography and Gender in Western Civilization,* ed. Jane Slaughter and Melissa K. Bokovoy, pp. 179–180. Copyright © 2003 by Houghton Mifflin Company. Used by permission.

She also waged a fierce battle against the harsh laws directed against prostitutes. Annie Wood Besant (1847–1933) became an active social reformer on behalf of the poor. Arguing that poor women suffered from excessive childbearing and that their children died too often because of their poverty, she and Charles Bradlaugh (1833–1891) republished a pamphlet that contained information on birth control. British authorities called the publication pornographic and brought Besant and Bradlaugh to trial in 1877. After being found guilty, Bradlaugh and Besant won the case on appeal. In 1888 Besant turned her attention to protecting the health of young women workers, and in 1893 she went to India to establish schools for girls, educate widows, and agitate for Indian home rule. (See the box "The Continuing Experiment: Annie Besant Argues for the Right of Free Discussion.")

In Catholic and Protestant countries, the Christian churches traditionally had identified with the rights of employers and seemed to ignore the lot of the workers. However, a number of Christians, lay and clerical, began to emphasize the church's need to address social issues. Pope Leo XIII (r. 1878–1903) reflected this trend and reinforced it among Catholics when in 1891 he issued his encyclical *Rerum novarum* (Of New Things), which defined the moral responsibility of Christians for the well-being of the poor. He declared, "Rich men and masters should remember this—that to exercise pressure for the sake of gain upon the indigent and the destitute and to make one's profit out of the need of another is condemned by all laws, human and divine." His message was taken up in France, Italy, and Spain among what became known as "social Catholics." In England Protestants' concern for the poor was evidenced by the founding of the Salvation Army in 1878. Religious groups also hoped they could win converts among the less privileged by alleviating their plight.

Increasingly, municipalities, volunteer groups, and churches accepted responsibility for the well-being of others. Among their many activities, private charitable groups furnished cheap housing for the poor; church groups visited them, providing advice and some material assistance; and municipalities opened free medical dispensaries. In many cases these pioneering efforts in aiding the poor were later taken over by the state, which, in amplified form, led to the development of the welfare state in much of twentieth-century Europe.

Educational and Cultural Opportunities

At the beginning of the nineteenth century, governments took little responsibility for providing education. Some upper-class children were educated with private tutors, and others attended elite schools. All schools were segregated by social class, and all but the very few existing charity schools for the poor charged tuition. In England the education of the masses became a national responsibility after the Second Reform Bill of 1867. This legislation extended the vote to the artisan classes and prompted a movement to ensure that the new voters were educated. In 1870 the English government began to provide significant subsidies for education, to set educational standards, and to establish a national inspection system to enforce them. England and France initiated mandatory primary school education in the 1880s for boys and girls.

Public education included not only reading, writing, and arithmetic but other skills as well. By insisting on punctuality and obliging students to carry out repetitive tasks such as copying letters, words, or sentences, schools encouraged people to fit into the emerging industrial society. The obedience and respect for authority learned at school shaped the soldiers and factory workers of the future. And regardless of political inclination, each regime took advantage of its control of the educational system to inculcate in the young the love of country and of its form of government.

Secondary education was, on the whole, available only to the privileged few in the upper middle classes. It confirmed their social status and won them access to the universities and the professions. For a very small number from the lower middle classes, secondary school attendance provided the means to ascend socially. The lower middle class was sparsely represented in universities, and the children of workers and peasants were totally absent.

Public education spread from the schools to other institutions, which made culture available to the masses in new ways. Between 1840 and 1880 the number of large libraries in Europe increased from forty to five hundred. The French national public library, the *Bibliothèque nationale,* was established in Paris in the 1860s. This iron and glass building, radical for its time, was an impressive monument to the desire to make reading available to an expanded public. Many provincial cities, as well as the glittering capitals of Europe, were endowed with new libraries. Less grandiose, but probably more important for mostly rural populations, were the traveling libraries.

Museums and art galleries, which in the previous century had been open to only a select few, gradually became accessible to the general public. The first museum to open to the public was the Louvre in Paris after the French Revolution. Other European countries lagged behind in making their cultural heritages available to the masses, but even the poorer classes gained access to these temples of culture by the late nineteenth century.

Culture in an Age of Optimism

THE improving economic and material conditions of the second half of the nineteenth century buoyed European thinkers. Many believed that men and women were becoming more enlightened, and they expressed faith in humankind's ability to transform the world with a parade of scientific and technological breakthroughs. The world seemed knowable and perfectible. This faith advanced secularism while it undermined the certainties of traditional religion. The arts reflected these new values, emphasizing realism and science—as well as an underlying foreboding about the dark side of this "age of optimism."

Darwin and Evolution

By midcentury most thinkers accepted the notion of the change and transformation of society—and, by analogy, of the natural environment. The French thinker Auguste Comte championed the notion that human development—human history—proceeded through distinct and irreversible stages. Human progress, inscribed in the laws of nature, leads inexorably upward to the final and highest stage of development, the positive—or scientific—stage. Widely read throughout Europe and Latin America, Comte's writings helped bolster the era's faith in science, and the very progress science made seemed to confirm its precepts. Comte's philosophy, known as "positivism," dominated the era. Whereas the romantics had emphasized feeling, the positivists upheld the significance of the measurable, the palpable, the verifiable. Scientific methods, the positivists were confident, would ensure the continued progress of humanity.

In the field of geology the Englishman Charles Lyell (1797–1875) maintained that the earth was far older than the biblical story of Genesis suggested. He argued that its geological formations—the mountains, valleys, and seas—were subject to natural forces that, over hundreds of thousands, even millions, of years, had shaped them. Most educated people accepted his theory, which led many to wonder if it might also be true that the animal kingdom had evolved gradually over long periods of time.

Although evolution in the biological realm had been suggested as early as the end of the eighteenth century, Charles Darwin (1809–1882) was the first to offer a plau-

Charles Darwin, Proponent of Evolution   This portrait was made in 1840, when the young scientist was wrestling with the meaning of the evidence he had collected in the Galápagos Islands. His observations there became the basis for *On the Origin of Species by Means of Natural Selection* (1859), the most important scientific work of the nineteenth century. *(Down House/The Bridgeman Art Library)*

sible explanation of the process. As the naturalist on an official British scientific expedition in the 1830s, he had visited the Galápagos Islands off the western coast of South America. On these islands he found species similar to but different from those on the mainland, and even different from one another. Could they be the results of separate creations? Or was it more likely that in varying environments they had adapted differently? Darwin proposed that closely related species compete for food and living space. In this struggle, those in each species that are better adapted to the environment have the advantage over the others and hence are more likely to survive. In the "struggle for existence," only the fittest endure.

READING SOURCES

DARWIN'S BASIC LAWS OF EVOLUTION

Writing in an age of vast transformations, Darwin could imagine the mutability of all nature, including species, over time. And like his contemporaries, he could imagine that evolution would lead to improvement, to increasing "perfection" of various species. A religious man who lost much of his faith as a result of his scientific investigations, Darwin was anxious to reassure Christians, hence his attempt to portray evolution as part of God's divine plan.

Nothing at first can appear more difficult to believe than that the more complex organs and instincts have been perfected, not by means superior to, though analogous with, human reason, but by the accumulation of innumerable slight variations, each good for the individual possessor. Nevertheless, this difficulty, though appearing to our imagination insuperably great, cannot be considered real if we admit the following propositions, namely, that all parts of the organisation and instincts offer, at least, individual differences—that there is a struggle for existence leading to the preservation of profitable deviations of structure or instinct—and, lastly, that gradations in the state of perfection of each organ may have existed, each good of its kind. The truth of these propositions cannot, I think, be disputed. . . .

As geology plainly proclaims that each land has undergone great physical changes, we might have expected to find that organic beings have varied under nature, in the same way as they have varied under domestication. And if there has been any variability under nature, it would be an unaccountable fact if natural selection had not come into play. . . .

There is grandeur in this view of life, with its several powers, having been originally breathed by the Creator into a few forms or into one; and that, whilst this planet has gone cycling on according to the fixed law of gravity, from so simple a beginning endless forms most beautiful and most wonderful have been, and are being evolved.

Source: Charles Darwin, *On the Origin of Species by Means of Natural Selection*, 6th ed., vol. 2 (1872; repr., New York: Appleton, 1923), pp. 267–268, 279, 305–306.

Those surviving, Darwin surmised, pass on the positive traits to their offspring. He called the mechanism that explained the evolution and development of new species "natural selection," a process that he proposed was imperceptible but continuous. (See the box "Reading Sources: Darwin's Basic Laws of Evolution.")

Darwin's theory of the inevitability of evolution in nature echoes the era's confidence in change and its conviction that the present represented a more developed stage of the past. His work was seen as confirming the notion that societies—like species—were preordained to evolve toward progressively higher stages. Darwin at first avoided the question of whether human beings, too, are affected by the laws of evolution. To do so would be to question humanity's uniqueness, its separation from the rest of creation by its possession (in the Christian view) of a soul. But in *The Descent of Man* (1871), Darwin did confront this issue, clearly stating his belief that humanity, too, is subject to these natural laws. The recognition that human beings are members of the animal kingdom like other species disturbed him, and the admission, he wrote, "is like confessing a murder." Nonetheless, for Darwin scientific evidence took precedence over all other considerations.

Many Christians were shocked by these assertions, and some denounced the new scientific findings. Some argued that science and faith belonged to two different worlds. Others claimed that there was no reason why God could not have created the world through natural forces. In the long run, however, Darwinism seemed to undermine the certainties of religious orthodoxies by showing their incompatibility with scientific discovery.

Some contemporaries applied Darwin's theories to human society. Social Darwinists argued that human societies evolve in the same way as plants and animals. Just as species, so some human societies—races, classes, nations—are destined to survive, while others are condemned to fade away. And from these harsh laws, a better humanity will evolve. The British social theorist Herbert Spencer (1820–1903), who coined the expression "survival of the fittest," believed that society should be established in such a way that the strongest and most resourceful will survive. The weak, poor, and improvident are not worthy of survival, and if the state helps them survive—for instance, by providing welfare—it will only perpetuate the unfit. Poverty is a sign of biological inferiority, wealth a sign of success in the struggle for survival. In Europe and the United States (where Spencer was extremely popular, selling hundreds of thousands of books), Social Darwinism was thus used to justify callousness toward the poor at home and imperial conquest abroad. Since in the colonizing game the white races were the subjugators of Africans and Asians and not vice versa, whites were clearly superior, argued Social Darwinists. People of color were seen as inferior, poorly endowed to compete in the race for survival (see Chapter 24).

Physics, Chemistry, and Medicine

Dramatic scientific breakthroughs occurred in the nineteenth century, confirming the prevalent belief that human beings could understand and control nature. Since the seventeenth century, scientists had attempted to study nature by careful observation, by seeking regularities in nature, and by developing theories to explain what they had observed. Scientific truths had their own rules, independent of the investigator, who had to remain impartial and objective. The scientific method yielded major breakthroughs in the nineteenth century. In physics, laws regarding electricity and magnetism were articulated by Michael Faraday (1791–1867) and James Clerk Maxwell (1831–1879) in the 1830s and 1850s, respectively. Their work established the field of electrical science. In the 1840s Hermann von Helmholtz (1821–1894) in Germany and James Joule (1818–1889) in Great Britain defined the nature of energy in the laws of thermodynamics. In chemistry, new elements were discovered almost every year, and individual findings contributed to the understanding of larger patterns. In 1869 Russian chemist Dmitri Mendeleev° (1834–1907) developed the periodic table, in which the elements are arranged by their atomic weight. He left blank spaces for elements still unknown but that he was confident existed. Within ten years, three of these elements were discovered, affirming the belief that scientific knowledge not only can be experimentally tested but also has predictive value. Such triumphs further enhanced science's prestige.

Mendeleev (men-del-LAY-ef)

Prolific research yielded discoveries in one field of knowledge that could be transferred to another. For example, chemists produced new color dyes, enabling biologists to stain slides of microorganisms and better study their evolution. Scientific breakthroughs also led to technical achievements. For instance, inventions in chemistry led to the development of the first artificial fertilizers in 1842, while in physics the discovery of electromagnetism formed the basis of the telegraph and later the commercial uses of electricity.

Science also became increasingly specialized. In the eighteenth century, the scientist had been a learned amateur practicing a hobby. In the nineteenth century, as the state and industry became more involved in promoting scientific research, the scientist became a professional employed by a university, a hospital, or some other institution. New theories and discoveries were disseminated by scientific journals and at meetings of scientific associations and congresses. Around midcentury a number of important breakthroughs occurred in medicine. Before the development of anesthesia, surgical intervention was limited. With only alcohol to dull the patient's pain, even the swiftest surgeons could perform only modest surgical procedures. In the 1840s, however, the introduction of ether and then chloroform allowed people to undergo more extensive surgery. It also was used to relieve pain in more routine procedures and in childbirth; Queen Victoria asked for chloroform when in labor.

Increasingly, the experimental method in science was applied to medicine, and as a result physicians became concerned not simply with treating diseases but with discovering their origins. Louis Pasteur (1822–1895) achieved notable breakthroughs when he discovered that microbes, small organisms invisible to the naked eye, cause various diseases. Pasteur found that heating milk to a certain temperature kills disease-carrying organisms. This process, called pasteurization, reduced the incidence of certain diseases that were particularly harmful to children. Pasteur initiated other advances as well in the prevention of disease. Vaccination against smallpox had started in England in the eighteenth century, but Pasteur invented vaccines for other diseases and was able to explain the process by which the body, inoculated with a weak form of bacilli, developed antibodies that successfully overcame more serious infections. In England the surgeon Joseph Lister (1827–1912) developed an effective disinfectant, carbolic acid, to kill the germs that cause gangrene and other infections in surgical patients. Lister's development of germ-free procedures transformed the science of surgery. By reducing the patient's risk, more ambitious surgery could be attempted. Eventually midwives and doctors, by washing their hands and sterilizing their instruments, began to reduce the incidence of the puerperal, or "childbed," fever that killed so many women after childbirth. The increasingly scientific base of medicine and its visible success in combating disease improved its reputation.

Science was now fashionable. In 1869 Empress Eugénie in France had Louis Pasteur come to tea, draw blood from her finger, and examine it under a microscope, all to the astonishment of her guests. Some frogs, brought in for experimentation, escaped down palace corridors. The spectacle of science as the chic entertainment of an empress was a reminder of the increasing authority it commanded in the later nineteenth century.

Birth of the Social Sciences

The scientific method, so dramatically effective in uncovering the mysteries of nature, was also applied to the human enterprise. Just as the secrets of nature were unlocked, the workings of society, it was thought, could be understood in a scientific manner.

No field in the human sciences flourished as much in the nineteenth century as history. In an era undergoing vast transformations, many people became interested in change over time. They were eager to employ the methods of the scientist to explore their past. The father of modern historical writing is the German Leopold von Ranke° (1795–1886). Departing from the tradition of earlier historians, who explained the past as the ongoing fulfillment of an overarching purpose—divine will, the liberation of humanity, or some other goal—Ranke insisted that the role of the historian was to "show how things actually were." Like a scientist, the historian must be objective and dispassionate. By viewing humankind of all eras and environments on their own terms, and not those of others, historians could arrive at a better understanding of humanity.

This perspective transformed the study of history into a discipline with recognizable common standards of evidence. Historians studied and interpreted original (or "primary") sources; they collected and published their findings; they founded professional organizations and published major journals.

Other social sciences also developed in this period. Anthropology, the comparative study of people in different societies, had been the subject of speculative literature for hundreds of years. Increased contacts with

non-European societies in the nineteenth century—the effect of burgeoning trade, exploration, and missionary activities—stimulated anthropological curiosity. In 1844 the Society of Ethnology was founded in Paris, followed by the Anthropological Society (1859). London, Berlin, and Vienna quickly followed suit, establishing similar societies in the 1860s. Consisting of medical doctors, biologists, and travelers, these societies speculated on the causes of the perceived differences among human races, mainly attributing the variations to their physical structures. Anthropologists gave apparent "scientific" backing to the era's racism, explaining that non-Europeans were condemned to an existence inferior to the white races.

In Britain the main anthropological theorist was Edward Tylor (1832–1917), the son of a brass manufacturer. Through his travels Tylor came into contact with non-European peoples, who aroused his curiosity. Strongly influenced by the evolutionary doctrines of his day, Tylor believed that the various societies of humankind were subject to discoverable scientific laws. Tylor posited that if one could travel back in time, one would find humankind increasingly unsophisticated. So, too, the farther one traveled from Europe, the more primitive humankind became. The contemporary African was at a level of development similar to that of Europeans in an earlier era.

Tylor was not technically a racist, since he argued that the conditions of non-Europeans were not due to biology but rather were a function of their institutions. Eventually they would "evolve" and become akin to Europeans. Like racists, however, evolutionists believed in the superiority of the European over other races. Anthropology gave "scientific" sanction to the idea of a single European people, sharing either a similar biological structure or a common stage of social development, which distinguished them from non-Europeans.

Anthropology gradually gained recognition and legitimacy as a profession. In 1872 in France, Paul Broca founded a journal devoted to physical anthropology. In 1876 he founded a school of anthropology with six chaired professors. In 1884 Tylor—who was so closely identified with anthropology it was called "Mr. Tylor's science"—was appointed to the first university chair in anthropology in Britain.

The term *sociology* was coined by Auguste Comte. A number of ambitious thinkers, among them the English "social philosopher" Herbert Spencer (see page 797), had considered how individuals are affected by the society in which they live. In the 1840s various social reformers published detailed statistical investigations revealing

---

von Ranke (fon RANG-key)

relationships between, for instance, income and disease and death rates. A few decades later the theoretical principles underlying sociology were spelled out. Among the first researchers to do so was Emile Durkheim° (1858–1917), who insisted that sociology was a verifiable science. He occupied the first chair of sociology at a French university in 1887. A few years later he founded a journal of sociology and mentored a corps of disciples who ensured the success of sociology as a professionalized discipline.

Whereas in the past history, anthropology, and sociology were the purview of amateurs, now professional historians, anthropologists, and sociologists were engaged full-time in research and teaching at universities or research institutes. The professionalization that had occurred in medicine and physics also transformed the social sciences. Professionalization and specialization led to significant advances in several disciplines, but it also led to the fragmentation and compartmentalization of knowledge. People of broad learning and expertise became far less common.

The Challenge to Religion

The scientific claims of the era seemed to clash with the traditions of religion. A number of scientists, including Darwin himself, found their Christian faith undermined by theories on evolution. Although most Europeans continued to be strongly influenced by traditional religious beliefs, they appeared less confident than in earlier eras.

After the revolutions of 1848, religion was seen as a bulwark of order. In France Napoleon III gave the Catholic Church new powers over education, and the bourgeoisie flocked to worship. In Spain moderates who had been anticlerical (opposed to the clergy) began to support the church, and in 1851 they signed a concordat (an agreement with the papacy) declaring Roman Catholicism "the only religion of the Spanish nation." In Austria in 1855, the state surrendered powers it had acquired in the 1780s, returning to bishops full control over the clergy, the seminaries, and the administration of marriage laws.

In 1848 the papacy had been nearly overthrown by revolution, and in 1860 it lost most of its domains to Italy. Thus Pope Pius IX became a sworn enemy of liberalism, and in 1864, in the *Syllabus of Errors,* he condemned a long list of perceived errors, among them "progress," "liberalism," and "modern civilization." To establish full control over the clergy and believers, the Lateran Council

in 1870 issued the controversial doctrine of papal infallibility, declaring that the pope, when speaking officially on matters of faith and morals, was incapable of error. This doctrine became a target of anticlerical opinion.

The political alliance the Catholic Church struck with reactionary forces meant that when new political groups came to power, they moved against the church. In Italy, since the church had discouraged national unification, conflict raged between the church and the new state. In Germany Catholics had either held on to their regional loyalties or favored unification under Austrian auspices. When Protestant Prussia unified Germany, Chancellor Bismarck viewed the Catholics with suspicion as unpatriotic and launched a campaign against them, the *Kulturkampf°* ("cultural struggle"). Bismarck expelled the Jesuits and attempted to establish state control over the Catholic schools and appointment of bishops. Not satisfied, he seized church property and imprisoned or exiled eighteen hundred priests.

In France the republicans, who finally won the upper hand over the monarchists in 1879, bitterly resented the church's support of the monarchist party. They were also strongly influenced by Comte's ideas of positivism, believing that France would not be a free country until the power of the church was diminished and its nonscientific or antiscientific disposition was overcome. The republican regime reduced the role of the church in education as well as some other clerical privileges.

Greater religious tolerance, or perhaps indifference to religion in general, led to more acceptance of religious diversity. In 1854 and 1871 England opened university admission and teaching posts at all universities to non-Anglicans. Anti-Catholicism, at times a popular and virulent movement, declined in the 1870s. In France, too, the position of religious minorities improved. Some of the highest officials of the Second Empire were Protestants, as were some early leaders of the Third Republic and some important business leaders and scientists.

Legal emancipation of Jews, started in France in 1791, subsequently spread to the rest of the Continent. England removed restrictions on Jews when the House of Commons, in 1858, and the House of Lords, the following decade, allowed Jews to hold parliamentary seats. In the 1860s Germany and Austria-Hungary granted Jews the rights of citizenship. Social discrimination continued, however, and Jews were not accepted as social equals in most of European society. Although some Jews occupied high office in France and Italy, they had to convert before they could aspire to such positions in Ger-

---

Durkheim (DIRK-hime)

Kulturkampf (KOOL-toor-kampf)

many and Austria-Hungary. In other fields access was easier. Some of the major European banking houses were founded by Jews—the Rothschilds in France, Britain, and Germany, and the Warburgs in Germany, for instance.

In the expanding economy of western Europe, where the condition of most people was improving, the enhanced opportunity of a previously despised minority aroused relatively little attention. In other parts of Europe, Jews were not so fortunate. When they seized economic opportunities in eastern Europe and moved into commerce, industry, and the professions, they were resented. Outbreaks of violence against them, called *pogroms,* occurred in Bucharest, the capital of Romania, in 1866 and in the Russian seaport of Odessa in 1871. Although economic rivalries may have fueled anti-Jewish feelings, they do not completely explain it. In most cases anti-Jewish sentiment occurred in the areas of Europe least exposed to liberal ideas of human equality and human rights.

The emphasis on science and reason transformed religion in the nineteenth century, but as the continued anti-Semitism demonstrates, it by no means always led to increased tolerance or weakened religious fervor. On the contrary, in certain cases religiosity grew. French people reported frequent sightings of the Virgin Mary. In 1858 a shepherd girl claimed to have seen and spoken with her at Lourdes°, which became an especially important shrine whose waters were reputed to heal the lame and the sick. In 1872 construction of a rail line allowed 100,000 people a year to visit the town.

Church attendance continued to be high, especially in rural areas. In England villagers usually attended church, many twice or more each Sunday. Children dutifully attended Sunday schools. Advances in printing made it possible to distribute large quantities of inexpensive religious tracts to a sizable and avid readership. The faithful eagerly funded proselytizing, sending large numbers of missionaries into all corners of the globe.

Culture in the Age of Material Change

The era's admiration of technology and science and its idolization of progress were reflected in the arts. Some artists optimistically believed they could more accurately portray reality by adopting the methods of the scientist, coolly depicting their subjects. A minority, however, were disillusioned by the materialism of the age and warned against its loss of values.

Photography had a direct impact on painting. Various experiments in the late eighteenth century, plus the inventions of the Frenchman Louis Daguerre° (1789–1851), made the camera relatively usable by the 1830s. It was still a large, cumbersome object, however, until the dry plate and the miniature camera were introduced in the 1870s. Twenty years later, with the invention of celluloid film, the camera came into wide use, the best-known mass-produced version being the Kodak camera invented by the American George Eastman (1854–1932). Unlike painting and sculpture, photography was affordable for the public. Photographic services were in high demand; by the 1860s, thirty thousand people in Paris made a living from photography and allied fields. Many Europeans became amateur photographers—Queen Victoria and Prince Albert had a darkroom at Windsor Castle. (See "Weighing the Evidence: The Modern City and Photography.")

The ability of photography to depict a scene with exactitude had a significant impact on art. On the one hand, it encouraged many artists to be true to reality, to reproduce on the canvas a visual image akin to that of a photograph. On the other hand, some artists felt that such realism was no longer necessary in their sphere. However, the great majority of the public, which now had wide access to museum exhibitions, was accustomed to photographic accuracy and desired art that was representative and intelligible. Realistic works of art met this need, at least superficially.

Discarding myths and symbols, many artists portrayed the world as it actually was, or at least as it appeared to them—a world without illusions, everyday life in all its grimness. The realist painter Gustave Courbet° (1819–1877) proclaimed himself "without ideals and without religion." His fellow Frenchman Jean-François Millet° (1814–1875) held a similar opinion. Instead of romanticizing peasants in the manner of earlier artists, he painted the harsh physical conditions under which they labored yet still made the peasants sufficiently presentable so the middle classes could hang the paintings in their living rooms. In England the so-called pre-Raphaelites took as their model the painters of Renaissance Italy prior to Raphael, who presumably had depicted the realistic simplicity of nature. In painting historical scenes, these artists emphasized meticulous research of the landscape, architecture, fauna, and costumes of their subjects. To paint the Dead Sea in *The Scapegoat,* the English artist Holman Hunt (1827–1910)

Lourdes (LOORD)

Daguerre (dah-GAIR) **Courbet** (koor-BAY)
Millet (mil-LAY)

Courbet: The Stone Breakers   This realistic 1849 painting depicts the rough existence of manual laborers. The bleakness of the subject matter and the style in which it was carried out characterized much of the realist school of art.   *(Staatliche Kunstsammulungen, Dresden/The Bridgeman Art Library)*

traveled all the way to Palestine to guarantee an accurate portrayal of the site.

In the past artists had been concerned about composition and perspective. But under the influence of photography, they began to paint incomplete, off-center pictures. *Orchestra of the Paris Opera* by the French artist Edgar Degas looks as if it has been cropped, with only half a musician showing on each edge and the top half of the ballet dancers missing.

On April 15, 1874, six French artists—Edgar Degas (1834–1917), Claude Monet° (1840–1926), Camille Pissarro (1830–1903), Auguste Renoir° (1840–1919), Alfred Sisley (1839–1899), and Berthe Morisot° (1841–1895)—opened an exhibition in Paris that a critic disparagingly called "impressionist," after the title of one of Monet's paintings, *Impression: Sunrise.* The impressionists were

influenced by new theories of physics that claimed images were transmitted to the brain as small light particles that the brain then reconstituted. The impressionists wanted their paintings to capture what things looked like before they had been "distorted" by the brain. Impressionist painters ceased painting in their studios and increasingly went outdoors to paint objects exactly as they looked when light hit them at a certain angle. Monet, for example, emphasized outdoor painting and the need for spontaneity—for reproducing subjects without preconceptions about how earlier artists had depicted them—and seeking to show exactly how the colors and shapes struck the eye. Monet was particularly interested in creating multiple paintings of the same scene—from different viewpoints, under different weather conditions, at different times of day—to underscore that no single "correct" depiction could possibly capture a subject.

The school of realism also influenced literature, especially the novel. In realist novels, life was not glorified

Monet (moh-NAY)   Renoir (ren-WOIR)
Morisot (mor-ee-SO)

READING
SOURCES   # EMILE ZOLA ON THE NOVELIST AS SCIENTIST

Emile Zola believed that the novelist should act like a scientist, experimenting with characters' reactions to different circumstances in order to determine the laws that govern thought and emotion. Zola wanted to be the literary equivalent of the great French scientist Claude Bernard (1813–1878), one of the founders of experimental science. The title of this essay, "The Experimental Novel," published in 1880, echoes the title of Bernard's Introduction to Experimental Medicine *(1865).*

Here you have scientific progress. In the last century, a more exact application of the experimental method creates chemistry and physics which free themselves from the irrational and the supernatural. Profound studies lead to the discovery that there are established laws; phenomena are mastered. Then a fresh step is taken. Living bodies, in which the vitalists still admitted a mysterious influence, are in their turn reduced to the general mechanism of matter.

Science proves that the conditions of life of all phenomena are the same in matter and in living bodies; hence, physiology gradually acquires the same certitude as chemistry and physics. But will we stop at that? Evidently not.

When we have proved that the body of man is a machine, which we shall one day be able to take to pieces and put together again at the experimenter's will, then it will be time to pass on to the sentimental and intellectual activities of man. This means that we should enter a realm which, until now, belonged wholly to philosophy and literature; it will be the decisive victory of science over the hypotheses of philosophers and writers. We already have experimental chemistry and physics; we are going to have experimental physiology; and then, later, we shall have the experimental novel. This is a necessary progression, and one whose end can easily be foreseen today. Everything is related, one had to start from the determinism of matter to arrive at the determinism of living bodies. . . . The same determinism must rule the stones in the roadway and the brains of man. . . .

It follows that science already enters our domain— the domain of writers like us, who are at the moment the students of man in his private and social activities. By our observations, by our experiments, we carry forward the work of the physiologist who had continued that of physicists and chemists.

Source: *Movements, Currents, Trends: Aspects of European Thought in the Nineteenth and Twentieth Centuries,* ed. Eugen Weber. Copyright © 1992 by D. C. Heath and Company. Reprinted by permission of Houghton Mifflin Company.

or infused with mythical elements; the stark existence of daily life was seen as a suitable subject. Charles Dickens (1812–1870), who came from a poor background and had personally experienced the inhumanity of the London underworld, wrote novels depicting the lot of the poor with humor and sympathy. The appalling social conditions he described helped educate his large middle-class audience on the state of the poor. He also provided numerous examples of individuals who by hard work were able to rise above their circumstances. In fact, the income from Dickens's many novels provided him with a comfortable income; by the pen he was able to join the middle class himself.

Another realist, the French novelist Gustave Flaubert° (1821–1880), consciously debunked the romanti-

cism of his elders. His famous novel, *Madame Bovary°,* describes middle-class life as bleak, boring, and meaningless. The heroine seeks to escape the narrow confines of provincial life by adulterous and disastrous affairs.

Emile Zola (1840–1902), another Frenchman, belonged to the naturalist school of literature. The writer, he declared, should be like a surgeon or chemist, providing a scientific cause and record of human behavior. His work, in Zola's words, is similar to "the analysis that surgeons make on cadavers." (See the box "Reading Sources: Emile Zola on the Novelist as Scientist.") Zola's Rougon-Macquart° series, which includes the novels *Nana* and *Germinal,* describes in detail the experience of several generations of a family. His major theme is the impact of

Flaubert (flo-BEAR)

Bovary (bo-vah-REE)
Rougon-Macquart (roo-ZHON–mah-KAR)

A Chinese Official's Views of European Material Progress

Educated in European universities, Ku Hung-Ming rose to become a high official in the Chinese court. His essays were penned under the impact of the European military intervention in China during the Boxer Rebellion in 1900. Ku denounced European notions of superiority over Asia, arguing that material progress is an inappropriate measure of a civilization's value.

In order to estimate the value of a civilization, it seems to me, the question we must finally ask is not what great cities, what magnificent houses, what fine roads it has built and is able to build; what beautiful and comfortable furniture, what clever and useful implements, tools and instruments it has made and is able to make; no, not even what institutions, what arts and sciences it has invested: the question we must ask, in order to estimate the value of a civilization,—is, what type of humanity, what kind of men and women it has been able to produce. In fact, the man and woman,—the type of human beings—which a civilization produces, it is this which shows the essence, the personality, so to speak, the soul of that civilization. Now if the men and women of a civilization show the essence, the personality and soul of that civilization, the language which the men and women in that civilization speak, shows the essence, the personality, the soul of the men and women of that civilization. . . .

To Europeans, and especially to unthinking practical Englishmen, who are accustomed to take what modern political economists call "the standard of living" as the test of the moral culture of or civilization of a people, the actual life of the Chinese and of the people of the East at the present day, will no doubt appear very sordid and undesirable. But the standard of living by itself is not a proper test of the civilization of a people. The standard of living in America at the present day, is, I believe, much higher than it is in Germany. But although the son of an American millionaire, who regards the simple and comparatively low standard of living among the professors of a German University, may doubt the value of the education in such a University, yet no educated man, I believe, who has travelled in both countries, will admit that the Germans are a less civilized people than the Americans.

QUESTIONS

1. How does the Chinese official define civilization? How does his view differ from the European view?

2. What is Ku Hung-Ming's idea of a hierarchy of civilization?

3. According to the ideas in this reading, what is the connection between progress and civilization?

SOURCE: Ku Hung-Ming, *The Spirit of the Chinese People*, 2d ed. (Beijing: Commercial Press, 1922), pp. 1, 144–145.

---

environment and heredity on his characters' lives of degradation and vice, in which they seem locked in a Darwinian struggle for survival: some are doomed by the laws of biology to succeed, others to succumb.

The Russian novelist Leo Tolstoy (1828–1910) brought a new perspective to the historical novel in *War and Peace*. Instead of a heroic approach to battle, he showed individuals trapped by forces beyond their control. Small and insignificant events as well as major ones seemed to govern human destiny. Another Russian novelist often associated with the realist school, Feodor Dostoyevsky (1821–1881), aimed to portray realistically the psychological dimensions of his characters in novels such as *Crime and Punishment* (1866), *The Idiot* (1868), and *The Brothers Karamazov* (1879–1880).

In music realism was less evident. Johannes Brahms (1833–1897), though not sympathetic to some of the romantic composers, himself wrote music that evoked folk themes, such as his *Hungarian Dances* or his *Love Songs*, just as the romantics had done. The major musician whose work might be labeled as paralleling the realist movement in the other arts is the Russian Modest Mussorgsky (1839–1881), whose music was consciously realistic. Mussorgsky attempted to capture the accents of natural speech, gestures, and the sound of crowds in piano pieces such as *Pictures at an Exhibition* and the opera *Boris Godunov*.

Although this era generally celebrated material progress, a number of intellectuals reacted against it. They were alarmed by the prospect of the popular masses achieving political power through winning the vote and by mass production and consumption. They denounced the smug and the self-satisfied, who saw happiness in acquisition and consumption. Some condemned the age in severe terms. Dostoyevsky railed against the materialism and egotism of the West, branding its civilization as driven by "trade, shipping, markets, factories." In Britain— the nation that seemed to embody progress—the historian Thomas Carlyle (1795–1881) berated his age as one not of progress but of selfishness. He saw parliamentarism as a sham, and he called for a strong leader to save the nation from endless debates and compromises. Unlike most of his contemporaries, who saw in material plenty a sign of progress, Carlyle saw the era as one of decline, bereft of spiritual values.

Another Englishman, John Ruskin (1819–1900), looked back to the Middle Ages as an ideal era in human history. People then did not produce with machines but exercised a fine sense of craftsmanship. People then supposedly had a better sense of community and labored for the common good. Ruskin was one of the founders of the arts and crafts movement, which aimed to produce goods for daily use with an eye for beauty and originality. "Industry without art is brutality," Ruskin warned.

In France republicans saw in the ostentation of the Second Empire a sign of depravity and decline. Defeat in war in 1870 and the outbreak of the Paris Commune contributed to the mood of pessimism among many intellectuals. Flaubert detested his own age, seeing it as petty and mean. The characters in Zola's Rougon-Macquart novels slide steadily downward as each generation's mental faculties, social positions, and morals degenerate. Some people abroad also were unimpressed with developments in Europe. (See the box "Global Encounters: A Chinese Official's Views of European Material Progress.")

Not all were optimistic in this age of optimism. If many people celebrated what they viewed as an age of progress, others claimed that under the outer trappings of material comfort lay a frightening ignorance of aesthetic, moral, and spiritual values.

Summary

DURING the second half of the nineteenth century, advances in industry created for many Westerners an era of material plenty, providing more riches and comforts to a larger population than ever before. This self-confident age believed in progress and anticipated further improvements in its material and intellectual environment. It appeared to be an age of unbounded optimism.

Economic changes transformed the class structure of many European countries, and middle-class values and tastes defined the second half of the century. The new wealth and technologies led to improvements in both the countryside and the cities; in both, life became more comfortable and safer. Governments provided new services, such as public education, cultural facilities, and expanded welfare services.

The material changes in society were reflected in intellectual currents. Change and evolution were embraced as an explanation for the origin of species. A new confidence in scientific research led to many scientific and technological breakthroughs. Novelists and painters aimed to dissect like scientists the world around them, adopting realism in the arts. Some intellectuals, however, were repulsed by the crass self-satisfaction of the bourgeoisie, and they despised their age's worship of industry and materialism.

Progress, as Europeans were to learn in a later era, was two-edged: the very forces that improved life for many also threatened it. The same breakthroughs in chemistry that led to the development of artificial fertilizers also provided more powerful military explosives. The expansion of education and the reduction of illiteracy meant an end to ignorance but also the creation of a public that could more easily absorb messages of hate against a rival nation or against religious or ethnic minorities at home. Material progress and well-being continued, but there were new forces in the shadows that would ultimately undermine the comforts, self-assurance, and peace of this age.

■ Suggested Reading

Auerbach, Jeffrey A. *The Great Exhibition of 1851*. 1999. Brings alive this international exposition.

Cannadine, David. *The Rise and Fall of Class in Britain*. 1999. Reveals the importance of class in nineteenth-century British society.

Clark, Linda L. *The Rise of Professional Women in France*. 2000. A fine study delineating the increasing role of women in the professions, especially public administration.

Goodman, David, and Colin Chant, eds. *European Cities and Technology Reader*. 1999. Emphasizes the importance of technological breakthroughs in the modernization of cities.

Hobsbawm, Eric J. *The Age of Capital, 1848–1875*. 1979. Particularly strong on social and economic developments.

Nord, Philip. *Impressionists and Politics*. 2000. Sets the French impressionists in their political and social contexts.

Standage, Tom. *The Victorian Internet*. 1998. A brief, popular history of the telegraph.

 For a searchable list of additional readings for this chapter, go to college.hmco.com/students.

The Modern City and Photography

This photo of Piccadilly Square in Manchester was taken in 1886. It documents the modernization of the nineteenth-century city and at the same time conveys the sense of immediacy that a new means of representation, the photograph, provided.

Manchester in the nineteenth century became a wealthy textile city, manufacturing and marketing textiles to the rest of Britain and the world. The first rail lines in Britain were built in Manchester; by 1840 six rail lines connected it to the rest of the kingdom. The city grew dramatically, from 43,000 in 1774 to 271,000 in 1831. By 1900 it had reached the 600,000 mark.

Piccadilly, the commercial center of Manchester, had warehouses and offices where buyers purchased textiles that they would in turn sell to retail consumers. Fancy stores were also located here, and in some cases elegant dwellings were situated in the upper floors. Piccadilly was a large open square allowing for the easy movement of pedestrians and wagons. City planners in the nineteenth century created squares and broad, straight avenues, such as those gracing Piccadilly, by tearing down old slums and narrow alleys. These broad avenues eased the flow of traffic and admitted fresh air and sunlight, which diminished exposure to killer diseases such as cholera and tuberculosis.

As it grew, Manchester needed public transportation to move people quickly on the broad new avenues. Notice the rails for the horse-drawn tramways. Horse-drawn carriages called omnibuses, which had been introduced in the 1820s, were the first means of mass transportation within the city. Trams ran on rails that reduced friction and allowed a horse to pull a far greater load. In this case the tram, located in the center of the photo, is a double-decker.

An industrial town, Manchester was not a particularly pleasant city to live in. Visitors complained of its grime, pollution, and foul smells. Many members of the commercial classes lived in wealthy suburbs and commuted by tram to work in the center. Sometime after this picture was taken, the horse-drawn tram was replaced by the electrical tram, which could transport more people faster than its predecessor. Its lower cost also meant that it was accessible even to most workers. With the advent of the electrical tram, workers also began to move to the suburbs, making the center less crowded.

The large modern city required ease of communication at night as well as in the daytime. Street lighting provided that convenience, as well as making the streets more secure by discouraging crime. Streetlamps became the norm in large cities, especially in the better neighborhoods. The elegant gaslights that adorn the square were replaced a few years later by electrical ones that were cheaper to operate and allowed for the spread of city lighting. In lighting, public transport, police, sanitation, and other municipal services, it was quite common to discriminate in favor of the richer neighborhoods while neglecting the poorer ones. The latter were usually the last to be served. By the 1880s, when the franchise was enlarged, municipalities became more sensitive to the needs of new voters of every class. In Manchester, as in many British cities, public services such as lighting, water supplies, and tram systems were municipalized, thus reducing the cost of these amenities and making them available to a larger proportion of the citizenry.

This photo,* taken in the 1880s, is also evidence of the great progress that had taken place in photography since its invention half a century earlier. In 1839 Louis Daguerre publicized the method of fixing an image on silvered copperplate. At first the cameras and equipment were so cumbersome that photography was confined to studios; photographers could not take pictures anywhere else. Thus the only images were portraits of people and the occasional still life. As the camera became simpler, photographers could leave the studio and take pictures outdoors. Improvements in film, most significantly the introduction of the dry plate method in the 1870s, made it far more sensitive to light, reducing exposure time to a fraction of a second. Now a photograph could capture movement without reducing it to a blur, as in this bustling city scene.

Originally photography had been regarded as a more exact, and less expensive, form of illustration and so was influenced by the conventions of painting. Most early photographs, even outdoor shots, were staged. Given the slowness of taking pictures and the obvious presence of the photographer with all the equipment, it

---

*The advice of Thomas Prasch in the choice of this photo is gratefully acknowledged.

could hardly have been different. But soon thereafter, thanks to technical innovations, photographers could capture a scene even without the cooperation of the subject. None of the subjects in this photo has eye contact with the camera. In fact, they seem unaware of the presence of the photographer as they go about their daily business.

If the modern photograph was different from a painting, photography still adhered to some of the traditions of painting—notably composition. The photographer has composed this image, has made choices as to what to put in the foreground. We get a sense of the harried merchant crossing the well-ordered street with its backdrop of amenities.

The new chemical and optical breakthroughs that made the camera such an effective new tool were implemented by inventors in cities such as London, Paris, and Berlin. Photographers in turn took pictures of some of the great technical feats of their era. The modern aspects of the city, such as this scene, were frequent subjects for the photographer's lens. With a modern device, the camera, the photographer captured the new modern metropolis that was so much more efficient—and exciting—than its predecessor.

Piccadilly Square, Manchester, ca. 1886   *(Topham Picturepoint/The Image Works)*

CHAPTER 24

Escalating Tensions 1880–1914

IN April 1912 the *Titanic*, the largest and most technologically advanced passenger ship ever built, sailed from Southampton, England, for New York. Its owners, the White Star Line, boasted that the building of this majestic vessel testified to "the progress of mankind" and would "rank high in the achievements of the twentieth century." Hailed as "virtually unsinkable," the *Titanic* struck an iceberg on the night of April 12, south of Newfoundland, and rapidly sank. More than 1,500 of the 2,100 people aboard perished in the icy North Atlantic waters. The overconfident captain had not taken warnings of icebergs in the ship's path seriously enough.

Two years later European society was hit by a major disaster—the outbreak of a world war. That such a disaster would end the era called by contemporaries the *belle époque°*, or "beautiful epoch," was as unimaginable as the *Titanic*'s fate. The booming economy had been expanding opportunities for many. The arts flourished and were celebrated. Parliamentary government continued to spread, and more nations seemed to be adapting to democracy as suffrage was extended. Yet hand in hand with these trends of apparent progress appeared troubling tendencies. Under the surface were forces threatening the stability of European society. There was peace, but in 1914 a lone assassin's bullet set off a series of reactions that ultimately led to war and the crash of the pre-1914 world.

In many societies, governing became more complex as populations increased. The population of Europe jumped from 330 million in 1880 to 460 million by 1914. A larger population coupled with

---

belle époque (BELL eh-POK)

The *Titanic* proudly announces its maiden voyage.
(Corbis)

extended suffrage meant that more men participated in the political system, but it became harder to reach a consensus. The example of democracy in some countries led to discontent in the autocratic ones at their failure to move toward freer institutions. In the same way that prosperity and economic growth aroused resentment in those who did not share in the benefits, women and some other groups became frustrated by their exclusion from the political system.

Intellectuals revolted against what they viewed as the smug self-assuredness of earlier years. They no longer felt certain that the world was knowable, stable, or subject to comprehension and, ultimately, to mastery by rational human beings. Some jettisoned rationality, imagining that they had made strides in sophistication by glorifying emotion, irrationality, and in some cases violence. The works of painters and writers seemed to anticipate the impending destruction of world order.

The anxieties and tensions that beset many Europeans took a variety of forms. Ethnic minorities became targets of hatred. European states embarked on a race for empire throughout the world, forcibly putting non-Europeans under white domination. On the Continent states felt increasingly insecure, worried that they would be subject to attack. They established standing armies, shifted alliances, drafted war plans, and, in the end, went to war.

QUESTIONS TO CONSIDER

- What were the main motivations for European imperialism?
- In what ways did the world-view of intellectuals living in the belle époque differ from that of a generation earlier?
- In what ways did British and Russian political institutions reveal an inability to resolve the issues facing society?
- To what extent did social problems undermine the Russian regime?
- What responsibility did each of the Great Powers have for the outbreak of war in 1914?

TERMS TO KNOW

new imperialism	suffragists
Second International	Weltpolitik
anti-Semitism	Bolshevik
Zionism	Triple Alliance
Sigmund Freud	Triple Entente
avant-garde	

THE NEW IMPERIALISM AND THE SPREAD OF EUROPE'S POPULATION

PART of Europe's self-confidence during the period from the 1880s to 1914 was based on the unchallenged sway it held over the rest of the globe. Europeans brought under political control large swaths of land across the seas and also marked the globe by massive migrations.

The age of empire building that started in Europe in the sixteenth century seemed to have ended by 1750. Then, in the 1880s, the European states launched a new era of expansionism, conquering an unprecedented amount of territory. In only twenty-five years Europeans subjugated 500 million people—one-half of the world's non-European population. European expansion was also manifest in a massive movement of people: between 1870 and 1914, 55 million Europeans moved overseas, mainly to Australia, the United States, Canada, and Argentina.

This era of ambitious conquest is often called the "new imperialism," to differentiate it from the earlier stage of empire building. Whereas the earlier imperialism focused on the Americas, nineteenth-century imperialism centered on Africa and Asia. And unlike the colonizing of the earlier period, the new imperialism occurred in an age of mass participation in politics and was accompanied by expressions of popular enthusiasm.

Economic and Social Motives

The hope of profit overseas was crucial in the dynamic of the new imperialism. Much of this hope was illusory, but the desire for huge markets was instrumental in stirring an interest in empire. Colonies, it was believed, would provide eager buyers for European goods that would stimulate production at home. "Colonial policy is the daughter of industrial policy," declared the French prime minister Jules Ferry° in 1884. Yet colonies did not represent large markets for the mother countries. In 1914 France's colonies represented only 12 percent of its foreign trade. Great Britain's trade with its colonies represented a considerable one-third of its foreign trade, but most of that was with the settlement colonies, such as Canada and Australia, not those acquired in the era of the new imperialism. As for Germany, colonial trade represented less than 1 percent of its exports. Even protective tariffs imposed on colonies by no means secured monopoly of trade. Far more than their colonies, France, Germany, and Great Britain continued to be one another's best customers.

Some proponents of empire, known as social imperialists, argued that possession of an empire could resolve social as well as economic issues. An empire could be an outlet for a variety of domestic frustrations, especially for those nations concerned about overpopulation. German and Italian imperialists often argued that their nations needed colonies in which to resettle their multiplying poor. Once the overseas territories were acquired, however, few found them attractive for settlement.

Nationalistic Motives

To a large extent, empire building was triggered by the desire to assert national power. At the end of the nineteenth century, two major powers emerged, Russia and the United States. Compared with these giants, western European nations seemed small and insignificant, and many of their leaders believed that to compete effectively on the world stage, they needed to become large territorial entities. Empires would enable them to achieve that goal.

The British Empire, with India as its crown jewel, constituted the largest, most powerful, and apparently

Ferry (feh-REE)

CHRONOLOGY

1873	Three Emperors' League
1882	Britain seizes Egypt
	Triple Alliance of Germany, Italy, and Austria-Hungary
1884	Three Emperors' League renewed
1890	Kaiser Wilhelm II dismisses Bismarck as chancellor
1894	Franco-Russian Alliance
	Beginning of the Dreyfus affair
1900	King of Italy assassinated
1903	Emmeline Pankhurst founds the Women's Social and Political Union
1904	Anglo-French Entente
1905	Einstein proposes theory of relativity
	Revolution in Russia
1907	Anglo-Russian Entente
1908	Young Turk rebellion in Ottoman Empire
1911	Italy grabs Libya
	Second Moroccan crisis
June 28, 1914	Archduke Franz Ferdinand is assassinated
August 4, 1914	With the entry of Britain, Europe is at war

wealthiest of all the European domains. It was the envy of Europe. Although the real source of Britain's wealth and power was the country's industrial economy, many people believed that possession of a vast empire explained Britain's success. And so the British example stimulated other nations to carve out empires. Their activities in turn triggered British anxieties. Britain and France unleashed a scramble for Africa and Asia; in Asia Britain also competed with Russia.

France, defeated by Prussia in 1870, found in its colonies proof that it was still a Great Power. Germany and Italy, which formed their national identities relatively late, cast a jealous eye on the British and French empires and decided that if they were to be counted as Great Powers,

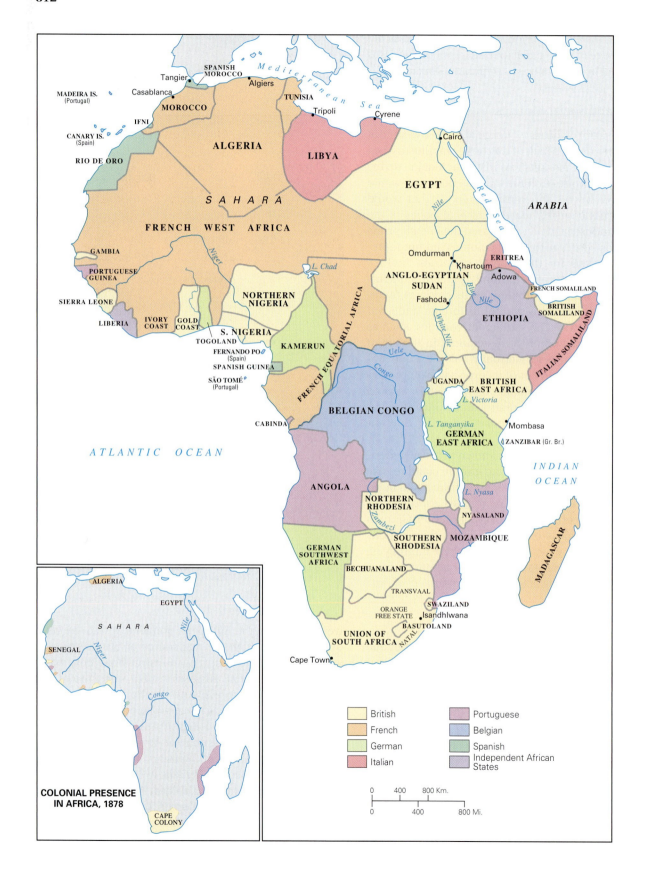

Mediterranean Sea

SPANISH MOROCCO
Tangier
Casablanca
MADEIRA IS. (Portugal)
Algiers
TUNISIA
Tripoli
Cyrene
Cairo
MOROCCO
IFNI
CANARY IS. (Spain)
RIO DE ORO
ALGERIA
LIBYA
EGYPT
ARABIA
SAHARA
Nile
Red Sea
FRENCH WEST AFRICA
GAMBIA
Niger
L. Chad
Omdurman
Khartoum
ERITREA
FRENCH SOMALILAND
PORTUGUESE GUINEA
NORTHERN NIGERIA
ANGLO-EGYPTIAN SUDAN
Adowa
BRITISH SOMALILAND
SIERRA LEONE
Fashoda
Blue Nile
ETHIOPIA
LIBERIA
IVORY COAST
GOLD COAST
S. NIGERIA
FRENCH EQUATORIAL AFRICA
White Nile
ITALIAN SOMALILAND
TOGOLAND
FERNANDO PO (Spain)
KAMERUN
Uele
SPANISH GUINEA
Congo
UGANDA
BRITISH EAST AFRICA
SÃO TOMÉ (Portugal)
BELGIAN CONGO
L. Victoria
CABINDA
L. Tanganyika
GERMAN EAST AFRICA
Mombasa
ZANZIBAR (Gr. Br.)
ATLANTIC OCEAN
INDIAN OCEAN
ANGOLA
NORTHERN RHODESIA
L. Nyasa
NYASALAND
Zambezi
MADAGASCAR
GERMAN SOUTHWEST AFRICA
SOUTHERN RHODESIA
MOZAMBIQUE
BECHUANALAND
TRANSVAAL
SWAZILAND
Isandhlwana
ORANGE FREE STATE
BASUTOLAND
Natal
UNION OF SOUTH AFRICA
Cape Town

Legend:
British
French
German
Italian
Portuguese
Belgian
Spanish
Independent African States

0 400 800 Km.
0 400 800 Mi.

COLONIAL PRESENCE IN AFRICA, 1878

ALGERIA
EGYPT
SAHARA
Nile
SENEGAL
Niger
Congo
CAPE COLONY

they too would need overseas colonies. Belgium's King Leopold II (r. 1876–1909) spun out various plans to acquire colonies to compensate for his nation's small size. And Britain, anxious at the emergence of rival economic and political powers in the late nineteenth century, found in its colonies a guarantee for the future.

In the race for colonies, worldwide strategic concerns stimulated expansion. Because the Suez Canal ensured the route to India, the British established a protectorate over Egypt in 1882. Beginning in the next decade, fearing that a rival power might threaten their position by encroaching on the Nile, they established control over the Nile Valley all the way south to Uganda (see Map 24.1). Russian expansion southward into central Asia toward Afghanistan was intended to avert a British takeover of this area, while the British movement northwestward to Afghanistan had the opposite intention—to prevent Russia from encroaching on India. The "great game" played by Russia and Britain in central Asia lasted the entire nineteenth century, ending only in 1907, with the signing of the Anglo-Russian Entente.

Much of this expansion was driven by the desire to control the often-turbulent frontiers of newly acquired areas. Once those frontiers had been brought under control, there were, of course, new frontiers that had to be subdued. As a Russian foreign minister said of such an incentive for expansion, "The chief difficulty is to know where to stop." The imperial powers rarely did.

The bitter rivalry among the Great Powers helps explain the division of the globe, but it also protected some regions from falling under European domination. In an effort to contain their rivalry in southeast Asia, Britain and France established Siam (now Thailand) as a buffer state. Russia seriously violated China's sovereignty by usurping large chunks of territory as it moved southward and eastward. The Western powers seized Chinese "treaty ports" and insisted on the right of their merchants and missionaries to move freely through the country. Yet most of China survived because the European powers held one another's ambitions in check. No state alone could conquer all of China; none would allow the others to do so either.

Map 24.1 Africa in 1914 European powers in the late nineteenth century conquered most of Africa. Only Liberia and Ethiopia were left unoccupied at the start of World War I.

Other Ideological Motives

In addition to the search for profit and nationalistic pride, Europeans developed a strong rationalization for imperialism. Because Europeans had gained technological and scientific know-how, many imperialists believed it was Europe's duty to develop Africa and Asia for the benefit of colonizer and colonized. Railroads, telegraphs, hospitals, and schools would transform colonial peoples by opening them to what were seen as the beneficent influences of Europe. If necessary, these changes would be realized by force.

At the same time that Europeans were making substantial material progress as a result of industrialization, their wide-scale expansion overseas brought them into contact with Africans and Asians who had not created an industrial economy. They assumed that the dramatic disparity between their own material culture and that of colonial peoples was proof of their own innate superiority. They viewed Africans and Asians as primitive, inferior peoples, still in their evolutionary "infancy." (See the feature "Weighing the Evidence: The Layout of the British Museum" on pages 840–841.)

Influenced by Darwin and his theory of the struggle for survival (see pages 796–798), many argued that just as competition among species existed in nature, so did groups of humans struggle for survival. Dubbed "Social Darwinists," these thinkers envisioned a world of fierce competition. They believed that the most serious struggle was among the races and, further, that the outcome was predetermined: the white race was destined to succeed, the nonwhites to succumb.

Many Europeans paternalistically believed they had a duty to "develop" these "infant" peoples. The British bard of imperialism, Rudyard Kipling (1865–1936), celebrated this view in his poem "White Man's Burden" (1899):

> Take up the White Man's burden—
> Send forth the best ye breed—
> Go bind your sons to exile
> To serve your captives' need.

Each nation was certain that providence had chosen it for a colonial mission. France, its leaders announced, had a civilizing mission to fulfill in the world; Prime Minister Ferry declared it the duty of his country "to civilize the inferior races." Although European states were colonial rivals, they also believed they were engaged in a joint mission overseas. Empire building underscored the belief in a common European destiny, as opposed to the ascribed savagery and backwardness of non-Europeans.

Dutch Colonial Officials in the Dutch East Indies   In this club in an outpost of empire (in present-day Indonesia), the comforts of European bourgeois life were lovingly re-created. Absent from this photo are the countless Indonesian servants who were part of the colonial officials' lives.   *(Royal Tropical Institute, Amsterdam)*

Pointing to historical antecedents, imperialists colored their activities with a hue of heroism. Many Europeans took satisfaction in the idea that their country performed feats akin to those of ancient Rome or the Crusaders, spreading "civilization" to far-flung empires. Colonial literature celebrated white men of action who, by their heroism, conquered and administered what had been large kingdoms or empires in Africa and Asia. Even novelists such as Kipling who tried to be sympathetic to "natives" nonetheless portrayed them as simple, almost childlike people, thus reinforcing European superiority.

Colonial acquisitions triggered public support for further expansion of the empire—support that was expressed by the founding of various colonial societies. Britain's Primrose League, which lobbied for empire as well as other patriotic goals, had 1 million members. The German Colonial Society, founded in 1888, had 43,000 members by 1914. The French and Italian groups were limited in size but had influential contacts with policy-makers. Colonial societies generally drew their membership from the professional middle classes—civil servants, professors, and journalists—who were quite open to nationalist arguments. These societies produced a steady stream of propaganda favoring empire building.

Much of the literature celebrating empire building described it in masculine terms. European men were seen as proving their virility by going overseas, conquering, and running empires. They contrasted their manliness with the supposed effeminacy of the colonial peoples. And in building empires, Europeans asserted their manliness in comparison with their wives, sisters, or mothers. Women were to stay home; if later they came overseas, it was as helpmates to male colonial officials or as missionaries. Believing that they would have a positive influence on the world, women missionaries, either as members of a religious order or joining their husbands, went to the colonies to spread Western religions and European values. A few women heroically explored

Mary Kingsley Defends Imperialism

Imperialism and the Europeans' belief in their superiority marked much of politics and culture in the decades from 1880 to 1914. During this time many men and some intrepid women travelers and missionaries, eager to export European values, voyaged overseas to the colonies. Mary Kingsley traveled to western Africa as a naturalist, studying and observing the different environments and cultures. She concluded that Africans were different from Europeans, inferior in some respects and excelling in others. Kingsley based her views on differences of culture rather than biology. She suggested that because Africans were less developed than Europeans, Britain had a special duty and obligation to them. In the nineteenth century, European nations carved up much of Africa and Asia, creating global empires. But in the twentieth century, most of those former colonies fought for and obtained their independence.

I openly and honestly own I sincerely detest touching on this race question. For one thing, Science has not finished with it; for another, it belongs to a group of enormous magnitude, upon which I have no opinion, but merely feelings, and those of a nature which I am informed by superior people would barely be a credit to a cave man of the paleolithic period. . . . I am often cornered for the detail view, whether I can reconcile my admiration for Africans with my statement that they are a different kind of human being to white men. Naturally I can, to my own satisfaction, just as I can admire an oak tree or a palm; but it is an uncommonly difficult thing to explain. All that I can say is, that when I come back from a spell in Africa, the thing that makes me proud of being one of the English is not the manners of customs up here, certainly not the houses or the climate; but it is the thing embodied in a great railway engine. I once came home on a ship with an Englishman who had been in South West Africa, for seven unbroken years; he was sane and in his right mind. But no sooner did we get ashore at Liverpool, than he rushed at and threw his arms round a postman, to that official's embarrassment and surprise. Well, that is how I feel about the first magnificent bit of machinery I come across: it is the manifestation of the superiority of my race.

In philosophic moments I call superiority difference, from a feeling that it is not mine to judge the grade in these things. Careful scientific study has enforced on me, as it has on other students, the recognition that the African mind naturally approaches all things from a spiritual point of view. . . . [H]is mind works along the line that things happen because of the action of spirit upon spirit. . . . We think along the line that things happen from action of matter upon matter. . . . This steady sticking to the material side of things, I think, has given our race its dominion over matter; the want of it has caused the African to be notably behind us in this. . . .

This seems to me simply to lay upon us English for the sake of our honour that we keep clean hands and a cool head, and be careful of Justice; to do this we must know what there is we wish to wipe out of the African, and what there is we wish to put in, and so we must not content ourselves by relying materially on our superior wealth and power, and morally on catch phrases. All we need to look to is justice.

QUESTIONS

1. On what does Kingsley base her contention that hers is a superior race? How might the specific areas of advancement that she mentions have assisted the British in controlling their colonies?

2. What is her justification for England's presence in Africa? How might that have created tensions between the British and the indigenous populations? What does her use of terms such as "justice" and "honor" communicate about how she felt concerning imperialism?

3. Where do you think Kingsley's position would have fallen in the spectrum of attitudes toward race and colonization at the time? Can people defend imperialism if they oppose racism? How successful was imperialism?

SOURCE: Mary H. Kingsley, *West African Studies* (London: Macmillan, 1899), pp. 329–331.

distant lands; the Englishwoman Mary Kingsley (1862–1900) went on two exploration trips into Africa. (See the box "The Continuing Experiment: Mary Kingsley Defends Imperialism.") Her popular books focused British interest on overseas territories, but they in no way shook the established view that empire was a man's enterprise.

Conquest, Administration, and Westernization

Industrialization gave Europeans the means to conquer overseas territories. They manufactured rapid-fire weapons. Their steam-driven gunboats and oceangoing vessels effectively projected power overseas. Telegraphic communications tied the whole world into a single network, allowing Europeans to gather information and co-ordinate military and political decision making. (See the feature "Information Technology: The Telegraph" on pages 780–781 in Chapter 23.) Such advantages made Europeans virtually invincible in a colonial conflict. One remarkable exception was the defeat of the Italians in Adowa in 1896 at the hands of an Ethiopian force that was not only superior in numbers but better armed.

Conquest was often brutal. In September 1898 British-led forces at the Battle of Omdurman slaughtered 20,000 Sudanese. From 1904 to 1908 an uprising in southwest Africa against German rule led to the killing of an estimated 60,000 of the Herero people. The German general, who had expressly given an order to exterminate the whole population, was awarded a medal by Kaiser Wilhelm II.

Colonial governments could be brutally insensitive to the needs of the indigenous peoples. (See the box "Global Encounters: Chief Montshiwa Petitions Queen Victoria.") To save administrative costs in the 1890s, France put large tracts of land in the French Congo under the control of private rubber companies, which systematically and savagely coerced the local people to collect the sap of the rubber trees. When the scandal broke in Paris, the concessionary companies were abolished, and the French state re-established its control. The most notorious example of exploitation, terror, and mass killings was connected with the Belgian Congo. Leopold II of Belgium had acquired it as a personal empire. It was his private domain, and he was not accountable to anyone for his actions there. To his shame, Leopold mercilessly exploited the Congo and its people. An international chorus of condemnation finally forced the king to surrender his empire and put it under the administration of the Belgian government, which abolished some of the worst features of Leopold's rule.

Brutal and abusive, imperialism spread Western technologies, institutions, and values. By 1914 Great Britain had built 40,000 miles of rail lines in India—nearly twice as much as in Britain. In India and Egypt, the British erected hydraulic systems that irrigated previously arid lands. Colonials built cities often modeled on the European grid system. In some cases they were graced with large, tree-lined avenues, and some neighborhoods were equipped with running water and modern sanitation. Schools, patterned after those in Europe,

Empire and Advertising   Empire had become so much a part of European life that advertisements for biscuits included colonial scenes. Media such as advertising made colonial domination seem normal, part of the natural order of things.   *(The Robert Opie Collection)*

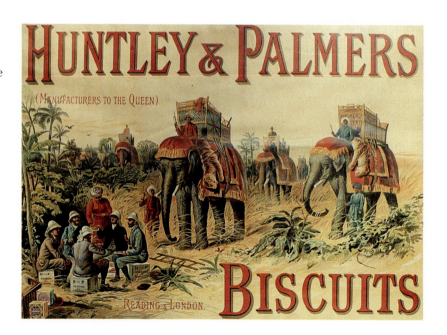

Chief Montshiwa Petitions Queen Victoria

In 1885 Bechuanaland, in southern Africa, became a British protectorate. The Bechuana leaders saw British protection as a means to prevent takeover by the Boers, Dutch-speaking white settlers who were aggressively expanding in South Africa. The British were cavalier about their responsibilities, however, and a few years later allowed the British South Africa Company, a particularly exploitive enterprise, to take control of Bechuanaland. In protest, Chief Montshiwa (1815–1896), a major chief of the Baralong people, petitioned Queen Victoria for redress. His petition was supported by missionary lobbying, and most of Bechuanaland was saved from the clutches of the company.

Mafeking, 16 August 1895

To the Queen of England and Her Ministers:

We send greetings and pray that you are all living nicely. You will know us; we are not strangers. We have been your children since 1885.

Your Government has been good, and under it we have received much blessing, prosperity, and peace. . . .

We Baralong are very astonished because we hear that the Queen's Government wants to give away our country in the Protectorate to the Chartered Company; we mean the B[ritish] S[outh] A[frica] Company.

Our land there is a good land, our fathers lived in it and buried in it, and we keep all our cattle in it. What will we do if you give our land away? My people are increasing very fast and are filling the land.

We keep all the laws of the great Queen; we have fought for her; we have always been the friends of her people; we are not idle; we build houses; we plough many gardens; we sow. . . .

Why are you tired of ruling us? Why do you want to throw us away? We do not fight against your laws. We keep them and are living nicely.

Our words are No: No. The Queen's Government must not give my people's land in the Protectorate to the Chartered Company. . . .

Peace to you all, we greet you;
Please send a good word back.
I am etc,

Montshiwa

QUESTIONS

1. What are Chief Montshiwa's grievances?
2. Why did the missionaries lend their support to the chief?
3. How does Montshiwa view the relationship between his people and the queen?

SOURCE: S. M. Molema, *Montshiwa, 1815–1896* (Cape Town: G. Struik, 1966), pp. 181–182.

---

taught the imperial language and spread Western ideas and scientific knowledge—though only to a small percentage of the local population.

The European empire builders created political units that had never existed before. In many parts of Africa they ignored tribal and indigenous differences, which had serious repercussions in the postcolonial world. Although there had been many efforts in the past to join the whole Indian subcontinent under a single authority, the British were the first to accomplish this feat (see Map 24.2). Through a common administration, rail network, and trade, Britain gave Indians the sense of a common condition, leading in 1885 to the founding of the India Congress Party. The Congress Party platform included the demand for constitutional government, representative assemblies, and the rule of law—concepts all based on Western theory and practice. Though initially demanding reforms within the British colonial system, the Congress Party eventually became India's major nationalist group.

In contact with the colonizers, intellectuals in colonial societies adopted a European ideology, nationalism. Nationalism was one of the major values Europeans successfully exported to their overseas possessions. In India it was those Indians who had been most exposed to British influence, by having studied in British schools or visited Britain, who were most likely to be nationalists. They founded a movement, known as "Young India," harking back to "Young Italy" and other European nationalist movements founded during the mid-1800s (see page 715). Similarly, in French Algeria before World War I, a movement named "Young Algerians" sprang up.

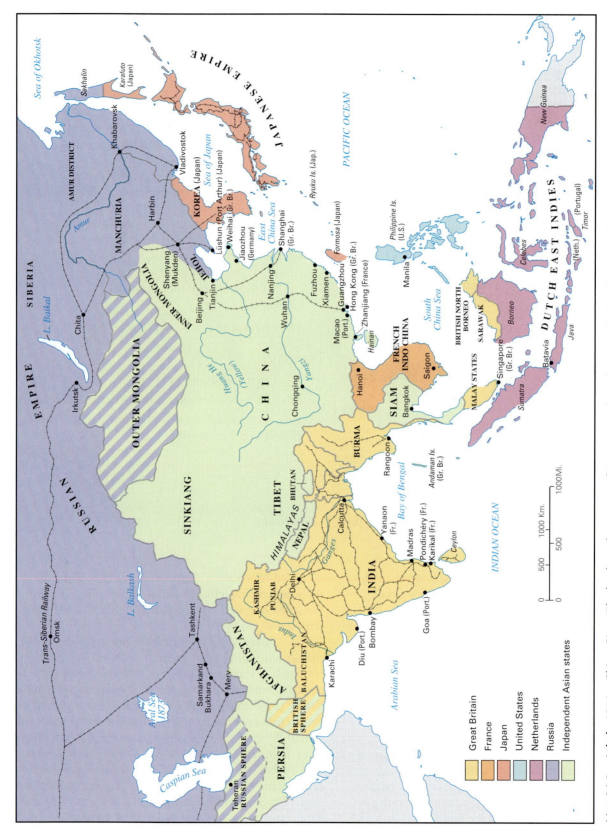

Map 24.2 Asia in 1914 China, Siam (Thailand), and a portion of Persia were the only parts of Asia still independent after the Great Powers, including the United States and Japan, subjugated the continent to alien rule.

Petersen: Emigrants Preparing to Depart Edward Petersen's 1890 painting depicts Danish emigrants preparing to leave their homeland. Between 1860 and 1914, 300,000 people emigrated from the small country of Denmark, most of them to the United States. *(Courtesy of the Aarhus Kunstmuseum. Reproduced with permission of Thomas, Poul, and Ole Hein Pedersen, Aarhus.)*

It was to be several decades before nationalism successfully challenged the European empires. In the meantime, Europeans took great satisfaction in their achievements overseas, confirming their sense of themselves as agents of progress, building a new and better world. Europeans arrogantly believed that they knew what was best for other people, and they accepted force as a means of implementing their ideas. Such attitudes may have colored the increasingly caustic relations between European states.

The ties of empire affected metropolitan cultures. The Hindi word for *bandit* became the English word *thug;* the Hindi number five, denoting the five ingredients necessary for a particular drink, became *punch.* Scenes from the colonial world often were the themes of European art, such as Paul Gauguin's° paintings of Tahiti

and advertising posters for products as different as soap and whiskey. After the turn of the century, Pablo Picasso's° cubism reflected his growing familiarity with African art. In running the largest empire in the world, the British emphasized the need to develop masculine virtues. They cultivated competitive sports and stern schooling, which, they believed, would develop "character" and leadership. To administer their overseas colonies, Europeans developed sophisticated means of gathering and managing information that benefited metropolitan societies. A growing number of people from the colonies also came to live in European cities. By 1900 some former colonial subjects, despite various forms of discrimination, had become full participants in the lives of their host countries; two Indians won election to the British Parliament in the 1890s.

Gauguin (go-GEYN)

Picasso (pih-KAH-so)

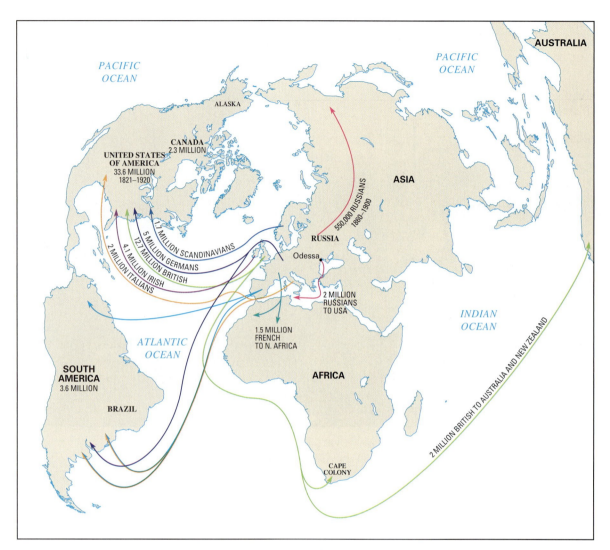

Map 24.3   European Migrations, 1820–1910   Throughout the nineteenth century, millions of Europeans left home for overseas; most headed for the United States.   *(Source: The Times Atlas of World History, 3rd ed. (Times Books). Reprinted by permission of HarperCollins Publishers, Ltd. © HarperCollins Publishers, Ltd. Some data from Eric Hobsbawm, The Age of Empire, 1875–1914 [New York: Pantheon, 1987].)*

Overseas Migrations and the Spread of European Values

The nineteenth century saw a phenomenal expansion in European overseas migrations, adding to Europe's impact on other societies (see Map 24.3). Europeans had always migrated. They left villages for towns or, in the case of migrant farm laborers, traveled from village to village as the seasons changed and different crops needed to be harvested. With the expansion of European power abroad beginning in the sixteenth century, Europeans migrated overseas. Between the sixteenth

and eighteenth centuries, around 6 million people left Europe. These numbers pale, however, when compared with the nineteenth-century figures. Between 1870 and 1914, 55 million Europeans left the Continent for the Americas, Australia, and New Zealand.

Certain European groups migrated to specific areas. Scandinavians settled in the upper midwestern United States, Italians in Argentina, Germans in Paraguay, Britons in South Africa, and Portuguese in Brazil, with each group leaving its imprint on its adopted land. The upper Midwest was known as "the great desert," but Scandinavians used farming techniques from their homelands to cultivate these dry lands. German Mennonites settled in Kansas and brought with them a strain of wheat that became the basis of the state's prosperity. Immigrants had a similar impact on urban areas. Durban, South Africa, looks like an English city, and some towns in Paraguay resemble Alpine villages of southern Germany. The Germans who came to Milwaukee, Wisconsin, made it a city of beer and strong socialist convictions, reminiscent of home.

Emigration scattered peoples and extended cultures overseas. By 1914 nearly half of all Irish and Portuguese lived outside Europe. The settlers consumed many European goods and in turn produced for the European market, increasing the centrality of Europe in the world economy. The migrations around the globe reinforced imperial conquest, further putting Europe's stamp on peoples and societies abroad.

If Europe appeared triumphant, its supremacy rested on frail foundations—mainly force. From the start, local resistance and even expressions of proto-nationalist sentiments challenged Europe's supremacy. Imperial powers, worried that their European rivals or their colonial subjects might cause trouble, looked to force to ensure the future of their empires.

FROM OPTIMISM TO ANXIETY: POLITICS AND CULTURE

ANY of the beliefs and institutions that had seemed so solid in the "age of optimism" found themselves under attack in the next generation. Forces hostile to liberalism became increasingly vocal. In the arts and philosophy, the earlier confidence was replaced by doubt, relativism, and a desire to flee the routines of everyday life.

The Erosion of the Liberal Consensus

In 1850 liberalism appeared to be the ascendant ideology, and liberals assumed that with the passage of time more and more people would be won over to their world-view. By 1900, however, liberalism faced serious challenges. Principles eroded within the liberal camp, and various ideas and movements—some new, some rooted in the past—chipped away at the liberal consensus. Prominent among these were socialism, anarchism, a new political right, racism, and anti-Semitism.

The undermining of the liberal consensus began among liberals themselves, who, in the face of changing circumstances, retreated from some of their basic tenets. For example, one of the principal emphases of liberalism had always been free trade. But under the pressure of economic competition, liberals supported tariffs at home and created closed markets for the mother country overseas in the empire.

Historically, liberals had typically stood for an expansion of civil liberties, yet several groups were denied their rights. Power remained an exclusively male domain, and liberal males saw nothing wrong or inconsistent in continuing to deny women both the vote and free access to education and professional advancement. In the face of labor agitation, many liberals no longer unconditionally supported civil liberties for workers and favored instead the violent crushing of strikes.

Similarly, liberals had always upheld the sanctity of private property, but under the pressure of events, they abandoned this principle as an absolute goal. To ensure workers' safety, they placed limits on employers by passing legislation on working conditions. In some countries, some liberals supported progressive income taxes, which other liberals perceived as a serious invasion of private property. When it became clear that a free market was unable to meet many human needs, welfare programs were instituted in several countries. These reforms were intended to strengthen the state by winning support from the masses and by fostering the growth of a healthy population through limited aid to mothers and children. But because they reflected the liberals' willingness to breach fundamental principles, especially pertaining to women, these measures also revealed the apparent inability of liberal ideology to deal with the real-life problems of the day.

The Growth of Socialism and Anarchism

Among the groups challenging the power and liberal ideology of the middle classes were the socialist parties, both Marxist and non-Marxist, whose goal was to win the support of workers by espousing their causes. Socialists varied in their notions of how their goals should be achieved: some favored pursuing objectives gradually and peacefully; others were dedicated to a violent overthrow of capitalist society.

In Britain, where the Liberal Party was more open to the needs of workers than in other European states, a separate socialist party, the Independent Labour Party, was established relatively late, in 1893. Not until the 1920s did this party gain any particular electoral success. More influential in the late nineteenth century was the Fabian Society, founded in 1884 and named after the

Roman general Fabian, who was noted for winning by avoiding open, pitched battles. The Fabians criticized the capitalist system as inefficient, wasteful, and unjust. They believed that by gradual, democratic means, Parliament could transfer factories and land from the private sector to the state, which would manage them for the benefit of society as a whole. Socialism was a desirable system that would replace capitalism because it was more efficient and more just. It would come into being not through class war but through enlightened ideas. This gradualist approach became the hallmark of British socialism, shaping the ideology of the Labour Party.

In Germany various strands of socialism came together when a single united party was formed in 1875. But within a few years a debate that was to break out in most socialist parties rent the German party: could socialism come about by gradual democratic means, or, as Marx had contended, would it require a violent revolution? The German socialist leader Eduard Bernstein° (1850–1932), who had visited England and had soaked up the influence of the Fabians, argued for gradualism in a book with the telling English title *Evolutionary Socialism* (1898). Marx had been wrong, said Bernstein, to suggest that capitalism necessarily led to the increasing wretchedness of the working class. The capitalist economy had in fact expanded and been able to provide for steadily improved conditions. Workers would not need to seize power by some cataclysmic act. Rather, by piecemeal democratic action, they could win more power and legislate on behalf of their interests. Since he argued for a revision of Marxist theory, Bernstein was labeled a "revisionist." Opposing him in this great debate was the party theoretician, Karl Kautsky° (1854–1938). Kautsky insisted that nothing short of a revolution would institute socialism.

Like most other socialists in Europe, the German socialists rejected revisionism and claimed to embrace the doctrine of a violent proletarian revolution. In fact, however, they pursued revisionist policies. Socialists in practice had become another parliamentary party that hoped to reach its goals through legislation.

Another movement that sought to liberate the downtrodden was anarchism, which proclaimed that humans could be free only when the state had been abolished. According to anarchist theory, in a stateless society people would naturally join together in communes and share the fruits of their labor. Some anarchists believed they could achieve their goal by educating people. Others were more impatient and hoped to speed up the process by making direct attacks on existing authority.

Jean Jaurès   An ideological moderate, the French socialist leader Jean Jaurès° (1859–1914) was a firebrand as a speaker, one of France's greatest orators. Much of his socialism was based on ethical notions about social justice, rather than on Maxist doctrine. Here Jaurès addresses a social gathering in 1913.   *(Roger-Viollet/Getty Images)*

The Russian nobleman Michael Bakunin° (1814–1876), frustrated at the authoritarianism of his homeland, became a lifelong anarchist. He challenged tsarism at home and participated in the 1848 revolutions throughout Europe. He viewed all governments as repressive and declared unilateral war on them: "The passion for destruction is also a creative passion." His ideas were particularly influential in Italy, Spain, and parts of France, especially among the artisan classes.

Many anarchists of this period wanted to bring about the new society by "propaganda of the deed." An attack on the bastions of power, these anarchists believed, could bring about the dissolution of the state. They formed secret terrorist organizations that assassinated heads of state or those close to them. Between

Bernstein (BURN-stine)   **Kautsky** (KOUT-skee)

Jaurès (Zhaw-REZ)   **Bakunin** (bah-KOO-neen)

1894 and 1901 anarchists killed a president of France, a prime minister of Spain, an empress of Austria, a king of Italy, and a president of the United States. These murders fixed the popular image of anarchism as a violence-prone ideology. More important, such manifestations of the "propaganda of the deed" produced no particular improvement in the lives of the working-class people on whose behalf these deadly campaigns had supposedly been launched.

Without accepting the anarchists' methods, some in the labor movement shared their hostility toward parliamentary institutions. A working-class program, labor activists argued, could be implemented only by a pure workers' movement, such as unionization. Workers should shun the political arena and concentrate on direct action. According to this line of thought, known as "syndicalism°" (after the French word for unions), workers should amass their power in unions and at the right moment carry out a general strike, crippling capitalist society and bringing it down. Syndicalism was particularly popular in Mediterranean countries, where its more militant form, anarcho-syndicalism, radicalized labor and made a sizable number of workers hostile to parliamentarism.

European socialism also attempted an international presence. In 1864 Marx had participated in the founding of the International Workers' Association, which fell prey to internal dissension and dissolved after a few years. Known as the First International, it was followed by a more robust organization, the Second International, in 1889. The International met yearly and debated issues of concern to socialists in general, including the worsening relations among European states. As early as 1893 the International urged European states to resolve their conflicts by mandatory arbitration. In 1907, sensing impending war, the International called on workers to strike and refuse military service in case of international conflict. The International saw itself as a bulwark of peace; it did not realize that once war broke out, Europeans, including socialists, would be swept up in nationalist fervor and would willingly go to war. Although most socialists advocated peace at home and abroad, many had contributed to a militant discourse with their class war rhetoric.

The New Right, Racism, and Anti-Semitism

The traditional opponents of liberalism on the political right were the conservatives, wedded to preserving the existing order. Beginning in the 1880s, however, a "new right" emerged that was populist and demagogic. Although conservatives had been wary of nationalism, the new right embraced it. Alienated by industry, democracy, and social egalitarianism, many in this new right rejected doctrines of human equality and embraced racist ideologies.

Racist thinking was common in the nineteenth century. Many Europeans believed that human races were not only different physiologically but also—as a result of these biological variations—differently endowed in intelligence and other qualities (see pages 799–800). Europeans were often ethnocentric, convinced they were the epitome of humankind, whereas members of other races belonged to lesser groups. At midcentury the Frenchman Arthur de Gobineau° (1816–1882) published his *Essay on the Inequality of Human Races,* declaring that race "dominates all other problems and is the key to it." Biologists and early anthropologists made similar statements, thus giving racism a "scientific" aura. Throughout the second half of the nineteenth century, race was thought to be the principal explanation for the differences that were discovered among human groupings.

These racist ideas helped fuel anti-Semitism. For centuries Jews had been the object of suspicion and bigotry. Originally, the basis of the prejudice was religious. As early as the Middle Ages, however, the argument emerged that "Jewish blood" was different. And with the popularization of pseudoscientific racist thinking in the nineteenth century, Jews were commonly viewed as a separate, inferior race, unworthy of the same rights as the majority of the population.

Historically, Christians had relegated the Jews in their midst to marginal positions. In the Middle Ages, when land was the basis of wealth and prestige, Jews had been confined to such urban trades as cattle trading and moneylending. They incurred high risks by lending money: they often were not paid back and faced unsympathetic courts when they tried to collect their debts. To counteract these risks, Jewish moneylenders charged high interest rates that earned them their unpopular reputation as usurers.

The emancipation of the Jews, which began in France with the Revolution and spread to Germany and Austria by the 1860s, provided them opportunities they had not had before. Some members of society found it hard to adjust to the prominence a few Jews gained. Because their increased social standing and success were concurrent with the wrenching social transformations

---

syndicalism (SIN-dih-ka-lizm)   **Gobineau** (go-bee-NO)

brought by industrialization and urbanization, anti-Semites pointed to the Jews as the perpetrators of these unsettling changes.

Many people perceived Jews as prototypical of the new capitalist class. Although most Jews were of modest means, resentment of the rich often was aimed at Jews. Earlier in the century many anti-Semites were socialists, speaking on behalf of the working class. Later they came from among the petite bourgeoisie—small shopkeepers and artisans—who felt threatened by economic change.

Political movements based on anti-Semitism were founded in the 1880s. They depicted Jews as dangerous and wicked and called for their exclusion from the political arena and from certain professions. In some cases proponents suggested that Jews be expelled from the state. Karl Lueger (1844–1928) was elected mayor of Vienna on an anti-Semitic platform. In Berlin the emperor's chaplain, Adolf Stöcker° (1835–1909), founded an anti-Semitic party, hoping to make political inroads among the working-class supporters of socialism. In France Edouard Drumont (1844–1917) published one of the bestsellers of the second half of the nineteenth century, *Jewish France*, in which he blamed all the nation's misfortunes on the Jews.

In Russia organized *pogroms,* or mass attacks, on Jews killed two thousand in the 1880s and one thousand in 1905, frightening two million Jews into exile, mostly to the United States. Russian Jews lived under social as well as legal disabilities. Condemned to second-class citizenship, they won full emancipation only with the Bolshevik Revolution of 1917. (See the box "Reading Sources: Mary Antin Faces Anti-Semitism in Russia.")

In the face of growing hostility, some Jews speculated that they would be safe only in their own nation. The Austrian Jewish journalist Theodore Herzl° (1860–1904), outraged by the Dreyfus affair in France, in which a Jewish officer was imprisoned on trumped-up charges of treason (see page 830), founded the Zionist movement. He advocated establishing a Jewish state in the Jews' ancient homeland of Israel. In the beginning, the Zionist movement won a following only in eastern Europe, where the Jews were particularly ill-treated, but by 1948 Zionism culminated in the creation of the state of Israel.

Various manifestations of anti-Semitism revealed the vulnerability of tolerance, one of the basic ideas of liberalism. It became eminently clear that racism, with its penchant for irrationality and violence, could easily be aroused.

Irrationality and Uncertainty

In contrast to the confidence in reason and science that had prevailed at midcentury, the era starting in the 1880s was characterized by a sense of irrationality and uncertainty—in philosophy, in the arts, even in religion. The positivism of the earlier era had emphasized the surface reality of "progress" but had neglected inner meaning and ignored the emotional and intuitive aspects of life. By the 1890s a neo-romantic mood, emphasizing emotion and feeling, stirred major intellectual movements. The spotlight was no longer on reason, but on instinct.

In philosophy the tension between reason and emotion was vividly expressed in the work of the German philosopher Friedrich Nietzsche° (1844–1900), who proclaimed that rationality had led humankind into a meaningless abyss. Reason would not resolve human problems, nor would any preconceived ideas. "God is dead," Nietzsche announced. Furthermore, he said, "we philosophers and 'free spirits' feel as if a new dawn were shining on us when we receive the tidings that 'the old god is dead'; our heart overflows with gratitude, amazement, anticipation, expectation." With no God, humankind was free of all outside constraints, free to overthrow all conventions. Nietzsche admonished his readers to challenge existing institutions and accepted truths and to create new ones.

The French philosopher Henri Bergson° (1859–1940) argued that science—and indeed life—must be interpreted not rationally but intuitively. "Science," Bergson declared, "can teach us nothing of the truth; it can only serve as a rule of action." Humans could best understand meaningful truths—such as the truth of religion, literature, and art—by relying on their feelings.

Various disciplines of knowledge subscribed to the notion that humans are often irrational, motivated by deep-seated instinctive forces. The Austro-Hungarian Sigmund Freud° (1856–1939) founded psychoanalysis, a method of treating psychic disorders by exploring the unconscious. Freud believed that people were motivated not only by observed reality but also by their unconscious feelings and emotions. Whereas earlier physicians had described the mental condition of "hysteria," a frequent diagnosis of women's illness, as a physical ailment, Freud saw its roots as psychological, the result of unresolved inner conflicts. Although Freud's work was influenced by rational methods, he stressed that irrational forces played a significant role in human behavior.

Stöcker (SHTOE-kur)   Herzl (HER-tsl)

Friedrich Nietzsche (FREED-reesh NEET-sheh)
Bergson (BERK-sohn)   Freud (FROYD)

MARY ANTIN FACES ANTI-SEMITISM IN RUSSIA

Mary Antin (1881–1949) grew up in a small town in an area known as the Pale of Settlement. The Pale comprised designated regions of the Russian Empire, from the Baltic to the Black Sea, where the tsarist regimes required Jews to live. Some Jews, such as artisans, could live in specified areas outside the Pale if they paid high fees and bribes, but they were subject to harassment by the authorities. In 1894 Antin immigrated with her family to the United States during the wave of migration resulting from Russian anti-Semitism and pogroms. She excelled in the Boston public schools and then went on to college, publishing her major book, The Promised Land, *in 1912. In this selection Antin points out how the Russian government severely restricted life for Jews, determining where they could live and work and whether they could go to school.*

The Gentiles used to wonder at us because we cared so much about religious things, about food and Sabbath and teaching the children Hebrew. They were angry with us for our obstinacy, as they called it, and mocked us and ridiculed the most sacred things. There were wise Gentiles who understood. These were educated people. . . . They were always respectful and openly admired some of our ways. But most of the Gentiles were ignorant. . . . If you did not keep on good terms with your Gentile neighbors, they had a hundred ways of molesting you. If you chased their pigs when they came rooting up your garden, or objected to their children maltreating your children, they might complain against you to the police, stuffing their case with false accusations and false witnesses. If you had not made friends with the police, the case might go to court; and there you lost before the trial was called unless the judge had reason to befriend you. . . .

The czar always got his dues, no matter if it ruined a family. There was a poor locksmith who owed the czar three hundred rubles, because his brother had escaped from Russia before serving his time in the army. . . . Now the locksmith never could have so much money, and he had no valuables to pawn. The police came and attached his household goods, everything he had, including his bride's trousseau; and the sale of the goods brought thirty-five rubles. After a year's time the police came again, looking for the balance of the czar's dues. . . . That fine of three hundred rubles was a sentence of life-long slavery for the poor locksmith, unless he could free himself by some trick. As fast as he could collect a few rags and sticks, the police would be after them. . . .

There was one public school for boys, and one for girls, but Jewish children were admitted in limited numbers. . . . I used to stand in the doorway of my father's store munching an apple that did not taste good any more, and watch the pupils going home from school in twos and threes; the girls in neat brown dresses and black aprons and little stiff hats, the boys in trim uniforms with many buttons. They had ever so many books in the satchels on their backs. . . . But those whom I envied had their troubles, as I often heard. Their school life was one struggle against injustice from instructors, spiteful treatment from fellow students, and insults from everybody. They were rejected at the universities, where they were admitted in the ratio of three Jews to a hundred Gentiles. . . . No, the czar did not want us in the schools.

Source: *Modern History Sourcebook: Mary Antin: A Little Jewish Girl in Russia, 1890,* http://www.Fordham.edu/halstall/mod/1890antin.html. From Eva March Tappan, ed., *The World's Story: A History of the World in Story, Song and Art,* vol. 6, Russia, Austria-Hungary, the Balkan States, and Turkey (Boston: Houghton Mifflin, 1914), pp. 243–247.

The social theorist Gaetano Mosca (1858–1941), in his book *Elements of Political Science* (1891), posited that in all societies—even democratic ones—an elite minority rules over the majority. The desire to dominate is a basic part of human nature; even in democratic or socialist societies, this thirst for power is never slaked. Beneath slogans touting the public good lies selfish ambition. Thus, as did Freud, Mosca suggested that surface appearances are deceptive and that irrational forces guide human behavior.

Freud in 1909   Although much of Sigmund Freud's career still lay ahead of him, he already had established a reputation as the founder of modern psychology.   *(Sigmund Freud Copyrights/Mary Evans Picture Library)*

In the arts, the idea of being *avant-garde*—French for "forefront"—took hold among creative people. Breaking the taboos of society and the conventions of one's craft seemed to be signs of artistic creativity. Artistic movements proclaimed idiosyncratic manifestoes and constantly called for the rejection of existing forms of expression and the creation of new ones. The symbolists in France and Italy, the expressionists in Germany, the futurists in Italy, and the secessionists in Austria all reflected the sense that they were living through a fractured period.

In protest against the mass culture of their day, artists focused on images that were unique. Unlike earlier art, which had a clear message, the art of this era did not. Many artists no longer believed their role was to portray or spread ideals. Rather, they tended to be introspective and even self-absorbed. The public at large

found it difficult to decipher the meaning of the new art, but bewildered or not, a number of patrons supported the avant-garde artists' talent and insight.

Unlike the realists who preceded them, artists in the 1890s surrendered to neo-romanticism, trying to investigate and express inner forces. As the French painter Paul Gauguin (1848–1903) noted, the purpose of painting is to communicate not how things look but the emotions they convey. The Russian Wassily Kandinsky° (1866–1944) asked viewers of his art to "look at the picture as a graphic representation of a mood and not as a representation of objects." Artists appeared to be examining the hidden anxieties of society. The Frenchman Gustave Moreau° (1826–1898) displayed monsters—creations of nightmare and byproducts of the unconscious. The Austrian artist Egon Schiele° (1890–1918) and the Norwegian painter Edvard Munch° (1863–1944) emphasized scenes of violence, fear, and sheer horror.

Musicians, too, stretched the traditional forms of their art. Claude Debussy° (1862–1918) defied the established rules of tone and harmony in Western music and its use of orchestral instruments in works such as *Prelude* and *Afternoon of a Faun* (1894) and his opera *Pelléas and Mélisande* (1902). Rather than being cerebral, he insisted, his work was instinctive.

Religion felt the effects of intellectual challenge as well. Although large numbers of people still held traditional religious beliefs and followed traditional practices, indifference to organized religion spread. In urban areas of western Europe, church attendance declined. As these regions urbanized, they became increasingly secular. With the decline of traditional Christian practices, various forms of mysticism became more widespread. Some people were attracted to Eastern religions such as Buddhism and Hinduism and to other mystical beliefs. These attitudes may have reflected a loss of faith in Western culture itself. As the century came to an end, a number of intellectuals argued that their culture, like the century, was destined for decline.

Scientists of this period questioned long-held commonsense beliefs. During the last week of the century, the German physicist Max Planck (1858–1947) suggested that light and other kinds of electromagnetic radiation, such as radio waves, which had always been considered continuous trains of waves, actually consist of individual packages of well-defined energy, which he called "quanta."

Wassily Kandinsky (vass-IH-lee kan-DIN-skee)
Moreau (mo-RO)   **Egon Schiele** (EYE-gohn SHE-lee)
Munch (MOONGK)   **Debussy** (duh-bew-SEE)

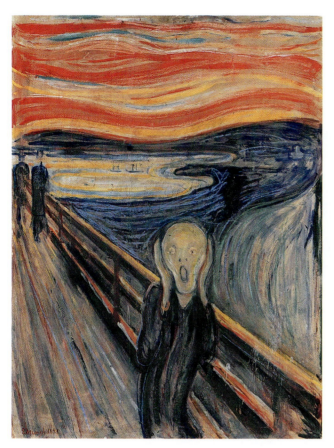

Munch: The Scream Painted in 1893, this work reflects the fear and horror that some intellectuals experienced at the end of the nineteenth century. *(Nasjonalgalleriet, Oslo/Erich Lessing/Art Resource, NY. © 2002 Artists Rights Society (ARS), New York/ADAGP, Paris)*

In 1905 Albert Einstein (1879–1955) proposed the theory of relativity, which required a drastic change in fundamental ideas about space and time. Time became a fourth companion of the three dimensions of space—length, breadth, and width. These ideas in physics, though necessary to explain certain new phenomena such as x-rays, were not easily understood because they were foreign to common experience. Ideas of uncertainty in physics came in the 1920s with the work of the German physicist Werner Heisenberg° (1901–1976). The old concept of a fixed cause tied to a fixed effect did not hold, because even though things happen predictably, they also happen randomly.

VULNERABLE DEMOCRACIES

BY the end of the nineteenth century, most of Europe's political systems floundered in crisis. The major powers with democratic institutions—Great Britain, France, and Italy—confronted volatile public opinion and had difficulty winning a broad consensus for their policies. They struggled with new challenges emerging from an expanded electorate that was at times frustrated by the failure of the system to respond to its demands. Turning away from the democratic precept of resolving differences through the ballot and legislation, many people—both in government and out—were willing to resort to extraparliamentary means, including violence, to see their interests prevail.

Great Britain

In Great Britain the Reform Bill of 1884 transformed the political landscape by giving the vote to two of every three adult men, doubling suffrage to five million. The appeal of this enlarged electorate tempted politicians to make demagogic promises, which were often broken later, to the exasperation of their constituents. It was also more difficult to reach compromises in a Parliament that no longer consisted of a fairly limited class of people with common interests and values. The British political system was faced with issues it was unable to resolve peacefully, and it was obliged—uncharacteristically—to resort to force or the threat of force.

As in earlier periods, Ireland proved to be a persistent problem. The political consciousness of the Irish had risen considerably, and they seethed under alien rule. In an attempt to quell Irish opposition in 1886, Prime Minister William Gladstone° proposed autonomy, or "home rule," for Ireland. There were many objections to such a plan, the most serious being that if Ireland, a predominantly Catholic country, ruled itself, the local Protestant majority in Ulster, the northeast part of the island, would be overwhelmed and likely to fall under Catholic control. "Home rule is Rome rule," chanted the supporters of Ulster Protestantism. Among Gladstone's own Liberals, many opposed changing the existing relationship between England and its neighboring possession. They seceded from the Liberals and formed the Unionist Party, which, in coalition with the Conservatives, ruled the

---

Werner Heisenberg (VER-ner HI-zen-berg)

Gladstone (GLAD-sten)

A Suffragist Attempts to Chain Herself to the Gates of Buckingham Palace, London, 1914 In their effort to win the vote, women resorted to public protests, and police often violently intervened. *(Popperfoto/Retrofile.com)*

country from 1886 to 1905. When the Liberals returned to power in 1906, they again proposed home rule. In 1911 the House of Commons finally passed a home rule bill, but it was obstructed in the House of Lords and was not slated to go into effect until September 1914.

In the process of wrangling over the Irish issue, many segments of British society showed they were willing to resort to extralegal and even violent means. Fearing Catholic domination, Protestants in northern Ireland armed themselves, determined to resist home rule. In the rest of Ireland, Catholic groups took up arms, too, insisting on the unity of the island. They were ready to fight for home rule for the whole of Ireland. The Conservative Party in Britain, which opposed home rule, called on Ulster to revolt. British officers threatened to resign their commissions rather than fight Ulster. The behavior of the Conservatives and the army indicated a breakdown of order and authority—a disregard for tradition by two of its bulwarks. Only the outbreak of world war in 1914 delayed a showdown over Ireland, and then by only a few years.

Once back in power in 1906, the Liberals committed themselves to an impressive array of social reforms but were frustrated by the difficulty of getting their program through the House of Lords. The feisty Liberal chancellor of the exchequer, David Lloyd George (1863–1945), expressed his outrage that the will of the people was being thwarted by a handful of magnates in the House of Lords, sitting there not by election but by hereditary right.

The Liberals' social reform program included old-age pensions. To finance them, Lloyd George proposed raising income taxes and death duties and levying a tax on landed wealth. A bill with these measures easily passed the House of Commons in 1909 but was stymied in the upper chamber, where many members were prominent landowners. The House of Lords technically had the power to amend or reject a bill passed by Commons, but for nearly 250 years it had been tacitly understood that the Lords did not have the right to reject a money bill. Nonetheless, motivated by economic self-interest and personal spite against the Liberals, a major-

READING SOURCES — PANKHURST TESTIFIES ON WOMEN'S RIGHTS

In 1908 the suffragists, led by Emmeline Pankhurst, issued a handbill calling on the people of London to "rush" Parliament and win the vote for women. The legal authorities interpreted their action as a violation of the peace, and several suffragists, including Pankhurst, were put on trial. They put up a spirited defense, in which Pankhurst movingly explained her motives for leading the suffragist cause.

I want you to realise how we women feel; because we are women, because we are not men, we need some legitimate influence to bear upon our law-makers. Now, we have tried every way. We have presented larger petitions than were ever presented for any other reform, we have succeeded in holding greater public meetings than men have ever had for any reform, in spite of the difficulty which women have in throwing off their natural diffidence, that desire to escape publicity which we have inherited from generations of our foremothers; we have broken through that. We have faced hostile mobs at street corners, because we were told that we could not have that representation for our taxes which men have won unless we converted the whole of the country to our side. Because we have done this, we have been misrepresented, we have been ridiculed, we have had contempt poured upon us. The ignorant mob at the street corner has been incited to offer us violence, which we have faced unarmed and unprotected by the safeguards which Cabinet Ministers have. We know that we need the protection of the vote even more than men have needed it. . . .

We believe that if we get the vote it will mean better conditions for our unfortunate sisters. We know what the condition of the woman worker is . . . and we have been driven to the conclusion that only through legislation can any improvement be effected, and that that legislation can never be effected until we have the same power as men have to bring pressure to bear upon our representatives and upon Governments to give us the necessary legislation. . . .

I should never be here if I had the same kind of power that the very meanest and commonest of men have—the same power that the wife-beater has, the same power that the drunkard has. I should never be here if I had that power, and I speak for all the women who have come before you and other magistrates. . . .

If you had power to send us to prison, not for six months, but for six years, for sixteen years, or for the whole of our lives, the Government must not think that they can stop this agitation. It will go on. . . .

We are here not because we are law-breakers; we are here in our efforts to become lawmakers.

Source: F. W. Pethick Lawrence, ed., *The Trial of the Suffragette Leaders* (London: The Women's Press, 1909), pp. 21–24.

---

ity in the House of Lords disregarded convention and voted against the bill. This decision provoked a major constitutional crisis.

The Liberal government wanted not only to pass its bill but also to reduce the power of the Lords. In 1911 it sponsored a bill, quickly passed by the House of Commons, to limit the House of Lords to a suspensive veto. This would mean that a bill defeated in the House of Lords could be prevented from going into effect for only a predetermined period—in this case, two years. The House of Lords refused at first to pass such a law. But at the request of the government, the king threatened to appoint four hundred new lords. Reluctantly, the House of Lords passed the bill.

During the debate over the bill, Conservatives—the representatives of British traditionalism and the upholders of decorum—resorted to brawling and refused to let the prime minister speak. It was the first time in British parliamentary history that such a breach of conduct had occurred. The British Parliament, considered the model for supporters of free institutions, had shown itself unable to resolve issues in a civil manner.

Violence also appeared in another unlikely place: the women's suffrage movement. Most liberal males, when speaking of the need to extend human liberty, had excluded women. Toward the end of the nineteenth century, that bastion, too, was under siege. Women began to organize into groups devoted to winning the vote but had little initial success. In 1903 Emmeline Pankhurst (1858–1928) and her two daughters founded the Women's Social and Political Union, whose goal was immediate suffrage.

Angered and frustrated by their lack of progress, the suffragists (often referred to by contemporaries as "suffragettes"), led by the Pankhursts, began a more militant program of protest in 1906—disturbing proceedings in Parliament, breaking windows at the prime minister's residence, slashing canvases at the National Gallery, burning down empty houses, dropping acid into mailboxes, and throwing bombs. They even threatened the lives of the prime minister and the king. Suffragists who were arrested often engaged in hunger strikes. Fearing they would die, the authorities force-fed the women—a painful and humiliating procedure. Female protesters were also physically attacked by male thugs. (See the box "Reading Sources: Pankhurst Testifies on Women's Rights.") That women would resort to violence, and that men inside and outside government would retaliate in kind, demonstrated how widespread the cult of force had become. When war broke out in 1914, the suffragists ceased their violent demonstrations and rallied to support their nation.

France

The Third Republic, founded in 1870 after France's humiliating military defeat at the hands of the Prussians, also struggled with an ongoing series of crises. Challenged by enemies on the political left and right who continually called for the abolition of democracy, the regime found itself buffeted from all sides.

The French government itself contributed to the unstable political situation by its lack of strong leadership. The need to build coalitions among the several parties in the parliament rewarded those politicians who had moderate programs and were flexible. Thus there was little premium on firm ideas and commitments, and the prime minister was often more a conciliator than a leader. Further, lackluster leadership appealed to republicans, who continued to fear that a popular leader might—as Louis Napoleon had in 1851—exploit his support to make himself dictator.

The regime seemed to lurch from scandal to scandal. The most notorious was the Dreyfus affair. In October 1894 Captain Alfred Dreyfus° (1859–1935) of the French army was arrested and charged with passing military secrets to the German embassy. Dreyfus seems to have attracted suspicion because he was the only Jewish

---

Dreyfus (DRY-fooss)

officer on the general staff. The evidence was flimsy—a handwritten letter that some thought Dreyfus had penned, although other experts testified that the handwriting was not that of the young officer.

This letter, and materials that later turned out to be forged, led the French army to court-martial Dreyfus and sentence him to life imprisonment on Devil's Island off the coast of South America. By March 1896 the general staff had evidence that another officer, Major Esterhazy, was actually the spy. But to reopen the case would be to admit the army had made an error, and the general staff refused to do this.

By late 1897, when the apparent miscarriage of justice became widely known, French society split over "the affair." The political left, including many intellectuals, argued for reopening the case. For them it was crucial that justice be carried out. The army and its supporters, right-wing politicians, royalists, and zealous Catholics, argued that the decision should stand. As the bulwark against internal and foreign threats, the army should be above the law, and the fate of a single man—guilty or innocent—was immaterial.

The affair unleashed a swirl of controversy and rioting, which led the government to order a retrial in 1899. But the court again found Dreyfus guilty—this time with "extenuating circumstances" and the recommendation that he be pardoned. Finally, in 1906, Dreyfus was fully exonerated. He ended his days as a general in the army that had subjected him to so much suffering.

The strong encouragement many Catholics gave to those who supported the original verdict confirmed the republicans' belief that the church was a menace to the regime. The Radical Party, the staunchest backers of Dreyfus, won the elections in 1898. Despite its title, the Radical Party backed moderate social reforms. It was uncompromising, however, in its anticlericalism, determined to wreak vengeance on Catholics and end the influence of the church once and for all. In 1905 the parliament passed a law separating church and state, thus ending the privileged position the Catholic Church had enjoyed. Violent language and physical confrontations on both sides accompanied this division. Catholics trying to prevent state officials from entering churches to take required inventories sometimes resorted to force, using weapons or, in one case, a bear chained to the church. Armed soldiers broke down church doors and dragged priests away.

Labor problems also triggered repeated confrontations with the government. Increased labor militancy produced long, drawn-out strikes, which in 1904 alone led to the loss of four million workdays. There was agitation in the countryside, too, particularly in 1907 in the Midi, the south of France. This region suffered from a crisis in the wine industry caused by a disease that attacked the vines, competition from cheap foreign wines, and fraud. More important, the region witnessed increased rural proletarianization as the population grew and larger landholdings were concentrated in fewer hands. Rural militancy led to a revolt in 1907. Troops were sent in, killing dozens and winning for the Radical regime the title "government of assassins."

Italy

The third major power in Europe to adopt parliamentary government also had grave problems. Although unification took place in 1860, Italy found genuine unity elusive. Regionalism, social strife, and an unrepresentative political system plagued the country. As in the past, the south especially challenged the central government. Assertive regionalism, crime, and poverty made this area resistant to most government programs.

The parliamentary system established in 1860 was far from democratic. Property qualifications limited suffrage to less than 3 percent of the population. And as a result of the persistence of *trasformismo* (see page 750)—the practice by which government corrupted and co-opted the opposition—electoral choice was short-circuited.

Between 1870 and 1890 the Italian government introduced some important reforms, but it was difficult to improve the general standard of living for a people undergoing rapid population growth. In the fifty years after unification, the population increased from 25 million to 35 million, and the country had limited resources to deal with such growth. In the south a few wealthy landowners held large *latifundia*°, or private estates, while the majority of the peasants were landless and forced to work the land for minimum wages. In the north industrialization had started, but the region was not rich in coal or iron. To be competitive, industry paid very low wages, and the workers lived in abject misery.

Conditions on the land and in the factories led to widespread protests, followed by stern government repression. In 1893 a Sicilian labor movement won the adherence of 300,000 members, who seized land and attacked government offices. The government responded with massive force and declared martial law. In 1896, with unrest spreading throughout the peninsula, the government placed half of the provinces under military rule. A cycle of violence and counterviolence gripped the nation. In this turbulent atmosphere, an anarchist killed King Umberto I on July 29, 1900.

Riots in Italian Parliament   Party strife and conflicts between individuals in the Italian parliament were so severe that often they degenerated into fisticuffs. This illustration catches a particularly violent moment of a parliamentary debate. *(Madeline Grimoldi)*

After the turn of the century, a new prime minister, Giovanni Giolitti° (1842–1928), tried to bring an end to the upheaval. He used government force more sparingly and showed a spirit of cooperation toward the workers. Seeking to broaden his popularity by an appeal to nationalist fervor, Giolitti launched an attack on Libya in 1911, wresting it from the ailing Ottoman Empire. The territory was arid and bereft of economic promise, but its conquest was championed as a test of national virility and the foundation of national greatness. The imperialists proudly proclaimed force the arbiter of the nation's future.

Domestically, the nation also returned to force. A wave of workers' discontent seized the nation again, and in June 1914 a national strike led to rioting and workers' seizing power in several municipalities. In the Romagna,

---

latifundia (lah-tee-FOON-dya)

Giovanni Giolitti (jo-VAH-nee jo-LEE-tee)

in northern Italy, an independent workers' republic was proclaimed. It took 100,000 government troops ten days to restore order. The workers' restlessness and brazen defiance led some nationalist right-wing extremists to form groups of "volunteers for the defense of order," anticipating the vigilante thugs who were to make up the early bands of Italian fascism.

AUTOCRACIES IN CRISIS

FOUR major autocracies dominated central and eastern Europe: Germany, Austria-Hungary, the Ottoman Empire, and Russia. If the democracies encountered difficulties in these years, the autocracies faced even more vehement opposition. Although many groups in the parliamentary regimes grew impatient at the slowness of change, theoretically at least they could believe that someday their goals would be realized. Not so in the autocracies. In authoritarian states, the demands for more democracy were growing louder. Opponents sought by all means, including violence, to challenge the existing order. Governments in turn were willing to use violence to maintain themselves.

The severity of autocratic rule varied from state to state, ranging from the absolutism of the Ottoman Empire to the semiparliamentary regime of Germany, but the ruler had the final political say in all of the states. Resistance to the autocracies included broad popular challenges to the German imperial system, the reduction of Austria-Hungary to a nearly ungovernable empire, and revolution in the Russian and Ottoman Empires.

Germany

Although Germany had a parliament, the government was answerable to the kaiser, not the people's electoral representatives. And in the late nineteenth century, Prussia, the most reactionary part of the country, continued to dominate.

To rule effectively, Chancellor Otto von Bismarck maneuvered and intrigued to quell opposition. In the face of socialist growth, he used an attempt to assassinate the emperor as the excuse to ban the Socialist Party in 1879. He succeeded in simultaneously winning over conservative agrarian and liberal industrial interests by supporting tariffs on both imported foodstuffs and industrial goods. He also turned against the Catholics, who were lukewarm toward Protestant Prussia, persecuting them and their institutions. These measures, however, did not prevent the growth of the Socialist and Catholic Center Parties.

Wilhelm II The German emperor liked to be viewed in a heroic and military posture. His crippled left hand is turned away from the viewer. *(Landesarchiv Berlin)*

Unfortunately for Bismarck, whose tenure in office depended on the goodwill of the emperor, Wilhelm I died in 1888, to be succeeded first by his son, Friedrich, who ruled only a few months, and then by his grandson, Wilhelm II (r. 1888–1918). The young Kaiser Wilhelm intended to rule as well as reign, but he was ill fit to govern. Convinced of his own infallibility, he bothered to learn very little. Born with a crippled hand, Wilhelm seemed to want to compensate for this infirmity by appearing forceful, even brutal. He hated any hint of limitation to his power, announcing, "There is only one ruler in the Reich and I am he. I tolerate no other." A restless individual, Wilhelm changed uniforms eight times daily and traveled ceaselessly among his seventy-five castles and palaces. Dismayed by Bismarck's proposals of reprisals against the socialists and the chancellor's unwillingness to take on a clearly pro-Austrian and anti-Russian foreign policy, the kaiser dismissed him. But he also did so to rid himself of a formidable, intimidating individual.

Wilhelm II was determined to make Germany a world power whose foreign policy would have a global impact. He wanted Germany to have colonies, a navy, and major influence among the Great Powers. This policy, *Weltpolitik,* or "world politics," greatly troubled Germany's neighbors, partly because they already worried about a new, assertive power in central Europe and partly because German moves were accompanied by the kaiser's bombastic threats. Within Germany, however, Weltpolitik won support. Steel manufacturers and shipbuilders received lucrative contracts; workers, in some industries at least, seemed assured of employment.

Although the nationalist appeals impressed many Germans, the nation could not be easily managed. The emperor's autocratic style was challenged, and his behavior was increasingly viewed as irresponsible. In the elections of 1912 one-third of all Germans voted for Socialist Party candidates. Thus the largest single party in the Reichstag was at least rhetorically committed to the downfall of the capitalist system and autocracy. Labor militancy also reached new heights. In 1912 one million workers—a record number—went on strike. More and more Germans pressed for a parliamentary system with a government accountable to the people's elected representatives.

The emperor could not tolerate criticism of his behavior. He had come to Bismarck's conclusions and frequently talked about using the military to crush socialists and the parliament. These violent thoughts were echoed in the officer corps and in government circles. To some observers it seemed likely that the days of German autocracy were numbered—or that the army and the people would come to blows.

Austria-Hungary

The neighboring Austro-Hungarian Empire was also wracked by a series of crises. In an age of intense nationalism, a multinational empire was an anomaly, as the emperor Franz Joseph (r. 1848–1916) himself acknowledged. Although the relationship between the two halves of the empire was regulated by the Compromise of 1867 (see page 755), the agreement did not prevent conflict between Austria and Hungary, particularly over control of their joint army. The insistence on separate Hungarian interests had developed to such a degree that, had it not been for the outbreak of the world war, Hungary probably would have broken loose from the dual monarchy.

In the Hungarian half of the empire, the Magyars found it increasingly difficult to maintain control. Other nationalities opposed Magyarization—the imposition of the Magyar language and institutions—and insisted on the right to use their own languages in their schools and administrations. The Hungarian government resorted to censorship and jailings to silence nationalist leaders. In the Austrian half of the empire, the treatment of nationalities was less harsh, but the government was equally strife-ridden.

There were no easy solutions to the many conflicts the empire faced. Since middle-class intellectuals led much of the national agitation, the Habsburg government introduced universal male suffrage in 1907 in an effort to undercut their influence. The result was an empire even more difficult to govern. It became nearly impossible to find a workable majority within a parliament that included thirty ethnically based political parties.

The virulence of debate based on nationality and class divisions grew to unprecedented extremes. Within the parliament, deputies threw inkwells at each other, rang sleigh bells, and sounded bugles. Parliament ceased to be relevant. By 1914 the emperor had dissolved it and several regional assemblies. Austria was being ruled by decree. Emperor Franz Joseph feared that the empire would not survive him.

Ottoman Empire

In the generation before 1914, no political system in Europe suffered from so advanced a case of dissolution as the Ottoman Empire, undermined by both secessionist movements within its borders and aggression from other European powers. Sultan Abdul Hamid° II (r. 1876–1909) ruled the country as a despot and authorized mass carnage against those who contested his rule, earning him the title "the Great Assassin."

Young, Western-educated Turks—the so-called Young Turks—disgusted at one-man rule and the continuing loss of territory and influence, overthrew Abdul Hamid in a coup in July 1908. They set up a government responsible to an elected parliament. The Young Turks hoped to stem the loss of territory by establishing firmer central control, but their efforts had the opposite effect. The various nationalities of the empire resented the attempts at "Turkification," the imposition of Turkish education and administration. Renewed agitation broke out in Macedonia, in Albania, and among the Armenians. The government carried out severely repressive measures to end the unrest, massacring thousands of Armenians.

To foreign powers, the moment seemed propitious to plunder the weakened empire. In 1911 Italy occupied Libya, an Ottoman province. Greece, Bulgaria, and Serbia—impatient to enlarge their territories—formed

---

Abdul Hamid (ab-DOOL ah-MEED)

an alliance, the Balkan League, which in 1912 prosecuted a successful war against the empire. Albania became independent, and Macedonia was partitioned among members of the league. Thus, except for the capital, Constantinople, and a narrow band of surrounding land, the empire was stripped of most of its European possessions.

Russia

Through the Great Reforms of the 1860s, the Russian autocracy had attempted to resolve many of the problems troubling its empire and people. But the reforms and the major social changes of the period unleashed new forces, making it even more difficult for the tsars to rule.

The needs of a modernizing country led to an increase in the number of universities and students. The newly educated Russian youths almost instantly began an ardent, sustained critique of autocracy. In the absence of a large group upholding liberal, advanced ideas, university students and graduates, who came to be known as the *intelligentsia,* saw it as their mission to transform Russia.

In the 1870s university youths by the thousands organized a populist movement, hoping to bring change to the countryside. These young idealists, both men and women, intended to educate the peasants and make them more politically aware. But they met with suspicion from the peasantry and repression by the government. Large numbers of populists were arrested and put on trial. Frustrated at the difficulty of bringing about change from below by transforming the people, disaffected radicals formed the People's Will, which turned to murdering public officials to hasten the day of revolution.

Although the regime intensified repression, it also sought to broaden its public support. In 1881 Tsar Alexander II decided to create an advisory committee that some thought would eventually lead to a parliamentary form of government. In March 1881, as he was about to sign the decree establishing this committee, the tsar was assassinated by members of the People's Will.

The new ruler, Tsar Alexander III (r. 1881–1894), who had witnessed the assassination, blamed his father's leniency for his death. By contrast, he was determined to uphold autocracy firmly. He sought to weaken his father's reforms, reducing local self-rule in the process.

When Alexander's son, Nicholas II (r. 1894–1917), succeeded Alexander to the throne in 1894, he declared that he would be as autocratic as his father. However, he lacked the methodical, consistent temperament such a pledge required. A pleasant man, he wanted to be liked, and he lacked the forcefulness to establish a coherent policy for his troubled country.

Since the Great Reforms serious problems had accumulated that threatened the stability of the regime. In the countryside the situation worsened steadily as the population exploded and pressure on the land increased. The provisions that had accompanied the freeing of the serfs left considerable discontent. The peasants were not free to come and go as they pleased; they had to have the permission of the village council. Agriculture remained inefficient, far inferior to that of western Europe. Hence the allotted land was insufficient to feed the peasants, creating a constant demand for more land.

Although Russia remained largely agrarian, there were pockets of industrial growth. Some factories and mining concerns were unusually large, with as many as six thousand employees. When workers grew incensed at their condition and insistent on winning the same rights and protection as their counterparts in western Europe, they engaged in massive strikes that crippled industry.

Political dissatisfaction with the autocracy grew. Members of the expanding middle classes began to clamor that, like their contemporaries in western Europe, they should be given the opportunity to participate in governance. Increasingly, aristocrats also demanded a right to political participation.

Various revolutionary groups committed to socialism continued to flourish. The heirs to the People's Will were the Socialist Revolutionaries, who emerged as a political force in the 1890s. They believed that the peasants would bring socialism to Russia. In 1898 the Russian Social Democratic Party was founded. A Marxist party, it promoted the industrial working class as the harbinger of socialism. In 1903 that party split into the Menshevik and Bolshevik factions. The Mensheviks insisted that Russia had to go through the stages of history Marx had outlined—to witness the full development of capitalism and its subsequent collapse before the socialists could come to power. The Bolsheviks, a minority group, were led by Vladimir Ilich Lenin (1870–1924), a zealous revolutionary and Marxist. Rather than wait for historical forces to undermine capitalism, he insisted that a revolutionary cadre could seize power on behalf of the working class. Lenin favored a small, disciplined, conspiratorial party, like the People's Will, while the Mensheviks favored a more open, democratic party. (See the box "Reading Sources: Lenin Urges a Conspiratorial Revolutionary Party.")

At the turn of the century these groups were still quite small and played a limited role in the mounting opposition to tsarism. But popular opposition soon grew in the face of Russian military ineptitude in the war against Japan, which had broken out in February 1904 in a dispute over control of northern Korea. Antagonism to

READING SOURCES

LENIN URGES A CONSPIRATORIAL REVOLUTIONARY PARTY

The Russian Socialist Party was wracked by internal debates over the direction and means by which a socialist revolution could be created. The majority favored a broad-based party, but in his 1902 essay "What Is to Be Done?" Lenin explained why revolution in Russia could succeed only if it were led by a cadre of professional revolutionaries, organized into a tightly knit conspiratorial group. As Lenin presses for a tightly organized party, notice the practical reasons he enumerates as well as the self-serving nature of his argument.

We must have a committee of professional revolutionaries . . . irrespective of whether they are students or working men. I assert: 1) That no movement can be durable without a stable organization of leaders to maintain continuity; 2) that the more widely the masses are drawn into the struggle and form the basis of the movement, the more necessary it is to have such an organization and the more stable it must be—otherwise it is much easier for demagogues to sidetrack the more backward sections of the masses; 3) that the organization must consist chiefly of persons engaged in revolution as a profession; 4) that in a country with a despotic government, the more we restrict the membership of this organization to persons who are engaged in revolution as a profession and who have been professionally trained in the art of combating the political police, the more difficult will it be to catch the organization; and 5) the wider will be the circle of men and women of the working class or of other classes of society able to join the movement and perform active work in it. . . .

It is . . . argued against us that the views on organization here expounded contradict the "principles of democracy."

Ponder a little over the real meaning of the high-sounding phrase . . . and you will realize that "broad democracy" in party organization, amidst the gloom of autocracy and the domination of the gendarmes, is nothing more than a useless and harmful toy. It is a useless toy, because as a matter of fact, no revolutionary organization has ever practiced broad democracy, nor could it, however much it desired to do so.

The only serious organizational principle the active workers of our movement can accept is: Strict secrecy, strict selection of members and the training of professional revolutionists.

Source: Vladimir Ilich Lenin, "What Is to Be Done?" in *Collected Works*, vol. 4 (New York: International Publishers, 1929), pp. 198–199, 210–213.

 For additional information on this topic, go to college.hmco.com/students.

the tsarist regime escalated as a result of social tensions, heightened by an economic slowdown.

Beginning in January 1905 a series of demonstrations, strikes, and other acts of collective violence erupted. Together they were dubbed "the revolution of 1905." One Sunday in January 1905, 400,000 workers seeking redress of their grievances gathered in front of the tsar's St. Petersburg palace. Rather than hear their protests, officials ordered soldiers to fire on them, resulting in 150 deaths and hundreds more wounded. "Bloody Sunday" inflamed the populace. The tsar, instead of being viewed as an understanding, paternal authority, had become the murderer of his people. Unrest spread to most of the country. As reports reached Russia of more defeats in the war with Japan, the regime's prestige deteriorated further. By September 1905 Russia had to sue for peace and admit defeat. Challenged in the capital, where independent workers' councils called *soviets* had sprung up, the government also lost control over the countryside, the site of widespread peasant uprisings.

Fearing for his regime, Nicholas hoped to disarm the forces challenging tsarism by meeting the demands for parliamentary government and granting major constitutional and civil liberties, including freedom of religion, speech, assembly, and association. At the end of October the tsar established an elective assembly, the Duma, with restricted male suffrage and limited political power. It was far from the Western-style parliament that Russian liberals had desired, but it quickly became the arena for criticism of autocracy. Wanting to create a more pliant instrument, the tsar suspended the assembly, changing its electoral base and its rules of operation. Even many

Workers' Demonstration in Moscow, 1905   In 1905 workers as well as peasants protested against the Russian autocracy. To bring the revolution under control, Nicholas II was obliged to grant several concessions.   *(Novosti)*

conservatives were disillusioned with the tsar's back-tracking and his breach of the promise he had made in 1905 to establish constitutionalism and parliamentarism.

The government reduced the peasants' financial obligations; weakened the power of the commune, or *mir* (see pages 760–761); and extended local self-rule to the peasants. But these changes did little to alleviate a worsening relationship between population and land. Between emancipation and 1914 the peasant population grew by 50 percent, but it acquired only 10 percent more land. In 1891 famine broke out in twenty provinces, killing a quarter of a million people. Rural poverty and discontent were widespread.

Labor unrest also mounted among industrial workers. In 1912 walkouts had involved 725,000 strikers, but by the first half of 1914 that number had doubled. When the French president visited St. Petersburg on the eve of the outbreak of the First World War, barricades were rising in the workers' neighborhoods.

Internally, the authoritarian states of Europe were fighting strong challenges. It was unclear how long they could maintain their respective grips.

THE COMING WAR

NSTABILITY and upheaval characterized international relations in the years between 1880 and 1914. But the outbreak of war was by no means inevitable. Good common sense dictated against it, and some intelligent people predicted that in the new modern era, war would become so destructive that it would be unthinkable. Finally, no European state wanted a war, although the Great Powers carried on policies that brought them to its brink.

Power Alignments

Germany enjoyed an unchallenged position in the international order of the 1870s and 1880s. It was united in an alliance with the two other eastern conservative states—Russia and Austria-Hungary—in the Three Emperors' League, formed in 1873 and renewed by treaty in 1884. And it was part of the Triple Alliance with Austria and Italy. France stood alone, without allies. Britain, with little interest in continental affairs, appeared to be enjoying a "splendid isolation."

However, Germany's alliance system was not free from problems. Two of its allies, Austria-Hungary and Russia, were at loggerheads over control of the Balkans. How could Germany be the friend of both? Wary of apparent German preference for Austria, Bismarck signed the Reinsurance Treaty in 1887, assuring Russia that Germany would not honor its alliance with Austria if the latter attacked Russia. After Bismarck's resignation in 1890, Kaiser Wilhelm allowed the Reinsurance Treaty to lapse. Alarmed, the Russians turned to France and, in January 1894, signed the Franco-Russian Alliance, by which each side pledged to help the other should either be attacked by Germany.

The Great Powers on the Continent were now divided into two alliances, the Triple Alliance and the

Franco-Russian Alliance. Britain formally belonged to neither, but if it favored any side, it would be the German-led alliance. Britain's strongest competitors in the 1880s and 1890s were France and Russia. Both rivaled Britain for influence in Asia, while France vied with Britain for control of Africa.

By its actions in the 1890s Germany lost British goodwill. Launching his Weltpolitik, Wilhelm II built up the German navy. Over the years Britain had developed a navy second to none. An island nation dependent on international trade for its economic survival, Britain saw a strong navy as a necessity and the German naval buildup as a threat to its security.

In the face of what Britain and France viewed as a mounting German menace, they decided to settle their differences overseas. In 1904 they signed an understanding, or *entente,* resolving their rivalries in Egypt. In 1907 Great Britain and Russia regulated their competition for influence in Persia (present-day Iran) with the Anglo-Russian Entente. Europe was still loosely divided into two groups, but now according to a different configuration: the Triple Alliance of Germany, Austria-Hungary, and Italy, and the Triple Entente of Great Britain, France, and Russia.

The Momentum Toward War

Only through a series of crises did these alignments solidify to the point where their members were willing to go to war to save them. France's attempts to take over Morocco twice led to conflict with Germany. In 1905 Germany insisted that an international conference discuss the issue and deny France this kingdom adjacent to its colony of Algeria. When France grabbed Morocco anyway, in 1911, Germany accepted the situation only after extorting compensation from the French, who deeply resented what they viewed as German bullying.

The heightened international rivalry forced the European states to increase their arms expenditures, which added in turn to their sense of insecurity. In 1906 Britain introduced a new class of ships with the launching of the *Dreadnought.* Powered by steam turbines, it was the fastest ship afloat; heavily armored, it could not be sunk easily; and its ten 12-inch guns made it a menace on the seas. The British had thought the Germans could not build equivalent ships, but they did, wiping out British supremacy. Older British ships could now easily be sunk by German dreadnoughts. No longer able to depend on its past supremacy, Britain was feeling less secure than at any time since the Napoleonic Wars, and it continued an expensive and feverish naval race with Germany.

In Germany the growing war-making capacity of Russia created great anxieties. The Japanese defeat of the tsarist empire in 1905 revealed the Russian military to be inferior—a lumbering giant, slow to mobilize and maneuver. As a result, Germany had not been particularly afraid of its eastern neighbor. But stung by its humiliation in 1905, Russia quickly rebuilt its army and planned an extensive rail network in the west. To many in Germany, their country now appeared encircled by a hostile Russia to the east and an equally unfriendly France to the west. Germany became genuinely worried, and beginning in 1912 many in the military and within the government started thinking about a preventive war. If war was inevitable, many Germans argued, it should occur before Russia became even stronger. Fear of the future military balance made some of the highest policymakers see the crisis that broke out in the summer of 1914 as an opportunity to go to war and throttle Russia.

Many political leaders viewed the escalating arms race as a form of madness. Between 1904 and 1913 French and Russian arms expenditures increased by 80 percent, those of Germany by 120 percent, those of Austria-Hungary by 50 percent, and those of Italy by 100 percent. British foreign secretary Sir Edward Grey (1862–1933) warned that if the arms race continued, "it will submerge civilization." But no way was found to stop it.

On the whole, warfare was not feared. Except for short victorious colonial wars, the Western powers had not experienced a major conflict since the Crimean War (1854–1856). Russia had successfully warred against the Ottoman Empire in 1876. Its war against Japan in 1905 had been a calamity, but Russia refused to believe that such a disaster would happen again. Most policymakers believed that the next war would be short. The wars that had so dramatically changed the borders of European states in the second half of the nineteenth century, notably the Austro-Prussian War of 1866 and the Franco-Prussian War of 1870, had been decided within a few weeks. Few imagined that the next war, if it came, would be very brutal or very lengthy, and therefore many of Europe's leaders did not dread war enough to make a major effort to prevent or avoid it.

It was the territorial rivalry between Austria and Russia that triggered international disaster. For decades enmity had been growing between the two empires over control of the Balkans (see Map 24.4). In 1903, following a bloody military coup that killed the king and queen of Serbia, a pro-Russian party took control of the Serbian government. In 1908 Russia, still not recovered from its defeat in 1905, was surprised when Austria unilaterally declared the annexation of the province of Bosnia (which it had administered since the Congress of Berlin in 1878; see page 757). The annexation appeared to spell an end to Serbia's dream of annexing Bosnia, which had

Map 24.4 **The Balkans in 1914** By 1914 the Ottoman Empire was much diminished, containing virtually no European territory. Political boundaries did not follow nationality lines. Serbia was committed to unite all Serbs at the expense of the Austro-Hungarian Empire.

many Serb inhabitants. Fearing war, Russia had to accept diplomatic defeat and abandoned its ally, Serbia. But Russia was determined not to cave in again.

Undeterred, Serbia spread anti-Austrian propaganda and sought to unify under its banner Slavs living in the Balkans, including those under Austrian rule. As a result, many Austrian officials were convinced that the survival of the Austro-Hungarian Empire required the destruction of Serbia. Talk of an attack on Serbia filled the Austrian court in 1914.

On June 28, 1914, the heir to the Habsburg throne, Archduke Franz Ferdinand, visited Sarajevo in Austrian-ruled Bosnia. A young Bosnian-Serb nationalist hostile to Austrian rule, who had been trained and armed by a Serb terrorist group called the Black Hand, assassinated the archduke and his wife.

The assassination of the heir to the throne provided Austria with an ideal pretext for military action. The German kaiser, fearing that failure to support Vienna would lead to Austrian collapse and a Germany bereft of any allies, urged Austria to attack Serbia. On July 23 Austria issued an ultimatum to Serbia, deliberately worded in such a way as to be unacceptable. When Serbia refused the ultimatum, Austria declared war on July 28.

Perceived self-interest motivated each state's behavior in the ensuing crisis. Although in the past Russia had failed to protect Serbia, now it was resolved to help. Russia's status as a Great Power demanded that it not allow its client state to be humiliated, much less obliterated. In the past the French government had acted as a brake on Russian ambitions in the Balkans. On the eve of the war in 1914, France counseled restraint, but it did not withhold its aid. Since 1911 France had increasingly feared

The Shot Heard Round the World The young Serb nationalist Gavril Princip shoots Franz Ferdinand, the heir to the Austro-Hungarian throne, and his consort. The assassination unleashed the outbreak of World War I. *(Österreichische Nationalbibliothek, Vienna)*

isolation in the face of what it perceived as growing German aggression. Its only ally on the Continent was Russia. To remain a Great Power, France needed to preserve its friendship with Russia and help that country maintain its own Great Power status.

Germany could not allow Austria, its only ally, to be destroyed. Its leaders may also have seen the crisis as a propitious moment to begin a war that was going to occur sooner or later anyway. The Germans no doubt thought it expedient to strike before the entente powers, especially Russia, became stronger. As the German prime minister put it, his country was about to take "a leap in the dark," and he declared war on Russia. Assuming that France would come to the aid of Russia, Germany invaded France through Belgium. The British, concerned by the threat to their ally France and outraged by the violation of Belgian neutrality, to which all the Great Powers had been signatories since 1839, declared war on Germany. Events hurtled forward between the Austrian declaration of war on Serbia on July 28 and the British decision on August 4. Europe was at war. Eventually so would be much of the world.

SUMMARY

O N the surface, the years 1880 to 1914 seemed comfortable. More people than ever before enjoyed material advantages and improved standards of living. Literacy spread. Death rates went down. Life expectancy rose.

Europe appeared to dominate the globe. In their relations with Africa and Asia, Europeans resorted to force to an unprecedented degree, conquering most of Africa and much of Asia. Europe intended to exploit the new empires as sources of wealth, trade, and the trappings of power. But colonial rivals and subjects challenged the future of these empires, leading to various anxieties.

With improved conditions in Europe, a revolution of rising expectations had been created. People grew more demanding, insisting in sometimes violent ways on their political and economic rights. Although mass movements such as socialism and the women's suffrage movement generally used peaceful means in their campaigns to change society, some of their members advocated and employed force. Anarchism appeared to stalk Europe. In turn, states did not hesitate to use force in efforts to quell various protest movements, even resorting to martial law.

Reflecting these trends, intellectuals such as Freud and Bergson and artists such as Munch and Moreau suggested that a hidden, irrational dimension of life lurked beneath the tranquil surface. Behind the façade of security and conformity lay many disturbing impulses, such as racism, anti-Semitism, and tyranny.

Although most Europeans were confident and optimistic about their futures, such self-assuredness was not universally shared. Intellectuals spoke of decadence and decline. Policymakers worried about the future of their countries and, anxious to avoid the threat of decline, resorted to extreme measures such as empire building overseas and armed competition in Europe. Among European thinkers and leaders, force had become widely accepted as the means to an end; some leaders—notably those of Austria-Hungary and Germany—favored war over negotiation in July 1914.

The major powers—except Britain, confident in its naval dominance—built up large standing armies with millions of men and lethal modern equipment. Europe's network of alliances led inexorably to the larger conflict. If some leaders still feared war, more dreaded the consequences of not fighting, believing that war would save their regimes from the internal and external challenges they faced. Few could foresee the dire consequences of such a choice.

■ Suggested Reading

Burrow, J. W. *The Crisis of Reason: European Thought, 1848–1914.* 2000. A strong emphasis on individual intellectuals and their contributions.

Carrère d'Encausse, Hélène. *Nicholas II.* 2000. A biography of the tsar, set within the context of an increasingly difficult country to govern.

Hobsbawm, Eric. *The Age of Empire, 1875–1914.* 1987. A fine survey emphasizing social change, by a leading British historian.

Hochschild, Adam. *King Leopold's Ghost.* 1998. A dramatic account of Leopold II's brutal rule over the Congo.

Jay, Mike, and Michael Neve, eds. *1900: A Fin-de-Siècle Reader.* 1999. A rich collection of documents on how people imagined the new century.

Johnson, Martin P. *The Dreyfus Affair.* 1999. A brisk review of the major events shaping the affair.

Joll, James. *The Origins of the First World War.* 1984. A clear, concise, readable history tracing how strategic interests and nationalist passions led to the outbreak of war.

Schorske, Carl E. *Fin de Siècle Vienna: Politics and Culture.* 1980. A critically acclaimed work on the arts and social and political thought in the Habsburg capital at the turn of the century.

 For a searchable list of additional readings for this chapter, go to college.hmco.com/students.

The Layout of the British Museum

The British Museum was founded in the mid-eighteenth century when the government acquired some private collections. The museum increased the size of its collections, largely through donations, bringing in objects from around the world. In its early years the museum was located in a converted private mansion. Then in 1847, to house its growing collection, the museum moved into a monumental building with a neoclassical façade. Until the 1830s public access was limited to the upper classes, mainly the learned. By the mid-nineteenth century, however, a million people a year were visiting the museum. Displays of materials gathered from non-European cultures drew particularly large audiences.

Consider how the exhibits reflected British imperialism. In the first half of the nineteenth century, objects from Oceania, reflecting British activities in the Pacific, were acquired. African materials became more plentiful with the British conquest of much of Africa after the 1880s. The British military expedition to Nigeria in 1897 led to the acquisition of the fabulous Benin bronzes.

While imperial adventures were shaping the museum collection, the museum in turn was supporting imperialism. Museum officials declared that increased knowledge about regions overseas would fuel enthusiasm for the imperial venture and make the British people better fit to rule their new subjects.

The manner in which the British Museum displayed some of its possessions reflected the intellectual currents of the times. In the late eighteenth and early nineteenth centuries, the museum grouped its non-European objects with "natural history": non-Europeans were associ-

Plan of the Upper Floor of the British Museum, ca. 1880 *(Based on map in Henry C. Shelley,*
The British Museum: Its History and Treasures [Boston: L. C. Page, 1911], pp. 274–275.)

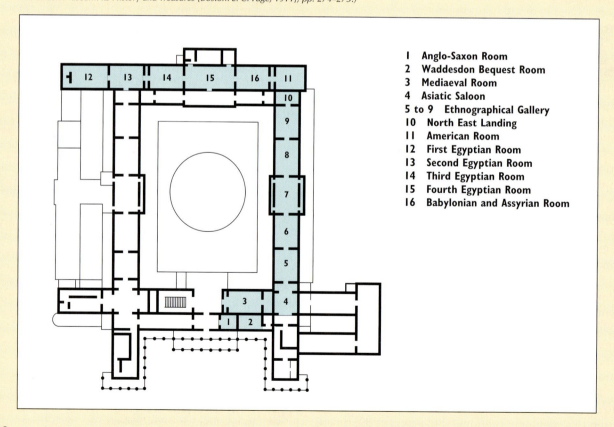

1 Anglo-Saxon Room
2 Waddesdon Bequest Room
3 Mediaeval Room
4 Asiatic Saloon
5 to 9 Ethnographical Gallery
10 North East Landing
11 American Room
12 First Egyptian Room
13 Second Egyptian Room
14 Third Egyptian Room
15 Fourth Egyptian Room
16 Babylonian and Assyrian Room

ated with nature, with the beasts of the earth. Running out of space, the museum moved the natural history collection to a separate Natural Museum in South Kensington, and in the 1880s ethnography, the branch of anthropology devoted to human cultures, constituted a separate collection.

The late-nineteenth-century plan of the upper floor of the museum shown here reflects the racial views of imperial Britain. After climbing the stairs from the ground floor, we start at the room labeled 1, the Anglo-Saxon Room, which celebrates England's early history. Then comes the Waddesdon Bequest Room, which houses various artifacts of ancient and medieval English and European history (the room is named after the Rothschild mansion, where the collection was previously housed). Next we arrive at the Mediaeval Room. Using the route most visitors would then take, we come to the Asiatic Saloon, filled with pottery, porcelain, and other works of art from Japan, China, Persia, and India.

What is the significance of this juxtaposition of rooms? The British and other Europeans had developed an ethnocentric view of the human races, believing that the white race was by far superior to all others. This belief seemed confirmed by the material accomplishments of Europeans, especially impressive in the nineteenth century. Of the non-Europeans, the Asians had won the grudging respect of the British and other Europeans. China, with its thousands of years of recorded history and sophisticated government structures, was one of several Asian societies that impressed them. Because many African societies lacked a written culture and had government and religious systems dramatically different from the Europeans', the British and other Europeans often considered Africans ignorant and primitive.

Biologists, anthropologists, and others speculating about the human races offered two different explanations for racial variations. These hypotheses competed with each other for public acceptance. According to the first, biology determined the level of civilization of each people. According to the second, different peoples were at different levels of development. In this view Europeans were most developed, Africans least; but eventually Asians and Africans would progress and reach a level similar to that of Europeans. In the meantime non-Europeans illustrated European life at earlier stages of development.

It is interesting that the Asiatic Saloon, with its swords, shields, and other elaborate Asian objects, was next to the Mediaeval Room. The positioning invites consideration that some nineteenth-century Asian societies were at a level of development akin to medieval England.

An empty corridor separated this part of the museum from the Ethnographical Gallery, giving visitors the sense that what they would view was separate from medieval England and selected Asian societies. The Ethnographical Gallery displayed objects from Asia, Oceania, Africa, and the Americas. They tended to be objects of daily life, such as household wares, weapons, and clothing. The stress was on their simplicity and primitiveness—presumably reflections of the primitive culture of their makers. The objects were not differentiated chronologically; pre-Columbian artifacts from the Americas were displayed beside modern African crafts. Ethnographic items were seldom dated, implying that the peoples who created them did not develop and had no history. The museum guidebook invited nineteenth-century viewers to consider how close the development of these peoples was to that of the earliest Europeans.

After passing through the Ethnographical Gallery, a visitor would arrive at the North East Landing and then enter the American Room. It contained items from Eskimos, Native Americans, and other peoples whom Victorians considered "primitives," but it also included artifacts from the Aztecs and Incas, whom the British considered to have been highly developed.

The Aztec and Inca collections abutted the room devoted to two ancient civilizations with monumental architecture, the Babylonian and Assyrian Room. Next came four Egyptian rooms. In the nineteenth century, the greatness of ancient Egyptian culture was recognized. The British Museum allotted ancient Egypt ample space far removed from what were seen as the "primitive" peoples represented in the Ethnographical Gallery.

In 1972 the ethnographic collection was moved out of the British Museum and now constitutes the Museum of Mankind. With the loss of empire and the decline of confidence in the superiority of the white race, the old uses for the objects collected overseas had become obsolete.*

---

*The author is grateful to Thomas Prasch, Washburn University, for his help and advice and for making available two of his unpublished papers on this subject.

CHAPTER 25

War and Revolution 1914–1919

MUD. It was not what soldiers had in mind when they headed off to war in August 1914 amid visions of glory, gallantry—and quick victory. But after heavy rain and constant shelling, mud was a fact of life for those fighting on the western front—Belgium and northern France—during the fall of 1917. The mud was so pervasive, in fact, that soldiers literally drowned in it. These Canadian troops are holding the line on November 14, 1917, at the end of the Battle of Passchendaele°, a British-led assault that began late in July. That assault pushed the Germans back a mere 5 miles—at the cost of 300,000 lives. There was no end to the war in sight.

Some had thought a major war impossible in rational, civilized Europe. Others had devoutly wished for war—precisely to break out of the stifling bourgeois conventions of rational, civilized Europe. When war actually began early in August 1914, the European mood was generally enthusiastic, even festive. No one was prepared for what this war would bring, including the hellish scenes of mud, smoke, artillery craters, blasted trees, decaying bodies, and ruined buildings that came to frame the daily experience of those on the western front. A far wider and more destructive war would follow within a generation, but it was World War I, known to contemporaries as "the Great War," that shattered the old European order, with its comfortable assumptions of superiority, rationality, and progress. After this war, neither Westerners nor non-Westerners could still believe in the privileged place of Western civilization in quite the same way.

The war that began in August was supposed to be over by Christmas. The British government promised "business as usual." But the

---

Passchendaele (PAH-shun-dale)

Passchendaele, Belgium, 1917.
(By courtesy of the Trustees of the Imperial War Museum)

843

fighting bogged down in a stalemate during the fall of 1914, then continued for four more years. By the time it ended, in November 1918, the war had strained the whole fabric of life, affecting everything from economic organization to literary vocabulary, from journalistic techniques to the role of women.

Partly because the war grew to become the first "world war," it proved the beginning of the end of European hegemony. The intervention of the United States in 1917 affected the military balance and seemed to give the war more idealistic and democratic purposes. The geographic reach of the war was itself unprecedented, especially after the intervention of the Ottoman Empire spread the fighting to the Middle East. Because of European colonial networks, the war also involved many other non-Europeans in combat or support roles. Although the old colonialism continued into the postwar era, the war nourished the forces that would later overthrow it.

Because of all the strains it entailed, the war had many unintended consequences. Revolutions dramatically changed the political landscape first in Russia, then in Germany. The Habsburg and Ottoman Empires collapsed. So when the victors met early in 1919 to shape the peace, they confronted a situation that could not have been foreseen in 1914. And their effort to determine the contours of the postwar world, and thus the immediate meaning of the war, left much unresolved.

QUESTIONS TO CONSIDER

- How did geography affect the shape and outcome of World War I?

- Why did this prove a total war, making necessary new forms of socioeconomic coordination and even systematic propaganda?

- What was the relationship between the war and the two revolutions in Russia in 1917?

- What factors shaped the peace settlement that the victors imposed on Germany in 1919?

TERMS TO KNOW

Sacred Union	provisional government
British blockade	Vladimir Lenin
total war	Wilson's "Fourteen Points"
Kriegsrohstoff-	Treaty of Brest-Litovsk
abteilung (KRA),	"stab in the back" myth
war raw materials	Treaty of Versailles
office	League of Nations
Petrograd Soviet	

THE UNFORESEEN STALEMATE, 1914–1917

WHEN the war began in August 1914, enthusiasm and high morale, based on expectations of quick victory, marked both sides. But fighting on the crucial western front led to a stalemate by the end of 1914, and the brutal encounters of 1916 made it clear that this was not the sort of war most had expected. By early 1917 the difficulties of the war experience brought to the surface underlying questions about what all the fighting was for—and whether it was worth the price.

August 1914: The Domestic and Military Setting

Although some, including Helmuth von Moltke° (1848–1916), chief of the German general staff, worried that this would prove a long, destructive war testing the very fabric of Western civilization, the outbreak of fighting early in August produced a wave of euphoria and a remarkable degree of domestic unity. To many, war came almost as a relief; at last, the issues that had produced tension and intermittent crisis for the past decade would find a definitive solution. Especially among educated young people,

---

Moltke (MOLT-kuh)

this settling of accounts seemed to offer the prospect of renewal, even a kind of redemption, for themselves and their societies. The war promised an escape from the stifling bourgeois world and, in response to the common danger, an end to the bickering and divisiveness of everyday politics. (See the box "Reading Sources: The Joys of August 1914.")

An unexpected display of patriotism from the socialist left reinforced the sense of domestic unity and high morale. Forgetting their customary rhetoric about international proletarian solidarity, members of the socialist parties of the Second International rallied to their respective national war efforts almost everywhere in Europe. To socialists and workers, national defense against a more backward aggressor seemed essential to the eventual creation of socialism. French Socialists had to defend France's democratic republic against autocratic and militaristic Germany; German Socialists had to defend German institutions, and the strong socialist organizations that had proven possible within them, against repressive tsarist Russia. When, on August 4, the German Socialist Party delegation in the Reichstag voted with the other parties to give the government the budgetary authority to wage war, it was clear that the Second International had failed in its long-standing commitment to keep the workers of Europe from slaughtering each other.

In France, the government had planned, as a precaution, to arrest roughly one thousand trade union and socialist leaders in the event of war, but no such arrests were necessary. The order of the day was "Sacred Union," which meant that French leaders from across the political spectrum agreed to cooperate for the duration of the war. Rather than seek to sabotage the war, Socialist leaders joined the new government of national defense. Germany enjoyed a comparable "Fortress Truce," including an agreement to suspend labor conflict during the war, although no Socialist was invited to join the war cabinet.

In 1914 the forces of the Triple Entente outnumbered those of Germany and Austria-Hungary. Russia had an army of over 1 million men, the largest in Europe, and France had 700,000. Britain, which did not introduce conscription until 1916, had about 250,000. Germany led the Central Powers with 850,000; Austria-Hungary contributed 450,000. Though outnumbered, the Central Powers had potential advantages in equipment, coordination, and speed over their more dispersed adversaries. The outcome was hardly a foregone conclusion in August 1914.

After the fighting began, a second group of nations intervened one by one, expanding the war's scope and complicating the strategic alternatives. In November

CHRONOLOGY

August 1914	Fighting begins
September 1914	French forces hold off the German assault at the Marne
August–September 1914	German victories repel Russian invasion on eastern front
May 1915	Italy declares war on Austria-Hungary
February–December 1916	Battle of Verdun
July–November 1916	Battle of the Somme
January 1917	Germans resume unrestricted submarine warfare
March 1917	First Russian revolution: fall of the tsar
April 1917	U.S. declaration of war
July 1917	German Reichstag war aims resolution
November 1917	Second Russian revolution: the Bolsheviks take power
March 1918	Treaty of Brest-Litovsk between Germany and Russia
March–July 1918	Germany's last western offensive
June 1918	Initial outbreak of the "Spanish flu"
July 1918	Second Battle of the Marne
November 1918	Armistice: fighting ends
January 1919	Paris Peace Conference convenes
June 1919	Victors impose Treaty of Versailles on Germany

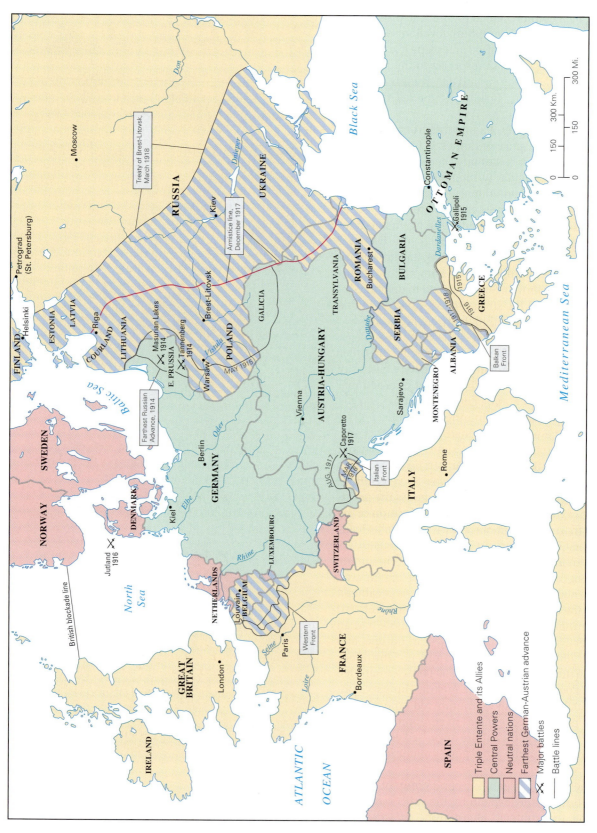

Map 25.1   Major Fronts of World War I   Although World War I included engagements in East Asia and the Middle East, it was essentially a European conflict, encompassing fighting on a number of fronts. A vast territory was contested in the east, but on the western front, which proved decisive, fighting was concentrated in a relatively small area.

READING SOURCES

THE JOYS OF AUGUST 1914

In an autobiography published in 1943, the writer Stefan Zweig (1881–1942) recalled the remarkable enthusiasm that accompanied the outbreak of war in his native Vienna in 1914. The popular mood reflected a naive faith, yet Zweig sensed that something more troubling was at work as well.

In Vienna I found the entire city in a tumult. The first shock at the news of war—the war that no one, people or government, had wanted—the war which had slipped, much against their will, out of the clumsy hands of the diplomats who had been bluffing and toying with it, had suddenly been transformed into enthusiasm. There were parades in the streets, flags, ribbons, and music burst forth everywhere, young recruits were marching triumphantly, their faces lighting up at the cheering. . . .

And to be truthful, I must acknowledge that there was a majestic, rapturous, and even seductive something in this first outbreak of the people from which one could escape only with difficulty. And in spite of all my hatred and aversion for war, I should not like to have missed the memory of those first days. As never before, thousands and hundreds of thousands felt what they should have felt in peace time, that they belonged together. A city of two million, a country of nearly fifty million, in that hour felt that they were participating in world history, in a moment which would never recur, and that each one was called upon to cast his infinitesimal self into the glowing mass, there to be purified of all selfishness. All differences of class, rank, and language were flooded over at that moment by the rushing feeling of fraternity. Strangers spoke to one another in the streets, people who had avoided each other for years shook hands. . . . The clerk, the cobbler, had suddenly achieved a romantic possibility in life; he could become a hero, and everyone who wore a uniform was already being cheered by the women. . . . But it is quite possible that a deeper, more secret power was at work in this frenzy. So deeply, so quickly did the tide break over humanity that, foaming over the surface, it churned up the depths, the subconscious primitive instincts of the human animal—that which Freud so meaningfully calls "the revulsion from culture," the desire to break out of the conventional bourgeois world of codes and statutes, and to permit the primitive instincts of the blood to rage at will.

. . . The people had unqualified confidence in their leaders; no one in Austria would have ventured the thought that the all-high ruler Emperor Franz Josef, in his eighty-third year, would have called his people to war unless from direct necessity, would have demanded such a sacrifice of blood unless evil, sinister, and criminal foes were threatening the peace of the Empire.

Source: Stefan Zweig, *The World of Yesterday: An Autobiography*, translated by Helmut Ripperger. Copyright © 1943 by the Viking Press, Inc. Used by permission of Viking Penguin, a division of Penguin Group (USA), Inc.

 For additional information on this topic, go to college.hmco.com/students.

1914 the Ottoman Empire, fearful of Russia, joined the Central Powers, thereby extending the war along the Russo-Turkish border and on to Mesopotamia and the approaches to the Suez Canal in the Middle East. For Arabs disaffected with Ottoman Turkish rule, the war presented an opportunity to take up arms—with the active support of Britain and France. Italy, after dickering with both sides, committed itself to the Entente in the Treaty of London of April 1915. This secret agreement specified the territories Italy would receive—primarily the Italian-speaking areas still within Austria-Hungary—in the event of Entente victory. In September 1915 Bulgaria entered the war on the side of the Central Powers, seeking territorial advantages at the expense of Serbia, which had defeated Bulgaria in the Second Balkan War in 1913. Finally, in August 1916, Romania intervened on the side of the Entente, hoping to gain Transylvania, then part of Hungary.

Thus the war was fought on a variety of fronts (see Map 25.1). This fact, combined with uncertainties about the role of sea power, led to ongoing debate among military decision makers about strategic priorities. Because of the antagonism that the prewar German naval buildup had caused, some expected that Britain and Germany

No Trenches in Sight   Spirits were high early in August 1914, as soldiers like these in Paris marched off to war. None foresaw what fighting this war would be like. None grasped the long-term impact the war would have.   *(Giraudon/Art Resource, NY)*

would quickly be drawn into a decisive naval battle. Britain promptly instituted an effective naval blockade on imports to Germany, but the great showdown on the seas never materialized. Even the most significant naval encounter between them, the Battle of Jutland in 1916, was inconclusive. Despite the naval rivalry of the prewar years, World War I proved fundamentally a land war.

Germany faced not only the long-anticipated two-front war against Russia in the east and France and Britain in the west; it also had to look to the southeast, given the precarious situation of its ally Austria-Hungary, which was fighting Serbia and Russia, then also Italy and Romania as well. On the eastern front, Germany was largely successful, forcing first Russia, then Romania, to seek a separate peace by mid-1918. But it was the western front that proved decisive.

Into the Nightmare, 1914

With the lessons of the wars of German unification in mind, both sides had planned for a short war based on rapid offensives, a war of movement. According to the Schlieffen° Plan, drafted in 1905, Germany would concen-

trate first on France, devoting but one-eighth of its forces to containing the Russians, who would need longer to mobilize. After taking just six weeks to knock France out of the war, Germany would then concentrate on Russia. French strategy, crafted by General Joseph Joffre° (1852–1931), the commander-in-chief of the French forces, similarly relied on rapid offensives. The boys would be home by Christmas—or so it was thought.

Although German troops encountered more opposition than expected from the formerly neutral Belgians, they moved swiftly through Belgium into northern France during August. By the first week of September they had reached the Marne River, threatening Paris and forcing the French government to retreat south to Bordeaux°. But French and British troops under Joffre counterattacked from September 6 to 10, forcing the Germans to fall back and begin digging in along the Aisne° River. By holding off the German offensive at this first Battle of the Marne, the Entente had undercut the Schlieffen Plan—and with it, it turned out, any chance of a speedy victory by either side.

During the rest of the fall of 1914, each side tried—unsuccessfully—to outflank the other. When, by the end

---

Schlieffen (SHLEE-fyn)

Joffre (JOFF-ruh)   **Bordeaux** (bor-DOH)   **Aisne** (ENN)

Trench Warfare Grim though they were, the trenches proved effective for defensive purposes. Here a British soldier guards a trench at Ovillers, on the Somme, in July 1916. *(Courtesy of the trustees of the Imperial War Museum)*

of November, active fighting ceased for the winter, a military front of about 300 miles had been established, all the way from Switzerland to the coast of the North Sea in Belgium (see Map 25.2 on page 863). This line failed to shift more than 10 miles in either direction over the next three years. The result of the first six weeks of fighting on the western front was not a gallant victory but a grim and unforeseen stalemate.

Virtually from the start, the war took a fiercely destructive turn. In northern France in September 1914, the Germans fired on the cathedral at Reims°, severely damaging its roof and nave, because they believed— apparently correctly—that the French were using one of its towers as an observation post. If such a catastrophe could happen to one of the great monuments in Europe, what else might this war bring?

The two sides were forced to settle into a war of attrition relying on an elaborate network of defensive trenches. Although separated by as much as 5 miles in some places, enemy trenches were sometimes within shouting distance, so there was occasionally banter back and forth, even attempts to entertain the other side. But the trenches quickly became almost unimaginably

Reims (RAANZ)

gruesome—filthy, ridden with rats and lice, noisy and smoky from artillery fire, and foul-smelling, partly from the odor of decaying bodies.

As defensive instruments, however, the trenches proved quite effective. Each side quickly learned to take advantage of barbed wire, mines, and especially machine guns to defend its positions. A mass of barbed wire, 3 to 5 feet high and 30 yards wide, guarded a typical trench. The machine gun had been developed before the war as an offensive weapon; few foresaw the decided advantage it would give the defense. But with machine guns, soldiers could defend trenches even against massive assaults—and inflict heavy casualties on the attackers.

In 1916 the British sent the first shipment of tanks to France as an antidote to the machine gun, but, as skeptics had warned, tanks proved too ungainly and unreliable to be widely effective. Although the French used them to advantage in the decisive Allied offensive in 1918, tanks were not crucial to the outcome of the war.

Though the defensive trenches had formidable advantages, neither side could give up the vision of a decisive offensive to break through on the western front. Thus the troops were periodically called on to go "over the top" and then across "no man's land" to assault the dug-in enemy. Again and again, however, such offensives

READING SOURCES

INTO THE TRENCHES

As the initial offensives on the western front turned into stalemate, ordinary soldiers on both sides began to experience unprecedented forms of warfare in an eerie new landscape. Writing home to his family from France in November 1914, a young German soldier, Fritz Franke (1892–1915), sought to convey what this new war was like. He was killed six months later.

Yesterday we didn't feel sure that a single one of us would come through alive. You can't possibly picture to yourselves what such a battle-field looks like. It is impossible to describe it, and even now, when it is a day behind us, I myself can hardly believe that such bestial barbarity and unspeakable suffering are possible. Every foot of ground contested; every hundred yards another trench; and everywhere bodies—rows of them! All the trees shot to pieces; the whole ground churned up a yard deep by the heaviest shells; dead animals; houses and churches so utterly destroyed by shellfire that they can never be of the least use again. And every troop that advances in support must pass through a mile of this chaos, through this gigantic burial ground and the reek of corpses.

In this way we advanced on Tuesday, marching for three hours, a silent column, in the moonlight, toward the Front and into a trench as Reserve, two to three hundred yards from the English, close behind our own infantry.

There we lay the whole day, a yard and a half to two yards below the level of the ground, crouching in the narrow trench on a thin layer of straw, in an overpowering din which never ceased all day or the greater part of the night—the whole ground trembling and shaking! There is every variety of sound—whistling, whining, ringing, crashing, rolling . . . [ellipses in the original] the beastly things pitch right above one and burst and the fragments buzz in all directions, and the only question one asks is: "Why doesn't one get me?" Often the things land within a hand's breath and one just looks on. One gets so hardened to it that at the most one ducks one's head a little if a great, big naval-gun shell comes a bit too near and its grey-green stink is a bit too thick. Otherwise one soon just lies there and thinks of other things. . . .

One just lives from one hour to the next. For instance, if one starts to prepare some food, one never knows if one may'nt have to leave it behind within an hour. . . .

. . . Above all one acquires a knowledge of human nature! We all live so naturally and unconventionally here, every one according to his own instincts. That brings much that is good and much that is ugly to the surface.

Source: A. F. Wedd, ed., *German Students' War Letters,* translated and arranged from the original edition of Dr. Philipp Witkop (London: Methuen, 1929), pp. 123–125.

---

proved futile, producing incredibly heavy casualties: "Whole regiments gambled away eternity for ten yards of wasteland."[1]

For the soldiers on the western front, the war became a nightmarish experience in a hellish landscape. Bombardment by new, heavier forms of artillery scarred the terrain with craters, which became muddy, turning the landscape into a near swamp. (See the box "Reading Sources: Into the Trenches.") Beginning early in 1915, tear gas, chlorine gas, and finally mustard gas found use on both sides. Although the development of gas masks significantly reduced the impact of this menacing new chemical warfare, the threat of poison gas added another nightmarish element to the experience of those who fought the war.

The notions of patriotism, comradeship, duty, and glory that had been prevalent in 1914 gradually dissolved as soldiers experienced the horrors of warfare. A French soldier, questioning his own reactions after battle in 1916, responded with sarcasm and irony: "What sublime emotion inspires you at the moment of assault? I thought of nothing other than dragging my feet out of the mud encasing them. What did you feel after surviving the attack? I grumbled because I would have to remain several days more without *pinard* [wine]. Is not one's first act to kneel down and thank God? No. One relieves oneself."[2]

Although the Germans had been denied their quick victory in the west, by the end of 1914 they occupied much of Belgium and almost one-tenth of France, including major industrial areas and mines producing most of

France's coal and iron. On the eastern front, as well, the Germans won some substantial advantages in 1914—but not a decisive victory.

The first season of fighting in the east suggested that the pattern there would not be trench warfare but rapid movement across a vast but thinly held front. When the fighting began in August, the Russians mustered more quickly than anticipated, confronting an outnumbered German force in a menacing, if reckless, invasion of East Prussia. But by mid-September German forces under General Paul von Hindenburg (1847–1934) and his chief of staff, General Erich Ludendorff (1865–1937), repelled the Russian advance, taking a huge number of prisoners and seriously demoralizing the Russians.

As a result of their victory in East Prussia, Hindenburg and Ludendorff emerged as heroes, and they would play major roles in German public life thereafter. Hindenburg, the senior partner, became chief of staff of the entire German army in August 1916, and the able and energetic Ludendorff remained at his side. Ludendorff proved to be the key figure as this powerful duo gradually assumed undisputed control of the whole German war effort, both military and domestic.

Seeking a Breakthrough, 1915–1917

After the campaigns of 1915 proved inconclusive, German leaders decided to concentrate in 1916 on a massive offensive against the great French fortress at Verdun, intending to inflict a definitive defeat on France. To assault the fortress, the Germans gathered 1,220 pieces of artillery for attack along an 8-mile front. Included were thirteen "Big Bertha" siege guns, weapons so large that nine tractors were required to position each of them; a crane was necessary to insert the shell, which weighed over a ton. The level of heavy artillery firepower that the Germans applied at Verdun was unprecedented in the history of warfare.

German forces attacked on February 21, taking the outer defenses of the fortress, and appeared poised for victory. The tide turned, however, when General Philippe Pétain (1856–1951) assumed control of the French defense at Verdun. Pétain had the patience and skill necessary to organize supply networks for a long and difficult siege. Furthermore, he proved able, through considerate treatment, to inspire affection and confidence among his men. By mid-July the French army had repelled the

Paul von Hindenburg and Erich Ludendorff
The talents of Hindenburg (*left*) and Ludendorff meshed effectively to carry them from success on the eastern front in 1914 to a predominant role in the German war effort. They are shown here at a reception in honor of Hindenburg's seventieth birthday in October 1917.   (*akg-images*)

German offensive, although only in December did the French retake the outer defenses of the fortress. The French had held firm in what would prove the war's longest, most trying battle—one that killed over 700,000 people. For the French the Battle of Verdun would remain the epitome of the horrors of World War I.

To relieve pressure on Verdun, the British led a major attack at the Somme River on July 1, 1916. On that day alone the British suffered almost 60,000 casualties, including 21,000 killed. Fighting continued into the fall, but the offensive proved futile in the end. One-third of those involved, or over 1 million soldiers, ended up dead, missing, or wounded.

Dominated by the devastating battles at Verdun and the Somme, the campaigns of 1916 finally extinguished the high spirits of the summer of 1914. Both sides suffered huge losses—apparently for nothing. By the end of 1916, the front had shifted only a few miles from its location at the beginning of the year.

In light of the frustrating outcome so far, the French turned to new military leadership, replacing Joffre as commander-in-chief with Robert Nivelle (1856–1924), who promptly sought to prove himself with a new offensive during the spring of 1917. Persisting even as it became clear that this effort had no chance of success, Nivelle provoked increasing resistance among French soldiers, some of whom were refusing to follow orders by the end of April.

With the French war effort in danger of collapse, the French government replaced Nivelle with General Pétain°, the hero of the defense of Verdun. Pétain reestablished discipline by adopting a conciliatory approach—improving food and rest, visiting the troops in the field, listening, offering encouragement, urging patience, even dealing relatively mercifully with most of the resisters themselves. To be sure, many of the soldiers who had participated in this near mutiny were court-martialed, and over 3,400 were convicted. But of the 554 sentenced to death, only 49 were actually executed.

After the failure of the Nivelle offensive, the initiative fell to the British under General Douglas Haig (1861–1928), who was convinced, despite skepticism in the British cabinet, that Nivelle's offensive had failed simply because of tactical mistakes. Beginning near Ypres° in Belgium on July 31, 1917, and continuing until November, the British attacked. As before, the effort yielded only minimal territorial gains—about 50 square miles—at a horrifying cost, including 300,000 British and Canadian casualties. Known as the Battle of Passchendaele,

the British offensive of 1917 ranks with the Battles of Verdun and the Somme as the bloodiest of the war.

1917 as a Turning Point

Meanwhile, the Germans decided to concentrate on the eastern front in 1917 in an effort to knock Russia out of the war. This intensified German military pressure helped spark revolution in Russia, and in December 1917 Russia's new revolutionary regime asked for a separate peace (see page 861). The defeat of Russia freed the Germans at last to concentrate on the west, but by this time France and Britain had a new ally.

On April 6, 1917, the United States entered the war on the side of the Entente, in response to Germany's controversial use of submarines. Germany did not have enough surface ships to respond to Britain's naval blockade, whether by attacking the British fleet directly or by mounting a comparable blockade of the British Isles. So the Germans decided to use submarines to interfere with shipping to Britain. Submarines, however, were too vulnerable to be able to surface and confiscate goods, so the Germans had to settle for sinking suspect ships with torpedoes. In February 1915 they declared the waters around the British Isles a war zone and served notice that they would torpedo not only enemy ships but also neutral ships carrying goods to Britain.

The German response was harsh, but so was the British blockade, which violated a number of earlier international agreements about the rights of neutral shipping and the scope of wartime blockades. The British had agreed that only military goods such as munitions and certain raw materials, not such everyday goods as food and clothing, were to be subject to confiscation. Yet in blockading Germany, the British refused to make this distinction, prompting the sarcastic German quip that Britannia not only rules the waves but waives the rules.[3]

In May 1915 a German sub torpedoed the *Lusitania*, a British passenger liner, killing almost 1,200 people and producing widespread indignation. Partly because 128 of those killed were Americans, U.S. president Woodrow Wilson issued a severe warning, which contributed to the German decision in September 1915 to pull back from unrestricted submarine warfare. But as German suffering under the British blockade increased, pressure mounted on Berlin to put the subs back into action.

The issue provoked bitter debate. Chancellor Theobald von Bethmann-Hollweg° (1856–1921) and the civilian authorities opposed resumption out of fear it would

---

Pétain (puh-TANH) **Ypres** (EE-pray)

Bethmann-Hollweg (BETT-mahn–HOHL-veg)

provoke the United States to enter the war. But Ludendorff and the military finally prevailed, partly with the argument that even if the United States did intervene, U.S. troops could not get to Europe in sufficient numbers, and in sufficient haste, to have a major impact. Germany announced it would resume unrestricted submarine warfare on January 31, 1917, and the United States responded with a declaration of war on April 6.

Many on both sides doubted that U.S. intervention would make a pivotal difference; most assumed—correctly—that it would take at least a year for the American presence to materialize in force. Still, the entry of the United States gave the Entente at least the promise of more fighting power. And the United States seemed capable of renewing the sense of purpose on the Entente side, showing that the war had a meaning that could justify the unexpected costs and sacrifice.

THE EXPERIENCE OF TOTAL WAR

AS the war dragged on, the distinction between the military and civilian spheres blurred. Suffering increased on the home front, and unprecedented governmental mobilization of society proved necessary to wage war on the scale that had come to be required. Because it became "total" in this way, the war decisively altered not only the old political and diplomatic order, but also culture, society, and the patterns of everyday life.

Hardship on the Home Front

The war meant food shortages, and thus malnutrition, for ordinary people in the belligerent countries, although Britain and France, with their more favorable geographic positions, suffered considerably less than others. Germany was especially vulnerable, and the British naval blockade exacerbated an already dire situation. With military needs taking priority, the Germans encountered shortages of the chemical fertilizers, farm machinery, and draft animals necessary for agricultural production. The government began rationing bread, meat, and fats during 1915. The increasing scarcity of food produced sharp increases in diseases such as rickets and tuberculosis and in infant and childhood mortality rates.

The need to pay for the war produced economic dislocations as well. Government borrowing covered some of the cost for the short term, but to underwrite the rest, governments all over Europe found it more palatable to

inflate the currency, by printing more money, than to raise taxes. The notion that the enemy would be made to pay once victory had been won seemed to justify this decision. But this way of financing the war meant rising prices and severe erosion of purchasing power for ordinary people all over Europe. In France and Germany, the labor truces of 1914 gave way to increasing strike activity during 1916.

With an especially severe winter in 1916–1917 adding to the misery, there were serious instances of domestic disorder, including strikes and food riots, in many parts of Europe during 1917. In Italy, major strikes developed in Turin and other cities over wages and access to foodstuffs. The revolution that overthrew the tsarist autocracy in Russia that same year began with comparable protests over wartime food shortages.

The strains of war even fanned the flames in Ireland, where an uneasy truce over the home-rule controversy accompanied the British decision for war in 1914. Partly because of German efforts to stir up domestic trouble for Britain, unrest built up again in Ireland, culminating in the Easter Rebellion in Dublin in 1916. The brutality with which British forces crushed the uprising intensified demands for full independence—precisely what Britain would be forced to yield to the Irish republic shortly after the war.

Moreover, new technologies made civilians ever less immune to wartime violence. Although bombing from aircraft began with an immediate military aim—to destroy industrial targets or to provide tactical support for other military units—it quickly became clear that night bombing, especially, might demoralize civilian populations. In 1915 German airplanes began bombing English cities, provoking British retaliation against cities in the German Ruhr and Rhineland areas. These raids had little effect on the course of the war, but they showed that new technologies could make warfare more destructive even for civilians.

Domestic Mobilization

Once it became clear that the war would not be over quickly, leaders on both sides also realized that the outcome would not be determined on the battlefield alone. Victory required mobilizing all of the nation's resources and energies. So World War I became a total war, involving the entire society.

The British naval blockade on Germany, which made no distinction between military and nonmilitary goods, was a stratagem characteristic of total war. The blockade would not affect Germany's immediate strength on the battlefield, but it could damage Germany's long-term war-making capacity. The blockade was effective partly because Germany had not made adequate preparations—including stockpiling—for a protracted war of attrition.

In peacetime, Germany had depended on imports of food, fats, oils, and chemicals, including the nitrates needed for ammunition. With the onset of war, these goods were immediately in short supply, as was labor. Thus Germany seemed to need stringent economic coordination and control. By the end of 1916, the country had developed a militarized economy, with all aspects of economic life coordinated for the war effort. Under the supervision of the military, state agencies, big business, and the trade unions were brought into close collaboration. The new system included rationing, price controls, and compulsory labor arbitration, as well as a national service law enabling the military to channel workers into jobs deemed vital to the war effort.

The Germans did not hesitate to exploit the economy of occupied Belgium, requisitioning foodstuffs even to the point of causing starvation among the Belgians themselves. They forced sixty-two thousand Belgians to work in German factories under conditions of virtual slave labor. By the time this practice was stopped in February 1917, nearly a thousand Belgian workers had died in German labor camps.

The body coordinating Germany's war economy was the *Kriegsrohstoffabteilung*° (KRA), or war raw materials office. Led initially by the able Jewish industrialist Walther Rathenau° (1867–1922), this agency came to symbolize the unprecedented coordination of the German economy for war. Recognizing that Germany lacked the raw materials for a long war, Rathenau devised an imaginative program that included the development of synthetic substitute products and the creation of new mixed (private and government) companies to allocate raw materials. The KRA's effort was remarkably successful—a model for later economic planning and coordination in Germany and elsewhere.

Although Germany presented the most dramatic example of domestic coordination, the same pattern was evident everywhere. In Britain, the central figure was David Lloyd George (1863–1945), appointed to the newly created post of minister of munitions in 1915. During his year in that office, ninety-five new factories opened, soon overcoming the shortage of guns and ammunition that

had impeded the British war effort until then. His performance made Lloyd George seem the one person who could organize Britain for victory. Succeeding Herbert Asquith as prime minister in December 1916, he would direct the British war effort to its victorious conclusion.

Accelerating Socioeconomic Change

Everywhere the war effort quickened the long-term socioeconomic change associated with industrialization. Government orders for war materiel fueled industrial expansion. In France, the Paris region became a center of heavy industry for the first time. The needs of war spawned new technologies—advances in food processing and medical treatment, for example—that would carry over into peacetime.

With so many men needed for military service, women were called on to assume new economic roles—such as running farms in France, or working in the new munitions factories in Britain. (See the box "Reading Sources: Domestic Mobilization and the Role of Women.") During the course of the war, the number of women employed in Britain rose from 3.25 million to 5 million. In Italy, 200,000 women had war-related jobs by 1917. Women also played indispensable roles at the front, especially in nursing units.

The expanded opportunities of wartime intensified the debate over the sociopolitical role of women that the movement for women's suffrage had stimulated. The outbreak of war led some antiwar feminists to argue that women would be better able than men to prevent wars, which were essentially masculine undertakings. Women should have full access to public life, not because they could be expected to respond as men did but because they had a distinctive—and valuable—role to play. At the same time, by giving women jobs and the opportunity to do many of the same things men did, the war undermined the stereotypes that had long justified restrictions on women's political roles and life choices.

For many women, doing a difficult job well, serving their country in this emergency situation, afforded a new sense of accomplishment, as well as a new taste of independence. Women were now much more likely to have their own residences and to go out on their own, eating in restaurants, even smoking and drinking. Yet while many seized new opportunities and learned new skills, women frequently had to combine paid employment with housework and child rearing, and those who left home—to serve in nursing units, for example—often felt guilty about neglecting their traditional family roles.

Kriegsrohstoffabteilung (kreegs-roh-stoff-AHB-ty-loong)
Rathenau (RAT-un-ow)

DOMESTIC MOBILIZATION AND THE ROLE OF WOMEN

Early in 1917, the British writer Gilbert Stone published a remarkable collection of statements intended to illuminate the new experiences that British women were encountering in the workplace. The following passage by Naomi Loughnan, a well-to-do woman who worked in a munitions factory, makes it clear that the new work experience during the war provoked new questions about both gender and class.

Engineering mankind is possessed of the unshakable opinion that no woman can have the mechanical sense. If one of us asks humbly why such and such an alteration is not made to prevent this or that drawback to a machine, she is told, with a superior smile, that a man has worked her machine before her for years, and that therefore if there were any improvement possible it would have been made. As long as we do exactly as we are told and do not attempt to use our brains, we give entire satisfaction, and are treated as nice, good children. Any swerving from the easy path prepared for us by our males arouses the most scathing contempt in their manly bosoms. . . . Women have, however, proved that their entry into the munitions world has increased the output. Employers who forget things personal in their patriotic desire for large results are enthusiastic over the success of women in the shops. But their workmen have to be handled with the utmost tenderness and caution lest they should actually imagine it was being suggested that women could do their work equally well, given equal conditions of training—at least where muscle is not the driving force. This undercurrent of jealousy rises to the surface rather often, but as a general rule the men behave with much kindness, and are ready to help with muscle and advice whenever called upon. If eyes are very bright and hair inclined to curl, the muscle and advice do not even wait for a call.

The coming of the mixed classes of women into the factory is slowly but surely having an educative effect upon the men. "Language" is almost unconsciously becoming subdued. There are fiery exceptions who make our hair stand up on end under our close-fitting caps, but a sharp rebuke or a look of horror will often bring to book the most truculent. . . . It is grievous to hear the girls also swearing and using disgusting language. Shoulder to shoulder with the children of the slums, the upper classes are having their eyes pried open at last to the awful conditions among which their sisters have dwelt. Foul language, immorality, and many other evils are but the natural outcome of overcrowding and bitter poverty. If some of us, still blind and ignorant of our responsibilities, shrink horrified and repelled from the rougher set, the compliment is returned with open derision and ribald laughter. . . . On the other hand, attempts at friendliness from the more understanding are treated with the utmost suspicion, though once that suspicion is overcome and friendship is established, it is unshakable.

Source: Naomi Loughnan, "Munition Work," in *Women War Workers: Accounts Contributed by Representative Workers of the Work Done by Women in the More Important Branches of War Employment*, ed. Gilbert Stone (New York: Thomas Y. Crowell, 1917), pp. 35–38.

Propaganda and the "Mobilization of Enthusiasm"

Because the domestic front was crucial to sustaining a long war of attrition, it became ever more important to shore up civilian morale as the war dragged on. The result was what the historian Elie Halévy called the "mobilization of enthusiasm"—the deliberate manipulation of collective passions by national governments on an unprecedented scale. Every country instituted extensive censorship, even of soldiers' letters from the front. Because of concerns about civilian morale, the French press carried no news of the Battle of Verdun, with its horrifying numbers of casualties. In addition, systematic propaganda included not only patriotic themes but also attempts to discredit the enemy, even through outright falsification of the news. British anti-German propaganda helped draw the United States into the war in 1917.

At the outset of the war, the brutal behavior of the German armies in Belgium made it easy for the French and the British to demonize the Germans. Having

ВСЕ ДЛЯ ВОЙНЫ!

ПОДПИСЫВАЙТЕСЬ НА 5½%

ВОЕННЫЙ ЗАЕМЪ.

Working Women and the War   All over Europe, governments recruited women to work in munitions factories. This Russian government poster uses an image of working women to rally support for the war. The text reads, "Everything for the war effort! Subscribe to the war loans at 5½ percent." *(Eileen Tweedy/The Art Archive)*

expected to pass through neutral Belgium unopposed, the Germans were infuriated by the Belgian resistance they encountered. At Louvain late in August 1914 they responded to alleged Belgian sniping by shooting a number of hostages and setting the town on fire, destroying the famous old library at the university. This notorious episode led the *London Times* to characterize the Germans as "Huns," a reference to the central Asian tribe that began invading Europe in the fourth century. Stories about German soldiers eating Belgian babies began to circulate.

In October 1914 ninety-three German intellectuals, artists, and scientists signed a manifesto, addressed to "the world of culture," justifying Germany's conduct in Belgium and its larger purposes in the war. As passions heated up, major intellectuals on both sides—from the German theologian Adolf von Harnack (1851–1930) to the French philosopher Henri Bergson (1859–1941)— began denigrating the culture of the enemy and claiming a monopoly of virtue for their own sides.

As the war dragged on, some came to believe that real peace with an adversary so evil, so abnormally different, was simply not possible. There must be no compromise but rather total victory, no matter what the cost. At the same time, however, war-weariness produced a countervailing tendency to seek a "white peace," a peace without victory for either side. But in 1917, as Europeans began earnestly debating war aims, the Russian Revolution and the intervention of the United States changed the war's meaning for all the belligerents.

Devastation at Louvain   Unexpected destruction at the outset of the war fanned the flames of hatred and changed the stakes of the conflict. Located in the path of the first German advance, the Belgian city of Louvain was particularly hard hit.   *(Courtesy of the trustees of the Imperial War Museum)*

TWO REVOLUTIONS IN RUSSIA: MARCH AND NOVEMBER 1917

STRAINED by war, the old European order cracked first in Russia in 1917. Initially the overthrow of the tsarist autocracy seemed to lay the foundations for parliamentary democracy. But by the end of the year, the Bolsheviks, the smallest and most extreme of Russia's major socialist parties, had taken power, an outcome that was hardly conceivable when the revolution began.

The Wartime Crisis of the Russian Autocracy

The Russian army performed better than many had expected during the first year of the war. As late as June 1916, it mounted a successful offensive against Austria-Hungary. Russia had industrialized sufficiently by 1914 to sustain a modern war, at least for a while, and the country's war production increased significantly by 1916. But Russia suffered from problems of leadership and organization—in transportation, for example—that made it less prepared for a long war than the other belligerents. Even early in 1915, perhaps a fourth of Russia's newly conscripted troops were sent to the front without weapons; they were told to pick up rifles and supplies from the dead.

In August 1915, Tsar Nicholas II (1868–1918) assumed personal command of the army, but his absence from the capital only accelerated the deterioration in government and deepened the divisions within the ruling clique. With the tsar away, the illiterate but charismatic Siberian "holy man" Grigori Rasputin (ca. 1872–1916) emerged as the key political power within the circle of the German-born Empress Alexandra (1872–1918). He won her confidence because of his alleged ability to control the bleeding of her hemophiliac son, Alexis, the heir to the throne. Led by Rasputin, those around the empress made a shambles of the state administration. Many educated Russians, appalled at what was happening, assumed—incorrectly—that pro-German elements at court were responsible for the eclipse of the tsar and the increasing chaos in the government. Asked one Duma deputy of the government's performance, "Is this stupidity, or is it treason?"

Finally, late in December 1916, Rasputin was assassinated by aristocrats seeking to save the autocracy from these apparently pro-German influences. This act indicated how desperate the situation was becoming, but eliminating Rasputin made little difference.

By the end of 1916, the difficulties of war had combined with the strains of rapid wartime industrialization to produce a revolutionary situation in Russia. The country's urban population had mushroomed, and now, partly because of transport problems, the cities faced severe food shortages. Strikes and demonstrations spread from Petrograd (the former St. Petersburg—a name abandoned as too German at the start of the war) to other cities during the first two months of 1917. In March renewed demonstrations in Petrograd, spearheaded by women protesting the lack of bread and coal, led to revolution.

The March Revolution and the Fate of the Provisional Government

At first, the agitation that began in Petrograd on March 8, 1917, appeared to be just another bread riot. Even when it turned into a wave of strikes, the revolutionary parties (see page 834) expected it to be crushed by the government troops stationed at the Petrograd garrison. But when they were called out to help the police break up the demonstrations, the soldiers generally avoided firing at the strikers. Within days, they were sharing weapons and ammunition with the workers; the garrison was going over to what was now becoming a revolution.

Late in the afternoon of March 12, leaders of the strike committees, delegates elected by factory workers, and representatives of the socialist parties formed a *soviet*, or council, following the example of the revolution of 1905, when such soviets had first appeared. Regiments of the Petrograd garrison also began electing representatives, soon to be admitted to the Petrograd Soviet, which officially became the Council of Workers' and Soldiers' Deputies. This soviet was now the ruling power in the Russian capital. It had been elected and was genuinely representative—though of a limited constituency of workers and soldiers. Following the lead of Petrograd, Russians elsewhere promptly began forming soviets, so that over 350 local units were represented when the first All-Russian Council of Soviets met in Petrograd in April. The overwhelming majority of their representatives were Mensheviks and Socialist Revolutionaries; about one-sixth were Bolsheviks.

On March 14 a committee of the Duma, recognizing that the tsar's authority had been lost for good, persuaded Nicholas to abdicate, then formed a new provisional government. This government was to be strictly temporary, paving the way for an elected constituent assembly, which would write a constitution and establish fully legitimate governmental institutions.

Considering the strains in the autocratic system that had produced the revolution of 1905 after the Russo-Japanese War, it was hardly surprising that the system would shatter now, in light of this far more trying war and the resulting disarray within the tsarist government. Russia had apparently experienced, at last, the bourgeois political revolution necessary to develop a Western-style parliamentary democracy. Even from an orthodox Marxist perspective, the immediate priority was to help consolidate the new democratic order, which would then provide the framework for the longer-term pursuit of socialism.

Although the fall of the tsarist order produced widespread relief, Russia's new leaders faced difficult questions about priorities. Should they focus their efforts on revitalizing the Russian war effort? Or, given the widespread war-weariness in the country, should they focus on domestic political reform? For now, the Petrograd Soviet was prepared to give the provisional government a chance to govern. But the soviet was a potential rival for power if the new government failed to address Russia's immediate problems.

The provisional government took important steps toward Western-style liberal democracy, establishing universal suffrage, civil liberties, autonomy for ethnic minorities, and labor legislation, including provision for an eight-hour workday. But the government failed in two key areas, fostering discontents that the Bolsheviks soon exploited. First, it persisted in fighting the war. Second, it dragged its feet on agrarian reform.

The provisional government's determination to renew the war effort stemmed from genuine concern about Russia's obligations to its allies, about the country's national honor and position among the great powers. The long-standing goal of Russian diplomacy—an outlet to the Mediterranean Sea through the Dardanelles—seemed

Lenin as Leader   Although he was in exile during much of 1917, Lenin's leadership was crucial to the Bolshevik success in Russia. He is shown here addressing a May Day rally in Red Square, Moscow, on May 1, 1919. *(ITAR-TASS/Sovfoto)*

within reach if Russia could continue the war and contribute to an Entente victory. The educated, well-to-do Russians who led the new government expected that ordinary citizens, now free, would fight with renewed enthusiasm, like the armies that had grown from the French Revolution over a century before. These leaders failed to grasp how desperate the situation of ordinary people had become.

Although the March revolution began in the cities, the peasantry soon moved into action as well, seizing land, sometimes burning the houses of their landlords. By midsummer, a full-scale peasant war seemed to be in the offing in the countryside, and calls for radical agrarian reform became increasingly urgent. Partly from expediency, partly from genuine concern for social justice, the provisional government promised a major redistribution of land. But it insisted that the reform be carried out legally—not by the present provisional government, but by a duly elected constituent assembly.

Calling for elections would thus seem to have been the first priority. The new political leaders kept putting it off, however, waiting for the situation to cool before giving up power to a newly elected assembly. But playing for time was a luxury they could ill afford. As unrest grew in the countryside, the authority of the provisional government diminished and the soviets gained in stature. But what role were the soviets to play?

The Bolsheviks Come to Power

In the immediate aftermath of the March revolution, the Bolsheviks had not seemed to differ substantially from their rivals within the socialist movement, at least on matters of immediate concern—the war, land reform, and the character of the revolution itself. But the situation began to change in April when Lenin, assisted by the German military, returned from exile in Switzerland. The Germans assumed—correctly, it turned out—that the Bolsheviks would help undermine the Russian war effort. Largely through the force of Lenin's leadership, the Bolsheviks soon took the initiative within the still-developing revolution in Russia.

Lenin (1870–1924), born Vladimir Ilich Ulianov, came from a comfortable upper-middle-class family. He was university-educated and trained as a lawyer. But after an older brother was executed in 1887 for participating in a plot against the tsar's life, Lenin followed him into revolutionary activity. Arrested for the first time in 1895, he was confined to Siberia until 1900. He then lived in exile abroad for almost the entire period before his return to Russia in 1917.

The Bolshevik Party was identified with Lenin from its beginning in 1903, when it emerged from the schism in Russian Marxist socialism. Because of his emphases, Bolshevism came to mean discipline, organization, and a special leadership role for a revolutionary vanguard. (See the box "Reading Sources: Lenin Urges a Conspiratorial Revolutionary Party" on page 835 in Chapter 24.) Lenin proved effective because he was a stern and somewhat forbidding figure, disciplined, fiercely intelligent, sometimes ruthless. As a Bolshevik colleague put it, Lenin was "the one indisputable leader . . . a man of iron will, inexhaustible energy, combining a fanatical faith in the movement, in the cause, with an equal faith in himself."[4]

Still, Lenin's reading of the situation when he returned to Petrograd in April astonished even many Bolsheviks. He argued that the revolution was about to pass from the present bourgeois-democratic stage to a socialist phase, involving dictatorship of the proletariat in the form of government by the soviets. So the Bolsheviks should begin actively opposing the provisional government, especially by denouncing the war as fundamentally imperialist and by demanding the distribution of land from the large estates to the peasants. This latter measure had long been identified with the Socialist Revolutionaries; most Bolsheviks had envisioned collectivization and nationalization instead.

As Lenin saw it, under the strains of war, all of Europe was becoming ripe for revolution. A revolution in Russia would provide the spark to ignite a wider proletarian revolution, especially in Germany. He did not envision backward Russia seeking to create socialism on its own. Although some remained skeptical of Lenin's strategy, he promptly won over most of his fellow Bolsheviks. And thus the Bolsheviks began actively seeking wider support by promising peace, land, and bread.

In April 1917 moderate socialists still had majority support in the soviets, so the Bolsheviks sought to build support gradually, postponing any decisive test of strength. But events escaped the control of the Bolshevik leadership in mid-July when impatient workers, largely Bolshevik in sympathy, took to the streets of Petrograd on their own. The Petrograd Soviet refused to support the uprising, and the provisional government had no difficulty getting military units to put it down, killing two hundred in the process. Though the uprising had developed spontaneously, Bolshevik leaders felt compelled to offer public support, and this gave the government an excuse to crack down on the Bolshevik leadership. Lenin managed to escape to Finland, but a number of his colleagues were arrested and jailed.

With the Bolsheviks on the defensive, counterrevolutionary elements in the Russian military decided to seize the initiative with a march on Petrograd in September. To resist this attempted coup, the provisional government, now led by the young Socialist Revolutionary Alexander Kerensky (1881–1970), had to rely on whoever could of-

fer help, including the Bolsheviks. And thanks to Bolshevik propaganda, the soldiers under the command of the counterrevolutionaries refused to fight against the upholders of the revolution in Petrograd. Thus the coup was thwarted. Within days, the Bolsheviks won their first clear-cut majority in the Petrograd Soviet, then shortly gained majorities in most of the other soviets as well.

During the fall of 1917, the situation became increasingly volatile, eluding control by anyone. People looted food from shops; peasants seized land, sometimes murdering their landlords. Desertions and the murder of officers increased within the Russian military.

With the Bolsheviks now the dominant power in the soviets, and with the government's control diminishing, Lenin, from his hideout in Finland, urged the Bolshevik central committee to prepare for armed insurrection. Although some found this step too risky, the majority accepted Lenin's argument that the provisional government would continue dragging its feet, inadvertently giving right-wing officer cadres time for another coup.

Because Lenin remained in hiding, the task of organizing the seizure of power fell to Leon Trotsky (1870–1940), who skillfully modified Lenin's aggressive strategy. Lenin wanted the Bolsheviks to rise in their own name, in opposition to the provisional government, but Trotsky linked the insurrection to the cause of the soviets and played up its defensive character against the ongoing danger of a counterrevolutionary coup. With the political center at an impasse, the only alternative to such a coup seemed to be a Bolshevik initiative to preserve the Petrograd Soviet, by now the sole viable institutional embodiment of the revolution and its promise. Trotsky's interpretation led people who wanted simply to defend the soviet to support the Bolsheviks' initiative.

During the night of November 9, armed Bolsheviks and regular army regiments occupied key points in Petrograd, including railroad stations, post offices, telephone exchanges, power stations, and the national bank. Able to muster only token resistance, the provisional government collapsed. Kerensky escaped and mounted what quickly proved to be a futile effort to rally troops at the front for a counterattack against the Bolsheviks. In contrast to the March revolution, which had taken about a week, the Bolsheviks took over the capital, overthrowing the Kerensky government, literally overnight and almost without bloodshed.

But though the Bolsheviks enjoyed considerable support in the network of soviets, it was not clear that they could extend their control across the whole Russian Empire. Moreover, from their own perspective, the revolution's immediate prospects, and its potential wider impact, were bound up with the course of the war. Would the Bolshevik Revolution in Russia prove the spark for revolution elsewhere in war-weary Europe, as Lenin anticipated?

The Russian Revolution and the War

Having stood for peace throughout the revolution, the Bolsheviks promptly moved to get Russia out of the war, agreeing to an armistice with Germany in December 1917. They hoped that Russia's withdrawal would speed the collapse of the war effort on all sides and that this, in turn, would intensify the movement toward revolution elsewhere in Europe. The Russian Revolution was but a chapter in this larger story. As Lenin noted to Trotsky, "If it were necessary for us to go under to assure the success of the German revolution, we should have to do it. The German revolution is vastly more important than ours." Indeed, said Lenin to the Bolsheviks' party congress of March 1918, "It is an absolute truth that we will go under without the German revolution."[5]

After assuming control in November, the Bolsheviks published the tsarist government's secret agreements specifying how the spoils were to be divided in the event of a Russian victory. They hoped to inflame revolutionary sentiment elsewhere by demonstrating that the war had been, all along, an imperialist offensive on behalf of capitalist interests. This Bolshevik initiative added fuel to the controversy already developing in all the belligerent countries over the war's purpose and significance.

THE NEW WAR AND THE ALLIED VICTORY, 1917–1918

BECAUSE the stakes of the war changed during 1917, the outcome, once peace finally came in November 1918, included consequences that Europeans could not have foreseen in 1914. German defeat brought revolution against the monarchy and the beginning of a new democracy. Austro-Hungarian defeat brought the collapse of the Habsburg monarchy and thus the opportunity for its national minorities to form nations of their own. As the old European order fell, grandiose new visions competed to shape the postwar world.

The Debate over War Aims

The French and British governments publicly welcomed the March revolution in Russia, partly because they expected Russia's military performance to improve under new leadership, but also because the change of regime seemed to have highly favorable psychological implications. With Russia no longer an autocracy, the war could be portrayed—and experienced—as a crusade for democracy. At the same time, the March revolution could only sow confusion among the many Germans who had understood their own war effort as a matter of self-defense against reactionary Russia. But the November revolution required a deeper reconsideration by all the belligerents.

Allied war aims agreements, such as the Treaty of London that brought Italy into the war in 1915, had remained secret until the Bolsheviks published the tsarist documents. Products of old-style diplomacy, those agreements had been made by a restricted foreign policy elite within the governing circles of each country; even members of the elected parliaments generally did not know their contents. The debate over war aims that developed in 1917 thus became a debate over decision making as well. Many assumed that a more democratic approach to foreign policy would minimize the chances of war since the people would not agree to wars for dynastic or business interests. In addition, there were exhortations for all the parties in the present war to renounce annexations and settle for a white peace. It was time to call the whole thing off and bring the soldiers home.

Seeking to counter such sentiments, especially the Russian contention that the war was not worth continuing, the idealistic U.S. president, Woodrow Wilson (1856–1924), insisted on the great potential significance of an Allied victory. First in his State of the Union speech of January 1918, and in several declarations thereafter, Wilson developed the "Fourteen Points" that he proposed should guide the new international order. Notable among them were open diplomacy, free trade, reduced armaments, self-determination for nationalities, a league of nations, and a recasting of the colonial system to ensure equal rights for the indigenous populations.

Lenin and Wilson, then, offered radically different interpretations of the war, with radically different implications for present priorities. Yet, compared with the old diplomacy, they had something in common. Together, they seemed to represent a whole new approach to international relations—and the possibility of a more peaceful world. Thus they found an eager audience among the war-weary peoples of Europe.

Despite the strains of the war, Sacred Union in France did not weaken substantially until April 1917, with General Nivelle's disastrous offensive. But then, as near mutiny began to develop within the army, rank-and-file pressures forced socialist leaders to demand clarification, and perhaps revision, of French war aims. Suddenly the French government was under pressure to suggest that the war had idealistic and democratic purposes. Doubts about the government's goals were threatening to turn into active opposition to the war.

The same pressures were at work in Germany. Antiwar sentiment grew steadily within the Social Democratic Party (SPD) until the antiwar faction split off and formed the Independent Socialist Party (USPD) in April 1917. A large-scale debate over war aims, linked to considerations of domestic political reform, developed in the Reichstag by the summer of 1917. On July 19, a solid 60 percent majority passed a new war aims resolution, which affirmed that Germany's purposes were solely defensive, that Germany had no territorial ambitions. Germany, too, seemed open to a white peace.

But just as the dramatic events of 1917 interjected new pressures for moderation and peace, pressures in the opposite direction also mounted as the war dragged on. It seemed to some that this war was only the beginning of a new era of cutthroat international competition; the old rules would no longer apply. War aims grew more grandiose as nations tried to gain the leverage for success in the postwar world. The present war offered a precious opportunity to secure advantages for that more contentious world, which would surely entail further war before long.

The shape of the current war convinced top German officials that Germany's geography and dependence on imports made it especially vulnerable in a long war. So Germany had to seize the present opportunity to conquer the means to fight the next war on a more favorable footing. Responding in February 1918 to calls for a white peace, General Ludendorff stressed that "if Germany makes peace without profit, it has lost the war." Germany, insisted Ludendorff, must win the military and economic basis for future security—to "enable us to contemplate confidently some future defensive war."[6] Many German officials believed that Germany could achieve parity with Britain, and thus the basis for security and peace, only if it maintained control of the Belgian coast. German expansion into Russian Poland and up the Baltic coast of Lithuania and Latvia seemed essential as well.

When, in response to the Russian request for an armistice, Germany was able to dictate the peace terms, as specified in the Treaty of Brest-Litovsk of March 1918, it became clear how radically annexationist Germany's war aims had become. European Russia was to be largely dismembered, leaving Germany in direct or indirect control of 27 percent of Russia's European territory, 40 percent of its population, and 75 percent of its iron and coal. All the Reichstag parties except the Socialists accepted the terms of the treaty, which, in fact, produced a renewed determination to push on to victory after the dis-

illusionment that had led to the Reichstag war aims resolution of July 1917.

France, less vulnerable geographically than Germany, tended to be more modest. But news of the terms the Germans had imposed at Brest-Litovsk inflamed the French, reinforcing their determination to fight on to an unqualified victory. Only thus could France secure the advantages necessary to ward off an ongoing German menace.

The Renewal of the French War Effort

The domestic division in France that followed the failure of Nivelle's offensive reached its peak during the fall of 1917. In November, with pressure for a white peace intensifying and France's ability to continue fighting in doubt, President Raymond Poincaré° (1860–1934) called on Georges Clemenceau° (1841–1929) to lead a new government. The 76-year-old Clemenceau was known as a "hawk"; his appointment portended a stepped-up prosecution of the war. His message was simple as he appeared before the Chamber of Deputies on November 20, 1917: "If you ask me about my war aims, I reply: my aim is to be victorious." For the remainder of the war, France was under the virtual dictatorship of Clemenceau and his cabinet.

Clemenceau moved decisively on both the domestic and military fronts. By cracking down on the antiwar movement—imprisoning antiwar leaders, suppressing defeatist newspapers—he stiffened morale on the home front. Understanding that lack of coordination between French and British military leaders had hampered the Allied effort on the battlefield, Clemenceau persuaded the British to accept the French general Ferdinand Foch° (1851–1929) as the first supreme commander of all Allied forces in the west. In choosing Foch, known for his commitment to aggressive offensives, Clemenceau was pointedly bypassing Pétain, whom he found too passive, even defeatist. After some initial friction, Clemenceau let Foch have his way on the military level, and the two proved an effective leadership combination.

The German Gamble, 1918

As the military campaigns of 1918 began, Germany seemed in a relatively favorable position: Russia had been knocked out of the war, and American troops were yet to arrive. Moderates in Germany wanted to seize the

---

Poincaré (pwan-cah-RAY)   **Clemenceau** (klem-ahn-SOH)
Foch (FOHSH)

opportunity to work out a compromise peace while there was still a chance. But the military leadership persuaded Kaiser Wilhelm II that Germany could win a definitive victory on the western front if it struck quickly, before U.S. help became significant. Since Germany would be out of reserves by summer, the alternative to decisive victory in the west would be total German defeat.

The German gamble almost succeeded. From March to June 1918, German forces seized the initiative with four months of sustained and effective attacks. By May 30 they had again reached the Marne, where they had been held in 1914. Paris, only 37 miles away, had to be evacuated again (see Map 25.2). As late as mid-July, Ludendorff remained confident of victory, but by mid-August it was becoming clear that Germany lacked the manpower to exploit the successes of the first several months of 1918.

Those successes had caused mutual suspicion between the French and the British at first, but under Foch's leadership the Western allies eventually managed fuller and more effective coordination. By mid-1918 American involvement was also becoming a factor. On June 4, over a year after the U.S. declaration of war, American troops went into action for the first time, bolstering French forces along the Marne. This was a small operation, in which the Americans' performance was amateurish when compared with that of their battle-seasoned allies. But as the Allied counterattack proceeded, 250,000 U.S. troops were arriving per month, considerably boosting Allied morale and battlefield strength.

By June 1918 Europe was experiencing the first outbreak of a virulent new influenza virus, promptly dubbed the "Spanish flu," though it had originated in South Africa. Because of their inferior diets, German soldiers proved far more susceptible to the disease than their adversaries, a fact that significantly affected Germany's combat performance during the crucial summer of 1918.

Germany lost the initiative for good during the second Battle of the Marne, which began on July 15 with yet another German attack. Foch launched a sustained counterattack on July 18, using tanks to good advantage, and maintained the momentum thereafter. By early August the whole western front began to roll back. With astonishing suddenness, the outcome was no longer in doubt, although most expected the war to drag on into 1919. Few realized how desperate Germany's situation had become.

Map 25.2 Stalemate and Decision on the Western Front On the western front, in northern France and Belgium, trench warfare developed and the best-known battles of the war were fought. Notable sites include Verdun, Passchendaele, and the Marne and Somme Rivers.

Meanwhile, Germany's allies began falling one by one. In the Balkans an Allied offensive broke through the German-Bulgarian line in September, prompting the Bulgarians to ask for an armistice. The Turkish military effort collapsed in October. With the defeat of Russia in 1917, German troops joined the Austrians on the Italian front, breaking through the Italian line at Caporetto late in 1917 and almost inflicting a decisive defeat. But after retreating, the Italians managed to regroup and hold— and eventually to drive the Austrians back. The Italian victory at Vittorio Veneto forced Austria's unconditional surrender on November 3, 1918. But by this point the armies of the Habsburg empire, a central pillar of the old European order, were disintegrating along nationality lines. And the impending collapse of this centuries-old empire gave its various national minorities the chance to form states of their own.

Military Defeat and Political Change in Germany

By late September it was clear to Ludendorff that his armies could not stop the Allied advance. On September 29 he informed the government that to avoid invasion, Germany would have to seek an immediate armistice. Hoping to secure favorable peace terms and to foist responsibility for the defeat onto the parliamentary politicians, Hindenburg and Ludendorff asked that a government based on greater popular support be formed. A leading moderate, Prince Max von Baden° (1867–1929), became chancellor, and he promptly replaced Ludendorff with General Wilhelm Groener° (1867–1939), who seemed more democratic in orientation. By now it was clear that ending the war could not be separated from the push for political change in Germany, especially because it was widely assumed that a more democratic Germany could expect more favorable peace terms.

After securing a written request for an armistice from Hindenburg, Prince Max sent a peace note to President Wilson early in October, asking for an armistice based on Wilson's Fourteen Points. During the month that followed, Prince Max engineered a series of measures, passed by the Reichstag and approved by the emperor, that reformed the constitution, abolishing the three-class voting system in Prussia and making the chancellor responsible to the Reichstag. At last Germany had a constitutional monarchy. Not completely satisfied, President Wilson encouraged speculation that Germany could expect better peace terms if Wilhelm II were to abdicate and Germany became a republic.

But a far more radical outcome seemed possible during late 1918 and early 1919. As negotiations for an armistice proceeded in October, the continuing war effort produced instances of mutiny in the navy and breaches of discipline in the army. By early November workers' and soldiers' councils were being formed all over Germany, just as in Russia the year before. On November 7, antiwar socialists in Munich led an uprising of workers and soldiers that expelled the king of Bavaria and proclaimed a new Bavarian republic. Its provisional government promptly sought its own peace negotiations with the Allies. On November 9, thousands of workers took to the streets of Berlin to demand immediate peace, and the authorities could not muster enough military resources to move against them.

The senior army leadership grew concerned that the collapse of government authority would undermine the ability of officers even to march their troops home. So Hindenburg and Groener persuaded the emperor to abdicate. Having lost the support of the army, Wilhelm II accepted the inevitable and left for exile in the Netherlands.

With the German right, including the military, in disarray, and with the centrist parties discredited by their support for what had become an annexationist war, the initiative passed to the socialists. They, at least, had been in the forefront of the movement for peace. But the socialists had divided in 1917, mostly over the question of response to the war. The mainstream of the SPD, by supporting the war for so long, had irrevocably alienated the party's leftist socialist wing. The most militant of these leftist socialists, led by Karl Liebknecht (1871–1919) and Rosa Luxemburg (1870–1919), envisioned using the workers' and soldiers' councils as the basis for a full-scale revolution, more or less on the Bolshevik model.

The SPD, on the other hand, clung to its reformist heritage and insisted on working within parliamentary institutions. Party leaders argued that a Bolshevik-style revolution was neither appropriate nor necessary under the circumstances. So SPD moderates proclaimed a parliamentary republic on November 9, just hours before the revolutionaries proclaimed a soviet-style republic. The next day the soldiers' and workers' councils in Berlin elected a provisional executive committee, to be led by the moderate socialist Friedrich Ebert° (1871–1925). As the new republic sought to consolidate itself, the radical leftists continued to promote further revolution. For Germany the end of the war meant a leap into an unfamiliar democratic republic, which had to establish itself in con-

---

Baden (BAH-dyn)   **Groener** (GREU-nur)

Ebert (A-bairt)

Rosa Luxemburg   Long a leader in the radical wing of the German Social Democratic Party, Luxemburg was at the center of the revolutionary activity in Berlin that immediately followed Germany's defeat in the war. She and her colleague, Karl Liebknecht, were murdered after their capture by anti-revolutionary forces in January 1919.   *(Centralne Archivum, Warsaw)*

ditions not only of military defeat and economic hardship but also of incipient revolution on the extreme left.

Birth from military defeat was especially disabling for the new republic because the German people were so little prepared for defeat when it came. Vigorous censorship had kept the public in the dark about Germany's real situation, so the request for an armistice early in October came as a shock. At no time during the war had Germany been invaded from the west, and by mid-1918 the German army had seemed on the brink of victory. It appeared inconceivable that Germany had lost a military decision, plain and simple. Thus the "stab in the back" myth, the notion that political intrigue and revolution at home had sabotaged the German military effort, developed to explain what otherwise seemed an inexplicable defeat. This notion would prove a heavy burden for Germany's new democracy to bear.

THE OUTCOME AND THE IMPACT

AFTER the armistice officially ended the fighting on November 11, 1918, it was up to the war's four victors—France, Britain, Italy, and the United States—to establish the terms of peace and, it was to be hoped, a new basis for order at the same time. But the peacemakers had to deal with a radically new political and territorial situation. Revolution had undermined, or threatened to undermine, the old political order in much of Europe. And the war had come to involve non-European powers and peoples in unprecedented ways. After all that had happened since August 1914, it was not clear what a restoration of peace and order would require. But it was evident that Europe would no longer dominate world affairs in quite the way it had.

The Costs of War

Raw casualty figures do not begin to convey the war's human toll, but they afford some sense of the magnitude of the catastrophe that had befallen Europe and much of the world. Estimates differ, but it is generally agreed that from 10 million to 13 million military men lost their lives, with another 20 million wounded. In addition, between 7 million and 10 million civilians died as a result of the war and its hardships. In the defeated countries especially, food shortages and malnutrition continued well after the end of the fighting. Thus the Spanish flu that had affected the balance on the battlefield early in the summer of 1918 returned with particularly devastating results during the fall. The influenza pandemic killed perhaps 30 million people worldwide.

Germany suffered the highest number of military casualties, but France suffered the most in proportional terms. Two million Germans were killed, with another 4 million wounded. Military deaths per capita for France were roughly 15 percent higher than for Germany—and twice as severe as for Britain. Of 8 million Frenchmen mobilized, over 5 million were killed or wounded. Roughly 1.5 million French soldiers, or 10 percent of the active male population, were killed—and this in a country already concerned about demographic decline. The other belligerents suffered less, but still in great numbers. Among the military personnel killed were 2 million Russians, 500,000 Italians, and 114,000 Americans.

Economic costs were heavy as well. In addition to the privations suffered during the years of war, Europeans found themselves reeling from inflation and saddled with debt, especially to the United States, once the war was over. Although the immediate transition to a peacetime economy did not prove as difficult as many had feared, the war and its aftermath produced an economic disequilibrium that lingered, helping to produce a worldwide depression by the 1930s.

The Search for Peace in a Revolutionary Era

The war had begun because of an unmanageable nationality problem in Austria-Hungary, and it led not simply to military defeat for Austria-Hungary but to the breakup of the Habsburg system (see Map 25.3). In east-central Europe, the end of the war brought bright hopes for self-determination to peoples like the Czechs, Slovaks, Poles, Serbs, and Croats. Even before the peacemakers opened deliberations in January 1919, some of these ethnic groups had begun creating a new order on their own. For example, a popular movement of Czechs and Slovaks established a Czechoslovak republic on October 29, 1918, and a new Yugoslavia and an independent Hungary similarly emerged from indigenous movements. Czechoslovakia and Yugoslavia were made up of different ethnic groups that found cooperation advantageous now but that might well disagree in the future. Moreover, many of these countries lacked traditions of self-government, and they had reason to feud among themselves. With the Habsburg system no longer imposing one form of stability, a power vacuum seemed likely in this potentially volatile part of Europe.

The Bolshevik Revolution in Russia immeasurably complicated the situation. The unsettled conditions in Germany and the former Habsburg territories in the wake of defeat seemed to invite the spread of revolution—precisely according to Lenin's script. Shortly after taking power, Lenin and his party had begun calling themselves "communists," partly to jettison the provincial Russian term *bolshevik*, but especially to underline their departure from the old reformist socialism of the Second International. In adopting "communism," they wanted to make it clear that they stood for a revolutionary alternative, and they actively sought to inspire revolution elsewhere.

Outside Russia, the greatest communist success in the wake of the war was in Hungary, where a communist regime under Béla Kun (1885–1937) governed Budapest and other parts of the country from March to August 1919, when it was put down by Allied-sponsored forces. At about the same time, communist republics lasted for months in the Slovak part of Czechoslovakia and in the important German state of Bavaria. Even in Italy, which had shared in the victory, socialists infatuated with the Bolshevik example claimed that the substantial labor

unrest that developed during 1919 and 1920 was the beginning of full-scale revolution.

Meanwhile, fears that the Russian Revolution might spread had fueled foreign intervention in Russia itself beginning in June 1918, when 24,000 French and British troops landed at Murmansk, in northern Russia. As long as the war with Germany lasted, military concerns helped justify this course, but after the armistice of November 1918, the intervention became overtly anticommunist, intended to help topple the new regime and undercut its efforts to export revolution.

Further complicating the postwar situation were the defeat and dissolution of the Turkish Ottoman Empire, which had controlled much of the Middle East in 1914. The Arab revolt against the Turks that developed in the Arabian peninsula in 1916 did not achieve its major military aims, though it endured, causing some disruption to the Turkish war effort. Its success was due partly to the collaboration of a young British officer, T. E. Lawrence (1888–1935), who proved an effective military leader and an impassioned advocate of the Arab cause. The support that Britain had offered the Arabs suggested that independence, perhaps even a single Arab kingdom, might follow from a defeat of the Ottoman Empire.

But British policy toward the Arabs was uncertain and contradictory. Concerned about the Suez Canal, the British government sought to tighten its control in Egypt by declaring it a protectorate in 1914, triggering increased anti-British sentiment in the region. The secret Sykes-Picot Agreement of May 1916, named for the British and French diplomats who negotiated it, projected a division of the Ottoman territories of the Middle East into colonial spheres of influence. France would control Syria and Lebanon, while Britain would rule Palestine and Mesopotamia, or present-day Iraq.

Potentially complicating the situation in the region was Zionism, the movement to establish a Jewish state in Palestine. Led by Chaim Weizmann (1874–1952), a remarkable Russian-born British chemist, the Zionists reached an important milestone when British foreign secretary Arthur Balfour (1848–1930) cautiously announced, in the Balfour Declaration of November 1917, that the British government "looked with favor" on the prospect of a "Jewish home" in Palestine. At this point

Map 25.3 The Impact of the War: The Territorial Settlement in Europe and the Middle East   The defeat of Russia, Austria-Hungary, Germany, and Ottoman Turkey opened the way to major changes in the map of east-central Europe and the Middle East. A number of new nations emerged in east-central Europe, while in the Arab world the end of Ottoman rule meant not independence but new roles for European powers.

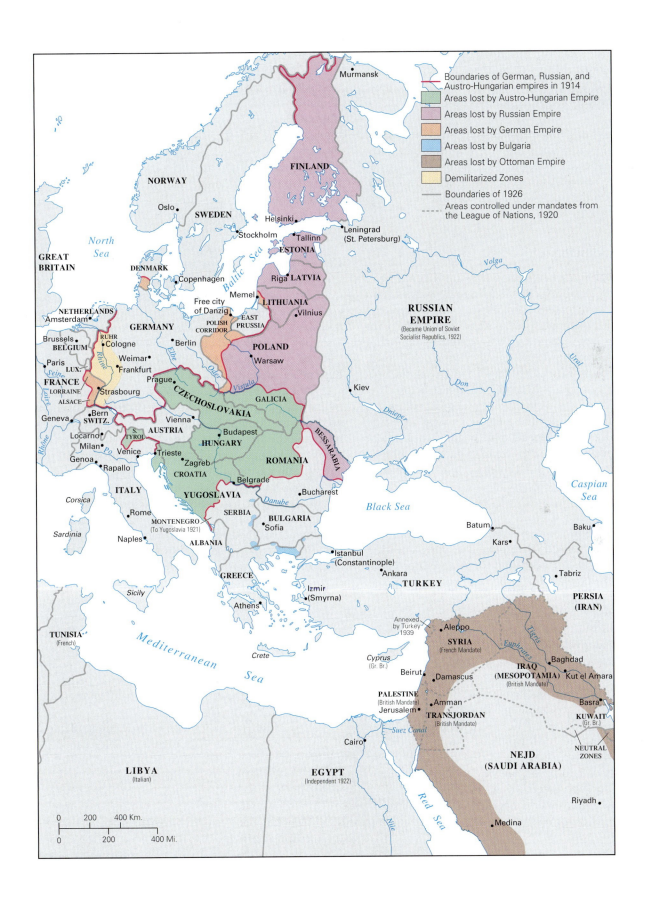

Boundaries of German, Russian, and Austro-Hungarian empires in 1914

Areas lost by Austro-Hungarian Empire

Areas lost by Russian Empire

Areas lost by German Empire

Areas lost by Bulgaria

Areas lost by Ottoman Empire

Demilitarized Zones

Boundaries of 1926

Areas controlled under mandates from the League of Nations, 1920

Murmansk

FINLAND

NORWAY

Oslo

SWEDEN

Stockholm

Helsinki

Leningrad (St. Petersburg)

Tallinn

ESTONIA

Riga LATVIA

RUSSIAN EMPIRE
(Became Union of Soviet Socialist Republics, 1922)

GREAT BRITAIN

North Sea

DENMARK

Copenhagen

Memel

Free city of Danzig

LITHUANIA

Vilnius

NETHERLANDS

Amsterdam

GERMANY

POLISH CORRIDOR

EAST PRUSSIA

Brussels

BELGIUM

RUHR

Cologne

Berlin

POLAND

Warsaw

Kiev

Paris

LUX.

Weimar

Frankfurt

FRANCE

LORRAINE

Strasbourg

Prague

CZECHOSLOVAKIA

GALICIA

ALSACE

Geneva

Bern

SWITZ.

Vienna

AUSTRIA

Budapest

HUNGARY

BESSARABIA

Locarno

S. TYROL

Milan

Venice

Trieste

Zagreb

CROATIA

ROMANIA

Genoa

Rapallo

ITALY

YUGOSLAVIA

Belgrade

Bucharest

Corsica

Rome

SERBIA

BULGARIA

Sofia

Black Sea

Caspian Sea

Batum

Baku

Sardinia

Naples

MONTENEGRO
(To Yugoslavia 1921)

ALBANIA

Kars

GREECE

Istanbul (Constantinople)

Ankara

Tabriz

TURKEY

Izmir (Smyrna)

Sicily

Athens

Crete

Mediterranean Sea

TUNISIA
(French)

Cyprus
(Gr. Br.)

PERSIA (IRAN)

Annexed by Turkey 1939

Aleppo

SYRIA
(French Mandate)

Baghdad

Beirut

IRAQ (MESOPOTAMIA)
(British Mandate)

Kut el Amara

PALESTINE
(British Mandate)

Damascus

Basra

Jerusalem

Amman

TRANSJORDAN
(British Mandate)

KUWAIT
(Gr. Br.)

NEUTRAL ZONES

Cairo

NEJD (SAUDI ARABIA)

LIBYA
(Italian)

EGYPT
(Independent 1922)

Red Sea

Riyadh

Medina

0   200   400 Km.

0   200   400 Mi.

Oder

Elbe

Vistula

Rhine

Seine

Loire

Rhône

Po

Danube

Dnieper

Don

Volga

Ural

Baltic Sea

Nile

Tigris

Euphrates

Suez Canal

Jews were only 10 percent of the population in Palestine, but British leaders sympathetic to Zionism saw no conflict in simultaneously embracing the cause of the Arabs against the Ottoman Turks. Indeed, Arabs and Jews, each seeking self-determination, could be expected to collaborate.

In the heat of war, the British established their policy for the former Ottoman territories without careful study. Thus they made promises and agreements that were not entirely compatible. After the war, the victors' efforts to install a new order in the Middle East would create fresh conflicts.

The Peace Settlement

The peace conference took place in Paris, beginning in January 1919. Its labors led to five separate treaties, with each of the five defeated states, known collectively as the Paris peace settlement. The first and most significant was the Treaty of Versailles with Germany, signed in the Hall of Mirrors of the Versailles Palace on June 28, 1919. Treaties were also worked out, in turn, with Austria, Bulgaria, Hungary, and finally Turkey, in August 1920.

This was to be a dictated, not a negotiated, peace. Germany and its allies were excluded, as was renegade Russia. The passions unleashed by the long war had dissolved the possibility of a more conciliatory outcome, a genuinely negotiated peace. Having won the war, France, Britain, the United States, and Italy were to call the shots on their own, with the future of Europe and much of the world in the balance. However, spokesmen for many groups—from Slovaks and Croats to Arabs, Jews, and pan-Africanists—were in Paris as well, seeking a hearing for their respective causes. Both the Arab Prince Faisal (1885–1933), who would later become king of Iraq, and Colonel T. E. Lawrence were on hand to plead for an independent Arab kingdom. (See the box "Global Encounters: Prince Faisal at the Peace Conference.") The African American leader W. E. B. Du Bois° (1868–1963), who took his Ph.D. at Harvard in 1895, led a major pan-African congress in Paris concurrently with the peace conference.

The fundamental challenge for the peacemakers was to reconcile the conflicting visions of the postwar world that had emerged by the end of the war. U.S. president Wilson represented the promise of a new order that could give this terrible war a lasting meaning. As he toured parts of Europe on his way to the peace conference, Wilson was greeted as a hero. Clemenceau, in contrast, was a hard-liner concerned with French security and dismissive of Wilsonian ideals. Since becoming

prime minister in 1917, he had stressed that only permanent French military superiority over Germany, and not some utopian league of nations, could guarantee a lasting peace. The negotiations at Paris centered on this fundamental difference between Wilson and Clemenceau. Although Britain's Lloyd George took a hard line on certain issues, he also sought to mediate, helping engineer the somewhat awkward compromise that resulted. When, after the peace conference, he encountered criticism for the outcome, Lloyd George replied, "I think I did as well as might be expected, seated as I was between Jesus Christ and Napoleon Bonaparte."[7]

In Article 231 of the final treaty, the peacemakers sought to establish a moral basis for their treatment of Germany by assigning responsibility for the war to Germany and its allies. On this basis, the Germans were required to pay reparations to reimburse the victors for the costs of the war, although the actual amount was not established until 1921. The determination to make the loser pay for what had ended up a fabulously expensive war was one of the factors militating against a compromise peace on both sides by 1917.

Germany was also forced to dismantle much of its military apparatus. The army was to be limited to a hundred thousand men, all volunteers. The treaty severely restricted the size of the German navy as well, and Germany was forbidden to manufacture or possess military aircraft, submarines, tanks, heavy artillery, or poison gas.

France took back Alsace and Lorraine, the provinces it had lost to Germany in 1871 (see Map 25.3). But for France, the crucial security provision of the 1919 peace settlement was the treatment of the adjacent Rhineland section of Germany itself. For fifteen years Allied troops were to occupy the west bank of the Rhine River in Germany—the usual military occupation of a defeated adversary. But this would only be temporary. The long-term advantage for France was to be the permanent demilitarization of all German territory west of the Rhine and a strip of 50 kilometers along its east bank. Germany was to maintain no troops on this part of its own soil; in the event of hostilities French forces would be able to march unopposed into this economically vital area of Germany.

French interests also helped shape the settlement in east-central Europe. Wilsonian principles called for self-determination, but in this area of great ethnic complexity, ethnic differences were not readily sorted out geographically. This made it easier for the French to bring their own strategic concerns to bear on the situation. To ensure that Germany would again face potential enemies from both the east and the west, French leaders envisioned building a network of allies in east-central

---

Du Bois (doo BOYS)

An Arab in Paris   Prince Faisal (*foreground*) attended the Paris Peace Conference, where he lobbied for the creation of an independent Arab kingdom from part of the former Ottoman Turkish holdings in the Middle East. Among his supporters was the British officer T. E. Lawrence (*middle row, second from the right*), on his way to legend as "Lawrence of Arabia."   (*Courtesy of the trustees of the Imperial War Museum*)

Europe. The first was the new Poland, created from Polish territories formerly in the German, Russian, and Austro-Hungarian Empires. That network might come to include Czechoslovakia, Yugoslavia, and Romania as well. These states would be weak enough to remain under French influence but, taken together, strong enough to replace Russia as a significant force against Germany.

Partly as a result of French priorities, Poland, Czechoslovakia, Yugoslavia, and Romania ended up as large as possible, either by combining ethnic groups or by incorporating minorities that, on ethnic grounds, belonged with neighboring states. The new Czechoslovakia included not only Czechs and Slovaks but also numerous Germans and Magyars. Indeed, Germans, mostly from the old Bohemia, made up 22 percent of the population of Czechoslovakia. By contrast, Austria, Hungary, and Bulgaria, as defeated powers, found themselves diminished (see Map 25.4). What remained of Austria, the German part of the old Habsburg empire, was prohibited from choosing to join Germany, an obvious violation of the Wilsonian principle of self-determination.

Desires to contain and weaken communist Russia were also at work in the settlement in east-central Europe. A band of states in east-central Europe, led by France, could serve not only as a check to Germany but also as a shield against the Russian threat. Romania's

The Victors and the Peace   In June 1919 the leaders of the major victorious powers exude confidence after signing with Germany the Treaty of Versailles, the most important of the five treaties that resulted from the Paris Peace Conference. From the left are David Lloyd George of Britain, Georges Clemenceau of France, and Woodrow Wilson of the United States.   (*Bettmann/Corbis*)

Prince Faisal at the Peace Conference

With the war nearing its end in October 1918, British authorities, in line with provisions of the Sykes-Picot agreement, permitted Faisal ibn-Husayn (1885–1933) to set up a provisional Arab state, with its capital at Damascus. As head of a delegation from this area to the Paris Peace Conference, Faisal claimed to speak for all Arab Asia, but some on the Arabian peninsula challenged his claim. In the memorandum of January 1919 that follows, he outlined the Arab position, mixing pride and assertiveness with a recognition that the Arabs would continue to need the support and help of Western powers. After the peace was concluded, Faisal found himself caught up in British and French rivalries as he was installed as king first of Syria, then of Iraq [Mesopotamia]. But his efforts were central to the eventual achievement of Arab independence in the Middle East.

We believe that our ideal of Arab unity in Asia is justified beyond need of argument. If argument is required, we would point to the general principles accepted by the Allies when the United States joined them, to our splendid past, to the tenacity with which our race has for 600 years resisted Turkish attempts to absorb us, and, in a lesser degree, to what we tried our best to do in this war as one of the Allies. . . .

The various provinces of Arab Asia—Syria, Irak, Jezireh, Hedjaz, Nejd, Yemen—are very different economically and socially, and it is impossible to constrain them into one frame of government.

We believe that Syria, an agricultural and industrial area thickly peopled with sedentary classes, is sufficiently advanced politically to manage her own internal affairs. We feel also that foreign technical advice and help will be a most valuable factor in our national growth. We are willing to pay for this help in cash; we cannot sacrifice for it any part of the freedom we have just won for ourselves by force of arms.

. . . The world wishes to exploit Mesopotamia rapidly, and we therefore believe that the system of government

there will have to be buttressed by the men and material resources of a great foreign Power. We ask, however, that the Government be Arab, in principle and spirit, the selective rather than the elective principle being necessarily followed in the neglected districts, until time makes the broader basis possible. . . .

In Palestine the enormous majority of the people are Arabs. The Jews are very close to the Arabs in blood, and there is no conflict of character between the two races. In principles we are absolutely at one. Nevertheless, the Arabs cannot risk assuming the responsibility of holding level the scales in the clash of races and religions that have, in this one province, so often involved the world in difficulties. They would wish for the effective super-position of a great trustee, so long as a representative local administration commended itself by actively promoting the material prosperity of the country. . . .

In our opinion, if our independence be conceded and our local competence established, the natural influences of race, language, and interest will soon draw us together into one people; but for this the Great Powers will have to ensure us open internal frontiers, common railways and telegraphs, and uniform systems of education. To achieve this they must lay aside the thought of individual profits, and of their old jealousies. In a word, we ask you not to force your whole civilisation upon us, but to help us to pick out what serves us from your experience. In return we can offer you little but gratitude.

QUESTIONS

1. How does Prince Faisal assess the prospects for unity among the diverse Arab peoples of Asia?

2. What role does Prince Faisal envision for the Western powers in Arab Asia?

Source: J. C. Hurewitz, *Diplomacy in the Near and Middle East: A Documentary Record: 1914–1956,* vol. 2 (Princeton, N.J.: D. Van Nostrand, 1956), pp. 38–39. Reprinted by Archive Editions, UK, 1987.

aggrandizement came partly at the expense of the Russian Empire, as did the creation of the new Poland. Finland, Latvia, Estonia, and Lithuania, all part of the Russian Empire for over a century, became independent states (see Map 25.3).

The territorial settlement cost Germany almost 15 percent of its prewar territory, but German bitterness over the peace terms stemmed above all from a sense of betrayal. In requesting an armistice, German authorities had appealed to Wilson, who had not emphasized war guilt and reparations. He seemed to be saying that the whole prewar international system, not one side or the other, had been responsible for the current conflict. Yet the peacemakers now placed the primary blame on Germany, so for Germans the terms of the peace greatly intensified the sting of defeat.

Wilson had been forced to compromise with French interests in dealing with east-central Europe, but he achieved a potentially significant success in exchange—the establishment of a League of Nations, embodying the widespread hope for a new international order. (See the box "The Continuing Experiment: The League of Nations.") According to the League covenant worked out by April, disputes among member states were no longer to be settled by war but by mechanisms established by the new assembly. Other members were to participate in sanctions, from economic blockade to military action, against a member that went to war in violation of League provisions.

How could Wilsonian hopes for a new international order be squared with the imperialist system, which seemed utterly at odds with the ideal of self-determination? Elites among the colonial peoples had tended to support the war efforts of their imperial rulers, but often in the hope of winning greater autonomy or even independence. The Indian leader Mohandas Gandhi (1869–1948), who had been educated in the West and admitted to the English bar in 1889, even helped recruit Indians to fight on the British side. But his aim was to speed Indian independence, and he led demonstrations that embarrassed the British during the war. (See the box "Global Encounters: Gandhi Advocates Nonviolence" on page 920 in Chapter 27.)

Colonial peoples participated directly in the war on both sides. In sub-Saharan Africa, for example, German-led Africans fought against Africans under British or French command. France brought colonial subjects from West and North Africa into front-line service during the war. But the resulting expansion of political consciousness led more of those subject to European imperialism to question the whole system.

The hope that support for the Western powers in wartime would eventually be rewarded led China and Siam (now Thailand) to associate with the Allied side in 1917, in an effort to enhance their international stature. Each was seeking to restore full sovereignty in the face of increasing Western influence. China sent 200,000 people to work in France to help ease France's wartime labor shortage.

At the peace conference, spokesmen for the non-Western world tended to be moderate in their demands.

Map 25.4   Ethnicity in East-Central Europe, 1919
Ethnic diversity made it hard to create homogeneous nation-states in east-central Europe. The new states that emerged after World War I mixed ethnic groups, and ethnic tensions would contribute to future problems.

And prodded by Wilson, the peacemakers made some concessions. German colonies and Ottoman territories were not simply taken over by the victors, in the old-fashioned way, but were placed under the authority of the League. The League then assigned them as mandates to one of the victorious powers, which was to report to the League annually on conditions in the area in question. Classes of mandates varied, based on how prepared for sovereignty the area was judged to be. In devising this system, the Western powers formally recognized for the first time that non-Western peoples under Western control had rights and interests of their own and that, in principle, they were progressing toward independence.

The League of Nations

In its very first part, before treating defeated Germany, the Treaty of Versailles established a new "League of Nations," outlining its aims and procedures as well as the obligations of its members. With this bold experiment, the war's victors sought to organize international relations on a radically new basis. The League's overriding aim was to settle international disputes without resort to war. But the League was also to fulfill an international responsibility, newly recognized here, for the gradual departure from colonialism. Although it instilled great hope at first, the League's inability to prevent aggression and war became clear during the 1930s. Even so, its failure prompted a still more determined effort to order international affairs with the creation of the United Nations in the aftermath of World War II.

The High Contracting Parties,

In order to promote international co-operation and to achieve international peace and security

by the acceptance of obligations not to resort to war,

by the prescription of open, just and honourable relations between nations,

by the firm establishment of the understandings of international law as the actual rule of conduct among Governments, and

by the maintenance of justice and a scrupulous respect for all treaty obligations in the dealings of organised peoples with one another,

Agree to this Covenant of the League of Nations. . . .

Article 12.

The Members of the League agree that if there should arise between them any dispute likely to lead to a rupture, they will submit the matter either to arbitration or to inquiry by the Council, and they agree in no case to resort to war until three months after the award by the arbitrators or the report by the Council. . . .

Article 16.

Should any Member of the League resort to war in disregard of its convenants under Articles 12, 13, or 15, it shall *ipso facto* be deemed to have committed an act of war against all other Members of the League, which hereby undertake immediately to subject it to the severance of all trade or financial relations, the prohibition of all intercourse between their nations and the nationals of the covenant-breaking State, and the prevention of all financial, commercial, or personal intercourse between the nationals of the covenant-breaking State and the nationals of any other State, whether a Member of the League or not. . . .

Article 22.

To those colonies and territories which as a consequence of the late war have ceased to be under the sovereignty of the States which formerly governed them and which are inhabited by peoples not yet able to stand by themselves under the strenuous conditions of the modern world, there should be applied the principle that the well-being and development of such peoples form a sacred trust of civilisation and that securities for the performance of this trust should be embodied in this Covenant.

The best method of giving practical effect to this principle is that the tutelage of such peoples should be entrusted to advanced nations who by reason of their resources, their experience or their geographical position can best undertake this responsibility, and who are willing to accept it, and that this tutelage should be exercised by them as Mandatories on behalf of the League.

QUESTIONS

1. How did the League of Nations expect to minimize the resort to war?

2. On what grounds did the League assume responsibility for overseeing the development of the former colonies of the defeated German and Ottoman Empires?

SOURCE: *The Treaties of Peace, 1919–1923,* vol. 1 (New York: The Carnegie Endowment for International Peace, 1924), pp. 10, 14, 17, 19.

Still, the mandate approach to the colonial question was a halting departure at best. Although Britain granted considerable sovereignty to Iraq in 1932, the victorious powers generally operated as before, assimilating the new territories into their existing systems of colonial possessions. After the hopes for independence raised in the Arab world during the war, this outcome produced a sense of betrayal among Arab leaders.

The Chinese similarly felt betrayed. Despite China's contributions to the Allied war effort, the victors acquiesced in special rights for Japan in China, causing a renewed sense of humiliation among Chinese elites and provoking popular demonstrations and a boycott of Japanese goods. Although Western leaders were allowing a non-Western power, Japan, access to the imperial club, they were hardly departing from imperialism. For Chinese, Arabs, and others, the West appeared hypocritical. Those whose political consciousness had been raised by the war came to believe not only that colonialism should end, but that the colonial peoples would themselves have to take the lead in ending it.

The incongruities of the postwar settlement prompted Marshal Foch to proclaim, "This is not peace. It is an armistice for twenty years."[8] Would the principal victors have the resolve, and the capacity, to preserve the new order they had solidified at Paris? Debate over the American role promptly developed in the United States as President Wilson sought Senate ratification of the Versailles treaty, which entailed U.S. membership in the League of Nations as well as commitments to France and Britain. Wilson's opponents worried that League membership would compromise U.S. sovereignty, but other nations managed to overcome such concerns and join the new organization. American reluctance stemmed especially from the isolationist backlash that was developing against the U.S. intervention in the European war. Late in 1919, at the height of the debate, Wilson suffered a disabling stroke. The Senate then refused to ratify the peace treaty, thereby keeping the United States out of the League of Nations.

American disengagement stemmed partly from doubts about the wisdom of the peace settlement that quickly developed in both Britain and the United States. During the peace conference, a member of the British delegation, the economist John Maynard Keynes° (1883–1946), resigned to write *The Economic Consequences of the Peace* (1920), which helped undermine confidence in the whole settlement. (See the box "The Continuing Experiment: The Government's Role in Managing a Free-Market Economy" on page 919 in Chapter 27.) Keynes charged that the shortsighted, vindictive policy of the French, by crippling Germany with a punishing reparations burden, threatened the European economy and thus the long-term peace of Europe. For some, then, the challenge was not to enforce the Versailles treaty but to revise it. This lack of consensus about the legitimacy of the peace made it especially hard to anticipate the longer-term consequences of the war.

The Cultural Impact of the Great War

The war touched virtually everyone, but it marked for life those who had experienced the nightmare of the trenches. At first, traditional notions of glory, heroism, and patriotic duty combined with images of fellowship and regeneration to enable the soldiers to make a certain sense of their wartime experience. But as the war dragged on, such sentiments gradually eroded, giving way, in many cases, to resignation and cynicism. (See the feature "Weighing the Evidence: The Poetry of World War I" on pages 876–877.) But others, such as the young German soldier and writer Ernst Jünger (1895–1998), lauded the war as the catalyst for a welcome new era of steel, hardness, discipline, organization, and machine precision.

After the war, many of those who had fought it felt a sense of ironic betrayal. Their prewar upbringing, the values and assumptions they had inherited, had not equipped them to make sense of what they had lived through. But the effort to find meaning involved not only the survivors but also the families and friends of those killed or maimed. There was much effort to recast traditional, often-religious categories and images for the near-universal experience of bereavement, which transcended national and class divisions.

Beginning in the late 1920s a wave of writings about the war appeared. Many were memoirs, such as *Goodbye to All That* by the English writer Robert Graves (1895–1985) and *Testament of Youth* by Vera Brittain (1893–1970), who had served as a British army nurse at the front. But easily the most famous retrospective was the novel *All Quiet on the Western Front* (1929) by the German Erich Maria Remarque (1898–1970), which sold 2.5 million copies in twenty-five languages in its first eighteen months in print. Remarque provided a gripping portrait of the experience of ordinary soldiers on the western front, but his book also reflected the disillusionment that had come to surround the memory of the war by the late 1920s. Not only were many friends dead or maimed for life, but all the sacrifices seemed to have been largely in vain, a sentiment that fueled determination to avoid another war in the future.

The novel forms of warfare introduced during World War I intensified fears of renewed war. Thanks to modern technology, which had been central to the West's confident belief in progress, Europeans had now experienced machine-gun fire, poison gas attacks, and the terror-bombing of civilians from airplanes. A generation

---

Keynes (KAINZ)

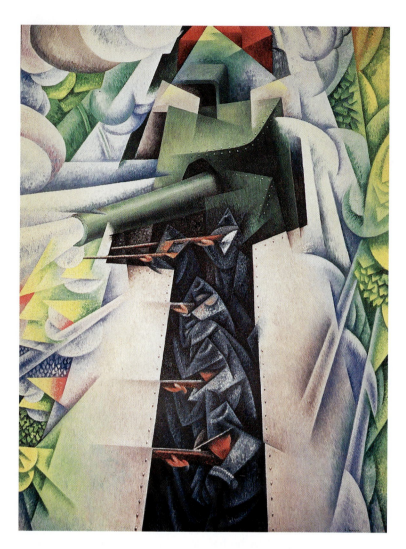

Severini: Armoured Train   In this painting from 1915, the Italian futurist Gino Severini (1883–1996) conveys the hard, steel-like imagery and the sense of disciplined modern efficiency that became associated with war, making it attractive to some young Europeans. *(Richard S. Zeisler Collection, New York/The Bridgeman Art Library. © 2001 Artists Rights Society [ARS], New York/ADAGP, Paris)*

later, to be sure, the advent of the nuclear age occasioned a measure of terror hardly imaginable earlier, but the experience of World War I was the turning point, the end of an earlier innocence.

What followed from the war, most fundamentally, was a new sense that Western civilization was neither as secure nor as superior as it had seemed. The celebrated French poet Paul Valéry (1871–1945), speaking at Oxford shortly after the war, observed that "we modern civilizations have learned to recognize that we are mortal like the others. We had heard . . . of whole worlds vanished, of empires foundered. . . . Elam, Nineveh, Babylon were vague and splendid names; the total ruin of these worlds, for us, meant as little as did their existence. But France, England, Russia . . . these names, too, are splendid. . . . And now we see that the abyss of history is deep enough to bury all the world. We feel that a civilization is as fragile as a life."[9] Valéry went on to warn that the com-

ing transition to peace would be even more difficult and disorienting than the war itself. So traumatic might be the convulsion that Europe might lose its leadership and be shown up for what it was in fact—a pathetically small corner of the world, a mere cape on the Asiatic landmass. Astounding words for a European, yet even Valéry, for all his foresight, could not anticipate what Europe would experience in the decades to follow.

SUMMARY

HE war that began in August 1914 was supposed to be over in a few months, but it quickly bogged down in stalemate in the west, which proved the decisive military front. Germany had to fight a two-front war, and it almost immediately began suffering under Britain's naval blockade. But the Germans defeated Russia in 1917 and then, in 1918, mounted a last-ditch offensive in the west that came close to succeeding as well. By 1918, however, lack of food, provisions, and manpower was fatally weakening the German effort, and U.S. intervention gave the anti-German coalition the long-term advantage in any case. Though it entailed far more sacrifice than anyone had expected at the outset, the war reached a definitive outcome with the defeat of Germany and its allies by November 1918.

So great were the strains of the war that radical political changes accompanied military defeat, first in Russia, then in Turkey, Austria-Hungary, and Germany. In destroying the Habsburg empire and the imperial regime in Germany, that outcome addressed the problems that seemed to have caused the war in the first place. But with so many pillars of the old order falling in the wake of the war, the future remained uncertain indeed, even after the major provisions of the peace settlement were established in 1919.

Because it was so much longer and more difficult than expected, this first "world war" proved a total war, calling forth new forms of socioeconomic coordination and even systematic propaganda. Partly as a result, the war accelerated processes, from technological development to women's suffrage, that many deemed progressive. But coming after a century of relative peace and apparent progress, this long and brutal war ended up shaking Europe's social and cultural foundations. The number of casualties, the advent of terrifying new weapons, the destruction of famous old monuments—all gave the war an apocalyptic aura that heightened its psychological impact. So despite a widespread desire to return to normal once the war was over, many were plagued by a deeper sense that the world could never be the same again. Troubling new uncertainties mixed with exciting new possibilities as Europe and the West looked to the future.

■ Notes

1. Thus wrote the German poet Ivan Goll in 1917; quoted in Modris Eksteins, *Rites of Spring: The Great War and the Birth of the Modern Age* (Boston: Houghton Mifflin, 1989), p. 144.

2. The remarks of Raymond Joubert, as quoted in John Ellis, *Eye-Deep in Hell: Trench Warfare in World War I* (Baltimore: Johns Hopkins University Press, 1989), p. 104.

3. Brian Bond, *War and Society in Europe, 1870–1970* (New York: Oxford University Press, 1986), p. 114.

4. A. N. Potresov, quoted in Richard Pipes, *The Russian Revolution* (New York: Random House, Vintage, 1991), p. 348.

5. Both statements are quoted in Koppel S. Pinson, *Modern Germany: Its History and Civilization*, 2d ed. (New York: Macmillan, 1966), p. 337.

6. Quoted in Arno J. Mayer, *Political Origins of the New Diplo-macy, 1917–18* (New York: Random House, Vintage, 1970), p. 135.

7. Quoted in Walter Arnstein, *Britain Yesterday and Today: 1830 to the Present*, 6th ed. (Lexington, Mass.: D. C. Heath, 1992), p. 266.

8. Quoted in P. M. H. Bell, *The Origins of the Second World War* (London and New York: Longman, 1986), p. 14.

9. Paul Valéry, *Variety*, 1st series (New York: Harcourt, Brace, 1938), pp. 3–4.

■ Suggested Reading

Beckett, Ian F. W. *The Great War, 1914–1918.* 2001. A thematically organized treatment; especially good on the global dimensions of the conflict.

Boemke, Manfred F., Gerald D. Feldman, and Elisabeth Glaser, eds. *The Treaty of Versailles: A Reassessment After 75 Years.* 1998. Scholars from a number of countries reassess all aspects of the treaty in a major collection of essays.

Chickering, Roger. *Imperial Germany and the Great War, 1914–1918.* 1998. A balanced, comprehensive introduction to the German war effort and experience; especially good on the interpenetration of military and sociopolitical concerns.

Ellis, John. *Eye-Deep in Hell: Trench Warfare in World War I.* 1989. A compelling account of life and death in the trenches, covering topics from trench construction to eating, drinking, and sex; includes striking photographs.

Figes, Orlando. *A People's Tragedy: The Russian Revolution, 1891–1924.* 1997. A lengthy, comprehensive, and gripping account of the revolutionary trajectory, from the famine of 1891 to the death of Lenin in 1924. Seeks to reveal the complexity of the whole process, its many episodes and forms of agency.

Fitzpatrick, Sheila. *The Russian Revolution, 1917–1932.* 2d ed. 1994. An ideal introductory work that places the events of 1917 in the sweep of Russian history.

Holquist, Peter. *Making War, Forging Revolution: Russia's Continuum of Crisis, 1914–1921.* 2002. By focusing on a particular region, this work shows how the Bolsheviks used the tools of mobilization and coercion already called forth by the war in their effort to reshape Russian society.

Keegan, John. *The First World War.* 1999. A comprehensive and accessible study by a widely read military historian.

Sharp, Alan. *The Versailles Settlement: Peacemaking in Paris, 1919.* 1991. A brief, clear, and balanced overview that seeks to do justice to the magnitude of the task the peacemakers faced.

Winter, J. M. *The Experience of World War I.* 1989. A beautifully illustrated work that proceeds via concentric circles from politicians to generals to soldiers to civilians, then to the war's longer-term effects.

Winter, Jay. *Sites of Memory, Sites of Mourning.* 1995. Using an effective comparative approach, a leading authority argues that Europeans relied on relatively traditional means of making sense of the bloodletting of World War I.

 For a searchable list of additional readings for this chapter, go to college.hmco.com/students.

The Poetry of World War I

We don't normally think of poetry and war together, and World War I, with its unexpected brutality and severe hardship, may seem the least poetic of wars. Yet even during the war, soldiers like Englishmen Rupert Brooke (1887–1915) and Wilfred Owen (1893–1918) sought to shape their experiences into poetic imagery. What does such poetry tell us about what the war meant to those who fought it? How has poetic testimony affected our understanding of the place of World War I in the Western experience?

In Brooke's wartime poetry, what strikes us first is his gratitude that his generation had come of age at this dramatic historical moment:

> Now, God be thanked Who has matched us with His
> hour,
> And caught our youth, and wakened us from sleeping

But why would a young man like Brooke welcome war? He seemed to envision release, deliverance—but from what?

When the war broke out, Brooke promptly volunteered, even pulling strings to get into a combat unit. Seeing action for the first time, in Belgium in October 1914, he was excited by the intensity of battle and pleased by his own calm self-control. Back in England for further training shortly thereafter, he wrote several sonnets, including "Peace," the one reproduced here, expressing his feelings about the war. But he died of blood poisoning on the way to battle in April 1915—without ever fully experiencing trench warfare.

Although most of the young Englishmen who took up arms with such enthusiasm in 1914 assumed that their country was in the right and that Germany was at fault, they gave little thought to the purposes of the war or the larger historical impact it might have. Brooke understood that the war would not accomplish all that was claimed for it, but he was grateful for the personal experience it made possible. Somehow it meant "peace," as the title of his sonnet suggests, and even cleanliness:

> To turn, as swimmers into cleanness leaping,
> Glad from a world grown old and cold and weary

Brooke's sense of deliverance responded to personal frustrations, yet he spoke for others of his generation who also were finding it difficult to assume a place in adult society at that particular time. Though they came from educated, upper-middle-class families, they were contemptuous of the routines and compromises of the respectable, everyday world to which they were expected to adjust. Thus Brooke welcomed the chance to

Rupert Brooke (1887–1915) *(Mansell Collection/ Getty Images)*

PEACE

Now, God be thanked Who has matched us with His hour,
   And caught our youth, and wakened us from sleeping,
With hand made sure, clear eye, and sharpened power,
   To turn, as swimmers into cleanness leaping,
Glad from a world grown old and cold and weary,
   Leave the sick hearts that honour could not move,
And half-men, and their dirty songs and dreary,
   And all the little emptiness of love!

Oh! we, who have known shame, we have found release there,
   Where there's no ill, no grief, but sleep has mending.
     Naught broken save this body, lost but breath;
Nothing to shake the laughing heart's long peace there
   But only agony, and that has ending;
     And the worst friend and enemy is but Death.

Rupert Brooke

Wilfred Owen (1893–1918) *(Hulton-Deutsch Collection/Corbis)*

ANTHEM FOR DOOMED YOUTH

What passing-bells for these who die as cattle?
　—Only the monstrous anger of the guns.
　Only the stuttering rifles' rapid rattle
Can patter out their hasty orisons.
No mockeries now for them; no prayers nor bells;
　Nor any voice of mourning save the choirs;—
The shrill, demented choirs of wailing shells;
　And bugles calling for them from sad shires.

What candles may be held to speed them all?
　Not in the hands of boys but in their eyes
Shall shine the holy glimmers of goodbyes.
　The pallor of girls' brows shall be their pall;
Their flowers the tenderness of patient minds,
And each slow dusk a drawing-down of blinds.

　　　　　　　　　Wilfred Owen

Leave the sick hearts that honour could not move,
And half-men, and their dirty songs and dreary

Yet those of Brooke's generation were equally troubled by their own uncertainty about values and commitments—to marriage, career, a place in society. Thanks to the overwhelming, inescapable reality of the war, values that had seemed empty—honor, country, duty, fellowship—now seemed meaningful after all. To his surprise and relief, Brooke found that he himself was capable of courage, commitment, and sacrifice. With its promise of cleanliness and renewal, the war was worth even its highest price, which was merely death.

Unlike Brooke, Wilfred Owen hated the war from the start. He was quickly struck by its sheer ugliness, as manifested in the landscape, the noise, the coarse language of the soldiers themselves. Yet he served with distinction, was decorated for bravery, and was killed by machine-gun fire just one week before the armistice in November 1918.

Owen, then, experienced the reality of World War I in a way that Brooke did not. The sonnet here, "Anthem for Doomed Youth," was written during September and October 1917, after the war had come to entail a terrible bloodletting. Thus Owen sought to shape sentiments very different from Brooke's—a sense of waste, of loss, of incongruity between suffering endured and results achieved. Whereas Brooke had brushed aside the possibility of death, Owen saw death as relentless, carrying off a generation of innocent youth, dying like cattle.

In a sense, even the dignity of death had become a casualty of the war. Thus Owen mixed funeral images with the new horror that this war had brought forth: the only mourning was "The shrill, demented choirs of wailing shells." Mocking the ongoing effort to sweeten the reality of death at the front through reference to nobility and sacrifice, Owen drowned out his initial suggestion of bells with the new and awful sounds of machine-gun fire:

—Only the monstrous anger of the guns.
Only the stuttering rifles' rapid rattle

Quite apart from its military and political outcome, World War I has assumed a particular place in our collective memory, thanks partly to those like Brooke and Owen who managed to frame their wartime experiences in the memorable language of poetry. At first, Brooke's poetry helped to justify the alarming slaughter to those who began questioning the war's purpose as it claimed the lives of their sons. Yet by now we find it hard to grasp the ideals that inspired his poetic testimony, for they were in one sense consumed by the war and the era of violence that it began. We still live in the world that emerged from that war, so Owen, with his tragic cynicism, is far more our contemporary. Brooke may still reveal for us something of the innocence that was lost, but it is especially through Owen's way of conveying the tragedy, the sense of betrayal and lost innocence, that World War I has continued to haunt the memory of Western civilization.

CHAPTER 26

The Illusion of Stability 1919–1930

IN 1925 Josephine Baker (1906–1975), a black entertainer from St. Louis, moved from the chorus lines of New York to the bistros of Paris, where she quickly became a singing and dancing sensation. Also a favorite in Germany, she was the most famous of the African American entertainers who took the cultural capitals of Europe by storm during the 1920s. After the disillusioning experience of war, many Europeans found a valuable infusion of vitality in Baker's jazz music, exotic costumes, and "savage," uninhibited dancing (see the photo on page 897).

The European attraction to African Americans as primitive, vital, and sensual reflected a good deal of racial stereotyping, but there really *was* something fresh and uninhibited about American culture, especially its African American variant. And even as they played to those stereotypes, black performers like Baker had great fun ironically subverting them. Many realized they could enjoy opportunities in parts of Europe that were still denied them in the United States. Baker herself was a woman of great sophistication who became a French citizen in 1937, participated in progressive causes, and was decorated for her secret intelligence work in the anti-Nazi resistance during World War II.

The prominence of African Americans in European popular culture was part of a wider infatuation with things American as Europeans embraced the new during the 1920s. Lacking the cultural baggage of Europe, America seemed to offer revitalization and modernity at the same time. With so many old conventions shattered by the war, the ideal of being "modern" became widespread among Europeans, affecting everything from sex education to furniture design. "Modern" meant no-nonsense efficiency, mass production, and a vital popular

Kees van Dongen, *Au cabaret nègre* (detail).
(Collection Christie's/Edimedia)

culture, expressed in jazz, movies, sport, and even advertising. (See the feature "Weighing the Evidence: Advertising" on pages 910–911.)

But Europeans themselves had pioneered modernism in many areas of the arts and sciences, and innovation continued after the war. Paris held its own as an international cultural center, hosting a decorative arts exhibition in 1925 that produced art deco, the sleek, "modernistic" style that helped give the decade its distinctive flavor. And in the unsettled conditions of postwar Germany, Berlin emerged to rival Paris for cultural leadership during what Germans called "the Golden Twenties." Innovations ranged from avant-garde drama to a sophisticated cabaret scene with a prominent homosexual dimension.

Still, there was something dizzying, even unnerving, about the eager embrace of the new during the 1920s. The war had accelerated the long-term modernization process toward large industries, cities, and bureaucracies, and toward mass politics, society, and culture. That process was positive, even liberating, in certain respects, but it was also disruptive and disturbing. Some Europeans viewed the vogue of black American entertainers as a symptom of decadence that would only undermine further the best of European civilization. In this sense, the postwar sense of release and excitement combined with an anxious longing for stability, for a return to order—or at least to ordering. Even in embracing the new, many were seeking a new basis for order and security, but where their efforts would lead remained unclear.

Although the immediate disruptions of wartime carried over to 1923, a more hopeful era of relative prosperity and international conciliation followed, continuing until 1929. But there was much that called into question the ideal of a "world safe for democracy" that had surrounded the end of the war. Revolutionary Russia remained an uncertain force, even as it began seeking to build socialism on its own. In Italy, the democracy that had emerged in the nineteenth century gave way to the first regime to call itself fascist, and some of the new democracies in east-central Europe did not survive the decade. The postwar efforts at economic restabilization, apparently successful for a while, masked growing strains in the international economy. In one sphere after another, postwar restabilization was fragile—and could quickly unravel.

QUESTIONS TO CONSIDER

- How did the differing priorities of Britain and France affect international relations during the 1920s?

- How and why did the priorities of the Russian communist regime change from 1919 to 1930?

- Why did Italy turn from parliamentary democracy to fascism even after sharing in the victory in World War I?

- What factors produced the political instability that made the future of the new German democracy so uncertain during the 1920s?

TERMS TO KNOW

Maginot Line
fascism
Benito Mussolini
Comintern (Third, or
   Communist,
   International)
New Economic Policy (NEP)
Joseph Stalin

Matteotti murder
corporative state,
   corporativism
Gustav Stresemann
Treaty of Locarno
surrealism
Bauhaus

THE WEST AND THE WORLD AFTER THE GREAT WAR

ALTHOUGH the United States and Japan were becoming important, the major international players before 1914 had been the European powers, who had apportioned much of the non-Western world in imperial networks. But the war and the peace had weakened—and to some extent discredited—the belligerent countries of Europe, who now found themselves saddled with foreign debts and unbalanced economies. Though the United States pulled back from a direct political role in Europe in 1919, it became far more active in world affairs, helping to engineer major conferences on arms limitation and international economic relations during the 1920s. But in crucial respects, the shape of the postwar international order still depended on Europeans. And colonial concerns continued to affect the balance of power in Europe, where it fell to the two major victors in the war, France and Britain, to enforce the controversial peace settlement.

The Erosion of European Power

Emerging from the war as the principal power in East Asia was a non-Western country, Japan, whose claims to the German bases in the region and to special rights in China were formally recognized at the Paris Peace Conference. With the Washington treaty of 1922, Japan won naval parity with Britain and the United States in East Asia. The Western nations were recognizing Japan as a peer, a great power—even a threat. Aspects of the Washington agreements were intended to block Japanese expansion in East Asia. If a new international system was to emerge, it would not be centered in Europe to the extent the old one had been.

After the slaughter of the war and the hypocrisy of the peace, Europeans could no longer claim to embody civilization with the same arrogance. And as the old Europe lost prestige, President Wilson's ideals of self-determination and democracy were greeted enthusiastically outside the West—in China, for example. At the same time, the Russian revolutionary model appealed to those in the colonial world seeking to understand the mainsprings of Western imperialism—and the means of overcoming it. To some Chinese intellectuals by the early 1920s, Leninism was attractive because it showed the scope for mass mobilization by a revolutionary vanguard.

CHRONOLOGY	
March 1919	Founding of the Italian fascist movement
November 1920	Russian civil war ends
March 1921	New Economic Policy announced at Russian Communist Party congress
October 1922	Mussolini becomes Italian prime minister
January 1923	French-led occupation of the Ruhr
November 1923	Peak of inflation in Germany
January 1924	First Labour government in Britain Death of Lenin
August 1924	Acceptance of the Dawes Plan on German reparations
October 1925	Treaty of Locarno
May 1926	Pilsudski's coup d'état in Poland Beginning of general strike in Britain
May 1927	Lindbergh completes first transatlantic solo flight
January 1929	Stalin forces banishment of Trotsky from Soviet Union
April 1929	Soviets adopt first economic Five-Year Plan
August 1929	Acceptance of the Young Plan on German reparations
October 1929	Death of Stresemann

Non-Western elites were learning to pick and choose from among the elements of the Western tradition. In the 1920s, ever greater numbers of colonial subjects were traveling to western Europe, often for education. Paris was a favored destination, partly because France made an effort to assimilate its colonial peoples. Although those educated in Europe were subject to Westernization, that did not necessarily make them more supportive of Western rule. Many began not only to question colonialism but also to take a fresh look at their own traditions, asking how they might serve the quest for a postcolonial order.

Reinforcing Imperialist Rule In response to episodes of anticolonialist violence in Amritsar, India, early in 1919, the British brutally cracked down, most notably in the massacre of April 1919. Here British authorities enforce a decree in the wake of the beating of a female British doctor on this road—forcing any Indian using the road to crawl along it. *(National Army Museum, London)*

By the 1920s, a generation of anticolonialist, nationalist intellectuals was emerging to lead the non-Western world. Some were more radical than others, but most agreed that the challenge was to learn from the West and to modernize, but without simply copying the West and losing distinctive cultural identities. It was imperative to sift through tradition, determining what needed to be changed and what was worth preserving. The pioneering Chinese nationalist Sun Yixien (Sun Yat-sen, 1866–1925) was typical in recognizing the need to adopt the science and technology of the West. But China, he insisted, could do so in its own way, without sacrificing its unique cultural and political traditions. (See the box "Global Encounters: Sun Yixien on Chinese Nationalism.")

As the greatest imperial power, Britain was especially vulnerable to the growing anticolonial sentiment. The struggle to hang on to its empire drew British energies away from the problems of Europe after the peace settlement.

In light of the strong Indian support for the British war effort, the British government promised in 1917 to extend the scope for Indian involvement in the colonial administration in India. Growing expectations as the war was ending provoked episodes of violence against the British, whose troops retaliated brutally in April 1919, firing indiscriminately into an unarmed crowd. This Amritsar Massacre helped galvanize India's independence movement, even though the British, seeking conciliation in the aftermath, extended self-rule by entrusting certain less essential government services to Indians. Another milestone was reached in 1921, when Mohandas Gandhi, the British-educated leader of the Indian independence movement, shed his European clothes in favor of simple Indian attire. But it was on the basis of Western egalitarianism, not some indigenous value, that Gandhi demanded political rights for the "untouchables," the lowest group in India's long-standing caste system. (See the box "Global Encounters: Gandhi Advocates Nonviolence" on page 920 in Chapter 27.)

In Egypt a full-scale anti-British insurrection broke out in 1919. After British troops suppressed the rebellion, British authorities offered to grant moderate conces-

Sun Yixien on Chinese Nationalism

Sun Yixien (Sun Yat-sen), widely regarded as the father of modern China, founded the Guomindang (Kuomintang), the Chinese nationalist movement, in 1912. Educated by Western missionaries in China, he lived in the United States for extended periods and came to admire the West in important respects. But he insisted that China, to make the best use of what the West offered, had to reconnect with its own unique traditions. Variations on this argument would be heard for decades as the rest of the world sought to come to terms with the seemingly more advanced West. The following passages are from an influential series of lectures that Sun Yixien presented in China in the early 1920s.

What is the standing of our nation in the world? In comparison with other nations we have the greatest population and the oldest culture, of four thousand years' duration. We ought to be advancing in line with the nations of Europe and America. But the Chinese people have only family and clan groups; there is no national spirit. Consequently, in spite of four hundred million people gathered together in one China, we are in fact but a sheet of loose sand. We are the poorest and weakest state in the world, occupying the lowest position in international affairs; the rest of mankind is the carving knife and the serving dish, while we are the fish and the meat. Our position now is extremely perilous; if we do not earnestly promote nationalism and weld together our four hundred millions into a strong nation, we face a tragedy—the loss of our country and the destruction of our race. To ward off this danger, we must espouse Nationalism and employ the national spirit to save the country. . . .

But even if we succeed in reviving our ancient morality, learning, and powers, we will still not be able, in this modern world, to advance China to a first place among the nations. . . . [W]e will still need to learn the strong points of Europe and America before we can progress at an equal rate with them. Unless we do study the best from foreign countries, we will go backward. With our own fine foundation of knowledge and our age-long culture, with our own native intelligence besides, we should be able to acquire all the best things from abroad. The strongest point of the West is its science. . . .

As soon as we learn Western machinery we can use it anytime, anywhere; electric lights, for example, can be installed and used in any kind of Chinese house. But Western social customs and sentiments are different from ours in innumerable points; if, without regard to customs and popular feelings in China, we try to apply Western methods of social control as we would Western machinery—in a hard and fast way—we shall be making a serious mistake. . . .

. . . For the governmental machinery of the United States and France still has many defects, and does not satisfy the desires of the people nor give them a complete measure of happiness. So we in our proposed reconstruction must not think that if we imitate the West of today we shall reach the last stage of progress and be perfectly contented. . . .

Only in recent times has Western culture advanced beyond ours, and the passion for this new civilization has stimulated our revolution. Now that the revolution is a reality, we naturally desire to see China excel the West and build up the newest and most progressive state in the world. We certainly possess the qualifications necessary to reach this ideal, but we must not merely imitate the democratic systems of the West.

QUESTIONS

1. Why does Sun Yixien think China, despite its ancient and sophisticated culture, has fallen behind the West?

2. Why does Sun Yixien insist that nationalism is essential for the Chinese to address their present challenge?

3. On what grounds does Sun Yixien consider it necessary for China to study Western culture, as opposed to relying on its own traditions?

Source: Sun Yat-sen, *San Min Chu I: The Three Principles of the People* (Taipei, Taiwan: China Cultural Service, 1953), pp. 5, 46, 109–113, 136, 138–139.

sions, as in India. But Egyptian nationalists demanded independence, which was finally granted in 1922. Egypt gradually evolved into a constitutional monarchy, with representative government and universal suffrage. But Britain retained a predominant influence in Egypt until the nationalist revolution of 1952 (see page 1007).

At the same time, nationalism was growing among West Africans who had studied in England. In March 1919 Western-educated Africans in the Gold Coast asked the British governor to establish representative institutions so that Africans could at least be consulted about governmental affairs. The West African National Congress, formed in 1920, made similar demands. The British agreed to new constitutions for Nigeria in 1923 and the Gold Coast in 1925 that took significant steps in that direction. They also agreed to build more schools, though they tended to promote practical education, including African languages and agriculture, whereas the African leaders wanted students to learn the Western classics that "made gentlemen." Such conflicting priorities indicate the complexities of the relationships between colonial rulers and the emerging elites among the colonized peoples.

Enforcing the Versailles Settlement

It was up to France and Britain to make sure the new international order worked, but it was not clear that either had the will and resources to do so. Cooperation between them was essential, yet sometimes their differences— in geography, in values, and in perceptions—seemed to doom them to work at cross-purposes.

France was the dominant power on the European continent after World War I, and until well into the 1930s it boasted the strongest army in the world. Yet even in the early 1920s a sense of artificiality surrounded France's image of strength—thus the shrillness and the defensiveness that came to mark French thinking and French policy.

In light of Germany's larger population and stronger industrial base, France's long-term security seemed to require certain measures to tip the scales in its favor. By imposing German disarmament and the demilitarization of the Rhineland, the Versailles treaty gave France immediate military advantages. Yet how long could these measures be maintained, once the passions of war had died down and Germany no longer seemed such a threat? France had hoped for British help in enforcing the treaty, but Britain was pulling back from the Continent to concentrate on its empire, just as it had after other major European wars.

In particular, the British wanted to avoid getting dragged into the uncertain situation in east-central Europe, where vital national interests did not seem to be at stake. Yet the French, to replace their earlier link with Russia, promptly developed an alliance system with several of the new or expanded states of the region, including Poland, Czechoslovakia, Romania, and Yugoslavia. France's ties to east-central Europe made the British especially wary of binding agreements with the French.

At first, France felt confident enough to take strong steps even without British support. In response to German foot-dragging in paying reparations, Prime Minister Raymond Poincaré decided to get tough in January 1923. Declaring the Germans in default, he sent French troops at the head of an international force to occupy the Ruhr industrial area and force German compliance. But the move backfired. The Germans adopted a policy of passive resistance in response, and the costs of the occupation more than offset the increase in reparations that France received. The French government ended up having to raise taxes to pay for the venture. Moreover, the move alienated the British, whose lack of support bordered on active hostility.

British leaders now viewed French policy as unnecessarily vindictive and bellicose, and they increasingly saw the Versailles treaty as counterproductive. Instead, they placed great store in the League of Nations and in the international arms reduction effort gaining momentum by the later 1920s. So France found itself with ever less support from its wartime allies as it sought to enforce the peace settlement. The Ruhr occupation of 1923 proved the last time the French dared to go it alone.

From that point on, France gradually lost the advantages it had gained by defeating Germany, and self-confidence gave way to defensiveness and resignation. The defensive mentality found physical embodiment in the Maginot° Line, a system of fortifications on the country's eastern border. Remembering the defensive warfare of World War I and determined to preclude the sort of invasion France had suffered in 1914, the military convinced France's political leaders to adopt a defensive strategy based on a fortified line. Construction began in 1929, and the Maginot system reached preliminary completion in 1935, when it extended along France's border with Germany from Switzerland to the border with Belgium.

This defensive system was not consistent with the other major strands of French policy, especially its alliances with states in east-central Europe. If France emphasized defense behind an impregnable system of forts, what good were French security guarantees to such new allies as Poland and Czechoslovakia?

Still, the situation remained fluid during the 1920s. In France, as in Britain, national elections in 1924 produced a victory for the moderate left, ending a period of conservative nationalist dominance since the war. In each country, international relations became a major issue in the elections, and the outcome heralded a more conciliatory tack, especially in relations with Germany.

Maginot (MAH-zhih-noh)

COMMUNISM, FASCISM, AND THE NEW POLITICAL SPECTRUM

IN making their revolution in 1917, the Russian Bolsheviks had expected to spark wider revolution, and hopes—and fears—that the revolution would spread were palpable in the immediate postwar period. The Russian communists initially enjoyed extraordinary prestige on the European left; but as the nature of Leninist communism became clearer, some Marxists grew skeptical or hostile, and the Russian model eventually produced a damaging split in international socialism. By the end of the 1920s revolution elsewhere was nowhere in sight, and it seemed that, for the foreseeable future, the communist regime in Russia would have to go it alone.

By then, a new and unexpected political movement had emerged in Italy, expanding the political spectrum in a different direction. This was the first fascism, which brought Benito Mussolini to power in 1922. Emerging directly from the war, Italian fascism was violent and antidemocratic—and thus disturbing to many. Stressing national solidarity and discipline, the fascists were hostile not only to liberal individualism and the parliamentary system, but also to Marxist socialism, with its emphasis on class struggle and the special role of the working class. Claiming to offer a modern alternative to both, Italian fascism quickly attracted the attention of those in other countries who were disillusioned with parliamentary politics and hostile to the Marxist left. The interplay of communism and fascism, as new political experiments, added to the uncertainties of the novel postwar world.

Changing Priorities in Communist Russia, 1918–1921

Even after leading the revolution that toppled the provisional government in November 1917, the Bolsheviks could not claim majority support in Russia. When the long-delayed elections to select a constituent assembly were held a few weeks after the revolution, the Socialist Revolutionaries won a clear majority, while the Bolsheviks ended up with fewer than one-quarter of the seats. But the Bolsheviks dispersed the assembly by force when it met in January 1918. And over the next three years the Communists, as the Bolsheviks renamed themselves, gradually consolidated their power, establishing a centralized and nondemocratic regime. Power lay not with the soviets, nor with some coalition of socialist parties, but solely with the Communist Party.

During its first years, the new communist regime encountered a genuine emergency that especially seemed to require such a monopoly of power. During 1918 to 1920, in what became a brutal civil war, the communist "Reds" battled counterrevolutionary "Whites," people who had been dispossessed by the revolution or who had grown disillusioned with the Communist Party. Moreover, foreigners eager to topple the communist regime began to intervene militarily. At the same time, several of the non-Russian nationalities of the old Russian Empire sought to take advantage of the unsettled situation to free themselves from Russian and communist control. Appointed "People's Commissar for War" in April 1918, Leon Trotsky forged a loyal and disciplined Red Army in an effort to master the difficult situation.

A series of thrusts, involving troops from fourteen countries at one time or another, struck at Russia from a variety of points along its huge border. The Whites and the foreign troops never forged a coordinated strategy, but the dogged counterrevolutionary assault seriously threatened the young communist regime and the territorial basis of the state it had inherited from the tsarist autocracy. In the final analysis, however, the Whites proved unable to rally much popular support. Peasants feared, plausibly enough, that a White victory would mean a restoration of the old order, including the return of their newly won lands to the former landlords. By the end of active fighting in November 1920, the communist regime had not only survived but regained most of the territory it had lost early in the civil war (see Map 26.1).

The need to launch the new communist regime in this way, fighting counterrevolutionaries supported by foreign troops, inevitably affected Communists' perceptions and priorities. Separatist sentiment might continue to feed counterrevolutionary efforts, so the new regime exerted careful control over the non-Russian nationalities. Thus, when the Union of Soviet Socialist Republics (USSR) was organized in December 1922, it was only nominally a federation of autonomous republics; strong centralization from the communist regime's new capital in Moscow was the rule from the start.

In the midst of the civil war the Russian Communists founded the Third, or Communist, International—widely known as the Comintern—in March 1919, to make clear their break with the seemingly discredited strategies of the Second International. Through the Comintern, the Russian Communists expected to translate their success in Russia into leadership of the international socialist movement. However, many old-line Marxists elsewhere were not prepared to admit that the leadership of European socialism had passed to the Bolshevik rulers of

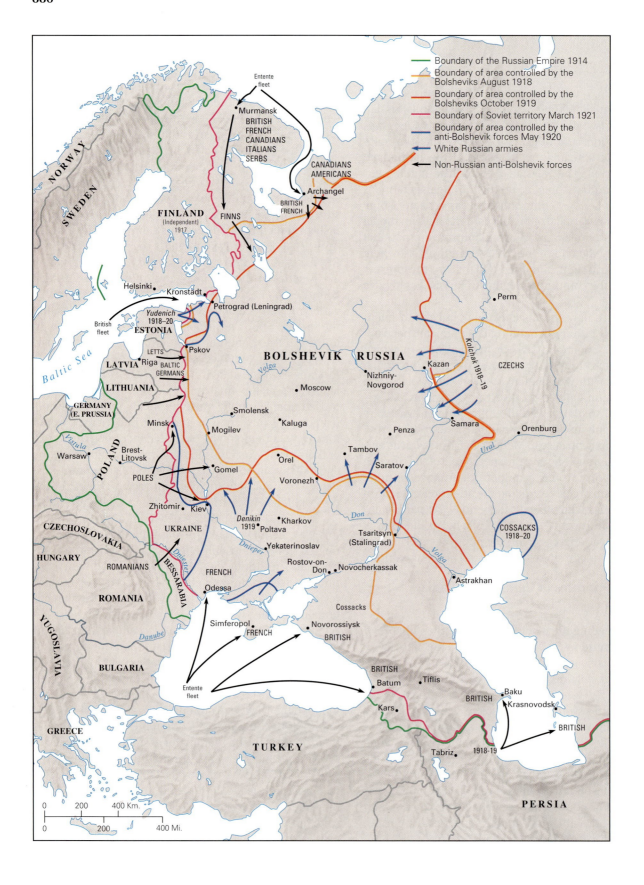

Boundary of the Russian Empire 1914
Boundary of area controlled by the Bolsheviks August 1918
Boundary of area controlled by the Bolsheviks October 1919
Boundary of Soviet territory March 1921
Boundary of area controlled by the anti-Bolshevik forces May 1920
White Russian armies
Non-Russian anti-Bolshevik forces

NORWAY

SWEDEN

FINLAND
(Independent)
1917

Entente
fleet

Murmansk
BRITISH
FRENCH
CANADIANS
ITALIANS
SERBS

FINNS

CANADIANS
AMERICANS

Archangel

BRITISH
FRENCH

Helsinki

Kronstadt

Petrograd (Leningrad)

Perm

Yudenich
1918–20

British
fleet

ESTONIA

Baltic Sea

LETTS

Pskov

LATVIA Riga

BALTIC
GERMANS

LITHUANIA

GERMANY
(E. PRUSSIA)

Minsk

Vistula

Brest-
Litovsk

Warsaw

POLAND

POLES

Zhitomir

Kiev

CZECHOSLOVAKIA

HUNGARY

ROMANIANS

BESSARABIA

UKRAINE

ROMANIA

Dniester

Odessa

FRENCH

Simferopol
FRENCH

YUGOSLAVIA

Danube

BULGARIA

GREECE

Smolensk

Mogilev

Gomel

Zhitomir

Denikin
1919

Kharkov

Poltava

Yekaterinoslav

Dnieper

BOLSHEVIK RUSSIA

Volga

Moscow

Nizhniy-
Novgorod

Kaluga

Orel

Voronezh

Tambov

Saratov

Don

Penza

Kazan

Samara

CZECHS

Orenburg

Ural

Kolchak 1918–19

Tsaritsyn
(Stalingrad)

COSSACKS
1918–20

Volga

Astrakhan

Rostov-on-
Don

Novocherkassak

Cossacks

Novorossiysk
BRITISH

BRITISH

Batum

Tiflis

Baku

Krasnovodsk
BRITISH

Entente
fleet

Kars

BRITISH

Tabriz

1918–19

TURKEY

PERSIA

0   200   400 Km.

0   200   400 Mi.

backward Russia. As early as 1919, the German Karl Kautsky (1854–1938), who had been the leading spokesman for orthodox Marxism after the death of Friedrich Engels in 1895, harshly criticized Leninist communism as a heretical departure that would lead to despotism and severely damage international socialism.

From its founding in March 1919 until the spring of 1920, as a wave of leftist political agitation and labor unrest swept Europe, the Comintern actively promoted the wider revolution that Lenin had envisioned. Seeking to win mass support, the organization accented leftist solidarity and reached out to the rank and file in the labor unions. By the spring of 1920, however, it seemed clear that further revolution was not imminent. Thus Comintern leaders began concentrating on improving organization and discipline for a more protracted revolutionary struggle.

The Russians felt that poor organization and planning had undermined the wider revolutionary possibility in Europe during 1919 and 1920. The Comintern would cut through all the revolutionary romanticism to show what the Leninist strategy, or communism, meant in fact. The Russians themselves would have to call the shots because what communism meant, above all, was tight organization and discipline.

The second Comintern congress, during the summer of 1920, devised twenty-one conditions for Comintern affiliation. Most notably, any socialist party seeking membership had to accept the Comintern's authority, adopt a centralized organization, and purge its reformists. By early 1921, the Comintern's aggressive claim to leadership had split the international socialist movement, for the Comintern attracted some, but not all, of the members of the existing socialist parties. Those who now called themselves "communists" accepted the Leninist model and affiliated with the Comintern. Those who retained the "socialist" label rejected Comintern leadership; they still claimed to be Marxists but declined to embrace the Bolshevik strategy for taking power.

Map 26.1   Foreign Intervention and Civil War in Revolutionary Russia, 1918–1920   By mid-1918 the new communist regime was under attack from many sides, by both foreign troops and anticommunist Russians. Bolshevik-held territory shrank during 1919, but over the next year the Red Army managed to regain much of what had been lost and to secure the new communist state. Anton Denikin, Alexander Kolchak, and Nicholas Yudenich commanded the most significant counterrevolutionary forces.   *(Source: Adapted from The Times Atlas of World History, 3d ed. Reprinted by permission of HarperCollins Publishers Ltd, © 1989.)*

At first, many European socialists had difficulty assessing the Comintern objectively. The Russian Communists enjoyed great prestige because they had made a real revolution, while elsewhere socialists had talked and compromised, even getting swept up in wartime patriotism. When the French Socialist Party debated Comintern membership at its national congress in December 1920, about 70 percent of the delegates voted to join and accept the twenty-one points, while a minority walked out to form a new socialist party. But as the implications of Comintern membership became clearer over the next few years, the balance shifted in favor of the socialists. Membership in the French Communist Party, which stood at 131,000 in 1921, declined to 28,000 by 1932.

Late in 1923 the Comintern finally concluded that revolution elsewhere could not be expected any time soon. The immediate enemy was not capitalism or the bourgeoisie, but the socialists, the communists' rivals for working-class support. The communists' incessant criticism of the socialists, whom they eventually dubbed "social fascists," demoralized and weakened the European left, especially in the face of the growing threat of fascism by the early 1930s. The schism on the left remained an essential fact of European political life for half a century.

From Lenin to Stalin, 1921–1929

To win the civil war, the communist regime had adopted a policy of "war communism," a rough-and-ready controlled economy in which food and supplies were commandeered for the Red Army. At the beginning of 1921, the economy was in crisis. Industrial production equaled only about one-fifth the 1913 total, workers in key factories went on strike, and peasants were resisting further requisitions of grain. In March 1921 sailors at the Kronstadt naval base near Petrograd mutinied, suffering considerable loss of life as governmental control was reestablished.

With the very survival of the revolution in question, Lenin replaced war communism with the New Economic Policy (NEP) in March 1921. Although transport, banking, heavy industry, and wholesale commerce remained under state control, the NEP restored considerable scope for private enterprise, especially in the retail sector and in agriculture. Peasants could again sell some of their harvest. The economy quickly began to revive and by 1927 was producing at prewar levels.

But what about the longer term? If revolution elsewhere was not on the immediate horizon, could the Soviet Union—relatively backward economically and scarred by over a decade of upheaval—build a genuinely

Rivals for the Soviet Leadership   In July 1926 in Moscow, Soviet leaders carry the coffin of Feliks Dzerzhinsky, the first head of the secret police. Among them are Trotsky (*with glasses, center left*), Stalin (*right foreground*), and Bukharin (*with mustache, at far right*), rivals for the Soviet leadership after Lenin's death. The winner, Stalin, would eventually have his two competitors killed. *(David King Collection)*

socialist order on its own? Certain measures were obvious: The new regime engineered rapid improvements in literacy, for example. But the Marxist understanding of historical progress required industrialization, and so debate focused on how to promote industrial development under Soviet conditions. That Soviet industrialization was somehow bound up with the creation of socialism was taken for granted.

This debate about priorities became intertwined with questions about the leadership of the new regime. Lenin suffered the first of a series of strokes in May 1922 and then died in January 1924, setting off a struggle among his possible successors. Leon Trotsky, an effective organizer and powerful thinker, was by most measures Lenin's heir apparent. Although he favored tighter economic controls to speed industrial development, Trotsky insisted that the Soviet Union's top priority should be spreading the revolution to other countries.

In contrast, Nikolai Bukharin (1888–1938) wanted to concentrate on the gradual development of the Soviet Union, based on a more open and conciliatory strategy than Trotsky envisioned. (See the box "The Continuing Experiment: Seeking to Build Socialism in the Soviet Union.") Rather than tightening controls to squeeze a surplus from agricultural producers, the government

should promote purchasing power by allowing producers to profit. By the time of his death Lenin had apparently begun thinking along the same lines. And he had come to have considerable misgivings about the man who would win this struggle to direct the fragile new Soviet regime, Joseph Stalin (1879–1953).

Stalin was born Josef Djugashvili into a lower-class family in Georgia, in the Caucasus region. As an ethnic Georgian, he did not learn to speak Russian until he was 11 years old. From the position of party secretary, which he had assumed in 1922, Stalin established his control within the Soviet system by 1929. Though he lacked Trotsky's charisma and knew little of economics, he was highly intelligent and proved a master of backstage political maneuvering. Stalin first outmaneuvered Trotsky and his allies, removing them from positions of power and forcing Trotsky himself into exile in 1929. Bitterly critical of Stalin to the end, Trotsky was finally murdered by Stalin's agents in Mexico in 1940. Stalin's victory over those like Bukharin was more gradual, but ultimately just as complete. And his victory proved decisive for the fate of Soviet communism.

By the later 1920s, those who believed in the communist experiment were growing disillusioned with the compromises of the NEP. It was time for the Soviet Union

Tatlin: Monument to the Third International   Vladimir Tatlin created this model for a monument to the Third International, or Comintern, during 1919 and 1920. He envisioned a revolving structure, made of glass and iron, and twice as tall as the later Empire State Building. Although the monument was never built, Tatlin's bold, dynamic form symbolizes the utopian aspirations of the early years of the communist experiment in Russia.   *(David King Collection)*

to push ahead to a new order, leaving capitalism behind altogether. Even if revolution was not imminent elsewhere, the Soviet Union could seize the lead and build "socialism in one country." Genuine enthusiasm greeted the regime's turn to centralized economic planning in 1927 and its subsequent adoption of the first Five-Year Plan early in 1929. Central planning led to a program of crash industrialization, favoring heavy industry, by the end of that year. But this new, more radical direction was not fully thought through, and it soon caused incredible suffering.

To buy the necessary plant and equipment, the state seemed to require better control of agricultural output than had been possible under the NEP. The key was to squeeze the agricultural surplus from the peasantry on terms more favorable to the government. By forcing peasants into large, state-controlled collective farms, government leaders could more readily extract the surplus, which would then be sold abroad, earning the money to finance factories, dams, and power plants.

Stalin's effort to mobilize society for the great task of rapid industrialization affected the whole shape of the regime—including cultural and artistic policy. During the 1920s, the possibility of building a new socialist society in the Soviet Union had attracted a number of modernist artists, who assumed that artistic innovation went hand in hand with the radical socioeconomic transformation the Communists were seeking to engineer. These artists wanted to make art more socially useful and more central to the lives of ordinary people. With Soviet cultural officials welcoming their experiments, such Soviet artists as Vladimir Tatlin (1885–1956) and Alexander Rodchenko (1891–1956) developed striking new cultural forms.

But in 1929 Soviet officials began mobilizing the cultural realm to serve the grandiose task of building socialism in one country. No longer welcoming experiment and innovation, they demanded "socialist realism," which portrayed the achievements of the ongoing Soviet revolution in an inspiring, heroic light. Modernism, in contrast, they denounced as decadent and counterrevolutionary.

In retrospect, it is clear that a Stalinist revolution within the Soviet regime began in 1929, but where it was to lead was by no means certain—not even to Stalin himself. Still, the Soviet Union was pulling back, going its own way by the end of the 1920s. For the foreseeable future, the presence of a revolutionary regime in the old Russia would apparently be less disruptive for the rest of Europe than it had first appeared.

The Crisis of Liberal Italy and the Creation of Fascism, 1919–1925

Fascism emerged directly from the Italian experience of World War I, which proved especially controversial because the Italians could have avoided it altogether. No one attacked Italy in 1914, and the country could have received significant territorial benefits just by remaining neutral. Yet it seemed to many, including leading intellectuals and educated young people, that Italy could not stand idly by in a European war, especially one involving Austria-Hungary, which still controlled significant Italian-speaking areas. To participate in this major war would be the test of Italy's maturity as a nation. In May 1915 Italy finally intervened on the side of the Triple

Seeking to Build Socialism in the Soviet Union

Once the Bolshevik Revolution failed to spread after 1917, it was not at all clear what might develop from the communist experiment in the Soviet Union. Anticommunists gloated, and some communists worried, that the compromises of Lenin's New Economic Policy (NEP) would lead back to capitalism. Nikolai Bukharin was the chief spokesman for those who argued that the NEP provided the framework for the gradual creation of a socialist society. Although elements of class struggle between workers and peasants persisted temporarily, the communists could proceed through cooperation, competition, and persuasion, without further coercion or rupture. After the triumph of Joseph Stalin, however, the communist experiment took a radically different direction, and Bukharin was executed in the wake of a show trial in 1938.

By harnessing the private economic interests of the small producer—through cooperation—it is possible to lead him gradually toward socialism. This can be done without suddenly and abruptly violating the established pattern of life and without thus exciting either hostility on the basis of petit bourgeois traditions or superstition on the part of the broad masses of the laboring peasantry. . . .

. . . Suffering from its "smallness," . . . the small peasant farm will compensate for this inadequacy with its *cooperative organization*. Supported by the proletarian state power, it will similarly win for itself all the advantages of any large-scale association and will use these advantages and benefits, deriving from cooperation, *in its struggle against the private farm of the kulak. Through struggle in the market, through market relations, and through competition* state enterprises and cooperatives will displace their competitor, i.e., private capital. In the final analysis, developing market relations will bring on their own destruction. On the soil of these market relations, . . . state industry and the cooperatives will gradually prevail over all other forms of economy and squeeze them out entirely. As this happens, the market itself will sooner or later wither away, being replaced by the state-cooperative distribution of everything that is produced.

Thus, our conception of the development toward socialism has changed significantly. But these changes do not in the least imply retreat from a proletarian policy. On the contrary, they represent the summation of a great revolutionary experience. In the New Economic Policy we discovered for the first time the proper combination of the private interests of the small producer with the general cause of socialist construction. *The New Economic Policy is not a betrayal of the proletarian line, but the only correct proletarian policy. . . .*

The development of present-day society in the direction of socialism is guaranteed by the fact that the working class holds power and that we have *a revolutionary dictatorship, or undivided rule*. The general significance of the proletarian dictatorship, is, first, that it is a weapon for suppressing the exploiters and any attempt they might make to regain power and, second, that it serves as a basic lever for the economic transformation of society. The working class uses its control over the machinery of state power in order *continu-*

Entente. The government's decision stemmed not from vague visions of renewal but from the commitment of tangible territorial gains that France and Britain made to Italy with the secret Treaty of London in April.

Despite the near collapse of the Italian armies late in 1917, Italy lasted out the war and contributed to the victory over Austria-Hungary. Supporters of the war felt that this success could lead to a thoroughgoing renewal of Italian public life. Yet many Italians had been skeptical of claims for the war from the outset, and the fact that it proved so much more difficult than expected hardly won them over. To socialists, Catholics, and many left-leaning liberals, intervention itself had been a tragic mistake.

Thus, despite Italy's participation in the victory, division over the war's significance immensely complicated the Italian political situation after the war was over.

Their skepticism was only confirmed when Italy did not secure all the gains it sought at the Paris Peace Conference. Italy got most of what it had been promised in the Treaty of London, but appetites increased with the dissolution of the Austro-Hungarian Empire. To some Italians, the disappointing outcome of the peace conference simply confirmed that the war had been a mistake, its benefits not worth the costs. But others were outraged at what seemed a denigration of the Italian contribution by France, Britain, and the United States. The outcome

ously to reform the economic relations of society in a socialist manner. . . .

The real task of the working class is to *reform the broad popular strata,* the *peasantry* in particular. Unwaveringly approaching this objective, and drawing the rest of society in its wake, the proletariat must reeducate the peasantry in a socialist manner, constantly elevating it and pulling it upward to the same material, economic, and cultural-political level as that of the leading strata of the proletarian population. As broad strata of the peasantry are reformed and reeducated, *they will increasingly become comparable with the proletariat,* merge with it, and be transformed into equal members of socialist society. The difference between the two classes will steadily disappear. In this way the broad masses of the peasantry, "changing their own nature," will blend with the workers of the city; and the dictatorship of the proletariat, as the dictatorship of a particular class, will increasingly wither away. . . .

. . . It is now necessary to outgrow *the methods of issuing commands or orders. What we need is a decisive, total, and unconditional switch to methods of persuasion.* . . .

And if we look even further into our future, we see a time when all the barriers among classes will disappear, when the division between town and country workers will be eliminated, when the need for all state organs of compulsion will vanish (assuming that capitalist states in other countries of the world will have been overthrown), and when all politics will completely die out. Then politics will be replaced by scientific leadership and scientific management of the social economy. . . .

. . . The advantages of *large-scale production* will become more and more apparent; steadily greater economies and benefits will accrue to the state economy from the growth of *planning,* i.e., from a more thoroughly planned and expedient use of all the material resources and labor power at the economy's disposal; and even greater sums will be available to the state power, which will be in a position to provide a broader range of assistance in the matter of organizing the peasantry through the construction of cooperatives, etc.

As a matter of fact, we have already demonstrated that we can build socialism even *without any direct technical-economic aid from other countries.* It is true that the forms of our socialism in the coming period of construction will inevitably be those of a backward socialism. But that does not matter, because even these forms guarantee a continuing movement toward other forms of socialism, which are more full and complete.

QUESTIONS

1. On what grounds does Bukharin argue that the Soviet Union can create a socialist society simply by following the logic of the present NEP?

2. How would decisions be made once the conflict of interests between the workers and the peasants was finally overcome altogether?

SOURCE: N. I. Bukharin, *Selected Writings on the State and the Transition to Socialism,* ed. Richard B. Day (Armonk, N.Y.: M. E. Sharpe, 1982), pp. 260–261, 263, 266, 273, 285, 292. Copyright © 1982 by M. E. Sharpe, Inc. Reprinted with permission.

---

fanned resentment not only of Italy's allies but also of the country's political leaders, who seemed too weak to deliver on what they had pledged.

The established leaders of Italy's parliamentary democracy also failed at the task of renewing the country's political system in light of the war experience. To be sure, in a spirit of democratic reform, Italy adopted proportional representation to replace the old system of small, single-member constituencies in 1919. The new system meant a greater premium on mass parties and party discipline at the expense of the one-to-one bargaining that had characterized the earlier *trasformismo.* But the new multiparty system quickly reached an

impasse—partly because of the stance of the Italian Socialist Party.

In contrast to the French and German parties, the Italian Socialists had never supported the war, and they did not accept the notion that the war experience could yield political renewal in the aftermath. So rather than reaching out to idealistic but discontented war veterans, Socialist leaders talked of imitating the Bolshevik Revolution. And the Italian situation seemed at least potentially revolutionary during 1919 and 1920, when a wave of national strikes culminated in a series of factory occupations. But despite their revolutionary rhetoric, Italy's Socialist leaders did not understand the practical

Benito Mussolini   The founder of fascism is shown with other fascist leaders in 1922, as he becomes prime minister of Italy. Standing at Mussolini's right (*with beard*) is Italo Balbo, later a pioneering aviator and fascist Italy's air force minister.   *(Corbis)*

aspects of Leninism and did not carry out the planning and organization that might have produced an Italian revolution.

The established parliamentary system was at an impasse, and the Socialist Party seemed at once too inflexible and too romantic to lead some sort of radical transformation. It was in this context that fascism emerged, claiming to offer a third way. It was bound to oppose the Socialists and the socialist working class because of conflict over the meaning of the war and the kind of transformation Italy needed. And this antisocialist posture made fascism open to exploitation by reactionary interests. By early 1921 landowners in northern and central Italy were footing the bill as bands of young fascists drove around the countryside in trucks, beating up workers and burning down socialist meeting halls. But fascist spokesmen claimed to offer something other than mere reaction—a new politics that all Italians, including the workers, would eventually find superior.

At the same time, important sectors of Italian industry, which had grown rapidly thanks to government orders during the war, looked with apprehension toward the more competitive international economy that loomed after the war. With its relative lack of capital and raw materials, Italy seemed to face an especially difficult situation. Nationalist thinkers and business spokesmen questioned the capacity of the present parliamentary system to provide the vigorous leadership that Italy needed. Prone to short-term bickering and partisanship, ordinary politicians lacked the vision to pursue Italy's international economic interests and the will to impose the necessary discipline on the domestic level. Thus the government's response to the labor unrest of 1919 and 1920 was hesitant and weak. (See the box "Reading Sources: Toward Fascism: Alfredo Rocco on the Weakness of the Liberal Democratic State.")

Postwar Italy, then, witnessed widespread discontent with established forms of politics, but those discon-

READING
SOURCES

TOWARD FASCISM: ALFREDO ROCCO ON THE WEAKNESS OF THE LIBERAL DEMOCRATIC STATE

As Italy's minister of justice from 1925 to 1932, the Italian legal scholar Alfredo Rocco (1875–1935) spearheaded the construction of the new fascist state. Speaking in November 1920, he revealed why he would seek to replace parliamentary democracy with a new, stronger form of government. Rocco was troubled, most immediately, by the apparent weakness of the liberal state in the face of strikes by unions, or syndicates, of public service employees. But the deeper problem he saw was liberal individualism, linked to shortsighted pursuit of personal advantage.

There is a crisis within the state; day by day, the state is dissolving into a mass of small particles, parties, associations, groups and syndicates that are binding it in chains and paralysing and stifling its activity: one by one, with increasing speed, the state is losing its attributes of sovereignty. . . . The conflict of interests between groups and classes is now being settled by the use of private force alone. . . . The state stands by impassively watching these conflicts which involve countless violations of public and private rights. This neutrality which, in liberal doctrine, was intended to allow free play for economic law in the clash of interests between the classes is now being interpreted as allowing the state to abandon its essential function of guardian of public order and agent of justice. . . .

. . . The eighteenth-century reaction against the state . . . came to a head politically in the explosion of the French Revolution. . . . From that time onwards, the claims of individualism knew no bounds. The masses of individuals wanted to govern the state and govern it in accordance with their own individual interests. The state, a living organism with a continuous existence over the centuries that extends beyond successive generations and as such the guardian of the immanent historical interests of the species, was turned into a monopoly to serve the individual interests of each separate generation. . . .

Now there can be no doubt that one of the most serious consequences of liberal agnosticism was the emergence of syndicalism, a syndicalism that was at once violent, subversive, and opposed to the state.

. . . The state must return to its traditions, interrupted by the triumph of liberal ideology, and treat the modern syndicates exactly as it treated the medieval corporations. It must absorb them and make them part of the state. . . . On the one hand, syndicates must be recognized as essential and on the other they must be placed firmly beneath the control of the state. . . . But above all, it is necessary to change them from aggressive bodies defending particular interests into a means of collaboration to achieve common aims.

Source: *Italian Fascisms from Pareto to Gentile*, ed. Adrian Lyttelton. Copyright © Adrian Lyttelton 1975. Used by permission of PFD on behalf of the author.

tented were socially disparate, and their aims were not entirely compatible. Some had been socialists before the war, others nationalists hostile to socialism. While some envisioned a more intense kind of mass politics, others thought the masses already had too much power. Still, these discontented groups agreed on the need for an alternative to both conventional parliamentary politics and conventional Marxist socialism. And all found the germs of that alternative in the Italian war experience.

The person who seemed able to translate these aspirations into a new political force was Benito Mussolini (1883–1945), who had been a prominent socialist journalist before the war. Indeed, he was so talented that he was made editor of the Socialist Party's national newspaper in 1912, when he was only 29 years old. At that point many saw him as the fresh face needed to revitalize Italian socialism.

His concern with renewal made Mussolini an unorthodox socialist even before 1914, and he was prominent among those on the Italian left who began calling for Italian intervention once the war began. The fact that socialists in France, Germany, and elsewhere had immediately rallied to their respective national war efforts raised new questions about conventional socialism, based on international proletarian solidarity. But the Italian Socialist Party refused to follow his call for intervention, remaining neutralist and aloof, so Mussolini found himself cut off from his earlier constituency.

However, through his new newspaper, *Il popolo d'Italia* (*The People of Italy*), Mussolini helped rally the disparate groups that advocated Italian participation in the war. He saw military service once Italy intervened, and after the war he seemed a credible spokesman for those who wanted to translate the war experience into a new form of politics. Amid growing political unrest, he founded the fascist movement in March 1919, taking the term *fascism* from the ancient Roman *fasces,* a bundle of rods surrounding an ax that guards carried at state occasions as a symbol of power and unity.

But fascism found little success at first. And even as it gathered force in violent reaction against the socialist labor organizations by 1921, the movement's direction was something of a mystery. Although young fascist militants wanted to replace the established parliamentary system with a new political order, Mussolini seemed ever more prone to use fascism as his personal instrument to achieve power within the existing system. When his maneuvering finally won him the prime minister's post in October 1922, it was not at all clear that a change of regime, or a one-party dictatorship, was at hand.

At that point, Mussolini, like most Italians, emphasized normalization and legality. Fascism had apparently been absorbed within the political system, perhaps to provide an infusion of youthful vitality after the war. With Mussolini as prime minister, there would be changes, but not revolutionary changes. Government would become more vigorous and efficient; the swollen Italian bureaucracy would be streamlined; the trains would run on time. But those who had envisioned more sweeping change were frustrated that nothing more had come of fascism than this.

A crisis in 1924 forced Mussolini's hand. In June the moderate socialist Giacomo Matteotti° rose in parliament to denounce the renewed fascist violence that had accompanied recent national elections. His murder by fascist thugs shortly thereafter produced a great public outcry, though the responsibility of Mussolini and his government was unclear. Many establishment figures who had tolerated Mussolini as the man who could keep order now deserted him. A growing chorus called for his resignation.

Mussolini sought at first to be conciliatory, but more radical fascists saw the crisis as an opportunity to end the compromise with the old liberal order and to begin creating a whole new political system. The crisis came to a head on December 31, 1924, when thirty-three militants called on Mussolini to demand that he make up his mind. In their view, the way out of the crisis was not to de-

limit the scope of fascism but to expand it. Mussolini was not an ordinary prime minister but the leader of fascism, *Il Duce*°. In that role he would have to accept responsibility even for his movement's violent excesses and finally begin implementing a full-scale fascist revolution.

Mussolini committed himself to this more radical course in a speech to the Chamber of Deputies a few days later, on January 3, 1925. Defiantly claiming the "full political, moral, and historical responsibility for all that has happened," including "all the acts of violence," he promised to accelerate the transformation that he claimed to have initiated with his agitation for intervention in 1914 and 1915.[1] And now began the creation of a new fascist state, although the compromises continued and the direction was never as clear as committed fascists desired.

Innovation and Compromise in Fascist Italy, 1925–1930

Early in 1925, the fascist government began to undermine the existing democratic system by imprisoning or exiling opposition leaders and outlawing nonfascist parties and labor unions. But fascism was not seeking simply a conventional monopoly of political power; the new fascist state was to be totalitarian, all-encompassing, limitless in its reach. Under the old liberal regime, the fascists charged, the state had been too weak to promote the national interest, and Italian society had been too fragmented to achieve its full potential. So Mussolini's regime both expanded the state's sovereignty and mobilized the society to create a deeper sense of national identity and shared purpose. To settle labor disputes, a new system of labor judges replaced the right to strike, which, the fascists claimed, had fostered neither productivity nor long-term working-class interests. New organizations— for youth, for women, for leisure-time activities—were to make possible new forms of public participation.

The centerpiece of the new fascist state was corporativism, which entailed mobilizing people as producers, through organization of the workplace. Groupings based on occupation, or economic function, were gradually to replace parliament as the basis for political participation and decision making. Beginning in 1926, corporativist institutions were established in stages until a Chamber of Fasces and Corporations at last replaced the old Chamber of Deputies in 1939.

Especially through this corporative state, the fascists claimed to be fulfilling their grandiose mission and providing the world with a third way, beyond both outmoded democracy and misguided communism. The practice of

---

Matteotti (mah-tay-OH-tee)

Il Duce (eel DOO-chay)

corporativism never lived up to such rhetoric, but the effort to devise new forms of political participation and decision making was central to fascism's self-understanding and its quest for legitimacy. And that effort attracted much attention abroad, especially with the Great Depression of the 1930s.

Despite the commitment to a new regime, however, fascism continued to compromise with pre-existing elites and institutions. The accommodation was especially evident in the arrangements with the Catholic Church that Mussolini worked out in 1929, formally ending the dispute between the church and the Italian state that had festered since national unification in 1870. With the Lateran Pact, Mussolini restored a measure of sovereignty to the Vatican; with the Concordat, he conceded to the church autonomy in education and supremacy in marriage law.

This settlement of an old and thorny dispute afforded Mussolini a good deal of prestige among nonfascists at home and abroad. But compromise with the church could only displease committed fascists, who complained that giving this powerful, autonomous institution a role in Italian public life compromised fascism's totalitarian ideal. Such complaints led to a partial crackdown on Catholic youth organizations in 1931, as Mussolini continued trying to juggle traditionalist compromise and revolutionary pretension.

By the end of the 1920s, then, it remained unclear whether Italian fascism was a form of restoration or a form of revolution. It had restored order in Italy, overcoming the labor unrest of the immediate postwar years, but it was order on a new, antidemocratic basis. Yet the fascists claimed to be implementing a revolution of their own at the same time. Fascism could be violent and disruptive, dictatorial and repressive, but Mussolini's regime seemed dynamic and innovative. Though its ultimate direction remained nebulous, fascism attracted those elsewhere who were discontented with liberal democracy and Marxist socialism. It thus fed the volatility and ideological polarization that marked the European political order after World War I.

TOWARD MASS SOCIETY

AFTER a few years of wild economic swings just after the war, Europe enjoyed renewed prosperity by the later 1920s. Common involvement in the war had blurred class lines and accelerated the trend toward what contemporaries began to call "mass society." As the new prosperity spread the fruits of industrialization more widely, ordinary people increasingly set the cultural tone, partly through new mass media such as film and radio. To some, the advent of mass society portended a welcome revitalization of culture and a more authentic kind of democracy, whereas others saw only a debasement of cultural standards and a susceptibility to populist demagoguery. But though the contours of mass society now became evident, social change did not keep up with the promise of—and the requirements for—democratic politics.

Economic Readjustment and the New Prosperity

In their effort to return to normal, governments were quick to dismantle wartime planning and control mechanisms. But the needs of war had stimulated innovations that helped fuel the renewed economic growth of the 1920s. The civilian air industry, for example, developed rapidly during the decade by taking advantage of wartime work on aviation for military purposes. More generally, newer industries such as chemicals, electricity, and advanced machinery led the way to a new prosperity in the 1920s, which significantly altered patterns of life in the more industrialized parts of the West. The automobile, a luxury plaything for the wealthy before the war, began to be mass-produced in western Europe. In France, automobile production shot up dramatically, from 40,000 in 1920 to 254,000 in 1929.

But the heady pace masked problems that lay beneath the relative prosperity of the 1920s, even in victorious Britain and France. While new industries prospered, old ones declined in the face of new technologies and stronger foreign competition. In Britain, the sectors responsible for Britain's earlier industrial pre-eminence—textiles, coal, shipbuilding, and iron and steel—were now having trouble competing. Rather than investing in new technologies, companies in these industries demanded government protection and imposed lower wages and longer hours on their workers. At the same time, British labor unions resisted the mechanization necessary to make these older industries more competitive.

Rather than realistically assessing Britain's prospects in the more competitive international economy, British leaders sought to return to the prewar situation, based on the gold standard, with London the world's financial center. For many Britons, the government's announcement in 1925 that the British pound was again freely convertible to gold at 1914 exchange rates was the long-awaited indication that normality had returned at last. Yet the return to 1914 exchange rates overvalued the pound relative to the U.S. dollar, making British goods more expensive on export markets and making it still

Surviving the German Inflation   A woman in Berlin lights her stove with worthless German paper money late in 1923. With inflation reaching 2,500 percent per month, the German government introduced a currency reform in November that soon stabilized prices. But the inflation wiped out the savings of many ordinary Germans and left a legacy of suspicion and bitterness.   *(Corbis)*

more difficult for aging British industries to compete. Further, Britain no longer had sufficient capital to act as the world's banker. By trying to do so, Britain became all the more vulnerable when the international economy reached a crisis in 1929.

The structural decline of older industries was clearest in Britain, but inflation and its psychological impact was most prominent in Germany and France. By the summer of 1923, Germany's response to the French occupation of the Ruhr had transformed an already serious inflationary problem, stemming from wartime deficit spending, into one of the great hyperinflations in history. At its height in November, when it took 4.2 trillion marks to equal a dollar, Germans were forced to cart wheelbarrows of paper money to stores to buy ordinary grocery items. By the end of 1923, the government managed to stabilize prices through currency reform and drastically reduced government spending—a combination that elicited greater cooperation from the victors. But the rampant inflation, and the readjustment necessary to control it, had wiped out the life savings of ordinary people while profiting speculators and those in debt, including some large industrialists. This inequity left scars that remained even as Germany enjoyed a measure of prosperity in the years that followed.

Inflation was less dramatic in France, but there, too, it affected perceptions and priorities in significant ways. For over a century, from the Napoleonic era to the outbreak of war in 1914, the value of the French franc had remained stable. But the war started France on an inflationary cycle that shattered the security of its many small savers—those, such as teachers and shopkeepers, who had been the backbone of the Third Republic. To repay war debts and rebuild war-damaged industries, the French government continued to run budget deficits, and thereby cause inflation, even after 1918. Runaway inflation threatened during 1925 and 1926, but the franc was finally restabilized in 1928, though at only about one-fifth its prewar value.

On the international level, war debts and reparations strained the financial system, creating problems with the financing of trade. But in the course of the 1920s, experts made adjustments that seemed to be returning the international exchange system to equilibrium. Only in retrospect, after the international capitalist system fell into crisis late in 1929, did it become clear how potent those strains were—and how inadequate the efforts at readjustment.

Work, Leisure, and the New Popular Culture

The wartime spur to industrialization produced a large increase in the industrial labor force all over Europe, and a good deal of labor unrest accompanied the transition to peacetime. Some of that agitation challenged factory discipline and authority relationships. Seeking to reestablish authority on a new basis for the competitive postwar world, business leaders and publicists fostered a new cult of efficiency and productivity, partly by adapting Taylorism and Fordism, influential American ideas about mass production. On the basis of his "time-and-motion" studies of factory labor, Frederick W. Taylor (1856–1915) argued that breaking down assembly-line production into small, repetitive tasks was the key to maximizing worker efficiency. In contrast, Henry Ford (1863–1947) linked the gospel of mass production to mass consumption. In exchange for accepting the discipline of the assembly line, the workers should be paid well enough to be able to buy the products they produced—even automobiles. Sharing in the prosperity that mass production made possible, factory workers would be loyal to the companies that employed them. Not all Europeans, however, welcomed the new ideas from America. In the new cult of efficiency and mass production, some saw an unwelcome sameness and a debasement of cultural standards.

In light of the major role women had played in the wartime labor force, the demand for women's suffrage proved irresistible in Britain, Germany, and much of Europe, though not yet in France or Italy. In Britain, where the call for women's suffrage had earlier met with controversy (see page 829), the right to vote was readily conceded in 1918, though at first only to women over 30. By now women no longer seemed a threat to the political system. And in fact British women, once they could vote, simply flowed into the existing parties, countering earlier hopes—and fears—that a specifically feminist political agenda would follow from women's suffrage.

Although there was much discussion of the "new woman," especially in Germany, the wider place of women in society and politics was uncertain during the 1920s, as the new sense of openness clashed with the desire to return to normal. (See the feature "Weighing the Evidence: Advertising" on pages 910–911.) Female employment remained higher than before the war, but many women—willingly or not—returned home, yielding their jobs to the returning soldiers. The need to replace the men killed in the war lent renewed force to the traditional notion that women served society, and fulfilled themselves, by marrying and rearing families. More generally, some men found the emancipated "new woman" threatening, and after all the disruptions of war, male leaders sometimes assumed that the very stability of the political sphere depended on conventional gender roles. Still, the decade's innovative impulse brought into the public arena subjects—largely taboo before the war— that might portend changes in gender roles later on. The desire to be "modern" produced, for example, a more open, unsentimental, even scientific discussion of sexuality and reproduction.

The new "rationalization of sexuality" fed demands that governments provide access to sex counseling, birth control, and even abortion as they assumed ever greater responsibilities for promoting social health. This trend was especially prominent in Germany, although German innovators learned from experiments in the new Soviet Union and from the birth control movement that Margaret Sanger (1883–1966) was spearheading in the United States.

The Sensational Josephine Baker   After moving from the United States to Paris in 1925, Baker quickly created a sensation as a cabaret dancer and singer. Her exotic costumes played on the European association of Africa with the wild and uninhibited. This poster advertises her appearance at the Folies-Bergère, a famed Parisian music hall.   *(The Granger Collection, New York)*

The more open and tolerant attitude toward sexuality affected popular entertainment—for example, Josephine Baker's dancing and costumes, which would have been unthinkable before the war. Another result was the emergence of a more visible gay subculture, prominent

Weimar Cinema   This poster advertises Fritz Lang's film *Metropolis,* which explored the dehumanization and exploitation of the modern city.   *(Schulz-Neudamm, Metropolis, 1926. Lithograph, 83″ × 36½″. Gift of Universum-Film-Aktiengesellschaft. Photograph © 1997 The Museum of Modern Art, New York/Art Resource, NY)*

especially in the vibrant cabaret scene in Berlin during the 1920s.

Mass consumption followed from the mass production that created the new prosperity of the 1920s. As it became possible to mass-produce the products of the second industrial transformation, more people could afford automobiles, electrical gadgets such as radios and phonographs, and clothing of synthetic fabrics, developed through innovations in chemistry. First came rayon, produced in small quantities since 1891 but mass-produced beginning in the 1920s. In this new artificial form, silk, long one of the trappings of wealth, was now within the means of ordinary people.

With the eight-hour workday increasingly the norm, growing attention was devoted to leisure as a positive source of human fulfillment—for everyone, not just the wealthy. European beach resorts grew crowded as more people had the time, and the means, to take vacations. An explosion of interest in soccer among Europeans paralleled the growth of professional baseball and college football in the United States. Huge stadiums were built across Europe.

The growth of leisure was linked to the development of mass media and mass culture. During the early 1920s radio became a commercial venture, reaching a mass audience in Europe, as in the United States and Canada. Although movies had begun to emerge as vehicles of popular entertainment even before the war, they came into their own during the 1920s, when the names of film stars became household words for the first time.

The rapid development of film showed that new, more accessible media could nurture extraordinary innovation. Germany led the way with such films as *The Cabinet of Dr. Caligari* (1920), *Metropolis* (1927), and *The Blue Angel* (1930), but the Russian Sergei Eisenstein (1898–1948) became perhaps the most admired film maker of the era with *Battleship Potemkin* (1925), his brilliant portrayal of the Russian revolution of 1905. In some spheres, however, America was beginning to outdo both Paris and Berlin. Marlene Dietrich (1901–1992), famous as Lola Lola in *The Blue Angel,* was among a number of German film celebrities who went to Hollywood.

Exploiting the new popular fascination with air travel, the American Charles Lindbergh (1902–1974) captured the European imagination in 1927 with the first solo flight across the Atlantic. Lindbergh's feat epitomized the affirmative side of the decade—the sense that there were new worlds to conquer and that there still were heroes to admire, despite the ironies of the war and the ambiguities of the peace.

Society and Politics in the Victorious Democracies

France and Britain seemed the best positioned of the major European countries to take advantage of renewed peace and stability to confront the sociopolitical problems of the postwar era. And during the 1920s, each seemed to return to normal. But was normal good enough, in light of the rupture of the war and the challenges of the emerging mass society?

Victory in the Great War seemed to belie France's prewar concerns about decadence and decline. In the immediate aftermath of the war, Clemenceau and other French leaders were confident in dealing with radical labor unrest and aggressive in translating the battlefield victory into a dominant position on the European continent. But the tremendous loss of French lives had produced a new fear—that France could not withstand another such challenge. The renewed confidence thus proved hollow.

Although some in prewar France had worried about falling behind rapidly industrializing Germany, victory seemed to have vindicated France's more cautious, balanced economy, with its blend of industry and agriculture. Thus the prewar mistrust of rapid industrial development continued. Rather than foster a program of economic modernization that might have promoted genuine security, the French pulled back even from the measure of state responsibility for the economy that had developed during the war.

To be sure, in France, as elsewhere, the 1920s was a decade of relative prosperity. Led by the oil and electricity industries, the economy grew at an annual rate of 4.6 percent between 1923 and 1929, double the prewar rate. Industrial production by 1929 was 40 percent higher than it had been in 1913. But, with the exception of Britain, other Western economies grew more rapidly during the 1920s, and the opportunity that growth afforded to modernize the French economy was not seized. Although government grants helped reconstruct almost eight thousand factories, most were simply rebuilt as they had been before the war. Moreover, the working class benefited little from the relative prosperity of the 1920s. Housing remained poor, wages failed to keep up with inflation, and France continued to lag behind other countries in social legislation.

Britain, too, made certain adjustments after the war but missed the chance to make others. The government's handling of the Easter Rebellion in Ireland in 1916 (see page 853) intensified anti-British feeling and fed further violence. But the British finally forged at least a provisional resolution. The first step was to partition Ireland, creating a separate Ulster, or Northern Ireland, from those counties with Protestant majorities. Ulster then remained under the British crown when a new independent Republic of Ireland was established in the larger, majority-Catholic part of the island in 1922.

The British political system remained stable between the wars, although the Labour Party supplanted the Liberals to become the dominant alternative to the Conservatives by the early 1920s. The Labour Party even got a brief taste of power when Ramsay MacDonald (1866–1937) formed Britain's first Labour government in January 1924. The coming of Labour to power resulted in a significant expansion of the governmental elite to incorporate those, like MacDonald himself, with genuinely working-class backgrounds.

The rise of Labour was striking, but it was the Conservative leader, Stanley Baldwin (1867–1947), who set the tone for British politics between the wars in three stints as prime minister during the years 1923 to 1937. Although he was the wealthy son of a steel manufacturer, Baldwin deliberately departed from the old aristocratic style of British Conservative politics. More down-to-earth and pragmatic than his predecessors, he was the first British prime minister to use radio effectively, and he made an effort to foster good relations with workers. Yet Baldwin's era was one of growing social tension.

With exports declining, unemployment remained high in Britain throughout the interwar period, never falling below 10 percent. The coal industry, though still the country's largest employer, had become a particular trouble spot in the British economy. As coal exports declined, British mine owners became ever more aggressive in their dealings with labor, finally, in 1926, insisting on a longer workday and a wage cut of 13 percent to restore competitiveness. The result was a coal miners' strike in May that promptly turned into a general strike, involving almost all of organized labor—about four million workers—in the most notable display of trade-union solidarity Britain had ever seen. For nine days the economy stood at a virtual standstill. But threats of arrest and a growing public backlash forced the union leadership to accept a compromise. The miners continued the strike on their own, but they finally returned to work six months later at considerably lower wages.

Although for somewhat different reasons, Britain and France both failed during the 1920s to take advantage of what would soon seem, in retrospect, to have been a precious opportunity to adjust their economies, heal social wounds, and create more genuinely democratic political systems. The lost opportunity would mean growing social tensions once the relative prosperity of the decade had ended.

WEIMAR GERMANY AND THE TRIALS OF THE NEW DEMOCRACIES

THE war was supposed to have paved the way for democracy, and the fall of the monarchies in Russia, Germany, and Austria-Hungary seemed almost made-to-order invitations. But events quickly overwhelmed the new democracy in Russia in 1917. After the war was over, circumstances seemed more favorable in Germany, Poland, and elsewhere in central Europe, but almost everywhere the new democracies led tortured lives and soon gave way to more authoritarian forms of government. So the postwar decade did not see the extension and consolidation of the political democracy that optimistic observers associated with the emerging mass society.

The most significant test took place in Germany, where a new democracy emerged from the republic proclaimed in November 1918. Elections in January 1919 produced a constituent assembly that convened in Weimar, a town associated with what seemed the most humane German cultural traditions. The assembly gave this new Weimar Republic, as it came to be called, Germany's first fully democratic constitution. But the Weimar democracy had great difficulty establishing its legitimacy, and it was suffering serious strains by 1930.

Democracy Aborted in East-Central Europe

New democracies were established in much of central and eastern Europe after the war, but except in Czechoslovakia and Finland, the practice of parliamentary government did not match the initial promise. Democracy seemed divisive and ineffective, so one country after another adopted a more authoritarian alternative during the 1920s and early 1930s.

Poland offers the most dramatic example. Although its democratic constitution of 1921 established a cabinet responsible to a parliamentary majority, the parliament fragmented into so many parties that instability proved endemic from the start. Poland had fourteen different ministries from November 1918 to May 1926, when Marshal Josef Pilsudski led a coup d'état that replaced parliamentary government with an authoritarian regime stressing national unity. This suppression of democracy came as a relief to many Poles—and was welcomed even

by the trade unions. After Pilsudski's death in 1935, a group of colonels ruled Poland until the country was conquered by Nazi Germany in 1939.

Democracy proved hard to manage in east-central Europe partly because of the economic difficulties resulting from the breakup of the Habsburg system. New national borders meant new economic barriers that disrupted long-standing economic relationships. Industrial centers such as Vienna and Budapest found themselves cut off from their traditional markets and sources of raw materials. In what was now Poland, Silesians had long been oriented toward Germany, Galicians toward Vienna, and those in eastern Poland toward Russia. Thus the new Polish nation-state was hardly a cohesive economic unit.

The countries of east-central Europe remained overwhelmingly agrarian, and this, too, proved unconducive to democracy. Land reform that accompanied the transition to democracy made small properties the norm in much of the region. But because these units were often too small to be efficient, agricultural output actually decreased after land was redistributed, most dramatically in Romania and Yugoslavia. When agricultural prices declined in the late 1920s, many peasants had no choice but to sell out to larger landowners. What had seemed a progressive and democratic reform thus failed to provide a stable agrarian smallholder base for democracy.

Germany's Cautious Revolution, 1919–1920

Meanwhile, in Germany, the Weimar Republic began under particularly difficult circumstances. Born of military defeat, it was promptly forced to take responsibility for the harsh Treaty of Versailles in 1919. During its first years, moreover, the regime encountered severe economic dislocation, culminating in the hyperinflation of 1923, as well as ideological polarization that threatened to tear the country apart.

Although Germany had strong military and authoritarian traditions, the initial threat to the new democracy came not from the right, disoriented and discredited, but from the left, stimulated by the Russian example. Those seeking further revolution, and those who feared it, could easily equate the proclamation of a German republic with the first revolution in Russia; as in Russia, the new, more democratic order could prove a mere prelude to communist revolution.

Spearheaded by Karl Liebknecht and Rosa Luxemburg in Berlin, revolutionary unrest reached its peak in Germany during December 1918 and January 1919. But even after Liebknecht and Luxemburg were captured and murdered in January, a serious chance of further revolution persisted through May 1919, and communist revolutionary agitation continued to flare up until the end of 1923.

As it turned out, there was no further revolution, partly because the parallel between Germany and Russia carried only so far. The new German government had made peace, whereas the leaders of the provisional government in Russia had sought to continue the war. Furthermore, those who ended up controlling the councils that sprang up in Germany during the fall of 1918 favored political democracy, not communist revolution, and therefore they supported the provisional government.

Even so, the revolutionary minority constituted a credible threat. And the new government made repression of the extreme left a priority—even if it meant leaving in place some of the institutions and personnel of the old imperial system. In November 1918, at the birth of the new republic, the moderate socialist leader Friedrich Ebert had agreed with General Wilhelm Groener, the new army head, to preserve the old imperial officer corps to help prevent further revolution. But when the regular army, weakened by war and defeat, proved unable to control radical agitation in Berlin in December, it seemed the republic would have to take extraordinary measures to defend itself from the revolutionary left. With the support of Ebert and Groener, Gustav Noske (1868–1946), the minister of national defense, began to organize "Free Corps," volunteer paramilitary groups to be used against the revolutionaries. Noske, who was a socialist, but one long supportive of the military, noted that "somebody will have to be the bloodhound—I won't shirk the responsibility."[2]

During the first five months of 1919, the government unleashed the Free Corps to crush leftist movements all over Germany, often with wanton brutality. In relying on right-wing paramilitary groups, the republic's leaders were playing with fire, but the immediate threat at this point came from the left. In 1920, however, the government faced a right-wing coup attempt, the Kapp Putsch. The army declined to defend the republic, but the government managed to survive thanks largely to a general strike by leftist workers. The republic's early leaders had to juggle both extremes because, as one of them put it, the Weimar Republic was "a candle burning at both ends."

Though sporadic street fighting by paramilitary groups continued, the republic survived its traumatic birth and achieved an uneasy stability by 1924. But Germany's postwar revolution had remained confined to the political level. There was no program to break up the cartels, with their concentrations of economic power. Even on the level of government personnel, continuity was more striking than change. There was no effort to build a loyal republican army, and no attempt to purge the bureaucracy and the judiciary of antidemocratic elements from the old imperial order. When right-wing extremists assassinated prominent leaders, such as the Jewish industrialist Walther Rathenau in 1922, the courts often proved unwilling to prosecute those responsible. In general, those who ran the new government day to day were often skeptical of democracy, even hostile to the new regime.

In light of the republic's eventual failure, the willingness of its early leaders to leave intact so much from the old order has made them easy targets of criticism. It can be argued, however, that the course they followed—heading off the extreme left, reassuring the established elites, and playing for time—was the republic's best chance for success. The new regime might establish its legitimacy by inertia, much like the Third Republic in France, which had similarly been born of defeat. Even lacking the sentimental fervor that had earlier surrounded democratic ideals, Germans might gradually become "republicans of reason," recognizing that this regime could be a framework for prosperity and renewed German prominence in international affairs. In the event of an early crisis, however, a republic consolidating itself in this cautious way might well find fewer defenders than opponents.

The constituent assembly elections of January 1919 took place before the peace conference had produced the widely detested Treaty of Versailles. When the first regular parliamentary elections finally were held in June 1920, the three moderate parties that had led the new government, and that had been forced to accept the treaty, suffered a major defeat, together dropping from 76 to 47 percent of the seats. These were the parties most committed to democratic institutions, but they were never again to achieve a parliamentary majority.

The 1920 elections revealed the problems of polarization and lack of consensus that would bedevil, and eventually ruin, the Weimar Republic. Because the electorate found it difficult to agree, or even to compromise, Germany settled into a multiparty system that led to unstable coalition government. And the strength, or potential strength, of the extremes immeasurably complicated political life for those trying to make the new democracy work. On the left, the Communist Party constantly criticized the more moderate Socialist Party for supporting the republic. On the right, the Nationalist Party (DNVP) played on nationalist resentments and fears of the extreme left—but the result was similarly to dilute support for the new republic. To the right even of the Nationalists were Adolf Hitler's National Socialists, or Nazis, who were noisy and often violent, but they attracted little electoral support before 1930.

Gustav Stresemann and the Scope for Gradual Consolidation

All was not necessarily lost for the republic when the three moderate, pro-Weimar parties were defeated in 1920. Germans who were unsupportive or hostile at first might be gradually won over. After the death of President Ebert in 1925, Paul von Hindenburg, the emperor's field marshal, was elected president. Depending on the circumstances, having a conservative military leader from the old order in this role could prove advantageous, or damaging, for the future of democracy. As long as there was scope for consolidation, Hindenburg's presidency might help persuade skeptics that the new regime was legitimate and a worthy object of German patriotism. But when crisis came by 1930, Hindenburg was quick to give up on parliamentary government—with devastating results.

The individual who best exemplified the possibility of winning converts to the Weimar Republic was Gustav Stresemann° (1878–1929), the leader of the German People's Party (DVP), a conservative party that did not support the republic at the outset. But it was relatively flexible and offered at least the possibility of broadening the republic's base of support. As chancellor, and especially as foreign minister, Stresemann proved the republic's leading statesman.

Stresemann's background and instincts were not democratic, but by the end of 1920 Germany's postwar political volatility had convinced him that if the new republic should go under, the outcome would not be the conservative monarchy he preferred but the triumph of the extreme left. Moreover, it had become clear that the new democratic republic was not likely to be revolutionary on the socioeconomic level. It made sense, then, to work actively to make the new regime succeed. From within this framework Germany could pursue its international aims, negotiating modifications of the Versailles treaty and returning to great power status.

Stresemann became chancellor in August 1923, when inflation was raging out of control. Within months

Stresemann (STRAY-zuh-mahn)

Hopes for Peace   Foreign ministers Aristide Briand (*left*) of France and Gustav Stresemann of Germany spearheaded the improved international relations that bred optimism during the late 1920s.   *(Corbis)*

his government managed to get the German economy functioning effectively again, partly because the French agreed that an international commission should review the reparations question, specifying realistic amounts based on Germany's ability to pay. During the summer of 1924, a commission led by the American financier Charles G. Dawes produced the Dawes Plan, which remained in force until 1929. The plan worked well by pinpointing revenue sources, lowering payments, providing loans, and securing the stability of the German currency. With the expiration of the Dawes Plan in 1929, the Young Plan, conceived by American businessman Owen D. Young, removed Allied controls over the German economy and specified that Germany pay reparations until 1988. The annual amount was less than Germany had been paying, so it was expected that this plan constituted a permanent, and reasonable, settlement.

Quite apart from the immediate economic issue, Stresemann understood that better relations with the victors, starting with France, had to be a priority if Germany was to return to the councils of the great powers. French foreign minister Aristide Briand° (1862–1932) shared Stresemann's desire for improved relations, and together they engineered a new, more conciliatory spirit in international affairs. Its most substantial fruit was the Treaty of Locarno of 1925. France and Germany accepted the postwar border between the two countries, which meant that Germany gave up any claim to Alsace-Lorraine. France, for its part, renounced the sort of direct military intervention in Germany that it had attempted with the Ruhr invasion of 1923 and agreed to begin withdrawing troops from the Rhineland ahead of schedule. Germany freely accepted France's key advantage, the demilitarization of the Rhineland, and Britain and Italy now explicitly guaranteed the measure.

By accepting the status quo in the west, Stresemann was freeing Germany to concentrate on eastern Europe, where he envisioned gradual but substantial revision in the territorial settlement that had resulted from the war. Especially with the creation of Poland, that settlement had come partly at Germany's expense. Stresemann, then, was pursuing German interests, not subordinating them to some larger European vision. But he was willing to compromise and, for the most part, to play by the rules as he did so.

With the Locarno treaty, the victors accepted Germany as a diplomatic equal for the first time since the war. Germany's return to good graces culminated in its entry into the League of Nations in 1926. The new spirit of reconciliation was widely welcomed. Indeed, Stresemann and Briand were joint winners of the Nobel Peace Prize for 1926.

Still, those to the right in Germany continually exploited German resentments by criticizing Stresemann's compromises with Germany's former enemies—in accepting the Dawes and Young Plans, for example. Even when successful from Stresemann's own perspective, these negotiations cost his party electoral support. The controversy that surrounded Stresemann, a German conservative pursuing conventional national interests, indicates how volatile the German political situation remained, even with the improved economic and diplomatic climate of the later 1920s. Still, Stresemann's diplomatic successes were considerable, and his death in October 1929, at the age of 51, was a severe blow to the republic.

Briand (bree-AHN)

An Uncertain Balance Sheet

Although Weimar Germany was considerably better off in 1929 than it had been in 1923, the political consensus remained weak, the political party system remained fragmented, and unstable coalition government remained the rule. Although the immediate threat from the extreme left had been overcome by 1923, many German conservatives continued to fear that the unstable Weimar democracy would eventually open the way to a socialist or communist regime.

The Weimar Republic epitomized the overall European situation during the 1920s. As long as prosperity and international cooperation continued, the new democracy in Germany might endure, even come to thrive. But the new institutions in Germany, like the wider framework of prosperity and stability, were fragile indeed. At the first opportunity, antidemocratic elites, taking advantage of their access to President Hindenburg, would begin plotting to replace the Weimar Republic with a more authoritarian alternative.

THE SEARCH FOR MEANING IN A DISORDERED WORLD

FOR all its vitality, the new culture of the 1920s had something brittle about it. The forces that produced a sense of openness, liberation, and innovation were disruptive and disturbing at the same time. Perhaps the frenetic pace only masked a deeper sense that things had started to come apart and might well get worse. The era called forth some notable diagnoses and prescriptions, but, not surprisingly, they differed dramatically.

Anxiety, Alienation, and Disillusionment

Concern about the dangers of the emerging mass civilization was especially clear in the *Revolt of the Masses* (1930), by the influential Spanish thinker José Ortega y Gasset (1883–1955). In his view, contemporary experience had shown that ordinary people were incapable of creating standards and remained content with the least common denominator. Communism and fascism indicated the violent, intolerant, and ultimately barbaric quality of the new mass age. But Ortega found the same tendencies in American-style democracy. Much of Europe seemed to be moving toward the mass politics and culture of the United States, but, as far as Ortega was concerned, that was a symptom of the deeper problem, not a solution.

Concern with cultural decline was part of a wider pessimism about the condition of the West, which stood in stark contrast to the belief in progress, and the attendant confidence in Western superiority, that had been essential to Western self-understanding before 1914. The German thinker Oswald Spengler (1880–1936) made concern with decline almost fashionable with his bestseller of the immediate postwar years, *The Decline of the West* (1918), which offered a cyclical theory purporting to explain how spirituality and creativity were giving way to a materialistic mass-based culture in the West.

To Sigmund Freud (1856–1939), the eruption of violence and hatred during the war and afterward indicated a deep, instinctual problem in the human makeup (see page 824). In his gloomy essay *Civilization and Its Discontents* (1930), Freud suggested that the progress of civilization requires individuals to bottle up their aggressive instincts, which are directed inward as guilt but may erupt in violent outbursts. This notion raised fundamental questions not only about the scope for continued progress but also about the plausibility of the Wilsonian ideals that had surrounded the end of the war. Perhaps, with civilization growing more complex, the Great War had been only the beginning of a new era of hatred and violence. (See the box "Reading Sources: Probing the Limits of Civilization and Progress.")

The sense that something incomprehensible, even nightmarish, haunted modern civilization, with its ever more complex bureaucracies, technologies, and cities, found vivid expression in the work of the Czech Jewish writer Franz Kafka (1883–1924), most notably in the novels *The Trial* and *The Castle*, published posthumously in the mid-1920s. In a world that claimed to be increasingly rational, Kafka's individual is the lonely, fragile plaything of forces utterly beyond reason, comprehension, and control. In such a world, the quest for law, or meaning, or God, is futile, ridiculous.

Especially in the unsettled conditions of Weimar Germany, the anxiety of the 1920s tended to take extreme forms, from irrational activism to a preoccupation with death. Suicides among students increased dramatically. Youthful alienation prompted the novelist Jakob Wassermann (1873–1934) to caution German young people in 1932 that not all action is good simply because it is action, that feeling is not always better than reason and discipline, and that youth is not in itself a badge of superiority.

Recasting the Tradition

Expressions of disillusionment revealed something about human experience in the unsettled new world, but they were sometimes morbid and self-indulgent. Other cultural leaders sought to be more positive; the challenge was not to give vent to new anxieties but to find antidotes to them. One direction was to recast traditional categories—in the arts, in religion, in politics—to make them relevant to contemporary experience. Although not all were optimistic about human prospects, many found such a renewal of tradition to be the best hope for responding to the disarray of the postwar world.

Among artists, even those who had been prominent in the modernist avant-garde before the war now pulled back from headlong experimentation and sought to pull things back together, though on a new basis. In music, composers as different as Igor Stravinsky (1882–1971) and Paul Hindemith (1895–1963) adapted earlier styles, although often in a somewhat ironic spirit, as they sought to weave new means of expression into familiar forms. The overall tendency toward neoclassicism during the period was an effort to give musical composition a renewed basis of order.

One of the most striking responses to the anxieties of this increasingly secular age was a wave of neo-orthodox religious thinking, most prominent in Protestants like the German-Swiss theologian Karl Barth (1886–1968). In his *Epistle to the Romans* (1919), Barth reacted against the liberal theology, the attempt to marry religious categories to secular progress, that had become prominent by the later nineteenth century. The war, especially, had seemed to shatter the liberal notion that the hand of God was at work in history, and Barth emphasized the radical cleft between God and our human, historical world, sunken in sin. Recalling the arguments of Augustine and Luther, he portrayed humanity as utterly lost, capable only of a difficult relationship with God, through faith, grace, and revelation.

With democracy faring poorly in parts of Europe, and with fascism and communism claiming to offer superior alternatives, some sought to make new sense of the liberal democratic tradition. In Italy, Benedetto Croce° (1866–1952) agreed with critics that the old justifications, based on natural law or utilitarianism, were deeply inadequate, but he also became one of Europe's most influential antifascists. The most significant innovations in modern thought, he argued, show us why

---

Croce (CROH-chay)

READING SOURCES

PROBING THE LIMITS OF CIVILIZATION AND PROGRESS

Writing at the end of the 1920s, Sigmund Freud, the founder of psychoanalysis, sought to probe the sources, and the wider implications, of the violence and aggressiveness that had been unleashed by the war and that had continued into the 1920s. His account of the wellsprings of violence challenged the long-standing Western belief in continued progress based on human rationality.

[Human beings] are not gentle creatures who want to be loved, and who at the most can defend themselves if they are attacked; they are, on the contrary, creatures among whose instinctual endowments is to be reckoned a powerful share of aggressiveness. As a result, their neighbor is for them not only a potential helper or sexual object, but also someone who tempts them to satisfy their aggressiveness on him, to exploit his capacity to work without compensation, to use him sexually without his consent, to seize his possessions, to humiliate him, to cause him pain, to torture and kill him. . . . Anyone who calls to mind the atrocities committed during the racial migrations or the invasion of the Huns, . . . or at the capture of Jerusalem by the pious Crusaders, or even, indeed, the horrors of the recent World War—anyone who recalls these things to mind will have to bow humbly before the truth of this view.

. . . In consequence of this primary mutual hostility of human beings, civilized society is perpetually threatened with disintegration. The interest of work in common would not hold it together; instinctual passions are stronger than reasonable interests. Civilization has to use its utmost efforts in order to set limits to man's aggressive instincts and to hold the manifestations of them in check. . . .

The communists believe that they have found the path to deliverance from our evils. According to them, man is wholly good and is well-disposed to his neighbor; but the institution of private property has corrupted his nature. . . . I have no concern with any economic criticisms of the communist system. . . . But I am able to recognize that the psychological premises on which the system is based are an untenable illusion. In abolishing private property we deprive the human love of aggression of one of its instruments, . . . but we have in no way altered the differences in power and influence which are misused by aggressiveness, nor have we altered anything in its nature. Aggressiveness was not created by property. It reigned almost without limit in primitive times, when property was still very scanty, and it already shows itself in the nursery. . . .

. . . It is precisely communities with adjoining territories, and related to each other in other ways as well, who are engaged in constant feuds and in ridiculing each other—like the Spaniards and the Portuguese, for instance, the North Germans and South Germans, the English and Scotch, and so on. I gave this phenomenon the name of "the narcissism of minor differences." . . . We can now see that it is a convenient and relatively harmless satisfaction of the inclination to aggression, by means of which cohesion between the members of a community is made easier.

. . . We may expect gradually to carry through such alterations in our civilization as will better satisfy our needs and will escape our criticisms. But perhaps we may also familiarize ourselves with the idea that there are difficulties attaching to the nature of civilization which will not yield to any attempt at reform.

Source: Sigmund Freud, *Civilization and Its Discontents*, trans. James Strachey. Copyright © 1961 by James Strachey, renewed 1989 by Alix Strachey. Used by permission of W. W. Norton & Company, Inc., and The Random House Group Limited.

democratic values, institutions, and practices are precisely what we need. We human beings are free, creative agents of a history that we make as best we can, without quite understanding what will result from what we do. Humility, tolerance, and equal access to political participation are essential to the process whereby the world is endlessly remade.

The new political challenges also stimulated fresh thinking within the Marxist tradition. By showing that Marxism could encompass consciousness as well as economic relationships, the Hungarian Georg Lukács (1885–1971) invited a far more sophisticated Marxist analysis of capitalist culture than had been possible before. Lukács accented the progressive role of realistic fiction

Croce's Antifascism Already internationally known as a philosopher of art and history, the Italian thinker Benedetto Croce began speaking out against fascism in 1925. His subsequent efforts to revitalize liberal democracy helped inspire the Italian resistance to fascism and made him one of the world's most respected intellectuals. He is shown here in a relaxed moment with three of his daughters in 1943. *(Bettmann/Corbis)*

and attacked the disordered fictional world of Kafka, which seemed to abandon all hope for human understanding of the forces of history. Though more eclectic, the Institute for Social Research, founded in Frankfurt, Germany, in 1923, gave rise to an influential tradition of criticism of capitalist civilization in what came to be known as the Frankfurt School. These innovations helped give the Marxist tradition a new lease on life in the West, even as it was developing in unforeseen ways in the Soviet Union.

The Search for a New Tradition

While some intellectuals sought renewal from within the European tradition, others insisted that a more radical break was needed—but also that the elements for a viable new cultural tradition were available.

Reflecting on the situation of women writers in 1928, the British novelist Virginia Woolf (1882–1941) showed how women in the past had suffered from the absence of a tradition of writing by women. By the 1920s, women had made important strides, but Woolf suggested that further advance required a more self-conscious effort by women to develop their own tradition. Most basically, women needed greater financial independence so that they could have the time for scholarship, the leisure for cultivated conversation and travel, and the privacy of "a room of one's own." Woolf also envisioned a new sort of historical inquiry, focusing on how ordinary women lived their lives, that could show contemporary women where they came from—and thus deepen their sense of identity. (See the box "Reading Sources: Tradition and Women: The Conditions of Independence.")

A very different effort to establish a new tradition developed in Paris, where the poet André Breton (1896–1966) spearheaded the surrealist movement in literature and the visual arts. Surrealism grew directly from Dada, an artistic movement that had emerged in neutral Zurich, Switzerland, and elsewhere during the war. Radically hostile to the war, Dada artists developed shocking, sometimes nihilistic forms to deal with a reality that now seemed senseless and out of control. Some made collages from gutter trash; others indulged in nonsense or relied on chance to guide their art. By the early 1920s, however, the surrealists felt it was time to create a new and deeper basis of order after the willful disordering of Dada. Hav-

TRADITION AND WOMEN: THE CONDITIONS OF INDEPENDENCE

Speaking in 1928 about the situation of women writers, the British novelist Virginia Woolf raised questions that were relevant to all women seeking the opportunity to realize their potential. Indeed, her reflections about the value of difference and the need for particular traditions inspired those seeking equal opportunity for decades to come. And her question about why we know so little about women's lives in the past helped stimulate later historians to investigate the experiences of ordinary people.

Woman . . . pervades poetry from cover to cover; she is all but absent from history. . . .

Occasionally an individual woman is mentioned, an Elizabeth, or a Mary; a queen or a great lady. But by no possible means could middle-class women with nothing but brains and character at their command have taken part in any one of the great movements which, brought together, constitute the historian's view of the past. . . . What one wants . . . is a mass of information; at what age did she marry; how many children had she as a rule; what was her house like; had she a room to herself; did she do the cooking; would she be likely to have a servant? All these facts lie somewhere, presumably, in parish registers and account books; the life of the average Elizabethan woman must be scattered about somewhere, could one collect it and make a book of it. It would be ambitious beyond my daring, I thought, looking about the shelves for books that were not there, to suggest to the students of those famous colleges that they should re-

write history, though I own that it often seems a little queer as it is, unreal, lop-sided. . . .

But whatever effect discouragement and criticism had upon their writing—and I believe they had a very great effect—that was unimportant compared with the other difficulty which faced them (I was still considering those early nineteenth-century novelists) when they came to set their thoughts on paper—that is that they had no tradition behind them, or one so short and partial that it was of little help. For we think back through our mothers if we are women. It is useless to go to the great men writers for help, however much one may go to them for pleasure. . . .

. . . Women have sat indoors all these millions of years, so that by this time the very walls are permeated by their creative force, which has, indeed, so overcharged the capacity of bricks and mortar that it must needs harness itself to pens and brushes and business and politics. But this creative power differs greatly from the creative power of men. And one must conclude that it would be a thousand pities if it were hindered or wasted, for it was won by centuries of the most drastic discipline, and there is nothing to take its place. It would be a thousand pities if women wrote like men, or lived like men, or looked like men. . . . Ought not education to bring out and fortify the differences rather than the similarities?

Source: Virginia Woolf, *A Room of One's Own* (San Diego: Harcourt Brace Jovanovich, Harvest/HBJ, 1989), pp. 43–45, 76, 87–88.

 For additional information on this topic, go to college.hmco.com/students.

---

ing learned from Freud about the subconscious, they sought to adapt Dada's novel techniques—especially the use of chance—to gain access to the subconscious mind, which they believed contains a deeper truth, without the overlay of logic, reason, and conscious control.

But other artists, seeking to embrace the modern industrial world in a more positive spirit, found surrealism merely escapist. Among them was Walter Gropius (1883–1969), a pioneering modernist architect and leader of an influential German art school, the Bauhaus, during the 1920s. Gropius held that it was possible to establish new

forms of culture, even a new tradition, that could be affirmative and reassuring in the face of the postwar cultural disarray. Rather than putting up familiar neoclassical or neo-Gothic buildings, "feigning a culture that has long since disappeared," society had to face up to the kind of civilization it had become—industrial, technological, efficient, urban, democratic, mass-based. If people picked and chose carefully from among the elements of this new machine-based civilization, they could again have a culture that worked, an "integrated pattern for living."[3]

The Bauhaus Building, Dessau   The Bauhaus, an influential but controversial German art school, was established in Weimar in 1919 and then moved to Dessau in 1925. Walter Gropius, its founding director, spearheaded the design of its new headquarters building, constructed in 1925–1926. The building immediately became a symbol of the Weimar modernism that some admired and others detested.   *(Vanni/Art Resource, NY)*

This "constructive," pro-modern impulse was particularly prominent in Germany, but it could be found all over—in the modernists of the Russian Revolution, in the French painter Fernand Léger° (1881–1955), in the Swiss architect Le Corbusier° (1887–1965). Whereas many of their contemporaries were at best ambivalent about the masses, these artists sought to bring high art and mass society together in the interests of both. And they welcomed the new patterns of life that seemed to be emerging in the modern world of mass production and fast-paced cities.

SUMMARY

THE 1920s proved a contradictory period of vitality and despair, pacifism and violence, restabilization and instability. The era began with bright hopes for democracy, yet the outcome of the dem-

Léger (leh-ZHAY)   Le Corbusier (luh cor-BOO-zee-ay)

ocratic experiment in central and eastern Europe was disappointing. In Germany, the improved economic and diplomatic situation by 1924 enhanced the prospects for democracy, but the new Weimar Republic remained fragile, unstable, and on the defensive. Even Italy, heir to a respectable tradition of democracy, gave rise to the troubling new phenomenon of fascism. A hopeful new spirit of international conciliation drew France and Germany closer together by the end of 1925, but France and Britain seemed to drift apart as the British, preoccupied with colonial concerns, distanced themselves from politics on the Continent.

Still, Europe seemed on its way to restabilization by early 1929. Of the three most volatile and potentially disruptive of the major countries, Italy and Germany seemed to be settling down, and the Soviet Union, though embarking on an unprecedented experiment in socioeconomic engineering, was by now looking inward rather than seeking to export revolution. When the decade is taken on its own terms, it is clear that the vitality, the renewed prosperity, and the diplomatic goodwill were all real. But so were the unresolved problems that made the

1920s a prelude to the more difficult 1930s, when the notion that Europe had returned to normal came to seem but a fairy tale.

■ Notes

1. Benito Mussolini, speech to the Italian Chamber of Deputies, January 3, 1925, from Charles F. Delzell, ed., *Mediterranean Fascism, 1919–1945* (New York: Harper & Row, 1970), pp. 59–60.
2. Quoted in Robert G. L. Waite, *Vanguard of Nazism: The Free Corps Movement in Postwar Germany, 1918–1923* (New York: W. W. Norton, 1969), pp. 14–15.
3. Walter Gropius, *Scope of Total Architecture* (New York: Collier Books, 1962), pp. 15, 67.

■ Suggested Reading

Bush, Barbara. *Imperialism, Race, and Resistance: Africa and Britain, 1919–1945*. 1999. Focuses on western and southern Africa; probes the changing nature of British colonial rule in light of growing resistance during the pivotal interwar period.

Gay, Peter. *Weimar Culture: The Outsider as Insider.* 1970. An influential study providing a good sense of the conflicting impulses—the embrace of modernity, the nostalgia for wholeness, the sense of foreboding—that made German culture so intense and vital during the 1920s.

Gentile, Emilio. *The Sacralization of Politics in Fascist Italy.* 1996. An engaging account of the rituals, symbols, and myths that, beginning in Italy during the 1920s, fed the first overtly totalitarian experiment.

Kolb, Eberhard. *The Weimar Republic.* 1988. Provides a good overall survey, then pinpoints the recent trends in research and the questions at issue among historians of the period.

Morgan, Philip. *Italian Fascism, 1919–1945.* 1995. A good introductory survey.

Pedersen, Susan. *Family, Dependence, and the Origins of the Welfare State: Britain and France, 1914–1945.* 1993. An effective comparative study showing how concerns about gender roles and family relations helped shape discussion and policy as government assumed greater responsibility for social welfare. Detailed but readable; a landmark in the new gender history.

Peukert, Detlev. *The Weimar Republic: The Crisis of Classical Modernity.* 1992. An accessible interpretive study, accenting the strains stemming from the rapid modernization of the 1920s. Stresses the loss of political legitimacy even before the onset of the Depression.

Stites, Richard. *Revolutionary Dreams: Utopian Visions and Experimental Life in the Russian Revolution.* 1989. A vivid account of the utopian aspirations that gave the new communist regime emotional force from 1917 to 1930.

Tucker, Robert C. *Stalin as Revolutionary, 1879–1929: A Study in History and Personality.* 1973. A pioneering account of Stalin's early years and rise to power, probing the sources of the elements of character and personality that helped shape his subsequent rule.

Wright, Jonathan. *Gustav Stresemann: Weimar's Greatest Statesman.* 2002. A balanced, thoroughly researched treatment. Though sensitive to the tensions in Stresemann's policies, it concludes that his willingness to play by the democratic rules was important in giving Weimar democracy a chance.

 For a searchable list of additional readings for this chapter, go to college.hmco.com/students.

Advertising

A sleek new automobile. A stylish "new woman" who'd adore a Christmas gift of jewelry. These images from the 1920s catch our eye even today, but why? The designs look "modern" somehow, and they convey particular messages about efficiency and the good life. What do such advertisements tell us about the changes at work in Western culture after World War I?

Advertising in one form or another is as old as civilization itself. But the advent of printing expanded possibilities, and the second industrial revolution led to a big boost in advertising by the 1890s, as ads for new products like bicycles and sewing machines appeared in newspapers and magazines. But it was during the 1920s that modern advertising came into its own. As mass consumption grew, advertising budgets expanded dramatically, and professional ad agencies emerged to study tastes and determine how to shape the desires of consumers. Moreover, the advent of commercial radio in 1920 opened a whole new set of possibilities, including the scope for musical jingles.

Mass consumption required advertising to show people what to want. And during the 1920s, ad agencies began offering images of the good life, seeking to define the popular sense of what it meant to be "modern." They often drew from the United States, which stood for efficiency and a fast-paced life of fun, pleasure, and consumerist abundance. So eager were the Germans to follow the U.S. lead in advertising that they adopted the term *sex appeal,* leaving it untranslated.

The new products featured in the print and broadcast media ran the gamut from automobiles to cosmetics, from rayon apparel to chewing gum. When the Wrigley Company of Chicago opened a factory in Germany in 1925, chewing gum quickly became associated with Americanization—and its use increased dramatically. But luxury goods were prominent as well, as in elegant ads such as the two shown here. Even for the many who could not afford expensive jewelry or the six-cylinder Opel, images of the good life stimulated the desire to buy less costly versions. Automobile consumption rose sharply during the 1920s, thanks also to the new techniques of mass production that Henry Ford had pioneered in the United States.

Although advertising served the economic interests of business by stimulating consumption, many began to view it as an art form as well. Far more attention was paid to its design, so the advertising "look" of the 1920s differed dramatically from anything seen before. As in the examples here, the new ads were often self-consciously modern, using simplified typefaces and stylized images suggesting the sleek efficiency and precision of the new machine age. The jewelry ad features an elegant contemporary typeface, and the German automobile ad of 1928 relies on crisp, bold forms and a clean, modern design.

The new prominence of advertising raised issues that were debated all over, but especially in Weimar Germany, where conditions remained unsettled even as a measure of prosperity returned by 1924. From cultural standards to gender roles, much was being called into question, and the wider implications of advertising were central to the "culture wars" of the period.

At an international advertising congress in Berlin in 1929, critics charged that advertising was furthering the debasement of standards already associated with mass culture and Americanization. Defenders countered that advertising was rejuvenating the mainstream culture, which had grown either stale and conventional or overblown and elitist. The fact that advertising served a commercial purpose need not mean cultural debasement. On the contrary, they argued, this new meshing of the best design with popular culture was healthy. In 1928 G. F. Hartlaub, a leading German art dealer, summed up a widespread view when he observed that advertising was a "truly social, collective, mass art, the only one we now have. It shapes the visual habits of that anonymous collectivity, the public. Little by little an artistic attitude is hammered into the mass soul by billboards."*

A particular advertising target was the "new woman," with her bobbed hair, short skirts, and freer lifestyle. But the image of women in advertisements was controversial, especially in Weimar Germany. Partly because of the simplification of female attire, images of the new woman in popular magazines provoked much concern about the "masculinization" of women by the mid-1920s. Some men found such images aggressive, even threatening.

Yet at the same time, advertising often assumed women to be master consumers—or perhaps merely mindless shoppers. In the holiday advertisement here,

---

*Quoted in John Willett, *Art and Politics in the Weimar Period: The New Sobriety, 1917–1933* (New York: Pantheon, 1978), p. 137. Translation modified slightly.

the woman is chic and liberated in one sense, but she is urged to drape herself with jewelry—to indulge in conventional ornament. This was also an age that claimed to value efficiency purified of ornament, as with the stripped-down typeface in the automobile ad. So though gender differentiation and women's roles were very much at issue in advertising, the relationship between portrayals of the new woman and genuine liberation remained uncertain.

Despite tensions and contradictions, advertising helped bring new issues to center stage after World War I. Although the ads of the 1920s assumed a prosperity that proved fleeting, the cultural change proved enduring. Eye-catching images of the sleek, the chic, the new—all bathed in "sex appeal"—became the staples of twentieth-century advertising, bound up with the new culture of mass consumption.

Advertising the Six-Cylinder Opel   As the ad says, the Opel triumphantly hit the jackpot in 1928.   *(From Bärbel Schrader and Jürgen Schebera, The "Golden" Twenties: Art and Literature in the Weimar Republic [New Haven: Yale University Press, 1990]. Reproduced with permission.)*

"Wear jewelry—It makes you a winner. And it's the ideal Christmas gift."   Such were the advertising messages for the chic "new woman" in Germany during the 1920s.   *(akg-images)*

CHAPTER 27

The Tortured Decade 1930–1939

"THEY shall not pass," proclaimed the charismatic Spanish communist Dolores Ibarruri° (1895–1989), whose impassioned speeches and radio broadcasts helped inspire the heroic defense of Madrid during the civil war that gripped Spain, and captured the attention of the world, during the later 1930s. Known as *La Pasionaria*—the passion flower—Ibarruri became a living legend for her role in defending the Spanish republic against the antidemocratic Nationalists seeking to overthrow it. But the Republican side lost, and she spent thirty-eight years in exile before returning to Spain in 1977, after the end of the military dictatorship that had resulted from the Spanish civil war.

In her effort to rally the Republican side, Ibarruri stressed the political power of women, and indeed women were prominent in the citizen militias defending Madrid and other Spanish cities. Women fought for the republic partly because it seemed to open new opportunities for them, especially as it became more radical by 1936. But just as some women welcomed the new direction, others became politically active on the opposing Nationalist side—to support the church, to combat divorce, to defend a separate sphere for women as the guardians of private life and family values.

The ideological polarization that characterized the Spanish civil war reflected the expanding reach of politics in the 1930s, when economic depression and the challenge from new, antidemocratic governments immeasurably complicated the European situation. The mechanisms used to realign the international economy after World War I had seemed effective for most of the 1920s, but by 1929 they were beginning to backfire, helping to trigger the Great Depression. During the early 1930s the economic crisis intensified sociopolitical

Ibarruri (ee-bah-RUHR-ee)

¡No pasarán! ("They shall not pass") Defending the democratic republic during the Spanish civil war.
(Biblioteca Nacional, Madrid)

913

strains all over the Western world—and beyond, heightening anti-Western feeling. In Germany the Depression helped undermine the Weimar Republic and opened the way for the new Nazi regime under Adolf Hitler, whose policies led through a series of diplomatic crises to a new European war.

German Nazism paralleled Italian fascism in its reliance on a single charismatic leader, its willingness to use violence, and its hostility to both parliamentary democracy and Marxist socialism. But Nazism emphasized racism and anti-Semitism in a way that Italian fascism did not, and it more radically transformed its society.

At the same time, Stalin's communist regime in the Soviet Union seemed to converge, in some ways, with these new fascist regimes—especially with German Nazism. So though they expressed widely different aims, Stalinism and Nazism are sometimes lumped together as instances of "totalitarianism." Both apparently sought control over all aspects of society, partly through the use of secret police agencies. But on closer inspection, the forms of coercion and violence in the Soviet and German regimes by the later 1930s were quite different, and the extent to which each can be understood as an instance of totalitarianism remains controversial.

Fascism, Nazism, and communism seemed able to sidestep—or surmount—the ills of the Depression, yet they stood opposed to the parliamentary democracy that had long seemed the direction of progressive political change. So the democratic movement appeared to lose its momentum in the face of the political and economic challenges of the 1930s. The defeat, by early 1939, of the democratic republic in Spain by the authoritarian Nationalists seemed to exemplify the political direction of the decade.

QUESTIONS TO CONSIDER

- How did the new international economic interdependence after World War I help produce the Great Depression?

- Why did the Stalinist attempt to build "socialism in one country" lead to the "terror-famine" of 1932–1933 and the "great terror" of 1937–1938?

- Through what measures did the Nazi regime claim to be improving the quality of the German population?

- Why did the other major countries not stop Hitler's Germany before it was strong enough to start a new European war in 1939?

TERMS TO KNOW

collectivization	"euthanasia" program
show trials	popular front
gulag	Rome-Berlin Axis
Adolf Hitler	remilitarization of the
National Socialist	Rhineland
(Nazi) Party	appeasement
Schutzstaffel (SS)	Nazi-Soviet Pact
Crystal Night	
(Kristallnacht)	

THE GREAT DEPRESSION

IF any single event can be said to have triggered the world economic crisis of the early 1930s, it was the stock market crash of October 1929 in the United States. But that crash had such an impact only because the new international economic order after World War I was extremely fragile. By October 1929, in fact, production was already declining in all the major Western countries except France.

The economies of Germany and the states of east-central Europe remained particularly vulnerable after the war, and in the increasingly interdependent economic world, their weaknesses magnified problems that started elsewhere. The crash of the U.S. stock market led to a restriction of credit in central Europe, which triggered a more general contraction in production and trade. Facing cruel dilemmas, policymakers proved unable to master the situation for the first few years of the crisis. The consequences—both human and political— were profound.

Sources of the Economic Contraction

Certain economic sectors, especially coal mining and agriculture, were already suffering severe problems by the mid-1920s, well before the stock market crash. British coal exports fell partly because oil and hydroelectricity were rapidly developing as alternatives. Unemployment in Britain was never less than 10 percent even in the best of times between the wars. In agriculture high prices worldwide during the war produced oversupply, which, in turn, led to a sharp drop in prices once the war was over. During the later 1920s, bumper harvests of grain and rice in many parts of the world renewed the downward pressure on prices. The result of low agricultural prices was a diminished demand for industrial goods, which impeded growth in the world economy.

Throughout the 1920s, finance ministers and central bankers had difficulty juggling the economic imbalances created by the war, centering on war debts to the United States and German reparations obligations to France, Britain, and Belgium. The strains in the system finally caught up with policymakers by 1929, when an international restriction of credit forced an end to the international economic cooperation that had been attempted throughout the decade.

The shaky postwar economic system depended on U.S. bank loans to Germany, funneled partly by international agreements but also drawn by high interest rates. By 1928, however, U.S. investors were rapidly withdrawing their capital from Germany in search of the higher returns that could be made in the booming U.S. stock market. This shift tightened credit in Germany. And then the crash of the overpriced U.S. market in October 1929 deepened the problem by forcing suddenly strapped American investors to pull still more of their funds out of Germany. This process continued over the next two years, weakening the major banks in Germany and the other countries of central Europe, which were closely tied to the German economy. In May 1931 the bankruptcy of Vienna's most powerful bank, the Credit-Anstalt, made it clear that a crisis of potentially catastrophic proportions was in progress.

Despite attempts at adjustment on the international level, fears of bank failure or currency devaluation led to runs on the banks and currencies of Germany and east-central Europe. To maintain the value of the domestic currency in world markets, and thereby to resist the withdrawal of capital, government policymakers raised interest rates. This measure was not sufficient to stem the capital hemorrhage, but by restricting credit still more, it further dampened domestic economic activity.

CHRONOLOGY

October 1929	U.S. stock market crash helps trigger Great Depression
December 1929	Forced collectivization in Soviet agriculture begins
June 1930	Smoot-Hawley Tariff Act (U.S.)
May 1931	Bankruptcy of Vienna's Credit-Anstalt
January 1933	Hitler becomes German chancellor
December 1934	Assassination of Kirov
March 1935	Hitler announces rearmament
October 1935	Italy invades Ethiopia
March 1936	Germany remilitarizes the Rhineland
May 1936	Blum becomes French popular front prime minister
July 1936	Spanish civil war begins
March 1938	Third Moscow show trial; Bukharin and others convicted and executed Anschluss: Germany absorbs Austria
September 1938	"Appeasement": Munich conference ends Sudetenland crisis
November 1938	Crystal Night pogrom
March 1939	Dismemberment of Czechoslovakia
May 1939	Pact of Steel binds fascist Italy and Nazi Germany
August 23, 1939	Nazi-Soviet Pact
September 1, 1939	Germany invades Poland
September 3, 1939	Britain and France declare war on Germany

Unemployment in Britain
The Depression hit Britain hard—and its effects continued to be felt throughout the 1930s. These unemployed shipyard workers from Jarrow, in northeastern England, are marching to London in 1936 to present a protest petition.
(Hulton Archive & Getty Images)

Finally, the Germans seemed to have no choice but to freeze foreign assets—that is, to cease allowing conversion of assets held in German marks to other currencies. In this atmosphere, investors seeking the safest place for their capital tried to cash in currency for gold—or for British pounds, which could then be converted to gold. Europe's flight to gold, however, soon put such pressure on the British currency that Britain was forced to devalue the pound and sever it from the gold standard in September 1931. This proved the definitive end of the worldwide system of economic exchange based on the gold standard that had gradually crystallized during the nineteenth century.

The absence of a single standard of exchange, combined with various currency restrictions, made foreign trade more difficult, thereby diminishing it further. So did the scramble for tariff protection that proved a widespread response to the developing crisis. Crucial was the U.S. Smoot-Hawley Tariff Act of June 1930, which raised taxes on imports by 50 to 100 percent, forcing other nations to take comparable steps. Even Britain, long a bastion of free trade, adopted a peacetime tariff for the first time in nearly a century with the Import Duties Act of 1932, which imposed a 10 percent tax on most imports.

The decline of trade spread depression throughout the world economic system. By 1933 most major European countries were able to export no more than two-thirds, and in some cases as little as one-third, of the amount they had sold in 1929. At the same time, losses from international bank failures contracted credit and purchasing power and furthered the downward spiral, until by 1932 the European economies had shrunk to a little over half their 1929 size. This was the astonishing outcome of the short-lived prosperity of the 1920s.

Consequences and Responses

The Depression was essentially a radical contraction in economic activity; with less being produced and sold, demand for labor declined sharply. In Germany industrial production by early 1933 was only half what it had been in 1929, and roughly six million Germans, or one-third of the labor force, were unemployed.

Although its timing and severity varied, the Depression profoundly affected the lives of ordinary people throughout the Western world and beyond. (See the box "Reading Sources: Working-Class Life During the Great Depression.") Unemployment produced widespread malnutrition, which led, in turn, to sharp increases in such diseases as tuberculosis, scarlet fever, and rickets. The decline in employment opportunities helped produce a backlash against the ideal of the "new woman," working outside the home, which had been a prominent aspect of the new freedom of the 1920s in Germany and elsewhere. Even those men and women who hung on to jobs suffered from growing insecurity. In his aptly titled *Little*

READING
SOURCES

WORKING-CLASS LIFE DURING THE GREAT DEPRESSION

During the Depression, the Left Book Club, an important movement of left-leaning British intellectuals, commissioned George Orwell (1903–1950) to write a report on the conditions of unemployed miners in the north of England. Published in 1937, Orwell's study of responses to the Depression offered pioneering insights into the dynamics of relative poverty in the modern world. The P.A.C. to which he refers is the British Public Assistance, or welfare, system.

It is noticeable everywhere that the anomalous position created by unemployment—the man being out of work while the woman's work continues as before—has not altered the relative status of the sexes. . . . Practically never . . . will you see the man doing a stroke of the housework. Unemployment has not changed this convention, which on the face of it seems a little unfair. The man is idle from morning to night but the woman is as busy as ever—more so, indeed, because she has to manage with less money. Yet so far as my experience goes the women do not protest. I believe that they, as well as the men, feel that a man would lose his manhood if, merely because he was out of work, he developed into a "Mary Ann."

But there is no doubt about the deadening, debilitating effect of unemployment on everybody, married or single, and upon men more than women. . . .

I remember the shock of astonishment it gave me, when I first mingled with tramps and beggars, to find that a fair proportion, perhaps a quarter, of these beings whom I had been taught to regard as cynical parasites, were decent young miners and cotton-workers gazing at their destiny with the same sort of dumb amazement as an animal in a trap. They simply could not understand what was happening to them. They had been brought up to work, and behold! it seemed as though they were never going to have the chance of working again. In their circumstances it was inevitable, at first, that they should be haunted by a feeling of personal degradation. That was the attitude toward unemployment in those days: it was a disaster which happened to *you* as an individual and for which *you* were to blame. . . .

. . . When people live on the dole for years at a time they grow used to it, and drawing the dole, though it remains unpleasant, ceases to be shameful. . . . In the back streets of Wigan and Barnley I saw every kind of privation, but I probably saw less *conscious* misery than I should have seen ten years ago. The people have at any rate grasped that unemployment is a thing they cannot help. It is not only Alf Smith who is out of work now; Bert Jones is out of work as well, and both of them have been "out" for years. It makes a great deal of difference when things are the same for everybody.

So you have whole populations settling down, as it were, to a lifetime on the P.A.C. And what I think is admirable, perhaps even hopeful, is that they have managed to do it without going spiritually to pieces. . . . [T]hey realize that losing your job does not mean that you cease to be a human being. So that in one way things in the distressed areas are not so bad as they might be. Life is still fairly normal, more normal than one really has the right to expect. Families are impoverished, but the family-system has not broken up. The people are in effect living a reduced version of their former lives. . . .

But they don't necessarily lower their standards by cutting out luxuries and concentrating on necessities; more often it is the other way about—the more natural way, if you come to think of it. Hence the fact that in a decade of unparalleled depression, the consumption of all cheap luxuries has increased. The two things that have probably made the greatest difference of all are the movies and the mass-production of cheap smart clothes since the war. . . . You may have three halfpence in your pocket and not a prospect in the world, and only the corner of a leaky bedroom to go home to; but in your new clothes you can stand on the street corner, indulging in a private daydream of yourself as Clark Gable or Greta Garbo, which compensates for a great deal.

Man, What Now? (1932), the German novelist Hans Fallada (1893–1947) explored the effects of the Depression on members of the lower middle class—store clerks, shop owners, civil servants. Such people were first resentful, then resigned, as their dreams of security, of "order and cleanliness," fell apart.

During the first years of the Depression, central bankers everywhere sought to balance budgets in order to reassure investors and stabilize currencies. With economies contracting and tax revenues declining, the only way to balance the budget was to sharply reduce government spending. In addition, governments responded to the decline in exports by forcing wages down, seeking to enhance competitiveness abroad. But by cutting purchasing power at home, both these measures reinforced the slowdown in economic activity.

Economic policymakers based their responses on the "classical" economic model that had developed from the ideas of Adam Smith in the eighteenth century (see page 715). According to this model, a benign "invisible hand" ensured that a free-market price for labor, for capital, and for goods and services would produce an ongoing tendency toward economic equilibrium. A downturn in the business cycle was a normal and necessary adjustment; government interference would only upset this self-adjusting mechanism.

By 1932, however, it was clear that the conventional response was not working, and governments began seeking more actively to stimulate the economy. Although the British economist John Maynard Keynes would outline the rationale for governmental intervention in technical economic terms in 1936, governments could only experiment, and strategies varied widely. (See the box, "The Continuing Experiment: The Government's Role in Managing a Free-Market Economy.") In the United States, Franklin D. Roosevelt (1882–1945) defeated the incumbent president, Herbert Hoover, in 1932 with the promise of a New Deal—a commitment to increase government spending to restore purchasing power. In fascist Italy, a state agency created to infuse capital into failing companies proved a reasonably effective basis for collaboration between government and business. In Germany, economics minister Hjalmar Schacht (1877–1970) mounted an energetic assault on the economic problem after Hitler came to power in 1933. Government measures sealed off the German mark from international fluctuations, stimulated public spending—partly on rearmament—and kept wages low. By 1935 Germany was back to full employment. This success added tremendously to Hitler's popularity.

High unemployment in Norway, Sweden, and Denmark helped social democrats win power in all three of these Scandinavian countries by the mid-1930s. The new left-leaning governments responded to the economic crisis not by a frontal assault on capitalism but by pioneering the "welfare state," providing such benefits as health care, unemployment insurance, and family allowances. To pay for the new welfare safety net, the Scandinavian countries adopted a high level of progressive taxation and pared military expenditures to a minimum. The turn to a welfare state eased the immediate human costs of the Depression and helped restore production by stimulating demand. At the same time, the Scandinavian model attracted much admiration as a "third way" between free-market capitalism and the various dictatorial extremes.

In the other European democracies the Depression proved more intractable. Although Britain saw some recovery by the mid-1930s, it was especially the rearmament of the later 1930s, financed by borrowing, or deficit spending, that got the British economy growing again. France, less dependent on international trade, experienced the consequences of the world crisis only gradually. But by the early 1930s, France, too, was suffering its effects, which lingered to the end of the decade, helping to poison the political atmosphere.

The Depression also had a major impact on the non-Western world and its relations with the West. The radical restriction of international trade meant a sharp decline in demand for the basic commodities that colonial and other regions exported to the industrialized West. Economic strains fed nationalist, anti-Western sentiments in colonial nations. The increase in misery among rural villagers in India, for example, spread the movement for national independence from urban elites to the rural masses. In this context Mohandas Gandhi°, who had become known by 1920 for advocating noncooperation with the British, became the first leader to win a mass following throughout the Indian subcontinent (see pages 882 and 978). Encouraging villagers to boycott British goods, Gandhi accented simplicity, self-reliance, and an overall strategy of nonviolent civil disobedience based on Indian traditions. (See the box "Global Encounters: Gandhi Advocates Nonviolence.")

In Japan, the strains of the Great Depression helped produce precisely the turn to imperialist violence that Gandhi sought to counter. Densely populated yet lacking raw materials, Japan was particularly dependent on international trade and reacted strongly as increasing tariffs elsewhere cut sharply into Japanese exports. Led by young army officers who were already eager for their

---

Gandhi (GAHN-dee)

The Government's Role in Managing a Free-Market Economy

In 1936, at the height of the Depression, the British economist John Maynard Keynes published *The General Theory of Employment, Interest and Money,* which proved the most influential work in economics of the twentieth century. While recognizing the advantages of a free-market economy, Keynes noted that capitalism seemed to entail a built-in tendency toward unemployment, dramatically evident in the Depression. Thus some people were attracted to socialist or statist alternatives, which might include, for example, the wholesale nationalization of industry. But Keynes insisted that a more active role for government in managing the capitalist economy could overcome the tendency toward unemployment while preserving a democratic framework and the advantages of a market economy. Government could manage the economy especially through the "socialization of investment"—absorbing money through taxation and spending it to stimulate the economy toward full employment.

The outstanding faults of the economic society in which we live are its failure to provide for full employment and its arbitrary and inequitable distribution of wealth and incomes. . . .

. . . I conceive, therefore, that a somewhat comprehensive socialisation of investment will prove the only means of securing an approximation to full employment; though this need not exclude all manner of compromises and of devices by which public authority will co-operate with private initiative. But beyond this no obvious case is made out for a system of State Socialism which would embrace most of the economic life of the community. It is not the ownership of the instruments of production which it is important for the State to assume. If the State is able to determine the aggregate amount of resources devoted to augmenting the instruments and the basic rate of reward to those who own them, it will have accomplished all that is necessary. Moreover, the necessary measures of socialisation can be introduced gradually and without a break in the general traditions of society. . . .

. . . The central controls necessary to ensure full employment will, of course, involve a large extension of the traditional functions of government. Furthermore, the modern classical theory has itself called attention to various conditions in which the free play of economic forces may need to be curbed or guided. But there will still remain a wide field for the exercise of private initiative and responsibility. Within this field the traditional advantages of individualism will still hold good.

Let us stop for a moment to remind ourselves what these advantages are. They are partly advantages of efficiency—the advantages of decentralisation and of the play of self-interest. . . .

Whilst, therefore, the enlargement of the functions of government, involved in the task of adjusting to one another the propensity to consume and inducement to invest, would seem to a nineteenth-century publicist or to a contemporary American financier to be a terrific encroachment on individualism, I defend it, on the contrary, both as the only practicable means of avoiding the destruction of existing economic forms in their entirety and as the condition of the successful functioning of individual initiative. . . .

The authoritarian state systems of to-day seem to solve the problem of unemployment at the expense of efficiency and of freedom. It is certain that the world will not much longer tolerate the unemployment which, apart from brief intervals of excitement, is associated—and, in my opinion, inevitably associated—with present-day capitalistic individualism. But it may be possible by a right analysis of the problem to cure the disease whilst preserving efficiency and freedom.

QUESTIONS

1. Why does Keynes argue for a considerably expanded role for government in coordinating the capitalist economy?

2. In what sense is Keynes trying to save free-market capitalism in light of the Depression and the appeal of the alternatives emerging in Italy, Germany, and the Soviet Union?

SOURCE: John Maynard Keynes, *The General Theory of Employment, Interest and Money* (New York: Harcourt, Brace & World, n.d.), pp. 372, 378–381. Reprinted by permission of J. S. Dring.

Gandhi Advocates Nonviolence

Mohandas Gandhi, a successful English-educated lawyer, emerged as a major force in the movement for Indian independence just after World War I. Calling first for a strategy of noncooperation with the British colonial overlords, Gandhi gradually developed a philosophy of nonviolent civil disobedience, which won widespread sympathy for the cause of Indian independence. The following excerpts from articles published in 1935 and 1939—years notable for outbreaks of violence elsewhere—explain the significance of nonviolence to Gandhi's overall strategy.

Non-violence to be a creed has to be all-pervasive. I cannot be non-violent about one activity of mine and violent about others. That would be a policy, not a life-force. That being so, I cannot be indifferent about the war that Italy is now waging against Abyssinia. . . . India has an unbroken tradition of non-violence from times immemorial. But at no time in her ancient history, as far as I know it, has it had complete non-violence in action pervading the whole land. Nevertheless, it is my unshakeable belief that her destiny is to deliver the message of non-violence to mankind. . . .

. . . India as a nation is not non-violent in the full sense of the term. . . . Her non-violence is that of the weak. . . . She lacks the ability to offer physical resistance. She has no consciousness of strength. She is conscious only of her weakness. If she were otherwise, there would be no communal problems, nor political. If she were non-violent in the consciousness of her strength, Englishmen would lose their role of distrustful conquerors. We may talk politically as we like and often legitimately blame the English rulers. But if we, as Indians, could but for a moment visualize ourselves as a strong people disdaining to strike, we should cease to fear Englishmen whether as soldiers, traders or administrators, and they to distrust us. Therefore if we became truly non-violent we should carry Englishmen with us in all we might do. In other words, we being millions would be the greatest moral force in the world, and Italy would listen to our friendly word. . . .

. . . [W]hen society is deliberately constructed in accordance with the law of non-violence, its structure will be different in material particulars from what it is today. But I cannot say in advance what the government based wholly on non-violence will be like.

What is happening today is disregard of the law of non-violence and enthronement of violence as if it were an eternal law. The democracies, therefore, that we see at work in England, America and France are only so called, because they are no less based on violence than Nazi Germany, Fascist Italy or even Soviet Russia. The only difference is that the violence of the last three is much better organized than that of the three democratic powers. Nevertheless we see today a mad race for outdoing one another in the matter of armaments. And if and when the clash comes, as it is bound to come one day, the democracies win, they will do so only because they will have the backing of their peoples who imagine that they have a voice in their own government whereas in the other three cases the peoples might rebel against their own dictatorships.

Holding the view that without the recognition of non-violence on a national scale there is no such thing as a constitutional or democratic government, I devote my energy to the propagation of non-violence as the law of our life—individual, social, political, national and international. I fancy that I have seen the light, though dimly. I write cautiously, for I do not profess to know the whole of the Law. If I know the successes of my experiments, I know also my failures. But the successes are enough to fill me with undying hope. I have often said that if one takes care of the means, the end will take care of itself. Non-violence is the means, the end for every nation is complete independence.

QUESTIONS

1. What is the difference between "strong" and "weak" nonviolence in Gandhi's thinking?

2. Why does Gandhi play down the difference between the democracies and the dictatorships of the West?

SOURCE: Raghavan Iyer, ed., *The Essential Writings of Mahatma Gandhi* (Delhi: Oxford University Press, 1991), pp. 245–247, 262–263. Copyright © 1991 by Navajivan Trust. Reprinted by permission of Navajivan Trust.

 For additional information on this topic, go to college.hmco.com/students.

country to embrace a less subservient form of Westernization, Japan turned to aggressive imperialism. As justification, the Japanese began arguing that they were spearheading a wider struggle to free East Asia from Western imperialism. (See the box "Global Encounters: Japan's 'Pan-Asian' Mission" on page 964 in Chapter 28.) Attacking in 1931, Japanese forces quickly reduced Manchuria to a puppet state, but the Japanese met stubborn resistance when they began seeking to extend this conquest to the rest of China in 1937.

Japanese pressure indirectly advanced the rise of the Chinese communist movement, led by Mao Zedong (Mao Tse-tung, 1893–1976). Securing a base in the Yanan district in 1936, Mao began seeking to apply Marxism-Leninism to China through land reform and other measures to link the Communist Party elite to the Chinese peasantry. Mao was notable among those adapting Western ideas to build an indigenous movement that would at once overcome Western imperialism and create an alternative to Western liberal capitalism.

The Depression, and the halting responses of the democracies in dealing with it, enhanced the prestige of the new regimes in the Soviet Union, Italy, and Germany. These three despotic powers appeared either to have avoided the economic crisis or to be dealing with it more creatively. But each of these new regimes was an experiment, and the innovations of each added to the uncertainties of the decade.

THE STALINIST REVOLUTION IN THE SOVIET UNION

THOUGH it won the admiration of some, the Soviet Union, in particular, experienced a decade of unprecedented upheaval during the 1930s. Seeking to build "socialism in one country," Joseph Stalin led the Soviet Union during the 1930s through an astounding transformation that mixed achievement with brutality and terror in often tragic ways. The resulting governmental system, which gave Stalin unprecedented power, proved crucial to the outcome of the great experiment that had begun with the Russian Revolution of 1917. But whether the fateful turn of the 1930s had been implicit in the Leninist revolutionary model all along or stemmed mostly from unforeseen circumstances and Stalin's idiosyncratic personality remains uncertain.

Crash Industrialization and Forced Collectivization

Stalin's program of rapid industrialization based on forced collectivization in agriculture began in earnest at the beginning of 1930. It entailed an assault on the better-off peasants, or *kulaks,* who were often sent to labor camps in Siberia while their lands were taken over by the

Collectivization in Soviet Agriculture   At the "New Life" collective farm, not far from Moscow, women stand for the morning roll call. The Soviet collectivization effort of the 1930s rested in important measure on the forced mobilization of peasant women.
(Endeavor Group UK)

government. The remaining peasants were herded into new government-controlled collective farms. So unpopular was this measure that many peasants simply killed their livestock or smashed their farm implements rather than have them collectivized. During the first two months of 1930, as many as fourteen million head of cattle were slaughtered, resulting in an orgy of meat eating and a shortage of draft animals. By 1934 the number of cattle in the Soviet Union was barely half what it had been in 1928.

Collectivization served, as intended, to squeeze from the peasantry the resources needed to finance industrialization, but it was carried out with extreme brutality. What was being squeezed was not merely a surplus—the state's extractions cut into subsistence. So while Soviet agricultural exports increased after 1930, large numbers of peasants starved to death. The great famine that developed during 1932–1933 resulted in between five million and six million deaths, over half of them in Ukraine. This "terror-famine" went unrecorded in the Soviet press, and the Soviets refused help from international relief agencies. (See the box "Reading Sources: Carrying Out the Stalinist Revolution.")

By 1937 almost all Soviet agriculture took place on collective farms—or on state farms set up in areas not previously under agriculture. However, restrictions on private plots and livestock ownership were eased slightly after 1933, and partly as a result, agriculture rebounded and living standards began to rise. By the late 1930s, moreover, significant increases in industrial output had established solid foundations in heavy industry, including the bases for military production.

In pursuing this program, Stalin played up the great historical drama surrounding the Soviet experiment, with its incredible targets and goals. Suggestions by some that the pace could not be maintained only proved grist for Stalin's mill: "No, comrades," he told a workers' conference early in 1931, "the tempo must not be reduced. On the contrary, we must increase it as much as is within our powers and capabilities. . . . To slow the tempo would mean falling behind. And those who fall behind get beaten. . . . Do you want our socialist fatherland to be beaten and to lose its independence? . . . We are fifty or a hundred years behind the advanced countries. We must make good this distance in ten years. Either we do this or they will crush us."[1]

Soviet propaganda, including art in the official socialist realist style, glorified the achievements of the new Soviet industrial and agricultural workers. "Stakhanovism°," named for a coal miner who had heroically exceeded his production quota in 1935, became the term for the prodigious economic achievements that the regime valued as it proclaimed the superiority of the communist system. Indeed, the fact that in the Soviet Union state management seemed to produce results while much of the world languished in depression helps explain the prestige that communism developed among intellectuals, in both the Western and non-Western worlds, during the 1930s.

But whatever its successes, this forced development program created many inefficiencies and entailed tremendous human costs. The Soviet Union could probably have done at least as well, with much less suffering, through other strategies of industrial development. Moreover, Stalin's program departed from certain socialist principles—egalitarianism in wages, for example—that the regime had taken very seriously during the late 1920s. By 1931, bureaucratic managers, concerned simply with maximizing output, were openly favoring workers in certain industries. Collective bargaining and the right to strike had vanished from the workers' arsenal.

From Opposition to Terror, 1932–1938

Stalin's radical course, with its brutality and uncertain economic justification, quickly provoked opposition. During the summer of 1932, a group centered on M. N. Ryutin° (1890–1937) circulated among party leaders a two-hundred-page tract calling for a retreat from Stalin's economic program and a return to democracy within the party. It advocated readmitting those who had been expelled—including Stalin's archenemy, Leon Trotsky. Moreover, the document strongly condemned Stalin personally, describing him as "the evil genius of the Russian Revolution, who, motivated by a personal desire for power and revenge, brought the Revolution to the verge of ruin."[2]

Stalin promptly had Ryutin and his associates ousted from the party, then arrested and imprisoned. But especially as the international situation grew menacing during the 1930s, Stalin became ever more preoccupied with the scope for further opposition. Both Germany and Japan exhibited expansionist aims that might threaten Soviet territories. Trotsky from exile might work with foreign agents and Soviet dissidents to sabotage the Soviet development effort.

In December 1934 the assassination of Sergei Kirov° (1888–1934), party leader of Leningrad (the former Petrograd), gave Stalin an excuse to intensify the crackdown against actual and potential opponents. The eventual re-

---

Stakhanovism (stah-KAH-nov-izm)

Ryutin (ree-YOU-tin)   **Kirov** (KIH-roff)

READING
SOURCES

CARRYING OUT THE STALINIST REVOLUTION

Lev Kopelev (1912–1997), who came from a middle-class Jewish family, was an enthusiastic Communist as a young man. Believing that the Soviet Communist Party embodied the progressive movement of history, he eagerly assisted in the forced collectivization drive of the early 1930s, which caused such suffering and death in his native Ukraine. But after World War II, he became critical of Soviet communism, and he was finally exiled from the Soviet Union in 1980.

Our great goal was the universal triumph of Communism, and for the sake of that goal everything was permissible. . . . And to hesitate or doubt about all this was to give in to "intellectual squeamishness" and "stupid liberalism," the attributes of people who "could not see the forest for the trees."

. . . I saw what "total collectivization" meant—how . . . mercilessly they stripped the peasants in the winter of 1932–33. I took part in this myself, scouring the countryside, searching for hidden grain, testing the earth with an iron rod for loose spots that might lead to buried grain. With the others, I emptied out the old folks' storage chests, stopping my ears to the children's crying and the women's wails. For I was convinced that I was accomplishing the great and necessary transformation of the countryside; that in the days to come the people who lived there would be better off for it; that their distress and suffering were a result of their own ignorance or the machinations of the class enemy; that those who sent me—and I myself—knew better than the peasants how they should live, what they should sow and when they should plow.

In the terrible spring of 1933 I saw people dying from hunger. I saw women and children with distended bellies, turning blue, still breathing but with vacant, lifeless eyes. . . .

Nor did I lose my faith. As before, I believed because I wanted to believe. Thus from time immemorial men have believed when possessed by a desire to serve powers and values above and beyond humanity. . . .

That was how we thought and acted—we, the fanatical disciples of the all-saving ideals of communism. When we saw the base and cruel acts that were committed in the name of our exalted notions of good, and when we ourselves took part in those actions, what we feared most was to lose our heads, fall into doubt or heresy and forfeit our unbounded faith. . . .

. . . The concepts of conscience, honor, humaneness we dismissed as idealistic prejudices, "intellectual" or "bourgeois," and, hence, perverse.

Source: No Jail for Thought by Lev Kopelev. Translated and edited by Anthony Austin (London: Secker & Warburg, 1977), pp. 11–13.

---

sult was a series of bizarre show trials, deadly purges, and, ultimately, a kind of terror, with several categories of Soviet citizens vulnerable to arbitrary arrest by the secret police. By the time it wound down, early in 1939, this "great terror" had significantly changed the communist regime—and Soviet society. But though the bare facts are clear, what to make of them is not.

In the three Moscow show trials, which took place during a twenty-month period from 1936 to 1938, noted Bolsheviks, including Nikolai Bukharin and major functionaries such as Genrikh Yagoda, recently removed as chief of the secret police, confessed to a series of sensational trumped-up charges: that they had been behind the assassination of Kirov, that they would like to have killed Stalin, that they constituted an "anti-Soviet, Trotskyite center," spying for Germany and Japan and preparing to sabotage Soviet industry in the event of war. Almost all the accused, including Bukharin and others who had been central to the 1917 revolution, were convicted and executed. Soviet authorities did not dare risk public trial for the few who refused, even in the face of torture, to play their assigned roles and confess. Among them was Ryutin, who was shot in secret early in 1937.

During 1937 a purge wiped out much of the top ranks of the army, with half the entire officer corps shot or imprisoned in response to unfounded charges of spying and treason. The Communist Party underwent several purges, culminating in the great purge of 1937 and 1938. Of the roughly two thousand delegates to the 1934 congress of the Communist Party, over half were shot during the next few years. The most prominent were especially vulnerable. Indeed, 114 of the 139 central committee members elected at the 1934 party congress had been shot or sent to a forced labor camp by 1939.

The first such camps were established under Lenin in 1918, during the civil war, but the camp system expanded exponentially under Stalin during the 1930s, coming to play a major economic role. This network of forced labor camps—there were eventually at least 476 of them—became known as the *gulag,* originally an acronym for "main camp administration."

Although considerable controversy remains over the number of victims of the gulag, and of the Stalinist revolution more generally, the totals are staggering. According to one influential high-end estimate, 8.5 million of the approximately 160 million people in the Soviet Union were arrested during 1937 and 1938, and of these perhaps 1 million were executed by shooting. Half of those belonging to the Communist Party—1.2 million people—were arrested; of these, 600,000 were executed, and most of the rest died in gulag camps. Altogether, the terror surrounding the several purges resulted in approximately 8 million deaths. Estimates of the death toll from all of Stalin's policies of the 1930s, including the forced collectivizations, range as high as 20 million.

Communism and Stalinism

What was going on in this bizarre and lethal combination of episodes? Obviously Stalinism was one possible outcome of Leninist communism, but was it the logical, even the inevitable, outcome? Leninism had accented centralized authority and the scope for human will to force events, so it may have created a framework in which Stalinism was likely to emerge. Yet Stalin's personal idiosyncrasies and growing paranoia seem to have been crucial for the Soviet system to develop as it did. But though he ended up the regime's undisputed leader, Stalin was part of a wider dynamic.

It was long assumed that Stalin was pursuing a coordinated policy of terror to create a system of total control. Yet recent research has shown that he was often merely improvising, responding to a situation that had become chaotic, out of control, as the Communists tried to carry through a revolution in a backward country. No one had ever attempted this sort of forced industrialization based on a centrally planned economy. At once idealistic, inexperienced, and suspicious, the regime's leaders really believed that failures must be due to sabotage—that "wreckers" were seeking to undermine the heroic Soviet experiment. Moreover, though Stalin tended to blow them out of proportion, there were genuine threats to the Soviet regime and his own leadership by the mid-1930s.

Whereas the terror was long viewed as almost random, it is now clearer that those in the upper and middle reaches of the Soviet system were the most vulnerable. Top officials encouraged ordinary workers to provide information about plant managers and local party officials who seemed incompetent or corrupt. And whether to serve the revolution or to vent personal resentments, such workers often took the initiative in denouncing their superiors, thereby playing important roles in the dynamic that developed.

But what explains the "confessions" that invariably resulted from the bizarre show trials? The accused sometimes succumbed to torture, and to threats to their families. But some, at least, offered false confessions because they believed that in doing so they were still serving the communist cause. All along, the revolution had required a willingness to compromise personal scruples, including "bourgeois" concerns about personal honor and dignity. Even though false, these confessions could help the communist regime ward off the genuine dangers it faced. So in confessing, the accused would be serving the long-term cause, which they believed to be bigger than Stalin and the issues of the moment. What some could not see—or admit—was that the triumph of Stalinism was fatally compromising the original revolutionary vision.

Surrounded by great propaganda, the show trials were central to the unending talk of foreign intrigues, assassination plots, and "wrecking" by the later 1930s. And all the talk had its effect, leading many ordinary citizens to believe that a vast conspiracy was indeed at work, responsible for the shortages and economic misfortunes that had accompanied the crash industrialization program.

Although much was unplanned and even out of control, Stalin's ultimate responsibility for the lethal dynamic of the later 1930s is undeniable. At the height of the terror, he personally approved lists for execution, and he took advantage of the chain of events to crush all actual or imagined opposition. By 1939 Stalin loyalists constituted the entire party leadership.

In a sense, the outcome was the triumph of Stalin over the Communist Party, which had held to the original Bolshevik ideal of collective leadership by a revolutionary vanguard. But even this outcome did not snuff out the revolutionary idealism that had helped carry the communist regime through the upheavals of the 1930s. Though some turned away in disillusionment or despair, others found the regime's ruthlessness in rooting out its apparent enemies evidence of its ongoing revolutionary purpose. And whereas Stalin was not a charismatic leader like Hitler or Mussolini, he was coming for many to embody the ongoing promise of the communist experiment.

HITLER AND NAZISM IN GERMANY

BESET with problems from the start, the Weimar Republic lay gravely wounded by 1932. Various antidemocratic groups competed to replace it. The winner was the Nazi movement, led by Adolf Hitler, who became chancellor in January 1933. It was especially Hitler's new regime in Germany that made the 1930s so tortured, for Hitler not only radically transformed German society but fundamentally altered the power balance in Europe.

Nazism took inspiration from Italian fascism, but Hitler's regime proved more dynamic—and more troubling—than Mussolini's. Nazism was not conventionally revolutionary, in the sense of mounting a frontal challenge to the existing socioeconomic order. Some of its themes were traditionalist and even antimodernizing. But in the final analysis Nazism was anything but conservative. Indeed, it constituted a direct assault on what had long been held as the best of Western civilization.

The Emergence of Nazism and the Crisis of the Weimar Republic

The National Socialist German Workers' Party (NSDAP), or Nazism, emerged from the turbulent situation in Munich just after the war. A center of leftist agitation, the city also became a hotbed of the radical right, nurturing a number of new nationalist, militantly anticommunist political groups. One of them, a workers' party founded under the aegis of the right-wing Thule Society early in 1919, attracted the attention of Adolf Hitler, who soon gave it his personal stamp.

Adolf Hitler (1889–1945) had been born not German but Austrian, the son of a middling government official. As a young man he had gone to Vienna, hoping to become an artist, but he failed to gain admission to the Viennese Academy of Fine Arts. By 1913 he had become a German nationalist hostile to the multinational Habsburg empire, and he emigrated to Germany to escape service in the Austrian army. He was not opposed to military service per se, however, and when war broke out in 1914, he immediately volunteered for service in the German army.

Corporal Hitler experienced firsthand the fighting at the front and, as a courier, performed bravely and effectively. Indeed, he was in a field hospital being treated for gas poisoning when the war ended. Although his fellow soldiers considered him quirky and introverted, Hitler found the war experience crucial; it was during the war, he said later, that he "found himself."

Following his release from the hospital, Hitler worked for the army in routine surveillance of extremist groups in Munich. In this role he joined the infant German Workers' Party late in 1919. When his first political speech at a rally in February 1920 proved a resounding success, Hitler began to believe he could play a special political role. From this point, he gradually developed the confidence to lead a new nationalist, anticommunist, and anti-Weimar movement.

But Hitler jumped the gun in November 1923 when, with Erich Ludendorff at his side, he led the Beer Hall Putsch in Munich, an abortive attempt to launch a march on Berlin to overthrow the republic. On trial after this effort failed, Hitler gained greater national visibility as he denounced the Versailles treaty and the Weimar government. Still, *Mein Kampf* (*My Battle*), the political tract that he wrote while in prison during 1924, sold poorly. To most, Hitler was simply a right-wing rabble-rouser whose views were not worth taking seriously.

His failure in 1923 convinced Hitler that he should exploit the existing political system, but not challenge it directly, in his quest for power on the national level. Yet Hitler did not view the NSDAP as just another political party, playing by the same rules as the others within the Weimar system. Thus, most notably, the Nazi Party maintained a paramilitary arm, the *Sturmabteilung* (SA), which provoked a good deal of antileftist street violence. Still, the Nazis remained confined to the margins of national politics in 1928, when they attracted only 2.6 percent of the vote in elections to the Reichstag.

The onset of the economic depression by the end of 1929 produced problems that the Weimar democracy could not handle—and that radically changed the German political framework. The pivotal issue was unemployment insurance, which became a tremendous financial burden for the government as unemployment grew. The governing coalition fell apart over the issue in March 1930, and this proved to be the end of normal parliamentary government in Weimar Germany.

President Paul von Hindenburg called on Heinrich Brüning (1885–1970), an expert on economics from the Catholic Center Party, to become chancellor. Brüning was to spearhead a hard-nosed, deflationary economic program intended to stimulate exports by lowering prices. Like most of the German middle classes, Brüning feared inflation, disliked unemployment insurance, and believed that Germany could not afford public works projects to pump up demand—the obvious alternative to his deflationary policy. But when he presented his program to the Reichstag, he encountered opposition not only from those on the left but also from conservatives, eager to undermine the republic altogether. As a result, Brüning could get no parliamentary majority. Rather than resigning or seeking a compromise, he invoked Article 48, the emergency provision of the Weimar constitution, which enabled him to govern under presidential decree.

When this expedient provoked strenuous protests, Brüning dissolved the Reichstag and scheduled new elections for September 1930. At this point there was still some chance that a more conciliatory tack would have enabled the chancellor to build a new parliamentary majority—and save parliamentary government. The Socialists were seeking to be more cooperative in the face of the deepening economic crisis and the prospect of new parliamentary elections, which, under these difficult circumstances, seemed to invite trouble. However, Brüning persisted, believing the electorate would vindicate him.

In fact, the outcome of the elections of September 1930 was disastrous—for Brüning, and ultimately for Germany as well. While two of the democratic, pro-Weimar parties lost heavily, the two extremes, the Communists and the Nazis, improved their totals considerably. Indeed, this was a major breakthrough for the Nazis, whose share of the vote jumped from 2.6 percent to 18.3 percent of the total.

Brüning continued to govern, still relying on President Hindenburg and Article 48 rather than majority support in the Reichstag. But his program of raising taxes and decreasing government spending failed to revive the economy. Meanwhile, the growth of the political extremes helped fuel an intensification of the political violence and street fighting that had bedeviled the Weimar Republic from the beginning. As scuffles between Nazis and Communists sometimes approached pitched battles, the inability of the government to keep order further damaged the prestige of the republic. And as the crisis deepened in 1932, conservative fears of a Marxist outcome played into Hitler's hands.

By this point, conservatives close to Hindenburg sensed the chance to replace the fragmented parliamentary system with some form of authoritarian government. A new, tougher regime would not only attack the economic crisis but also stiffen governmental resistance against the apparent threat from the extreme left. In May 1932 those advisers finally persuaded Hindenburg to dump Brüning, and two of them, Franz von Papen° (1878–1969) and General Kurt von Schleicher° (1882–1934), each got a chance to govern in the months that followed. But neither succeeded, partly because of the daring strategy Hitler adopted.

When, following the ouster of Brüning, new elections were held in July 1932, the Nazis won 37.3 percent of the vote and the Communists 14.3 percent. Together, the two extremes controlled a majority of the seats in the Reichstag. Hitler, as the leader of what was now the Reichstag's largest party, refused to join any coalition—unless he could lead it as chancellor. Meanwhile, the authoritarian conservatives around President Hindenburg wanted to take advantage of the Nazis' mass support for antidemocratic purposes. Finally, in January 1933, with government at an impasse, Papen lined up a new coalition that he proposed to Hindenburg to replace Schleicher's government. Hitler would be chancellor, Papen himself vice chancellor, and Alfred Hugenberg (1865–1951), the leader of the Nationalist Party, finance minister. For months, Hindenburg had resisted giving Hitler a chance to govern, but he felt this combination might work to establish a parliamentary majority, to box out the left and to contain Nazism. So Hindenburg named Hitler Germany's chancellor on January 30, 1933.

It became clear virtually at once that the outcome of the crisis was a dramatic change of regime, the triumph of Hitler and Nazism. But though the Nazis had always wanted to destroy the Weimar Republic, they were not directly responsible for overthrowing it. The rise of Nazism was more a symptom than a cause of the crisis of Weimar democracy.

In one sense, the Weimar Republic collapsed from within, largely because the German people disagreed fundamentally about priorities after the war—and then again with the onset of the Depression. Thus the new democracy produced unstable government based on multiparty coalitions, and it fell into virtual paralysis when faced with the economic crisis by 1930. At the same time, however, those around Hindenburg were particularly quick to begin undercutting democratic government in 1930, as the economic crisis seemed to intensify the threat from the extreme left.

As unemployment grew during the first years of the 1930s, both the Nazis and the Communists gained electoral support, but the Germans voting for the Nazis were not simply those most threatened economically. Nor did

Papen (PAH-pin) **Schleicher** (SHLY-shur)

Initial Steps in the Nazi Revolution   On May 10, 1933, just months after Hitler came to power, university students in Berlin parade toward the plaza in front of the opera house where, in a huge bonfire, they would burn books by Jews and others deemed incompatible with the spirit of the National Socialist revolution. Comparable book burnings took place that night in university towns all over Germany.   *(akg-images)*

the Nazi Party appeal primarily to the uneducated or socially marginal. Rather, the party served as a focus of opposition for those growing alienated from the Weimar Republic itself. Although the Nazis did relatively poorly among Catholics and industrial workers, they put together a broad, fairly diverse base of electoral support, ranging from artisans and small shopkeepers to university students and civil servants. But though Hitler was clearly anti-Weimar, anticommunist, and anti-Versailles, his positive program remained vague, so those who voted for the Nazis were not clear what they might be getting. In light of economic depression and political impasse, however, it seemed time to try something new.

The Consolidation of Hitler's Power, 1933–1934

When Hitler became chancellor, it was not obvious that a change of regime was beginning. Like his predecessors,

he could govern only with the president's approval, and governmental institutions like the army, the judiciary, and the diplomatic corps, though hardly bastions of democracy, were not in the hands of committed Nazis. But even though an element of caution and cultivated ambiguity remained, a revolution quickly began, creating a new regime, the Third Reich.

On February 23, just weeks after Hitler became chancellor, a fire engulfed the Reichstag building in Berlin. It was set by a young Dutch communist acting on his own, but it seemed to suggest that a communist uprising was imminent. This sense of emergency gave the new Hitler government an excuse to restrict civil liberties and imprison leftist leaders, including the entire Communist parliamentary delegation. Even in this atmosphere of crisis, the Nazis could not win a majority in the Reichstag elections of March 5. But support from the Nationalists and the Catholic Center Party enabled the Nazis to win Reichstag approval for an enabling act granting Hitler the power to make laws on his own for the next four years, bypassing both the Reichstag and the president.

Although the Weimar Republic was never formally abolished, the laws that followed fundamentally altered government, politics, and public life in Germany. The other parties were either outlawed or persuaded to dissolve, so that in July 1933 the Nazi Party was declared the only legal party. When President Hindenburg died in August 1934, the offices of chancellor and president were merged, and Germany had just one leader, Adolf Hitler, holding unprecedented power. Members of the German armed forces now swore loyalty to him personally.

During this period of power consolidation, Hitler acted decisively but carefully, generally accenting normalization. To be sure, his methods occasionally gave conservatives pause, most notably when he had several hundred people murdered in the "blood purge" of June 30, 1934. But this purge was directed especially against the SA, led by Ernst Röhm (1887–1934), who had had pretensions of controlling the army. His removal seemed evidence that Hitler was taming the radical elements in his own movement. In fact, however, this purge led to the ascendancy of the *Schutzstaffel*, or SS, the select Nazi elite, led by Heinrich Himmler (1900–1945). Linked to the Gestapo, the secret political police, the SS became the institutional basis for the most troubling aspects of Nazism.

Hitler's World-View and the Dynamics of Nazi Practice

In achieving the chancellorship and in expanding his power thereafter, Hitler showed himself an adept politician, but he was hardly a mere opportunist, seeking to amass power for its own sake. Power was only the instrument for the grandiose transformation he believed necessary. And the most troubling aspects of Nazism, from personal dictatorship to the eventual effort to exterminate the Jews of Europe, stemmed from an overall vision of the world that radiated from Hitler himself. It had coalesced in Hitler's mind by about 1924.

This is not to say that Hitler was an original thinker or that his ideas were true—or even plausible. But he sought to make systematic sense of things, and the most disturbing features of his political activity stemmed directly from the resulting world-view. His most committed followers shared certain of his ideas, although fanatical loyalty to Hitler himself was more important for some of them. The central components of Hitler's thinking—geopolitics, biological racism, anti-Semitism, and Social Darwinism— were by no means specifically German. They could be found all over the Western world by the early twentieth century.

Geopolitics claimed to offer a scientific understanding of world power relationships based on geographical determinism. In his writings of the 1920s, Hitler warned that Germany faced imminent decline unless it confronted its geopolitical limitations. To remain fully sovereign in the emerging new era of global superpowers like the United States, Germany would have to act quickly to expand its territory. Otherwise it would end up like Switzerland or the Netherlands.

For decades German imperialists had argued about whether Germany was better advised to seek overseas colonies or to expand its reach in Europe. As Hitler saw it, Germany's failure to make a clear choice had led to its defeat in World War I. Now choice was imperative, and current geopolitical thinking suggested the direction for expansion. Far-flung empires relying on naval support were said to be in decline. The future lay with land-based states—unified, geographically contiguous, with the space necessary for self-sufficiency. By expanding eastward into Poland and the Soviet Union, Germany could conquer the living space, or *Lebensraum*, necessary for agricultural-industrial balance—and ultimately for self-sufficiency.

Though limited and mechanistic, this geopolitical way of thinking is at least comprehensible, in light of the German vulnerabilities that had become evident during World War I. The other three strands of Hitler's world-view were much less plausible, though each had become prominent during the second half of the nineteenth century. Biological racism insisted that built-in racial characteristics determine what is most important about any individual. Anti-Semitism went beyond racism in claiming that Jews had played, and continued to play, a special and negative role in history. The fact that the Jews were dispersed and often landless indicated that they were different—and parasitical. Finally, Social Darwinism, especially in its German incarnation, accented the positive role of struggle—not among individuals, as in a prominent American strand, but among racial groups.

The dominant current of racist thinking labeled the "Aryans" as healthy, creative, superior. Originally the Sanskrit term for "noble," *Aryan* gradually came to indicate the ancient language assumed to have been the common source of the modern Indo-European languages. An Aryan was simply a speaker of one of those languages. By the late nineteenth century, however, the term had become supremely ill defined. In much racist thinking, Germanic peoples were somehow especially Aryan, but race mixing had produced impurity—and thus degeneration. Success in struggle with the other races was the ultimate measure of vitality, the only proof of racial superiority for the future.

Hitler brought these themes together by emphasizing that humanity is not special, but simply part of nature, subject to the same laws of struggle and selection as the other animal species. Humanitarian ideals are thus dangerous illusions. As he put it to a group of officer cadets in 1944:

> Nature is always teaching us . . . that she is governed by the principle of selection: that victory is to the strong and that the weak must go to the wall. She teaches us that what may seem cruel to us, because it affects us personally or because we have been brought up in ignorance of her laws, is nevertheless often essential if a higher way of life is to be attained. Nature . . . knows nothing of the notion of humanitarianism, which signifies that the weak must at all costs be protected and preserved even at the expense of the strong.
>
> Nature does not see in weakness any extenuating reasons . . . on the contrary, weakness calls for condemnation.[3]

To Hitler, the Jews were not simply another of the races involved in this endless struggle. Rather, as landless parasites, they embodied the principles—from humanitarianism to class struggle—that were antithetical to the healthy natural struggle among unified racial groups. "Jewishness" was bound up with the negative, critical intellect that dared suggest things ought to be not natural but just, even that it was up to human beings to change the world, to make it just. The Jews were the virus keeping the community from a healthy natural footing. Marxist communism, embodying divisive class struggle as well as utopian humanitarian ideals, was fundamentally Jewish.

The central features of Nazism in practice, from personal dictatorship to the extermination of the Jews, followed from Hitler's view of the world. First, the racial community must organize itself politically for this ceaseless struggle. Individuals are but instruments for the success of the racial community. Parliamentary democracy, reflecting short-term individual interests, fosters selfish materialism and division, thereby weakening that community. The political order must rest instead on a charismatic leader, united with the whole people through bonds of common blood.

Nazi Aims and German Society

Although Hitler's world-view provided the underlying momentum for the Nazi regime, it did not specify a con-

sistent program that could be implemented all at once. Moreover, the regime sometimes found it necessary to adopt short-term expedients that conflicted with its long-term aims. Thus it was possible for Germans living under Nazi rule in the 1930s to embrace aspects of Nazism in practice without seeing where it was all leading.

To create a genuine racial community, or *Volksgemeinschaft,* it was necessary to unify society and instill Nazi values, thereby making the individual feel part of the whole—and ultimately an instrument to serve the whole. This entailed more or less forced participation in an array of Nazi groupings, from the Women's Organization to the Hitler Youth, from the Labor Front to the

Hitler and Children   Adolf Hitler was often portrayed as the friend of children. This photograph accompanied a story for an elementary school reader that described how Hitler, told it was this young girl's birthday, picked her from a crowd of well-wishers to treat her "to cake and strawberries with thick, sweet cream."   *(From* Jugend um Hitler. *Heinrich Hoffman © "Zeitgeschichte" Verlag und Vertriebs-Gesellschaft Berlin. Reproduced with permission. Photo courtesy Wiener Library, London)*

Strength Through Joy leisure-time organization. Common participation meant shared experiences such as weekend hikes and a weekly one-dish meal. Even the most ordinary, once-private activities took on a public or political dimension. Moreover, the Nazis devised unprecedented ways to stage-manage public life, using rituals like the Hitler salute, symbols like the swastika, new media like radio and film, and carefully orchestrated party rallies—all in an effort to foster this sense of belonging. (See the feature "Weighing the Evidence: Film as Propaganda" on pages 944–945.)

The Nazi regime enjoyed considerable popular support, but even after Hitler was well entrenched in power, most Germans did not grasp the regime's deeper dynamic. Some welcomed the sense of unity, the feeling of belonging and participation, especially after what had seemed the alienation and divisiveness of the Weimar years. Moreover, Hitler himself was immensely popular, partly because of his personal charisma, partly because his apparently decisive leadership was a welcome departure from the near paralysis of the Weimar parliamentary system. But most important, before the coming of war in 1939, he seemed to go from success to success, surmounting the Depression and repudiating the major terms of the hated Versailles treaty.

Hitler's propaganda minister, Joseph Goebbels (1897–1945), played on these successes to create a "Hitler myth," which made Hitler seem at once a hero and a man of the people, even the embodiment of healthy German ideals against the excesses and corruption that could be attributed to the Nazi Party. This myth became central to the Nazi regime, but it merely provided a façade behind which the real Hitler could pursue partially hidden, longer-term aims. These aims were not publicized directly because the German people did not seem ready for them. In this sense, then, support for Hitler and his regime was broad but shallow during the 1930s.

Moreover, resistance increased as the regime became more intrusive. Youth gangs actively opposed the official Hitler Youth organization as it became more overbearing and militaristic by the late 1930s. But people resisted especially by minimizing their involvement with the regime, retreating into the private realm, in response to the Nazi attempt to make everything public.

Did such people feel constantly under threat of the Gestapo, the secret police? In principle, the Gestapo could interpret the will of the *Führer*, or leader, and decide whether any individual citizen was "guilty" or not. And the Gestapo was not concerned about due process; on occasion it simply bypassed the regular court system. But the Gestapo did not terrorize Germans at random.

Its victims were generally members of specific groups, people suspected of active opposition, or people who protected those the Gestapo had targeted.

Moreover, changes and contradictions in Nazi goals allowed considerable space for personal choice. During the struggle for power, the Nazis had emphasized the woman's role as wife and mother and deplored the ongoing emancipation of women. Once Hitler came to power, concerns about unemployment reinforced these views. (See the box "Reading Sources: The Nazi Revolution and the Role of Women.") Almost immediately Hitler's government began offering interest-free loans to help couples set up housekeeping if the woman agreed to leave the labor force. Such efforts to increase the German birthrate reinforced the emphasis on child rearing in Nazi women's organizations. Nonetheless, the size of the family continued to decrease in Germany as elsewhere in the industrialized world during the 1930s.

Beginning in 1936, when rapid rearmament began to produce labor shortages, the regime did an about-face and began seeking to attract women back to the workplace, especially into jobs central to military preparation. These efforts were not notably successful, and by 1940 the military was calling for the conscription of women into war industries.

Further, the Nazis valued the family only insofar as it was congruent with the "health" of the racial community, and efforts to promote that health also compromised traditional family values. The regime regulated marriage and sought actively to eliminate the "unhealthy," those deemed unfit. Just months after coming to power in 1933, Hitler brushed aside the objections of Vice Chancellor Franz von Papen, a Catholic, and engineered a law mandating the compulsory sterilization of persons suffering from certain allegedly hereditary diseases. Medical personnel sterilized some 400,000 people, the vast majority of them "Aryan" Germans, during the Nazi years.

Hitler's regime also began immediately to single out the Jews, although Nazi Jewish policy remained an improvised hodgepodge prior to World War II. Within weeks after Hitler became chancellor in 1933, new restrictions limited Jewish participation in the civil service, in the professions, and in German cultural life—and quickly drew censure from the League of Nations. The Nuremberg Laws, announced at a party rally in 1935, included prohibition of sexual relations and marriage between Jews and non-Jewish Germans. Beginning in 1938, the Jews had to carry special identification cards and to add "Sarah" or "Israel" to their given names.

But though Hitler and other Nazi leaders claimed periodically to be seeking a definitive solution to Germany's

READING SOURCES

THE NAZI REVOLUTION AND THE ROLE OF WOMEN

Hitler and the Nazis trumpeted a highly traditionalist conception of women's roles. In doing so, they were reacting sharply against the emancipation of women that had been a hallmark of the 1920s, especially in Germany. Although a shortage of labor would force some compromise later in the decade, Hitler made the official Nazi view of women unmistakably clear in a speech to the women's section of the Nazi Party on September 8, 1934.

The slogan "Emancipation of women" was invented by Jewish intellectuals and its content was formed by the same spirit. In the really good times of German life the German woman had no need to emancipate herself. She possessed exactly what nature had necessarily given her to administer and preserve; just as the man in his good times had no need to fear that he would be ousted from his position in relation to the woman.

In fact the woman was least likely to challenge his position. Only when he was not absolutely certain in his knowledge of his task did the eternal instinct of self and race-preservation begin to rebel in women. There then grew from this rebellion a state of affairs which was unnatural and which lasted until both sexes returned to the respective spheres which an eternally wise providence had preordained for them.

If the man's world is said to be the State, his struggle, his readiness to devote his powers to the service of the community, then it may perhaps be said that the woman's is a smaller world. For her world is her husband, her family, her children, and her home. But what would become of the greater world if there were no one to tend and care for the smaller one? . . . Only on the basis of this smaller world can the man's world be formed and built up. The two worlds are not antagonistic. They complement each other, they belong together just as man and woman belong together.

We do not consider it correct for the woman to interfere in the world of the man, in his main sphere. We consider it natural if these two worlds remain distinct. To the one belongs the strength of feeling, the strength of the soul. To the other belongs the strength of vision, of toughness, of decision, and of the willingness to act. In the one case this strength demands the willingness of the woman to risk her life to preserve this important cell and to multiply it, and in the other case it demands from the man the readiness to safeguard life.

The sacrifices which the man makes in the struggle of his nation, the woman makes in the preservation of that nation in individual cases. What the man gives in courage on the battlefield, the woman gives in eternal self-sacrifice, in eternal pain and suffering. Every child that a woman brings into the world is a battle, a battle waged for the existence of her people. And both must therefore mutually value and respect each other when they see that each performs the task that Nature and Providence have ordained. And this mutual respect will necessarily result from this separation of the functions of each.

It is not true, as Jewish intellectuals assert, that respect depends on the overlapping of the spheres of activity of the sexes; this respect demands that neither sex should try to do that which belongs to the sphere of the other. It lies in the last resort in the fact that each knows that the other is doing everything necessary to maintain the whole community. . . .

So our women's movement is for us not something which inscribes on its banner as its programme the fight against men, but something which has as its programme the common fight together with men. For the new National Socialist national community acquires a firm basis precisely because we have gained the trust of millions of women as fanatical fellow-combatants, women who have fought for the common life in the service of the common task of preserving life, who in that combat did not set their sights on the rights which a Jewish intellectualism put before their eyes, but rather on the duties imposed by nature on all of us in common.

Source: *Nazism: A History in Documents and Eyewitness Accounts, 1919–1945*, vol. 2, *State Economy and Society, 1933–1939*, edited by J. Noakes and G. Pridham, new edition with index, pp. 255–256. Copyright © 2000. Reprinted by permission of the University of Exeter Press.

"Jewish problem," the dominant objective during the 1930s was to force German Jews to emigrate. About 60,000 of Germany's 550,000 Jews left the country during 1933 and 1934, and perhaps 25 percent had gotten out by 1938. The fact that the regime stripped emigrating Jews of their assets made emigration more difficult. Potential host countries, concerned about unemployment during the Depression, were especially unwilling to take in substantial numbers of Jews if they were penniless.

On November 9, 1938, using the assassination of a German diplomat in Paris as a pretext, the Nazis staged the *Kristallnacht* (Crystal Night) pogrom, during which almost all the synagogues in Germany and about seven thousand Jewish-owned stores were destroyed. Between 30,000 and 50,000 relatively prosperous Jews were arrested and forced to emigrate after their property was confiscated. Although the German public had generally acquiesced in the earlier restrictions on Jews, this pogrom, with its wanton violation of private property, shocked many Germans.

Concentration camps—supplementary detention centers—had become a feature of the Nazi regime virtually at once, but prior to 1938 they were used primarily to hold political prisoners. As part of the Crystal Night pogrom, about 35,000 Jews were rounded up and sent to the camps, but most were soon released as long as they could document their intention to emigrate. When World War II began in 1939, the total camp population was about 25,000. The systematic physical extermination of the Jews began only during World War II.

However, the killing of others deemed superfluous or threatening to the racial community began earlier, with the so-called euthanasia program initiated under volunteer medical teams in 1939. Its aim was to eliminate chronic mental patients, the incurably ill, and people with severe physical handicaps. Those subject to such treatment were overwhelmingly ethnic Germans, not Jews or foreigners. Although the regime did all it could to make it appear the victims had died naturally, a public outcry developed, especially among relatives and church leaders by 1941, when the program was largely discontinued. But by then it had claimed 100,000 lives and seems essentially to have achieved its initial objectives.

This "euthanasia" program was based on the sense, fundamental to radical Nazism, that war was the norm and readiness for war the essential societal imperative. In war, societies send individuals to their deaths and, on the battlefield, make difficult distinctions among the wounded, letting some die in order to save those most likely to survive and return to battle. Struggle necessitates selection, which requires overcoming humanitarian scruples—especially the notion that "weakness" calls for special protection. Thus it was desirable to kill even ethnic Germans who were deemed unfit, as "life unworthy of life."

Preparation for war was the core of Nazism in practice. The conquest of living space in the east would make possible a more advantageous agricultural-industrial balance. The result would be not only the self-sufficiency necessary for sovereignty but also the land-rootedness necessary for racial health. Such a war of conquest would strike not only the allegedly inferior Slavic peoples of the region but also detested communism, centered in the Soviet Union.

The point of domestic reorganization was to marshal the community's energies and resources for war. Because German business interests generally seemed congruent with Nazi purposes, Nazi aims did not appear to require some revolutionary assault on business elites or the capitalist economy. But the Nazis had their own road to travel, and beginning in 1936 they proved quite prepared to bend the economy, and to coordinate big business, to serve their longer-term aims of war-making.

The Nazi drive toward war during the 1930s transformed international relations in Europe. The other European powers sought to understand Hitler's Germany in terms of the increasingly polarized political context of the period. Before considering the fortunes of Hitler's foreign policy, we must consider fascism as a wider phenomenon—and the efforts of the democracies, on the one hand, and the Soviet Union, on the other, to come to terms with it.

FASCIST CHALLENGE AND ANTIFASCIST RESPONSE, 1934–1939

COMMUNISM, fascism, and Nazism all repudiated the parliamentary democracy that had been the West's political norm. Each seemed subject to violence and excess, yet each had features that some found attractive, especially in light of the difficult socioeconomic circumstances of the 1930s. But communists and adherents of the various forms of fascism were bitterly hostile to each other, and the very presence of these new political systems caused polarization all over Europe.

Beginning in 1934 communists sought to join with anyone who would work with them to defend the democratic framework against further fascist assaults. Without democracy, the very survival of communist parties was in doubt. This effort led to new antifascist coalition governments in Spain and France. In each case, however, the Depression restricted maneuvering room, and these governments ended up furthering the polarization they were seeking to avoid. By mid-1940, democracy had fallen in Spain, after a brutal civil war, and even in France, in the wake of military defeat.

European Fascism and the Popular Front Response

Although fascism attracted some of those elsewhere who were disaffected with democracy and hostile to communism, the line between fascism and conservative authoritarianism blurred in the volatile political climate of the 1930s. To some, any retreat from democracy appeared a step toward fascism.

In east-central Europe, political distinctions became especially problematic. Movements like the Arrow Cross in Hungary and the Legion of the Archangel Michael in Romania modeled themselves on the Italian and German prototypes, but they never achieved political power. Those who controlled the antidemocratic governments in Hungary and Romania, as in Poland, Bulgaria, and Yugoslavia, were authoritarian traditionalists, not fascists. Still, many government leaders in the region welcomed the closer economic ties with Germany that Hitler's economics minister, Hjalmar Schacht, engineered. The difference between authoritarianism and fascism remained clearest in Austria, where Catholic conservatives undermined democracy during 1933 and 1934. They were actively hostile to the growing pro-Nazi agitation in Austria, partly because they wanted to keep Austria independent.

In France various nationalist, anticommunist, and anti-Semitic leagues gathered momentum during the early 1930s. They covered a spectrum from monarchism to outspoken pro-fascism, but together they constituted at least a potential threat to French democracy. In February 1934, right-wing demonstrations against the Chamber of Deputies provoked a bloody clash with police and forced a change of ministry. As it began to seem that even France might be vulnerable, those from the center and left of the political spectrum began to consider collaborating to resist fascism. The Communists, especially, took the initiative by promoting "popular fronts" of all those seeking to preserve democracy.

This was a dramatic change in strategy for international communism. Even as Hitler was closing in on the German chancellorship in the early 1930s, German Communists, following Comintern policy, continued to attack their socialist rivals rather than seek a unified response to Nazism. From the communist perspective,

Ideological Confrontation   At a major international exhibition in Paris in 1937, the new antidemocratic political regimes of the interwar period made bold propaganda statements. With a sculpture from fascist Italy's pavilion in the foreground, we look across the Seine River to a classic representation of the ideological warfare of the 1930s: the Soviet Pavilion, on the left, facing the German Pavilion, on the right. *(AP/Wide World Photos)*

fascism represented the crisis phase of monopoly capitalism, so a Nazi government would actually be useful to strip away the democratic façade hiding class oppression in Germany. But by 1934 the threat of fascism seemed so pressing that Communists began actively promoting electoral alliances and governing coalitions with socialists and even liberal democrats to resist its further spread. From 1934 until 1939, Communists everywhere consistently pursued this "popular front" strategy.

By the 1930s, however, it was becoming ever harder to know what was fascist, what was dangerous, what might lead where. As fears intensified, perceptions became as important as realities. Popular front governments, intended to preserve democracy against what appeared to be fascism, could seem to conservatives to be leaning too far to the left. Ideological polarization made democracy extraordinarily difficult. The archetypal example proved to be Spain, where a tragedy of classical proportions was played out.

From Democracy to Civil War in Spain, 1931–1939

Spain became a center of attention in the 1930s, when its promising new parliamentary democracy, launched in 1931, led to civil war in 1936 and the triumph of a repressive authoritarian regime in 1939. An earlier effort at constitutional monarchy had fizzled by 1923, when King Alfonso XIII (1886–1941) supported a new military dictatorship. But growing opposition led first to the resignation of the dictator in 1930 and then, in April 1931, to the end of the monarchy and the proclamation of a republic. The elections for a constituent assembly that followed in June produced a solid victory for a coalition of liberal democrats and Socialists, as well as much hope for substantial reform.

A significant agrarian reform law was passed in 1932, but partly because of the difficult economic context, the new government was slow to implement it. Feeling betrayed, Socialists and agricultural workers became increasingly radical, producing growing upheaval in the countryside. Radicalism on the left made it harder for the moderates to govern and, at the same time, stimulated conservatives to become more politically active.

A right-wing coalition known as the CEDA, led by José Maria Gil Robles° (1898–1980), grew in strength, becoming the largest party in parliament with the elections of November 1933. In light of its parliamentary strength, the CEDA had a plausible claim to a government role, but it was kept from participation in government until October 1934. It seemed to the left, in the ideologically charged atmosphere of the time, that the growing role of the CEDA was a prelude to fascism. To let the CEDA into the government would be to hand the republic over to its enemies.

A strong Catholic from the traditional Spanish right, Gil Robles refused to endorse the democratic republic as a form of government, but he and the CEDA were willing to work within it. So the Spanish left may have been too quick to see the CEDA as fascist—and to react when the CEDA finally got its government role. However, Mussolini and Hitler had each come to power more or less legally, from within parliamentary institutions. The German left had been criticized for its passive response to the advent of Hitler; the Spanish left wanted to avoid the same mistake.

Thus, when the CEDA finally got a role in the government, the left responded during the fall of 1934 with quasi-revolutionary uprisings in Catalonia and Asturias, where a miners' commune was put down only after two weeks of heavy fighting. In the aftermath, the right-leaning government of 1935 began undoing some of the reforms of the left-leaning government of 1931–1933, though still legally, within the framework of the parliamentary republic.

In February 1936 a popular front coalition to ward off fascism won a narrow electoral victory, sufficient for an absolute majority in parliament. As would be true in France a few months later, electoral victory produced popular expectations that went well beyond the essentially defensive purposes of the popular front. Hoping to win back the leftist rank and head off what seemed a dangerous attempt at revolution, the new popular front government began to implement a progressive program, now including the land reform that had been promised but not implemented earlier. But it was too late to undercut the growing radicalization of the masses.

A wave of land seizures began in March 1936, followed by the most extensive strike movement in Spanish history, which by June was becoming clearly revolutionary in character. To many, the government's inability to keep order had become the immediate issue. By the early summer of 1936, leaders of the democratic republic had become isolated between the extremes of left and right, each preparing an extralegal solution.

Finally, in mid-July, several army officers initiated a military uprising against the government. Soon led by General Francisco Franco (1892–1975), these Nationalist insurgents took control of substantial parts of Spain. Elsewhere they failed to overcome the resistance of the Republicans, or Loyalists, those determined to defend the republic. So the result was not the intended military takeover but a brutal civil war (see Map 27.1). The substantial Italian fascist and Nazi German intervention on the Nationalist side by the end of 1936 intensified the war's ideological ramifications. At the same time, the remarkable, often heroic resistance of the Loyalists captured the imagination of the world. Indeed, forty thousand volunteers came from abroad to fight to preserve the Spanish republic.

It proved a war of stunning brutality on both sides. Loyalist anticlericalism led to the murder of twelve bishops and perhaps one-eighth of the parish clergy in Spain.

Gil Robles (heel ROH-blayce)

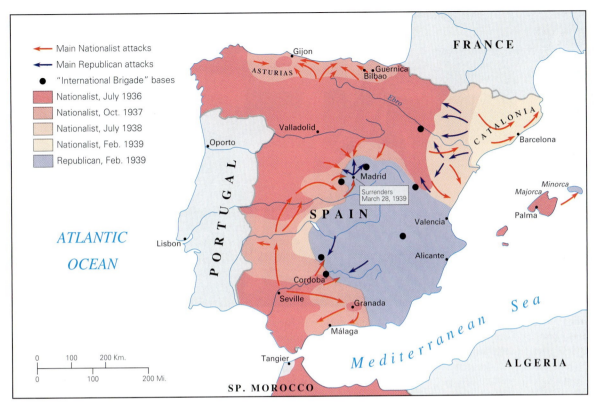

Map 27.1   The Spanish Civil War, 1936–1939   The Nationalist insurgents quickly took over most of northern and eastern Spain in 1936 and then gradually expanded their territory. The fall of Madrid early in 1939 marked the end of the fighting. The revolutionary effort of 1936 and 1937 within the Republican zone was centered in Barcelona.   *(Source: Adapted from* The Times Atlas of World History, *3d ed. Reprinted by permission of HarperCollins Publishers Ltd.)*

On the other side, the German bombing of the Basque town of Guernica° on a crowded market day in April 1937, represented unforgettably in Pablo Picasso's painting, came to symbolize the violence and suffering of the whole era.

Republican Loyalists assumed that Franco and the Nationalists represented another instance of fascism. In fact, however, Franco was no fascist, but rather a traditional military man whose leadership role did not rest on personal charisma. He was an authoritarian emphasizing discipline, order, and Spain's Catholic traditions.

Still, in their effort to rally support during the civil war, Franco's forces found it expedient to take advantage of the appeal of the Falange°, a genuinely fascist movement that had emerged under the leadership of the charismatic young José Antonio Primo de Rivera (1903–1936). Although extremely weak at the time of the elec-

---

Guernica (gher-NEE-kah, in Spanish; GWAIR-nee-kah, as customarily rendered in English)   **Falange** (fah-LAHN-hay)

tions in February 1936, the Falange grew rapidly in opposition to the leftist radicalism that followed the popular front victory. As street fighting between left and right intensified that spring, the republic arrested José Antonio, as he was called, and he was in prison when the civil war began.

José Antonio decided that his best hope was alliance with the military. Although he was contemptuous of their shortsighted conservatism, he felt that their very absence of ideas afforded an opening for the Falange to provide direction, a genuine alternative. But it worked out the other way. In November 1936, the government tried and executed José Antonio for conspiring to overthrow the republic. The Nationalists promptly began invoking his memory, and using other trappings of the Falange, to increase their popular appeal.

Meanwhile, the republic's leaders had to fight a civil war while dealing with continuing revolution in their own ranks. Developing especially in Catalonia from the uprisings of 1936, that revolution was not communist

Picasso: Guernica   Created for the Spanish Pavilion at the famed 1937 Paris Exhibition, Picasso's painting conveys horror and outrage—his response to the German bombing of Guernica on a crowded market day in 1937, during the Spanish civil war. Picasso's stark, elemental imagery helped define this era of violence and suffering for the generations that followed.   *(Pablo Picasso,* Guernica *[1937, May–early June]. Oil on canvas. Art Resource, NY. © 2002 Artists Rights Society [ARS], New York/ADAGP, Paris)*

but anarchist and syndicalist in orientation. The Communists, true to popular front principles, insisted that this was no time for such "infantile leftist" revolutionary experiments. What mattered, throughout the Republican zone, was the factory discipline necessary to produce essential war materiel. So the Communists, under Stalin's orders, were instrumental in putting down the anarchist revolution in Catalonia in June 1937.

Under these extraordinary circumstances, the Communists, at first a distinct minority on the Spanish left, gradually gained ascendancy on the Republican side, partly because they were disciplined and effective, partly because Soviet assistance enhanced their prestige. However, this single-minded prosecution of the civil war did not prove enough to defeat the military insurgency, despite the considerable heroism on the Loyalist side. The war ended with the fall of Madrid to the Nationalists in March 1939. General Franco's authoritarian regime governed Spain until his death in 1975.

In Spain, as in Weimar Germany, the lack of consensus in a new republic made parliamentary democracy difficult, and the wider ideological framework magnified the difficulties. With the political boiling point so low, the left and the right each saw the other in extreme terms and assumed that extraordinary response to the other was necessary. Thus the left tended to view even con-

servatives operating within a parliamentary framework as "fascist," and both sides were relatively quick to give up on a democratic republic that seemed to be tilting too far in the wrong direction.

France in the Era of the Popular Front

In France, as in Spain, concern to arrest the spread of fascism led to a popular front coalition, here including Socialists, Communists, and Radicals, that governed the country from 1936 to 1938. Although it did not lead to civil war, the popular front was central to the French experience of the 1930s, producing polarization and resignation and undermining confidence in the Third Republic.

Beginning in 1934, the French Communists took the initiative in approaching first the Socialists, then the Radicals, to develop a popular front coalition against fascism. In reaching out to the Radicals, the Communists stressed French patriotism and made no demand for significant economic reforms. Stalin gave this effort a major push in 1935 when, in a stunning change in the communist line, he stressed the legitimacy of national defense and explicitly endorsed French rearmament.

In the elections of April and May 1936, the popular front won a sizable majority in the Chamber of Deputies, putting the Socialists' leader, Léon Blum (1872–1950), in line to become France's first Socialist prime minister. The Communists pledged full support of the new Blum government, but to avoid fanning fears, they did not participate directly. However, despite the popular front's moderate and essentially defensive aims, the situation quickly began to polarize after the elections.

Fearing that the new Blum government would be forced to devalue the French currency, and thereby diminish the value of assets denominated in francs, French investors immediately began moving their capital abroad. At the same time, the popular front victory produced a wave of enthusiasm among workers that escaped the control of popular front leaders and culminated in a spontaneous strike movement, the largest France had ever seen. By early June it had spread to all major industries nationwide. Although the workers' demands—for collective bargaining, a forty-hour workweek, and paid vacations—were not extraordinary, the movement involved sit-down strikes as well as the normal walkouts and thus seemed quasi-revolutionary in character. The major trade union confederation, the Communists, and most Socialists, including Blum himself, saw the strikes as a danger to the popular front, with its more modest aims of defending the republic, and eagerly pursued a settlement.

That settlement, the Matignon° Agreement of June 8, 1936, was a major victory for the French working class. Having been genuinely frightened by the strikes and now reassured that the popular front government would at least uphold the law, French industrialists were willing to make significant concessions. So the workers got collective bargaining, elected shop stewards, and wage increases as a direct result of Matignon, then a forty-hour workweek and paid vacations in a reform package promptly passed by the parliament.

In the enthusiasm of the summer of 1936, other reforms were enacted as well, but after that the popular front was forced onto the defensive. Two problems undermined its energy and cohesion: the noncooperation of French business and the Spanish civil war. The cautious response of Blum, the Socialist prime minister, is striking in each case, but he faced a situation with little maneuvering room.

From the outset Blum stressed that he had no mandate for revolution, and as France's first Socialist prime minister, he felt it essential to prove that a Socialist could govern responsibly. Thus Blum did not respond energetically to the capital flight, even though it produced serious currency and budgetary difficulties. Perhaps, as critics suggest, he should have acted more aggressively

Matignon (mah-tin-YAWN)

Sit-Down Strikes in France The Popular Front victory in the French elections of 1936 prompted a wave of sit-down strikes that won a forty-hour workweek and other benefits for the workers. But the strikes also proved deeply polarizing as France sought to prepare for the possible return of war. These workers have taken over a factory in a Paris suburb in June 1936. *(David Seymour/Magnum Photos)*

to overhaul the French banking and credit system. But Blum shied away from any such drastic measures, both to prove he could be moderate and to avoid antagonizing business.

Blum was also uncertain as he faced the dilemmas surrounding the Spanish civil war. The key question was whether the French government should help the beleaguered Spanish republic, at least by sending supplies. Although he initially favored such help, Blum changed his mind under pressure from three sides. The Conservative government of Stanley Baldwin in Britain was against it. So was the French right; some even suggested that French intervention would provoke a comparable civil war in France. Moreover, the Radicals in his own coalition were generally opposed to helping the Spanish republic, so intervention would jeopardize the cohesion of the popular front itself.

Thus, rather than help supply the Spanish republic, Blum promoted a nonintervention agreement among the major powers, including Italy and Germany. Many Socialists and Communists disliked Blum's cautious policy, especially as it became clear that Mussolini and Hitler were violating their hands-off pledges. As Blum stuck to nonintervention, the moral force of the popular front dissolved.

In 1938 a new government under the Radical Edouard Daladier° (1884–1970), still nominally a creature of the popular front, began dismantling some of the key gains of 1936, even attacking the forty-hour week. Citing productivity and national security concerns, Daladier adopted pro-business policies and succeeded in attracting capital back to France. But workers, watching the gains they had won in 1936 slip away, felt betrayed. At the same time, businessmen and conservatives began blaming the workers' gains—such as the five-day week— for slowing French rearmament. Although such charges were not entirely fair, they indicated how poisoned the atmosphere in France had become in the wake of the popular front.

As France began to face the possibility of a new war, the popular front was widely blamed for French weakness. When war came at last, resignation and division were prevalent, in contrast with the patriotic unity and high spirits of 1914. It was partly for that reason that France was so easily defeated by Germany in 1940. And when France fell, the democratic Third Republic fell with it.

THE COMING OF WORLD WAR II, 1935–1939

EVEN as the Great Depression added to their burdens, Western leaders faced the challenge of maintaining the peace during the 1930s. But despite the promising adjustments of the 1920s, many of the problems that accompanied the World War I peace settlement were still in place when Hitler came to power. And Hitler had consistently trumpeted his intention to overturn that settlement. What scope was there for peaceful revision? Could the threat of war stop Hitler? By the last years of the 1930s, these questions tortured the Western world as Hitler went from one success to an-

Daladier (dah-lah-dee-YAY)

other, raising the possibility of a new and more destructive war. And the power balance rested on the responses not only of the Western democracies, but of fascist Italy and the communist Soviet Union as well.

The Reorientation of Fascist Italy

During its first decade in power, Benito Mussolini's fascist regime in Italy concentrated on domestic reconstruction, especially the effort to mobilize people through their roles as producers within a new corporative state (see pages 894–895). But though corporativist institutions were gradually constructed, with great rhetorical fanfare, they bogged down in bureaucratic meddling. Corporativism proved more the vehicle for regimentation than for a more genuine kind of participation. Mussolini offered assurances that, despite the necessary compromises, fascism's corporativist revolution was continuing, but many committed fascists were sharply critical of the new system. Fascism seemed to have stalled, partly as the result of compromise with prefascist elites and institutions, and partly as the result of its own internal contradictions.

Mussolini was never merely the instrument of the established elites, but neither was he a consistent ideologue like Hitler. By the early 1930s, he sometimes seemed satisfied with ritual, spectacle, and the cult of his own infallibility as he juggled the contending forces in fascist Italy. But the limitations he had encountered on the domestic level increasingly frustrated him. On the international level, in contrast, the new context after Hitler came to power offered some welcome space for maneuver. So as the fascist revolution in Italy faltered, Mussolini concentrated increasingly on foreign policy.

Though Italy, like Germany, remained dissatisfied with the territorial status quo, it was not obvious that fascist Italy and Nazi Germany had to end up in the same camp. For one thing, Italy was anxious to preserve an independent Austria as a buffer with Germany, whereas many Germans and Austrians favored the unification of the two countries. Such a greater Germany might then threaten the gains Italy had won at the peace conference at Austria's expense. When, in 1934, Germany seemed poised to absorb Austria, Mussolini helped stiffen the resistance of Austria's leaders and played a part in forcing Hitler to back down. Mussolini even warned that Nazism, with its racist orientation, posed a significant threat to the best of European civilization.

As it began to appear that France and Britain might have to work with the Soviet Union to check Hitler's Germany, French and British conservatives pushed for good relations with Mussolini's Italy to provide ideological balance. So Italy was well positioned to play off both sides as Hitler began shaking things up on the international level after 1933. In 1935, just after Hitler announced significant rearmament measures, unilaterally repudiating provisions of the Versailles treaty for the first time, Mussolini hosted a meeting with the French and British prime ministers at Stresa, in northern Italy. In an overt warning to Hitler's Germany, the three powers agreed to resist "any unilateral repudiation of treaties which may endanger the peace of Europe."

However, Mussolini was already preparing to extend Italy's possessions in East Africa to encompass Ethiopia (formerly called Abyssinia). He assumed that the French and British, who needed his support against Hitler, would not offer significant opposition. Ethiopia had become a League of Nations member in 1923—sponsored by Italy, but opposed by Britain and France because it still practiced slavery. After a border incident in December 1934, Italian troops invaded in October 1935, prompting the League to announce sanctions against Italy.

These sanctions were applied haphazardly, largely because France and Britain wanted to avoid irreparable damage to their longer-term relations with Italy. In any case, the sanctions did not deter Mussolini, whose forces prevailed through the use of aircraft and poison gas by May 1936. But they did make Italy receptive to German overtures in the aftermath of its victory. And the victory made Mussolini more restless. Rather than seeking to play again the enviable role of European balancer, he sent Italian troops and materiel to aid the Nationalists in the Spanish civil war, thereby further alienating democratic opinion elsewhere.

Conservatives in Britain and France continued to push for accommodation with Italy, hoping to revive the "Stresa front" against Hitler. Some even defended Italian imperialism in East Africa. But Italy continued its drift toward Germany. Late in 1936 Mussolini spoke of a new Rome-Berlin Axis for the first time. During 1937 and 1938 he and Hitler exchanged visits. Finally, in May 1939, Italy joined Germany in an open-ended military alliance, the Pact of Steel, but Mussolini made it clear that Italy could not be ready for a major European war before 1943.

Partly to cement this developing relationship, fascist Italy adopted anti-Semitic racial laws, even though Italian fascism had not originally been anti-Semitic. Indeed, the party had attracted Jewish Italians to its membership in about the same proportion as non-Jews. Although the imperial venture in Ethiopia had been popular among the Italian people, the increasing subservience to Nazi Germany displeased even many committed fascists. Such opposition helped keep Mussolini from intervention when war broke out in September 1939.

Restoring German Sovereignty, 1935–1936

During his first years in power, through 1936, Hitler could be understood as merely restoring German sovereignty, revising a postwar settlement that had been misconceived in the first place. However uncouth and abrasive he might seem, it was hard to find a basis for opposing him. Yet in commencing German rearmament in 1935, and especially in remilitarizing the Rhineland in March 1936, Hitler fundamentally reversed the power balance established in France's favor at the peace conference.

France's special advantage had been the demilitarization of the entire German territory west of the Rhine River and a 50-kilometer strip on the east bank. The measure had been reaffirmed at Locarno in 1925, now with Germany's free agreement, and it was guaranteed by Britain and Italy. Yet on a Saturday morning in March 1936, that advantage disappeared as German troops moved into the forbidden area. The French and British acquiesced, uncertain of what else to do. After all, Hitler was only restoring Germany to full sovereignty.

But Hitler was not likely to stop there. As a result of the war and the peace, three new countries—Austria, Czechoslovakia, and Poland—bordered Germany (see Map 27.2). In each, the peace settlement had left trouble spots involving the status of ethnic Germans; in each, the status quo was open to question.

Austria, Czechoslovakia, and Appeasement

As early as 1934, Hitler had moved to encompass his homeland, Austria, but strenuous opposition from Italy led him to back down. The developing understanding with Italy by 1936 enabled Hitler to focus again on Austria—initiating the second, more radical phase of his prewar foreign policy. On a pretext in March 1938, German troops moved into Austria, which was promptly incorporated into Germany. This time Mussolini was willing to acquiesce, and Hitler was genuinely grateful.

The Treaty of Versailles had explicitly prohibited this *Anschluss*, or unity of Austria with Germany, though that prohibition violated the principle of self-determination. It was widely believed in the West, no doubt correctly, that most Austrians favored unity with Germany now that the Habsburg empire had broken up. The *Anschluss* could thus be justified as revising a misconceived aspect of the peace settlement.

Czechoslovakia presented quite a different situation. Although it had preserved democratic institutions, the country included restive minorities of Magyars, Ruthenians, Poles, and—concentrated especially in the Sudetenland, along the German and Austrian borders—about

Map 27.2   The Expansion of Nazi Germany, 1936–1939   Especially with the remilitarization of the Rhineland in 1936, Hitler's Germany began moving, step by step, to alter the European power balance. In September 1939 the Soviet Union also began annexing territory, capitalizing on its agreement with Germany the month before.

3.25 million Germans. After having been part of the dominant nationality in the old Habsburg empire, those Germans were frustrated with their minority status in the new Czechoslovakia. Worse, they seemed to suffer disproportionately from the Depression. Hitler's agents actively stirred up their resentments.

Leading the West's response, when Hitler began making an issue of Czechoslovakia, was Neville Chamberlain (1869–1940), who followed Stanley Baldwin as

Britain's prime minister in May 1937. An intelligent, vigorous, and public-spirited man from the progressive wing of the Conservative Party, Chamberlain has long been derided as the architect of the "appeasement" of Hitler at the Munich conference of 1938, which settled the crisis over Czechoslovakia. Trumpeted as the key to peace, the Munich agreement proved but a step to the war that broke out less than a year later. Yet though it failed, Chamberlain's policy of appeasement stemmed

The Illusion of Peace Neville Chamberlain, returning home to Britain from Munich to a hero's welcome, waves the peace declaration that was supposed to have brought "peace in our time." This was late September 1938. Less than a year later, Europe was again at war. *(Hulton Archive/Getty Images)*

not from cowardice or mere drift, and certainly not from some unspoken pro-Nazi sentiment.

Rather than let events spin out of control, as seemed to have happened in 1914, Chamberlain sought to master the difficult international situation through creative bargaining. Surely, he felt, the excesses of Hitler's policy resulted from the mistakes of Versailles; redo the settlement on a more realistic basis, and Germany would behave responsibly. The key was to pinpoint the sources of Germany's frustrations and, as Chamberlain put it, "to remove the danger spots one by one."

Moreover, in Britain as elsewhere, there were some who saw Hitler's resurgent Germany as a bulwark against communism, which might spread into east-central Europe—especially in the event of another war. Indeed, the victor in another war might well be the revolutionary left. To prevent such an outcome was worth a few concessions to Hitler.

The Czechs, led by Eduard Beneš° (1884–1948), made some attempt to liberalize their nationality policy. But by April 1938 they were becoming ever less sympathetic to Sudeten German demands for autonomy, especially as

***

Beneš (BAY-naish)

German bullying came to accompany them. Tensions between Czechoslovakia and Germany mounted, and by late September 1938 war appeared imminent, despite Chamberlain's efforts to mediate. Both the French and the British began mobilizing, with French troops manning the Maginot Line for the first time.

A 1924 treaty bound France to come to the aid of Czechoslovakia in the event of aggression. Moreover, the Soviet Union, according to a treaty of 1935, was bound to assist Czechoslovakia if the French did so. And throughout the crisis, the Soviets pushed for a strong stand in defense of Czechoslovakia against German aggression. For both ideological and military reasons, however, the British and French were reluctant to line up for war on the side of the Soviet Union. The value of the Soviet military was uncertain, at best, at a time when the Soviet officer corps had just been purged.

By September, Hitler seemed eager to smash the Czechs by force, but when Mussolini proposed a four-power conference, he was persuaded to talk again. At Munich late in September, Britain, France, Italy, and Germany settled the matter, with Czechoslovakia—and the Soviet Union—excluded. Determined not to risk war over what seemed Czech intransigence, the British ended up agreeing to what Hitler had wanted all along—not merely autonomy for the Sudeten Germans but German annexation of the Sudetenland.

The Munich agreement specified that all Sudeten areas with German majorities be transferred to Germany. Plebiscites were to be held in areas with large German minorities, and Hitler pledged to respect the sovereignty of the now diminished Czechoslovak state. Chamberlain and his French counterpart, Edouard Daladier, each returned home to a hero's welcome, having transformed what had seemed certain war to, in Chamberlain's soon-to-be-notorious phrase, "peace in our time."

Rather than settle the nationality questions bedeviling Czechoslovakia, the Munich agreement only provoked further unrest. Poland and Hungary, eager to exploit the new weakness of Czechoslovakia, agitated successfully to annex disputed areas with large numbers of their respective nationalities. Then unrest stemming from Slovak separatism afforded a pretext for Germany to send troops into Prague in March 1939. The Slovak areas were spun off as a separate nation, while the Czech areas became the Protectorate of Bohemia and Moravia. Less than six months after the Munich conference, most of what had been Czechoslovakia had landed firmly within the Nazi orbit (see Map 27.2). It was no longer possible to justify Hitler's actions as an effort to unite all Germans in one state.

Poland, the Nazi-Soviet Pact, and the Coming of War

With Poland, the German grievance was still more serious, for the new Polish state had been created partly at German expense. Especially galling to Germans was the Polish corridor, which cut off East Prussia from the bulk of Germany in order to give Poland access to the sea. The city of Danzig (now Gdansk), historically Polish but part of Germany before World War I, was left a "free city," supervised by the League of Nations.

Disillusioned by Hitler's dismemberment of Czechoslovakia and angered by the Germans' menacing rhetoric regarding Poland, Chamberlain announced to the House of Commons on March 31, 1939, that Britain and France would intervene militarily should Poland's independence be threatened. Chamberlain was not only abandoning the policy of appeasement; he was making a clear commitment to the Continent, of the sort that British governments had resisted since 1919. He could do so partly because Britain was rapidly rearming. By early 1940, in fact, Britain was spending nearly as large a share of its national income on the military as Germany was.

Chamberlain's assertive statement was not enough

to deter Hitler, who seems to have been determined to settle the Polish question by force. In an effort to localize the conflict, however, Hitler continued to insist that German aims were limited and reasonable. Germany simply wanted Danzig and German transit across the corridor; it was the Polish stance that was rigid and unreasonable. Hitler apparently believed that Polish stubbornness would alienate the British and French, undercutting their support. And as the crisis developed by mid-1939, doubts were increasingly expressed, on all sides, that the British and French were really prepared to aid Poland militarily—that they had the will "to die for Danzig."

Although they had been lukewarm to Soviet proposals for a military alliance, Britain and France began to negotiate with the Soviet Union more seriously during the spring and summer of 1939. But reservations about the value of a Soviet alliance continued to gnaw at Western leaders. For one thing, Soviet troops could gain access to Germany only by moving through Poland or Romania. But each had territory gained at the expense of Russia in the postwar settlement, so the British and French, suspicious of Soviet designs, were reluctant to insist that Soviet troops be allowed to pass through either country.

Even as negotiations between the Soviet Union and the democracies continued, the Soviets came to their own agreement with Nazi Germany on August 23, 1939, in a pact that astonished the world. Each side had been denouncing the other, and although Hitler had explored the possibility of Soviet neutrality in May, serious negotiations began only that August, when the Soviets got the clear signal that a German invasion of Poland was inevitable. It now appeared that no Soviet alliance with Britain and France could prevent war. Under these circumstances, a nonaggression pact with Germany seemed better to serve Soviet interests than a problematic war on the side of Britain and France. So the Soviets agreed with the Germans that each would remain neutral in the event that either became involved in a war with some other nation.

The Soviet flip-flop stemmed partly from disillusionment with the British and French response to the accelerating threat of Nazism. The democracies seemed no more trustworthy, and potentially no less hostile, than Nazi Germany. But the Soviets were playing their own double game. A secret protocol to the Nazi-Soviet Pact apportioned major areas of east-central Europe between the Soviet Union and Germany. As a result, the Soviets soon regained much of what they had lost after World War I, when Poland, Finland, and other states had been created or aggrandized with territories that had formerly been part of the Russian Empire.

The Nazi-Soviet Pact seemed to give Hitler the free hand he wanted in Poland. With the dramatic change in alignment, the democracies were surely much less likely to intervene. But Chamberlain, again determined to avoid the hesitations of 1914, publicly reaffirmed the British guarantee to Poland on August 25. Britain would indeed intervene if Germany attacked. And after Hitler ordered the German invasion of Poland on September 1, the British and French responded with declarations of war on September 3.

With each step on the path to war, Hitler had vacillated between apparent reasonableness and wanton aggressiveness. Sometimes he accented the plausibility of his demands in light of problems with the postwar settlement; sometimes he seemed to be actively seeking war. Even in invading Poland, he apparently still hoped to localize hostilities. But he was certainly willing to risk a more general European war, and the deepest thrust of his policy was toward an all-out war of conquest—first against Poland, but ultimately against the Soviet Union. War was essential to the Nazi vision, and only when the assault on Poland became a full-scale war did the underlying purposes of Nazism become clear.

SUMMARY

THE 1930s made a cruel mockery of the hopes for restabilization that had followed World War I. The Depression and the challenges from new political regimes called both capitalism and democracy into question. Hitler's Germany, especially, presented an unprecedented challenge to the European order, but the leading democracies, Britain and France, were slow to respond. Eagerness to avoid another war affected their reactions, as did the ideological polarization of the decade. Led by Britain, the democracies began seriously resisting the Nazi challenge only in 1939.

During the 1930s the democracies had to respond to three novel regimes—Italian fascism, German Nazism, and Stalinist communism—that did not play by the expected rules. Although their originating purposes differed, each was totalitarian in seeking the total political mobilization of the population, so that even leisure-time activities took on a public or political dimension. And each claimed to be superior partly because of its capacity to mobilize people for great collective projects as democratic regimes could not. But though they did involve ordinary people in new ways, each of the three regimes concentrated power in the hands of dictators. Thus they were at once dynamic and unpredictable—and thus, in part, the hesitancy and uncertainty of the democracies in dealing with them.

At the same time, the hesitations of the democracies during the 1930s tended to confirm the view of the three dictators that democracy was weak, decadent, passé. Such contempt inclined Mussolini and Hitler to ever greater recklessness, and persuaded Stalin finally to make his own deal with the Nazis in August 1939. When he invaded Poland on September 1, Hitler believed the democracies would let him have his way. It was hardly clear that this would end up another European war, let alone the most destructive, cataclysmic war the world had ever seen.

■ Notes

1. Quoted in Martin McCauley, *The Soviet Union Since 1917* (London and New York: Longman, 1981), pp. 72–73.
2. Quoted in Robert Conquest, *The Great Terror: A Reassessment* (New York: Oxford University Press, 1990), p. 24.
3. Quoted in Helmut Krausnick et al., *Anatomy of the SS State* (New York: Walker, 1968), p. 13.

■ Suggested Reading

Applebaum, Anne. *Gulag: A History*. 2003. A major survey of the Soviet camp network, based on extensive new research. Comprehensive, but sensitive and accessible.

Bell, P. M. H. *The Origins of the Second World War in Europe*. 2d ed. 1997. A well-organized and fair-minded survey.

Burleigh, Michael. *The Third Reich: A New History*. 2000. A lengthy reinterpretation by a major authority on Nazi Germany, making effective use of the notions of totalitarianism and political religion to place the Nazi experience within the wider context of the era.

Burleigh, Michael, and Wolfgang Wippermann. *The Racial State: Germany 1933–1945*. 1991. An influential, thoroughly researched study of the Nazi quest for "race hygiene."

Fitzpatrick, Sheila. *Everyday Stalinism, Ordinary Life in Extraordinary Times: Soviet Russia in the 1930s*. 1999. An engaging, balanced account of urban life in the Soviet Union in the context of the upheavals of the 1930s.

Kershaw, Ian. *Hitler*, vol. 1, *1889–1936, Hubris*, and vol. 2, *1936–1945, Nemesis*. 1999, 2000. Thorough and readable, the most important biography of Hitler.

Payne, Stanley G. *A History of Fascism, 1914–1945*. 1995. A comprehensive account with historical and interpretive sections, as well as an epilogue on the scope for neofascism.

Stephenson, Jill. *Women in Nazi Germany*. 2001. An up-to-date survey by a pioneering expert on the topic.

Watt, Donald Cameron. *How War Came: The Immediate Origins of the Second World War, 1938–1939*. 1989. A detailed but readable narrative account, based on thorough research.

Weber, Eugen. *The Hollow Years: France in the 1930s*. 1994. A lively account of French life and manners during a decade that led to humiliation and defeat.

 For a searchable list of additional readings for this chapter, go to college.hmco.com/students.

Film as Propaganda

One of the extraordinary pieces of evidence from the Nazi period is *Triumph of the Will*, a documentary film on the sixth Nazi Party rally, which took place from September 4 to 10, 1934, in the historic city of Nuremberg, by this time the official site for such party rallies. Directed by a talented young woman named Leni Riefenstahl (1902–2003), *Triumph of the Will* has long been recognized as one of the most compelling propaganda films ever made. What can we learn from this film about how the Nazis understood and used propaganda? What was the Nazi regime trying to convey in sponsoring the film, with the particular images it contained?

A sense of the scope for political propaganda was one of the defining features of the Nazi movement virtually from its inception. In his quest for power Hitler allotted an especially significant role to his future propaganda minister, Joseph Goebbels. Both Hitler and Goebbels saw that new media and carefully orchestrated events might be used to shape the political views of masses of people.

The Nazi Party held the first of what would become annual conventions in Nuremberg in 1927. From the start, these meetings were rallies of the faithful, intended to give the Nazi movement a sense of cohesion and common purpose; but they increasingly became carefully staged propaganda spectacles, with banners and searchlights, parades and speeches. When, by 1934, the regime had completed the task of immediate power consolidation, it seemed time to seize the potential of the film medium to carry the spectacle beyond those present in Nuremberg. The intention to make a film thus influenced the staging of the 1934 rally. Film would transform the six-day event into a single potent work of art.

When Hitler came to power, Goebbels, as propaganda minister, assumed control of the German film industry, and he was particularly jealous of his prerogatives in this sphere. If there was to be a film of one of the Nuremberg rallies, he assumed that he would be in charge. So he objected strenuously when Hitler decided that Riefenstahl, who was not even a party member, should film the 1934 rally.

Already popular as an actress, Riefenstahl had established her own film-making company in 1931, before she turned 30. Her first film won the admiration of Hitler, who sought her out and eventually proposed that she direct the film of the party rally. Although she was an artist with no special interest in politics, Riefenstahl, like many Germans, believed at this point that Hitler might be able to revive Germany's fortunes. So despite considerable reluctance, she bowed to Hitler's persistence and agreed to do the film—though only after she was guaranteed final control over editing. Her relations with Goebbels remained strained, but Hitler continued to support her as she made *Triumph of the Will*.

Riefenstahl developed the 107-minute film by editing 61 hours of footage that covered everything from Hitler's arrival and motorcade to the closing parades and speeches. As depicted on film, the party rally does not convey an overt ideological message. We hear Hitler simply trumpeting German renewal, not attacking Jews or glorifying conquest. Most striking in Riefenstahl's portrayal are the unity and epic monumentality that Nazism had apparently brought to Germany thanks to Hitler's leadership.

The film opens as Hitler emerges from dramatic cloud formations to arrive by airplane, descending from the sky like a god. He appears throughout the film as an almost superhuman figure, even, as in the shot shown here, as inspired, possessed, uncanny. Above all, he is a creator who shapes reality by blending will and art, forging masses of anonymous individuals into one people, one racial community, ready for anything. Those individuals seem, from one perspective, to lose their individuality in a monolithic mass, as in the shot of the parade grounds. But their sense of involvement in grandiose

As seen in *Triumph of the Will*, the Leader . . .

. . . and the Disciplined, Tightly Knit Community of Followers   *(Both photos from the Museum of Modern Art/Film Stills Archive)*

purposes charges them emotionally, even gives them a kind of ecstasy. The symbols, the massed banners, the ritualistic show of conformity, all strengthened this sense of participation in the new people's community. But unity and community were not ends in themselves; the film exalted military values and depicted a disciplined society organized for war.

Triumph of the Will extended participation in the spectacle to those who were not actually present in Nuremberg. Because the film chiseled the sprawling event into a work of art, seeing the film was in some ways more effective than being there. The Nazis looked for every means possible to involve the whole society in ritualistic spectacles that could promote a sense of belonging and unity. In addition to film, they made effective use of radio, even subsidizing the purchase of radio sets, or "people's receivers." Such new media were to help ordinary Germans feel a more meaningful kind of belonging

than possible under the democracy of the Weimar Republic. But this was only an emotional involvement, not the active participation of free citizens invited to make rational choices.

Triumph of the Will had its premiere in March 1935, with Hitler in the audience. It won several prizes in Germany and abroad but enjoyed only mixed success with the German public, especially outside the large cities. For some, it was altogether too artistic, and the Nazi regime did not use it widely for overt propaganda purposes. Still, the Nazis commissioned no other film about Hitler, for *Triumph of the Will* captured the way he wanted to be seen. Indeed, Hitler praised the film as an "incomparable glorification of the power and beauty of our Movement."

 For additional information on this topic, go to college.hmco.com/students.

CHAPTER 28

The Era of the Second World War 1939–1949

THE effects could well be called unprecedented, magnificent, beautiful, stupendous and terrifying. No man-made phenomenon of such tremendous power had ever occurred before. . . . Thirty seconds after the explosion came first, the air blast pressing hard against the people and things, to be followed almost immediately by the strong, sustained, awesome roar which warned of doomsday and made us feel that we puny things were blasphemous to dare tamper with the forces heretofore reserved to The Almighty."[1]

So wrote Brigadier General Thomas F. Farrell, who had just witnessed the birth of the atomic age. On July 16, 1945, watching from a shelter 10,000 yards away, Farrell had seen the first explosion of an atomic bomb at a remote, top-secret U.S. government testing ground near Alamogordo, New Mexico. Such a weapon had been little more than a theoretical possibility when World War II began, and it required a remarkable concentration of effort, centered first in Britain, then in the United States, to make possible the awesome spectacle that confronted General Farrell. Exceeding most expectations, the test revealed a weapon of unprecedented power and destructiveness.

Within weeks, the United States dropped two other atomic bombs—first on Hiroshima, then on Nagasaki—to force the surrender of Japan in August 1945. Thus ended the Second World War, the conflict that had begun six long years earlier with the German invasion of Poland. At first Germany enjoyed remarkable success, prompting Italy to intervene and encouraging Japanese aggressiveness as well. But Britain held on even after its ally, France, fell to Germany in 1940. Then the war changed character in 1941 when Germany attacked the Soviet Union and Japan attacked the United States.

Atomic bombing of Nagasaki, August 9, 1945. When this photo was taken, from an observation plane 6 miles up, thirty-five thousand people on the ground had already died.
(By courtesy of the Trustees of the Imperial War Museum)

Britain, the United States, and the Soviet Union quickly came together in a "Grand Alliance," which spearheaded the victorious struggle against the Axis powers—Germany, Italy, and Japan. In Europe, the Soviet victory in a brutal land war with Germany proved decisive. In East Asia and the Pacific, the Americans gradually prevailed against Japan. The American use of the atomic bomb to end the war was the final stage in an escalation of violence that made World War II the most destructive war in history. What the advent of this terrifying new weapon would mean for the future remained unclear in the war's immediate aftermath.

The ironic outcome of the Second World War was a new cold war between two of the victors, the United States and the Soviet Union. Emerging from the war with far greater power and prestige, each assumed a world role that would have been hard to imagine just a few years earlier. By the end of the 1940s, these two new superpowers had divided Europe into competing spheres of influence. Indeed, the competition between the United States and the Soviet Union almost immediately became global in scope, creating a bipolar world. And the cold war between them was especially terrifying because, seeking military advantage, they raced to stockpile ever more destructive nuclear weapons. Thus the threat of nuclear annihilation helped define the cold war era.

World War II led to the defeat of Italy, Germany, and Japan and in this sense resolved the conflicts that had caused it. But the experience of this particular war changed the world forever. Before finally meeting defeat, the Nazis were sufficiently successful to begin implementing their "new order" in Europe, especially in the territories they conquered to the east. As part of this effort, in what has become known as the Holocaust, they began systematically murdering Jews in extermination camps, eventually killing as many as six million. The most destructive of the camps was at Auschwitz°, in what had been Poland. Often paired after the war, Auschwitz and Hiroshima came to stand for the incredible new forms of death and destruction that the war had spawned—and that continued to haunt the world long after it had ended, posing new questions about the meaning of Western civilization.

QUESTIONS TO CONSIDER

- How did the Allies manage to defeat Germany in World War II, after Germany's remarkable success during the war's first two years?

- Does it make sense to link the Holocaust and the atomic bombing of Japan as radically new forms of violence emerging from the Second World War, or are they better seen as fundamentally dissimilar?

- What are the arguments for and against the Allied policy of forcing Nazi leaders to stand trial after Germany's military defeat?

- What was the relationship between the Allied victory in World War II and the coming of the cold war?

TERMS TO KNOW

Vichy France	D-Day
Charles de Gaulle	Yalta conference
Winston Churchill	United Nations
Auschwitz-Birkenau	Potsdam conference
Stalingrad	Nuremberg trials
"the Great Patriotic War"	iron curtain
Franklin Delano Roosevelt	cold war
Lend-Lease Act	Truman Doctrine

Auschwitz (OWSH-vits)

THE VICTORY OF NAZI GERMANY, 1939–1941

INSTEAD of the enthusiasm evident in 1914, the German invasion of Poland on September 1, 1939, produced a grim sense of foreboding, even in Germany. Well-publicized incidents such as the German bombing of civilians during the Spanish civil war and the Italian use of poison gas in Ethiopia suggested that the frightening new technologies introduced in World War I would now be used on a far greater scale. The new conflict would be a much uglier war, more directly involving civilians.

Still, as in 1914, there were hopes that this war could be localized and brief—that it would not become a "world war." Hitler and the Germans envisioned a *Blitzkrieg,* or "lightning war," and the initial outcome seemed to confirm these expectations. Poland fell quickly, and Hitler publicly offered peace to Britain and France, seriously thinking that might be the end of it. The British and French refused to call off the war, but from 1939 through 1941 the Nazis won victory after victory, establishing the foundation for their new order in Europe.

Initial Conquests and "Phony War"

The Polish army was large enough to have given the Germans a serious battle. But in adapting the technological innovations of World War I, Germany had developed a new military strategy based on rapid mobility. This Blitzkrieg strategy employed swift, highly concentrated offensives based on mobile tanks covered with concentrated air support, including dive-bombers that struck just ahead of the tanks. In Poland this strategy proved decisive. The French could offer only token help, and the last Polish unit surrendered on October 2, barely a month after the fighting had begun. The speed of the German victory stunned the world.

Meanwhile, the Soviets began cashing in on the pact they had made with Nazi Germany a few weeks before. It offered a precious opportunity to undo provisions of the World War I settlement that had significantly diminished the western territories of the former Russian Empire. On September 17, with the German victory in Poland assured, Stalin sent Soviet forces westward to share in the spoils. Soon Poland was again divided between Germany and Russia, just as most of it had been before 1914. The Baltic states of Estonia, Latvia, and Lithuania soon fell as well.

When Finland proved less pliable, the Soviets invaded in November 1939. In the ensuing "Winter War,"

CHRONOLOGY	
September 1, 1939	Germany invades Poland
1939–1940	Soviets wage "Winter War" against Finland
1940	Germany attacks Denmark and Norway (April)
	Germany attacks the Netherlands, Belgium, and France (May 10)
1941	Germany attacks the Soviet Union (June 22)
	Churchill and Roosevelt agree to the Atlantic Charter (August)
December 7, 1941	Japan attacks Pearl Harbor
August 1942–February 1943	Battle of Stalingrad
November 1942	Allied landings in North Africa
1943	Warsaw ghetto revolt (April–May)
	Soviet victory in Battle of Kursk-Orel (July)
	Allied landings in Sicily; fall of Mussolini; Italy asks for an armistice (July)
	Teheran conference (November)
June 6, 1944	D-Day: Allied landings in Normandy
February 1945	Yalta conference
May 7–8, 1945	Germany surrenders
June 1945	Founding of the United Nations
July–August 1945	Potsdam conference
August 6, 1945	U.S. atomic bombing of Hiroshima
August 14, 1945	Japan surrenders
March 1947	Truman Doctrine
June 1948–May 1949	Berlin blockade and airlift
August 1949	First Soviet atomic bomb
September 1949	Founding of the Federal Republic in West Germany

950

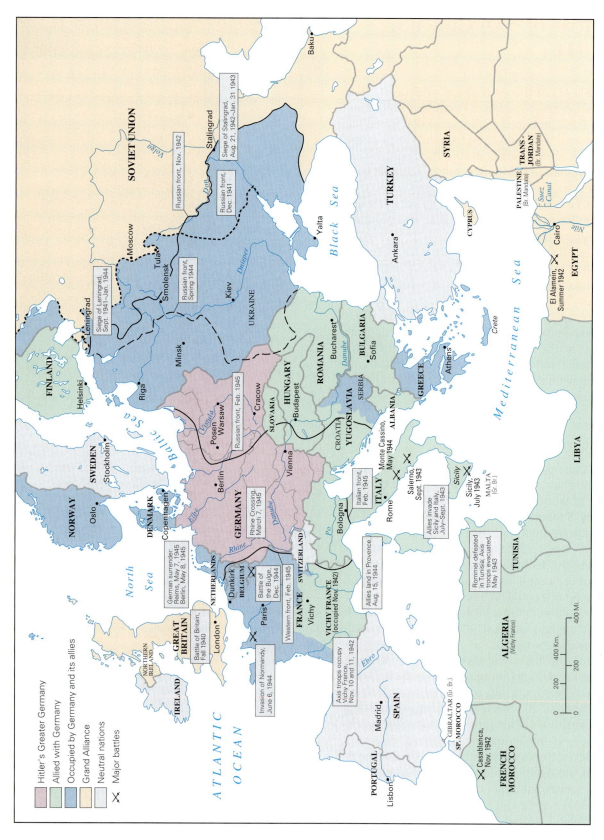

Map 28.1 **World War II: European Theaters** Much of Europe saw fighting during World War II, although different fronts were important at different times. What proved decisive was the fighting that ensued in the vast expanse of the Soviet Union after the Germans invaded in June 1941.

Hitler's Greater Germany
Allied with Germany
Occupied by Germany and its allies
Grand Alliance
Neutral nations
Major battles

SOVIET UNION

Baku

Stalingrad
Siege of Stalingrad, Aug. 21, 1942–Jan. 31 1943
Russian front, Nov. 1942
Russian front, Dec. 1941

Moscow
Tula
Smolensk
Russian front, Spring 1944
Kiev
UKRAINE

Leningrad
Siege of Leningrad, Sept. 1941–Jan. 1944

FINLAND
Helsinki

Riga
Minsk

SWEDEN
Stockholm

NORWAY
Oslo

DENMARK
Copenhagen

Posen
Warsaw
Cracow
Russian front, Feb. 1945
Vistula

GERMANY
Berlin
Rhine Crossing, March 7, 1945
German surrender: Reims, May 7, 1945 Berlin, May 8, 1945

Elbe
Rhine
Danube

SLOVAKIA
Vienna

HUNGARY
Budapest

ROMANIA
Bucharest
Danube

BULGARIA
Sofia

YUGOSLAVIA
SERBIA
CROATIA

GREECE
Athens

ALBANIA

Monte Cassino, May 1944
Salerno, Sept. 1943
Allies invade Sicily and Italy, July–Sept. 1943

ITALY
Rome
Bologna
Po
Italian front, Feb. 1945

Sicily
Sicily, July 1943
MALTA (Gr. Br.)

Crete

TURKEY
Ankara

CYPRUS

SYRIA

TRANS-JORDAN (Br. Mandate)

PALESTINE (Br. Mandate)
Suez Canal
Nile

EGYPT
Cairo
El Alamein, Summer 1942

LIBYA

Mediterranean Sea

Black Sea
Yalta

Baltic Sea

North Sea

Atlantic Ocean

GREAT BRITAIN
London
Battle of Britain, Fall 1940

NORTHERN IRELAND

IRELAND

NETHERLANDS
Dunkirk
BELGIUM
Battle of the Bulge, Dec. 1944

FRANCE
Paris
Western front, Feb. 1945

SWITZERLAND

VICHY FRANCE (occupied Nov. 1942)
Vichy

Invasion of Normandy, June 6, 1944

Allies land in Provence, Aug. 15, 1944

Axis troops occupy Vichy France, Nov. 10 and 11, 1942

Ebro

SPAIN
Madrid

PORTUGAL
Lisbon

GIBRALTAR (Gr. Br.)
SP. MOROCCO

FRENCH MOROCCO
Casablanca, Nov. 1942

ALGERIA (Vichy France)

TUNISIA
Rommel defeated in Tunisia; Axis troops evacuated, May 1943

Don
Volga
Dnieper

0   200   400 Mi.
0   200   400 Km.

the Finns held out bravely, and the Soviets managed to prevail by March 1940 only by taking heavy casualties. The difficult course of the war in Finland seemed to confirm suspicions that Stalin's purge during the mid-1930s had substantially weakened the Soviet army. Still, by midsummer 1940, the Soviet Union had regained much of the territory it had lost during the upheavals that followed the revolution of 1917.

In the west, little happened during the strained winter of 1939–1940, known as the "Phony War." Then, on April 9, 1940, the Germans attacked Norway and Denmark in a surprise move to preempt a British and French scheme to cut off the major route for the shipment of Swedish iron ore to Germany. Denmark fell almost at once, while the staunch resistance in Norway was effectively broken by the end of April. The stage was set for the German assault on France.

The Fall of France, 1940

The war in the west began in earnest on May 10, 1940, when Germany attacked France and the Low Countries. The Germans launched their assault on France through the Ardennes Forest, above the northern end of the Maginot Line—terrain so difficult the French had discounted the possibility of an enemy strike there (see page 884). As in 1914, northern France quickly became the focus of a major war pitting French forces and their British allies against invading Germans. But this time, in startling contrast to World War I, the Battle of France was over in less than six weeks, a humiliating defeat for the French.

The problem for France was not lack of men and materiel, but strategy. Germany had only a slight numerical advantage in tanks but used mobile tanks and dive-bombers to mount rapid, highly concentrated offensives. Anticipating another long, defensive war, France had dispersed its tanks among infantry units along a broad front. Once the German tank column broke through the French lines, it quickly cut through northern France and moved toward the North Sea. France's poor showing convinced the British that rather than commit troops and planes to a hopeless battle in France, they should get out and regroup for a longer global war. Finally, in early June, 200,000 British troops—as well as 130,000 French—escaped German encirclement and capture through a difficult evacuation at Dunkirk (see Map 28.1).

By mid-June, Germany had won a decisive victory. As the French military collapsed, the French cabinet resigned, to be replaced by a new government under Marshal Philippe Pétain, who had led the successful French effort in the Battle of Verdun during World War I. Pétain's government first asked for an armistice and then engi-

neered a change of regime. The French parliament voted by an overwhelming majority to give Pétain exceptional powers, including the power to draw up a new constitution. So ended the parliamentary democracy of the Third Republic, which seemed responsible for France's weakness. The republic gave way to the more authoritarian Vichy° regime, named after the resort city to which the government retreated as the Germans moved into Paris. The end of the fighting in France resulted in a kind of antidemocratic revolution, but one in which the French people, stunned by military defeat, at first acquiesced.

According to the armistice agreement, the French government was not only to cease hostilities but also to collaborate with the victorious Germans. French resistance began immediately, however. In a radio broadcast from London on June 18, Charles de Gaulle° (1890–1970), the youngest general in the French army, called on French forces to rally to him to continue the fight against Nazi Germany. The military forces stationed in the French colonies, as well as the French troops that had been evacuated at Dunkirk, could form the nucleus of a new French army. Under the present circumstances of military defeat and political change, de Gaulle's appeal seemed quixotic at best. Most French colonies went along with what seemed the legitimate French government at Vichy—to which de Gaulle was a traitor. Yet a new Free French force grew from de Gaulle's remarkable appeal, and its subsequent role in the war compensated, in some measure, for France's humiliating defeat in 1940.

Winston Churchill and the Battle of Britain

With the defeat of France, Hitler seems to have expected that Britain, now apparently vulnerable to German invasion, would come to terms. And certainly some prominent Britons questioned the wisdom of remaining at war. But the British war effort found a new and effective champion in Winston Churchill (1874–1965), who replaced Neville Chamberlain as prime minister on May 10, when the German invasion of western Europe began. Although Churchill had been prominent in British public life for years, his career to this point had not been noteworthy for either judgment or success. He was obstinate, difficult, something of a curmudgeon. Yet he rose to the wartime challenge, becoming one of the notable leaders of the modern era. In speeches to the House of Commons during the remainder of 1940, he inspired his nation with some of the most memorable words of the war. Though some found a negotiated settlement with Germany even more sensible in light of the outcome in

Vichy (VEE-shee) **de Gaulle** (duh GOHL)

France, Churchill's dogged promise of "blood, toil, tears, and sweat" helped rally the British people, so that later he could say, without exaggeration, that "this was their nest hour."

After the fall of France, Churchill's Britain promptly moved to full mobilization for a protracted war. Indeed, Britain developed the most thoroughly coordinated war economy of all the belligerents, producing more tanks, aircraft, and machine guns than Germany did between 1940 and 1942. The National Service Act of 1941 subjected men ages 18 to 50 and women ages 20 to 30 to military or civilian war service. The upper age limits were subsequently raised to meet the demand for labor. Almost 70 percent of the three million people added to the British work force during the war were women.

Britain, then, intended to continue the fight even after France fell. Hitler weighed his options and decided to attack. In light of British naval superiority, he hoped to rely on aerial bombardment to knock the British out of the war without an actual invasion. The ensuing Battle of Britain culminated in the nightly bombing of London from September 7 through November 2, 1940, killing fifteen thousand people and destroying thousands of buildings. But the British held. Ordinary people holed up in cellars and subway stations, while the fighter planes of the Royal Air Force fought back effectively, inflicting heavy losses against German aircraft over Britain.

Although the bombing continued into 1941, the British had withstood the worst the Germans could de-liver, and Hitler began looking to the east, his ultimate objective all along. In December 1940 he ordered preparations for Operation Barbarossa, the assault on the Soviet Union. Rather than continuing the attack on Britain directly, Germany would use submarines to cut off shipping—and thus the supplies the British needed for a long war. Once Germany had defeated the Soviet Union, it would enjoy the geopolitical basis for world power, while Britain, as an island nation relying on a dispersed empire, would sooner or later be forced to come to terms.

Italian Intervention and the Spread of the War

Lacking sufficient domestic support, and unready for a major war, Mussolini could only look on as the war began in 1939. But as the Battle of France neared its end, it seemed safe for Italy to intervene, sharing in the spoils of what appeared certain victory. Thus in June 1940 Italy entered the war, expecting to secure territorial advantages in the Mediterranean, starting with Corsica, Nice, and Tunisia, at the expense of France. Italy also hoped eventually to supplant Britain in the region—and even to take the Suez Canal.

Although Hitler and Mussolini got along reasonably well, their relationship was sensitive. When Hitler seemed to be proceeding without Italy during the first year of the war, Mussolini grew determined to show his independence. Finally, in October 1940, he ordered Italian forces to attack Greece. But the Greeks mounted a strong resis-

British Resistance At the height of the German bombing of Britain in 1940, Winston Churchill and his wife, Clementine, survey the damage in London. *(Hulton Archive/ Getty Images)*

tance, thanks partly to the help of British forces from North Africa.

Meanwhile, Germany had established its hegemony in much of east-central Europe without military force, often by exploiting grievances over the outcome of the Paris Peace Conference in 1919. In November 1940 Romania and Hungary joined the Axis camp, and Bulgaria followed a few months later. But in March 1941, just after Yugoslavia had similarly committed to the Axis, a coup overthrew the pro-Axis government in Yugoslavia, and the new Yugoslav government prepared to aid the Allies.

By this point Hitler had decided it was expedient to push into the Balkans with German troops, both to reinforce the Italians and to consolidate Axis control of the area. As the war's geographic extent expanded, its stakes increased, yet the Germans continued to meet every challenge. By the end of May 1941 they had taken Yugoslavia and Greece (see Map 28.1).

At the same time, the war was spreading to North Africa and the Middle East because of European colonial ties. The native peoples of the area sought to take advantage of the conflict among the Europeans to pursue their own independence. Iraq and Syria became involved as the Germans, operating from Syria, which was administered by Vichy France, aided anti-British Arab nationalists in Iraq. But most important proved to be North Africa, where Libya, an Italian colony since 1912, lay adjacent to Egypt, where the British presence remained strong.

In September 1940 the Italian army drove 65 miles into Egypt, initiating almost three years of fighting across the North African desert. A British counteroffensive from December 1940 to February 1941 drove the Italians back 340 miles into Libya, prompting Germany to send some of its forces from the Balkans into North Africa. Under General Erwin Rommel (1891–1944), the famous "Desert Fox," Axis forces won remarkable victories in North Africa from February to May 1941. But successful though they had been, the German forays into North Africa and the Balkans had delayed the crucial attack on the Soviet Union.

THE ASSAULT ON THE SOVIET UNION AND THE NAZI NEW ORDER

ERMAN troops invaded the Soviet Union on June 22, 1941, initiating what proved to be the decisive confrontation of World War II. Although the Nazis enjoyed the expected successes for a while, the Soviets eventually prevailed, spearheading the Allied victory in Europe. Supplies from their new Allies—Britain and eventually the United States—aided the Soviet cause, but the surprising strength of the Soviet military effort was the most important factor in the eventual outcome. In the process, the Soviets suffered incredible casualties, and after they gained the initiative, they proceeded with particular brutality as they forced the invading Germans back into Germany.

In doing so, the Soviets were responding to the unprecedented form of warfare that the Nazis had unleashed. While preparing for the attack on the Soviet Union, Hitler had made it clear to the Nazi leadership that this was to be no ordinary military engagement but a war of racial-ideological extermination. The Germans penetrated well into the Soviet Union, reaching the apex of their power late in 1942. German conquests by that point enabled Hitler to begin constructing the new, race-based European order he had dreamed of. Although in western Europe the Nazis generally sought the collaboration of local leaders, in the Soviet Union, as in Poland, the new order meant brutal subjugation of local populations. As part of this process, the Nazis began systematically killing Jews, first by shooting, then by mass-gassing them in specially constructed death camps.

An Ambiguous Outcome, 1941–1942

In ordering preparations for Operation Barbarossa in December 1940, Hitler decided to risk attacking the Soviet Union before knocking Britain out of the war. Then he invaded the Balkans and North Africa in what may have been an unnecessary diversion. In retrospect, it is easy to pinpoint that combination as his fatal mistake. But in light of the Soviet purges of the 1930s and what seemed the poor performance of the Soviet army against Finland, Hitler had reason to believe the Soviet Union would crack relatively easily. Western military experts had come to similar conclusions, estimating that German forces would need but six weeks to take Moscow. And if Germany were to defeat the Soviet Union with another Blitzkrieg, it could gain control of the oil and other resources required for a longer war against Britain and, if necessary, the United States.

Attacking the Soviet Union on June 22, 1941, German forces achieved notable successes during the first month of fighting, partly because Stalin was so unprepared for this German betrayal. Ignoring warnings of an impending German assault, he had continued to live up to his end of the 1939 bargain with Hitler, even supplying the Germans with oil and grain. After the attack, Russia's defenses were at first totally disorganized, and by late November German forces were within 20 miles of Moscow.

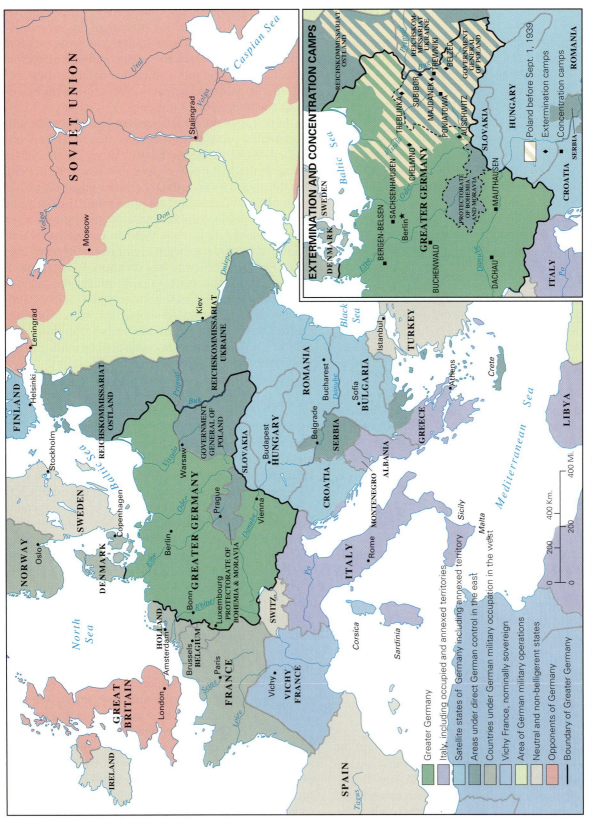

EXTERMINATION AND CONCENTRATION CAMPS

SOVIET UNION

Ural

Caspian Sea

Stalingrad

Volga

Don

Moscow

Volga

FINLAND

Helsinki

Leningrad

Kiev

REICHSKOMMISSARIAT OSTLAND

REICHSKOMMISSARIAT UKRAINE

Pripet

Bug

Black Sea

Istanbul

TURKEY

SWEDEN

Stockholm

Baltic Sea

Warsaw

GOVERNMENT GENERAL OF POLAND

Vistula

Odra

SLOVAKIA

Budapest

HUNGARY

ROMANIA

Bucharest

Danube

Sofia

BULGARIA

Belgrade

SERBIA

GREECE

Athens

Crete

NORWAY

Oslo

Copenhagen

DENMARK

Berlin

Prague

Vienna

Elbe

Rhine

Oder

Danube

GREATER GERMANY

PROTECTORATE OF BOHEMIA & MORAVIA

Bonn

Luxembourg

CROATIA

MONTENEGRO

ALBANIA

Mediterranean Sea

LIBYA

North Sea

HOLLAND

Amsterdam

BELGIUM

Brussels

Paris

FRANCE

Seine

Loire

SWITZ.

Vichy

VICHY FRANCE

ITALY

Rome

Po

Sicily

Malta

Corsica

Sardinia

GREAT BRITAIN

London

IRELAND

SPAIN

Tagus

400 Mi.

400 Km.

200

200

0

0

Greater Germany

Italy, including occupied and annexed territories

Satellite states of Germany including annexed territory

Areas under direct German control in the east

Countries under German military occupation in the west

Vichy France, nominally sovereign

Area of German military operations

Neutral and non-belligerent states

Opponents of Germany

Boundary of Greater Germany

Inset:

EXTERMINATION AND CONCENTRATION CAMPS

REICHSKOMMISSARIAT OSTLAND

REICHSKOMMISSARIAT UKRAINE

Pripet

Bug

TREBLINKA

SOBIBOR

MAJDANEK

PONIATOWA

BELZEC

GOVERNMENT GENERAL OF POLAND

ROMANIA

Baltic Sea

Vistula

Oder

AUSCHWITZ

HUNGARY

SLOVAKIA

SWEDEN

DENMARK

BERGEN-BELSEN

SACHSENHAUSEN

CHELMNO

Berlin

GREATER GERMANY

BUCHENWALD

PROTECTORATE OF BOHEMIA AND MORAVIA

MAUTHAUSEN

DACHAU

Elbe

Danube

ITALY

Po

CROATIA

SERBIA

Poland before Sept. 1, 1939

Extermination camps

Concentration camps

Map 28.2   The Nazi New Order in Europe, 1942   At the zenith of its power in 1942, Nazi Germany controlled much of Europe. Concerned most immediately with winning the war, the Nazis sought to coordinate the economies of their satellite states and conquered territories. But they also began establishing what was supposed to be an enduring new order in eastern Europe. The inset shows the locations of the major Nazi concentration camps and the six extermination camps the Nazis constructed in what had been Poland.

Forgive me, comrade . . .   On June 23, 1941, the day after Nazi Germany attacked the Soviet Union, the *London Daily Mail* published this cartoon depicting Hitler's betrayal of his 1939 pact with Stalin.   *(Daily Mail, London, 23 June 1941. Reprinted with permission of Solo Syndication Limited)*

But the Germans were ill-equipped for Russian weather, and as an early and severe winter descended, the German offensive bogged down. In December the Soviets mounted a formidable surprise counterattack near Moscow. The German Blitzkrieg, which had seemed a sure thing in July, had failed. Germany might still prevail, but a different strategy would be required.

Although their initial assault had stalled, the Germans still had the advantage. German forces failed to take the key city of Leningrad in 1941, but they cut it off by blockade and, until early 1944, kept it under siege with relentless bombing and shelling. During the summer of 1942, they mounted another offensive, moving more deeply into the Soviet Union than before, reaching Stalingrad in November. But this proved the deepest penetration of German forces—and the zenith of Nazi power in Europe.

Hitler's New Order

By the summer of 1942, Nazi Germany dominated the European continent as no power had before (see Map 28.2). German military successes allowed the Nazi regime to begin building a new order in the territories under German domination. Satellite states in Slovakia and Croatia, and client governments in Romania and Hungary, owed their existence to Nazi Germany and readily adapted themselves to the Nazi system. Elsewhere in the Nazi orbit, some countries proved eager collaborators; others did their best to resist; still others were given no opportunity to collaborate but were ruthlessly subjugated instead.

The Nazis' immediate aim was simply to exploit the conquered territories to serve the continuing war effort. Precisely as envisioned, access to the resources of so much of Europe made Germany considerably less vulnerable to naval blockade than during World War I. France proved a particularly valuable source of raw materials; by 1943, for example, 75 percent of French iron ore went to German factories.

But the deeper purposes of the war were also clear in the way the Nazis treated the territories under their control, especially in the difference between east and west. Western Europe experienced plenty of atrocities, but Nazi victory there still led to something like conventional military occupation. The Germans tried to enlist the cooperation of local authorities in countries like Denmark, the Netherlands, and France, though with mixed results. And whereas the Nazis exploited the economy of France, for example, it never became clear what role France might play in Europe after a Nazi victory. However, in Poland and later in the conquered parts of the Soviet Union, there was no pretense of cooperation, and it was immediately clear what the Nazi order would entail.

After the conquest of Poland, the Germans annexed the western part of the country outright and promptly executed, jailed, or expelled members of the Polish elite—professionals, journalists, business leaders, and priests. The Nazis prohibited the Poles from entering the professions and restricted even their right to marry. All the Polish schools and most of the churches were simply closed.

In the rest of Poland, known as the General Government, Nazi policy was slightly less brutal at first. Most churches remained open, and Poles were allowed to practice the professions, but the Nazis closed most schools above the fourth grade, as well as libraries, theaters, and museums, as they sought to root out every expression of Polish culture. Some Poles in this area were forced into slave labor, but a final decision as to whether the Polish population was to be exterminated, enslaved, or shipped off to Siberia was postponed—to be made after the wider war had been won. (See the box "Reading Sources: Toward the Nazi New Order.")

With the conquest of Poland, Nazi leaders proclaimed that a new era of monumental resettlement in eastern Europe had begun for Germany. Germans selected for their racial characteristics were now resettled in the part of Poland annexed to Germany. Most were ethnic Germans who had been living outside Germany. During the fall of 1942, Heinrich Himmler's *Schutzstaffel* (SS), the select Nazi elite, began to arrest and expel peasants from the rest of Poland to make way for further German resettlement. By 1943 perhaps one million Germans had been moved into what had been Poland.

After the assault on the Soviet Union, Hitler made it clear that eastern Europe as far as the Ural Mountains was to be opened for German settlement. War veterans were to be given priority, partly because the German settlers would have to be tough to resist the Slavs, who would be concentrated east of the Urals. To prepare for German colonization, Himmler told SS leaders that Germany would have to exterminate thirty million Slavs in the Soviet Union. After the German invasion, the SS promptly began executing prisoners of war, as well as any Soviet leaders they could find. However, the Nazis expected that several generations would be required for the resettlement of European Russia.

The Holocaust

Conquest of the east also opened the way to a more radical solution to the "Jewish problem" than the Nazis had contemplated before. Under the cover of war, they began actually killing the Jews within their orbit. Thus began the process, and the experience, that has come to be known as the Holocaust.

When and why this radical policy was chosen remains controversial. Although prewar Nazi rhetoric occasionally suggested the possibility of actual physical extermination, talk of a "final solution to the Jewish problem" seemed to mean forced emigration. Although the precise chain of events that led to a more radical approach will no doubt remain uncertain, it was surely bound up with the fortunes of the war.

The conquest of Poland, with a Jewish population of 3.3 million, gave the Nazis control over a far greater number of Jews than ever before. In 1940, as part of their effort to create a new order, the Nazis began confining Polish Jews to ghettos set up in Warsaw and five other cities. Although much brutality and many deaths accompanied this process, the Nazis had not yet adopted a policy of systematic killing. Indeed, at first no one knew what was to become of these Jews. At this point Nazi authorities were concentrating on removing, or even killing, non-Jewish Poles to make way for German resettlement into former Polish lands. The fate of the Jews would be decided later.

After the defeat of France, Himmler and the SS made tentative plans to develop a kind of superghetto for perhaps four million Jews on the island of Madagascar, at that point still a French colony, once the war had been won. However, as the Polish ghettos grew more crowded and difficult to manage, Nazi officials in Poland began pressing for a more immediate solution.

At the same time, Hitler made it clear that the invasion of the Soviet Union would launch something new, a racial-ideological war of annihilation. Accompanying the military forces were specially trained SS units, essentially mobile killing squads, assigned to get rid of Communist Party officials and adult male Jews. But soon some began murdering Jewish women and children as well. By late November 1941, the Nazis had killed 136,000 Jews, most by shooting, in the invaded Soviet territories. But this mode of killing proved both inefficient and psychologically burdensome—even for these specially trained killers. Their experience in the Soviet Union combined with the problems in the Polish ghettos to lead Nazi leaders to begin seeking a more systematic and impersonal method of mass extermination by late summer 1941.

The most likely scenario is that Hitler settled on physical extermination of the Jews in the thrill of what seemed impending victory over the Soviet Union. At the end of July 1941, Reinhard Heydrich of the SS began developing a detailed plan, and by the fall the Nazis were sending German and Austrian Jews to the ghettos in Poland and actively impeding further Jewish emigration from Europe.

Heydrich explained his plan for the extermination of the Jews in January 1942 at a conference of high-ranking officials at Wannsee, a suburb of Berlin. The conference had been postponed from November, and by January the operation had already begun. The Nazis took advantage of the personnel and the methods—especially the deadly Zyklon-B gas—that had proven effective during the "euthanasia" campaign of 1939 through 1941 in Germany (see page 932). By March 1942 they had constructed several extermination camps with gas chambers and crematoria, intended to kill large numbers of Jews and dispose of their bodies as efficiently as possible. Now they began full-scale mass killing, targeting first the Polish Jews who

READING
SOURCES

TOWARD THE NAZI NEW ORDER

After Nazi Germany conquered much of Poland in 1939, the SS assumed major responsibility for creating a new Nazi order in the conquered territories. In a memorandum dated May 15, 1940, and endorsed by Hitler, the SS leader Heinrich Himmler offered "some thoughts on the treatment of the alien population in the east." The passages that follow make clear the racist basis of Nazi wartime policy.

In our treatment of the foreign ethnic groups in the east we must . . . fish out the racially valuable people from this mishmash, take them to Germany and assimilate them there.

. . . The non-German population of the eastern territories must not receive any education higher than that of elementary school with four forms [grades]. The objective of this elementary school must simply be to teach: simple arithmetic up to 500 at the most, how to write one's name, and to teach that it is God's commandment to be obedient to the Germans and to be honest, hard-working, and well-behaved. I consider it unnecessary to teach reading.

There must be no schools at all in the east apart from this type of school. Parents who wish to provide their children with a better education both in the elementary school and later in a secondary school, must make an application to the higher SS and Police Leader. . . . If we recognize such a child as being of our blood then the parents will be informed that the child will be placed in a school in Germany and will remain in Germany indefinitely. . . .

The parents of these children of good blood will be given the choice of either giving up their child . . . or they would have to agree to go to Germany and become loyal citizens there. . . .

Apart from the examination of the petitions which parents put forward for a better education, all 6–10 year olds will be sifted each year to sort out those with valuable blood and those with worthless blood. Those who are selected as valuable will be treated in the same way as the children who are admitted on the basis of the approval of the parents' petition.

. . . The moment the children and parents arrive in Germany they should not be treated in school and life as outcasts but—after changing their names and despite being treated with vigilance—should be integrated into German life on the basis of trust. The children must not be made to feel rejected; for, after all, we believe in our own blood, which through the mistakes of German history has flowed into a foreign nation, and are convinced that our ideology and ideals will find an echo in the souls of these children which are racially identical to our own. . . . Abusive expressions such as "Polack" or "Ukrainian" and such like must be out of the question. . . .

After these measures have been systematically implemented during the next ten years, the population of the General Government will inevitably consist of an inferior remnant. . . . This population will be available as a leaderless laboring class and provide Germany with migrant and seasonal labor for special work projects (road-building, quarries, construction); even then they will get more to eat and have more from life than under Polish rule.

Source: *Nazism, 1919–1945: A Documentary Reader*, vol. 3, *Foreign Policy, War and Racial Extermination*, edited by J. Noakes and G. Pridham, new edition with index. Copyright © 2001. Reprinted by permission of the University of Exeter Press.

had already been confined to ghettos. The Nazis brutally suppressed attempts at resistance, like the Warsaw ghetto uprising of April and May 1943.

During the war the Nazis constructed six full-scale death camps, although not all were operating at peak capacity at the same time. All six were located in what had been Poland (see inset, Map 28.2). Horrifying though they were, the concentration camps in Germany, such as

Dachau, Buchenwald, and Bergen-Belsen, were not extermination camps, although many Jews died in them late in the war.

The largest of the six death camps was the Auschwitz-Birkenau complex, which became the principal extermination center in 1943. The Nazis shipped Jews from all over Europe to Auschwitz, which was killing about twelve thousand people a day at the height of its operation in

The End of the Warsaw Ghetto   In April 1943 the sixty thousand Jews remaining in the Warsaw ghetto revolted rather than face shipment to the extermination camps. Many died in the ensuing fighting; others perished as the Germans set fire to the ghetto. Almost all the rest were captured and sent to their deaths at Treblinka. Before it was put down in May, the uprising killed at least three hundred Germans.   *(AP/Wide World Photos)*

1944. Auschwitz was one of two extermination camps that included affiliated slave-labor factories, in which Jews considered most able to work were often literally worked to death. Among the companies profiting from the arrangement were two of Germany's best known, Krupp and IG Farben.

The Jews typically arrived at one of the camps crammed into cattle cars on special trains. SS medical doctors subjected new arrivals to "selection," picking some for labor assignments and sending the others, including most women and children, to the gas chambers. Camp personnel made every effort to deceive the Jews who were about to be killed, to lead them to believe they were to be showered and deloused. Even in camps without forced-labor factories, Jews were compelled to do much of the dirty work of the extermination operation. But under the brutal conditions of the camps, those initially assigned to work inevitably weakened; most were then deemed unfit and put to death.

The Nazis took every precaution to hide what was going on in the death camps. The SS personnel involved were sworn to silence. Himmler insisted that if secrecy was to be maintained, the operation would have to be quick—and total, to include women and children, "so that no Jews will remain to take revenge on our sons and grandsons." Himmler constantly sought to accelerate the process, even though it required labor and transport facilities desperately needed for the war effort. Indeed, as the fortunes of war turned against Germany, the extermination of the Jews became a kind of end in itself.

Himmler and the other major SS officials, such as Rudolf Höss°, the commandant at Auschwitz, or Adolf Eichmann°, who organized the transport of the Jews to the camps, were not simply sadists who enjoyed humiliating their victims. Rather, they took satisfaction in doing what they believed was their duty without flinching, without signs of weakness. Addressing a group of SS members in 1943, Himmler portrayed the extermination of the Jews as a difficult "historical task" that they, the Nazi elite, must do for their racial community: "Most

---

Höss (HOESS)   **Eichmann** (IKE-mahn)

Face-to-Face Killing in the Holocaust
It is estimated that a little over half the Jewish victims of the Holocaust died in gas chambers. Almost a quarter died of starvation and disease, resulting from deprivation and ill treatment at the hands of the Germans. But another quarter died close-up, mostly by shooting. The perpetrators sometimes humiliated their victims first—and even documented what they were doing in photos like this one, from Lukow, Poland. It was probably taken in the fall of 1942, when a branch of the German police liquidated the ghetto there.   *(Yad Vashem Film and Photo Archive)*

of you know what it means to see a hundred corpses piled up, or five hundred, or a thousand. To have gone through this and—except for cases of human weakness—to have remained decent, that has made us tough. This is an unwritten, never to be written, page of glory in our history."[2]

However, as Himmler's casual reference to "cases of human weakness" suggests, a minority of camp guards and others failed to live up to this image and indulged in wanton cruelty toward their helpless victims. For some, the extermination process became the occasion to act out sadistic fantasies. But though this dimension is surely horrifying, the bureaucratic, factory-like nature of the extermination process has seemed still more troubling in some respects, for it raises questions about the nature of modern rationality itself. The mass killing of Jews required the expertise of scientists, doctors, and lawyers; it required the bureaucratic organization of the modern state—all to provide the most efficient means to a monstrous end.

Despite the overriding emphasis on secrecy, reports of the genocide reached the West almost immediately in 1942. At first, however, most tended to discount them as wartime propaganda of the sort that had circulated during World War I, when stories about Germans eating Belgian babies whipped up war fever. Skepticism about extermination reports was easier because there were a few concentration camps, like Theresienstadt° in the former Czechoslovakia, that housed Jews who had been selected for special treatment. These camps were not used

for extermination and were not secret; the Red Cross was even allowed to inspect Theresienstadt several times. Those outside, and the German people as well, were led to believe that all the Jews were being interned, for the duration of the war, in camps like these, much as Japanese Americans were being interned in camps in the western United States at the same time. But even as the evidence grew, Allied governments, citing military priorities, refused pleas from Jewish leaders in 1944 to bomb the rail line into Auschwitz.

The Nazis' policy of actually murdering persons deemed undesirable or superfluous did not start with, and was not limited to, the Jews. First came the "euthanasia" program in Germany, and the war afforded the Nazis the chance to do away with an array of other "undesirables," including Poles, Sinti and Roma ("Gypsies"), communists, homosexuals, and vagrants. The Nazis also systematically killed perhaps 2 million Soviet prisoners of war. So the most radical and appalling aspect of Nazism did not stem from anti-Semitism alone. This must not be forgotten, but neither must the fact that the Jews constituted by far the largest group of victims—perhaps 5.7 to 6 million, almost two-thirds of the Jews in Europe. (See the feature "Weighing the Evidence: Holocaust Testimony" on pages 982–983.)

Collaboration in Nazi Europe

In rounding up Jews for extermination, and in establishing their new order in Europe, the Nazis found willing collaborators among some of the countries within their orbit. Several of them found collaboration with the

---

Theresienstadt (teh-REZ-ay-en-shtat)

victorious Nazi regime the best way to pursue their own nationalist agendas. Croatia, earlier part of the new state of Yugoslavia, was eager to round up Jews and Gypsies, as well as to attack Serbs, as part of its effort to establish itself as a nation-state. But national circumstances varied across Europe, and so did degrees of collaboration. In Denmark, Norway, and the Netherlands, the Nazis thought racial kinship would matter, but they never found sufficient support to make possible genuinely independent collaborationist governments. Denmark did especially well at resisting the German effort to round up Jews, as did Italy and Bulgaria.

Vichy France was somewhere in the middle, and thus it has remained particularly controversial. When the Vichy regime was launched during the summer of 1940, Marshal Pétain, its 84-year-old chief of state, enjoyed widespread support. Pétain promised to maximize French sovereignty and shield his people from the worst aspects of Nazi occupation. At the same time, the Vichy government claimed to be implementing its own "national revolution," returning France to authority, discipline, and tradition after the shambles of the Third Republic. Vichy's revolution was anti-Semitic and hostile to the left, so it seemed compatible, up to a point, with Nazism. And at first Germany seemed likely to win the war. Thus, Pétain's second-in-command, Pierre Laval (1883–1945), was willing to collaborate actively with the Nazis. The Vichy regime ended up doing much of the Nazis' dirty work for them—rounding up workers for forced shipment to German factories, hunting down members of the anti-German resistance, and picking up Jews to be sent to the Nazi extermination camps.

After the war, Pétain, Laval, and others were found guilty of treason by the new French government. Because of his advanced age, Pétain was merely imprisoned, while Laval and others were executed. Despite the contributions of de Gaulle's Free French and the French resistance, the shame of Vichy collaboration continued to haunt France, deepening the humiliation of the defeat in 1940.

Toward the Soviet Triumph

The import of what happened elsewhere in Europe depended on the outcome of the main event, the German invasion of the Soviet Union. Although the German Sixth Army, numbering almost 300,000 men, reached Stalingrad by late 1942, the Germans could not achieve a knockout. The Soviets managed to defend the city in what was arguably the pivotal military engagement of World War II. While some Soviet troops fought street by street, house by house, others counterattacked, encircling the attacking German force. Hitler refused a strategic retreat, but his doggedness backfired. By the end of January 1943, the Soviets had captured what remained of the German force, about 100,000 men, very few of whom survived to return to Germany. Perhaps 240,000 German soldiers died in the Battle of Stalingrad or as prisoners afterward. But the price to the Soviets for their victory was far greater: a million Soviet soldiers and civilians died at Stalingrad.

Although the Germans resumed the offensive on several fronts during the summer of 1943, the Soviets won the tank battle of Kursk-Orel in July, and from then on Stalin's Red Army moved relentlessly westward, forcing the Germans to retreat. By February 1944 Soviet troops had pushed the Germans back to the Polish border, and the outcome of the war was no longer in doubt.

The Soviet victory on what proved the decisive front of World War II was incredible, in light of the upheavals of the 1930s and the low esteem in which most held the Soviet military in 1941. Portraying the struggle as "the Great Patriotic War" for national defense, Stalin managed to rally the Soviet people as the Germans attacked. Rather than emphasize communist themes, he recalled the heroic defenses mounted against invaders in tsarist times, including the resistance to Napoleon in 1812. But though the Soviets ultimately prevailed, the cost in death, destruction, and suffering was almost unimaginable. For example, by the time Soviet forces finally broke the siege of Leningrad in January 1944, a million people in the city had died, most from starvation, freezing, or disease. And the Soviets won on the battlefield partly by taking incredible numbers of casualties.

The invading Germans gained access to major areas of Soviet industry and oil supply, and by the end of 1941 the country's industrial output had been cut in half. Yet the Soviet Union was able to weather this blow and go on to triumph. Outside help contributed, but only 5 to 15 percent of Soviet supplies came from the West. Between 1939 and 1941, Soviet leaders had begun building a new industrial base east of the Urals. And when the Germans invaded in 1941, the plant and equipment of 1,500 enterprises were dismantled and shipped by rail for reassembly farther east, out of reach of German attack. Then, beginning in 1942, thousands of brand-new factories were constructed in eastern regions as well.

Moreover, the earlier purges of the armed forces proved to have done less long-term damage than outside observers had expected. If anything, the removal of so many in the top ranks of the military hierarchy made it easier for talented young officers like Georgi Zhukov (1896–1974), who would become the country's top military commander, to rise quickly into major leadership positions.

Stalingrad, November 1942   From September 1942 until the German surrender early in February 1943, this city on the Volga River saw some of the heaviest fighting of World War II. The Soviet victory, in the face of incredible casualties, was arguably the turning point of the war in Europe.   *(Sovfoto/Eastfoto)*

When the United States entered the war in December 1941, the Soviets were fighting for survival. They immediately began pressuring the United States and Britain to open another front in Europe, preferably by landing in northern France, where an Allied assault could be expected to have the greatest impact. But the Allies did not invade northern France and open a major second front until June 1944. By then the Soviets had turned the tide in Europe on their own.

A GLOBAL WAR, 1941–1944

WORLD War II proved unprecedented in its level of violence partly because it eclipsed even World War I in its geographical reach. The European colonial presence quickly drew the war to North Africa and the Middle East. But the war's early results in Europe also altered the power balance in East Asia and the Pacific, where the Russians and the Japanese had long been antagonists. During the 1930s, the United States had also become involved in friction with Japan. By 1941 President Franklin Roosevelt was openly favoring the anti-Axis cause, though it took a surprise attack by the Japanese in December 1941 to bring the United States into the war.

Japan and the Origins of the Pacific War

As a densely populated island nation lacking the raw materials essential for industry, Japan had been especially concerned about foreign trade and spheres of economic influence as it modernized after 1868. By the interwar period, the Japanese had become unusually reliant on exports of textiles and other products. During the Depression of the 1930s, when countries all over the world adopted protectionist policies, Japan suffered from increasing tariffs against its exports. This situation tilted the balance in Japanese ruling circles from free-trade proponents to those who favored a military-imperialist solution.

To gain economic hegemony by force, Japan could choose either of two directions. The northern strategy, concentrating on China, would risk Soviet opposition as well as strong local resistance. The southern strategy, focusing on southeast Asia and the East Indies, would encounter the imperial presence of Britain, France, the Netherlands, and the United States.

Japan opted for the northern strategy in 1931, when it took control of Manchuria, in northeastern China. But the Japanese attempt to conquer the rest of China, beginning in 1937, led only to an impasse by 1940. Japanese aggression in China drew the increasing hostility of the United States, a strong supporter of the Chinese nationalist leader Jiang Jieshi (Chiang Kai-shek) (1887–1975), as well as the active opposition of the Soviet Union. Clashes with Soviet troops along the border between Mongolia and Manchuria led to significant defeats for the Japanese in 1938 and 1939. The combination of China and the Soviet Union seemed more than Japan could handle.

By 1941, Germany's victories in Europe had seriously weakened Britain, France, and the Netherlands, the major European colonial powers in southeast Asia and the East Indies. The time seemed right for Japan to shift to a southern strategy. To keep the Soviets at bay, Japan agreed to a neutrality pact with the Soviet Union in April 1941. Rather than worry about China and the areas of dispute with the Soviet Union, the Japanese would seek control of southeast Asia, a region rich in such raw materials as oil, rubber, and tin—precisely what Japan lacked.

Japan had already joined with Nazi Germany and fascist Italy in an anticommunist agreement in 1936. In September 1940, the three agreed to a formal military alliance. For the Germans, alliance with Japan was useful to help discourage U.S. intervention in the European war. Japan, for its part, could expect the major share of the spoils of the European empires in Asia. However, diplomatic and military coordination between Germany and Japan remained minimal.

The United States began imposing embargoes on certain exports to Japan in 1938, in response to the Japanese aggression in China. After Japan had assumed control of Indochina, nominally held by Vichy France, by the summer of 1941, the United States imposed total sanctions, and the British and Dutch followed, forcing Japan to begin rapidly drawing down its oil reserves. Conquest of the oil fields of the Dutch East Indies now seemed a matter of life and death to the Japanese.

These economic sanctions heightened the determination of Japanese leaders to press forward aggressively now, when the country's likely enemies were weakened or distracted. But the Japanese did not expect to achieve a definitive victory over the United States in a long, drawn-out war. Rather, they anticipated, first, that their initial successes would enable them to grab the resources to sustain a longer war if necessary, and, second, that Germany would defeat Britain, leading the United States to accept a compromise peace allowing the Japanese what they wanted—a secure sphere of economic hegemony in southeast Asia.

Some Japanese leaders—diplomats, businessmen, naval officers, and even the emperor and some of his circle—were dismayed by the prospect of war with the United States. But as the influence of the military grew during the 1930s, it became ever more difficult for those opposing Japan's new imperialist direction to make themselves heard. By 1941, a conformist confidence in victory was demanded, and dissenters dared not speak out for fear of being labeled traitors.

The Japanese finally provoked a showdown on December 7, 1941, with a surprise attack on Pearl Harbor, a U.S. naval base in Hawaii. The next day, Japanese forces seized Hong Kong and Malaya, both British colonies, and Wake Island and the Philippines, both under U.S. control. The United States promptly declared war; in response, Hitler kept an earlier promise to Japan and declared war on the United States. World War II was now unprecedented in its geographic scope (see Map 28.3).

Much like their German counterparts, Japanese forces got off to a remarkably good start. By the summer of 1942, Japan had taken Thailand, the Dutch East Indies, the Philippines, and the Malay Peninsula. Having won much of what they had been seeking, the Japanese began devising the Greater East Asia Co-Prosperity Sphere, their own new order in the conquered territories. (See the box "Global Encounters: Japan's 'Pan-Asian' Mission.")

The United States in Europe and the Pacific

During the first years of the war in Europe, the United States did not have armed forces commensurate with its economic strength; in 1940, in fact, its army was smaller than Belgium's. But the United States could be a supplier in the short term and, if it chose to intervene, a major player over the longer term. With the Lend-Lease Act of March 1941, intended to provide war materiel without the economic dislocations of World War I, the United States lined up on the side of Britain against the Axis powers. In August 1941 a meeting between Churchill and Roosevelt aboard a cruiser off the coast of Newfoundland produced the Atlantic Charter, the first tentative agreement about the aims and ideals that were to guide the anti-Axis war effort. The Americans extended lend-lease to the Soviet Union the next month.

But though Roosevelt was deeply committed to the anti-Axis cause, isolationist sentiment remained strong in the United States. The Japanese attack on Pearl Harbor in December inflamed American opinion and enabled Roosevelt at last to bring his country into the war as an active belligerent. By May 1942 the United States had joined with Britain and the Soviet Union in a formal military alliance against the Axis powers.

The two democracies had joined with Stalin's Soviet Union in a marriage of expediency, and mutual suspi-

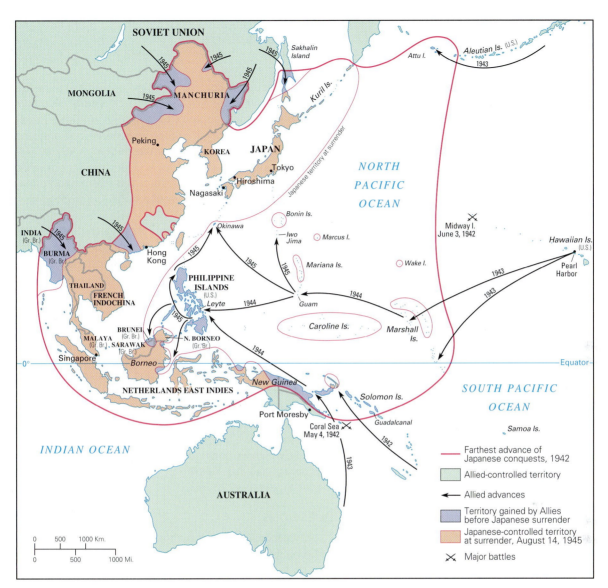

Map 28.3   The War in East Asia and the Pacific   After a series of conquests in 1941 and 1942, the Japanese were forced gradually to fall back before advancing U.S. forces. When the war abruptly ended in August 1945, however, the Japanese still controlled much of the territory they had conquered.

cions marked the relationship from the start. Initially, Britain and the United States feared that the Soviet Union might even seek a separate peace, as Russia had in World War I. The Soviets, for their part, worried that these new-found allies, with their long-standing anticommunism, might hold back from full commitment or even seek to undermine the Soviet Union.

In response to pressure from Stalin, Britain and the United States agreed to open a second front in Europe as soon as possible. But the Nazis dominated the Conti-

nent, so opening such a front required landing troops from the outside. It proved far more difficult to mount an effective assault on Europe than either Churchill or Roosevelt anticipated in 1942. The resulting delays furthered Stalin's suspicions that his allies were only too eager to have the Soviets do the bulk of the fighting against Nazi Germany—and weaken themselves in the process.

The United States agreed with its new allies to give priority to the war in Europe. But because it had to respond to the direct Japanese assault in the Pacific, the

Japan's "Pan-Asian" Mission

With the coming of war against the Western powers in 1941, the Japanese could claim to be freeing Asians from Western imperialism and establishing a new economic order in East Asia and the Pacific. This selection from an essay titled "Our Present War and Its Cultural Significance," written just after the bombing of Pearl Harbor by the well-known author Nagayo Yoshio (1888–1961), accents Japan's anti-Western mission in the region. Yoshio understood, especially from his country's recent experience in China, that Asians might find Japanese hegemony just as oppressive as Western domination. Although it served Japan's own economic interests and was often applied brutally, Japanese "pan-Asianism" helped fuel the reaction against Western imperialism in Asia and the Pacific, with lasting results after the war.

Whenever Japan has faced a powerful enemy it has been the *yamato damashii* [Japanese national spirit] which provided the basis of our courage. Now that we can talk in retrospect of the Sino-Japanese War, I am afraid our national spirit has not been given a proper chance to be aroused, due to the deplorable fact that we had to fight with China, our sister nation, with no foreseeable conclusion to look forward to. . . . While desperately fighting with a country which we made our enemy only reluctantly we were trying to find out a principle, an ethic based upon a new view of the world, which would justify our course of action. . . . The China incident was not only insufficient to fulfill this goal but also met with insurmountable obstacles. Consequently, time and opportunity ripened to declare war against the United States and England. . . .

. . . We would have nothing to say for ourselves if we were merely to follow the examples of the imperialistic and capitalistic exploitation of Greater East-Asia by Europe and the United States. . . .

. . . It is true that the science of war is one manifestation of a nation's culture. But from this time on we have to realize the increasing responsibility on our part if we are to deserve the respect of the people of East-Asian countries as their leaders, in the sphere of culture in general (not only the mere fusion and continuance of Western and Oriental cultures but something surpassing and elevating them while making the most out of them) such as the formation of national character, refinement, intellect, training to become a world citizen, etc. . . .

The sense of awe and respect with which the Orientals have held the white race, especially the Anglo-Saxons, for three hundred years is deep-rooted almost beyond our imagination. It is our task to realize this fact and deal with this servility at its root, find out why the white people became the objects of such reverence. It goes without saying that we cannot conclude simplemindedly that their shrewdness is the cause. Also we have to be very careful not to impose the *hakko ichiu* [the gathering of the whole world under one roof] spirit arbitrarily upon the Asians. If we make this kind of mistake we might antagonize those who could have become our compatriots and thus might also blaspheme our Imperial rule. . . .

To sum up, we have finally witnessed the dawn of a new principle which we had been searching for over ten years. . . . The phrase "Greater East-Asian Coprosperity Sphere" is no longer a mere abstract idea.

QUESTIONS

1. Why, according to the author, did the Japanese effort in China sow confusion about Japan's wider aims?

2. What role was Japan to play in southeast Asia if it was *not* merely to replace Western imperialistic exploitation with another form?

SOURCE: "Our Present War and Its Cultural Significance" by Nagayo Yashiofrom, translated by Mitsuko Iriye, in *Modern Asia and Africa*, edited by William H. McNeill and Mitsuko Iriye (New York: Oxford University Press, 1971), pp. 232–236.

United States was not prepared to act militarily in Europe right away. What it could do, however, was supply the British with the ships needed to overcome German submarines, which seriously threatened shipping to Britain by 1942.

In the Pacific theater, in contrast, it was immediately clear that the United States would bear the brunt of the fighting against Japan. Although the Japanese went from one success to another during the first months of the war, they lacked the long-term resources to exploit their initial victories. In May 1942 the Battle of Coral Sea—off New Guinea, north of Australia—ended in a stalemate, stopping the string of Japanese successes. Then in June, the United States defeated the Japanese navy for the first time in the Battle of Midway, northwest of Hawaii. After the United States stopped attempted Japanese advances in the Solomon Islands and New Guinea early in 1943, U.S. forces began steadily advancing across the islands of the Pacific toward Japan (see Map 28.3).

The Search for a Second Front in Europe

As the Soviet army fought the Germans in the Soviet Union, the United States and Britain tried to determine how they could help tip the scales in Europe, now an almost impregnable German fortress. Stalin kept urging a direct assault across the English Channel, which, if successful, would have the greatest immediate impact. Churchill, however, advocated attacking the underbelly of the Axis empire by way of the Mediterranean, which would first require winning control of North Africa. And it was that strategy the Allies tried first, starting in 1942.

By May 1943, step one of Churchill's plan had succeeded, but North Africa was valuable only as a staging ground for an Allied attempt to penetrate Europe from the south (see Map 28.1). Meeting at the Moroccan city of Casablanca in January 1943, Churchill and Roosevelt agreed that British and American forces would proceed from North Africa to Sicily and on up through Italy. The Soviets, still pushing for an invasion across the English Channel into France, objected that the Germans could easily block an Allied advance through the long, mountainous Italian peninsula.

Crossing from North Africa, Allied troops landed in Sicily in July 1943, prompting the arrest of Mussolini and the collapse of the fascist regime. Supported by King Victor Emmanuel III, the Italian military commander, Pietro Badoglio°, formed a new government to seek an armistice. Meanwhile, Allied forces moved on to the Italian mainland, but the Germans quickly occupied much of Italy in response. They even managed a daring rescue of Mussolini and promptly re-established him as puppet leader of a new rump republic in northern Italy, now under German control. Just as the Soviets had warned, the Germans sought to block the Italian peninsula, and it was not until nine months later, in June 1944, that the Allies reached Rome. So Churchill's strategy of assaulting Europe from the south proved less than decisive.

Badoglio (bah-DOHL-yo)

Only when Churchill, Roosevelt, and Stalin met for the first time, at Teheran, Iran, in November 1943, did they agree that the next step would be to invade western Europe from Britain. Preparations had been underway since early 1942, but the operation was complex and hazardous in the extreme. Finally, Allied troops crossed the English Channel to make an amphibious landing on the beaches of Normandy, in northern France, on June 6, 1944, known to history as D-Day. Partly by deceiving the Germans seeking to defend the area, they were quickly able to consolidate their positions.

The success of the D-Day invasion opened a major second front in Europe at last. Now American-led forces from the west and Soviet forces from the east worked systematically toward Germany. The one substantial German counterattack in the west, the Battle of the Bulge in December 1944, slowed the Allies' advance, but on March 7, 1945, Allied troops crossed the Rhine River (see Map 28.1).

By June 1944, when Allied forces landed at Normandy, Soviet forces had already crossed the 1939 border with Poland as they moved steadily westward. But in August the Soviets stopped before reaching Warsaw, allowing the Nazis to crush a notable uprising by the Polish resistance from August to October. The Polish Home Army, as it was called, was seeking to liberate Warsaw on its own, without waiting for the Soviets, who seemed likely to impose communism on Poland. In putting down the uprising, the German occupying forces suffered ten thousand casualties, then destroyed much of the city in retaliation. Meanwhile, the major Soviet thrust began cutting south, through Romania, which surrendered in August, and on into the Danube Valley in Hungary and Yugoslavia during the fall. The Soviets resumed their advance, taking Warsaw and moving westward toward Germany, only in January 1945.

Now, with the defeat of Germany simply a matter of time, Allied concern shifted to the postwar order. Churchill, especially, worried about the implications of the Soviet advances in east-central Europe and the Balkans. As a supplement to the D-Day landings, he wanted to strike from Italy through Yugoslavia into east-central Europe. But the Americans resisted; Churchill's priorities, they felt, reflected old-fashioned concerns over spheres of influence that were no longer appropriate. So the Allies concentrated instead on a secondary landing in southern France in August 1944. This assault, in which Free French forces were prominent, led quickly to the liberation of Paris. But because the Allies made both their landings in France, and not in southeastern Europe, the

D-Day, 1944   Allied forces land at Normandy, early in the morning of June 6, 1944, at last opening a major second front in Europe.   *(National Archives, Washington)*

Western democracies were involved only in the liberation of western Europe. It was the Soviets who drove the Germans from east-central Europe and the Balkans. This fact, and the resulting geographic distribution of military strength, fundamentally affected the postwar order in Europe.

THE SHAPE OF THE ALLIED VICTORY, 1944–1945

THE leaders of the Soviet Union, Britain, and the United States sought to mold that postwar order at two notable conferences in 1945. Even as they brought different aspirations for the postwar world, they had to deal together with the legacy of a war of unprecedented violence and destruction. At the same time, they also had to face the hard military realities that had resulted from the fighting so far: each country had armies in certain places but not in others. The result was an informal division of Europe into spheres of influence among the victors.

The most serious question the Allies faced concerned Germany, which was widely held responsible for the two world wars, as well as for Nazism with all its atrocities—including the concentration and extermination camps, discovered with shock and horror by the advancing Allied armies in 1945. Germany was to be forced to surrender unconditionally; there would be no negotiation or armistice. But what should be done with the country over the longer term?

In the Pacific theater, as in Europe, the way the war ended had major implications for the postwar world. The United States decided to use the atomic bomb, a weapon so destructive that it forced a quick Japanese surrender. The suddenness of the ending helped determine the fate of the European empires in Asia.

The Yalta Conference: Shaping the Postwar World

When Stalin, Roosevelt, and Churchill met at Yalta, a Soviet Black Sea resort, in February 1945, Allied victory was assured, and the three leaders accomplished a great deal. Yet controversy has long surrounded the Yalta conference. Western critics have charged that the concessions made there to Stalin consigned east-central Europe to communist domination and opened the way to the dangerous cold war of the next forty years. At the time, however, the anticipation of victory produced a relatively cooperative spirit among the Allies. Thus they firmed up plans for military occupation of Germany in separate zones, for joint occupation of Berlin, and for an Allied Control Council, composed of the military commanders-in-chief, which would make policy for all of Germany by unanimous agreement.

Each of the Allies had special concerns, but each got much of what it was seeking at Yalta. Roosevelt was eager for Soviet help against Japan as soon as possible, and he won Soviet commitment to an agreement tentatively worked out earlier. In exchange for territorial concessions in Asia and the Pacific, Stalin agreed to declare war on Japan within three months of the German surrender.

Churchill, meanwhile, worried about the future of Europe in light of the American intention, which Roosevelt announced at Yalta, to maintain occupation troops in Europe for only two years after the war. To help balance Soviet power on the Continent, Churchill felt it essential to restore France as a great power. To this end, he urged that France be granted a share in the occupation of Germany and a permanent seat on the Security Council of the proposed new international organization, the United Nations (see page 974). Roosevelt agreed, even though he had little use for Charles de Gaulle or what he viewed as the pretensions of the French.

It seemed to the Americans that both Britain and the Soviet Union remained too wedded to traditional conceptions of national interest as they sought to shape the postwar world. Hence one of Roosevelt's major priorities was to secure British and Soviet commitment to the United Nations before the three allies began to disagree over particular issues. He won that commitment at Yalta, but only by giving in to Churchill on the sensitive matter of British colonies.

Because anti-imperial sentiment worked to Japan's advantage in Asia, the United States had pestered Britain on the colonial issue since early in the war. Roosevelt even asked Churchill in 1941 about British intentions in India. So prickly was Churchill that he proclaimed in 1942, "I have not become the King's First Minister in order to preside over the liquidation of the British Empire." The parties agreed at Yalta that the British Empire would be exempt from an anticipated measure to bring former colonies under United Nations trusteeship after the war.

Although it was not the only question on the table, the future of the former Axis territories was central to the seaside deliberations. By the time of the conference, those territories were already being divided into spheres of influence among the Allies, and in light of the location of Allied troops, the eventual alignment was probably inevitable. In Italy, where U.S. and British troops held sway,

The Big Three at Yalta   With victory over Nazi Germany assured, Churchill, Roosevelt, and Stalin were in reasonably good spirits when they met at Yalta, a Black Sea resort in the Soviet Union, in February 1945. Important sources of friction among them were evident at the meeting, but the differences that led to the cold war did not seem paramount at this point. The Yalta conference proved to be the last meeting of the three leaders.   *(F.D.R. Library)*

968

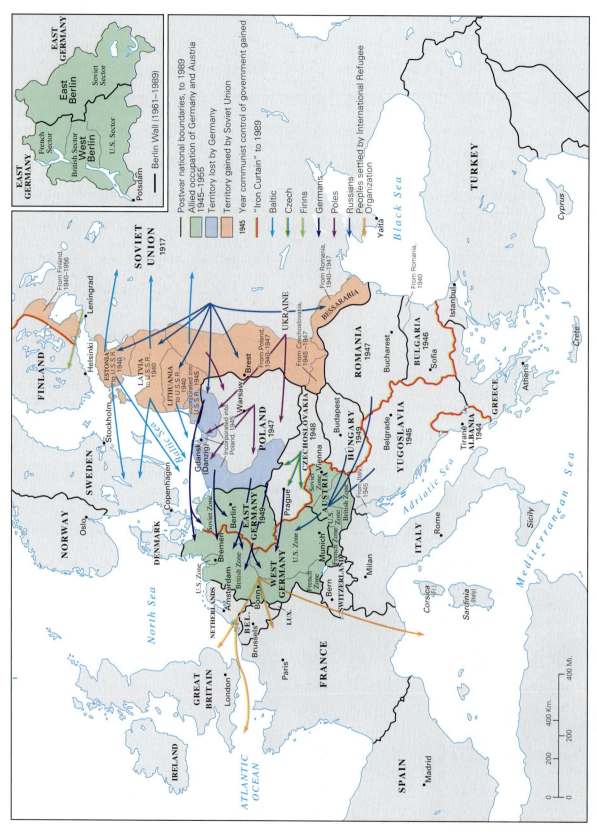

Map 28.4 The Impact of World War II in Europe As a result of World War II, the Soviet Union expanded its western borders and Poland shifted westward at the expense of Germany. Territorial changes added to the wartime disruption and produced a flood of refugees. The cold war division of Europe did not depend on immediate territorial changes, but soon Germany itself came to be divided along east-west lines.

the two democracies had successfully resisted Stalin's claim for a share in the administration. In east-central Europe, however, the Soviet army was in control. Still, the United States, with its vision of a new world order, objected to spheres of influence and insisted that democratic principles be applied everywhere. At Yalta this American priority led to an awkward compromise over east-central Europe: the new governments in the area were to be both democratic and friendly to the Soviet Union.

Most important to the Soviets was Poland, with its crucial location between Russia and Germany. Although the they insisted that communists lead the new Polish government at the outset, the Soviets compromised by allowing a role for the noncommunist Polish government-in-exile in London and by promising free elections down the road. The Allies agreed that Poland would gain substantial German territory to its west to make up for the eastern territory it had already lost to the USSR (see Map 28.4).

In addition, the United States and Britain were to have a role in committees set up to engineer the transition to democracy in the rest of east-central Europe. However, only the Soviets had troops in the area, and those committees proved essentially powerless. The sources of future tension were already at work at Yalta, but they generally remained hidden by the high spirits of approaching victory.

Victory in Europe

Although the tide had turned in 1943, Germany managed to continue the war by exploiting its conquered territories and by more effectively allocating its domestic resources for war production. Thanks partly to the efforts of armaments minister Albert Speer, war production grew sharply between 1941 and 1944, so Germany had plenty of weapons even as the war was ending. The Germans even proved able to withstand the systematic bombing of cities that the British, especially, had thought might prove decisive.

Beginning in 1942, British-led bombing attacks destroyed an average of half the built-up area of seventy German cities, sometimes producing huge firestorms. The bombing of the historic city of Dresden in February 1945 killed at least sixty thousand civilians in the most destructive air assault of the war in Europe. But despite this widespread destruction, such bombing did not undermine morale or disrupt production to the extent expected. Even in the face of steady Allied bombing, Germany increased its war production during 1943 and 1944.

But Germany encountered two crucial bottlenecks that finally crippled its military effort: it was running out of both oil and military personnel. Despite making effective use of synthetics, the Nazi war machine depended heavily on oil from Romania. Late in August 1944, however, Soviet troops crossed into Romania, taking control of the oil fields. And though the terror bombing of cities did not have the anticipated impact, the more precisely targeted bombing favored by U.S. strategists significantly affected the outcome. In May 1944 the United States began bombing oil fields in Romania and refineries and synthetic oil plants in Germany. Soon Germany lacked enough fuel even to train pilots. So serious were the bottlenecks by 1945 that the German air force could not use all the aircraft that German industry was producing.

Soviet troops moving westward finally met U.S. troops moving eastward at the Elbe River in Germany on April 26, 1945. With his regime now thoroughly defeated and much of his country in ruins, Hitler committed suicide in his underground military headquarters in Berlin on April 30, 1945. The war in Europe finally ended with the German surrender to General Dwight D. Eisenhower (1890–1969) at Reims, France, on May 7 and to Marshal Zhukov at Berlin on May 8. The world celebrated the end of the fighting in Europe, but an element of uncertainty surrounded the Allied victory. East-West differences were increasingly coming to the fore within the anti-German alliance.

The Potsdam Conference and the Question of Germany

The immediate question for the victorious Allies was the fate of Germany, which they confronted at the last of their notable wartime conferences, at Potsdam, just outside Berlin, from July 17 to August 2, 1945. The circumstances were dramatically different from those at Yalta just months before. With Hitler dead and Germany defeated, no common military aim provided unity. And of the three Allied leaders who had been at Yalta, only Stalin remained. President Roosevelt had died in April, so his successor, Harry Truman (1884–1972), represented the United States. In Britain, Churchill's Conservatives lost the general election during the first days of the conference, so Clement Attlee (1883–1967), the new Labour prime minister, assumed the leadership of the British delegation.

At Potsdam the Allies had to determine how to implement their earlier agreements about Germany, which, devastated by bombing and devoid of a government, depended on the Allied occupying forces even for its

The Soviet Victory in Europe
After forcing the Germans back for almost two years, Soviet troops reached Berlin in April 1945. After a day of heavy fighting and bombardment, the Soviets took the Reichstag building, in the heart of the devastated German capital, on April 30. Here two Soviet sergeants, Yegorov and Kantariya, plant the Soviet flag atop the Reichstag, symbolizing the Soviet victory in the decisive encounter of World War II in Europe. *(ITAR-TAS/Sovfoto)*

day-to-day survival. For a time, U.S. policymakers had even considered destroying Germany's industrial capacity in perpetuity. However, cooler heads understood that the deindustrialization, or "pastoralization," of Germany would not be in anyone's economic interests. Moreover, as the democracies grew increasingly suspicious about Soviet intentions, an economically healthy Germany seemed necessary to help in the balance against the Soviet Union.

For their part, the Soviets had reason to take a much harder line against Germany. Having been ravaged by invading German forces twice within living memory, the Soviet Union wanted to weaken Germany both territorially and economically. And of the three victors, the Soviets had suffered a greatly disproportionate share of the wartime destruction and economic loss, so they also sought to exploit the remaining resources of Germany by exacting heavy reparations. Moreover, the British and the Americans accepted the Soviet proposal that Germany's eastern border with Poland be shifted substantially westward, to the line formed by the Oder and Neisse° Rivers. But just as Poland gained at the expense of Germany, the Soviet Union kept a substantial slice of what had been eastern Poland (see Map 28.4).

Each of the three Allies had responsibility for administering a particular zone of occupation, but they were supposed to coordinate their activities in a common policy toward Germany. This effort was to include de-

Nazification, demilitarization, and an assault on concentrations of economic power—to root out what seemed to have been the sources of Germany's antidemocratic and aggressive tendencies. But East-West disagreements over economic policy soon undermined the pretense of joint government.

The Atomic Bomb and the Capitulation of Japan

In the Pacific, Japan had been forced onto the defensive by September 1943, and though it mounted two major counterattacks during 1944, the Japanese navy was crippled by shortages of ships and fuel by the end of the year. However, as the situation grew more desperate for Japan, Japanese ground soldiers battled ever more fiercely, often fighting to the death or taking their own lives rather than surrendering. Beginning late in 1944, aircraft pilots practiced *kamikaze*°, suicidally crashing planes filled with explosives into U.S. targets. The Japanese used this tactic especially as the Americans sought to take Okinawa in the spring of 1945. The U.S. forces finally prevailed in June, but only after the most bitter combat of the Pacific war (see Map 28.3).

In conquering Okinawa, American forces got close enough for air raids on the Japanese home islands. But

Neisse (NYE-suh)　**kamikaze** (kah-mih-KAH-zee)

though the United States was now clearly in control, it seemed likely that an actual invasion of Japan would be necessary to force a Japanese surrender. Some estimated that, because the Japanese could be expected to fight even more desperately to defend their own soil, invasion might well cost the United States one million additional casualties. It was especially for this reason that the Americans decided to try to end the war in an altogether different way—by using an atomic bomb.

In 1939 scientists in several countries, including Germany, had started to advise their governments that new, immensely destructive weapons based on thermonuclear fission were theoretically possible. The German economics ministry began seeking uranium as early as 1939, but Hitler promoted jet- and rocket-propelled terror weaponry instead, especially the V-2 rocket bombs that the Germans began showering on England in the fall of 1944. Still, fear that the Nazis were developing atomic weapons lurked behind the Allied effort to produce the ultra-lethal bomb as quickly as possible.

Although the British were the first to initiate an atomic weapons program, by late 1941 the Americans were building on what they knew of British findings to develop their own crash program, known as the Manhattan Project. Constructing an atomic bomb proved far more difficult and costly than most had expected in 1941, and it took a concerted effort by the United States to have atomic weapons ready for use by mid-1945.

The U.S. decision to use the atomic bomb on Japanese civilians has been one of the most controversial of modern history. The decision fell to the new president, Harry Truman, who had known nothing of the bomb project when Roosevelt died in April 1945. During the next few months, Truman listened to spirited disagreement among American policymakers. Was it necessary to drop the bomb to force the Japanese to surrender? Since the ultimate victory of the United States was not in doubt, some argued that it would be enough simply to demonstrate the new weapon to the Japanese in a test firing.

By July, when the Allies met at Potsdam, the United States was prepared to use the bomb. But President Truman first warned Japan that if it did not surrender at once, it would be subjected to destruction immeasurably greater than Germany had just suffered. The Japanese ignored the warning, although the United States had begun area-bombing Japanese cities a few months before. The bombing of Tokyo in March produced a firestorm that gutted one-fourth of the city and killed over 80,000 people. In light of the Japanese refusal to surrender, the use of the atomic bomb seemed to Truman to be the logical next step.

At 8:15 on the morning of August 6, 1945, from a height of 32,000 feet above the Japanese city of Hiroshima, an American pilot released the first atomic bomb to be used against an enemy target. The bomb exploded after 45 seconds, 2,000 feet above the ground, killing 80,000 people outright and leaving tens of thousands more to die in the aftermath. Three days later, on August 9, the Americans exploded a second atomic bomb over Nagasaki, killing perhaps 50,000 people. Although sectors of the Japanese military held out for continued resistance, Emperor Hirohito° (1901–1989) finally surrendered on August 15. The bombing of civilians had discredited the Japanese military, which not only had proved unable to defend the country but had systematically misled the Japanese people about their country's prospects.

The war in the Pacific ended more suddenly than had seemed possible just a few months earlier (see Map 28.3). This worked in favor of the various national liberation or decolonization movements that had developed in Asia during the war, for the Europeans had little opportunity to re-establish their dominance in the colonial territories they had earlier lost to the Japanese. In the Dutch East Indies, the Japanese had encouraged anticolonial sentiment, even helping local nationalists create patriotic militias. After the war, the Dutch were never able to reassert their control against this Indonesian nationalist movement. But though the war had severely weakened the old Western imperialism in Asia and the Pacific, what would replace it remained unclear.

Death, Disruption, and the Question of Guilt

World War II left as many as 60 million people dead—three times as many as World War I. About that same number were left homeless for some length of time, or found themselves forced onto the mercies of others as refugees. The Soviet Union and Germany suffered by far the highest casualty figures; for each, the figure was considerably higher than in World War I. An appalling 23 million Soviet citizens died, of whom 12 million to 13 million were civilians. Poland lost over 6 million, the vast majority civilians, including perhaps 3 millions Jews. Germany lost 5 million to 6 million, including perhaps 2 million civilians.

In contrast, casualty rates for Italy, Britain, and France were lower than in World War I. Italy suffered 200,000 military and 200,000 civilian deaths. Total British losses, including civilians, numbered 450,000, to which

Hirohito (hee-roh-HEE-toh)

Reconstruction Begins
Shortly after the end of the war, women in Berlin pass pails of rubble along a line to dump. Wartime bombing had severely damaged cities throughout much of Europe, although destruction was greatest in Germany.   *(Hulton Archive/ Getty Images)*

must be added 120,000 from the British Empire. Despite its quick defeat, France lost more lives than Britain because of the ravages of German occupation: the 350,000 deaths among French civilians considerably exceeded the British figure, closer to 100,000.

The United States lost 300,000 servicemen and 5,000 civilians. Figures for Japan are problematic, partly because the Japanese claim that 300,000 of those who surrendered to the Soviets in 1945 have remained unaccounted for. Apart from this number, 1.74 million Japanese servicemen died from 1941 to 1945, more from hunger and disease than from combat, and 300,000 civilians died in Japan, most from U.S. bombing.

During the war, Jews, Poles, and others deemed undesirable by the Nazis had been rounded up and shipped to ghettos or camps, where the great majority had died. Of those Jews who were still alive when the Nazi camps were liberated, almost half died within a few weeks. Even those who managed to return home sometimes faced pogroms during the difficult months that followed; forty Jews were killed in the worst of them, at Kielce°, Poland, in 1946.

Late in the war, as German forces in the east retreated, ethnic Germans living in Poland, Czechoslovakia, Hungary, and elsewhere in east-central Europe began

seeking refuge in Germany. They were fleeing the Soviet advance but also seeking to escape the growing wave of anti-German resentment in those countries. Once the war was over, the Poles began expelling ethnic Germans from the historically German areas that were now to become Polish. These Germans were sometimes sent to detention camps, and when they were shipped out, it was often in cattle cars. According to some estimates, as many as two million died in the process. At the same time, the uprooting of Poles that had begun during the war continued as Poles were systematically forced from the Polish territories incorporated into the Soviet Union.

In Czechoslovakia the government expelled 3.5 million Germans from the Sudetenland area by 1947. All told, at least 7 million German refugees moved west into the shrunken territory of the new Germany by 1947. They were among the 16 million Europeans who were permanently uprooted and transplanted during the war and its immediate wake. And the process continued at a diminished rate thereafter. By 1958 perhaps 10 million Germans had either left or been forced out of the new Poland, leaving only about 1 million Germans still living there.

As the end of the war approached, Europeans began attempting to assess guilt and punish those responsible for the disasters of the era. In the climate of violence, resistance forces in France, Italy, and elsewhere often subjected fascists and collaborators to summary justice,

Kielce (KYEL-tsuh)

sometimes through quick trials in ad hoc courts. In Italy this process led to 15,000 executions, in France 10,000. French women accused of sleeping with German soldiers were shamed by having their heads shaved.

The most sensitive confrontation with the recent past took place in Germany, where the occupying powers imposed a program of de-Nazification. In the western zones, German citizens were required to attend lectures on the virtues of democracy and to view the corpses of the victims of Nazism. In this context, the Allies determined to identify and bring to justice those responsible for the crimes of Hitler's regime. This effort led to the Nuremberg trials of 1945 and 1946, the most famous of a number of war crimes trials held in Germany and the occupied countries after the war.

Although Hitler, Himmler, and Goebbels had committed suicide, the occupying authorities apprehended for trial twenty-four individuals who had played important but very different roles in Hitler's Third Reich. All but three were convicted of war crimes and "crimes against humanity." Twelve were sentenced to death; of those, two committed suicide, and the other ten were executed.

Questions about their legitimacy dogged the Nuremberg trials from the start. To a considerable extent the accused were being judged according to law made after the fact. The notion of "crimes against humanity" remained vague. Moreover, even insofar as a measure of international law was in force, it was arguably binding only on states, not individuals. But in light of the unprecedented atrocities of the Nazi regime, there was widespread agreement among the victors that the Nazi leaders could not be treated simply as defeated adversaries.

INTO THE POSTWAR WORLD

EVEN after the fighting stopped in 1945, remarkable changes continued as the forces unleashed by the war played themselves out. In a number of war-torn countries, the legacies of wartime resistance movements helped shape the political order and priorities for beginning anew. At the same time, differences between the Soviets and the Western democracies began to undermine the wartime alliance, soon producing the division of Germany and a bipolar Europe. Thus the conclusion of World War II led directly to the danger of a third world war, which might involve nuclear weapons and thus prove immeasurably more destructive than the last.

In addition to the dramatic changes in Europe, the wider effects of the war brought to the forefront a whole new set of issues, from anticolonialism to the Arab-Israeli conflict to the spread of communism within the non-Western world. These issues would remain central for decades. By 1949, however, it was already possible to discern the contours of the new postwar world, a world with new sources of hope but also with conflicts and dangers hardly imaginable ten years earlier.

Resistance and Renewal

Though the Nazis had found some willing collaborators, the great majority of those living under German occupation came to despise the Nazis as their brutality became ever clearer. Nazi rule meant pillage, forced labor in Germany, and the random killing of hostages in reprisal for resistance activity. In one extreme case, the Germans destroyed the Czech village of Lidice°, killing all its inhabitants, in retaliation for the assassination of SS security chief Reinhard Heydrich in 1942.

Clandestine movements of resistance to the occupying Nazi forces gradually developed all over Europe. In western Europe, resistance was especially prominent in France and, beginning in 1943, northern Italy, which was subjected to German occupation after the Allies defeated Mussolini's regime. But the anti-German resistance was strongest in Yugoslavia, Poland, and the occupied portions of the Soviet Union, where full-scale guerrilla war against the Germans and their collaborators produced the highest civilian casualties of World War II. The Polish resistance achieved some notable successes in sabotaging roads and railroads, although it met disastrous defeat when it sought to tackle the Germans head-on in Warsaw in 1944.

The role of the resistance proved most significant in Yugoslavia, where the Croatian Marxist Josip Broz, taking the pseudonym Tito (1892–1980), forged the opponents of the Axis powers into a broadly based guerrilla army. Its initial foe was the inflated Croatian state that the Germans, early in 1941, carved from Yugoslavia and entrusted to the pro-Axis Croatian separatist movement, the Ustashe°. But Tito's forces soon came up against a rival resistance movement, led by Serb officers, that tended to be pro-Serb, monarchist, and anticommunist. By 1943 Tito led 250,000 men and women in what had become a vicious civil war, one that deepened ethnic divisions and left a legacy of bitterness. Tito's forces prevailed, enabling him to create a communist-led government in Yugoslavia late in the war.

In France and Italy as well, communists played leading roles in the wartime resistance movements. As a

---

Lidice (LIH-dyit-seh)   **Ustashe** (oo-STAH-zhiy)

result, the Communist Party in each country overcame the disarray that followed from the Nazi-Soviet Pact of 1939, and after the war each enjoyed a level of prestige that would have been unthinkable earlier.

In the French case, the indigenous resistance, with its significant communist component, generally worked well with de Gaulle and the Free French, operating outside France until August 1944. Still, de Gaulle took pains to cement his own leadership in the overall struggle. Among the measures to this end, he decreed women's suffrage for France, partly because women were playing a major role in the resistance. After the liberation of France in 1944, he sought to control a potentially volatile situation by disarming the resistance as quickly as possible.

The western European resistance movements are easily romanticized, their extent and importance overstated. Compared with regular troops, resistance forces were poorly trained, equipped, and disciplined. In France fewer than 30 percent of the nearly 400,000 active resisters had firearms in 1944. But though the Allies never tried to use them in a systematic way, the resistance movements made at least some military contribution, especially through sabotage. And they boosted national self-esteem for the longer term, helping countries humiliated by defeat and occupation make a fresh start after the war.

But had governments and institutions outside Germany done all they could—especially as the dimensions of the Nazi exterminations began to come into focus? For example, President Roosevelt, in the face of appeals from Jewish groups, declined to try to disrupt the Nazi killing machine by bombing rail lines to Auschwitz. As he saw it, the way to save as many Jews as possible was to win the war as quickly as possible.

Especially controversial has been the response of Pope Pius XII (r. 1939–1958), who declined to take the moral high ground and denounce Nazi atrocities explicitly. He felt that he could not censure the Nazis without also censuring the Soviets, at that point allies in the anti-Nazi cause. He also feared for the fortunes of the Catholic Church as an institution in areas under German control, including Rome itself during the pivotal nine months from September 1943 to June 1944. The mission of the church was not merely to save lives but above all to save souls—and for that the institution was essential. Many felt, however, that stronger moral leadership by the Catholic Church would have stiffened resistance to the Nazis, stimulated aid to individual Jews, and enhanced the overall self-confidence of the West as it faced the post-Holocaust future.

Conflicting Visions and the Coming of the Cold War

Starting with the Atlantic Charter conference of 1941, Roosevelt had sought to ensure that the common effort against the Axis powers would lead to a firmer basis for peace, to be framed through a new international organization after the war. At a conference at Dumbarton Oaks in Washington, D.C., in September 1944, the United States proposed the structure for a new "United Nations." Meeting in San Francisco from April to June 1945, delegates from almost fifty anti-Axis countries translated that proposal into a charter for the new organization. As Roosevelt had envisioned, the major powers were given a privileged position in the organization as permanent members of the Security Council, each with veto power. To dramatize its departure from the Geneva-based League of Nations, which the United States had refused to join, the United Nations was headquartered in New York. In July 1945 the U.S. Senate approved U.S. membership in the international body almost unanimously.

By the end of the war, several international meetings had used the United Nations title. In July 1944 the United Nations Monetary and Financial Conference at Bretton Woods, New Hampshire, brought together delegates from forty-four nations to deal with problems of currency and exchange rates. Although it produced only recommendations subject to ratification by the individual states, the conference indicated a new determination to cooperate on the international level after the failures of the interwar period. The outcome of the conference, the Bretton Woods Agreement, laid the foundation for international economic exchange in the noncommunist world for the crucial quarter century of economic recovery after the war. In addition, the conference gave birth to the International Monetary Fund and the International Bank for Reconstruction and Development, which played major roles in the decades that followed.

Whereas the United States envisioned a world order based on the ongoing cooperation of the three victors, the Soviet Union had a different agenda. Its top priority was to create a buffer zone of friendly states in east-central Europe, especially as a bulwark against Germany. While seeking this sphere of influence in east-central Europe, Stalin gave the British a free hand to settle the civil war between communists and anticommunists in Greece, and he did not push for revolution in western Europe. The strong Communist Parties that had emerged from the resistance movements in Italy and France were directed by Moscow to work within broad-based democratic fronts rather than try to take power. Although no formal deal was made, Stalin saw this moderate position in western and southern Europe as a tacit exchange with the West for a free hand in east-central Europe.

The Division of Germany

The site of greatest potential stress between the Soviets and the democracies was Germany. At first, the Western Allies were concerned especially to root out the sources of Germany's antidemocratic, aggressive behavior, but that concern faded as communism, not Nazism, came to seem the immediate menace. And it was especially conflict over Germany that cemented the developing division of Europe. Neither the democracies nor the Soviets lived up to all their agreements concerning Germany, but in light of the fundamental differences in priorities, cooperation between the two sides was bound to be difficult at best.

Disagreements over economic policy proved the major source of the eventual split. At Potsdam, the West had accepted Soviet demands for German reparations, but rather than wait for payment, the Soviets began removing German factories and equipment for reassembly in the Soviet Union. To ensure that they got their due, the Soviets wanted access to the economic resources not simply of the Russian occupation zone but of the whole of Germany. The United States and Britain, in contrast, gave priority to economic reconstruction and quickly began integrating the economies of the Western zones for that purpose.

Friction developed from 1945 to 1948 as the West insisted on reduced reparations and a higher level of industrial production than the Soviets wanted. Finally, as part of their effort to spur economic recovery, the United States and Britain violated Allied agreements by introducing a new currency without Soviet consent. Stalin answered in June 1948 by blockading the city of Berlin, cutting its western sectors off from the main Western occupation zones, almost 200 miles west (see Map 28.4). The Western Allies responded with a massive airlift that kept their sectors of Berlin supplied for almost a year, until May 1949, when the Soviets finally backed down.

By 1948 two separate German states began emerging from the Allied occupation zones. The Western occupying powers had begun restoring local government immediately after the war, to create the administrative framework necessary to provide public utilities and food distribution. Gradually a governing structure was built from the ground up in the Western zones, which were increasingly coordinated.

With Allied support, a "parliamentary council" of West German leaders met during 1948 and 1949 and produced a document that, when ratified in September 1949, became the "Basic Law" of a new Federal Republic of Germany, with its capital at Bonn. This founding document was termed simply the Basic Law, as opposed to the constitution, to emphasize the provisional character of the new West German state. To create a state limited to the west was not to foreclose the future reunification of Germany. But as it became clear that a new state was being created in the Western zones, the Soviets settled for a new state in their zone, in eastern Germany. Thus the Communist-led German Democratic Republic, with its capital in East Berlin, was born in October 1949.

The "Iron Curtain" and the Emergence of a Bipolar World

In east-central Europe, only Yugoslavia and Albania had achieved liberation on their own, and the communist leaders of their resistance movements had a plausible claim to political power. Elsewhere, the Soviet army had provided liberation, and the Soviet military presence remained the decisive political fact as the war ended. In much of the region, authoritarianism and collaboration had been the rule for a decade or more, so there was no possibility of returning to a clearly legitimate prewar political order. To be sure, each country had local political groups, some representing former governments in exile, that now claimed a governing role, but their standing in relation to the Soviet army was uncertain.

Under these circumstances, the Soviets were able to work with local communists to install new communist-led regimes friendly to the Soviet Union in most of east-central Europe. But though Churchill warned as early as 1946 that "an iron curtain" was descending from the Baltic to the Adriatic, the process of Soviet power consolidation was not easy, and it took place gradually, in discrete steps over several years. (See the two boxes "Reading Sources: Discerning the Iron Curtain" and "Reading Sources: Churchill as Warmonger: Stalin's Response to the 'Iron Curtain' Speech.") The Communist-led government of Poland held elections in January 1947—but rigged them to guarantee a favorable outcome. In Czechoslovakia the Communist Party anticipated serious losses in upcoming elections and so finally took power outright in 1948. By 1949 communist governments, relying on Soviet support, controlled Poland, Czechoslovakia, East Germany, Hungary, Romania, and Bulgaria, with Yugoslavia and Albania also communist but capable of a more independent line.

Communism might have spread still farther in Europe, and perhaps beyond, but the West drew the line at Greece. There, as in Yugoslavia, an indigenous, communist-led resistance movement had become strong

READING SOURCES

DISCERNING THE IRON CURTAIN

Winston Churchill, out of office and touring the United States, sought to explain the postwar international situation in a speech at Westminster College in Fulton, Missouri, on March 5, 1946. To characterize the developing division of Europe, Churchill referred to "an iron curtain," a term that attracted immediate attention and dramatically affected public opinion in both the United States and western Europe. Some have suggested that Churchill was overdramatizing the situation in an effort to keep the United States engaged in Europe.

A shadow has fallen upon the scenes so lately lighted by the Allied victory. Nobody knows what Soviet Russia and its Communist international organization intend to do in the immediate future, or what are the limits, if any, to their expansive and proselytizing tendencies. . . . We understand the Russian need to be secure on her western frontiers by the removal of all possibility of German aggression. We welcome her to her rightful place among the leading nations of the world. . . . It is my duty, however, to place before you certain facts. . . .

From Stettin in the Baltic to Trieste in the Adriatic, an iron curtain has descended across the Continent. Behind that line lie all the capitals of the ancient states of central and eastern Europe. Warsaw, Berlin, Prague, Vienna, Budapest, Belgrade, Bucharest, and Sofia, all these famous cities and the populations around them lie in what I must call the Soviet sphere, and all are subject in one form or another, not only to Soviet influence but to a very high and, in many cases, increasing measure of control from Moscow. Athens alone—Greece with its immortal glories—is free to decide its future at an election under British, American and French observation. The Russian-dominated Polish Government has been encouraged to make enormous and wrongful inroads upon Germany, and mass expulsions of millions of Germans on a scale grievous and undreamed-of are now taking place. The Communist parties, which were very small in all these Eastern States of Europe, have been raised to pre-eminence and power far beyond their numbers and are seeking everywhere to obtain totalitarian control. . . .

If now the Soviet Government tries, by separate action, to build up a pro-Communist Germany in their areas, this will cause new serious difficulties in the British and American zones, and will give the defeated Germans the power of putting themselves up to auction between the Soviets and the Western Democracies. Whatever conclusions may be drawn from these facts—and facts they are—this is certainly not the Liberated Europe we fought to build up. Nor is it one which contains the essentials of permanent peace. . . .

. . . I do not believe that Soviet Russia desires war. What they desire is the fruits of war and the indefinite expansion of their power and doctrines. But what we have to consider here to-day while time remains, is the permanent prevention of war and the establishment of the conditions of freedom and democracy as rapidly as possible in all countries. . . .

From what I have seen of our Russian friends and allies during the war, I am convinced that there is nothing they admire so much as strength, and there is nothing for which they have less respect than for weakness, especially military weakness.

Source: *Winston S. Churchill: His Complete Speeches, 1897–1963,* vol. 7, *1943–1949,* ed. Robert Rhodes James (New York: Chelsea House, 1974), pp. 7290–7292. Copyright © 1974 Chelsea House Publishers. Reprinted by permission of the publisher.

 For additional information on this topic, go to college.hmco.com/students.

---

enough to contend for political power by late 1944. But when it sought to oust the monarchical government that had just returned to Greece from exile, the British intervened, helping the monarchy put down the leftist uprising. Although Stalin gave the Greek communists little help, communist guerrilla activity continued, thanks partly to support from Tito's Yugoslavia. In 1946 a renewed communist insurgency escalated into civil war.

As U.S.-Soviet friction turned into a cold war, both countries began taking a more active interest in the Greek conflict, though Soviet intentions remained uncertain. After the financially strapped Labour government in Britain reduced its involvement early in 1947, the United States stepped in to support the Greek monarchy against the communists. American policymakers feared that communism would progress from the Balkans

| READING SOURCES | CHURCHILL AS WARMONGER: STALIN'S RESPONSE TO THE "IRON CURTAIN" SPEECH |

Soviet leader Joseph Stalin was quick to respond to Churchill's speech. In an interview in the official Soviet newspaper Pravda *eight days later (March 13, 1946), he accused Churchill of calling for war on the Soviet Union. But Stalin also revealed the more subtle concerns that were causing the divergence between the Soviets and their former allies, Britain and the United States. The three countries had joined forces against Hitler, but the Soviets' geographical situation and recent historical experience contrasted sharply with U.S. and British circumstances. These dissimilarities, perhaps even more than ideological differences, led Stalin to his antithetical interpretation of the outcomes and lessons of the recent war.*

Question: How do you appraise Mr. Churchill's latest speech in the United States of America?

Answer: I appraise it as a dangerous act, calculated to sow the seeds of dissension among the Allied states and impede their collaboration. . . .

. . . Mr. Churchill now takes the stand of the warmongers. . . .

. . . The German race theory led Hitler and his friends to the conclusion that the Germans, as the only superior nation, should rule over other nations. The English race theory leads Mr. Churchill and his friends to the conclusion that the English-speaking nations, as the only superior nations, should rule over the rest of the nations of the world. . . .

Question: How do you appraise the part of Mr. Churchill's speech in which he attacks the democratic systems in the European states bordering upon us, and criticizes the good neighborly relations established between these states and the Soviet Union?

Answer: This part of Mr. Churchill's speech is compounded of elements of slander and elements of discourtesy and tactlessness. . . .

. . . The following circumstances should not be forgotten. The Germans made their invasion of the U.S.S.R. through Finland, Poland, Rumania, Bulgaria, and Hungary. The Germans were able to make their invasion through these countries because, at the time, governments hostile to the Soviet Union existed in these countries. As a result of the German invasion the Soviet Union has lost irretrievably in the fighting against the Germans, and also through the German occupation and the deportation of Soviet citizens to German servitude, a total of about seven million people. In other words, the Soviet Union's loss of life has been several times greater than that of Britain and the United States of America put together. Possibly in some quarters an inclination is felt to forget about these colossal sacrifices of the Soviet people which secured the liberation of Europe from the Hitlerite yoke. But the Soviet Union cannot forget about them. And so what can there be surprising about the fact that the Soviet Union, anxious for its future safety, is trying to see to it that governments loyal in their attitude to the Soviet Union should exist in these countries? How can anyone, who has not taken leave of his wits, describe these peaceful aspirations of the Soviet Union as expansionist tendencies on the part of our state? . . .

Mr. Churchill comes somewhere near the truth when he speaks of the increasing influence of the Communist parties in eastern Europe. It must be remarked, however, that he is not quite accurate. The influence of the Communist parties has grown not only in eastern Europe, but in nearly all the countries of Europe which were previously under fascist rule . . . or which experienced German, Italian, or Hungarian occupation. . . .

The increased influence of the Communists cannot be considered fortuitous. It is a perfectly logical thing. The influence of the Communists has grown because, in the years of the rule of fascism in Europe, the Communists showed themselves trusty, fearless, self-sacrificing fighters against the fascist regime for the liberty of the peoples.

Source: Josef Stalin, "Churchill's Speech Is a Call for War on Russia," in *The Origins of the Cold War, 1941–1947: A Historical Problem with Interpretations and Documents*, ed. Walter LaFeber (New York: John Wiley and Sons, Inc., 1971).

through Greece to the Middle East. Thus, in March 1947, President Truman announced the Truman Doctrine, which committed the United States to the "containment" of communism throughout the world. (See the box "The Continuing Experiment: 'Containment' as a Cold War Strategy.") American advisers now began re-equipping the anticommunist forces in Greece. Faced with this determined opposition from the West, Stalin again pulled back, but the Greek communists, with their strong indigenous support, were not defeated until 1949.

Thus the wartime marriage of expediency between the Soviet Union and the Western democracies gradually fell apart in the war's aftermath. Only in Austria, jointly occupied by the Soviets and the Western democracies, were the former Allies able to arrange the postwar transition in a reasonably amicable way. The Soviets accepted the neutralization of a democratic Austria as the occupying powers left in 1955. Elsewhere, Europe was divided into two antagonistic power blocs.

The antagonism between the two superpowers became more menacing when the Soviets exploded their first atomic bomb in August 1949, intensifying the postwar arms race. By then, in fact, the United States was on its way to the more destructive hydrogen bomb. The split between these two nations, unmistakable by 1949, established the framework for world affairs for the next forty years.

The West and the New World Agenda

At the same time, other dramatic changes around the world suggested that, with or without the cold war, the postwar political scene would be hard to manage. Events in India in 1947, in Israel in 1948, and in China in 1949 epitomized the wider new hopes and uncertainties spawned by World War II.

Although the British, under U.S. pressure, had reluctantly promised independence for India in order to elicit Indian support during the war, British authorities and Indian leaders had continued to skirmish. Mohandas Gandhi was twice jailed for resisting British demands and threatening a massive program of nonviolent resistance to British rule. But by 1946 the British lacked the will and the financial resources to maintain their control on the subcontinent. Thus Britain acquiesced as the new independent states of India and Pakistan emerged on August 15, 1947. Allowing independence to India, long the jewel of the British Empire, raised questions about Britain's role in the postwar world and portended a wider disintegration of the European colonial system. There would be new countries, many of them poor—and resentful of Western imperialism. What would that mean for the new world order, centering on the United Nations, that Roosevelt had envisioned?

Questions about the fate of the Jews, who had suffered so grievously during World War II, were inevitable as well. Almost two-thirds of the Jews of Europe had been killed, and many of the survivors either had no place to go or had decided that they could never again live as a minority in Europe. Many concluded that the Jews must have a homeland of their own. For decades such Zionist sentiment (see page 866) had centered on the biblical area of Israel, in what had become, after

Gandhi and Anticolonialism An apostle of nonviolence, Mohandas Gandhi became one of the most admired individuals of the century as he spearheaded the movement for Indian independence. He is pictured (*center*) in December 1942 with the British stateman Sir Stafford Cripps (*left*), who had come to India to offer a plan for Indian self-government. Despite the good spirit evident here, Cripps's mission failed; Gandhi and his movement held out for full independence. *(Corbis)*

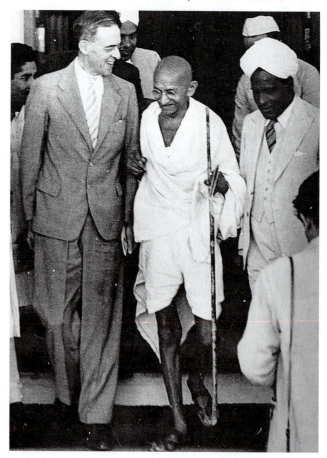

"Containment" as a Cold War Strategy

As a foreign service officer, George F. Kennan (b. 1904) emerged as the U.S. government's leading authority on the dynamics of Soviet foreign policy by the later 1940s. After analyzing Soviet postwar objectives in his now-famous "long telegram" from Moscow to the U.S. State Department in 1946, Kennan returned to the United States to become director of the State Department's Policy Planning Staff from 1947 to 1949. With hawks pondering a preemptive strike on the Soviet Union and doves stressing mutual accommodation, Kennan forcefully advocated a middle position, a strategy of "containment," in an article published anonymously in the journal *Foreign Affairs* in 1947. And his views prevailed. An uncertain experiment when it began in 1947, containment proved successful—arguably for the reasons Kennan anticipated.

[The Soviet Union] is under no ideological compulsion to accomplish its purposes in a hurry. . . . Thus the Kremlin has no compunction about retreating in the face of superior force. And being under the compulsion of no timetable, it does not get panicky under the necessity for such retreat. Its political action is a fluid stream which moves constantly, wherever it is permitted to move, toward a given goal. . . .

. . . The patient persistence by which it is animated means that it can be effectively countered not by sporadic acts which represent the momentary whims of democratic opinion but only by intelligent long-range policies on the part of Russia's adversaries—policies no less steady in their purpose, and no less variegated and resourceful in their application, than those of the Soviet Union itself.

In these circumstances it is clear that the main element of any United States policy toward the Soviet Union must be that of a long-term, patient but firm and vigilant containment of Russian expansive tendencies. It is important to note, however, that such a policy has nothing to do with outward histrionics: with threats or blustering or superfluous gestures of outward "toughness." While the Kremlin is basically flexible in its reaction to political realities, it is by no means unamenable to considerations of prestige. . . . It is a *sine qua non* of successful dealing with Russia that the foreign government in question should remain at all times cool and collected and that its demands on Russian policy should be put forward in such a manner as to leave the way open for a compliance not too detrimental to Russian prestige.

In the light of the above, it will be clearly seen that the Soviet pressure against the free institutions of the western world is something that can be contained by the adroit and vigilant application of counter-force at a series of constantly shifting geographical and political points, corresponding to the shifts and manœuvres of Soviet policy, but which cannot be charmed or talked out of existence. . . .

. . . Soviet power is only a crust concealing an amorphous mass of human beings among whom no independent organizational structure is tolerated. . . . If, consequently, anything were ever to occur to disrupt the unity and efficacy of the Party as a political instrument, Soviet Russia might be changed overnight from one of the strongest to one of the weakest and most pitiable of national societies. . . .

. . . It is . . . a question of the degree to which the United States can create among the peoples of the world generally the impression of a country which knows what it wants, which is coping successfully with the problems of its internal life and with the responsibilities of a World Power, and which has a spiritual vitality capable of holding its own among the major ideological currents of the time. To the extent that such an impression can be created and maintained, the aims of Russian Communism must appear sterile and quixotic, the hopes and enthusiasm of Moscow's supporters must wane, and added strain must be imposed on the Kremlin's foreign policies. For the palsied decrepitude of the capitalist world is the keystone of Communist philosophy. . . .

. . . The United States has it in its power to increase enormously the strains under which Soviet policy must operate, to force upon the Kremlin a far greater degree of moderation and circumspection than it has had to observe in recent years, and in this way to promote tendencies which must eventually find their outlet in either the break-up or the gradual mellowing of Soviet power.

QUESTIONS

1. What conception of the Soviet Union and its aims led Kennan to propose a policy of containment?

2. What would containment actually entail on a practical level as a response to Soviet moves?

3. Why did Kennan believe that the United States had to be unified, consistent, and principled in everything it did if it was eventually to prevail in the cold war?

SOURCE: "X" [George F. Kennan], "The Sources of Soviet Conduct," *Foreign Affairs* 25, no. 4 (July 1947). Reprinted by permission of FOREIGN AFFAIRS. Copyright 1947 by the Council on Foreign Relations, Inc.

World War I, the British mandate of Palestine. Jewish immigration to the area accelerated during the interwar period, but it caused increasing friction between the Jews and the Palestinian Arabs.

Concerned about access to Middle Eastern oil, the British sought to cultivate good relations with the Arab world after the war. Thus they opposed further immigration of Jews to Palestine, as well as proposals to carve an independent Jewish state from the area. The United States, however, was considerably more sympathetic to the Zionist cause. As tensions built, Jewish terrorists blew up the British headquarters in Jerusalem, and the British decided to abandon what seemed a no-win situation. In September 1947 they announced their intention to withdraw from Palestine, leaving its future to the United Nations. In November the UN voted to partition Palestine, creating both a Jewish and a new Arab Palestinian state (see Map 28.5).

Skirmishing between Jews and Arabs became full-scale war in December 1947, and in that context the Jews declared their independence as the new state of Israel on May 14, 1948. When the fighting ended in 1949, the Israelis had conquered more territory than had been envisioned in the original partition plan, and the remaining Arab territories fell to Egypt and Jordan, rather than forming an independent Palestinian state. Thus was born the new state of Israel, partly a product of the assault on the Jews during World War II. Yet it was born amid Arab hostility and Western concerns about oil, and so its long-term prospects remained uncertain.

In 1949 the communist insurgency in China under Mao Zedong (Mao Tse-tung) (see page 921) finally triumphed over the Chinese Nationalists under Jiang Jieshi (Chiang Kai-shek), who fled to the island of Taiwan. During the war, the Communists had done better than the Nationalists at identifying themselves with the Chinese cause against both Japanese and Western imperialism. And after their victory, the Chinese Communists enjoyed great prestige among other "national liberation" movements struggling against Western colonialists. To many in the West, however, the outcome in China by 1949 simply intensified fears that communism was poised to infect the unsettled postwar world.

SUMMARY

HE war that began in Europe in 1939 gradually spread to become by far the widest and most destructive in history. Driven by expansionist

Map 28.5   The Proposed Partition of Palestine and the Birth of the State of Israel   In November 1947 the United Nations offered a plan to partition the British mandate of Palestine, but complications immediately arose. The Jews of the area won their own state, Israel, but the Palestinian Arabs were left stateless. Thus tensions continued in the area.

aims, the aggressors—first Germany and then Japan—won impressive victories at the start. Then a Grand Alliance of Britain, the Soviet Union, and the United States gradually came together and won the war in both Europe and Asia by August 1945. But the war brought unprecedented death and destruction and troubling new forms of violence, from factory-like genocide to the nuclear bombing of civilians.

As a result of the war, the two major fascist powers collapsed, and fascist forms of politics, with their hostility to democracy and their tendencies toward violence and war, stood discredited. But it was not clear whether Germany and Italy, and, for that matter, much of the rest of Europe, would be able to develop effective democratic political systems amid defeat and destruction.

The Soviets had borne the brunt of the war in Europe, and the Soviet Union—and its communist system—emerged with enhanced prestige. At the same time, an overseas war had again drawn the United States, which was prepared in the aftermath, as it had not been after World War I, to play an ongoing leadership role in world affairs. The Soviet Union and the United States offered competing visions of the future, and during the decades that followed, their competition helped shape everything from Italian domestic politics to the decolonization struggle in southern Africa.

By 1949 the division of Europe, the advent of nuclear weapons, and the symptomatic events in India, Israel, and China made it clear that the world's agenda had been radically transformed in the ten years since the beginning of World War II. With the Soviet Union and the United States emerging from the war as superpowers, and with the once-dominant European countries weakened and chastened, the center of gravity in the West changed dramatically. Thus the relationship between the West and the world was bound to be radically different.

Whereas there had been, for a while, some illusion of a "return to normal" after World War I, it was obvious after World War II that the old Europe was gone forever. Indeed, much of Europe's proud culture, on the basis of which it had claimed to lead the world, lay in the ruins of war, apparently exhausted. What role could Europe play in Western civilization, and in the wider world, after all that had happened? What lessons had been learned, and what foundations for the future could be found, as the experiment continued?

■ Notes

1. From Farrell's full account as related by General Leslie Groves in his "Memorandum to the Secretary of War," dated July 18, 1945, in *The American Atom: A Documentary History of Nuclear Policies from the Discovery of Fission to the Present,* ed. Philip L. Cantelon, Richard G. Hewlett, and Robert C. Williams, 2d ed. (Philadelphia: University of Pennsylvania Press, 1991), pp. 56–57.
2. Quoted in Karl Dietrich Bracher, *The German Dictatorship: The Origins, Structure, and Effects of National Socialism,* trans. Jean Steinberg (New York: Praeger, 1970), p. 423.

■ Suggested Reading

Browning, Christopher R. *Ordinary Men: Reserve Police Battalion 101 and the Final Solution in Poland.* With a new afterword. 1998. A case study approach to the role of ordinary Germans in the Holocaust.

Campbell, John, ed. *The Experience of World War II.* 1989. Focusing on the experience of those touched by the war, this collaborative volume covers everything from prisoners of war to the uses of the arts for propaganda purposes; large format, with superb illustrations and maps.

Gaddis, John Lewis. *We Now Know: Rethinking Cold War History.* 1997. Taking advantage of newly available Russian and Chinese documents, a leading authority reassesses the cold war, from its origins to the Cuban missile crisis of 1962.

Hilberg, Raul. *Perpetrators, Victims, Bystanders: The Jewish Catastrophe, 1933–1945.* 1992. The dean of Holocaust historians offers an accessible, compelling account by weaving capsule portraits delineating the many layers of involvement and responsibility at issue in the Holocaust.

Jackson, Julian. *The Fall of France: The Nazi Invasion of 1940.* 2003. After assessing causes and consequences from a variety of angles, this major study of a long-standing problem concludes that, in light of the anomalous Nazi determination to wage war, the fall of France was not a "strange defeat."

_____. *France: The Dark Years, 1940–1944.* 2001. A major reassessment of the Vichy period, set within the broader sweep of modern French history.

Keegan, John. *The Second World War.* 1989. A detailed but readable study featuring military operations; well illustrated.

Overy, Richard J. *Why the Allies Won.* 1995. Denying that the sheer weight of numbers made the outcome inevitable, this account focuses on the differences in political, economic, and even moral mobilization to explain why the Allies defeated the Axis powers.

Parker, R. A. C. *Struggle for Survival: The History of the Second World War.* 1990. An accessible, comprehensive, and well-balanced survey, especially good on debates over strategy and the wider implications of the strategies chosen.

Trachtenberg, Marc. *A Constructed Peace: The Making of the European Settlement, 1945–1963.* 1999. An original work that pushes beyond the long-standing cold war framework to argue that concerns about Germany and nuclear weapons were central to the postwar settlement.

Weinberg, Gerhard L. *A World at Arms: A Global History of World War II.* 1994. An enlightening global approach by a leading historian of the period that stresses the interrelationship among simultaneous events and decisions in the various theaters of the war around the world.

 For a searchable list of additional readings for this chapter, go to college.hmco.com/students.

Holocaust Testimony

There were loud announcements, but it was all fairly restrained: nobody did anything to us. I followed the crowd: "Men to the right, women and children to the left," we had been told. The women and children disappeared into a barrack further to the left and we were told to undress. One of the SS men—later I knew his name, Küttner—told us in a chatty sort of tone that we were going into a disinfection bath and afterwards would be assigned work. Clothes, he said, could be left in a heap on the floor, and we'd find them again later. . . .

The queue began to move and I suddenly noticed several men fully dressed standing near another barrack further back, and I was wondering who they were. And just then another SS man (Miete was his name) came by me and said, "Come on, you, get back into your clothes, quick, special work." That was the first time I was frightened. Everything was very quiet, you know. And when he said that to me, the others turned around and looked at me—and I thought, my God, why me, why does he pick on me? When I had got back into my clothes, the line had moved on and I noticed that several other young men had also been picked out and were dressing. We were taken through to the "work-barrack," most of which was filled from floor to ceiling with clothes, stacked up in layers. . . . You understand, there was no time, not a moment between the instant we were taken in there and put to work, to talk to anyone, to take stock of what was happening . . . [ellipses in the original] and of course never forget that we had no idea at all what this whole installation was for. One saw these stacks of clothing—I suppose the thought must have entered our minds, where do they come from, what are they? We must have connected them with the clothes all of us had just taken off outside . . . [ellipses in the original] but I cannot remember doing that. I only remember starting work at once making bundles.*

This is the voice of Richard Glazar, recalling when, as a young Jewish student from Prague, he arrived at the Nazi extermination camp at Treblinka in October 1942.

---

*The testimony of Richard Glazar is from Gitta Sereny, *Into That Darkness: An Examination of Conscience* (New York: Random House, Vintage Books, 1983), pp. 176–179, 183.

Glazar was telling his story in 1972 to the British journalist Gitta Sereny, who had been covering the trial in Germany of the commandant of the Treblinka camp, Franz Stangl. Seeking to understand Stangl, Sereny tracked down a number of those who had come into contact with him, including survivors like Glazar.

Glazar's recollections are part of a rich body of testimony by Jewish survivors of the Holocaust, testimony that is often moving, gripping, terrifying. Some accounts offer direct personal recollections. Others integrate personal remembrance into literature. Still others use the insights of social psychology in an effort to explain the special features of the camp experience.

Even with all this evidence, we wonder if we can ever really grasp what millions of Jews experienced at the hands of the Nazis in the extermination camps. But listening to witnesses like Glazar, we gain some sense of the uncertainty and fear, the suffering and humiliation, that helped define that experience. And we recognize the determination, the affirmation of life, that marked the Jewish response.

We may be surprised at Glazar's insistence that "we had no idea at all what this whole installation was for." Didn't the Jews understand what the camps held for them? In fact, some Jews had a better idea than others, but in most cases only through rumor, and no one could know the whole story as it was unfolding. Over a year before, Glazar's family had sent him to work in the country, where they assumed he would be safe, so he had been relatively isolated. But what one knew, or could surmise, also depended on what one was prepared to believe was possible, what the world could hold. Some simply could not believe the rumors.

Once they were in the camps, however, the Jews could only come to terms with the unprecedented situation as best they could. Let us listen further to Glazar, whose insights into the minds of the SS overseers help us better to grasp the terrible capriciousness of the situation:

One must not forget their incredible power, their autonomy within their narrow and yet, as far as we were concerned, unlimited field; but also the isolation created by their unique situation and by what they—and hardly anyone else even within the German or Nazi community—had in common. Perhaps if this isolation had been the result of good rather than evil deeds, their own relationship towards each other would have been different. As it was, most of them seemed to hate and despise each other and do anything—almost anything—to "get at" each other. Thus, if one of them selected a man out of a new transport for work, in other words to stay alive at least for a while, it could perfectly easily happen . . . that one of his rivals . . . would come along and kill that man just to spite him. . . . All this created a virtually indescribable atmosphere of fear. The most important thing for a prisoner at Treblinka, you see, was not to make himself conspicuous.

But what, then, can be said about the human attributes that such conditions called forth—and that enabled some, at least, to survive?

Our daily life? It was in a way very directed, very specific. . . . It was essential to fill oneself completely with a determination to survive; it was essential to create in oneself a capacity for dissociating oneself to some extent from Treblinka; it was important not to adapt completely to it. . . .
It wasn't *ruthlessness* that enabled an individual to survive—it was an intangible quality, not peculiar to educated or sophisticated individuals. Anyone might have it. It is perhaps best described as an overriding thirst—perhaps, too, a talent for life, and a faith in life.

Glazar, of course, was speaking thirty years later, and despite the engaging spontaneity of his testimony, he may have forgotten things, or the experiences of the intervening years may have colored his memory. Moreover, he could only tell what he recalled through the categories of language, which may be inadequate to convey, to those who were not there, what it was like to be sent to a Nazi extermination camp. Perhaps survivors called upon years later to put their recollections into words are bound to impose too much order, even to romanticize, by using categories their listeners can understand—or want to hear. Glazar was clearly stretching to find the words. Does "talent for life" ring true? We will continue to wonder.

As for Glazar himself, he escaped from Treblinka in an uprising in August 1943 and then made his way to Germany, where he managed to survive the war disguised as a foreign laborer. When Sereny reached him in 1972, he was living in Switzerland, working as an engineer.

Arrival at the Auschwitz Extermination Camp
(Corbis)

CHAPTER 29

An Anxious Stability: The Age of the Cold War 1949–1989

THE atmosphere was festive, euphoric. Those who came to celebrate could hardly believe it was happening, for it had been unthinkable just a few months before. Yet happening it was, one of the defining events of the twentieth century, live on television. This was November 1989, and the Berlin Wall was coming down.

Erected to stop emigration from communist East Germany to the West in 1961, the wall had become an all-too-tangible symbol of the division of Europe, and much of the world, for more than four decades after World War II. The two superpowers that had emerged from the war, the Soviet Union and the United States, had settled into a cold war marked by ideological competition, an arms race, and nuclear stalemate.

As a physical barrier of concrete and barbed wire, the Berlin Wall had divided families and caused much human suffering. Indeed, 191 people died and 5,000 were arrested trying to cross it. But the East German government, by 1989 desperate to preserve its legitimacy, opened the wall on November 9 and began dismantling it within days. However, it proved too late. The communist regime in East Germany collapsed as part of a wider anticommunist revolution that finally enveloped even the Soviet Union in 1991. The anxious cold war era was suddenly over; virtually no one had foreseen its abrupt ending.

Although Berlin had been a particular hot spot, the cold war was global in scope. It seemed that confrontation between the Soviet Union and the United States might take place almost anywhere, sparking the cold war into a hot war threatening nuclear annihilation. And indeed confrontation came closest not over Berlin but over Soviet missiles in Cuba in 1962. That crisis was surmounted, and

East Germans (*backs to camera*) stream through the dismantled Berlin Wall into West Berlin.
(*Lionel Cironneau/AP/Wide World Photos*)

The Search for Cultural Bearings

Prosperity and Democracy in Western Europe

The Communist Bloc: From Consolidation to Stagnation

Europe, the West, and the World

The Collapse of the Soviet System, 1975–1991

East-West relations alternately warmed and cooled during the quarter century that followed.

Both halves of Europe had to operate within the bipolar framework, but the Western and Soviet blocs confronted different challenges and evolved in different ways. The countries of western Europe adjusted to a diminished international role as they recognized their dependence on U.S. leadership and gradually lost their overseas colonies. The change in scale led many politicians and intellectuals to advocate some form of European union, which might eventually enable the western Europeans to deal with the superpowers on a more equal basis. On the domestic level, the immediate postwar situation was so unsettled that few western European countries could simply return to the prewar norm. Postwar reconstruction rested on a new consensus that government must play a more active role in promoting economic growth and social welfare. By the 1960s the promise of shared prosperity was realized to a remarkable extent. But changing circumstances by the early 1970s threatened the consensus that postwar prosperity had made possible.

Although the Soviet Union had suffered immensely in winning World War II, the communist regime emerged from the war with renewed legitimacy. During the 1950s and 1960s, the Soviet system achieved some significant successes, but its efforts to outgrow its Stalinist framework were halt-ing. By 1980 the system was becoming rigid and stagnant. And thus the dramatic changes in the Soviet bloc that came to a head in 1989, leading to the opening of the Berlin Wall and, by 1991, to the end of communism in Europe. Only as it was ending, more than four decades after World War II, did observers realize that the anxious cold war era had been one of relative stability and peace.

QUESTIONS TO CONSIDER

- ✑ **What factors led to the surprisingly rapid restoration of democracy in much of continental western Europe after World War II?**

- ✑ **How did the place of western Europe in world affairs change during the cold war era?**

- ✑ **What caused the new sociopolitical discontents evident in western Europe by the end of the 1960s?**

- ✑ **What led to the collapse of the communist system in the Soviet Union and its satellite states?**

TERMS TO KNOW

existentialism	**Prague Spring**
North Atlantic Treaty	**Suez crisis**
Organization (NATO)	**European Economic**
welfare state	**Community (EEC)**
Konrad Adenauer	**Helsinki Accords**
Willy Brandt	**Solidarity**
Warsaw Pact	**Mikhail Gorbachev**

THE SEARCH FOR CULTURAL BEARINGS

THE events from World War I to the cold war added up to an unprecedented period of disaster for Europe. Europeans were bound to ask what had gone wrong and what could be salvaged from the ruins of a culture that had made possible the most destructive wars in history, as well as fascism, totalitarianism, and the Holocaust. With so much discredited or called into question, Europeans faced an unprecedented period of experiment.

The cold war framework crucially shaped responses all over the Western world. Some embraced the Soviet Union or sought a renewed Marxism. Opposition to communism helped stimulate others to return to religious or classical traditions or to embrace new ideas associated with America's recent successes. In western Europe, at least, this effort to take stock led promptly to the renewed determination and fresh ideas that helped produce the dramatically successful reconstruction of the postwar years. But the anxieties stemming from superpower rivalry, and especially the nuclear arms race, were bound to temper any renewed optimism.

Absurdity and Commitment in Existentialism

The postwar mood of exhaustion and despair found classic expression in the work of the Irish-born writer Samuel Beckett (1906–1989), especially in his plays *Waiting for Godot* (1952) and *Endgame* (1957). Through Beckett's characters, we see ourselves going through the motions, with nothing worth saying or doing, ludicrously manipulating the husks of a worn-out culture. The only redeeming element is the comic pathos we feel as we watch ourselves.

The same sense of anxiety and despair led to the vogue of existentialism, a movement that marked philosophy, the arts, and popular culture from the later 1940s until well into the 1950s. Existentialism developed from the ideas of the German thinker Martin Heidegger (1889–1976), especially *Being and Time* (1927), one of the most influential philosophical works of the century. Though it was a philosophy of sorts, existentialism was most significant as a broader cultural tendency, finding expression in novels and films. The existentialists explored what it means to be human in a world cast adrift from its cultural moorings, with no mutually accepted guideposts, standards, or values.

The most influential postwar existentialists were the Frenchmen Jean-Paul Sartre° (1905–1980) and Albert Camus° (1913–1960), each of whom had been involved in the French resistance, Camus in a particularly central role as editor of an underground newspaper. For both, an authentic human response to a world spinning out of control entails engagement, commitment, and responsibility—even though every action is fraught with risk.

Rather than accept the bleak, ludicrously comic vision of Beckett's plays, Camus sought to show how we might go on living in a positive, affirmative spirit, even in a world that seemed simply absurd in one sense, especially after the recent disasters in Europe. Conventional values like friendship and tolerance could be made usable again, based on the simple fact that we human beings are all caught up in this unmasterable situation together. People suffer and die, but as we come together to help as best we can, we might at least learn to stop killing one another.

Camus split from Sartre in a disagreement over the ongoing value of Marxism and the communist experiment in the Soviet Union. Though never an orthodox communist, Sartre found potential for human liberation in the working class, in communist political parties, even in the Soviet Union itself, which he saw as the strongest alternative to U.S. imperialism. By the 1950s he was

Sartre (SAH-truh)   Camus (kah-MOO)

CHRONOLOGY

1947	India and Pakistan achieve independence
	Marshall Plan announced
1949	Formation of NATO
1951	Formation of the European Coal and Steel Community
1953	Death of Stalin
	Workers' revolt in East Germany
1955	West Germany joins NATO
	Warsaw Pact
1956	Khrushchev de-Stalinization speech
	Suez crisis
	Hungarian reform movement crushed
1957	*Sputnik I* launched
	Common Market established
1958	Beginning of Fifth Republic in France
1959	Bad Godesberg congress: reorientation of German socialism
1961	Berlin Wall erected
1962	Algerian independence from France
	Cuban missile crisis
1964	Ouster of Khrushchev
1968	Days of May uprising in France
	Prague Spring reform movement crushed
1969	Brandt becomes West German chancellor
1973	First OPEC oil crisis
1975	Communist victory in Vietnam
1979	Election of Pope John Paul II
1980	Formation of Solidarity in Poland
	Formation of independent Zimbabwe from Southern Rhodesia
1982	Death of Brezhnev
1985	Gorbachev comes to power in the Soviet Union
1986	Chernobyl disaster
1989	Collapse of communism in east-central Europe
1991	Collapse of communism in the Soviet Union
	Dissolution of the Soviet Union

Sartre and de Beauvoir Among the most influential intellectual couples of the century, Jean-Paul Sartre and Simone de Beauvoir emerged as leaders of French existentialism by the later 1940s. See the box on page 994. *(Corbis Sygma)*

portraying existentialism as fundamentally a way to revitalize Marxism.

By contrast, Camus, who had started as a communist in the 1930s, had grown disillusioned with communism even before the war, and his major political tract, *The Rebel* (1951), was partly an attack on Marxism and communism. Establishing new bases for human happiness and solidarity meant recognizing limits to what human beings could accomplish, limits even to our demands for freedom and justice. These were precisely the limits that the new political movements of the century had so disastrously overstepped. Communism, like fascism, was part of the problem, not the solution.

Marxists and Traditionalists

Sartre was among the many European intellectuals who believed that Marxism had won a new lease on life from the wartime resistance. As they saw it, Marxism could be revamped for the West, without the Stalinist excesses of the Soviet Union. Marxism remained a significant strand in Western political culture throughout the cold war era, but it also attracted periodic waves of denunciation.

In Italy, as in France, the communists' major role in the resistance enhanced their prestige, preparing the way for the extraordinary posthumous influence of Antonio Gramsci° (1891–1937), a founder of the Italian Commu-

nist Party who had spent most of the fascist period in prison. His *Prison Notebooks,* published during the late 1940s, became influential throughout the world and helped make Marxism a powerful force in postwar Italian culture. Seeking to learn the lessons of the fascist triumph in Italy, Gramsci pointed Marxists toward a flexible political strategy, attuned to the special historical circumstances of each country. Thanks partly to Gramsci's legacy, Italy had the most innovative and important communist party outside the communist world for several decades after the war.

Loosely Marxist ideas were central to the renewal of political activism in the West by the late 1960s, although Marxism proved more effective as a critique of capitalism than as a blueprint for change. The best-known spokesman for a renewed radicalism on both sides of the Atlantic during the late 1960s and early 1970s was the German-born social thinker Herbert Marcuse° (1898–1979), who explored the cultural mechanisms through which capitalism perpetuates itself in *One-Dimensional Man* (1964).

Even during the late 1940s, however, others, like Camus, denied that any recasting could overcome the inherent flaws in Marxism. Damaging revelations about the excesses of Stalinism during the 1930s seemed to confirm this view. Such writers as the Hungarian-born Arthur Koestler° (1905–1983) who had believed in communism during the 1930s now denounced it as "the God that failed." Whatever its initial promise, Marxism anywhere would inevitably lead to the kind of tyranny that had developed in the Soviet Union. In his futuristic novel *Nineteen Eighty-Four,* published in 1949, the British intellectual George Orwell, long a partisan of leftist causes, chillingly portrayed the dehumanization that totalitarianism—and, by association, communism—seemed bound to entail.

By the mid-1970s, the disturbing portrait of the Soviet gulag, or forced-labor-camp system, by the exiled Soviet writer Alexander Solzhenitsyn° (b. 1918) stimulated another wave of anticommunist thinking. And whether or not Marxism was necessarily Stalinist and repressive in implication, its relevance to the increasingly prosperous industrial democracies of western Europe was open to question. By the early 1980s, many had come to believe that the Marxist understanding of capitalism and class relations was simply passé.

Those hostile to Marxism often insisted that the West had to reconnect with older traditions if it were to

---

Gramsci (GRAHM-she)

Marcuse (mar-KOO-zuh)   Koestler (KEST-lur)
Solzhenitsyn (soul-zhen-IT-sin)

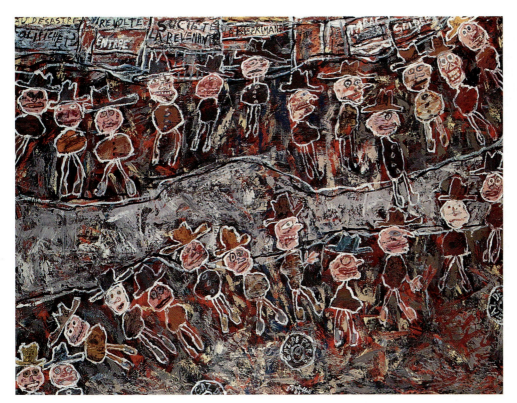

Dubuffet: Spinning Round Seeking to depart from the European tradition of sophisticated, well-made art, Jean Dubuffet developed imagery that was at once crude and primitive, playful and whimsical. *(Tate Gallery, London/Art Resource, NY. © 2003 Artists Rights Society [ARS], New York/ADAGP, Paris)*

avoid further horrors like those it had just been through. Especially in the first years after the war, many, like the French Catholic thinker Jacques Maritain° (1882–1973), held that only a return to religious traditions would suffice. For the American-born British writer T. S. Eliot (1888–1965), the essential return to tradition had to embrace family and locality, as well as religion. Without a return to tradition, Eliot warned, the West could expect more excesses such as fascism and totalitarianism in the future.

The Intellectual Migration and Americanism

The extraordinary migration of European artists and intellectuals to the United States to escape persecution during the 1930s and 1940s profoundly affected the cultural life of the postwar period. An array of luminaries arrived on American shores, from the composer Igor Stravinsky to the theoretical physicist Albert Einstein, from the architect Walter Gropius to the radical social theorist Herbert Marcuse.

Before this cross-fertilization, American culture had remained somewhat provincial, sometimes proudly and

self-consciously so. All the direct contact with these Europeans by the 1940s helped propel the United States into the Western cultural mainstream. No longer could "Western" culture be identified primarily with Europe. In some spheres—painting, for example—Americans were now confident enough to claim the leadership for the first time.

With the abstract expressionism of the later 1940s, American painters began creating visual images the likes of which had never been seen in Europe. In comparison with the raw, energetic painting of Jackson Pollock (1912–1956), the work of the Europeans seemed merely "pretty"—and the newly brash Americans were not shy about telling them so. Now New York began to supplant Paris as the art capital of the Western world.

But the American achievement owed something to European existentialism, and it became possible only because so many of the most innovative European painters had come to New York, where the Americans had been able to learn their lessons firsthand. At the same time, European painters such as Jean Dubuffet° (1901–1985) in France and Francis Bacon (1910–1992) in Britain created new forms of their own—sometimes

---

Maritain (mar-eh-TAHN)

Dubuffet (doo-boo-FAY)

playful, sometimes brutal—as they sought the startling new visual imagery that seemed appropriate to Western culture after the era of fascism and war. Even in the United States, artists began reacting against the deep seriousness of abstract expressionism during the mid-1950s. One new direction led by the early 1960s to "pop art," which was "American" in a different sense, featuring the ordinary objects and mass-produced images of modern consumerist culture. (See the feature "Weighing the Evidence: Pop Art" on pages 1020–1021.)

Some Europeans were eager to embrace what seemed distinctively American because America had remained relatively free of the political ideologies that seemed to have led Europe to totalitarianism and ruin. By the 1950s, there was much talk of "the end of ideology," with America indicating a healthier alternative combining technology, value-free social science, and scientific management. Whereas the old European way led either to mere theorizing, to political extremism, or to polarization and impasse, the American approach got results by tackling problems one at a time, so that they could be solved by managerial or technical experts.

Such Americanism fed the notion that Europe needed a clean break based on technological values. If such a break was necessary, however, what was to become of the European tradition, for centuries the center of gravity of the West and until recently dominant in the world? Did anything distinctively European remain, or was Europe doomed to lick its wounds in the shadow of America? These questions lurked in the background as Europeans faced the difficult task of economic and political restoration.

PROSPERITY AND DEMOCRACY IN WESTERN EUROPE

BY 1941 democracy seemed to be dying on the European continent, yet it quickly revived in western Europe after World War II, taking root more easily than most had thought possible. The bipolar international framework helped. The United States actively encouraged democracy, and Europeans nervous about communism and the Soviet Union were happy to follow the American lead. Success at economic reconstruction was important as well. Not only was there greater prosperity, but governments could afford to deliver on promises of enhanced security, social welfare, and equal opportunity. It also mattered that western Europeans learned from past mistakes.

Economic Reconstruction and the Atlantic Orientation

It is hard to imagine how desperate the situation in much of western Europe had become by 1945. Major cities like Rotterdam, Hamburg, and Le Havre lay largely in ruins, and normal routines suffered radical disruption. Production had declined to perhaps 25 percent of the prewar level in Italy, to 20 percent in France, and to a mere 5 percent in southern Germany. Cigarettes, often gained through barter from American soldiers, served widely as a medium of exchange.

Although the U.S. commitment to assist European reconstruction was not originally a cold war measure, the developing cold war context made it seem all the more necessary for the United States to help the Europeans get their economies running again. The key was the Marshall Plan, which U.S. secretary of state General George Marshall outlined in 1947 and which channeled $13.5 billion in aid to western Europe by 1951.

Cold war concerns deepened the partnership in April 1949, when the United States spearheaded a military alliance, the North Atlantic Treaty Organization (NATO), that included much of western Europe. The Soviets were tightening their grip on their satellite states in east-central Europe, and the NATO alliance was intended to check any Soviet expansion westward. The Soviets had considerable superiority in conventional forces, which had ready access to western Europe, but U.S. nuclear superiority provided a balance. Indeed, the American nuclear guarantee to western Europe was the cornerstone of the NATO alliance. Thus it seemed crucial for the United States to maintain its superiority in nuclear weapons, a fact that fueled the continuing arms race and nuclear buildup.

On the economic level, the western Europeans quickly proved worthy partners. So impressive was the recovery in continental western Europe by the 1950s that some dubbed it an "economic miracle." Western Europeans took advantage of the need to rebuild by adopting up-to-date methods and technologies, though economic strategies differed from one country to the next. The new German government cut state aid to business and limited the long-standing power of cartels—organizations of private businesses that regulated the production, pricing, and marketing of goods. The state was permitted to intervene in the economy only to ensure free competition. In France, by contrast, many were determined to use government to modernize the country, thereby overcoming the weakness that had led to defeat. So France adopted a flexible, pragmatic form of government-led economic planning.

Ban the Bomb   As nuclear tension escalated during the 1950s, some people built air-raid shelters; others took to the streets in antinuclear protests. The protest movement was especially prominent in Britain, where the noted philosopher Bertrand Russell (1872–1970) played a central role. Here, at the right of those seated, he awaits arrest during a sit-in demonstration outside the British Defense Ministry.   *(Hulton Archive/Getty Images)*

In 1946 Jean Monnet° (1888–1979) launched the first of the French postwar economic plans, which brought government and business leaders together to agree on production targets. Economic planning enabled France to make especially effective use of the capital that the Marshall Plan provided. By 1951 French industrial production had returned to its prewar peak, and by 1957 it had risen to twice the level of 1938.

Strong and sustained rates of economic growth were achieved throughout much of western Europe until the late 1960s. From 1953 to 1964, annual rates of growth averaged 6 percent in Germany, 5.6 percent in Italy, and 4.9 percent in France. Britain, however, lagged considerably, averaging only 2.7 percent growth annually during that same period.

As part of the new postwar consensus, labor was supposed to be brought more fully into economic decision making. Thus, for example, the trade unions participated in the planning process in France. In Germany the codetermination law of 1951 provided for labor participation in management decisions in heavy industry, and labor representatives were given access to company books and full voting memberships on boards of directors. This measure ultimately made little difference in

the functioning of the affected firms, but it helped head off any return to trade-union radicalism.

During the first years of rapid economic growth, the labor movement remained fairly passive in western Europe, even though wages stayed relatively low. After an era of depression, fascist repression, and war, workers were grateful simply to have jobs, free trade unions, and at least the promise of greater prosperity in the future. By the 1960s, however, it seemed time to redeem that promise; labor began demanding—generally with success—to share more fully in the new prosperity. Now, rather abruptly, much of western Europe took on the look of a consumer society, with widespread ownership of automobiles, televisions, and other household appliances.

Social Welfare and the Issue of Gender

Western governments began to adopt social welfare measures on a large scale late in the nineteenth century (see page 793), and by the 1940s some degree of governmental responsibility for unemployment insurance, workplace safety, and old-age pensions was widely accepted. Some Europeans, seeking renewal after the war, found attractive models in Sweden and Denmark, where the outlines of a welfare state had emerged by the 1930s. Sweden, especially, drew attention as a "middle way" that

Monnet (moh-NAY)

avoided the extremes of either Soviet Marxism, with its coercive statism, or American-style capitalism, with its brash commercialism and selfish individualism.

Sweden's economy remained fundamentally capitalist, based on private ownership; even after World War II, its nationalized, or government-run, sector was not large by European standards. But the system of social insurance in Sweden was the most extensive in Europe, and the government worked actively with business to promote full employment and to steer the economy in directions deemed socially desirable. Moreover, the welfare state came to mean a major role for the Swedish trade unions, which won relatively high wages for workers and even enjoyed a quasi-veto power over legislation.

At the same time, the Swedish government began playing a more active role in spheres of life that had formerly been private, from sexuality to child rearing. Thus, for example, drugstores were required to carry contraceptives beginning in 1946. Sweden was the first country to provide sex education in the public schools; optional beginning in 1942, it became compulsory in 1955. By 1979 the Swedes were limiting corporal punishment— the right to spank—and prohibiting the sale of war toys. This deprivatization of the family stemmed from a sense, especially pronounced in Sweden, that society is collectively responsible for the well-being of its children.

Although the Swedish model was extreme in certain respects, most of western Europe moved in the same direction in an effort to restore consensus and establish the foundations for democratic renewal after the war. Even Britain, one of the war's major victors, quickly began constructing a welfare state, dumping Winston Churchill in the process.

Early in the war most Britons began to take it for granted that major socioeconomic changes would follow from victory. Greater collective responsibility for the well-being of all British citizens seemed appropriate in light of the shared hardships the war had imposed. Moreover, the successes of government planning and control during the wartime emergency suggested that once the war was over, government could assume responsibility for the basic needs of the British people, guaranteeing full employment and providing a national health service. But the Labour Party, led by Clement Attlee (1883–1967), seemed better equipped to deliver on that promise than the Conservatives, whose leader, Churchill, was in fact quite hostile to welfare state notions. So when Britain held its first postwar elections, in July 1945, Churchill's Conservatives suffered a crushing loss to Labour, which promptly began creating the British welfare state.

Although some expected, and others feared, that the result would be a form of socialism, the new direction

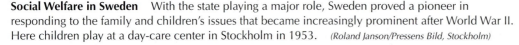

Social Welfare in Sweden   With the state playing a major role, Sweden proved a pioneer in responding to the family and children's issues that became increasingly prominent after World War II. Here children play at a day-care center in Stockholm in 1953.   *(Roland Janson/Pressens Bild, Stockholm)*

did not undermine the capitalist economic system. The Labour government nationalized some key industries, but 80 percent of the British work force remained employed in private firms in 1948. Moreover, even under Labour, the British government did not seek the kind of economic planning role that government was playing in France. Much like the United States, Britain relied on monetary and fiscal policy to coordinate its economy.

The core of the British departure was a set of government-sponsored social welfare measures that significantly affected the lives of ordinary people. These included old-age pensions; insurance against unemployment, sickness, and disability; and allowances for pregnancy, child rearing, widowhood, and burial. The heart of the system was free medical care, to be provided by the National Health Service, created in November 1946 and operating by 1948.

In Britain, as elsewhere, gender roles were inevitably at issue as government welfare measures were debated and adopted. Were married women to have access to the welfare system as individual citizens or as members of a family unit, responsible for child rearing and dependent on their husbands as breadwinners? Should government seek to enable women to be both mothers and workers, or should government help make it possible for mothers not to have to work outside the home? Women themselves did not always agree on priorities, and some instructive differences in accent were evident across national boundaries.

As during the First World War, the percentage of women in the work force had increased significantly during World War II, but both women and men proved eager to embrace the security of traditional domestic patterns once the war was over. So the war did not change gender patterns of work even to the extent that World War I had done. In Britain women made up about 30 percent of the labor force in 1931, 31 percent in 1951. The percentage of women in the U.S. work force increased from 26 percent to 36 percent during the war years, but by 1947 it had returned to 28 percent. Thus the embrace of welfare measures took place at a time of renewed conservatism in conceptions of gender roles.

British feminists initially welcomed provisions of the British welfare state that recognized the special role of women as mothers. The government was to ease burdens by providing family allowances, to be paid directly to mothers of more than one child to enable them to stay home with their children. This seemed a more progressive step than the perpetual British trade-union demand for a "family wage," sufficient to enable the male breadwinner to support a family so that his wife would not have to work. But though women were now to be com-

pensated directly for their role as mothers, the assumptions about gender roles remained essentially the same.

In France, which had refused even to grant women the vote after World War I, the very different situation after 1945 stimulated an especially innovative response to gender and family issues. After the experience of defeat, collaboration, and resistance, the French were determined to pursue both economic dynamism and individual justice. But they also remained concerned with population growth, so they combined incentives to encourage large families with measures to promote equal opportunity and economic independence for women.

As they expanded the role of government after the war, the French tended more than the British to assume that paid employment for women was healthy and desirable. New laws gave French women equal access to civil service jobs and guaranteed equal pay for equal work. However, the French recognized at the same time both that women had special needs as mothers and that husbands shared the responsibility for parenting. So the French system provided benefits for women during and after pregnancy but also family allowances that treated the two parents as equally essential. At the same time, the system viewed women as individual citizens, regardless of marital or economic status. Thus all were equally entitled to pensions, health services, and job-related benefits.

Although female participation in the paid labor force declined just after the war, it began rising throughout the West during the 1950s, then accelerated during the 1960s, reaching new highs in the 1970s and 1980s. Thanks partly to the expansion of government, the greatest job growth was in the service sector—in social work, health care, and education, for example—and many of these new jobs went to women. From about 1960 to 1988, the percentage of women ages 25 to 34 in the labor force rose from 30 to 67 in Britain, from 42 to 75 in France, and from 49 to 87 in Germany.

These statistics reflect significant changes in women's lives, but even as their choices expanded in some respects, women became more deeply aware of enduring limits to their opportunities. Thus a new feminist movement emerged by the early 1970s, drawing intellectual inspiration from *The Second Sex*, a pioneering work published in 1949 by the French existentialist Simone de Beauvoir (1908–1986). (See page 988 and the box "The Continuing Experiment: Female Freedom and the Future of Gender Relations.")

The Restoration of Democracy

Much of continental western Europe faced the challenge of rebuilding democracy after defeat and humiliation.

Female Freedom and the Future of Gender Relations

In her pioneering book *The Second Sex,* first published in 1949, Simone de Beauvoir considered the present situation of women, and the meaning of sexual difference, from an existentialist perspective. While recognizing the societal obstacles that women faced, she suggested that women had too often settled for subordinate roles, thereby avoiding the responsibility and risk that human freedom entails. The insights of existentialism could help women to seize responsibility for their own lives—and to join with men as equal partners in the ongoing human experiment. This would not be to deny the differences between men and women, but to expand human relationships and open new ways of expressing, valuing, and enjoying those differences. This book inspired not only the renewed feminism that emerged during the later 1960s but also the wider thinking about gender roles and the meaning of sexual difference that continued for decades thereafter.

The nature of things is no more immutably given, once for all, than is historical reality. If woman seems to be the inessential which never becomes the essential, it is because she herself fails to bring about this change. . . .

To decline to be the Other, to refuse to be a party to the deal—this would be for women to renounce all the advantages conferred upon them by their alliance with the superior caste. Man-the-sovereign will provide woman-the-liege with material protection and will undertake the moral justification of her existence; thus she can evade at once both economic risk and the metaphysical risk of a liberty in which ends and aims must be contrived without assistance. Indeed, along with the ethical urge of each individual to affirm his subjective existence, there is also the temptation to forgo liberty and become a thing. . . .

If a caste is kept in a state of inferiority, no doubt it remains inferior; but liberty can break the circle. Let negroes vote, and they become worthy of having the vote; let woman be given responsibilities and she is able to assume them. . . .

. . . There will be some to object that . . . when woman is "the same" as her male, life will lose its salt and spice. . . .

. . . And it is true that the evolution now in progress threatens more than feminine charm alone: in beginning to exist for herself, woman will relinquish the function as double and mediator to which she owes her privileged place in the masculine universe. . . . There is no denying that feminine dependence, inferiority, woe, give women their special character; assuredly woman's autonomy, if it spares men many troubles, will also deny them many conveniences; assuredly there are certain forms of the sexual adventure which will be lost in the world of tomorrow. But this does not mean that love, happiness, poetry, dream, will be banished from it.

. . . New relations of flesh and sentiment of which we have no conception will arise between the sexes; already, indeed, there have appeared between men and women friendships, rivalries, complicities, comradeships—chaste or sensual—which past centuries could not have conceived. . . .

. . . There will always be certain differences between man and woman; her eroticism, and therefore her sexual world, have a special form of their own and therefore cannot fail to engender a sensuality, a sensitivity, of a special nature. . . .

. . . To emancipate woman is to refuse to confine her to the relations she bears to man, not to deny them to her; let her have her independent existence and she will continue none the less to exist for him *also:* mutually recognizing each other as subject, each will yet remain for the other an *other.* . . . When we abolish the slavery of half of humanity, together with the whole system of hypocrisy that it implies, then the "division" of humanity will reveal its genuine significance and the human couple will find its true form.

QUESTIONS

1. What does de Beauvoir find to be the challenge—and opportunity—facing women?
2. Why does she insist that female emancipation will lead not to a bland sameness but to entirely new modes of relationship between men and women?

With the developing cold war complicating the situation, the prospects for democracy were by no means certain in the late 1940s. Although the division of Germany weakened communism in the new Federal Republic, in France and Italy strong Communist Parties had emerged from the wartime resistance and claimed to point the way beyond conventional democracy altogether.

The new Federal Republic of Germany held its first election under the Basic Law in August 1949, launching what proved to be a stable and successful democracy. Partly to counter the Soviet Union, but also to avoid what seemed the disastrous mistake of the harsh peace settlement after World War I, the victors sought to help get West Germany back on its feet as quickly as possible. At the same time, West German political leaders, determined to avoid the mistakes of the Weimar years, now better understood the need to compromise, to take responsibility for governing the whole nation.

To prevent the instability that had plagued the Weimar Republic, the creators of the new government strengthened the chancellor in relation to the Bundestag, the lower house of parliament. In the same way, the Basic Law helped establish a stable party system by discouraging splinter parties and by empowering the courts to outlaw extremist parties. And the courts found reason to outlaw both the Communist Party and a Neo-Nazi Party during the formative years of the new German democracy.

The West German republic proved more stable than the earlier Weimar Republic partly because the political party system was now considerably simpler. Two mass parties, the Christian Democratic Union (CDU) and the Social Democratic Party (SPD), were immediately predominant, although a third, the much smaller Free Democratic Party (FDP), proved important for coalition purposes.

Konrad Adenauer (1876–1967), head of the CDU, the largest party in 1949, immediately emerged as West Germany's leading statesman. A Catholic who had been mayor of Cologne under Weimar, he had withdrawn from active politics during the Nazi period, but he reemerged after the war to lead the council that drafted the Basic Law. As chancellor from 1949 to 1963, he oriented the new German democracy toward western Europe and the Atlantic bloc, led by the United States.

The new bipolar world confronted West Germany with a cruel choice. By accepting the bipolar framework, the country could become a full partner within the Atlantic bloc. But by straddling the fence instead, it could keep open the possibility that Germany could be reunified as a neutral and disarmed state. When the outbreak of war in Korea in 1950 intensified the cold war, the United States pressured West Germany to rearm and join the Western bloc. Although some West Germans resisted, Adenauer prevailed, committing the Federal Republic to NATO in 1955. Adenauer was eager to anchor the new Federal Republic to the West, partly to buttress the new democracy in West Germany, but also to cement U.S. support in the face of what seemed an ongoing Soviet threat to German security.

By the late 1950s the West German economy was recovering nicely, and the country was a valued member of the Western alliance. Adenauer's CDU seemed so potent that the other major party, the SPD, appeared to be consigned to permanent—and sterile—opposition. Frustrated with its outsider status, the SPD began to shed its Marxist trappings in an effort to widen its appeal. Prominent among those pushing in this direction was Willy Brandt (1913–1992), who became mayor of West Berlin in 1957, and who would become the party's leader in 1963. At its watershed national congress at Bad Godesberg in 1959, the party officially gave up talk of the class struggle and adopted a more moderate program.

Adenauer stepped down in 1963 at the age of 87, after fourteen years as chancellor. The contrast with Weimar, which had known twenty-one different cabinets in a comparable fourteen-year period, could not be more striking. The Adenauer years proved to Germans that democracy could mean effective government, economic prosperity, and foreign policy success. Still, Adenauer had become somewhat authoritarian by his later years, and it was arguable that West Germany had become overly reliant on him and his party.

During the years from 1963 to 1969, the CDU proved it could govern without Adenauer, and the SPD came to seem ever more respectable, even joining as the junior partner in a government coalition with the CDU in 1966. Finally, in October 1969, new parliamentary elections brought Brandt to the chancellorship, and the SPD became responsible for governing West Germany for the first time since the war.

Brandt sought to provide a genuine alternative to the CDU without undermining the consensus that had developed around the new regime since 1949. He wanted especially to improve relations between West Germany and the Soviet bloc, but this required a more independent foreign policy than Adenauer and his successors had followed. Under Adenauer, the Federal Republic had refused to deal with East Germany at all. So Brandt's opening to the East, or *Ostpolitik*°, was risky for a socialist chancellor seeking to prove his respectability. But he pursued it with skill and success.

Ostpolitik (OST-po-luh-teek)

Franco-German Cooperation
French president Charles de Gaulle (*left*) and West German chancellor Konrad Adenauer (*right*) draw an enthusiastic crowd in Bonn in September 1963. De Gaulle was in the West German capital for the first formal meeting after France and West Germany had signed a friendship treaty in January. Each of the two leaders strongly advocated the new cooperation between their countries, and that cooperation proved a cornerstone of the unprecedented peace and prosperity in western Europe after World War II.
(akg-images)

In treaties with the Soviet Union, Czechoslovakia, and Poland during the early 1970s, West Germany accepted the main lines of the postwar settlement. This was to abandon any claim to the former German territory east of the Oder-Neisse° line, now in Poland. Brandt also managed to improve relations with East Germany. After the two countries finally agreed to mutual diplomatic recognition, each was admitted to the United Nations in 1973. Brandt's overtures made possible closer economic ties between them, and even broader opportunities for ordinary citizens to interact across the east-west border. His *Ostpolitik* was widely popular and helped deepen the postwar consensus in West Germany.

In France and Italy, unlike West Germany, the communists constituted a potent force in light of their major roles in wartime resistance movements. The presence of Western troops in France and Italy gave the leverage to noncommunists, however, and Moscow directed the communists in both countries to settle for the moderate course of participation in broad political coalitions. But as new democracies took root in each nation, the United States intervened persistently to minimize the communists' role. Though support for the communists in France continued to grow until 1949, the French Communist Party settled into a particularly doctrinaire position,

maintaining strict subservience to the Soviet Union, and found itself increasingly marginalized thereafter.

As the leader of the French resistance effort, Charles de Gaulle immediately assumed the dominant political role after the liberation of France in August 1944. But he withdrew, disillusioned, from active politics early in 1946, as the new Fourth Republic returned to the unstable multiparty coalitions that had marked the later years of the Third Republic. Still, governmental decision making changed significantly as the nonpolitical, technocratic side of the French state gained power in areas such as economic planning. And government technocrats survived the fall of the Fourth Republic in 1958, when de Gaulle returned to politics in a situation of crisis stemming from France's war to maintain control of Algeria (see page 1008).

Although de Gaulle became prime minister within the Fourth Republic at this point, it was clear that his return signified a change of regime. The French legislature promptly gave his government full powers for six months. Taking up the mandate, the regime drafted a new constitution, which was then approved by referendum in the fall of 1958. The result was the new Fifth Republic, which featured a stronger executive—and soon a president elected directly by the people and not dependent on the Chamber of Deputies. It was only in 1958, with the return of de Gaulle and the advent of the Fifth Republic, that government in postwar France began to assume definitive contours.

Oder-Neisse (OH-dur–NYE-suh)

Italy's political challenge, after more than twenty years of fascism, was even more dramatic than France's. Shortly after the war, the Italians adopted a new democratic constitution and voted to end the monarchy, thereby making modern Italy a republic for the first time. But much depended on the balance of political forces, which quickly crystallized around the Christian Democratic Party (DC), oriented toward the Catholic Church, and the strong Communist Party. Many Italian moderates with little attachment to the church supported the Christian Democrats as the chief bulwark against communism. And though they consistently had to work with smaller parties to attain a parliamentary majority, the Christian Democrats promptly assumed the dominant role, which they maintained until the early 1990s.

The Communists continued to offer the major opposition, typically winning 25 to 35 percent of the vote in national elections. Taking their cue from Gramsci's writings, they adopted a proactive strategy to make their presence felt in Italian life and to demonstrate the superiority of their diagnoses and prescriptions. And they found considerable success as they organized profit-making cooperatives for sharecroppers, ran local and regional governments, and garnered the support of intellectuals, journalists, and publishers. But though they had proven capable of operating constructively within a democratic framework, their longer-term role remained unclear into the 1970s. What were the Communists trying to accomplish on the national level, and how long was it supposed to take? Could they function as part of a majority governing coalition within a democratic political system?

By the 1960s the new democracies in Germany, France, and Italy seemed firmly rooted, and during the 1970s Greece, Spain, and Portugal also established workable democracies after periods of dictatorial rule. Following the death of Francisco Franco in 1975, almost forty years after his triumph in the Spanish civil war, democracy returned to Spain more smoothly than most had dared hope. Franco ordained that a restoration of the monarchy would follow his death, and King Juan Carlos (b. 1938; r. 1975–) served as an effective catalyst in the transition to democracy. The new constitution of 1978 dismantled what was left of the Franco system so that, for example, Catholicism was no longer recognized as the official religion of the Spanish state.

New Discontents and New Directions

Even as democracy seemed to be thriving in western Europe, political disaffection began to threaten the consensus in the more established democracies by the late 1960s.

Such frustration deepened in the more difficult economic environment of the 1970s, when Britain, for example, began finding it could no longer afford its welfare state. But when disaffection first emerged, in the late 1960s, western Europe was at the height of the new prosperity, and so the discontent did not stem from immediate economic circumstances alone. A new radicalism similarly emerged in the United States during the 1960s. Although this American radicalism developed especially from the civil rights movement and from opposition to the U.S. war in Vietnam, a sense that ordinary people were not truly empowered by contemporary democratic institutions fed the new radicalism on both sides of the Atlantic.

Long in gestation, the American civil rights movement sought to overcome racial segregation and other limitations on the rights of African Americans in the United States. It gathered momentum during the 1950s, inspired partly by decolonization struggles elsewhere. A Baptist minister, Martin Luther King, Jr. (1929–1968), emerged as the movement's best-known leader after he spearheaded a successful bus boycott in Montgomery, Alabama, during 1955 and 1956. Professing the technique of non-violence that Mohandas Gandhi had practiced in India (see the box "Global Encounters: Gandhi Advocates Nonviolence" on page 920 in Chapter 27), King won widespread sympathy for the movement among American whites. In 1963 he led a mixed-race throng of 200,000 in a march on Washington, D.C., that helped produce the landmark Civil Rights Act of 1964 and other legislation ending segregation and overt forms of racial discrimination. The civil rights movement fragmented by the late 1960s, as some African Americans rejected nonviolence and even the desirability of integration. Although discrimination and de facto segregation could still be found thereafter, the civil rights movement transformed American society and helped stimulate movements for change around the world for decades thereafter.

The most dramatic instance of radical protest in western Europe was the "Days of May" uprising of students and workers that shook France during May and June of 1968. The movement's aims were amorphous or utopian, and cooperation between students and workers proved sporadic. But the episode gave vent to growing discontent with the aloofness of the technocratic leaders and the unevenness of the modernization effort in de Gaulle's France. Despite the impressive economic growth, many ordinary people were coming to feel left out as public services were neglected and problems worsened in such areas as housing and education. French universities were a particular target, drawing protests and even full-scale takeovers by radical students. (See the box "Reading Sources: Students and Revolution: The 'Days of May' in Paris, 1968.")

Enrollment in French universities more than doubled between 1939 and 1960, then more than doubled again between 1960 and 1967. Apart from a few highly selective *grandes écoles,* the institutions of the state-run university system were open to anyone who passed a standard examination. To limit enrollments by restricting access did not seem politically feasible. Instead, the government tried to build to keep up with demand—thereby creating vast, impersonal institutions with professors increasingly inaccessible to students. But overcrowding persisted, and the value of a university degree diminished, leaving graduates with uncertain job prospects.

In Italy frustration with the stagnation of the political system bred radical labor unrest by 1969 and then a major wave of terrorism during the 1970s. By this time many radical young people found the Communists too caught up in the system to be genuinely innovative, yet still too weak to break the Christian Democrats' lock on power. Because the Italian Communists, unlike the German Social Democrats, never established their credibility as a national governing party, the Christian Democrats grew ever more entrenched, becoming increasingly arrogant and corrupt.

In Germany the Green movement formed by peace and environmental activists during the late 1970s took pains to avoid acting like a conventional party. Concerned that Germany, with its central location, would end up the devastated battleground in any superpower confrontation, the Greens opposed deployment of additional U.S. missiles on German soil and called for an alternative to the endless arms race. The SPD, as the governing party in an important NATO state, seemed unable to confront this issue and lost members as a result.

Prominent among the new political currents emerging by the early 1970s was the renewed feminist movement, which recalled the earlier movement for women's suffrage. This drive for "women's liberation" sought equal opportunities for women in education and employment. It was striking, for example, that despite major steps toward equal educational opportunity in postwar France, the country's prestigious engineering schools were still not admitting women in the late 1960s and would begin doing so only during the 1980s. But feminists also forced new issues onto the political stage as they worked, for example, to liberalize divorce and abortion laws.

At the same time, women faced new questions after a generation of experience with the activist postwar state. In Britain, where government had sought to free mothers from the necessity of employment outside the home, feminists increasingly blamed the welfare state for their ongoing second-class status. But the tradeoffs were complex, and discussion continued, making gender issues central to public policy and personal choice all over the Western world by the last two decades of the century.

Days of May   French students use garbage-can covers as shields just minutes before a violent confrontation with police near the Gare de Lyon in Paris on May 25, 1968. The student-led protest movement revealed a reservoir of resentment that had built up in French society despite the democracy and prosperity of the postwar period.   *(Marc Riboud/Magnum Photos)*

STUDENTS AND REVOLUTION: THE "DAYS OF MAY" IN PARIS, 1968

As part of the radical demonstrations in Paris in May 1968, the Sorbonne, the most famous university on the European continent, became the focus of student demonstrations. Despite a series of arrests, students took over and occupied the university on May 13. A month later, on June 13, the Occupation Committee of the Sorbonne issued a manifesto reviewing what had happened and specifying the course for the future. The police retook the Sorbonne three days later, but the interplay of frustrations and aspirations evident in this manifesto continued to shape debate and influence policy thereafter.

It was during the evening of 13 May after a week of fighting that we finally reoccupied the Sorbonne. We then realised more than ever that things would never again be as they had been. From that day onwards a new era had begun for the university. During the general strike and factory occupations, hundreds of thousands of students occupied their faculties, transforming them into red centres of support for the workers' struggle and for reflection on the future of the university.

Today, now that the majority of workers have, for the time being, returned to work, where has it all got us? Assemblies and committees have discussed the reforms for the university, the principles of university administration and teaching. We have witnessed the collapse of the academic authorities, the disappearance of rectors. We have heard the professors, the former landlords, shout about their sudden willingness for dialogue! . . .

Everyone knows that in the present circumstances a pure and simple reform of the university structures will by no means suffice. By calling the Sorbonne the "People's University," we have simply said that before changing the internal structures of the university, we must be sure for whom and with what aim it will be used. It took five centuries for the priests and then the bourgeoisie to build their university. It is therefore to be expected that in one month we cannot transform their university into one for the workers. . . .

. . . The Sorbonne should be called "the University at the Service of the Revolution":

a. Not only university reform, but also the political atmosphere which conditions it, should be examined during the six-month study programme. All problems concerning society will be examined, studied and discussed. Seminars will be arranged, enquiries carried out. Reports will be prepared. At the Sorbonne, we will talk about social living conditions, about the power of management, about underdevelopment, as well as imperialistic wars, advertising and immigrant workers. . . .

d. It should be an open forum for workers, farm workers, employees, all those wishing to give their opinion on the university of tomorrow. The Sorbonne could be used to help them in their struggle in their factory or profession against capitalism. . . .

THE FORMER REGIME IS DEAD, HELP US TO BUILD A NEW ORDER!

Source: Vladimir Fišera, *Writing on the Wall: May 1968: A Documentary History*, pp. 245–247. Copyright © 1979. Reprinted with permission of St. Martin's Press.

THE COMMUNIST BLOC: FROM CONSOLIDATION TO STAGNATION

By the late 1950s, policymakers in the West were increasingly concerned that the Soviet Union, though rigid and inhumane in important respects, might have significant advantages in the race with the capitalist democracies. Westerners worried especially about producing enough scientists and engineers to match the Soviets. With the Great Depression still in mem-ory, some economists held that central planning might prove more efficient, and more likely to serve social justice, than capitalism. The Soviet effort constituted a highly visible chapter in the continuing experiment in the West, and it was not clear what the outcome might be. The sense that the communist system offered formidable competition added to the anxieties in the U.S.-led Atlantic bloc.

Nonetheless, the awed political and economic order that had emerged under Stalin continued in the Soviet Union. And when it was imposed on the countries within the Soviet orbit after the war, it produced widespread

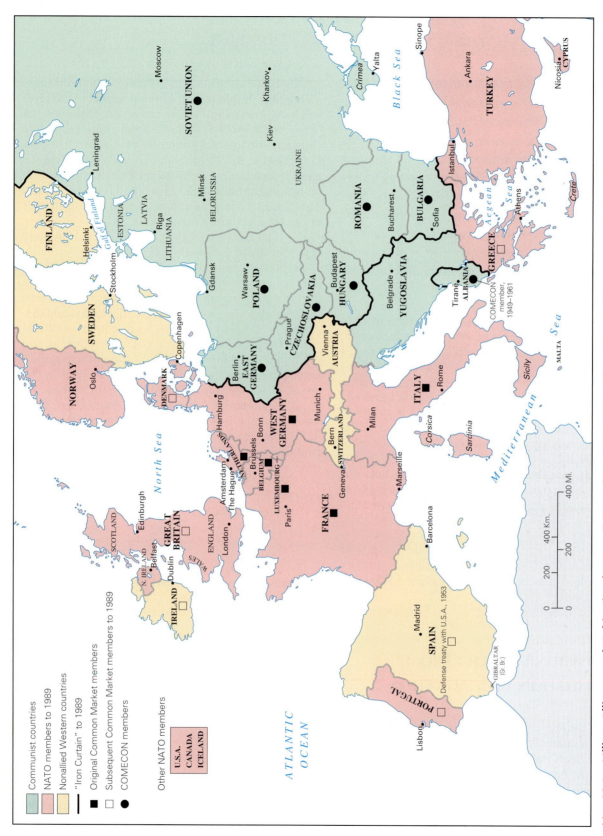

Map 29.1 Military Alliances and Multinational Economic Groupings, 1949–1989 The cold war split was reflected especially in the two military alliances: NATO, formed in 1949, and the Warsaw Pact, formed in 1955. Each side also had its own multinational economic organization, but the membership of the EEC, or Common Market, was not identical to that of NATO. Although communist, Yugoslavia remained outside Soviet-led organizations, as did Albania for part of the period.

resentment—and new dilemmas for Soviet leaders. Efforts to make communism more flexible after Stalin's death in 1953 proved sporadic at best. The Soviet suppression of the reform movement in Czechoslovakia during the "Prague Spring" of 1968 seemed to prove the inherent rigidity of the Soviet system.

Dilemmas of the Soviet System in Postwar Europe, 1949–1955

Even in victory, the Soviet Union had suffered enormously in the war with Nazi Germany. Especially in the more developed western part of the country, thousands of factories and even whole towns lay destroyed, and there were severe shortages of everything from labor to housing. Yet the developing cold war seemed to require that military spending remain high.

At the same time, the Soviet Union faced the challenge of solidifying the new system of satellite states it had put together in east-central Europe. Most of the region had no desirable interwar past to reclaim, and thus there was widespread sentiment for significant change. Even in Czechoslovakia, which had been the most prosperous and democratic state in the region, considerable nationalization of industry was completed even before the communist takeover in 1948. And whatever integration into the new Soviet bloc might mean politically, it was not clear in the late 1940s that it had to be economically disadvantageous over the long term. The Soviet system seemed to have proved itself in standing up to the Nazis, and many believed that a socialist economic system could be made to work.

Partly in response to U.S. initiatives in western Europe, the Soviets sought to mold the new communist states into a secure, coordinated bloc of allies. In the economic sphere, the Soviets founded a new organization, COMECON, as part of their effort to lead the economies of the satellite states away from their earlier ties to the West and toward the Soviet Union (see Map 29.1). In the military-diplomatic sphere, the Soviets countered NATO in 1955 by bringing the Soviet bloc countries together in a formal alliance, the Warsaw Pact, which provided for a joint military command and mutual military assistance. The Warsaw Pact established a new basis for the continuing presence of Soviet troops in the satellite states, but the tensions within the Soviet-dominated system in east-central Europe soon raised questions about what the pact meant.

From the start, Yugoslavia had been a point of vulnerability for the Soviet system. Communist-led partisans under Josip Tito had liberated Yugoslavia from the Axis on their own, and they had not needed the Red Army to begin constructing a new communist regime (see page 973). Tito was willing to work with the Soviets, but because he had his own legitimacy, he could be considerably more independent than those elsewhere whose power rested on Soviet support. Thus the Soviets deemed it essential to bring Tito to heel, lest his example encourage too much independence in the other communist states. When Soviet demands became intolerably meddlesome from the Yugoslav point of view, Tito broke with the Soviet Union altogether in 1948. Yugoslavia then began developing a more flexible socialist economic system, with greater scope for local initiatives.

Stalin's response to Tito's defection was a crackdown on potential opponents throughout the Soviet bloc. Though the terror did not approach the massive scale of 1937–1938 (see pages 923–924), again the secret police executed those suspected of deviation, inspiring fear even among the top leadership. As such repression proceeded in the satellite states, opposition strikes and demonstrations developed as well, finally reaching a crisis point in East Germany in 1953.

In East Berlin a workers' protest against a provision to increase output or face wage cuts promptly led to political demands, including free elections and the withdrawal of Soviet troops. Disturbances soon spread to the other East German cities. Though this spontaneous uprising was not well coordinated, Soviet military forces had to intervene to save the East German communist regime. But the East German protest helped stimulate strikes and antigovernment demonstrations elsewhere in the Soviet bloc as well, convincing Soviet leaders that something had to be done. However, at this point the leadership of the Soviet Union was again being sorted out, for Stalin had died early in 1953, a few months before the crisis in East Germany came to a head.

De-Stalinization Under Khrushchev, 1955–1964

Although a struggle for succession followed Stalin's death, the political infighting involved a reasonable degree of give-and-take, as opposed to terror and violence. To be sure, the contestants quickly ganged up on the hated secret police chief, who was tried and executed within months, but this stemmed from their prior agreement to limit the role of the secret police. Moreover, although one of the eventual losers was sent to Siberia to run a power station and the other was made ambassador to Outer Mongolia, it was a major departure that the winner, Nikita Khrushchev° (1894–1971), ordered neither of them exiled or executed.

Khrushchev (KROOSH-choff)

Slightly crude, even something of a buffoon, Khrushchev outmaneuvered his rivals by 1955 partly because they repeatedly underestimated him. Although his period of leadership was brief, it was eventful indeed—and in some ways the Soviet system's best chance for renewal.

At a closed session of the Soviet Communist Party's twentieth national congress in February 1956, Khrushchev made a dramatic late-night speech denouncing the criminal excesses of the Stalinist system and the "cult of personality" that had developed around Stalin himself. (See the box "Reading Sources: Khrushchev Denounces the Crimes of Stalinism.") Khrushchev's immediate aim was to undercut his hard-line rivals, but he also insisted that key features of Stalinism had amounted to an unnecessary deviation from Marxism-Leninism. So the advent of Khrushchev suggested that there might be liberalization and reform.

At the same time, however, the growing popular discontent in the satellite states placed the whole system in crisis. In the face of the East German uprising of 1953, the Soviets backed off from hard-line Stalinism, making room for more moderate communists they had previously shunned, such as the Hungarian Imre Nagy° (1896–1958). Khrushchev even sought to patch things up with Tito, exchanging visits with him in 1955 and 1956. In his speech to the party congress in 1956, Khrushchev suggested that different countries might take different routes to communism.

But could liberalization be contained within the larger framework of Soviet leadership, or were openness and innovation bound to threaten the system itself? The test case proved to be Hungary, where reformers led by the moderate communist Nagy had taken advantage of the liberalizing atmosphere by mid-1956 to begin dismantling collective farms and moving toward a multiparty political system. They even called for Soviet troops to withdraw, to enable Hungary to leave the Warsaw Pact and become neutral. These were not changes within the system, but challenges to the system itself. When a democratic coalition government was set up by November, the Soviets used tanks to crush the Hungarian reform movement. Thousands were killed during the fighting or subsequently executed, and 200,000 Hungarians fled to the West.

Yet even the crackdown in Hungary did not mean a return to the old days of Stalinist rigidity in the Soviet bloc. The Soviets understood that the system had to become more palatable, but liberalization was to be contained within certain limits. Above all, it could not challenge communist monopoly rule and the Warsaw

Pact. After 1956 the satellites were granted greater leeway, and showed greater diversity, than had previously seemed possible. Hungary's new leader, János Kádár (1912–1989), collectivized agriculture more fully than before, but he also engineered a measure of economic decentralization, allowing scope for local initiatives and market mechanisms.

In East Germany, in contrast, Walter Ulbricht (1893–1973) concentrated on central planning and heavy industry in orthodox fashion. The East German economy became the most successful in the Soviet bloc, primarily because here the new communist regime fell heir to a skilled industrial labor force. Still, that economic growth was built on low wages, so East German workers were tempted to emigrate to West Germany as the West German economic miracle gleamed ever brighter during the 1950s. The special position of Berlin, in the heart of East Germany yet still divided among the occupying powers, made such emigration relatively easy, and 2.6 million East Germans left for the West between 1950 and 1962. With a population of only 17.1 million, East Germany could not afford to let this hemorrhaging continue. Thus, in August 1961 the Ulbricht regime erected the Berlin Wall, an ugly symbol of the cold war division of Europe.

From Liberalization to Stagnation

As a domestic leader, Khrushchev proved erratic, but he was an energetic innovator, willing to experiment. He jettisoned the worst features of the police state apparatus, including some of the infamous forced-labor camps, and offered several amnesties for prisoners. He also liberalized cultural life and gave workers greater freedom to move from one job to another. The economic planning apparatus was decentralized somewhat, affording more scope for local initiatives and placing greater emphasis on consumer goods. The government expanded medical and educational facilities and, between 1955 and 1964, doubled the nation's housing stock, substantially alleviating a severe housing shortage.

Though living standards remained relatively low, Khrushchev's reforms helped improve the lives of ordinary people. Even his claim in 1961 that the Soviet Union would surpass the Western standard of living within twenty years did not seem to be an idle boast. The Soviets had launched *Sputnik I* in 1957, assuming the lead in the ensuing space race, and they sent the first human into space in 1961. Such achievements suggested that even ordinary Soviet citizens had reason for optimism. More generally, the communist regimes throughout the Soviet bloc entered the 1960s with confidence after having achieved excellent rates of economic growth during the 1950s.

Nagy (NAHZH)

READING SOURCES

KHRUSHCHEV DENOUNCES THE CRIMES OF STALINISM

In his speech to the Soviet Communist Party's national congress in 1956, Nikita Khrushchev repeatedly contrasted Stalin with Lenin, seeking to show that Stalinism had been an unfortunate and unnecessary deviation, not the logical outcome of the communist revolution. Khrushchev's denunciation of Stalin produced considerable commotion in the hall.

It is impermissible and foreign to the spirit of Marxism-Leninism to elevate one person, to transform him into a superman possessing supernatural characteristics akin to those of a god. . . .

Such a belief about a man, and specifically about Stalin, was cultivated among us for many years. . . .

While ascribing great importance to the role of the leaders and organizers of the masses, Lenin at the same time mercilessly stigmatized every manifestation of the cult of the individual. . . .

Stalin originated the concept "enemy of the people." This term . . . made possible the usage of the most cruel repression, violating all norms of revolutionary legality, against anyone who in any way disagreed with Stalin, against those who were only suspected of hostile intent, against those who had bad reputations. This concept, "enemy of the people," actually eliminated the possibility of any kind of ideological fight or the making of one's views known on this or that issue, even those of a practical character.

In the main, and in actuality, the only proof of guilt used, against all norms of current legal science, was the "confession" of the accused himself; and, as subsequent probing proved, "confessions" were acquired through physical torture against the accused. . . .

Arbitrary behavior by one person encouraged and permitted arbitrariness in others. Mass arrests and deportations of many thousands of people, execution without trial and without normal investigation created conditions of insecurity, fear and even desperation. . . .

Lenin used severe methods only in the most necessary cases, when the exploiting classes were still in existence and were vigorously opposing the revolution, when the struggle for survival was decidedly assuming the sharpest forms, even including a civil war. Stalin, on the other hand, used extreme methods and mass repressions at a time when the revolution was already victorious, when the Soviet state was strengthened, when the exploiting classes were already liquidated. . . . It is clear that here Stalin showed in a whole series of cases his intolerance, his brutality and his abuse of power. . . .

Source: *The Anti-Stalin Campaign and International Communism: A Selection of Documents*, edited by the Russian Institute, Columbia University. Copyright © 1956. Reprinted by permission.

 For additional information on this topic, go to college.hmco.com/students.

Yet Khrushchev had made enemies with his erratic reform effort, and this led to his forced retirement in October 1964. After the unending experiment in the economy, his opponents wanted to consolidate, to return to stability and predictability. But not until 1968 did it become clear that the liberalization and innovation of the Khrushchev era were over.

By early 1968 a significant reform movement had developed within the Communist Party in Prague, the capital of Czechoslovakia. Determined to avoid the fate of the Hungarian effort in 1956, the reformers emphasized that Czechoslovakia was to remain a communist state and a full member of the Warsaw Pact. But within that framework, they felt, it should be possible to invite freer cultural expression, democratize the Communist Party's procedures, and broaden participation in public life.

However, efforts to reassure the Soviets alienated some of the movement's supporters, who stepped up their demands. As earlier in Hungary, the desire for change seemed to outstrip the intentions of the movement's organizers. Finally, in August 1968, Soviet leaders decided to crack down, sending Soviet tanks into Prague to crush the reform movement. This end of the "Prague Spring" closed the era of relative flexibility and cautious innovation in the Soviet bloc that had begun in 1953.

A period of relative stagnation followed under Leonid Brezhnev° (1906–1982), a careful, consensus-seeking bureaucrat. In dealing with the United States, Brezhnev helped engineer significant moves toward arms control and an easing of tensions. But despite this *détente,* the

Brezhnev (BREZH-nef)

The End of the Prague Spring   Moving tanks into Prague in August 1968, Soviet leaders ended the widely admired reform movement in Czechoslovakia. Though there were protests, as shown here on August 20, the outcome was a foregone conclusion once the Soviets decided to intervene. Although life soon returned to "normal" in the Czechoslovak capital, the ending of the Prague Spring proved a watershed for the fate of communism in Europe.   *(Josef Kondelka/Magnum Photos)*

"Brezhnev Doctrine" specified in no uncertain terms that the Soviet Union would intervene as necessary to help established communist regimes remain in power. For the Soviet satellite states, there seemed to be no further hope of reform from within. But even as resignation marked the first years after 1968, forces soon emerged that undermined the whole communist system.

EUROPE, THE WEST, AND THE WORLD

B Y the early 1950s, the old Europe seemed dwarfed by the two superpowers and, for the foreseeable future, divided by the conflict between them. The colonial networks that had manifested

European predominance unraveled rapidly at the same time. One obvious response was some form of European integration. A unified Europe might eventually become a global superpower in its own right. Although the first steps toward European unity did not go as far as visionaries had hoped, a new group of leaders established lasting foundations by the late 1950s. Still, the cold war framework limited the new union's geographical extent and the scope of its activity for decades.

The Cold War Framework

That cold war tensions could produce dangerous military conflict quickly became clear as superpower divisions over Korea, which had been jointly liberated from the Japanese by the Americans and the Soviets, helped produce the complex Korean War (1950–1953). Although the United States had previously declared Korea outside the U.S. defense perimeter, it intervened in support of noncommunist South Korea in the face of an attempt by communist North Korea, encouraged by Stalin, to unify Korea as a communist state. The war was inconclusive, leaving the Korean peninsula divided more or less as before, but it prompted the United States to extend containment on a global level and to step up military production.

In retrospect, however, it is clear that the most intense phase of the cold war ended with Stalin's death in 1953. In his speech to the twentieth party congress in 1956, Khrushchev repudiated the previous Soviet tenet that the very existence of Western capitalist imperialism made a military showdown with the communist world inevitable. During a visit to the United States in 1959, he stressed that the ongoing competition between the two sides could be peaceful. However, despite summit conferences and sporadic efforts at better relations, friction between the Soviet Union and the United States continued to define the era.

Indeed, a new peak of tension was reached in October 1962, when the Soviets began placing missiles in Cuba, just 90 miles from the United States. Cuba had developed close ties with the Soviet Union after a 1959 revolution led by Fidel Castro (b. 1926). With Castro beginning to develop a communist system, a U.S.-supported force of Cuban exiles sought to invade Cuba and foment insurrection against the new regime in April 1961. This effort proved a fiasco, but it demonstrated to the Soviets that the new Cuban regime was vulnerable to overthrow from the United States.

Although the United States had placed offensive missiles in NATO member Turkey, adjacent to the Soviet Union, the Soviet attempt to base missiles in Cuba seemed an intolerable challenge to the U.S. administration. President John F. Kennedy (1917–1963) responded with a naval blockade of Cuba, and for several days the superpowers seemed on the verge of military confrontation. Finally, the Soviets agreed to withdraw their missiles in exchange for a U.S. promise not to seek to overthrow the communist government of Cuba. The Americans also agreed informally to remove their offensive missiles from Turkey. Khrushchev's willingness to retreat antagonized hard-liners in the Soviet military and contributed to his ouster from power two years later. Yet Khrushchev himself viewed the outcome in Cuba as a victory. By challenging the United States with missiles, the Soviets had helped secure the survival of the Cuban communist regime, which was now less vulnerable to overthrow by the United States. The long-term significance of the outcome was not clear in 1962, but the Cuban missile crisis produced anxiety on all sides. This was the closest the superpowers came to direct, armed confrontation during the cold war period.

At the same time, it became increasingly clear that international communism was not the monolithic force it had once seemed. The most dramatic indication was the Sino-Soviet split, which developed during the 1950s as the Chinese Communist Party under Mao Zedong solidified its power. In the long struggle that led to their victory in 1949, the Chinese Communists had often had no choice but to go their own way, and during the 1940s especially, Stalin had been willing to subordinate any concern for their cause to Soviet national interests. After taking power in 1949, the Chinese Communists pursued their own path to development without worrying about the Soviet model. Not without reason, the Soviets feared that the independent, innovative Chinese might be prepared to challenge Soviet leadership in international communism. By the early 1960s, the Chinese Communists' path had become appealing to many in the non-Western world, though it attracted dissident communists in the West as well.

The Varieties of Decolonization

The advent of a new world configuration, with a circumscribed place for Europe, found dramatic expression in the rapid disintegration of the European colonial empires after World War II (see Map 29.2). The war itself had been a major catalyst for independence movements throughout the world. In southeast Asia and the Pacific, quick Japanese conquests revealed the tenuous hold of France, the Netherlands, and Britain on their domains. And it was not colonial reconquest that marked the end of the war, but the atomic bomb and the victory of the United States, which took a dim view of conventional European colonialism.

The effort of the Netherlands to regain control of the Dutch East Indies led to four years of military struggle against the Indonesian nationalist insurgency. Although most independent observers felt that the Dutch could not win, the Dutch were reluctant to relinquish control of the East Indies, which had been in their hands since the seventeenth century. Especially after the humiliations of defeat and occupation during World War II, many of the Dutch took pride in their imperial role. The struggle lasted from 1945 to 1949, when the Dutch finally had to yield as their former colony became independent Indonesia.

Unlike the Netherlands, Britain was still a great power in the twentieth century, and its empire had long seemed

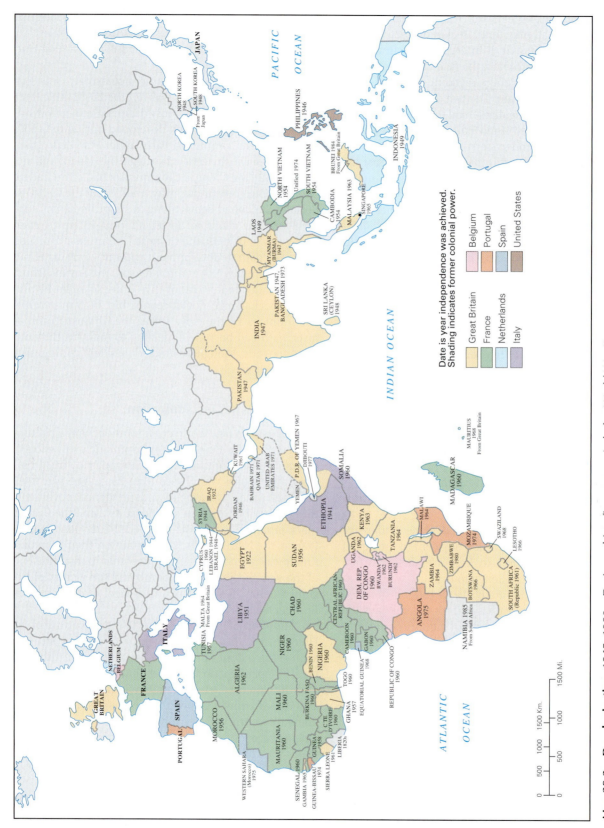

Map 29.2 Decolonization, 1945–1980 During a thirty-five-year period after World War II, the European empires in Africa, Asia, and the Pacific gradually came apart as the former colonies became independent nations.

essential to its stature. But the structure of the British Empire had been evolving for decades before World War II. With the Statute of Westminster, passed by the British Parliament in 1931, such dominions as Canada, Australia, New Zealand, and South Africa became truly independent, controlling their own foreign policies and joining the League of Nations. This statute was essentially the founding document of the British Commonwealth of Nations. Though it initially encompassed only former British possessions dominated by people of European origin, the commonwealth provided the basis for relatively orderly decolonization after World War II.

In granting independence to India and Pakistan in 1947, the British understood that traditional colonial arrangements were ending, but they envisioned playing an ongoing leadership role by incorporating their former colonies into the British Commonwealth. However, the commonwealth idea proved to have little appeal for those winning independence, and the British Commonwealth proved to be little more than a voluntary cooperative association. Still, Britain was the most realistic of the European colonial powers, grasping the need to compromise and work with emerging national leaders in light of decolonization pressures.

Nevertheless, even Britain decided to resist in 1956, when it provoked an international crisis over the status of the Suez Canal in Egypt (see Map 28.1 on page 950). Once a British protectorate, Egypt had remained under heavy British influence even after nominally becoming sovereign in 1922. But a revolution in 1952 produced a new government of Arab nationalists, led by the charismatic Colonel Gamal Abdel Nasser (1918–1970). In 1954 Britain agreed with Egypt to leave the Suez Canal zone within twenty months, though the zone was to be international, not Egyptian, and Britain was to retain special rights there in the event of war. In 1956, however, Nasser announced the nationalization of the canal, partly so that Egypt could use its revenues to finance public works projects.

Led by the Conservative Anthony Eden (1897–1977), Britain decided on a showdown. Eden won the support of Israel and France, each of which had reason to fear the pan-Arab nationalism that Nasser's Egypt was now spearheading. Israel had remained at odds with its Arab neighbors since its founding in 1948, and Nasser was helping the Arabs who were beginning to take up arms against French rule in Algeria.

Late in 1956 Britain, Israel, and France orchestrated a surprise attack on Egypt. After the Israelis invaded, the British and French bombed military targets, then landed troops to take the canal. But the troops met stubborn Egyptian resistance, and the British and French encountered decisive defeat in the diplomatic maneuvering that accompanied the outbreak of fighting. Both the United States and the Soviet Union opposed the Anglo-French-Israeli move, as did world opinion. The old European powers had sought to act on their own, by the old rules, but the outcome of this Suez crisis demonstrated how limited their reach had become.

Still, the 1956 debacle did not convince France to abandon its struggle to retain Algeria. And that struggle proved the most wrenching experience that any European country was to have with decolonization. For the French the process started not in North Africa but in Indochina, in southeast Asia, during World War II.

Led by the communist Ho Chi Minh (1890–1969), the Indochinese anticolonialist movement gained strength resisting the Japanese during the war. Then, before the French could return, Ho established a political base in northern Vietnam in 1945. Although the French reestablished control in the South, negotiations between the French and the Vietnamese nationalists seemed at first to be moving toward some form of self-government for Vietnam. But in 1946 French authorities in Indochina deliberately provoked an incident to undercut negotiations and start hostilities. Eight years of difficult guerrilla war followed, creating a major drain on the French economy.

With its strongly anticolonialist posture, the United States was unsympathetic to the French cause at first. But the communist takeover in China in 1949 and the outbreak of war in Korea in 1950 made the French struggle in Indochina seem to be a battle in a larger war against communism in Asia. By 1954 the United States was covering 75 percent of the cost of the French effort in Indochina. Nonetheless, when the fall of the fortified area at Dien Bien Phu in May 1954 signaled a decisive French defeat, the United States decided to pull back and accept a negotiated settlement. Partly at the urging of its European allies, the United States had concluded that the Soviet threat in Europe must remain its principal concern.

France worked out the terms of independence for Vietnam in 1955. The solution, however, entailed a North-South partition to separate the communist and anticommunist forces, pending elections to unify the country. The anticommunist regime the United States sponsored in the South resisted holding the elections, so the country remained divided (see Map 29.2). With the Americans providing first advisers, then, beginning in 1964, active military support, South Vietnam sought unsuccessfully to defeat a guerilla insurgency supported by the communist North. After finally defeating the United States and South Vietnam in 1975, the communist heirs of those who had fought the French assumed the leadership of a reunified Vietnam.

In France the defeat in Indochina in 1954 left a legacy of bitterness, especially among army officers, many of whom felt that French forces could have won had they not been undercut by politicians at home. When the outcome in Indochina emboldened Arab nationalists in North Africa to take up arms against the French colonial power, the French army was anxious for a second chance—and the French government was willing to give it to them. Algeria had been under French control since 1830, and it had a substantial minority of ethnic Europeans, totaling over a million, or 10 percent of the population.

Although France gradually committed 500,000 troops to Algeria, the war bogged down into what threatened to become a lengthy stalemate, with increasing brutality on both sides. (See the box "Global Encounters: At the Height of the Anticolonialist Struggle.") As it drained French lives and resources, the war became a highly contentious political issue in France. The situation came to a head during the spring of 1958, when the advent of a new ministry, rumored to favor a compromise settlement, led to violent demonstrations, engineered by the sectors of the French army in Algeria. Military intervention in France itself seemed likely to follow—and with it the danger of civil war.

It was at this moment of genuine emergency that Charles de Gaulle returned to lead the change to the Fifth Republic. Those determined to hold Algeria welcomed him as their savior. But de Gaulle fooled them, working out a compromise with the nationalist rebels that ended the war and made Algeria independent in 1962. Only de Gaulle could have engineered this outcome without provoking still deeper political division in France.

By the end of the 1950s, the colonialist impulse, which had still been significant immediately after World War II, was waning noticeably all over Europe. But resistance remained, though its forms varied considerably, as the colonies of sub-Saharan Africa continued to move toward independence. Outcomes depended on several factors: the number and intransigence of European settlers, the extent to which local elites had emerged, and the confidence of the Europeans that they could retain their influence if they agreed to independence. Of the major imperial powers in the region, Britain had done best at preparing local leaders for self-government and proved the most willing to work with indigenous elites. The two smallest countries, Belgium and Portugal, were less certain they could maintain their influence, and they proved the most reluctant to give up their imperial status.

The transition was smoothest in British West Africa, where the Gold Coast achieved independence as Ghana, first as a commonwealth dominion in 1957, then as a fully independent republic in 1960. Few British settlers lived in that part of Africa, and the small, relatively cohesive African elite favored a moderate transition, not revolution. Where British settlers were relatively numerous, however, the transition to independence was much more difficult. The very presence of Europeans had impeded the development of cohesive local elites, so movements for independence in those areas tended to become more radical, threatening the expropriation of European-held property. In Southern Rhodesia, unyielding European

Independence for Ghana Government leaders carry Prime Minister Kwame Nkrumah on April 14, 1957, just after Ghana (the former Gold Coast) obtained its independence from Britain. As the first postcolonial black government leader in Africa, Nkrumah proved a role model for other African leaders before being deposed in a military coup in 1966. *(Bettmann/Corbis)*

At the Height of the Anticolonialist Struggle

The unsuccessful struggle of the French to maintain control of Algeria, in the face of the rebellion that began in 1954, proved especially bitter and divisive—and a watershed as Western opinion turned decisively against imperialism. Although there were atrocities on both sides, the brutality of the French response called into question France's self-proclaimed civilizing mission even among many of the French themselves. Speaking on October 31, 1960, the eve of the sixth anniversary of the beginning of the war, Ferhat Abbas (1899–1985), prime minister of the provisional government of the Algerian republic, expressed confidence in victory because of the widespread support the anticolonialist movement had garnered around the world. In 1962 the French abandoned the struggle, and Algeria became independent.

People of Algeria,

Tomorrow, November 1, 1960, the war in Algeria will enter its seventh year. The fight for liberty and independence will continue with its inevitable wake of suffering and sacrifice.

A great deal has been said and written about the war in Algeria. Never will its unjust nature, its horrors, its crimes be sufficiently denounced. With this war of colonial reconquest, designed to perpetuate French domination over an Arab and African country, imperialism has plundered, wrought terror and famine—its principal arms in the attempt to bring our people to their knees. . . .

The colonial regime is the very negation of justice and law. It is useless to think that what was usurped by force can be restored other than by force. Imperialism has never given liberty to its victims as a gift. As I have said, independence is not offered, it is obtained by force. . . .

The capitulation which the French Government attempts in vain to obtain through alleged negotiations on a ceasefire is madness. We only took up arms as a last resort, when all peaceful means were found to be unworkable. We are not going to lay them down on the basis of vague promises of a self-determination whose implementation is entrusted to an army, an administration and a police which condemns the very principle of self-determination.

That would be to betray our dead, our martyrs and our flag. It would mean condemning our country to a neocolonialism as pernicious as the former. . . .

. . . While French imperialism is increasingly disapproved of and isolated, we receive messages of sympathy and tangible proofs of active solidarity from all over the world.

As dawn breaks on the seventh year of war, the international juncture is not unfavorable to us. . . .

. . . The Algerian people, which is an African people, is fighting for its freedom and its independence. We are convinced that whatever happens, the African peoples who have waged the same battle will continue to show their solidarity for our cause.

Public opinion in Europe and in South America is more and more sensitive to the struggle of the Algerian people. All those who have fought for freedom identify our struggle with theirs. Even in France, the French people, more and more conscious of their responsibilities, denounce the war of colonial reconquest and vigorously demand peace in Algeria. We salute that French youth, those workers, intellectuals and all those fighting against the continuation of the war in our country. . . .

The war in Algeria is a fight for freedom. The Algerian people which has suffered colonial domination for more than 130 years, which has shed its blood generously for the last six years, is conscious of the price of its struggle. It is aware of the occult forces which lust after the riches of its soil. The policy of the lie and of dupery will no longer affect it. All the Algerian people, men and women, children and old people, are aware of colonial realities.

And so the people will continue their struggle until victory, that is, until the liberation of Algeria.

QUESTIONS

1. Why does Abbas insist that independence must be won by force?
2. Why does Abbas seem so confident that Algeria will prevail in its struggle against French colonialism?

SOURCE: Louis L. Snyder, *The Imperialism Reader: Documents and Readings on Modern Expansionism* (Princeton, N.J.: D. Van Nostrand, 1962), pp. 519–524.

settlers resisted the British government's efforts to promote a compromise. A white supremacist government declared its independence from Britain in 1965, fueling a guerrilla war. The Africans won independence as Zimbabwe only in 1980.

The process of decolonization led to a remarkable transformation in the thirty-five years after World War II. Forms of colonial rule that had been taken for granted before World War I stood discredited, virtually without defenders, by the late twentieth century. Europeans were now accepting the principle of national self-determination for non-Europeans. But decolonization hardly offered a neat and definitive solution. In formerly colonial territories, new political boundaries often stemmed from the ways Europeans had carved things up, rather than from indigenous ethnic or national patterns. Moreover, questions remained about the longer-term economic relationships between the Europeans and their former colonies.

Economic Integration and the Origins of the European Union

As the old colonialism increasingly fell into disrepute, many found in European unity the best prospect for the future. Although hopes for full-scale political unification were soon frustrated, the movement for European integration achieved significant successes in the economic sphere, especially through the European Economic Community, or Common Market, established in 1957.

The impetus for economic integration came especially from a new breed of "Eurocrats"—technocrats with a supranational, or pan-European, outlook. A notable example was Robert Schuman (1886–1963), a native of Lorraine, which had passed between France and Germany four times between 1870 and 1945. After serving as a German officer in World War I, he was elected to the French Chamber of Deputies in 1919 just after Lorraine was returned to France. As French foreign minister after World War II, Schuman was responsible for a 1950 plan to coordinate French and German production of coal and steel. The Schuman Plan quickly encompassed Italy, Belgium, the Netherlands, and Luxembourg to become the European Coal and Steel Community (ECSC) in 1951. Working closely with Schuman was Jean Monnet, who served as the ECSC's first president. From this position, he pushed for more thoroughgoing economic integration. The successes of the ECSC led the same six countries to agree to a wider "Common Market," officially known as the European Economic Community (EEC), in 1957.

After the merger of the governing institutions of the several European supranational organizations in 1967,

the term *European Community* (EC) and later *European Union* (EU) came to indicate the institutional web that had emerged since the launching of the European Coal and Steel Community in 1951. Meanwhile, its membership gradually expanded, encompassing Denmark, Ireland, and Britain in 1973, Greece in 1981, Spain and Portugal in 1986, and Austria, Finland, and Sweden in 1995 (see Map 29.1). For newly democratic countries like Spain, Portugal, and Greece, Common Market membership became a pillar of the solidifying democratic consensus.

The immediate aim of the original EEC was to facilitate trade by eliminating customs duties between its member countries and by establishing common tariffs on imports from the rest of the world. For each member of the EEC, tariff reduction meant access to wider markets abroad, but also the risks of new competition in its own domestic market. So it was hard to be sure who might gain and who might lose from the move. However, the EEC proved advantageous to so many that tariff reduction proceeded well ahead of schedule. By 1968 the last internal tariffs had been eliminated.

With tariffs dropping, trade among the member countries nearly doubled between 1958 and 1962. For example, French exports of automobiles and chemicals to Germany increased more than eightfold. Partly because the increasing competition stimulated initiative and productivity, industrial production within the EEC increased at a robust annual rate of 7.6 percent during those years.

Despite these successes, vigorous debate accompanied the development of the EEC during the 1960s. To enable goods, capital, and labor to move freely among the member countries, some coordination of social and economic policy was required. But were the member states prepared to give up some of their own sovereignty to the Common Market to make that coordination possible?

In the mid-1960s French president de Gaulle forced some of the underlying uncertainties to the fore. Though he had willingly turned from the old colonialism, de Gaulle was not prepared to compromise French sovereignty, and he was not persuaded that supranational integration offered the best course for postwar Europe. With the end of the Algerian war in 1962, France began playing an assertively independent role in international affairs. Thus, for example, de Gaulle developed an independent French nuclear force, curtailed the French role in NATO, and recognized the communist People's Republic of China.

This determination to assert France's sovereignty led to friction between de Gaulle and the supranational Eurocrats of the Common Market. Matters came to a head in 1965, when a confrontation developed over agricultural policy. The immediate result was a compromise, but de Gaulle's tough stance served to check the increasing supranationalism evident in the EEC until then. As the economic context became more difficult during the 1970s, it became still harder to maintain the EEC's cohesion. So though the Common Market was an important departure, it did not overcome traditional national sovereignty or give western Europe a more muscular world role during the first decades after World War II.

The Energy Crisis and the Changing Economic Framework

As the political situation in western Europe became more volatile by the early 1970s, events outside Europe made it clear how interdependent the world had become—and that the West did not hold all the trump cards. In the fall of 1973, Egypt and Syria attacked Israel, seeking to recover the losses they had suffered in a brief war in 1967. Although the assault failed, the Arab nations of the oil-rich Middle East came together in the aftermath to retaliate against the Western bloc for supporting Israel. By restricting the output and distribution of the oil its members controlled, the Arab-led Organization of Petroleum Exporting Countries (OPEC) produced a sharp increase in oil prices and a severe economic disruption all over the industrialized world. Western Europe, which was heavily dependent on Middle Eastern oil, was especially hard hit. By January 1975 the price of oil was six times what it had been in 1973, before the embargo, and this increase remained a source of inflationary pressure throughout the Western world until the early 1980s.

The 1970s proved to be an unprecedented period of "stagflation"—sharply reduced rates of growth combined with inflation and rising unemployment. The economic miracle was over, partly because the process soon to be known as globalization was now taking off. The European economies were subject to growing competition from non-Western countries, most notably Japan. In light of increasing global competition and rising unemployment, the labor movement was suddenly on the defensive throughout the industrialized West. And the changing circumstances inevitably strained the social compact that had enabled western Europe to make a fresh start after the war.

THE COLLAPSE OF THE SOVIET SYSTEM, 1975–1991

THOUGH the reasons were different, the Soviet Union also encountered economic stagnation during the 1970s. The deteriorating situation finally produced a major reform effort by the mid-1980s. At the same time, Soviet leaders began encouraging liberalization in the satellite states, where new forms of opposition had developed after the crushing of the Prague reform movement in 1968. But the liberalization effort unleashed forces that led to the unraveling of the satellite system in 1989, then to the collapse of the Soviet communist regime in 1991.

The disintegration of the communist system stunned Western observers, who had come to take the anxious stability of the cold war framework for granted. But that

Oil, the West, and the World
Led by several oil-rich Arab states, OPEC drove up world oil prices by restricting production during the 1970s. The power of the oil cartel made it clear that decisions by non-Westerners could vitally affect the industrialized West. OPEC delegates are shown here in Algiers in 1975. *(Corbis Sygma)*

Women's Work in the Soviet Union   This cartoon adapts the caryatid form from ancient sculpture to depict the special burdens that were coming to wear more heavily on women as the Soviet economy bogged down. Intended to commemorate International Women's Day, the image appeared in the Soviet magazine *Krokodil* in 1984.   *(Krokodil Magazine, March 1984)*

framework rested on a kind of balance between the superpowers, with their parallel, even competing experiments. By the 1980s those experiments had produced radically different results. Thus the balance was lost, and the framework of anxious stability dissolved.

Economic Stagnation in the Soviet Bloc

The impressive rates of economic growth achieved in the Soviet Union and several of the satellite states continued into the 1960s. However, much of that success came from adding labor—women and underemployed peasants—to the industrial work force. By the end of the 1960s that process was reaching its limits, so increasingly the challenge for the Soviet bloc was to boost productivity through technological innovation.

By the late 1970s, however, the Soviets were falling seriously behind the West as a new technological revolution gathered force. The state-directed Soviet economy had proven quite capable of technological leadership when marshaling resources for a particular task was required. Thus the Soviets led the way in space travel, for example. But continuing development in high technology demanded the freedom to experiment and exchange ideas and the flexibility to anticipate innovation and shift resources. In these areas, the Soviet system, with its direction from the top, proved too rigid to compete with the free-market systems of the Atlantic bloc. Moreover, as the Soviet system bogged down, the expense of the arms race with the United States dragged ever more seriously on the Soviet economy. Ordinary Soviet citizens grew increasingly frustrated as the communist economy proved erratic in providing the most basic consumer goods. Yet major functionaries now enjoyed access to special shops and other privileges.

In satellite countries such as Poland and Hungary, the communist governments managed for a while to win mass support by borrowing from foreign banks to provide meat and other consumer goods at artificially low prices—"sausage-stuffing," some called it. But as the lending banks came to realize, by the end of the 1970s, that such loans were not being used to foster modernization and productivity, these governments found it much harder to borrow. Thus they began having to impose greater austerity.

Throughout the Soviet bloc, frustration grew especially among women, who seemed to bear a disproportionate share of the burdens. Women were more likely to be employed outside the home in the communist countries than in the West. About 90 percent of adult women in the Soviet Union and East Germany had paid jobs outside the home by 1980. In 1984, 50 percent of the East German work force was female, compared with 39 percent in West Germany. Yet not only were these women concentrated in jobs with low pay and prestige, but they also still bore the major responsibility for child-care, housework, and shopping. They had few of the labor-saving devices available in the West, and they often had to spend hours in line to buy ordinary consumer items. Dissatisfaction among women fed a new underground protest movement that began developing in the Soviet bloc in the mid-1970s—an indication of the growing strains in the overall system.

The Crisis of Communism in the Satellite States

For many intellectuals in the Soviet bloc, the Soviet suppression of the Prague Spring in 1968 ended any hope that communism could be made to work. The immediate outcome was a sense of hopelessness, but by the mid-1970s a new opposition movement had begun to take shape, especially in Hungary, Poland, and Czechoslovakia. It centered initially on underground (or *samizdat*) publications, privately circulated writings—sometimes mimeographed in as few as five or six copies—that enabled dissidents to share ideas critical of the regime.

In one sense, these dissidents realized, intellectuals and ordinary people alike were powerless in the face of heavy-handed communist government. But they came to believe they could make a difference simply by "living the truth," ceasing to participate in the empty rituals of communist rule. And mere individual honesty could have political potential especially because of the Helsinki Accords on human rights that the Soviet bloc countries had accepted in 1975.

The meeting of thirty-five countries in Helsinki, Finland, in 1975 was one of the most important fruits of the *Ostpolitik,* or opening to the East, that Willy Brandt began pursuing after becoming West Germany's chancellor in 1969 (see page 995). Eager to grasp Brandt's offer to regularize the status of East Germany and to confirm the

western border of Poland, the Soviet bloc found it expedient to accept the detailed agreement on human rights—the Helsinki Accords—that resulted from the meeting.

Though merely symbolic in one sense, that agreement proved a touchstone for initiatives that would help bring the whole Soviet system crashing down. Through various "Helsinki Watch" groups monitoring civil liberties, anticommunists in the satellite states managed to assume the moral leadership. By demanding that the communist governments live up to their agreements, by noting the gap between idealistic pretense and grim reality, opposition intellectuals began to cast doubts on the very legitimacy of the communist regimes.

The most significant such group was Charter 77, which emerged in Czechoslovakia in response to the arrest of a rock group called "The Plastic People of the Universe." Longhaired and anti-establishment like their counterparts in the West, the Plastic People were deemed filthy, obscene, and disrespectful of society by the repressive Czechoslovak regime. In 1977, protesting the crackdown on the group, 243 individuals signed "Charter 77"—using their own names and addresses, living the truth, acting as if they were free to register such an opinion.

A leader in Charter 77 was the writer Václav Havel° (b. 1936), who noted that after 1968 the notion of reforming the communist system through direct political action was dead. (See the box "Reading Sources: Power from Below: Living the Truth.") Hopes for change depended on people organizing themselves, outside the structures of the party-state, in diverse, independent social groupings. Havel and a number of his associates were in and out of jail as the government sought to stave off this protest movement. And despite their efforts, government remained particularly repressive and ordinary people relatively passive in Czechoslovakia until the late 1980s. For quite different reasons, Hungary and Poland offered greater scope for change.

Even after the failed reform effort of 1956, Hungary proved the most innovative of the European communist countries. Partly because its government allowed small-scale initiatives outside the central planning apparatus, Hungary was able to respond more flexibly to the growing economic stagnation. By the mid-1980s various alternative forms of ownership were responsible for one-third of Hungary's economic output.

This openness to economic experiment enabled reformers within the Hungarian Communist Party to gain

---

Havel (HA-vul)

READING SOURCES

POWER FROM BELOW: LIVING THE TRUTH

Considering the scope for change in the communist world by the late 1970s, Václav Havel imagines a conformist grocer who routinely puts a sign in his window with the slogan "Workers of the world, unite!" simply because it is expected. That same grocer, says Havel, has the power to break the system, which rests on innumerable acts of everyday compliance.

The real meaning of the greengrocer's slogan has nothing to do with what the text of the slogan actually says. Even so, this real meaning is quite clear and generally comprehensible because the code is so familiar: the greengrocer declares his loyalty . . . in the only way the regime is capable of hearing; that is, by accepting the prescribed *ritual,* by accepting appearances as reality, by accepting the given rules of the game. In doing so, however, he has himself become a player in the game, thus making it possible for the game to go on, for it to exist in the first place. . . .

Let us now imagine that one day something in our greengrocer snaps and he stops putting up the slogans merely to ingratiate himself. He stops voting in elections he knows are a farce. He begins to say what he really thinks at political meetings. . . . He rejects the ritual and breaks the rules of the game. He discovers once more his suppressed identity and dignity. . . .

. . . He has shown everyone that it *is* possible to live within the truth. Living within the lie can constitute the system only if it is universal. The principle must embrace and permeate everything. There are no terms whatsoever on which it can coexist with living within the truth, and therefore everyone who steps out of line *denies it in principle and threatens it in its entirety.* . . .

And since all genuine problems and matters of critical importance are hidden beneath a thick crust of lies, it is never quite clear when the proverbial last straw will fall, or what that straw will be. This . . . is why the regime prosecutes, almost as a reflex action preventively, even the most modest attempts to live within the truth.

. . . The crust presented by the life of lies is made of strange stuff. As long as it seals off hermetically the entire society, it appears to be made of stone. But the moment someone breaks through in one place, when one person cries out, "The emperor is naked!"—when a single person breaks the rules of the game, thus exposing it as a game—everything suddenly appears in another light and the whole crust seems then to be made of a tissue on the point of tearing and disintegrating uncontrollably.

Source: Václav Havel et al., *The Power of the Powerless: Citizens Against the State in Central-Eastern Europe* (Armonk, N.Y.: M. E. Sharpe, 1985), pp. 31, 37, 39–40, 42–43. Reprinted by permission from M. E. Sharpe, Inc., Armonk, NY 10504.

---

the upper hand. Amid growing talk of "socialist pluralism," the Hungarian elections of 1985 introduced an element of genuine democracy. Increasingly open to a variety of viewpoints, the Hungarian Communists gradually pulled back from their long-standing claim to a monopoly of power.

The reform effort that built gradually in Hungary stemmed especially from aspirations within the governing elite. More dramatic was the course of change in Poland, where workers and intellectuals, at odds even as recently as 1968, managed to come together during the 1970s. When Polish workers struck in 1976, in response to a cut in food subsidies, intellectuals formed a committee to defend them. This alliance had become possible because dissident intellectuals were coming to emphasize the importance of grass-roots efforts that challenged the logic of the communist system without attacking it directly.

An extra ingredient from an unexpected quarter also affected the situation in Poland, perhaps in a decisive way. In 1978 the College of Cardinals of the Roman Catholic Church departed from long tradition and, for the first time since 1522, elected a non-Italian pope. Even more startling was the fact that the new pope was from Poland, behind the iron curtain. He was Karol Cardinal Wojtyla° (b. 1920), the archbishop of Cracow, who took the name John Paul II.

After World War II, the Polish Catholic Church had been unique among the major churches of east-central Europe in maintaining and even enhancing its position. It worked just enough with the ruling Communists to be allowed to carve out a measure of autonomy. For many Poles, the church thus remained a tangible institutional alternative to communism and the focus of national self-

---

Wojtyla (voy-TILL-ah)

Lech Walesa and Solidarity   A shipyard electrician, Walesa spearheaded the dissident Polish trade union, Solidarity, formed in 1980, and then emerged from prison to lead the movement that eventually toppled the communist regime in Poland in 1989. Here he addresses a rally during a strike at the Lenin shipyard in Gdansk in August 1988.   *(Corbis Sygma)*

consciousness in the face of Soviet domination. Thus the new pope's visit to Poland in 1979 had an electrifying effect on ordinary Poles, who took to the streets by the millions to greet him—and found they were not alone. This boost in self-confidence provided the catalyst for the founding of a new trade union, Solidarity, in August 1980.

Led by the remarkable shipyard electrician Lech Walesa° (b. 1944), Solidarity emerged from labor discontent in the vast Lenin shipyard in Gdansk, on the Baltic Sea (see Map 29.1). Demanding the right to form their own independent unions, seventy thousand workers took over the shipyard, winning support both from their intellectual allies and from the Catholic Church. Support for Solidarity grew partly because the government, facing the crisis of its "sausage-stuffing" strategy, was cutting subsidies and raising food prices. But the new union developed such force because it placed moral demands first—independent labor organizations, the right to strike, and freedom of expression. Reflecting the wider opposition thinking in east-central Europe, Solidarity was not to be bought off with lower meat prices, even had the government been able to deliver them.

After over a year of negotiation, compromise, and broken promises, the tense situation came to a head in December 1981, when the government under General Wojciech Jaruzelski° (b. 1923) declared martial law and outlawed Solidarity, imprisoning its leaders. Strikes in protest were crushed by military force. So much for that, it seemed: another lost cause, another reform effort colliding with inflexible communist power in east-central Europe, as in 1953, 1956, and 1968. But this time it was different, thanks especially to developments in the Soviet Union.

The Quest for Reform in the Soviet Union

The death of Leonid Brezhnev in 1982 paved the way for a concerted reform effort that began in earnest when Mikhail Gorbachev° (b. 1931) became Soviet Communist Party secretary in 1985. Gorbachev's effort encompassed four intersecting initiatives: arms reduction; liberalization in the satellite states; *glasnost*°, or "openness" to discussion and criticism; and *perestroika*°, or economic "restructuring." This was to be a reform within the Soviet system. There was no thought of giving up the Communist Party's monopoly on power or embracing a free-market economy. The reformers still took it for granted

Walesa (va-WEN-sah)

Jaruzelski (yah-roo-ZELL-skee)   Gorbachev (GOR-ba-choff)
glasnost (GLAHZ-nost)   perestroika (pair-es-TROY-kah)

that communism could point the way beyond Western capitalism, with its shallow consumerism, its illegal drugs, its widespread crime. A measure of idealism guided the reformers' efforts, but they had to make communism work.

Gorbachev understood that "openness" was a prerequisite for "restructuring." The freedom to criticize was essential to check abuses of power, which, in turn, was necessary to overcome the cynicism of the workers and improve productivity. Openness was also imperative to gain the full participation of the country's most creative people, whose contributions were critical if the Soviet Union was to become competitive in advanced technology.

The main thrust of perestroika was to depart from the rigid economic planning mechanism by giving local managers more autonomy. The alternative did not have to entail privatization or a return to free-market capitalism. It could mean, for example, letting workers elect factory managers. But any restructuring was bound to encounter resistance, especially from those with careers tied to the central planning apparatus. And Gorbachev's program made only partial headway in this crucial sector.

The Anticommunist Revolution in East-Central Europe

Meanwhile, in Poland, Walesa remained a powerfully effective leader even from prison. He was able to keep his heterogeneous movement together as the ideas of Solidarity continued to spread underground. Then the advent of Gorbachev in 1985 changed the overall framework, for Gorbachev was convinced that restructuring the Soviet system required reform in the satellites as well. As the Polish economy, already in difficulty by 1980, reached a crisis in 1987, Solidarity began stepping up its efforts.

When proposed price increases were rejected in a referendum, the Polish government imposed them by fiat. Strikes demanding the relegalization of Solidarity followed during the spring of 1988. The government again responded with military force, but Solidarity-led strikes in August forced government leaders to send signals that they might be prepared to negotiate. With the economy nearing collapse, the government recognized that it could no longer govern on its own.

The negotiations that followed early in 1989 proved pivotal. When they began, Walesa and his advisers wanted primarily to regain legal status for Solidarity within the Communist-dominated system, still under Jaruzelski. In exchange, they assumed they would have to help legiti-

mate a rigged election to approve painful but necessary economic measures. But as these "Round Table" negotiations proceeded, the government gave ever more in exchange for Solidarity's cooperation. Not only did it consent to legalize Solidarity, but it agreed to make the forthcoming elections free enough for the opposition genuinely to participate.

The elections of June 1989 produced an overwhelming repudiation of Poland's communist government. Even government leaders running unopposed failed to win election as voters crossed out their names. In the aftermath of the elections, President Jaruzelski was forced to give Solidarity a chance to lead. Not all members of the opposition felt it wise to accept government responsibility under such difficult economic circumstances, but finally Tadeusz Mazowiecki° (b. 1927), Walesa's choice and one of the movement's most distinguished intellectuals, agreed to form a government.

The chain of events in Poland culminated in one of the extraordinary events of modern history—the negotiated end of communist rule. That a communist government might give up power voluntarily had been utterly unforeseen. It happened partly because the Soviet Union under Gorbachev was seeking reform and thus had become much less likely to intervene militarily. It also helped that the Polish Catholic Church was available to act as mediator, hosting meetings, reminding both sides of their shared responsibilities in the difficult situation facing their country. By some accounts, General Jaruzelski, who seemed for most of the 1980s to be just another military strongman and Soviet lackey, had proved to be a national hero for his grace, perhaps even ingenuity, in yielding power to the opposition. But most important was the courage, the persistence, and the vision of Solidarity itself.

Although the Hungarians were already breaking out of the communist mold, it was especially the Polish example that suggested to others in the Soviet bloc that the whole system was open to challenge. During 1989 demands for reform and, increasingly, for an end to communist rule spread through east-central Europe by means of the domino effect that had preoccupied the Soviets from the start. By the end of that year, the Soviet satellite system was in ruins (see Map 30.1 on page 1026).

A marked increase in illegal emigration from East Germany to the West had been one manifestation that the system was starting to unravel. During 1989 the reform-minded Hungarian Communists decided to stop impeding East Germans, many of whom vacationed in Hungary, from emigrating to the West at the Hungarian

---

Mazowiecki (mah-zo-VYETS-kee)

border with Austria. If the communist reformers in East Germany were to have any chance of turning the situation around, they had to relax restrictions on travel and even grant the right to emigrate. They began preparing to do both as part of a host of reforms intended to save the system. On November 9, 1989, the East German communist regime did the unthinkable and opened the Berlin Wall, which was promptly dismantled altogether. Germans now traveled freely back and forth between East and West. Although the fate of the Soviet Union itself remained uncertain, the opening of the wall signaled the end of the cold war. It was no longer a bipolar world.

This liberalization effort came too late, however. By now, discontented East Germans envisioned not simply reforming the communist system but ending it altogether. Within weeks it was clear that the rhythm of events was beyond the control of East Germany's reform communists, who opened the way for German reunification in 1990. Despite some nervousness, the four postwar occupying powers—the United States, Britain, France, and the Soviet Union—gave their blessing as the Federal Republic simply incorporated the five East German states. The communist system in East Germany simply dissolved.

Although some in West Germany were hesitant about immediate reunification, especially because of the economic costs that seemed likely, West German chancellor Helmut Kohl° (b. 1930) sought to complete the process as quickly as possible. By early 1990 the emigration of East Germans to the West had become a flood. West German law treated these Germans as citizens, entitled to social benefits, so their arrival in such numbers presented a considerable financial burden. It seemed imperative for West Germany to regularize the situation as quickly as possible, assuming responsibility for the East and restoring its economy.

The division of Germany, symbolized by the Berlin Wall, had been the central fact of the bipolar cold war world. Now Germany was a unified country for the first time since Nazism and the Second World War. What would it mean?

The End of the Soviet Union

Meanwhile, in the Soviet Union, what began as a restructuring of the communist system became a struggle for survival of the system itself. The much-trumpeted glasnost produced greater freedom in Soviet culture and politics, but Gorbachev sought to avoid alienating hard-line Communists, so he compromised, watering down the

Kohl (KOLE)

economic reforms essential to perestroika. The result proved a set of half measures that only made things worse. Because so little was done to force the entrenched Soviet bureaucracy to go along, the pace of economic reform was lethargic. The essential structures of the command economy weakened, but free-market forms of exchange among producers, distributors, and consumers did not emerge to replace them.

In 1986 an accidental explosion at the Soviet nuclear power plant at Chernobyl, in Ukraine (see Map 29.3), released two hundred times as much radiation as the atomic bombs dropped on Hiroshima and Nagasaki combined. The accident contaminated food supplies and forced the abandonment of villages and thousands of square miles of formerly productive land. The radioactivity released would eventually hasten the deaths of at least 100,000 Soviet citizens. Despite his commitment to openness, Gorbachev reverted to old-fashioned Soviet secrecy for several weeks after the accident, in an effort to minimize what had happened. As a result, the eventual toll was far greater than it need have been. The accident and its aftermath seemed stark manifestation of all that was wrong with the Soviet system—its arrogance and secrecy, its premium on cutting corners to achieve targets imposed from above.

By the end of the 1980s, Soviet citizens felt betrayed by their earlier faith that Soviet communism was leading to a better future. A popular slogan spoke sarcastically of "seventy years on the road to nowhere." The economic situation was deteriorating, yet people were free to discuss alternatives as never before. As the discussion came to include once-unthinkable possibilities such as privatization and a market economy, it became clear that the whole communist system was in jeopardy.

By mid-1990, moreover, the union of Soviet republics itself tottered on the verge of collapse. Lithuania led the way in calling for outright independence. But the stakes were raised enormously when the Russian republic, the largest and most important in the USSR, followed Lithuania's lead. In June 1990 the newly elected chairman of Russia's parliament, Boris Yeltsin (b. 1931), persuaded the Russian republic to declare its sovereignty. Yeltsin had grown impatient with the slow pace of economic and political change, and by threatening that Russia might go its own way, he hoped to force Gorbachev's reform effort beyond the present impasse. As a further challenge to Gorbachev, Yeltsin dramatically resigned from the Communist Party during its televised national congress in July 1990. When, in June 1991, free elections in the Russian republic offered the first clear contest between communists determined to preserve the system and those seeking to replace it, the anticommunist

Yeltsin was elected the republic's president by a surprising margin.

After tilting toward the hard-liners late in 1990, Gorbachev sought a return to reform after Yeltsin's dramatic election as Russia's president in June 1991. He even engineered a new party charter that jettisoned much of the Marxist-Leninist doctrine that had guided communist practice since the revolution. In August the hard-liners struck back with a coup that forced Gorbachev from power—but only for a few days. Yeltsin, supported by ordinary people in Moscow, stood up to the conspirators, while the secret police refused to follow orders to arrest Yeltsin and other opposition leaders. The coup quickly fizzled, but the episode galvanized the anticommunist movement and radically accelerated the pace of change.

Although Gorbachev was restored as head of the Soviet Union, the winner was Yeltsin, who quickly mounted an effort to dismantle the party apparatus before it could regroup. Anticommunist demonstrations across much of the Soviet Union toppled statues of Lenin and dissolved local party networks. In a referendum in December 1991, Ukraine, the second most populous Soviet republic, overwhelmingly voted for independence. Not only the communist system but the Soviet Union itself was simply disintegrating. Late in December, Gorbachev finally resigned, paving the way for the official dissolution of the Soviet Union on January 1, 1992 (see Map 29.3). The European map again included Russia, as well as, in a matter of months, fourteen other sovereign states from what had been the Soviet Union.

One of the notable experiments in the history of the West, nourished by the hopes and ideals of generations, the communist regime in the Soviet Union had proved a resounding failure.

Map 29.3   The Dissolution of the Soviet Union   As crisis gripped the Soviet system by the late 1980s, the republics of the Soviet Union began declaring first their sovereignty, then their independence. Most of the fifteen republics that had made up the Soviet Union became part of a much looser confederation, the Commonwealth of Independent States, in 1991 and 1992.

SUMMARY

N the decades that followed World War II, a bipolar framework, dominated by the United States and the Soviet Union, shaped world affairs. The states of western Europe declined in influence, even losing their remaining colonial possessions. They had to follow the U.S. lead, especially in matters of national security. From within that framework, however, they were able to achieve remarkable prosperity and significant steps toward multinational integration.

In the Soviet bloc, Stalin's death in 1953 brought an end to the most repressive features of the communist system. Under his successor, Nikita Khrushchev, the Soviet Union seemed able to compete with the United States in areas from education to space travel. But the experiment with various forms of central planning in the Soviet bloc proved ever less successful. At the same time, the crushing of a series of opposition and reform efforts, from East Berlin in 1953 to Prague in 1968, made it clear that the Soviets intended to keep their European satellites on a tight leash.

In western Europe, the shared experience of wartime led to a new social compact based on greater government responsibility for economic well-being and social welfare. By 1968, however, strains began to appear in the Western democracies, and the slowdown in economic growth during the 1970s only made them worse. Though the economic improvement remained remarkable, many western Europeans came to feel left out as the key decisions fell to party leaders or technocratic planners. Still, western Europe had come to take for granted a substantial measure of prosperity and political legitimacy, while in the communist countries of eastern Europe, growing economic stagnation fueled a much deeper form of political disaffection during the 1970s and 1980s. The parallel experiments were turning out very differently. Discontent in the Soviet bloc produced forces for change that led the whole communist system to unravel by the end of 1991.

Thus ended the cold war era. The immediate response in the West was euphoria, for the anxieties that had resulted from the rivalries and mutual suspicions of the superpowers seemed to vanish almost overnight. But what would follow remained unclear. Reformers in the former communist countries claimed to want individual freedom, political democracy, and free-market capitalism, but it would be necessary to build these on the ruins of the now-discredited communist system, a task never confronted before. And what sort of international order might replace the dangerous but stable bipolar framework that had stood since World War II?

■ Suggested Reading

Bark, Dennis L., and David R. Gress. *A History of West Germany,* vol. 1, *From Shadow to Substance, 1945–1963,* and vol. 2, *Democracy and Its Discontents, 1963–1991.* 2d ed. 1993. A favorable account of West Germany's democracy and its Atlantic and European roles in the face of ongoing suspicion and criticism.

Chamberlain, M. E. *Decolonization: The Fall of the European Empires.* 2d ed. 1999. An updated edition of a highly regarded overview.

Crockatt, Richard. *The Fifty Years' War: The United States and the Soviet Union in World Politics, 1941–1991.* 1995. A balanced history of U.S.-Soviet relations, showing the global impact of their cold war rivalry.

Dedman, Martin J. *The Origins and Development of the European Union, 1945–95: A History of European Integration.* 1996. A concise and accessible introductory work.

Hitchcock, William I. *The Struggle for Europe: The Turbulent History of a Divided Continent, 1945–2002.* 2003. A highly regarded survey—comprehensive, balanced, and engaging.

Laqueur, Walter. *Europe in Our Time: A History, 1945–1992.* 1992. A comprehensive, well-balanced survey by a leading authority on twentieth-century Europe.

Marwick, Arthur. *The Sixties: Cultural Revolution in Britain, France, Italy, and the United States, c. 1958–c. 1974.* 1998. A lengthy but gripping portrait of a pivotal decade.

Schulze, Max-Stephan, ed. *Western Europe: Economic and Social Change Since 1945.* 1999. A superior collection of essays accenting economic change; some treat individual countries, others overarching topics.

Springhall, John. *Decolonization Since 1945: The Collapse of European Overseas Empires.* 2001. An accessible and comprehensive survey.

Stokes, Gale. *The Walls Came Tumbling Down: The Collapse of Communism in Eastern Europe.* 1993. Dramatic and comprehensive, the first standard account of the dissolution of communism in east-central Europe.

 For a searchable list of additional readings for this chapter, go to college.hmco.com/students.

Pop Art

Hamburgers, comic strips, soup-can labels, familiar images of entertainment icons—such was the stuff of "pop art," which burst onto the New York art scene in the early 1960s and came to exert a widespread cultural influence. Indeed, with their imaginative renderings of familiar images and whimsical sculptures of everyday objects, artists like Andy Warhol (1928–1987), Roy Lichtenstein (1923–1997), and Claes Oldenburg (b. 1929) helped shape the experience of the later twentieth century. But was this serious art or simply a joke, a parody, a put-on? Were the pop artists poking fun at the triviality of modern society, or were they deepening our encounter with defining aspects of contemporary culture? Whatever their intent, what does this striking new art form tell us about the direction of Western culture in the decades after World War II?

The term *pop art* was coined in England in the 1950s, when a group of artists and critics became interested in bridging the cultural gap between "fine art" and the emerging popular culture of mass media and machine-produced images, of advertising and automobiles. Like everyone else, they associated that consumerist mass culture with America—the America of Hollywood, Detroit, and Madison Avenue. And they found it more vital than the conventional fine art of the period. The American pop artists were similarly fascinated by the impersonal, mass-produced, often expendable quality of the objects and images that have come to surround us.

Pop art was part of a wider reaction against the deeply serious abstract expressionist painting that emerged in New York just after the Second World War. By the early 1950s, abstract expressionists like Jackson Pollock (1912–1956) and Mark Rothko (1903–1970) had created images of unprecedented power, whether seeking to forge an artistic identity in the face of nothingness or to transcend selfhood in a cosmic wholeness. In the mid-1950s, however, younger artists, "tired of the stink of artists' egos," began reacting against the self-importance of abstract expressionism. For these younger artists, art did not have to be a vehicle for the psychological expression of the artist or a quest for "the tragic and timeless." Although the reaction took several forms, pop art proved the most influential. The pop art movement emerged especially in the United States, and it interested Europeans as typically American—fresh and fascinating or garish and vulgar, depending on one's point of view.

Whereas the abstract expressionists had sought to rise above the everyday world, Claes Oldenburg's sculptures played with the scale and context of the most ordinary objects—a mixer, a three-pronged plug, a lipstick, a hamburger—to deepen our involvement with the everyday things that surround us. In this sense, the aim of pop art was not simply to parody or satirize, but to affirm our relationship with the trappings of ordinary life. Hollywood, Detroit, and Madison Avenue were all right after all; indeed, they had become the centers of Western culture by the later twentieth century.

Though anonymous and impersonal, the modern world of mass production, mass consumption, and mass media is "popular" because its images and objects are accessible to us all. In fact, they bombard us from all directions, giving shared shape and definition to our everyday lives. This is our world, the pop artists were saying, and they were creating the art appropriate to our time. They invite us to relax and enjoy that world, but they also enhance our experience by making art from it, thereby awakening us to its novelty and vitality.

But some viewers have found an element of melancholy, nostalgia, even tragedy just beneath pop art's eye-catching surface. In a world of mass media and reproduced images, more of our experience becomes secondhand and literally superficial. Likewise, pop subjects, from fast food to billboards, have no deeper meaning, no expressive personal agenda. With his multiplied image

Oldenburg: Floor Burger, 1962 *(Claes Oldenburg [American, b. 1929], Floor Burger, 1962. Canvas filled with foam rubber and cardboard boxes, painted with acrylic paint, 132.1 x 213.4 cm. Art Gallery of Ontario, Toronto. Reproduced with permission of Claes Oldenburg.)*

Warhol: Marilyn Diptych, 1962   *(© Copyright ARS, NY. Tate Gallery, London/Art Resource, NY)*

of Marilyn Monroe, Andy Warhol dealt not with the actress herself but with the obsessive familiarity of her image. He cultivated a deadpan, detached style that reflected the machine-made quality of his subject matter—the quality that made the images he started with so familiar in the first place. But even as, on one level, he embraced aspects of the new mass culture, Warhol was exploring precisely the emotional detachment—and the accompanying trivialization of emotion—at work in the culture that had produced the images he adapted. Especially in his paintings treating impersonal newspaper images of disaster and death, Warhol bore witness to our indifference—and perhaps to a cosmic meaninglessness as well. One expert has noted that "in Warhol's pictures of the material objects and other false idols that most of us worship, the pain lies just below the bright surfaces of the images and waits passively to engage us."*

The advent of pop art provoked a series of questions that remain unanswered: Is the embrace of the mass-produced and commercial, at the expense of traditional "fine art" values, a symptom of exhaustion or a healthy affirmation of contemporary popular culture, so bound up with the commercial world? Or is pop art perhaps a valuable comment on the emptiness of that culture, with its impersonal conformity, garish commercialism, and mechanical repetition? In the final analysis, were the pop artists abandoning the artist's lofty mission and giving in to the ordinary? Or were they the first to show us what "Western civilization" had come to mean by the late twentieth century?

---

*Eric Shanes, *Warhol* (New York: Portland House, 1991), p. 41.

 For additional information on this topic, go to college.hmco.com/students.

CHAPTER 30

The West and the World Since 1989

O N January 17, 2004, ten thousand people, most of them Muslim women, marched through Paris protesting a proposed law to ban conspicuous religious displays in French public schools, hospitals, and other governmental buildings. Similar demonstrations took place throughout France and in a number of major cities throughout the world. Although large Christian crosses and Jewish yarmulkes, or skullcaps, were also at issue, the law seemed especially to target the headscarves traditionally worn by Muslim women. Yet the French National Assembly adopted the law by an overwhelming margin the next month. The controversy made it strikingly clear that matters of citizenship, assimilation, and cultural diversity had come to center stage as the West wrestled with the riddles of a newly multicultural world.

The headscarf issue prompted demonstrations in France as early as 1989, when three teenaged Muslim girls were suspended from school on the grounds that, in wearing the scarves, they were violating an existing law banning religious displays in public schools. The girls insisted they were not seeking to flaunt their religion or to convert others; the point was simply that Islamic teaching required women to cover their heads in public as a sign of modesty. Yet in the eyes of some Westerners, that practice reflected the second-class status of women in Islamic civilization. To defend the right to wear the scarves was thus to condone the oppression of women.

An uncertain compromise resulted from this earlier "affair of the scarves," but the issue continued to smolder, becoming more intense as the Muslim presence in France increased and tensions between Muslims and non-Muslims grew. By 2004 France had about five million Muslims, constituting 8 percent of the population. Often living in

At the center of worldwide demonstrations in January 2004, French Muslim women in Paris demand the right to wear the traditional Muslim headscarf in public schools and other public buildings. Their banners carry such slogans as "Modesty!" "My scarf, my choice," and "France, homeland of human rights." *(AP/Wide World Photos)*

blighted housing projects, young Muslims, especially, claimed to suffer from job discrimination and police harassment. But thus, it was feared, they were increasingly prone to militancy or Islamic fundamentalism.

Polls indicated that whereas 69 percent of the French backed the new law, these issues divided the French Muslim community. Muslim support for the ban on the headscarf reflected a fear of backlash against indications of Islamic separatism, but a genuine desire for assimilation was also at work. However, many Muslims were reluctant to accept full assimilation if it was to mean the gradual loss of their religious identity in France's secular society. Many non-Muslims supported the right of women to wear the scarf precisely on the grounds of pluralism, tolerance, and freedom of expression. Yet some of those opposing the new law sought not to preserve diversity but to keep Islamic girls in the public schools to expose them to secular influence and to promote assimilation. By restricting religious expression, they argued, the new law would spawn separate Islamic schools, thereby deepening the divisions already evident in France.

This tangled issue arose from within a process known first as modernization, or "Westernization," then, by the 1990s, as "globalization." Whatever the term, at issue was the process through which ever more of the world was drawn into the competitive global market economy that had gradually spread from Europe over the previous millennium. By the end of the twentieth century, globalization entailed complex patterns of emulation and resistance, envy and resentment, increasingly focused on the global reach of the United States. The backlash included not only the embrace of traditional cultural expressions like the Muslim headscarf but also, on occasion, violence and terrorism.

Although the issue, up to a point, was the West's relationship with the wider world, the West itself seemed to be fragmenting in new ways by the middle of the first decade of the twenty-first century. Such splintering became possible only with the end of the cold war, which had overshadowed all else for four decades after World War II.

With the collapse of communism, the West was no longer divided into rival power blocs representing competing experiments. The former communist countries scrambled to institute Western-style democratic capitalism, and by the first decade of the twenty-first century many of them had been encompassed into the European Union (EU). But even in the established Western democracies, unprecedented economic and technological change raised new questions, some of which threatened to challenge the political consensus that had crystallized since World War II.

QUESTIONS TO CONSIDER

- Why and how did the relationship between western Europe and the United States change after the end of the cold war?

- What can we learn from the experience of the postcommunist countries about the health of modern democracy?

- Why did concerns about immigration, citizenship, assimilation, and cultural diversity become central throughout much of the Western world by the beginning of the twenty-first century?

- What questions emerged as the West began playing a more active role in confronting crises all over the globe during the 1990s?

TERMS TO KNOW

European Union (EU)	information technology
G-8 (Group of 8)	Margaret Thatcher
Maastricht agreements	World Trade
euro	Organization (WTO)
Common Agricultural	digital divide
Policy (CAP)	nongovernmental
ethnic cleansing	organizations (NGOs)
unilateralism	social market economy
Vladimir Putin	

THE UNCERTAIN INTERNATIONAL FRAMEWORK AFTER THE COLD WAR

The disintegration of the Soviet system from 1989 to 1991 meant the swift, unexpected end of the bipolar cold war framework that had defined the era since World War II (see Map 30.1). What international roles would the Western democracies be prepared to play, together or separately, now that resisting communism was no longer the central preoccupation? And what place would the former communist countries, most notably Russia, assume in whatever new order emerged?

An immediate and troubling outcome of the end of the cold war was renewed ethnic conflict in parts of Europe. Although Czechoslovakia divided peacefully into two nations, the Czech Republic and Slovakia, on January 1, 1993, ethnic concerns elsewhere produced violence and massive human rights violations. Violence also found expression in increased international terrorism by the early twenty-first century.

Efforts to address the unforeseen problems of the post–cold war world raised questions about respective roles of multinational entities such as the UN, NATO, and the EU, which was both expanding and proceeding toward deeper European integration. Although the need to respond to those problems unified the West up to a point, by the early twenty-first century differences surfaced that threatened to fragment the West as never before since World War II.

New Power Relationships in the West

That the end of the cold war had left the United States "the world's only superpower" quickly became a cliché, and the United States continued to offer leadership through the framework they had established after World War II. Although NATO's role was less clear with the end of the Soviet threat, NATO expanded first in 1999, then in 2004, to encompass most of the former Soviet satellite states of eastern Europe, from Poland to Bulgaria. To the former communist countries, NATO membership meant the definitive repudiation of the cold war division of Europe.

At first some found such NATO expansion a needless provocation to Russia, now, in its postcommunist guise, an especially uncertain player on the international scene. Whereas the collapse of communism meant renewed pride and independence for the former satellite states,

CHRONOLOGY	
1979	Thatcher becomes prime minister of Britain
	First direct elections to European parliament
1981	Mitterrand elected president of France
1990	Reunification of Germany
1991	Beginning of fighting in Yugoslavia
	Maastricht agreements expand scope of European Union
1996	Peace in Bosnia
	Yeltsin re-elected as president of Russia
1997	Blair becomes prime minister of Britain
1998	UN establishes international criminal court in The Hague
	Socialist-led coalition under Schröder replaces Kohl's conservative government in Germany
1999	Euro launched as currency of European Union
	NATO bombing of Serbia in response to Serb policies in Kosovo
	Renewal of Russia's war with Chechnya
	Protests at WTO meeting in Seattle
2000	Putin elected president of Russia
2001	Serbian government sends Milosevic for trial before the international war crimes tribunal in The Hague
	Terrorist attack on United States
2003	U.S.- and British-led forces overthrow Saddam Hussein's regime in Iraq
	WTO meeting in Cancun, Mexico, breaks up amid protests
2004	EU adds ten new member countries, for a total of twenty-five

Russia felt humiliated as a onetime superpower that was now poor, diminished in size, and seemingly ignored in world affairs. But the West was anxious not to alienate the new Russia. Germany and France each developed strong bilateral relations with the former communist power. Moreover, Russia was invited to join the informal grouping of the world's seven largest economic powers (the United States, Japan, Germany, France, Britain, Italy, and Canada), which had begun meeting during the

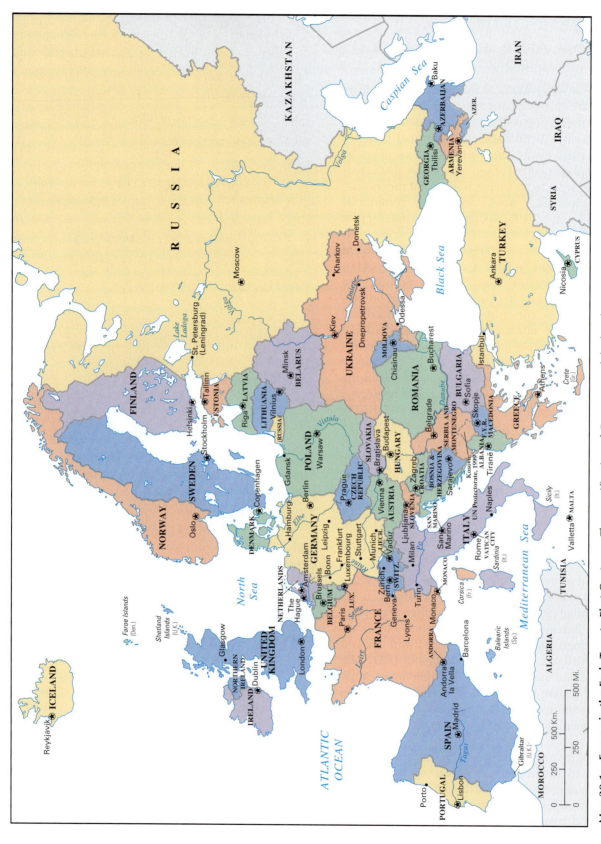

Map 30.1 Europe in the Early Twenty-First Century The reunification of Germany and the breakup of the Soviet Union, Yugoslavia, and Czechoslovakia fundamentally altered the map of Europe during the 1990s.

The Democratic Reichstag, Berlin
The centerpiece of the renovation of the German parliament building, undertaken by the noted British architect Norman Foster and completed in 1999, was the addition of a glass dome, intended to manifest the openness of Germany's democracy as its capital moved from Bonn to Berlin.
(Reimer Wulf/akg-images)

1970s in an effort to coordinate economic policies. Although the present size of the Russian economy did not warrant inclusion in this "Group of Seven," or G-7, it seemed worthwhile to give the new Russia a voice in what thus became the G-8.

Germany, which promptly reunified as communism collapsed in the East, seemed a major beneficiary of the end of the cold war. Whereas some worried that the new Germany might return to bullying and aggressiveness, others—Germans and non-Germans alike—were eager to have Germany assume a stronger diplomatic role, and thus the responsibilities commensurate with its economic strength.

The Federal Republic officially moved its capital from quiet, provincial Bonn to Berlin in 1999, when a costly makeover of the old parliament (Reichstag) building by the British architect Norman Foster had been completed. (See the box "Reading Sources: Reconstructing Berlin: The New German Capital After the Cold War.") As it happened, precisely as the refurbished building was opened, German forces were involved in their first combat roles since World War II, participating in NATO air strikes responding to what seemed genocidal aggression in Yugoslavia. German chancellor Gerhard Schroeder, a socialist, insisted that Germany, in light of its recent history, could not turn away but indeed had a particular responsibility to respond. Still, though Germany contributed significantly to international peacekeeping efforts, many Germans remained reluctant to support an expanded international military role. German military spending remained low compared with that of the United States, Britain, and France.

The European Union

As the European Union continued to expand and deepen by the early twenty-first century, it became clear that it constituted one of the notable experiments in Western history. Though still very much in progress, that experiment produced a complex web of institutional arrangements that were bizarre and complex in one sense, bold and innovative in another.

After the oil crises of the 1970s, and amid increasing concern about "Eurosclerosis," or lack of innovation and competitiveness, the EU's twelve members committed themselves in 1985 to creating a true single market with genuinely free competition by the end of 1992. Goods, services, and money would circulate freely among the member countries; manufacturing would conform to uniform product standards; and equal competition for government contracts would apply.

Meeting at Maastricht, in the Netherlands, in 1991, leaders of the member countries agreed to a new Treaty on European Union, which, among other things, provided for a common policy on workers' rights and committed members to a common currency and a common central banking structure by 1999. Although the EU's members eventually ratified most of the Maastricht

READING SOURCES

RECONSTRUCTING BERLIN: THE NEW GERMAN CAPITAL AFTER THE COLD WAR

Berlin was a city like none other in modern history. Associated with Prussian militarism, then with German nationalism, and finally with the worst features of Nazi aggression, the city ended up divided by the cold war—and the Wall—then restored as the capital of the reunified Germany in 1999. How could the democratic Federal Republic, modestly headquartered in provincial Bonn since its inception in 1949, best embrace Berlin, with all its historical connotations? Jane Kramer, one of the most authoritative journalistic analysts of contemporary Europe, conveyed what Berlin was like in 1999 as it remade itself to be the capital of an established democracy.

One morning in Berlin this spring, on my way to an interview with a city planner, I stopped at the new Galeries Lafayette, in the east of the city on Friedrichstrasse, to pick up a croissant at the basement supermarket. By then, I had been in Berlin for at least a week. I had tried counting the construction cranes—seven hundred of them, the papers said—dipping over the born-again capital of a united Germany. I had prowled the sites of that construction, tracing the path of a wall and a no man's land that only ten years ago had split the city down its center. I had toured the Chancellery and some of the other new government buildings going up around the Reichstag, itself restored with a new glass dome. I had been through the Potsdamer Platz, where Sony and DaimlerChrysler were hosting a real-estate-development potlatch on twenty-eight acres of what used to be bombed-out desert. And I had seen the Schlossplatz, in East Berlin, where people were still arguing about the fate of an immense and incontestably ugly building called the Palace of the Republic, which until November of 1989, when the Wall came down, had housed the East German parliament. I had dug up the figures: five thousand six hundred and forty architects practicing in Berlin; a hundred and thirty thousand workers officially rebuilding Berlin (and no one knows how many unregistered foreign crews still bunking in converted shipping-container dormitories on the big sites); six thousand bureaucrats drawing salaries to (depending on who's talking) contribute to or complicate the process. I had heard all about "the architecture of the European city," "the architecture of the Berlin Republic," "the architecture of civil society," "the architecture of public space," and "the architecture of democratic transparency." I had spent so much time looking at buildings, thinking about buildings, listening to people whose job it was to try to redeem or redefine or reinvent "Germanness" through the new buildings of the capital, that my trip to the Galeries Lafayette was the first time I had actually used any of those buildings in what for me could be considered a normal way. . . .

. . . It's safe to say that only in Berlin will you hear that a middle-sized, medium-priced department store with seventeen brands of tights and fresh breakfast pastries in the basement is a field of battle for nothing less than the soul of Germany—and not even because of its assault on your pocketbook (Germans call it "consumer terrorism") but because of a cone-shaped glass-and-steel atrium that a planner found "authoritarian," and not the "agora" he had hoped for.

The change in Berlin over the past few years has been astonishing, and, with this sort of architectural anguish (it's endemic now), the most astonishing part may be that anything gets built at all.

. . . Every city creates a market in its own obsessions, and right now in Berlin the obsession is architecture—or, more accurately, how to make a credible Berlin out of a city with no consensual idea of itself, and no common history beyond a negative one.

Source: Adapted from "Living with Berlin" by Jane Kramer. Originally published in *The New Yorker*, July 5, 1999, pp. 50–52. Copyright © 1999 by Jane Kramer. Reprinted by permission of the author.

agreements, member countries could essentially opt out of certain provisions. Even as the new common currency, the euro, was introduced in two major steps, in 1999 and 2002, four of the fifteen EU members, including Britain, remained outside the common currency mechanism. Still, the common currency facilitated a notable increase in supranational mergers and takeovers—a trend that threatened some but promised greater efficiency and international competitiveness for European firms.

So successful was the EU that others clamored to join. At its summit in Athens in April 2003, the EU accepted ten countries, eight of them recently communist, for full membership in 2004. With this single step, membership would jump from fifteen countries to twenty-five—a remarkable increase from the original six that had launched the European Economic Community (EEC) in 1957 (see page 1010). The lure of membership significantly strengthened democracy in the candidate states, for the EU insisted on democratic institutions and alignment with EU laws and procedures as a condition of membership. Eager to be accepted, Romania, Bulgaria, and Croatia took serious steps to meet the criteria for membership, and by 2003 it was even possible to ask when Serbia and Albania might be ready.

Especially problematic was the case of Turkey, long a key NATO member and long interested in joining the EU. Although its tradition of secular government was well established, Turkey was a predominantly Islamic country at a time of growing concerns about militant Islamic fundamentalism. The Turkish candidacy raised questions about how far the EU was prepared to expand, even about the meaning of "Europe."

With expansion, long-standing questions about the EU's structure and functioning became more pressing. Although the EU made democracy a condition for membership, it had its own "democratic deficit": major decisions were made by an unelected policy elite. Still, the issue of openness and accountability was tricky because of the EU's institutional complexity.

By the early twenty-first century, the EU included a network of five interlocking core institutions, variously seated in Brussels, Strasbourg, Luxembourg, and Frankfurt. The executive branch was the Commission in Brussels, consisting of twenty appointed members, but with a professional staff of sixteen thousand. Charged to pursue the wider interests of the community, not to represent national interests, the Commission had considerable power to initiate and enforce EU legislation. The question was whether these unelected "Eurocrats" had too much power.

The legislative branch of the EU was the Council of Ministers, composed of ministers from the governments of the member countries. On routine matters, the Council voted by majority, weighted by the size of each country's population. More sensitive issues required unanimity; thus each member country had veto power. Especially as the EU prepared to expand, reformers sought to extend the role of majority rule and minimize the scope for veto.

EU membership entailed some loss of national sovereignty, thanks especially to the increasingly powerful role of the judicial branch, the European Court of Justice, headquartered in Luxembourg. In a landmark 1988 case, the court struck down a German law on beer purity,

which it found to have been an instance of disguised protectionism. The German government complied with the court's ruling. This precedent made it clear that EU agreements had priority over national legislation, and thereafter the court proved increasingly willing to interpret EU treaties broadly, at the expense of national prerogatives.

In contrast, the power of the European Parliament, which had developed from the assembly of the European Coal and Steel Community, and which divided its time between Strasbourg and Brussels, was more potential than actual. Although it had some oversight over budget and expanding powers to block or amend legislation, the parliament remained the weakest of the core EU institutions in 2003. As a result, despite the genuinely democratic character of this body, voters in the member countries demonstrated little interest in the election of its members.

The fifth core institution, the European Central Bank, headquartered in Frankfurt, was born with the commitment to a common monetary policy and currency in 1991. Like central banks everywhere, it sought to regulate the money supply and thereby to help the EU's economies function in a smooth and coordinated way.

Through gradual, incremental change over more than fifty years, the EU had become an established and powerful entity by the early twenty-first century. By this time "Europe" was a hybrid, at once a genuinely supranational entity and a collection of sovereign states. There had never been anything quite like it before. In spheres such as trade, agriculture, and the environment, the EU was dominant; national governments had little freedom of action. But other spheres, such as defense, taxation, and criminal justice, remained mostly national prerogatives. The question was whether the EU would continue to expand its sphere of competence—and in what directions. For example, there was not yet a true single market for services, though services accounted for 70 percent of economic activity in the EU. Thus reformers advocated that the EU specify uniform standards for professional qualifications.

The creation of an internal customs union, benign though it seemed, had never committed the EU to freer trade with nonmember countries—the United States, for example, or the developing nations of the non-Western world. Indeed, half the EU budget at the end of the 1990s went to the widely criticized Common Agricultural Policy (CAP), entailing subsidies to protect farmers from outside competition. By 2003 the EU Commission was trying to reform the CAP to make it less wasteful and protectionist. But the possibility of lower supports had led to several massive demonstrations by French farmers

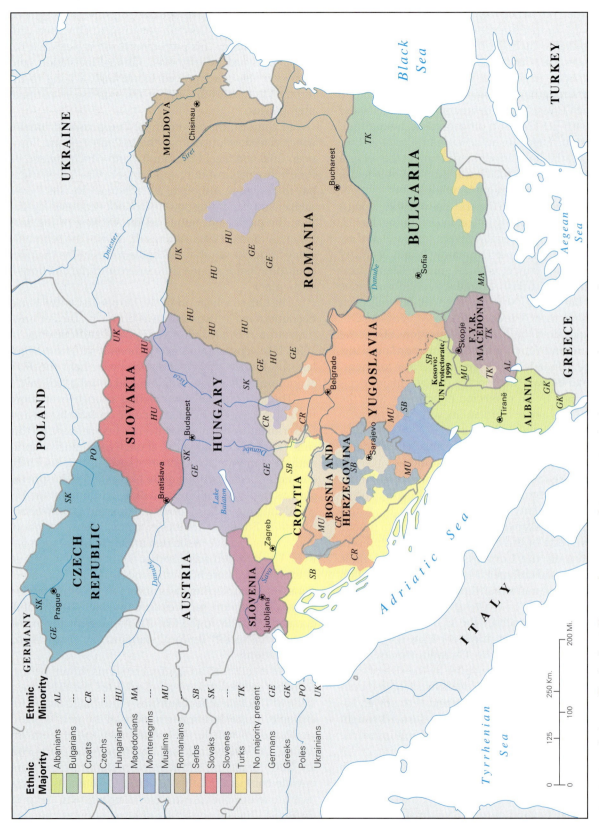

Map 30.2 Ethnic Conflict in the Balkans and East-Central Europe   Much of east-central Europe, and particularly the Balkans, has long been an area of complex ethnic mixture. The end of communist rule opened the way to ethnic conflict, most tragically in what had been Yugoslavia. This map shows ethnic distribution in the region in the mid-1990s.

Ethnic Majority

Ethnic Minority

Albanians	AL
Bulgarians	---
Croats	CR
Czechs	---
Hungarians	HU
Macedonians	MA
Montenegrins	---
Muslims	MU
Romanians	---
Serbs	SB
Slovaks	SK
Slovenes	---
Turks	TK
No majority present	
Germans	GE
Greeks	GK
Poles	PO
Ukrainians	UK

during the 1990s, and in light of the fierce ongoing political opposition to change, the scope for reform remained unclear.

The anticipated expansion of 2004 demanded that the EU both clarify and streamline procedures. Thus in 2002 it charged a committee, chaired by former French president Valéry Giscard d'Estaing, to draft a formal constitution. Although an initial draft won broad general endorsement at the EU summit in June 2003, it raised various objections. Adoption of the final constitution was promised before June 2004, but the process faced significant hurdles. Many people worried that whereas more democracy was desirable in principle, it would make the EU more beholden to shortsighted, parochially national concerns—and thus less successful.

Ethnic Conflict and Peacekeeping Roles

As the members of the European Union struggled to create a supranational entity, forces in the opposite direction—subnational, religious, ethnic, tribal—grew more powerful in parts of the West, sometimes producing violent conflict. Beginning in 1969, the British had to use troops in Northern Ireland to keep order in the face of ongoing threats from Irish Catholics seeking the end of British rule and unification with the Republic of Ireland. The result was more than three decades of conflict between Protestants and Catholics that eluded definitive solution into the twenty-first century. A movement to separate French-speaking Quebec from the rest of Canada periodically became prominent, almost succeeding in 1995.

Still, the most dramatic situation was in postcommunist Yugoslavia, where ethnic and religious conflict led to the disintegration of the country in a series of brutal wars among Serbs, Croats, Bosnian Muslims, and ethnically Albanian Kosovars (see Map 30.2). Defining events of the 1990s, these wars proved a major challenge for the new international order after the cold war.

Although much was made of ancient ethnic and religious differences once Yugoslavia began falling apart, the area had long traditions of pluralism and tolerance. Ethnic relations had been poisoned, however, by recent events, especially the civil war during World War II (see page 973). The situation had remained reasonably stable under Josip Tito's independent communist regime, which insisted on Yugoslav unity while affording some measure of regional autonomy. But within a few years of Tito's death in 1980, intellectuals concerned about cultural distinctiveness began undermining the wider Yugoslav identity that Tito had sought to foster.

After the fall of communism, Slovenia and Croatia declared themselves independent of Yugoslavia in May 1991. At the same time, the Serb leader of the remaining Yugoslavia, Slobodan Milosevic° (b. 1941), a former communist, embraced Serb nationalism at least partly to maintain his own power. His aim was to unite all the Serbs, two million of whom lived outside Serbia, mostly in Croatia and Bosnia-Herzegovina. He would start by taking over the substantial parts of Croatia with Serb majorities, then divide Bosnia-Herzegovina with Croatia.

Starting in 1991, Milosevic proceeded with extreme brutality, fostering "ethnic cleansing"—forced relocation or mass killing to rid the territory in question of non-Serb inhabitants. In the Bosnian capital, Sarajevo, a culturally diverse city long known for its tolerant, cosmopolitan atmosphere, more than 10,000 civilians, including 1,500 children, were killed by shelling and sniper fire during a Serb siege from 1992 to early 1996.

When a Serb mortar killed thirty-seven civilians in a marketplace in Sarajevo in August 1995, NATO forces responded with air strikes that led to peace accords and the end of fighting by early 1996. Although the peace agreement envisioned a unified Bosnian state, the contending Serbs, Croats, and Bosnian Muslims quickly began carving out separate spheres, violating agreements about repatriation and the rights of minorities. By 2003 Bosnia remained an ethnically divided international protectorate, still dependent on the international peacekeeping force stationed there.

The next phase of the Yugoslav tragedy centered on the province of Kosovo, which Serbs viewed as the cradle of their nationhood (see Map 30.2). For complex historical reasons, however, Serbs had long constituted only a minority of its population. The majority were ethnically Albanian, and by the late 1980s they were talking independence—and sometimes mistreating the minority Serbs. As part of his effort to foster Serb nationalism, Milosevic countered by suspending autonomy for Kosovo within the Yugoslav confederation in 1991. The fissuring of Yugoslavia over the next few years emboldened the Kosovars, who had come to envision full independence, as opposed to mere autonomy within the Serbian part of what remained of Yugoslavia. By provoking Serb intransigence, they could expect to win international support as they demanded independence.

When Milosevic struck against the Kosovars in the spring of 1999, ruthlessly pursuing ethnic cleansing, the Western powers again intervened, first convening a

Milosevic (mih-LO-suh-vitch)

After the Fighting in Kosovo
In Pristina, capital of the province of Kosovo in the former Yugoslavia, an ethnic Albanian child plays in the former dwellings of Serbs and Roma ("Gypsies") in April 2001. The houses had been wrecked by Albanians returning from expulsion by the Serbs in 1999. *(Thomas Dworzak, Magnum Photos)*

meeting with Serb and Kosovar leaders on Kosovo's future. When the Serb-led remnant of Yugoslavia refused to sign, NATO made good on its threats to bomb Serbia in retaliation. The bombing, concentrated on such economic targets as bridges and power stations, continued for eleven weeks in late 1999.

Critics argued that it set a dubious precedent to attack Serbia for refusing a settlement that would have ceded territory and opened the rest of Serbia to quasi-occupation by NATO. No one denied that Kosovo was part of Serbia, so the NATO action was an overt interference in the internal affairs of a sovereign state. Even the notion that the operation was a humanitarian response to genocide seemed hypocritical to some, who asked why the international community had done nothing in response to the far more systematic genocide in Rwanda in 1994, when 800,000 people had been killed in a hundred days. Defenders countered that it was partly because of the soul-searching in the aftermath of Rwanda that the Western countries were now changing the rules and taking responsibility for concerted action.

Once the NATO bombing began, the Serbs intensified their ethnic cleansing of Kosovo, burning homes, forcing 800,000 refugees to flee into neighboring Macedonia and Albania. But the bombing finally led both the Serbs and the Kosovars to pull back from their more extreme demands, and Russia agreed to join in the multinational peacekeeping force in Kosovo in the aftermath.

Still, the outcome bore little relationship to the multiethnic pluralism NATO had been seeking. As Kosovars came to dominate the now-ravaged territory, the rule was ethnic separation, portending some sort of division. Moreover, the new Kosovo was dominated first by lawless gangs, then increasingly by criminal organizations that the peacekeepers proved powerless to control.

Although Milosevic was the first sitting head of state to be indicted for war crimes, he proved resilient, initially surviving his defeat in Kosovo in 1999. He lost the presidential election in September 2000, however, and the following year, under pressure from the international community, the Serbian government within the rump Yugoslav confederation turned him over to the international war crimes tribunal in The Hague. Meanwhile, those who led Serbia after Milosevic's defeat fought a difficult battle against systematic corruption and organized crime as they sought to make their country worthy of membership in the European Union.

Responding to Global Terrorism

Further complicating international relations after the cold war was an increase in the scale and extent of terrorism, sometimes pitting non-Westerners against the West. European venues ranged from Northern Ireland to the Basque region of northern Spain to the rebellious Russian republic of Chechnya. In the United States right-wing extremists bombed a federal government building in Oklahoma City in 1995, and U.S. embassies in Kenya and Tanzania were subjected to terrorist attacks in 1998.

With this new terror already erupting, an unprecedented suicide attack shook the United States on September 11, 2001. Hijackers seized four large airliners, crashing one into each of the towers of the World Trade Center in New York City and another into the Pentagon, just outside Washington, D.C. The fourth plane, apparently also headed for Washington, crashed in Pennsylvania. The World Trade Center crashes collapsed both towers, which had been among the world's most visible landmarks. The concerted attack claimed the lives of over three thousand people from eighty-two countries.

The United States proclaimed the attack an act of war, and the NATO alliance invoked Article 5 for the first time: the attack on one of its members was to be treated as an attack against all. U.S. leaders promptly assigned responsibility to al Qaeda, an international terrorist network led by the wealthy Saudi Arabian Osama bin Laden, who was living in exile in Afghanistan. There he and others of his network were protected by the Taliban regime, whose extreme, radically fundamentalist version of Islam they shared in certain respects.

Led by President George W. Bush, the United States initiated military action against the Taliban regime later in 2001. Several weeks of U.S. bombing enabled Afghan opposition forces to oust the Taliban and force al Qaeda onto the defensive. But bin Laden seemed to have survived, and al Qaeda regrouped sufficiently to launch terrorist attacks against Western interests in Morocco and Saudi Arabia in 2002 and 2003. Unlikely to be eradicated by military force alone, such terrorism posed an ongoing threat to Western security and complicated the West's relations with the non-Western world.

The Controversial Iraq War of 2003

The United States won widespread support, not only in the West, for its effort to root out international terrorist networks, especially al Qaeda. But the Americans encountered formidable opposition in 2002 when the Bush administration began to call for the overthrow of Saddam Hussein in Iraq. Saddam was charged with stockpiling chemical and biological weapons of mass destruction in violation of the UN peace agreement that followed the Persian Gulf War of 1991. In that war a broad, U.S.-led coalition defeated an Iraqi effort to conquer Kuwait. Iraq was also accused of developing a nuclear weapons program and supporting terrorist networks like al Qaeda. Moreover, Saddam had long tyrannized the Iraqi people.

Terror in New York City, September 11, 2001   With one of the twin towers of the World Trade Center burning from an attack at 8:45 A.M., a second hijacked plane crashed into the second tower less than an hour later. By the end of the morning, both towers had collapsed.   *(Chao Soi Cheong/AP/Wide World Photos)*

As it began to appear that the United States might be prepared to act unilaterally, the Iraq issue became one of the most divisive in recent history, straining the Western alliance like nothing before. No one denied that the Iraqi regime was a brutal dictatorship that had developed, and even used, weapons of mass destruction in the past. But as the United States began to press the issue, an array of countries, with France, Germany, Russia, and China in the forefront, insisted that UN weapons inspectors be given more time to assess Iraq's compliance with the peace terms. Moreover, they held that any punitive action in the event of noncompliance be directed by the UN Security Council, not the United States acting unilaterally.

Yet the Americans won a good deal of international support. The governments of Britain, Italy, Spain, Denmark, Poland, Hungary, and the Czech Republic sent a letter to the *Wall Street Journal* supporting Bush's get-tough policy. Most important, British prime minister Tony Blair, despite considerable opposition from within his own Labour government, made Britain a full partner of the United States. Romania and Bulgaria cooperated, even letting their military bases be used as staging points

Protesting the Impending War in Iraq   The run-up to the U.S.-led invasion of Iraq provoked large demonstrations in much of Europe. Here, on February 15, 2003, antiwar protesters pass the Colosseum in Rome carrying a large rainbow flag inscribed with the word "peace" in many languages.   *(Fabio Sardella/AP/Wide World Photos)*

for the ensuing U.S. assault on Iraq. Each hoped to gain not only NATO membership but also permanent American bases as the United States contemplated redeploying some of its forces in Europe in light of the changing international configuration. But even in countries with governments supporting U.S. policy, the public tended to be strongly opposed to a military showdown in Iraq.

When it became clear the United States and Britain could not win UN Security Council endorsement, they sent military forces into Iraq in March 2003 and toppled Saddam Hussein's regime within six weeks. The military success proved easier than most people had expected, but the tasks of reconstruction proved more difficult than U.S. officials had envisioned. Months after the United States declared active hostilities ended on May 1, 2003, the occupying forces suffered almost daily casualties. As it gradually became clear that Iraq had had no active program to develop weapons of mass destruction on the eve of invasion, fresh questions about the justification for the war inevitably emerged. In addition, there was evidence that both the U.S. and British governments had relied to some extent on faulty intelligence or had used intelligence selectively to justify the invasion.

In April 2003, with the defeat of Saddam assured, the leaders of Russia, France, and Germany met in St. Petersburg, Russia, to seek a common policy toward the reconstruction of Iraq. Although they claimed to be seeking cooperation with the United States and Britain, they called for the UN to play the central role in rebuilding Iraq. The United States opposed this policy. As the magnitude and expense of rebuilding Iraq became clearer, however, the United States sought the support of both the United Nations and Western allies. Finding a workable basis for cooperation proved difficult, and it was not clear how long the United States could bear the major burden of engineering the political transition in Iraq.

The U.S. effort received a boost with the capture of Saddam Hussein himself in December 2003. Photos of this now disheveled figure, who had been hiding literally in a hole in the ground, made it clear that his regime had been decisively ended. But in March 2004 a coordinated series of terrorist bombings on commuter trains in Madrid killed over 200 people on the eve of Spanish elections. Preliminary evidence suggested al Qaeda responsibility. In the elections that followed, the Spanish electorate repudiated the governing conservatives in favor of the Socialists, whose leader, José Luis Rodríguez Zapatero, charged that the U.S.-led occupation of Iraq was becoming a fiasco. He promptly reaffirmed an earlier pledge to withdraw the 1300 Spanish troops from Iraq if the reconstruction effort were not entrusted to the United Nations. As the question of Iraq continued to sow division in the West, some feared, and others hoped, that the Spanish example would lead other members of the U.S.-led coalition to rethink their commitments.

NEW OUTCOMES OF THE CONTINUING DEMOCRATIC EXPERIMENT

The issue for western Europe since World War II had been the restoration or renewal of democracy, and democracy had become the unchallenged norm in the region by the 1980s. The postwar history of eastern Europe had been very different, but after the fall of communism the former Soviet bloc countries scrambled to adopt the western European model that had settled out since World War II. Although the problems of adjustment were especially dramatic, and even tragic, in Russia, patterns in most of the former communist countries increasingly approximated those of the mature democracies of western Europe.

The mainstream tendency was toward democratic procedures, the rule of law, and an orderly alternation of competing political parties within a framework of stability, consensus, and tolerance. But technological change and globalization were altering the socioeconomic framework at the same time, producing new challenges for governments and even threatening the socioeconomic compact that had emerged after World War II.

The Postcommunist Experiment

Although the former communist countries were generally eager to join the mainstream capitalist democracies, the area had little experience with the give-and-take of democratic politics, and the fragile new political systems had to engineer the difficult transition from a command to a free-market economy. The economies in the former communist satellite states were close to chaos as the transition began, and their attempts to construct market economies brought on unemployment, inflation, and widespread corruption. No longer could ordinary people count on the subsidized consumer goods or the welfare safety net the communist regimes had provided. While many suffered great hardship, some former communist functionaries quickly got rich by taking over state-owned companies.

The pattern of change and the degree of success varied considerably from country to country, and the region lagged dramatically in per capita income. But by the mid-1990s, the transition to a market economy seemed to be working (see Map 30.3). Partly thanks to the lure of EU membership, possible only for fully functioning democracies, most of the postcommunist countries made considerable progress toward mainstream democracy. Even the election of former Communists in Poland and Hungary during the mid-1990s did not compromise democracy or the market economy. Even so, in Poland, for example, public spending was widely held to be poorly managed, services were poor, and the tax system was full of loopholes.

In Russia, where communism had far deeper roots than elsewhere in the former Soviet bloc, the transition from communism proved especially difficult. Although privatization proceeded rapidly in Russia, even more than elsewhere, it mostly benefited former Communist Party functionaries, some of whom became instant multimillionaires. By the mid-1990s Russia had evolved a kind of "crony capitalism," with a small group of economic oligarchs manipulating much of the economy through dubious banking practices and outright extortion—and paying no taxes. Shrinking every year after the fall of communism, the Russian economy had decreased by perhaps half after ten years. The results inevitably included a sharp decline in living standards and the decay of the infrastructure, including roads, schools, and hospitals. Especially sobering were the demographic effects: Russians were dying young and having few children. By 2001 the population had dropped to 143 million—a decline of 6 million people in ten years.

The combination of economic stringency and governmental weakness produced a chilling increase in street crime, from muggings to auto theft. By the end of the 1990s, moreover, dozens of journalists, politicians, and business leaders had been murdered gangland style, with the killers never apprehended. Particularly appalling was the death of Galina Starovoitova°, a widely admired liberal legislator and potential presidential candidate who was gunned down outside her St. Petersburg apartment in 1998. (See the box "Reading Sources: Lawlessness in Postcommunist Russia.")

As Russia's president during the first postcommunist years, Boris Yeltsin seemed a committed reformer—surely the best hope for an orderly transition to democracy and a market economy. He enjoyed widespread support from the Western democracies, but among Russians the

---

Starovoitova (stah-ro-VOY-to-vah)

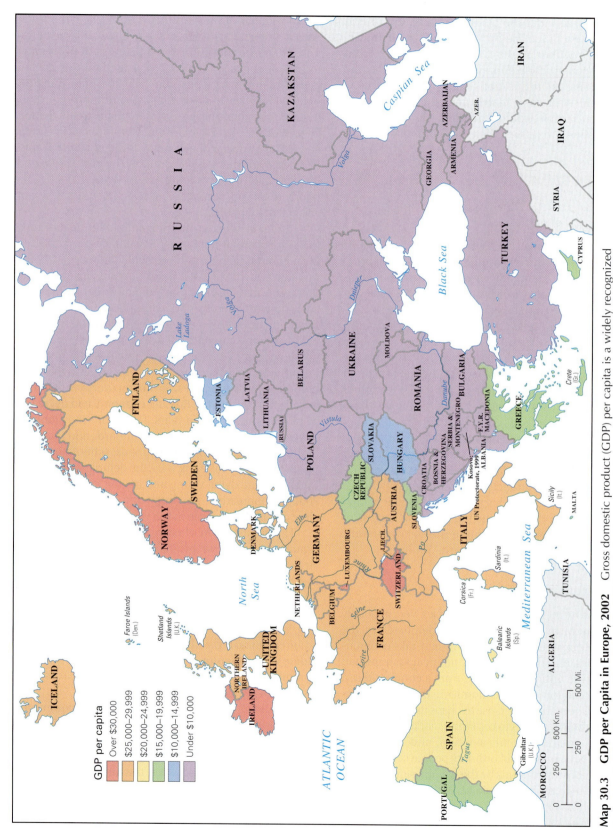

GDP per capita

- Over $30,000
- $25,000–29,999
- $20,000–24,999
- $15,000–19,999
- $10,000–14,999
- Under $10,000

Map 30.3 GDP per Capita in Europe, 2002   Gross domestic product (GDP) per capita is a widely recognized measure of national economic success. By 2002, this measure varied dramatically among the European countries, revealing the wide disparity in economic well-being across the Continent. The former communist countries continued to lag, even as some were growing at impressive rates. The U.S. figure was $37,600, and Canada's was $29,400.

READING SOURCES   LAWLESSNESS IN POSTCOMMUNIST RUSSIA

The extent of the breakdown in Russia that followed the collapse of communism surprised almost everyone. In this passage, Eleanor Randolph, a U.S. newspaper correspondent who spent much of the 1990s covering developments in Russia, provides a vivid sense of the debilitating lawlessness that became widespread in all reaches of Russian society.

The new freedoms that meant liberty for some meant lawlessness for others. Crime rates in Russia soared, and they stunned a nation of former Soviet citizens who were accustomed to feeling safe and protected. It was an old safety that most Westerners and many Soviets found suffocating because its price was a totalitarian government that tried to control every aspect of human life. But when it was gone, evaporating in late 1991, some Russians said they felt like youngsters whose capricious and dictatorial parent had suddenly disappeared. They were trained in the fine art of dodging the rules and tricking the rulers. Suddenly they were in charge of their own lives, forced to find their way in a strange and often hostile new world, to figure out their own forms of survival. Although there were plenty of rules and guidelines and laws on the books—old Soviet laws and new Russian laws scrambled in an incomprehensible legal jumble—Russia in 1991 essentially became a lawless society.

The lawlessness spread steadily to all levels—from the big-time criminals who disregarded the law to get rich to ordinary people who were forced to break the law to stay alive. For many Russians, the "true" criminals were at the top level, either the *mafiya* or the wealthy new businessmen, terms that were often considered synonymous among working people still trying to figure out the difference between legal and illegal capitalism. The ordinary person who disobeyed the law accidentally or as a matter of necessity was not a real criminal, according to these Russians; he was simply a survivor. . . .

There had been lawlessness and corruption in the old days, of course. . . .

Now, however, the corruption was open and shameless. From a nation that made the pretense of equality, Russia changed into a country where the haves were waving their money haughtily at the have-nots. Mobsters, whose names became household words, patrolled the city streets with their lights flashing, bullying other drivers out of their way. A new class of rich Russians, whose means of making money fell somewhere between business and grand larceny, built large, expensive fortresses in the suburbs. Casinos, with their garish Las Vegas–style lights blinking into the dark city streets, lured the men who looked like the cartoon-character Kapitalist from the old Soviet propaganda sheets. Fat, oily, covered with diamonds and draped with long-legged women, these men took whatever they could get, with the greediness of people who feared it could all be taken away with the stroke of a pen, a knock at the door. . . .

The Russian people, literate, intelligent, and canny, learned to cope in ways that many of them saw as demeaning, immoral, and necessary. . . .

The feeling that one should take one's fair share of the old Soviet state began to seep into all levels of the new society. . . .

. . . Gangs of townspeople in several areas a few hours outside [Moscow] would work together to unload freight trains traveling through their territory. One group would cut the electrical current just as a line of railroad cars approached their area. When the train slid to a stop, an army of townspeople would descend on the cars, plucking whatever could be used, traded, or sold. Armed guards, often about four of them per train, were reluctant to fire on their fellow citizens—especially since these gangs were made up of women, old people and children. . . .

Get it while you can had become the golden rule. . . .

What was perhaps most amazing in this era was that there were still millions of Russians who did not steal, who did not murder their neighbors to get what they wanted. . . . There was still enough honesty ingrained in enough people that the entire fabric of the nation had not yet disintegrated into a society of looters and inveterate cheats. . . .

Most Russians clearly did not want this lawlessness. . . . Like all of us, they wanted some feeling that if certain rules were obeyed, everything would be more or less normal. They wanted the security of knowing they were operating in the right.

Source: Reprinted with the permission of Simon & Schuster Adult Publishing Group from *Waking the Tempest: Ordinary Life in the New Russia* by Eleanor Randolph. Copyright © 1996 by Eleanor Randolph.

difficult circumstances produced disenchantment with reform, nostalgia for the stability of communism, and much resentment of the West.

As it sought to engineer the transition to democratic capitalism, the Yeltsin government had to deal with the attempted defection of Chechnya°, a small, largely Muslim republic located in the Caucasus (see Map 29.3 on page 1018). Long restive under Russian control, the Chechens began demanding independence after the collapse of the Soviet Union in 1991, finally provoking war with Russia in 1994. In the aftermath of a compromise in 1996, Chechen hard-liners oppressed the Russian minority, kidnapping and enslaving some, and even killed journalists and international aid workers. When Islamic militants began spreading the anti-Russian message from Chechnya to adjacent Dagestan, Russia renewed full-scale war with Chechnya in 1999.

This renewed confrontation made possible the rise of Vladimir Putin°, who had been director of Russia's secret police, though he was virtually unknown in political circles. Calling for a tough stance on Chechnya, Putin was Yeltsin's choice for prime minister in 1999, and he immediately delivered on his promise to clear Dagestan of Chechen terrorists. Whereas most Russians had disliked the earlier confrontation with Chechnya, by now they had had enough—not only of Chechen defiance but also of Russia's weakness. Putin's popularity soared as he talked tough and acted tougher. A brutal Russian assault late in 1999 left much of Chechnya, especially the capital, Grozny, in ruins.

In poor health and increasingly erratic, Yeltsin resigned at the end of 1999, essentially to make way for Putin, who was elected president early in 2000. His police background and harsh rhetoric caused concern in the West. Indeed, prominent international observers began lamenting that Russia had been "lost" to democracy and the Western community, the result of the facile assumption that the turn to a free-market economy would be a panacea.

By 2003, however, there were some signs of progress under Putin. Tax collection had improved, some well-run companies had emerged, and the middle class was clearly expanding. But the political order still suffered from secrecy and governmental inaccessibility. The media were increasingly concentrated and subject to restrictions and controls. The postcommunist experiment in Russia remained particularly uncertain by the middle of the first decade of the twenty-first century.

Chechnya (CHECH-nyah)   **Putin** (POO-tin)

The Changing Socioeconomic Framework

Although the established Western democracies enjoyed renewed economic growth during the 1980s, technological change and globalization raised new questions about what governments should try to do, and could afford to do, that remained central to the West's agenda in the twenty-first century. Moreover, even as globalization and new technologies promised a different prosperity over the long term, they threatened some of the bases of postwar prosperity in the short term.

Although the technological revolution encompassed everything from robotics to fiber optics, it was based especially on the computer, or what soon came to be summed up as "information technology." (See the feature "Information Technology: The Internet.") Some new firms were able to exploit technology and start from scratch, while older competitors often faced problems of redundant workers or outmoded plants and equipment. In all cases, manufacturing jobs were lost, as competition forced the industrial sector to become more efficient through computers and automation. In the German steel industry, which had spearheaded a remarkable industrial transformation a century before, more than half the jobs disappeared during the 1970s and 1980s.

Even with the renewed prosperity of the 1980s, unemployment reached levels not seen since the Great Depression. During the 1990s high unemployment persisted in much of western Europe, even as it declined to postwar lows in the United States. In Germany, for example, unemployment stood at more than 10 percent in 2003, compared with 6 percent in the United States. Most people attributed the difference in unemployment rates to the different structure of labor markets and, more generally, to the greater flexibility of the U.S. economy. As a result of laws, labor agreements, and the postwar consensus now in place, European workers who had jobs were more secure than their American counterparts. But European employers were less able to adapt to changing conditions by laying off workers or hiring new ones with different skills. During the 1980s American firms were more likely to restructure or downsize in response to technological change and increasing global competition. As a result, the U.S. economy was better at creating new jobs as new opportunities emerged during the 1990s.

Changing labor patterns reinforced the decline of organized labor, which was decidedly on the defensive throughout western Europe and the United States by the 1980s. The increasing danger of unemployment undercut the leverage of the unions. And as the economy grew more complex, workers were less likely to think of themselves as members of a single, unified working class.

Still, union membership varied considerably from country to country, and some unions exerted influence in new ways. In a survey of union membership as a percentage of the work force in twelve industrialized countries in 2001, Denmark and Sweden had the highest figures—around 80 percent. The figures for Italy, Germany, and Britain were all around 30 percent. The lowest figures were in France (10 percent) and the United States (14 percent). Despite some much-publicized militancy in resisting government efforts at pension reform, the unions generally had moved beyond their earlier confrontational posture to an increasing pragmatism.

In Germany local union councils were more willing to make informal agreements with big companies that, while technically violating Germany's restrictive labor regulations, helped keep jobs in Germany. At the same time, some German-based multinational companies such as Volkswagen actively sought to head off trouble with German unions by agreeing to guidelines specifying how they would operate worldwide. By committing itself to offering workers proper pay and working conditions and the right to unionize, Volkswagen was saying that it would not merely seek the lowest bidder, as globalization sometimes seemed to demand. In this respect, too, the unions were still making a difference.

Rethinking the Welfare State

Government welfare measures had helped establish the new political consensus in western Europe since World War II. Indeed, most western European countries moved well beyond the United States in providing everything from health care to pensions. But beginning as early as the 1970s, some began to question both the monetary costs of such measures and their implications for European competitiveness in the global economy.

Although much publicity surrounded the postwar British welfare state, by the early 1970s the percentage of the British economy devoted to public expenditure for welfare, housing, and education—18.2 percent—was about average for the industrialized nations of the West. Sweden had the highest figure at 23.7 percent, and by that point 40 percent of Sweden's national income was devoted to taxes to finance the system—the highest rate of taxation in the world. But pressures on the welfare state were especially striking in Sweden at the same time. Swedish opinion-makers grew increasingly doubtful that a welfare state could nurture the initiative and productivity needed for success in the increasingly com-

Thatcher's Conservative Revolution   As British prime minister from 1979 to 1990, Margaret Thatcher led an assault on the welfare state and a renewed embrace of free-market economics in Britain. Together with U.S. president Ronald Reagan, who greatly admired her, she came to symbolize the retreat from government that marked the 1980s. Thatcher is shown at a political rally in London in 1987.   *(D. Hudson/Corbis Sygma)*

petitive global economy. Sweden found itself less competitive, both because its wages were high and because it was not keeping abreast of technological developments.

In Britain a dramatic assault on the welfare state began developing at the same time, especially because the postwar British economy, having lagged behind the others of the industrialized West, suffered especially with the more difficult economic circumstances of the 1970s. Between 1968 and 1976, the country lost one million manufacturing jobs. By the mid-1970s this economic decline threatened to shatter Britain's postwar consensus around the welfare state as the British people could not agree on how to apportion the pain of the necessary austerity measures.

During the 1970s each of Britain's two major political parties made a serious effort to come to grips with the situation, but neither succeeded, especially because neither could deal effectively with Britain's strong trade unions. But when the militantly conservative Margaret Thatcher (b. 1925) became prime minister in 1979, it was clear that Britain was embarking on a radically different course.

Thatcher insisted that Britain could reverse its economic decline only by fostering a new "enterprise culture," restoring the individual initiative that had been sapped, as she saw it, by decades of dependence on

The Internet

In the late 1960s the U.S. Department of Defense commissioned some bright graduate students to develop a way to share information on computers with university researchers. The program they devised enabled computers to use existing telephone lines to send files from one machine to another. The resulting protocol, or set of rules, included the little-used "at" symbol—@—which soon became the pivot in every electronic mail (e-mail) address in the world.

Thus was born the Internet—not in some Silicon Valley garage but at the U.S. Defense Department, which made the new program freely available to universities to facilitate research. At first the impact was limited. Computers were big, clunky machines, and only governments, universities, and large businesses could afford them. All of this changed during the 1980s, when IBM began marketing the small, affordable personal computer (PC). The potential to share information on computers was now available to individuals—in their professional or working roles, but also as consumers, correspondents, hobbyists, political activists, or simply as human beings curious about their world. Anyone could put information on a computer that others might want to access. The potential magnitude of such sharing became clear only gradually, but by the end of the 1990s the Internet had taken definite form, encompassing an array of possibilities from e-mail to the World Wide Web.

The Internet seemed to overcome physical distance by opening a whole new "cyberspace"—a term derived from *cybernetics,* coined in 1948 to indicate the comparative study of control systems, from the brain to the computer. Since antiquity people had been able to go to physical places—libraries—to access physical objects containing information. But as the Internet made possible access to all networked computers, and as more people found it advan-

tageous to make more information available, Internet users could find a great deal of information more quickly than ever before. Thus, for example, stock markets became more open and democratic, and interactive learning across physical distance became possible. By bringing buyers and sellers together regardless of physical separation, auction sites such as eBay created more efficient markets. At the same time, "chatrooms" made it possible to express opinions, reach an audience, and participate in a wider conversation, often with persons otherwise unknown. Businesses improved productivity through more efficient procurement and inventory control.

As the possibilities dawned, an array of young "high-tech" companies emerged by the end of the 1990s, spearheading what seemed a whole "new economy." Stock prices soared for companies having anything to do with the Internet. But this proved to be a speculative bubble that burst, sending stocks plummeting in 2001. A similar pattern had accompanied earlier technological revolutions—the advent of the railroad in early-nineteenth-century Britain, for example. But whereas many aspiring young Internet firms went belly-up in 2001, a number of the pioneers quickly re-emerged stronger than ever.

Avoiding the speculative swings was Google, launched as a privately held company in 1998, and quickly the most widely used search engine. The company's announced aim by 2003 was remarkably sweeping: "Our whole mission is to organize the world's information."* Google even sought ways to personalize searches: by keeping track of what you had sought before, Google could better understand what you were likely to be seeking this time. But such potential added to concerns about privacy as activity on the web increased. Third parties could keep track of sites accessed and

government. So her government made substantial cuts in taxes and corresponding cuts in spending for education, national health, and public housing. It also fostered privatization, selling off an array of state-owned firms from Rolls-Royce to British Airways. The government even sold public housing to tenants, at as much as 50 percent below market value, a measure that helped win considerable working-class support.

At the same time, several new laws curtailed trade-union power, and Thatcher refused to consult with union leaders as her predecessors had done since the war. A

showdown was reached with the yearlong coal miners' strike of 1984 and 1985, one of the most bitter and violent European strikes of the century. Its failure in the face of government intransigence further discredited the labor movement and enhanced Thatcher's prestige. Still, the violent encounters between police and picketing strikers, carried nationwide on television, indicated the cracks in the relative social harmony that Britain had long enjoyed.

Even critics admitted that Thatcher's policies, especially her willingness to curb the unions, had produced a significant change in British attitudes in favor of enter-

An Internet Café With the sudden popularity of the Internet by the mid-1990s, "Internet cafés" emerged all over the world. They offered Internet access, along with coffee, to those who did not own personal computers. London's Cyberia café was typical. *(Martyn Hayhow/SIPA Press)*

purchases made and then develop a profile of interests, buying habits, health concerns—whether for marketing or some less elevated purpose.

Some people suggested that the Internet made possible greater democracy by bypassing the "gatekeepers" in journalism, publishing, or academics, but others grew anxious about quality as the Internet made ever more unedited information available. At the same time, the scope for delivering information via the Internet raised complex intellectual property issues, which came dramatically to a head over access to recorded music. By the year 2000, ten million people were using the Napster website to download recorded music from a network of fellow users, bypassing traditional methods of distribution and remuneration. The recording industry first filed suit to recover millions of dollars in lost compact disk sales, then began prosecuting individuals accused of downloading music illegally. At the same time, record companies scrambled to find new ways to distribute music over the Internet. The challenge was to find ways for users to compensate the creators of music and other forms of intellectual property that were now more readily available through the Internet.

As organizations and individuals became ever more dependent on the Internet, they also became more vulnerable.

Viruses and worms, introduced by individuals bent on mischief for whatever reason, could paralyze businesses and other organizations. Sheer volume was another concern. Some experts predicted gigantic cyber traffic jams, even gridlock. Part of the problem was an explosion of unwanted junk e-mails, sent in bulk from forged names and addresses to Internet users worldwide. As such "spam" threatened to overwhelm not only the e-mail system but the Internet itself, filtering spam became big business. Spearheaded by the European Union, some governments adopted tough laws in an effort to restrict spam, but regulations proved difficult to enforce in light of the Internet's extension across borders and cultures.

Although the Internet's very popularity produced vulnerability, frustration, and new problems, there was no turning back from this powerful means of accessing and sharing information. By the early twenty-first century, the ongoing Internet revolution had become central to the continuing experiment with information technology.

---

*Elizabeth Millard, "Google's Next Step," interview with Google spokesperson Nate Tyler, *E-Commerce Times*, October 20, 2003, http://www.ccommercetimes.com/perl/story/31868.html.

prise and competition. The number of new businesses reflected a revival of entrepreneurship—apparently the basis for Britain's improved economic performance during the 1990s. But the gap between rich and poor widened, and the old industrial regions of the north were left ever farther behind.

Even as the welfare state receded in Sweden and Britain, the reach of government expanded elsewhere. In Italy reforms during the 1970s made available a wider range of state services—from kindergarten and medical care to sports and recreational facilities—than ever

before. In France by the mid-1990s, five-week paid vacations were mandatory, with the government sometimes subsidizing the cost of transportation to seaside or mountain resorts. Indeed, the French welfare system had emerged as a model. In 2000 the UN's World Health Organization rated the French health care system the world's best. Moreover, social services in France were delivered with less paperwork and intrusiveness than elsewhere.

Accustomed to a strong government role in society, Europeans had difficulty understanding how measures such as government-sponsored health care could cause such controversy among Americans. But as global economic competition intensified, governments throughout western Europe found it more difficult to pay for all the benefits they had gradually come to promise.

Generous pensions, especially for government workers, had been one aspect of the postwar compact. By 2003 Italy and Austria were devoting 15 percent of their economies to public-sector pensions, the highest figures in Europe. Few Austrians worked past age 60. But the need for reform was becoming obvious by the 1980s, especially as falling birth rates and aging populations meant that relatively fewer workers would have to foot the bill for increasing numbers of pensioners.

By the early twenty-first century, pension reform had become a major issue in much of Europe. Although most agreed that reform was necessary, massive union-led demonstrations against government proposals for pension reform brought France almost to a halt in May 2003. Comparable protests greeted reform proposals in Germany, Italy, and Austria. The issue had come up earlier in France, in 1995, and union demonstrations had forced the government to back down. But in 2003 Prime Minister Jean-Pierre Raffarin insisted that the very survival of the French republic depended on reform.

Higher education was another area of contention. After more than thirty years of free higher education in Germany, by the early twenty-first century universities and state governments were increasingly calling for student fees to ease overcrowding, update ill-equipped libraries, and improve declining research performance. In Britain, too, higher fees seemed likely, and comparable pressures developed all over the Western world.

Left, Right, and the Democratic Consensus

The continental European political system remained more complex than that of the United States, with smaller minority parties periodically playing significant roles. Still, the dominant tendency in western Europe was toward some form of two-party system after World War II. With the radical right largely discredited after the war, the challenge, or potential for challenge, to the system itself had come mostly from the socialist left. But by the late 1980s, the left seemed to have been domesticated for good; it no longer claimed to offer a systematic alternative. In important respects, in fact, social democrats and conservatives sounded more and more alike. For instance, after Willy Brandt became chancellor of West Germany in 1969, the Socialists led the government for thirteen years, finally meeting electoral defeat in 1982. By that point, Socialists and conservatives agreed

on the essentials, squabbling only about degrees. The Socialists had completed the turn to moderation that they had begun in the late 1950s, leaving Germany with essentially a two-party system.

The political mainstream seemed to offer fewer choices, however, and the resulting frustration fed the new radicalism evident by the early 1970s. As the established Marxist left seemed unable to deal persuasively with contemporary concerns, new coalitions developed around newly politicized issues such as abortion and the environment. The successes of this new left fed renewed hopes for a more systematic change in socioeconomic relations by the early 1980s, when revitalized socialist parties in France, Spain, and Italy marginalized the communists and, for a time, seemed poised to reorient government, even to spearhead that systematic change.

The pivotal case was France, where François Mitterrand° (1916–1996) was elected president in 1981, promising to create the first genuinely democratic socialism. Despite a vigorous start, however, he gradually abandoned any talk of socialism in the face of economic and political pressures. By the end of the 1980s, he was questioning the relevance of long-standing socialist tenets and playing up the virtues of entrepreneurship, the profit mechanism, and free-market competition. Mitterrand realized that France, like the other industrial democracies, had to operate in an increasingly competitive international economy, which seemed to impose the same rules on all.

As French socialism seemed to lose its sense of direction, the party met massive defeats at the polls in 1993 and 1995. Still, the Socialists had proved they could work within the system, and a Socialist-led coalition regained the parliamentary majority in 1997. Much like Germany, France seemed to have settled into a two-party system, which meant stability but also a narrowing of discussion and choice. Even Italy, long notorious for the surface instability of its government, moved toward a system of alternating left-leaning and right-leaning coalitions after major scandals during the early 1990s undermined the long-standing political establishment.

Although the socialist left had won reforms that were now central to the consensus around democratic capitalism, by the 1990s it had abandoned much of what it had stood for—from class struggle and revolution to state ownership and a centrally planned economy. It could apparently serve only as the mildly left-leaning alternative within the framework of capitalist democracy. When the Labour Party returned to power in Britain in 1997, the popular new prime minister, Tony Blair, did not

Mitterrand (MEE-tuh-rahn)

offer a bold new program or reverse key Thatcherite measures like privatization.

With the decline of socialism as a political alternative, and with the welfare state increasingly open to question, a new right gained prominence by the mid-1990s. Though differing considerably in priorities, respectability, and success, leaders such as José María Aznar in Spain, Jean-Marie Le Pen in France, Jörg Haider° in Austria, Gianfranco Fini° in Italy, and Pim Fortuyn in the Netherlands tapped into political frustration and economic uncertainty. Some were absorbed into the mainstream, while others provoked renewed political division.

In addressing economic anxieties, the new conservatives sometimes articulated problems that mainstream politicians ignored, but they often disagreed among themselves—over the relative merits of free trade and protectionism, for example. On one issue, however, they were in clear agreement. This was the issue of assimilation, citizenship, and national identity as globalization proceeded and immigration increased. Though typically winning only 15 to 20 percent of the vote in national elections, figures like Le Pen, Haider, and Fortuyn articulated a growing concern that the influx of immigrants was responsible not only for increasing crime but also for a weakening of the common values necessary to sustain society. The value of diversity, the scope for belonging, and the meaning of citizenship were becoming mainstream concerns, bound up with wider issues of personal and national identity.

LIFESTYLES AND IDENTITIES

By the mid-1960s, the remarkable postwar economic growth had created a secular, consumerist society throughout much of the West, establishing patterns of life that continued into the twenty-first century, when cell phones and personal computers were commonplace. But changing lifestyles dictated new choices, and the new affluence challenged traditional sources of personal identity in sometimes unexpected ways. There was concern, and sometimes conflict, over issues from education to gender roles to the environment.

By the early twenty-first century, this newly secular, consumerist society had become one of the defining aspects of the West. The allure of this society fueled the increased immigration from the non-Western world to the more developed countries of the West. But immigrants often retained aspects of their non-Western cultural identities, prompting new questions about diversity, assimilation, and community in the West. Moreover, important groups of non-Westerners rejected Western secular consumerism altogether. For the various forms of Islamic fundamentalism, it was nothing less than an abomination.

Family Life and Gender Roles

The new affluence significantly affected demographic patterns, partly because contraception became more readily available. Indeed, the advent of the birth control pill, widely obtainable by the late 1960s, fostered a sexual revolution that was central to the emerging secular lifestyle.

In western Europe, as in the United States, a remarkable baby boom had followed the end of World War II and carried into the early 1960s. But the birthrate declined rapidly thereafter, so family size had diminished markedly by 1990. In Italy the number of births in 1987 was barely half the number in 1964, when the postwar baby boom reached its peak. Between 1993 and 2003, Italy's population increased by but 0.01 percent, to 57.5 million, and it was expected to shrink to 56 million by 2010. By 1995 the population was not sustaining itself in a number of European countries (see Map 30.4). These demographic patterns suggested that there would not long be enough people of working age to support the massive numbers of pensioners on the horizon.

The feminist movement that had re-emerged in the late 1960s gradually expanded its focus beyond the quest for formal equality of opportunity. Examining subtle cultural obstacles to equality led feminists to the more general issue of gender—the way societies make sense of sexual difference and allocate social roles on that basis. There was much interest in the ideas of the French existentialist Simone de Beauvoir, who had addressed in 1949 many of the issues concerning gender roles that came to the fore during the 1980s. (See the box "The Continuing Experiment: Female Freedom and the Future of Gender Relations" on page 994 in Chapter 29.) And as the debate expanded from "women's issues" to gender roles, the self-understanding of men was inevitably at issue as well. By the late twentieth century, gender was central not only to public policy but also to private relationships and life choices in much of the Western world.

By the 1970s women sought measures such as government-subsidized day care that would enable them to combine paid employment with raising a family. At the same time, governments increasingly understood

---

Haider (HY-dur)   **Fini** (FEE-nee)

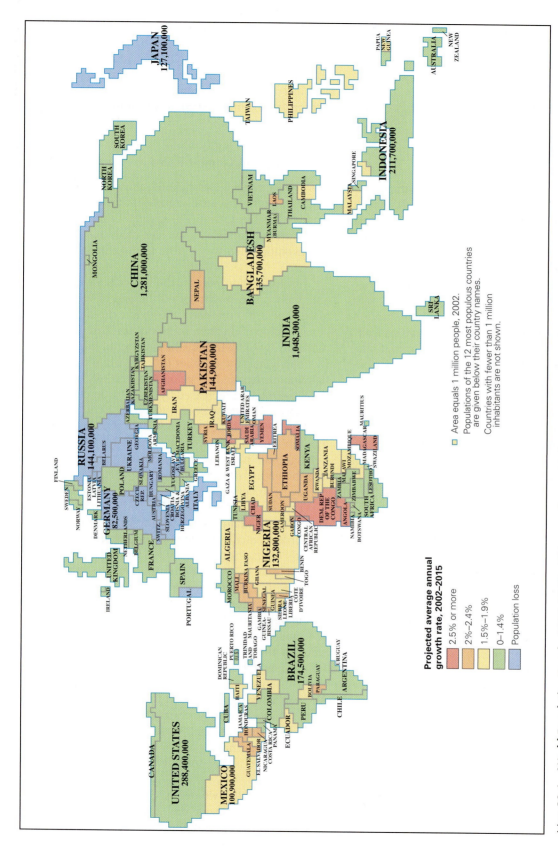

Map 30.4 World Population Trends, 2002–2015 This map shows populations in 2002, as well as projected average annual growth rates from 2002 to 2015, in countries throughout the world. In the developed countries of the West, populations are relatively high but growing slowing, if at all. Most of the world's population growth is occurring in the less developed countries outside the West. *(Source: Data from www.worldbank.org.)*

the value of policies to encourage both productive working parents with effective childhood development. Setting the pace was France, where the government began making quality day care available to all during the 1980s. Government subsidies kept costs within reach for ordinary working families. In addition, 95 percent of French children ages 3 to 6 were enrolled in the free public nursery schools available by the early 1990s. The figures for Italy (85 percent) and Germany (65 to 70 percent) were also relatively high, but Britain lagged behind (35 to 40 percent).

As some saw it, the increasing reliance on child-care at once reflected and reinforced a decline in the socializing role of the traditional family. Concerns about "latchkey children" and the decline of "quality time" for families became prominent in the popular media. But the social changes at work were complex, and their longer-term implications for the well-being of parents, children, and society itself remained unclear. Some studies showed that an early day-care experience enhanced the socialization of children. Others cautioned against romanticizing the traditional nuclear family, which had been less prevalent than widely believed and not always successful in any case. Moreover, the responsibilities of parenting did not have to fall primarily on mothers. The biological difference in childbearing and nursing remained, however, and even committed feminists disagreed about whether parenting entailed a special role for women and, if so, about the implications for public policy.

Although much remained contested or uncertain, the scope for greater sharing of parental responsibilities and the need for equal career opportunities across gender lines were widely recognized by the 1990s. The French model seemed to work well in combining child support with equal opportunity for paid employment. In simultaneously offering day care and allowances to concentrate on parenting, French government programs seemed to give French mothers a genuine choice as to whether to work outside the home. French family policy was widely popular; the key question by 2003 was whether France could afford it.

Also much at issue, and highly controversial, by the early twenty-first century were the rights of homosexual couples—to adopt children, for example, or to have their partnerships legally recognized as marriage. Whether married or not, were homosexual partners entitled to job benefits such as health care, which often were available to heterosexual couples?

The interrelationship of family, gender, sexuality, and personal self-realization, never static, was evolving in new ways—a crucial aspect of the ongoing experiment in the West.

Economic Growth and Environmental Concerns

The impact of rapid economic growth on the European landscape and cityscape provoked ever greater concern by the last third of the twentieth century. The number of automobiles in western Europe increased from 6 million in 1939 to 16 million by 1959 to 42 million by 1969. Almost overnight, traffic and air pollution fundamentally changed the face of Europe's old cities. In 1976 five statues that had supported the Eastern Portico of the Erectheum Temple on the Acropolis in Athens since the fifth century B.C. were replaced by replicas and put in a museum to save them from the rapid decay that air pollution was causing.

With the end of communist rule, it became obvious that the years of communism had produced environmental degradation on an appalling scale in the Soviet bloc. The damage was the byproduct not of affluence, but of the lure of affluence, as communists sought to surpass the West. Even with the fall of communism, it was hard to break from the old polluting patterns because jobs and energy sources often depended on them. For years Ukraine could not afford to replace the remaining nuclear reactors at Chernobyl, despite safety and environmental risks that the 1986 accident had only worsened (see page 1017). International aid finally enabled Ukraine to close the plant in 2000.

The greater affluence in Western Europe made possible, and sometimes dictated, more creative responses to pollution. Many cities adopted pedestrian-only zones to restrict automobile traffic. In February 2003 London initiated the world's most ambitious road-pricing experiment in an effort to reduce traffic by 15 percent, thereby cutting congestion, wasted time, and air pollution. Those driving into an 8-square-mile area of the central city from 7:00 a.m. to 6:30 p.m. on weekdays—at that point, 250,000 cars daily—were charged a fee of $8 a day. The system relied on two hundred surveillance cameras, linked to a computer database, that read the license plates of entering cars. More ambitious possibilities for using global positioning satellites to implement variable pricing, with fees for using roads and highways to depend on patterns of traffic congestion, also were being discussed in many parts of the West.

It was not only the urban environment that proved vulnerable to the byproducts of the new affluence. By the early 1980s acid rain had damaged one-third of the forests of West Germany, including the famous Black Forest of the southwest. Water pollution was a major problem from the Rhine to the Mediterranean to the Black Sea.

Differences in response to environmental concerns sometimes produced friction among Western countries or complicated the West's relations with the non-Western world. Especially symptomatic was the controversy over genetically altered foods, widely consumed in the United States since 1996. European concerns over safety led the EU to impose a moratorium on genetically modified products, including imports from the United States, in 1998. The United States considered the moratorium illegal under existing trade agreements and, joined by Canada, Argentina, and Egypt, filed suit with the World Trade Organization (WTO) in 2003 to compel the EU to lift the moratorium.

In May 2003, on the eve of the annual G-8 meeting, U.S. president George W. Bush charged that European restrictions on genetically altered foods were undercutting efforts to provide food aid to Africa. The European example had led Africans to avoid investments in such crops. Moreover, some famine-ridden African countries had refused U.S. food aid because of European-induced concerns about safety. Partly at issue was the fear that genetically modified crops might infiltrate native crops and thereby jeopardize African exports to Europe. Americans countered that Europeans were using a bogus issue to help limit U.S. food exports to Europe—and hurting African development in the process. Some U.S. officials even called European policy "genocidal."

The United States had joined the other industrialized nations in signing the Kyoto agreement of 1997, designed to limit emissions of the "greenhouse gases" widely held by scientists to be causing global warming, with potentially catastrophic consequences. But questioning the scientific evidence and citing concerns about economic growth, the Bush administration pulled the United States out of the agreement in 2001, causing much resentment in Europe and elsewhere.

Religious Identities

Whereas religious affiliation and church or synagogue attendance remained relatively stable in the United States, Europeans abandoned churches in droves after the mid-1950s. As church attendance dropped, popular culture revolved less around religious festivals and holy days. Moreover, in assuming responsibility for social welfare, European governments had gradually taken over much of the charitable role that the churches had long played.

Seeking to change with the times, the Catholic Church undertook a notable modernization effort under the popular Pope John XXIII (r. 1958–1963). But under his more conservative successors, the church became caught up in controversy, especially over issues such as abortion that women had forced to the fore. By the 1990s

its conservative social policy had put the Catholic Church on the defensive.

In such traditionally Catholic countries as France, Italy, and Spain, many people considered themselves "cultural Catholics" and ignored church rulings they found inappropriate, especially those concerning sexuality, marriage, and gender roles. In referenda in 1974 and 1981, two-thirds of Italians defied the Vatican by voting to legalize divorce and approve abortion rights. Even in heavily Catholic Ireland, the electorate approved, though narrowly, the legalization of divorce in 1995, after having defeated it overwhelmingly in a referendum just nine years before.

When surveys showed that 80 percent of Spaniards considered themselves Catholic early in the twenty-first century, even the cardinal-bishop of Madrid admitted that for many, "Catholic" was not a way of life but merely a label, perhaps linked to national identity. Other surveys showed that whereas in 1975, the year of Francisco Franco's death, 61 percent of Spaniards reported regular church attendance, that figure had dropped to 19 percent by the early twenty-first century. Even 46 percent of those calling themselves Catholic admitted that they almost never went to church.

A survey of church attendance in eleven western European countries in 1999–2000 found Spain somewhere in the middle, with 25 percent of the population saying they had been to church at least once a month. Ireland had the highest rate of attendance (58 percent), followed by Italy (about 40 percent). The lowest rates were in Denmark (3 percent) and Sweden (4 percent). Other surveys suggested that such self-responses probably doubled the actual rate of church attendance. While religious affiliations weakened in western Europe, the Russian Orthodox Church experienced a notable revival after the collapse of communism and the breakup of the Soviet Union.

In parts of the West, religious and ethnic identities blurred, sometimes enhancing the potential for conflict. Most at issue by the beginning of the twenty-first century was the place of Muslims in Europe. Even after the breakup of the wider Soviet Union gave independence to the predominantly Muslim central Asian republics, the remaining Russian Federation included more than twenty million Muslims, or about 15 percent of the overall population. In both absolute numbers and percentage terms, this was the largest Muslim population in Europe. Included were those who identified themselves as Muslims in cultural terms even if they did not practice the Islamic religion.

A significant Islamic revival among Russian Muslims followed the collapse of communism, producing increasing friction with the central authorities. In 2002 the interior ministry banned women from wearing headscarves in photos for official documents. The Russian supreme court upheld the ban in the face of an appeal from Islamic women that it violated Russia's constitutionally guaranteed freedom of religion. At the same time, the Russian army refused to allow Muslim services on military bases.

Immigration, Assimilation, and Citizenship

Whereas Russia's Muslims predated the majority Orthodox Christians, Muslims in western Europe were generally recent immigrants or members of immigrant families established since World War II. France, with 8 percent, had the largest Muslim population in western Europe by 2003. Most of these Muslims came from Algeria and other former French colonies in Africa. By the time of the "affair of the scarves" in 1989 (see page 1023), the place of Muslims had become a central and volatile issue. Indeed, concerns about national community, cultural diversity, and the meaning of citizenship were taking center stage all over Europe. During the 1990s the arrival of refugees from the former Yugoslavia and other trouble spots added another dimension to the issue.

By 1995, 11 million legal resident immigrants were living in the countries of the European Union—including, as the largest contingent, 2.6 million Turks (see Map 30.5). There were also as many as 4 million illegal immigrants. At issue throughout Europe was not only new immigration but also the status of immigrant families already resident, in some cases for several generations since World War II. Because of differences in tradition and their own historical experiences, individual countries tended to conceive the issues—and the alternatives—differently.

Germany had actively recruited foreign workers during the decades of economic boom and labor shortage that followed the war. By 1973 noncitizens constituted 2.6 million workers, or 11.9 percent of the work force. At first these "guest workers" were viewed not as immigrants but as temporary, almost migrant, laborers. But as they remained in Germany, their family patterns came to approximate those of the rest of the population, although their birthrates were considerably higher. By the 1980s Germany had a large and increasingly settled population of non-Germans, many of them born and educated there.

In addition, the German Federal Republic had adopted a generous asylum law in an effort to atone for the crimes of the Nazi period. With the turmoil surrounding the end of communism in the Soviet bloc, the newly

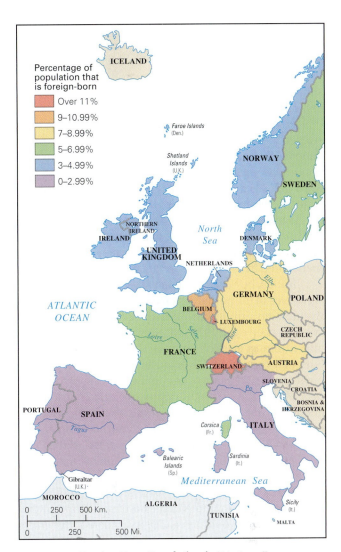

Map 30.5   Foreign-Born Population in Western Europe
Increasing immigration prompted resentment against foreigners and concerns about assimilation in much of western Europe during the 1980s and 1990s. This map indicates the percentage of the population that was foreign-born in each of the countries of western Europe as of 1997.   *(Source:* New York Times, *September 24, 2000. Copyright © 2000 by the New York Times Co. Reprinted by permission.)*

reunified Germany found 60,000 new arrivals seeking asylum every month by 1993. At that point Germany had a large foreign population of 6.4 million, or roughly 8 percent of the population.

The law governing citizenship for immigrants and their descendants had originated in 1913 and reflected a long-standing German assumption that citizenship presupposed German ethnicity—or at least full assimilation. Thus ethnic Germans—more than a million of whom moved to Germany from the former Soviet bloc between 1988 and 1991—were immediately accorded German citizenship. But the many Turks, for example, who had been born in Germany were denied citizenship. Precisely because citizenship seemed to entail full assimilation, some Germans opposed giving it to "foreigners" out of respect for cultural diversity.

As the new wave of immigration from the east swelled the "foreign" population in Germany, more mundane motives came to the fore. Germans subject to economic pressures felt that immigrants and asylum-seekers were getting a better deal than Germans themselves were. Resentments simmered and sometimes boiled over. Two thousand attacks on foreigners, some of them fatal, were reported in 1992 alone. As reaction against refugees and foreign workers grew, the German parliament voted in 1993 to restrict the right of asylum.

In 1999, however, after defeating Helmut Kohl's conservatives in the parliamentary elections the year before, the new governing coalition of Socialists and Greens voted to shelve the 1913 law. Citizenship was now available to almost everyone born in Germany or whose parents had resided and worked in Germany for at least eight years. Still, controversy and even violence continued. During the year 2000, right-wing attacks on foreigners and synagogues reached levels not seen since the immediate aftermath of German reunification in the early 1990s. On November 9, the anniversary of the Crystal Night pogrom of 1938, 200,000 Germans marched in Berlin to protest the violence and support equal rights.

French law accorded citizenship automatically to second-generation immigrants, on the assumption that these offspring would be readily assimilated. But critics such as Jean-Marie Le Pen charged that many recent immigrants did not want to assimilate. Whereas the French left defended cultural diversity and its compatibility with citizenship, the right complained that citizenship was being devalued as a mere convenience, requiring no real commitment to the national community.

By the early twenty-first century, the tendency all over Europe was to push assimilation—the formation of national citizens. Whereas some conflated the impulse with racism, others insisted that, on the contrary, anyone could belong, regardless of race or ethnicity, but that belonging required a positive commitment, adopting the mainstream values of the national community, not holding to cultural differences.

Amid concern about the weakening of Danish national identity, Denmark pioneered a proactive, carrot-and-stick approach in the first years of the new century. If immigrants were to qualify for welfare benefits, they had to take language and civics courses and to accept compulsory job placement as necessary. Norway and Germany moved in the same direction, while France continued to stress assimilation around common republican and secular values. Among the major western European nations, Britain was becoming the exception in settling for a laissez-faire approach, accepting multiculturalism and eschewing any compulsory acculturation. British cities, however, had experienced racial tension and violence during the 1980s and 1990s.

Supranational, National, and Subnational Identities

By the late 1980s consumerism and the widening impact of American popular culture—from blue jeans and American TV to shopping malls and theme parks—suggested a growing homogenization in the capitalist democracies. A Euro-Disneyland opened in France in 1992 and, after a slow start, proved increasingly popular. American fast-food chains such as McDonald's, adopting some European ways and even serving beer and wine, satisfied hungry locals in cities all over Europe.

But Americanization threatened long-standing European identities, and Europeans sometimes adopted special measures to preserve distinctiveness. The EU specified that EU television programming had to be at least 40 percent EU-made, while the French mandated that at least every third popular song played on the radio had to be French.

Prominent among European critics of Americanization was José Bové, the outspoken leader of France's small farmers. When he stood trial in 2000 for vandalizing a McDonald's restaurant in France, thirty thousand people turned out to demonstrate their support. His book *The World Is Not for Sale* became a bestseller. (See the box "Reading Sources: The Reaction Against Globalization.") Typically equating globalization with Americanization, Bové articulated a widespread concern for French distinctiveness and identity in the face of U.S. "cultural imperialism," as France seemed increasingly overrun by American films, television, music, even novels in French translation.

But were quotas and mandates really necessary to preserve distinctiveness? Even as many were coming to assume that American pop culture was irresistible, it became clear that European viewers were increasingly picking local TV programming on their own, quite apart from quotas. Between 1996 and 2002, the number of hours of American TV programming fell 26 percent in Spain, 17 percent in Germany, and 9 percent in Italy. By 2003 every EU country was well above the 40 percent

By the early twenty-first century, the flamboyant French farmer José Bové was emerging as a major spokesman for those concerned about the implications of globalization. But Bové's concerns made clear how different, even incompatible, the aims of antiglobalization activists often were. While poorer countries called on the European Union and the United States to end the agricultural subsidies that, in their view, unfairly skewed world trade, Bové found protection in agriculture essential to resist the distorting influence of large multinational corporations on the world's agricultural production and food supply. Here Bové and his colleague François Dufour outline their views in a widely read interview published in 2000.

Could you sum up your proposals?

Dufour: In the first place, we reaffirmed people's rights to control what they eat and to choose their form of agriculture freely and democratically. The abundance of goods and food has reached unprecedented levels, but so have the number of homeless, unemployed, or undernourished people. Europe based its agricultural policy on the concept of food self-sufficiency by protecting its markets from external competition. We believe that this was legitimate, and that all other countries—or groups of countries—in the world should be allowed to choose which crops they want to protect from competition to ensure self-sufficiency in food, and maintain a balance between town and countryside.

This has to include having the power to oppose the relocation of agricultural production that European agribusiness is currently undertaking—setting up pig and chicken farms, and greenhouses for the cultivation of vegetables, in countries where costs are lower and labour and environmental regulations are barely enforced. In the majority of instances, these practices have distorted local agriculture, destroyed the environment, reduced natural resources and threatened food safety. When large agricultural enterprises replace a thousand farmers, while simultaneously increasing production and selling it on the world market, national food policies are jeopardized. . . . Each country—or group of countries—is entitled to protect its food resources. This is the basic tenet of food sovereignty; it means that protection

from imports is an indispensable condition for international fair trade.

Bové: That was our second principle: all international exchanges should be governed by the principle of fair trade. Fair trade means buying goods at their real production cost, instead of the situation today, where world prices are the result of "dumping"; low prices are set by the wealthiest countries using big handouts to cut export costs and other disguised internal financial help. Powerful companies frequently adopt such practices in order to undermine the prices in the countries they intend to move into next. Once they've swept the local agriculture out of the way, they raise prices again. . . .

Some of those experiencing the destabilizing effects of globalization seem ready to retreat into nationalism. How do you differ from these chauvinists?

Bové: Their idea of sovereignty relates to the nation-state, and theirs is a selfish, frightened and irrational response. Since the fall of the Berlin Wall, the pace of world trade has accelerated, and needs to be regulated. Our concept of sovereignty enables people to think for themselves, without any imposed model for agriculture or society, and to live in solidarity with each other. This sovereignty means independent access to food: to be self-sufficient and to be able to choose what we eat.

Furthermore, the globalization of trade must be counteracted on the same level—that is to say, on a world scale rather than on a narrow-minded nation-state basis. . . .

The French Prime Minister, Lionel Jospin, falls between two stools when he tries simultaneously to promote sustainable farming and France as a major agricultural exporter. Nationalists want strong borders so that the French multinationals, especially those concerned with food, are masters at home and bosses everywhere else—on our money, of course.

It's dangerous and illusory to take pride in the fact that France is the leading exporter of farm produce in Europe, when 90 per cent of our exports are subsidized. . . .

Source: José Bové and François Dufour (interviewed by Gilles Luneau), *The World Is Not for Sale: Farmers Against Junk Food*, trans. Anna de Casparis (London: Verso, 2001), pp. 152–154, 159. Reproduced by permission.

 For additional information on this topic, go to college.hmco.com/students.

minimum for local programming, with the average at 62 percent.

Meanwhile, the growing prominence of the supranational EU, and doubts about the import of national politics, nourished a renewed premium on subnational identities in such distinctive European regions as Flanders, Corsica, Scotland, and Catalonia. Flemings and Corsicans, Scots and Catalans, actively sought to preserve some measure of their distinct cultures and languages in the face of all the contemporary pressures toward standardization. In Britain Tony Blair fostered the "devolution" of powers from the central government in London to Scottish and Welsh assemblies in 1999.

National sentiment grew especially uncertain in Italy, which had had a relatively brief and problematic history as a unified nation. Although its movement for national unification had drawn widespread enthusiasm throughout the Western world in the nineteenth century (see pages 745–750), by the 1990s disillusionment with national politics made many Italians particularly eager to embrace the EU, while others turned in the opposite direction, renewing their identification with region or locality. Resentful of the national government's ties to the less prosperous south, a new political movement, the Northern League, emerged during the 1990s to push for the north to become an independent state. Whatever the seriousness of such literal separatism, the Northern League's persistent strength suggested that "Italian" was becoming less important as a basis of individual identity in Italy's prosperous north.

Some historical sense is typically central to any group identity, but the place of history became espe-

Kiefer: Osiris and Isis   The German artist Anselm Kiefer combined unusual materials to create haunting images that often suggested the horrors of recent history. In this work, dated 1985–1987, the interpenetrating layers of human culture include images of ruin and death, hope and resurrection.   *(Anselm Kiefer,* Osiris und Isis, *1985–1987. Mixed media on canvas, 150" x 220½" x 6½". San Francisco Museum of Modern Art. Purchased through a gift of Jean Stein by exchange, the Mrs. Paul L. Wattis Fund, and the Doris and Don Fisher Fund. Photo: Ben Blackwell)*

cially problematic in much of Europe with the disruptions and disasters of the twentieth century. At the same time, the radical transformation in the half century since World War II in some ways cut Europeans off from their own traditions. The uneasy contemporary relationship with the past, especially the traumatic past of the earlier twentieth century, took especially pointed form in the neo-expressionist painting prominent in Germany and Italy by the 1980s.

For a generation after World War II European artists, unsure of their direction, had tended to follow the lead of New York. But by the late 1960s, the new generation that included such artists as the German Anselm Kiefer (b. 1945) and the Italian Sandro Chia (b. 1946) sought to confront the recent past—and thus the meaning of a tradition that now included fascism, total war, and the Holocaust. What did it mean to be German or Italian in light of this difficult past and the globalizing present and future? Wrestling with the interface of recent history and national identity, Kiefer and Chia conveyed the paradox and ambiguity that many felt as the rapidly changing West encountered the layers of the Western cultural tradition.

THE WEST IN A GLOBAL AGE

By the early twenty-first century, the West was part of a world that, in one sense, was dramatically less Eurocentric than it had been a century before, when European imperialism was at its peak. Events in the West competed for attention with OPEC oil prices, Chinese trade practices, and North Korea's nuclear program. Decisions vitally affecting, or demanding the response of, the industrialized countries of the West might be made anywhere. Just as capital and information flowed more quickly than ever across national borders, so could epidemic diseases emerging in some distant forest or jungle. This was the reverse side of the new interconnectedness of a global world. A planetary culture, a threatened environment, an interdependent economy, and an increasing sense of international responsibility required people to think in global terms as never before. (See the box "Global Encounters: Nelson Mandela and the Universality of Human Values.")

Uniformity and Diversity in the "Global Village"

By the last decades of the twentieth century, as the web of interaction thickened, a kind of global culture began

to emerge for the first time. Indeed, talk of a single "global village" became commonplace. But just as "Americanization" produced concerns about preserving distinctiveness elsewhere in the West, "globalization" produced comparable concerns on a global level. Although the process promised a better life for many people in less developed countries, valuable diversity was seemingly being lost in an ever more uniform world. For instance, half of the world's 6,500 languages were expected to disappear during the twenty-first century.

Skyscrapers in booming Asian cities looked much like skyscrapers in the West. Indeed, they were often designed by the same architects. Businessmen in conservative Western dress made postwar Japan the world's second-largest economy. American firms transferred billing and even customer service operations to lower-cost India, even as India was becoming a major player in computer technology. "Americanization" made products such as Coca-Cola and McDonald's burgers familiar not just in Europe but worldwide. Especially among urban youth, a common style emerged that owed much to American popular culture. Meanwhile, for everyone from scientists to business leaders to airline pilots, English became the language of international intercourse.

At work, however, was not simply Western or American cultural imperialism. What resulted in many spheres, from food to popular music, was not merely homogenization but a more complex kind of fusion, as elements from diverse cultures interpenetrated and enriched one another while retaining distinctive features. The British tourist board declared Indian curry to be the official British dish, testimony to the number of Indian restaurants in Britain—itself testimony to the enduring cultural interchange between Britain and its former colony. Although diversity sometimes produced tension and misunderstanding as interaction deepened, it was also increasingly valued.

Even multinational media conglomerates increasingly accented local content. When Viacom launched MTV in the 1980s, the producers assumed that since the pop music culture was universal, a single channel would succeed everywhere. But it quickly became evident that success required local variation. Between 2001 and 2003, MTV launched fourteen new channels, for a total of thirty-eight around the world. Each was tailored to local tastes, with no emphasis on an American link. One MTV executive observed, "we don't even call it an adaptation of American content: it's local content creation. . . . The American thing is irrelevant."[1] So whereas the advent of MTV had initially seemed to entail overt cultural imperialism, the program's evolution manifested—

Nelson Mandela and the Universality of Human Values

For all the admiration that continued to surround those who had helped undermine Soviet-style communism, the most revered person in the West and the world at the beginning of the twenty-first century was surely the black South African Nelson Mandela (b. 1918). As a militant in the African National Congress, which was seeking to overcome the brutally segregationist apartheid system in South Africa, he spent twenty-seven years in prison. He was released in 1990 as part of a wider amnesty granted by South Africa's new president, F. W. De Klerk (b. 1936). Responding to international pressures, including effective trade sanctions, De Klerk wanted Mandela's help in restructuring the South African system. The two were central to the ensuing negotiations that repealed apartheid and began the transition to a nonracial democracy in South Africa. When the first elections were held under the new system in 1994, Mandela was elected president of South Africa. In this passage from the conclusion to his autobiography, he articulates the idealism that inspired his remarkable achievement and made him a symbol of shared human values to Westerners and non-Westerners alike.

On the day of the inauguration, I was overwhelmed with a sense of history. In the first decade of the twentieth century, a few years after the bitter Anglo-Boer War and before my own birth, the white-skinned peoples of South Africa patched up their differences and erected a system of racial domination against the dark-skinned peoples of their own land. The structure they created formed the basis of one of the harshest, most inhumane societies the world has ever known. Now, in the last decade of the twentieth century, and my own eighth decade as a man, that system had been overturned forever and replaced by one that recognized the rights and freedoms of all peoples regardless of the color of their skin.

That day had come about through the unimaginable sacrifices of thousands of my people, people whose suffering and courage can never be counted or repaid. I felt that day, as I have on so many other days, that I was simply the sum of all those African patriots who had gone before me. That long and noble line ended and now began again with me. I was pained that I was not able to thank them and that they were not able to see what their sacrifices had wrought. . . .

I never lost hope that this great transformation would occur. Not only because of the great heroes I have already cited, but because of the courage of the ordinary men and women of my country. I always knew that deep down in every human heart, there is mercy and generosity. No one is born hating another person because of the color of his skin, or his background, or his religion. People must learn to hate, and if they can learn to hate, they can be taught to love, for love comes more naturally to the human heart than its opposite. Even in the grimmest times in prison, when my comrades and I were pushed to our limits, I would see a glimmer of humanity in one of the guards, perhaps just for a second, but it easy enough to reassure me and keep me going. . . .

I was not born with a hunger to be free. I was born free—free in every way that I could know. . . .

---

and contributed to—the more complex global cross-fertilization in process. As one product of an American culture that itself reflected fusion, MTV promoted new local variation and diversity around the world.

The "North-South" Divide and Mutual Interdependence

Beginning especially in the 1970s, western Europe and North America encountered formidable economic competition first from Japan and then from other countries of the East Asian Pacific rim. What increasingly mattered, as globalization proceeded, was the difference between the industrialized, relatively affluent "North" and the less developed "South," including much of Africa, Latin America, southern Asia, and the Middle East. Indeed, "North-South" tensions, resulting from demographic and economic patterns, quickly moved to center stage to replace the East-West tensions that had ended with the cold war. World population reached six billion in 1999, having doubled since 1960. This was the fastest rate of world population growth ever, and by the 1990s virtually all of that growth was in Africa, Asia, and Latin America (see Map 30.4).

But then I slowly saw that not only was I not free, but my brothers and sisters were not free. I saw that it was not just my freedom that was curtailed, but the freedom of everyone who looked like I did. That is when I joined the African National Congress, and that is when the hunger for my own freedom became the greater hunger for the freedom of my people. It was this desire for the freedom of my people to live their lives with dignity and self-respect that animated my life, that transformed a frightened young man into a bold one, that drove a law-abiding attorney to become a criminal, that turned a family-loving husband into a man without a home, that forced a life-loving man to live like a monk. I am no more virtuous or self-sacrificing than the next man, but I found that I could not even enjoy the poor and limited freedoms I was allowed when I knew my people were not free. Freedom is indivisible; the chains on any one of my people were the chains on all of them, the chains on all of my people were the chains on me.

It was during those long and lonely years that my hunger for the freedom of my own people became a hunger for the freedom of all people, white and black. I knew as well as I knew anything that the oppressor must be liberated just as surely as the oppressed. A man who takes away another man's freedom is a prisoner of hatred, he is locked behind the bars of prejudice and narrow-mindedness. I am not truly free if I am taking away someone else's freedom, just as surely as I am not free when my freedom is taken from me. The oppressed and the oppressor alike are robbed of their humanity.

When I walked out of prison, that was my mission, to liberate the oppressed and the oppressor both. Some say that has now been achieved. But I know that that is not the case. The truth is that we are not yet free; we have merely achieved the freedom to be free, the right not to be oppressed. We have not taken the final step of our journey, but the first step on a longer and even more difficult road. For to be free is not merely to cast off one's chains, but to live in a way that respects and enhances the freedom of others. The true test of our devotion to freedom is just beginning.

. . . After climbing a great hill, one only finds that there are many more hills to climb. I have taken a moment here to rest, to steal a view of the glorious vista that surrounds me, to look back on the distance I have come. But I can rest only for a moment, for with freedom comes responsibilities, and I dare not linger, for my long walk is not yet ended.

QUESTIONS

1. In what sense is Mandela appealing to human values, as opposed to the values or special circumstances of a particular group?

2. On what basis does Mandela claim to be seeking the liberation of the oppressors as well as the oppressed?

3. Why does Mandela suggest that the struggle for freedom is essentially endless?

SOURCE: *Long Walk to Freedom* by Nelson Mandela. Copyright © 1994 by Nelson Rolihlahla Mandela. Reprinted by permission of Little, Brown and Company (Inc.).

As the population exploded in the less developed world, the gap between rich and poor nations widened. One aspect of this process, producing much concern by the early twenty-first century, was the growing "digital divide"—the disparity in access to the computing and Internet technologies that seemed essential to compete in the global economy. New technologies were not bridging, but rather widening, the gap between the richer and poorer nations of the world.

The West recognized some responsibility to assist economic development in the developing world, but individual countries differed considerably in the ways they claimed to be doing so. Whereas most Americans assumed that they led the world in foreign aid, the United States, among the twenty-one richest countries, actually devoted the smallest percentage of its overall economy to direct foreign aid as of 2002. The most generous countries—Denmark, Norway, and the Netherlands—gave almost seven times as much. But such direct aid was only one measure of the ways the developed world might assist development elsewhere. Also important were direct investment, trade policy, and a willingness to accept immigrants, who often sent money back to their countries of origin, thereby providing essential foreign exchange. As the least protectionist of the wealthy nations, the United States was most helpful on trade because its markets were more open to products from developing countries.

Growing concern about the environment intensified the sense of global interdependence and pointed to the need for international cooperation. Problems such as global warming, the loss of biodiversity, and the deterioration of the ozone layer were inherently supranational in scope. Yet environmental concerns also complicated relations between the industrialized nations and the rest of the world. Countries seeking to industrialize encountered environmental constraints that had not been at issue when the West industrialized. The challenge for the West was to foster protection of the environment in poorer regions of the globe without imposing unfair limitations on economic growth.

Also bringing home mutual interdependence was the rapid spread of disease with the intensification of contacts around the world. Moreover, there was evidence that new diseases were emerging more frequently as the world grew more crowded. The human population intruded into previously untouched jungles and forests, intensifying interaction among species that had formerly remained largely separated. The crowding of animals for food production also fed the genesis and spread of new diseases.

AIDS (acquired immune deficiency syndrome), a sexually transmitted disease caused by the HIV virus, had apparently spread from chimpanzees to humans in Africa earlier in the twentieth century, although it began to be recognized only in the late 1970s. It then spread throughout the world beginning in the 1980s. Particularly devastating in Africa, AIDS remained a major concern in the early twenty-first century.

In the late 1990s, West Nile virus and monkeypox appeared at almost the same time. SARS (severe acute respiratory syndrome), a highly contagious and often fatal disease, was first reported in southern China in 2003, apparently contracted by a human being from a civet cat. The disease reached epidemic proportions in some areas of China and was carried elsewhere by travelers. The fact that Toronto, one of the most successful North American cities, was especially hard hit made clear the wider vulnerability of the West in this age of rapid transport and communication.

At the same time, responses to the SARS outbreak raised questions about local and multinational responsibilities and the interface between them. In this case, the poor initial Chinese response exacerbated the threat to the wider world. Uncertainty also surrounded the efforts of the UN's World Health Organization (WHO) to coordinate efforts to contain the disease. At first a WHO warning concerning travel to Toronto prompted criticism

New Diseases in a Global World
Modern, cosmopolitan Toronto was especially hard hit by SARS, which spread from China in 2003. In light of the quarantine that had to be imposed, even emergency rooms were forced to close, as this photo of North York General Hospital on May 26, 2003, makes clear.
(CP, Kevin Frayer/AP/Wide World Photos)

from Canadian officials that the organization was over-reacting, even overstepping its authority. Yet the WHO insisted that it needed wider authority to coordinate the international response to such diseases. A flare-up of SARS in Toronto after the WHO warning was lifted suggested that, if anything, the organization's measures had not been stringent enough.

The Controversy over Economic Globalization

Although many forces fed globalization, arguably the most potent, and increasingly controversial, was international capitalism itself. The capitalist ideal of free and open markets sounded appealing, and economic models, based on comparative advantage, could explain how everybody wins through expanded international economic exchange. The world economy was not a zero-sum game. But whatever the virtues of free global markets in principle, experience showed globalization to be a multi-edged sword, producing complex, often-contradictory results.

In 2003 France's Peugeot Citroën chose Trnava, a town in western Slovakia, for a site of a major auto-mobile assembly plant, to start turning out cars in 2006. The same firm was also embarking on a joint venture with Japan's Toyota to build cars in the Czech Republic. At the same time, the British firm MG Rover was making a major investment in Poland, and France's Renault was launching a new budget model at its factory in Romania. The former communist countries of east-central Europe were proving tremendously appealing to automakers elsewhere. Although the communist system had not proved competitive over the long term, it had left a reasonably good infrastructure, as well as a skilled and disciplined labor force costing only about 20 percent as much as the EU labor force. Moreover, these countries offered prime locations within the soon-to-be-enlarged EU.

Yet for western European firms to shift investment in new plants and equipment toward the east often meant an immediate blow to southern European members of the EU, who no longer could offer the cheapest labor. Thus, for example, Volkswagen announced in 2002 that it was eliminating jobs in Spain as it shifted part of its production to Slovakia. With such tempting possibilities for the big manufacturers in east-central Europe, the chairman of Renault predicted that a new Toyota factory that opened in northern France in 2001 would be "the last large car plant in Western Europe."[2] Such was the relentless dynamic of international capitalism in the increasingly global marketplace.

Those most immediately disadvantaged by such shifts were the workers losing their jobs and the government entities losing tax revenues. In theory, in overall economic terms, these workers could be more effectively employed in jobs requiring higher skill levels, so the solution was to retrain them for jobs possible only in the richer, more technologically advanced countries. At the same time, the countries attracting the investment, and the workers getting the new jobs, seemed to be the immediate winners. Still, lower labor costs would mean some combination of higher profits for the companies involved and lower auto prices for consumers.

Whatever its theoretical justification, globalization bred increasingly vocal opposition, fueled by concerns over fairness, exploitation, and the "Americanization" of the world. Meetings of the G-8 proved prominent targets of opposition, but at least as important was the network of supranational agencies, starting with the World Bank and the International Monetary Fund (IMF), that had developed from the Bretton Woods agreement near the end of World War II (see page 974). Also central, especially in promoting free trade, was the World Trade Organization (WTO), which grew from a multilateral trade agreement in 1947.

These organizations had been major vehicles for the influence of the wealthy nations, centered in the West, on those trying to catch up. In that role they often sought to influence domestic policies—by refusing, for example, to lend to countries spending heavily on armaments. And these organizations had long drawn praise for helping to keep the world economy stable and growing. By the late 1990s, however, they had come to constitute a focal point for the growing concerns about accelerating economic globalization.

Meetings of the WTO in Seattle in 1999 and of the World Bank and IMF in Washington, D.C., in 2000 drew large demonstrations. Riots accompanied G-8 meetings in 2001 and 2003. Those protesting were often naive about economics and the benefits of free trade. But their protests raised significant questions about wages, working conditions, environmental impact, and international financial arrangements that were not always adequately addressed in the prevailing economic models. The French activist José Bové (see page 1048) insisted that the food supply was too fundamental to be left to a free global market, which would yield a dominating role for international agribusiness—and thus bland uniformity. Most fundamentally at issue was whether it made sense to foster free trade and globalization without greater consistency in social and environmental policy. In the absence

Opposing Globalization   By the late 1990s, globalization sparked periodic protests, especially against the multinational organizations that seemed especially to promote it. This activist demonstrates at the WTO meeting in Cancún, Mexico, on September 14, 2003.   *(EPA Photo/EFE/David de la Paz/AP/ Wide World Photos)*

of common standards, free trade was not likely to be fair trade. The challenge was to find some balance between free trade and regulation within an increasingly global economy.

In September 2003 the WTO meeting in Cancún, Mexico, broke up amid much bitterness. A group of twenty-one poorer nations, led by Brazil, India, and China, walked out, accusing the United States and the EU of hypocrisy in calling for freer trade while still subsidizing their own farmers. By helping the richer countries export agricultural products at lower prices, such subsidies made it harder for poorer countries to develop their own crops and to sell them to the richer countries. West African cotton farmers suffered as the United States spent more than $3 billion a year on subsidies to 25,000 U.S. cotton growers, helping to make the United States the world's largest cotton exporter and depressing cotton prices worldwide. The United States claimed to be eager to cut farm subsidies, but only as part of a more systematic reduction that would also involve Japan and the EU, which was devoting 40 percent of its budget to such subsidies. The surprising cohesiveness of the new group of poorer countries—the G-21, as it was promptly dubbed—seemed to indicate the dawn of a more confrontational era in world trade. Some worried that the whole framework of international trade that had emerged from the agreement of 1947 was coming apart.

The Question of Global Responsibility

If people were forced to think in global terms as never before, how far did global responsibility extend in a world that remained divided into sovereign nation-states? The series of brutal, sometimes genocidal conflicts from Yugoslavia to Rwanda to Liberia that marked the post–cold war period fostered a growing sense of collective responsibility on the part of what was increasingly called "the international community." Amorphous though it was, that entity seemed to take on real existence by the end of the 1990s. But who or what constituted "the international community" and the conditions under which it should act remained uncertain.

Of course, a prominent international organization was already in place—the United Nations, the fruit of the hopes for a better world in light of World War II. By the 1990s no one denied that it had achieved significant successes in areas such as nutrition, health, and education. Kofi Annan (b. 1938) of Ghana, who became its secretary-general in 1997, was highly regarded worldwide. Indeed, he, together with the UN itself, was awarded the Nobel Peace Prize in 2001. Still, UN forces were often overburdened as they took on the often-incompatible objectives of peacekeeping and humanitarian relief—sometimes in areas where there was no real peace to keep. And the organization's members, especially its leaders on the Security Council, were frequently divided about what should be done. When Serbs in a UN "safe area" around Srebrenica°, in Bosnia, massacred as many as twenty thousand people in 1995, torturing or burying alive a number of the victims, the Security Council refused the UN secretary-general's pleas for additional troops.

But the UN remained an important, or potentially important, player even as concerns for national sovereignty continued to compromise its ability to act. UN inspectors had assumed the burden of policing Iraqi compliance with the peace that followed the Persian Gulf War of 1991. After ad hoc UN war crimes tribunals began dealing with atrocities in the Balkans and Rwanda, the UN established its permanent international criminal court in The Hague in 1998. Its charge was to bring to justice those responsible for war crimes or crimes against humanity.

Whatever its center of gravity, the international community rested on the commitment and initiative of the rich Western countries because only they had the means to act globally in response to natural or human-made disasters. Supplementing the efforts of governments was a network of nongovernmental organizations (NGOs), such as the Red Cross, Amnesty International, and Doctors Without Borders, that had emerged over the years to deal with humanitarian relief or human rights issues. Collectively they were a major presence on the international scene by the early twenty-first century and central to the international community.

The conflicts that developed in hot spots around the world after the cold war spawned an increasing sense that it was up to the Western-led international community to "do something." But do what—and at what cost? What aims were realistic? Those seeking to provide aid or maintain peace were often forced to deal with semi-criminal elements who diverted humanitarian aid to buy weapons or who took peacekeepers and aid workers hostage—or even killed them. In 1994, for the first time, more UN civilian aid workers (twenty-four) than peacekeeping soldiers were killed in the line of duty. And the death toll for aid workers rose rapidly during the decade.

Whereas the rich countries of the West increasingly felt a responsibility to confront troubles elsewhere, the question was whether they were willing to supply the means, to take the risks, even to suffer the casualties necessary to do so effectively. (See the box "The Continuing Experiment: The Question of Western Responsibility.") The response of the United States and much of the

West to the terrorist attack of September 11, 2001, and to Saddam Hussein's regime in Iraq indicated an increased willingness to intervene, but questions remained about the conditions under which the Western powers, in whatever combination, would act. How immediately did their own national interests have to be affected?

THE UNCERTAIN MEANING OF THE WEST

Although in one sense "globalization" essentially meant "Westernization" to many advocates and critics alike, its accelerating pace bred deeper uncertainty about what was specifically Western—about the meaning and value of the Western tradition. During the cold war, the West had offered two competing visions to the world. But with the fall of communism, one of them stood discredited, and democratic capitalism emerged the clear winner. As the end of the cold war also ended the division of Europe and removed the common adversary, the ties that had helped bind western Europe to the United States loosened. Indeed, the need to respond both to the challenges of the competitive global economy and to the increasingly volatile international environment occasioned friction and fragmentation within the West. By the early twenty-first century, it was no longer clear what the West stood for or who spoke for the West. In this continuing experiment, even something so apparently solid as the Western alliance or "the Atlantic orientation" was not cut in stone.

Most obviously at work were differences in priorities, especially at the interface of capitalism and democracy, that reflected the diversity of possible human values. At the same time, growing U.S. unilateralism alienated many Europeans. The whole way of thinking multilaterally that had bound together the United States and western Europe since the Second World War was changing. Those who lamented this change agreed that there was blame on both sides.

The United States, Europe, and the West

Although the cultural relationship between western Europe and the United States had been long and complex, entailing much stereotyping on both sides, it became especially tricky with the changes that resulted from World War II. For decades thereafter, western Europeans seemed to have no choice but to follow the U.S. lead. But such subservience was troubling to them, and a kind

---

Srebrenica (shreb-reh-NEET-sah)

The Question of Western Responsibility

The end of the cold war helped open the way to ethnic conflict, terrorism, and, in some areas, the breakdown of government as violent warlords fought for control. With the world more interconnected than ever before, it was increasingly assumed that "the international community," spearheaded by the rich countries of the West, ought to respond to tragedy anywhere. But quite apart from the difficult questions of leadership and coordination, it was not clear what level of risk, and expense, the West was prepared to assume. In the following excerpt, Brian Urquhart, born in Britain in 1919 and long a senior official of the United Nations, offers a pointed analysis of the issues that came to the fore as the West experimented with a more active response to tragedies around the world.

What is to be done when hundreds of thousands of people in a hitherto little-known region of the world are hounded from their homes, massacred, or starved to death in a brutal civil war, or even in a deliberate act of genocide? To our credit, we no longer turn away from the face of evil, but we still don't know how to control it. As the new century dawns, one of the biggest problems for international organizations and their member governments is to learn how to react to the great human emergencies that still seem to occur regularly in many parts of the world. . . .

The so-called "international community" is anything but a constitutional system. As far as it is organized at all, it is an institutional arrangement, unpredictable and slow to act. It usually responds only when disaster has already struck and when its members, usually in the UN Security Council, can agree to take action. Even then, since the UN has no standing forces or substantial resources of its own, its action, if it can be agreed upon, is likely to be too little and too late.

In his opening address to the General Assembly on September 20, 1999, Secretary-General Kofi Annan made an impassioned plea for UN intervention in cases of gross violations of human rights. The reactions of governments to Annan's remarks showed very clearly how far the world still has to go before evil can be systematically dealt with internationally. Most comments on Annan's speech were critical and stressed the paramount importance of national sovereignty; some even saw humanitarian intervention as a cloak for American or Western hegemony or neocolonialism. Only a small minority of Western countries supported Sweden's position that the collective conscience of mankind demands action.

A new idea of "human security" has now taken its place alongside the much older concept of "international peace and security." It has emerged as the result of a vaguely defined and fitful international conscience on the part of the liberal democracies, and it has been encouraged both by the prodigious growth of nongovernmental organizations and by the communications revolution. However, the rules and the means for protecting human security are still tentative and controversial, not least because virtually any situation threatening human security is likely to raise questions of national sovereignty. No government wants to set up a system which may, at some point in the future, be invoked against itself.

. . . Humanitarian action as it emerged in the aftermath of World War II was principally concerned with refugee resettlement and the reconstruction of war-shattered countries. In those innocent days, humanitarian relief was seen as a nonpolitical activity, dictated by the needs of the afflicted and by the resources and expertise available to meet them. . . . That relatively nonpolitical concept of humanitarianism has come to a brutal end with the rising importance of warlords and the conflicts within states of the post–cold war world. The international sponsors of humanitarian aid are no longer dealing with more or less responsible governments. . . .

. . . "The whole aid community has been overtaken by a new reality," the IRC [International Rescue Committee] stated. "Humanitarianism has become a resource . . . and people are manipulating it as never before. Sometimes we just shouldn't show up for a disaster." . . .

QUESTIONS

1. Why did the West find it so difficult to respond to the sorts of disasters that came to the fore after the cold war?

2. Why did even humanitarian aid come to seem increasingly ineffective under certain circumstances?

SOURCE: "In the Name of Humanity" by Brian Urquhart, *The New York Review of Books,* April 27, 2000, pp. 19–21. Reprinted with permission from *The New York Review of Books.* Copyright © 2000 NYREV, Inc.

of love-hate relationship with the United States developed in western Europe. At the same time, the two regions' very different experiences of recent history, especially the events surrounding the two world wars, inevitably produced some differences in perceptions and priorities.

Even after Europe's postwar economic recovery, the United States was clearly setting the pace in high-technology industries, prompting concerns by the 1960s that western Europe, despite its remarkable postwar recovery, was becoming a mere economic satellite of the United States. Europe seemed to be caught in a dilemma: to retain its distinctiveness over the long term, it had to become more competitive—which apparently meant becoming more like America in the short term. The French writer Jean-Jacques Servan-Schreiber° (b. 1924) made this case in 1967 in *The American Challenge,* the classic statement of postwar Europe's ambivalent attitude toward Americanization. Haunted by the decline of earlier civilizations, Servan-Schreiber warned that if Europeans failed to become sufficiently dynamic to compete with the Americans, Europe would gradually sink into decadence without ever understanding why it had happened.

By the 1980s much of western Europe had caught up with the United States in standard of living, and western Europeans set the pace in confronting some of the new problems that resulted from ongoing socioeconomic change. The French day-care system was one example. The size of the EU economy was about equal to that of the United States by the end of the 1990s, and the Europeans proved quite competitive in certain fields. For example, Europe's Airbus did well in head-to-head competition with American aircraft manufacturer Boeing.

It was increasingly clear, in fact, that two models of democratic capitalism were at work—and to some extent in competition. The U.S. model, largely shared by Britain since the Thatcher years, placed greater emphasis on free enterprise and the market, whereas continental western Europe had evolved a "social market economy," with greater commitment to security, consensus, and communitarian values. The European model provided a more substantial safety net—in health care, for example—as well as a stronger commitment to subsidized transportation and day care.

But the social market economy of continental Europe was increasingly on the defensive during the 1990s, a period of remarkable prosperity for the United States, which forcefully asserted its leadership in the "new economy" revolving around information technology. As the American model came to seem better at fostering in-

novation and competitiveness, western Europeans again worried about falling behind, even as they also sought to preserve European distinctiveness in the face of Americanization. Superior as it might seem in principle, the European model, with its costly welfare provisions, seemed to obstruct the adaptability necessary for success in the competitive global economy. One symptom was the consistently higher rate of unemployment, especially among young people, in Europe.

The question by the early twenty-first century was clear: Could Europe maintain and even extend its more socially oriented model while becoming more economically competitive? Or, in light of globalization and the third industrial revolution, was Europe bound to adapt the leaner and meaner American model?

Still, differences in values and priorities were ingrained and likely to survive whatever adjustments Europeans might find necessary. In some respects, in fact, it was almost as if the Americans and Europeans had passed in the night in the decades since World War II. In the United States, which had long prided itself on its egalitarianism vis-à-vis class-bound Europe, disparities between rich and poor had become greater than anywhere in the developed world by the early twenty-first century. In the business world, the ratio of executive compensation to worker salaries was dramatically higher in the United States than in Europe.

Perhaps still more significant was the difference in attitudes toward such disparities. Wary of extreme inequalities of income, Europeans tended to view unrestricted competition more as a threat than an opportunity. Whereas most Europeans found the inequalities and insecurities of American life unacceptable, Americans accented the scope for upward mobility that their system offered. As long as anyone could get rich, it did not matter that some were much richer than others. Americans were much more likely than Europeans to see themselves as moving up.

At the same time, Americans had grown more skeptical about government and its capacity to provide social services. Whereas 62 percent of those surveyed in Britain in 2002 said they would accept higher taxes for better services, less than 1 percent of those in the United States held this view. Friction over particular policies from pollution control to product testing reflected similar differences in priorities and values. The United States was more likely than Europe to rely on unfettered freedom, competition, and the market. Europe was more cautious—more willing to err on the side of health and the environment.

A good deal of sniping back and forth accompanied the increasing competition between Europe and the United States in the early twenty-first century. Whether

---

Servan-Schreiber (SAIR-vahn–SHRY-bay)

this was just the usual squabbling within a family or the sign of a deeper split remained unclear.

U.S. Unilateralism

A major source of friction between the United States and Europe was growing U.S. unilateralism—the willingness, even determination, to go its own way in the world on the basis of what it took to be its own interests. Uniquely situated as the world's economic engine and military-diplomatic superpower, the United States was increasingly prone to unilateralism during the 1990s. The country moved more decisively in that direction when George W. Bush became president in January 2001 and especially in the aftermath of the terrorist attacks on September 11. In pursuing its own course, the United States was departing from the multilateral international system that it had fostered since World War II. Foreshadowed in the Atlantic Charter of 1941 (see page 962), such multilateralism found expression in NATO, the economic organizations growing from the Bretton Woods agreement, and a whole array of multilateral understandings and institutions governing matters such as arms control and war crimes.

While an overwhelming majority of nations—120, to be exact—supported the establishment of the UN international criminal court in The Hague in 1998, the United States was among only 7 (including China, Israel, Iraq, and Libya) that opposed it. As efforts to establish the court followed, the United States sought an exemption for itself because it worried that American peacekeepers might be especially tempting targets of false accusations of war crimes. Such concerns were not groundless, and they indicated the unique problems the United States faced as the world's undisputed, and often resented, superpower. But many found it disturbing that the United States did not want to play by the same rules as virtually everyone else.

Against this backdrop of sociocultural difference and increasing U.S. unilateralism, the divisions over the Iraq War of 2003 produced much vituperation, including a good deal of sloganeering and stereotyping. Whereas Europeans were "Euroweenies," full of excuses for backing away from a fight, Americans were gun-toting, shoot-'em-up cowboys.

In his best-selling book *After the Empire: The Breakdown of the American Order,*[3] the French writer Emmanuel Todd argues that whereas the United States had been a benevolent and needed world presence from 1950 to 1989, by the early twenty-first century it was past its prime. Though militarily powerful, it was musclebound in a world of increasing economic interdependence. Offering a socioeconomic model that appealed to few elsewhere, its leadership claims had grown hollow. Whatever the value of such analyses, they brought into sharper relief the wider differences in values between Europe and America that were already becoming evident.

As the United States seemed not only uniquely powerful but also increasingly willing to act on its own, many critics proclaimed a unipolar world to be inherently unhealthy, even for the hegemonic power. U.S. unilateral-

Europe on Its Own?   France's Jacques Chirac, Russia's Vladimir Putin, and Germany's Gerhard Schroeder (*left to right*) were the most prominent of the European leaders to oppose the U.S.-led invasion of Iraq. With the fighting in progress, they met in St. Petersburg, Russia, in April 2003 to coordinate their response. The meeting both symbolized the gulf that had developed over Iraq between the United States and much of Europe and suggested that new alignments within the West might be emerging. (*Alexander Zemlianichenko/AP/Wide World Photos*)

ism seemed even to reflect a messianism that some found frightening. Belgian prime minister Guy Verhofstadt found the United States to be "a deeply wounded power that has now become very dangerous and thinks it must take over the whole Arab world."[4] Some Europeans continued to look to the UN to limit the American imperium, but others, including many non-Europeans, found a stronger European military and diplomatic presence the only potential balance to the United States.

Although Europeans were not pacifists, they were much less willing than Americans to resort to force. Whereas the United States was devoting 3 percent of its economy to its armed forces by 2003, France and Britain were each devoting 2.5 percent and Germany 1.6 percent. The gap in military muscle was still more striking, and arguably growing, if what the money bought was considered. Americans tended to buy new high-tech equipment; Europeans devoted more resources to pay and pensions. Although Germans played a significant role in peacekeeping efforts, Germany had to lease planes from Ukraine to transport its troops to Afghanistan for that purpose in 2002.

Some suggested that Europeans had grown soft in their reliance on the United States since World War II. Now they were simply talking out of both sides of their mouths, agreeing that, in principle, the West must be prepared to fight on occasion, but unwilling to pay if it meant cutting the welfare benefits they had come to expect. Surveys suggested that most Europeans—63 percent of Italians, for example, and 69 percent of Poles—opposed increased defense spending to enhance Europe's standing as a world power. Moreover, Europeans had failed to achieve a unified military and diplomatic policy. It was attractive for a variety of reasons to let the United States shoulder the military burden in a dangerous world—while criticizing from a stance of haughty superiority.

What Had the West Come to Mean?

A certain triumphalism in the West, encompassing *western* Europe, accompanied the failure of the communist experiment in the Soviet Union by 1991. A particular Western model, based on democratic capitalism, had proved superior to the communist alternative; victory bred renewed confidence in the winning model. Now even Russia was seeking to align with the democratic capitalism of the West, no longer claiming to point the way beyond it. But the effort to move from communism to democratic capitalism was itself an unprecedented experiment, which might even make clearer what was required to make democratic capitalism work.

Whatever might prove true in the longer term, the results in Russia by the turn of the century were sobering indeed. Russia demonstrated that under certain circumstances, even a turn to freedom and a market economy could yield an exploitative and brutal "gangster capitalism." If democracy and a market economy were to be socially beneficial, a deeper consensus around civic responsibility and the rule of law was required. People had to be willing to pay taxes, and the state had to be strong enough to collect taxes, to limit corruption, and to sustain genuinely open markets and an orderly banking system. "Negative liberty," getting government out of the way, was not sufficient. Indeed, this new Russian experiment demonstrated that a single-minded focus on free markets was no less utopian than Soviet Russia's single-minded insistence on central planning and command from above.

But there were differences in the capitalist economies even of the most successful democracies. Whereas the crisis over Iraq splintered the EU, it also prompted deeper reflection among Europeans about what they offered the world, especially as the United States seemed to claim privilege in articulating Western values, even the meaning of freedom. To many thinking Europeans, it was self-evident that European economic practices and social legislation were more congenial and more readily exportable to the non-Western world than U.S. policies.

Still, the U.S. model was widely admired, partly for the openness and transparency of its markets and the full disclosure demanded of its publicly traded companies. In this respect, the United States tended to be much ahead of Europe and Japan, not to mention the "emerging markets" of the Pacific rim. Americans actively pushed others to develop comparable openness and disclosure. Yet American-style capitalism also proved to be subject to excess and abuse by the first years of the twenty-first century.

During the 1990s U.S. stock markets boomed, and top corporate executives, enjoying soaring compensation, became celebrities. But then an unprecedented series of scandals involving accounting practices and stock price manipulation hit several major U.S. firms, most famously Enron and WorldCom. In principle, oversight from corporate boards of directors, independent auditors, and government regulators was supposed to prevent the sorts of abuses that came to light. But directors and accountants were subject to conflicts of interest, as were brokerage firms that recommended stocks to the public. Government regulators, if not simply lax, were underfunded and overextended.

The continuing experiment had demonstrated the remarkable capacities of the free-market system to foster innovation and generate wealth—especially in comparison with its onetime communist rival. But these scandals, a decade after the collapse of Soviet communism, prompted renewed questions about the Western model. Above all, could the institutions of a pluralistic democracy check the tendencies to excess in free-market capitalism that the experiment had also revealed?

Governments sometimes seemed to lack the muscle, or the will, to address not only the immediate problems of capitalist corporate accounting but also wider problems following from globalization and technological change. Even within the democratic political systems, the increasingly obvious role of money—needed to finance campaigns and win elections—raised doubts about the capacity of elected governments to pursue some common public interest. The political cynicism fed by the prominence of money in politics produced declining voter turnouts all over the Western world by the late 1990s.

Although corruption was worst in the former communist countries, and although its incidence varied considerably in the more established democracies, it was a worrisome tendency in much of the West. In Italy the increasingly systematic corruption bred by the need for political money finally came to light in 1992, discrediting much of the entrenched political class and producing a wholesale turnover in the political elite. Some leading French Socialists got caught up in corruption scandals in the early 1990s, and by the end of the decade even former German chancellor Helmut Kohl, long one of Europe's most respected leaders, stood partly discredited for accepting illegal campaign contributions.

Whatever the patterns of divergence and convergence within the West, what was ultimately at issue, after its roughly two-hundred-year experiment with liberal capitalism, was the scope for creating and maintaining a genuine public sphere and a government worthy of public trust. That rested, in turn, on the capacity for citizenship. On this level, the democracy that the West held up as a model for the non-Western world remained very much an experiment in progress.

CONCLUSION: LEARNING FROM WESTERN CIVILIZATION IN A GLOBAL AGE

Was "the West" still a meaningful category by the early twenty-first century, when talk of globalization and cultural fusion was rampant? For several decades bitter debate had raged in the West over the legitimacy of "Western civilization" as a concept. Some critics highlighted the geographical imprecision of "the West" and claimed that the words *Western* and *civilization* had been juxtaposed simply to justify conquest and domination. Even among those who recognized a distinctive Western cultural tradition, some found it elitist and limiting. In their view, Western culture had defined itself around a group of artifacts—writings, paintings, monuments—that reflected the experience of a very restricted circle.

Others countered that imperialism and assumptions of superiority had not been confined to the West. Moreover, they continued, the West had been the source of ideas—the "rights of man," the scope for eliminating exploitation—that were now being eagerly embraced in the non-Western world. Even the charges of cultural elitism directed against the Western tradition stemmed from a democratic impulse that had itself grown, and could only have grown, from within that Western tradition. By the last decades of the twentieth century, that impulse was prompting historians to focus on ordinary people and a far wider circle of cultural interpreters, thereby expanding the "canon"—the body of works considered worthy of our attention.

Questions about the Western tradition and its contemporary relevance were bound up with the advent of *postmodernism,* a term widely used by the early 1990s for a cultural orientation that had been gathering force for decades. (See the feature "Weighing the Evidence: Postmodern Architecture" on pages 1064–1065.) Postmodernism reflected a certain conception of what *modernism* had meant, even a sense that modernism had defined an era that was ending. But what was ending—and how was it bound up with the debate over Western civilization—was not so clear.

Postmodernism emerged partly as confidence in the scope for a neutral, objective social science began to decline during the 1960s. That confidence had reflected the belief in reason that had emerged from the Scientific Revolution and the Enlightenment. Reason had seemed universal, not limited to any particular culture, and it was assumed to be applicable to the human as well as the natural world.

To apply reason seemed "modern," and the West, having progressed by applying reason, had long understood itself to be in the forefront of modernity. Everyone else was scrambling to catch up through the universal process of modernization. Such was the "master narrative" through which the West had understood its place in the world as it set the agenda during the modern era. It had been that conception of the world, and the sense of

Old and New in Contemporary Europe
Especially with the transformation of Europe since World War II, new styles intersect with living artifacts from the past to form sometimes ironic combinations. Here, in a neighborhood in Milan, Italy, teenagers wearing blue jeans and backpacks seem oblivious to the legacies of Roman antiquity and Christianity that are prominent around them.   *(© 1993 George Steinmetz)*

superiority underlying it, that had seemed to justify Western imperialism.

But even as globalization proceeded during the late twentieth century, Western thinkers retreated from this long-standing master narrative. There was no question that capitalism had spread from Europe, but the West was not necessarily the model, the standard of development. Indeed, a growing interest in the non-Western world and an increasing respect for its diverse traditions came to mark Western culture.

Postmodernists questioned claims of certainty, objective truth, and intrinsic meaning in language, in works of art, and ultimately in all cultural expressions. Some held that such claims were assertions of privilege in what was essentially a political struggle for power—the power to set the wider social agenda. Especially in the U.S., the postmodernist reaction led by the 1980s to the vogue of the French philosopher and historian Michel Foucault°

(1926–1984), who showed that the power to specify what counts as knowledge was the key to social or political power. Since all knowledge was suspect, Foucault's accents invited mistrust and disruption. At the same time, however, an array of equally innovative thinkers, from the German Jürgen Habermas (b. 1929) to the American Richard Rorty (b. 1931), sought a more constructive orientation based on a renewed, no longer arrogant understanding of Western traditions, including the place of reason and democracy.

For those embracing this more constructive approach, the point was not to celebrate Western civilization but simply to understand it—as the framework that continued to shape the West and, less directly, the world. That tradition included much that might be criticized, and its present outcome entailed much that might be changed. Habermas, in particular, was a persistent and often radical critic of what he saw as the disparity

Foucault (foo-KOH)

(continued on page 1066)

Postmodern Architecture

Three building complexes, one by an Italian working in Japan, another by an American working in Germany, and a third by a Spaniard working in Spain: they look dramatically different, yet they were built at roughly the same time. Do they have anything in common? In fact, each was rejecting earlier "modern" architecture, and each expressed what came to be known as "post-modernism" by the last two decades of the twentieth century.

Modernism in architecture, design, and urban planning had emerged especially during the 1920s from sources like the German Bauhaus, which turned resolutely from tradition to embrace the modern industrial age (see page 907–908). During the first two decades after World War II, this modernist approach triumphed at last, transforming cities throughout the world. Now known as "the international style," it reflected the wider self-understanding of the modern world, centered in the West. "Modern" meant rationality and efficiency, clarity and regularity, machine precision and mass culture. Ornament, decoration, symbolism, and historical reference had little or no place.

At issue, in fact, was not just a particular style of building but a new relationship with history. As modern, we seemed to be living on the cutting edge of history, in the eternal present, endlessly being cut off from our past. Henry Ford, widely taken as the personification of modernity in his time, put the matter directly: "History is bunk."

But by the 1960s, a reaction began to develop in architecture and urban planning, reflecting deeper thinking about history, about what it meant to be modern, and about the contemporary relationship with cultural traditions, including older buildings. In 1977 the architectural critic Charles Jencks, in his book *The Language of Post-Modern Architecture,* used the term "post-modernism" to characterize what now seemed to be a new movement or direction.

The earlier notion of modernity was coming to seem dubious in an emerging world of global interchange and plural perspectives. Memory, history, and the presence of the past were more, not less, important as accelerating technological change made possible instant communication and constant access to information across the globe. Yet there was sometimes irony, uncertainty, or paradox in the coexistence of old and new.

Postmodernist architects did not merely reject the earlier modernism, and certainly their aim was not simply to revive previous styles such as classical or Gothic, though elements of them, as embodiments of our living history, might be incorporated in postmodern buildings. For example, look at the photo below of the Palazzo Hotel, designed by the Italian Aldo Rossi (1931–1997). Set in a Japanese city, the hotel clearly recalls Italian buildings, even those of the fascist period, themselves ambiguously modern, with references to the classical tradition and especially ancient Rome. For the façade, constructed of red marble and brick crossed with green steel moldings, Rossi combined contrasting materials, uncertain scale, and historical reference in a striking, even uncanny way.

Moreover, postmodernist architects were just as committed to modern techniques and materials as the modernists. They reacted, however, against the modernist pretense of a single right way, the rejection of ornament and history, and the reduction of architecture to function and the logic of machines. Postmodernists did not simply accept but actively celebrated messiness,

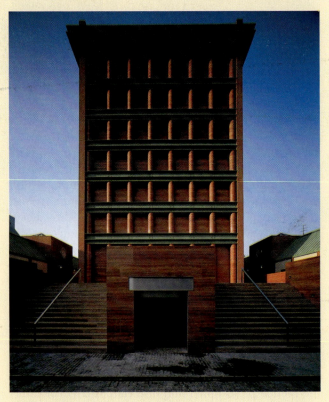

Aldo Rossi: Il Palazzo Hotel, Fukuoka, Japan *(Courtesy, Nacasa & Partners, Inc.)*

**Frank Gehry: Der Neue Zollhof
(The New Customs House),
Düsseldorf, Germany**

(Thomas Mayer, photographer)

**Santiago Calatrava: City of Arts
and Sciences, Valencia, Spain**

(Barbara Burg and Oliver Schuh, Palladium
Photodesign, Cologne, Germany)

variety, mixture, and complexity. The American Frank Gehry (b. 1929) suggested impermanence as well as postmodern pluralism in his complex of three office buildings in Düsseldorf, Germany. Notice how the project incorporates modernist elements—flat roofs, identical prefabricated windows—but provides remarkable variety and contrast by cladding one of the units in red brick, one in mirror-polished stainless steel, and the third in white plaster. At the same time, the uniform, angled windows contrast with the curved surfaces. None of the three is the right way; rather, they play evocatively against one another.

Unlike Rossi and Gehry, Santiago Calatrava (b. 1951) designed buildings that drew on a wider frame of reference to create forms that were never before part of our built environment. Calatrava used highly sculptured forms for the building shown here (above right)—the centerpiece of a science museum complex built in the bed of a diverted river in his native Valencia, Spain. Taking advantage of his engineering background, he created unexpected spaces and sculptural surfaces that went beyond tradition altogether. With structures suggesting bones and tendons, he conveyed the dynamics of movement, of folding, opening, and closing—even the opening and closing of an eye.

So dramatically different though they appear, these three architectural statements share the wider postmodern framework. Rossi invokes the past to resist change; Gehry plays with the past, even the recent modernist past, while suggesting impermanence; Calatrava transcends the present outcome of the past, but without the limitations, the particular discipline, that modernism imposed. Rather than submit to the logic of the machine, he felt free to experiment more boldly, devising radically new forms. Each of the three architects represents a strand in the wider, complex, and contradictory postmodernist approach to history and tradition, including the tradition of modernism itself.

between Western democratic ideals and contemporary social and political practices. But effective criticism had to rest on free inquiry and rational understanding, as opposed to prejudice or wishful thinking. The invitation to think freely about the Western tradition, to criticize and change it, rested on precisely that tradition; indeed, the scope for such criticism and change had been central to the Western belief in reason. That openness remained perhaps the West's most fundamental legacy.

■ Notes

1. Quoted in *The Economist,* April 5, 2003, p. 59.
2. Quoted in *The Economist,* March 29, 2003, p. 58.
3. New York: Columbia University Press, 2004. The original French edition was published in 2002.
4. Quoted in *The Economist,* April 12, 2003, p. 50.

■ Suggested Reading

Ardagh, John. *France in the New Century: Portrait of a Changing Society.* 1999. An updated edition of a lively, perceptive survey of the remarkable changes in French life since World War II.

Brubaker, Rogers. *Citizenship and Nationhood in France and Germany.* 1992. A lucid comparative study showing how very different conceptions of citizenship emerged in these two countries as a result of their contrasting historical experiences over the past two centuries.

Calleo, David P. *Rethinking Europe's Future.* 2001. Against a carefully drawn historical backdrop, this important work pinpoints the key issues in the evolving partnership between Europe and the United States and stresses the potential for a greater European contribution to world affairs.

Fehrenbach, Heide, and Uta G. Poigner, eds. *Transactions, Transgressions, Transformations: American Culture in West-*

ern Europe and Japan. 2000. A superior collection of essays reassessing the United States' cultural impact on Europe and Japan. Several of the essays treat film or popular music, while others are more comparative or synthetic in approach.

Garton Ash, Timothy. *In Europe's Name: Germany and the Divided Continent.* 1993. A searching essay on Germany's place in Europe and the world, from the years of division to reunification to the post–cold war order.

Guttman, Robert J., ed. *Europe in the New Century: Visions of an Emerging Superpower.* 2001. An assessment of Europe's strengths and weaknesses by leading European politicians and journalists, who also seek to envision what the new century will bring.

Hoffman, David E. *The Oligarchs: Wealth and Power in the New Russia.* 2002. Through the interweaving biographies of six central figures, traces the emergence of the new oligarchic capitalism in postcommunist Russia. Illuminates the political influence of the oligarchs in an unprecedented situation between legality and criminality.

McCormick, John. *Understanding the European Union: A Concise Introduction.* 1999. A clear introduction to the history, structure, and functioning of the central institutions of the EU.

Ramet, Sabrina, and Christine Ingebritsen, eds. *Coming In from the Cold War: Changes in U.S.-European Interactions Since 1980.* 2002. Essays assessing the impact of the end of the cold war on varied aspects the U.S.–western European relationship.

Shawcross, William. *Deliver Us from Evil: Peacekeepers, Warlords, and a World of Endless Conflict.* 2000. Accents the limits and contradictions of the Western response to crises in areas lacking an indigenous political class.

 For a searchable list of additional readings for this chapter, go to college.hmco.com/students.

Glossary

This Glossary covers the complete text, Chapters 1 through 30.

absolutism Extraordinary concentration of power in royal hands, achieved particularly by the kings of France, most notably **Louis XIV,** in the seventeenth century. Proponents argued that hereditary monarchy was the divinely ordained form of government. *(Ch. 16)*

Act of Supremacy (1534) Act of the English Parliament during the Protestant Reformation that finalized the break with the Catholic Church by declaring the king to be head of the Church of England. Henry VIII required a public oath supporting the act, which Sir **Thomas More** refused to take; More was then executed for treason. *(Ch. 14)*

Adenauer, Konrad (1876–1967) Leading statesman of post–World War II Germany. As chancellor (1949–1963), he oriented the country toward western Europe and the United States and proved to Germans that democracy could mean effective government, economic prosperity, and foreign policy success. *(Ch. 29)*

agricultural revolution Dramatic increase in food production from the sixteenth to eighteenth centuries, brought about by changes in agricultural practices, cultivation of new crops, greater availability of animal manure, and introduction of the nutrient-rich potato from the Americas. *(Ch. 18)*

Alexander the Great (356–323 B.C.) King of **Macedon** (r. 336–323) and conqueror of the **Persian Empire.** Son of **Philip II** of Macedon, Alexander was an ingenious warrior who, in the course of his conquests, spread Greek civilization to western Asia, Egypt, and India. His despotism and ruler-worship set a precedent for later monarchs, including many Roman emperors. *(Ch. 4)*

Alexandria Mediterranean seaport in northern Egypt founded by **Alexander the Great** in 332 B.C. It was a thriving Hellenistic city with great harbors, marketplaces, banks, inns, courts, shipbuilding facilities, and a renowned library. *(Ch. 4)*

Amarna reform Term for the ancient Egyptian king Amenhotep IV's seizure of power from temple priests by replacing the god Amun-Re with Aten and renaming himself Akhenaten. After Akhenaten's death, the Amun-Re cult regained power. *(Ch. 1)*

Anabaptists Radical religious reformers in Germany and Switzerland during the Reformation. They rejected the practice of infant baptism, believing that baptism should occur only after confession of sin. They also believed that Christians should live apart in communities of the truly redeemed. Mennonites and Hutterites are their modern descendants. *(Ch. 14)*

Antigonids Dynasty of Macedonian rulers founded in 276 B.C. by Antigonus Gonatas, grandson of Antigonus the One-Eyed, a general of **Alexander the Great.** The Antigonid dynasty lasted about 140 years, until the Roman conquest. *(Ch. 4)*

Antioch Greatest of the cities founded by Seleucus, a general of **Alexander the Great.** Located near the present-day Turkish-Syrian border, it became one of the wealthiest and most luxurious of all eastern Mediterranean cities. *(Ch. 4)*

anti-Semitism Centuries-old prejudice against and demonization of Jews. Anti-Semitism became virulent in Europe in the 1880s with the emergence of the ultranationalist and racist "New Right" ideologies and political movements. An essential part of the Nazi world-view, it led to the Holocaust. *(Ch. 24)*

appeasement The term for the policy employed by Britain's prime minister, Neville Chamberlain, to defuse the 1938 crisis with Germany's **Adolf Hitler.** Chamberlain acquiesced to Hitler's demands to annex the Sudetenland portion of Czechoslovakia, which proved a giant step toward the war that broke out less than a year later. *(Ch. 27)*

Aquinas, Thomas (1225–1274) Dominican friar and theologian. In his two most famous works, *Summa Contra Gentiles* and *Summa Theologiae,* he distinguished between natural truth, or what a person could know by reasoning, and revealed truths, which can be known only through faith in God's revelation. No one before him had so rigorously followed the dialectical method of reasoning through a whole field of knowledge. *(Ch. 10)*

Archaic Greece Period of ancient Greek history from around 700 to 500 B.C. Archaic Greece was characterized by artistic achievement, increased individualism amid communal solidarity, and a moving away from divine and toward abstract, mechanistic explanations. The Western philosophical tradition began during this period. *(Ch. 3)*

Arianism Popular heresy advocated by the priest Arius (ca. 250–336), emphasizing that Jesus was the "first born of all creation." It sought to preserve and purify Christianity's monotheism by making Jesus slightly subordinate to the Father. It was condemned by the **Council of Nicaea.** *(Ch. 7)*

Aristotle (384–322 B.C.) Ancient Greek philosopher, student of **Plato** and tutor of **Alexander the Great.** Aristotle emphasized the goal (*telos* in Greek) of change; in his view the entire cosmos is teleological, and every one of its parts has an essential purpose. Aristotle's scientific writings were the most influential philosophical classics of Greek and Roman civilization and remained so during the Middle Ages. *(Ch. 3)*

Armada (1588) Massive fleet of Spanish warships sent against England by **Philip II** but defeated by the English navy and bad weather. The tactics used by the English helped set the future course of naval warfare. *(Ch. 15)*

Assyrians Warlike people who ruled the ancient Near East during the first millennium B.C. Their innovations included using cavalry as their main striking force and having weapons and armor made of iron. *(Ch. 2)*

Augsburg Confession (1532) Document written by Philip Melanchthon (1497–1560), with the approval of **Martin Luther,** that became the most widely accepted statement of the Lutheran faith. It constitutes part of the creedal basis for today's Lutheran churches. *(Ch. 14)*

Augustine (354–430) North African bishop and one of the most influential Christian thinkers. Augustine wrote that all people were sinners in need of God's redemption, that history is the struggle between those who call on divine grace and those who sin, and that learning was useful only to the extent that it equipped individuals to read and understand the Bible's message of salvation. *(Ch. 7)*

Augustus (63 B.C.–A.D. 14) Honorific title of Gaius Julius Caesar Octavianus, grandnephew of **Julius Caesar** and first Roman emperor. After defeating Mark Antony and Cleopatra at the Battle of Actium (31 B.C.), Augustus ruled the empire for forty-five years. His rule laid the foundations of two hundred years of prosperous Roman peace. See also **Principate.** *(Ch. 6)*

Auschwitz-Birkenau The largest and principal extermination center of Nazi Germany's six death camps, all of which were located in what had been Poland. The Nazis shipped Jews from all over Europe to Auschwitz, which killed about twelve thousand people a day at the height of its operation in 1944. *(Ch. 28)*

avant-garde French for "forefront," the term refers to early-twentieth-century artists who, inspired by novel or unconventional techniques, considered themselves precursors of new styles. Avant-garde movements proclaimed idiosyncratic manifestos and constantly called for the rejection of existing forms of expression and the creation of new ones. *(Ch. 24)*

Aztecs Amerindian people that dominated central Mexico from the fourteenth through the sixteenth centuries from their capital Tenochtitlán (present-day Mexico City). Weakened by exposure to virulent Old World diseases, they were conquered in 1521–1523 by Spanish forces led by **Hernán Cortés.** *(Ch. 13)*

Babylonian Captivity of the Papacy Term used to describe the period from 1308 to 1378 when popes resided north of the Alps rather than in central Italy or Rome, where the pope was the bishop. The term refers to the period when the tribes of Israel lived in exile. *(Ch. 11)*

Bacon, Francis (1561–1626) England's lord chancellor during the reign of James I and author of a utopian essay extolling science's benefits for a peaceful society and human happiness. His influential works encouraged the empirical method and inductive reasoning. See also **empirical method.** *(Ch. 17)*

barbarian kingship Central institution in a succession of kingdoms (ca. 300–600) ruled by barbarian (non-Roman) leaders, which evolved from former Roman provinces. Most such kings had been political or military leaders under Roman authority before becoming independent rulers. *(Ch. 7)*

baroque Style of European art and architecture popular from the late sixteenth to early eighteenth century. Baroque artists, such as Peter Paul Rubens, modified Renaissance techniques, adding dynamism and emotional energy. Baroque painting used light to portray dramatic illusion, and baroque churches were both impressively grand and emotionally engaging. *(Ch. 15)*

Bauhaus An influential German art school, founded in 1919, that sought to adopt contemporary materials to develop new forms of architecture, design, and urban planning in response to the cultural uncertainty that followed World War I. Though it arguably failed in its immediate German context, the Bauhaus helped shape the whole idea of "the modern" in the West and throughout the world for decades to come. *(Ch. 26)*

Bernard of Clairvaux (1090–1153) Monk, church reformer, and influential adviser to kings and popes. Bernard believed that faith and divine inspiration were more important than dialectical reasoning. He was instrumental in the success of the Cistercian religious order. *(Ch. 10)*

Bismarck, Otto von (1815–1898) Nineteenth-century German statesman. A Prussian aristocrat, Bismarck was the autocratic architect who, through a series of aggressive wars, united Germany and served as the nation's first chancellor. He administered an emperor-controlled country that became the dominant power in Europe. See also **Realpolitik.** *(Ch. 22)*

Black Death (1348–1351) First of a series of epidemics, probably bubonic plague, that raged in Europe and western Asia for three centuries. The Black Death killed about 60 percent of those infected. The huge population decline fueled the economic and social transformations of the late Middle Ages. *(Ch. 11)*

Bolsheviks Members of a faction of the Russian Socialist Party led by **Vladimir Ilich Lenin** (1870–1924), a zealous Marxist who insisted that a revolutionary cadre could seize power on behalf of the working class. The Bolsheviks gained control of Russia in November 1917. *(Ch. 24)*

Bonaparte, Napoleon. See **Napoleon Bonaparte.**

bourgeois century Characterization of the nineteenth century, especially the latter half. In western Europe, the bourgeois elites (middle classes), which had expanded dramatically in the wake of industrialization, helped fashion much of society. *(Ch. 23)*

Brandenburg-Prussia Group of German territories ruled by the Hohenzollern family that became one of Europe's most powerful states in the seventeenth century. Its military strength was supported by its hereditary landowners, who were granted autonomy in their territories. *(Ch. 16)*

Brandt, Willy (1913–1992) Socialist West German chancellor (r. 1969–1974). Brandt's widely popular policy of opening to the East, or *Ostpolitik,* made possible closer economic ties between West and East Germany and broader opportunities for ordinary citizens to interact across the east-west border. *(Ch. 29)*

Brest-Litovsk, Treaty of (1918) Treaty in which Russia accepted its defeat by Germany and its allies in World War I. The treaty forced the Russians to cede much of European Russia to Germany. After Germany's defeat by the Allies later in the year, the **Bolsheviks** recaptured Ukraine and the Caucasus region. *(Ch. 25)*

British blockade Britain's naval blockade of Germany during World War I. By means of this tactic, which cut off supplies to Germany but which also violated several provisions of international law, the British seriously impeded the German war effort. *(Ch. 25)*

Caesar, Gaius Julius (100–44 B.C.) Roman general gifted at war and politics. Named dictator in 49 B.C., he was assassinated by the members of the **senate** in 44 B.C. He introduced to Europe the calendar of 365¼ days. He was succeeded as ruler by his grandnephew Octavian (**Augustus**). Later Roman emperors were also called *caesar.* *(Ch. 5)*

caliphate Arab empire established by the successors of **Muhammad;** *caliph* means "successor to the prophet." The Umayyad caliphate, with its capital in Damascus, ruled from 661 to 750; the Abbasid caliphate, based in Baghdad, from 750 to 1258. *(Ch. 8)*

Calvin, John (1509–1564) Franco-Swiss theologian and founder of the Reformed Church in Geneva. Calvin's theological writings, most notably *Institutes of the Christian Religion* (1536), were widely disseminated and hugely influential. Calvin stressed the absolute power of God and the need for moral reform of the Christian community. *(Ch. 14)*

canon law   Collection of orderly rules for the government of the Catholic Church, based on papal decrees and decisions of church councils. In 1140 the monk Gratian published the *Decretum,* the first systematic collection of canon law. *(Ch. 10)*

Carlowitz, Treaty of (1699)   Treaty imposed by the European allies on a weakening Ottoman Empire. The Habsburgs, Venetians, Russians, and Poles gained territory and power at the Turks' expense. *(Ch. 16)*

Carolingian Renaissance   Major revival of learning, combined with reform of religious and political institutions, that occurred under **Charlemagne** and his successors. The revival encompassed the founding of schools in religious institutions, production of textbooks, dissemination of early church teachings and of **canon law,** as well as secular reforms such as regularization of royal estates. *(Ch. 8)*

Catherine the Great (r. 1762–1796)   Empress of Russia. Through an astute policy of wars and alliances, Catherine expanded her country's borders south to the Black Sea and west into Europe. An "enlightened despot," she advanced the westernizing reforms begun by **Peter the Great.** *(Ch. 18)*

Cato the Censor (234–149 B.C.)   Marcus Portius Cato, Roman general and statesman. Known as Cato the Censor because he denounced luxury goods, he was the first Roman historian to write in Latin. *(Ch. 5)*

Charlemagne   Frankish king (r. 768–814), crowned emperor in 800. He carried out a program of legal and ecclesiastical reform, patronized learning, and revitalized the western Roman Empire. See also **Carolingian Renaissance.** *(Ch. 8)*

Charles V (r. 1519–1558)   Holy Roman emperor and, as Charles I, king of Spain. His empire included Spain, Italy, the Low Countries, and Germany. Though he vigorously opposed the spread of Protestantism during the Reformation, he was forced to sign the Religious Peace of Augsburg in 1555, which acknowledged the right of German princes to choose the religion to be practiced in their territories, Lutheran or Catholic. Charles abdicated his imperial and royal titles the next year, ceding the empire to his brother Ferdinand and his Spanish possessions to his son **Philip II.** *(Ch. 14)*

Chartism   Nineteenth-century British political movement whose goal was to transform Britain from an oligarchy to a democracy. The Chartists' demands were contained in the 1838 "people's charter," which called for universal male suffrage, electoral districts with equal population, salaries and the abolition of property qualifications for Members of Parliament, the secret ballot, and annual general elections. The movement failed, but most of its measures eventually became law. See also **Second Reform Bill.** *(Ch. 21)*

chivalry   Initially, a medieval code of conduct for mounted warriors, focusing on military prowess, open-handed generosity, and earning a glorious reputation. Later it evolved into an elaborate set of rules governing relations between men and women. *(Ch. 10)*

Christianity   Sect originally rooted in Judaism that emerged as a fully separate religion by around A.D. 200. Emphasizing belief in one God and the mission of his son, **Jesus of Nazareth,** as savior, Christianity offered salvation in the next world and a caring community in the present one. A mes-sianic religion, Christianity emphasized Christ's return, leading to the beginning of a heavenly kingdom on earth. *(Ch. 6)*

Churchill, Winston (1874–1965)   British prime minister (1940–1945; 1951–1955). As the leader of his country during World War II, Churchill's courage, decisiveness, memorable words, and boundless energy made him widely seen as one of Britain's greatest leaders of the twentieth century. See also **Yalta conference.** *(Ch. 28)*

Cicero, Marcus Tullius (106–43 B.C.)   Philosopher, writer, and statesman who was Rome's greatest orator. He was crucial in making the Latin language a vessel for the heritage of Greek thought. *(Ch. 5)*

city-state   State consisting of an independent city and the surrounding territory under its control. Early examples were the Sumerian city-states in the third millennium B.C. *(Ch. 1)*

civic humanism   An ideology, championed by Florentine writers and public officials during the Renaissance, that emphasized their city's classical republican virtues and history. They argued that a moral and ethical value was intrinsic to public life. *(Ch. 12)*

Civil Code   Law code established under Napoleon in 1801 that included limited acceptance of revolutionary gains, such as a guarantee of equality before the law and taxation of all social classes. Also known as the Napoleonic Code, it enshrined modern forms of property ownership and civil contracts, enhanced paternal control of families, outlawed divorce in most circumstances, and placed women under the legal domination of fathers and husbands. *(Ch. 19)*

Classical Greece   Period of ancient Greek history from about 480 to 323 B.C. Classical Greek culture emphasized public life as the central theme of art and literature, and its sculpture was the most anatomically precise yet. Classical Greece set many standards for modern Western culture. See also **demokratia.** *(Ch. 3)*

Cluny (Cluniacs)   A spiritual reform begun in 910 in central France. The movement emphasized strict adherence to the Benedictine Rule, as well as the ideas that the church should pray for the world without being deeply involved in it and must be free from lay control. *(Ch. 10)*

cold war   The hostile standoff between the Soviet Union and the United States that began after World War II, when communist governments, relying on Soviet support, took control of most of east-central Europe. The Soviets' first atomic bomb explosion in 1949 intensified the conflict, which shaped world affairs for the next forty years. *(Ch. 28)*

collectivization   The program that reshaped agriculture in the Soviet Union under **Joseph Stalin** during the early 1930s. By forcing peasants into government-controlled collective farms, the Soviet regime sought to take control of agricultural production in order better to finance rapid industrialization. *(Ch. 27)*

Columbian Exchange   Historians' term for the blending of cultures between the Old World and the New after Christopher Columbus's arrival in the New World in 1492. The Spanish and other Europeans brought their plants, domesticated animals, and diseases to the Americas. The Americas contributed New World crops, most notably maize (corn) and potatoes, transforming the Old World diet. *(Ch. 13)*

Comintern (Third, or Communist, International)   An association founded in March 1919 by the communists (formerly

Bolsheviks) to translate their success in Russia into leadership of the international socialist movement. Its program of tight organization and discipline under Russian leadership produced a schism between communists and socialists in Europe and throughout the world. *(Ch. 26)*

Common Agricultural Policy (CAP) A major pillar of the **European Union,** accounting for half of its budget by 2000, the Common Agricultural Policy entailed subsidies to protect farmers from outside competition. The CAP was widely criticized by advocates of freer world trade. *(Ch. 30)*

communes Form of government in Italian towns that rose in the eleventh century. Despite numerous local variations, communes involved common decision making by local notables, including both landed aristocrats and wealthy merchants or industrialists. *(Ch. 9)*

Compromise of 1867 Agreement that divided the Habsburg Empire into Austria in the west and Hungary in the east, a dual monarchy under Emperor Franz Joseph called Austria-Hungary. The compromise confirmed Magyar dominance in Hungary. *(Ch. 22)*

conciliarists These people argued that the pope was not a universal monarch, but rather the first among equals in the Church. Thus, church councils had the right and duty to reform and correct even the pope. *(Ch. 11)*

congress system System of European international relations in the first half of the nineteenth century in which the major European states cooperated to preserve the balance of power. This system disappeared as political leaders increasingly used force to pursue their narrow interests. *(Ch. 22)*

Congress of Vienna (1814–1815) Conference called by the victorious powers—Austria, Great Britain, Prussia, and Russia—who defeated Napoleon. Guided by the Austrian foreign minister, Prince Metternich, the Great Powers drew new territorial boundaries advantageous to themselves. They also attempted to provide long-term stability on the European continent and restored some of the rulers who had been overthrown. See also **congress system.** *(Ch. 21)*

conservatism Ideology underlying the order established in Europe in 1815. Conservatives emphasized resistance to change and preservation of the existing order of monarchy, aristocracy, and an established church. *(Ch. 21)*

Copernicus, Nicholas (1473–1543) Polish astronomer who initiated the Scientific Revolution by proposing that the earth and other planets orbit the sun, a theory called the heliocentric, or sun-centered, system. See also **heliocentric theory.** *(Ch. 17)*

corporative state, corporativism The system established in fascist Italy beginning in 1926 that sought to involve people in public life not as citizens but as producers, through their roles in the economy. A system based on such occupational groupings eventually replaced parliament as the basis of political representation in fascist Italy. *(Ch. 26)*

Cortés, Hernán (1485–1546) Spanish commander who conquered the **Aztecs** and claimed the Valley of Mexico for Spain. Cortés had only five hundred men but was aided by an outbreak of smallpox and the help of Amerindian peoples eager to end Aztec control. *(Ch. 13)*

Cossacks Originally the term (from a Russian word meaning "free man" or "adventurer") for peoples of Tater origin who inhabited the hinterland of the Black and Caspian seas. Their numbers swelled, after 1500, by peasants who fled serfdom in Poland-Lithuania and the growing Russian state. The Cossacks helped to provide a military buffer between the Polish-Lithuanian and Russian states and the Ottomans to the south, and resisted Polish domination in the seventeenth century, but slowly lost their autonomy to the expanding Russian state in the eighteenth century. *(Ch. 16)*

Council of Constance (1414–1418) Assembly convened by Holy Roman Emperor Sigismund to heal deep religious and civil divisions. The council declared that its rulings were binding even on the pope. Its selection of Pope Martin V ended the **Great Schism.** *(Ch. 11)*

Council of the Indies Body established by the king of Spain in 1524 to oversee Spain's colonial possessions. Located at court, eventually in Madrid, it supervised all legal, administrative, and commercial activity in the colonies until the early eighteenth century. *(Ch. 13)*

Council of Nicaea (325) History's first ecumenical, or "all-church," council, convened by the emperor Constantine. The council condemned **Arianism** and proclaimed key elements of the Nicene Creed, especially the doctrine that Christ was "one in being with the Father," co-equal and co-eternal. *(Ch. 7)*

Council of Trent (1545–1563) Ecumenical council of the Roman Catholic Church during the Reformation. Though rejecting many Protestant positions, the council reformed and reorganized the church partly in response to Protestant criticisms. Its decrees reaffirmed and defined the basic tenets of Roman Catholicism for the next four hundred years. *(Ch. 14)*

covenant As told in the Hebrew Bible, the pact God made with Abraham, the first patriarch of **Israel.** In return for the land of Canaan and the promise of becoming a great nation, the Israelites agreed to worship no other gods. *(Ch. 2)*

Cromwell, Oliver (1599–1658) English Puritan general and statesman. A military genius and leader in the English Civil War, Cromwell governed as Lord Protector during the Interregnum from 1653 to 1658. *(Ch. 16)*

Crusades (1095–1270) A series of largely unsuccessful wars waged by western European Christians to recapture the Holy Land from the Muslims and ensure the safety of Christian pilgrims to Jerusalem. Later, the term came to designate any military effort by Europeans against non-Christians. *(Ch. 9)*

Crystal Night (*Kristallnacht*) Organized Nazi assault on Jewish businesses and synagogues during the night of November 9–10, 1938, following the assassination of a German diplomat in Paris. Almost all the synagogues in Germany and about seven thousand Jewish-owned stores were destroyed. The broken shop windows gave the episode its name. Although the German public generally deplored this wanton destruction of property, the Crystal Night pogrom initiated a more radical phase of Nazi anti-Jewish policy. *(Ch. 27)*

cuneiform First writing system in Mesopotamia, consisting of wedge-shaped impressions in soft clay. Named from the Latin word for "wedge-shaped," it was developed about 3500–3100 B.C. *(Ch. 1)*

Darwinism Profoundly influential theory of biological evolution, first put forth by Charles Darwin (1809–1882). He proposed that all forms of life continuously develop through natural selection, whereby those that are better adapted to the environment have the advantage and are more likely to survive and pass on their beneficial traits to their offspring. *(Ch. 23)*

D-Day The complex Allied amphibious landings in Normandy, France, on June 6, 1944, that opened a second major European front in World War II. In the aftermath of this invasion, American-led forces in the west began moving toward Germany, completing the Soviet effort, which was already forcing the Germans back on the eastern front. *(Ch. 28)*

Decembrists Group of Russian military officers who led the December 1825 rebellion after the death of Tsar Alexander I, seeking to install a constitutional monarchy with Alexander's eldest brother, Constantine, as tsar. They were defeated and executed by Constantine's younger brother, Nicholas. The Decembrists were seen as martyrs by later Russian revolutionaries. *(Ch. 21)*

Declaration of the Rights of Man and the Citizen (1789) Document issued by the **National Assembly** of France in August 1789. Modeled on the U.S. Constitution, the declaration set forth the basis for the new French government and asserted "the natural, inalienable and sacred rights of man." *(Ch. 19)*

De Gaulle, Charles (1890–1970) The youngest general in the French army, he called on French forces to follow his lead and continue the fight against Nazi Germany after the fall of France in June 1940. As the leader of the new Free French force that emerged thereafter, he won renewed respect for France as a major power and sought to exercise political leadership after France's liberation in 1944. Though he retired from public life in 1946, disillusioned with politics, he returned in 1958 to spearhead the creation of the new Fifth Republic. He served as its president from 1958 to 1969. *(Ch. 28)*

demokratia Term coined in Athens in the fifth century B.C. to describe the city's system of direct government. It means "the power *(kratos)* of the people *(demos)*." Athenian society pioneered today's key democratic principles, including freedom, equality, universal citizenship, and the rule of law. *(Ch. 3)*

Descartes, René (1596–1650) French philosopher, scientist, and mathematician. Descartes emphasized skepticism and deductive reasoning in his most influential treatise, *Discourse on Method.* He offered the first alternative physical explanation of matter after the Copernican revolution. *(Ch. 17)*

digital divide A term for the disparity in access to the computing and Internet technologies that seemed essential to compete in the twenty-first-century global economy. It was one way that new technologies were widening the gap between the world's haves and have-nots. *(Ch. 30)*

Directory French revolutionary government from 1795 to 1799, consisting of an executive council of five men chosen by the upper house of the legislature. It was overthrown in a coup led by **Napoleon Bonaparte.** *(Ch. 19)*

Dominic Dominic de Guzman (1170–1221), Spanish priest and founder of the spiritually influential Dominican mendicant order. The order was known for the irreproachable life of its members, its learning, and its desire to emulate the apostolic life of the early church by poverty and preaching. *(Ch. 10)*

Dutch East India Company Commercially innovative Dutch company formed in 1602 that combined government management of trade with both public and private investment.

The formation of the company created a permanent pool of capital to sustain trade and resulted in a dramatic expansion of commerce with Asia. *(Ch. 16)*

Edict of Milan (313) Proclamation issued primarily by Emperor Constantine that made Christianity a legal religion in the Roman Empire. Constantine promoted the Christian church, granting it tax immunities and relieving the clergy of military service. *(Ch. 7)*

Edict of Nantes (1598) Edict of Henry IV granting France's Protestants **(Huguenots)** the right to practice their faith and maintain defensive garrisons. They were also guaranteed access to schools, hospitals, royal appointments, and separate judicial institutions. The edict was revoked by **Louis XIV** in 1685. *(Ch. 15)*

Elizabeth I (r. 1558–1603) First woman to occupy the English throne successfully. Elizabeth's adroit rule brought stability to England after the turmoil of previous reigns. She firmly established Protestantism in England, encouraged English commerce, defended the nation against the Spanish **Armada,** and fostered the English Renaissance in poetry and drama. *(Ch. 15)*

empirical method Philosophical view developed by the seventeenth-century English philosophers **Francis Bacon** and **John Locke,** asserting that all knowledge is based on observation and experimentation and that general principles should be derived from particular facts. *(Ch. 17)*

encomienda A Spanish royal grant of protectorship over a group of Amerindians. The receivers of the grants (encomenderos) were obliged to Christianize the people under their charge, but instead most forced the natives to work as virtual slaves in mines and on Spanish lands. See also **Bartolomé de Las Casas.** *(Ch. 13)*

enlightened despotism Term for the reform-oriented rule of eighteenth-century monarchs such as **Frederick the Great,** Joseph II of Austria, and **Catherine the Great.** Enlightened despots applied Enlightenment remedies to economic problems, encouraged education and legal reform, and improved agricultural productivity by enabling some peasants to own the land they worked. *(Ch. 18)*

entrepreneurs People who assume the risks of organizing and investing in a new business venture. Entrepreneurship is closely connected with the inventions and innovations made during the industrial age. *(Ch. 20)*

Epicureans Adherents of the Athenian philosopher Epicurus (341–270 B.C.), who taught that the soul is made up of atoms that do not exist after death. Epicureans emphasized the avoidance of pain and the pursuit of intellectual pleasure. *(Ch. 4)*

Erasmus, Desiderius (1466–1536) Prominent Dutch humanist during the Renaissance, best known for his satire *Praise of Folly.* Erasmus's works reinterpreted Greek and Roman wisdom and emphasized tolerance, reason, and faith in the goodness and educability of the individual. *(Ch. 12)*

ethnic cleansing A term describing attempts to remove an unwanted ethnic group from an area, which can include forced relocation and mass killing. Beginning in 1991, this tactic was implemented by Yugoslavian ruler Slobodan Milosevic (b. 1941) to unite all Serbs, many of whom lived in neighboring Croatia, Bosnia-Herzegovina, and **Kosovo.** *(Ch. 30)*

Etruscans Inhabitants of twelve loosely confederated city-states north of Rome in Etruria that flourished in the seventh to sixth centuries B.C. They were conquered by the Romans by the early third century B.C. *(Ch. 5)*

euro The common currency launched by the **European Union** in 1999 to eliminate the cost of currency exchange and boost trade and economic interaction. As of January 1, 2002, it replaced the national currencies of the participating countries (the "Eurozone"). *(Ch. 30)*

European Economic Community (EEC) (1957–1967) Common market formed by Belgium, France, West Germany, Italy, Luxembourg, and the Netherlands to promote free trade. The EEC was replaced by the European Community (EC) in 1967. *(Ch. 29)*

European Union (EU) New name for the European Community after the **Maastricht agreement** of 1991. By 2001 the European Union had nine members in addition to the original six members of the **European Economic Community:** Britain, Denmark, Ireland (joined 1973); Greece (joined 1981); Portugal, Spain (joined 1985); and Austria, Finland, Sweden (joined 1995). See also **euro.** *(Ch. 30)*

"euthanasia" program The Nazi program of systematically killing people, overwhelmingly ethnic Germans, whom the Nazis deemed superfluous or threatening to the German racial health. Victims included chronic mental patients, the incurably ill, and people with severe physical handicaps. Initiated in 1939, the program had claimed 100,000 lives by the time it was discontinued in 1941. *(Ch. 27)*

existentialism A philosophical and cultural movement, influential from the late 1940s into the 1950s, that explored life in a world cast adrift from its cultural moorings. Highly influential were the Frenchmen Jean Paul Sartre (1905–1980) and Albert Camus (1913–1960), for whom an authentic human response to an apparently meaningless universe entailed commitment and responsibility. *(Ch. 29)*

factories Centralized workplaces where a number of people cooperate to mass-produce goods. The first factories of industrializing Europe were made possible by the development of the **steam engine** as a central power source. The mechanized production of factories led to huge productivity increases in the nineteenth century. See also **industrialization, mass production.** *(Ch. 20)*

fascism A violent, antidemocratic movement founded by **Benito Mussolini** in Italy in 1919. The term is widely used to encompass Hitler's Nazi regime in Germany and other movements stressing disciplined national solidarity and hostile to liberal individualism, the parliamentary system, and Marxist socialism. *(Ch. 26)*

February Patent (1861) Enactment issued in February 1861 by the Austrian emperor Franz Joseph (r. 1848–1916) that established a constitutional monarchy in the old Austrian Empire. The patent guaranteed civil liberties and provided for local self-government and an elected parliament. *(Ch. 22)*

feudal revolution The societal change in tenth-century France from prince-dominated territories with loyal, reliable, but few vassals to the advent of many locally powerful magnates with numerous vassals whose fidelity was uncertain and who primarily provided military service. *(Ch. 9)*

Five Pillars of Islam The basic teachings of Islam: (1) the profession of faith, "There is no God but Allah and **Muhammad** is His Prophet"; (2) individual prayer five times daily, plus group prayers at noon on Friday; (3) the sunup-to-sundown fast during the month of Ramadan; (4) giving generous alms to the poor; and (5) pilgrimage to Mecca at least once in a person's lifetime. *(Ch. 8)*

Flavians Dynasty of the Roman emperors Vespasian (r. 69–79), Titus (r. 79–81), and Domitian (r. 81–96), whose rule was a time of relative peace and good government. Unlike the Julio-Claudians, the Flavians descended from Italian landowners, not old Roman nobility. Domitian persecuted the nobility and was assassinated. *(Ch. 6)*

Fourteen Points Proposals by U.S. president Woodrow Wilson (1856–1924) to guide the new international order that would follow an Allied victory in World War I. Specifics included open diplomacy, free trade, reduced armaments, self-determination for nationalities, and a league of nations. *(Ch. 25)*

Francis of Assisi (1181–1226) Italian monk and founder of a new order of friars ("brothers," from the Latin *fratres*). Francis was born wealthy but adopted a life based on the scriptural ideals of poverty, preaching, and service. His apostolate to the urban poor was highly popular. *(Ch. 10)*

Frankfurt Assembly (1848–1849) Popularly elected national assembly that attempted to create a unified German state. The assembly drew up a constitution and offered the German throne to Friedrich Wilhelm IV, king of Prussia, who declined, fearing a war with Austria and not wanting an office offered by representatives of the people. *(Ch. 21)*

Frederick the Great (r. 1740–1786) Autocratic king of Prussia who transformed the country into a major military power, acquired Polish Prussia, and waged three wars against Austria. He participated in and encouraged the study of philosophy, history, poetry, and French literature. *(Ch. 18)*

Freud, Sigmund (1856–1939) Austrian founder of psychoanalysis, a method of treating psychic disorders by exploring the unconscious. Freud believed that people were motivated in part by their unconscious feelings and drives. He helped call attention to the concept that irrational forces play a significant role in human behavior. *(Ch. 24)*

friendly societies Nineteenth-century organizations formed by workers; members pooled their resources to provide mutual aid. Combining business activity with feasts, drinking bouts, and other social functions, friendly societies promoted group solidarity and a sense of working-class identity. *(Ch. 20)*

G-8 (Group of 8) Originally a Group of Seven, or G-7, this informal association of the world's seven largest economic powers (the United States, Japan, Germany, France, Britain, Italy, and Canada) began meeting during the 1970s in an effort to coordinate economic policies. After the fall of communism, the group added Russia, thereby becoming the G-8. *(Ch. 30)*

Galileo Galilei (1564–1642) Italian physicist and astronomer who provided evidence supporting the **heliocentric theory** of **Nicholas Copernicus** and helped develop the physics of mechanics. His publication of his astronomical observations and his subsequent condemnation by the Catholic Church spurred popular debate and greatly influenced the future of science. *(Ch. 17)*

gentry Class of wealthy, educated, and socially ambitious families in western Europe, especially England, whose political and economic power was greatly enhanced during the sixteenth century. They shared with traditional old-family warrior-aristocrats certain legal privileges, security of landownership, and a cooperative relationship with the monarchy. See also **price revolution.** *(Ch. 15)*

Girondins Political faction during the French Revolution. Republicans and members of the Jacobin Club, the Girondins dominated the French Legislative Assembly when it began to meet in 1791. They favored an activist government but were less radical than other members of the club, called the **Jacobins.** The Girondins were purged from the National Convention in 1793, and many were executed during the **Terror.** *(Ch. 19)*

glasnost Russian term meaning "greater openness." Glasnost was the leading motif in the Great Reforms begun in 1861 by Tsar Alexander II (r. 1855–1881), who sought to strengthen Russia by restructuring its institutions in the wake of defeat in the Crimean War. Glasnost was also part of the reform efforts of **Mikhail Gorbachev** in the Soviet Union during the 1980s. *(Ch. 22)*

Glorious Revolution (1688) Bloodless English revolution in which Parliament replaced the Catholic King James II with William (of Orange) and his wife Mary (James's Protestant daughter). Parliament imposed on the new sovereigns a Bill of Rights that confirmed Parliament's power and protected freedom of speech. *(Ch. 16)*

Golden Bull of 1356 Edict of Holy Roman Emperor Charles IV establishing the method of electing a new emperor. It acknowledged the political autonomy of Germany's seven regional princes. *(Ch. 11)*

Gorbachev, Mikhail (b. 1931) The Soviet Communist Party secretary who, beginning in 1985, attempted to reform the Soviet communist system through arms reduction; liberalization in the satellite states; **glasnost,** or "openness" to discussion and criticism; and *perestroika,* or economic "restructuring." Though widely admired in the West, these measures failed, and Gorbachev ended up presiding over the end of the Soviet communist regime. *(Ch. 29)*

Gothic Period in European architecture, sculpture, and painting from the twelfth to early sixteenth centuries. Gothic architecture was distinguished by the pointed arch, ribbed vault, and point support, which produced a building characterized by verticality and translucency. Examples are the Cathedral of Notre-Dame of Paris and the royal portal at Chartres Cathedral. *(Ch. 10)*

Gracchi Ancient Roman faction led by Tiberius Sempronius Gracchus (163–133 B.C.) and later his brother, Gaius (153–121 B.C.), both of whom were killed by their political opponents. They challenged the conservative **senate** on behalf of the poor. *(Ch. 5)*

"the Great Patriotic War" Term for World War II devised by **Joseph Stalin** to rally Soviet citizens against the German invasion. Stalin appealed to Russian nationalism and recalled past heroic defenses of Russia rather than communist themes. *(Ch. 28)*

Great Reform Bill (1832) British law that broadened the franchise and provided parliamentary seats for new urban areas that had not previously been represented. The bill was a major victory for the government and middle classes over the aristocracy. *(Ch. 21)*

Great Schism (1378–1417) Period during which two, then three, rival popes claimed to rule the Christian Church. The schism ended when the **Council of Constance** deposed all three competing previous popes and elected Martin V as the new pope. *(Ch. 11)*

guilds Merchant groups and associations of crafts and trades established in European cities and towns beginning in the thirteenth century. Guilds expanded greatly during the later Middle Ages. They provided economic benefits, fostered a sense of community, and served as mutual assistance societies. *(Ch. 9)*

gulag Network of 476 forced labor camps for political prisoners in the Soviet Union. The *gulag* (an acronym for "main camp administration") was first used by Lenin in 1918 but was greatly expanded by **Joseph Stalin** in the 1930s. *(Ch. 27)*

Gutenberg, Johann (ca. 1399–1468) German inventor of movable metal type. His innovations led to the publication of the first printed book in Europe, the Gutenberg Bible, in the 1450s. Printed books and broadsheets played a critical role in disseminating the ideas of the Renaissance and the Reformation. *(Ch. 12)*

Hagia Sophia Largest Christian church ever built, constructed in Constantinople from 532 to 537 for the Roman emperor **Justinian.** The church consists of two intersecting rectangular basilicas that incorporate arches; the whole is surmounted by a huge dome. *(Ch. 7)*

Hanseatic League Late medieval association of over a hundred trading cities, centered on the German city of Lübeck. The league dominated coastal trade in northern Europe from the fourteenth to the fifteenth centuries, until Dutch, English, and south German merchants finally gained shares of the wool, grain, and fur trades. *(Ch. 11)*

heliocentric theory Theory advanced by **Nicholas Copernicus** that the earth and other planets orbit the sun. Supported by the scientific and mathematical discoveries of **Johannes Kepler** and **Galileo Galilei,** heliocentrism, which means "sun-centered," won acceptance by the end of the seventeenth century. *(Ch. 17)*

Hellenism Term used to designate ancient Greece's language, culture, and civilization, especially after **Alexander the Great** spread them to other parts of the Mediterranean, western Asia, and North Africa. *(Ch. 4)*

Helsinki Accords (1975) Agreements signed by thirty-five countries in Helsinki, Finland, that committed the signatories to recognize existing borders, to increase economic and environmental cooperation, and to promote freedom of expression, religion, and travel. Dissidents in Soviet bloc countries soon fastened on these provisions to highlight the lack of human rights and to discredit the ruling communist governments. *(Ch. 29)*

Henry VIII (r. 1509–1547) King of England. Initially a defender of traditional Christianity, Henry broke with the papacy over the issue of his divorce. He needed a divorce, he argued, in order to marry a younger woman who might be able to produce a male heir to the kingdom. As a result of the dispute, Henry supported Reformers in the English Church. *(Ch. 14)*

Henry "the Navigator" (1394–1460) Portuguese prince and director of Portugal's exploration and colonization of Africa's western coast. The Portuguese quickly established trading stations in the region, laying the foundations for their overseas empire. *(Ch. 13)*

Herodotus (ca. 485–425 B.C.) Ancient Greek historian; with **Thucydides,** a founder of history-writing in the West. The word *history* comes from a word used by Herodotus, *historiai,* meaning "inquiries" or "research." In his history of the Persian Wars, Herodotus saw the fall of the Persian Empire as part of a perpetual cycle of the rise and fall of empires. *(Ch. 3)*

Hildegard of Bingen (1098–1179) German abbess who was perhaps the most profound psychological thinker of her age. More than anyone before her, Hildegard opened up for discussion the feminine aspects of divinity. She was also adept in music and biblical studies. *(Ch. 10)*

Hitler, Adolf (1889–1945) The German dictator who, after being legally named chancellor in 1933, militarized Germany and started World War II in 1939, leading the country to defeat in 1945. His enforcement of state-sponsored **anti-Semitism** and racial purity among German people led to the murder of millions of Jews, Gypsies, and Slavic peoples. *(Ch. 27)*

Hobbes, Thomas (1588–1679) English philosopher. In his treatise *Leviathan,* Hobbes asserted that people are made up of mechanistic appetites and so need a strong ruler to hold them in check. However, he also envisioned citizens as potentially equal and constrained neither by morality nor by natural obedience to authority. *(Ch. 17)*

Homer Greatest ancient Greek poet, credited as the author of the epics the *Iliad* and the *Odyssey,* both written during the eighth century B.C. His dramatic stories inspired, moved, and educated the Greeks. *(Ch. 2)*

hominids The primate family *Hominidae,* which includes humans. The modern human being, *Homo sapiens sapiens,* is the only species of this family still in existence. *(Ch. 1)*

hoplite phalanx Battlefield tactic of **Archaic Greece** that relied on a tightly ordered unit of heavily armed, pike-bearing infantrymen. It was the dominant military force in western Asia and the Mediterranean region until 197 B.C. *(Ch. 3)*

Huguenots French Protestants, followers of the teachings of **John Calvin.** Huguenots battled Catholics throughout the sixteenth and seventeenth centuries. Many emigrated to other western European countries and England's American colonies, especially after the revocation of the **Edict of Nantes.** French Protestants gained full religious freedom in the nineteenth century. *(Ch. 15)*

humanism Western European literary and cultural movement of the fourteenth and fifteenth centuries. Humanists emphasized the superiority of ancient Greek and Roman literature, history, and politics, and focused on learning and personal and public duty. See also **Desiderius Erasmus, Francesco Petrarch, Thomas More.** *(Ch. 12)*

Hundred Years' War (1337–1453) Series of conflicts between the ruling families of France and England over territory in France and the succession to the French crown. Sporadic raids and battles devastated the French countryside and checked population growth. The inspirational leadership of **Joan of Arc** contributed to France's eventual success in expelling the English from nearly all of the disputed land. *(Ch. 11)*

hunter-gatherers Food-collecting society in which people live by hunting, fishing, and gathering fruits and nuts, with no crops or livestock being raised for food. During the **Neolithic Revolution,** some hunter-gatherers developed agriculture. *(Ch. 1)*

Hus, Jan (ca. 1370–1415) Czech religious reformer who strongly attacked clerical power and privileges and advocated reform of church practice. His execution for heresy at the **Council of Constance** provoked a civil war in Prague and Bohemia. *(Ch. 11)*

iconoclasm Rejection of, or even the destruction of, religious images in worship. Iconoclasm was the official policy of the Byzantine Empire from 726 to 843 and played a role in the continuing estrangement of Byzantium from the West. *(Ch. 8)*

impressionism Late-nineteenth-century style of painting pioneered by the French artists Degas, Monet, Pissarro, Renoir, Sisley, and Morisot. Influenced by new theories that images were transmitted to the brain as small light particles, which the brain then reconstituted, the impressionists sought to capture what things looked like before they were "distorted" by the brain. *(Ch. 23)*

Inca A flourishing sixteenth-century empire administered from the mountains of Peru and extending from modern Ecuador to Chile. It was conquered for Spain by Francisco Pizzaro (1470–1541), aided by a smallpox epidemic and native peoples seeking to end Inca domination. *(Ch. 13)*

Index of Prohibited Books A list of books banned by the Roman Catholic Church because of moral or doctrinal error. First announced in 1559, it was only sporadically enforced and had little effect. The Index was suppressed in 1966. *(Ch. 14)*

industrialization Beginning in Britain in the later eighteenth century, a system of **mass production** of goods in which specialization and mechanization made manufacturing efficient and profitable. Early industrialization enabled Britain to become the dominant world power in the nineteenth century. See also **factories.** *(Ch. 20)*

information technology Term for the revolution in information availability and communications resulting from the late-twentieth-century development of personal computers and the Internet. See also **digital divide.** *(Ch. 30)*

Interregnum (1649–1660) Literally "between reigns," the period in English history from the execution of Charles I to the restoration of Charles II. During these years England was a republic—a Commonwealth—ruled by **Oliver Cromwell,** who became Lord Protector in 1653. *(Ch. 16)*

iron curtain Term used by Winston Churchill in a speech on March 5, 1946, to warn that, thanks to Soviet policy, a formidable de facto barrier was emerging in Europe, cutting the Soviet sphere off from the West and threatening the long-term division of the continent. Though the term was not coined by Churchill, his phrasing dramatically affected public opinion in the west. The "iron curtain" suggested both the division of Europe and Soviet culpability throughout the cold war period. *(Ch. 28)*

Israel People who settled on the eastern shore of the Mediterranean around 1200 B.C., or perhaps earlier. Their belief in one God directly influenced the faith of Christians, Muslims, and modern Jews. See also **monotheism.** *(Ch. 2)*

Ivan IV, "the Terrible" (r. 1533–1584) First Russian ruler routinely to use the title "tsar" (Russian for "Caesar"), he presided over the expansion and centralization of the Russian state. Ivan continued Moscow's expansion, begun by his grandfather Ivan III, south and east against Mongol-controlled states. Under Ivan IV, Russians moved east across Siberia for the first time. Within his expanding empire, Ivan ruled as an autocrat; he was able to bypass noble participation and intensify the centralization of government by creating ranks of officials loyal only to himself. *(Ch. 15)*

Jacobins In revolutionary France, a political club named for a monastic order. One of the most radical of republican groups, the Jacobins purged the **Girondins,** originally fellow members of the club, from the National Convention in 1793.

Leaders of the **Terror,** such as **Maximilien Robespierre,** came from their ranks. *(Ch. 19)*

Jesus of Nazareth (ca. 4 B.C.–A.D. 30) Founder of **Christianity.** A forceful preacher and reformer who, to his followers, was Christ, "the anointed one" (from the Greek *Christos*), foretold in the Hebrew Bible as the redeemer of Israel who would initiate the kingdom of heaven. The dynamism and popularity of his teachings led to a clash with Jewish and Roman authorities in Jerusalem and to his crucifixion by the Romans. *(Ch. 6)*

Joan of Arc (d. 1431) Charismatic French military leader during the **Hundred Years' War.** A late medieval mystic, Joan heard "voices" telling her to assist in driving the English from France. She was captured and burned as a heretic by the English. Later she was canonized as Saint Joan, patron saint of France. *(Ch. 11)*

Julio-Claudians Dynasty of Roman emperors founded by **Augustus** and ruling from A.D. 14 to 68. The succession consisted of Augustus's stepson Tiberius, great-grandson Caligula, grandnephew Claudius, and great-great-grandson Nero. For elite Romans, this era was one of decadence and scandal; for ordinary people, it was a time of stability and peace. *(Ch. 6)*

July Revolution (1830) Uprising in Paris in July 1830 that forced King Charles X to abdicate and signaled a victory for constitutional reform over an absolute monarchy. The liberal Louis Philippe was proclaimed "King of the French," with limited powers, by the chamber of deputies. The revolution sparked democratic uprisings in Belgium, Germany, Italy, and Russian Poland and helped persuade British peers to vote for the **Great Reform Bill.** *(Ch. 21)*

justification by faith Doctrine professed by **Martin Luther** that Christians can be saved (justified) only by faith, a free gift of God, and not by penitential acts or good works. Luther's doctrine directly challenged the authority and fundamental practices of the Roman Catholic Church. *(Ch. 14)*

Justinian (r. 527–565) One of the greatest of all Rome's emperors. His comprehensive collection of Roman law is the most influential legal collection in human history. He built **Hagia Sophia,** reformed the imperial administration, and fought constant wars to expand the empire. *(Ch. 7)*

Kepler, Johannes (1571–1630) German astronomer. Kepler developed the three laws of planetary motion, known as Kepler's Laws, which are still accepted, and mathematically confirmed the Copernican **heliocentric theory.** *(Ch. 17)*

Kriegsrohstoffabteilung (KRA) The "War Raw Materials Office" that coordinated Germany's World War I economy. The KRA produced synthetic substitute products and created new mixed (private and government) companies to allocate raw materials. This body served as a model for later economic planning and coordination in Germany and elsewhere. *(Ch. 25)*

Kristallnacht See **Crystal Night.**

laissez faire French term meaning "to leave alone," it was applied to the economic doctrine put forward by **Adam Smith** in 1776. Smith advocated freeing national economies from the fetters of the state and allowing supply and demand to shape the marketplace. Laissez-faire ideas contributed to the drive to lower tariffs in the nineteenth century. See also **liberalism.** *(Ch. 21)*

Las Casas, Bartolomé de (1474–1566) First bishop of Chiapas, in southern Mexico. A former *encomendero*, Las Casas passionately condemned the brutality of the Spanish conquests. In 1542 King Charles accepted Las Casas's criticisms, abolishing Indian slavery and greatly restricting the transfer of **encomiendas.** *(Ch. 13)*

Latin Indo-European language of ancient Rome and its empire, from which today's Romance languages developed. *(Ch. 5)*

laws of motion The natural laws of gravity, planetary motion, and inertia first laid out in the seventeenth century by **Isaac Newton.** Newton demonstrated that these laws apply to the solar system and could be used to predict the existence of an as-yet-unseen planet. *(Ch. 17)*

lay investiture Control of church appointments by laymen. Emperor Henry IV (1066–1106) and Pope Gregory VII (1073–1085) disputed who should have this authority in the Christian world. The 1122 Concordat of Worms stipulated that bishops could be invested by kings only after a free church election. *(Ch. 9)*

League of Nations (1919–1946) An international alliance established at the end of World War I without the membership of the United States. Though its covenant called for the peaceful settlement of disputes among member states and for sanctions against a member that went to war in violation of League provisions, it failed to prevent the escalating violence that culminated in World War II. *(Ch. 25)*

legion Innovative and highly successful ancient Roman battle formation. The legion included many flexible, adaptable, and semi-independent groups that broke their enemies' order with javelins at long range, then charged with sword and shield. *(Ch. 5)*

Lend-Lease Act (1941) Act by the U.S. Congress authorizing President **Franklin Roosevelt** to lend or lease weapons or other aid to countries the president designated. A major declaration of American support for the threatened British, lend-lease was later extended to several other countries. *(Ch. 28)*

Lenin, Vladimir Ilyich (1870–1924) Russian revolutionary. Leader of the **Bolsheviks** since 1903, he launched the November 1917 revolution that overthrew the **provisional government.** He concluded the **Treaty of Brest-Litovsk** with Germany and began the establishment of communism in the Soviet Union. See also **New Economic Policy.** *(Ch. 25)*

Leonardo da Vinci (1452–1519) A painter, engineer, and scientist, da Vinci rejected arguments and ideas based on imitation of the ancients. Rather, he advocated careful study of the natural world. *(Ch. 12)*

liberalism Nineteenth-century economic and political theory that called for reducing government powers to a minimum. Liberals worked to impose constitutional limits on government, establish the rule of law, eliminate state regulation of the economy, and ensure a voice in government for men of property and education. *(Ch. 21)*

linear perspective Revolutionary technique developed by early-fifteenth-century Florentine painters for representing three-dimensional objects on a two-dimensional plane. The technique is based in part on the observation that as parallel lines recede, they appear to converge. *(Ch. 12)*

Livia (58 B.C.–A.D. 29) Wife of **Augustus** and mother of Tiberius, his successor. As one of Augustus's main advisers, she intrigued to secure the succession for Tiberius and was suspected of poisoning several family members, including Augustus himself. *(Ch. 6)*

Locarno, Treaty of (1925) Treaty that introduced a new, more conciliatory spirit in international affairs. France and Germany accepted the postwar border between them, and Germany was again accepted as a diplomatic equal and entered the League of Nations in 1926. *(Ch. 26)*

Locke, John (1632–1704) English philosopher. In his influential *Two Treatises of Government,* Locke asserted that the state arises from a contract that individuals freely endorse. Therefore, because sovereignty resides with the people, rebellion against abuse of power is justified—a revolutionary vision of a political society based on human rights. See also **empirical method.** *(Ch. 17)*

Louis XIV (r. 1643–1715) Longest-reigning ruler in European history, who imposed absolute rule on France and waged several wars attempting to dominate Europe. He was known as the Sun King, and his reign marked a great flowering of French culture. *(Ch. 16)*

Loyola, Ignatius (1491–1556) Spanish nobleman and founder of the Society of Jesus, or Jesuits, which has been called the vanguard of the Catholic reform movement. After papal approval of the order, the Jesuits focused primarily on educating Catholics and reconverting Protestants. *(Ch. 14)*

Luddites Organized groups of British workers formed in 1811–1812, who smashed machines and rioted to protest against industrialization, which they felt would threaten their livelihood. The name comes from their mythical leader, General Ned Ludd. *(Ch. 20)*

Luther, Martin (1483–1546) German theologian and religious reformer. Luther began the Protestant Reformation in 1517 with the publication of his *Ninety-Five Theses,* which challenged indulgences and Catholic teachings on penitential acts. His translation of the Bible into German in 1522 standardized the modern German language. See also **Augsburg Confession, justification by faith, sola scriptura.** *(Ch. 14)*

Maastricht agreement (1991) Agreement among twelve European Community countries at Maastricht, the Netherlands, to form the **European Union.** The member states agreed to expand cooperation on social, foreign, judicial, and security matters and adopted a timetable for a common policy on workers' rights, a common currency (the **euro**), and a common central banking structure. *(Ch. 30)*

Maccabees Traditionalist Jews led by the Hasmonean family, who in 168 B.C. revolted against Hellenizing laws and influences. Their success is celebrated today during the Jewish holiday of Hanukkah. *(Ch. 4)*

Macedon Weaker, less culturally advanced state on Greece's northern border. It was unified and led to power by **Philip II** and **Alexander the Great,** who became rulers of Greece. *(Ch. 4)*

Machiavelli, Niccolò (1469–1527) Florentine politician and political theorist. His most famous work, *The Prince,* describes the methods a prince can use to acquire and maintain power. Often misunderstood as a defender of despotism, Machiavelli emphasized that a successful ruler needed to anticipate and consider the consequences of his actions. *(Ch. 12)*

Magellan, Ferdinand (1480?–1521) Portuguese-born Spanish explorer who led the first expedition to sail around the world. After finding the South American passage to the Pacific Ocean, he sailed to the Philippines, where he was killed by natives. Survivors on one of his ships completed the circumnavigation. *(Ch. 13)*

Maginot Line A 200-mile system of elaborate permanent fortifications on France's eastern border, named for war minister André Maginot, and built primarily during the 1930s. It was a defense against German frontal assault; in 1940 the Germans invaded by flanking the line. *(Ch. 26)*

Magna Carta (1215) Momentous document that England's barons forced King John to sign. It required the king to respect the rights of feudal lords, not abuse his judicial powers, and consult the barons—in essence, it put the king under the law, not above it. *(Ch. 9)*

manifest destiny Term coined in 1845 for the belief that the expanding United States was destined to occupy the North American continent from coast to coast. The rhetoric of manifest destiny was invoked to justify war with Mexico in 1846 and the acquisition of California and the southwest from Mexico in 1848. *(Ch. 22)*

manor In western Europe, a type of estate that developed under the Carolingians. One-quarter to one-half of the land was set aside as a reserve (or demesne), to be worked on behalf of the landlord; the remainder was divided into tenancies worked by individual peasants for their own support. *(Ch. 8)*

Maria Theresa (r. 1740–1780) Habsburg archduchess of Austria and queen of Hungary and Bohemia. After successfully defending her right to the Austrian throne against attacks by **Frederick the Great** and others, she reformed and centralized the administration of her Austrian and Bohemian lands. *(Ch. 18)*

Marina, Doña (Malintzin) (1501–1550) An Aztec by birth, she was sold to the Mayas and eventually became a translator and guide for the Spanish. After her critical role in the conquest, she married a Spaniard and lived as a Spanish noblewoman. *(Ch. 13)*

Marxism Political and economic theories of the two German philosophers and revolutionaries, Karl Marx (1818–1883) and Friedrich Engels (1820–1895), which they called scientific **socialism** and which gave birth to modern communism. Marxism argued that the oppressed working class should and inevitably would rebel against the capitalist owners and build a communist society. *(Ch. 21)*

mass production System in which great numbers of people work in centralized, mechanized **factories** to produce large quantities of goods; an essential feature of **industrialization.** A series of eighteenth-century inventions, culminating in the **steam engine,** enabled Britain to mass-produce textiles and benefit from the resulting increases in productivity. *(Ch. 20)*

Matteotti murder The 1924 killing by fascist thugs of Italian moderate socialist Giacomo Matteotti after he denounced the fascist violence accompanying national elections. The public outcry following the murder eventually led **Mussolini** to commit to a more radical direction, which included the creation of a new fascist state. *(Ch. 26)*

mechanistic world-view Seventeenth-century philosophical view that saw the world as a machine that functions in strict obedience to physical laws, without purpose or will. Experience and reason were regarded as the standards of truth. *(Ch. 17)*

Mehmed II (r. 1451–1481) Ottoman sultan who completed the conquest of the Byzantine Empire by capturing Constantinople in 1453. Mehmed established Constantinople as the Ottoman capital and repopulated the city with a mix of Greek, Armenian, Jewish, and Muslim communities. *(Ch. 11)*

mercantilism Economic policy pursued by western European states in the seventeenth and eighteenth centuries, stressing self-sufficiency in manufactured goods, tight government control of trade to foster the domestic economy, protectionist policies, and the absolute value of bullion. *(Ch. 16)*

Minoans Society that flourished between 2000 and 1375 B.C. on the Aegean island of Crete, where Greece's first civilization appeared. Their sophisticated culture and economy were administered from their magnificent palaces. See also **Mycenaeans.** *(Ch. 2)*

mir Russian peasant commune. After Tsar Alexander II freed the serfs in 1861, the mir determined land use and paid the government mortgages and taxes. Peasants could leave the land only with the mir's permission. *(Ch. 22)*

monasticism Ascetic way of life. Christian monasticism was founded by an Egyptian layman, Anthony (d. 356), who renounced all worldliness and pursued a life of prayer in the desert. A more communal form of monasticism was created by Pachomius (290–346), who wrote the first monastic Rule—a code for daily living in a monastic community. Monasticism quickly spread throughout the Christian world. *(Ch. 7)*

Monophysitism Fifth-century theological doctrine emphasizing the divine nature of **Jesus of Nazareth.** The Council of Chalcedon condemned monophysitism and pronounced that Christ had two authentic natures—he was true God and true man. *(Ch. 7)*

monotheism Belief that there is only one God. The Hebrew Bible places this belief as originating about 2000–1500 B.C., when God commanded Abraham to give up Mesopotamian polytheism for belief in one God. *(Ch. 2)*

More, Thomas (1478–1535) Chancellor of England under Henry VIII. More's best-known work, *Utopia,* was highly critical of contemporary European kingdoms. It describes a fictional land of peace and harmony that has outlawed private property and all forms of wealth. More was executed when he refused to take an oath to support the **Act of Supremacy.** See also **humanism.** *(Ch. 12)*

Muhammad (570–632) Prophet and founder of Islam. In 610 he began to receive revelations commanding him to teach all people a new faith that called for an unquestioned belief in one god, Allah, and a deep commitment to social justice for believers. Before his death, he had converted most of Arabia. See also **Five Pillars of Islam, Quran.** *(Ch. 8)*

Mussolini, Benito (1883–1945) Italian fascist dictator. Mussolini founded the fascist movement in 1919 and took power in 1922. He replaced Italy's parliamentary democracy with a **corporative state** and pursued an expansionist foreign policy. He concluded the Pact of Steel with **Adolf Hitler** in 1939 and took Italy into World War II in 1940. Deposed in 1943, he was killed by partisans in 1945. *(Ch. 26)*

Mycenaeans Militaristic people from the Greek mainland who conquered the *Minoans* around 1550–1375 B.C. Mycenaean civilization was a center of Bronze Age culture until its destruction around 1100 B.C. *(Ch. 2)*

mystery religions Popular Hellenistic cults featuring the initiation of worshipers into secret doctrines. Mystery religions replaced the traditional Greek religion of the Olympian gods. Some ancient Egyptian cults were recast as mystery religions, influencing early Christianity. *(Ch. 4)*

Napoleon Bonaparte (1769–1821) Emperor of the French (r. 1804–1815). A French general who took part in a coup in 1799 against the **Directory,** Napoleon consolidated power as first consul and proclaimed himself emperor with the approval of a national plebiscite in 1804. His military conquests exported French revolutionary reforms to the rest of Europe. He was finally defeated and exiled in 1815. *(Ch. 19)*

National Assembly (1789–1791) Legislative body formed in France in 1789 after the Third Estate insisted on being certified as members of the Estates General as a whole. The National Assembly drafted the **Declaration of the Rights of Man and the Citizen** and a constitution that called for a constitutional (not absolute) monarchy. *(Ch. 19)*

National Socialist (Nazi) Party The political party that grew from the movement that German dictator **Adolf Hitler** made his vehicle to power. Originating from the radical right in Munich in 1919, the Nazi Party won voting support during the early 1930s, paving the way for Hitler to be named German chancellor in 1933. *(Ch. 27)*

nationalism Belief arising in the eighteenth century that people derive their identity from their nation and owe it their primary loyalty. The criteria for nationhood typically included a common language, religion, and political authority, as well as common traditions and shared historical experiences. Nationalism was a major force in most of the revolutions of 1848 and in the subsequent unification of Italy and of Germany. *(Ch. 21)*

Nazi-Soviet Pact (1939) Surprise agreement between the Soviet Union and Nazi Germany in August 1939 that each would remain neutral if either got into a war with some other nation. The pact freed Germany to attack Poland a few days later without fear of Soviet reprisal. *(Ch. 27)*

Neo-Babylonians Rulers of western Asia between 612 and 539 B.C. who elaborately rebuilt Babylon, creating the famous Hanging Gardens. They destroyed Jerusalem, deporting many Judeans in what is known as the Babylonian Captivity. *(Ch. 2)*

Neolithic Revolution Human discovery and spread of agriculture, between about 13,000 and 5000 B.C. People first domesticated dogs and other animals and then learned how to cultivate crops. *(Ch. 1)*

New Economic Policy (NEP) (1921–1928) A Russian economic liberalization measure aimed at reviving an economy in crisis. The NEP restored considerable scope for private enterprise and allowed peasants to sell some of their harvest. After initial economic success, it was eventually considered a threat to the socialist state and was replaced by state-controlled central planning. *(Ch. 26)*

new imperialism Era of European overseas expansion launched in the 1880s. In the following decades, Europeans subjugated 500 million people in Africa and Asia—one half of the world's non-European population. *(Ch. 24)*

Newton, Isaac (1643–1727) English physicist, mathematician, and natural philosopher. Newton's mathematical computation of the laws of gravity and planetary motion, which he combined with a fully developed theory of inertia, completed the explanation for motion initiated by **Nicholas Copernicus.** See also **laws of motion.** *(Ch. 17)*

nongovernmental organizations (NGOs) A network of organizations unaffiliated with governments but central to the international community, such as the Red Cross, Amnesty International, and Doctors Without Borders, that had gradually emerged by the early twenty-first century to deal with humanitarian relief and human rights issues. *(Ch. 30)*

North Atlantic Treaty Organization (NATO) An alliance for regional defense, created in 1949 by the United States, Canada, and western European nations, whose members agree to defend one another from attack by nonmember countries. Its original aim was to contain the Soviet Union. *(Ch. 29)*

Nuremberg trials The war crimes trials conducted in Nuremberg, Germany. Most of the twenty-four defendants were convicted of war crimes and "crimes against humanity." *(Ch. 28)*

On the Donation of Constantine Work by Lorenzo Valla (1407–1457) proving that the *Donation of Constantine* was not written at the time of the emperor Constantine. The forged *Donation* purported to record Constantine's transfer to the pope of jurisdiction over Rome and the western half of the empire. Valla's work undermined the papacy's claim to political rule in central Italy. *(Ch. 12)*

Orthodoxy The Catholic Christian faith of Byzantium. It differed from Roman Catholicism by its use of Greek instead of Latin, the inclusion of icons in worship, an adherence to the Greek church fathers, some differences in basic theology, and many differences in customs and practices. *(Ch. 8)*

papacy Name for the institution ruled by the bishop of Rome who, in Roman Catholic tradition, is the successor to Peter, the most prominent apostle. Since Peter was believed to be the leader of the original followers of Christ, his successors, the popes (from *papa* by the fourth century), were believed to be the leaders of the whole church. *(Ch. 7)*

Papal Monarchy Period during the twelfth and thirteenth centuries when the power of the Catholic Church was increasingly expanded and centralized in the hands of the popes, as papal policy focused on recovering lost lands and rights in central Italy. *(Ch. 9)*

Papal States Beginning in the eighth century, territories held by the popes in central Italy under the protection of the Frankish kings. *(Ch. 8)*

papyrus Paperlike writing material used by the ancient Egyptians, Greeks, and Romans. Made primarily in Egypt from the papyrus plant, it was durable, flexible, and easy to write on. *(Ch. 1)*

Paris Commune (1871) Parisian workers' uprising intended to establish a workers' government under home rule. Stemming from labor discontent and the radicalization of workers during the siege of Paris in the Franco-Prussian War, the commune was suppressed by the army of the conservative French government. *(Ch. 22)*

Parliament English legislative institution, consisting of a House of Lords and a House of Commons, whose ancestors were the royal courts that met in 1265 and 1295. The king considered the courts a device to win support for royal agendas; the barons viewed them as opportunities to play a real policymaking role in government. In the late sixteenth and early seventeenth centuries, Parliament used control over monies to bargain with the crown over foreign and domestic policies, leading to resistance to and eventual deposition of Charles I. The power of parliament within the government was definitively established when it forced William and Mary to accept its role in government in the Glorious Revolution (1688.) See also **Glorious Revolution.** *(Ch. 9, 16)*

paterfamilias Oldest living male in an ancient Roman family, who had supreme legal power within the household. Only the paterfamilias could own property free and clear. *(Ch. 5)*

Paul of Tarsus (d. ca. 67) Christian apostle and saint. A Jew from Anatolia and a Roman citizen, Paul first persecuted the Christians but became a believer around A.D. 36. Paul taught that the life and resurrection of **Jesus of Nazareth** offered all humanity the hope of salvation through faith. Under Paul, **Christianity** began its complete separation from Judaism. *(Ch. 6)*

pax Romana Latin for "Roman peace," the term refers to the period of peace and prosperity in the Roman Empire from A.D. 69 to 180. During this time the emperors emphasized extending citizenship and spreading prosperity throughout the provinces, and Italy was no longer the tyrant of the Mediterranean. See also **Flavians.** *(Ch. 6)*

Peace of Westphalia (1648) Treaty that ended the **Thirty Years' War.** The principalities within the Holy Roman Empire were recognized as virtually autonomous, severely weakening the power of the emperor. Calvinism joined Catholicism and Lutheranism as tolerated faiths within the empire, and the treaty closed the age of religious wars. *(Ch. 15)*

Pericles Leader of fifth-century-B.C. Athens when **demokratia** became entrenched as the government and way of life. Distinguished for his oratory and honesty, he established Athens as a great center of art and literature as well as a great empire. *(Ch. 3)*

Persian Empire Vast, prosperous, and law-abiding West Asian empire, from about 550 B.C. to its conquest by **Alexander the Great** around 330 B.C. The relatively tolerant rule of the Persian emperors represented the greatest success yet of a universal kingship. The Persians also built the first great navy. *(Ch. 2)*

Peter the Great (r. 1682–1725) Russian tsar. Brilliant, energetic, and tyrannical, Peter revolutionized Russian society by his determined efforts to westernize his nation culturally, economically, and politically. He modernized the army and navy, secured seaports, and made Russia into a great power. *(Ch. 16)*

Petrarch, Francesco (1304–1374) Influential Italian poet, biographer, and humanist during the Renaissance. Petrarch advocated imitating the actions, values, and culture of the ancient Romans to reform the excesses of the present world. *(Ch. 12)*

Petrograd Soviet The *soviet* (council) of leaders of strike committees and army regiments elected in March 1917, when Petrograd's workers protested in response to severe wartime food and coal shortages. Central to the Bolshevik Revolution of 1917, the soviet eventually became the ruling power in the Russian capital—but only temporarily. *(Ch. 25)*

pharaoh Ancient Egyptians' title for their king, an absolute, all-powerful, and all-providing ruler. It was believed that the ruler represented the ancestors and guaranteed the fertility of the soil. *(Ch. 1)*

Philip II (382–336 B.C.) King of **Macedon.** A brilliant soldier and statesman, Philip conquered the Greek world. He developed a well-trained, professional year-round army and mastered the technology of siegecraft. He was succeeded by his son, **Alexander the Great.** *(Ch. 4)*

Philip II (r. 1556–1598) King of Spain, son of **Charles V.** An avid Roman Catholic, he ruled Spain at the height of its influence. Philip dispatched the ill-fated **Armada** to invade England and attempted to quash the revolt of the Netherlands. *(Ch. 15)*

philosophes French term referring to thinkers and critics of the Enlightenment era, including **Voltaire** and Diderot. Philosophes applied to political and social thought the confidence in human reason and the intelligibility of natural law that **Isaac Newton** and other scientists had recently achieved. *(Ch. 18)*

Phoenicians Canaanites whose civilization flourished about 1000–750 B.C. in present-day coastal Syria, where they established major trading ports. Master sailors, they planted colonies around the Mediterranean, many of which, including Carthage, became independent states. The Phoenicians exported the civilization of western Asia—including the Phoenician alphabet, derived from **Ugarit**—to the Mediterranean world. *(Ch. 2)*

plantation system Agricultural practices developed by the fifteenth-century Portuguese to produce sugar on their island colonies in the Atlantic using involuntarily transported slaves from Africa. Portugal's prototype—wealthy absentee landlords and masses of forced labor producing cash crops on vast tracts of land—was the model for the New World plantation system. In seventeenth- and eighteenth-century French and English colonies in the Caribbean, large sugar plantations owned by wealthy, often absentee, landlords replaced smaller-scale independent farming. See also **slave trade.** *(Chs. 13, 16)*

Plato (427–348 B.C.) Ancient Greek philosopher, student of **Socrates.** One of Western philosophy's greatest exponents of idealism, Plato believed that the senses are misleading and that truth can therefore be attained only by training the mind to overcome commonsense evidence. In the *Republic,* Plato describes an ideal state in which philosophers rule as kings, benevolently and unselfishly. *(Ch. 3)*

polis Term for an ancient Greek city-state, a system that reached its height around 700–300 B.C. The ideological and political organization of the polis emphasized equality and a shared community life for all citizens, not just the elite. *(Ch. 3)*

popular front A term for antifascist electoral alliances and governing coalitions that communists promoted from 1934 until 1939 to resist the further spread of fascism. Popular front coalitions won control of government in both Spain and France during 1936. *(Ch. 27)*

positivism Philosophy of the French thinker Auguste Comte (1798–1857). Comte asserted that human history progressed through distinct and irreversible stages, leading inexorably upward to the final and highest stage of development, the positive—or scientific—stage. Positivism and its optimistic outlook for human progress were influential in both Europe and Latin America during the nineteenth century. *(Ch. 23)*

Potsdam conference A July–August 1945 meeting held at Potsdam, Germany, between the USSR, the United States, and Great Britain to implement their earlier agreements concerning the treatment of defeated Germany. Many of the agreements reached were later abandoned amid growing hostility between the USSR and the Western democracies. *(Ch. 28)*

Prague Spring The attempt by Czechoslovakian reformers in 1968 to gain freer cultural expression, democratization of Communist Party procedures, and broader participation in public life within the framework of a communist state. The forcible suppression of the movement by Soviet leaders seemed to signal the end of any hope for flexibility and openness within the Soviet sphere. *(Ch. 29)*

price revolution Steady rise in prices in the sixteenth and seventeenth centuries, resulting from population growth and the influx of precious metals from Spain's New World territories. As wages lost one-tenth to one-fourth of their value, people sought new work, protested against taxes, and attacked scapegoats. The price revolution concentrated wealth in fewer hands and contributed to the rise of a new **gentry** class. *(Ch. 15)*

primogeniture A legal inheritance system that provided the first born, usually the first-born son, the right to inherit all the family land and farm. *(Ch. 20)*

Principate The constitutional monarchy of the Early Roman Empire, from 31 B.C. to A.D. 192. The term comes from *Princeps,* or "first citizen," an old title of respect used in the **senate.** See also **Augustus, Flavians.** *(Ch. 6)*

professionalization Establishment in the nineteenth century of common standards and requirements, especially in medicine, law, architecture, and engineering. Professionalization brought either government or self-regulation to vocations whose prestige rested on the claim of exclusive expertise in their fields. *(Ch. 23)*

proletariat Term used by Karl Marx to describe the new class of industrial workers who owned none of the means of production and were totally dependent on factory owners for their livelihoods. In Marxist thought, capitalists were destined to be overthrown by the proletariat. See also **Marxism.** *(Ch. 20)*

provisional government The body that ruled Russia from March to November 1917, in the wake of the revolution that overthrew the tsarist regime. Originally intended to be a temporary step to an elected constituent assembly, its policies caused discontents that the **Bolsheviks** were quick to exploit. *(Ch. 25)*

Ptolemies Dynasty of Egyptian kings who ruled from 304 to 30 B.C., founded by Ptolemy I, a Macedonian general of **Alexander the Great.** It was the wealthiest, most sophisticated, and longest lasting of the Hellenistic kingdoms. See also **Alexandria.** *(Ch. 4)*

Punic Wars (264–146 B.C.) Three wars during which the Roman Empire eventually destroyed Carthage. The Romans later adopted the Carthaginians' plantation system using massive numbers of slaves. *(Ch. 5)*

Puritans Radical Protestants in late-sixteenth- and seventeenth-century England. Puritans emphasized Bible reading, preaching, private scrutiny of conscience, and de-emphasized institutional ritual and clerical authority. Puritans became a majority in Parliament during the reign of Charles I and led the campaign against the king during the English Civil War. *(Ch. 15)*

Putin, Vladimir Elected president of Russia early in 2000, he had been director of Russia's secret police before coming to political prominence as prime minister in 1999. He cracked down on the insurgency in Chechnya and, as president, proved more energetic in dealing with Russia's problems than his predecessor, Boris Yeltsin. *(Ch. 30)*

putting-out system The production in country homes of thread and cloth by spinners and weavers for an entrepreneur who bought raw materials and "put them out" to be finished by individual workers. This cottage industry system expanded in eighteenth-century Europe as increased numbers of agricultural laborers needed more nonfarm work in off-seasons. *(Ch. 18)*

Quran Islamic sacred writings, which **Muhammad** communicated in the form of "recitations," insisting that he was transmitting a direct revelation from Allah. After Muhammad's death, his followers arranged the recitations into 114 *Suras,* or chapters, containing legal and wisdom literature and moral teaching. *(Ch. 8)*

rabbinic Judaism Main form of Judaism, which emerged during the first century A.D. under the leadership of the rabbis, the spiritual descendants of the Pharisees. Rabbinic Judaism amplified and interpreted the Hebrew Bible to clarify Jewish practice, elevated the oral law to equal authority with the written **Torah,** and enabled Judaism to evolve flexibly. *(Ch. 6)*

Realpolitik Style of governing that uses all means, including war, to expand the influence and power of a state. The best-known practitioner of Realpolitik was Prussian chancellor **Otto von Bismarck.** *(Ch. 22)*

Reconquista Wars of reconquest in the Iberian Peninsula from the eleventh to fifteenth centuries. Spanish and Portuguese rulers seized territories from the weakening Muslim regime. By awarding reconquered lands to their nobles, Christian kings enhanced their own status and power. *(Ch. 9)*

remilitarization of the Rhineland The reoccupation of Germany's Rhineland territory by German troops in March 1936, in clear violation of the **Treaty of Versailles.** When the French and British did not resist the German move, **Adolf Hitler** was emboldened to additional acts of aggression elsewhere. *(Ch. 27)*

Renaissance Term derived from the French word for "rebirth" used to describe a period of intense creativity between 1350 and 1500 when cultural values were based on imitation of classical Greek and Roman norms. *(Ch. 12)*

res publica Romans' concept of their republic, which uniquely influenced Western political institutions. *Res publica* is Latin for "public thing," as opposed to *res privata,* "private thing," as the Romans characterized monarchy. *(Ch. 5)*

revisionism Late-nineteenth-century argument that **socialism** could and should come about by gradual, democratic means. This idea was a "revision" of Marx's contention that socialism would require a violent revolution. Most European socialists claimed to reject revisionism while at the same time pursuing revisionist policies. *(Ch. 24)*

risorgimento Italian term, beginning in the late eighteenth century, for the political and cultural renewal of Italy. It later came to describe the political and military events that led to the unification of Italy in 1861. *(Ch. 22)*

Robespierre, Maximilien (1758–1794) French lawyer and revolutionary leader. A **Jacobin** who joined the Committee of Public Safety in 1793, Robespierre called for the **Terror** to suppress internal dissent. *(Ch. 19)*

Romanesque Meaning "in the Roman style," this nineteenth-century term characterized the transitional architecture and painting of the period between the waning of Carolingian art and the full emergence of **Gothic** art in the twelfth century. Distinctive features of Romanesque churches are their exuberant decoration and ornament. *(Ch. 10)*

romanticism Artistic movement, prevalent from the 1760s to 1840s, that rebelled against rationalism. Writers, painters, and composers rejected the Enlightenment and its rationalist values, instead praising emotion and sensitivity, and worshiping nature for its inherent beauty. *(Ch. 21)*

Rome-Berlin Axis Alliance between Hitler's Nazi Germany and Mussolini's fascist Italy. Beginning as an informal understanding by 1936, it was cemented by an anti-Comintern agreement and eventually by an open-ended military alliance, the Pact of Steel, in 1939. *(Ch. 27)*

Roosevelt, Franklin Delano (1882–1945) U.S. president who served from 1933 to 1945, through the Great Depression of the 1930s and World War II. His New Deal program, including large public works projects, was an innovative response to the Depression. *(Ch. 28)*

Rousseau, Jean-Jacques (1712–1778) French writer and philosopher. In his 1762 work, *The Social Contract,* Rousseau depicted a hypothetical state with direct democracy in which citizens have inalienable rights to wide-ranging liberties. He was influential as a critic of an elite society still dominated by status, patronage, and privilege. *(Ch. 18)*

Sacred Union An agreement made between French leaders of different political groups to cooperate during World War I. The French government had initially feared that the Socialists might sabotage the war, when, in fact, they were eager to join the new government of national defense. *(Ch. 25)*

salons Regular gatherings in eighteenth-century Parisian private homes, where **Voltaire** and other **philosophes** read and discussed their works in progress, with the exchange of ideas facilitated by female s*alonnières* (salon leaders). Anyone with appropriate manners could participate as an equal, enabling conversation to shift from maintaining the status quo to questioning it. *(Ch. 18)*

sans-culottes Ordinary citizens of revolutionary Paris, whose derisive nickname referred to their inability to afford fashionable knee pants ("culottes"). Because of their effective political organization, they were able to influence the direction of the French Revolution through pressure on the government as well as direct action, such as to overthrow the monarchy in August 1792. *(Ch. 19)*

Sappho (fl. ca. 625 B.C.) Ancient Greek poet from the island of Lesbos. Sappho wrote odes, wedding songs, and hymns expressing intimate feelings, including love for other women. She wrote of female sexuality in a male-dominated culture. *(Ch. 3)*

second industrial revolution Interrelated economic changes that resulted in a significant speedup in production in western Europe after 1850. Key factors were the introduction of new products, new methods of manufacture, and new materials such as mass-produced steel, synthetic dyes, and aluminum. *(Ch. 23)*

Second International International socialist organization founded in 1889 that met yearly to debate issues of broad concern. Beginning in 1907, it called for workers to strike and to refuse military service in case of international conflict. *(Ch. 24)*

Second Reform Bill (1867) British legislation that extended suffrage by lowering property qualifications and set equal population requirements for all parliamentary districts. The legislation bolstered the existing system, as the newly enfranchised clerks, artisans, and other skilled workers felt more a part of society. *(Ch. 22)*

Seleucids Dynasty of rulers of Asia Minor from 312 to 64 B.C. Founded by Seleucus (ca. 358–281 B.C.), a general of **Alexander the Great,** the kingdom spread **Hellenism** by establishing seventy colonies throughout the Near East. *(Ch. 4)*

senate In the ancient Roman Republic and Empire, the powerful council of elders that advised the monarchs (Latin: *senatus*, from *senex*, "old man"). Romans spoke of the senate's *auctoritas*, a quasi-religious prestige. *(Ch. 5)*

separate spheres Notion, especially prevalent in the mid-nineteenth century, of two distinct sets of roles—one male and public, the other female and private. While the man was out in the world advancing his career, the bourgeois woman was to run her home, providing her family with an orderly, comfortable shelter. *(Ch. 23)*

Seven Years' War (1756–1763) The first major war between European nations started and fought largely in their overseas empires, the Seven Years' War was in part a conflict between Britain and France for control of overseas possessions. Britain emerged the decisive winner in this phase of the conflict, partly because France was simultaneously involved in the conflict on the European continent, in which France and Austria tried to contain the aggressive Prussia. *(Ch. 18)*

show trials Trials staged for ideological and propaganda reasons in the USSR. In the most famous, orchestrated by **Joseph Stalin** from 1936 to 1938, major communist figures were made to confess to trumped-up charges and executed. These trials helped persuade Soviet citizens that a high-level conspiracy was responsible for the USSR's economic woes. *(Ch. 27)*

Sistine Chapel Chapel at the Vatican Palace commissioned by Pope Sixtus IV in 1475, best known for Michelangelo's magnificent paintings of the Creation and Last Judgment. The monument vividly captures the cultural, religious, and ideological program of the papacy. *(Ch. 12)*

slave trade Europeans' trade with Africa in which involuntary laborers were bought and shipped to the Americas to be sold primarily to owners of plantations where sugar and other commodities were produced. The trade reached its peak in the eighteenth century, when approximately 7 million Africans were shipped across the Atlantic. The slave trade was an integral part of the "triangle trade" by which Europe, Africa, and the Americas were connected. See also **plantation system**. *(Chs. 13, 16, 18)*

Smith, Adam (1723–1790) Scottish economist who developed the doctrine of **laissez faire.** In his treatise *The Wealth of Nations* (1776), Smith argued that an economy regulates itself better without interference by government and without monopolies and other economic privileges. Smith suggested that people's economic activities are often "led by an invisible hand" to benefit society as a whole. *(Ch. 18)*

social Catholics Catholics in western Europe who believed that society bore responsibility for the well-being of the poor. They were following the ideas set out in 1891 by Pope Leo XIII (r. 1878–1903) in his encyclical *Rerum novarum* ("Of New Things"). *(Ch. 23)*

Social Darwinism Theory of social evolution first articulated by Herbert Spencer (1820–1902). According to Social Darwinists, human societies evolve in the same way as plants and animals, and the weak, poor, and improvident are not worthy of survival. Social Darwinism was used to justify callousness toward the poor at home and imperialist conquest abroad. See also **Darwinism.** *(Ch. 23)*

social market economy The late-twentieth-century socially-oriented model of capitalism practiced in continental western Europe, providing a substantial safety net in health care and a commitment to public services such as transportation and day care. It competed with the U.S. model, shared by Britain, which emphasized free enterprise. *(Ch. 30)*

socialism Nineteenth-century economic and social doctrine and political movement that opposed private ownership and control of the means of production. Socialists believed that the "social" or state ownership of property, unlike private ownership, would benefit society as a whole, creating a more just system. *(Ch. 21)*

Society of Jesus (Jesuits) Founded in 1534 by **Ignatius Loyola** (1491–1556), the Jesuits soon became leaders in the Catholic Counter Reformation. The Jesuits were famed for their schools and work as spiritual advisers. *(Ch. 14)*

Society of Revolutionary Republican Women In revolutionary France, a powerful political club that represented the interests of female **sans-culottes.** The society was included in a general ban on political participation by women that the Committee of Public Safety instituted in October 1793. *(Ch. 19)*

Socrates (469–399 B.C.) Ancient Greek philosopher, a founder of the Western philosophical tradition. Socrates changed the emphasis of philosophy from the natural world to human ethics. He believed that no one who truly understood goodness would ever choose to do evil. Accused of being an atheist and corrupting the young, Socrates was executed in 399. Socrates' teachings were recorded and transmitted by his students, including **Plato.** *(Ch. 3)*

sola scriptura Doctrine put forward by **Martin Luther** in *On the Babylonian Captivity of the Church* (1520) that church authority had to be based on biblical teachings. In particular he argued that the sacraments of the Catholic Church—other than baptism and communion—were not found in the Bible. *(Ch. 14)*

solidarism Late-nineteenth-century policy of conservative and liberal parties to blunt the appeal of socialism. Solidarism emphasized the mutual responsibility of classes and individuals for one another's well-being and led to the passage of laws and benefits to improve the lot of the working class. *(Ch. 23)*

Solidarity A trade union formed from a movement of shipyard workers in communist Poland in 1980. It became the nucleus of widespread demands for change—including independent labor organizations, the right to strike, and freedom of expression. Though forced underground in 1981, the movement eventually proved crucial to the downfall of the communist regime in Poland. *(Ch. 29)*

Solon (ca. 630–560 B.C.) Statesman of early Athens. Appointed to a one-year term as sole archon in 594 B.C., Solon transformed Greek society through mediation, moderation, respect for law, and measures that liberated the poor and downtrodden. His economic reforms sparked a commercial boom. *(Ch. 3)*

Spanish Inquisition Church court that began in 1478 when King Ferdinand and Queen Isabella obtained papal approval to control the grand inquisitor. The Spanish Inquisition investigated and condemned many former Jews and Muslims who were believed to have insincerely converted to Christianity. It became an important and lucrative instrument to expand state power. *(Ch. 11)*

SS *(Schutzstaffel)* Nazi elite troops, led by Heinrich Himmler. Linked to the Gestapo, the secret political police, the SS specialized in institutionalized terror tactics and were responsible for some of the worst atrocities of the Nazi regime. *(Ch. 27)*

"stab in the back" myth The notion, widely held among Germans after their unexpected loss in World War I, that political intrigue and revolution at home had sabotaged the German military effort. It helped alienate Germans from their new democratic government. *(Ch. 25)*

Stalin, Joseph (1879–1953) Soviet dictator. Secretary of the Communist Party since 1922, Stalin outmaneuvered his rivals after the death of Lenin to take control of the Soviet government by 1929. Stalin jettisoned the **New Economic Policy** and instituted a program of crash industrialization and agricultural **collectivization.** He concluded the **Nazi-Soviet Pact** in 1939 but joined the Allies after the German invasion of the Soviet Union in 1941. Victorious in World War II, Stalin sponsored the takeover of governments in eastern Europe by communist regimes, contributing to the development of the **cold war.** See also **"the Great Patriotic War," gulag, Potsdam conference, show trials, Yalta conference.** *(Ch. 26)*

Stalingrad (1942–1943) Decisive World War II battle. The Soviet Union, at immense cost in lives, launched repeated counterattacks on Germany's Sixth Army, stopping it from advancing farther and finally forcing it to surrender. The battle is often considered the turning point of World War II in Europe. *(Ch. 28)*

steam engine Machine invented in England in its modern form by James Watt in 1777. The steam engine provided mechanized power for manufacturing and made **factories** and **mass production** possible. *(Ch. 20)*

Stoics Believers in a philosophical system begun in Athens by Zeno (335–263 B.C.). Stoicism emphasized the pursuit of wisdom, the reliability of sensory experience, and freedom from all passion. Stoics focused on intentions as well as the results of actions. *(Ch. 4)*

Streseman, Gustav (1878–1929) German statesman of the Weimar Republic. Leader of the conservative German People's Party, Streseman served briefly as chancellor in 1923, then as foreign secretary from 1923 to 1929. He secured a reduction of Germany's reparations payments and negotiated the **Treaty of Locarno,** paving the way for Germany's entry to the League of Nations in 1926. His death in 1929 was a blow to hopes for the development of democracy in Germany and peace in Europe. *(Ch. 26)*

Suez crisis (1956) Crisis prompted by Egypt's nationalization of the British-owned Suez Canal. The effort of Britain, France, and Israel to seize the canal prompted a strong negative reaction in world opinion, forcing them to withdraw. The episode demonstrated the newly limited reach of the western European powers in world affairs. *(Ch. 29)*

suffragists Activists who, beginning in the late nineteenth century, organized to win the vote for women. Adopting increasingly violent tactics, English suffragists (often referred to by contemporaries as "suffragettes") endured attacks by male thugs, were arrested, engaged in hunger strikes, and were force-fed. *(Ch. 24)*

Sumerians Dominant inhabitants of Mesopotamia in the third millennium B.C. They established the world's first civilization, thirty flourishing city-states with a common culture, commerce, and tendency to make war on one another. *(Ch. 1)*

summa An encyclopedic compendium of carefully arrayed knowledge on a particular subject. Examples are the two most famous works of **Thomas Aquinas,** the *Summa Contra Gentiles* and the *Summa Theologiae. (Ch. 10)*

surrealism A movement in literature and the visual arts that emerged in Paris in the early 1920s. Though indebted to dada and its mocking defiance of convention, surrealism sought to find something positive by exploring the realm of the subconscious, partly by following some of **Sigmund Freud**'s insights about access to the subconscious. *(Ch. 26)*

Tacitus, Cornelius (ca. A.D. 55–120) Roman historian of the "Silver Age." Tacitus lauded the simple virtues of the German tribes and expressed nostalgia for the Republic. His greatest works were *The Histories,* on the civil wars of A.D. 69, and *The Annals,* chronicling the emperors from Tiberius through Nero. *(Ch. 6)*

Tanzimat Turkish term, meaning "restructuring," for the reform movements in the Ottoman Empire beginning in 1839. Reforms included security of property, equity in taxation, and equality before the law regardless of religion. Government officials were given fixed salaries and subjected to regular inspections. *(Ch. 22)*

Tennis Court Oath (1789) Pledge signed by all but one Third Estate deputy of the Estates General of France on June 20, 1789. The deputies swore to continue to meet until a constitution was drafted. *(Ch. 19)*

Terror (1793–1794) Systematic repression of internal enemies undertaken by revolutionary tribunals across France at the urging of **Maximilien Robespierre.** Approximately fourteen thousand people were executed, including aristocrats, **Girondins,** and **sans-culottes.** The Terror ended with the arrest and execution of Robespierre in July 1794. *(Ch. 19)*

tetrarchy Government ruled by four leaders. Emperor Diocletian established a tetrarchy in about 293 to address the Roman Empire's political instability, huge size, and complexity, as well as to promote experienced men and provide an orderly imperial succession. *(Ch. 7)*

Thatcher, Margaret (b. 1925) As Conservative prime minister of Britain from 1979 to 1990, she spearheaded a number of measures to promote privatization and free enterprise at the expense of the welfare state and the British labor unions. So dramatic was the resulting change in direction that it is sometimes characterized as Thatcher's conservative revolution. *(Ch. 30)*

third-century crisis Period from A.D. 235 to 284, when the Roman Empire suffered barbarian invasions, domestic economic problems, plague, assassinations, and urban decline. Attempting to fend off invasions at opposite fronts, the emperors devalued the currency, leading to massive inflation. *(Ch. 6)*

Third Estate In France, the common people, as distinct from the nobles (First Estate) and clergy (Second Estate). In the Estates General in 1789, it was presumed that the votes of the First and Second Estates would overrule those of the Third Estate, although the commoners vastly outnumbered the nobles and clergy. *(Ch. 19)*

Thirty Years' War (1618–1648) Destructive war, involving most European countries but fought in Germany, resulting from sixteenth-century religious tensions, regionalism versus centralizing forces, and dynastic and strategic rivalries between rulers. See also **Peace of Westphalia.** *(Ch. 15)*

Thucydides (ca. 455–397 B.C.) Ancient Greek historian; with **Herodotus,** a founder of history-writing in the West. A failed Athenian general, Thucydides made a careful study of the Peloponnesian War and prided himself on the accuracy of his account of the prolonged conflict. *(Ch. 3)*

Torah First five books of the Bible. Accepted as sacred by the Hebrews around 425 B.C., it relates the working out of God's pact, or **covenant,** with the Hebrews, his chosen people. *(Ch. 2)*

Tordesillas, Treaty of (1494) Treaty by which Pope Alexander VI divided the rights of colonization of the newly identified lands between Portugal and Spain. He had intended to give Africa to the Portuguese and the New Worlds to Spain, but by a miscalculation Brazil remained in the Portuguese area. *(Ch. 13)*

total war The concept, first associated with World War I, that war requires the mobilization of all a nation's resources and energies. The unexpected need to wage total war during World War I accelerated social and economic processes, from technological development to women's suffrage. *(Ch. 25)*

Toussaint-Louverture, François (1743–1803) Former slave who governed the island of Saint Domingue (Haiti) as an independent state after the slave revolt of 1791. In 1802 French forces captured Toussaint-Louverture, who died in prison. *(Ch. 19)*

trading-post empire Commercial system developed by Portugal in the sixteenth century to dominate trade in the Indian Ocean through fortified, strategically placed naval bases. All merchants were expected to acquire export licenses and ship products through Portuguese ports. *(Ch. 13)*

tragedy Serious play with an unhappy ending. Greek tragedy emerged and reached its height in the fifth century B.C. in the works of Aeschylus, Sophocles, and Euripides. The essence of Greek tragedy is the nobility in the spectacle of a great man or woman failing because of a "fatal flaw," but learning from failure. *(Ch. 3)*

trasformismo System of political manipulation used by Count Camillo di Cavour (1810–1861), Piedmont's prime minister, to create majorities in parliament to support his cabinet. The practice of using cajolery and bribery to transform foes into supporters would continue to characterize Italian government in the late nineteenth century. *(Ch. 22)*

Triple Alliance Military alliance established in 1882 among Germany, Austria-Hungary, and Italy to counter the Franco-Russian Alliance (later the **Triple Entente**). The system of rival alliances contributed to the escalation of international tensions. *(Ch. 24)*

Triple Entente Military alliance between Great Britain, France, and Russia, completed in 1907, countering the **Triple Alliance.** The system of rival alliances eventually brought all of Europe into World War I. *(Ch. 24)*

triumph Elaborate procession through the streets of ancient Rome. Triumphs were voted by the **senate** to salute a general's victory over a foreign army. *(Ch. 5)*

Truman Doctrine The U.S. policy of containment, or limiting communist expansion, as outlined by President Harry Truman in 1947. Intended most immediately to deter any communist designs on Greece or Turkey, the doctrine was used thereafter to support any country that the United States considered threatened by communism during the **cold war.** *(Ch. 28)*

Ugarit Cosmopolitan port on northern Syria's Mediterranean coast that was a thriving trading center, especially around 1400–1200 B.C. The alphabet invented by Ugaritic scribes is the source of today's widely used Roman alphabet. *(Ch. 1)*

unilateralism Term describing the increasing willingness of the United States to go its own way in world affairs after the end of the cold war, and especially after the terrorist attack on the United States in September 2001. In pursuing its own course, the United States was departing from the multilateral international system that it had sought to foster since World War II. This departure alienated many Europeans. *(Ch. 30)*

United Nations International organization of nations founded in 1945 to encourage peace, cooperation, and recognition of human rights. The major powers—China, France, Great Britain, the Soviet Union, and the United States—were given a privileged position as permanent members of the Security Council, each with veto power. *(Ch. 28)*

urbanization Term related to the growth of cities, largely connected to the **industrialization** of the late eighteenth and nineteenth centuries. Cities aided industry by providing markets for goods and a concentrated source of workers. However, with urbanization came a host of new problems such as urban slums, lack of sanitation, and pollution. *(Ch. 20)*

utilitarianism Political theory of Jeremy Bentham (1748–1832). Bentham argued that the purpose of government is to provide "the greatest happiness of the greatest number" and that the test of government is its usefulness. Democracy was implicit in Bentham's philosophy: the greatest number could ensure its own happiness only by voting for its rulers. *(Ch. 21)*

Vasco da Gama (1460?–1524) Pioneering Portuguese explorer and trader whose voyage from 1497 to 1499 around the Cape of Good Hope to Mozambique and India inaugurated a four-hundred-year-long Portuguese presence in the Indian Ocean region. *(Ch. 13)*

vassal Drawing on both Roman and Germanic customs, vassalage linked two men—lord and vassal—in an honorable, reciprocal bond based on loyalty and service. Eventually leading nobles and their vassals formed a social and political elite. *(Ch. 8)*

Versailles, Treaty of (1919) Peace treaty between the victorious Allies and defeated Germany after World War I. The harsh terms of this dictated peace produced a sense of bitterness and betrayal in Germany. *(Ch. 25)*

Vichy France The term for the repressive French government that followed the Third Republic after France's defeat by Nazi Germany in 1940. Headquartered in the resort town of Vichy, the government collaborated with the victorious Germans, who occupied Paris. *(Ch. 28)*

Victorian morality Nineteenth-century ethos wherein the values of the dominant middle class, which emphasized strict moral principles, especially regarding sex and drink, became the social norms. In Queen Victoria, who reigned for two-thirds of the century, the middle classes saw a reflection of their own values. *(Ch. 23)*

Virgil Roman poet whose works contributed to the Augustan renewal. In the *Eclogues,* Virgil (Publius Vergilius Maro, 70–19 B.C.) describes the blessings of peace under **Augustus;** in the *Georgics,* he glorifies Italian agriculture. His *Aeneid* mythologizes Rome and describes both the burden and glory of empire. *(Ch. 6)*

Visigoths Germanic people who served as allied troops for the Romans. When threatened by the Huns, the Visigoths crossed the Danube and settled in the Balkans. Eventually they sacked Rome in 410 and expanded their rule to parts of Spain and southern France. *(Ch. 7)*

Voltaire (François-Marie Arouet, 1694–1778) Prolific French writer, critic, and reformer who embodied the spirit of eighteenth-century rationalism: its confidence, its increasingly practical bent, its wit and sophistication. His satires and philosophical critiques targeted Christianity, intolerance, and tyranny. See also **philosophes.** *(Ch. 18)*

Vulgate Bible Latin version of new translations of the Hebrew Scriptures and Greek New Testament written by Jerome (331–420) for Pope Damasus. It was called the Vulgate because it was the Bible for the "people" (*vulgus*), whose language was Latin. *(Ch. 7)*

Warsaw Pact (1955–1991) Military-diplomatic alliance of Soviet bloc countries, created to counter NATO. The pact established a joint military command and mutual military assistance, as well as a new basis for the continuing presence of Soviet troops in the satellite states. See also **cold war.** *(Ch. 29)*

welfare state The concept, especially prevalent in western countries after World War II, that government should adopt large-scale social welfare measures, while maintaining a primarily capitalistic economy. Among the welfare measures usually adopted were a national health service, old-age pensions, and insurance against unemployment, sickness, and disability. *(Ch. 29)*

Weltpolitik Meaning "world politics," the term describes the policy pursued by Kaiser **Wilhelm II** (r. 1888–1918) to make Germany a world power, with colonies, a navy, and major influence among the Great Powers. The kaiser implemented his ambitious agenda with nationalistic appeals and bombastic threats. *(Ch. 24)*

Wilhelm II (r. 1888–1918) German kaiser (emperor) whose aggressive diplomatic, commercial, and military policies helped trigger World War I. His pursuit of *Weltpolitik* severely aggravated international tensions. See also **Weltpolitik.** *(Ch. 24)*

World Trade Organization (WTO) Growing from a multilateral trade agreement in 1947, it sought, with mixed success, to promote freer trade throughout the world. By the end of the 1990s WTO meetings were drawing large demonstrations by anti-globalization activists, most notably in Seattle in 1999 and in Cancún, Mexico, in 2003. *(Ch. 30)*

Yalta conference The meeting in February 1945 at Yalta, a Soviet Black Sea resort, between Stalin, Roosevelt, and Churchill. With Allied victory assured, they began outlining plans for the postwar order, including the military occupation of Germany. See also **Potsdam conference.** *(Ch. 28)*

Young Turks Term describing the young intellectuals who wanted to transform the Ottoman Empire into a more modern, Westernized state. Self-exiled in the late 1860s in Paris and London, they overthrew the sultan and seized power in 1908. The expression has subsequently come to designate any group of activists pushing for political change. *(Ch. 22)*

Zionism Nationalist Jewish movement. In the late nineteenth century, faced with growing **anti-Semitism,** some Jews argued that they would be safe only in their own nation. Zionism advocated establishing a Jewish state in the Jews' ancient homeland of Palestine, an idea that became reality with the creation of Israel in 1948. *(Ch. 24)*

Zoroastrianism Religion founded about 1000–550 B.C. by the Persian prophet Zarathustra (*Zoroaster* in Greek). Zoroastrians believe in a supreme deity and a cosmic contest between good and evil within each individual. *(Ch. 2)*

Zwingli, Huldrych (1484–1531) Town preacher of Zurich, Zwingli became a leader of the urban reformation in Switzerland and southwest Germany, emphasizing the importance of the community in the salvation of individuals. *(Ch. 14)*

Index